W9-CTW-423

# Contemporary
# Literary Criticism

# Guide to Gale Literary Criticism Series

**When you need to review criticism of literary works, these are the Gale series to use:**

| If the author's death date is: | You should turn to: |
| --- | --- |
| After Dec. 31, 1959 (or author is still living) | **CONTEMPORARY LITERARY CRITICISM**<br>for example: Jorge Luis Borges, Anthony Burgess, William Faulkner, Mary Gordon, Ernest Hemingway, Iris Murdoch |
| 1900 through 1959 | **TWENTIETH-CENTURY LITERARY CRITICISM**<br>for example: Willa Cather, F. Scott Fitzgerald, Henry James, Mark Twain, Virginia Woolf |
| 1800 through 1899 | **NINETEENTH-CENTURY LITERATURE CRITICISM**<br>for example: Fedor Dostoevski, Nathaniel Hawthorne, George Sand, William Wordsworth |
| 1400 through 1799 | **LITERATURE CRITICISM FROM 1400 TO 1800** **(excluding Shakespeare)**<br>for example: Anne Bradstreet, Daniel Defoe, Alexander Pope, François Rabelais, Jonathan Swift, Phillis Wheatley |
| | **SHAKESPEAREAN CRITICISM**<br>Shakespeare's plays and poetry |
| Antiquity through 1399 | **CLASSICAL AND MEDIEVAL LITERATURE CRITICISM**<br>for example: Dante, Homer, Plato, Sophocles, Vergil, the Beowulf Poet |

---

## Gale also publishes related criticism series:

**CHILDREN'S LITERATURE REVIEW**

This series covers authors of all eras who have written for the preschool through high school audience.

**SHORT STORY CRITICISM**

This series covers the major short fiction writers of all nationalities and periods of literary history.

**POETRY CRITICISM**

This series covers poets of all nationalities, movements, and periods of literary history.

ISSN 0091-3421

Volume 64

# Contemporary Literary Criticism

Excerpts from Criticism of the
Works of Today's Novelists, Poets,
Playwrights, Short Story Writers, Scriptwriters,
and Other Creative Writers

**Roger Matuz**
EDITOR

**Cathy Falk**
**Mary K. Gillis**
**Sean R. Pollock**
**David Segal**
ASSOCIATE EDITORS

**Gale Research Inc.** · DETROIT · LONDON

## STAFF

Roger Matuz, *Editor*

Cathy Falk, Mary K. Gillis, Marie Lazzari, Sean R. Pollock, David Segal,
Robyn V. Young, *Associate Editors*

Jennifer Brostrom, Ian Goodhall, Susan M. Peters, Janet M. Witalec, *Assistant Editors*

Jeanne A. Gough, *Production & Permissions Manager*
Linda M. Pugliese, *Production Supervisor*
Maureen A. Puhl, Jennifer VanSickle, *Editorial Associates*
Donna Craft, Paul Lewon, Lorna Mabunda, Camille P. Robinson, *Editorial Assistants*

Victoria B. Cariappa, *Research Manager*
Maureen Richards, *Research Supervisor*
Paula Cutcher–Jackson, Judy L. Gale, *Editorial Associates*
Amy Kaechele, Robin Lupa, Mary Beth McElmeel,
Tamara C. Nott, *Editorial Assistants*

Sandra C. Davis, *Permissions Supervisor (Text)*
Josephine M. Keene, Denise M. Singleton, Kimberly F. Smilay, *Permissions Associates*
Maria L. Franklin, Michele Lonoconus, Shalice Shah, Nancy K. Sheridan,
Rebecca A. Stanko, *Permissions Assistants*
Shelly Rakoczy, *Student Co-op Assistant*

Patricia A. Seefelt, *Permissions Supervisor (Pictures)*
Margaret A. Chamberlain, *Permissions Associate*
Pamela A. Hayes, Keith Reed, *Permissions Assistants*

Mary Beth Trimper, *Production Manager*
Shanna G. Philpott, *External Production Associate*

Art Chartow, *Art Director*
C. J. Jonik, *Keyliner*

Copyright © 1991
Gale Research Inc.
835 Penobscot Bldg.
Detroit, MI 48226-4094

Library of Congress Catalog Card Number 76-38938
ISBN 0-8103-4438-6
ISSN 0091-3421

Printed in the United States of America

Published simultaneously in the United Kingdom
by Gale Research International Limited
(An affiliated company of Gale Research Inc.)

# Contents

Preface   vii

Acknowledgments   xi

**Anna Akhmatova** 1889-1966 ................... 1
*Russian poet*

**Maya Angelou** 1928- ........................... 23
*American autobiographer*

**John Cheever** 1912-1982 ..................... 42
*American short story writer
and novelist*

**E. M. Cioran** 1911- ............................ 72
*Rumanian-born philosopher*

**W. E. B. Du Bois** 1868-1963 ............... 101
*American nonfiction writer*

**Steve Erickson** 1950- .......................... 136
*American novelist*

**Jules Feiffer** 1929- ............................. 147
*American playwright and cartoonist*

**Sylvia Fraser** 1935- ............................ 165
*Canadian novelist*

**Nikki Giovanni** 1943- .......................... 181
*American poet*

**Doris Grumbach** 1918- ........................ 197
*American novelist*

**Ken Kesey** 1935- .................................. 206
*American novelist; entry devoted to
One Flew over the Cuckoo's Nest*

**Hanif Kureishi** 1954- ........................... 245
*English scriptwriter and novelist*

**Philip Larkin** 1922-1985 ...................... 256
*English poet; entry devoted to
Collected Poems*

**Craig Lucas** 19??- ................................ 288
*American playwright*

**Peter Matthiessen** 1927- ...................... 300
*American novelist and nonfiction
writer*

**Vladimir Nabokov** 1899-1977 .............. 330
*Russian-born American novelist;
entry devoted to Lolita*

**Tom Robbins** 1936- ............................. 370
*American novelist*

**Iain Crichton Smith** 1928- ................... 386
*Scottish poet*

**John Kennedy Toole** 1937-1969 .......... 403
*American novelist*

**Jeanette Winterson** 1959- .................... 425
*English novelist*

**Tobias Wolff** 1945- .............................. 445
*American novelist and short story
writer*

Literary Criticism Series Cumulative Author Index   465

*CLC* Cumulative Nationality Index   517

*CLC-64* Title Index   531

# Preface

Named "one of the twenty-five most distinguished reference titles published during the past twenty-five years" by *Reference Quarterly,* the *Contemporary Literary Criticism (CLC)* series provides readers with critical commentary and general information on more than 2,000 authors now living or who died after December 31, 1959. Previous to the publication of the first volume of *CLC* in 1973, there was no ongoing digest monitoring scholarly and popular sources of critical opinion and explication of modern literature. *CLC,* therefore, has fulfilled an essential need, particularly since the complexity and variety of contemporary literature makes the function of criticism especially important to today's reader.

## Scope of the Series

*CLC* presents significant passages from published criticism of works by creative writers. Since many of the authors covered by *CLC* inspire continual critical commentary, writers are often represented in more than one volume. There is, of course, no duplication of reprinted criticism.

Authors are selected for inclusion for a variety of reasons, among them the publication or dramatic production of a critically acclaimed new work, the reception of a major literary award, revival of interest in past writings, or the adaptation of a literary work to film or television.

The present volume of *CLC* includes W. E. B. Du Bois, a major force in helping define African-American social and political causes in the United States; Craig Lucas, whose *Prelude to a Kiss* won the 1990 Obie Award for best off-Broadway play; and Peter Matthiessen and Tom Robbins, authors of the recent popular and critically respected novels *Killing Mr. Watson* and *Skinny Legs and All,* respectively.

Perhaps most importantly, works that frequently appear on the syllabuses of high school and college literature courses are represented by individual entries in *CLC.* Ken Kesey's *One Flew over the Cuckoo's Nest* and Vladimir Nabokov's *Lolita* are examples of works of this stature appearing in *CLC,* Volume 64.

Attention is also given to several other groups of writers—authors of considerable public interest—about whose work criticism is often difficult to locate. These include mystery and science fiction writers, literary and social critics, foreign writers, and authors who represent particular ethnic groups within the United States.

## Format of the Book

Altogether there are about 500 individual excerpts in each volume—with approximately seventeen excerpts per author—taken from hundreds of book review periodicals, general magazines, scholarly journals, monographs, and books. Entries include critical evaluations spanning from the beginning of an author's career to the most current commentary. Interviews, feature articles, and other published writings that offer insight into the author's works are also presented. Students, teachers, librarians, and researchers will find that the generous excerpts and supplementary material in *CLC* provides them with vital information needed to write a term paper, analyze a poem, or lead a book discussion group. In addition, complete bibliographical citations note the original source and all of the information necessary for a term paper footnote or bibliography.

## Features

A *CLC* author entry consists of the following elements:

• The **author heading** cites the form under which the author has most commonly published, followed by birth date, and death date when applicable. Uncertainty as to a birth or death date is indicated by a question mark.

• A **portrait** of the author is included when available.

• A brief **biographical and critical introduction** to the author and his or her work precedes the excerpted criticism. The first line of the introduction provides the author's full name, pseudonyms (if applicable), nationality, and a listing of genres in which the author has written. Since *CLC* is not intended to be a definitive biographical source, cross-references have been included to direct readers to these useful sources published by Gale Research: *Short Story Criticism* and *Children's Literature Review,* which provide excerpts of criticism on the works of short story writers and authors of books for young people, respectively; *Contemporary Authors,* which includes detailed biographical and bibliographical sketches of nearly 97,000 authors; *Something about the Author,* which contains heavily illustrated biographical sketches of writers and illustrators who create books for children and young adults; *Dictionary of Literary Biography,* which provides original evaluations and detailed biographies of authors important to literary history; and *Contemporary Authors Autobiography Series* and *Something about the Author Autobiography Series,* which offer autobiographical essays by prominent writers for adults and those of interest to young readers, respectively. Previous volumes of *CLC* in which the author has been featured are also listed in the introduction.

• A list of **principal works,** arranged chronologically and, if applicable, divided into genre categories, notes the most important works by the author.

• The **excerpted criticism** represents various kinds of critical writing, ranging in form from the brief review to the scholarly exegesis. Essays are selected by the editors to reflect the spectrum of opinion about a specific work or about an author's literary career in general. The excerpts are presented chronologically, adding a useful perspective to the entry. All titles by the author featured in the entry are printed in boldface type, which enables the reader to easily identify the works being discussed. Publication information (such as publisher names and book prices) and parenthetical numerical references (such as footnotes or page and line references to specific editions of a work) have been deleted at the editor's discretion to provide smoother reading of the text.

• A complete **bibliographical citation** designed to help the user find the original essay or book follows each excerpt.

• A **further reading** section appears at the end of entries on authors who have generated a significant amount of criticism other than the pieces reprinted in *CLC.* In some cases, it includes references to material for which the editors could not obtain reprint rights.

## Other Features

• An **Acknowledgments** section lists the copyright holders who have granted permission to reprint material in this volume of *CLC.* It does not, however, list every book or periodical reprinted or consulted during the preparation of the volume.

• A **Cumulative Author Index** lists all the authors who have appeared in the various literary criticism series published by Gale Research, with cross-references to Gale's biographical and autobiographical series. A full listing of the series referenced in the index appears on page 465 of this volume. Readers will welcome this cumulated author index as a useful tool for locating an author within the various series. The index, which lists birth and death dates when available, will be particularly valuable for those authors who are identified with a certain period but whose death date causes them to be placed in another, or for those authors whose careers span two periods. For example, Ernest Hemingway is found in *CLC,* yet a writer often associated with him, F. Scott Fitzgerald, is found in *Twentieth-Century Literary Criticism.*

• A **Cumulative Nationality Index** alphabetically lists all authors featured in *CLC* by nationality, followed by numbers corresponding to the volumes in which they appear.

• A **Title Index** alphabetically lists all titles reviewed in the current volume of *CLC.* Listings are followed by the author's name and the corresponding page numbers where the titles are discussed. English translations of foreign titles and variations of titles are cross-referenced to the title under which a work was originally published. Titles of novels, novellas, dramas, films, record albums, and poetry, short story, and essay collections are printed in italics, while all individual poems, short stories, essays, and songs are printed in roman type within quotation marks; when published separately (e.g., T.S. Eliot's poem *The Waste Land* ), the title will also be printed in italics.

• In response to numerous suggestions from librarians, Gale has also produced a **special paperbound edition** of the *CLC* title index. This annual cumulation, which alphabetically lists all titles reviewed in the series, is available to all customers and will be published with the first volume of *CLC* issued in each calendar year. Additional copies of the index are available upon request. Librarians and patrons will welcome this separate index: it saves shelf space, is easy to use, and is disposable upon receipt of the following year's cumulation.

## A Note to the Reader

When writing papers, students who quote directly from any volume in the Literary Criticism Series may use the following general forms to footnote reprinted criticism. The first example pertains to material drawn from periodicals, the second to material reprinted from books:

[1]Anne Tyler, "Manic Monologue," *The New Republic* 200 (April 17, 1989), 44-6; excerpted and

reprinted in *Contemporary Literary Criticism,* Vol. 58, ed. Roger Matuz (Detroit: Gale Research, 1990), p. 325.

[2]Patrick Reilly, *The Literature of Guilt: From 'Gulliver' to Golding* (University of Iowa Press, 1988); excerpted and reprinted in *Contemporary Literary Criticism,* Vol. 58, ed. Roger Matuz (Detroit: Gale Research, 1990), pp. 206-12.

## Suggestions Are Welcome

The editors welcome the comments and suggestions of readers to expand the coverage and enhance the usefulness of the series.

# ACKNOWLEDGMENTS

The editors wish to thank the copyright holders of the excerpted criticism included in this volume, the permissions managers of many book and magazine publishing companies for assisting us in securing reprint rights, and Anthony Bogucki for assistance with copyright research. We are also grateful to the staffs of the Detroit Public Library, Wayne State University Purdy/Kresge Library Complex, and the University of Michigan Libraries for making their resources available to us. Following is a list of the copyright holders who have granted us permission to reprint material in this volume of *CLC*. Every effort has been made to trace copyright, but if omissions have been made, please let us know.

## COPYRIGHTED EXCERPTS IN *CLC*, VOLUME 64, WERE REPRINTED FROM THE FOLLOWING PERIODICALS:

*America*, v. 161, November 25, 1989 for a review of "On the River Styx" by Andre Dubus, III. © 1989. All rights reserved. Reprinted by permission of the author./ v. 126, February 19, 1972. © 1972. All rights reserved. Reprinted with permission of American Press, Inc., 106 West 56th Street, New York, NY 10019.—*The American Book Review*, v. 12, March-April, 1990. © 1990 by *The American Book Review*. Reprinted by permission of the publisher.— *American Literature*, v. 47, November, 1975; v. 51, March, 1979. Copyright © 1975, 1979 Duke University Press, Durham, NC. Both reprinted with permission of the publisher.—*The American Poetry Review*, v. 19, May-June, 1990 for "Sacred Days: The Collected Poems of Philip Larkin" by Elizabeth Spires. Copyright © 1990 by World Poetry, Inc. Reprinted by permission of the author.—*The American Spectator*, v. 15, January, 1982. Copyright © *The American Spectator* 1982. Reprinted by permission of the publisher.—*The Annals of the American Academy of Political and Social Science*, v. 376, March, 1968 for "Attitudes Toward Sex in American 'High Culture' " by Robert Boyers. © 1968, by The American Academy of Political and Social Science. Reprinted by permission of the publisher and the author.—*The Antioch Review*, v. 24, Summer, 1964. Copyright © 1964 by the Antioch Review Inc. Reprinted by permission of the Editors.—*The Atlantic Monthly*, v. 227, March, 1971 for "The Peripatetic Reviewer" by Edward Weeks; v. 202, September, 1958 for a review of "Lolita" by Charles Rolo. Copyright 1971; 1958, renewed 1986 by The Atlantic Monthly Company, Boston, MA. Both reprinted by permission of the Literary Estates of the respective authors.—*Ball State University Forum*, v. XXVII, Winter, 1986. © 1986 Ball State University. Reprinted by permission of the publisher.—*Belles Lettres: A Review of Books by Women*, v. 5, Summer, 1990. Reprinted by permission of the publisher.—*Best Sellers*, v. 41, November, 1981. Copyright © 1981 Helen Dwight Reid Educational Foundation. Reprinted by permission of the publisher.—*Black American Literature Forum*, v. 17, Fall, 1983 for "Displacement and Autobiographical Style in Maya Angelou's 'The Heart of a Woman' " by Carol E. Neubauer. Copyright © 1983 Indian State University. Reprinted by permission of *Black American Literature Forum* and the author.—*The Bloomsbury Review*, v. 10, May-June, 1990 for a review of "On the River Styx and Other Stories" by Paul W. Rea; v. 10, September-October, 1990 for "A Life Reimagined" by Tim McNulty. Copyright © by Owaissa Communications Company, Inc. 1990. Both reprinted by permission of the respective authors.—*Book World—The Washington Post*, September 22, 1968. © 1968 Postrib Corp. Reprinted by courtesy of the *Chicago Tribune* and *The Washington Post*./July 25, 1976; June 19, 1977; April 19, 1981; September 30, 1984; November 3, 1985; May 11, 1986; June 29, 1986; January 4, 1987; February 14, 1988; January 22, 1989; April 30, 1989; May 7, 1989; March 25, 1990. © 1976, 1977, 1981, 1984, 1985, 1986, 1987, 1988, 1989, 1990, *The Washington Post*. All reprinted by permission of the publisher.—*Books*, New York, February 25, 1962. © 1962 I.H.T. Corporation. Reprinted by permission of the publisher.—*Books in Canada*, v. 9, April, 1980 for "Where Have All Deflowerers Gone?" by I. M. Owen; v. 19, August-September, 1990 for "The Soul of Russia" by Al Purdy. Both reprinted by permission of the respective authors.—*Boston Review*, v. X, December, 1985 for a review of "Back in the World" by Matthew Gilbert. Copyright © 1985 by the Boston Critic, Inc. Reprinted by permission of the author.—*British Book News*, February, 1984. © *British Book News*, 1984. Courtesy of *British Book News*.— *Canadian Literature*, n. 60, Spring, 1974 for "Rationality in Mind" by Pat Barclay; n. 71, Winter, 1976 for "A Better Hard Centre" by Francis Mansbridge; n. 89, Summer, 1981 for "Assembly Line Stories: Pastiche in Sylvia Fraser's 'The Candy Factory' "by Lorna Irvine; n. 107, Winter, 1985 for "Cold War" by R. B. Hatch. All reprinted by permission of the respective authors.—*The CEA Critic*, v. 45, March-May, 1983. Copyright © 1983 by the College English Association, Inc. Reprinted by permission of the publisher.—*Chicago Tribune—Books*, January 18, 1987 for "In Doris Grumbach's Novel, to Be Human Is to Be a Freak" by David Holahan; November 8, 1987 for "Rollicking 'Oranges' Uses Its Daring Humor to Get Religion" by Joseph Olshan; January 22, 1989 for "Seeking A Self" by Richard Russo. © copyrighted 1987, 1989, Chicago Tribune Company. All rights reserved. All reprinted by permission of the respective authors./June 25, 1989; April 1, 1990. © copyrighted 1989, 1990, Chicago Tribune Company. All rights reserved. Both used with permission.—*The Christian Science Monitor*, February 26, 1987

## COPYRIGHTED EXCERPTS IN *CLC,* VOLUME 64, WERE REPRINTED FROM THE FOLLOWING BOOKS:

**PHOTOGRAPHS APPEARING IN *CLC*, VOLUME 64, WERE RECEIVED FROM THE FOLLOWING SOURCES:**

# Anna Akhmatova

## 1889-1966

(Pseudonym of Anna Andreevna Gorenko; also transliterated as Anna Axmatova.) Russian poet, translator, and essayist.

Akhmatova is considered one of the finest Russian poets of the twentieth century for her poetic range, technical skill, and her artistic and personal integrity. A founding member of the Acmeists—writers who attempted to restore clarity to poetic language and who utilized ordinary objects and events of daily life for their subject— Akhmatova wrote poetry distinguished by concrete imagery and simple language. Her early volumes contain brief, intimate lyrics that often present the trials of unhappy love. Akhmatova's most frequent subjects include the passage of time, loss, emotional vicissitudes, regret, and nostalgia. Although her *oeuvre* is considered consistently mature, in each successive early volume Akhmatova's tone became more weighty and dignified as the effects of the First World War and then the Russian Revolution entered her poetic consciousness. Akhmatova garnered both popular and critical acclaim for rendering these and other representative experiences in personal terms, and for creating a unique blend of sonorous traditional rhythms, meters, and forms. Sam Driver acknowledged: "Much of the stir caused by [Akhmatova's poetry] derived precisely from the tension between the very ordinaryness of the settings and diction on the one hand and the sophistication in rhythms and sound patterning on the other."

Akhmatova was born in a coastal town off the Black Sea. She moved with her family at a young age to Tsarskoye Selo, or Czar's Village, near St. Petersburg, where she was raised. Akhmatova began writing poetry after surviving a mysterious illness that nearly killed her as a young girl. She became friends with Nikolai Gumilyov, a young poet who later helped form the Acmeist group and became one of its most eloquent spokespersons. Gumilyov's teacher at the Tsarskoye Selo Boys' Academy was Innokenty Annensky, a scholar of Greek whose posthumous collection *The Cypress Chest* greatly influenced both young poets. Gumilyov and Akhmatova were married in 1910, and Akhmatova gave birth to a son, Lev, in 1912. The marriage was unhappy, however, and the couple spent much time apart as he travelled in Africa and she in Europe. Akhmatova and Gumilyov were divorced in 1918. Akhmatova's early collections of poetry, notably, *Vecher, Chyotki,* and *Belaya staya* (*The White Flock*), contain lyric self-portraits and personal reflections on love and love's sorrows. As war and revolution spread through Russia, Akhmatova wrote of both her own losses and those suffered by all Russian people. By 1917, the year of publication of *The White Flock,* the occasional religious imagery of the earlier volumes predominates as Akhmatova's persona prays for an end to the cataclysms of war.

Akhmatova's next collections, including *Podorozhnik* and

*Anno Domini MCMXXI,* drew unfavorable commentary from Soviet government officials. Her high status before the Revolution and the grave, mournful tone of pieces bewailing the death, poverty, and fear of wartime put her at odds with the demands of the state for uplifting, public-spirited art. An unofficial ban on the publication of her works went into effect in 1925. Although Akhmatova continued to write poetry, to translate verse, and to publish critical essays on the Russian poet Aleksander Pushkin after the ban went into effect, she did not publish another collection of original verse until *Iz shesti knig* appeared in 1940. In this period of relative silence she suffered great personal tragedy; she lost many friends to Stalin's persecution and death camps, and her son was repeatedly arrested. Much of Akhmatova's work of this period existed for years only in the poet's memory. These verses reflect her anguish over her misfortunes and the changes that time and history had wrought upon her country.

From the beginning of her career through the 1950s and '60s, Akhmatova's reputation was based almost solely on the love lyrics she composed in her youth. Since her gradual rehabilitation by the state following the death of Stalin in 1953, a concerted effort has been made to publish the entirety of her works and to trace her innovations through critical studies. Her current reputation rests primarily on the lengthy poem sequences *Rekviem: Tsikl stikhotvorenii* and *Poema bez geroya: Triptykh (Poem without a Hero: Triptych)*. *Rekviem* comprises short poems that form a kind of narrative alluding to the Crucifixion. On a more literal level, these poems record Akhmatova's feelings and, by extension, those of her fellow citizens, who too were notified of the arrest, sentencing, imprisonment and exile of loved ones. Some of the most moving of these verses concern the fate of those women who waited outside the gates of the state prisons for months on end, hoping to see, and to pass some food or clothing to their sons and husbands. *Rekviem* is honored for its grave and majestic tone, which stems from Akhmatova's subtle, complex rhythms. John Bayley commented: "In her long poem sequences, Akhmatova uses meters of great robustness and subtlety in the Russian which when transposed into English can often sound all too like Shelley or Poe at their most ebullient. The strong accents and stresses of Russian have a variety and flexibility that iron out a regular beat that would otherwise dominate the more docile English syllables."

Beginning in 1940, Akhmatova composed and revised *Poema Bez Geroya (Poem without a Hero)* over the course of two decades. *Poem without a Hero* is more elaborately conceived than any of Akhmatova's earlier works and features a cast of masked party-goers—a fictional premise more common to the works of the Symbolists of Akhmatova's youth than to those of the Acmeists. Set in 1913, the poem takes as its catalyst the suicide of a callow young officer who despairs when his beloved takes another man as her lover. Akhmatova invests this incident from her youth with forebodings of the senseless brutality of the war, revolution, and civil strife that successively struck Russia beginning in 1914. Peter France remarked: "In [*Poem without a Hero*, Akhmatova] looks back from the 'high tower of the year 1940' to what has become a remote past, conjuring up images of the dead and seeking to exorcise her own sense of guilt. . . . It is a magnificent achievement."

(See also *CLC*, Vols. 11, 25; *Contemporary Authors*, Vols. 17-20 rev. ed. and Vols. 25-28, [obituary]; and *Contemporary Authors Permanent Series*, Vol. 1.)

## PRINCIPAL WORKS

*Vecher*   1912
*Chetki*   1914
*Belaya Staya*   1917
   [*The White Flock*,   1978]
*U Samovo Morya*   1921
*Podorozhnik*   1921
*Anno Domini MCMXXI*   1923
*Forty-Seven Love Songs*   1927
*Iz Shesti Knig*   1940
*Stikhotyoreniya, 1909-1957*   1958
*Poema Bez Geroya: Triptykh*   1960
   [*A Poem without a Hero*,   1973]
*Stikhi, 1909-1960*   1961
*Collected Poems: 1912-1963*   1963

*Rekviem: Tsikl Stikhotvorenii*   1964
*Poeziya*   1964
*Beg Vremeni*   1965
*Stikhotvoreniia, 1909-1965*   1965
*Sochineniya*. 2 vols.   1965, 1968
*Selected Poems*   1969
*Poems of Akhmatova*   1973
*Tale without a Hero and Twenty-two Poems by Anna Akhmatova*   1973
*Requiem and Poem without a Hero*   1976
*Selected Poems*   1976
*Way of All the Earth*   1979
*Anna Akhmatova: Poems*   1983
*Sochineniia v dvukh tomakh*. 2 vols.   1986
*Poems*   1988
*Severnye elegii: stikhotvoreniia, poety, o poetakh*   1989
*The Complete Poems of Anna Akhmatova*. 2 vols.   1990

## Joseph Brodsky

[*The essay excerpted below was originally published in 1983 as the Introduction to* Anna Akhmatova: Poems.]

When her father learned that his daughter was about to publish a selection of her poems in a St. Petersburg magazine, he called her in and told her that although he had nothing against her writing poetry, he'd urge her "not to befoul a good respected name" and to use a pseudonym. The daughter agreed, and this is how "Anna Akhmatova" entered Russian literature instead of Anna Gorenko.

The reason for this acquiescence was neither uncertainty about the elected occupation and her actual gifts nor anticipation of the benefits that a split identity can provide a writer. It was done simply for the sake of "maintaining appearances," because among families belonging to the nobility—and the Gorenkos were one—the literary profession was generally regarded as somewhat unseemly and befitting those of more humble origins who didn't have a better way of making a name.

Still, the father's request was a bit of an overstatement. After all, the Gorenkos weren't princes. But then again the family lived in Tsarskoe Selo—Tsar's Village—which was the summer residence of the imperial family, and this sort of topography could have influenced the man. For his seventeen-year-old daughter, however, the place had a different significance. Tsarskoe was the seat of the Lyceum in whose gardens a century ago "carelessly blossomed" young Pushkin.

As for the pseudonym itself, its choice had to do with the maternal ancestry of Anna Gorenko, which could be traced back to the last khan of the Golden Horde: to Achmat Khan, descendant of Jenghiz Khan. "I am a Jenghizite," she used to remark not without a touch of pride; and for a Russian ear "Akhmatova" has a distinct Oriental, Tatar to be precise, flavor. She didn't mean to be exotic, though, if only because in Russia a name with a Tatar overtone meets not curiosity but prejudice.

All the same, the five open *a*'s of Anna Akhmatova had a hypnotic effect and put this name's carrier firmly at the top of the alphabet of Russian poetry. In a sense, it was her first successful line; memorable in its acoustic inevitability, with its *Ah* sponsored less by sentiment than by history. This tells you a lot about the intuition and quality of the ear of this seventeen-year-old girl who soon after her first publication began to sign her letters and legal papers as Anna Akhmatova. In its suggestion of identity derived from the fusion of sound and time, the choice of the pseudonym turned out to be prophetic.

Anna Akhmatova belongs to the category of poets who have neither genealogy nor discernible "development." She is the kind of poet that simply "happens"; that arrives in the world with an already established diction and his/her own unique sensibility. She came fully equipped, and she never resembled anyone. What was perhaps more significant is that none of her countless imitators was ever capable of producing a convincing Akhmatova pastiche either; they'd end up resembling one another more than her. (pp. 34-5)

Akhmatova is the poet of strict meters, exact rhymes, and short sentences. Her syntax is simple and free of subordinate clauses whose gnomic convolutions are responsible for most of Russian literature; in fact, in its simplicity, her syntax resembles English. From the very threshold of her career to its very end she was always perfectly clear and coherent. Among her contemporaries, she is a Jane Austen. In any case, if her sayings were dark, it wasn't due to her grammar.

In an era marked by so much technical experimentation in poetry, she was blatantly non-avant-garde. If anything, her means were visually similar to what prompted that wave of innovations in Russian poetry, as everywhere else, at the turn of the century: to the Symbolists' quatrains, ubiquitous as grass. Yet this visual resemblance was maintained by Akhmatova deliberately: through it she sought not the simplification of her task but a worsening of the odds. She simply wanted to play the game straight, without bending or inventing the rules. In short, she wanted her verse to maintain appearances.

Nothing reveals a poet's weaknesses like classical verse, and that's why it's so universally dodged. To make a couple of lines sound unpredictable without producing a comic effect or echoing someone else is an extremely perplexing affair. This echo aspect of strict meters is most nagging, and no amount of oversaturating the line with concrete physical detail sets one free. Akhmatova sounds so independent because from the outset she knew how to exploit the enemy.

She did it by a collage-like diversification of the content. Often within just one stanza she'd cover a variety of seemingly unrelated things. When a person talks in the same breath about the gravity of her emotion, gooseberry blossoms, and pulling the left-hand glove onto her right hand—that compromises the breath—which is, in the poem, its meter—to the degree that one forgets about its pedigree. The echo, in other words, gets subordinated to the discrepancy of objects and in effect provides them with a common denominator; it ceases to be a form and becomes a norm of locution.

Sooner or later this always happens to the echo as well as to the diversity of things themselves—in Russian verse it was done by Akhmatova; more exactly, by that self which bore her name. One can't help thinking that while its inner part hears what, by means of rhyme, the language itself suggests about the proximity of those disparate objects, the outer one literally sees that proximity from the vantage point of her actual height. She simply couples what has been already joined: in the language and in the circumstances of her life, if not, as they say, in heaven.

Hence the nobility of her diction, for she doesn't lay claim to her discoveries. Her rhymes are not assertive, the meter is not insistent. Sometimes she'd drop a syllable or two in a stanza's last or penultimate line in order to create the effect of a choked throat, or that of unwitting awkwardness caused by emotional tension. But that would be as far as she'd go, for she felt very much at home within the confines of classical verse, thereby suggesting that her raptures and revelations don't require an extraordinary formal treatment, that they are not any greater than those of her predecessors who used these meters before. (pp. 36-8)

If Akhmatova was reticent, it was at least partly because she was carrying the heritage of her predecessors into the art of this century. This obviously was but an homage to them, since it was precisely that heritage which made her this century's poet. She simply regarded herself, with her raptures and revelations, as a postscript to their message, to what they recorded about their lives. The lives were tragic, and so was the message. If the postscript looks dark, it's because the message was absorbed fully. If she never screams or showers her head with ashes, it's because they didn't.

Such were the cue and the key with which she started. Her first collections were tremendously successful with both the critics and the public. In general, the response to a poet's work should be considered last, for it is a poet's last consideration. However, Akhmatova's success was in this respect remarkable if one takes into account its timing, especially in the case of her second and third volumes: 1914 (the outbreak of World War I) and 1917 (the October Revolution in Russia). On the other hand, perhaps it was precisely this deafening background thunder of world events that rendered the private tremolo of this young poet all the more discernible and vital. In that sense again, the beginning of this poetic career contained a prophecy of the course it came to run for half a century. What increases the sense of prophecy is that for a Russian ear at the time the thunder of world events was compounded by the incessant and quite meaningless mumbling of the Symbolists. Eventually these two noises shrunk and merged into the threatening incoherent drone of the new era against which Akhmatova was destined to speak for the rest of her life.

Those early collections (***Evening, Rosary,*** and ***White Flock***) dealt mostly with the sentiment which is *de rigueur* for early collections; with that of love. The poems in those books had a diary-like intimacy and immediacy; they'd describe no more than one actual or psychological event and were short—sixteen to twenty lines at best. As such they could be committed to memory in a flash, as indeed they were—and still are—by generations and generations of Russians.

Still, it was neither their compactness nor their subject matter that made one's memory desire to appropriate them; those features were quite familiar to an experienced reader. The news came in the form of a sensibility which manifested itself in the author's treatment of her theme. Betrayed, tormented by either jealousy or guilt, the wounded heroine of these poems speaks more frequently in self-reproach than in anger, forgives more eloquently than accuses, prays rather than screams. She displays all the emotional subtlety and psychological complexity of nineteenth-century Russian prose and all the dignity that the poetry of the same century taught her. Apart from these, there is also a great deal of irony and detachment which are strictly her own and products of her metaphysics rather than shortcuts to resignation. (pp. 39-40)

The intensely personal lyricism of **White Flock** is tinged with the note that was destined to become her imprimatur: the note of controlled terror. The mechanism designed to keep in check emotions of a romantic nature proved to be as effective when applied to mortal fears. The latter was increasingly intertwined with the former until they resulted in emotional tautology, and **White Flock** marks the beginning of this process. With this collection, Russian poetry hit "the real, non-calendar twentieth century" but didn't disintegrate on impact. (p. 41)

She remained true to her diction, to its private timbre, to refracting rather than reflecting life through the prism of the individual heart. Except that the choice of detail whose role in a poem previously was to shift attention from an emotionally pregnant issue presently began to be less and less of a solace, overshadowing the issue itself.

She didn't reject the Revolution: a defiant pose wasn't for her either. Using latter-day locution, she internalized it. She simply took it for what it was: a terrible national upheaval which meant a tremendous increase of grief per individual. She understood this not only because her own share went too high but first and foremost through her very craft. The poet is a born democrat not thanks to the precariousness of his position only but because he caters to the entire nation and employs its language. So does tragedy, and hence their affinity. Akhmatova, whose verse always gravitated to the vernacular, to the idiom of folk song, could identify with the people more thoroughly than those who were pushing at the time their literary or other programs: she simply recognized grief.

Moreover, to say that she identified with the people is to introduce a rationalization which never took place because of its inevitable redundancy. She was a part of the whole, and the pseudonym just furthered her class anonymity. In addition, she always disdained the air of superiority present in the word "poet." "I don't understand these big words," she used to say, "poet, billiard." This wasn't humility; this was the result of the sober perspective in which she kept her existence. The very persistence of love as the theme of her poetry indicates her proximity

to the average person. If she differed from her public it was in that her ethics weren't subject to historical adjustment. (pp. 41-2)

In any case, there is no psychological difference between Akhmatova's "civic" poems of World War I and the revolutionary period, and those written a good thirty years later during World War II. Indeed, without the date underneath them, poems like **"Prayer"** could be attributed to virtually any moment of Russian history in this century which justifies that particular poem's title. Apart from the sensitivity of her membrane, though, this proves that the quality of history for the last eighty years has somewhat simplified the poet's job. It did so to the degree that a poet would spurn a line containing a prophetic possibility and prefer a plain description of a fact or sensation.

Hence the nominative character of Akhmatova's lines in general and at that period in particular. She knew not only that the emotions and perceptions she dealt with were fairly common but also that time, true to its repetitive nature, would render them universal. She sensed that history, like its objects, has very limited options. What was more important, however, was that those "civic" poems were but fragments borne by her general lyrical current, which made their "we" practically indistinguishable from the more frequent, emotionally charged "I." Because of their over-lapping, both pronouns were gaining in verisimilitude. Since the name of the current was "love," the poems about the homeland and the epoch were shot through with almost inappropriate intimacy; similarly, those about sentiment itself were acquiring an epic timbre. The latter meant the current's widening.

Later in her life, Akhmatova always resented attempts by critics and scholars to confine her significance to her love poetry of the teens of this century. She was perfectly right, because the output of the subsequent forty years outweighs her first decade both numerically and qualitatively. Still, one can understand those scholars and critics, since after 1922 until her death in 1966 Akhmatova simply couldn't publish a book of her own, and they were forced to deal with what was available. (pp. 43-4)

Akhmatova's love poems, naturally, were in the first place just poems. Apart from anything else, they had a terrific novelistic quality, and a reader could have had a wonderful time explicating the various tribulations and trials of their heroine. (Some did just that, and on the basis of those poems, the heated public imagination would have their author "romantically involved" with Alexander Blok—the poet of the period—as well as with His Imperial Majesty himself, although she was a far better poet than the former and a good six inches taller than the latter.) Half self-portrait, half mask, their poetic persona would augment an actual drama with the fatality of theater, thus probing both her own and pain's possible limits. Happier states would be subjected to the same probing. Realism, in short, was employed as the means of transportation to a metaphysical destination. Still, all this would have amounted to animating the genre's tradition were it not for the sheer quantity of poems dealing with the said sentiment.

That quantity denies both biographical and Freudian approaches, for it overshoots the addressees' concreteness and renders them as pretexts for the author's speech. What art and sexuality have in common is that both are sublimations of one's creative energy, and that denies them hierarchy. The nearly idiosyncratic persistence of the early Akhmatova love poems suggests not so much the recurrence of passion as the frequency of prayer. Correspondingly, different though their imagined or real protagonists are, these poems display a considerable stylistic similarity because love as content is in the habit of limiting formal patterns. The same goes for faith. After all, there are only so many adequate manifestations for truly strong sentiments: which, in the end, is what explains rituals.

It is the finite's nostalgia for the infinite that accounts for the recurrence of the love theme in Akhmatova's verse, not the actual entanglements. Love indeed has become for her a language, a code to record time's messages or, at least, to convey their tune; she simply heard them better this way. For what interested this poet most was not her own life but precisely time and the effects of its monotone on the human psyche and on her own diction in particular. If she later resented attempts to reduce her to her early writing, it was not because she disliked the status of the habitually love-sick girl: it was because her diction and, with it, the code, subsequently changed a great deal in order to make the monotone of the infinite more audible.

In fact, it was already quite distinct in *Anno Domini MCMXXI*—her fifth and technically speaking last collection. In some of its poems, that monotone merges with the author's voice to the point that she has to sharpen the concreteness of detail or image in order to save them, and by the same token her own mind, from the inhuman neutrality of the meter. Their fusion, or rather the former's subordination to the latter, came later. In the meantime, she was trying to save her own notions of existence from being overtaken by those supplied to her by prosody: for prosody knows more about time than a human being would like to reckon with.

Close exposure to this knowledge, or more accurately to this memory of time restructured, results in an inordinate mental acceleration that robs insights that come from the actual reality of their novelty, if not of their gravity. No poet can ever close this gap, but a conscientious one may lower his pitch or muffle his diction so as to downplay his estrangement from real life. This is done sometimes for purely aesthetic purposes: to make one's voice less theatrical, less *bel canto*-like. More frequently, though, the purpose of this camouflage is, again, to retain sanity, and Akhmatova, a poet of strict meters, was using it precisely to that end. But the more she did so, the more inexorably her voice was approaching the impersonal tonality of time itself, until they merged into something that makes one shudder trying to guess—as in her **"Northern Elegies"**— who is hiding behind the pronoun "I."

What happened to pronouns was happening to other parts of speech, which would peter out or loom large in the perspective of time supplied by prosody. Akhmatova was a very concrete poet, but the more concrete the image, the more extemporary it would become because of the accompanying meter. No poem is ever written for its story line's

sake only, just as no life is lived for the sake of an obituary. What is called the music of a poem is essentially time restructured in such a way that it brings this poem's content into a linguistically inevitable, memorable focus.

Sound, in other words, is the seat of time in the poem, a background against which its content acquires a stereoscopic quality. The power of Akhmatova's lines comes from her ability to convey the music's impersonal epic sweep, which more than matched their actual content, especially from the twenties on. The effect of her instrumentation upon her themes was akin to that of somebody used to being put against the wall being suddenly put against the horizon. (pp. 44-7)

*Anno Domini MCMXXI* was her last collection: in the forty-four years that followed she had no book of her own. In the postwar period there were, technically speaking, two slim editions of her work, consisting mainly of a few reprinted early lyrics plus genuinely patriotic war poems and doggerel bits extolling the arrival of peace. These last ones were written by her in order to win the release of her son from the labor camps, in which he nonetheless spent eighteen years. These publications in no way can be regarded as her own, for the poems were selected by the editors of the state-run publishing house and their aim was to convince the public (especially those abroad) that Akhmatova was alive, well, and loyal. They totaled some fifty pieces and had nothing in common with her output during those four decades.

For a poet of Akhmatova's stature this meant being buried alive, with a couple of slabs marking the mound. Her going under was a product of several forces, mostly that of history, whose chief element is vulgarity and whose immediate agent is the state. Now, by MCMXXI, which means 1921, the new state could already be at odds with Akhmatova, whose first husband, poet Nikolai Gumilyov, was executed by its security forces, allegedly on the direct order of the state's head, Vladimir Lenin. A spin-off of a didactic, eye-for-eye mentality, the new state could expect from Akhmatova nothing but retaliation, especially given her reputed tendency for an autobiographical touch.

Such was, presumably, the state's logic, furthered by the destruction in the subsequent decade and a half of her entire circle (including her closest friends, poets Vladimir Narbut and Osip Mandelstam). It culminated in the arrests of her son, Lev Gumilyov, and her third husband, art-historian Nikolai Punin, who soon died in prison. Then came World War II.

Those fifteen years preceding the war were perhaps the darkest in the whole of Russian history; undoubtedly they were so in Akhmatova's own life. It's the material which this period supplied, or more accurately the lives it subtracted, that made her eventually earn the title of the Keening Muse. This period simply replaced the frequency of poems about love with that of poems in memoriam. Death, which she would previously evoke as a solution for this or that emotional tension, became too real for any emotion to matter. From a figure of speech it became a figure that leaves you speechless.

If she proceeded to write, it's because prosody absorbs

death, and because she felt guilty that she survived. The pieces that constitute her **"Wreath for the Dead"** are simply attempts to let those whom she outlived absorb or at least join prosody. It's not that she tried to "immortalize" her dead: most of them were the pride of Russian literature already and thus had immortalized themselves enough. She simply tried to manage the meaninglessness of existence, which suddenly gaped before her because of the destruction of the sources of its meaning, to domesticate the reprehensible infinity by inhabiting it with familiar shadows. Besides, addressing the dead was the only way of preventing speech from slipping into a howl.

The elements of howl, however, are quite audible in other Akhmatova poems of the period and later. They'd appear either in the form of idiosyncratic excessive rhyming or as a non sequitur line interjected in an otherwise coherent narrative. Nevertheless, the poems dealing directly with someone's death are free of anything of this sort, as though the author doesn't want to offend her addressees with her emotional extremes. This refusal to exploit the ultimate opportunity to impose herself upon them echoes, of course, the practice of her lyric poetry. But by continuing to address the dead as though they were alive, by not adjusting her diction to "the occasion," she also refuses the opportunity to exploit the dead as those ideal, absolute interlocutors that every poet seeks and finds either in the dead or among angels.

As a theme, death is a good litmus test for a poet's ethics. The "in memoriam" genre is frequently used to exercise self-pity or for metaphysical trips that denote the subconscious superiority of survivor over victim, of majority (of the alive) over minority (of the dead). Akhmatova would have none of that. She particularizes her fallen instead of generalizing about them, since she writes for a minority with which it's easier for her to identify in any case. She simply continues to treat them as individuals whom she knew and who, she senses, wouldn't like to be used as the point of departure for no matter how spectacular a destination.

Naturally enough, poems of this sort couldn't be published, nor could they even be written down or retyped. They could only be memorized by the author and by some seven other people, since she didn't trust her own memory. From time to time, she'd meet a person privately and would ask him or her to recite quietly this or that selection as a means of inventory. This precaution was far from being excessive: people would disappear forever for smaller things than a piece of paper with a few lines on it. Besides, she feared not so much for her own life as for that of her son, who was in a camp and whose release she desperately tried to obtain for eighteen years. A little piece of paper with a few lines on it could cost a lot, and more to him than to her, who could lose only hope and, perhaps, mind.

The days of both, however, would have been numbered had the authorities found her **Requiem,** a cycle of poems describing the ordeal of a woman whose son is arrested and who waits under prison walls with a parcel for him and scurries about the thresholds of state offices to find out about his fate. Now, this time around she was autobio-

graphical indeed, yet the power of **Requiem** lies in the fact that Akhmatova's biography was all too common. This requiem mourns the mourners: mothers losing sons, wives turning widows, sometimes both, as was the author's case. This is a tragedy where the chorus perishes before the hero.

The degree of compassion with which the various voices of **Requiem** are rendered can be explained only by the author's Orthodox faith; the degree of understanding and forgiveness which accounts for this work's piercing, almost unbearable lyricism, only by the uniqueness of her heart, her self, and this self's sense of time. No creed would help to understand, much less forgive, let alone survive this double widowhood at the hands of the regime, this fate of her son, these forty years of being silenced and ostracized. No Anna Gorenko would be able to take it. Anna Akhmatova did, and it's as though she knew what was in store when she took this pen name.

At certain periods of history it is only poetry that is capable of dealing with reality by condensing it into something graspable, something that otherwise couldn't be retained by the mind. In that sense, the whole nation took up the pen name of Akhmatova—which explains her popularity and which, more importantly, enabled her to speak for the nation as well as to tell it something it didn't know. She was, essentially, a poet of human ties: cherished, strained, severed. She showed these evolutions first through the prism of the individual heart, then through the prism of history, such as it was. This is about as much as one gets in the way of optics anyway.

These two perspectives were brought into sharp focus through prosody, which is simply a repository of time within language. Hence, by the way, her ability to forgive—because forgiveness is not a virtue postulated by creed but a property of time in both its mundane and metaphysical senses. This is also why her verses are to survive whether published or not: because of the prosody, because they are charged with time in both those senses. They will survive because language is older than state and because prosody always survives history. In fact, it hardly needs history; all it needs is a poet, and Akhmatova was just that. (pp. 48-52)

*Joseph Brodsky, "The Keening Muse," in his* Less than One: Selected Essays, *Farrar, Straus and Giroux, 1986, pp. 34-52.*

### David McDuff

Born in 1889 in a Black Sea coastal town, one of five children of a naval engineer, [Anna Gorenko] had been taken by her family at the age of eleven months first to Pavlovsk, then to Tsarskoye Selo. When Anna was five, her sister Rika, one year younger than herself, died of tuberculosis. At the age of ten, Anna herself became seriously ill, though the doctors were unable to find the reason for the illness. It was after this illness that she began to write poetry. By the time she was thirteen she had learned French and was already familiar with the poetry of Baudelaire and Verlaine, as well as with that of many of the "Parnassians and *poètes maudits*". . . . At about this time she befriended another young poet, three years older than herself, Nikolay Gumilyov; Gumilyov had attended the Tsarskoye Selo Men's Academy, where one of his teachers was Innokenty Annensky. Gumilyov, who shared Anna's passion for French Symbolist poetry, fell in love with her, casting her in the role of mermaid and tragic princess as a foil to his own poetic persona of "conquistador" and romantic visionary.

In January 1905 the Gorenkos were shaken by the news of the destruction of the entire Russian fleet by the Japanese at Tsushima. The disaster made a particularly deep impression on Anna; she described it later as "a shock to last one's whole lifetime." At Easter of the same year Gumilyov tried to kill himself in despair at her refusal to take his love for her seriously, and she broke off relations with him. In the summer her parents separated, and she was taken to the south of Russia by her mother. There this fateful year ended for her with the ominous and distant news of the abortive 1905 revolution. It was the year in which for the first time she experienced catastrophe on both a private and a public level and, as she studied for her final-year school exams, she began to write poetry in earnest.

In 1906, Anna Gorenko became Anna Akhmatova. During her lifetime, the poet herself gave several accounts of the events that led up to the choice of this pseudonym. Some aspects of those events remain unclear, however, and they are still surrounded by a certain enigma. The most straightforward version of the story is that Anna's father objected to her using the family name to sign her "decadent" poems, as he feared it might bring it into disrepute. His daughter bowed to this objection, and went in search of a pseudonym. In the end, she chose the family name of her Tatar great grandmother, which was also the name of the last Tatar princes of the Golden Horde. The story may not, however, have been quite as simple as this. Although there is no direct evidence that Annensky, another pseudonymous poet, was in any way directly involved in his pupil's choice of *nom de plume*, certain remarks she made in the course of her life lead one to suppose that this may in fact been the case. Annensky's significance for Akhmatova's development as a poet cannot be overestimated. His personality and writings together constituted the single most important influence on her poetic art. She considered him her "teacher" in every sense of the word. This is a fact that is sometimes ignored by students of her work, but it is one that repays attention. So strong was the link between these two poets that Akhmatova herself tended only to allude to it, out of a kind of emotional reserve: her poetry is filled with fleeting allusions to Annensky's poems; not surprisingly, her conversation also contained hints and clues that pointed to Annensky's role in her life as an artist. (pp. 55-7)

The year 1910 was a fateful one for Akhmatova. During it she made the first of several pre-World War I visits to Western Europe, and in particular to Paris, where she was to meet, among other people, the then unknown young painter Modigliani. (Two years later, partly as a result of Modigliani's influence, she would visit Northern Italy, where the impression she received from the medieval

painting and architecture was, in her own words, "like a dream you remember all your life.")

1910 also saw the release, by the Moscow publishing house *Grif,* of Annensky's posthumous collection *Kiparisovy larets—The Cypress Chest.* Akhmatova recalls coming back to St. Petersburg from Kiev with Gumilyov, whom she had finally consented to marry, in the spring of that year. Together the two poets paid a visit to the Russian Museum. Gumilyov had with him a set of the proofs of *The Cypress Chest.* He gave Akhmatova the poems of his former headmaster to read. She was stunned by them, and read the book right through there and then, in her own words "forgetting everything else in the world." (pp. 57-8)

Akhmatova's poetry proceeds directly from that of Annensky. In one sense her art may be said to represent a completion of Annensky's unfinished labor. Such a claim would be in keeping with a remark made by Akhmatova to Nikita Struve towards the end of her life: "Yes, Innokenty Annensky is an immense (*grandioznyy*) poet, we all came out of him. No one could come out of Blok, he was too complete. . . . " Or again, in a conversation with Lidiya Chukovskaya: "All the poets came out of him: Osip, Pasternak, myself, even Mayakovsky."

Histories of Russian literature generally tend toward the view that modern Russian poetry—and in particular the poetry of the famous "quartet" made up of Akhmatova, Mandelstam, Pasternak, and Tsvetayeva—took its origins in the various literary movements such as Symbolism, Acmeism, and Futurism that flourished in St. Petersburg and Moscow during the early years of this century. Although there is of course some truth in this assertion, it is misleading in that it distracts attention both from the essentially private, individual character of one important element in that poetry, and from the public, general, non-literary character of another of its constituents, an equally important one. The literary squabbling and programism that marked these now largely forgotten guilds and sodalities had in fact rather little to do with the mainstream development of Russian poetry. Much more important to that development was the confrontation between the traditions, literary and non-literary, of the Russian past, and the onslaught of the modern era, with its revolutions, labor camps, and sense of a moral abyss. In Annensky's poetry this conflict is already present in the form of a terrible presentiment sparked by the revolution of 1905. A similar intuition can be found in the poetry of Blok and some of the other symbolists: but nowhere in their poems is it coupled, as it is in Annensky's, with such a profound sense of the cultural and historical past, or with such a burden of guilt and uneasy conscience.

This is, I believe, one of the meanings of Akhmatova's statement that "we all came out of " Annensky. The statement is perhaps more true of herself and of Mandelstam than it is of Pasternak or Tsvetayeva. The latter were Muscovites, whereas Mandelstam, like Akhmatova, spent much of his youth in the vicinity of St. Petersburg. Annensky's poem *Peterburg,* first published in 1910, was the model for their own extensive treatment of this urban poetic genre, in which the image of stone, and stones, is inextricably linked with the name "Peter" in both its New Testament and its Russian historical contexts. The emphasis on stone is also linked to the unique circumstances of the city's inception, in particular the issuing of ukases by Peter forbidding the use of stone for building purposes anywhere else in Russia, and commanding all who entered the city to bring stones with them—these directives were seen at the time as a sinister attempt to play God and defy the dispositions of nature. Annensky's vision of the city is filled with a sense of foreboding and impending catastrophe. . . . (pp. 59-60)

Akhmatova, like Mandelstam, took from Annensky this essentially negative characterization of St. Petersburg and transformed it into the spiritual and psychological ambience of her poetry. The result is an architectural, lapidary, yet utterly simple verse, the ultimate concerns of which are ethical and moral. The plainness of style is matched by quiet, regular meters and rhymes. Once again it is the Verlainean *chanson grise* that comes to mind, but filtered through a Russian historical consciousness.

It is all too easy to read the early work of Akhmatova as "love poetry." Such was the temptation to weave imaginary romances around the poems of **Vecher (Evening)**, **Chyotki (Rosary)**, and **Belaya Staya (White Flock)** that early reviewers and commentators put all kinds of stories and rumors into circulation. The poems were assumed to refer not only to the poet's relations with Gumilyov, but also to supposed affairs with Aleksandr Blok and even with Tsar Nicholas II. Empty speculation of this kind ran rife among émigré literary circles in the years after the 1917 revolution, and for many years it made a proper assessment of Akhmatova's poetry from this period difficult, if not impossible. Fortunately, the poet was herself able eventually to put to rest most of the wilder rumors—indeed, since the publication of Lidiya Chukovskaya's extensive and valuable memoirs there is little or no room left for such imaginative exercises. While it is true that a small number of the early poems are addressed to Gumilyov, and that others contain references to Knyazev, Nedobrovo, Anrep, and other friends, Akhmatova's purpose is not to provide an open diary of her private emotional life. The *ty* ("thou") of these poems is not an individual human being—it is rather a blending of individual humanity with time, of the concrete and personal with the abstract and impersonal. Akhmatova conducts her conversation with time and destiny as though she were speaking to a being of flesh and blood that may also be something else—a fusion of identities that includes all "I's," one of the [*miriovooi*], the possessors of a myriad of souls, among which their own is lost. As Annensky expresses it at the beginning of his Dostoyevskian poem "The Double": "Not I, and not he, and not you, / And the same as I, yet not the same. . . . "

As in the case of Annensky, it is prose fiction and the condition of fictional characters that suggest themselves as a literary equivalent here. In particular, the techniques of Marcel Proust come to mind: again and again an event, a moment of psychological unease or of emotional nearness, is brought with great clarity before the all-seeing lens of the poet's memory. It is the details of the scene that re-

main—the people themselves have long since gone their separate ways:

> The final meeting: I stood on the road.
> The house was as dark as shame.
> Only in the bedroom, candles showed
> An indifferent yellow flame.
>             **("The Song of the Final Meeting")**

> How could I forget? He went out, reeling.
> His mouth dreadful, twisted, grim . . .
>             **("I pressed my hands together . . . ")**

In these poems what is important is not so much the actuality of the experience as its historicity, its association with an irrevocably vanished past. Many of the poems are written in the past tense, which accentuates the general sense of loss and muted grief. Even those written in the present tense have a curiously time-locked quality. The fisherman who makes the girl fishers blush belongs to the moment in which he is observed—he will go on fishing there, while the shoals of "fish" (the girls) pass on like the flowing of the river—or of time. The three poems in **Evening** grouped together and devoted to Tsarskoye Selo describe the place not in terms of the present but of the past, first in the form of what appears to be a memory of Annensky ("a soul suffocated / In the delirium before death"), then as a comparison of the poet herself with the statue of Peace in the Yekaterininsky Park (Annensky had also written a poem about this statue), and finally as an imaginary memory of Pushkin ("Here's where he put his three-cornered hat / And a rumpled book of poems by Parny"). Thus the three poems become, with their backward glance, a part of Tsarskoye Selo itself, sharing in its remembering present.

The function of remembering, of memory, is such an important one in Akhmatova's poetry that it needs special consideration. Pushkin's famous poem "Remembrance," which ends: "I complain bitterly, and shed bitter tears, / But do not wash away the sorry lines" might stand as an epigraph over much of Akhmatova's work. Annensky had already begun to develop this theme in poems such as "Anguish of Remembrance," where the act of remembering becomes identical with the act of creation. Akhmatova makes this creative, individual pursuit of memory into the foundation of her poetic art. For all her apparent concern with relationships and emotional involvements, she speaks out of a condition that is profoundly solitary. It is a solitariness that implies a deeper solidarity than that of love relationships. The woman in these poems is conscious of being unable to fulfill the expectations of men—she is not entirely a being of the here and now: part of her is turned into the face of time. She cannot speak in a voice that is wholly personal; her "I" is fused with other "I" 's in other times and other places. Perhaps she is indeed a mermaid, or a fairytale princess who does not need, cannot respond to earthly affection. At times her sense of unearthliness grows so strong that she appears to herself, in her physical incarnation, as a doll, or a toy:

> And now I have become toylike
> Like my roseate friend cockatoo.

Akhmatova's absorption in memory and the processes of time led her away from any danger of fascination with her personal experience and united her with the wider, shared experience of a public reality. One of the primary aspects of that absorption and that enlarged experience as they express themselves in her poems is the city of St. Petersburg. In many of the early poems, personal, individual time is supplanted by the time of the city. The city's stone architecture absorbs the fates and lives of its individual citizens and projects them toward the condition of art and history:

> My heart sustains its even beat,
> What could the long years give to me?
> Beneath the arch on Gallery Street
> Our shadows will forever be.
> **("Poems About St. Petersburg," II)**

***Rosary,*** the collection from which the lines above are quoted, was published in the spring of 1914. The war that broke out later that year was in many ways instrumental in bringing Akhmatova a resolution of the tension she had experienced between the 'public-poetic' and the private aspects of her life. Her marriage to Gumilyov had hardly been a marriage at all, in many respects, since much of their time had been spent apart—Gumilyov in Africa, Akhmatova in Russia. Although in 1912 she had given birth to a son, Lev, she had not continued to look after him herself, but had entrusted him to the care of Gumilyov's mother. By so doing, she considered she had "lost" him. With the outbreak of war, Gumilyov immediately enlisted and went off to the front. Left alone in Slepnyovo, the small estate owned by Gumilyov's parents, Akhmatova contemplated the onslaught of what later she was to call "The True Twentieth Century."

***White Flock,*** which appeared in 1917 and which contains the poems that give Akhmatova's immediate reactions to the war and to the atmosphere of the period that led up to the 1917 revolution, bears as its epigraph a line from Annensky's sinister poem *Sweetheart* (*Milaya*). This story of a mother who has drowned her child echoes the Gretchen fable in Goethe's *Faust*. Akhmatova develops the theme in her poem **"Where, tall girl, is your gypsy babe"** (**"Gde, vysokaya, tvoy tsyganyonok"**). She reflects that "I was not worthy / To bear the lot of a mother—that bright torture," as she wanders from room to room, looking for her son's cradle.

This acute sense of guilt, grief, and loss was to be reiterated on a very much larger scale in Akhmatova's poems. As Mother Russia began to lose her sons to "The True Twentieth Century," Akhmatova's voice took on a new, tragic note. An intonation of prayer, already present in her earlier work, now became predominant, as personal and public misfortune merged into one. In a poem written in 1916, she says that her first reaction to the news of the outbreak of war was to pray to God and to beg him to destroy her before the first battle. Subsequently this desire for self-immolation became a readiness for self-sacrifice in order to save Russia:

> Give me illness for years on end,
> Shortness of breath, insomnia, fever.
> Take away my child and friend,
> The gift of song, my last believer.
> I pray according to Your rite,
> After many wearisome days,—
> That the storm cloud over Russia might

Turn white and bask in a glory of rays.

The other important theme of **White Flock** is private friendship and love. It is significant, however, that in addressing those human beings for whom she has particular affection, Akhmatova points away from the context of emotional fulfillment and "happy" love toward a wider, tragic arena, and sometimes toward objects and images that are openly religious in character. The poem **"Statue at Tsarskoye Selo,"** dedicated to Nikolay Nedobrovo, invokes the ponds, autumn leaves, and swans of the Yekaterininsky Park, and the "celebrated girl" with her "unshiveringly crossed legs" who looks out across the pathways from her plinth of "northern stone." Akhmatova says that she feels a "dark fear" as she looks at the statue. "And how could I forgive her," she asks Nedobrovo, "the enthusiasm of your enamoured praise? Look, elegantly naked like that, she's happy to be sad." In another poem, **"When in the gloomiest of capitals"** (**"Kogda v mrachneyshey iz stolits"**), the poet describes how at the time of her flight from St. Petersburg in the summer of 1916—motivated by tuberculosis—the only thing she took with her was the altar cross she had received from her friend Boris Anrep on "the day of betrayal." Feeling guilty because she is unable to love Anrep in the way he loves her, Akhmatova tells him how the cross preserves her from "bitter ravings," and helps her to remember everything—even the "last day," when she left both him and the city.

In these "personal" poems, too, there is the Akhmatovan sacrifice of self, of private identity. It is a sacrifice that involves at once an intensification of pain and a distancing of it. In Akhmatova's poetry, as in that of Dante, the details of individual grief are subsumed by a consciousness of the movements of the spheres, and by a striving to comprehend the Divine will in terms of a moral quest. The 1917 October revolution was experienced by Akhmatova as a catastrophe, a moral disaster—but her love for Russia was far too immense, too absolute for her to be able to turn her back on the calamity. She accepted it as yet another, though colossal, intensification of suffering, another stage in the sacrifice of her nation. Even though it opened the way to the lower circles of Hell, she still believed, like Dante, that the poet can traverse Hell and even redeem it, and that this task is a sacred one:

> When in suicidal anguish
> The nation awaited its German guests
> And the stern spirit of Byzantium
> Had deserted the Russian Church;
> When the capital by the Nevá
> Had forgotten its majesty
> And like a drunken prostitute
> Did not know who would take it next,
> I heard a voice call consolingly.
> It was saying: "Come to me here,
> Leave your remote and sinful country,
> Leave Russia behind forever.
> I will wash your hands of blood
> Take the black shame from your heart
> And cover up with another name
> The pain of insult and defeat."
> But with indifference, peacefully,
> I covered my ears with my palms,
> So that these unworthy words

Should not sully my mournful spirit.

This poem, with its simplicity of feeling, its directness achieved without the smallest sacrifice of intellectual complexity, and its dark-toned lyrical stoicism, stands like an inscription over the work that Akhmatova was to produce during the next half-century. It marks the inauguration of her later style, which is Dantean, not in any grandiose or "sculptural" sense, but in the sense in which Mandelstam characterized the poetry of Dante: "Imagine a monument made of granite or marble, the symbolic idea of which is not to depict a steed or a horseman, but to reveal the inner structure of granite or marble . . . imagine a monument of granite, erected in honour of granite and in order to reveal its essence. . . . "

In his essay on Akhmatova, published in 1915, Nikolay Nedobrovo had counselled her to follow Pushkin's exhortation to the poet to "go where your secret dreams lead you." This advice served to strengthen within Akhmatova her allegiance to Pushkin's spirit and example, an allegiance already well established by her childhood in Tsarskoye Selo and her apprenticeship to Annensky. The tradition represented by Pushkin was to be of vital importance to her during the years that followed the October revolution. It was thanks to this inspiration that she was able to avoid the twin perils of becoming, as a poet, either exclusively preoccupied with herself or with the upheaval in the outside world. (pp. 60-6)

Nothing could be further removed from the style and spirit of her poetry than the "confessional" mode of versewriting. It was the critic Boris Eykhenbaum who pointed out that the personal, diary-like quality of Akhmatova's poetry is an illustory one: after careful reading, we become aware that these "diary entries" are, in fact, thoroughly impersonal. Their unvarnished concision, their spirituality that is somehow in the world, are the attributes of a poetry that has transcended the illusion of personality and has allied its softly speaking voice to an iron-hard objective knowledge of the limits of the human, a level-headed humility in the face of God's purpose, and a consciousness and understanding of human weakness and frailty. Akhmatova's poems of the revolutionary and immediate postrevolutionary period, published in the collections *Plantain* (1921) and *Anno Domini* (1922) contain no ecstatic or apocalyptic utterances, nor do they represent a withdrawal into the self, into "private life"; what they express above all is grief, and a sense of guilt:

> I called death down on the heads of those I cherished.
> One after the other, their deaths occurred.
> I cannot bear to think how many perished.
> These graves were all predicted by my word.

The event that was uppermost in the poet's consciousness, and conscience, when she wrote these lines was undoubtedly the death of Gumilyov. Akhmatova had divorced her husband in 1918 and had married the Assyriologist Vladimir Shileyko, with whom, however, she had soon parted company, going to live with the composer Artur Lourié and the actress and dancer Olga Sudeykina in a house on the Fontanka. In August 1921, Gumilyov was arrested and shot for his part in an anti-Bolshevik conspiracy.

Akhmatova was deeply horrified: her poems began to reflect, for the first time, a creeping sense of fear and dread:

> A sound beyond the wall, muffled yet stark—
> A ghost? A rat? The door? Did I latch it?

With the dread was mingled grief that so many of those whom she had loved and who had loved her—from the young poet Knyazev, who had committed suicide, to Gumilyov himself—had met violent and unnatural deaths. Yet the grief goes beyond even this: it extends into a lament for her entire generation and for the whole of suffering Russia. Love is for Akhmatova, as for Annensky, synonymous with suffering, and in the tragic music of separation, betrayal, fear, and death there is a continued echo of "the bow and the strings":

> As ravens circle above the place
> Where they smell fresh-blooded limbs,
> So my love, with its triumphant face,
> Inflicted its wild hymns.

In the years before the revolution, Akhmatova had built a very considerable literary reputation. Her poems had received wide circulation—she had even become, to some extent, a "popular" poet. After the 1917 revolution, all that began to change. *Plantain* and *Anno Domini* drew hostile criticism from the newly established commissars of the literary left: Akhmatova's poems were felt by them to belong to an age that was past, too exclusively concerned with the problems of personal existence and insufficiently engaged with the themes of "revolutionary" reality. This superficial and blinkered view of her writing was to become all too familiar in the years to come. Matters were not helped by the fact that many of those who had been the poet's most perceptive and sensitive readers were now leaving Russia and going to live in the West. Akhmatova did not follow them. As we have seen, she felt that her place was in Russia, whatever the sufferings she might have to endure there. "I am not with those who have abandoned their land / To be torn apart by its enemies," she wrote at the beginning of a famous poem from *Anno Domini.* In the same poem, however, she professes "eternal sympathy" for the exile, as she does for prisoners, or the sick:

> Dark is your road, wanderer,
> And the foreign bread smells of wormwood.

Indeed, she herself was now to become an exile, although an inner one. The deaths of Nedobrovo (1919), Gumilyov (1921), and Blok (1921) left her feeling isolated, and the hostile comment her books attracted in the new, harsh, and utterly changed political climate meant that she could not hope to continue to publish. The banning order that in 1925 was passed on her in the form of an unofficial Communist Party resolution meant that for the next fifteen years none of her poetry was published in the Soviet Union, and that it was forty years before she was allowed to publish a new book of her own. She was now treated by literary critics and public alike as essentially a voice from the past, and her literary career was considered to be at an end. (pp. 67-9)

Although Akhmatova did not stop writing poetry altogether in the inter-war years, she wrote significantly less in them than she had done previously. She began, for the first time, to take an interest in family life. The twelve years (from 1926 until 1938) during which she lived with the art critic and historian Nikolay Punin in Fontannyy Dom were the nearest she ever came to living a settled existence. Desperately poor—the "old age" pension issued to her at the age of thirty-six by the Soviet authorities was barely enough to keep her in cigarettes and matches, according to Nadezhda Mandelstam—Akhmatova had little option but to attempt to find security in the traditional female rôle of wife and mother. Her son Lev, now aged sixteen, came to live with her, Punin, and Punin's daughter, and something approaching a family was formed. But Akhmatova's life with Punin was not a happy one, and as early as 1930 she tried to leave him. Economic necessity and the emotional demands made on her by Punin dictated otherwise, however, and she adopted a stoical attitude to her situation. She became immersed in the study of the architecture of St. Petersburg, and in Pushkin scholarship, treating this as Pushkin himself had treated the study of history—as an antidote to the trials of domestic life. But the study of Pushkin was for her much more than this: as we have already seen, it was a source of inner strength and was the most obvious outward sign that her deep and lasting preoccupation with poetic word and with the poet's function as a moral remembrancer had not ceased. (pp. 69-70)

Love and respect for the poetic word as an instrument of moral education, as a means of combating the debasement of spirit and language entailed by history's obsession with power and the "useful," and by the individual's involuntary acquiescence in that obsession, are as characteristic of Akhmatova's poetry as they are of Annensky's. In the essay already quoted, Nedobrovo had written of her poems: " . . . that they are constructed on the word may be shown on the example of a poem like the following, which is in no way untypical of ***Rosary.*** " The poem in question is **"True Tenderness"**:

> There's no confusing true tenderness
> With anything else—it's at rest.
> No good your being so solicitous
> As you drape my furs round my breast.
> No good your talking to me
> Submissively of first love.
> I know those looks, stubborn and hungry,
> I know what you're thinking of.

Nedobrovo remarks: "The voice here is so simple and conversational that one may perhaps wonder whether this is poetry at all. But if we read the poem again, we may observe that if all our conversations were like this, it would be enough, in order to exhaust the possibilities of most human relationships, to exchange them for two or three eight-line stanzas—and the result would be a reign of silence."

This concentration and distillation of the colloquial was to remain a fundamental characteristic of Akhmatova's poetry right to the end, even when, later in life, she adopted large-scale forms in order to confront the terrible events of wartime and the darkness of the postwar world. Her refusal to abandon the mode of intimate conversation may be likened to that of Mandelstam, to whom Akhmatova

was close during the 1920s and 1930s (their friendship is chronicled in the two volumes of Nadezhda Mandelstam's memoirs), and who in his essay *On the Nature of the Word* (1923) wrote of Annensky as the teacher of "an inner Hellenism, adequate to the spirit of the Russian language, as it were, a domestic Hellenism." Mandelstam's emphasis on the home, on a domestic world outlook, his insistence that

> the happy repository of heaven
> is a lifelong house that you can carry
> anywhere

is very similar to Akhmatova's; both poets were lifelong outcasts and wanderers; neither of them, after childhood, ever really knew a settled existence. Coextensive with the linguistic concern in their poetry is a concern with St. Petersburg as a spiritual home, and an essentially Christian attitude toward people and objects as being ultimately capable of redemption and authenticity.

"I have no use for odic hosts, / The charms of elegiac flights," wrote Akhmatova in a poem of 1940. In the same poem, she gave a thoroughly Annenskian description of the poet's task, derived in part from memories of the lanes and backyards of her Tsarskoye Selo childhood:

> If you but knew the kind of sweepings
> Verses grow from, with no reticence,
> Like weeds—the burdock and the goosefoot,
> The yellow dandelion by the fence.

For all his preoccupation with the intimate lyric, with the "sweepings" of existence, Annensky had at times had recourse to large-scale forms—notably the prose poem and the verse tragedy—and in the last third of her life, Akhmatova, too, addressed the challenge of enlarged formal conceptions. This was in part a response to the massive scale of the catastrophes that had overtaken the world, but it was also an inevitable development of the cyclical character of much of her earlier work. Although Akhmatova did not make use of the *trilistnik,* the miniature tripartite cycle so beloved of Annensky, until very late in her poetic career, the cyclical grouping of poems according to mood, theme, and element was a technique dear to her, and it was by means of it that she was able to approach the building of larger prosodic structures. She had, it is true, taken some steps in this direction as early as 1914, in the autobiographical *poema,* ***By the Seashore;*** but it is ***Requiem*** and the extended poems that make up the central achievement of Akhmatova's later years, and possibly of her art as a whole, the enigmatic and monumental ***Poem Without a Hero,*** in which the fruits of this endeavor are to be seen. Although these poems, like others of the same period, are still essentially "chamber music," the forms they employ are increasingly symphonic in their grandeur and complexity.

The first great manifestation of Akhmatova's late style, in which a restrained colloquialism is made to convey the mingling of the individual's fate with the events of history, is the cycle ***Requiem*** which, although it was not published in the West until 1963 (and has never been published in the Soviet Union), consists for the most part of the poems Akhmatova wrote between 1935 and 1940 in response to the arrest and imprisonment of her son, Lev, by the Soviet authorities. The city is still present in these poems, as before, except that now St. Petersburg has been replaced by Leningrad, which is a projection of Russia's past onto its present and of its present onto its past. It is also, in a sense that St. Petersburg is in Annensky's poem, a city of death:

> . . . the hosts of those convicted
> Marched by, mad, tormented throngs,
> And train whistles are restricted
> To singing separation songs.
> The stars of death stood overhead,
> And guiltless Russia, that pariah,
> Writhed under boots, all blood-bespattered,
> And the wheels of many a black maria.

In this requiem for all the women who, like the poet herself, stood in the queues outside the Leningrad prisons, trying to visit their husbands and children, and for all the people who perished in the camps, Akhmatova subordinates her own grief to the public woe. Facing death and madness, talking to them on intimate terms, she leaves behind the realm of the living and approaches the land of the dead. The cycle of poems is conceived as a progress along the stations of the Cross (some of the poems bear titles such as **"The Judgment"** and **"The Crucifixion"**). (pp. 71-4)

These poems are, in the first instance, Akhmatova's own "stations of the Cross." But as the cycle progresses, it acquires an even more profound dimension. The image of the lonely woman waiting at the prison gate is assimilated first to the image of *all* the women, and eventually to the image of Mary Magdalene. The sufferings of the Russian people are identified with the agony of the crucified Christ. Yet nowhere does the writing become abstract or emblematic—the scene is simple, direct, and concrete:

> The choir of angels glorified the mighty hour
> And all the heavens melted into fire.
> To his Father he said: "Why hast thou forsaken
> me?"
> And to his Mother: "Weep not for me . . . "
>
> Mary sobbed, and beat her breast.
> His favorite disciple stood still as stone.
> But no one dared to cast a glance
> At where the silent Mother stood alone.

The individual, pictorial quality of these scenes is vital: such suffering can only be redeemed in the sacred act of remembrance; the memory of the epoch must not be allowed to fade in people's consciousness, and the poet prays that if ever a monument is raised to her it should be placed not by the sea, or in the park at Tsarskoye Selo, but

> here where for three hundred years I had to
> wait,
> And still they didn't open that certain gate.

In ***Requiem*** all the attributes and characteristics of Akhmatova's earlier poetry—the intimate, conversational manner, the struggle with conscience and guilt (at one point in the cycle the poet construes her present sufferings as a punishment for her frivolous girlhood), the brooding presence of the city, the meditation on the themes of love, death, and time, and the concept of poetic inspiration as

prayer—fuse together and move forward into a new dimension of transfigured suffering. The nearness of extinction in Leningrad, the city of death, makes the barriers of time irrelevant. What matter now are the absolute, timeless qualities of a grief that has transcended itself and become a monument:

> Let from the lids of bronze, unmoving eyes
> Snow melt and stream like the tears each human
> cries.

Returning in 1946 to Tsarskoye Selo (it had been renamed "Pushkin" some eight years previously by Stalin), Akhmatova found the town in ruins: "They've burnt my little toy town / And I've no loophole back to the past," begins the poem she wrote as an immediate reaction to her loss. This sense of the door to the past having irrevocably slammed shut had already been confirmed by a number of cataclysmic events, which included the siege of Leningrad in 1941 by the German army, the death of Mandelstam in a labor camp, and Tsvetayeva's suicide. The end of the war saw an intensification of the officially approved campaign against Akhmatova and her work. She was subjected to crude abuse in the press—all hope that she would ever be able to publish seemed to be lost. This, in spite of the fact that during the war she had acted in the most heroic, patriotic manner, broadcasting to the people of Leningrad to give them courage, and dedicating a cycle of poems to the city in its state of siege.

In 1940, aware that a world was coming to an end, Akhmatova had begun to jot down the first sketches of a poem about the eve of the Russian revolution. It was a work she had been thinking about since as early as 1923, when she had made allusion to a long poem she planned to write "in which there is not a single hero." All during 1941, even at the height of the terrible artillery attacks and bombing raids, she continued, weak and ill, to work at this poem. It was to become a characterization in verse of a whole era, conceived as a dialogue of the temporal-historical with the eternal. With its three dedications (to Knyazev / Mandelstam, to Sudeykina, and to Isaiah Berlin, whom Akhmatova had befriended in 1945 when he was a diplomat in Moscow); with its invocation of the year 1913, of the world and Russia as they were on the eve of "The True Twentieth Century," and the poet's friends, surrounded by the shades of the past dressed as mummers; with its intermezzo, bearing an epigraph inspired by T. S. Eliot's *Four Quartets,* "My future is in my past"; and its epilogue, dedicated to the city of Leningrad under siege, the poem presents a complex refracting mirror to the face of history. . . .

The mirror that recurs throughout the poem is the eye of conscience: the poet takes upon herself not only her own sins but also the sins of an entire epoch. The personal hell she has traversed is also the hell of man's inhumanity to man. Past, present, and future momentarily coincide, and as they do so, time and history are brought to an end—eternity, in the shape of Russia's mysterious fate, calls through suffering from afar:

> Lowering her dry eyes
> And wringing her hands, Russia
> Walked before me into the East.

In Akhmatova's "Poem of Memory," or "Poem of Conscience," as the literary critic A. I. Pavlovsky called it, there is no hero, only the voice of the age and the voice of God. In this work the guilt of an individual past is overcome and expiated in the recognition of a shared, generational suffering, a Way of the Cross that is the same for those of the poet's contemporaries who stayed in Russia, for those who were exiled to Central Asia or Siberia, and for those who went abroad, to the West:

> Some in Tashkent, some in New York,
>    And the air of exile has a bitter smack
>       Like poisoned wine.

*Poem Without A Hero* is the expression of a great inner freedom: in it, space and time are transcended, and the threads of the poet's life are brought together in her complete identification with the destiny of her nation and her people. It is also a defiance of the labor camps, of the Terror, a rendering powerless of the evil forces that had laid siege to her own life and the lives of her contemporaries. It is a supreme act of allegiance to the spirit of Russian literary culture and its power of moral education, in particular as that spirit is expressed in the poetry of Derzhavin, Pushkin, and Annensky. And, like the Yekaterininsky Park, which Annensky described in his Pushkin centenary address at Tsarskoye Selo as "the park of memories," it is a public and national monument of enduring beauty.

In the *Poem* an insuperable obstacle to further creation seems to have been overcome, an almost cosmic guilt atoned for. The guilt the poet has felt at the deaths of Knyazev and Gumilyov, at having been spared the fate of Mandelstam, of Tsvetayeva, at being alive at all—all this is lifted in a sudden recognition that she is, after all, an heir to the noble Russian poetic tradition. A poem written in 1958, **"The Heiress,"** describes a walk in the grounds of Tsarskoye Selo in the following terms:

> Among these halls, standing deserted,
> A song was what I seemed to hear.
> Who could have told me in that year
> That this was what I should inherit:
> The swans, the bridges of those times,
> Felitsa, all of her chinoiseries,
> The palaces' ethereal galleries,
> Miraculous beauty of the limes.
> My shadow, even, that fear's wave
> Distorted beyond recognition,
> The hairshirt of the heart's contrition,
> The lilac of beyond the grave.

In the last years of her life, Akhmatova continued to write poetry of undiminished clarity, severity, and grace. By now her fame had penetrated far beyond the boundaries of her native land. Her meeting with Robert Frost in 1962, and her visit to Oxford in 1965, had helped to establish her international reputation as the greatest living Russian poet. Sadly, however, Western translations of her work were still few in number. In 1964, Robert Lowell published his translation (with Olga Carlisle) of *Requiem,* and in 1965 D. M. Thomas offered an English version of the same poem. French, German, and Italian translations were also published at about the same time. It was not until several years after Akhmatova's death in 1966, however, that any substantial account of her work appeared

in English translation, the first being Richard McKane's Penguin selection (1969). During the 1970s a relatively large number of translated selections appeared, perhaps the finest of them being Stanley Kunitz' and Max Hayward's *Poems of Akhmatova* (1974). Neither McKane nor Kunitz / Hayward make any consistent attempt to reproduce in their translations the formal, prosodic, and musical qualities of Akhmatova's verse, however, but concentrate primarily on meanings, although Kunitz / Hayward do make an occasional gesture in the direction of rhyme and meter. While these plain but generally accurate versions may be of great assistance to readers with only a partial knowledge of Russian, they—like those of W. Arndt (1976)—are surely intended as an adjunct to the original poems rather than as independent translations (the Kunitz / Hayward versions face the Russian texts). D. M. Thomas' *Way of All the Earth* (1979) makes a more determined move toward the formal attributes of the original poems; some of his versions manage to retain both meaning and structure, and to stand on their own as poems. Others in the volume are weaker, however, and some should simply not have been included at all.

Lyn Coffin's translations of Akhmatova's poetry are the first I have seen to attempt a consistent deployment of rhyme and meter over the whole range of the poet's output. The results come as near, I think, to the sense and form of the originals as may be possible in the English language. In saying this, I do not mean to imply that these versions are by any means perfect; their deficiencies are, however, ones imposed by culture, language, geography, and time, and not by any attempt by the translator to impose her own personality on her subject, or to make Akhmatova more "assimilable" for Western readers. The selection, although relatively short, is a careful one, and covers all periods of Akhmatova's creative life. Among the longer poem sequences and cycles, only a part of *Requiem* is translated, and *Poem Without A Hero* is not represented at all; but there is a fine rendering of the weirdly hermetic **"Midnight Verses"** of 1963, presented in their entirety. The book [*Poems* by Anna Akhmatova] has an Introduction by the poet Joseph Brodsky, who was close to Akhmatova during the last years of her life and whom she helped at the time of his victimization and exile by the Soviet authorities. This concise and powerful essay brings Coffin's translations nearer to Akhmatova's spirit and to the spirit of classical Russian poetry than can be said to be the case with other available translated selections. In particular, it points up just how far from adequate is the type of approach adopted by a translator like Mary Maddock, who in her *Three Russian Women Poets* includes a number of Akhmatova versions that, while they express at least some of the original meaning, are conceived in literary terms so alien to the spirit of the Russian that they miss the essence of the poems altogether. (pp. 75-81)

Writing in 1923 about Innokenty Annensky, Osip Mandelstam expressed himself in the following terms:

> Gumilyov called Annensky a great European poet. It seems to me that when the Europeans find out about him, having meekly educated their generations in the study of the Russian language, just as previous generations were educat-

ed in the study of the ancient languages and classical poetry, they will be inspired with fear by the insolence of this regal plunderer, who abducted the dove Eurydice from them and took her to the snows of Russia, who tore the classical shawl from the shoulders of Phaedra and tenderly placed, as befits a Russian poet, an animal skin on an Ovid who was still shivering from cold.

Mandelstam's words might be made equally well to apply to Akhmatova, and to the sense of wonder with which future generations of non-Russians will one day greet her work. (pp. 81-2)

&#x20;

> David McDuff, "Anna Akhmatova," in Parnassus: Poetry in Review, Vol. 11, No. 2, Fall-Winter, 1983, pp. 51-82.

## John Bayley

Anna Akhmatova had been in her youth one of the "Acmeist" poets, along with her husband Gumilev and Mandelstam. Acmeism was essentially a reaction against the symbolist movement in Russian poetry, a movement that tended, as such things do in Russia, to extremes, in this case extremes of uplift, mysticism, apocalypse. Acmeism by contrast was concerned with poetry as architecture, and poems as objects of weight and mass-produced as if in a workshop (the poets' guild or workshop was one of the group's other names for itself). The most important early influence on Akhmatova was her discovery of the poems of Innokenti Annensky, an expert translator and scholar of ancient Greek, who had written—they were published posthumously—a volume of verses called The Cypress Box. Her early poems are precise evocations of places, moments, loves, deceptive intensities of being, carved out with reticence and a kind of inner dignity.

It is significant that the Russian symbolist poets, notably Blok and Bryusov, hailed the revolution of 1917 in their whole consciousness. They were fascinated by the idea of such a thing. Their attitude was not unlike that of Yeats in "The Second Coming" and "Lapis Lazuli," joyfully greeting the end of order and the coming of the "rough beast" in a spirit of "gaiety transfiguring all that dread." Terror was merely an exciting and poetical idea to them, as the rough beast slouching toward Bethlehem was for Yeats. The Acmeists' reaction was very different: they recognized facts and truths when they saw them. Pasternak in Dr. Zhivago refers to Blok's line, "we children of Russia's terrible years," and he remarks dryly that those years really had been terrible for those who had been killed, bereaved, or imprisoned. The symbolic status of revolution was not the same thing as what actually occurred, and the Acmeists were only interested in what actually occurred.

Because of this common sense, as one has to call it, Akhmatova, like Mandelstam, can write about virtually anything. It is hard to think of any poetry in English, and certainly of none written in the last century, that has the range of hers, and the amazing power to rise to an occasion. Mandelstam said that great poetry was often a response to total disaster, and it is true that we may think of Milton, blind and at the mercy of his political enemies,

setting out to write Paradise Lost. True in some heroic ages perhaps, but not much in our own, when poets in their sufferings have been more apt to lose themselves, like Pound muttering in his Cantos, or to say with Yeats: "I think it better that in times like these / A poet's mouth be silent." With her husband shot and her son imprisoned, Akhmatova wrote her poem Requiem between 1935 and 1940, telling of her experiences in the Yezhov terror. (p. 21)

Rare indeed for a poet to rise like that to such a challenge. But the whole poem has about it the dignity of utter simplicity, without false modesty or any attempt at the common touch. She describes her experiences as if they happened to her only, like words in a gospel, the equivalent in art of what she called the severe and shapely spirit of Russian orthodoxy. In this spirit she concludes by saying that if her countrymen ever want to make a monument to her she would consent if they put it outside the prison gates where she had stood, and where the news she longed for never came through the door.

> And may the melting snow drop like tears
> From my motionless bronze eyelids,
> And the prison pigeons coo above me
> And the ships sail slowly down the Neva.

That is D. M. Thomas's translation, from a rendering of Requiem and Poem Without a Hero published in 1976. In her new version from a selection of Akhmatova's poems, [entitled Poems,] Lyn Coffin attempts, and not without success, the flowing meter of the original.

> Let from the lids of bronze, unmoving eyes
> Snow melt and stream like the tears each human cries,
> And let in the distance the prison pigeons coo,
> While along the Neva, ships pass quietly through.

That has the movement but not the weight, or the calm simplicity. Thomas is better at giving an idea of that. As usual the problem is insoluble, but never mind: Coffin's is a good try that deserves as much credit as the cautious versions, or more. In her long poem sequences Akhmatova uses meters of great robustness and subtlety in the Russian which when transposed into English can often sound all too like Shelley or Poe at their most ebullient. The strong accents and stresses of Russian have a variety and flexibility that iron out a regular beat that would otherwise dominate the more docile English syllables. The meter of Poem Without a Hero, for example, has an extraordinarily commanding and stately rhythm, reminiscent of the Dies Irae, which could be Englished with its rhyme scheme as follows (the section refers to the ponderous march of the twentieth century, "the real not the calendar one," advancing on Petersburg like the stone effigy of the commander in Don Juan):

> Thus up every street there came drumming,
>   So past every porch it was coming,
>     The shape finding its way in the gloom.
> Gusts tore the placards off the palings,
>   Smoke spun a dance over the railings,
>     And the lilac flowers smelt of the tomb.

It was the metrical movement, percussive and minatory,

that first started itself in Akhmatova's head, so she tells us, before any words came. In the Russian it sounds measured and relaxed, as calm as the stride of a great cat. The experts would say that the Akhmatovan line here consists of two anapests with an amphilbrach, or two with an iamb, a combination so rare as to be virtually extinct, and certainly never found before on this scale. Annensky would no doubt have appreciated it, but it seems unlikely that Akhmatova herself would or could have worked it out theoretically.

The most complex and enigmatic of her works, *Poem Without a Hero (Poema bez geroia)*, combines the personal and the historical somewhat in the manner of *The Waste Land,* but a great deal more dramatically. It is a poem of expiation, both for the personal sins she felt she and her contemporaries in St. Petersburg were guilty of, and for the national sorrows and horrors in part expunged by the great struggle for liberation against the Germans. It is certainly an arcane poem—Akhmatova called it "a Chinese box with a triple base," but its personal and literary allusions do not distrub its majestic liturgical flow. Even more than *The Waste Land* it is a poem that seems to call for explanations and yet does not really need them. It is essentially a voice poem, in the tradition that Pushkin stylized in the figure of the "Improvisatore" in "Egyptian Nights," who denies any idea of how complex verse can suddenly come into his head, rhymed and in regular feet, so that it can be instantly declaimed. Like many Russian masterpieces, especially by Pushkin, of whom Akhmatova was a profound student and critic, her *Poema* has the form of an open secret, at once spontaneous and enigmatic.

"I hear certain absurd interpretations of *Poem Without a Hero,*" she writes in the foreword. "And I have been advised to make it clearer. This I decline to do. It contains no third, seventh or twenty-ninth thoughts. I shall neither explain nor change anything. What is written is written." And not in her voice alone, or that of her muse. She wrote the poem at intervals over twenty years, committing it entirely to memory because she feared to write it down, and it ends with a dedication to "its first audience," the fellow citizens who died in Leningrad during the siege. "Their voices I hear, and I remember them when I read my poem aloud, and for me this secret chorus has become a permanent justification of the work."

This combination of unashamed individuality with a public voice is characteristic of the best Russian poetry since Pushkin, who drew a sharp distinction between himself as an ordinary, idle, and fashionable man about town, gambling with friends and running after women, and himself as the vehicle for an unknown and inexplicable inspiration, a voice that might speak with the accents of private friendship or of public authority. Akhmatova had something of the same dual persona: the dandy of Petersburg society, the arrogant beauty involved in bohemian intrigues at poets' cafés like the Stray Dog, and at the same time the grave poetic voice of conscience and religious awe, the voice of Russia's severe and disciplined spirit, silenced for a while by the anarchic envy and clamor of revolution, but speaking out in the fine series of poems dedicated to London at war (unprinted and unheard of, of

course, while Soviet Russia was the ally of Nazi Germany), and in the sonorous poem **"Courage,"** a summons not to the Soviets but to her fellow Russians, which actually appeared in *Pravda* a few months after the German invasion.

She was a Russian Orthodox believer and a Russian patriot. Her poetry flowed from both kinds of faith, and as the opening lines of **Requiem** pronounce, she was deeply proud, too, of having remained in Russia while so many others of her class and kind had fled into emigration. The four lines are very simple, but their tone sets a notorious problem for the translator:

> No foreign sky protected me,
> no stranger's wing shielded my face.
> I stand as witness to the common lot,
> survivor of that time, that place.

This attempt by Stanley Kunitz Americanizes the translation, and makes one realize how deep and subtle is the difference between "great simple verses" in the American tradition and in the Russian. The difference was even more marked when Robert Lowell reconstituted the lines in his own fashion.

> I wasn't under a new sky,
> its birds were the old familiar birds.
> They still spoke Russian. Misery
> spoke familiar Russian words.

Those are wholly American words, and an American tone. Lyn Coffin is the best at getting some equivalent of the original's weight and *gravitas*.

> No, it wasn't under a foreign heaven,
> It wasn't under the wing of a foreign power,—
> I was there among my countrymen,
> I was where my people, unfortunately, were.

"Unfortunately" could have been an unfortunate word, but its complex English connotations in fact just provide the right note, stopping just this side of the ironic. "Unhappily" would have verged on the portentous. (pp. 21-2)

Lyn Coffin is probably wise not to attempt [to translate Akhmatova's *Poem Without a Hero*], for her rhymed versions could not come near it, though they are frequently and rather unexpectedly effective when she renders in this way the shorter and earlier poems. Early Akhmatova often has a crisply matter-of-fact quality, which transposes well into an American idiom. Here is Coffin's version of one of Akhmatova's earliest poems, **"While Reading Hamlet."**

> A dust-covered patch to the right of the cemetery.
> Beyond that, a river of unfolding blue.
> "Get thee to a nunnery," you said, "Or marry
> An idiot—It's up to you."
> That's the sort of thing princes always say,
> But I won't forget it as I grow older.
> May your words kccp flowing as ccnturies wear away,
> Like an ermine mantle tossed over someone's shoulder.

"But I won't forget it as I grow older" hits just the right note, more so than Kunitz's more sober and impersonal "but these are words that one remembers." (Kunitz's version, though, had the Russian on the other side of the page—an excellent arrangement—and the added advantage of an essay by Max Hayward, by far the best and most concise introduction to Akhmatova yet written for readers in English') [see Further Reading List].

Lyn Coffin succeeds again in the short, tart poem in which Akhmatova glances at her unhappy relations with her husband, the poet Gumilev. She married him in 1910, after many proposals by him, one of them accompanied by a suicide attempt. Although an original poet, an explorer, and a gallant soldier (after the war he was shot by the Bolsheviks for alleged conspiracy); Gumilev was clearly not an easy man to live with, and Akhmatova herself seems to have been quite innocent of all the ordinary domestic virtues.

They had one son who because of his name was arrested in the purges, and for whom his mother spent the hours of anguish outside the Leningrad jail which are commemorated in *Requiem.* Released to fight in the war, he was re-arrested after it. Sadly, after his final release he became estranged from his mother. The son of the poet Tsvetaeva, who hanged herself in 1941, had done the same. Even in a situation of apocalypse the gap between life and art can often have the same dreadful old commonplaceness about it. Had it not been for revolution, tyranny, and violent death, Gumilev and Akhmatova would no doubt have quarreled, been jealous of each other's loves and poems, and finally separated like any other writers anywhere. As it is the little poem written only months after her marriage has a terse clarity about it which includes, even if it does not foretell, the future. There is humor in it too, as well as sympathy and a kind of wry fellow-feeling.

> The three things he loved most in life
> Were white peacocks, music at mass,
> And tattered maps of America.
> He didn't like kids who cried and he
> Didn't like raspberry jam with tea
> Or womanish hysteria.
> . . . And I was, like it or not, his wife.

Kunitz's version has rival virtues, but ends, "And he was tied to me"—which leaves the relationship ambiguous. Lyn Coffin cleverly gets her rhyme on the first and last line even though she has to pad out the latter. The Russian states merely: "And I was his wife."

There are some excellent versions too of the poems written during the first war and in the early days of the revolution, when Akhmatova was beginning, as it were, to rise to the occasion: **"I hear the oriole's voice," "The Tale of the Black Ring," "The Muse,"** and the magnificent **"Lot's Wife,"** which celebrates the woman who looked back at her old home in "red-towered Sodom," and deliberately paid the price. **"Dante,"** a poem on the same theme, was memorably rendered by Kunitz. The poet sends Florence "a curse from hell / and in heaven could not forget her": he refused to bow the knee to the town that was "perfidious, base, and irremediably home." Lyn Coffin's version weakens this somewhat, but her version of the almost equally memorable **"Cleopatra"** concludes well.

> Tomorrow they will chain her children. And yet
> She has something left in the world to do—one
>    more jest.
> And the little black snake, as if a parting regret,
> With an equable hand, she puts on her swarthy
>    breast.

In these poems Akhmatova invokes historical precedents for her fate without any scrap of pretension. The meter, unfortunately, is a mere jingle compared to the Russian, but nothing can be done about that. What comes faintly through is the quality that Joseph Brodsky isolates in his preface to this translation [see excerpt above]—the true classic. "Nothing reveals a poet's weaknesses like classic verse," he says, "and that's why it's so universally dodged." As a poet in the same tradition, he is the best possible perceiver of what gives Akhmatova's verse its inner strength.

Continually we hear echoes of the true classic in her verse, but they are neither assumed nor something she is trying to conceal; they are deliberate. As Brodsky says, "She came fully equipped, and she never resembled anyone." She did not have to make herself like Yeats: she knew what she was. She was Anna Akhmatova, not Anna Gorenko. Her father, a naval architect of aristocratic birth, told her to write poetry by all means, but not to "sully a good name" by publishing under it, so she adopted a name from the distant past of her mother's family, a name which, as Brodsky points out, has a distinctly Tatar flavor. It went with her appearance—"five feet eleven, dark-haired, fair-skinned, with pale grey-green eyes like those of snow leopards, slim and incredibly lithe, she was for half a century sketched, painted, cast, carved and photographed by a multitude of artists starting with Amadeo Modigliani." Bizarre, after this, that Brodsky compares her to Jane Austen (". . . her syntax resembles English. From the very threshold of her career to its very end she was always perfectly clear and coherent"), but the point is an exceptionally shrewd one. Neither cared in the least about originality, or even about being an "artist": they just were so. (pp. 23-4)

> *John Bayley, "Poems with a Heroine," in* The New York Review of Books, *Vol. XXX, Nos. 21 & 22, January 19, 1984, pp. 21-4.*

## Richard Eder

The ship dwindles to the horizon and disappears; it is the watcher on the shore whose heart is shrunk by absence. The sailor, for better or worse, is where he is, life-size.

The night of Stalin's repression has been told in all kinds of ways, most famously by Alexander Solzhenitsyn's books about the prison camps and their inmates. But in the literature of Soviet suffering there may be no pages more powerful than the cycle of poems by Anna Akhmatova entitled *Requiem.*

Nothing inside the prison walls so fiercely expresses deprivation and injustice—with such a large intensity that it stands for an entire order of human loss—as her chronicle of the women who stood, year after year, outside those walls. After the death of both hope and despair, they waited for word of the fate of those within, and for the chance to hand a knitted cap through, or a pair of shoes. Like the mothers of Argentina's Plaza de Mayo, years later, who turned the "disappeared" into a visible presence, the Russian women, by standing outside the city's jails, jailed the entire city:

> That was when the ones who smiled
> Were the dead, glad to be at rest . . .
> And like a useless appendage, Leningrad
> Swung from its prisons.

It is quite reasonable to think of Akhmatova, who died in 1966 at age 76, as the greatest woman poet in the Western World since Sappho. In a monumental endeavor, seemingly poised upon the frailest of underpinnings, the tiny Zephyr Press of Somerville, Mass., has brought out the first complete collection of her poems published anywhere in the world.

With original Russian versions and a supple translation that all but turns the facing pages warm to the touch, [*The Complete Poems of Anna Akhmatova*], more than 1,500 pages in length, includes more than 700 poems—some previously unprinted—copious notes, several introductions, prefaces and memoirs, and about 75 photographs and drawings. (p. 3)

Roberta Reeder, who edited the collection and the notes, contributes a monograph placing the poems in their historical and biographical context. Judith Hemschemeyer, the translator, provides additional commentary. Among her perceptive remarks is the point that Akhmatova's poetry, unlike that of many of her contemporaries, nearly always addresses a second person, explicitly or implicitly. The reader receives this burning gaze face to face.

Hemschemeyer's translations are not simply a work but a pilgrimage. A poet, she read a few of Akhmatova's poems in translation about 25 years ago. She then learned Russian so that, with the help of word-by-word literal versions, she could translate them all. "I became convinced that Akhmatova's poems should be translated in their entirety and by a woman, and that I was that person," she writes.

Akhmatova's imperial largeness of spirit is catching, clearly. So is a portion of her art. Hemschemeyer chose a very direct rendering, stressing clarity, intimacy and an unforced syntax over any effort to pursue the original's rhymes and sonorities. But she uses assonance and slant rhyme, and her seeming plain style is governed by a lyrical ear. In truth, her translations are not so much plain as transparent. If I did not know English, I would learn it to read them.

Akhmatova's life and her poetry were brutally cut in two by history. Born to a well-to-do family, living a privileged childhood, she became a glittering figure in the Bohemian literary world of pre-revolutionary St. Petersburg. She was a member of the Acmeist circle of poets—Osip Mandelstam, her lifelong brother in poetry and suffering, was another—and her first husband was a poet.

She was a flaming creature. Taking into account her bipolar candle-burning, and the long purgatory she underwent

later on, one thinks of Edna St. Vincent Millay turned into Mother Courage. Except that the poetry of her youth, hugely successful, was also incomparably better. She wrote of childhood, of the countryside, of the city, and of all varieties of love from girlish to adult and adulterous.

She had a blinding sense of place and time. She fused the richness of things and passions with a premonition—and later, the memory—of their transience. Thus, an early poem evokes her sumptuous childhood garden together with a stone bust, toppled beside the water: "He has given his face to the waters of the lake / And he's listening to the green rustling. / And bright rainwater washes / His clotted wound . . . / Cold one, white one, wait, / I'll become marble too."

There is the young girl considering her new-found sexuality: "In my room lives a beautiful / Slow black snake; / It is like me, just as lazy, / Just as cold . . . "

The quick desolation of an early marriage: "The heart's memory of the sun grows faint. / The grass is yellower. / A few early snowflakes blow in the wind, / Barely, barely . . . / The willow spreads its transparent fan / Against the empty sky. / Perhaps I should not have become / Your wife . . . "

The excitement and insomnia of an affair: "Both sides of the pillow / Are already hot. / Now even the second candle / Is going out, and the cry of the crows / Gets louder and louder. / I haven't slept all night / And now it's too late to think of sleep . . . / How unendurably white / Is the blind on the white window. / Hello."

There was the pride of a woman and a poet in her prime, addressing a no doubt not imaginary lover: "Oh it was a cold day / In Peter's miraculous city. / Like a crimson fire the sunset lay, / And slowly the shadow thickened. / Let him not desire my eyes, / Prophetic and fixed. / He will get a whole lifetime of poems / The prayer of my arrogant lips."

The revolution came, and suddenly poverty gnawed away her life and, worse, her writing went out of favor. Poetry had to be hard and elevating. By 1925, the literary leaders were saying that she should have had the intelligence to be dead.

Hardship and the impossibility of publishing; expulsion from the Writers Union. Worse was to come. The purges of the mid-1930s spared her, but her only son, Lev, was arrested. For a year-and-a-half, she joined the lines outside the Leningrad prison. And, in *Requiem,* she found a voice again: harsh with knowledge, powerful with anger, yet with all the lovely particularity of her youth. (pp. 3, 7)

> *Richard Eder, "The Greatest Woman Poet Since Sappho," in* Los Angeles Times Book Review, *March 18, 1990, pp. 3, 7.*

## John Bayley

It will be interesting to see how the coming of glasnost affects Russian poets and their poetry. Already so brilliant and talented a poet as Joseph Brodsky has become as much a cosmopolitan as a Russian poet, often writing in

English, and acclimated to the indifference of an open society where poetry is the preserve of academics and a few other enthusiasts. Nothing feels more separated from this than the poetry and personality of Anna Akhmatova, who in her old age was kind to Mr. Brodsky when he was young and befriended him before he had to leave the Soviet Union.

For most Soviet poets she preserved a steady if good-natured contempt. She was the high priestess of a Russian poetry that was almost an extension of the Russian Church—hieratic, gravely melodious, attracting a vast audience of devotees who knew much of the nation's poetry by heart in the same sense that they knew the Orthodox ritual. Her friend, the poet Osip Mandelstam, who died during the Stalinist purges in a distant eastern gulag, once remarked that poetry was taken so seriously in Russia that a poet could be killed for writing it. Pushkin would have understood that, and Mandelstam's satirical verse about Stalin signed his own death warrant. Akhmatova too was persecuted by the Soviet state: her former husband, the poet Nikolai Gumilyov, was shot in 1921, and their son was twice imprisoned for long periods for the crime of bearing his father's name.

But Russian poets, like martyrs of the church, have thrived on such treatment and on the holy status it gave their work. Akhmatova herself was very conscious of this status. In 1962, four years before Akhmatova died at the age of 76, Robert Frost visited the Soviet Union and paid a call on her at the *dacha* lent her for the occasion at the writers' colony near Leningrad. The two distinguished old poets sat side by side in wicker chairs and talked quietly, "And I kept thinking," Akhmatova wrote afterward,

> here are you, my dear, a national poet. Every year your books are published. . . . They praise you in all the newspapers and journals, they teach you in the schools, the President receives you as an honored guest. And all they've done is slander me! . . . I've had everything—poverty, prison lines, fear, poems remembered only by heart, and burnt poems. And humiliation and grief. And you don't know anything about this and wouldn't be able to understand it if I told you. . . . But now let's sit together, two old people, in wicker chairs. A single end awaits us. And perhaps the real difference is not actually so great?

But she knew it was. Great not so much in terms of suffering—bitter and prolonged as that had been—but in terms of the sheer necessity for poetry in such times, for the Russian poet and for his audience. In a happier country it is one of the amenities, not the needs. The culture that is optional and varied in a civilized society was for many in Stalin's country the only way to stay living and sane.

For this reason the poet must never forget, or allow the new barbarism to blot out the past. Akhmatova saw her poetic role as one of remembering and bearing witness. As Roberta Reeder points out in her admirable introduction to *The Complete Poems of Anna Akhmatova,* "for Akhmatova, to forget was to commit a mortal sin. Memory had become a moral category: one remembers one's misdeeds, atones, and achieves redemption." And in those

miserable years in which Soviet culture sought to impose a Communist stereotype on every aspect of society, the poet's personal memories were as communally precious as statements bearing witness to public events and universal suffering. Akhmatova's two great poems, *Requiem* and *Poem Without a Hero,* record, respectively, the time of terror and the purges and a more timeless vision of the past in which the dead and the living meet and change roles, and key events in the poet's own life become part of a public nightmare.

The central event of *Poem Without a Hero* is the suicide of a young friend, a cadet officer who had fallen in love with Olga Sudeikina, an actress who was a close friend of Akhmatova's. (There are excellent photographs in this collection of Akhmatova herself and of people in her life.) Sudeikina took parts in the decadent dramas put on in the group theaters and by St. Petersburg cabarets like the Stray Dog. She was also for a time the lover of the poet Aleksandr Blok, another close friend of Akhmatova's, and it was jealousy for this rival that caused the young soldier-poet Vsevolod Knyazev to shoot himself. Although this suicide occurred a year before World War I, it was for Akhmatova a symbol and foretaste of all the horrors to come. The figure of Knyazev mutates in the poem into that of the poet Mandelstam himself, who had said to Akhmatova shortly before his arrest: "I am ready to die." And in the carnival of the threatening 20th century ("The real—not the calendar— / Twentieth Century"), both merge with a "guest from the future," the Oxford professor Isaiah Berlin, who came to call on Akhmatova in 1945, when he was working in Moscow for the British Foreign Office.

Delighted as she was to see this admirer from the West, with whom she conversed for a whole night in her cramped garret near the Moika Canal, Akhmatova was always convinced that she owed to that visit her subsequent persecution by Andrei Zhdanov, Stalin's minister for culture, a pursuit that lasted till the tyrant's death and recalled some of her worst times during the purges before the war. In those days she had planned and begun to write *Requiem,* a great poem like a dirge or chant in Orthodox ritual, which was inspired by a woman who spoke to her as they waited in line outside the prison where their sons were held, saying, "Can you put this into your poetry?" Akhmatova replied that she could. *Requiem* wonderfully commemorates the horror of the time and without a trace of self-consciousness asks that if a statue of herself, the poet, is ever erected by her fellow countrymen it should stand here outside the prison wall by the Neva River, with the melted snow running from its bronze face like tears.

That section of the poem shows with what reverence, solemnity even, Akhmatova regarded her poetic calling, a dignity that makes the public posturing of such a poet in the West as W. B. Yeats seem tawdry by contrast. One of Akhmatova's most moving as well as most stately poems commemorates the death of Lot's wife, turned into a pillar of salt for the last glance she could not resist taking of her native town. . . .

Sonorous, calm, déliberate in movement, the Russian words can be transformed into no English equivalent; but in this admirably restrained and accurate translation by Judith Hemschemeyer, the sense and the message strike with all the weight of the original. To have rendered the whole corpus of such a poet into plain, proportioned, forceful English is a remarkable achievement; and Amanda Haight, the *doyenne* of Akhmatova studies, who died a year ago and to whom the volumes are dedicated, must have been proud of the project—the first complete collection of Akhmatova and, since it is printed here in both languages, also the first complete Russian edition—and she must have given it her blessing.

Just as one of Pushkin's finest long poems, "The Bronze Horseman," may have been conceived as a reply to his Polish friend Adam Mickiewicz, who had produced an anti-Petersburg poem in "Forefathers' Eve," so **Poem Without a Hero** may have been intended in one sense as Akhmatova's reproach to the poet Mikhail Kuzmin, who had been the lover of Knyazev and alluded to his suicide in his own poem published in 1929 called "The Trout Breaks the Ice." Ms. Reeder suggests that Kuzmin's malice and frivolity, and his wish to obliterate Knyazev's suicide from memory, seemed irresponsible to Akhmatova, and a symptom of the decline that had led to the Revolution. Certainly there is an air of almost religious expiation about Akhmatova's great poem, some of whose rhythms echo those of Kuzmin's much slighter work. There is also a very definite relationship with T. S. Eliot's "Four Quartets," with their blending of public and private images and their meditation on time future in time past. Like Eliot, Akhmatova used as a source of inspiration the motto of Mary, Queen of Scots: "In my end is my beginning."

Conscience, repentance, suffering, bearing witness—all these spiritual attributes have an effortless place in Akhmatova's poetry, and testify to the kinds of purgation the poet underwent in her work. Some of her gravest and most emphatic poems repeat her claim to have stood fast, accepted persecution, remained with her people, not sheltered "under a foreign wing." The philistine Zhdanov, and even Trotsky himself, sneered at her work as that of a hysterical female immersed in frivolous love affairs, who regarded God as a sort of benevolent gynecologist. Akhmatova was not in any modern sense a feminist, but she was proud to be a woman, and a woman speaking with authority in a world of men. One of her epigrams observes sardonically that she has given a voice to women and their feelings, and they have followed her lead all too well: "God grant that I could make them silent again." (pp. 9-10)

In old age she remained a dignified and benevolent presence, her aquiline features molded into a more placid cast, but her powers were undiminished, and her poems as strong, shapely and well made as ever. (p. 10)

> *John Bayley, "The Sheer Necessity for Poetry,"*
> *in* The New York Times Book Review, *May 13, 1990, pp. 9-10.*

## Al Purdy

A beautiful woman she was not, on the evidence of nearly a hundred photographs in these two books. She was majestic instead, her nose imperial Roman, unsmiling for every camera. She possessed immense natural dignity. Men fell in love with her continually. She married three times. Even in old age, her face and carriage were striking and received homage. Indeed, she expected homage, almost demanded it according to some who knew her well; and accepted it without surprise. The Grande Dame, yet rather pitiful in old age—although she rejected pity fiercely.

Anna Akhmatova. Born in 1889 of a well-to-do family, she was told by her father when she began to write poetry that he did not want his name (Gorenko) associated with "that trade." She changed hers to Akhmatova, the Tatar name of a maternal ancestor, and made the new name famous. . . .

Over the 10-year period between 1912 and 1922, which included the First World War and the Russian Revolution, Akhmatova published five books of poetry. These were mostly love poems, and were very popular with young people at the time. She claimed, of course, that the poems did not reflect her own life (most poets do claim that), and were not autobiographical—which is true, in a sense. But one learns much about the woman from these poems: her romantic yearning for the perfect human relationship, her work growing in intensity and depth of feeling, and expanding in its subject matter.

In 1922 Mayakovsky denounced Akhmatova's poetry publicly, although she was as non-political as it was possible to be after the Revolution. Mayakovsky's mistress of that time said later that he read Akhmatova constantly, every day. But the Communist regime, growing ever more puritanical and repressive, could not abide Akhmatova's love poems: at least that seems to be one possible reason for her disfavour. Also: some of her friends were actually engaged in "alarums and excursions" of counter-revolution. After 1925 she was not allowed to publish in the Soviet Union. (p. 31)

These two enormous [volumes, **The Complete Poems of Anna Akhmatova,**] amount to a complete galaxy of Akhmatova's poems, and much else besides. There's a full-length biography by Roberta Reeder, the editor; several memoirs by people who knew her well; a chronology; and many, many photographs. The translator, Judith Hemschemeyer, learned Russian for the task, and devoted several years to it, receiving encomiums for her work.

I have previously read several other books related to Akhmatova: Nadezhda Mandelstam's memoir, *Hope Against Hope;* Olga Ivinskaya's reminiscences (she was Pasternak's friend); and, more important, Olga Carlisle's anthology of Russian poets, *Poets on Streetcorners* (1968). There are many of Akhmatova's poems in *Streetcorners,* translated by various hands, including Stanley Kunitz, Adrienne Rich, Rose Styron, Richard Wilbur, and Robert Lowell. Lowell "adapted" Akhmatova's **Requiem,** written after her son Lev's last arrest and imprisonment in Leningrad.

This long 11-part poem is regarded by many, including myself, as Akhmatova's best. **Requiem** was first published, long after its composition, in Munich, Germany, in 1963. Lowell included his adaptation of the poem in his *Imita-*

*tions.* It begins in prose, with Akhmatova waiting, along with many other relatives and friends of the prisoners, in "the prison lines at Leningrad." Another woman, apparently recognizing the poet, whispered in her ear, "Could you describe this?" Akhmatova answered, "Yes, I can."

Lowell used quatrains, off-rhymes, and rough metrics in his adaptation; Hemschemeyer free verse in her translations. Using the latter method, I think it's much more difficult to make a poem memorable and meaningful. As a study in comparative translation then, here are the last five verses of Akhmatova's **Requiem** as adapted by each writer (spaces between stanzas omitted).

Lowell:

> Friends, if you want some monument
> gravestone or cross to stand for me,
> you have my blessing and consent,
> but do not place it by the sea.
> I was a sea-child, hardened by
> the polar Baltic's grinding dark;
> that tie is gone: I will not lie,
> a Tsar's child in the Tsarist park.
> Far from your ocean, Leningrad,
> I leave my body where I stood
> three hundred hours in lines with those
> who watched unlifted prison windows.
> Safe in death's arms, I lie awake,
> and hear the mother's animal roar,
> the black truck slamming on its brake,
> the senseless hammering of the door.
> Ah, the Bronze Horseman wipes his eye
> and melts, a prison pigeon coos,
> the ice goes out, the Neva goes
> with its slow barges to the sea.

(that is not the poetry of a "Grande Dame")

And Hemschemeyer:

> And if ever in this country
> They decide to erect a monument to me,
> I consent to that honor
> Under these conditions: that it stand
> Neither by the sea, where I was born:
> My last tie with the sea is broken,
> Nor in the Tsar's garden near the cherished pine
>     stump,
> Where an inconsolable shade looks for me,
> But here, where I stood three hundred hours,
> And where they never unbolted the doors for
>     me.
> This, lest in blissful death
> I forget the rumbling of the Black Marias,
> Forget how that detested door slammed shut
> And an old woman howled like a wounded ani-
>     mal.
> And may the melting snow stream like tears
> From my motionless lips of bronze,
> And a prison dove coo in the distance,
> And the ships of the Neva sail calmly on.

Lowell called his version of **Requiem** an "imitation," a free adaptation of Akhmatova; Hemschemeyer's is probably truer to the original, but nevertheless is still only an approximation.

After Stalin died in 1953, Akhmatova's verse was again published in the Soviet Union; and a reverence for her

began. Most of her friends were long dead, from imprisonment in Siberia, as victims of execution, or simply old age; but a new generation loved her poems. Joseph Brodsky, before he emigrated to the United States, was one of her protégés. Some critics have called her the greatest woman poet since Sappho; but it is impossible to judge Sappho's work accurately since so little of it remains. In any case, Akhmatova left behind a legend as well as her poems when she died in 1966, a woman who, in the minds of some admirers, is emblematic of the soul of Russia. And the **Requiem** suite (Lowell's version) is indelible in my own memory.

In a country where most of the citizens were prisoners, incarcerated or not, Akhmatova was a free woman and lived her life as one. I admire her immensely. During her lifetime she rarely had very much money. When her poems were banned she translated foreign literature for small remuneration. Her friends—Pasternak among them—helped her; she helped them. It may be thought that her life was tragic. Perhaps, but it was also a triumph: *Yes, I can.* (pp. 31-2)

*Al Purdy, "The Soul of Russia," in* Books in Canada, *Vol. XIX, No. 6, August-September, 1990, pp. 31-2.*

## Marjorie Perloff

[*The Complete Poems of Anna Akhamatova*], a bilingual edition, with extraordinary notes, biographies, photographs, illustrations, and facsimile pages, would be a bargain at twice the price. The poems themselves, of which more in a moment, are framed, in Volume I, by a Translator's Preface, in which Judith Hemschemeyer, herself a poet, provides valuable comments on Akhmatova's prosody and stylistic habits, and by the editor Roberta Reeder's 160-page critical biography of the poet, which could easily have been published as a separate book. Then in Volume II, there are further biographical memoirs, this time by Isaiah Berlin and by Akhamatova's protegé, the critic Anatoly Naiman. At the back of Volume II, following a group of 200 uncollected lyrics (some of Akhamatova's most brilliant poems, reproduced from V. M. Zhirmunsky's 1976 Leningrad edition), there are detailed scholarly notes on the poem and a full bibliography. The production job (the arrangement is chronological, the Russian on facing pages, with the fascinating photographs, lithographs, and drawings giving a very full picture of Akhamatova and her circle from childhood to old age, interspersed throughout) seems to me quite simply stunning.

For some reason, Akhmatova's poetry had never really penetrated my consciousness as had Khlebnikov's or Mayakovsky's or Pasternak's. I knew English versions of some of her famous poems like **"I Visited the poet. . ."** (to Alexander Blok) and **"The Tale of the Black Ring,"** but found her seemingly straightforward lyrics on love and sorrow and death too direct and "simple" to have the appeal that, say, Khlebnikov's complicated linguistic experiments had for me. But reading Akhmatova in these new translations (on the whole, *excellent* in capturing the poems' visual lay-out, tone, and sound quality—at least so it seems to a novice in the Russian language like me), in the light of Reeder's fascinating account of the poet's life has made me a total convert. (pp. 233-34)

Akhamatova's poetry uses very little figuration; it is primarily heightened natural speech presented in straightforward syntax in the rhythms of folk song and *dolnik* (a poem with a fixed number of stresses but not a fixed number of syllables, usually with a complicated rhyme scheme and echolalia). But, like Goethe's lyric, which it very much resembles, Akhamatova's is *occasional* poetry whose strength lies in capturing, by means of delicate verbal adjustments, the exact emotion of a particular moment. Here is a poem of 1915, dedicated to the critic and connoisseur N. V. Nedobrovo, a man with whom Akhamatova shared a great deal but with whom she was not in love:

> There is a sacred boundary between those who
>   are close,
> And it cannot be crossed by passion or love—
> Though lips fuse in dreadful silence
> And the heart shatters to pieces with love.
>
> Friendship is helpless here, and years
> Of exalted and ardent happiness,
> When the soul is free and a stranger
> To the slow languor of voluptuousness.
>
> Those who strive to reach it are mad, and those
> Who reach it—stricken by grief . . .
> Now you understand why my heart
> Does not beat faster under your hand.

If the English version cannot quite capture the rhythmic quality of the original, with its intricately sounded four-stress lines and prominent rhymes (*strasti / chasti; toskoio / rukoio*), it does convey the poet's startling admission that for her, love is not based on psychological or emotional communion but on "the slow languor of voluptuousness," that without that "slow languor," "my heart / Does not beat faster under your hand." This last phrase seems almost hackneyed until we stop to consider what it really means. For the poet is not making the standard Romantic speech about her inability to return her lover's passion; she is not gently but firmly refusing his suit. On the contrary, it is while she is letting him caress her breasts and having sex with him, that she tells this close friend and ardent lover that he just doesn't turn her on.

There is a cruel, almost a brutal element in such confession, and indeed one begins to see Akhamatova as anything but the "domestic" poet (Trotsky witheringly dismissed her as a "doctor of female ailments"), she is often taken to be. Her love poems (and her best poems *are* love poems) run the gamut from self-abasement to intense erotic satisfaction, from contempt for a husband to pity for a former lover and shyness in the face of a new encounter, from *schadenfreude* at the defeat of a rival to total despair at the rejection by a new love object. Indeed, the force and violence of the poet's response to the passions leads me to a second observation.

Akhamatova's lyric is animated by an assumption that goes counter to all current feminist talk of victimization at the hands of the patriarchy, of the second-class status of women, and so on. That assumption is that a woman can be as strong and powerful as any man. Akhamatova let nothing interfere with her work, a work she refused to distinguish from life, and especially from sexual love— neither marriage (a bond under which she chafed and repeatedly dissolved) nor motherhood (she left her only child Lev in the country to be brought up by relatives), nor the extreme poverty and deprivation that came after the Revolution, nor the censorship of her work under Stalin. When World War II broke out, she gave radio speeches, mobilizing the women of Leningrad. The poet Olga Beggolts recalls, "With a face severe and angry, a gas mask thrown over her shoulder, she took on the fire watch like a regular soldier. She sewed bags for sand which were put on the trenches." If she was not a "good" mother in her youth, she spent endless hours of her maturity trying to free her son, a prominent scholar, from arrest and exile, going so far as to write verses to Stalin so as to plead Lev's cause. Her efforts on behalf of her imprisoned friend Osip Mandelstam are legendary. In the fifties, during the final decade of her life, when she was ousted from the Union of Soviet Writers, she earned her living translating the works of Serbian, Armenian, and Ukrainian authors.

At a time when many of our own poets and artists are so obsessed by the NEA debacle that they seem to have forgotten why they became poets in the first place, Anna Akhamatova provides the most luminous example imaginable of *what can be done*. And further: at a time when the "woman artist" is too often represented as a Camille Claudel (the title of a recent film), who must choose between "art" and "love," it is refreshing to witness Akhamatova's life-long conviction that she had to have both and that one fed the other. Indeed, if one reads straight through from **Evening** (1912), published when Akhamatova was only twenty-three, to the lyrics of the sixties collected in **Seventh Book,** the image that emerges is of a powerful woman to whom every turn presents a formidable roadblock but who not only survives but triumphs. A highly improbable tale for the twentieth century and hence doubly rewarding. (pp. 234-36)

*Marjorie Perloff, in a review of "The Complete Poems of Anna Akhmatova," in* Sulfur, *Vol. XI, No. 27, Fall, 1990, pp. 233-37.*

---

## FURTHER READING

Berlin, Isaiah. "Conversations with Russian Poets." *The Times Literary Supplement,* No. 4,048 (31 October 1980): 1233-36.
   Recounts Berlin's fateful meetings with Anna Akhmatova in 1945 and 1956.

Birnbaum, Henrik. "Face to Face with Death: On a Recurrent Theme in the Poetry of Anna Akhmatova." *Scando-Slavica* 28 (1982): 5-17.
   Technical and thematic analysis of Akhmatova's poem "To Death."

Des Pres, Terrence. "Poetry and Politics." *Triquarterly* 65 (Winter 1986): 17-29.

    Incorporates a reading of Akhmatova's poem "Veronezh" into a discussion of the connection between poetry and politics in contemporary verse.

Gifford, Henry. "Writing for the Nation." *The Times Literary Supplement,* No. 4,223 (9 March 1984): 250.

    Gifford discusses the merits and flaws of Lyn Coffin's translation of Akhmatova's poetry.

Hayward, Max. "Anna Akhmatova." In *Poems of Akhmatova,* edited by Stanley Kunitz and Max Hayward. Boston: Little, Brown, 1973.

    Brief critical biography.

Ketchian, Sonia. "Metempsychosis in the Verse of Anna Axmatova." *Slavic and East European Journal* 25, No. 1 (Spring 1981): 44-60.

    Defines metempsychosis and examines its appearance in a variety of forms throughout Akhmatova's verse.

Kurt, Anna and John Crowfoot. "Akhmatova and Translation." *Soviet Literature* 6, No. 495 (1989): 177-81.

    Discusses Akhmatova's publishing history and various translations of her works into English.

Rosslyn, Wendy. "The Theme of Light in the Early Poetry of Anna Akhmatova." *Renaissance and Modern Studies* XXIV (1980): 79-91.

    Traces the various connotations of light in Akhmatova's first five volumes of poetry.

Young, David. "Mending What Can't Be Mended." *Field: Contemporary Poetry and Poetics* 39 (Fall 1988): 34-39.

    Analyses the fourth poem in Akhmatova's "Northern Elegies" sequence.

# Maya Angelou

## 1928-

(Born Marguerite Johnson) American autobiographer, poet, scriptwriter, dramatist, nonfiction writer, composer, and editor.

Hailed as one of the great voices of contemporary African-American literature, Angelou is best known for *I Know Why the Caged Bird Sings,* the first of her series of five autobiographical novels. In addition to her prose, Angelou has written poetry, performed as a singer and dancer, written, directed, and acted in plays and films, and has composed musical scores. Angelou's literary works have generated great interest because they reflect her tenacity in overcoming social obstacles and her struggle for self-acceptance. Critics particularly praise her dynamic prose style, poignant satire, and her universal messages. Angelou herself states: "I speak to the black experience but I am always talking about the human condition—about what we can endure, dream, fail at and still survive."

Angelou began producing her autobiographical works after friends, among them such notable writers as James Baldwin and Jules Feiffer, suggested she write about her childhood spent between rural, segregated Stamps, Arkansas, where her pious grandmother ran a general store, and St. Louis, Missouri, where her worldly, glamorous mother lived. *I Know Why the Caged Bird Sings,* which became a great critical and commercial success, chronicles Angelou's life up to age sixteen, providing a child's perspective of the perplexing world of adults. This volume contains the gruesome account of how Angelou, at the age of eight, was raped by her mother's lover; it ends with her attempts as a single, teen-aged mother to nurture and protect her newborn son. In addition to creating a trenchant account of a girl's coming-of-age, this work also affords insights into the social and political tensions pervading the 1930s.

The next four volumes of Angelou's autobiography—*Gather Together in My Name, Singin' and Swingin' and Gettin' Merry Like Christmas, The Heart of a Woman,* and *All God's Children Need Traveling Shoes*—continue to trace her psychological, spiritual, and political odyssey. As she emerges from a disturbing and oppressive childhood to become a prominent figure in contemporary American literature, Angelou's quest for self-identity and emotional fulfillment continues to result in extraordinary experiences. Her encounters with Malcolm X and Dr. Martin Luther King, Jr. are two examples of the many episodes contained in these volumes. Angelou's personal involvement with the civil rights and feminist movements both in the United States and in Africa, her developing relationship with her son, and her knowledge of the hardships associated with the lower class of American society

are recurrent elements in the series. The four subsequent works are generally considered inferior to *I Know Why the Caged Bird Sings*; critics cited lack of moral complexity and failure to generate empathy or universal appeal. However, they continued to praise Angelou's narrative skills and her impassioned responses to the challenges in her life.

*All God's Children Need Traveling Shoes,* Angelou's latest autobiographical installment, is distinctive in its examination of black America's intellectual and emotional connections with post-colonial Africa. In this work, Angelou describes her four-year stay in Ghana where she worked as a free-lance writer and editor. The overriding theme in this volume is the search for "home," or what Patrice Gaines-Carter terms "a place or condition of belonging." Angelou finds much to venerate about Africa, but gradually realizes that although she has cultural ties to the land of her ancestors, she is nevertheless distinctly American and in many ways isolated from traditional African society. Angelou observes: "If home was not what we had expected, nevermind, our need for belonging allowed us to ignore the obvious." Wanda Coleman mirrored the general critical opinion of *All God's Children Need Traveling Shoes* when she stated that Angelou's work is "an important document drawing much needed attention to the hidden history of a people both African and American."

Angelou has described the art of autobiography as a means for a writer to go back to the past and recover through imagination and invention what has been lost. Angelou stated that she is "not afraid of the ties [between past and present]. I cherish them, rather. It's the vulnerability. . . . It's allowing oneself to be hypnotized. That's frightening because we have no defenses, nothing. We've slipped down the well and every side is slippery. And how on earth are you going to come out? That's scary. But I've chosen it, and I've chosen this mode as my mode."

Angelou's poetry, fashioned almost entirely of short lyrics with jazz rhythms, addresses social issues pertaining to African-Americans. Although her poetry, which is collected in such volumes as *Just Give Me a Cool Drink of Water 'fore I Diiie* and *And Still I Rise,* has contributed to her reputation and is especially popular among young people, most commentators reserve their highest praise for her prose. Angelou's dependence on alliteration, her heavy use of short lines, and her conventional vocabulary led several critics to declare her poetry superficial and devoid of her celebrated humor. Nevertheless, some reviewers praise her poetic style as refreshing and graceful. J. T. Keefe describes Angelou's poems as "curving scimitars that skillfully pierce the hearts of their readers [with] enviable economy."

(See also *CLC,* Vols. 12, 35; *Contemporary Authors,* Vols. 65-68; *Contemporary Authors New Revision Series,* Vol. 19; *Something about the Author,* Vol. 49; and *Dictionary of Literary Biography,* Vol. 38.)

## PRINCIPAL WORKS

### AUTOBIOGRAPHIES

*I Know Why the Caged Bird Sings*   1970
*Gather Together in My Name*   1974
*Singin' and Swingin' and Gettin' Merry Like Christmas*   1976
*The Heart of a Woman*   1981
*All God's Children Need Traveling Shoes*   1986

### POETRY

*Just Give Me a Cool Drink of Water 'fore I Diiie*   1971
*Oh Pray My Wings Are Gonna Fit Me Well*   1975
*And Still I Rise*   1978
*Shaker, Why Don't You Sing?*   1983
*Now Sheba Sings the Song*   1987
*I Shall Not Be Moved*   1990

### PLAYS

*Cabaret for Freedom* [with Godfrey Cambridge]   1960
*The Least of These*   1966
*Ajax* [adaptor; from the drama *Ajax* by Sophocles]   1974

*And Still I Rise*   1976

### SCREENPLAYS

*Georgia, Georgia*   1972
*All Day Long*   1974

### TELEVISION SCRIPTS

*Black, Blues, Black* [series]   1968
*Assignment America* [series]   1975
"The Legacy"   1976
"The Inheritors"   1976
"Sister, Sister"   1982

### RECORDINGS

*Miss Calypso*   1957
*The Poetry of Maya Angelou*   1969
*An Evening with Maya Angelou*   1975
*Women in Business*   1981

---

### Carol E. Neubauer

When Maya Angelou started her autobiographical series in 1970 with *I Know Why the Caged Bird Sings,* she naturally chose her childhood as the organizing principle of her first volume. The story of *Caged Bird* begins when the three-year-old Angelou and her four-year-old brother, Bailey, are turned over to the care of their paternal grandmother in Stamps, Arkansas, and it ends with the birth of her son when she is seventeen years old. The next two volumes, *Gather Together In My Name* (1974) and *Singin' and Swingin' and Gettin' Merry Like Christmas* (1976), narrate Angelou's life along chronological lines for the most part, and one would expect that her most recent addition to the autobiographical sequence, *The Heart of a Woman* (1981), would proceed with the account of her career as entertainer, writer, and freedom fighter. In many ways, Angelou meets her readers' expectations as she follows her life forward chronologically in organizing the newest segment in the series. Yet it is interesting to note that at the beginning of *The Heart of a Woman,* as she continues the account of her son's youth, she returns to the story of her own childhood repeatedly. The references to her childhood serve partly to create a textual link for readers who might be unfamiliar with the earlier volumes and partly to emphasize the suggestive similarities between her own childhood and that of her son. Maya Angelou's overwhelming sense of displacement and instability is, ironically, her son's burden too.

The most significant similarity between their childhood years is the condition of displacement in a familial as well as a geographical sense. Both Angelou and Guy, her son, are displaced from their immediate families several times during their youth. They are placed in the care of relatives or family friends and are moved from neighborhood to neighborhood and state to state. In a brief flashback in the second chapter of *The Heart of a Woman,* the writer reminds us of the displacement which characterized her youth and links this aspect of her past with her son's present attitude. When Guy is fourteen, Angelou decides to move to New York. She does not bring Guy to New York until she has found a place for them to live, and when he arrives after a one-month separation, he initially resists her attempts to make a new home for them. . . . From this and similar encounters with Guy, Angelou learns that the continual displacement of her own childhood is something she cannot prevent from recurring in her son's life.

Rather than a unique cycle perpetuated only within her family, Angelou's individual story presents a clear pattern commonly shared and passed along to new generations continually. In fact she identifies her own situation and the threat of displacement as a common condition among black families in America and acknowledges the special responsibility of the black mother: "She questions whether she loves her children enough—or more terribly, does she love them too much? . . . In the face of these contradictions, she must provide a blanket of stability, which warms but does not suffocate, and she must tell her children the truth about the power of white power without suggesting that it cannot be challenged." Providing stability for the children as the family disintegrates is a virtually impossible task, not only for Angelou but for many women in similar situations. After the dissolution of the family, the single parent is often left with an overwhelming sense of guilt and inadequacy; and, for Angelou, the burden is all the more taxing, because she has been solely responsible for her son from the very beginning of his life. (pp. 123-24)

As Angelou narrates selected events that illustrate the periods of displacement in Guy's life, she adapts elements from both fiction and fantasy. Although she is clearly working within the genre of autobiography, Angelou freely borrows from these two traditionally more imaginative types of writing. On numerous occasions in her earlier volumes, she has employed what has become a rather personalized autobiographical style, a method which integrates ingredients from diverse modes of writing and gracefully crosses over traditionally static generic lines. One of the most memorable uses of fantasy in all of Angelou's writing is found in *Caged Bird* and involves a visit to a racist dentist in Stamps. As a child, she imagines that her grandmother grows to gigantic height and instantly gains superhuman strength to retaliate against the bigoted dentist who refuses to treat Angelou. In *Heart of a Woman,* she combines fiction and fantasy with the more standard biographical or historical mode to capture the subtleties of her relationship with her son and to emphasize the apparent similarities between their lives.

Examples of fictionalization in *Heart of a Woman* are quite varied. They range from rather common techniques, such as representational detail in description and reconstructed accounts of actual dialogue, to more specialized devices used to create a sense of history beyond the individual life story and to include other narratives from folklore within her own narrative. Each fictional technique contributes to the overall completeness and credibility of the autobiographical text.

In *Heart of a Woman,* Angelou deliberately strives to capture the individual conversational styles of her relatives and friends. In a sense, her friends and acquaintances be-

come "characters" in the story of her life, and like any good writer of fiction, she attempts to make their conversations realistic and convincing. With some of the people who figure in her autobiography, there is no objective measure for credibility other than the reader's critical appreciation for life itself. If the conversant in question is not well-known beyond the scope of the autobiography, Angelou need only ensure that the dialogue attributed to the individual be consistent with his character as delineated in the text itself. Yet many of her friends and associates were either highly successful celebrities or popular political figures, and the conversations recorded in her life story have points of reference beyond the autobiographical text. In other words, readers can test the degree of verisimilitude in the recorded dialogues with either firsthand knowledge or secondhand sources of information about the celebrities' lives.

It is highly probable, for example, that many of Angelou's readers are already familiar with the rhetorical styles of Martin Luther King, Jr., and Malcolm X, and the popular lyrics of Billie Holiday. In fact the lives of these three people in such accounts as *Why We Can't Wait, The Autobiography of Malcolm X,* and *Lady Sings the Blues* have in many ways become part of our contemporary folk history. Angelou adds a personalized quality to her recollections of conversations with these individuals and many others. The record of their conversations in *Heart of a Woman* brings them to life again, because the autobiographer is sensitive to and even somewhat self-conscious about the accurate reconstruction of their individual styles.

Since memory is not infallible, fictionalization comes into play whenever the autobiographer reconstructs or, perhaps more correctly, recreates conversation. While the autobiographer relies on invention, he or she creates the illusion of an infallible memory that records exactly the feel of a place and the words spoken there. Thus, when Angelou narrates visits with Billie Holiday in Laurel Canyon, she takes care to imitate her rather flamboyant verbal style. . . . As much as Angelou is shocked by the first words that tumble out of the famous entertainer's mouth, she is moved by Holiday's sensitivity in communicating with a precocious young boy who would be offended by any "off-color" phrases. "She carefully avoided profanity and each time she slipped, she'd excuse herself to Guy, saying, 'It's just another bad habit I got'." Holiday and Guy soon develop a balanced rapport and thoroughly enjoy the little time they spend together. Guy exuberantly tells her about his adventures and the books he has read, while she in turn sings her sorrowful songs to him as she relaxes and finds solace in the company of the child. In a sense, the anecdotes about Billie Holiday in *Heart of a Woman* form a tribute to her, for as Angelou admits, "I would remember forever the advice of a lonely sick woman, with a waterfront mouth, who sang pretty songs to a twelve-year-old boy."

In addition to using fictional techniques in the reconstruction of dialogue, Angelou turns to fictionalization to create a sense of history larger than the story of her own life. In her description of her meeting with Malcolm X, for example, Angelou combines the re-creation of credible dialogue with historical references that go beyond her individual life. Again there are points of reference beyond the writer's account that measure its accuracy.

In one scene, Angelou and her close friend Rosa Guy, both representatives of the Cultural Association of Women of African Heritage, decide to call on Malcolm X to ask for his help in controlling a potential riot situation brought about by their United Nations demonstration to protest the death of Lumumba. The following dialogue demonstrates her talent for remembering and recording their conversation as precisely as possible:

> I joined the telling, and we distributed our story equally, like the patter of a long-time vaudeville duo.
> "We—CAWAH . . . "
> "Cultural Association of Women of African Heritage."
> "Wanted to protest the murder of Lumumba so we—"
> "Planned a small demonstration. We didn't expect—"
> "More than fifty people—"
> "And thousands came."
> "That told us that the people of Harlem are angry and that they are more for Africa and Africans"
> "than they ever let on . . . "

Face to face with Malcolm X, Angelou and her friend, both extremely articulate women, are reduced to a stammering "vaudeville duo." The stichomythic rhythm in the reconstructed conversation suggests the degree of intimidation that the women experienced in the presence of Malcolm X. The power of his personality causes their initial uneasiness, which soon turns to disappointment as Malcolm X coolly refuses to involve his Muslim followers in public demonstration.

Angelou's unsuccessful interview with the Harlem leader provides a clear contrast with her first meeting with Martin Luther King. The larger historical context of their exchange expands the personal perimeter of her life story. At the time of her first conversation with King, Angelou has been working as Northern Coordinator of the Southern Christian Leadership Conference in New York. She has devoted the previous months to raising funds, boosting membership, and organizing volunteer labor both in the office and in the neighborhoods. When Dr. King pays his first visit to the New York office during her tenure, she does not have advance notice of his presence and rushes into her office one day after lunch to find him sitting at her desk. They begin to talk about her background and eventually focus their comments on her brother, Bailey:

> "Come on, take your seat back and tell me about yourself."
>
> . . . When I mentioned my brother Bailey, he asked what he was doing now.
>
> The question stopped me. He was friendly and understanding, but if I told him my brother was in prison, I couldn't be sure how long his understanding would last. I could lose my job. Even more important, I might lose his respect. Birds

of a feather and all that, but I took a chance and told him Bailey was in Sing Sing.

> He dropped his head and looked at his hands. . . .
>
> "I understand. Disappointment drives our young men to some desperate lengths." Sympathy and sadness kept his voice low. "That's why we must fight and win. We must save the Baileys of the world. And Maya, never stop loving him. Never give up on him. Never deny him. And remember, he is freer than those who hold him behind bars."

Angelou appreciates King's sympathy, and of course shares his hope that their work will make the world more fair and free. She recognizes the undeniable effects of displacement on Bailey's life and fervently hopes that her son, who has not escaped the pain of displacement, will be spared any further humiliation and rejection.

When Angelou extends her personal narrative to include anecdotes about well-known entertainers or political figures, or observations about significant historical events, she necessarily fictionalizes the story of her past. Fictionalization is clearly at play on both a conscious and an unconscious level in the act of remembering and transcribing key events from her private life, but it becomes virtually inevitable in recording her subjective impressions about a public event or person. Whenever there is more than one account of an event, as there usually is in the public or historical context, comparisons reveal inconsistencies or discrepancies that are the product of varied individual response. Thus fictionalization occurs when Angelou includes other narratives within the narrative of her life. Each borrowed story is usually a sampling of folklore, but is told in a slightly different context to achieve a special effect within the autobiography. (pp. 124-26)

[One example of this is when] she recalls the stories of several slave heroines while attending an informal gathering of African women in London. All of the women present are the wives of political activists in the struggle to end apartheid and second-class citizenship for black Africans. Although their national backgrounds are quite different, they share the same sense of frustration and ineffectualness in comparison with their husbands, who ironically enjoy more autonomy in the fight for freedom. To ease their sense of uselessness, they gather one day in the home of Mrs. Oliver Tambo, the wife of the leader of the African National Congress. Here the women narrate traditional tales from African folklore. Although Angelou initially feels somewhat estranged from the spontaneous ceremony, she is soon moved to share folktales from the tradition of slave narratives concerning women who led the fight for freedom in America.

Her first story narrates the history of Harriet Tubman, a model of the strong black women at the heart of American history, a woman who fought against devastating odds and suffered extraordinary personal sacrifice to free many of her people. Tubman is, therefore, an appropriate figure to celebrate in an international group of black women. Tubman, Angelou tells them, "stood on free ground, above a free sky, hundreds of miles from the chains and lashes of slavery and said, 'I must go back. With the help of God I will bring others to freedom,' and . . . although suffering brain damage from a slaver's blow, she walked back and forth through the lands of bondage time after time and brought hundreds of her people to freedom." Pleased with the success of her first tale, Angelou follows the inspiring story of Harriet Tubman with an even more dramatic presentation of the heroism of Sojourner Truth. Once again she selects the figure of a fearless black American woman who devoted her life to end slavery and to educate both Northerners and Southerners about the responsibilities of freedom. Sojourner Truth, like Harriet Tubman, is a fitting example of the essential strength of black American women to share with a group of African women celebrating the same heroic characteristics in their ancestors. The anecdote relates an equal rights meeting in the 1800s at which Truth addressed the group and was accused by a white man of being a man dressed as a woman:

> "Ain't I a woman? I have suckled your babes at this breast." Here she put her large hands on her bodice. Grabbing the cloth she pulled. The threads gave way, the blouse and her undergarments parted and her huge tits hung, pendulously free. She continued, her face unchanging and her voice never faltering, "And ain't I a woman?"

> When I finished the story, my hands tugging at the buttons of my blouse, the African women stood applauding, stamping their feet and crying. Proud of their sister whom they had not known a hundred years before.

The stories about Sojourner Truth and Harriet Tubman, like the folktale of Brer Rabbit, enlarge the scope of Angelou's autobiography and bring certain historical points of reference to the story of one person's life. Readers come to understand *Heart of a Woman* not only through the avenues of her life opened in the text but through the samplings of folklore that are included as well. Fictionalization comes into play as Angelou adapts these borrowed narratives and anecdotes to illustrate the theme of displacement in her life and her son's.

I have shown that Angelou adapts fictional techniques in *Heart of a Woman* to make her life story fully realistic and convincing, and to supplement the personal scope with the larger historical context. In addition Angelou uses elements of fantasy to illustrate disappointments and defeats she has experienced in life and to reveal the complexity of her relationship with her son. Her use of fantasy can be divided into two types: the narration of a fantasy that ends in illusion and suggests the autobiographer's somewhat ironic stance in examining her past and the narration of a fantasy that becomes reality and emphasizes her inability to protect her son and herself from harmful influences. With both types of fantasy, the writer stresses the importance of imagination when a situation does not measure up to one's expectations. (pp. 126-27)

The complex nature of her relationship with her son is at the heart of this most recent of Angelou's autobiographical volumes. At the end, Guy is seventeen and has just passed the matriculation exams at the University of Ghana. The last scene pictures Guy driving off to his new dormitory room with several fellow university students. The conclusion of *Heart of a Woman* announces a new beginning for Angelou and hope for her future relationship with Guy. In this sense, the newest volume in the series follows the pattern established by the conclusions of the earlier volumes. *Caged Bird* ends with the birth of Guy, *Gather Together* with the return to her mother's home in San Francisco after regaining her innocence through the lessons of a drug addict, and *Singin' and Swingin'* with the reunion of mother and son in a paradisiacal setting of a Hawaiian resort. The final scene of *Heart of a Woman* suggests that the future will bring more balance between dependence and independence in their relationship and that both will have significant personal successes as their lives begin to take different courses. Although Guy has assumed that he has been fully "grown up" for years, they have at last reached a point where they can treat each other as adults and allow one another the chance to live independently. Many of Angelou's victories are reflected in Guy in the last scene, for, although Guy is the same age she is at the end of *Caged Bird,* his young life promises many more opportunities and rewards as a result of his mother's perseverance and her belief "that life loved the person who dared to live it." Moreover, Angelou shares Guy's fresh sense of liberation; she too is embarking on a new period of strength and independence as she begins her life yet again—on her own and in a new land. It is from this position of security that Maya Angelou looks back to record her life story and to compensate for the years of distance and displacement through the autobiographical act. (p. 129)

> *Carol E. Neubauer, "Displacement and Autobiographical Style in Maya Angelou's 'The Heart of a Woman',"* in Black American Literature Forum, *Vol. 17, No. 3, Fall, 1983, pp. 123-29.*

## Selwyn R. Cudjoe

The Afro-American autobiographical statement is the most Afro-American of all Afro-American literary pursuits. During the eighteenth and nineteenth centuries, thousands of autobiographies of Afro-American slaves appeared expressing their sentiments about slavery, the most cruel of American institutions. The practice of the autobiographical statement, up until the contemporary era, remains the quintessential literary genre for capturing the cadences of the Afro-American being, revealing its deepest aspirations and tracing the evolution of the Afro-American psyche under the impact of slavery and modern U.S. imperialism. (p. 6)

There is nothing in the autobiographical statement that makes it essentially different from fiction except, of course, that which has been erected by convention. Michael Ryan, picking up on the observations of Jacques Derrida, has argued that inherent in the structure of the autobiographical statement is the necessary death of the author as a condition for the existence of the referential machinery. "The writing," he states, "must be capable, from the outset, of functioning independently of the subject, of being repeated in the absence of the subject. Strictly speaking, then, its referent is always 'ideal' of fictional—produced and sustained by convention."

To the degree, however, that the referent is present in the autobiography (it being absent or "ideal" in fiction), there is really nothing in the autobiography that guarantees that it will not be read as fiction or vice versa. In fact, any discussion on the Afro-American autobiography is always likely to raise this question: "Is it really true?" and almost always the author must present strong evidence that the work is unquestionably autobiographical. . . . (p. 7)

Autobiography and fiction, then, are simply different means of arriving at, or (re)cognizing the same truth: the reality of American life and the position of the Afro-American subject in that life. Neither genre should be given a privileged position in our literary history and each should be judged on its ability to speak honestly and perceptively about Black experience in this land. (p. 8)

[Maya Angelou's] *I Know Why the Caged Bird Sings* . . . explores growing up Black and female in the American South during the second quarter of this century. . . . The world to which Angelou introduces us is embroidered with *humiliation, violation, displacement,* and *loss.* From the outset Angelou sounds the pervading themes when she declares: "If growing up is painful for the Southern Black girl, being aware of her displacement is the rust on the razor that threatens the throat. It is an unnecessary insult." From this introduction she wends her way to the end of her work, where she concludes: "The Black female is assaulted in her tender years by all those common forces of nature at the same time that she is caught in the tripartite crossfire of *masculine prejudice, white illogical hate* and *Black lack of power.*"

This is the burden of the work: to demonstrate the manner in which the Black female is violated, by all of the forces above, in her tender years and to demonstrate the "unnecessary insult" of Southern girlhood in her movement to adolescence.

Southern life, as Angelou demonstrates, is one of harshness and brutality. It is exemplified by the conditions under which the workers of Stamps lived, the fear engendered by the Ku Klux Klan, the wanton murder of Black folks (which led Mother Henderson to send Maya and her brother Bailey to their mother in California), the racial separation of the town, and the innumerable incidents of denigration which made life in the South an abomination against God and man. Not that moments of happiness were entirely absent from her childhood life, but such moments came, as Thomas Hardy characterized them in *The Mayor of Casterbridge,* as but "the occasional episode[s] in a general drama of pain."

Such cruelty led to a well-defined pattern of behavior on the part of the South's citizens and the adoption of certain necessary codes if one was to exist in that part of the country. As Angelou points out: "The less you say to white folks (or even powhitetrash) the better." The insults of the powhitetrash had to be accepted and the spiritual and emotional manner in which the whites tried to debase the Blacks had to be fended off at each moment of existence.

As the text charts Angelou's movement from *innocence* to *awareness,* from childhood to an ever quickening sense of adolescence, there were certain ideological apparatuses, inserted into the social fabric, which Angelou had to overcome in order to maintain a sense of relative liberation and autonomy. It is the virtue of Angelou and the strength of the statement that, as she develops, she is able to detect the presence of these apparatuses, to challenge them and to withstand their pervasive and naturalizing tendencies.

In this country, as in any other capitalist country, religion, education, and sports are supposed to function in certain ideological ways so that the subject accepts certain well-defined practices. Thus, while religion is designed to keep the Afro-American in an oppressed condition, here Black people subverted that institution and used it to assist them to withstand the cruelty of the American experience. (pp. 11-13)

One of the most poignant moments of ideological unveiling comes when Angelou describes her graduation exercises of 1940 at Lafayette County Training School. As she listens to the condescending and racist manner in which Mr. Edward Donleavy, the featured speaker, insulted the intelligence of her class, hearing the approving "amens" of her elders as he made his invidious comparisons with Central, the white school of the area, Angelou, a young sensitive Black female, could only think: "It was awful to be Negro and have no control over my life. It was brutal to be young and already trained to sit quietly and listen to charges brought against my color with no chance of defense. We should all be dead. I thought I should like to see us all dead, one on top of the other."

And here the sense of collective responsibility, a sensibility charged by the disparagement of the group, is reflected. In the impotence of childhood there is nothing she can do, but the charges which have been leveled against her people will not be soon forgotten.

Indeed, the act colors the texture of her world; she realizes the emptiness of the sentiments which were expressed in the valedictory address: "I am master of my fate, I am captain of my soul." Observing the inherent falsehood of the statement "To be or not to be," she could only observe in ironic tones: "Hadn't he heard the whitefolks? We couldn't *be,* so the question was a waste of time." It is out of this web of reality that she takes her first, fumbling steps toward her social development in Stamps, Arkansas.

According to the text, . . . the major crime of the society is that it attempts to reduce all Negroes to a sense of impotence and nothingness. This is the internal "rust" which threatens the "personhood" of Black people (young and old) in all of America. It is the inherent homicidal tendency of an oppressive and racist society which pushes these young people to the brink of spiritual waste and physical destruction. For Maya, such a milieu becomes the point of departure from which she struggles to salvage a sense of dignity and personhood, the necessary prerequisite before any sense of femaleness can be expressed.

Maya Angelou understands that to be Black and female is to be faced with a special quality of violence and violation. This peculiarity is brought into sharp focus when

Maya goes to live with her mother and is subsequently raped by her mother's boyfriend. When she is faced with this catastrophe, her first reaction is to withdraw into herself. Yet because of the strength of her individual will, she is able to work herself back to a point where she can function in a seemingly productive manner in her social world. Nevertheless, the rape of this eight-year-old by an almost impotent adult Black male—who, it would seem, was unable to enjoy a relatively mature and respectful relationship with an adult Black woman—can be seen as symbolic of only one aspect of this internal dimension of Black life. (pp. 14-15)

Angelou wants to suggest that the power, the energy, and the honesty which characterized our examination of our relationship with our oppressor (i.e., at the external level) must now be turned inward in an examination of some of the problems which seem to have inhibited our own level of social development and our quest for liberation. In other words, the problem of Afro-American liberation is to be seen as both an *internal* and an *external* reality, the former of which must be our exclusive concern. It is this internal probing which characterizes [*I Know Why the Caged Bird Sings*] and marks the writings of the Black female writer.

One cannot, however, simply read the shortcomings of Black life back into the text and forget the complicity of white society, which is the major causative agent of Black denigration. On the larger canvas from which this life is drawn, the villain is to be recognized as a society which reduces men to impotence, women to lives of whoredom, and children to victimization by their fathers' lust and impotence. Indeed, it is the perception of what constitutes femininity and beauty which leads Maya into a sexual liaison that eventually produces an unplanned pregnancy. Certainly at the age of sixteen she was not prepared financially or emotionally to take care of a child.

But to argue for the cruelty and brutality of the society does not deny the episodes of beauty which relieve the monotony of life in Stamps or the violence of California. Nor can one deny the progressive tendency of the religious life of Stamps's Black community. It is to argue, however, that the cruelty so overwhelms the sensibility of the Black person in the South that it makes it very difficult for him/her to exist in the society. For a Black woman it further demonstrates the pain which growth and awareness demand. As Angelou says: "Without willing it, I had gone from being ignorant of being ignorant to being aware of being aware. And the worst part of my awareness was that I didn't know what I was aware of." This realization of her status is bought at a price: her subjection to the tripartite force of which she speaks (masculine prejudice, white illogical hate, and Black powerlessness).

One of the shortcomings of the text revolves around the manner in which the story is told from the point of view of an adult, who imposes the imagination, logic, and language of an adult upon the work and thus prevents the reader from participating in the unfolding of childhood consciousness as it grows into maturity. The tone of the work is even and constant, which causes the text to be almost predictable in its development. The rationalization of later years tends almost to destroy the flow of the text. Indeed many times one is forced to question the authenticity of her response to incidents in her life. (pp. 15-16)

The task of autobiography . . . does not consist in the mere reproduction of naturalistic detail but, because it involves the creative organization of ideas and situations and makes an ethical and moral statement about the society, must generate that which is purposeful and significant for our liberation. . . .

The intense solidity and moral center which we observed in *Caged Bird* is not to be found in *Gather Together in My Name.* . . . The richly textured ethical life of the Black people of the rural South and the dignity with which they live their lives are all but broken as we enter the *alienated* and *fragmented* lives which the urban world of America engenders. It is these conditions of *alienation* and *fragmentation* which characterize the life of Maya Angelou as she seeks to situate herself in urban California during her sixteenth to nineteenth years. (pp. 16-17)

*Gather Together* reveals a more selective vision of Afro-American life. In this work, the author writes about one particular kind of Afro-American whom she meets through the kind of work she does. When one considers that Angelou has been a short-order cook, a waitress at a nightclub, a madam in charge of her own house of prostitution, a nightclub dancer, a prostitute, and the lover of a drug addict who stole dresses for a living, it becomes apparent that the range of characters whom she encountered during this period of emotional and social upheaval were indeed limited to the declassed elements of the society. And this is what differentiates *Gather Together* from both *Caged Bird* and *Singin' and Swingin' and Gettin' Merry Like Christmas.*

The violation which began in *Caged Bird* takes on a much sharper focus in *Gather Together.* To be sure, the author is still concerned with the question of what it means to be Black and female in America, but her development is reflective of a particular type of Black woman at a specific moment of history and subjected to certain social forces which assault the Black woman with unusual intensity.

Thus when she arrives in Los Angeles she is aware that even her mother "hadn't the slightest idea that not only was I not a woman, but what passed for my mind was animal instinct. Like a tree or a river, I merely responded to the wind and the tides." In responding to the indifference of her mother's family to her immaturity, she complains most bitterly, "they were not equipped to understand that an eighteen-year-old mother is also an eighteen-year-old girl." Yet it is from this angle of vision—that of "a tree in the wind" possessing mostly "animal instinct" to an "unequipped" eighteen-year-old young woman—that we must prepare to respond to Angelou's story.

Neither politically nor linguistically innocent, *Gather Together* reflects the imposition of values of a later period in the author's life. Undoubtedly, in organizing the incidents of text in a coherent manner (i.e., having recourse to memorization, selection of incidents, etc.), the fictive principle of which we spoke in our introduction comes fully into play. The fact is that with time the perception of the subject changes, which demonstrates that the autobiographical statement indicates one's *attitudes* toward the fact, rather than the presentation of the facts (i.e., the incidents) as given and unalterable. It is that *attitude toward the facts* to which critics should respond.

For example, it is difficult for the reader to believe that the young Angelou set out to organize the prostitution of Johnnie Mae and Beatrice because she wanted to take revenge on those "inconsiderate, stupid bitches." Nor can we, for that matter, accept the fact that she turned tricks for L.D. because she believed that "there was nothing wrong with sex. I had no need for shame. Society dictated that sex was only licensed by marriage documents. Well, I didn't agree with that. Society is a conglomerate of human beings, and that's just what I was. A human being."

As a justification, it rings too hollow. Society is not a conglomeration merely of human beings. Society is a conglomeration of *social beings* whose acts make them *human* or *nonhuman.* To the degree that those acts *negate* our humanity, they can be considered wrong. To the degree that they *affirm* our humanity they can be considered correct. Such reasoning, though, is only to keep the argument within the context in which Maya Angelou has raised the question.

For me, the importance of the text—its social significance—lies in its capacity to signify to, and from, the larger social context from which it originates. Clearly, *Caged Bird* and *Gather Together* assume their largest meaning or meanings within the context of the larger society. As a consequence, one cannot reduce important attitudes of social behavior by mere strident comments of dissent. Such attitudes and values are derived from the larger *social* context of Afro-American life. Correspondingly, one questions Angelou's attitude toward Johnnie Mae when she cries out that she has been wounded: "And, ladies, you decided in the beginning that you were going to screw me one way or the other. Look at us now. Who did the screwing?" It is imperious, but is it correct?

In spite of this imperious attitude, and a certain degree of life-saving pride, Maya is an extremely lonely young woman; a young woman more isolated in bustling California than she was in the quietude of Stamps; a young woman who had to use both that imperious attitude and her life-saving pride to exist. . . . Yet precisely because she is drifting through this phase of her life, none of this advice is particularly fruitful to her nor does she seem particularly proud of her activity during those "few tense years" of sixteen through eighteen. Of course, it is not so much that these incidents took place; what is more important is what she made of these incidents in terms of her own social development. While this question cannot be answered here, we hesitate to accept in an unquestioning manner her interpretation of what these events meant to her life.

Finally, two horrendous and dramatic incidents make her realize how much on the brink of catastrophe she had been. The kidnapping of her child (i.e., the near-loss of her child, her most important and significant achievement thus far) and her being saved from a life of drugs by the generosity of Troubadour Martin really gave her that rebirth into innocence; a rebirth at a higher level of dialectical understanding.

Yet in a curious way the book seems not to succeed. Its lack of moral weight and ethical center deny it an organizing principle and rigor capable of keeping the work together. If I may be permitted, the incidents of the book appear merely gathered together in the name of Maya Angelou. They are not so organized that they may achieve a complex level of signification. In fact, it is the absence of these qualities which make the work conspicuously weak.

The language has begun to loosen up and this becomes the work's saving grace. Where there were mere patches of beautiful writing in *Caged Bird,* there is a much more consistent and sustained flow of eloquent and almost honey-dipped writing. The simplicity of the speech patterns remains, yet there is a much more controlled use of language. The writing flows and shimmers with beauty; only the rigorous, coherent and meaningful organization of experience is missing.

At the end of the work, the author attempts to recover some of the powerful ideological unfoldment of the society which we encountered in *Caged Bird.* Whereas, however, she presented herself as an integral part of the society in *Caged Bird,* in *Gather Together* she separates herself from the daily life and sufferings of her people and projects a strikingly individual ethos. . . . (pp. 17-20)

This kind of distance and assumption weakens the work because it begins to rely almost exclusively on individual exploits rather than to reflect the traditional collective wisdom and/or sufferings of the group. Because of this absence, the work reduces itself at times to a titillating account of a personal life bereft of the context of the larger society. The narrowly private existence of the subject is substituted for the *personal universalized* (which gives such great power to the Afro-American autobiographical statement), and the importance of *Gather Together* is diminished. (p. 20)

Thus, where she announces at the end of *Caged Bird* that she "had gone from being ignorant of being ignorant to being aware," at the end of *Gather Together* she declares for a certain type of innocence which cannot be really regarded in the same light as that which we found at the beginning of *Caged Bird.* It must be regarded as the (re)discovery of that primal innocence, at a higher level of consciousness, which was lost in her original encounter with the American dream. The sinking into the slime of the American abyss represents the necessary condition of regeneration and (re)birth into a new and, hopefully, more consciously liberated person. Thus, if *Caged Bird* sets the context for the subject, *Gather Together* presents itself as the necessary purgation through which the initiate must pass in order to (re)capture and to (re)define the social self to function in a relatively healthy manner in white America.

*Singin' and Swingin'* explores the adulthood of Maya Angelou, again major protagonist, as she moves back into and defines herself more centrally within the mainstream of the Black experience. In this work, she encounters the white world in a much fuller, more sensuous manner, seeking to answer, as she does, the major problem of her works: what it means to be Black and female in America. We would see that this quest, in the final analysis, reduces itself to what it means to be Black and person in America; the urgency of being Black and female collapses into what it means to be Black and person. In order to achieve this, the book is divided into two parts: part one, in which the writer works out her relationship with the white American world, and part two, in which she makes a statement about her own development through her participation in the opera *Porgy and Bess,* and her encounter with Europe and with Africa.

*Singin' and Swingin'* opens with a scene of displacement in which Angelou feels a sense of being "unanchored" as the family bonds of her youth are torn asunder under the impact of urban life in California. Under these new circumstances the author examines her feeling and her relationship with the larger white society as she encounters white people on an intimate personal level for the first time. As the reader will recall, Blacks and whites lived separately in Stamps and the occasion for shared and mutual relations did not exist. Before Angelou can enter into any relationship, though, she must dispense with all the stereotypical notions she has about white people. Indeed it is no longer possible to argue: "It wasn't nice to reveal one's feelings to strangers. And nothing on earth was stranger to me than a friendly white woman."

As the autobiography gradually unfolds, she observes that most of the stereotypical pictures which she has of whites are designed to protect her feelings from the cruelty of white hate and indifference. Yet as she grows into adulthood, these notions are punctured and eventually discarded, the biggest test coming when she is forced to make a decision about marrying Tosh, a white man, who is courting her through her son. Part of the difficulty arises from Angelou's awareness that whites had violated her people for centuries and that "Anger and guilt decided before my birth that *Black was Black and white was white* and although the two might share sex, they must never exchange love."

Angelou confronts the problem with a sort of evasion when she tells herself that Tosh "was Greek, not white American; therefore I needn't feel that I had betrayed my race by marrying one of the enemy, nor could white Americans believe that I had so forgiven them the past that I was ready to love a member of their tribe." She is not entirely satisfied by the truce she makes with her Blackness and for the rest of her marriage has to contend with the guilt created by her liaison with a white male.

With the end of her marriage, the tears came and the fright that she would be cast into "a maelstrom of rootlessness" momentarily embroidered her mind. Soon, however, it gave way to the knowledge that she would be ridiculed by her people in their belief that she was another victim of a "white man [who] had taken a Black woman's body and left her hopeless, helpless and alone." At the end of this encounter, however, she would be better prepared to deal with her own life, having gained a certain entrance

to the white world and possessing, already, the stubborn realities of Black life.

One of the significant facets of the author's relationship to Tosh revolves around the manner in which she effaces her own identity within the framework of the marriage. But the compromises which she makes to secure a stronger marriage cannot be seen only in the context of the *subjection* of wife to husband or Black female to white male. It can also be read as the subjection of the central values of the Black world (and, as a consequence, of the Black woman) to the dominant totality of white values.

In this context, it is to be noted that in spite of the fact that Angelou finds many aspects of white culture objectionable, most of the dominant images of perfection and beauty remain fashioned by the ethos of white society. Yet the tensions which keep the first section of the work together center around the general tendency of her wanting to be absorbed into the larger ambit of American culture (i.e., white culture) and her struggle to maintain a sense of her Black identity. (pp. 21-3)

As Angelou begins the second phase of her development (i.e., her evolution toward adulthood) her Southern origins became the necessary basis on which she begins to evaluate the major transformations which have taken place in her life thus far. . . . The identification of her people's sufferings in the minds of the ordinary European, their immediate identification of her with Joe Louis, the enthusiastic manner in which the Europeans welcomed the *Porgy* cast and the spirituals of her people, led to some of the most revealing moments of her development. The recognition that "Europeans often made as clear a distinction between Black and white Americans as did the most confirmed Southern bigot . . . [in that] Blacks were liked, whereas white Americans were not" did much to raise her self-esteem and a recognition of her emergent place in the world. (pp. 23-4)

It is, however, the success of *Porgy* which seemed paradigmatic of her evolution as an autonomous and fully liberated person. The pride which she takes in her company's professionalism, their discipline onstage, and the wellspring of spirituality that the opera emoted, all seem to conduce toward an organic harmony of her personal history as it intertwined with the social history of her people. The triumph of *Porgy,* therefore, speaks not only to the dramatic success of a Black company, it speaks, also, to the personal triumph of a remarkable Black woman. *Singin' and Swingin'* is a celebration of that triumph.

In 1970 Maya Angelou produced her first work, a volume concerned with what it meant to be Black and female in America. By 1976 she had enlarged her concerns to address what it meant to be Black and person in America, given the social, political, and economic constraints which militate against any achievement in contemporary America. (p. 24)

*Selwyn R. Cudjoe, "Maya Angelou and the Autobiographical Statement," in* Black Women Writers (1950-1980): A Critical Evaluation, *edited by Mari Evans, Anchor Press/Doubleday, 1984, pp. 3-37.*

## Priscilla R. Ramsey

Maya Angelou's physical shifts from Stamps, Arkansas' Lafayette County Public School to the Village Gate's stage in Manhattan and from New York to a teaching podium at Cairo University in Egypt represent an intellectual and psychological voyage of considerable complexity—one of unpredictably erratic cyclic movement. She has chronicled some of this voyage in her three autobiographies. . . . Additionally she has written three collections of poetry: *Oh Pray My Wings are Gonna Fit Me Well* (1975), *And Still I Rise* (1971), and *Just Give Me a Cool Drink of Water 'fore I Die* (1971). (p. 139)

The public achievements have been many and yet the private motivation out of which her writing generates extends beyond the mere search for words as metaphors for purely private experience. Her poetry becomes both political and confessional. Significantly, one sees in her autobiographies a role-modeling process—one paradigmatic for other women—while not allowing the didactic to become paramount in either the poetry or the autobiographies.

Her autobiographies and poetry reveal a vital need to transform the elements of a stultifying and destructive personal, social, political and historical milieu into a sensual and physical refuge. Loneliness and human distantiation pervade both her love and political poetry, but are counterposed by a glorification of life and sensuality which produces a transcendence over all which could otherwise destroy and create her despair. This world of sensuality becomes a fortress against potentially alienating forces, i.e., men, war, oppression of any kind, in the real world. This essay examines the outlines of this transcendence in selected examples from her love and political poetry. . . . (p. 140)

Drawing upon her scholarly and gifted understanding of poetic technique and rhetorical structure in modern Black poetry, Ruth Sheffey explains:

> Genuine rhetoric, indeed all verbal art, coexists with reason, truth, justice. All of the traditions of rational and moral speech are allied to the primitive idea of goodness, to the force of utterance. Because the past is functional in our lives when we neither forget it nor try to return to it, the new Black voices must reach the masses in increasingly communal ways, must penetrate those hidden crevices of our beings only recognizable and reachable by poetry.

Professor Sheffey speaks here to the fundamental meaning and significance Black poetry holds for its private community. Sheffey's remarks could not more appropriately describe Maya Angelou's poetic voice in terms of motive, content and audience. By way of example consider:

No No No No

No
the two legg'd beasts
that walk like men
play stink finger in their crusty asses
while crackling babies
in napalm coats
stretch mouths to receive
burning tears

on splitting tongues
JUST GIVE ME A COOL DRINK OF
    WATER 'FORE I DIE . . .

(pp. 140-41)

Her metynomic body imagery functions as poetic referent further chronicling and transporting her prophetic message: stop the assault on Black people and recognize their humanness. As prophecy, her succinct assertions for change beginning with napalmed babies, epitomized in hopeful dreams as the poem progresses—disintegrate ironically into the decayed emptiness of an old man's "gaping mouth." (pp. 142-43)

The audience, a Black one, cannot help but understand the universal message this poem imports. It is a collectively oriented statement (the persona's "I" operating synedochically for the group), and one of hope, although a hope which ironically collapses at poem's end.

A similar transcendence becomes the ironically complicated prophetic message in ["The Calling of Names"]:

> He went to being called a Colored man
> after answering to "hey nigger,"
> Now that's a big jump,
> anyway you figger,
>         Hey, Baby, Watch my smoke.
> From colored man to Negro.
>
> With the "N" in caps
> was like saying Japanese
> instead of saying Japs.
>
>     I mean, during the war.
>
> The next big step
> was change for true
> From Negro in caps
> to being a Jew.
>
>     Now, Sing Yiddish Mama.
>
> Light, Yello, Brown
> and Dark brown skin,
> were o.k. colors to
> describe him then,
>
>     He was a bouquet of Roses.
>
> He changed his seasons
> like an almanac,
> Now you'll get hurt
> if you don't call him "Black"
>
>     Nigguh, I ain't playin' this time.

As significant referents, words are used to recreate a personal reality, but as verbal discourse they remain very close to the writer's understanding of truth. Maya Angelou brings to the audience her own perceptions of historical change and their relationship to a new reality. With the exception of a long ago Phyllis Wheatley, whose poems speak almost exclusively of God, nature and man, few Black artists have focused their poetic gifts outside history, politics and their changing effects upon Black life. Here Maya Angelou engages in this lifelong tradition of speaking to the concerns of a historical and political Black presence in World War II, Voter and Civil Rights legislation of the fifties; finally the Black Power Movement of the sixties—these events name only a few of the historical and political meanings the synedochic imagery of naming has signalled for Blacks in America.

From the ancient African rituals which gave a child a name harmonious with his or her chi to the derogatory epithets coming out of slavery's master-servant relationships—naming has always held a reality redefining importance for black people. It has reached the level contemporarily with the recreation of one's destiny, an incantation signalling control over one's life. Hence the proliferation of African names with significant meanings.

But as the incantation and the structure of the poem's ideas have evolved out of historical and political event, one hears the old degrading epithets merging into new and more positive meanings.

Her title with its article "the" and preposition "of" signal, perhaps, the only formalizing or distancing aesthetic techniques in the poem. Her emphasis is primarily upon the concrete, the substantive movement back to a derogatory black history and a clearly assertive statement about a more positive future. Like many of the poems in this collection this one also works toward the notion of a positive identity, a positive assertion of what and who Black people have decided they will be. Her formal rhyme scheme here is one in which the initial stanzas rhyme the second and fourth lines, a rhyming pattern more constricted than in much of her other political poetry. Less metaphorical transformation and less abstraction appear in this poem, however, and while that makes it aesthetically less pleasing, its meaning speaks more directly to the concrete issues of evolving importance to Afro-American history and politics. The abstractions of metaphor perhaps then do not apply here. (pp. 143-44)

While Maya Angelou's political poetry suggests the irony of emotional distantiation by using bodily imagery as her objective correlative, her love poetry almost equally as often employs this series of patterns to capture an image, an instant, an emotional attitude. Moreover, fantasy often rounds out the missing parts of the human whole when reality fails to explain fully what she sees. Here in the following poem, **"To a Man"** she explores this mystery, this distantiation from the understanding of a man:

> My man is
> Black Golden Amber
> Changing.
> Warm mouths of Brandy Fine
> Cautious sunlight on a patterned rug
> Coughing laughter, rocked on a whirl of French
>    tobacco
> Graceful turns on wollen stilts
> Secretive?
> A cat's eye.
> Southern, Plump and tender with navy bean sul-
>    lenness
> And did I say "Tender?"
> The gentleness
> A big cat stalks through stubborn bush
> And did I mention "Amber"?
> The heatless fire consuming itself.
> Again. Anew. Into ever neverlessness.
> My man is Amber

> Changing
> Always into itself
> New. Now New.
> Still itself.
> Still

If indeed this poem talks about a man and not some more hidden and abstract object we cannot define, then **"To a Man"** explores the mysteries of a baffling and emotionally distant human being through a persona's fantasy, her worshipping recreation of an artifice rather than of any more luminous understanding of his many selves. And while she does not name him in the poem and he could be reminiscent of any of the men she knew, her description of him evokes a picture of Make, a South African freedom fighter and the man who became her second husband. She recounts this marriage and its end in her final autobiography, *The Heart of a Woman.* Whether a husband or not, his mystery constitutes her poem's ostensible statement, through her persona's particular visual gestalt, i.e., approach. The persona's failure to (penetrate) her subject's overpreoccupation with his own personal style as a wall against intimacy becomes a source of the poem's interesting aesthetic and emotional tension. Her subject cannot be captured, i.e., "understood" and he is cut off from the persona's concentrated engagement by this barrier that she creates—his personal style. The word choices she selects to describe or rather, guess at what she comprehends about him are words suggesting the altering and varying nature of his physical and psychic characteristics. She looks at him seeing only the qualities of an ambiance he creates around himself through the deliberateness of his studied poses. He moves "Cat like." She images his moving dynamism concretely in "woolen stilts" which both regalize and thrust him backward spatially and temporally to a time when he could have been a royal African chieftain dancing on tall stilts.

She magnificently combines the auditory, tactile and visual into the imagery of his " . . . coughing laughter rocked on a whirl of French tobacco" graphically capturing what we take to be—given all she has said before—still, his moving and elegant dynamism. His sight, sound, smell—even his smoke concretized in French rather than in some ordinary domestic. (pp. 146-47)

Like a musical recitative, she repeats in . . . **"To a Man,"** descriptions framed in rhetorical questions drawing attention all the more to his stolid mystery. In using the repeated rhetorical questions, she counterposes her technique against the traditional way in which modern Black poets use repetition. Modern Black poets use repetitious phrasing for emphasis, clarity and to signal an end to complexity. In Angelou's work the rhetorical questions increase tension and complexity and build upon his opaque mystery. Why?

Some of the explanation might lie in the fact that writers often repeat the issues and conflicts of their own lives throughout much of their art until either concrete conditions or the art brings insight and resolution. Witness Richard Wright's unending preoccupation with the Communist Party's orthodoxy and demanding control over his work, or Gwendolyn Brooks' mid-career, philosophical redirection after attending the Fisk University Black Writer's Conference. The seeds for a similar obsession lie in her autobiographies and project into Angelou's poetry. She berates herself for her overly romantic ability to place men on pedestals, to create a rose-colored fantasy around them at a distance only to later discover her cognitive error. Her relationships with men in **Caged Bird** and **Gather Together** have this fantasy quality where she over-elaborates their personalities in her own mind confusing their concrete behaviors with her day-dream. She does this, sometimes out of her own unconscious desire for their unconditional love—wanting almost a symbiotic object-subject attachment to them. In the final analysis, each of these men exploits her because all are morally and characterologically flawed in ways her own emotional neediness causes her to miss as her fantasy life recreates their personalities. One lover, temporarily stationed close to her home in San Diego, uses her companionship while his naval assignment lasts then leaves her. He returns to his wife. A fast living "sugar daddy" cons her into prostitution to "help" him with a non-existent gambling debt. Again concrete conditions force her into looking beneath the surface he presents. She finds that her "giving" provided pretty dresses for his wife. Nothing more! Finally, when at last she marries, and her fantasies tell her she has found nirvana in the white picket fenced-cottage she has dreamed of she learns its hidden price: she will become prisoner rather than mistress of the house and husband. (pp. 147-48)

The narcissistic male is always the one most attractive to [Angelou] and the one most mysterious—ultimately he will always turn out to be the man most destructive to her and her capacity to invest too much of her dependency and need in him too quickly. The wonder which underlies her perceptions in **"To a Man"** are not surprising provided one has read her autobiographies and identified this common psychic pattern she recurrently illustrates. What she identifies as mystery and wonder are part of the guardedness and distance he sustains—keeping her always at a safe length away from himself. One would expect anger from her rather than wonder.

Anger would have been more appropriate toward his self-protection and yet she does not express anger. Perhaps also the absence of anger affirms the passivity Lillian Arensberg has seen in Angelou's writing. We must, however, not overlook another important factor which accounts for what may be occurring here from an aesthetic and artistic rather than a purely psychic point of view. Her persona's opportunity to draw attention to it—rather than to her male subject. Thus, in doing this, she can draw upon her female audience's alleged universal bafflement with the mysterious male psyche. The poem would be better called "To a Woman" in that case, if one accepts this less direct reading of the poem. (pp. 149-50)

While Maya Angelou's poetry may not have taken us into every nook and cranny of her long and complex life starting with the Lafayette County Training School—its various movements and insights have nonetheless helped us understand the themes, the issues even some of the conflicts which have pervaded her inner life. Thus, while we could not share the objective events in all their entirety . . . , her various poetic stances have given us some lead into parts of that subjective voyage. (p. 151)

Her love poetry . . . suggests her relationship to a world which can be stultifying, mystifying and oppressive, but one she will not allow to become these things and overwhelm her. The voyage through her life has not been filled with soft and pliable steps each opening into another opportunity for self acceptance. Her voyage has instead been anything but that and yet she has filled those voids with fantasy, song, hope and the redefinition of her world's view through art. (p. 152)

> *Priscilla R. Ramsey, "Transcendence: The Poetry of Maya Angelou," in* A Current Bibliography on African Affairs, *Vol. 17, No. 2, 1984-5, pp. 139-53.*

## Lucinda H. MacKethan

The expression "Mother Wit" has three associations: according to Alan Dundes, it is, first, "a popular term in black speech referring to common sense"; secondly, it is "the kind of good sense not necessarily learned from books or in school"; and thirdly, "with its connotation of collective wisdom acquired by the experience of living and from generations past," it is "often expressed in folklore." In his collection of essays related to Afro-American folklore, Dundes consistently pairs mother wit with laughter and humor, for, as he says, "it is what makes a people laugh that reveals the soul of that people." When we look, however, at the word *mother,* in relation to mother wit, we might wonder how the term applies to the traditional experience of the Afro-American mother from slavery times forward; the question we could ask is, Why are these women laughing? . . . [The experiences of the black woman in the autobiographical works of] Maya Angelou [reveal] little cause for laughter. (p. 51)

Angelou's story of her girlhood is in many places a lyrical testament to language as providing her one saving image of self; from a childhood in which she tried to live wordlessly as a means of protecting herself against knowledge that was certain pain, Angelou emerged armed, she says, with a "secret word which called forth the djinn who was to serve me all my life: books."

The woman's brand of mother wit that we see in the works of . . . Angelou is tied to [her] special sense of the capacities of language as an enabling power. That power first reveals itself in the humor of caricature, in broad slaps of ridicule applied to the backsides of oppressors who include white men, white women, and black men too. Secondly, the power of language appears in the humor of exaggeration, a device which comes into play particularly when [Angelou portrays] the gulf that existed between what [she] had the right to expect and what the world was willing to allow. And finally, the power of mother wit resides perhaps most plentifully in . . . representations of [her] own mothers' words of wisdom; in [Angelou's] works mother figures offer the practical, loving, yet also tough and disciplining advice for life that they know their black daughters must acquire if they are to have any hope of being more than the mules of the world. . . . (pp. 52-3)

The development of verbal humor as a survival strategy . . . is a unifying device for the events of her life that Maya Angelou selected for *I Know Why the Caged Bird Sings.* Angelou the autobiographer takes her childhood self, who goes by many names, on a kind of quest for a name and for words. . . . The progress of this girl's life is made possible by a series of word-bringers—her brother, her teachers, her mother's con men friends, her mother herself—who gradually open to her the potential of language; words alone can free her from her fear of and dependency on others' conceptions. Thus, with no ability to raise the words she needs, Marguerite in the first scene is betrayed by the white world's view of beauty: "Because I was really white," she tries to think, "and because a cruel fairy stepmother, who was understandably jealous of my beauty, had turned me into a too-big Negro girl, with nappy black hair, broad feet, and a space between her teeth that would hold a number-two pencil." By the end of the book, Maya is not only talking but she has an edge on her white school mates; she and her friends "were alert to the gap separating the written word from the colloquial. We learned to slide out of one language and into another without being conscious of the effort."

The most important of the word-bringers in Maya's life is her mother—a savvy, sassy, street-wise Mama who makes Black beautiful and language a gift of the body as well as an art of the mind. Vivian Baxter Johnson can dance, can shoot a crooked business partner, can make her living in the tough blues joints of St. Louis and San Francisco. Yet most of all she can talk, and unlike Maya's conservative southern grandmother's, her talk is full of hope, irreverence for tradition, and scorn for anyone who thinks they can keep her down. When she repeats the old report, "They tell me the whitefolks still in the lead," she says it, Angelou tells us, "as if that was not quite the whole truth." Vivian's words are a compendium of mother wit: "She had a store of aphorisms," Angelou remarks, "which she dished out as the occasion demanded": "The Man upstairs, He don't make mistakes;" "It ain't no trouble when you pack double;" "Nothing beats a trial but a failure;" and perhaps most to our point, "Sympathy is next to shit in the dictionary, and I can't even read."

While we are given no explicit statement at the end of her story that Marguerite Johnson has fully absorbed what she needs of her mother's verbal capacities, Maya's own nascent motherhood, and her attitude toward becoming a mother, indicate that a survivor is coming into being. She tells us her feelings as a young, unwed mother who managed to hide her pregnancy from her family for almost eight months, and her words have a kind of triumph in them . . . . Gone is the girl who could see her Blackness only as some cruel fairy godmother's revenge. With a real mother, and mother wit, Maya has the preparation she needs to become the writer, the word-bringer, who created *I Know Why the Caged Bird Sings.*

One joke that the Black American community has shared for a long time shows a young black girl gazing into the fabled mirror to ask, "Who's the fairest of all?," where-upon the mirror, of course, answers back: "It's Snow White, you Black bitch, and don't you forget it." The joke, we can bet, is a trick on that tired white trope, locked as it is in the blind and self-reflexive looking glass of impotent white hate. The [autobiography of Maya Angelou reveals] . . . that, beginning in slavery times, women found the means, in the company of other nurturing women, to change the joke and slip the yoke. So indeed, they don't call it Mother Wit for nothing. (pp. 59-60)

> *Lucinda H. MacKethan, "Mother Wit: Humor in Afro-American Women's Autobiography," in* Studies in American Humor, *n.s. Vol. 4, Nos. 1 & 2, Spring & Summer, 1985, pp. 51-61.*

## Wanda Coleman

Celebrity autobiographies? Ugh! Too many are self-aggrandizements, elaborations of scanty press packets. Titillation and allusion shape the redundant seduction of the reader already seduced by fame. But after a dozen or so pages of Maya Angelou's [fifth volume of] autobiography, *All God's Children Need Traveling Shoes,* one is zipping uncritically along—captured in her embrace.

In this book, the noted black playwright picks up life in her mid-30s. It is the eve of the near-death of her only son; and, the metaphorical loss of a mother whose manchild claims independence. In self-conscious prose, Angelou recounts her adventures as an Afro-American expatriate in the Ghana of the mid-to-late 1960s. There she joins a disgruntled and confused group of black Americans at odds with the fatherland that rejects them as first-class citizens and the idealized motherland that fails to live up to their naive assumptions. . . .

In Kwame Nkrumah's Ghana "by accident," Angelou discovers a representative cross section of urban and rural blacks which she subdivides into four groups: teachers and farmers, American government reps, businessmen, and political emigres. She aligns herself with the latter.

This extravagant peopling of *All God's Children* is interwoven with adages and bits of folk/street wisdom salted with Angelou's reflections as she contrasts the black American and the black African:

> Was it possible that I and all American Blacks had been wrong . . . ? Could the cutting treatment we often experienced have been stimulated by something other than our features, our hair and color? Was the odor of old slavery so obvious that people were offended and lashed out at us automatically? Had what we judged as racial prejudice less to do with race and more to do with our particular ancestors' bad luck and having been caught, sold and driven like beasts?

The answer comes, ironically, later, from the splendid declaration of a black king: "We are black, BLACK! And we give no explanation, no apology."

Maya Angelou tends to play the coquette at moments and confession is forthcoming only by way of device. Angelou's pen wavers when the focus turns inward, and her language becomes careful. You can feel her not saying certain things. Her posture is discreet and ladylike as prescribed by Protestant tradition. Sans philosophical weight, Angelou nevertheless recreates her *attitude* with dramatic clarity. She evokes the temper of the civil rights era with unquestionable authenticity. While its language runs to the lay and not the literary, *I Know Why the Caged Bird Sings* remains my contender for Angelou's magnum opus. This should not and does not diminish *All God's Children Need Traveling Shoes* as a thoroughly enjoyable segment from the life of a celebrity. It is an important document drawing more much needed attention to the hidden history of a people both African and American.

> Wanda Coleman, in a review of "All God's Children Need Traveling Shoes," in Los Angeles Times Book Review, *April 13, 1986, p. 4.*

### Patrice Gaines-Carter

Because [*All God's Children Need Traveling Shoes*] is the fifth volume of Maya Angelou's autobiography, it's tempting to ask how one writer could stretch a life through so many works. The easy answer is that she can do so because her life has been more exciting, more adventurous, more fraught with challenge than most lives. But the truth is Maya Angelou could have probably written five volumes of her life if she had spent all of her days alone in a 12-by-12 room with nothing but a pen and paper.

She hasn't, of course. . . .

Yet what endears Angelou to us is both none of this adventure and exotic variety and all of it. It is not her actions, but the meaning she gives each of them that makes her life story important. There is always present her mother wit, her humor, her sincere search for significance where there seems to be none. She not only lives history but in a quiet way gives us her interpretation of it, never imposing herself, but always provoking thought.

Only occasionally is the writing in *All God's Children* brilliant, but when Angelou weaves her stylistic magic she does captivate: "The breezes of the West African night were intimate and shy, licking the hair, sweeping through cotton dresses with unseemly intimacy, then disappearing into the utter blackness." That is the first sentence of the book and one of the more memorable.

Her true strength is as a story teller, although her first vocation was as a dancer and actress. Just as Angelou the raconteur charms an audience today during lectures and readings, she charms her readers. She knows how to weave a tale, draw the most out of a moment, play an audience to the hilt. It is not the way Angelou strings words together that will be remembered when this book is put away, but the stories of her life, the anecdotes about famous people and her heartfelt search for what she calls "home."

This search for "home" centers on Angelou's realization that her son Guy has been a kind of personal home for her and she has been his home. The thought comes to her after Guy is in an automobile accident. Daily, she stands by his hospital bed, while he lies motionless in a body cast with one arm and one leg fractured and his neck broken. . . .

It was her son's accident that put Angelou in Ghana. The two had traveled from Cairo, where they had been living, to Ghana so Guy could attend the University of Ghana in Accra. Angelou planned to settle in Liberia.

But after the accident, needing to be near Guy in the hospital, Angelou joined the group of black American immigrants with ease, sharing with each member the need to find a "home" where they were neither hated nor abused because of their color. . . .

Frequently, the black immigrants were met with disdain from Africans, a reaction that grew out of cultural differences as well as years of miseducation about each other. Yet, on the surface, the two groups interpreted each other's actions as arrogance. (p. 11)

Despite the clashes between cultures, there are numerous times when the differences between the two groups dissolve and their histories mesh. In one incident, some Ghanaian women mistake Angelou for one of their own. So sure are they of their assessment that they speak to her in their native tongue and wait for her answer. Tearfully, they recount for her the story of how years ago many adults were dragged from their village by slave traders while the children escaped by hiding in the woods.

"They are sure you are descended from those stolen mothers and fathers," an interpreter explains to Angelou, as the writer trembles with joy, tears trickling down her cheeks.

In all of its manifestations Angelou's search for "home"—a place or condition of belonging—should be a universal journey understood by most readers. Although her story is one of an actual journey to another continent, it is also the story of a spiritual search that takes place inside every person who quests after self-knowledge. (p. 12)

> Patrice Gaines-Carter, "Home Is Where the Heart Is," in Book World—The Washington Post, *May 11, 1986, pp. 11-12.*

### Sharron Freeman

I feel very uncomfortable with my critical reactions to Maya Angelou's fifth autobiographical narrative, [*All God's Children Need Traveling Shoes,*] especially since I loved *I Know Why the Caged Bird Sings, Singin' and Swingin' and Gettin' Merry Like Christmas* and *Gather Together in My Name* (the fourth was *The Heart of a Woman*). Somehow, I feel responsible for supporting her work with positive reviews, because of her outstanding contributions to literature.

But—I was left cold by this rambling account of her time spent in Ghana trying to fit in as a black American woman in a foreign black culture. Her descriptions weren't complete enough to take me, the reader, back in time to *both* this period in history and her life. At times, I felt as if I were merely reading a recitation of the names and places that made up her memories of spending her 33rd through 35th year in West Africa. She meets famous people . . . but doesn't flesh out their impact on her life in enough detail to recreate the experience on paper as fully as she has done in her past recreations.

The realities of being an American on African soil in the early sixties . . . is clearly presented as are the realities of the fact that just being black doesn't make one an instant member of African culture. Angelou describes how she comes to the realization that she can't continue living in Africa and must return to the United States to keep her struggle alive and moving, even though her son and part of her heart are firmly embedded in Africa.

Her life is so interesting and unusual . . . that I am incredibly awed by her account of her achievements, in the face of the odds that might have stifled her. This comes across in the book . . . , but sounds better when I write about it than it was to read.

This period in history is such an important one for adolescents to understand, that I'm aware that a book such as this could offer them a valuable peek into the times. I'm not advocating total rejection of this title, but I can foresee a problem with this sometimes-breezy account. (pp. 170-71)

*Sharron Freeman, in a review of "All God's Children Need Traveling Shoes," in* Voice of Youth Advocates, *Vol. 9, Nos. 3 & 4, August & October, 1986, pp. 170-71.*

## Deborah E. McDowell

No genre has captured the Afro-American literary imagination as has autobiography. Beginning with the slave narratives—Frederick Douglass' *Narrative of the Life of Frederick Douglass* (1845) and Linda Brent's *Incidents in the Life of a Slave Girl* (1861) among the best examples—Afro-American writers have returned compellingly to the genre that selects and records the incidents of a life and shapes them into an image of self. . . .

To this collection, Maya Angelou has added five volumes, a number unequalled, to my knowledge, by any other Afro-American writer. ***All God's Children Need Traveling Shoes*** is the latest of the chronicle which began with the very popular and justly acclaimed ***I Know Why the Caged Bird Sings*** (1970). These volumes cover miles of geographical territory and milestones of personal history. . . .

This latest installment departs from the singular constant of Afro-American autobiography: the confrontation of a Black self with a racist American society that ever threatens to destroy it. Angelou's first four volumes record that confrontation, illuminating an aspect unique to the Black woman. In her life, the oppression of race joins with the oppression of gender to create "the rust on the razor that threatens [her] throat." Taken together, Angelou's autobiographies show a self that defies the rusted razor, a self that—true to the demands of the genre—survives and triumphs.

The personal survival and triumph recorded in ***All God's Children Need Traveling Shoes*** are not the consequence of a confrontation with a racist American social structure. This is, rather, a confrontation with an African heritage, a heritage she has viewed primarily in abstract and sentimental terms: Africa was an "ancient tribal soul," "an all

sepia paradise," a mother into whose arms she could "snuggle down" much as "a baby snuggles in a mother's arms." The book records the sometimes painful process of exchanging that faulty and naive understanding of Africa for one more realistic and complex. Its unifying, if sometimes overdrawn theme and metaphor, is *home.*

Like so many Afro-Americans in the sixties, Angelou regarded Africa as a haven from racist America. They formed an "unceasing parade of naive travelers who thought that an airline ticket to Africa would erase the past and open wide the gates to a perfect future." In Africa they would be received in "the welcoming arms of the family . . . bathed, clothed with fine raiment and seated at the welcoming table." In other words, Africa would be the home that America never was and could never be. But this fantasy is shattered soon after Angelou's arrival in Ghana. . . .

[Angelou] arrives in a Ghana basking in its five-year-old independence and lauding the achievement and promise of its president, Kwame Nkrumah. W. E. B. DuBois is already living there as an expatriate; Malcolm X visits, enlisting support for his newly-formed Organization of Afro-American Unity, designed to link the civil rights struggles of Black Americans with newly-independent African nations.

Against this backdrop of progressive politics, Angelou's most startling and disappointing experiences stand out and take on added significance. When she looks for employment at the Ghana Broadcasting Office, she is first patronized then scornfully treated by a receptionist who volunteers that "American Negroes are always crude." . . . The receptionist's scorn seems mild, however, compared to the treatment of Black Americans when they are suspected of involvement in an attempt on Nkrumah's life.

Not all of Angelou's experiences deal with the sober hardships of rejection and displacement, however. She is warmly welcomed, befriended and supported by some Africans, including the writer Efua Sutherland. Her accounts of these relationships are leavening, at times even funny. In one episode she hires an African beautician to braid her hair "Ghanaian fashion"; instead, the woman gives her a style like that worn by pickaninnies "to teach [her] a lesson on the foolishness of trying to 'go native.'"

For a little over one-third of the book, Angelou manages to capture convincingly these and other complexities of Black Americans living in Africa. She portrays with telling candor the Africa of shattered fantasies, the Africa that did not greet her homecoming with open arms. But finally, perhaps because of some vestigial longing for "home," Angelou is seduced by those same fantasies, creating, at the end of the book, an "illusory place, befitting [her] imagination." The latter part of the book seems to wash over all the earlier convincingly rendered details of rejection, unrecognition and displacement as it rushes to an unearned and unconvincing conclusion—an embrace, if you will, with the African mother who had earlier closed her arms. Blending clichés and stereotypes (however much their basis is in historical fact), Angelou fashions a reconciliation that seems schematic and false, the stuff of textbooks, robbed of feeling.

For example, on a weekend trip into the bush, she stops for gas in Cape Coast, the inglorious site of a former holding fort for captured slaves. Having avoided the place for a year, she hurries out of the town back onto the highway, but she cannot escape; "history had invaded [her] little car." . . .

But these passages seem prefabricated, dead to the feeling that the reader has come to expect of Angelou's record of her African sojourn. It is their cumulative effect that creates a sense of inauthenticity and contributes to the reader's detachment from her story.

Shortly before returning to America, Angelou visits Eastern Ghana and is given a tour of Keta, a town whose population was nearly decimated by the slave trade. There she is accosted by an Ewe woman who "had the wide face and slanted eyes of my grandmother." The woman appears hostile, but because of the language barrier she and Angelou are unable to communicate. The guide comes to the rescue, explaining that the woman has mistaken Angelou for the daughter of a friend, for a descendant "from those stolen mothers and fathers" from the village of Keta. Angelou sums up this experience in terms that have a disappointingly generic ring:

> I had not consciously come to Ghana to find the roots of my beginnings, but I had continually and accidentally tripped over them or fallen upon them in my everyday life . . . And here in my last days in Africa, descendants of a pillaged past saw their history in my face and heard their ancestors speak through my voice. . . . The women wept and I wept. I too cried for the lost people, their ancestors and mine. But I was also weeping with a curious joy. Despite the murders, rapes and suicides, we had survived. The middle passage and the auction block had not erased us. . . . There was much to cry for, much to mourn, but in my heart I felt exalted knowing there was much to celebrate. Although separated from our languages, our families and customs, we had dared to continue to live. We had crossed the unknowable ocean in chains and had written its mystery into "Deep River, my home is over Jordan."

It could be argued that what I'm calling a generic summary is simply evidence that the slave experience is so embedded in the collective unconscious of all Black Americans that images evoking that experience are inevitable and to be expected. That notwithstanding, I had hoped to find a sharper, more quickened personal idiom amid this collective story of slave-trading, the Middle Passage and the auction block. But then, perhaps it is impossible to mine and inscribe a personal idiom, given that story's weight and complexity.

In this sense, *All God's Children Need Traveling Shoes* fits squarely in the tradition of Afro-American autobiography. As one student of the genre has observed, the "self" of Afro-American autobiography is not an "individual with a private career, but a soldier in a long, historic march toward Canaan."

*Deborah E. McDowell, "Traveling Hopefully," in* The Women's Review of Books, *Vol. IV, No. 1, October, 1986, p. 17.*

### Publishers Weekly

[Tom] Feelings's 84 sepia and black-and-white illustrations of black women were drawn in Africa, the U.S., South America and the Caribbean. They inspired Angelou . . . to write [*Now Sheba Sings the Song,* a] poem celebrating black women's strength, dignity, exuberance and sexuality. Pictures and verse complement each other in this slender offering. . . . The verses sometimes successfully mingle natural speech rhythms with a literary diction that filters the voice of African-American woman's centuries of struggle and perseverance. An often eloquent poem is trapped amid prosaic pictures.

*A review of "Now Sheba Sings the Song," in* Publishers Weekly, *Vol. 231, No. 7, February 20, 1987, p. 65.*

### Maya Angelou (interview with Carol E. Neubauer)

*[Neubauer]: I see autobiography in general as a way for a writer to go back to her past and try to present what is left in memory but also to recover what has been lost through imagination and invention.*

[Angelou]: Autobiography is for me a beloved which, like all beloveds, one is not given by family. One happens upon. You know, you turn the corner to the left instead of to the right. Stop in the parking lot and meet a beloved, or someone who becomes a beloved. And by the time I was half finished with *Caged Bird* I knew I loved the form—that I wanted to try to see what I could do with the form. Strangely enough, not as a cathartic force, not really; at any rate I never thought that really I was interested or am interested in autobiography for its recuperative power. I liked the form—the literary form—and by the time I started *Gather Together* I had gone back and reread Frederick Douglass' slave narrative. Anyway, I love the idea of the slave narrative, using the first person singular, really meaning always the third person plural. I love that. And I see it all the time in the black literature, in the blues and spirituals and the poetry, in essays James Baldwin uses it. But I've tried in each book to let the new voice come through and that's what makes it very difficult for me not to impose the voice of 1980 onto the voice I'm writing from 1950, possibly.

*And so when you say you look for a new voice you don't mean the voice of the present or the time of writing the autobiographical account, but rather of that period of your past. That must be difficult.*

Very. Very difficult, but I think that in writing autobiography that that's what is necessary to really move it from almost an "as told to" to an "as remembered" state. And really for it to be a creative and artistic literary art form. I believe I came close to recreating the voice in *Gather Together* of that young girl—eratic, sporadic, fractured. I think in each case I've come close. Rather a sassy person in *Singin' and Swingin'*.

*It seemed that in* **The Heart of a Woman,** *either the voice was more complex or else there was more than one voice at work. There seemed to be the voice of that time in your life and yet another voice commenting on that time.*

It seems so, but I looked at that quite carefully and at the period I think it is the voice because I was really coming into a security about who I was and what I was about, but the security lasted sometimes for three or four days or maybe through a love affair or into a love affair or into a job. I think it would be like smoke in a room. It would just dissipate and I would suddenly be edgewalking again. I would be one of those children in the rye, playing very perilously close to the precipice and aware of it. I tried very hard for the voice. I remember the woman very well.

*What I saw in* **Heart of a Woman** *was not so much that there were two voices talking against one another, but rather that a voice from a more recent time commented ironically on the predominant voice of that time in the past. The irony of you as the writer and the autobiographical presence coming through.*

It is really one of the most difficult. First, well, I don't know what comes first in that case. Whether it is the insistence to write well while trying to speak in a voice thirty years ago. I'm now writing a new book and trying to speak in that voice—the voice of 1963 and what I know about writing in 1984. It really is difficult.

*Does it become more difficult the closer you get to the present?*

Yes, absolutely. Because by '63 my command of English was *almost* what it is today and I had been very much influenced by Vus Make. He had really influenced my thinking, and his English was exquisite. My reading in other languages also by that time had very much influenced my speaking and I was concerned about eloquence by 1960. So this book is really the most difficult and I've been ducking and dodging it too. I know this morning I should call my editor and tell him I have not forgotten him. He's very much on my mind and the work is very much on my mind. I don't know what I'm going to do when I finish this book. I *may* try to go back and pick up some of the incidents that I left out of maybe *Caged Bird* or *Gather Together* or any of the books. I don't know how to do that.

*Are you thinking of autobiography?*

Yes.

*That's fascinating. One of the things I'm interested in particularly is how the present influences the autobiographical past. I think what you're engaged in doing now and have been since* **Caged Bird** *is something that's never been done before in this scope. Each volume of yours is a whole and has a unity that works for that volume alone. If you were to go back to the period of* **Caged Bird** *that would add another wrinkle in this question of time and different voices.*

I don't know how I will do it, and I don't know if I'll be able to do it. But I think there are facets. When I look at a stained glass window, it's very much like this book. I have an idea that the books are very much like the Everyman stories so that there is greed and kindness and generosity and cruelty, oppression, and sloth. And I think of the period I'm going to write about and I try to see which of the incidents in which greed, say it's green, which of these that happened to me during that period will most demonstrate that particular condition. Now some are more rich, but I refuse them. I do not select them because it's very hard to write drama without falling into melodrama. So the incidents I reject, I find myself unable to write about without becoming melodramatic. I just can't see how to write it. In *Gather Together* there is an incident in which a man almost killed me—tried to, in fact—and kept me for three days and he was a mad man, literally. My escape was so incredible, literally incredible, that there was no way to write it, absolutely, to make it credible and not melodramatic.

*Have you ever chosen to take another incident in that case, perhaps one that might not have even happened, and use that as a substitute?*

No, because there are others which worked, which did happen, and which showed either cruelty or the irony of escape. So I was able to write that rather than the other.

*I see. So you didn't have to sacrifice the core of the experience.*

No, I never sacrificed. It's just choosing which of those greens or which of those reds to make that kind of feeling.

*It's a beautiful metaphor, the greens, the reds and the light coming through the window. Because in a sense, memory works that way; it filters out past work. And yet an autobiographer has a double task—at least double, probably triple or quadruple—in some ways the filtering has been done beyond your control on an unconscious level. But as a writer working in the present you, too, are making selections or choices, which complicate the experience.*

There is so much to talk to you about on this subject. I have, I think, due to all those years of not talking, which again, I chose to minimize in *Caged Bird* because it's hard to write that without, again, the melodramas leaking in. But because of those years of muteness, I think my memory was developed in queer ways, because I remember—I have total recall—or I have none at all. None. And there is no pattern to the memory, so that I would forget all the good and the bad of a certain time, or I will remember *only* the bad of a certain time, or I will remember *only* the good. But when I remember it, I will remember *everything* about it. *Everything.* The outside noises, the odors in the room, the way my clothes were feeling—everything. I just have it, or I remember nothing. I am sure that is a part of the sort of psychological problems I was having and how the memory went about its business knitting itself.

*Almost as a treasure chest or a defense.*

Yes, both, I guess. But in a sense, not really a defense, because some of the marvelous things I've not remembered. For instance, one of the promises I've exacted from every lover or husband who promised to be a permanent fixture was that *if* I die in the house, if something happened, get me outside. Please don't let me die in the room, or open the window and let me see some rolling hills. Let me see, please. Now, my memory of Stamps, Arkansas, is flat, dirt, the trees around the pond. But everything just flat and mean. When I agreed to go to join Bill Moyers for his creativity program, I flew to Dallas and decided to drive to Stamps because I wanted to sneak up on Stamps. It's, I guess, 200 miles or more. When I drove out of Texas into Arkansas, Stamps is 30 miles from Texas. I began to see the undulating hills. I couldn't believe it! I couldn't believe it! It's beautiful! It's what I love. But the memory had completely gone.

*When you're working, for example, on your present book, are there things that help you remember that period or any period in the past better?*

Well, a curious thing has happened to me with every book. When I start to work—start to plan it—I encounter people whom I have known in that time, which is really queer. I've wondered if I would encounter them anyway, or if it's a case of "when the student is ready the teacher appears." If I simply wouldn't see their value if I would encounter them and wouldn't see their value for what I'm working on, because I wouldn't be working on that. That is one of the very interesting things. I'm working on Ghana now and this summer I went to London to write a play. I saw a sister friend there from Ghana and suddenly about fifteen Ghanaians; soon I was speaking Fanti again and they were reminding me, "Do you remember that time when?" and suddenly it all came right up my nostrils. But what I do is just pull myself away from everything and everybody and then begin the most frightening of the work. And that is going back. I'm always afraid I'll never come out. Every morning I wake up, usually about 5:30 and try to get to my work room. I keep a little room in a hotel. Nothing on the walls, nothing belonging to me, nothing. I go in and I try to be in by 6:30 and try to get back, get back. Always, for the first half hour is spent wondering if anybody cares for me enough to come and pull me out. Suppose I can't get out?

*That's a difficult road to retrace—to find.*

Like an enchanted . . . I know that sounds romatic, but you know how I mean. But I do get back and I remember one thing and I think, "Yes, and what are the other things like that that happened?" And maybe a second one will come. It's all there. *All of it* is there.

*Even down to the finest details and the dialogues, what you said to the people you were with.*

The sound of the voices. And I write wurrrrrrrrrrrrrrr.

*How long do you write if you go in at 6:30?*

Well, I'm out by 12:30, unless it's really happening. If it's really happening I'll stay till 2:00, but no longer. No longer. And then get out and go home and shower and make a lovely lunch and drink a lot of wine and try to come down. Get back. Stop in a shop, "Hi, how are you? Fine. . . ." So I can ascertain that I do live and people remember me.

*Do you leave it in the middle of an incident so that you have a way back, or do you write to the end of each one?*

No, I can't write to the end of the incident. I will write to a place that's safe. Nothing will leak away now; I've got it. Then at night I'll read it and try to edit it.

*The same night?*

The same night. Try to edit it for writing, a little of it. And then begin again the next day. Lordy.

*Is it a frightening journey because of the deep roots from that time to the present? Do you feel a kind of vulnerability?*

I am not afraid of the ties. I cherish them, rather. It's the vulnerability. It's like using drugs or something. It's allowing oneself to be hypnotized. That's frightening, because then we have no defenses, nothing. We've slipped down the well and every side is slippery. And how on earth are you going to come out? That's scary. But I've chosen it, and I've chosen this mode as my mode.

*How far will the fifth volume go?*

Actually, it's a new kind. It's really quite a new voice. I'm looking at the black American resident, me and the other black American residents in Ghana, and trying to see all the magic of the eternal quest of human beings to go home again. That is maybe what life is anyway. To return to the Creator. All of that naiveté, the innocence of trying to. That awful rowing towards God, whatever it is. Whether it's to return to your village or the lover you lost or the youth that some people want to return to or the beauty that some want to return to.

*Writing autobiography frequently involves this quest to return to the past, to the home. Sometimes, if the home can't be found, if it can't be located again, then that home or that love or that family, whatever has been lost, is recreated or invented.*

Yes, of course. That's it! That's what I'm seeing in this trek back to Africa. That in so many cases that idealized home of course is non-existent. In so many cases some black Americans created it on the spot. On the spot. And I did too. Created something, looked, seemed like what we have idealized very far from reality. It's going to be a painful, hard book to write, in that not only all the stuff that it cost me to write it, but there will be a number of people who will be disappointed. So I have to deal with that once the book is out. The main thing is getting it out. (pp. 286-91)

*Maya Angelou and Carol E. Neubauer, in an interview in* The Massachusetts Review, *Vol. XXVIII, No. 2, Summer, 1987, pp. 286-92.*

### Publishers Weekly

Angelou's poems [in *I Shall Not be Moved*] embrace opposite poles: the laughter of old folks who "generously forgive life for happening to them," and the "helpless hope" on the faces of starving children. Though she can be directly political, as in a stinging letter to **"These Yet to Be United States,"** more often, a political dimension emerges naturally from ordinary lives observed with keen irony ("Even minimal people can't survive on minimal wage"). Angelou's themes include loss of love and youth, human oneness in diversity, the strength of blacks in the face of racism and adversity. The book's title is also the refrain of **"Our Grandmothers,"** a moving history poem about the struggles of black women. Some of these lyrics are free-form, while others use conventional rhyme and meter to good effect. Angelou . . . writes with poise and grace.

*A review of "I Shall Not Be Moved: Poems," in* Publishers Weekly, *Vol. 237, No. 12, March 23, 1990, p. 69.*

### Lenard D. Moore

[In *I Shall Not be Moved*] Angelou speaks eloquently of black life, unfolding a significant history in poems that are highly controlled and yet powerful: "She lay, skin down on the moist dirt, / the canebrake rustling / with the whispers of leaves, and / loud longing of hounds and / the ransack of hunters crackling the near branches." Here, the language is precise and filled with imagery. Like Gwendolyn Brooks, Angelou's poems are sparsely written while still revealing painful truths to the reader: "She stands / before the abortion clinic, / confounded by the lack of choices. / In the Welfare line, / reduced to the pity of handouts." [This is an] important new collection from one of the most distinctive writers at work today.

*Lenard D. Moore, in a review of "I Shall Not Be Moved," in* Library Journal, *Vol. 115, No. 10, June 10, 1990, p. 132.*

---

## FURTHER READING

Lupton, Mary Jane. "Singing the Black Mother: Maya Angelou and Autobiographical Continuity." *Black American Literature Forum* 24, No. 2 (Summer 1990): 257-76.
> Examination of the uniqueness of Angelou's autobiographical method. Lupton states that Angelou is unconventional in that throughout her volumes she denies closure and continues her narrative.

Tate, Claudia, ed. "Maya Angelou." In her *Black Woman Writers at Work,* pp. 1-11. New York: Continuum Publishing Company, 1983.
> Interview with Angelou in which she discusses the nature of her poetry and prose works.

Washington, Carla. "Maya Angelou's Angelic Aura." *The Christian Century* 105, No. 3 (23 November 1988): 1031-32.
> Discusses Angelou's spirituality as evidenced in her poetry and autobiographies.

# John Cheever

## 1912-1982

American short story writer and novelist.

Cheever is considered one of the most important twentieth-century American writers of short fiction. His well-
crafted chronicles of upper-middle-class manners and
mores, which describe the psychic unrest underlying suburban living, earned him the appellation "the Chekhov of
the exurbs." Although such stories as "The Swimmer,"
"The Enormous Radio," and "The Housebreaker of
Shady Hill" established Cheever as a skillful storyteller
and a trenchant social commentator, the republication of
sixty-one of his best stories in the 1978 collection *The Stories of John Cheever*—which received the Pulitzer Prize,
the National Book Award, and the National Book Critics
Circle Award—prompted serious scholarly appraisals of
his works. Critics particularly noted Cheever's thematic
interest in human morality and spirituality, and praised
his compassion and abiding belief in the redemptive power
of love.

Cheever was born in Quincy, Massachusetts. His New England background is evident in the settings of his stories
and in the traditions and values that inform them. He attended Thayer Academy, a preparatory school in Massachusetts, but his formal education ended when he was expelled at seventeen for smoking. The short story he wrote
about the experience, "Expelled," published in 1930 in the
*New Republic,* marked the beginning of Cheever's literary
career. The theme of this piece, the conflict between the
necessity for order and propriety and the desire for adventure and pleasure, recurs throughout Cheever's work.
During the next several years, Cheever lived mainly in
New York City, supporting himself with odd jobs, including a stint of writing book synopses for the Metro-
Goldwyn-Mayer film studio while remaining primarily interested in writing fiction. During the 1930s his short stories appeared in such magazines as the *Atlantic, Colliers,
Story,* the *Yale Review,* and, especially, the *New Yorker.*
Cheever's connection with the *New Yorker* began in 1935
and lasted his entire life; well over one hundred of his stories were originally published in that magazine. Despite its
advantages, this alliance also had a detrimental effect on
Cheever's reputation, for critics associated his stories with
the stereotypical *New Yorker* style: slick, facile, and self-
conscious.

Cheever was serving in the United States Army during
World War II when his first collection, *The Way Some
People Live,* was published in 1943. Composed of thirty
stories, many of them little more than sketches, the book
garnered several positive reviews. After the war, Cheever
wrote scripts for television series, including "Life with Father." In 1953 his second collection, *The Enormous Radio
and Other Stories,* appeared. This volume illustrates Cheever's movement toward longer, more fully developed
works. Mostly set in New York City, these pieces usually

concern optimistic but naive individuals who experience
culture shock after coming to the city. The much-
anthologized title story exemplifies one of Cheever's predominant themes: that social proprieties and conventions
cannot subdue emotional conflicts.

Cheever's fictional world commonly portrays individuals
in conflict with their communities and often with themselves. His stories are remarkably homogenous, and most
share similar settings and characters. The typical Cheever
protagonist is an affluent, socially prominent, and emotionally troubled upper-middle-class WASP who com-
mutes to his professional job in the city from his home in
suburbia. Cheever's description of this milieu is realistic,
but his stories extend beyond accurate depictions of a particular way of life. Into each picture of his idyllic suburbia,
Cheever injected an element of emotional tension arising
from the gap between the serene environment and individual passion and discontent. While this tension may take
many forms, the most common problem in a Cheever
story concerns marital conflict. Adultery, real or fantasized, is a motif, as Cheever's characters struggle with
their simultaneous desires for emotional fulfillment and
domestic and societal order. Cheever does not judge his

characters; rather, he treats them with understanding and compassion. Although he obviously intended to satirize the stifling and hypocritical aspects of the lifestyle he depicts, Cheever clearly recognized that while the values of affluent suburbia may not address the individual's deepest concerns, they do reflect an admirable effort to impose stability on a chaotic world. Commentators observe that since Cheever's characters are ambivalent in their desires, so the stories themselves are ambiguous, and present no clear resolution. The stories are generally realistic in setting and technique, but they are less complete tales than isolated slices of life briefly illuminated.

Recent critics have noted subtle but important phases in Cheever's short fiction career. With *The Housebreaker of Shady Hill and Other Stories* Cheever moved his settings from New York City to the suburban world commonly associated with his work, and irony, wit, and narrative detachment become more evident. In *Some People, Places, and Things That Will Not Appear in My Next Novel,* stories with European backdrops begin to appear. Critics noted a darker tone in *The Brigadier and the Golf Widow,* in addition to a more experimental technique, particularly in "The Swimmer." Often regarded as Cheever's finest story, "The Swimmer" blends realism and myth as it follows Neddy Merrill's eight-mile journey, during which he attempts to swim in all the swimming pools of Westchester County. The image of the old athlete who tries to regain his lost youth through physical endeavor is common in Cheever's fiction. *The World of Apples* also has been termed somber, but some critics dispute this description, citing the title story as an unequivocal celebration of the triumph of human decency.

Cheever's novels share thematic concerns with his short fiction. *The Wapshot Chronicle,* which won the National Book Award in 1958, episodically traces the disintegration of the eccentric Wapshot family in St. Botolphs, a small town in Massachusetts. The novel is divided into four parts: part one centers on Leander's feelings of uprootedness and subsequent loss of self-esteem induced by his sister and wife; parts two and three focus on his sons, Moses and Coverly, who leave their hometown for Washington, D. C. and New York only to find themselves comically ill-suited for big city life; and part four ends optimistically, with both brothers producing their own sons, thus perpetuating the Wapshot lineage. In this work, as in its sequel, *The Wapshot Scandal,* Cheever stressed the importance of family relationships and traditions. *The Wapshot Scandal,* often considered his darkest book, concerns the pervasive fear of death in contemporary life, which includes threats from nuclear weapons, auto accidents, cancer, as well as spiritual death from boredom and meaninglessness. Cheever's third novel, *Bullet Park,* also presents a pessimistic view of contemporary America. The first section of the novel concerns Eliot Nailles, the archetypal suburban conformist, and his troubled relationship with his rebellious son, Tony. The experiences of Paul Hammer, the illegitimate son of a wealthy but unreliable businessman, are chronicled in the second section through his journal entries, which reveal his growing insanity. Hammer randomly chooses to crucify Tony Nailles as a sacrificial act he hopes will shake the suburban community of

Bullet Park from its insular complacency. Mr. Nailles saves his son, however, and Hammer is institutionalized in a state hospital. The novel's conclusion suggests that Hammer's action has not affected Bullet Park. Several critics viewed in *Bullet Park* a shift in focus from Cheever's investigations of suburban manners to a greater interest in mythical and religious matters.

Cheever's next novel, *Falconer,* introduces several changes into his fiction: a seamy environment, extensive Christian symbolism, and coarse language. In this work, a former college professor incarcerated in Falconer Prison for murdering his brother experiences rebirth and redemption through overcoming his heroin addiction, engaging in a homosexual relationship, and miraculously escaping from prison. Janet Groth remarked: "[In] *Falconer,* John Cheever has written a stunning meditation on all the forms of confinement and liberation that can be visited upon the human spirit." Cheever's final work, the novella *Oh What a Paradise It Seems,* centers on businessman Lemuel Sears's crusade to save a pond that represents the healthy innocence of his youth from industrial contamination. Sears's campaign is disrupted by heterosexual and homosexual affairs but he eventually resumes his interest in the cause and, with the help of a fanatical housewife, succeeds in thwarting the polluters and reviving the health of the lake.

(See also *CLC,* Vols. 3, 7, 8, 11, 15, 25; *Short Story Criticism,* Vol. 1; *Contemporary Authors,* Vols. 5-8, rev. ed., Vol. 106 [obituary]; *Contemporary Authors New Revision Series,* Vols. 5, 27; *Contemporary Authors Bibliographical Series,* Vol. 1; *Dictionary of Literary Biography,* Vol. 2; *Dictionary of Literary Biography Yearbook: 1980, 1982;* and *Concise Dictionary of American Literary Biography: The New Consciousness, 1941-1968.*)

## PRINCIPAL WORKS

SHORT FICTION COLLECTIONS

*The Way Some People Live: A Book of Stories*   1943
*The Enormous Radio and Other Stories*   1953
*The Housebreaker of Shady Hill and Other Stories*   1958
*Some People, Places, and Things That Will Not Appear in My Next Novel*   1961
*The Brigadier and the Golf Widow*   1964
*The World of Apples*   1973
*The Stories of John Cheever*   1978

OTHER

*The Wapshot Chronicle*   (novel)   1957
*The Wapshot Scandal*   (novel)   1964
*Bullet Park*   (novel)   1969
*Falconer*   (novel)   1977
*Oh What a Paradise It Seems*   (novella)   1982

---

### Cynthia Ozick

What is the difference between a minor and a major writer? Certainly it is not subject-matter: *The Wapshot Scandal* and *Anna Karenina* are both about adultery. Nor is it a question of control—John Cheever has an aerialist's sly command over just how taut the line of a sentence should be, and just how much power must be applied or withheld in the risk of ascent. Nor can the disparity be uncovered, finally, in any theory of what sustains an original characterization—the plain fact is that Leander Wapshot and Honora Wapshot are among those figures who continue to stand even after the novels that housed them have disintegrated into total non-recall. They outlive and overwhelm every artifact and sunset on the premises, and the reason is the premises are exactly that—not merely a farm and a house in a New England port town called St. Botolphs, but the premises and hypotheses of Cheever's idea of America. It is not that major writers work from major premises and minor writers from minor ones—Chekov alone is evidence for the opposite. The difference is simply this: those writers we must ultimately regard (*regard,* not dismiss) as minor do not believe in what they are showing us. Major writers believe. Minor writers record not societies, or even allegories of societies, but vapid dreams and pageants of desire.

Now in an earlier, pre-Wapshot era, Cheever was celebrated as our supreme cicerone and Virgil of the suburbs—conductor on those commuters' trains carrying us to that eery but fine place known as Shady Hill, and, when we arrived, canny conductor once again, this time of the ladies' cocktail orchestra hidden in the forsythia. Everyone applauded, but everyone said: "Limited. Give us more; become major," and those prosperous, self-consciously self-improving communities along the New Haven tracks, with their amiable lusts, lawns, loves, lushes, and of course their babysitters and assembly nights and conjugalities, were abandoned for nothing less than the Yankee Heritage itself. Or so it seemed—*The Wapshot Chronicle* appeared to be both a Departure and a Widening-of-Compass. That Moses and Melissa Wapshot at length settled in Proxmire Manor, Shady Hill under another name, was only accident, and irrelevant; Cheever, in moving from the short story to the novel, had given up the breadth of a finger-nail for the roominess of all the Russian steppes. And as if that were not bravery enough, we have in *The Wapshot Scandal* a sequel, suggesting perhaps an American cycle, family epic, documentary, even, of the national or free-world tone: it is true that the *Scandal* chases us all the way from a missile center (with gantries on the horizon) somewhere in the "real" American West to a sale of male prostitutes just on the other side of the Bay of Naples, where Melissa buys her old lover (who happens also to be her old grocery-boy), to Rome, where, in good Yankee-heritage Edmund Wilson style, Honora is caught up with for non-payment of Federal taxes. The canvas looks wide enough at last—surely Shady Hill is finally too specialized to count, surely St. Botolphs is left far behind, veiled in its miasma of not-being-with-it?

But the canvas, just because it *is* so "contemporary," is deceptive; you can turn it upside-down and see something else, perhaps the very note the artist most needed to hide from himself and us—that suddenly clear figure in the abstraction which gives everything away. The *Chronicle*

began overtly as an idyll, so that it might end cunningly as an idyll mocking at its own elements. But the *Scandal,* to prove its even shrewder ironies, begins with the mockery itself: Coverly Wapshot, spending the night in the empty house of his childhood, thinks he sees the ghost of Leander. "Oh, Father, Father, why have you come back?" he cries, and cries it still, even when he is safely back in the missile center which is his home, and which, like all appurtenances of the up-to-date, is thoroughly ghost-free.—"Oh, Father, Father, why have you come back?"

The answer is that in Cheever Father (Father Time, in fact) always comes back because he only pretended not to be there in the first place. Cheever's suburbs are not really suburbs at all; they are a willed and altogether self-deluding reconstruction of a dream of St. Botolphs. And St. Botolphs is not really what we are meant to take it for, a dying New England village redolent of its sailing-glory days—it too is a fabrication, a sort of Norman Rockwell cover done in the manner of Braque: Cheever's deliberately wistful, self-indulgent and sleight-of-hand dream of a ruined history and temperament. It is the history and temperament of the "quaint," commemorated and typified in fake widow's walks on top of those ubiquitous antique shoppes which seek to reproduce Our New England Legacy in places like Mojave Desert naval stations or the Florida swamps. Under this system of pretense we all landed at Plymouth Rock, and that is why Dr. Cameron, the missile master of the *Scandal,* is shamed by having to reveal that he was born not a Cameron, but a Bracciani. Cheever's Yankee Heritage, for most Americans, never existed, and even the few who are entitled to it have long ago repudiated it for the acceptable salvations of our coast-to-coast parking lot, with its separate traffic lanes for shopping carts and baby carriages. This is the supermarket America we all daily smell, and this is the America which the suburbs, those stage-sets of our grassy and decently small-town beginnings, play at forsaking and often denying. The trouble is not just homesickness, but meretricious homesickness. We long for the white clapboard house behind the picket fence, we have need of going to Grandma's for Thanksgiving, and in our plasterboard-walled version of the American Dream Past we tell each other lies about the land around us. The suburbs are not St. Botolphs, they cannot be St. Botolphs, because there is no St. Botolphs any more—and for most of us there never was. We too were born Bracciani.

All of this Cheever knows, and his knowledge is his irony—but there is no iron in it. The problem stems partly from the beauty of his prose—I can think of only four or five other novelists who match his crystal and perfectionist dedication to the weight of a word, and, except for Nabokov, they are all embossers, cameo-workers in the extreme. Cheever's is a prose on which the ironic has been forced by conscience and will: so that often enough the second half of a sentence will contrive to betray the first half—whether by anti-climax, an unexpected intrusion of the mundane or a sly shift of tonality from the oratorical to the humble, or a shudder of fatalism suddenly laid on the glory of the perceived world. (pp. 62-4)

"This was the place where he [Coverly] had been conceived and born, where he had awakened to the excellence of life," Cheever says of St. Botolphs, "and there was some keen chagrin at finding the scene of so many dazzling memories smelling of decay; but this, he knew, was the instinctual foolishness that leads us to love permanence where there is none." This explicit rebuttal of all his charge of instruments, games, ceremonies, and exaltations of love is rare in Cheever; he eschews statement and leaves it to the falling tread of his elegiac lines. Among these his disbelief must be *detected,* for he covers everything over with a burden of beauty and sensibility. Exquisite apprehension of one's condition cancels failure; "some intensely human balance of love and misgiving" cancels brutality. Eloquence cancels all things inscrutable. All the same it is no surprise that Cheever does not believe in St. Botolphs and its cardboard replicas, including the houses and lives girdled by the gantries. He does not pretend to believe in them; he only wishes they were real. The luminiferous quality of his wishing follows his sentences like a nimbus, and in the end he fails to move because he moves us *all the time,* from moment to moment, from poignancy to poignancy. In Cheever, even adultery is less an act than an emblem of promise and peace. In every instance rapture overwhelms chagrin; over every person and incident he throws his coruscating net of allusion: to the past, to other lives, other possibilities, other hopes—so that his novels have no unitary *now* out of which the next event can naturally rise. I mentioned Chekhov as an example of a writer who, though self-limiting, is not minor, and it is Chekhov who gives the final word on the relation of manner to emotion. For language to be moving, Chekhov said, coldness is essential—a style should always be colder than its material. Cheever's infirmity is not that he is often episodic (he progresses like a radiant yet never static mediaeval triptych), and not even that his people are frequently tiresome innocents (through whom he has the terrifying trick of making evil seem picturesque); but he has not heeded Chekhov. It is no use arguing that he has justified and ameliorated his nostalgia by mocking it. The mockery is weaker than the nostalgia and is in every case overcome by it. And the nostalgia, like those wagon-wheels on suburban lawns, like old Mr. Jowett, the stationmaster of St. Botolphs with his yellow lantern, is fraudulent and baseless, a lie told not out of malice or self-interest, but worse, out of sentiment and wholesale self-pity.

It is all a part of the American piety. It is a ritual exercise in an emptied-out culture—the so-called Yankee Heritage has no willing legatees. "Oh, Father, Father, why have you come back?" But in reality, and in America especially, he does not come back, and Cheever, in his anguish over this absence, this unyielding and mutilating absence, settles for ghosts. There is no Yankee sociology, there is no Yankee anthropology, there is only a Yankee archaeology, and, perhaps, a Yankee mythology, more comic-strip cliché than compelling legend. The latter subsumes an image of a Europe ruined, brilliant, erotic, and past. It is on account of the abundant yet barren supermarket present that Cheever needs this sensuous and fertile make-believe past—how else can he complicate and enrich? Mere eccentricity, like Honora Wapshot's, will not do—eccentricity is a function of a secure and complacent society, but Cheever is so out of sorts and so out of sympathy with Happy

America that he has been driven to invent a Happier America. It is a sad country where a decision—a return, a renewal, a reprieve—is made not because anything has *happened,* but because something is all at once *felt:* an epiphany of the spirit, a revelation without relevance. Smell the rain! see how the light slants!—and suddenly restoration is achieved, forgiveness flows from the spleen. It is a country so splendid and melancholy, so like an artificial (though thoroughly artistic) rose, that anyone writing in it can measure his stature by the inchworm. Oh, it is hard to be a Yankee—if only the Wapshots were, if not Braccianis, then Wapsteins—how they might then truly suffer! And we might truly feel. (pp. 65-6)

*Cynthia Ozick, "Cheever's Yankee Heritage,"* in Critical Essays on John Cheever, *edited by R. G. Collins, G. K. Hall & Co., 1982, pp. 62-6.*

**Kathryn Riley**

Commentators on the fiction of John Cheever invariably conclude that a visionary quality is one of the central features of that fiction. For example, Samuel Coale [see *CLC,* Vol. 25] observes that

> Cheever's darker tales conjure up the strange powers that objects may have over the unenlightened mind. His lyric tales celebrate those moments of beauty and spiritual illumination that can occur only within the sound moral framework of an ordered and disciplined way of life.

Similarly, Lynne Waldeland characterizes Cheever as "basically a romantic and a moralist," noting his awareness of "life-enhancing and life-diminishing qualities both in people and in the world which can thwart the full humanity of his characters" [see *CLC,* Vol. 25]. (p. 21)

Within this general orientation, however, Cheever's critics have had to come to terms with another quality of his work, one suggested by the passages from Coale and Waldeland: namely, the darker, more negative side of his vision. For a significant amount of Cheever's fiction explores neither affirmation nor triumph nor transcendence. Instead, we are frequently confronted with characters who achieve, at best, a qualified success or, at worst, unqualified defeat.

Given Cheever's avowed mistrust of "plot," . . . many readers have assumed that a somewhat fatalistic or unpredictable strain runs through Cheever's predominantly affirmative vision. Scott Donaldson relates this quality to the disorienting modern world that Cheever's characters inhabit:

> In his fiction, Cheever warns, Jeremiah-like, against the boredom and depression, drugs and suicide, that will surely follow the suburbanite on the cruel journey of commutation, unless. . . . But the answers he leaves to us.

[Eugene] Chesnick [see *CLC,* Vol. 7] discerns a similar "recognizable form" in Cheever's fiction,

> the depiction of what appears to be a more or less satisfactory life and the abrupt revelation of

genuine frustration. Some people live, it would seem, in a condition of considerable anxiety.

Other assessments of this darker vision can be found in Wadeland, Bracher and Clinton S. Burhans, Jr. The arguments of these readers can be summarized, in most cases, as follows: Cheever's characters live in a world that is confusing, absurd, or potentially menacing. The source of dramatic conflict in Cheever's works is, typically, unexpected and unexplainable by the laws of logic. Correspondingly, the direction in which this conflict is resolved (that is, toward affirmation or toward defeat) often seems equally governed by chance or by unpredictable sources of good and evil. Therefore, we can infer that Cheever's central message involves the need to sustain a personal vision in the face of contradictory evidence, and that characters whose personal vision results in defeat serve to illustrate the operation of chance or evil.

My departure from such readings has to do with the second, third, and fourth points of the argument outlined above: the source of dramatic conflict in Cheever's work, the resolution of it, and the thematic inferences that should be drawn when that resolution results in a character's defeat. Specifically, I will use three of Cheever's stories to illustrate that, although a sense of vision marks many of Cheever's most praiseworthy characters, he does not give blanket approval to this quality *per se*. Instead, the protagonists of **"O Youth and Beauty!"**, **"The Swimmer,"** and **"The Geometry of Love"** are defeated precisely because they imprison themselves by withdrawing into a vision that amounts to a solipsistic fantasy.

**"O Youth and Beauty!"** traces the downfall of one character who attempts to defy the constrictions of reality on his life. Cash Bentley, a forty-year-old former track star, customarily ends Shady Hill parties with a hurdle race, using the host's furniture as his obstacle course. During such an exhibition one night, he breaks his leg, which leaves him disabled in both body and spirit. Cash attempts his next hurdle race several months later. Although he succeeds in finishing the course, the changes that age and illness have wrought on him are apparent:

> His face was strained. His mouth huge open. The tendons of his neck protruded hideously. . . . People held their breath when he approached the final sofa, but he cleared it and landed on his feet. Louise ran to his side. His clothes were soaked with sweat and he gasped for breath.

The next evening, Cash stages a hurdle race in his own living room. He enlists Louise to fire the shot signalling the start of the race, but the gun doesn't go off at first because he hasn't told her to release the safety:

> "It's that little lever," he said. "Press that little lever." Then in his impatience, he hurdled the sofa anyway.
>
> The pistol went off and she got him in mid-air. She shot him dead.

This story's ending—like that, as Waldeland has noted, of Hemingway's "The Short Happy Life of Francis Macomber"—leaves the matter of Louise's guilt ambiguous. On the one hand is her "exacting and monotonous" life as Cash's wife and the mother of their four children. The family's financial and marital problems nag her even as she sleeps: "Snowsuits, shoes, baths, and groceries seemed to have permeated her subconscious. . . . 'I can't afford veal cutlets,' she said one night." Offsetting this possible motive for murder, however, is her simple ignorance of how to handle the pistol; and just before Cash asks Louise to fire it we see her upstairs, "cutting out of the current copy of *Life* those scenes of mayhem, disaster, and violent death that she felt might corrupt her children. She always did this."

Of more interest than the problem of Louise's guilt is Cash's struggle to escape the temporal confinements that constantly threaten to beat down his spirit. He is a fairly sympathetic character; "he was never aggressive or tiresome about his brilliant past" and was "one of the best-liked men in Shady Hill." He and Louise manage to keep their marriage and their finances above water—not without some backsliding, but they manage. Yet an irreversible change comes over Cash after his accident and subsequent stay in the hospital. He begins to see the world through images of death and decay: rotting meat, cobwebs, an old whore standing in the rain, decomposing roses. His wife and friends irritate and disappoint him. He seems, in short, to have lost "the thing that had preserved his equilibrium."

That "thing" has to do, of course, with Cash's sense of his own vitality. Having lost the link to his youth, he has nothing to replace it with except, perhaps, the martinis that Louise finds him drinking in the cellar one Saturday afternoon. Simultaneously, his perception of Shady Hill changes. Cheever describes "a wonderful summer night" in which the suburb sits "in a bath of placid golden light" and the air is "a delicious element to walk through." But Cash is seized by "such savage and bitter jealousy [of his neighbors] that he feels ill." He reminds the reader less of Francis Macomber than of a figure suddenly thrust out of the "Cold Pastoral" portrayed on Keat's Grecian urn. He can exist happily only when the "mad pursuit" and "struggle to escape" take place outside of time. Ironically, he can reenter this timeless state only through death.

As shown by Cash Bentley's fate, protagonists who attempt to deny reality and to escape totally into a private vision do not succeed when that vision cuts them off from social and personal bonds and responsibilities or from a realistic assessment of their own limitations. In similar attempts to evade reality, Neddy Merrill of **"The Swimmer"** and Charlie Mallory of **"The Geometry of Love"** withdraw into solipsistic illusions. These lead to their eventual downfall because such illusions do not hold up when tested against the external order.

**"The Swimmer,"** widely anthologized and discussed because of Cheever's masterful handling of both the realistic and mythic levels of the story, traces Neddy Merrill's odyssey across Westchester County after he decides to return home from a neighbor's party by swimming the intervening backyard pools. Like Young Goodman Brown (this story echoes Hawthorne's in that it takes place on a Sunday and one of the "longest days of the year"), Merrill starts out eager to explore his world and confident in his ability to conquer it. And also like that character, his final revelation comes unexpectedly to both himself and the reader.

As Cortland Auser and Stephen C. Moore point out, Merrill begins his journey with an heroic vision:

> He was not a practical joker nor was he a fool but he was determinedly original and had a vague and modest idea of himself as a legendary figure. The day was beautiful and it seemed to him that a long swim might enlarge and celebrate its beauty.

(Neddy's vision, we should note, has also been tempered by his consumption of gin at the afternoon party.) When he begins his journey he is described in appropriately heroic language, as "a pilgrim, an explorer, a man with a destiny." But as he crosses pool after pool, the hard light of reality gradually shines more strongly. The first neighbors whose pool he arrives at greet him hospitably, offering him a drink. But then he encounters a dry pool (the owners had moved); someone throws a beer can at him as he is crossing a highway; a neighbor tells him that" "We've been *terribly* sorry to hear about all your misfortunes' "; he gets thrown out as a gatecrasher by some people who "did not belong to Neddy's set"; and his former mistress refuses even to give him a drink.

Finally, upon reaching his own home, he finds it dark and deserted:

> Had Lucinda stayed at the Westerhazys' for supper? Had the girls joined her there or gone someplace else? . . . He tried the garage doors to see what cars were in but the doors were locked and the rust came off the handles onto his hands. . . . The house was locked, and he thought that the stupid cook or the stupid maid must have locked the place up until he remembered that it had been some time since they had employed a maid or a cook. He shouted, pounded on the door, tried to force it with his shoulder, and then, looking in at the windows, saw that the place was empty.

Waldeland defines Cheever's purpose here as the portrayal of "social realities that emerge as the story progresses, realities that have to do with the role wealth and social status play in the world which Neddy wishes to invest with legendary meaning and beauty." Coale finds, similarly, that Neddy's voyage "reveals not only the beauty of the landscape, as well as the self-righteous and snobbish social hierarchy of the place, but also his expulsion from it."

These interpretations, however, fail to consider Merrill's own unsympathetic qualities. True, several of his encounters are with people who "cut" him. But at the same time, Cheever suggests that Merrill has been guilty of the same sins. Merrill feels, for instance, that the Biswangers will be "honored" to give him a drink, all the time knowing that the couple "invited him and Lucinda for dinner four times a year, six weeks in advance. They were always rebuffed and yet they continued to send out their invitations, unwilling to comprehend the rigid and undemocratic realities of their society." Likewise, he approaches his former

mistress arrogantly: "It was he who had broken it off, . . . and he stepped through the gate of the wall that surrounded her pool with nothing so considered as self-confidence. It seemed in a way to be his pool, as the lover . . . enjoys the possession of his mistress with an authority unknown to holy matrimony." But she, too, rebuffs him. Thus, while Cheever does outline for us the rigid social hierarchy of Bullet Park, he also reveals Merrill's transgressions to be offenses against some more universal code of behavior, not merely against arbitrary points of manners. Merrill's withdrawal into a private vision, therefore, should not be interpreted as a noble ambition; rather, it reflects his refusal to acknowledge some more essential, important connections with others.

Charlie Mallory's dilemma in **"The Geometry of Love"** . . . is a similar one with a more fatal outcome. A free-lance engineer faced with problems in understanding his wife, his colleagues, and his daily routine ("the boredom of a commuters' local, the stupidities in the evening paper, the rush to the parking lot"), he invents a geometry of the emotions, hoping that "If he could make a geometric analysis of his problems, mightn't he solve them, or at least create an atmosphere of solution?" Henceforth he works out his emotional crises with a slide rule, arriving at soothing, calming solutions capable of rendering even the desolate landscape of Gary, Indiana, harmless.

Eventually, though, Mallory falls victim to an unnamed illness and undergoes an operation that leaves him in critical condition. After a disturbing visit from his wife, who "could not conceal the fact that she considered his collapse to be selfish," he works out "a simple, geometrical analogy between his love for Mathilda and his fear of death." This holds him until a few days later when he looks into a mirror for the first time since his operation: "His emaciation forced him back to geometry, and he tried to equate the voracity of his appetite, the boundlessness of his hopes, and the frailty of his carcass." The equation does not balance, however; he dies that afternoon.

Mallory, like Cash Bentley and Neddy Merrill, has tried to construct a stay against confusion that, by its nature, is temporary at best. Mallory has more sympathetic qualities than does Merrill, for the people whom he staves off with his geometry—his brooding wife, a drunk business associate who puts a kitten in a blender—are, indeed, "rude, damp, and scurrilous." Perhaps as he does in his job as a free-lance engineer, Mallory hopes to balance freedom and chance with precision and grace; perhaps like the Englishman whose name his echoes, he wants to create a kind of Camelot ruled by the absolutes of geometry. Certainly the qualities he longs for are virtues in Cheever's world: "He wanted radiance, beauty, and order, no less." Yet achieving "an atmosphere of solution" requires a fatal step: ignoring the "vast number of inponderables" that threaten his delicate theorems.

To summarize, these three stories demonstrate that vision is not an inherently positive trait in Cheever's fictional world. Moreover, such an interpretation reveals a kind of continuum when we consider Cash Bentley, Neddy Merrill, and Charlie Mallory in light of other Cheever protagonists. In stories like **"The Sorrows of Gin"** and **"The**

Five-Forty-Eight," protagonists are defeated because they reject a spiritual world of youth and beauty. In **"O Youth and Beauty!"**, **"The Swimmer,"** and **"The Geometry of Love,"** protagonists are defeated, conversely, when they attempt to withdraw totally into such a world. The "success stories" among Cheever's characters—for example, Johnny Hake in **"The Housebreaker of Shady Hill"** or Moses Wapshot in **"The Death of Justina"**—become aware of the necessity to integrate and balance a visionary perspective on life with a realistic one.

It is true, as critics have pointed out, that Cheever's protagonists live in a potentially absurd or menacing world. When characters are defeated by this world, however, we should look again for the source of their defeat, rather than assigning the blame to the laws of chance, the force of social realities, or the power of evil. The decline of the three protagonists discussed in this essay suggests, instead, that their attempt to withdraw into a seemingly superior world has ironic and tragic consequences. Again recalling Hawthorne, Cheever reminds us that a character's denunciation of a crass material world can shade quickly and dangerously into self-righteousness and isolation, rather than transcendence. (pp. 21-5)

*Kathryn Riley, "John Cheever and the Limitations of Fantasy," in* The CEA Critic, *Vol. 45, Nos. 3-4, March-May, 1983, pp. 21-6.*

**Frederick R. Karl**

John Cheever's two Wapshot novels [*The Wapshot Chronicle* and *The Wapshot Scandal*]—and many of his short stories by implication—are shadowy existences of Hawthorne's sense of the flawed pastoral. In *The Scarlet Letter* and elsewhere, Hawthorne observed man as living in a "dispossessed garden," that is, in a garden of potential perfection upset by man's own imperfections. Hawthorne's sense of the mode is almost as archetypically American as is Emerson's "ideal realm," the latter leading to fantasies, the former to waste lands. For Hawthorne, the "perfect place" can never be free of evil or sin; the ideal must always be balanced by the dysfunctioning human, beset by some demonic force which he or she cannot resolve. Cheever's adaptation of this removes much of the fierce intensity, the fire of madness we perceive in Hawthorne's vision, and turns the material into a comically dispossessed pastoral: life remains appetizing although profoundly disturbed. He is concerned as much with "American dreams" as nightmares.

Cheever's dispossessed pastoral is St. Botolphs, an inland port in the great days of the Massachusetts sailing fleets; now it has been reduced to a small factory town. Yet even so, St. Botolphs has within it pastoral dimensions, so that proximity to nature in an unthreatening environment still obtains. There the Wapshot family lives in a pastoral balance: Leander, captain of the riverboat *Topaze,* Mrs. Sarah Wapshot, and their two sons, Coverly and Moses. The boys' names suggest the pastoral dimension, as well as the Hawthorne tradition.

When Moses and Coverly leave St. Botolphs for New York and Washington, respectively, their point of reference is not just home, represented by St. Botolphs, but a locale signifying for them a prior existence associated with Edenic, not just idyllic, life. Their memories include alternating trips with Leander into the wilderness, where they fish for trout and live in squalor. For the sake of the Edenic setting, they accommodate themselves to desperate camp conditions. Yet the period has its magical dimension: they are reliving, within distance of St. Botolphs, a wilderness life that contains no threat, no women, no social life—simply Leander and one son cooking hamburgers on a pot lid and trolling for trout, separate from the world, in a Garden of their own making, untouchable from the outside. That camp is like being present at the creation.

Yet even there, everything is decaying, a reminder that Eden is ephemeral. "Everything was dead; dead leaves, and branches, dead ferns, dead grass, all the obscenity of the woods death, stinking and moldy, was laid thickly on the trail. A little white light escaped from the clouds and passed fleetly over the woods, long enough for Moses to see his shadow, and then this was gone." Against this sense of dying and sere nature, still there is the wonder of the present.

The boys strike out to make their fortunes, but their inner life is turned back toward St. Botolphs by a kind of magnetic force. Although St. Botolphs is seriously flawed— Leander is a wastrel, Mrs. Wapshot caught in a marriage that has long since gone sour, old Honora lost in a disconnected time zone—even so, it is "some reminder of paradise—some happy authentication of the beauty of the summer countryside. . . . It was all real and they were flesh and blood."

Personal dimensions broaden into sociopolitical ones when Cheever contrasts Coverly's background with the places he is sent as a taper. As a man involved in computers, he is himself systematized, sent by way of a preselected program to locations he knows nothing about, then further programmed into government villages, also standardized. This institutionalization of life finds its lateral movement in the destruction of the *Topaze* on the rocks— Leander's quest for Byronic experience dashed on the shoals—and in the flawed quality of Clear Haven, the castle-like home where Moses pursues his fair Melissa. Thus, all three locations are faulted, with St. Botolphs the most resistant to the ravages of civilized change.

Clear Haven, despite recalling that "first place," is a prison of sorts, where Justina, Melissa's old aunt, rules as dictator, keeps all the inmates in thrall to her, and tries to prevent Melissa from functioning as an individual. Before Moses has insight into the castle, he sees it as a perfect place for the early months of his marriage. Since his conception of love and a relationship is intensely associated with sexual fulfillment, his dreams of paradise are filled with lovely women. Fair Haven is such a refuge: "even the benches in the garden were supported by women with enormous marble breasts and in the fall his eye fell repeatedly on naked and comely men and women in the pursuit of the glow of love."

But like everything else beyond the domain of St. Botolphs, life is infected by ego, self-indulgence, power games. Justina boasts of her own power: "I could be all these things [wicked, rude, boorish] and worse and there would still be plenty of people to lick my boots." As she smiles sweetly on Moses, he "saw for once how truly powerful this old dancing mistress had been in her heyday and how she was like an old Rhine princess, an exile from the abandoned duchies of upper Fifth Avenue and the dusty kingdoms of Riverside Drive." Moses perceives more than Eve; he sees, as if for the first time, evil.

The novel is of an ideological piece with Cheever's stories. For unlike Updike, with whom he can be superficially compared, Cheever is very conscious of the darkening sky that lies just beyond every endeavor to live and/or expand. The suburban railroad which runs through the center of so many of his stories is a monster of civilization, a freak which becomes indispensable, and a deceptive element in the life of every commuter. For while it is a lifeline, it is also a passage into anonymity. The railroad connects two forms of life: St. Botolphs, based on illusions, and its morbid replacements—Clear Haven and government villages. Near the end of the novel, a new cycle is about to begin, with the death of Leander by drowning and the birth of sons for Coverly and Moses. Leander's death clears the way for another round of illusions based on pastoral dreams. For the new generation, St. Botolphs will prove a magnet for their dreams; and they will repeat that alternation of refuge and escape which gives them vitality.

When Cheever returned to the Wapshot chronicle in *The Wapshot Scandal,* published six years later, in 1963, he sharpened the divisions. Here everything that disconnects the individual from St. Botolphs has within it forms of death, usually by way of machinery and technology. The Garden and the machine are in deadly conflict, and illusions gain in significance. In a key episode, Coverly has become attached to the team of Cameron, a man whose scientific achievements have made him an arbiter over life and death for much of the world. Yet Cameron is himself woefully incomplete, lacking a dimension, the archetype for Cheever of those who have made no progress "in solving the clash between night and day, between the head and the groin."

Coverly's dilemma is how to behave in a society which increasingly retreats from any values he can recognize or assimilate as forms of behavior. Old cousin Honora, also, no longer recognizes the familiar and must flee St. Botolphs in disgrace. Cheever is neither intense nor tragic about such conflicts between individual behavior and a world in which values no longer matter. But in his laid-back, suburban manner, he is reaching toward broad themes, what we find more comprehensively in books as different as *Giles Goat-Boy* (only a few years removed from [*The Wapshot Scandal* ] and *Gravity's Rainbow.* Barth and Pynchon are more panoramic novelists, but they limn similar experiences. And if we dip back into Barth's earlier career, before *Giles,* we see in his *The Floating Opera* and *The End of the Road* the same kind of world that Cheever has illuminated. The end is a rounding off, with Christmas Eve in St. Botolphs; in the end is the beginning. The brothers welcome a busload of blind people into Coverly's house,

and the seeing and the blind sit down to dinner together. With that, the omniscient narrator indicates that it is time to pull out. He leaves on an incantatory note, to the effect that all will fade, St. Botolphs and whatever it stands for—like Eden itself: "I will never come back, and if I do there will be nothing left, there will be nothing left but the headstones to record what has happened; there will really be nothing at all." Leander's final message, that man's soul is able to "endure every sort of good and every sort of evil," will become an idle fancy. Once the illusions pass, the machine has triumphed. (pp. 49-51)

> *Frederick R. Karl, "The Persistence of Pastoral," in his* American Fictions, 1940/1980: A Comprehensive History and Critical Evaluation, *Harper & Row, Publishers, 1983, pp. 42-74.*

## Robert G. Collins

Cheever's work was published over a fifty-year span. However, it is the later fiction, from ***Bullet Park*** through ***Falconer*** to the final ***Oh What a Paradise It Seems,*** as well as the stories that were studded through the same two decades, which reveal as an elaborately developed theme the breakdown of a pattern of mutual mating and the emergence of a new sexual definition for the individual. Even in the earlier Wapshot novels, Cheever had constantly presented his male and female characters as attracted to each other by sentiment but incapable of a permanently amiable, not to say loving, relationship. The rare pair who did get on together after the first flush of sexual attraction were almost determinedly mindless. Few of his female figures were protagonists; fewer still were developed personalities, though often the women were elusive mysteries to their mates. Virtually all of them, from a shadowed vantage point, were hostile to the men, who in turn were maudlin in their largely inexplicable love for the women and inevitably ineffective in dealing with them. In short, if we grant Cheever his *donnée,* it has generally been that of the fuddled, sincere male, whose woman is sentimentally cherished but, practically speaking, beyond his grasp, soon exasperated with him, eventually contemptuous of him, she is invariably a confirmation of his own ineffectuality rather than someone with whom a positive union can be accomplished.

Such was the Country Husband, the boozing, unhappy, mindbound fellow of Cheever's middle period. This protagonist looked as if he had little future other than taking up an anesthetizing hobby; yet, he would become the literal alien, the man who moved out of his skin, that restricting and soiled garment, and drifted into new worlds searching for a real image to correspond with his continuing need. In fact, in the later fiction, Cheever apparently goes beyond the picture of marriage as a trap to propose, implicitly, a more radical modern condition; that is, he seems to be questioning traditional mating practices at the very core. Marriage no longer serves the case; his figures move beyond it. Read carefully, he can be seen as articulating a new form of social reality, taking the tensions of modern marriage as an inexorable fact before which the alienated man now retreats, abandoning the engagement as a largely purposeless one, an anachronism in which he has been mired like a soul in mindless sin. In **Bullet Park,** the alter-ego protagonists, Nailles and Hammer, are respectively a doped-up solid citizen and a hysterically ineffective social conscience; the first is wed to a woman who might as well be lobotomized since she is only a female embodiment of his drug habit; the second is tied to a harridan who pointlessly rips the flesh off him with every word that she utters and so, too, is an avatar of his total life anguish. In neither case is there a real mating of two realized individuals; forced to view the story from the point of view of the male characters, we can see the women as drug or demon but little more.

The words of one of the characters in Cheever's last novel [*Oh, What a Paradise It Seems*] might well be a valid judgment upon the author himself: "You don't understand women at all." But that refrain may be less lament than acceptance. Lynne Waldeland has pointed out in considerable detail that Cheever has always short-changed women in his portrayal of them. The charge in itself is significant from her feminist point of view, but with respect to the work in general, it leaves us with all of the questions that such a situation raises. What does marriage mean to Cheever's characters, the traditional social generalizations aside? What does sex itself mean? What does the basis of separateness, or alienation of the characters, seen as a prevailing condition, suggest as a future prospect for them? Is Cheever talking about the end of marriage and family, mating in the connubial sense? In brief, what unfolds from these later male protagonists in their separate lives? (Waldeland is right, Cheever never really speaks from the female mind.)

Listen, for a moment, to Ezekial Farragut in **Falconer:** "There is nothing on earth as cruel as a rotten marriage." In itself a touching statement, certainly, yet in the later fiction one searches in vain for any *other* kind of marriage. Not unexpectedly, then, Cheever extends his bitterness into a generalization; again from **Falconer:** "as an incarnation of the vision of love, Holy Matrimony is only a taste of the hellish consequences involved in claiming that a vision can be represented by thought, word and deed." A "vision": the word is chosen with more reverence than appears at first glance. What displaces traditional marriage is precisely the chief factor in what makes Cheever's later work so little tied to explicit reality, precisely what makes it so "visionary." This vision as earthly fulfillment is of an amorous acceptance without possessiveness, the raising to a redemptive ritual of the casual masculine sexual encounter, the legitimization on carefully established grounds of lust as love, love in the only way that it can be had without the incurring of debt. If, as Cheever says through one of his characters, "lines of quarrel" are "as ritualistic as Holy Matrimony," in Cheever Country, marriage itself has become an outworn creed.

Interestingly, the word "creed," or rather its human antithesis, the "miscreant" or *unbeliever,* has been seen as particularly apt for Cheever's characters as first encountered in each story. The unbeliever who is guilty, or caught in sin, is one who cannot keep faith with a general belief: the miscreant is not simply an agnostic. The religious interpreters of Cheever, forming perhaps the largest single group of critics to appear in the last few years, have linked such "miscreancy" with a need for Christian redemption. It seems, however, equally possible to leave God out of it, and see the whole situation as a projection of a new approach to—or perhaps an imaginative retreat from—the conflict that began with the first mating in the Biblical garden. The miscreant of Cheever's late writings who purges himself of such sin by a sexual inversion, by discovering that his "pollution" is not, after all, impurity but only so when regarded as impure by one's self, such a *miscreant* becomes by definition a new form of *believer.*

A comparatively late story by Cheever, **"The World of Apples,"** is a work that is, in the plot itself, retrospective, meditative, explicitly tied to the need for confronting one's own sexual drive without tie to an actual and specific person as object of that physical desire. A comedy, it combines a freshness of atmosphere and a spontaneous vigor that is perfectly reflected in the title. Asa Bascomb, the octogenarian American poet whose lyric voice has celebrated nature magnificently for over a half century, reminds most readers of Robert Frost. However, this pastoral bard has long lived as a celebrated exile in an Italian villa, the object of literary pilgrims; the Vermont "World of Apples" is the world of his vanished youth, in fact. In certain ways, then, there is an element of the exiled Ezra Pound in his life style; in his emotional life, on the other hand, there are definite evocations of Walt Whitman. Nonetheless, this conglomerate personality emerges as quite a real Asa Bascomb.

Bascomb's problem can be stated simply. At the age of eighty-two, Bascomb has long been a widower. His dead wife has the quality of a mythic figure in his own life; when he thinks of her, it is with an automatic title, "his beloved Amelia," although she seems to have, even in retrospect, little flesh and blood about her—other than, we are told, having made "many of their decisions." In short, Bascomb's memory of his wife is at best a dutiful one. Shortly after we meet him, Bascomb on a holiday inadvertently stumbles upon a couple copulating in a wood. "They had not bothered to undress and the only flesh visible was the [male] stranger's hairy backside." This incident triggers the wave of sexual lust that besieges Bascomb for the better part of the story: "all he could think of was the stranger's back. It seemed to have more zeal and meaning than his celebrated search for truth." The scenes that follow are low comedy, ribald humor. Bascomb is serviced by his housekeeper, Maria, after dinner ("She was always happy to accommodate him although he always insisted that she take a bath"), which relieves him briefly although it does not satisfy him. The lust comes roaring back, and over the next ten days he composes dozens of pornographic tales and filthy limericks, which he destroys afterward, alternately wallowing in his lust and weeping at the way in which it blots out the fresh rain and crisp air of his own internal world of apples: "His mind had become unclean. . . . The welcoming universe, the rain wind that sounded through the world of apples had vanished. Filth was his destiny, his best self. . . . He glanced up at the mountains that had no cheering power—looked up at the meaningless blue sky. Where was the strength of decency?

Had it any reality at all? Was the gross bestiality that obsessed him a sovereign truth?"

Fleeing by bus from his rural villa to Rome, he wanders the streets, and in a public toilet has a brief but startling confrontation with a male whore who is exhibiting himself. The description is one that will, in fact, echo throughout the rest of the story, although Bascomb immediately flees the scene. "The man's face was idiotic—doped, drugged, and ugly—and yet, standing in his unsavory orisons, he seemed to old Bascomb angelic, armed with a flaming sword that might conquer banality and smash the glass of custom." The flaming sword of the penis is, of course, only a sword by penetration, and the encounter certainly has, despite Bascomb's horrified reaction, an element of homosexual responsiveness specifically because of the image in which he sees it. When he returns home, he reads Petronious and Juvenal and finds in them none of the sense of shame and spoliation that his own erotic impulses represent to him. "What was it that he had lost?" he asks himself; "He well knew his instincts to be rowdy, abundant, and indiscreet and had he allowed the world and all its tongues to impose upon him some structure of transparent values . . . ? . . . when had the facts of life become obscene, and what were the realities of this virtue . . . ?" The story continues with Bascomb going to visit the shrine of the Angel of Monte Giordano, who supposedly can cleanse "the thoughts of a man's heart."

After certain comic delays, he arrives there, presents the image, already buried in offerings of jewelry but not otherwise described, with his Lermontov medal, utters one of Cheever's fine comic prayers—which has, apparently, little to do with his problem, other than the possible relevance of the first two figures named: "God bless Walt Whitman. God bless Hart Crane. God bless Dylan Thomas. God bless William Faulkner, Scott Fitzgerald, and especially Ernest Hemingway." On his way home, Asa Bascomb sees a waterfall by the road, and remembers a scene from his childhood in which he had observed a white-haired old man—his father—strip himself and bathe under such a cataract, bellowing with pleasure. Inspired by the memory, the son, now himself an old man, duplicates the action—"When he stepped away from the water he seemed at last to be himself." The story ends with the elderly figure, restored to his world of apples, composing a lyric to "the inalienable dignity of light and air."

The above summary almost completely ignores those elements which make this story an indisputably effective comic piece, a triumph of style that charms the reader. However, that very quality is laid over the story line just described in such a way as to disguise its implications, while that story nonetheless remains as the scaffolding of the piece. Does the Angel of Monte Giordano "cure" Bascomb, when much of the rationale suggests that the real ailment is not his burst of Dionysian lust but his *sense* of it as lewdness? What of the angel who really is described, the Angel of the Flaming Sword in the public toilet, from whom Bascomb flees? Is the final bath in the torrent, which returns him to his world of apples, not so much a lyric epiphany, as a slightly hidden joke—the cold shower over the animal in heat?

If Asa Bascomb, having in some way outlived marriage and found a heterosexual relationship too utilitarian to serve his need, runs away from the Angel with the Flaming Sword, he is one of the last of Cheever's protagonists to do so. In his later years, after decades of prolific output as a short story writer, Cheever concentrated on longer works, producing two of his five novels in the last six years of his life. Both *Falconer* and *Oh What a Paradise It Seems* are products of his mature concerns, and both clearly demonstrate a post-marital world, a redefined personal morality that is seen as necessary and even sanctified.

In his own later life, Cheever was several times asked about a homosexual element in his work, although generally not in a direct way. In the interview with Susan Cheever Cowley, he laughingly dismissed it, referring to his own experience as having been limited to childhood experimentation during his Boy Scout days. (Twice, in *Falconer,* his protagonist makes a similar reference.) In another interview, held only ten months before his death, Cheever fulminated angrily against an unpublished Ph.D. dissertation that had traced homosexual references in his fiction, maintaining that the author of the study had been thoroughly "discredited," that he had taken advantage of Frederick, John Cheever's older brother, in his last years and encouraged him to suggest things that were totally imaginary from the earlier life of the brothers. Clearly, until the end of his life, Cheever was not prepared to accept the validity of homosexuality in itself, for itself. Yet, the last two novels involve the crucial presence of physical love between men, with physical relationships between the protagonists and women first falling away in each case. Equally clearly, then, Cheever saw such sexual legitimization as tied to a complex situation: the dilemma of Asa Bascomb reconsidered, without the cold shower as an efficacious cure, although the waterfall remains somehow in the background. (pp. 264-68)

Although after *Falconer,* Cheever might well have thought of himself as having now made his disguised statement, even if few readers immediately interpreted it, the cryptic, skeletal novel called *Oh What a Paradise It Seems* proves to be a final reassertion. Published in February 1982, just four months before Cheever's death, it shows us another man in search of a world that is purified of the foulness that is shot through and through the frenetic, over-fed and under-loved society in which we live. Again his protagonist is a symbolic figure, going through a symbolic journey in a post-marital era, where the old answers no longer suffice. Lemuel Sears, like Asa Bascomb, is a man who has survived into a re-grown bachelorhood. Twice married (the first time apparently to the same woman as Bascomb, since both remember "beloved Amelia," the second time to Estelle, a club woman who in her habits somewhat resembles the later Renée Herndon), Sears's wives are both dead, both nostalgically made up of chance memories that have little reality. A life-long New Yorker now at retirement age, Sears has paradoxically no visible friends that precede the story. A grown daughter is mentioned, but has no distinct role in the action, and there seems to be little real tie between them.

When we meet Sears, then, he is old but undefined in any ultimate way.

Two story lines exist, linked by Sears but with little connection between the secondary figures. The first is the story of Beasley Pond, its historic purity abruptly befouled by poisonous waste through the avarice of an unseen Mafia and the complicity of the town politicians. The Pond is restored to purity almost as rapidly as it was befouled, not because of Sears's futile efforts but through a completely improbable device introduced by the author. The other story line tells us of Sears's romance with a beautiful woman of thirty-five or forty, his initial success and devotion to her, with her subsequent casual dismissal of him, and his restoration to sexual and psychological happiness through an amorous relationship with another Angel with a Flaming Sword—the male elevator operator in the woman's building. As this brief summary indicates, the fouling of the pond and the sexual ambiguity of Sears are paralleled. The ultimate acceptance by Sears of his happiness with his male lover as a positive bonding of kindred spirits seems to be an obvious correlation to the health of Beasley Pond being restored, once the corrupt elements of society are forced to leave it alone.

The repetition of elements here from the earlier stories is so distinct as to make them overt symbols. The "beloved Amelia" is the outgrown female myth, which no longer serves the wanderer in search of a sexual and psychological identity. The woman, Renée Herndon, with whom Sears develops a sexual relationship from which she abruptly dismisses him, is like the earlier beautiful women, "a remarkably good-looking woman . . . splendid . . . stunning." . . . Like Marcia, Renée has a busy separate life that she makes no effort to communicate to him; like her, too, she largely ignores Sears and frequently speaks dismissively to him. An apparition of beauty, she leaves Sears floundering without explanation, although like Marcia on occasion when the mood is on her she can welcome Sears clad only in a rapidly discarded bathrobe. Perhaps most significantly, although he does not have to go through the purgatory of prison to burn away his guilt as an accomplice in the corruption of society as Farragut did, Sears like the earlier protagonist has been guilty of such complicity. Prior to his recent retirement he has been a computer expert, wiring together the modern world across a couple of continents.

The title of the novel, ***Oh What a Paradise It Seems,*** suggests the autumnal tone of the work, the retrospective and dramatically meditative nature of it. The initial reference to it comes when Sears first sees Renée Herndon in the bank before he speaks to her: "here was very definitely a declaration of paradise . . ."; and a moment later, "he felt that a profound and gratifying erotic consummation is a glimpse of another's immortal soul as one's own immortal soul is shown." But satisfying as some of their early sexual encounters are, they are not to be Adam and Eve. When we look at Sears's relationship with Renée, we realize that the word "Seems" in the title should thematically be "Seemed." He is generally frustrated in personal communication when not in sex, and only the fact that he is now fighting the pollution of Beasley Pond obscures that frus-

tration. The first thing she says to him, and she says it repeatedly, even interrupting oral sex once to say it—it is also the last thing she says in the book—is "You don't know the first thing about women!"

He doesn't, of course, for they are not to be known, at least not for Cheever's late protagonists. Sears goes directly from her to the arms of Eduardo, here shown to be comforting, sympathetic arms. Eduardo is a model citizen, happily married, with two grown children, and requires nothing whatsoever from Sears beyond their periodic happy love making. Even the lingering emotion of jealousy that Farragut had suffered from is absent for Sears; going to Canada on a lover's holiday with him, he can subsequently send Eduardo off to Florida with his wife, saying only in a cheery voice "Get a great tan!"

Nonetheless, as initiation into homosexual experience, the relationship sends Sears to a psychiatrist, a comic figure who turns out himself to be a homosexual with all of the hang-ups of guilt. Sears gently refuses the psychiatrist's interpretations, actually deriving a greater sense of ease about his relationship from the session and sufficient confidence to continue it. "[Eduardo] seems to offer me an understanding of modes of loneliness that are quite new to me and new I expect to other men . . ."

As with Farragut, the true development of the story seems to be Sears's acceptance of himself, and a reversing of the traditional view of the individual as polluted to one in which the society itself is befouled. As the environmentalist Horace Chisholm conducts Sears around Beasley Pond, chanting a litany of the plagues and poisons that have been spilled into it by the criminals and politicians that control the town, Sears's guilt dissolves proportionately. What a desecration of the living, breathing earth this despoiling represents!: "A trout stream in a forest, a traverse of potable water, seemed for Sears to be the bridge that spans that mysterious abyss between our spiritual and our carnal selves. How contemptible this made his panic about his own contamination. To accept one's self and all one's natural instincts as clean is to lead the way to the cleansing of the earth.

While on the last page or two we have a reference to Sears waking in bed with Renée, it is a *remembered* scene, and there is no indication that the affair with her has continued after the relationship with Eduardo falls into the comfortable and familiar pattern that it does. In any event, if the male/female relationship continues, it is outside real communication, since they have never engaged in a real conversation, one of openness and intimacy when they are together. With Eduardo, Sears remains the post-marital man, the solitary figure who can give and receive physical pleasure without debt or obligation ensuing, the man who has safely passed that choking noose of jealousy and accepted the world as a place of solitary men, regarding the golden dawn. On the last published page of Cheever's life work, we read: "It was the most powerful sense of our being alive on the planet. It was that most powerful sense of how singular, in the vastness of creation, is the richness of our opportunity. The sense of that hour was of an exquisite privilege, the great benefice of living here and renewing ourselves with love. What a paradise it seemed!"

As we listen to this lyric consciousness, we see Lemuel Sears, standing in the Garden. Alone. (pp. 275-77)

*Robert G. Collins, "Beyond Argument: Post-Marital Man in John Cheever's Later Fiction," in* Mosaic: A Journal for the Interdisciplinary Study of Literature, *Vol. XVII, No. 2, Spring, 1984, pp. 261-79.*

## George W. Hunt

In John Cheever's short story, **"A Vision of the World,"** we meet a very ordinary, somewhat complacent man who begins by telling us what happened on a Saturday afternoon a short while ago. He was spading his garden in peaceful contentment when he suddenly uncovered a buried shoepolish can with a note inside that reads: "I, Nils Jugstrum, promise myself that if I am not a member of the Gory Brook Country Club by the time I am twenty-five years old I will hang myself." The Saturday gardener is briefly shaken, but he quickly returns to peaceable thoughts because the sky is clear blue and the smell of grass fills the air. Then he notices black ants conquering the red ants and carrying off the corpses, a robin being pursued by blue jays, a cat scouting a sparrow, and finally a copperhead snake shedding its skin.

Vaguely disturbed, the narrator decides to drive to the supermarket in town. The supermarket is playing piped-in cha-cha music, so he asks a plain woman on the bakery line to dance. They do for a minute or two, and he becomes elated once more. On the drive home, he is stopped by a parade of marchers, but they carry no banners and seem to be marching for no discernible purpose or destination. Back home he then begins to reflect on this odd chain of events and wonders whether "reality" is actually more illogical, haphazard and illusory than our dream life, that "our external life has the quality of a dream and that in our dreams we find the virtues of conservatism."

On the nights following he has three dreams. In the first he discovers himself on a strange tropical island where he finds the native language difficult. When a waiter comes to his table for his order, the narrator says a gibberish phrase to him that begins "Porpozec ciebie nie prosze . . ." The waiter compliments him, and our narrator awakes. In the second dream he finds himself looking out on a beach from a bedroom window in a cottage on Nantucket. A single figure emerges, walking down the beach as the surf roars. It is a bishop, decked out in mitre, cope and chasuble in preparation for high Mass. The bishop sees him at the window and raises his hand in blessing and calls out "Porpozec ciebie . . ." In the third dream he is playing touch football on the winning side. His wife and children and those of his friends are sitting in improvised stands. When the winning touchdown is scored, they stand and cheer the words, "Rah, rah, rah. Porpozec ciebie . . ."

The untranslatable phrase triggers the "excitement of discovery" in him, but the next morning when his wife asks him to indicate his breakfast order on the Magic Tablet, he writes "Porpozec ciebie . . ." After he repeats the sentence with great eagerness, she begins to cry and recommends he take a vacation. He does so, flying to Sarasota, Florida. That night he dreams of a pretty woman kneeling in a field of wheat. She seems more real to him than all the hamburger joints and motels close by and she addresses him in the very words he anticipates she will say: "Porpozec ciebie." The story ends with the narrator awakened by rain:

> I think of some farmer who, hearing the noise of the rain, will stretch his lame bones and smile, feeling that the rain is falling into his lettuce and his cabbages, his hay and his oats, his parsnips and his corn. I think of some plumber who, waked by the rain, will smile at a vision of the world in which all the drains are miraculously cleansed and free. Right-angle drains, crooked drains, root-choked and rusty drains all gurgle and discharge their waters into the sea. I think that the rain will wake some old lady, who will wonder if she left her copy of *Dombey and Son* in the garden. Her shawl? Did she cover the chairs? And I know that the sound of the rain will wake some lovers, and that its sound will seem to be part of that force that has thrust them into one another's arms. Then I sit up in bed and exclaim aloud to myself, "Valor! Love! Virtue! Compassion! Splendor! Kindness! Wisdom! Beauty!" The words seem to have the colors of the earth, and as I recite them I feel hopefulness mount until I am contented and at peace with the night.

John Cheever (1912-1982) wrote better and more sophisticated stories (notably **"Goodbye My Brother," "The Country Husband," "The Swimmer," "The Death of Justina," "The World of Apples"**), but perhaps **"A Vision of the World"** illustrates best the multi-layered quality of his fiction wherein the comic, the moral, the magical and the religious unite in effortless fashion. This story also demonstrates those distinctive qualities that made Cheever the envy of his writing peers: remarkable inventiveness, humor, human compassion, and a musical, poetic style of such balanced cadence that his fiction cries out to be read aloud.

In a Cheever story comic tension is created by the disparity between the urbane, decorous, sensible narrative voice and the often eccentric and absurd episodes it must recount. As in this story, a typical Cheever tale usually begins with a rather commonplace man in a commonplace setting. Suddenly he encounters some totally unexpected disaster or inexplicable intrusion; then imperceptibly he and sometimes even the setting will metamorphose into the fabulous, and the casually told story will take on the thematic outlines of biblical or classical myth. **"A Vision of the World"** opens in a garden—Edenesque and peaceful, or so it seems. But then suicidal and murderous instincts (the snake's presence) become apparent in both the natural and the human worlds. Reality appears disrupted and corrupted to the narrator, and so he seeks in his dreams a revelation that will redeem reality for him. In the Bible, of course, dreams are often the unexpected media of revelation, mysterious hints of blessings to come—and yet they are intensely private and puzzling as in this story. To appreciate the climactic passage quoted above, one should recall that the Book of Revelation, the last book in the Bible, ends with the images of the tree and the waters of life being restored (Rv. 22:1-2), symbolically reversing the loss of the tree and the fountain of life in the Garden of Eden. Thus this tale, in subtle comic fashion, is the Bible's story in miniature, recapitulating the genesis, the sad interim, and the joyous culmination of Revelation, where love and virtue and dry bones and peace and the natural world are all restored. (pp. 174-75)

*George W. Hunt, "The Vision of John Cheever," in* New Catholic World, *Vol. 228, No. 1366, July-August, 1985, pp. 174-76.*

## Lynne Waldeland

One of the notable facts about the fiction of John Cheever is his choice of suburbia as his particular terrain within the landscape of American fiction. Many of his short stories and all of his novels are set in suburban locations, and the artifacts as well as the mores of the suburban way of life are attended to. But his outlook is finally not exclusively that of the chronicler of manners or the social critic, although those perspectives appear in his work. He, like many major American writers before him, is deeply interested in the crucial issue of the individual's need for freedom [over] society's inevitable restriction of that freedom, and Cheever's suburbia, as one more arena in which this basic conflict is played out, is similar in this way at least to Hester Prynne's Salem, Isabel Archer's "Europe," and Babbitt's Zenith.

Cheever's fictional practice links him in significant ways to writers like Hawthorne, James, and Lewis and the traditions in which they worked. He captures the feelings of isolation and rebellion of individuals restricted in society, as do most American romantic writers, including Hawthorne. At the same time, the texture of his work is largely realistic, and he is a master of the revelatory detail; consequently, he is often placed in the tradition of the realistic novel of manners with a writer like James. Furthermore, his view of American society in its suburban manifestation is often critical; Cheever's Shady Hill and Bullet Park are memorable satiric landmarks on the American literary landscape along with Lewis's Gopher Prairie and Zenith. And Cheever shares further perceptions with these writers. Like James, he shows that individual failures of perception and will share with social pressures and deceptions equal blame for the difficulties of the individual in his social world. Like Lewis, he blames society for failing to nurture human traits that would help people find and sustain personal freedom. But he is most significantly like Hawthorne in believing that the alienating effects of society on the individual are balanced by the fact that people need a social context in which to be fully human. Consequently, we read repeatedly in Cheever's work about people who feel isolated and unfulfilled in their social contexts and who sometimes rebel against the superficialities and restrictions of their suburban lives, and we often sympathize. But Cheever almost always reintegrates these characters into their societies before the story's end, just as Hawthorne does with Hester. And, although we may sometimes view the reintegration of a certain character as a defeat, more often we are led to believe, however reluc-

tantly, that whatever the deficiencies it may possess, society is the only viable context in which human beings can discover and develop their humanity.

Cheever's **"The Country Husband,"** first published in *The New Yorker* in 1954 and anthologized in *The Housebreaker of Shady Hill and Other Stories* in 1958, effectively demonstrates how he works with this issue. The protagonist, Francis Weed, lives in Shady Hill, a suburb of New York City, which, while not as severe as Hester's Salem, is nonetheless inhospitable to the full range of human needs and desires. It is a tranquil and orderly place, and most human emotions find only sublimated outlets. Anger is visible primarily in Mr. Nixon's running battle with squirrels who rob his bird-feeder, sentiment audible only in Donald Goslin's nightly rendition of Beethoven's "Moonlight Sonata," played mawkishly "like an outpouring of tearful petulance, lonesomeness, and self-pity—everything it was Beethoven's greatness not to know." Only Jupiter, a large black dog, is free, passionate, and undomesticated. In the sort of set-piece Cheever does so well, Jupiter's assaults on the tranquility of Shady Hill are catalogued. Ransacker of garbage pails and clotheslines, thief of the steaks that Donald Goslin barbecues regularly every Thursday night, disturber of garden parties and tennis matches, destroyer of Mr. Nixon's prize rose garden, he even gets tangled up in the processional at Christ Church on Sunday. But, we are assured, Jupiter's days are numbered; someone will soon poison him. Shady Hill will not long tolerate a being who undermines its order with passion and independence and vitality.

Two unusual events disturb the normal routine of Francis Weed's life, and he is unable to find a place for them in this world of Shady Hill. The title of "country husband" refers not only to his marital status and fatherhood but also to his commuting way of life; while he is returning from a business trip the plane he is on makes a crash landing in a cornfield outside Philadelphia. He is unhurt and makes his way by a variety of conveyances to New York just in time to catch his regular commuter train out to Shady Hill. Sitting with a neighbor, Trace Bearden, he tries to tell him of his experience, but "Francis had no powers that would let him recreate a brush with death—particularly in the atmosphere of a commuting train, journeying through a sunny countryside where already, in the slum gardens, there were signs of harvest. Trace picked up his newspaper, and Francis was left along with his thoughts." The calm of this environment is impervious to penetration by something so serious as the fact of death, and Francis is left to handle the trauma of it in isolation.

He has just as little success communicating his experience to his family; here his role of "country husband" and father of four repeatedly gets in the way of his personal need for understanding and sympathy. He has not gotten the first sentence of his story out when his children begin to fight, and he has to stop and try to restore order. He seems unable to get through to his wife, who fails to react to his news and instead sends him off on an errand to call his older daughter to dinner. He plans to tell her about the crash but discovers her reading a forbidden magazine and ends up scolding her. The dining table is alive with further quarrels waiting to happen, and after things reach a certain point of chaos, Francis asks petulantly why the children can't eat early. His wife, waiting for this, replies that she cannot cook two dinners; her youth and beauty have already been sacrificed to a life of homemaking. Long-submerged tensions find expression as the quarrel escalates:

> Francis says that he must be understood; he was nearly killed in an airplane crash, and he doesn't like to come home every night to a battlefield. Now Julia is deeply committed. Her voice trembles. He doesn't come home every night to a battlefield. The accusation is stupid and mean. Everything was tranquil until he arrived.

Dinner ends abruptly with everyone fleeing the table. The absence of a place where Francis could naturally express his fear and doubt and receive some uncomplicated sympathy has precipitated a foolish but alienating quarrel.

This one moment of discontinuity between Francis and his environment could probably be survived, but it is followed immediately by another. The next night, at a party, Francis notices that the maid passing drinks at the Farquarson's looks familiar, and he finally, with difficulty, places her. He had seen her at the end of World War II in Normandy, where she was undergoing a brutal public punishment for having lived with the German commandant during the occupation. The memory is vivid and unsettling, but Francis suddenly realizes that he cannot share it with anyone, including his wife. . . . Once again, the inadequacy of his social environment deprives Francis of a chance to articulate and hence possess his experience, and he feels frustrated and disconnected.

These experiences and his inability to find a place for them in his regular life set Francis up effectively for the crisis that follows, a crisis that leads him from these sensations of isolation to something close to a willed rebellion. That night he waits in the car to take the babysitter home, and instead of white-haired Mrs. Henlein, a beautiful young girl steps out into the lighted doorway.

> Now the world is full of beautiful young girls, but Francis saw here the difference between beauty and perfection. All those endearing flaws, moles, birthmarks, and healed wounds were missing, and he experienced in his consciousness that moment when music breaks glass, and felt a pang of recognition as strange, deep, and wonderful as anything in his life.

There is no evidence outside Francis Weed's perceptions that the substitute baby-sitter, Anne Murchison, is in any way extraordinary; the above passage makes clear that it is Francis's need for something fulfilling and perfect that is at work. And what Francis is missing in his life and thinks he finds in the girl is further revealed when he notices that she has been crying and politely inquires as to the cause. Instead of responding politely, she pours out her hurt and grief, having to do with an abusive alcoholic father, and finally breaks down and weeps with abandon in Francis's arms. At this point he is a goner. The absence of emotion and sympathy in his world, from which he has

been suffering, shows up in terrible relief against the openness and vulnerability of the girl weeping in his arms.

Cheever makes it clear that the resulting infatuation of Francis with the babysitter is all on his part. Except for a spontaneous kiss that first night, attributable to gratitude for his concern, Anne does nothing to lead Francis on, and, in fact, she repulses the one abortive advance he makes. At the same time, it is clear that Cheever does not want us to write off Francis's situation as the ridiculous wanderlust of a bored, middle-aged husband. The two moments of recognition in his life, coming fast upon each other as they have, and his realization that he cannot communicate them, have made him susceptible to the meanings he imposes on the girl, and his plight is only partly comic.

His first response to his new feeling is to spend an uneasy night of half-finished dreams. He fantasizes a life with Anne—crossing the ocean on the old *Mauretania,* living with her in Paris. The impoverished terms in which Cheever has Francis express his dream are telling; in the absence of real passion and spontaneity in his life, Francis is forced to rely on trite, second-hand structures for this new reality. In a waking moment, Francis—once again the country husband—tries to force himself to focus his mind on "some thing he desired to do that would injure no one," and he finally settles on skiing. It is hard to resist the idea that even here Francis is turning to a traditional American notion of getting away to nature as a way to regain control over one's life. At any rate, this dream turns revelatory too; the exhilaration of skiing turns to effort as Francis seeks "with ardor some simplicity of feeling and circumstance." This whole sequence focuses much less on the affair Francis is contemplating than on the various things that are missing in his life that would lead him to need this fantasy.

In the morning, memories of the *Mauretania* and Paris dominate, and the first social consequence of his new sense of freedom and rebellion occurs. On the platform while he waits for his train, old Mrs. Wrightson, social arbiter of the community, engages Francis in an endless and inane conversation about her difficulties in finding curtains. Her tale of woe ends with the confession that she simply doesn't know what to do with her living room windows.

> "I know what to do with them," Francis said.
> "What?"
> "Paint them black on the inside, and shut up."

Mrs. Wrightson limps away, wounded in the soul, and Francis has a moment of supreme exhilaration. But the insight that follows sobers him and indicates to us that we have witnessed something more than just an instance of gratuitous nastiness. Francis reflects:

> Among his friends and neighbors, there were brilliant and gifted people—he saw that—but many of them, also, were bores and fools, and he had made the mistake of listening to them all with equal attention. He had confused a lack of discrimination with Christian love, and the confusion seemed general and destructive.

In this scene Cheever points out not only the external

causes that have led Francis to this moment of isolation but also the ways in which Francis himself has been an accomplice in his fate.

In any event, the relationship he thinks he needs to have with Anne Murchison does not materialize. He buys her a bracelet, but never gets the chance to give it to her. He finds her in the foyer of his house one evening and attempts an embrace, only to be interrupted by a neighborhood child. He writes her love letters, only to be led to a painful awareness of "the abyss between his fantasy life and the practical world." At this point, Francis, set up by a series of disappointments as he was earlier by the two extraordinary events, reaches a breaking point. He learns accidentally that Anne is engaged to be married to a boy from Shady Hill. The next day he is asked by a neighbor to provide an employment reference for the boy, and he responds by doing his best to savage the young man's reputation and ruin his chance for the job. Moments later he is horrified at what he has done and thinks back over the chain of events that has brought him to this uncharacteristic behavior:

> There was nothing to mitigate his feelings—nothing that laughter or a game of softball with the children would change—and thinking back over the plane crash, the Farquarsons' new maid, and Anne Murchison's difficulties with her drunken father, he wondered how he could have avoided arriving at just where he was. He was in trouble. He had been lost once in his life, coming back from a trout stream in the north woods, and he had now the same bleak realization that no amount of cheerfulness or hopefulness or valor or perseverance could help him find, in the gathering dark, the path that he'd lost.

Francis considers his alternatives—religion, psychiatry, massage parlors, rape—and decides on psychiatry, domesticated suburbanite that he is. Once he makes this socially appropriate decision, a decision aimed at adjustment rather than change, it is pretty much all over for Francis's try at a more independent life. The last direct view we have of him occurs when he enters the doctor's office and, with tears in his eyes, confesses "I'm in love, Dr. Herzog." This section of the story conveys a certain ambivalence on Cheever's part about this situation. There is something of a comedown for Francis in seeking out a psychiatrist to help him accommodate to the given order of Shady Hill. Yet Cheever seems also to think that Francis in rebellion is Francis lost and that there is no possibility of his living a fulfilled life outside his social context.

The resolution of Francis's conflict is handled obliquely but tellingly. There is no further focus on him; instead, Cheever repeats his earlier catalogue of the doings and beings of Shady Hill. Mr. Nixon is again battling the squirrels; Donald Goslin is again misplaying the "Moonlight Sonata." But this time, Francis himself appears in the catalogue; he is down in his basement building a coffee table, a woodworking project suggested as therapy by Dr. Herzog. He has been reintegrated into the society of Shady Hill. The moment of rebellion is over.

Our understanding of Francis is completed in the final se-

quence of the story. While Julia Weed is working in her garden, a cat wanders in, "sunk in spiritual and physical discomfort," because someone has dressed it in doll clothes. Julia calls to it, intending to free it from these encumbrances, but "the cat gives her a skeptical look and stumbles away in its skirts." The cat might seem a humorous but gratuitous touch if it were not that Jupiter follows immediately, prancing through the tomatoes with the remnants of an evening slipper in his mouth. The juxtaposition of the two animals seems to provide one more illumination; Jupiter possesses the kind of freedom, passion, vitality, and social independence that Francis has yearned for, but that is finally unavailable to him. The cat, on the other hand, is similar to Francis; he too is made uncomfortable and restricted by things imposed on him from outside, but he is, like Francis, unable to divest himself of them. However, one supposes that the cat will eventually be rescued. We might ask whether Francis's reintegration is also a rescue rather than a defeat.

Cheever does not want us to perceive Francis's story too simply. The abortive nature of the affair Francis tries to pursue makes clear that it is important mostly as a catalyst for a more significant conflict in Francis's relationship to society, a conflict that, for all its brevity and its comic overtones, stands in a respected and crucial American tradition. In the brief span of a short story with its consequent limitation of scope, Cheever has put Francis through the same experience shared by characters like Isabel Archer, George Babbitt, and Hester Prynne. All four characters have searched through the experience of isolation for some sort of independence; all have been reintegrated into their social environments in the end. Francis's differences from and similarities to these other protagonists clarify where Cheever finally stands in this story and in most of his others. Unlike Isabel Archer, since Francis has not been greatly deceived by the world to which he now must accommodate, his reintegration lacks some of the tragic dimension that attends Isabel's fate. And although there may be some surface similarities between Babbitt's situation and Francis's, the reader does not feel the sense of Francis's inevitable defeat as one does Babbitt's; Francis is never as unthinking, insensitive, egotistical, or vulgar as Babbitt. The most instructive parallel for me, however, is between Francis and Hester Prynne. Both characters' rebellion is set in motion by the intrusion of passion into lives from which it is missing, and both live in societies hostile not only to passion but to most aspects of human vitality and personal freedom. Both societies in question are portrayed negatively, and the protagonists, because of their greater humanity, earn our understanding and sympathy. Nevertheless, in the end, Hawthorne and Cheever reintegrate their protagonists into their societies because, in fact, neither author really believes that there is any other arena for human fulfillment than that of human society. The claims of society on both Hester and Francis are real, despite the stifling aspects of life in society; and the reintegration of both characters, although not exactly a triumph, is not a defeat either but an accommodation to human reality that both authors regretfully accept. (pp. 5-11)

*Lynne Waldeland, "Isolation and Integration:*

John Cheever's 'The Country Husband'," in Ball State University Forum, *Vol. XXVII, No. 1, Winter, 1986, pp. 5-11.*

## Scott Donaldson

In *The Wapshot Chronicle* (1957), his first novel, Cheever contrasted a somewhat idealized and unrecapturable past with a less hospitable but not intolerable present. His tone ranged from genial to satirical without becoming bitter. Then, in his dark period of the 1960's, and particularly in *The Wapshot Scandal* (1964) and *Bullet Park* (1969), he adopted the narrative stance of a visiting anthropologist who, despite his apparent objectivity—"at the time of which I'm writing," the narrative voice would remark—regarded the ills of modernity with something verging on despair. Finally, in his last two novels—*Falconer* (1977) and *Oh What a Paradise It Seems* (1982)—this dismayed observer struggled toward acceptance of the deeply flawed universe, and even toward affirmation. Miracles could happen.

From these novels and from such well-known stories as **"The Death of Justina"** (1960) and **"The Angel of the Bridge"** and **"The Brigadier and the Golf Widow"** (both 1961), it would be easy to assemble a catalogue of the troubles besetting Americans in the third quarter of the 20th century. Technology can destroy the world. Our food, our entertainment, our homes, our very existences have become standardized and tasteless. We've lost our roots. Love gives way to lust, religion to psychiatry. Liquor and drugs anesthetize us against the fear of death. Cheever spells out no such bill of particulars, but it is implicit in the stories he tells and emerges through incident and conversation and symbol. Two dominant symbols in his work for this modern malaise are the superhighway and the supermarket.

Of the two, the superhighway is the most frequently and obviously invoked. Cheever's expressway that gouges through the landscape compares with the 19th-century railroad as the machine in the American garden. Emerson speculated that the railroad rides upon us and not the other way around, Thoreau feared that we had constructed a fateful engine beyond our capacity to control. A similar theme runs through much of Cheever's work, where the superhighway is the Atropos that levels the contours and obliterates the sights and smells of a fragrant past, and that in combination with trains and planes produces an incredible mobility at the expense of homelessness.

Uprootedness is at the heart of *The Wapshot Chronicle,* in which the two brothers Moses and Coverly Wapshot leave their native St. Botolphs to seek their fortunes in more thriving areas. All the young leave St. Botolphs, a dying seaport town. The movement is toward nomadism (a favorite Cheever term), toward a gypsy culture without roots, and the psychic costs—in loneliness and in yearning for roots—are heavy, especially for Coverly and his wife Betsey.

The young couple are assigned to Remsen Park, a government community where Coverly is employed in missile work, and Betsey—a small-town girl herself—is desperately lonely there. Bereft as she is, she is drawn to the supermarket, a modern artifact that has a more ambivalent symbolic import in Cheever's fiction than the superhighway.

> She walked out of Circle K and down 325th Street to the shopping center and went into the supermarket, not because she needed anything but because the atmosphere of the place pleased her.

There she strikes up a conversation with the pleasant young cashier who directs her to the electrical appliance store five doors down the street. There she strikes up a conversation with another man who promises to fix the cord on her iron and comes home, where she strikes up a conversation with a vacuum cleaner salesman who happens to ring her bell. Betsey can find friends only by way of these instrumental relations. Distraught, she decides to leave, and in her absence (for she will come back) Coverly "thought of her against scenes of travel—trains and platforms and hotels and asking strangers for help with her bags—and he felt great love and pity."

A relationship clearly exists between supertravel and supermarket. The fast cars and express trains and jet airplanes that make nomads of us all bear a certain affinity to the supermarket that is not really the friendly country store Betsey Wapshot wishes it were. (pp. 654-56)

The fear of death dominates *The Wapshot Scandal:* death by nuclear explosion, death by plane crash, death on the highway, death by cancer, above all the death-in-life of a meaningless and boring suburban existence that confronts Moses Wapshot's beautiful wife Melissa. Melissa, like the scientist Dr. Cameron who plays the violin while matter-of-factly contemplating the end of the world, seeks escape from mortality in lust. Dr. Cameron feels "the chill of death go off his bones" in the arms of his Roman mistress. Melissa purchases her own warmth in the form of the grocery boy Emile, and eventually they, too, go to Rome, on the wings of a supermarket promotion.

Fired from his job at an old-style grocery store because of his fornication with Melissa, Emile goes to work "at the new supermarket on the hill—the one with the steeple." To lure customers from the Grand Union and the A&P, the new store develops "an exploitation package." The store promises to distribute a thousand plastic eggs on Easter Eve, with certificates inside for a dozen real eggs, a bottle of French perfume, an outboard motor, and so on, with five golden eggs entitling the finders to "a three-week, all-expense vacation for two at a luxury hotel in Madrid, Paris, London, Venice or Rome." Emile is hired to hide the eggs between two and three on Easter morning, but word gets out and—in a scene Malcolm Cowley construed as "a Brueghel vision of hell"—he is pursued on his rounds by dozens of women in nightgowns and robes and curlers (they all appear "to be wearing crowns") who block the progress of his car and let the air out of his tires so that finally he is reduced to throwing eggs and dumping entire crates of them into a tract of empty land. But Emile keeps the golden egg for Rome in his pocket, on the way home leaves it on Melissa's lawn, and that—with bizarre complications—is why Melissa and Emile are living to-gether in the Eternal City as the novel ends.

In effect they are exiles rather than expatriates in Rome. Melissa's marriage has of course collapsed. The Italians whom she and Emile see socially treat them like the outcasts they are. She is last glimpsed in the Supra-Marketto Americano, pushing her way through the walls of food as solace for her bewilderment and grief. (pp. 658-9)

John Cheever was fully cognizant of the comic paradox of the supermarket in Rome, and liked to tell a story about meeting a rather assertive Bostonian at an embassy cocktail party there.

> "What do you do, Mr. Shivers?" the Bostonian asked, having missed the name.
>
> "Oh, I write. What do *you* do?"
>
> "I'm a manager for Minimax in Boston."
>
> "What brings you to Rome, then?"
>
> "Well, Mr. Shivers," the Bostonian declared, "Rome needs Minimax and Minimax needs Rome. We're going to build a supermarket in Rome that will put the Pantheon to shame."

Though hardly a rival to the Pantheon, Cheever's modern supermarket is rich and strange indeed. "Except for the shapes of the pastry," the narrator of the 1962 story, **"A Vision of the World,"** remarks during his Saturday afternoon visit to the supermarket, "there was nothing traditional to be seen at the pastry counter." Then, having purchased his brioches, he is inspired by the cha-cha music to dance briefly with a homely stranger. But no such humor, no such momentary gaiety brightens the picture of Melissa at the Supra-Marketto, like Ophelia grieving unto madness.

Despite the darkness of **The Wapshot Scandal,** Cheever insisted in the *Time* cover story that appeared a few weeks after the novel was published that he felt "an impulse to bring glad tidings to someone. My sense of literature is a sense of giving, not a diminishment." And he emphasized that he did not intend to belittle anyone trapped in contemporary culture, like the woman obsessed with collecting plaid stamps, for example. "It is quite possible that a woman who goes to sleep and dreams of getting a new plaid-stamp book is not quite as undignified as she appears to be. People actually sidestep the pain of death and despair by the thought of purchasing things. . . . The time for levity or even making fun of people who go to bed and dream of having 17 plaid-stamp books full is over." Josephine Herbst, a writer Cheever had known and respected since the mid-1930's, could not agree. "You may be right about the plaid stampbooks and the utility of buying to stave off thoughts of death," she wrote him, but she could not "imagine life, anywhere, at any time, so pared down to that necessity." He was, she thought, celebrating the wrong values, and besides, *Time* had him all wrong as a facile celebrant. "You don't just celebrate life out of nothing, but out of a deep pessimism. Which makes it the more valid, for our time, for any time." Herbst was absolutely right about that, for if in his later novels Cheever seems "suspended between a tragic pessimism and a raptured

expectancy . . . [seems] to be listening for the tone of angels, as the earth smoulders beneath him," it was the tension between these polar outlooks, and the attempt to resolve them, that gave his writing power and dignity. The resolution did not come easily. His nearly impossible task was to make the world of the supermarket (and the super-highway) "in which we must live, congenial to the sensibility that makes life worth living."

More than anything else Cheever wrote, 1969's **Bullet Park** sings the sorrows of excessive mobility. The title refers, rather ominously, to a suburb not unlike Proxmire Manor in its pretended immunity from the rigors of life, but in fact Bullet Park is a dangerous place to live and represents a permanent home for almost no one. "The people of Bullet Park," the anthropologizing narrator observes, intended "not so much to have arrived there as to have been planted and grown there, but this of course was untrue." Everything is in flux in this apparently comfortable world. The novel opens on the scene of a small railroad station, but this is not like the wistful way stations of the past. The building, designed "with some sense of the erotic and romantic essence of travel," is now "a warlike ruin." On the station platform one morning, a waiting commuter is sucked under the Chicago express, leaving only "a highly polished brown loafer" to signify his passing. On that same platform, co-protagonist Eliot Nailles waits in terror for his daily ride to New York City. He has made the trip a thousand times, but now a phobia overtakes him and he cannot board the train unless he dopes himself with a massive tranquilizer that will float him "down the tracks into Grand Central."

The other protagonist, Paul Hammer, is a world traveler who settles in Bullet Park to awaken the world by murdering Nailles' son Tony (Cheever is little concerned with credibility in his late fiction). Obviously unbalanced, Hammer is subject to attacks of melancholy that overtake him on trains and planes and drive him to the brink of suicide. Then, however, he remembers that he has been inspired by his insane mother to commit a ritual murder and so shock America out of its drugged stupor. He does not succeed. In the end, Nailles rescues his son as Hammer prepares to immolate him on the cross of Christ's Church and, in a curiously ambivalent ending, brings matters back to normal. "Tony went back to school on Monday and Nailles—drugged—went off to work and everything was as wonderful, wonderful, wonderful, wonderful as it had been."

"Never, in the history of civilization," Hammer's mother proclaims, "has one seen a great nation single-mindedly bent on drugging itself" like the United States. She chooses to live in Europe but on a trip to Los Angeles takes a ride on a freeway and there witnesses "another example of forgetfulness, suicide, municipal corruption and the debauchery of natural resources." Bullet Park itself averages 22 traffic casualties a year "because of a winding highway that seemed to have been drawn on the map by a child with a grease pencil." One Saturday morning, Nailles takes Hammer fishing, and they drive north on Route 61, one of the "most dangerous" and "most inhuman" of the new highways. (pp. 660-62)

Despite its emphasis on the stupefying effects of drugs and liquor and on the deadly pathways of rapid travel, ***Bullet Park*** offers a more hopeful picture than ***The Wapshot Scandal.*** Nailles is not terribly bright or capable, but he does manage to rescue his son. Moreover, as his reminiscence about the roads of yesterday suggests, he remains keenly attuned to nature. When he comes home to Bullet Park one night, the rain lets up, and he can distinguish the various sounds that the wind out of the northeast makes as it fills up different trees: "maple, birch, tulip and oak." What good is this knowledge? he reflects, and answers his own question. "Someone has to observe the world."

Exactly, and while he thinks this, the mysterious Swami Rutuola is upstairs with the teenager Tony who has troubles of his own, the murderous Hammer aside, and in a period of extended depression has refused to get out of bed. Neither conventional medicine nor psychiatry can rouse Tony, but Rutuola does. His method is to invoke an appealing image in Tony's mind and to reinforce that image with repetition. "I am in a house by the sea." the Swami has Tony repeat after him. "It is four o'clock and raining." "I am sitting in a ladderback chair with a book in my lap." "I have a girl I love who has gone on an errand but she will return." "I am sitting under an apple tree in clean clothes and I am content." Next the Swami coaches Tony in the "love" cheer and the "hope" cheer—he says "love" over and over, as many as a hundred times, and the same with "hope"—and miraculously the treatment works and Tony is restored to health.

In effect the whole Cheever program for coping with the ills of modernity is summed up in these few pages. "Someone has to observe the world." Restoration comes with mountain air, the wind in the trees, the rain at the seashore, the scent of apples. It comes through love. And it will not come if we succumb to despair.

Ezekiel Farragut in ***Falconer,*** Cheever's widely publicized 1977 novel set in prison, conquers his drug addiction and escapes from confinement—again, miraculously—through giving himself in love and persistently yearning toward the light. Farragut's release from addiction and imprisonment paralleled Cheever's own 1975 victory over the confinements of alcoholism. Thereafter the darkness that pervaded ***The Wapshot Scandal*** and, to a lesser degree, ***Bullet Park,*** gave way to radiance. Despite its forbidding subject matter, ***Falconer*** is full of blue sky, and there is nothing equivocal about its affirmative ending. Free at last, Farragut walks into the future in a coat a perfect stranger has just given him as protection against the rain and against detection. "Rejoice," he thinks to himself. "Rejoice." That there was more to celebrate than to bemoan became an article of belief for Cheever in his last years.

Yet as the title of ***Oh What a Paradise It Seems*** (1982) hints, the earth we inhabit is not really a paradise, or at least is not likely to remain one in an age of pollution. (pp. 663-64)

Cheever has been criticized for looking backward, for a nostalgia that by overvaluing a golden past ignores the question of how to confront the flawed present. But in his

later work that is not at all true. He was every bit as aware in 1980 as in 1960 of the depradations that nomadism and commercialism (symbolized by superhighway and supermarket) had worked upon his culture. Yet in his last fiction he rejected negation as a contemptible attitude. In his most optimistic moods, he looked to the future rather than the idealized past for relief. Perhaps, he thought, the "automobile dumps, polluted rivers, jerry-built ranch houses" of the present were "not, as they might seem to be, the ruins of our civilization but . . . the temporary encampments and outposts of the civilization we—you and I—shall build."

In any event, so long as people could see the blue sky, feel the sea breeze, smell the sweet grass, and love one another, they should not succumb to despair. Life itself was the greatest of gifts. What he aimed to do, in ***Falconer*** and ***Paradise,*** was "to study triumphs, the rediscoveries of love, all that I know in the world to be decent, radiant, and clear." Was his writing getting better, a particularly dense television interviewer asked him in 1979? Well, not necessarily better, he answered, but he hoped there was a growth "as if one were discovering more light, if light is what one is after." This observation silenced his interviewer entirely, but those who read Cheever's fiction carefully and admire it, like John Updike, knew what he was talking about.

When Updike read ***Paradise*** in proof, certain images stuck in his mind: "The ecstatic ice skating, the wind chimes, the exultant evocation of the supermarket. This last place especially needed you to sing it," he wrote Cheever in December 1981. The previous month, the two writers made a joint appearance on the Dick Cavett show, but Updike felt he had not managed to articulate for television what he most valued in his colleague's work. "I kept saying radiant on Cavett but it's more like the little star inside a snowball on a sunny day." What Cheever had done during the 1960's was to tell us how we lived. In his last two novels he went beyond that. "You do that elemental thing only the rarely good writer can do"—Updike summed up the accomplishment—you "tell us how we are alive." (pp. 667-68)

*Scott Donaldson, "Supermarket and Superhighway: John Cheever's America," in* The Virginia Quarterly Review, *Vol. 62, No. 4, Autumn, 1986, pp. 654-68.*

## Wayne Stengel

The 1984 publication of Susan Cheever's *Home before Dark,* a memoir by John Cheever's novelist daughter about Cheever's thirty-year struggle with alcoholism and bisexuality, reveals Cheever to be anything but a glib writer of *New Yorker* short stories of manners. In *Home before Dark,* Cheever emerges as a consistently brooding surrealist, a writer whose novels and stories frequently return to images of exile, family discord, and disruptive travel. The sense of displacement that these situations evokes haunted Cheever throughout his career. His writing therefore becomes the effort to bridge the gap, lessen the abyss between appearance and reality in both the world he recorded and the life he lived. As Susan Cheever quotes from the journal her father kept from the early 1930s until his death in 1982: "The bridge of language, metaphor, anecdote, and imagination that I build each morning to cross the incongruities in my life seems very frail indeed." Accordingly, the sense of psychological disorientation that plagued Cheever in the last five years of his life permeates all his art. This quality makes Cheever a master of fragmentary, anecdotal short stories and, for some critics, an unsatisfactory shaper of novelistic continuity and *durée*.

However, just this sense of obsolescence and disarray in the midst of the seemingly familiar, affluent, and secure creates the collage effect of much of Cheever's fiction. It also gives his writing as many affinities to postmodernism as to the more realistic milieu of an Updike or an Auchincloss. Moreover, *Home before Dark* should enable his audience to see Cheever as an unfailingly surreal lyricist of disorientation, a writer whose fictions are propelled by a perpetual sense of fear. Similarly, Cheever's joyous ecstasy in the physical world can be extinguished as quickly as a candle flame.

As Clinton S. Burhans, Jr., and Frederick Bracher have demonstrated, of all John Cheever's more than 100 short stories no single tale so closely reveals his point of view and philosophy of composition as **"A Vision of the World,"** first collected in *The Brigadier and the Golf Widow* in 1964. With this story, written in midcareer, Cheever literalizes the compunction he feels to bridge the gap. Here he creates a chain, arch, or bridge—and these are the words Cheever uses again and again in his fiction—between an absurdly affluent world of material possessions and the unsettling yet unifying force of his dreams. By midcentury, Cheever was convinced that the quotidian, grotesque realities of American life had grown uniformly hostile and threatening. In the nature of dream experience, he felt, lay the meaning and explanation for the grating disjunctures and incongruities of middle-class suburban life.

Any reader intrigued by Cheever's thought and writing can find repeated instances of his metaphoric use of the concept of the chain, arch, or link. This structuring device bridges the distance between the increasingly horrifying American nightmare and an idealized, seemingly Jungian dreamworld of archetypes, doubles, light and shadows, personae, and masks. Cheever believed this realm might give individual lives a vision of completeness and transcendence. In describing the shaping of his fiction to Christopher Lehmann-Haupt in 1969, Cheever said: "It's almost like shaping a dream . . . to give precisely the concord you want . . . the arch, really. It's almost the form of an arch." Or as R. G. Collins interprets Cheever's remark: "It seems an accurate description of Cheever's view of successful fiction, a dream that becomes an arch tying together the universe of the inner being." However, when one begins to explore the implications of this linkage, a reader is surprised at how thoroughly the metaphor runs through Cheever's writing. Nonetheless, Cheever's protagonists have enormous difficulty in making these bridges connect their dream visions with reality.

**"A Vision of the World"** develops more like a transcen-

dental essay by Emerson or Thoreau than a contemporary short story. The narrator, a suburban lord of the manor—much like Cheever in Ossining—describes a series of random events that frustrates all of his efforts to make order or purpose of his world. The absurd cha-cha musak that blares over the delicatessen counter of his neighborhood grocery induces the homely woman in front of him into his arms for a fleeting pas de deux. Gardening in his backyard, the narrator discovers a copperhead molting from its winter skin and suddenly experiences a prescience of the evil that his suburban enclave so wants to deny. Nearby, the narrator unearths a long-buried shoe-polish can containing a twenty-year-old note from a young social climber asserting that he will hang himself if he is not a member of the Gory Brook Country Club by the time he is twenty-five. Apprehensively, the narrator wonders how to make sense of this increasingly meaningless world. Interestingly, it is his wife, the dream-conscious, feminine principle who offers a solution:

> But I was grateful to my wife then for what she had said, for stating that the externals of her life had the quality of a dream. The uninhibited energies of the imagination had created the supermarket, the viper, and the note in the shoe-polish can. Compared to these, my wildest reveries had the literalness of double-entry bookkeeping. It pleased me to think that our external life has the quality of a dream and that in our dreams we find the virtues of conservatism.

With the aid of the feminine imagination, the narrator suddenly understands how to interpret reality so as to make it less threatening and distorted. If the human imagination finds Sixties' suburban life bizarre and disorienting, that same imagination can be used to interpret those qualities of the narrator's dreams that suggest harmony, security, and triumph. Suddenly, the protagonist discovers a narrative method which will generate the events of the story to come while reconstructing the chain of situations through which the tale has evolved. The narrator will use imagination and language to describe not a bridge of events, but that essence of his dreams which suggests wholeness and harmony in a deeply fragmented world.

> What I wanted to identify then was not a chain of facts but an essence—something like that indecipherable collision of contingencies that can produce exaltation or despair. What I wanted to do was to grant my dreams, in so incoherent a world, their legitimacy.

Many of Cheever's narrators use their imaginations and speech as mediation between senseless reality and an ironically coherent dreamworld. This process involves them in two immediate problems. First, the arch, bridge, or chain that is the Cheever protagonist's device for conveying the quality of dream may convey situations and plot, but it is grossly inadequate to reproduce the texture and essence of dream. These Jacob's ladders fall before even the most superficial Jungian analysis. Secondly, the language—gesture, intonation, and semiotic—of the dream state is hardly the articulated speech of contemporary Westchester. Therefore Cheever's narrators are always confronted with the dilemma of translating the speech and thoughts of dream into the language of surreal *Bullet Park*. Thus the Cheever protagonist desperately clings to his bridges and wants to destroy them; he or she desires passage between dream and debilitating reality while sensing that no means of satisfactory translation may ever be attainable.

Nonetheless, this narrator doggedly pursues his tranquilizing dreams and his effort to translate them into tormenting reality. The protagonist of **"A Vision of the World"** first dreams of arriving with a group of men on a desert island and of mastering the difficult language of this world while ordering a meal in a restaurant. He next dreams of seeing a priest or bishop walking along the edge of a seashore and of being greated by this holy man with the same sentence of this arcane language he used earlier in the restaurant. Finally, he dreams of playing on the winning team in a touch football game. Consistently, his wife and daughter, and the wives and daughters of the other team members who have formed a cheerleading squad for the players, hail their fathers and husbands with the same cheering phrase. "Porpozec ciebie nie prosze dorzanin albo zyolpocz ciwego," says the narrator to the waiter, the priest to the narrator, and the cheerleaders to the players. Like many Cheever stories, this repeated speech act is a linguistic attempt to carry the secure, unifying nature of dream to the discordant collage of middle-class American experience.

Typically, the Cheever protagonist can maintain a shaky equilibrium between dream essence and the baroque, discontinuous dreamland of American life as long as this narrator restricts his dreams and their uncommunicative language to his own consciousness. When these individuals strive, as Cheever the writer did daily, to bridge the gap between individual dream and desperate American dreamland, disaster ensues. Emotional breakdown, or *cafard,* that compulsive sense of dread that inflicts so many of Cheever's protagonists, results. In **"A Vision of the World"** this apocalyptic moment occurs when the narrator enters his wife's kitchen, a dreamland of "pink, washable walls, chilling lights, built-in television (where prayers were being said), and artificial potted plants." Fresh from his dream of being on the winning side of the football game, the narrator writes his breakfast order on the tablet the family reserves for their mealtime transcriptions. Without hesitation, the narrator writes, "Porpozec ciebie nie prosze dorzanin albo zyolpocz ciwego." Amused, then concerned, his wife asks him what these words mean. The protagonist responds by repeating the phrase over and over again. Immediately, his wife calls for help. The family doctor arrives and gives the narrator a sedative. Within hours, the narrator takes an afternoon plane to Florida to recuperate from nervous exhaustion.

Inevitably, dreams and dreamland pursue the protagonist to Florida. There the narrator transfers his frustration with his wife to a dream of a beautiful, alluring woman kneeling in a field of wheat. He recounts this dream in language that attempts to evoke the comfort of his dreams while bridging the gap between confusing reality and transcendent imagination. Describing this enticing, desirable woman much as Eliot describes the hyacinth girl in *The Waste Land,* the narrator says:

> And yet she seems real—more real than the Tamiami Trail four miles to east, with its Smorgorama and Giganticburger stands, more real than the back streets of Sarasota. I do not ask her who she is. I know what she will say. But then she smiles and starts to speak before I can turn away. "Porpozec ciebie . . . " she begins. Then either I awake in despair or am waked by the sound of rain on the palms. . . . I think of some plumber who, waked by the rain, will smile at a vision of the world in which all the drains are miraculously cleansed and free. Right-angle drains, crooked drains, root-choked and rusty drains all gargle and discharge their waters into the sea. . . . Then I sit up in bed and exclaim aloud to myself, "Valor! Love! Virtue! Compassion! Splendor! Kindness! Wisdom! Beauty!" The words seem to have the colors of the earth, and as I recite them I feel my hopefulness mount until I am contented and at peace with the night.

As this passage eloquently demonstrates, Cheever's persona believes many of the connecting links of twentieth-century life are inadequate to men's and women's expressive needs. If these chains and links are still in place, for many, they have become bonds and shackles rather than pathways to communication or love. The garish Tamiami Trail and the vulgar backstreets of Sarasota are convoluted thoroughfares for those who travel them. The woman in the narrator's dream has more reality for this dreamer than these roadways have. Moreover, Cheever's persona questions the purpose of love or eroticism in the modern world if it functions only as a dream. Often the communication attained with the object of desire is the same nonsense syllables of social approval, religious affirmation, or athletic victory the narrator has heard in other dreams.

In despair, the protagonist turns to the practical world and thoughts of a plumber wakened by rain from a pleasant dream of a world without clogged drains. This vision could only occur in a world where connections are made, arches arch, chains link, and our most soothing dreams flow into reality. Its sheer sublimity enables the protagonist to decode his linguistic puzzle. "Porpozec ciebie nie prosze dorzanin albo zyolpocz ciwego" means valor, love, virtue, compassion, splendor, kindness, wisdom, beauty. The narrator searches desperately for these qualities in the modern world. Yet he finds them only in this ersatz, Slavic language of his dreams. The tale ends with the narrator repeating these invaluable but diminishing attributes. In an almost religious epiphany, he forms an ecstatic chain of being reaching from earth to the heavens above him. The narrator could bridge the gap between the language of his dreams and the virtues those words represent if only these qualities were more abundant in the modern world.

**"A Vision of the World"** serves as a paradigm of a kind of Cheever story in which a narrator attempts to use his imagination to connect his tranquilizing dreams with the wilderness of twentieth-century existence. In these tales Cheever shapes fictive experience into the arch of a dream. One can also see how this story suggests interesting applications to other stories throughout Cheever's career. The arch-chain-bridge metaphor has immediate affinity with a frequently anthologized Cheever story, **"The Angel of the**

Bridge," from *The Brigadier and the Golf Widow* (1964). In this tale the bridge of the title is the Tappan Zee Bridge, a contemporary New York thoroughfare swirling with terrifying traffic and inhuman speed. The George Washington and the Triborough Bridges completely paralyze the protagonist's driving reflexes. However the Tappan Zee finally proves crossable when the narrator gives a ride to a female hitchhiker—a kind of angel—whose beautiful voice calms the narrator and enables him to travel the bridge.

What Cheever has done in this story is to forge a poetic bridge of correspondences that serves as a parallel to the frightening automotive bridges men and women have inherited from mid-twentieth century, machine-ridden technology. In **"A Vision of the World"** the protagonist attempts to translate the security of his dreams into the manic, incomprehensible dreamland of contemporary suburbia. Analogously in **"The Angel of the Bridge,"** the preconscious fear of its protagonist becomes that all the bridges in New York will collapse as he drives over them. This hysteria describes the interior life of a man whose dreams have given way to nightmares. This traumatized protagonist must maintain an almost impossible equilibrium between the terror unleashed by the mechanizations of suburban America and the spiritual vertigo he feels as an individual driven by this society.

The ultimate horror of this story is that not only the narrator but his mother and older brother have been afflicted by a similar *cafard,* a fear of the mechanization and change inherent in midcentury America. This phobia so intensifies that it transforms its victims into machines, automatons ruled and programmed by their dread. While the narrator is partially sympathetic to their fates, he also feels their conditions are ridiculous. His brother has become a man terrified of elevators because he believes all the skyscrapers in New York will fall on one another as he ascends from floor to floor. His mother's situation is equally grotesque. She is a woman so frightened of change that she spends her days skating on the rink at Rockefeller Center since it reminds her of her childhood in St. Botolphs, Massachusetts. The narrator's jealousy of his brother's social standing and his hostility to his mother's nostalgia for the past make family ties too emotionally ambiguous a chain for him to accept their *cafards.*

Only when he arrives at the highest point in the arc of a bridge does the narrator exhibit his own *cafard.* His frenzy shows how his own dreams have become nightmares about the ugliness and duplicity of American life. Such moments also reveal how deeply he hates the flimsy, hypocritical chains of appearance we erect to bridge the gaps between surfaces and reality. On a trip to southern California, the narrator observes the chaos of Sunset Boulevard at three a.m. In this epiphany, he discovers the connecting link between his vision of the world and his fear of bridges:

> But the height of bridges seemed to be one link
> I could not forge or fasten in this hypocritical
> chain of acceptances. The truth is, I hate free-
> ways and Buffalo Burgers. Expatriated palm
> trees and monotonous housing developments de-

press me. The continuous music on special-fare trains exacerbates my feelings. I detest the destruction of familiar landmarks. I am deeply troubled by the misery and drunkenness I find among my friends, I abhor the dishonest practices I see. And it was at the highest point in the arc of a bridge that I became aware suddenly of the depth and bitterness of my feelings about modern life, and of the profoundness of my yearnings for a more vivid, simple, and peaceable world.

The aesthetic tension of **"The Angel of the Bridge"** evolves from the emotion of a writer who realizes that despite his fear of bridges, he desperately needs these constructs. Cheever's consistent artistic quest was the effort to forge a bridge of correspondences between the grim, macabre realities of post-World War II American life and the dreams, aspirations, imaginative possibilities, and even nightmares that many Americans use to evade these actualities. The writer's task thus becomes the same as the individual dreamer's: to use the imagination to record the world of dreams and anxieties and to counterbalance a frighteningly technological world with structures of hope, imagination, and love.

**"The Angel of the Bridge"** is a particularly rich Cheever story. It examines the actual bridges of a menacing, industrialized world, the imaginative bridges of dream and language, and the hereditary bridges of family bonds and ties which haunted all of Cheever's life and art. At the highest arc of the Tappan Zee Bridge, the narrator confronts his most intense fear. All he can see before him is the sweating face of his brother in a claustrophobic elevator and his mother going around and around on the ice at Rockefeller Center. His family symbolizes those links that give him personal history but which also lock him into molds determined by blood and genes. He pulls to the side of the Tappan Zee and prays that his totally debilitating anguish will pass. Meanwhile he insists that all the bridges in the world are falling down. Yet as he relates the incident, this bridge of family weakness still stands, fixed in place before his harried consciousness:

> I remembered my brother's face, sallow and
> greasy with sweat in the elevator, and my moth-
> er in her red skirt, one leg held gracefully aloft
> as she coasted backward in the arms of a rink at-
> tendant and it seemed to me that we were all
> three characters in some bitter and sordid trage-
> dy, carrying impossible burdens and separated
> from the rest of mankind by our misfortunes.
> My life was over and it would never come back,
> everything that I loved—blue-sky courage, lusti-
> ness, the natural grasp of things. It would never
> come back. I would end up in the psychiatric
> ward of the county hospital, screaming that the
> bridges, all the bridges in the world, were falling
> down.

Once again, the essential dilemmas for the Cheever protagonist remain. Should he believe that the frail bridge of language he uses to recount his trauma might be an adequate means of opposing the horrors of reality? Is he justified in feeling that these bridges are inadequate, or that they have all collapsed? Finally, should he fear any bridge that attempts to link exterior, manufactured appearances with vulnerable human yearnings? Moreover, if these bridges are functional, how does the Cheever narrator translate the aspirations of his dreams? These are the qualities that Cheever calls in the preceding passage, "blue-sky courage, lustiness, the natural grasp of things." Unfortunately, they are found nowhere in the story. To triumph, these virtues must become forces that can effectively overwhelm the soulless mayhem of the highways or the agonizing *cafards* of his family and himself.

Cheever resolves the seemingly insoluble problem in **"The Angel of the Bridge"** with almost divine intervention. A young woman folksinger hitchhiking on the Tappan Zee interprets the narrator's stopped car as a sign that her signaling has been answered. She enters his car carrying a small harp in a cracked oilskin. Then she proceeds to sing to him the English folk ballad "I gave my love a cherry that had no stone." Listening to her music, the narrator miraculously finds the courage to cross the bridge. He records his almost ecstatic transformation as a nearly religious conversion:

> She sang me across a bridge that seemed to be an astonishingly sensible, durable, and even beautiful construction designed by intelligent men to simplify my travels, and the water of the Hudson below us was charming and tranquil. It all came back—blue-sky courage, the high spirits of lustiness, an ecstatic sereneness.

Similarly, in **"A Vision of the World,"** the repetition of a phrase in an invented language becomes a mystical, religious epiphany. This transformation parallels the appearance of the beautiful, pure-voiced angel in **"The Angel of the Bridge,"** whose song creates this story's musical dream vision. In both cases, the language of these events supplies the link, the bridge between the world of dream and the terrifying emptiness of modern life. Moreover, Cheever translates his protagonists' dreams. Their visions represent those sublime qualities of love, courage, and compassion found in our dreams but dwindling in an absurdly industrialized world. (pp. 223-31)

Ultimately, much of Cheever's writing as demonstrated in these two tales seems a continual search for the language and structure to contain his sacramental dream vision. As Clinton S. Burhans, Jr., defines Cheever's goal: "Cheever's writing since the mid-fifties . . . seems at its deepest levels of meaning and value to be his groping both for a conceptual framework to explain his apprehensions and also for a language and form to express them." Therefore, dream becomes the medium, while song or heightened language serves as the expression of this quest. Congruently, the arch, bridge, or link functions as the overriding shape of his dream vision. Consistently, ecstatic religious sensation seems his stories' goal. Likewise, feminine intuition emerges as the spark or goad that enables Cheever's narrators to span their linguistic distances. Throughout his career Cheever attempted to suffuse his surreal suburbs with qualities of love, courage, faith, and compassion. He found these attributes vanishing in midcentury America, and he desperately sought the words and vision to translate these virtues across his bridge of language. (p. 232)

*Wayne Stengel, "John Cheever's Surreal Vision and the Bridge of Language," in* Twentieth Century Literature, *Vol. 33, No. 2, Summer, 1987, pp. 223-33.*

## Loren C. Bell

The opening paragraph of John Cheever's **"The Swimmer"** establishes the common malady lingering poolside at the Westerhazys' that midsummer Sunday. "We all *drank* too much," said Lucinda Merrill. While the others talk about their hangovers, Neddy Merrill sits "by the green water, one hand in it, one around a glass of gin." Apparently instead of talking, Neddy "had been swimming and now he was breathing deeply, stertorously as if he could gulp into his lungs the components of that moment, the heat of the sun, the intenseness of his pleasure." Debilitated by his hangover and his swim, warmed by the hot sun and cold gin, his deep breathing resonant with heavy snoring sounds, Neddy slips into the most natural condition given the circumstances: he falls asleep. His pleasure invents a dream of heroic exploration which ends with a desolate vision within a midsummer's nightmare.

The invitation to transform *A Midsummer Night's Dream* into "a midsummer's nightmare" is tempting, first, because Cheever's references to midsummer seem insistent. The story begins, "It was one of those midsummer Sundays . . . ." About the midpoint, after the wind has stripped the Levys' maple tree of its autumnal leaves, Neddy reasons that "since it was midsummer the tree must be blighted . . . ." Near his journey's end, under a winter sky, Neddy wonders, "What had become of the constellations of midsummer?" A further link to the play is the mystifying confusion of the seasons:

> The spring, the summer,
> The childing autumn, angry winter, change
> Their wonted liveries; and the mazed world,
> By their increase, now knows not which is
> which.

The transformation seems more than ironic wordplay when we consider another connection to Shakespeare: Cheever's observation that Neddy "might have been compared to a summer's day, particularly the last hours of one. . . . " Despite his impression of "youth, sport, and clement weather," Neddy is not a likely subject for a sonnet, at least not for Sonnet 18: "Shall I compare thee to a summer's day? / Thou art more lovely and more temperate." Alcoholic, snobbish, adulterous, self-indulgent— Neddy is by no means mild or temperate, yet he is linked to the sonnet. He is the other subject of the poem, the inevitability of decline. Thus, he is compared to the last hours of a summer's day because, like the season, Neddy's "lease hath all too short a date." As "every fair from fair sometime declines, / By chance or nature's changing course untrimmed," so Neddy's "eternal summer"—his illusory youthful vigor and, more important, his illusion of success, his share in the tenuous American dream—will also fade. Whether or not he has actually lost his money and status, his house and family, in the context of his dream he seems to have lost "possession of that fair [he] owest." As his pilgrimage to that realization ends, we sense that

Neddy has indeed wandered through the valley of the shadow.

The dream motif (and its direction) having thus been suggested, Neddy snores beside the pool; "the components of that moment . . . seemed to flow into his chest." Here the narrative becomes internalized in Neddy. The dream itself begins and, with it, the "implied progression from day to night, summer to winter, vigorous manhood to old age."

The surrealistic quality of dreams insinuates itself throughout Neddy's journey. With his "discovery" of the Lucinda River, we see that superior point of view of the dreamer, suspended, detached, not quite real: "He seemed to see, with a cartographer's eye, that string of swimming pools, that quasi-subterranean stream that curved across the county." Removing "a sweater that was hung over his shoulders" (had it been hung there by someone else?), he plunges into the stream of his subconscious. "To be embraced and sustained by the light green water . . . seemed," to Neddy, to be "the resumption of a natural condition"; the dreamer floats on waves of sleep like the swimmer buoyed by light green water.

When Neddy hears the Bunkers' distant poolside party, "the water refracted the sound of voices and laughter and seemed to suspend it in midair," distant, disembodied voices made nearer by the trick of water and physics. It is one of those phenomena of reality that make us recall the dream distortion of sound as well as place and time. When he leaves the Bunkers', "the brilliant, watery sound of voices fade[s]," as if he leaves some bright sanctuary to pursue his darkening journey. Near the Lancaster public pool, "the effect of the water on voices, the illusion of brilliance and suspense, was the same . . . but the sounds here were louder, harsher, and more shrill . . . ." The distortion will recur at the Biswangers' with even harsher effects.

Another illustration of the dream motif is Neddy's sense of separation and detachment. As he surveys the scene at the Bunkers' pool, including the red de Haviland trainer "circling around and around and around in the sky with something like the glee of a child in a swing," he "felt a passing affection for the scene, a tenderness for the gathering, as if it was something he might touch." The ambiguity of the word *passing* is effective, Neddy's "passing affection" may be only transitory; his nightmare will show that what he holds dear is indeed fleeting. But given the tenderness with which he regards his own life and this scene of "prosperous men and women," *passing* suggests rather convincingly its archaic sense of "great" or "surpassing." For the moment he is held outside that circle rather like Hawthorne's Robin Molineux when the boy views his family gathered for vespers under the spreading tree in their dooryard. But the door will not be shut in Neddy's face—not just yet, for he enters this scene as a welcome guest and greets his fellow players (or playfellows) in a dizzying round of kisses and handshakes, even though the thunder has sounded.

"I had the *strangest* dream last night. I was standing on the shoulder of Route 424, waiting to cross, and I was *naked*. . . . " So Neddy, on some other day, waking from some other dream, might well have recounted that common dream image. But his vulnerability and exposure in this afternoon's dream will probably not be another amusing anecdote told at breakfast. When he reaches the highway, he is "close to naked," naked enough to be "exposed to all kinds of ridicule," but perhaps not naked enough to perceive any truths beyond his discomfort and his perplexing inability to turn back. He is genuinely naked when he steps out of his trunks and through the Hallorans' yellowed beech hedge to encounter something closer to the naked truth when Mrs. Halloran says,

> "We've been *terribly* sorry to hear about all your misfortunes, Neddy."
>
> "My misfortunes?" Ned asked. "I don't know what you mean."
>
> "Why, we heard that you'd sold the house and that your poor children. . . . "
>
> "I don't recall having sold the house," Ned said, "and the girls are at home."

Neddy's first response seems natural enough, yet when Mrs. Halloran begins to tell him precisely what she does mean, he interrupts her. Like unsettling, bright pinpoints of truth abruptly piercing an alcoholic blackout, her explanation hints at sharp truths that must ultimately be faced. Neddy's reply seems more an evasion than an answer, the suppression of a dark truth's glimmering. It also suggests the illogical, if not absurd, utterances of dreams.

To discern truth from within or without a dream is difficult enough, but to discern the dream itself from within is more difficult. For Neddy, it is impossible. Unprepared for the humiliation along Route 424, he is bewildered, but "he could not go back, he could not even recall with any clearness the green water at the Westerhazys', the sense of inhaling the day's components, the friendly and relaxed voices saying that they had *drunk* too much." Caught powerless and unaware in a nightmare that now controls him, he can only swim with its current. At the Sachses' pool, he still feels obliged to swim, "that he had no freedom of choice about his means of travel." Just two pools from his own house, obligation has become compulsion: "While he could have cut directly across the road to his home he went on to the Gilmartins' pool" and then "staggered with fatigue on his way to the Clydes."

It is in dreams that apple blossoms and roses are replaced with the "stubborn autumnal fragrance" of chrysanthemums or marigolds. It is in dreams that midsummer constellations become the stars of a winter sky, and slender, youngish Neddy Merrill goes "stooped" and "stupified" to whatever truth, whatever self-discovery, his nightmare has led him. "He had been immersed too long, and his nose and throat were sore from the water," a swimmer's complaint that might be shared by an afternoon sleeper whose snoring has been too long and loud, and whose dream is too frightening.

In *A Midsummer Night's Dream,* we are told that "the course of true love never did run smooth." Neddy's encounters with love would seem to bear witness. The easy familiarity with which he greeted his bronze Aphrodite that morning is rebuffed by Shirley Adams, his former mistress with "hair the color of brass." Despite Neddy's "passing affection," the course of his real love—his pursuit of the American dream of success and suburban happiness—runs no more smoothly. Perhaps it too is besieged,

> Making it momentary as a sound,
> Swift as a shadow, short as any dream;
> Brief as the lightning in the collied night,
> That, in a spleen, unfolds both heaven and earth,
> And ere a man hath power to say "Behold!"
> The jaws of darkness do devour it up.
> So quick bright things come to confusion.

In the nightmarish ruin of the "quick bright things" in Neddy's life, he has been led to the vision that his dream of wealth, status, and happiness is transitory, illusory, and fraught with perils. If our dreams are empty, what then are we? The use of that discovery, whether for reform or despair, is left to Neddy and to us. Perhaps he will mend his ways, or (as Prufrock fears) Neddy Merrill may awake from his watery dream only to drown—in one way or another. (pp. 433-36)

> *Loren C. Bell, " 'The Swimmer': A Midsummer's Nightmare," in* Studies in Short Fiction, *Vol. 24, No. 4, Fall, 1987, pp. 433-36.*

## L. S. Klepp

Railroad stations, with their pathos of arrival and departure, beginnings and endings, loom large in Cheever's fiction. You may remember the business executive in **"The Five-Forty-Eight,"** left prostrate and weeping in the coal dust as the victimized woman who has turned the tables on him walks toward the station platform. Or the little girl sitting with her cardboard suitcase in the waiting room as the ticket clerk phones the sodden father she has tried to run away from in **"The Sorrows of Gin."** A story called **"Of Love: A Testimony,"** written when Cheever was 22, evokes the melancholy future of a character by placing him alone on a station platform: "He has taken the wrong train and there is nobody there to meet him."

This early story marks perhaps the first appearance of Cheever's baffled and aching odd man out. We encounter him again and again in the stories and yet again in Scott Donaldson's *John Cheever: A Biography* and the newly published *Letters of John Cheever* (edited by his son, Benjamin), for Cheever himself seems to have often felt as if he had taken the wrong train. A gregarious, irresistibly charming and witty man who loved parties, with a wife, three children, many friends, and late in life, many lovers of both sexes, he was accompanied much of the time by a harrowing loneliness that most of us would require a Gobi or Sahara to achieve. This sense of exile in familiar surroundings carries over into nearly everything he wrote; it is the moral wilderness his wayward characters blunder into and try to find their way out of.

In the 1978 introduction to his stories, Cheever wrote: "The constants that I look for in this sometimes dated paraphernalia are a love of light and a determination to trace some moral chain of being." Moral chains of being are

scarce in our random, casual literary climate, and most critics didn't know one when they saw one. For a long time Cheever was praised or damned as a suburban realist, a specialist in nuances of class, ambition, and adultery in the manner of Marquand and O'Hara. His eye for the symbols and symptoms of such things was as sharp as theirs, but he had other fish to fry.

In Cheever's most characteristic fiction, realism quietly assumes the shape of fable. This turn began as early as **"The Enormous Radio"** (1947). A young couple acquires a radio that mysteriously begins picking up conversations in the other apartments in the building. They are baffled, amused, then appalled; the conversations reveal unsavory things behind the respectable appearance of the people they encounter in the elevator: duplicity and larcenous greed, petulance and wife-beating, an affair with the handyman on one floor and a high-class whore on another. Cast as the snake in the garden, the radio brings the couple unwelcome knowledge of good and evil, including their own. They quarrel, and the woman turns on the radio, seeking the consolation of the nursery rhymes she had heard being sung in one apartment, but it has stopped eavesdropping; she hears only the routine public rumors of the human condition, delivered in a "suave and noncommittal" voice. . . . (p. 27)

Later, in **"Metamorphoses,"** Cheever actually brought some Greek myths to Manhattan, making Antaeus an investment banker and Orpheus a singer of radio jingles who meets his Eurydice on the Fifth Avenue bus, but most of his ostensibly realistic stories are as mythic as his mythic ones. The titles alone often make the point: **"The Pot of Gold," "O City of Broken Dreams," "Clancy in the Tower of Babel."** The characters in these stories, realistic enough to get on the Fifth Avenue bus without exciting comment, retain a certain simplicity of outline that allows them to step quickly off and into the oblique fable as it picks up speed: faithful servants, cruel dowagers, the twinned good and bad brothers in **"Goodbye, My Brother,"** the seraphic hitchhiker-folksinger, complete with harp, in **"The Angel of the Bridge,"** the woman in bohemian black who might as well be carrying a scythe in **"Torch Song."**

If a bewildered sense of discord, exile, and lost innocence is the note struck most often in Cheever's fiction, it is nevertheless far from relentlessly bleak. The theme has its comic possibilities, as in **"Mene, Mene, Tekel, Upharsin,"** a story about a man who is dismayed by the pornography and brute violence that have taken over the bookstands and who finds that, by some law of cultural compensation, fragments of absurdly ornate and sentimental novels are being written on the walls of men's rooms. Comedy and satire are as elemental as elegy in Cheever's work, and so are the rapturous evocations of natural beauty—the sound and smell of summer rain or the sea, leaves drifting through an autumn twilight—that have for his characters a sacramental power. Another redemptive force is love— filial love in *The Wapshot Chronicle,* homosexual love in *Falconer,* heterosexual love *passim,* though only during the truces in the prevailing sex wars. Cheever's beatific visions are always intense and always fleeting. But then it is in the nature of paradise to be lost, and of literature to make the most of the resulting dramatic and poetic possibilities. It was never so well lost in Cheever's work as in his most famous story, **"The Swimmer"**: the transition—from summer afternoon to autumn night, from exuberance to an empty house—is so deft as to be nearly imperceptible.

The theme of paradise lost wasn't furnished for Cheever, as it was for Nabokov, by a childhood resembling a long golden afternoon. At some point while he was growing up in Quincy, Mass., his mother told him that he was an accident; had she not drunk two Manhattans one afternoon, he would never have been conceived, and his father wanted him aborted, going so far as to invite the local abortionist to dinner, an incident that reappears in both *The Wapshot Chronicle* and *Falconer.* His father, a shoe salesman, already 49 when John was born in 1912, lost his job in the decline of the New England shoe industry in the 1920s and took to drink. John's mother, born in England, was resolutely independent, dominated his father, and devoted herself to assorted good causes and then to the gift shop she opened to support the family, leaving little time for her younger son. Donaldson, quoting Cheever's wife, Mary, in support, concludes in his biography that Cheever was left with a permanent sense of being unloved. It is plausible, considering the number of forlorn and yearning men in his fiction, and the number of remote and implacable women. As his parents' marriage fell apart, he took the side of his defeated father rather than his resourceful mother.

Cheever's literary gifts arrived early. If his grade-school classmates did well, the teacher rewarded them by allowing John to tell them an improvised story. Like other children who grow up to be writers, he lived in a fantasy world of his own devising. Like others, he did badly at school. Unlike others, he turned his failure into a precocious literary success. **"Expelled,"** the thinly disguised story he wrote about his expulsion from Thayer Academy, was bought by Malcolm Cowley for *The New Republic* in 1930, when Cheever had just turned 18.

Donaldson's biography is especially useful for the light it sheds on Cheever's rather bohemian early years. After sharing a Boston apartment with his older brother, reinforcing an intensely ambivalent relationship that supplied him with another major fictional theme, Cheever spent the first of his many productive interludes at Yaddo. In 1934, he followed the advice of E. E. Cummings, the writer he most admired, and moved to New York, where he lived in a grim little room on Hudson Street that Walker Evans photographed. He worked on stories that didn't sell and a novel he couldn't finish, earned a few dollars summarizing novels for the MGM script department, and staved off starvation with stale bread and buttermilk. Cowley said that his stories were too long to be bought and told him to go home and write four stories in four days. It worked; two of the stories were sold to *The New Yorker,* the first of 121 he was to publish in the magazine.

These early stories, 30 of which were collected in his first book, *The Way Some People Live* (1943), are shadowed with muted sad ironies that fall a bit heavily on his hard-

up Hopperesque New Yorkers staring disconsolately out of their apartment windows. . . . Some of them are very slight, and Cheever left all of them out of his 1978 collection [*The Stories of John Cheever*], but the slightest still display the impeccable and graceful phrasing that Cheever developed into the most distinguished prose style in postwar American literature, and the best of them—**"Homage to Shakespeare,"** for instance, or **"The Edge of the World"**—can be placed alongside the best of his later work. (pp. 27-8)

He had frequent skirmishes with *The New Yorker* over its fiction rates, and he moved to a rented house in the Westchester suburbs in 1951 to save money, shortly after the power company shut off the electricity in his New York apartment. The move did more harm to his reputation than to his writing. His use of suburban material and association with *The New Yorker* were enough for some critics to deduce that he was mild-mannered and genteel. His work actually reveals a Dostoevskian streak, embracing misfits and brooding over guilt and redemption. Even his sunniest and most robustly comic novel, *The Wapshot Chronicle* (1957), a celebration of small-town Yankee eccentricity and sturdy integrity that owed much to his own family, has nothing to do with genteel nostalgia; it's too full of messy and baffling life.

After the success of the *Chronicle,* which won a National Book Award, Cheever acquired a measure of fame, and by 1964 he appeared, somewhat reluctantly, on the cover of *Time.* And then—like one of his hapless characters, struck down just as he clears a final hurdle—his life began to come apart. He was depressed about the way American life had evolved during the Cold War. "Life in the United States in 1960 is Hell," he declared at a literary symposium, and he elaborated on this anathema in *The Wapshot Scandal* (1964), his darkest novel, with its vision of a nomadic and spiritually bankrupt society dominated by missiles and half-mad technocrats. He was troubled by an increasingly contentious marriage and increasingly insistent homosexual impulses. But the main drama of this period was his struggle with alcoholism. . . .

The immediate result of his escape from alcohol was his novel of escape, *Falconer,* inspired by what he learned from the prisoners he had taught at Sing Sing a few years earlier. Escape, Donaldson suggests, had always been a preoccupation. He spent his life both seeking and seeking release from the middle-class security and respectability his family in Quincy hadn't been able to sustain. In the few years before his health began to fail (he died of cancer in 1982), he contemplated moving into a city apartment, traveled much, and found fitful fulfillment in the affairs with women and men that he had been carrying on for years. But he finally didn't walk away from his tense marriage and his old house in Ossining; they were all the order he had, and they offered refuge from the disheveled contingencies of escape. He devoutly believed in the ceremonial proprieties that confined him. Cheever was an acutely divided soul for whom resolution could come only in work. You carry away from his fiction, as you do from Hopper's painting, a sense of the order that can be made out of absence and loss.

If it is possible to be a Calvinist without Calvin's God and without Calvin, perhaps the chief signs of election are a bad conscience and a taste for allegory. Cheever, though a mildly devout Episcopalian, seems to have inherited both from a long line of New England ancestors. His parables of the elusiveness of grace were nicely compassed in the short-story form and were pulled off urbanely enough to be accommodated in *The New Yorker.* On these stories his reputation will largely rest; his best novel, **The Wapshot Chronicle,** is itself so episodic as to resemble a story sequence. The reputation of another, more adamant tracer of moral chains of being, Flannery O'Connor, also rests on short fiction, and perhaps the two reputations together will eventually topple the altar on which critics have placed the novel, for when the dust settles, it will, I think, become clear that no greater American writers have emerged in the postwar period. (p. 28)

> L. S. Klepp, "Autumn Sonata: John Cheever Stings Like a WASP," in VLS, No. 69, November, 1988, pp. 27-8.

## Malcom O. Magaw

*Falconer,* John Cheever's absorbing novel depicting the incarceration and the dramatic escape of its protagonist Ezekiel Farragut from Falconer prison, has aroused a considerable amount of critical attention and controversy ever since its publication in 1977. I would like to join that forum and propose an argument advancing a post-Camusian existential reading of the book.

"Farragut (fratricide, zip to ten, #734-508-32)," writes Cheever, "had been brought to this old iron place [Falconer] on a late summer's day. He wore no leg irons but was manacled to nine other men, four of them black and all of them younger than he." Thus begin the corrosive yet ultimately redeeming adventures and misadventures of Cheever's heroin-addicted, identity-muddled, memory-dissociated protagonist—a college professor, forty-eight years of age, married, and the father of a schoolboy son—who was sentenced to prison for the murder of his brother Eben. During an argument, Cheever recounts, Eben had screamed at Zeke, " '[Father] wanted you to be killed. Mother told me. He had an abortionist come out to the house. Your own father wanted you to be killed.' Then," says Cheever, "Farragut struck his brother with a fire iron. The widow testified that Farragut had struck his brother eighteen to twenty times, but she was a liar, and Farragut thought the doctor who corroborated this lie contemptible." In prison Farragut is assigned to cellblock F, where his methadone and placebo cure, his relationships with Tiny and Walton, the guards, and with the other prisoners there—namely, Ransome, Stone, Chicken Number Two, and Cuckold—and near where his sexual relationship with his best friend Jody all eventually, but not easily, lead him out of the lower depths of his dissociation and fragile identity to a sufficient degree of association and self-confidence to make his break, just as his lover and mentor Jody had done some months before him.

In my view, Farragut's escape from Falconer in the burial sack of his just deceased friend Chicken Number Two, his subsequent blood-letting emergence from that sack after it has been taken outside the walls of Falconer, and his bumbling yet ever-improving progress immediately thereafter are Cheever's metaphor for Farragut's first unsteady yet spirited steps out of his long recoil from the absurd into a purgatorial testing ground, from which he soon launches himself into existential freedom. On that premise, then, I would argue that *Falconer* can be read as a pivotal work in the evolution of the existential persona in modern literature, for its perspective on the human dilemma (and also the human potential) both derives from and takes issue with the assumptions and hypotheses advanced by Albert Camus in his classic essay *The Myth of Sisyphus* (1942) and the novels he wrote as correlatives to it. In Cheever's Farragut we see a late-century, interestingly modified version of the Sisyphean hero—namely, a protagonist who fits the Camusian mold up to the point of his having advanced from the brain-dead nonhero trapped in the absurd to the rebel and antihero awakened to and in recoil from the absurd, but who breaks out of that mold as he progresses from antihero to a considerably different kind of existential hero. In violation of the absolute integrity of Self that is the trademark of Camus's prototype, Cheever allows his existential initiate to depend on Other—indeed to find Other indispensable—in his recovery from an immobilizing recoil from the absurd. He also gives Farragut something practical to complement his Camusian "courage." He gives him "cunning," a special capacity which has the effect of reducing his Sisyphean vulnerability and increasing his potentiality for coming to terms with the absurd.

Victim that he has been for his entire life, Farragut is less the aggressive rebel relentlessly pushing the rock of absurdity, as he sets out to turn his life around, and more the seemingly passive yet cunning and opportunistic interceptor of benefits and coincidences that come his way. Farragut, in short, is an updated version of his Camusian prototype, one whose character is in key with a late-century, contemporary view of the existential hero. By drawing from Other rather than away from it, Farragut compromises some of the principles of his mid-century prototype and either makes things work to his advantage or allows them to do so as he moves ever closer to launching himself onto the rain-washed street of existential vitality in the last scene of the novel. His final existential awakening—his triumphant annunciation of Self—then, is viewed by Cheever as the direct result of a positive and complex involvement with Other. My point is that Farragut's joyful discovery of the Self—"Rejoice, he thought, rejoice"—could never have been achieved without his interaction with the absurd, that in Falconer prison Farragut displays a deference to the absurd that ultimately has the effect of equipping him to take sovereignty over it and to be free of its lies, illusions, and perversities forever. As Cheever himself said in an interview with John Firth, "All my work deals with confinement in one shape or another, and the struggle toward freedom. Do I mean freedom? Only as a metaphor . . . a sense of boundlessness, the possibility of rejoicing!"

Distant relatives though Sisyphus and Farragut may be, two strains of their kinship can be readily identified.

Camus and Cheever both view their protagonists as "victims" and the universe as "absurd." They tend to agree, then, that a man's declaration of independence from the meaningless world in which he finds himself and his adoption of the Self as his only authentic source of identity constitute the only self-respecting way for him to live his life. As Camus's Sisyphus himself states it, "Thus I draw from the absurd three consequences, which are my revolt, my freedom, and my passion." Built into that concept is a contemptuous renunciation of conventions and institutions and their preposterous claims to being the repository of "essence." There is no preexisting essence. There is only the essence one generates from his own existence. In Cheever's thought-provoking symbolism throughout *Falconer* these conventions and institutions are metaphorized as birds of prey—falcons, which are trained by the falconers of society to victimize human beings rather than to order and enrich their lives.

In effect, then, Farragut has been the victim of falconers long before he is taken to the prison of that name—indeed all the way back almost to his biological beginning. His father, we are told, had sought to have his birth aborted. That intention—its failure notwithstanding—is a signal to what is to follow. From that time on, Farragut is apparently somehow destined to be the victim of falconers. They make up the story of his life. His family are falconers: a maniacal and suicidal father, a zany mother, and a fratricidal brother—all of whom, he says, "dealt in contraband" otherwise known as "unlicensed spiritual, intellectual and erotic stimulants." Matrimony, another institution, fails him also, married as he is to the bitchy and vain Marcia who, as a bisexual, is a part-time wife at best. Then there is the institution of professional ethics; we see it holding out a symbolic, perverse hand when Farragut's drug-addicted department chairman at the university invites him to shoot up with him before each of them goes off to teach his class. One could go on and on. The point is that Farragut, like Camus's Sisyphus, is confronted with the absurd, and most of his life is spent in a retreat and zombielike removal from it because he has no inkling of the positive but latent force of existential energy he possesses. He has no inkling of this, that is, until Jody comes into his life at the prison.

And this brings me to the main point of my argument. Cheever's existential man of the last quarter of the century, unlike Camus's prototype of mid-century, does not learn to cope independently by coping independently. He does not teach himself—after a contemptuous repudiation of his absurd world—what an authentic existential selfhood is. Cheever complicates, and in a way confounds, the formula when he sets his middle-aged initiate on course toward an existential awakening by allowing Other rather than Self to show him the way. Farragut was not the kind of man, his high levels of intelligence and imagination notwithstanding, who could find his own way onto the high road of existentialism, and I seriously doubt that Cheever thought that anyone could. As stated above, to turn to Other for help, however, was, in the earlier mainstream of existential hypothesizing, of course a betrayal of the Self, a capitulation to the absurd, and therefore a serious violation of one's existential integrity. But Cheever seems to be presenting his novel from a less doctrinaire perspective of the absurd and the possible existential answer to it that has been evolving in a post-Camusian world. He invests his Sisyphean rock-pusher with a view to the practical and to a willingness to make compromises. He reasons that independent rock-pushing is probably the best kind there is in theory, but that no man can be expected to live by a rock-pushing principle that he does not understand; nor will that man understand it until he has had some briefing on its complexities from a seasoned mentor or two.

Farragut gets separate briefings from his friend Jody in the prison and from the nameless fellow traveler at the bus stop outside the prison in the last scene of the novel. As two indispensable practical aids from Other, they are not however all that Farragut needs from Other before he is ready to take that existential walk alone in the rain. He also needs the help of a miracle. In Camus's conceptualized absurd world there are no miracles, of course. But in Cheever's unphilosophized absurd world just about anything can happen, including miracles. To be specific, the death of Chicken Number Two is not just an everyday kind of death. It is an existential "Good Friday" kind of death, for it miraculously opens the way for Farragut's own psychological death, purgation, and rebirth. I am referring again to the miraculous presence of Chicken Number Two's burial sack, which, combined with Farragut's "cunning and courage," provides him with what turns out to be his rite of passage from a lifelong entrapment in falconry to a new life in existential freedom—put in other words, from the absurdity of Other to the authenticity of his essence-producing Self. Farragut's worthiness of a miracle is concisely expressed by Theo D'haen, who says, "He concerns himself with the fate of a fellow prisoner and eases the older man's dying hour. By this act of grace Farragut regains contact with the deepest wellsprings of his own humanity. When the old man's body is being removed for burial, Farragut takes his place and . . . is reborn into a new and brighter life."

But meanwhile the whole process is interestingly and ironically confounded by the glaring fact that Farragut, as I have just pointed out, has had to draw from Other in order to get sprung from Other. This assessment of Farragut's peculiarly evolving character is evidenced first in the manner in which he learned self-love. In Camus's terms, self-love is an absolute requirement for the achieving of an authentic existential selfhood. But it is something Farragut could never either have intuited or taught to himself; he needed Jody to teach him. Existential self-love, it should be understood, is more a matter of self-possession than of narcissism. But for someone whose self-image is as fragile as Farragut's, it might be necessary to put him through a phase of narcissism before he can be expected to reach the final goal of self-possession. With a long history of low self-esteem, Farragut at age forty-eight begins the journey to his existential awakening in a vacuum as it were and needs to learn how to be aggressive and seize love from another. He needs this in order to get a reasonably stable self-image established, and this is primarily what Jody's presence in his life at the prison accomplishes for him. He gives Farragut sufficient self-esteem to forge ahead to an authentic existential kind of self-love. That final goal is what Robert G. Collins expresses as a kind of self-actualizing self-love "in which the spirit is fulfilled in unison with the other, but [from which] it can separate afterward" and then proceed on its own independent way.

Jody's instruction begins with his attempt to teach Farragut how to smile. "I love you, Chicken, but you don't know how to smile," he tells Farragut and proceeds with a discourse in which the "smile" motif symbolizes an outlook on life of high expectancy—indeed of existential intensity. But it has to be a particular kind of smile—one that registers pleasure with oneself rather than with another. But Farragut doesn't catch on. He has a vague awareness of something important and different here, but he still has to look outside himself to find it. His problem is that he loves only Jody, not Jody and himself. Describing that exclusive dependence on Other for love, Cheever says, "Farragut lay on his cot. He wanted Jody. The longing began in his speechless genitals . . . then moved up to his viscera and from there to his heart, his soul, his mind, until his entire carcass was filled with longing." Indeed, a "carcass" is about all that a body can be in existential terms if its object of longing and affection is exclusively Other rather than Self in combination with Other. As their affair goes on, however, Farragut does eventually catch on, but only (as I keep insisting) with the help of Other—in this instance, Jody. The point is, he has to find out what Jody's capacity for self-love is before he can activate and celebrate the same impulse in himself. And the only way he can understand Jody's capacity for self-love is to love Jody. But the fact is, Farragut balks at the first hint he gets that his love for Jody is actually a projection of his love for himself. "If love was a chain of resemblances," he reasons, "there was, since Jody was a man, the danger that Farragut might be in love with himself." He views it as a "danger" because he has been conditioned to believe that self-love can be tolerated only in a woman, never in a man. "He had seen self-love [in a man] only once that he could remember," he says in the same passage, and to Farragut it had been repugnant.

But Farragut's meditation on the danger of self-love suddenly shifts to a time when Jody said to him after they had made love, " 'Man, you're beautiful. I mean you're practically senile and there isn't much light in here, but you look very beautiful to me,' " a compliment which Farragut calls a "whore's line," yet one to which he admits he was "helplessly susceptible." "It seemed," Farragut goes on, "that he had always known he was beautiful and had been waiting all his life to hear this," and a little later he ends his meditation on self-love by saying, "To love oneself would be . . . a delicious pursuit. How simple to love oneself!"

For Farragut, however, it is not actually all that "simple," and after his meditation he returns for a while to his dubious position on the acceptability of self-love. He does make progress later on, however, when he says at the end of their affair, "He could kiss Jody passionately, but not tenderly." That parting kiss was one that seized upon life but surrendered nothing in return—no tenderness, no ac-

tual giving, just a passionate taking. But this final emotional moment with Jody is clearly of such intensity that its sense of self-fulfillment and self-affection does not last. And it is in any case a brand of self-love viewed by Cheever as simply a temporary phase through which Farragut must pass to achieve the self-possession of an authentic, existential brand of self-love. For that, he needs help from Other again—this time to purge his ambivalent consciousness of its self-doubts.

This second agent of assistance comes, as I have said, in the miracle of Chicken Number Two's death. Miracle notwithstanding, Cheever has given us a signal much earlier to suggest its ultimate occurrence. In the love scenes just discussed, Jody repeatedly calls Farragut "Chicken," "a fitting soubriquet," observes George W. Hunt, "for one who will substitute himself for Chicken Number Two." The point is, Farragut's temporary entombment in, and subsequent rebirth from, his dead friend's shroud as it were launches him into a symbolic, stumbling walk through purgatory, a journeyman's bumbling progress in which he gradually strips away the doubts he has had about self-love as he encounters a night vision of symbolic sights that pertain to spiritual cleansing and subsequent existential mobility. The principle objects to which I am attributing symbolic meanings are seen surrealistically by Farragut first in states of disrepair and then later in top working order. For example, very early in his purgatorial journey he sees a three-legged washing machine and the husk of a wrecked car in a dump yard. Much later he sees the washing machine metamorphosed into efficiently operating washers (and driers) in a laundromat and the wrecked car into a smooth-running city bus, the same bus in fact that takes Farragut to the end of his journey through purgatory and to the starting line for his walk out onto the highway of existential self-consciousness and self-possession. Included also in this bizarre progress through purgatory is the ritual of the letting of blood. Farragut bleeds from cuts on his fingers and thigh made accidentally when he was cutting himself out of his burial bag with a razor blade. It is a significant ritual because of its existential implications. The point is, it is now Farragut's own blood that redeems him and initiates him into a new life, not the blood of Other. "His foot was wet with blood," he says, "but he didn't care." Instead of bleeding to death he is walking in his own blood to a new life. Existence precedes essence.

And so end the early and intermediate phases of Farragut's symbolic existential progress through purgatory. The two images that link these earlier phases with the final phase are the electric heater and the sky-blue motorcycle helmet, both of which belong to the amiable stranger at the bus stop and which Farragut, offering a hand, picks up and carries aboard the bus. The electric heater with its golden bowl shaped like the sun anticipates the high voltage of existential illumination that Farragut is soon to plug his consciousness into. The sky-blue helmet repeats the blue sky motif of freedom that recurs throughout the novel and that in this instance symbolizes both a potential cycling mobility and a cerebral crown of highly self-conscious freedom that he is soon to wear, helmeted as he will be with a faultless "cunning and courage."

But Farragut is not ready for his existential crown and his self-actualizing walk in the rain quite yet. He is still dependent on Other—in this instance, the man at the bus stop who owns the heater and the helmet. Farragut is still dependent on Other because he is still haunted by his fear of falling, an obsession he has had to deal with ever since his deranged brother pushed him out of an upstairs window several years earlier. It takes his third helpmate from Other to relieve Farragut of his vertigo, a disorder which symbolically suggests his incapacity to achieve existential equilibrium. As they board the bus the amiable stranger pays both fares and then leads Farragut to the third seat on the left side by the window. " 'Sit down here,' " he tells Farragut. Thus settled in this third seat on the left with his final mentor from Other, Farragut, almost at the end of his purgatorial journey, could perhaps see in his mind's eye the kindly ghosts of his first two mentors in the second and first seats directly ahead of him—Chicken Number Two and Jody, respectively—summoning him forward on the liberating (left) side and the trafficking (window) side of his consciousness to self-love, self-possession, and a rejoicing acknowledgment of his existential selfhood. Moments later, wearing his third mentor's coat to protect him from a possible overdose of existential energy and stimulation, Farragut steps off the bus, now his own man—indeed, now his own falconer in pursuit of the only prey worth hunting and possessing: his existential selfhood.

Cheever says of his new existential man, "Stepping from the bus onto the street, he saw that he had lost his fear of falling. . . . He walked along nicely. Rejoice, he thought, rejoice." Disengaged from Other, he can now say what Camus's Sisyphus says: "Knowing whether or not man is free doesn't interest me. I can experience only my own freedom." Yet implicit in that triumphant imperative to "rejoice" is Farragut's backward glance and wave of a hand of gratitude to his three mentors from Other whose presences were vital in the processes that took him from his recoil from the absurd to his existential awakening.

Cheever's existentialism, attuned as it is to contemporary life, modifies and complicates the prototype of modern existential man that evolved from Camus's doctrinaire assumptions and hypotheses on the absurd in the 1940s and 50s. Instead of defiantly rebelling against Other, Cheever's new existential man acknowledges the serviceability of Other to himself and to any other longtime bumbling victim of falconry in the modern world who has found the incentive at last to locate, identify, and enjoy a redeeming selfhood that has eluded him for the better part of a lifetime. (pp. 75-81)

> *Malcolm O. Magaw, "Cheever's New Existential Man in 'Falconer',"* in The International Fiction Review, *Vol. 17, No. 2, Summer, 1990, pp. 75-81.*

## FURTHER READING

Bosha, Francis J. *John Cheever: A Reference Guide.* Boston: G. K. Hall & Co., 1981, 125 p.
    Comprehensive bibliography covering Cheever's works up to 1979 and criticism of his fiction from 1943 to 1979. Includes a detailed introduction to Cheever's life and writings.

Cheever, John. "Fiction Is Our Most Intimate Means of Communication." *U. S. News & World Report* LXXXVI, No. 20 (21 May 1979): 92.
    Thoughtful remarks on the role and the meaning of literature in contemporary life. Cheever writes that in his own work, "urgency is what I principally seek," and that "I want to share with [the] reader the excitement of being alive or of comprehending the human condition."

Cheever, Susan. *Home Before Dark: A Biographical Memoir of John Cheever by His Daughter.* Boston: Houghton Mifflin Co., 1984, 243 p.
    Reminiscences by Cheever's novelist-daughter, who writes in the preface: "I wanted to tell the story of a man who fought to adhere to some moral standard until the end of his life." Includes excerpts from John Cheever's private journals as well as several pages of photographs.

Coale, Samuel. *John Cheever.* New York: Frederick Ungar Publishing Co., 1977, 130 p.
    Biographical and critical study that discusses several of Cheever's short stories and all of his novels. Includes brief bibliography.

Collins, R. G. "Fugitive Time: Dissolving Experience in the Later Fiction of Cheever." *Studies in American Fiction* 12, No. 2 (Autumn 1984): 175-88.
    Explores Cheever's treatment of time in the later short stories and in *Oh, What a Paradise It Seems.*

——, ed. *Critical Essays on John Cheever.* Boston: G. K. Hall & Co., 1982, 292 p.
    Collection of criticism including interviews with the author, a representative selection of short reviews of his stories and novels, and a number of longer critical studies on various aspects of his fiction.

Donaldson, Scott. *John Cheever: A Biography.* New York: Random House, 1988, 416 p.
    Thorough biography faulted as pedestrian by some critics.

Grant, Annette. "John Cheever: The Art of Fiction LXII." *The Paris Review* 17, No. 67 (Fall 1976): 39-66.
    Interview with Cheever addressing his work and life and the relationship between the two, his experiences in Hollywood and academia, and his feelings regarding the *New Yorker.*

Hunt, George W. *John Cheever: The Hobgoblin Company of Love.* Grand Rapids, Mich.: William B. Eerdmans Publishing Company, 1983, 326 p.
    Insightful study emphasizing the moral dimension of Cheever's fiction.

O'Hara, James E. *John Cheever: A Study of the Short Fiction.* Boston: Twayne Publishers, 1989, 161 p.
    Chronicles the growth of Cheever's short fiction, "examining a representative selection of his stories to clarify

significant developments in both the style and thematic
content of his work from 1930 to 1981."

# E. M. Cioran

## 1911-

(Full name Emil M. Cioran) Rumanian-born philosopher and essayist.

Cioran is considered a formidable successor to the tradition of personal, unsystematic philosophical discourse exemplified by Friedrich Nietzsche, Søren Kierkegaard, and Ludwig Wittgenstein. In his essays, Cioran employs irony, paradox, and aphoristic prose to subvert conventional thought on such topics as alienation, consciousness, history, language, literature, religion, and death. Calling his works "more or less autobiographical—a rather abstract form of autobiography," Cioran posits a comprehensively pessimistic view of existence, and is particularly censorious of Western civilization, tracing its decadence to the "exacerbation of the intellect and its corresponding diminution of instinct." John Pilling commented: "Cioran is fanatically devoted to disabusing us of the illusions and consoling fictions we have wilfully erected to prevent ourselves seeing what it is to be human. His 'exercise in anti-utopia' is everywhere haunted by the dream of restoring us to a status we have irretrievably lost."

The son of a Greek Orthodox priest, Cioran was born in Rasinari, Rumania. After studying philosophy at Bucharest University, he went to Paris in 1937 on a scholarship. Shortly thereafter, Cioran rejected traditional philosophy as well as his father's religion. He has remained in Paris without becoming a French citizen, explaining, "I have no nationality—the best possible status for an intellectual." As a young man, Cioran suffered from extreme insomnia, which he cites as a primary influence on his conception of consciousness and time. His sleeplessness also prompted him to realize "that in moments of great despair philosophy is no help at all and offers absolutely no answers."

Although he had published five volumes in Rumania, including *Peculmile disperării* (translated as *On the Summits of Despair*), which won the Prize for Young Rumanian Writers, Cioran did not publish in France until 1949. After undergoing the difficult process of learning a new language as an adult, Cioran printed his first work in French, *Précis de décomposition* (*A Short History of Decay*). This analysis of Western civilization from its origins to the present established Cioran as a consummate stylist and a writer of unmitigated pessimism. Cioran suggests that Western society is in irrevocable decline, its decay abetted by religion—or any cause—that inflames passions which inspire people to persecute dissenters or start wars. In his next collection of essays, *La tentation d'exister* (*The Temptation to Exist*), Cioran continues to explore the downfall of societies, most notably in "On a Winded Civilization." In this piece, which many critics believe is his finest essay, Cioran asserts that nations stop thriving once they become overrefined and relinquish barbaric impulses. Other essays in *The Temptation to Exist* examine such topics as self-consciousness, mystics, exile,

the history of Jewish people, and writing and language. David Stern remarked: "[Cioran] is the creator of a curving pessimism so profound and ironic as to almost meet a serious optimism at the other end of its arc. His aphorisms are lucid medicines that have no intent to cure. Thus, pure . . . , they are valuable remedies for the mind."

In *Histoire et utopie* (*History and Utopia*), Cioran surveys political regimes throughout history and concludes that all forms of government are flawed. Civilization, Cioran maintains, has hastened ruin by dissipating humanity's violent instincts, and therefore its vitality. *La chute dans le temps* (*The Fall into Time*), which offers a bleak portrait of history, denigrates "progress" as the scourge of humankind and advises an unwavering skepticism toward all political and belief systems as the only way for humanity to avert extinction. The six essays in *Le mauvais démiurge* (*The New Gods*) reprise many of Cioran's overriding concerns: "The New Gods" argues for the superiority of polytheism over monotheism; "Encounters with Suicide" explores his obsession with suicide; "The Undelivered" is a meditation on the life of the mystic and the concept of the void, which Cioran regards as a beneficial nothingness;

and "Paleontology," inspired by a musuem visit, reflects his horror of the body. Cioran's next two works, *Écartèlement* (*Drawn and Quartered*) and *De l'inconvénient d'être* (*The Trouble with Being Born*), exhibit his preference for a series of aphorisms over the traditionally structured essay as well as his growing pessimism about history and existence. Stephen Koch observed: "[*The Trouble with Being Born* is] a collection of aphorisms driven into existence by the throb of a panic fear of death and spiritual failure, turned against itself to meditate on the 'disaster' of birth—the beginning of the ordeal of consciousness, and far more 'horrible' than the end."

(See also *Contemporary Authors,* Vols. 25-28, rev. ed.)

## PRINCIPAL WORKS

ESSAY COLLECTIONS

*Précis de décomposition*   1949
   [*A Short History of Decay,* 1975]
*Syllogismes de l'amertume*   1952
*La tentation d'exister*   1956
   [*The Temptation to Exist,* 1968
*Histoire et utopie*   1960
   [*History and Utopia,* 1987]
*La chute dans le temps*   1964
   [*The Fall into Time,* 1970]
*Le mauvais démiurge*   1969
   [*The New Gods,* 1974]
*Écartèlement*   1971
   [*Drawn and Quartered,* 1983]
*De l'inconvénient d'être*   1973
   [*The Trouble with Being Born,* 1976]
*Exercices d'admiration*   1986
*Aveux et anathèmes*   1988

---

## Claude Mauriac

One of the best French writers today is a Rumanian in exile. So far, he is known only to a few admirers, who will be followed by many others. This is E. M. Cioran, author of three essays, ***Précis de décomposition*** (***A Short History of Decay;*** 1949), ***Syllogismes de l'amertume*** (Syllogisms of Bitterness; 1952), and ***La tentation d'exister*** (***The Temptation to Exist;*** 1956).

There are few French authors who know how to use our language with such mastery. Cioran, who believes in nothing, can't resist having faith in beautiful language. Attaching importance to words is one of the weaknesses he admits, one of the few breaks in the continuity of his skepticism. For him, the emptiness of the word corresponds to the emptiness of the world. The emptiness hidden by things is found also behind the names designating them. . . . Cioran doesn't forgive himself for continuing to write. He belongs to those who, aware that only silence has power, none the less cannot give up the word, especially writing. Cioran, the hopeless, is a man of letters, a contradiction that he feels keenly. It is another opportunity

to ridicule himself. While proceeding farther and farther into negation, time after time, within himself, Cioran comes across a bit of attachment to life which he cannot overcome.

No other language than French could have been so effective in his constantly renewed effort toward elucidation. Cioran has *espoused the genius of a language that specializes in sighs of the intellect, in which whatever is not cerebral is suspect or nil.* . . . The decadence of the West is particularly perceptible to Cioran. He associates himself with what is destroying little by little the civilization which supports him. France itself does not always escape his blasphemies. This wicked lucidity, this refusal to have hope in the future, this lack of indulgence, E. M. Cioran turns first of all against himself. It is a new opportunity to sink a little deeper into negation. By indicting what he loves, he hurts himself a little more. We might say he gives himself a little more pleasure; he is masochistic. No one can attain total indifference toward the world and himself. By reopening his wounds Cioran maintains a feeling of sensuality that makes peace of mind impossible for him as well as for others. (pp. 213-15)

The author of ***Le tentation d'exister*** thinks constantly about how to humiliate and trample on himself, and not without a secret pride: "Anxious to be covered with ignominy, I envied all who exposed themselves to the sarcasm and venom of others, and who, piling shame on shame, missed no opportunity for solitude. I thus reached the point of idealizing Judas. . . . " He often associates the word "voluptousness" with defeat, weakness, bitterness, and decay. It pleases him to destroy himself. He wishes us rare joys, queer delights:

> One day, who knows, perhaps you will experience the pleasure of aiming at an idea, shooting it, seeing it lie there, and then begin the exercise over again on another; on all of them; the desire to bend over an individual, to make him deviate from his old appetites, from his old vices, in order to impose new and more harmful ones on him so that he will perish from them; to become furious at a period or against a civilization, to rush at time and make martyrs of its moments; then, to turn against yourself, to torture your memories and ambitions, and, fouling your breath, infect the air the better to suffocate.

These dream illnesses are born of real anxieties, which in all probability are not all moral ones. He who evokes the lack of air so effectively and so many times must have suffocated already. As for the masochism, we find it tinged as usual with sadism. Cioran considers "our blood too tepid, our appetites too well mastered." He likes the fact that Christianity "at its good moments" was sanguinary, that it *excelled in massacre.* Vandalism charms him. The hysteria of the Middle Ages (or what he so labels) appears admirable to him. As for the anchorites, he envies them for having known so well how *to remedy the insufficiency of their troubles:* "Left to itself, the flesh encloses us in a contracted horizon. As we submit it to torture, it sharpens our perceptions and enlarges our perspectives: the mind is the result of the tortures it undergoes or inflicts." . . . Cioran dreams then "of an acid thought which would insinuate itself into things to disorganize them, perforate, traverse them; of a book whose syllables, infecting the paper, would eliminate literature and readers; of a book which would be the carnival and apocalypse of Letters, an ultimatum to the pestilence of the Word." A new theoretician of aliterature, he none the less continues his painstaking work.

With France exhausting itself more and more in the midst of a civilization itself in decay (as Cioran claims and we accept his postulate), its language cannot escape degeneration. The author of *La tentation d'exister* quotes these words of Joseph de Maistre: "All individual or national deterioration is immediately anticipated by a directly proportionate deterioration in language." About this deterioration E. M. Cioran writes some beautiful passages. Assuring us that French is declining, he proves the contrary by the beauty, precision, and cadence of a language which, even in classical times, was scarcely more perfect or efficient. We can say about him what he assures us about La Bruyère: that the semicolon was his obsession. If he uses it with artistry, he employs the exclamation point as rarely as possible, a recourse abused by the romantics.

That it is a Rumanian who handles the French language with such perfection may reassure the French, who might be disturbed or even hurt by the severity of Cioran's views about their country, a severity from which not only is no nation exempt (with the exception of the Jewish people) but nothing else in the world either, not even the world itself or his own country. This is said for the sake of those who might be disagreeably surprised by lines like these: "A nation's bad habits are as apparent as an individual's." Or again: "A nation of the gesture, a theatrical nation, France loved its acting as well as its audience. She has had her fill, she wants to leave the stage, and no longer aspires to anything but the *stage setting of oblivion*." This is open to argument, but because of his love for the theater Cioran is almost a naturalized citizen, he is one of us. He, too, has a tendency to pose. He has no objection to forcing his ideas a little if the cadences of a fine phrase demand it.

Only the Jews escape, then, from the declaration of failure which our author draws up with a pleasure too grating not to be desperate. The chapter that he devotes to them, **"Un peuple de solitaires"** ("A People of Solitaries"), is one of the most beautiful in *La tentation d'exister*. Nothing so intelligent or thorough has ever been written about this unfortunate and admirable race. It pained Cioran to belong to a nation without history. "How can one be a Rumanian?" was a question, he assures us, that he could only answer with perpetual mortification. "Hating my people, my country, its eternal peasants delighted with their torpor and almost bursting with stupidity, I blushed that I was descended from them, disclaimed them, refused to allow myself to accept their sub-eternity, their petrified larval convictions, their geological dreaming." His country, *whose existence obviously made no sense, seemed to him an epitome of non-being and a materialization of the inconceivable*: "To be part of it, what humiliation and irony! What a calamity! What leprosy!" Subsequently, Cioran became reconciled to Rumania, a connivance and complicity which, instead of raising them both, lowered

them even more in his estimation. To his country, Cioran owes not only his *peasant neurasthenia,* not only "his finest, surest defeats, but even his gift for covering his cowardice with make-up, for hoarding his remorse," a gift which we know (and he knows) he has all too great a tendency towards: "I realized the advantage of belonging to a small country, of living with no background, carefree as a buffoon, an idiot or a saint. . . . " Elsewhere, pretending to evoke Joseph de Maistre, he tells us a very personal secret: "A thinker enriches himself by everything that escapes him, everything that is hidden from him: if he happens to lose his country, what a piece of luck!"

But Cioran found someone more unfortunate (and more *exiled* ) than he: "To be a man is one tragedy; to be a Jew is another. So, the Jew has the privilege of living through our situation *twice*." It pleases him that Jews are unbeatable at jokes. He likes the idea that decadence doesn't bother them, since their history unfolds outside of History. A dead town is a town without Jews. Man is a Jew *who has not made the grade.* The Germans detested in the Jew the realization of their own dreams, the universality which they were unable to attain. Whatever they do and wherever they go, the mission of the Jews is to be on the lookout. In short, although they are in the world, they are really not of it. . . . At last they are trying to take their place in History and to escape "their immemorial status of stranger." E. M. Cioran, who never speaks other than of himself even when he comments on, sings about, and glorifies the great Jewish sorrow, Cioran, for whom there is no other secret or fate but his own, for he is one of those who are fascinated by their own death and can never think about anything else, Cioran confesses that he is grateful to "these vanquishers of the abyss" for having made him glimpse the advantage of not losing his grip, not giving way *to the voluptuousness of being a derelict:* "Meditating on their refusal to be shipwrecked, one vows to imitate them, knowing that it is a vain aspiration, that our lot is to sink to the bottom, to answer the call of the abyss." (pp. 215-20)

His appetite for being persisted, no matter how hard he tried to destroy everything solid that he had, while facing the certainty of non-being. Hence the final effort which gave the book its title, the acceptance of the inextinguishable, unsmotherable, unkillable *temptation to exist.* Utterly tired of "polemics with non-being," Cioran aspires *to regain the privileges of irrationality,* privileges, in fact, whose secrets he had never lost completely. "Existing is a habit which he does not despair of acquiring." Consolidating his position with his reverses, he makes believe that he is choosing what is forced upon him: an unuprootable hope. This is the struggle of a moribund man against death. We are all dying. We never stop. Cioran's struggle is the more ours according as we are of his lucid breed.

For it is a breed, and one that has many representatives. There are many of us who have renounced what Cioran calls the superstition of the Ego. Although we don't stop "leaning on ourselves for support," we no longer rehash "our differences." We know that nothing essential distinguishes us, that we are interchangeable, scarcely more or less intelligent than one another. As a result we all write the same books. To quote Cioran is to offer the best possible commentary on the modern novel or essay, Beckett's as well as Camus's. We find again the very words which we all use and which will carry our dearest, cruelest convictions. First and foremost, it should be understood that *we are nothing:*

> In revenge for our shortcomings in naïveté, freshness, hope, and simplicity, the "psychological sense," our greatest acquisition, has transformed us into spectators of ourselves. Our greatest acquisition? No doubt it is, taking into account our metaphysical incapacity, just as it is no doubt the only kind of depth of which we are capable. But if one goes beyond psychology, our whole "inner life" assumes the aspect of an emotional meteorology whose variations have no significance. Why be interested in the maneuvers of ghosts, in stages of semblance? . . . The "ego" is essentially the privilege only of those who do not make the most of their capabilities. . . . Suddenly, beyond everything, I glide toward the point of non-existence of each object. The ego: a label.

This results in a new conception of literature, or rather aliterature, which, from Beckett to Robbe-Grillet, through many more obscure researchers, and through Cioran, is in the process of renovating the act of writing. The time of futility is past, and also that of a certain professorial seriousness. In a period often devoid of religious faith, there are no longer any interesting writers except for philosophers. The novelist devotes himself exclusively to an essential that he knows to be relative and misleading, but whose appearance, the only reality within reach, fascinates him. "To reflect life in its details, to degrade our amazement into anecdotes, what a torture for the mind!" (pp. 220-21)

Cioran writes: "An artist describes best what he might have accomplished. He becomes his own critic." And further: "Also it is not without significance that the only novels worthy of interest are precisely those in which, once the universe is dismissed, nothing happens." True. But from here on I no longer agree with him as to novels "delightfully unreadable, without head or tail; they could just as well stop at the first sentence as contain tens of thousands of pages":

> A narration that eliminates what is narrated, the object, corresponds to a paroxysm of the intellect, a meditation *without content.* The mind sees itself reduced to the act by which it is mind and nothing more. All its activities lead back to itself, to a stationary unfolding that prevents it from clinging to things. No knowledge, no action. . . .

This *adventure in the unintelligible* does not tempt us. We preserve our yearning for understanding, for grasping. Hence our attention to objects that we refuse to excommunicate, following Robbe-Grillet's example. Hence our need to cling to things, at least to their appearances—and (but here Robbe-Grillet is no longer with us) to those other reflections, thoughts, born of sensations, which they command and comment upon. "*Meaning* begins to be dated." It is on this point that we believe it necessary to

part with Cioran and from certain writers whom he salutes without naming. "If the artist of today takes refuge in the obscure, it is because he can no longer innovate *with what he knows.*" Before Joyce and Proust this was already asserted. Well, Proust and Joyce came. Others will come. I shall not give up the idea of seeing and knowing more in what we already see and know.

Therefore, we reaffirm that even for the *alittérateurs* everything ends in literature. . . . Cioran denies the outer world, denouncing its unreality, scrutinizing his obsession with death, then, in the end, offers his despair a hope, even if it is false. But he never stops coming back to language problems. And I myself, reviewing his work, stress its literary character still more by dwelling on what refers only to the question of style. It is because in a universe where truth is dead, nothing consoles us, nothing amuses us, except the lullaby which we sing to ourselves and which can only be made of words. They are what Cioran, the metaphysician of non-being, calls *the axioms of twilight.* (pp. 222-23)

*Claude Mauriac, "E. M. Cioran," in his* The New Literature, *translated by Samuel I. Stone, George Braziller, Inc., 1959, pp. 213-24.*

## Richard Gilman

"In every delicate civilization there functions a radical disjunction between reality and the word," E. M. Cioran writes in an essay called **"Style as Risk,"** one of the dozen or so pieces that make up [*The Temptation to Exist* ]. This disharmony or lack of coherence between reality and language is the book's main theme, or rather its chief energizing force and occupation, since Cioran is so far from being a systematic thinker that even "theme" is too circumscribed and *official* a word to describe the kinds of tasks his mind sets itself. Impulsive, rash, extraordinarily subtle but also robust, immensely well provided with learning but never merely erudite, rapid, dizzying and dangerous, his writing constitutes that kind of achievement for which the European mind, but not the American, is celebrated: an "autobiography," as Cioran himself calls it, in the form of one's thoughts. . . .

He has a claim, although he would be the last to do anything to press it and might even think it horrifying, to be regarded as among the handful of forceful and original minds writing anywhere today.

He might think it horrifying because to be a writer even of genius is only the shakiest of triumphs. Writing, in his view, is an abyss that opens up each time one turns to language and thereby separates oneself more widely from life (an abyss only less deep perhaps than the one that opens if we abandon language altogether). What it means to write, beyond personality or psychology, writing as a form of *waging* existence, is Cioran's subject, which is in turn part of a wider ground and arena: the nature, status and destiny of consciousness. Consciousness as the supreme achievement and value of Western civilization, with the crisis that such celebration has brought about, is what Cioran addresses himself to in these essays, which by the very fact of their having been written participate in the crisis and bear all the marks of its bitter and ludicrous agony.

"To be conscious is to be divided from oneself, is to hate oneself. This hatred seethes at our roots at the same time as it furnishes sap to the Tree of Knowledge." Cioran, as Susan Sontag says in her illuminating introduction, is in one sense only the latest in "that melancholy parade of European intellectuals in revolt against the intellect." Yet he is also an elitist of the intellect, uncompromising in his insistence on standards and on daringness in thought, and committed with all the force of his intellect to struggle against the irreconcilabilities that the mind by its very nature opens up between men and the world. He embodies the dilemma in its most acute form and stands, as Miss Sontag says, halfway between a "reprise" of all the old gestures of complaint against the mind and a "genuine transvaluation" of them. (p. 25)

That reason, thought, is our curse, causing us to "acquire existence by division from our being," while at the same time it remains true that it is our very nature to reason, is Cioran's obsession. The "exacerbation of the intellect and its corresponding diminution of instinct" is the chief element in his reading of Western experience. Yet it isn't simply the dominance of mind at the expense of affective life that has brought us to what Cioran calls "our fate: to be incurables who protest." It is the way we have seized on our "incurability" while refusing finally to accept it, the way we have made our malaises—products of our consciousness—into the central principle of our self-regard, raising knowledge of our maladies to the status of a self-definition, honoring most those ancestors who have taught us how contented we are, all those "malcontents, triflers, fanatics whose disappointments and excesses we must continue." Among them Cioran includes nearly all the great rebels, the utopians, the literary geniuses of horrific vision, such as Baudelaire and Dostoevsky.

Yet Cioran has no brief for another kind of writer: classic, balanced, humane. "Discretion," he writes, "is deadly to genius, ruinous to talent." And again: "Examine the minds which manage to intrigue us: far from taking the way of the world into consideration, they defend *indefensible* positions." For Cioran, to defend indefensible positions is at the heart of more than strenuous literature; it constitutes the secret of keeping oneself in being. "We cannot be *normal* and *alive,*" he writes in one of the most brilliant essays in the book, **"On a Winded Civilization."** The manner in which he manages to distinguish this necessary abnormality from that which we cultivate as neurotic self-definition seems to me to be one of the primary sources of his originality.

Another is the way he manages to stand on a Platonic base and yet not build the structures one would expect to see rise. (This is a point on which I think Miss Sontag wrong. Rightfully seeing the dualisms in Cioran's thought as Platonic, she tasks him for not making a Nietzschean attempt to resolve them, without seeming to see how strenuous is his refusal to make a *Platonic* resolution of them.) He is stricken with consciousness of finiteness, of *specificity,* and speaks of the "degradation" involved in the "parceling out of the absolute" which takes place in every one of our ac-

tions. Yet he erects no system of "ideas" that can serve as absolutes, buttressing us—but only *mentally*—against the erosions of actuality. He exhibits no longing for this particular sort of Western escape through transcendence, and only a rueful, skeptical longing for the Eastern alternative. In the intersection of his hunger for the absolute and his consciousness of finiteness, of his resentment of ideas and his need to employ them, lies the instigation and sustaining force of his genius.

Cioran's attitude towards history is one of the most crucial aspects of his thought and one of the most relevant to us. Overwhelmed by history, sickened by our entrenched habit of thinking of ourselves as products, *results,* we're engaged now in trying to throw history off; this is the innermost meaning of the anti-authoritarian stance of the young. For Cioran, spread-eagled on a longer cross, history is "a monster we have called up against ourselves," and again, "man's aggression against himself." To this point there is nothing that clashes with what the young feel but are seldom able to articulate. But Cioran's thinking soon shows itself as being of a different temper and commitment.

History, for him is the annals of man's futility, the record of his existential anomaly, not the sum of the mistakes men have made; he is no progressive, much less a political radical, nor does his thought ever come to grips directly with political actualities. For him history is characterized by what he calls the "idolatry of becoming," that process of consciousness being transformed into thought and thought into futurity which Nietzsche had in mind when he castigated his own countrymen: poor Germans, "they never are, they're always becoming." To wish to become is to be dissatisfied with what is; it is what Cioran calls our "perpetual revolt," which involves "an irreverence towards ourselves, towards our powers." Against this wish to become Cioran hurls a wish to *un-become,* to find nothingness, no-action, silence, as plenitudes, inverted spurs to being.

This is the most difficult and also the coldest and most forbidding aspect of his thought, but its most crucial. To oppose the idolatry of becoming is for Cioran to wish to overthrow the worship of action, which he calls a "superstition" and a "curse." "Destruction awaits anyone," he writes, "who, answering to his vocation and fulfilling it, exerts himself within history; only the man who sacrifices every gift and talent escapes. . . ." Yet Cioran won't be fixed in what might seem a new quietism or a species of Eastern morale. The true implications of his thought, the balancing of contradictions, defense of the indefensible and therefore heroism, emerge in unmistakable ways, not as steps in an argument but as light struck off from his engagements with conditions. When he writes that the "only minds which seduce us are the minds which have destroyed themselves trying to give their lives a meaning," we become aware of how "meaning" inheres more nearly in such doomed enterprises than in solutions or *results,* those species of artifacts by which we fill up the void. And when he writes that, "Only the man who strives to fail deserves our trust: if he succeeds in this he will have killed the monster, the monster he was as long as he was concerned to act, to triumph."—we see that what he's addressing is the core of our idolatries and perversions, our aggression against existence in the name of mastery and success, our displacing the world by the ego, our thrusting forward of the self before being. An impossibilist of purity and the absolute, a lucid sufferer from the disease of finiteness, a man for whom the idea of non-being is the only sure clue to being, Cioran stands towards the rest of us—"ham actors of wisdom and madness"—as someone who will not be *taken in.*

In his rage against becoming, the deferring of life, Cioran can be seen now to have relevance to what is newest in our thinking about ourselves, what is not ham. His thought moves towards and illumines, from a cold, infinitely aristocratic perspective, the thought and action of the present as they concern rebellion against power, control, exploitation, against process and becoming. We *are,* is what members of the young, the illogical, the unmethodical and unimperialist, all those who refuse to be guilty on the one hand and acquisitive on the other, are trying to find the full right words to say.

Cioran is at an earlier stage of this desire. In him it still remains an ache, an impossible hope. As Miss Sontag points out, he is unable to move beyond history, or rather the attitudes of history; he is still a victim of time. There is no principle in his thought of relaxation, that letting go by means of which the self and the moment may announce themselves without need for justification by the future or the past. He writes of "the philosophy of unique moments, the only philosophy," but it remains a *philosophy,* a consolation and a substitute. What is needed, perhaps, is a newer kind of heroism than his, of the sort Miss Sontag touches on when she compares Cioran with John Cage and finds the latter more centrally involved in an act of freedom because of his less fierce will, his greater capacity to *forget.* Meanwhile Cioran is there to give us "this lesson in perplexity," this noble example of how, short of peace, the mind has to see to it that we don't mistake what we have, that we don't find it peaceful. (pp. 25-7)

*Richard Gilman, "The Revolt Against Becoming," in* The New Republic, *Vol. 158, No. 20, May 18, 1968, pp. 25-7.*

**William H. Gass**

Each of Cioran's essays [in *The Temptation to Exist* ] adopts the tone of the dilemma, even if none has Zeno's unflinching elegance of form, for Zeno was rapacious, the Attila of logic, and wished to win; he strove always for conclusions. Conclusions? Cioran seems to say, they are only vanities, and he repudiates them all . . . but again, not absolutely. Although he seems to have taken his aphoristic style from Nietzsche, as well as many of his ideas, he is never as wild or bold or positive as Nietzsche was. His work drones with disillusion. His complaints about the intellect, his stress on instinct, his references to time, remind one of similar attitudes in Schopenhauer and Bergson, as well as some of the moods of the existentialists; nor can one escape the feeling that he's been kissed, immoderately, by Spengler. However, principally he is a Platonist

unsure of which horse he should allow to lead, and regrets sometimes that the dark horse of desire has been tamed. Being, Non-Being, and Becoming: these ghosts haunt him, as do those ancient Greek divisions of the soul. His essays are exemplifications of the disease he says we suffer from: superbly written, economical, concerned with the very foundations of thought and being, they are nevertheless extraordinarily careless pieces of reasoning, travel from fallacy to fallacy with sovereign unconcern, deal almost wholly with borrowings, and spider down from dubious premises thick threads of purely *historical* associations. So evenly is Cioran divided against himself, on irony's behalf, that there is scarcely a line which does not contain truth by precisely a half. Yet it is the conditions these pieces reveal which justifies their claim (strong, though implicit), to picture our contemporary mind. What one essay says of Meister Eckhart perfectly applies to Cioran himself:

> Even in the Middle Ages, certain minds, tired of sifting the same themes, the same expressions, were obliged, in order to renew their piety and to emancipate it from the official terminology, to fall back on paradox, on the alluring, sometimes brutal, sometimes subtle formula . . . his style, rather than his ideas, gained him the honor of being convicted of heresy. . . . Like every heretic, he sinned on the side of form. An enemy of language, all orthodoxy, whether religious or political, postulates *the usual expression.*

Thus, as Susan Sontag points out in her exemplary Introduction, there is nothing fresh about Cioran's thought . . . except its formal *fury.* His book has all the beauty of pressed leaves, petals shut from their odors; yet what is retained has its own emotion, and here it is powerful and sustained. ***The Temptation to Exist*** is a philosophical romance on modern themes: alienation, absurdity, boredom, futility, decay, the tyranny of history, the vulgarities of change, awareness as agony, reason as disease.

E. M. Cioran is, in every way, an alien; he has no home, even in his own heart. Born in Rumania, that nebbish among nations, he was exiled from it before he left, though now he bitterly pretends to have come to terms with its history of failure and its Balkan sense of fatality: " . . . would I have been able, without my country, to waste my days in so exemplary a manner?" Living in Paris since 1937, he has abandoned his native language (alien, now, to that too), and composes his tight little essays in French; essays which he has no home in either, for he distrusts even his occupation ("To write books is to have a certain relation with original sin."), since a concern with the Word withdraws us from the World—we vanish inside our syllables. "At least," he addresses a prospective author, "I have the excuse of hating my actions, of performing them without believing in them," and although he loathes his own self-loathing, he often regards this emotion as the only way to redemption. Are we to take all these repudiations seriously? Not a bit. Just a little. Yes and no. Truths he utters ironically to expose the falsehood in them, while falsehoods receive the same treatment, so what soundness they have will shine through. He seems really to think that if he writes his lies *like* lies, that will excuse them, but what he risks by this tactic is revealing an essentially frivolous mind. At his worst he appears a world-weary wit out of Oscar Wilde, no more: "Self-doubt worked on human beings to such a point that they invented love as a remedy, a tacit pact between two unfortunates to overestimate and praise each other shamelessly." Consciousness, itself, he's quite alone in. Thought, as well—his sole addiction—takes him even further from the sources of vitality, and ruthlessly discloses its own futility—so much so that he says, "our strength can be measured by the sum of beliefs we abjure," and "each of us should wind up his career a deserter of all possible causes."

What Cioran would do without his belief in alienation, disease, and decline, is not clear; yet surely these ideas should be abandoned, unless he is willing to qualify them until they lose their usefulness to poetry. Indeed, all his causes are in the same sinking boat. He tells us that the only minds which intrigue us "defend indefensible positions," and that "the only minds which seduce us are the minds which have destroyed themselves trying to give their lives a meaning" (note how we are dragged by the *us* out to these extremities); yet there are other minds, other styles, which risk more (one essay is titled **"Style as Risk"**), those which dare to replace flamboyance with responsibility. If we ask ourselves soberly what such remarks mean, or what amount of truth they contain, musn't our answer honestly be: very little, and not much?

Although his treatment of the doctrine of Destiny is acid, and his feelings about determinism in general more than skeptical, the opposition between reason and instinct, between civilization and vitality, between time and freedom—the whole lot—is presented as inevitable, the decline of the West as inescapable; and he regularly throws his thought, which he properly describes as autobiographical (and which has only a subjective, a psychological, validity), into the first person plural, where it obtains the abstractness and rigidity of a mathematical model. Theories of decline and decay require a belief in Necessity as much as those which naïvely predict Progress; they both lean on history (which Cioran sourly regards as "man's aggression against himself"), and both depend heavily upon the use of terms (like *instinct, intellect, civilization*) which facilitate equivocation, and produce in the reader that effortless sense of depth and subtlety which is so rewarding and so inexpensive. Finally, both need eyes which blaze at the oncoming of contrary facts, and dazzle them into the ditch.

Nietzsche, who made so many of the same observations Cioran does, was altogether wiser: the Apollonian and Dionysian principles are only *possible* enemies; the health he was after required their unity, not their opposition. Cioran suffers from what Nietzsche called

> . . . the greatest and most disastrous of maladies, of which humanity has not to this day been cured: his sickness of himself, brought on by the violent severance from his animal past, by his sudden leap and fall into new layers and conditions of existence, by his declaration of war against the old instincts that had hitherto been the foundation of his power, his joy, and his awesomeness.

Cioran's diagnosis is the same, but he regards, even a little smugly (a condition, of course, he also recognizes), this disease as incurable; and therefore—some think bravely—perseveres in it, aggravates it, champions it. (pp. 18-19)

Our minds can grow their own bodies, become body, play a different Demiurge. We can swell with the world we take in. Otherwise we shrink and wrinkle like a prune. In the prune, contracting on its core, I sense small temptation, little reason, to exist. (p. 20)

*William H. Gass, "The Evil Demiurge," in* The New York Review of Books, *Vol. XI, No. 5, August 22, 1968, pp. 18-20.*

### Daniel Stern

[The positions taken in Cioran's] thought are more extreme than any claims that can be made for him. Cioran is a sort of final philosopher of Western civilization. In [*The Temptation to Exist*] you will find all the tired old arguments from alienation to crisis theology, all previously expressed in prose by Nietzsche, in poetry by Rilke and in individual essays by Camus and Sartre. But you will have to search carefully, because they have been transformed by the most subtle of ironic minds into statements that have the compression of poetry and the audacity of cosmic clowning. The difference between Cioran and his forerunners in the twilight of the gods our minds have been treated to for the last 70 years or so is that he has gone beyond them. They treated hopelessness: he breathes it as if it were air. They were concerned with the absence of usable values: he questions the very use of thought and language with which to couch either the loss of old values or the creation of new ones. Despair? Kid stuff. One feels in these rhythms an impatience with despair.

What is one to do with this man who wants the last word. But *really* the last word. One feels that when Beckett finally reaches the silence he has been reaching for, Cioran will quietly say, "But . . . " The measure of his spiritual ambitions can perhaps be sensed in this passage from **"Some Blind Alleys: A Letter,"** which is included in the book:

> Is futility, then, no more than an "ideal?" That is what I must fear, that is what I shall never be resigned to. Each time I catch myself assigning some importance to things, I incriminate my mind, I challenge it and suspect it of some weakness, of some depravity. I try to wrest myself from everything, to raise myself by uprooting myself; in order to become futile, we must sever our roots, must become metaphysically *alien*.

A protean enterprise? Perhaps a super-romantic Prometheus reversing myth and returning fire to the gods in exchange for a lucid futility? With Cioran we must be careful, for in his key essay in the book, **"On a Winded Civilization,"** he says: "Men's minds need a simple truth, an answer which delivers them from their questions, a gospel, a tomb. The moments of refinement conceal a death-principle: nothing is more fragile than subtlety."

This, then, is a mind in revolt against the Enlightenment, as Susan Sontag points out in her introduction [see Further Reading list]. But we have had lots of those, from Joseph de Maistre (on whom Cioran has written) to T. S. Eliot and T. E. Hulme and his metaphysical *Speculations*. But here is a mind not only in revolt against the Enlightenment, with its sterile rationalism, but against the metaphysical revolution that followed it and which we are still in the midst of (there is a measured attack on this in his essay **"Dealing with the Mystics"**); a mind in revolt against mind itself. He is the philosopher of ultimate suspicion.

"One does not abuse one's capacity to doubt with impunity. When the skeptic no longer extracts any active virtue from his problems and his interrogations, he approaches his denouement, indeed he seeks it out . . . let others settle his uncertainties, let someone else help him to succumb!" For students of history this is not, after all, such unfamiliar ground.

I envision this anti-philosopher, exiled in his Paris, brooding over the dying civilizations that people his world—and ours. But the world of his writing is almost as difficult as the world he seeks *not* to transform with his thought. Cioran, almost involuntarily, gives us an explanation in his essay **"Style as Risk"**:

> Every idolatry of style starts from the belief that reality is even more hollow than its verbal figuration, that the accent of an idea is worth more than the idea, a well-turned excuse more than a conviction, a skillful image more than an unconsidered explosion . . . A well-proportioned sentence, satisfied with its equilibrium or swollen with its sonority, all too often conceals the *malaise* of a mind incapable of acceding by *sensation* to an original universe. What is surprising if style should be simultaneously a mask and an admission?

Thus Cioran maintains a precarious balance between all the classic polarities of thought: style and fact, mind and body, history and individuality. The child of Nietzsche, he is the creator of a curving pessimism so profound and ironic as to almost meet a serious optimism at the other end of its arc. His aphorisms are lucid medicines that have no intent to cure. Thus, pure—sterile—in a world of false Messiahs, they are valuable remedies for the mind.

> Daniel Stern, *"Ironies of a Cosmic Clown," in* Book World—The Washington Post, *September 22, 1968, p. 6.*

### Bernard Murchland

In broad terms *The Temptation to Exist* can be classified as a contribution to our growing literature of exhaustion, focusing in a series of terse, apophatic essays on the reality of decay and the pleasures of the void. "The only free mind is one that plies its own vacuity," Cioran says. "Negation is the mind's first freedom." The fruits of rationality are poisonous; action is futile; to breathe is an effort. Indeed, even to bear a name is "to claim an exact mode of collapse."

Cioran's ability to sustain the mood of negativity is nothing short of amazing. All forms of culture and life are weighed and found not merely wanting but repulsive. We are urged to renounce the acquisitions of history (that monster we call up against ourselves) and reason (a sign of vital inadequacy) as a beggar renounces belongings. From Socrates and St. Paul to modern-day America and Russia the odyssey of our dissolution is delineated in detail. Not unsurprisingly, Cioran's reflections grow increasingly misanthropic. He detects self-hatred at the root of consciousness and suggests that man may be the last caprice of nature. There is no doubt that all of this gives expression to the apocalyptic imagination of our times. . . .

But Cioran is not content to remain in the abyss. From negation to negation he is led finally to affirmation. Just when it seems that no light is about to break, the reader realizes that the long journey through the tunnel has been a prelude to a revelation. (p. 446)

In a chapter entitled **"Dealing with the Mystics"** it becomes clear whom Cioran admires and what values he cherishes. Mysticism is viewed as an adventure which forays upwards and seizes another form of space and is thus superior to the doctrines of decadence. Eckhart, Silesius, John of the Cross and Suso emerge as the remedying heroes of existential *angst*. Cioran admires their wilful claim to divine status, their vitality and imbalance, especially their madness. By their conquest of a supreme illusion, he writes, they resolve the antinomies of existence. Beginning with the awareness that nothing is, they end with the conviction that everything is. "Contrary to that abstract, false void of the philosophers, the mystics' nothingness glistens with plenitude: delight out of this world, discharge of duration, a luminous annihilation beyond the limits of thought."

In her introduction to this book Susan Sontag says: "What is missing in Cioran's work is anything parallel to Nietzsche's heroic effort to surmount nihilism . . . All the venerable Platonic dualisms appear in his writings." I should argue that this judgment is patently false. Quite apart from the question of whether or not dualisms, venerable or otherwise, can be found in Plato's thought (in my view they cannot), it seems obvious that Cioran is proposing a transvaluation of all values that is just as radical as Nietzsche's. Both belong to that tradition of bold assertion that includes Augustine, Innocent III, Rousseau and Schopenhauer. "We can ascend to ecstasies as effective as those of the mystics and conquer this world," Cioran asserts, although he would want to do so in secular terms, without reference to God or the Beyond. But the dynamics of affirmation are the same in both cases; in both cases a therapy of madness is urged upon us. This is the basis of the author's final act of faith: "Everything which keeps us from self-dissolution, every lie which protects us against our unbreathable certitudes is religious. When I grant myself a share in eternity, when I conceive of a permanence which includes me, I trample underfoot the evidence of my friable, worthless being." Nothingness, he notes, would be easier; but it is our unhappy fate to yield to the temptation to exist and dissolve ourselves in being.

*The Temptation to Exist* evinces a radically voluntaristic conception of reality and as such is not particularly original. It is continuous with a long tradition of religious orthodoxy which views conflict as the metaphysical heart of the universe and values striving over achievement, anguish and tension over satisfaction and the eternal over the temporal. Faith is achieved at the price of negating the time-and-space bound media of our humanity. This view of the way things are transforms what Cioran presumably takes to be a self-transcending dialectic into a self-consuming dichotomy that burns itself out in the pursuit of impossible goals. There is no way in which temporal effort can be adequate to an absolute demand, no way in which meaning can be satisfactorily divorced from the given conditions of our human experience. Hegel-like attempts to embrace the absolute, all autonomous dialectics spun out of volitional determination are bound to prove disastrous. Nietzsche's madness stands as an enduring symbol to modern man of that inevitability.

One must, of course, grant Cioran the right to choose madness. That may conceivably be a form of salvation for him. But the imaginative failure of his vision must at the same time be noted. The materials of experience lend themselves to less strident resolutions and happier equations. Less apocalyptic options are open to modern man and I take it to be no small part of the work of reconstruction that faces us all to seek these out.

Cioran refuses to be taken in by our contemporary fetishisms. That is all to the good. Why, then, is he taken in by the oldest of man's idols: that yearning for immutability which Arthur Lovejoy has termed the eternalistic pathos? (pp. 446-47)

> *Bernard Murchland, in a review of "The Temptation to Exist," in* Commonweal, *Vol. LXXXIX, No. 13, December 27, 1968, pp. 446-47.*

## Edward W. Said

Along with only one other of the forms of writing the essay can afford to make no concessions to narrative description—it has no image in mind but itself—and to forsake what Hopkins called pitch, or utterly faithful accuracy, in the interests of play. Montaigne comes to mind immediately, also Oscar Wilde. In the modern perspective their essays are expatriations from things (as Wilde has one of his characters say, "things exist only to be argued about") and explorations in a language whose written version surprises by its wit, invention, sheer novelty. Writing, in other words, that delights in the mere fact of its being written cleverly, as if by a child first learning to scratch words on a page, seeing them as pretty and strangely meaningful bursts of script that transgress the unrelieved blankness of the paper. The epigram and the aphorism in the essay are what characters are to a play, or what philology is to literature. The subject of the essay does not exist beforehand, and neither does the subject go on existing after it—the subject is neither predictive nor prolonged beyond the essay, yet the subject is a choice made, as E. M. Cioran puts it, for "a break with the quietude of Unity." Thus some of his own essays, collected and translated under a title (*The Temptation to Exist* ) that preserves the essay's primitive hesitancy, "advance, dissociated from

[their own] footsteps," and what they undertake is to give "knowledge without information." Cioran's project in writing coexists admirably with what he calls "the essential tendency of the modern mind": "to pulverize the *acquired.*"

Such a project does not of course enhance the coherence of Cioran's work. Nevertheless he is an exquisitely intelligible writer who "prowls around the Absolute," preferring what he calls the fragility of subtlety to wholehearted sincerity that might obscure the very finest points. He cannot really be read consecutively, since his prose (to which Yeats's image of a fly struggling in marmalade is very suited) accomplishes turn after turn of dense thought that seems always to leave the reader elsewhere. Yet the vigilance of his writing is an expression of his, and his writing's, consciousness, and that is explicitly based on self-hatred. For what is the pulverization of the acquired but a desire to destroy the closest and the most intimate of our gained possessions, the self? "It is from self-hatred that consciousness emerges, hence it is in self-hatred that we must seek the point of departure of the human phenomenon. I hate myself: I am absolutely a man." When he charges us "to become a source, an origin, a starting point . . . to multiply by all means our *cosmogonic moments*" he urges us to convert our misanthropy into energy, and into spectacle. A desire consequently to be interesting is saturated with hatred, although interest is productive. Cioran's characteristic idiom then forges together consciousness (which includes being interesting, and hating it) with the production of thought and prose (which includes a wish to pulverize, and the means to work that end). As a form of provocation his writing deposits the reader into a maelstrom of discomforts. Here is an image from an essay (**"The Evil Demiurge"**) . . . that analogically turns back on the prose that delivers it: "We find it inadmissable that a god, *or for that matter a man,* could issue from a round of gymnastics consummated by a groan."

Cioran is peculiar enough to be a case, but not an example. His pages are dotted with impossible words like abulia, presbyopic, succedanea, aporia, mirific, obnubilation, incivism. Development, for example, is foreign to him, just as he is studiously foreign, actually and metaphysically, in everything he does. He is a Rumanian who writes French which, in Richard Howard's translation, comes over in English with very much the same jerky intellectual queerness. The essays that have been published over the past five years . . . emerged from other collections, but bearing the same marks of what Cioran calls the hybrid intellectual: a talent for "voyeurism of the void," the incapacity to emulate Eastern or mystical abstraction, the distraction that keeps his rages from final nihilism. He has written on Joseph de Maistre, Machiavelli, utopias, but above all on decomposition. Most of all, he thinks, he suffers from the inability "to take place." Like Rameau's nephew he sees the world, and his writing therefore acts out, a series of positions taken—but only for a short while. Then he abandons them all since "meaning," he avers, "is beginning to date." Inescapably the predicament returns him to an awareness of the impasse of writing itself:

> If today's artist takes refuge in obscurity, it is because he can no longer create with *what he*

*knows.* The extent of his information has turned him into a commentator, an Aristarchus without illusions. To safeguard his originality he has no recourse save an excursion into the unintelligible. He will therefore abandon the facts inflicted on him by an erudite and barren age. If he is a poet, he discovers that none of his words, in its legitimate acceptation, has a future; if he wants them to be viable, he must fracture their meaning, court impropriety. In the world of Letters as a whole, we are witnessing the capitulation of the Word which, curiously enough, is even more exhausted than we are. Let us follow the descending curve of its vitality, surrender to its degree of overwork and decrepitude, espouse the process of its agony. Paradoxically, it was never so free before; its submission is its triumph: emancipated from reality, from experience, it indulges in the final luxury of no longer expressing anything except the ambiguity of its own action.

Such a view of language makes it rather difficult to summarize systematically Cioran's own thought, although he is plainly a man of very strong dislikes, which include himself, other writers, and the novel preeminently. His attacks on Christianity, and on St. Paul in particular, are unlike Nietzsche's in that, first of all, they see the religion only as a bundle of depressing contradictions and, second of all, they cannot forgive Christianity for being *passé.* For Cioran, however, the premise of his withering criticism is not as it was for Marx in the criticism of religion, but rather in the attack upon time and history. Here Cioran rejoins the radical critique of writing of which I spoke earlier. For writing is a moving image of time: every word and letter is an addition to previous writing just as—to force the parallel a little closer—every moment adds to the prior sum. Whether as writer or as man, the urge to *add to,* which Cioran identifies as the demiurge in man, is a disease, the result "of centuries of attention to time":

> Instead of letting it erode us gradually, we decided to go time one better, to add to its moments *our own.* This new time grafted onto the old one, this time elaborated and projected, soon revealed its virulence: objectivized, it became history, a monster we have called up against ourselves, a fatality we cannot escape, even by recourse to the formulas of passivity, the recipes of wisdom.

In whatever we do, or write, we are acting against ourselves by remembering, rewriting (though digressively) the tired script of history. Thus "when a writer's gifts are exhausted, it is the ineptitude of a spiritual director that comes to fill the blanks of his inspiration." Such a man then is "a spoiler suspended between speech and silence." Most writing is fraudulent, a mask for the void behind it, and the novelist, because his fictions are the most exorbitant, is "an archeologist of absence."

The greatest justice that can be done Cioran is to apply these strictures to his own writings, to let his thought think against itself. His relish for extreme statement, as I suggested earlier, is always indulged; one statement first animates, then precipitates steps towards a new statement, equally extreme—this is what Cioran himself calls "the idolatry of becoming." The essays are a biography of

movements, in the way that an oscillograph conveys a version of music that is not the music itself. To be "up against itself at last," as he claims his work to be, means that Cioran's essays instead toss about at a remove from everything they attempt to touch. . . . A victim of its own temporal fixation, Cioran's writing is reduced to a particularly energetic variety of what Roland Barthes has called writing at the zero degree.

I find it difficult therefore to agree with Susan Sontag (who has provided a set of valiant, but not always pertinent, notes as an introduction [see Further Reading list]) when she claims Cioran for the tradition of Novalis, Rilke and Kafka. On the contrary, he seems a mocking ghost of all traditions, which in effect means that he mocks all writing in some of the same ways that Jacques Derrida, for example, has closed the world of writing by treating it as *mere* writing. Even less—and here Miss Sontag curiously implies this while stating the opposite—does Cioran resemble John Cage, for whom a kind of joyous freedom, *jouissance,* underlies every one of his efforts in either prose, music, or silence. Cioran, by his own admission, is "a fanatic *without convictions,*" firmly, even hysterically, committed to the amateurism of the insoluble. His prose is perfect for what it does, and it is airless as well; like the Europe he characterizes mercilessly, the prose becomes more interesting as it masters the art of surviving itself. His highest praise is bestowed on the Jews, for they, he thinks, have always represented what in a sense his writing wishes to accomplish, "failure on the move."

Cioran is to the essay what Borges, I think, is to fiction. That is, when we read both writers we are constantly in the presence of the mask and of the apocryphal utterance, one undercutting the other, and so on until we are tired out by the unceasing game. Borges' fable and what Cioran calls "abstract autobiography" are pretexts by which, as Cioran goes on to say, the writer "can continue to cry out: 'Anything, except my truths!'" We might call this the insomniac stage of writing, and were it not for the preservation of ironic hauteur, the stage seems a needless punishment. Yet the sustained pose of such a style—detached from and yet thoroughly implicated in its revulsions—gives one pause. For after all writing has triumphed, with

> the universe reduced to the articulations of the sentence, *prose as the unique reality,* the word self-absorbed, emancipated from the object and from the world: a sonority-in-itself, cut off from the exterior, the tragic ipseity of a language bound to its own finitude.

(pp. 770-73)

*Edward W. Said, "Amateur of the Insoluble,"* in The Hudson Review, *Vol. XXI, No. 4, Winter, 1968-69, pp. 769-73.*

## L. B. Cebik

Do not read only good books. The poor and mediocre are very often far more instructive. Intrinsically, E. M. Cioran's essays in **The Temptation to Exist** are obscure, often pointless, scarcely original, and they make little contribution either to philosophy or its understanding. They display great mastery of the jargon and rhetoric of existentialism; they touch upon all the requisite subjects: the critique of societies (**"On a Winded Civilization"**), the critique of cultures (**"A People of Solitaries"**), literary criticism (**"Beyond the Novel"**), and various esoteric wonders of the realm (**"Dealing with the Mystics"**). Some of the pieces even get around to a small bit of the self-analysis from which existentialism draws its reason and strength. Mostly, however, they wander in the style of existentialism, but punctiliously evade its issues. They want the fervor of a Kierkegaard, the power of a Nietzsche, or even the cool resolve of a Camus, and most certainly show nothing of Sartre's technical skill and subtlety. They show no sign of the lesser but useful analytic skill that one finds in the works of Jean Wahl and others of his academic family. For all these failures, there are genuine insights in Cioran's meanderings, though clearly all of them can be found verbatim in the writers so far mentioned, who are surely Cioran's masters, and in the medieval and reformation introspectivists, whom the twentieth century existentials take as soul mates.

Nevertheless, reading Cioran is instructive, perhaps even enlightening. Through him one can see the thorns which plagued his masters: betrayed subjectivity and resentful mediocrity. These are not so much harsh as useful judgments. Indeed, by every standard of a certain school of European and American intellectualism, Cioran's essays . . . are competent and perhaps laudable works. Through Cioran, the entire school appears. "I have no nationality," writes Cioran for the record, "the best possible status for an intellectual." His comrades-in-pens-and-typewriters must envy him the natural alienation, for it seems (and *seems* alone) to allow Cioran his commitment to ethical, political, social, and human non-commitment, his vacuous intellectualism. He suffers, and loves the suffering. His writing consequently is but a wallowing in self-stopping conflicts, the continual generation of the artificial *angst* necessary to his existence. Thus, he can rail at a now defunct hegelianism (we now call it marxism) as so many exercises in futility, because masters Kierkegaard and Nietzsche have done so, but he cannot see—he must not let himself see—that his own masters would dismiss him as more vile than the Eden asp. He seeks to seduce; he seeks (or pretends to seek) existential essences and wonders, and suffers, joyously at the impossible task.

To catch the culprit and thereby the entire genre of which Cioran is a distinctive representative, one must be on the lookout for the tell-tale signs. For example . . . "One always perishes by the self one assumes": note the word "assumes" and the absence of that dangerous and arduous task of becoming a self; mediocrity of intellect is often concommitant with laziness of soul. Not to suffer, says Cioran, is bad faith: again and again this appears, as if existence were pure suffering and never a suffering for. He rejects the "Cult of Truth" and attacks Voltaire for having only a half-knowledge; the contradiction suggests that what he actually hates is Voltaire's piercing and sarcastic acumen, his ability to see through shoddy intellectualization to the shoddy intellect. Voltaire, in the proper sense, *offends* Cioran, and the latter, interestingly enough, never uses this powerful existential category. Like Camus in *The*

*Fall*, Cioran disclaims the right to impose his convictions, but he proclaims, "the same is not true of my vacillations." Unlike Camus, for whom *The Fall* was but a first step to his work, Cioran is content to impose his own problem (if it is one); he does not want—he has vested interest in not wanting—to resolve it. Resolution would require a non-cognitive, non-intellectual act which would rob him of his comfortable status. Of course (we can almost read the whimper), the fault lies not with him, but rather with the age: health lies in the past. General bad health of the age accounts for our suffering, but makes it not so pressing a difficulty as needs resolution.

Cioran is threatened by novels, which he cannot write (he lacks an eye for people and the concrete), the Jews, which he cannot understand (same reason), and Being, for which he lacks the strength, will and rigor. He rests content in his pseudo-nothingness, in a purely negative existence. He knows from Nietzsche (poorly understood as a "sum of attitudes") to rail at "the obsession with system"; yet, logically he demands system. Success—the destruction of system—would be his own demise, the end of his work of generating paradox out of system. He dismisses discipline as merely a "submission to style," playing upon the ambiguity of the word (form without content and a "life style" which *is* content) to elude the problem. He generalizes— "the history of ideas is no more than a parade of labels converted into so many absolutes"—where only the particular, the narrowly circumscribed would be true or useful. He hates Paul as a traitor, perhaps because of all men Paul took on a new existence and knew his philosophy was only the shallowest excuse to lure men into what lay underneath. Paul offends the intellectual and arouses the *ressentiment* which Nietzsche despised and which Cioran exemplifies. Cioran goes so far as to defend self-pity as concealing strength. Pretension: that he can recognize "the naturally troubled soul," the categorically invisible. High pretension: that "reality itself remains, immobilized by my doubts." Supreme pretension: "to dissolve myself in Being" when he can talk about it.

The form, the rhetoric, the style: all is there save the content, the honest wrestling with genuine problems until either they give way to the force of will or they command complete and necessary resignation. One cannot help feeling that Cioran wants his empty self-sophistry. (pp. 400-02)

As a piece of philosophic illumination [***The Temptation to Exist***] holds little value. The value it has for the reader's own self-reflection will be proportional to the effort and honesty put into it. (p. 402)

*L. B. Cebik, in a review of "The Temptation to Exist," in* The Georgia Review, *Vol. XXIII, No. 3, Fall, 1969, pp. 400-02.*

## Charles Newman

To say that Cioran is a paradox would be only a half-truth. He is ambivalent even about the possibility of being self-contradictory, profoundly skeptical of irony itself. Nevertheless, he is, crabwise, on the attack. The obsessive theme of these interrelated essays [in ***The Fall into Time***] . . . is his revulsion against fashionable despair, that democratic access to bathos and absurdity which serves as the intellectual superstructure of our time.

Stop anyone over twelve on the street today and on a moment's notice he can provide a Spenglerian theory of our decline; any housewife can chart her loneliness in the grand tradition of Kafka and Kierkegaard. We have become proud of our pessimism, elevated our melancholy to the status of a metaphysic. Cioran's diagnosis is that while contemporary man has managed to begin "dying on his own," his pride is such that he cannot even sense the humiliation of the enterprise. Man is the only animal who can endure any metamorphosis by putatively *explaining* it, justify any loss without understanding its implications. This would be an incredible spectacle were there anyone else to watch it. As it stands, the Apocalypse becomes only another occasion for self-congratulation and theorizing; the *Angst* of our time, only the newest form of hubris.

It is the clichés of despair, the banality of the abyss which fuel Cioran's withering indifference. The progressive disrealization of the world which began in the Renaissance is for him an unutterable tragedy, a matter to be savored by an elitist of suffering, not popularized as the latest accessory to bourgeois idealism. The split between sensation and thinking is not a "frame of reference," a problem to be solved by "interdisciplinary studies," but an insomniacal agony, the very articulation of which only redoubles and regenerates our pain. In those few instances in which Cioran drops his lofty detachment, becomes an active complainer, he echoes [Antonin] Artaud: "All I ask is to feel my brain."

One can best understand Cioran as a phenomenon of the French language, as distinct from French culture, and French literary culture in particular. While he may be sloppily assigned to those long if thinning ranks of Pascalian skeptics or contemporary "existential" thinkers, his achievement lies in the repudiation of such influences—or, more precisely, in carrying the premises of their relativism to a logical if outrageous conclusion. Since Cioran does not engage in specific polemic nor acknowledge by name any other living writer, one can only imagine the extent of his contempt for the "committed" literature of a Sartre, for the systematic and relentless attempt to *justify* the duality of being and nonbeing, for the entire enterprise of attempting to resolve the ambiguities of literature and life. Similarly, one can see him jeering at the plight of Camus' Sisyphus, or for that matter at any other of those humorless existential trade unionists who compound their incompetence with stoicism, pit their solipsism against determinism and call it dignity. These "heroic" poses represent for Cioran only the latest revenge of the intellect against itself and confirm the loss of our best instincts. "To be human is no solution," as he says, "any more than ceasing to be so."

For Cioran, ontology itself is a specious problem, even an "ontology of nothingness," to use Michel Foucault's phrase, since reports of "the void" tend to be just as unverifiable as those about what we "know." There is nothing particularly affirmative about acknowledging the negative. Just because we hate ourselves, he observes apropos of Tolstoy, does not mean we still are not living a lie. The realization of "nothingness" is one thing—like going into a room and reporting that "nothing was there"—but one cannot begin at the beginning of nothingness any more than one can start at the beginning of any learning process; one cannot make assertions about language or nature from a hypothetical vantage point outside them. . . . (pp. 9-12)

The central concern of *The Temptation to Exist* . . . was to confirm the total disjunction between language and reality. That work represents a kind of final assault on the typology which has formed the basis of Western thought—the notion that the physical world embodies signs of metaphysical reality; and, more, that if human intelligence is pure, it can define these correspondences through language. "The works of God" as Jonathan Edwards had it, "are but a kind of voice or language to instruct beings in things pertaining to himself . . . wherever we are, and whatever we are about, we may see divine things excellently represented . . . *and* it will abundantly tend to confirm the Scriptures, for there is an excellent agreement between these things and the Scripture."

But for Cioran, language is a sticky symbolic net, an infinite regression from things cutting men off from the world, as they once cut themselves off from God; and so, to scramble the metaphor, humans are no more than shadows who project their images upon the mirror of infinity. ("A shadow grappling with images, a somnambulist who *sees himself* walking . . . ") What Edwards called the "images or shadows of divine things," Cioran would rearrange as 'divined images by shadows of no things.' This conclusion of *The Temptation to Exist* becomes the working hypothesis of *The Fall into Time.* Nothing divine, only the divined: language, insofar as it can reorient our behavior, perhaps slows the death of the species; but at the same time, in increasing our endless analogies for experience, it prevents us from being fully alive to ourselves. Neutralized by our uniqueness, we become incapable of capitalizing even on what sets us apart from the animals—our capacity for indifference. Style *is* the man—unfortunately for us. As Cioran puts it: "Consciousness is not lucidity. Lucidity, man's monopoly, represents the severance process between the mind and the world; it is necessarily consciousness of consciousness, and if we are to distinguish ourselves from the animals, it is lucidity alone which must receive the credit or the blame." (pp. 12-13)

Cioran would be appalled if anyone accused him of originality in thought, which would not be necessarily desirable even if it were possible. What *is* original is his personalization of these ideas through his style:

> Every idolatry of style starts from the belief that reality is even more hollow than its verbal figuration, that the accent of an idea is worth more than the idea, a well-turned excuse more than a conviction, a skillful image more than an unconsidered explosion. . . . A well-proportioned sentence, satisfied with its equilibrium or swollen with its sonority, all too often conceals the *malaise* of a mind incapable of acceding by *sensation* to an original universe. What is surprising if style should be simultaneously a mask and an admission?

French, that pluperfect language, is the perfect vehicle for Cioran, whose thought is circuitous without being tautological, whose circumvolved syntax can gather a point and discharge it in the same phrase. (p. 14)

While nothing in *The Fall into Time* offers as much of a lyrical *tour de force* as the essays **"A People of Solitaries"** or **"Beyond the Novel"** in *The Temptation to Exist, The Fall* represents an even more advanced process of compression, one might even say asphyxiation. The more Cioran attacks rationality, the more pellucid he becomes. There are no transitions, no breathing spaces between these paragraphs, no hiatus in these gnomic sentences, so classic in their density, yet touched with baroque recapitulations which heighten not the harmony but the irony. The book should end with a blank signature to hold the air that has been extruded from the text.

It is not difficult to translate Cioran's ideas, for their apothegmatic arrangement lends itself to facile reconstruction. The temptation is to *cease* his momentum, grasp him by the aphorism, make him into a kind of Gallic Oscar Wilde. The problem is to capture his complexity as well as his precision, both the acceleration and aphasia of his cyclic cadences, and this is the particular triumph of Richard Howard's translation. It is the decisiveness of Cioran's style which both accentuates and gives the lie to the ambivalence of his message; it is a style which does not embody his thoughts as much as it exemplifies the consequences of his thought. As Edward Said has pointed out [see excerpt above], Cioran is to the essay what Borges is to fiction.

For Cioran, sterility itself becomes a strategy. His method is calculated to defy introduction, his individual works serve to undermine his *oeuvre*. The parts are always more than the whole. But at the same time he infects us with what he insists is man's worst impulse—to append, explain, refute, to *add* to—to take language as seriously as we might take life were we abler. Other writers cry out for attention; one reads Cioran to be rid of him. One writes in order to ignore him. One is "fair" to him at one's peril. For his attenuation and ascesis demand that *we* justify those impure energies which activate our willingness to account for him, to put him *in context*—for in doing so, we confess our inability to take him at his word, becoming one of that "throng of readers, those omnipresent and invisible murderers." (pp. 14-16)

It is easy to understand why Cioran has been so uniformly ignored—his impossibilist vocabulary, his library of books which no one else has read, the cold elegance of his aphoristic syntax, his hatred for the present which makes liberals think he is a reactionary, the insistent *isolato* voice which makes conservatives think he is an anarchist, the effortless erudition which gains him the suspicion of scholars, the astringent elitism which can only put the wider audience he deserves hopelessly on the defensive. Too tough-minded to be considered tragic, too funny to be a true terrorist, the barbarian appears on the rim of the Carpathians to preside at the death of a civilization, only to be "civilized" in spite of himself, a redundant eremite, a specialist in the last gasp.

Given Cioran's enormous efforts to repudiate writing as a career, the contemporary reader may tend to underestimate what is most striking about his accomplishment. For the most difficult task for the writer is not how to "make a living," to ignore both insult and loneliness, but how to survive one's "circle," one's own supportive contemporaries. While most of the intelligentsia of Cioran's Sixth Arrondissement in the late '30's and '40's have long since repaired to their respective ministries of culture and/or ceased writing altogether, we still receive terse messages from one who has *stayed put*, made a profession of not being for sale, had the strength to let his talent mature at its own pace. (Cioran was thirty-six before he even decided to write in French.) As Edward Dahlberg, the only living writer I know of who has affinities with Cioran, says: "I don't think we write for anybody, just like we die for nobody . . . every time we compose a good line, a forest springs up in our hearts." Cioran could only concur with an imperceptible nod. Neither of them can forgive a society in which hermeticism is the only possible honesty. (pp. 24-5)

[Cioran] knows he could have become a great mystic—a connoisseur of that last frontier for Western will—for then his disdain of attention could have been given the texture of a tradition. But as much as he admires the vegetable, he knows we are incapable of surfeiting ourselves, even with pain. Western man is de-natured, and can only work himself back, not to *his* God, but His condition: "Amid his seamless hebetude, a single thought still agonizes [man]. . . . What did God do when he did nothing? How did He spend, before the Creation, His terrible leisure? . . . I was, I am, I will be, me is a question of grammar and not of existence."

Perhaps Cioran adopts the pose of a man without influence, since his own writing seems so totally without influences. Certainly, he can be best defined in terms of what he has *bypassed*. What other twentieth-century thinker is so untouched by either Marx or Freud? Partially, this is due to his assault on determinism—economic, erotic, or existential. It would be clearly preferable, he would say, to deny our freedom, that ugly knowledge that our paralysis is self-inflicted, or to adopt some utopian view of the past or an apocalyptic future. Then we could exist by either renouncing ourselves or denouncing our enemies. But the trick, in every sense, is to will "just enough to live," since our choice is between "impassivity and imposture," and though the finest thing about us is our rage, direct repudiation implies a "complicity with certainty," and as such denies our condition.

Reformist critiques of society, then, degenerate into equally profane analyses, instances only of our genius for turning back on ourselves—Marxism merely an involuted example of what capitalist societies have done to "backward" cultures. "The civilized man . . . in order to push them there . . . will inoculate them with the poison of anxiety and release them only when he has observed in them the same symptoms of haste as in himself." Cast by knowledge into time, it becomes doubly impossible for us to imagine a present; the future becomes only something to be remembered, "the past that is to come." No system, more than any man, is immune to the deceptions of technology, and our inhuman means of production are the consequence, not the cause, of our condition.

As for psychoanalysis, that "sadistic therapeutics . . . singularly expert in the art of substituting, for our naive discomforts, an intricate variety," why should we expect any more from health than from history since our will ejects us from both? If man is the unhappy animal because he asks himself too many questions, then of what use is that most interrogative of sciences? The promise of less anxiety is as dubious as that of more leisure. Our sickness, after all, is our only common bond; suffering, the created consciousness of the race. If we are defined by fear, then neither Marx or Freud can allay it, since the one offers a fall back into history to "encounter oneself"; the other, a retreat into the self to divine history. Our organism cannot be adapted to either, for in an "explained universe, nothing would still have a meaning but madness itself."

The problem is dictated neither by culture nor personality but by language. . . . Language, that which "outlives itself," is what prevents us from going beyond the boundaries of the self. This is Cioran's chant of shame. The poison of individualism has been with us from the beginning, and we must acknowledge our pain and sickness since they are the very preconditions of our consciousness. There is no going back to a pre-linguistic paradise, to a supremacy over time based upon some primordial stupidity, any more than we can decay into a future McLuhanite garden of undifferentiated consciousness, an apotheosis of silence where we can treat our wordlessness as innocence. And the writer's only dignity is that he should know this better than anyone, that in his banishment he stands for all men. Small consolation. "Our opinions are tumors which destroy the integrity of our nature and nature itself." (pp. 26-9)

Cioran is clearly a self-styled straddler of the modern and post-modern eras. In his rigor, his erudition, his hatred of the dissolution of language, his formalism which constitutes its own morality, he is a legitimate heir to the great European modernists. But whereas the modernists never doubted their capacity to construct imaginary edifices against a world which revolted them, the post-modern era is characterized by a revulsion against our very means and materials, a hatred of our minds coextensive with our hatred for what passes for the world. Cioran stands for us, then, as that rarest of thinkers—a crucial transitional figure who occupies not a place so much as a synapse in the devolution of Western thought. As Wilde, another more frivolous son of Nietzsche has elaborated, some critics might prefer to *explain* ideas, but the task is really to "deepen their mystery," combat one's doubts and certitudes with equal energy.

Cioran would agree with the Structuralists that language can be reduced to formal models which have no universal or synthetic consequences. Further, he would agree that words cut us off from our origins and have no direct instrumental relation to the world. But Cioran would also insist that professional detachment, literary or otherwise, is no cure for alienation. Exposing one's ignorance and limitations cannot be justified as either scientific or thera-

peutic. The absurd is not the amusing theater we have made it. If we insist on converting even our terror into constructive entertainment, then we shall have truly lost everything, consigned ourselves to that "wrong eternity."

The only thing, it would seem, that Cioran does not comprehend, or at least has not yet bothered to articulate, is his own delight in language in spite of himself, his obsession to *become* what he writes, the necessity to write "in order," as Le Clezio says, "to conquer the silence of other languages." For while he has perhaps succeeded in "falling out of time," he has failed to reach that Archimedean point, that privileged position outside of language "external to the world and to himself."

It is here that we must either confess with Pascal and Rousseau that we are trapped within language and dignify silence as the only nobility, or reassert our faith in the very plasticity of life, in its metalinguistic possibilities, as did Nietzsche and William James. In Cioran's words: "To realize oneself is to dedicate oneself to the intoxication of multiplicity." This is the duality which Cioran offers, and while he explicitly argues for Rousseau's penultimate silence, his conduct is contradictory, and marvelously so. For in the same gesture by which he denies himself existence, he affirms the power of speech, and this is the paradox which is, even for him, finally unassimilable.

It is true that we "live" in a circle of language, but it is simply a matter of rhetoric (which is to say free choice) whether we choose to describe that circle as vicious or magical. To assert either at the expense of the other, Cioran would pronounce absurd, but he is subtle enough to know that

> To produce, to create . . . is to have the courage or the luck not to perceive the lie of diversity, the deceptive character of the multiple . . . to produce a work is to espouse all those incompatibilities, all those fictive oppositions so dear to restless minds. More than anyone, the writer knows what he owes to these semblances, these deceptions, and should be aware of becoming indifferent to them. If he neglects or denounces them, he cuts the ground from his own feet . . . if he turns to the absolute, what he finds there will be, at best, a delectation in stupor. . . .

That point at which we cease thinking *about* language and willfully make best use of it—"anyone who is carried away by his reasoning *forgets* that he is using reason, and this forgetting is the condition of all creative thought . . . "—that is the point at which the critic becomes the artist, and Cioran has had both the "courage" and the "luck" to do so. (pp. 29-32)

*Charles Newman, in an introduction to* The Fall into Time *by E. M. Cioran, translated by Richard Howard, Quadrangle Books, 1970, pp. 9-32.*

### W. H. Auden

*The Fall into Time* can and, I think, should be read simultaneously in at least two ways, perhaps more. It can be read seriously as a sermon by a latter-day Jeremiah (it is not an accident, surely, that M. Cioran is the son of a Greek Orthodox priest) about The Fall of Man, a passionate denunciation of the mess he has made of his life, a condition which, the preacher says, is better accounted for by theology than by biology.

In listening to such a sermon, one naturally expects some exaggeration; if we are to be roused from our sloth and flattering illusions, the picture must be painted as black as possible. Man, says this preacher, is "an episode, a digression, a heresy, a kill-joy, a wastrel, a miscreant who has complicated everything." Consciousness is an evil, "the quintessence of decrepitude." Knowledge is an evil: "The more we yield to the desire to know, stamped as it is with perversity and corruption, the more incapable we become of remaining *inside* some reality, any reality." Language is an evil: "[Man] will never approach life's inviolate sources if he still has dealings with words."

The preacher, however, is in the anomalous position, of which M. Cioran, I'm sure, is well aware, of being unable to practice what he preaches. To denounce consciousness, he must appeal to the conscious minds of his audience; to denounce knowledge is to claim that he *knows* it is evil; to denounce language he has to use words. Chesterton wrote: "If it is not true that a divine being fell, then one can only say that one of the animals went entirely off its head." To understand Man, that is, individual men must share his madness. So M. Cioran says of one of his forerunners, Nietzsche: "We owe the diagnosis of our disease to a lunatic, more contaminated and scarred than any of us, to an avowed maniac, precursor and model of our own delirium."

M. Cioran, himself, however, is certainly sane by ordinary standards. Only now and again does he say something which, to me, seems crazy. I do not believe that he is a Manichaean, but occasionally he makes remarks which make him sound like one, as when he suggests that God fell when He created the Universe, or when he declares: "No one recovers from the disease of being born, a deadly wound if ever there was one." Then he says that, while everybody's secret wish is to be praised, which is true, we are all ashamed to admit it, which is, surely, false, though, of course, we want to be praised for the right reasons.

For the most part, however, M. Cioran carries me along with him. On the mental triad, Faith or Belief, Doubt, and Denial, he has fascinating things to say. Without beliefs of some kind, we cannot really live, far less act.

> Anyone who cherishes the equilibrium of his mind will avoid attacking certain essential superstitions. This is a vital necessity for thinking, despised only by the skeptic who, having nothing to preserve, respects neither the secrets nor the tabus indispensable to the duration of certitudes. . . .
> Skepticism has against it our reflexes, our appetites, our instincts. For all its declarations that being is a prejudice, this prejudice, older than ourselves, outdates man and life, resists our attacks, withstands reasoning and proof, since it is also true that whatever exists and manifests itself in duration is based on the undemonstrable and the unverifiable.

The capacity to affirm or believe proceeds, says M. Cioran, from "a depth of barbarism which the majority, which virtually the totality of men have the good fortune to preserve. . . ."

The term "barbarism" obviously has shock value, but I suspect there may be another reason why he uses it. He writes in French, and the French language has no equivalent to the English term "common sense." (*"Bon sense"* is not the same thing.)

M. Cioran distinguishes between two kinds of skeptic, the "pure" skeptic or Negator, and the Doubter. The negator is not really seeking for truth, his goal is endless interrogation and he rarely calls the act of negation in question. The doubter, on the other hand, frequently calls doubt into question.

> The drama of the doubter is greater than that of the negator, because to live without a goal is more difficult than to live for a bad cause.

But to regard M. Cioran solemnly as a preacher is not the only way of reading him. He can also be read playfully as a master of language who is having enormous fun handling words. In his most intelligent Introduction, Mr. Charles Newman speaks of the temptation to grasp M. Cioran by the aphorism, "to make him into a kind of Gallic Oscar Wilde." Provided one realizes that he is not simply that, I think it is a perfectly legitimate way of reading him.

He has said that all his books are autobiographical, but no writer could be less "confessional." He tells us that a man in good health is always disappointing, but I suspect his own health is good. I hope so, for his sake, since, if it is not, then by his own judgment he is a sadist. He says that, if only there were more boasters and flatterers around, the psychiatrist would be out of a job, but I'm pretty sure he indulges in neither activity. He declares that we should be better off if we were verminous like the animals and smelled of the stable, but I should be surprised to hear that he never takes a bath. He condemns lucidity:

> Consciousness is not lucidity. Lucidity, man's monopoly, represents the severance of consciousness: it is necessarily consciousness of consciousness, and, if we are to distinguish ourselves from the animals, it is lucidity alone which must receive the credit or the blame.

Yet the first thing one notices about these two sentences, or any others by M. Cioran, is how "lucid" they are. Never, in reading him, does one encounter, as one often does when reading Hegel or Heidegger, sentences which make one exclaim: "What the heck does this mean?" For me, the two most interesting authors writing in French who have emerged since the last war are M. Cioran and M. Malcolm de Chazal, both of them aphorists, a literary device which always gives me joy. When, for instance, I read

> He who has never envied the vegetable has missed the human drama

or

> Resign from the race? That would be to forget

that one is never so much a man as when one re-grets being so

they make me feel anything but gloomy.

*W. H. Auden, "The Anomalous Creature," in*
The New York Review of Books, *Vol. XVI,
No. 1, January 28, 1971, p. 20.*

## Peter Caws

[E. M. Cioran] is a brilliant and original exponent of a rare genre, the philosophical essay. The taste for such writing, and especially for Cioran's, can for most of us only be an acquired one, but it is well worth acquiring. Quite apart from the inherent satisfaction of encountering a genuine style, Cioran offers a form of intellectual experience that helps to balance the preoccupations of an uneasy time.

His titles are the first indication of the complex and quizzical attitude he takes toward the world. *The Temptation to Exist* was first published in France in 1956, at the tail-end of the popularity of existentialism and was published here in 1968; the phrase may be read as a commentary, as well as having a straightforward meaning when its terms are understood. What Cioran means by "exist" is best indicated by his use of it: "Carpathian shepherds have made a much deeper impression on me than the professors of Germany, the wits of Paris. I have seen Spanish beggars, and I should like to have been their hagiographer. They had no need to invent a life for themselves: they *existed;* which does not happen in civilization." Temptation, on the other hand, is what the saints suffered, against which they developed the practice of *askesis,* or spiritual exercise; they came to love their temptations, without which the exercises would no longer have made sense.

So Cioran, trapped—as we all are—in the inauthenticities of civilization and of language, represents to himself the authenticity of barbarism and of silence (the beggars, the shepherds) as a genuinely desirable state; and yet to relapse into it, into pure existence, would deprive him of the acute consciousness of his condition which is the object of his own *askesis.* Whatever the truth of that condition, even if it involves witnessing the disintegration of the Western World, he cannot renounce the satisfaction that comes from being aware—and being aware that he is aware—of the historical situation, of the character of men and of nations. Nor can he resist a second temptation, to write, even though he claims to hate his actions—and clearly savors the paradox this involves.

So the temptations are fortunate, and so—but not for the usual reasons—is the Fall. If God had had better foresight, the Fall might never have occurred: "No sooner had Adam tasted the forbidden fruit than God, understanding at last whom He was dealing with, lost His head. By putting the Tree of Knowledge in the middle of the Garden, by boasting of its merits, and especially its dangers, He had committed a grave imprudence, had anticipated his creature's innermost desire." The Fall was responsible for the gift of self-awareness Cioran so much values; it made history possible. "Cast by knowledge into time, we were thereby endowed with a destiny." *The Fall into Time* is

a meditation on the course of human history, which has, as Cioran sees it, produced not the slightest improvement in man's lot.

*The Temptation to Exist* is made up of shorter pieces, on Western civilization, on the Jews, on the writer, on the novel, on mystics and apostles and philosophers, all with Cioran's special brand of ambiguity, his taste for the indirect and the inverted. He comes to the defense of Judas ("He dreamed of equaling Jesus, of counterbalancing him in evil; in good, with such a competitor, there was no way for Judas to distinguish himself "), he excoriates St. Paul ("Accountable for our religious and ethical prejudices, he has determined the norms of our stupidity"). He is above all self-possessed, whether in amusement or anger.

The business of presenting Cioran to an English-speaking public has involved three other people, all with literary reputations of their own. Richard Howard's translations are superlatively good, so good that Cioran at once acquires a character in English, not spoiled by any intrusion of strangeness. A Rumanian by birth, he made a conscious decision, as an exile in Paris at the age of 36, to write in French. The self-discipline in which this involved him made him acutely aware of his writing, and this awareness pervades it and gives it an implicit double structure; to have brought this over into English is an accomplishment for which Mr. Howard cannot be too highly praised.

Susan Sontag and Charles Newman have contributed prefaces to *The Temptation to Exist* and *The Fall into Time* respectively. While Mr. Newman's essay, with its unnervingly appropriate epigraphs from Artaud, stands in its own right as a piece of critical literature worth reading alongside Cioran, Miss Sontag's should on no account be read until afterwards, if then. Only when Cioran has been absorbed can it be seen just how misleading her treatment of him is.

One has to be in the mood for Cioran, willing to suspend a certain critical attitude in order to see through his eyes. These philosophical essays are not after all essays in philosophy—they are at once too assertive and too casual. That is why the comparison with Nietzsche and Wittgenstein is so ludicrous: Cioran has none of Nietzsche's moral passion or concern for the future, none of Wittgenstein's painstaking care for distinctions of meaning.

"All my books," he says, "are more or less autobiographical—a rather abstract form of biography, I admit"; their value lies in their being the autobiography of a man whose sensibilities are more highly developed than and far in advance of our own. "In advance" relatively speaking—we may not think it either desirable or necessary to follow or agree with Cioran, we may not even like him much; he tends to overdo his detachment, his style may come to seem too rich, we may not wish to be distracted for long from our own less reflective involvement in the world.

But once read, Cioran cannot fail to provoke reflection; in fact, he insistently demands it. And that, given the usual pace of our lives, is no small service.

*Peter Caws, "When Adam Ate the Apple, God*

*Lost His Head," in* The New York Times
Book Review, *March 14, 1971, p. 28.*

## George Woodcock

France has a long history of philosophers who proceed by
self-analysis, psychological explorers who inevitably find,
as Cioran remarks, that they "cannot believe we are free
when we are always with ourselves, facing ourselves, *the
same.*" It is the condition of those who have, as the book's
title suggests [*The Fall into Time*], "fallen out of time."
For the earlier representatives of this tradition, there was
an escape route—albeit a narrow and perilous one—
toward eternity. Pascal followed it; so, more stumblingly,
did Maine de Biran.

Cioran treats God as a historic figure (though there are
times when one suspects him of giving grudging acknowledgment to a living Devil) and recognizes that Paradise is
receding with every step of progress. Thus his solution is
a passionate stoicism, a misanthropy—for who but Man
have men a right to despise—whose roots stem from a love
that pride is reluctant to lay bare.

He is not a systematic philosopher, and the critic who
tried to order his thought would be falling into a trap Cioran has thoughtfully prepared. He is less a metaphysician
than an introspective moralist, using the peculiar rhetoric
that has become almost mandatory in France for writers
of this kind. Occasionally he uses it hypnotically, like Malraux, or Camus at his rare worst, and the reader suddenly
awakens to find himself carried on a surge of grand abstractions that leave him wondering just where meaning
vanished.

Most often, however, Cioran manages the style with consummate agility, juggling its parentheses and paradoxes
with a grace and an irony assisted—in this edition—by a
sensitive translator: "And man, the weak and inadaptable
animal *par excellence,* finds his prerogative and his catastrophe in undertaking tasks incommensurable with his
powers, falling a victim to will, stigma of his imperfection,
the sure means of affirming himself and of coming to
nothing. . . . "

Cioran's prose is much too concise and aphoristic for
paraphrase; each of his parenthetical clauses adds a nuance of meaning. And it is as difficult to classify him as
it is to summarize him.

He is the reverse of an optimist. At times he seems to suggest that hope vanished for humanity with the triumph of
literacy. Man's "capacity to degenerate," he says, "is lim-
itless." Yet one cannot call him a pessimist, for he tells
also of the ways man can defy and evade the despoilment
that the loss of eternity and the extremity of wisdom have
brought upon him.

Cioran attacks and probes and criticizes constantly, baring our—or his—shamefulness in its most intimate forms;
he cries out against civilization, declaring that the "vestiges of humanity are still to be found only among the peoples who, outdistanced by history, are in no hurry to catch
up"; and, viewing the swelling populations of the world,
he asserts that "interchangeable, they justify by their num-

ber the aversion they inspire." One welcomes the scourg-
ing voice of the minatory prophet, only to perceive the
compassion of this despiser of Man—but perhaps not of
men—who can write with exemplary subtlety an essay
**"On Sickness"** that analyzes the function of pain as an element giving meaning to existence.

It is even hard to maintain the label of skeptic that often
seems appropriate to Cioran. For there is a difference between the true skeptic and the man who can say, "I become aware of myself, indeed I *am,* only when I deny."
Possibly the most striking essay in **The Fall into Time** is
**"Skeptic and Barbarian,"** the least personal and most historical piece in the book. Here Cioran analyzes the way
doubt weakens the spirit of cultures as well as the resolve
of individuals. Where the skeptic triumphs, he suggests,
the barbarian will always follow.

While Cioran carefully avoids drawing the moral in terms
of contemporary situations, a reader would have to be insensitive to the issues of the day not to name in his mind
the personalities to whom a statement such as this one applies: "Since the virtues of barbarians consist precisely in
the power of taking sides, of affirming or denying, they
will always be celebrated by declining periods. The nostalgia for barbarism is the last word of a civilization; and
thereby of skepticism." The skeptic who turns himself into
"a friend and accomplice of the hordes" is too evidently
among us for Cioran's warning to be without point or
value. That it is given outside history, outside the context
of our time, simply adds to its urgency.

Cioran has lived in the Thebaid of the perpetually self-
examining moralists. When such eremites, tempered by
solitude, appear in the city, we can only listen. They do
not ask us to act, but merely to question ourselves. (pp.
22-3)

*George Woodcock, "Combating Wisdom," in*
The New Leader, *Vol. LIV, No. 6, March 22,
1971, pp. 22-3.*

## David Bromwich

Called in French *Le mauvais démiurge, The New Gods* is
the third of his works to be translated and it has the
charm, vigor and fearlessness of the other volumes in his
"philosophical romance." One must admire an author like
Cioran and also, perhaps, dread him a little. He is the sub-
tlest living gazer into the abyss. His great subject of meditation has been the passage of mankind "from logic to epilepsy."

To write in a foreign language as Cioran writes in French
is to be shut out from certain temptations. Lucidity becomes the chief order of business. Quite possibly Cioran's
asceticism began as an effect of his style; he dislikes elegance of the approved variety, and prefers whatever is
odd. "From logic to epilepsy." The phrase might easily
come from Dostoevsky, Nietzsche, Baudelaire, Cioran's
patron saints of the 19th century. But they were at best im-
provising from a dark text, whereas Cioran is a consistent
and, when he can manage it without irony, a wholly convinced nihilist: "Thought is destruction in its essence.

More precisely: in its *principle.* You think, you begin to think, in order to break bonds, to dissolve affinities, to compromise the scaffolding of the 'real.' " That philosophy is truest which most cheerfully annihilates itself.

Self-consciousness, with its endless trek back to ground zero, dictates the form and content of everything Cioran writes. The habit of inversion has bred in him a notable facility for the aphorism, and hardly a sentence in *The New Gods* is without its small cue of astonishment. Thus, in **"Paleontology,"** which is about old bones in a museum of natural history: "I suspect that I would never have returned—in flesh or in spirit—so often to those premises if, evidently, they hadn't flattered my incapacity for illusion." One notices how, like fossil-words brought to life, "incapacity" and "flattered" perform a contrary dance around each other, first rewarding the narrator for his insight and then rapping him smartly for his conceit.

**"Encounters with Suicide,"** the finest essay in the book, offers a jagged image of life on the edge of things: "This passion in the middle of the night, this insistence on a final explanation with yourself, with the elements." The thought of death revives you even as it sets you to rest and, though you tremble, you walk on and "your blood seethes." ("You" for Cioran is almost always first person singular.) Only after the decision has been reached

> comes the reassuring impression which the absence of others inspires: everyone else is asleep. How to abandon a world in which you can still be alone? This night, which was to be the last, is the one you cannot part with, you do not conceive that it might be eliminated. And you would like to defend it against the day which undermines and soon submerges it.

Cioran speaks with the authority of a survivor. And for all his avowed misanthropy—he is "crabby by divine decree"—his alacrity in the unlovely job of thinking against himself is surely tonic. He is free of the small arbitrary prejudices which can discredit a prophet at home or away, and if he lays himself open to attack, it is on the ground of temperament: that his cast of characters, humanity as a whole, is too large; or perhaps that the mood which has to support the cast is psychologically too narrow.

"The moralist's primordial duty," Cioran writes, "is to depoeticize his prose; only then, to observe men." It may be said that he discharges the second of these duties admirably and the first with irregular success. Despite its idiosyncrasy his prose is often, if not poetic, at least artfully dramatizing. Yet self-consciousness is the modern disease, quite distinctively so, and meditation of this kind, precisely because of its self-regarding posture, can prevent it from becoming an ease. At times, like a character in Dostoevsky whom he must have studied, Cioran has the air of gently saluting and conversing with every bearer of bad tidings: Will you have some tea, Stavrogin?

> *David Bromwich, "Gazing Into the Abyss," in* The New York Times Book Review, *January 19, 1975, p. 24.*

## Edward Marcotte

The six essays contained in *The New Gods* range over all of Cioran's major themes: the price of knowledge, the infirmity of flesh, death, mysticism, terror, false attachments. **"Encounters with Suicide"** is a much more intimate investigation of this taboo subject than Camus's well-known posing of the question. **"The Undelivered"** considers the mystic's quest. **"The Demiurge"** is a meditation on our obsession with God; **"Strangled Thoughts"** a series of brief, disconnected paragraphs marked by rage, indignation, irony. **"The New Gods"** follows a more coherent argument than the other essays: relative advantages of polytheism over monotheism. **"Paleontology"** is a reflection on decay and death occasioned by a visit to a museum—a confrontation with "those empty sockets that stare at you more insistently than eyes, that rummage sale of skulls, that automatic sneer on every level of zoology."

In a time when practically everything is accepted, E.M. Cioran seems a likely candidate for unacceptability. Were he an American writing in English, Cioran might have a hard time getting his essays published in literary quarterlies, no philosophical journal would have him, and it may not be too far-fetched to picture him resorting to a vanity press. Though he is one of the outstanding thinkers writing today in the loose, personal tradition of Montaigne, Pascal, Kierkegaard, Nietzsche and Thoreau—touching on deeply spiritual matters from a nonpartisan, nonacademic, nontechnical viewpoint—his audience is not large. "Only the writer without a public," he remarks, "can allow himself the luxury of being sincere." . . .

[Cioran's] writing is endlessly quotable, phenomenally witty, entertaining, lucid. The pleasure of reading Cioran makes his relative neglect even more of a paradox. It may be that we are tired of hearing many of the things he has to say. He is often compared to Nietzsche, for example, and indeed resembles him in many ways. Another matter is Cioran's extreme darkness and cynicism. He should be ranked with the great pessimists and cynics of all time, a successor to Diogenes, Voltaire, Schopenhauer. A Swiftian misanthrope, he writes, "Let us block the way of all flesh. . . . " (p. 377)

Cioran takes a fanatical pleasure in reiterating with ever deepened insight and precision the horrors of existence, the traps of knowledge, consciousness and ego; yet he offers no program for deliverance. Eloquence and wit are poor routes to salvation. As Cioran confesses, " . . . all my metaphysical inclinations come up short against my frivolity."

Yet I suspect that Cioran speaks to a special self or region in many of us. Responding to him is a private thing—he is no thinker to discuss and share, or that only with a few close initiates. Pessimism (like the currently more popularized subject of death) is a primal taboo in our society. We feel a strong obligation to suppress any problems and questions that resist being appropriated under some social or practical heading. Those apparently insoluble problems of existence, we would like to think, are projections of neurosis or faulty ideology.

For someone who views literature or ideas from a social

or utilitarian standpoint, Cioran will seem to be a monument of self-indulgence. Even assuming that literature should not be judged primarily for its usefulness to society, we'd still want to ask what use Cioran himself hopes to derive from shaping such discomforting reflections into eloquent prose. And the question is best asked not in sarcasm but out of the curiosity of one who admires these writings and therefore seeks to plumb their ultimate wisdom: to know what barricade their author seeks to erect between himself and the discontents he writes of, what consolation he hopes to gain, what absolution, what balm. "If we make doubt a goal," he writes, "it can be as comforting as faith."

Susan Sontag, in her introduction to **The Temptation to Exist** [see Further Reading list], describes Cioran as politically conservative; I'd call him closer to apolitical. Political hopes are based on the belief that at least some of mankind's problems can be solved on that plane. But as Cioran has it, "The horrors that glut the universe constitute an integral part of its substance; without them, the universe would physically cease to exist."

Such a position is amenable only to mysticism. Yet despite his continuing argument and fascination with mysticism, Cioran refrains from any commitment. This indeed is a key feature of his position. His skepticism seems almost gratuitous at times. Cioran is well aware, and even obsessively so, how lucidity and skepticism preclude the surrender necessary for salvation. Is it that his skepticism reaches to the authenticity of transcendence itself, or is he stopped merely by his own confessed inequality to the task? May it not be that Cioran has reached the point of no return with lucidity and eloquence, the point at which they become sophistry; where—to turn one of his own insights against him—one proceeds from words to the actual, rather than vice versa, and where style is an object of idolatry and the presentation of an idea takes precedence over the idea itself?

Attitudes like Cioran's are signs of fanatical belief in one's own perceptions. That is to say, believing one's perceptions are authentic and infallible representations of *how it is*. Such a condition precludes either a religious leap of faith or consolation through trust in the perceptions of others. Doctrines and ideologies can't get to him, since the only acceptable dogma is his own awareness and judgment. And despite Cioran's undoubted perceptiveness, despite the depth and often uncanny precision of his intelligence, can we be sure that he does not in the end succumb to a sort of blindness? Considering the present hold exerted by epistemological relativism, when all world views, ideologies, positions have come to appear arbitrary, gratuitous, a matter of temperament or programming, such a position as Cioran's must indeed seem quaint, perhaps antiquated, and most significantly, *unnecessary.*

Yet Cioran himself has recognized this option but turned it to his own purposes: "Doubt too is capable of fervor, doubt too, in its way, triumphs over every perplexity, doubt too has an answer to everything." (pp. 377-78)

> *Edward Marcotte, "The Pleasures of Pessimism," in* The Nation, *New York, Vol. 221, No. 12, October 18, 1975, pp. 377-78.*

## Stephen Koch

[E.M. Cioran's **The Trouble with Being Born**] suggests more forcefully than ever how this crucial, distressing genius is producing a philosophical counterpart to the art of Samuel Beckett. Their books belong on the same shelf of the mind—right at the edge of the Abyss. They share analogous ambitions: both have consciously understood themselves as last survivors in the great, declining traditions of their respective disciplines; both are wretched, exalted, at the End.

Though he uses the language of discourse, Cioran like Beckett writes through an intensely lyric modality of impasse, contradiction, self-hatred and depression. Both share the theme of the death of culture, refracted through their own agonies, and remain obsessed with the endless entrapped monotony of their dilemmas, trying to end their endlessness. Trying to begin. Again. The literary forms of both, in search of authenticity and purity, grow progressively shorter—Cioran the essayist is now an aphorist—as they make their long anguished drive toward the absolute authenticity of silence. In his more strait-laced, philosopher's way, Cioran even shares some of Beckett's humor, learned I suppose from his master Nietzsche's clattering laughter among the Absolutes.

The title of **The Trouble with Being Born** sets the tone: a collection of aphorisms driven into existence by the throb of a panic fear of death and spiritual failure, turned against itself to meditate on the "disaster" of birth—the beginning of the ordeal of consciousness, and far more "horrible" than the end.

The aphorisms, grim as death, are often intellectually dazzling, sometimes shocking, sometimes infuriating. Cioran's entrapped, incandescent mind repeatedly insists on its embrace with disgust, weariness, panic, futility, self-hatred. The writing is superb, utterly nuanced with its quizzical irony and despair, and the intellectual pathos of cynicism. As an aphorist, Cioran states only his conclusions, fastidiously never revealing the experience whereby he has reached them. He is filled with the depressive's conviction that experience doesn't matter; things do not significantly change; to recount the story is therefore pointless. In every sense, Cioran has only *conclusions,* conclusions in an interminable and utterly inconclusive process of doubt. And so even the superlative elegance of his style is a function of his despair. . . .

**The Trouble with Being Born** compiles the emblazoned jottings of pessimism's ecstasy, a fierce ecstasy repeatedly undermined by Cioran's own coldly brilliant deflations. Cioran is an anti-ecstatic thirsting for the drunkenness of absolute negativity, claiming that the trouble with being born is that life won't let him enjoy that absolute. . . .

There is something horrible in the violent purity, self-cruelty and excess of this cautious, witty, brilliant man. The purity of intellectual extremes—his latter-day substitute for absolutes—has great prestige for Cioran; and indeed at such extremes, pessimism is the only possible position. As Cioran contemptuously points out again and again (confidently self-possessed with the full snobbishness of his despair), any optimistic view of the modern world, given its unlovely realities, *must* be relative, meliorist, humane, tolerant—a view that ignores extremes—otherwise it will be stupid or worse. And for Cioran as much as Nietzsche, the virtues of moderation are ultimately contemptible. Cioran writes the intellectual autobiography of his own sensibility, and his sensibility is miserable, self-hating, insomniac, chronically depressed and dazzling. My first reading of this book left me impressed, appalled and angry. My second reading left me still impressed, still appalled and a little angry, but joining in its startling laughter. To be sure, smiling even a little at this fierce, undismissible intellectual call to order, which can neither be accepted nor rejected—for the only way to live with it, *pace* Cioran, is with the tentative, humane values—falls in the category of cold comfort. But Cioran has prepared us for that: "An aphorism? Fire without flames. Understanding that no one tries to warm himself at it."

> Stephen Koch, *"I Think, Therefore I Die,"* in Book World—The Washington Post, *July 25, 1976, p. 63.*

### D. J. Enright

To offer a résumé of [*A Short History of Decay*] would no doubt be to simplify and coarsen it. Such a procedure might also offend by misrepresentation in another way: endowing it with more meaningfulness than it has. Of Rumanian origin, this French writer is much concerned with lucidity: in him, alas, *lucide* aspires towards the condition of *suicide*.

However, the very first item serves to bring out the flavour of E. M. Cioran's thought, his philosophy or anti-philosophy. 'Once man loses his *faculty of indifference* he becomes a potential murderer.' Ideals are dangerous—except perhaps for an ideal ideal, the like of which we shall wait for Cioran to invoke. 'Firm resolves draw the dagger; fiery eyes presage slaughter.' Better to be a Hamletist, a swindler, a con man, to whom can be imputed none of history's great convulsions . . . The idea (or anti-idea) is not a new one. . . . Yeats's celebrated lament that the best lack all conviction whereas the worst are full of passionate intensity—except that Cioran holds that the good *should*—are those *who*—lack all conviction.

To be sure, Cioran is a good deal more sophisticated than that. We shall not be allowed to sail for long under the colours of unresolution and nonconviction. Cioran (*Précis de décomposition* was originally published in 1949) is an addict, or prisoner, or celebrant, of Catch-22. 'I dream of an Eleusis of disabused hearts, of a lucid Mystery, without gods and without the vehemences of illusion.' That is, indeed, a dream, for the heart is never wholly disabused, the Mystery is never lucid. The only escape from Catch-22 is into paradoxes and aphorisms, into 'poetry'.

Cioran slates philosophers amusingly. 'Compared to music, mysticism, and poetry, philosophical activity proceeds from a diminished impulse and a suspect depth, prestigious only for the timid and the tepid.' His preferred poets are Shelley (except when he is out to do good), Shakespeare (who never 'served' anything), Hölderlin, Baudelaire and Rilke. The thought occurs that Cioran

himself is a Rimbaudian version of Alain: more given to overt provocation than Alain, more given to floweriness and violence, much less humane. (pp. 680-81)

In his most entertaining manner, the author develops a grudge against dreaming. 'If we could conserve the energy we lavish in that series of dreams we nightly leave behind us, the mind's depth and subtlety would reach unimaginable proportions.' Why, an imbecile 'who was not victimised by this waste' would be able 'to disentangle all the snags of the metaphysical lies or initiate himself into the most inextricable difficulties of mathematics'!

By this time, the reader has a fair idea of what Cioran would do with those unimaginable proportions, those metaphysical disentanglements and those mathematical initiations. For years, he says, he lived in the shadow of the great female saints. 'And then . . . I stopped loving them.' St Theresa was too interested in the colour of Jesus's eyes. As for Jesus: the objection is to his resuscitation. Without it, he would have been a splendid tragic hero. Even more so, had he had no followers. More so still—one wonders—if no one had ever heard of him?

Cioran has a way of putting things, sometimes a quaint way, which is all his own, and I suspect that Richard Howard has translated with skill and firm resolve. Love's one function, the author contends, is to 'help us endure those cruel and incommensurable Sunday afternoons which torment us for the rest of the week—and for eternity'. And 'without the allurement of the ancestral spasm, we should require a thousand eyes for hidden tears, or else nails to bite, mile-long nails'. But what—you may ask—about that much prized sloth?

Well, if Sunday afternoons were extended for months, the slothful, exasperated by having been right all along, and now *obviously* in the right, might be induced to lean over backwards and 'indulge in the degrading temptation of tasks'.

Though this is a short book, the *métaphysicien du néant* (as Claude Mauriac has called him) [see excerpt above] has written at too great length. His aperçus sink beneath the repeated hammer blows. 'In this world nothing is in its place, beginning with this world itself.' 'In the gamut of creatures, only man inspires a sustained disgust.' (In fact—or in my opinion—there isn't enough gamut in Cioran's neighbourhood.) Human existence is a dog's life, but dogs are preferable to humans. After the proclamation, in italics, 'All our humiliations come from the fact that we cannot bring ourselves to die of hunger,' there seems little point in saying anything else, however elegantly or wittily. From nihilism nihil comes. Quite often, reading this book, one can only murmur *'Touché';* quite often one adds: 'Yes, but he's more touched than I am *touché.'* (p. 681)

> D. J. Enright, *"Mile-Long Nails,"* in The Listener, *Vol. 96, No. 2485, November 25, 1976, pp. 680-81.*

### John Pilling

Each of Cioran's seven books (five translated into English) has its own tone and emphasis, but each forms part of an attempt at a systematic dismantling of Western philosophy, a controlled exercise in negation which makes other pessimists look half-hearted. But his writings are not so unreservedly negative, nor as merely diagnostic as some commentators would have us believe. He writes with too much fervour for this to be true, and the effect of reading him is too invigorating. Cioran is fanatically devoted to disabusing us of the illusions and consoling fictions we have wilfully erected to prevent ourselves seeing what it is to be human. His "exercise in anti-utopia" is everywhere haunted by the dream of restoring us to a status we have irretrievably lost. "There is no negator", as he says himself, "who is not famished for some catastrophic *yes.*"

Although his self-laceration is clearly genuine, it is also, I think, a strategy designed to obscure the idiosyncratic essence of what he is saying, to protect himself from our scorn by showing that he has been there before us. He is always presenting himself in the darkest possible light as a being "refractory to the slightest undertaking", who takes perverse delight in "[glossing] our fall from grace", an "addict of precariousness" whose only affection is for "the explosion and collapse of things." But his true position is more equivocal. Perhaps his most brilliant formulation of it is when he sees himself as "a terrorist who, going out into the street to perpetrate some outrage, stops on the way to consult Ecclesiastes or Epictetus." Cioran is fascinated by intellectually terrorist activity, but too much of a sceptic to commit himself to it. This means that it is quite possible to feel relatively secure at even his most outrageous and seemingly inhuman recommendations. He is a much more persistent ironist than Nietzsche. "Above Doubt", he writes in *Précis de décomposition,* "I rank only the delight which derives from it." However much the delights of the barbarian may fascinate him, and even excite him, he is never fooled by them, and never supports them without pointing out their limitations.

With such a confirmed addict of doubt, however, Doubt itself has sometimes had to go by the board. "Futility is the most difficult thing in the world," he writes in *The Temptation to Exist.* "I hoped to achieve it by the practice of scepticism. Yet scepticism adapts itself to our character . . . personalizes itself." When the sceptic in Cioran fades, the barbarian in him is likely to take over. But scepticism, "the faith of undulant minds", remains the one mental activity which can unfailingly bring him "the rapture of impasse", and only scepticism can always satisfy his desire to "remain forever in the equivocal" enunciating "an endless dialogue." Straightforward cynicism (notwithstanding his deep admiration for Diogenes) is clearly too unambiguous to do this. His compulsion towards the "congenital perplexity" of inertia overrules his affection for decisive acts of denial.

This is nowhere better demonstrated than in his attitude to suicide, a subject never far from his thoughts, since he locates it at the furthest remove from inertia and believes it can only be performed in a state of rage against the world. He is fascinated by suicide, but shrinks back from its finality. It is the need to vent his spleen that keeps him alive; for him "every book is a deferred suicide." The act of writing (which necessitates an abrogation of inertia and

forces one into violent utterance) is ultimately only a simulacrum of the infinitely more expressive and liberating act of killing oneself. "Without suicide," he says laconically in *Précis,* "no salvation."

But since "no one", not even the suicide, "recovers from the disease of being born," Cioran is forced to explore alternative, if less efficacious, forms of salvation. He does this with some diffidence, since one half of him believes that "salvation is the death of song, the negation of art and of the mind" and there are poems, pictures and philosophies he cannot help admiring. He cannot deny, in fact, that poetry, when it succeeds, "supplies, *for a moment,* our salvation" although he is deeply and justly suspicious of how aestheticism can turn into hagiography. Nor does he deny the attraction of "the only religion which has contributed a radical formulation for salvation," Buddhism. What he does deny is the validity of any comprehensive social or political solution: "It is hard to see how humanity might be saved *en bloc.*" He therefore confines himself to how it might save itself individually, since it has ignored the infallible recipe of mass simultaneous suicide.

Cioran is in no doubt that for us to be "saved" we must first of all free ourselves of our historicist illusions. History is a subject on which Cioran always speaks with withering scorn. For him it is "nothing but a procession of fake Absolutes," an "indecent alloy of banality and apocalypse," "the product of a race which stands." He knows, as any student of Bergson would have to know, that time "constitutes our vital element" but he also knows that time enchains us: "so long as we have not triumphed over time, we remain slaves." It is "the fall into time" which has ruined us, and only the fall out of it can redeem us. Cioran suggests that one way of triumphing over time is to regard history as an unalterable monolith, "an invariable total which cannot undergo any modification." This formulation, which effectively mummifies history, clearly attracts Cioran, but is open to the objection that history has demonstrably existed and is continuing to do so. Cioran is therefore forced to admit that history has happened, but to content himself with pointing out that it is only repeating itself endlessly and deteriorating as it does so. This enables him to equate present-day Europe with the Decadence and Alexandrianism that accompanied the fall of the Roman Empire, and at the same time to suggest that we are in a much worse plight. Time and again Cioran reminds us that we are living in a late period, a period close to total disappearance. It is "too late for humanity to be released from the illusion of action, too late for it to be raised to the sanctity of sloth," and "too late to be wise" above all. It is on this perception that he predicates the positive, or partially positive, elements of his thought.

The demystification of history obliges us, Cioran believes, to recognize that our natural, and indeed primordial, resting-place is the Void. If at this point he runs the risk of being mistaken for a latter-day Existentialist, it is a risk he is quite conscious of, and he counters it with considerable dexterity, if not with any terminological rigour. "In order to become futile," he writes in *The Temptation to Exist,* "we must sever our roots, must become metaphysically *alien.*" What we must avoid, as *The Fall into Time* warns us, is making negation a programme or system like those that have previously enchained us. The Void is an "*infinite* impasse", an "abyss without vertigo", not so much an idea as "what helps us rid ourselves of any idea." "The danger", Cioran writes in **The New Gods** (and we can hardly doubt that it is the existentialist philosophers that he is thinking of ), "is to convert the void into a substitute for being, and thereby to thwart its essential function, which is to impede the mechanism of attachment." Nothingness—and here Sartre is obviously being taken to task—is too substantial; it is only a "sordid version of the void." Only a state of absolute hebetude, of total stupefaction (like Flaubert's *bêtise*), will allow us entry into the nourishing climate of the Void. This is why Cioran is such an addict of our decadence, so keen to see it continue, for if it is "encouraged" (and thereby "exhausted") it will allow "new forms"—hopefully the Void—to come into existence.

Cioran's thirst for the Void is in essence religious, a residue of the Orthodox faith he long ago abandoned. "The experience of the Void," he writes in **The Temptation to Exist,** "is the unbeliever's mystic temptation." The Void is the nearest we may hope to come to the primordial unity of being that existed before Creation. Cioran has an immense "nostalgia for this time before time" that can obviously never be assuaged, and it gives his writing on the subject an almost tragic grandeur, although he is careful to point out that "the void . . . is, like every product of quietism, antitragic in essence." Cioran is yearning to be restored to the unity that pre-dated the dualisms he has been so strenuously exploring in his role as sceptic. He has "a craving for . . . the *first impasse*" quite as great as any of the Gnostic thinkers he often refers to. Being is, for him, quite literally, a crime for which he must atone: "It is as if, creeping into this world, I had profaned a mystery." One's separate existence is an "infraction committed against the undivided creation," the act of a "god without scruples, a feculent god," in short a Gnostic Demiurge.

This Gnostic strain in Cioran underpins his attitude to moral questions. Any personal creation of our own—artistic or procreative—can only mirror this primal curse and should be avoided if at all possible. It is typical of Cioran's latent aestheticism that he should find redeeming features in artistic creation: "To write a faultless page, or only a sentence, raises you above Becoming." On the other hand bringing people into the world, and thereby delaying the desired day of humanity's disappearance, is quite irredeemable: "One does not procreate on Patmos." It is characteristic of Cioran's bifocal attitude that, though he admires many thinkers and writers, he resents the fact that their creations have delayed our deliverance by their very originality. What Cioran is seeking to do is to inaugurate a period of what he considers absolute normality in which every man will be illiterate and sterile. Man, as at present constituted, is the "abnormal" animal; only Diogenes ("the most profoundly normal of men") and perhaps himself ("For a long while I have lived with the notion that I was the most normal being that ever existed") have genuinely striven to attain "an ideal lucidity, an ideal normalcy." Here most readers will find it hard to follow Cioran; these formulations smack of someone whose solipsism has

reached its apotheosis, replacing the complex relationships of social life with an arrogant assertion of self. But the key word here is "ideal". Cioran knows that this is his own peculiar day-dream, that we shall never inhabit a "universe exempt from celestial intoxications." Only an ideal moralist ("a combination of cynicism and lyric ardour") would be able to bring this universe into being: a mixture, as he says in one of many provocative pairings, of Vauvenargues and the Marquis de Sade.

It may seem perverse of Cioran to think of himself as a moralist. But it is difficult to see him in any other role. He has become progressively more suspicious of the saints and sages he has spent a lifetime reading, and he knows he is neither a saint nor a sage. "Life is the site of my infatuations: everything I wrest from indifference I give back almost at once. This is not the saints' method." The "demonic effervescence" of the saints and the heretical wildness of the Gnostics and Cathars have left an indelible mark on his own meditations, but he is quite without their faith in a transcendental solution, and a stranger to the delights of asceticism.

As moralist, however, Cioran is inevitably a kind of sage, and to make even an eccentric and incoherent philosophy out of such diverse influences should command our respect for a mind of the first order. Each of Cioran's aphoristic, fragmentary utterances demands our separate attention. If one fragment reminds us of Pascal and another of La Rochefoucauld, we can never say that they are not, first and foremost, Cioran's own. His desiccated and at times ethereal utterance, now savage, now strangely tranquil, always energized except where a studied limpidity can spring a sudden ironic trap on the reader—the very weariness with which he reiterates things he has said with the same dissatisfaction on countless other occasions—this is the special flavour of Cioran. Every paragraph is a testament to what he has called "the anomaly of writing." He does not, like many philosophers, take refuge in a hieratic style; his voice is characteristically broken, short-breathed, wrung from him, on the point of petering out. He is not a writer we enjoy a dialogue with. He has the stridency and arrogance of utter conviction. He can leave us, like Chamfort, spellbound by the sheer force of his intuition, or, again like the melancholy Frenchman, irritated by the obviousness of his bias or the triteness of his insight. However maxim-like his formulations may seem, we cannot regard them as the utterances of a disembodied sage remote from us. He himself sees his writings as "more or less autobiographical, a rather abstract form of autobiography, I admit." What he is seeking to enunciate is the perfectly true, and hence utterly devastating, insight into human misery, not in order that he may cease from speaking (though he would be happy if he could allow himself such a luxury of inactivity) but so that he may testify to the "decomposition" which is, for him, the essence of being human. It is because he is without consolation that he is also without project: the two are synonymous for him. He is unquestionably the greatest living master of "meditation without object" and if the elliptical gloom which the French call *cafard* cannot be expected to flourish in England, it is unthinkable we should continue to ignore entirely such a remarkable and compelling thinker. (pp. 15-17)

*John Pilling, "E. M. Cioran: An Introduction," in* PN Review, *Vol. 6, No. 1, 1979, pp. 14-17.*

## John Updike

*The New Gods* (no doubt a more salable title, in progressivist America, than the original French *Le mauvais demiurge*), though the smallest of Cioran's three collections in English, fairly represents him in its range of topic and quality. The first essay, or prose flight, **"The Demiurge,"** proposes with more fervor than irony the existence of "a wicked and woebegone god, a god accursed," who created this botched universe and whose "criminal injunction" to multiply Man is doomed to obey, at least until the happy day when "pregnant women will . . . be stoned to death." In its contemplation of the "dreadful miracle" of Creation, this essay is almost pious, and with his final hint of "*another* creator" Cioran might be one of those Jesuits who whip off the scoffer's mask to administer the sacraments. But the mask is his face. The next section, **"The New Gods,"** ends by lamenting Christianity's present mood of tolerance: "Its career finished, its hatred is finished too." The historical period of Rome's decline and the Church's emergence is one of the author's favorites; impossibly well read in the late Skeptics and the early Christians, he is a connoisseur of paganism's decadence, "the cumulus of inner defeats" that permitted the new religion to triumph. He is always interesting on this subject, which inspired, in an earlier volume, the maxim "Energy, privilege of the dregs, always comes from below." Cioran is consistently boring, on the other hand, on the subject of Buddhism and Oriental quietism. His longing for this particular brand of unattainable religiosity leads him to dwell, in **"The Undelivered,"** upon the thought of the void as fondly as a hen broods upon an egg, hatching such fuzzy aperçus as "The void is nothingness stripped of its negative qualifications, nothingness transfigured." **"Paleontology"** uses a visit to a museum to trip a meditation upon the loathsome flesh, "that layer of grease which keeps us from discerning what is *fundamental* in ourselves." Here, more than usual, Cioran seems irresponsibly extreme: is it really true, for instance, that "whatever is alive, the most repellent animal or insect, shudders with fear—does nothing but"? What is signified by "an abstract joy, an exaltation granted alike to being and to the absence of being"? And is it not a peculiar sort of nihilistic piffle to say that bones "grant me a glimpse of the day when I shall no longer have to endure the obsession of the human, of all shackles the most terrible"? **"Encounters with Suicide,"** the longest and what should be the most involving essay in the book, though touched with hints of personal experience and with a delicate poetry of the death wish, a wish "to run joyously toward our ghost," is vitiated by abstractness, as if the writer had felt suicide only as an idea in the brain and never as an action latent in the muscles. "A man does not kill himself, as is commonly supposed, in a fit of madness but rather in a fit of unendurable lucidity": perhaps this should be so, but we doubt that it is. Cio-

ran is at his most reflexively, coquettishly paradoxical with assertions like "When you have understood that nothing *is,* that things do not even deserve the status of appearances, you no longer need to be saved, you are saved, and miserable forever."

All his essays balk at flowing; they feel, rather, written from point to point, from shock to shock, cadenzas parading as melody. The frequent recourse to asterisks and fresh starts betrays the shifting perspectives of an intelligence committed only to itself. The best section of *The New Gods,* the most entertaining, concrete, and suggestive of Cioran's living mind, is the last—a string of disconnected aphorisms called **"Strangled Thoughts."** Thc title declares a congenial murderousness; he dreams, he has earlier written, of a language whose words will break jaws like fists. Here, his thoughts, freed of any need to harmonize with a context, stab:

> Refinement is the sign of deficient vitality, in art, in love, and in everything.

> First duty, on getting up in the morning: to blush for yourself.

> All our thoughts are a function of our ailments.

> The creator who becomes transparent to himself no longer creates: to know oneself is to smother one's endowments and one's demon.

> We are all deep in a hell each moment of which is a miracle.

Dignified by a defiant perfectionism of style, Cioran is of that type of intellectual outsider described by Thomas Mann in his short story "At the Prophet's": "A fevered and frightfully irritable ego here expanded itself . . . The solitary ego sang, raved, commanded. It would lose itself in confused pictures, go down in an eddy of logical error, to bob up again suddenly and startlingly in an entirely unexpected place. Blasphemies and hosannahs—a waft of incense and a reek of blood." Though advertised by his American sponsors as a "philosopher," Cioran lacks one-half of that word's etymology, which is *philos* ("loving") + *sophos* ("wise"). Wisdom devoid of love is sophistry. Read alongside another nervous, doubting paragrapher, such as Wittgenstein, Cioran conspicuously lacks two qualities the other in his thought possesses—gentleness and seriousness. He does not wish to relieve, through clarification, our irritations; he does not wish, like Nietzsche and Kierkegaard, to inflame them to the point of crisis and cure. He wishes only, with his nimble, sinister spidering amid the complexities of our cultural situation, to give us—one of his favorite words—*frissons;* the means seem disproportional to the ends. (pp. 600-02)

*John Updike, "A Monk Manqué," in his* Hugging the Shore: Essays and Criticism, *1983. Reprint by Vintage Books, 1984, pp. 597-602.*

## George Steiner

E. M. Cioran has, over the past four decades, established for himself an esoteric but undoubted reputation as an essayist and aphorist of historical-cultural despair. **Drawn** *and Quartered* is the translation of a text published in French, as *Écartèlement,* in 1971. The maxims and reflections that make up the main part of *Drawn and Quartered* are preceded by an apocalyptic prologue. Gazing upon the immigrants, the hybrids, the rootless flotsam of humanity that now tide through our anonymous cities, Cioran concludes that it is indeed—as Cyril Connolly proclaimed—"closing-time in the gardens of the West." We are Rome in its febrile and macabre decline: "Having governed two hemispheres, the West is now becoming their laughing-stock: subtle specters, end of the line in the literal sense, doomed to the status of pariahs, of flabby and faltering slaves, a status which perhaps the Russians will escape, those *last* White Men." But the dynamics of inevitable degradation extend far beyond the particular situation of the capitalist and technological Western sphere. It is history itself that is running down. . . .

The human species, intones Cioran, is beginning to put itself out of date. The only interest a *moraliste* and prophet of finality can take in man stems from the fact that "he is tracked and cornered, sinking ever deeper." If he continues on his doomed, sordid path, it is because he lacks the strength needed to capitulate, to commit rational suicide. Only one thing is absolutely certain of man: "He is stricken in his depths . . . he is rotten to the roots."

What, then, lies ahead? Cioran replies:

> We advance *en masse* toward a confusion without analogy, we shall rise up one against the other like convulsive defectives, like hallucinated puppets, because, everything having become impossible and unbreathable for us all, no one will deign to live except to liquidate and to liquidate himself. The sole frenzy we are still capable of is the frenzy of the end.

The sum of history is "a futile odyssey," and it is legitimate—indeed, compelling—"to wonder if humanity as it is would not be better off eliminating itself now rather than fading and foundering in expectation, exposing itself to an era of agony in which it would risk losing all ambition, even the ambition to vanish." After which rumination, Cioran bows out with a little pirouette of self-teasing irony: "Let us then renounce all prophecies, those frantic hypotheses, let us no longer allow ourselves to be deceived by the image of a remote and improbable future; let us abide by our certitudes, our indubitable abysses."

The quarrel with this kind of writing and pseudo thinking is not one of evidence. The century of Auschwitz and of the thermonuclear-arms race, of large-scale starvation and totalitarian madness may indeed be hastening toward a suicidal close. It is conceivable that human greed, the enigmatic necessities of mutual hatred which fuel both internal and external politics, and the sheer intricacy of economic-political problems may bring on catastrophic international conflicts, civil wars, and the inward collapse of aging as well as of immature societies. We all know this. . . .

No, the objections to be urged are twofold. The passages I have quoted bear witness to a massive, brutal oversimplification. The grain of human affairs is, always has been, tragicomic. . . . History and the lives of politics and of societies are far too manifold to be subsumed under any one grandiloquent pattern. The bestialities of our age, its potential for self-ruin are evident; but so is the plain fact that more men and women than ever before in the history of this planet are beginning to be adequately fed, housed, and medically cared for. Our politics are indeed those of mass murder; yet for the first time in recorded social history the notion is being articulated and realized that the human species has positive responsibilities toward the handicapped and the mentally infirm, toward animals and the environment. I have, often enough, written about the venom of current nationalism, about the virus of ethnic and parochial fury which impels men to slaughter their neighbors and reduce their own communities to ash (in the Middle East, in Africa, in Central America, in India). However, subtle but forceful countercurrents are beginning to emerge. Multinational organizations and businesses, the free-masonry of the natural and applied sciences, youth cultures, the revolution in the dissemination of information, and the popular arts are generating wholly novel chances and imperatives of coëxistence. They are eroding frontiers. The chances do remain slight; but it may be that they will come in time to inhibit the scenario of Armageddon. It would be fatuous arrogance to rule otherwise. (p. 155)

There is throughout Cioran's jeremiads an ominous *facility*. It requires no sustained analytic thought, no closeness or clarity of argument to pontificate on the "rottenness," on the "gangrene," of man, and on the terminal cancer of history. The pages on which I have drawn not only are easy to write, they *flatter* the writer with the tenebrous incense of the oracular. One need only turn to the work of Tocqueville, of Henry Adams, or of Schopenhauer to see the drastic difference. These are masters of a clairvoyant sadness no less comprehensive than Cioran's. Their reading of history is no rosier. But the cases they put are scrupulously argued, not declaimed; they are informed, at each node and articulation of proposal, with a just sense of the complex, contradictory nature of historical evidence. The doubts expressed by these thinkers, the qualifications brought to their own persuasions honor the reader. They call not for numbed assent or complaisant echo but for reëxamination and criticism. The question that remains is this: Do Cioran's apocalyptic convictions, his mortal pessimism and disgust occasion original and radical perceptions? Are the *pensées,* the aphorisms and maxims, that constitute his title to fame truly in the lineage of Pascal, of La Rochefoucauld, or of his immediate exemplar Nietzsche?

*Drawn and Quartered* contains numerous aphorisms on death. This is always a favorite topic for aphorists—for, indeed, is there ever much to be *said* about death? "Death is a state of perfection, the only one within a mortal's grasp" (the point implicit is a feeble, traditional wordplay on the Latin sense of "perfection"). "There is no one whose death I have not longed for, at one moment or another" (echoing La Rochefoucauld). "Death, what a dishonor! To become suddenly an *object*"—which is followed by the wholly unconvincing assertion that "nothing makes us modest, not even the sight of a corpse." The tone rises to a macabre chic: "Whatever is exempt from the funereal is necessarily vulgar." The climax of portentous silliness is this: "Death is the solidest thing life has invented, so far."

Let us try another theme, that of the acts of writing and of thought. "A book should open old wounds, even inflict new ones. A book should be a *danger*." Quite so—and said, a long time ago, almost verbatim, by Franz Kafka. "One does not write because one has something to say but because one *wants* to say something." Fair enough. "Existing is plagiarism." A witty, suggestive hit. "When we know what words are worth, the amazing thing is that we try to say anything at all, and that we manage to do so. This requires, it is true, a supernatural nerve." True enough; but professed often, and with irrefutable authority, by Kafka, by Karl Kraus, by Wittgenstein and Beckett. "The only *profound* thinkers are the ones who do not suffer from a sense of the ridiculous." Cf. Rousseau and Nietzsche, who arrived at the same finding, but with far greater circumstantial force. (To which caveat, Cioran might reply, "I have invented nothing, I have merely been the secretary of my sensations.") "An author who claims to write for posterity must be a bad one. We should never know *for whom* we write." The admonition may be unexceptionable; a moment's thought of Horace, Ovid, Dante, Shakespeare, or Stendhal reveals its shallowness.

Cioran is the author of an interesting essay on De Maistre, the great thinker of counterrevolution and anti-democratic pessimism. A number of aphorisms—and they are among the more substantial—point to this strain in Cioran's own nocturnal politics: "Never lose sight of the fact that the plebs regretted Nero." "All these people in the street make me think of exhausted gorillas, every one of them tired of imitating man!" "The basis of society, of any society, is a certain *pride in obedience*. When this pride no longer exists, the society collapses." "Whoever speaks the language of utopia is more alien to me than a reptile from another geological era." "Torquemada was *sincere*, hence inflexible, inhuman. The corrupt popes were charitable, like all who can be bought." I happen to believe that Cioran's stoic élitism, his rejection of meliorism *à l'américaine,* has more truth in it than most of the currently modish brands of ecumenical liberality. But nothing very fresh or arresting is being added here to the plea for darkness in De Maistre, in Nietzsche, or in the visionary politics of Dostoyevski. The aphorism on Torquemada, for instance, with its modish *frisson,* comes directly out of De Maistre's immensely powerful tractate in favor of the hangman.

The most revealing aphorisms are those in which Cioran testifies to his own bleak, fatigued condition: "All my ideas come down to various discomforts debased into generalities." "I feel effective, competent, likely to do something positive only when I lie down and abandon myself to an interrogation without object or end." There is a lucid pathos in Cioran's confession that he could more easily found an empire than a family, and immediate persuasion in his remark that original sin can be doubted only by those who have not had children. One instinctively trusts and ponders the proposition "I do not struggle against the world, I struggle against a greater force, against my *weari-*

*ness* of the world." But, as a British idiom has it, a little world-weariness does go a very long way. One hundred and eighty pages, climaxing in the (ludicrous) cry "Man is *unacceptable,*" leave one recalcitrant.

The trouble may well lie with Cioran's dictum that in aphorisms, as in poems, the single word is king. This may be true of certain types of poetry, mainly lyrical. It is not true of the great aphorists, for whom the *sententia* is sovereign, and sovereign precisely insofar as it compels on the reader's mind an internalized but elided wealth of historical, social, philosophic background. . . . No doubt there are better examples of Cioran's work, particularly from before the time when his writings turned into self-repetition. But a collection of this order. . . . does raise the question not so much whether the emperor has any clothes as whether there is any emperor. (pp. 156-58)

*George Steiner, "Short Shrift," in* The New Yorker, *Vol. LX, No. 9, April 16, 1984, pp. 152, 155-58.*

### Kirkus Reviews

"I have not had the decency, paltry individual that I am, to eliminate myself." So instead of swallowing poison, Cioran [in ***Drawn and Quartered***] chews his pessimistic cud through 192 pages of *pensées* on the nightmare of history, its approaching cataclysmic end, and, above all, the sickening void of existence. Readers of Cioran's earlier work . . . will find nothing new here; but if your tastes run to epigrammatic nihilism, then you may enjoy the shots of philosophical absinthe he serves up on this occasion. . . . For sober analysis, on the other hand, you'd better look elsewhere. Cioran apparently hopes to emulate such great masters of the aphorism as Pascal, Schopenhauer, and Nietzsche, but he's just not in their league. He's a failed Buddhist . . . , obsessed with absurdity (much like that other Frenchified Rumanian, Eugene Ionesco), but inclined less to protest than to morose delectation in the apocalyptic twilight—as he sees it—of civilization. Cioran, to be sure, can be sensible as well as silly. Though he anticipates the triumph of unconsciousness ("the one true paradise") rather complacently, he also displays a kind of moral outrage (illogical, perhaps, but it does him credit anyway) over the evils preceding or attending that triumph. And if not terribly profound, he's readable and sometimes witty. If the Me Generation ever starts feeling Sartrean nausea, it may find in Cioran a vivid—and vaguely masochistic—articulation of its distress.

*A review of "Drawn and Quartered," in* Kirkus Reviews, *Vol. XLIX, No. 14, July 15, 1987, p. 912.*

### Roger Kimball

**"Thinking against Oneself"** and **"On a Winded Civilization"**: the titles of the opening two essays of *The Temptation to Exist* may be said to epitomize the mood and general outlook of not only this volume but all of Cioran's work. Here, as elsewhere, what Cioran offers are not reasoned arguments or sustained reflections but a series of highly charged *aperçus* on the debacle of Western civilization, the fate of the intellectual in contemporary society, the end of the novel, the virtues of tyranny, the future of utopia, and other edifying topics. Yet behind these ostensible themes lies his one real abiding concern, a concern that [Susan Sontag in her introduction to *The Temptation to Exist* (see Further Reading list)] sums up admirably. "Cioran's subject: on being a *mind,* a consciousness tuned to the highest pitch of refinement." "In Cioran's writings," she adds, "the mind is a voyeur. But not of 'the world.' Of itself." With these last characterizations especially, we come close to the center of Cioran's thought.

The recent appearance of a translation of *Histoire et utopie*—a slim collection of six essays meditating on the virtues and liabilities of the utopian impulse, the imperfections of democracy, and the primacy of hate and rancor in the inventory of human emotions—offers an appropriate occasion on which to reassess Cioran's achievement. Is he the embattled intellectual hero that Miss Sontag presents, a lonely mind of "real power" courageously recording important truths that are too unpalatable for the majority of thinkers to acknowledge? Or is he more in the way of an intellectual *poseur,* a metaphysical aesthete who anatomizes his self-inflicted agonies not for the sake of any presumed truth but merely in order to provide himself with ever more exquisite spectacles of disbelief? Almost everything Cioran has written points to the latter conclusion.

Cioran's appeal does not rest only on the substance of his position; equally—if not more—important is his style, his epigrammatic tautness. His advertised labors with the French language have resulted in a style that blends an almost Olympian coolness and intellectuality with the appearance of passion bordering, at times, on hysteria. Like so much about Cioran, it is essentially an adolescent style: high-handed, confessional, histrionic, but nevertheless full of energy. His habitual use of the royal we—one of his most obvious rhetorical borrowings from Nietzsche—helps invest his writing with a patina of authority; and if one discounts context and forgets about picayune things like meaning, Cioran can be eminently quotable. But he clearly values the *effect* of his style over consistency of argument. One does not have to read far in his work before understanding Susan Sontag's enthusiasm: in Cioran she found a kindred spirit, an inspiration, a writer who preserved the appearance of serious intellectual inquiry while giving absolute priority to rhetorical gestures, verbal extravagances, and modishly provocative poses. (p. 38)

Cioran's favorite rhetorical gambit—his predominant bid for attention—is disarmingly simple: he takes conventional wisdom about politics, culture, or ethics and inverts it. In the hallowed tradition of *épater la bourgeoisie,* he sets out to shock, to unsettle, to provoke. Not that there is anything particularly new in Cioran's painstakingly contentious statements; mostly, they read like formulaic declarations of existentialist angst and venom. True, when one first dips into his work, it can seem brashly outrageous. How extraordinary to be told that philosophy is the "privilege of . . . *biologically* superficial peoples," to discover

that "we spend the prime of our sleepless nights in mentally mangling our enemies, rending their entrails, wringing their veins, trampling each organ to mush," or to learn that at the age of twenty Cioran supposed "that to become the enemy of the human race was the highest dignity to which one might aspire." (p. 39)

After two or three essays, such displays lose whatever novelty they originally had; and after slogging through several books, one realizes that Cioran's pose as intellectual provocateur is little more than a mask for a series of repetitious clichés. Thus he is everywhere at pains to extol dreams and madness as bastions of freedom and genius. In **"Thinking against Oneself "** he writes that "we are all geniuses when we dream, the butcher the poet's equal there. . . . Only the madman enjoys the privilege of passing smoothly from a nocturnal to a daylight existence." And a bit later: "It is the madman in us who forces us into adventure; once he abandons us, we are lost. . . . We cannot be *normal* and *alive* at the same time."

Beggars, too, are favored objects of Cioran's admiration, for in his view the beggar's "thought is resolved into his being and his being into his thought. He *has* nothing, he *is* himself, he endures: to live on a footing with eternity is to live from day to day, from hand to mouth." It's the old image of the poor fool turning out to be wiser than the educated philistine. Cioran treats us to this one a good deal. In an essay entitled **"Beyond the Novel,"** he admonishes us to dispense with the genre because it is too bookish and mundane to deal with what really matters.

> What interest can a mere life afford? What interest, books inspired by other books or minds dependent on other minds? Only the illiterate have given me that *frisson* of being which indicates the presence of truth. Carpathian shepherds have made a much deeper impression upon me than the professors of Germany, the wits of Paris. I have seen Spanish beggars, and I should like to have become their hagiographer. They had no need to invent a life for themselves: they *existed;* which does not happen in civilization.

What *does* happen in civilization? Cioran never really says. But one wonders if it really matters to him. As his quasi-metaphysical, yet nowhere defined, use of the term "existence" here suggests, he is not against using words primarily as emotional embroidery. And what about the "truth" that these illiterate Spanish peasants are said to possess? In another essay he scornfully summarizes his feelings about that dinosaur with a phrase: "The Truth? An adolescent fad or symptom of senility."

Clearly, Cioran's thought rests largely on a Romantic opposition of instinct to intellect, on a *preference* for instinct over intellect. "Whatever emanates from the inferior zones of our nature," he writes, "is invested with strength, whatever comes from below stimulates: we invariably produce and perform better out of jealousy and greed than out of nobility and disinterestedness." Hence his suspicion of reason as "the rust of our vitality," and his claim that "we are born to exist, not to know; to be, not to assert ourselves. Knowledge, having irritated and stimulated our appetite for power, will lead us inexorably to our ruin. . . . [K]nowledge taints the economy of a human being." No arguments are provided for these sentiments, possibly because, as he notes elsewhere, he is convinced that "the dynasty of intelligibility" is drawing to a close. What use are reasons and arguments in a realm of chaos and unintelligibility? (pp. 39-40)

It cannot be said that Cioran has improved or particularly matured with age. One of the most recent of his books to be translated into English, *The Trouble with Being Born* (1976), a collection of aphorisms published in French in 1973, strikes one as a series of rambling, disconnected thoughts culled from the journal of a well-read but deeply troubled teenager—that, or a collection of rejected entries from Woody Allen's parody of Kafka. (p. 40)

Cioran's attitude—not to say attitudinizing—toward violence and disaster epitomizes his efforts at self-dramatization. Often, he pauses to vent his spleen on himself. "I have hated myself in all the objects of my hatreds, I have imagined miracles of annihilation, pulverized my hours, tested the gangrenes of the intellect." But he saves most of his energy for others. In **"Odyssey of Rancor"** we are told that by nature man is saturated with murderous resentment. Hate is presented as mankind's guiding principle, yet most men, especially in the civilized West, "are not equal to their hatred." Only this keeps them from destroying one another at once. The "need to kill, inscribed in every cell," has been stymied by civilization, and this has vitiated man's primitive vigor and led to decadence and decline. For Cioran, "we become *good* only by destroying the best of our nature," and, similarly, "our imaginations function only in hope of others' misfortune." "We"? "Our"? How easily grammar insinuates complicity!

In essays like **"Russia and the Virus of Liberty"** and **"Learning from the Tyrants"** (both of which, with **"Odyssey of Rancor,"** appear in *History and Utopia*), Cioran elevates the themes of violence and hatred from the individual to the social and political level. Democratic liberalism appears not as a social and political achievement of the first order but as a concession to weakness and decay. "Freedoms prosper only in a sick body politic: tolerance and impotence are synonyms." Since he believes that "the passion to reduce others to the status of objects" is the key to understanding politics, he has profound respect for political tyrants. (p. 41)

Though he assures us that he "abominates tyrants," Cioran also admits that he "harbors a weakness for tyrants"—largely, one suspects, because he thinks that "a world without tyrants would be as boring as a zoo without hyenas." Indeed, he seems to believe that we all would behave as tyrants if only we had the courage, lucidity, and forcefulness. Hence tyrants are said to "reveal us to ourselves, they incarnate and illustrate our secrets." And hence Cioran regards the asperity and violence of his writing as a substitute for the physical violence he has been incapable of perpetrating: "Unable to render myself worthy of them [the tyrants] by action, I hoped to do so by words, by the practice of sophism and enormity: to be as odious with the means of mind as they were with those of power, to devastate by language, to blow up the word and with

it the world, to explode with one and the other, and finally to collapse under their debris!" Moreover, he envisions a great tyrant on the horizon, one who will forge the nations of the earth into a single entity. "The scattered human herd will be united under the guardianship of one pitiless shepherd, a kind of planetary monster before whom nations will prostrate themselves in an alarm bordering on ecstasy." Somehow, though, the decidedly unecstatic alarm one feels reading such professions is not assuaged by his blithe identification of Hitler as "the rough draft of our future," the harbinger of this envisioned "planetary monster."

Given his infatuation with exile, alienation, and historical catastrophe, one could have predicted that Cioran would sooner or later find himself moved to write about Judaism and the Jews. Among other things, **"A People of Solitaries,"** his essay on the Jews in *The Temptation to Exist,* is a perfect example of his simplifying hostility toward religion.

> For them, eternity was a pretext for convulsions, a spasm: vomiting imprecations and anthems, they wriggled before the eyes of a God insatiable for hysterias. This was a religion in which man's relations with his Creator are exhausted in a war of epithets, in a tension which keeps him from pondering, from emphasizing and thereby from remedying his differences, a religion based on adjectives, effects of language, and in which style constitutes the only hyphen between heaven and earth.

Not, one hastens to add, that he is much better on Christianity. "[W]e"—that inveigling plural again—"yawn over the Cross . . . To attempt to save Christianity, to prolong its career, would not occur to us; on occasion it awakens our . . . indifference." (The ellipses are Cioran's.)

But of course his chief interest in Judaism is not in its religious dimension but in the stereotype of the Jew as victim and scapegoat. And here, as in his frequent invocation of "biological capital" in other essays, Cioran betrays a species of race thinking that is tantamount to racism. For him, the Jews occupy a distinct ontological category that makes them different *toto genere* from "ordinary" human beings: "Let someone else do them the insult of making 'meaningful' statements about them! I cannot bring myself to do so: to apply our standards to them is to strip them of their privileges, to turn them into mere mortals, an ordinary variety of the human type." Professed admiration becomes a cloak for an extraordinarily patronizing presumptuousness. Did the Jews suffer untold barbarities at the hands of the Nazis? Well, Cioran airily dismisses the question, advising us to "leave aside regrets, or delirium. . . . The instinct of self-preservation mars individuals and collectivities alike." Perhaps it was this last observation that led even Miss Sontag to admit that Cioran's discussion of the Jews "displays a startling moral insensitivity to the contemporary aspects of his theme." (pp. 41-2)

[If] there is a wild inconsistency of argument in Cioran's work, there is nonetheless an almost rigid consistency of attitude; Cioran's positions and opinions shift from page to page; contradictions abound; but throughout it all he maintains his stance as extreme philosophical anarchist: "Bluntly: my rebellion is a faith to which I subscribe without believing in it," he writes, reasoning that "since the Absolute corresponds to a meaning we have not been able to cultivate, let us surrender to all rebellions: they will end by turning against themselves, against us. . . . " And this, you understand, is meant as a recommendation.

In a writer as unsystematic and (one assumes) deliberately inconsistent as Cioran, it will perhaps seem idle to look for the presuppositions of his position. But lurking behind much of his writing is the essentially Romantic glorification of absolute freedom—the *confusion,* that is to say, of indeterminate spontaneity with genuine freedom, which has meaning only when limited and determined by particular choices. Throughout Cioran's work one encounters the idea that *any* definite thought or action is an encroachment upon freedom that ought ideally to be resisted. "The sphere of consciousness shrinks in action," he writes in the lead essay of *The Temptation to Exist* ["**Thinking against Oneself**"]:

> no one who acts can lay claim to the universal, for to act is to cling to the properties of being at the expense of being itself, to a form of reality to reality's detriment. . . . If we would regain our freedom, we must shake off the burden of sensation, no longer react to the world by our senses, break our bonds. . . . The only free mind is the one that, pure of all intimacy with beings or objects, plies its own vacuity.

Elsewhere he speaks of "the illusory character, the nullity of all action" and concludes that "freedom can be manifested only in the void of beliefs, in the absence of axioms, and only where the laws have no more authority than a hypothesis." In other words, according to Cioran, freedom can be manifested only where it is impossible. For him, freedom is the elusive corollary of "Being" or "the Absolute," terms whose emptiness is not remedied simply by being capitalized.

At bottom, Cioran's main theme, the theme that he returns to again and again, the theme that more than any other has endeared him to leftist intellectuals like Miss Sontag and allowed them to overlook his otherwise unacceptable politics, is hatred of the West, its institutions, heritage, and legacy. Describing the West as "a sweet-smelling rottenness, a perfumed corpse," Cioran asserts that, having shed brutality, the West has also lost its strength. . . . Again and again he proclaims the end of Western culture. Even now the West is "preparing for its end," he tells us; "let us envisage chaos. Already, most of us are resigned to it."

Predictably, bourgeois society, being an enclave of liberal democratic thought, comes in for special criticism. In **"Letter to a Faraway Friend,"** the opening essay in *History and Utopia,* Cioran enlarges on the "lacunae of bourgeois society," coyly assuring his "faraway friend" that such a society is not "entirely and absolutely displeasing to me—you know my weakness for the horrible—but the expenditure of insensitivity it requires to be endured is out of all proportion to my reserves of cynicism." Expatiating

on the "curse" that has fallen upon the liberal West, he asks why the West "produces only these businessmen, these shopkeepers, these racketeers with their blank stares and atrophied smiles, to be met with everywhere, in Italy as in France, in England as in Germany? Is it with such vermin as this that a civilization so delicate and complex must come to an end?" Of course, anti-Western animus has been a stock-in-trade of fashionable intellectuals at least since the middle of the nineteenth century. But Cioran's vitriol attains a rare level of savagery and contempt. And one cannot help wondering if there isn't something in the rejoinder that Cioran quotes from an unnamed friend in **"Some Blind Alleys: A Letter":** " 'The West—you aren't even part of it.' "

Especially in his earlier work, Cioran's rhetoric recalls no one so much as Nietzsche, and one is not surprised to find that Miss Sontag observes—not without embarrassment, one suspects, for the observation cannot but dim her subject's claim to originality—that Nietzsche "set down almost all Cioran's position almost a century ago." In fact, though, this is only half true. There is no doubt that Cioran was deeply impressed by Nietzsche; his writing is permeated by the philosopher's themes, his perfervid prose, even his distinctive locutions and images. Nietzsche's infatuation with violence and power, his use of physiological metaphors to explain art and other cultural phenomena, his deliberate inversion of inherited moral categories, his vision of a stance "beyond good and evil": all this and more reappears predigested in Cioran's works.

But Cioran is less Nietzsche's disciple than his ape. He adopts the extravagant rhetorical gestures, glories in shocking conventional wisdom, and clearly would like to describe himself, as did Nietzsche, as intellectual "dynamite." But when one comes to examine the substance of Cioran's thought, one discovers that on almost every issue his position—insofar as he adopts a consistent position—is completely at odds with Nietzsche's teaching. Miss Sontag herself admits that "what's missing in Cioran's work is anything parallel to Nietzsche's heroic effort to surmount nihilism." Since the effort to surmount nihilism forms the core of Nietzsche's mature thought, its utter absence in Cioran's work already marks an important divergence from Nietzsche.

More generally, Cioran's gloomy flirtations with the void are diametrically opposed to Nietzsche's efforts to overcome the life-poisoning pessimism of (as he puts it in *The Gay Science*) the man who "revenges himself on all things by forcing his own image, the image of his torture, on them, branding them with it." Cioran's work proceeds from a disgust—or at least the pretense of a disgust—with life, especially the life of civilized man. Despite his own excesses, at the center of Nietzsche's thought is the ambition to woo modern man back from his disenchantment with life. "I should very much like," Nietzsche writes, "to do something that would make the thought of life even a hundred times more appealing." For Cioran, revenge is the lugubrious tonic that provides life with its chief fascination; for Nietzsche "the spirit of revenge" constitutes the main impediment to man's self-affirmation. Behind all the bravura, there is something terribly pathetic about Cioran.

"What a torment to be ordinary, a man among men!" he has exclaimed. But, as he put it in one of his most insightful observations, "nothing is more commonplace than the *ersatz* troubled soul, for everything can be learned, even *angst*." (pp. 42-4)

> *Roger Kimball, "The Anguishes of E. M. Cioran," in* The New Criterion, *Vol. VI, No. 7, March, 1988, pp. 37-44.*

---

## FURTHER READING

Messmer, Michael W. "In Complicity with Words: The Asymptotic Consciousness of E. M. Cioran." In *The Secular Mind: Transformations of Faith in Modern Europe,* edited by W. Warren Wagar, pp. 220-38. New York: Holmes & Meier, 1982.
    Examination of Cioran's career emphasizing his paradoxical orientation toward language, philosophy, and religion.

Sontag, Susan. Introduction to *The Temptation to Exist,* by E. M. Cioran, translated by Richard Howard, pp. 7-29. Chicago: Quadrangle Books, 1968.
    Analyzes Cioran's major concerns and praises him as the most distinguished contemporary thinker in the tradition of such "personal (even autobiographical), aphoristic, lyrical, anti-systematic" philosophers as Soren Kierkegaard, Friedrich Nietzsche, and Ludwig Wittgenstein.

Weiss, Jason. "An Interview with Cioran." *Grand Street* 5, No. 3 (Spring 1986): 105-40.
    Rare, wide-ranging interview in which Cioran discusses such topics as his work, other philosophers, his struggle to learn French, and how insomnia influenced his thought.

# W. E. B. Du Bois

## 1868-1963

(Full name William Edward Burghardt Du Bois) American historian, essayist, novelist, biographer, poet, autobiographer, and editor.

Du Bois was a major force in helping define African-American social and political causes in the United States. Alternately considered a leader and an outcast, Du Bois espoused controversial opinions early in his life and was regarded by many as a prophet. He is widely remembered for his conflict with Booker T. Washington over the role of blacks in American society—an issue that he treated at length in his famous essays collected in *The Souls of Black Folk*. A writer of important works in many genres, Du Bois is particularly known for his historiography and for his pioneering role in the study of black history. According to Herbert Aptheker, however, Du Bois was above all a "history maker," and his works and ideas continue to attract attention and generate controversy.

Du Bois had an almost idyllic childhood in Great Barrington, Massachusetts, where his family was part of a stable community of fifty blacks in the small town of 5,000. Class and race distinctions were slight in Great Barrington, and the town quickly recognized Du Bois as a youth of exceptional intelligence and ability. When his mother died soon after his high school graduation, some residents of the town gave Du Bois a scholarship on condition that he attend Fisk University, a southern school founded for the children of emancipated slaves. Although Du Bois had always dreamed of attending Harvard University, he accepted the scholarship. In 1885 Du Bois traveled to Fisk in Nashville, Tennessee—his first journey to the southern United States.

"No one but a Negro going into the South without previous experience of color caste can have any conception of its barbarism," Du Bois later wrote in his *Autobiography*. Yet Du Bois was "deliriously happy" at Fisk, where he met students of his own race. There he excelled at his studies, and during summers taught young blacks who lived in destitute rural areas of Tennessee. After graduating with honors from Fisk in three years, Du Bois entered Harvard in 1888 to receive a second bachelor's degree and then his doctorate. Although many fellow students treated him with animosity, Du Bois met several Harvard professors who would provide lifelong inspiration—Josiah Royce, George Santayana, Albert Bushnell Hart, and William James, who became a mentor and friend. With only his dissertation to complete to receive his doctorate in history, Du Bois enrolled at the University of Berlin in Germany; there he studied philosophy, sociology, and history for two years. Upon returning to the United States in 1894, however, he promptly rediscovered " 'nigger'-hating America," where the chances of a black history instructor finding a teaching position were slim. In 1895 Du Bois completed his dissertation, *The Suppression of the Af-*

*rican Slave-Trade to the United States of America, 1638-1870.* The work became the first volume of the Harvard Historical Studies series, and Du Bois became the first black American to receive his doctorate from Harvard. In 1899 Du Bois published the sociological study *The Philadelphia Negro,* the product of interviews with 5,000 black persons living in the "dirt, drunkenness, poverty, and crime" of Philadelphia. The work, commissioned by the University of Pennsylvania, pioneered the scholarly study of black Americans. The University, however, did not offer Du Bois a position on its faculty, one of several occasions when Du Bois was denied a key teaching position because of his color.

At the advent of the twentieth century, the champion of black Americans was Booker T. Washington, then the principal of Tuskegee Institute in Alabama and the most powerful black man in America. Washington laid the blame for blacks' social status on their inferior economic positions, and he was prepared to delay voting reforms until blacks contributed to the economy by learning trades in agriculture and industry. Du Bois, however, could not abide this stance. Francis L. Broderick wrote of Du Bois: "Long restive under Washington's acquiescence in second-class citizenship, Du Bois ordered the Negro to be a man and demanded that white America recognize him as such." The two men, diametrically opposed in their views toward education, each found supporters, and the historic conflict began. In 1903 Du Bois published his best-known work, a collection of fourteen essays titled *The Souls of Black Folk.* According to Arnold Rampersad, *Souls* became "perhaps the most influential work on blacks in America since *Uncle Tom's Cabin.*" In the essay "On Mr. Booker T. Washington and Others," Du Bois praised Washington for preaching "Thrift, Patience, and Industrial training," but condemned his apologies to those in power, maintaining that Washington "does not rightly value the privilege and duty of voting, belittles the emasculating effects of caste distinctions and opposes the higher training of our brighter minds." Other essays were largely autobiographical and discussed the "twoness" of being both American and black—"two warring ideals in one dark body, whose dogged strength alone keeps it from being torn asunder."

With the publication of *Souls,* Du Bois became inextricably involved with the fight for black equality. In 1905 Du Bois formed the Niagara Movement, the first black protest movement of the twentieth century. Du Bois helped institute a more lasting movement in 1909 when he became the only black founding member of the National Association for the Advancement of Colored People (NAACP). Du Bois launched and edited *Crisis,* the official publication of the NAACP, which soon became the most important magazine directed at a black audience. Du Bois contributed editorials condemning lynching and disenfranchisement, and his discussion of arts and letters in *Crisis* is considered a catalyst for the Harlem Renaissance literary movement. In 1918, however, Du Bois lost some credibility when he urged support for American involvement in World War I in the editorial "Close Ranks"; later, he discovered widespread racism in the armed forces in Europe. Many black Americans turned away from Du Bois's leadership at this time. This essay and his conflict with Marcus Garvey, the popular Jamaican leader of the Universal Negro Improvement Association and "back-to-Africa" movement, indicated Du Bois's alienation from a significant part of the black population in America.

"I would have been hailed with approval, if I had died at age fifty. At seventy-five my death was practically requested," said Du Bois of struggles later in his life, according to Addison Gayle, Jr. During the 1930s, Du Bois continued to write important works, including *Black Reconstruction,* in which he maintained that black Americans played a major role in the Reconstruction period, a theory ignored by previous historians. Du Bois also wrote several autobiographies; nevertheless, his popularity waned and resentment toward him grew. He was removed from the NAACP twice for ideological differences: once after opposing in *Crisis* the NAACP's idea of integration, and later for supporting Progressive party candidate Henry Wallace for president in 1948 while the NAACP's executive secretary, Walter White, unofficially campaigned for Harry S. Truman. In 1951 Du Bois was indicted as an unregistered "agent of a foreign principal" because of his involvement in the "subversive" Peace Information Center,

an organization that sought to inform Americans about international events and to abolish the atomic bomb. Although Du Bois was acquitted, his passport remained in the custody of the United States government. Awarded the International Lenin Prize in 1958, Du Bois became a member of the Communist Party of the United States in 1961, shortly before renouncing his American citizenship. He died at the age of ninety-five in Accra, Ghana.

"The problem of the twentieth century is the problem of the color line," declared Du Bois to the Pan-African Congress in 1900, and his famous statement, which became the introduction to *The Souls of Black Folk,* has been hailed as prophetic. Despite the controversy that surrounded his ideas and actions throughout his embattled lifetime, Du Bois continued to fight for equality between races. Arnold Rampersad wrote: "Far more powerfully than any other American intellectual, [Du Bois] explicated the mysteries of race in a nation which, proud of its racial pluralism, has just begun to show remorse for crimes inspired by racism."

(See also *CLC,* Vols. 1, 2, 13; *Contemporary Authors,* Vols. 85-88; *Something about the Author,* Vol. 42; *Dictionary of Literary Biography,* Vols. 47, 50, 91; *Concise Dictionary of Literary Biography,* 1865-1917; and *Black Writers.*)

## PRINCIPAL WORKS

*The Suppression of the African Slave-Trade to the United States of America, 1638-1870* (history) 1896
*The Philadelphia Negro: A Social Study* (essay) 1899
*The Souls of Black Folk: Essays and Sketches* (essays) 1905
*The Negro in the South, His Economic Progress in Relation to His Moral and Religious Development; Being the William Levi Bull Lectures for the Year 1907* [with Booker T. Washington] (lectures) 1907
*John Brown* (biography) 1909
*The Quest of the Silver Fleece* (novel) 1911
*The Negro* (history) 1915
*Darkwater: Voices from within the Veil* (poems, essays, and sketches) 1920
*The Gift of Black Folk: The Negroes in the Making of America* (history) 1924
*Dark Princess: A Romance* (novel) 1928
*Africa: Its Geography, People and Products* (history) 1930
*Africa: Its Place in Modern History* (history) 1930
*Black Reconstruction: An Essay Toward a History of the Part Which Black Folk Played in the Attempt to Reconstruct Democracy in America; 1860-1880* 1935
*Black Folk, Then and Now: An Essay in the History and Sociology of the Negro Race* 1939
*Dusk of Dawn: An Essay Toward an Autobiography of a Race Concept* (autobiography) 1940
*Color and Democracy: Colonies and Peace* (essay) 1945
*The World and Africa: An Inquiry into the Part Which Africa Has Played in World History* (criticism) 1947
*In Battle for Peace: The Story of My 83rd Birthday* (memoirs) 1952
*\*The Ordeal of Mansart* (novel) 1957

*Mansart Builds a School* (novel) 1959
*Worlds of Color* (novel) 1961
**Selected Poems* (poetry) 1964
*The Autobiography of W. E. B. Du Bois: A Soliloquy on Viewing My Life From the Last Decade of Its First Century* [edited by Herbert Aptheker] (autobiography) 1968
*W. E. B. Du Bois Speaks: Speeches and Addresses* [edited by Philip S. Foner] (speeches) 1970
*W. E. B. Du Bois: The Crisis Writing* [edited by Daniel Walden] (essays) 1972
*The Emerging Thought of W. E. B. Du Bois: Essays and Editorials From "The Crisis"* [edited by Henry Lee Moon] (essays) 1972
*The Education of Black People: Ten Critiques, 1906-1960* [edited by Herbert Aptheker] (essays) 1973

*These works are collectively referred to as the *Black Flame* trilogy.

**The publication date of this work is uncertain.

## The Nation

That so gifted a writer as the author of *Souls of Black Folk* should be tempted to write a new life of John Brown from the point of view of the negro is easily understood. It also goes without saying that [with *John Brown*,] Dr. Du Bois has made a readable volume of his appreciation of the martyr of 1859, the fiftieth anniversary of whose execution is now at hand. So little have the negroes themselves as yet done to honor the memory of John Brown that this book might have taken on a special significance. But Dr. Du Bois's work is disappointing in that it betrays no original research and abounds in inaccuracies. This is partly because he has relied upon his predecessors in the field. His is the eighth serious biography of John Brown to appear and unfortunately only one or two of these were written in the spirit or manner of the historian who desires to be impartial and to go to original sources for his information. Thus Col. R. J. Hinton's book is frankly a brief for Brown, and Mr. Sanborn's biography, a treasure-house of material, suffers from the author's association with the preparations for Harper's Ferry. It is, moreover, twenty-four years old and since its publication much has come to light, both in Kansas and elsewhere, which is of importance to the interpreter of Brown and his times.

For this and other reasons, Dr. Du Bois leaned upon untrustworthy staves, when he relied upon his predecessors. A few examples will suffice. He accepts Col. Hinton's attribution to Edmund Babb of Cincinnati of the anonymous letter of August 20, 1859, betraying Brown's exact plans to Secretary Floyd. But it has been known for years that David J. Gue, now living in New York city, was the author of that letter and that it was written not to injure Brown, but to save his life by heading off the raid. The full story Dr. Du Bois will find in Benjamin F. Gue's valuable *History of Iowa*, published in 1903. Again, he follows Redpath in accusing the Border Ruffians of wholesale assaulting of women in the early Kansas days. In the entire range of Kansas literature and manuscripts now available, there are but two recorded instances of this crime, and these are by no means wholly established, for at least one rests only

upon Redpath's word, when acting as correspondent of an Eastern newspaper. Dr. Du Bois also assumes, with another biographer, that John Brown's victims on the Pottowatomie had the benefit of some sort of trial. But not a scintilla of evidence has yet been produced to confirm this belief. Indeed, the facts all make against it. Again, Dr. Du Bois accepts without investigation the repeated statements that John Brown was descended from Peter Brown of the Mayflower, although this is denied by the foremost authorities on the Mayflower genealogies. Finally, it must be noted that Dr. Du Bois follows Sanborn, Hinton, and others in justifying the abominable Pottowatomie massacre, which, had it been perpetrated by Border Ruffians, would have been denounced as a crime against humanity.

But Dr. Du Bois's own errors are numerous enough. He makes of George B. Gill, Brown's Kansas follower, a Canadian, whereas he was an American; to Jeremiah G. Anderson of Indiana, born of sturdy, white farmer parentage, he attributes negro blood, and Lewis Sheridan Leary, a free-born negro, becomes slave-born on the same page and is dubbed Lewis Sherrard Leary as well. Of the twenty-two raiders, Dr. Du Bois says that "six or seven" were negroes; he adds John Anderson, a mythical raider, and Jeremiah G. Anderson to the five actual negroes, Leary, Copeland, O. P. Anderson, Green, and Newby. Incredible as it may seem, Dr. Du Bois records that seventeen negroes were "probably killed" in the raid, when, besides four of Brown's negroes, Leary, Copeland, Green, and Newby, but two slaves lost their lives, and neither of these while fighting. He accepts also, in all its absurdities, the narrative of O. P. Anderson, the negro who escaped, and endorses it as a trustworthy document. Yet Anderson insisted, for one thing, that there were thirty men killed on the Southern side, in the face of Col. Robert E. Lee's official report to President Buchanan that there were but five deaths, all told, in addition to John Brown's own losses; and Lee is yet to be accused of falsifying facts or failing to obtain them.

Dr. Du Bois is not, however, to be bound even by John Brown's words, for he evolves the astounding theory that the raid failed through the delay of the rear-guard in Maryland in moving the arms into Harper's Ferry before the trap into which Brown had walked was sprung. But, unfortunately for this, Brown repeatedly stated while in jail that he deserved to be hanged for his military blundering. . . . and he assured Gov. Wise and others that his care for his prisoners led him to delay too long, despite the warnings of his men that he must leave the town at once. Part of Dr. Du Bois's difficulty here is due to his belief that William Thompson, Brown's messenger to the rear-guard, failed to reach it. If he should read Terence Byrne's testimony before the Senate Committee of Inquiry and John E. Cook's confession, he would not only ascertain that Thompson did carry out his instructions but find many details with which he is now unacquainted.

Coming to John Brown's trial, Dr. Du Bois says that the jury "was empanelled without challenge," although, in fact, Brown's counsel used every peremptory challenge to which he was entitled. This is duly recorded in the minutes of the trial and attested by the presiding judge. Again, the author places Brown in Iowa in August, 1856, although he never entered the State at that time. But why continue? A page of the *Nation* would not suffice to record the other slips which make it impossible to accept this volume, readable as it is, as a reliable contribution to America's history. This is most regrettable because of Dr. Du Bois's valuable sociological studies, upon the accuracy of which no doubts have been cast. His last chapter in the book before us is a notable discussion of the race question as it stands to-day in the light of John Brown's sacrifice.

> *A review of "John Brown," in* The Nation, *New York, Vol. 89, No. 2313, October 28, 1909, pp. 405.*

## Oswald Garrison Villard

It was too much, we suppose, to expect that Mr. W. E. B. Du Bois should produce another book as great as his ***Souls of Black Folk.*** It was given to Harriet Beecher Stowe to write but one *Uncle Tom's Cabin*. The ***Souls of Black Folk*** burns with the passion for justice of a wronged and suffering nature, proud and sensitive, wounded to its depths by the cruel injustice of the color line. Only a genius could have compressed into another volume as much spiritual agony, as poignant an appeal to the conscience of his fellow-citizens. Yet there are essays in Mr. Du Bois's latest volume, ***Darkwater,*** that strike almost as compelling a note. Certainly his **"Litany at Atlanta"**, written in that city immediately after the rioting and the massacre of innocents, must take high rank as literature; and with it are other chapters of as genuine beauty as they are of unquestioned power. No other colored American has ever written like this and few white. There is a chapter in ***Darkwater*** on **"The Souls of White Folk"**, apropos of the white race's descent into Avernus on the fields of Europe, which all white folk ought to read. As for Jesus Christ in Texas, it is to be commended to no man or no woman who wishes to dismiss the Negro problem with an easy conscience. In brief, ***Darkwater*** carries its challenge on every page. America, conceited, self-satisfied, certain of its justice, its virtue, and the impossibility of bettering its form of government, would be abashed, indeed, if Mr. Du Bois's terrible indictment should penetrate deep into its inner consciousness. Some day it will—or there will be atonement in far greater bloodshed and death than goes on today where men draw the line that mocks fraternity, denies equality, defies democracy, and blasphemes liberty.

Why have Mr. Du Bois's shafts not struck deeper? Why are the withers of the American people so unwrung on the Negro problem? The causes are many; they go to the very roots of our social and our economic order, for the question of the Negro is but one phase of the necessary reconstruction of our society. Great as *The Souls of Black Folk* is, it has had not a tithe of the influence of "Uncle Tom's Cabin." There must be a conjunction of time and public excitement and author to insure such another success as Mrs. Stowe's. Slavery was an evil upon which public attention could be wholly focused. It was *the* fact that dominated all public life for decades. The present slavery is not to be isolated as a clear-cut phenomenon; it has innumerable phases, and none as yet seriously overshadows the whole life and thought of the nation. So the situation calls for a far greater book than an *Uncle Tom's Cabin* to stir similarly a nation beset not by one but by a hundred perplexities. Next, the colored people have yet to find themselves. They are a long way from effective race-consciousness. They are without the modern cohesiveness of the Jew; they lack sorely the power to organize; and their masters place every obstacle in the way. It is becoming daily more apparent that they must find their way out by taking their places with the white masses who struggle in economic bondage.

And as for Dr. Du Bois's power? It is a fact that his own ability to suffer and to feel the wrongs of his race so deeply is at once his strength, the reason for his leadership, and also his chief weakness. For it carries with it a note of bitterness, tinctured with hate, and the teaching of violence which often defeats his own purpose. Doubtless, few of us with sympathies so keen, with nerves so rasped, with wounds so raw, would do better. But still, some suppression of the ego, a lesser self-consciousness, and the omission of personal bitterness at all times would carry Mr. Du Bois and his cause much further. "Our cause," wrote Charles Sumner once, "is nobler than that of our fathers inasmuch as it is more exalted to struggle for the freedom of others than our own." It is a sentiment for Mr. Du Bois to take to heart.

We are not, of course, of those who would criticize Mr. Du Bois for demanding every right and every equality for his people. On the contrary, it is his great merit that he has refused to compromise. Booker T. Washington once said to the writer of this review that he envied him his freedom of speech, his ability to speak out about the wrongs of the Negroes without thought of consequences. He himself, he pointed out, could not do so while his work lay in the South. So Washington's life was essentially one of compromise and opportunism. Mr. Du Bois surrenders to neither; he rightly claims for his people every field of achievement which is anyone else's. Both men have been essential to the race. In the South progress must be slow—step by step—and Tuskegee, like Hampton, marks a great step forward; both are tolerated today largely because they teach trades and manual labor. Had Tuskegee aspired to anything higher it would have been burned to the ground before this. Hence Mr. Washington's leadership was confined to making good farmers, good business men, and good tradesmen. He rightly looked upon the problem of his race as an economic one, but only in the narrowest sense—the winning of good jobs, the buying of a little farm by industry and integrity, the purchasing of the good will of the masters by hard labor and a refusal to aspire to anything celestial. He never clearly visualized the problem as being merely a part of the great struggle of all the masses; he never saw that his battle was but a phase of the greater one, that the chief hope of freedom for his people rests in the freedom of all workers from the thralls that have held them down.

It is even now questionable whether the radicalism of Mr. Du Bois will not soon be made to appear conservative by contrast with the demands of the Negro group which in the *Messenger* and elsewhere has frankly joined the extremists in the labor field. Certainly there are now three parts to the Negro movement, with Mr. Du Bois nearly in the center, even though he has espoused the Socialist cause and does see the necessity of the solidarity and the international cooperation of labor.

Last year Mr. Du Bois took the initiative in calling the first international congress of colored peoples in Paris during the Peace Conference which so utterly ignored their rights. If this becomes a permanent biennial gathering it may prove to be one of Mr. Du Bois's chief claims to the gratitude of his people. He is but fifty; he has years of usefulness before him. If time can but mellow him; if the personal bitterness which so often mars his work can disappear; if a truer Christian spirit than now shines through his writings can guide him; if he desists from his recent dangerous advocacy of meeting force with force, and can bring himself to walk more in the manner of the Nazarene—the possibilities of his further usefulness seem great indeed. (pp. 726-27)

> *Oswald Garrison Villard, in a review of "Darkwater," in* The Nation, *New York, Vol. CX, No. 2865, May 29, 1920, pp. 726-27.*

## Sterling D. Spero

It is not surprising that the publication of this book should be hailed as a literary event. Dr. Du Bois is a great personality. He is the hero of one of the outstanding social controversies of recent American history—the great debate with Booker T. Washington, outwardly a clash of conflicting theories of education, actually a bitter political fight over the Negro's place in American society. In this fight Dr. Du Bois stood squarely and bravely for full educational opportunity and complete social and political equality, as against Washington's insistence upon the Negro's adjustment to the inferior status which the white world imposed upon him. While Dr. Du Bois, through his books, through the *Crisis* which he long edited, and through the National Association for the Advancement of Colored People, which he helped to found, has continued this fight without giving or asking quarter, the struggle has more and more been losing its reality. This is not because it has been attaining its objectives—these are almost as far away as at the start—but because Dr. Du Bois and the movements he has led have never realized the social basis of the things for which they were fighting. The suppression of civil liberties, no matter what racial complications it assumes in the case of the Negro, is primarily the suppression of the rights of labor. To Dr. Du Bois the issue was primarily racial. He never fully grasped the economic basis of racial discrimination, and he therefore never attempted to lead the National Association for the Advancement of Colored People to realize the need of working out an economic program. He has held to his racial approach to the Negro problem with increasing intensity, finally reaching the point where he is willing to accept segregation and an independent black economy inside white society as an instrument of Negro liberation.

And now as an old man Dr. Du Bois has turned to reading Marx. The child of this strange intellectual marriage is **Black Reconstruction.** Written with all the poetry and fervor of his ***Souls of Black Folk,*** one of the authentically important books of its generation, **Black Reconstruction** sets out to correct the false impressions and disprove the lies and slanders of the white historians of the Civil War and Reconstruction.

The Reconstruction, Dr. Du Bois points out, took place amid "the slime of [an] era of theft and corruption, which engulfed the nation and did not pass by the South. Legislators and public officials were bribed. Black men and white men were eager to get rich. In every Southern state white members of the old planter aristocracy were part and parcel of the new thieving and grafting." New York had its Tweed ring; other states had equally unsavory though less famous machines; the federal government experienced the worst period of corruption in its history, going through a series of scandals in which a Vice-President, a Speaker of the House, chairmen of leading Congressional committees, and Cabinet officers were involved. When the Negro Reconstruction governments showed similar corruption, the South blamed the situation on the Negro and "reiterated this charge until it became history." The Reconstruction governments, on the other hand, despite the inexperience of their members and the poverty of the states they governed, accomplished great and positive gains. They broadened the popular base of the government, they improved the criminal law, they laid the foundation of Southern public education. Much of their legislation still remains on the statute books. The constitutions which they adopted remained in force for years after the return of white control.

This book would have been an important contribution to historical literature if the author had been content to show by this method that the Negro "is an average and ordinary human being who under given environment develops like other human beings." But Du Bois's old race consciousness and new Marxism do not allow him to remain content with the demonstration of this major thesis; they lead him to transform the Negro plantation slaves into a revolutionary working class and make the Reconstruction legislatures into dictatorships of the proletariat.

Not satisfied to accept the fact that the emancipation of the Negro was the result of the defeat of the Southern planters by the Northern industrial capitalists, Du Bois insists that "the black worker won the war by a general strike which transferred his labor from the Confederate planter to the Northern invader." That the Negro participated in the Civil War is a historical fact beyond refutation, but the part he played can by no manipulation of terms be made to fit Du Bois's interpretation. About 178,000 Negroes—78,000 freemen and 100,000 former slaves—fought with the Union armies, and nearly 4,000,000 remained loyal to their slave masters, raising the food, making the supplies, transporting the troops to fight for their enslavement. Nearly 28,000 actually fought with the Southern armies. The Negro masses did not play a conscious and decisive role in their own emancipation. The hundred thousand black men who joined the Federal forces came largely from areas invaded and conquered by the Northern troops. Some joined freely; others were inducted by force, in a process more like the corvée than a general strike. Only on the theory of the last straw could we call these additions to the Northern armies decisive.

But even more fantastic than this thesis of Du Bois's is his insistence that the Reconstruction legislatures were proletarian dictatorships. He declares:

> . . . among Negroes, and particularly in the South, there was being put into force one of the most extraordinary experiments in Marxism that the world, before the Russian Revolution, had seen. That is, backed by the military power of the United States, a dictatorship of labor was to be attempted, and those who were leading the Negro race in this vast experiment were emphasizing the necessity of political power and organization backed by protective military power.

This is the central thesis of *Black Reconstruction.* A proletarian dictatorship resting on the military forces of victorious industrial capital! Indeed, this was "an extraordinary experiment in Marxism." Dictatorships the Reconstruction governments were, and the dictatorship here, as always, was a dictatorship of the power which controlled the military force.

Marx's hero was the proletariat. Du Bois's hero is the Negro. Du Bois, fresh from his reading of Marx, makes the Negro the proletariat. Everywhere throughout this book, in many ways an extraordinary work, Du Bois's race consciousness distorts his Marxism; so that the net result of *Black Reconstruction* is to add more confusion than light to the understanding of one of the crucial epochs of American history. (pp. 108-09)

> *Sterling D. Spero, in a review of "The Negro's Role," in* The Nation, *New York, Vol. CXLI, No. 3655, July 24, 1935, pp. 108-09.*

### Charles H. Wesley

Racial propaganda has been so interjected into the writing of history in the United States that the search for truth, which is the main pursuit of historical work, has been almost entirely obscured. Many historians have been propagandists in matters of race, either by direct action or by neglect. Some of them have been born in the South or nurtured in its tradition or they have been too diffident to emancipate their thinking and their research from the dominant racial views. They have striven to prove the obvious racial conclusion, to convert the public and to write that which their readers were desirous of believing. They have not sought for the open mind. They were lay preachers seeking to convert and were more concerned with the effects of their observations than with their accuracy. The scholar who attempts the type of special pleading designed to strengthen traditional beliefs soon loses in intellectual integrity. It is almost impossible for one who takes a partisan view of a question to be honest with himself and frank with the facts.

Propagandist influences have played active parts in shaping the contents of historical writing in relation to the South. In the days before and after the War for Southern Independence, the South felt that it was not treated fairly

by historians; and textbook writers were urged to produce books which were favorable to the slaveholding interests; and since the close of the war, textbooks were demanded which would justify the present racial attitude and social system of the South. By legislation and through the activity of public associations, the Southern states have prescribed the types of history which should be used in their schools and read by their youth. Southerners have undertaken an agitation for books which were different from those used in Northern schools, and they have succeeded. Textbook companies in the North have yielded to this demand and have produced books for Southern consumption. Historians along with novelists have entered this market in order to sell their products. They have trimmed their sails for the seas where sailing was easy.

The Civil War and Reconstruction periods have been the subjects of historical writing for decades, with Southern historians as the leading exponents of the subjects. While they have been zealous to create a sectional presentation of history favorable to the South, they have also made the special endeavor to place the Negro in an unfavorable light. This has been done so frequently that the Negro's subordinate place in history has become traditional in such works. This type of writing gave a basis for discrimination and disfranchisement. Under its influence, no loyal Southerner was expected to desire the return of the activity of the black citizen and politician. Even the white laborer must be taught to shun his possible black competitor. Therefore, the Negro must be kept in his place!

This background was the occasion for the writing and publication of *Black Reconstruction* by Dr. W. E. B. Du Bois. He has undertaken in this volume to present a picture of Reconstruction as it related to the life of the Negro people in this era. He has selected the twenty-year period, 1860-1880, and has described the work as "An Essay Towards a History of the Part which Black Folk Played in the Attempt to Reconstruct Democracy in America." In his foreword to the reader, Dr. Du Bois indicates that the reaction of the reader will depend on his view of the Negro when he begins to read the book.

If the Negro is regarded as an ordinary person, the facts will be permitted to speak for themselves but if, says the author, "he is regarded as an inferior creation, who can never successfully take a part in modern civilization and whose emancipation and enfranchisement were gestures against nature, then he will need something more than the sort of facts that I have set down." He also states that he is going to write about Negroes as though they were human beings, and that he does this conscious of the fact that this approach may curtail the number of his readers. He thus frankly begins by abandoning the concept of race and launches into the history of submerged Americans, who happen to be colored, during the Reconstruction period.

This approach and point of view have been laying dormant in the thinking of the author for several decades. He does not say so, but those of us who are familiar with historical contributions know of this fact. Twenty-five years ago he wrote for the American Historical Review an article under the title **"Reconstruction and Its Benefits."** It has taken a long time for him to secure the opportunity of placing in extended form the ideas which he described in the earlier period. Thanks to the Rosenwald Fund and the Carnegie Corporation, this opportunity was granted to him! Much has been said and written of Du Bois' apostasy in matters of race, but comparing the two studies, twenty-five years apart, one may see that the author at least in one respect has kept essential faith with his views through the passing years.

The historians of Reconstruction, Burgess, Dunning, Rhodes, Fleming and others have presented their partisan views and their disciples have not turned from the paths of their masters. Numerous studies and monographs, as well as a variety of histories have been published, describing the economic, political and social aspects of Reconstruction.

Just as slavery has been considered as a minor cause of the War for Southern Independence, the Negro has been regarded as a negligible factor in Reconstruction. No historian would write a comprehensive story of Reconstruction and place the Negro in a worthy setting. The abolitionists and Reconstruction Radicals were regarded as fanatics. No historian would risk his reputation among historians or his job in a Southern university by writing praiseworthy sentences about the work of these men. Rhodes, a retired business man and capitalist who had turned historian, published a carefully documented study, which was said to be a scholarly description of the period, although the Negro was neglected except as a lazy, shiftless, improvident element of Southern society. Bowers, a newspaper historian and politician, had written the last word, it was said, when he villified Sumner, Stevens and the Radicals, because they thought that Negroes should be citizens and the equals of other Americans. They wrote as historians who were expressing familiar opinions about the Negro participants and their friends in the Reconstruction drama. What more could any historian say?

However, a Negro historian, using these studies as a basis, presents a comprehensive survey of the field which they have surveyed and reaches entirely different conclusions. Without garnering any new facts or digging into primary manuscript and unpublished source materials, Du Bois has written a new interpretation of the old facts. He has seen that writers on Reconstruction have had causes to serve and axes to grind and have been swayed by prejudice and tradition. He has freed himself of these in order that he may tell the truth as it has been established through an examination of the evidence. He does not write as a Negro historian but as an impartial historian who does not propose to distort or discolor the facts but to present them in a discriminating monograph. It is a story retold with new emphasis, new points of view, richer detail and literary excellence. Some ultracritical reviewer may say that this book is also propaganda. This is by no means evident to impartial readers. But even if it were true, one might ask if it is not both fair and expedient to meet fire with fire in such instances? It is certain that the type of propaganda which builds faith into a people concerning themselves is more worthy than the type which robs them of it and causes them to regard themselves as inferiors to other men and women whose faces just happen to be fairer.

*Black Reconstruction* is divided into seventeen chapters covering the period of American History from the years of slavery to the so-called complete restoration of Home Rule in the South. The first three chapters treat the period prior to the war and constitute a background for the study. The war is covered in three chapters under the titles, "The General Strike," "The Coming of the Lord," and "Looking Backward." Three chapters treat the transition to freedom and the political struggles in Congress and the legislatures. Succeeding chapters localize the scenes and the reader sees "The Black Proletariat in South Carolina," "The Black Proletariat in Mississippi and Louisiana," "The White Proletariat in Alabama, Georgia and Florida," and "The Duel for Labor Control on Border and Frontier." Three chapters then follow dealing with "Counter-Revolution of Property," "Founding the Public School" and "Back Toward Slavery." The final chapter treats "The Propaganda of History."

Black workers and white workers, black voters and white voters vie for place in the study. Statesmen who were friends to the Negro and to the Republic march across the pages as stalwarts. Statesmen who were enemies to the Negro and to the Republic are displayed in all of their weaknesses. Democratic education as expressed in the public school is described as a distinct contribution of Black Reconstruction to the White South. In a comprehensive and well-balanced treatment, the author pursues his subpect through 746 pages. An abundant quantity of verbatim quotation contributes to the length of the work and the narrative is broken by its frequent use. At periods there seem to be repetitions of thought and expression but these are excusable because of the need for emphasis. As a whole the book is a vivid story of the part played by Negroes in the Reconstruction of the American States.

Dr. Du Bois has sought for themes which would serve as syntheses for the book, and he finds them in two ideas, the Marxism theory of the state and the Negro as the test of American Democracy. The concept of the class struggle is one of the accepted views which the author endeavors to read into the facts of the period. Reconstruction is to him an economic revolution as well as a political one. Moreover, if American Democracy cannot include Negroes mainly because they are black, the author would seem to ask, what is it good for? But it is the Du Bois fecundity of interpretation and expression rather than the historical narrative or the adherence to a theme which gives the book its special quality.

It is so much easier to criticize a good book, and especially a controversial one, than it is to write a good one! Reviewers should not therefore be taken too seriously. However, it may be observed that there is a tendency to dismiss the explanations of some events with all too brief a wave of the hand. In writing about the causes of the war and in explaining the prevalence of the "saving of the union" sentiment in the North and its influence on the Border states, the author states, "And yet they all knew that the only thing that really threatened the union was slavery and the only remedy was abolition." This is a broad generalization which demands more evidence and discussion. It was true that there were some few who knew of the fundamental cause of the conflict but it is certain that "all" did not know them, as they do not know now. Again, after describing the failure of Negro insurrections during the war, the author asserts that, "Such plans came to naught for the simple reason that there was an easier way involving freedom with less risk." This too is quite an insufficient explanation of these events, and yet with a brief flourish they are dismissed. Similar doubtful generalizations meet the reader in the pages of the book. One may not accept all of the author's conclusions, but it is difficult to escape the inferences which are drawn from the facts that Negroes were persons and that they were and are affected as other peoples when they are subjected to similar circumstances.

As the reader comes to the end of this volume, he regrets to admit, as does the author, that this experiment in democracy had come to an end so soon, and that it was "a splendid failure." Almost triumphantly, however, we join with him in saying that "it did not fail where it was expected to fail." It was not the Negro who occasioned the failure. It was not his lack of capacity. There was no connection between race and corruption at the ballot box or debts in the legislatures or any other maladjustment in this period. So timely a volume cannot fail to have influence in a period when American Democracy reluctantly seems almost on the verge of granting to the Negro population some of its citizenship privileges.

The book, barring its prolixity in quotation and literary expression, is almost as attractive as fiction. In many places, it more nearly resembles fictional writing than serious history. The author is frequently the poet who is writing prose. He is again producing the language and the imagery of the *Soul of Black Folk.* He is the lyric historian, stringing his lyre. He is the literary knight with the plumed pen. Accordingly, as an interpretation of the Negro's contribution to Reconstruction, this work is not only readable but also eloquent in its thought-provoking conclusions. It fills an important gap in our interpretative knowledge of Reconstruction and should prove useful, stimulating and ultimately popular. An all too brief bibliography gives the reader an introduction to a small number of Reconstruction studies evaluated by cryptic sentences at the head of each list.

For several decades, W. E. B. Du Bois has been among the pioneers who are leading in the advance of the social sciences as they relate to the Negro population. One of the major aspects of the Negro's status in the United States has developed out of the fact that the writing of history has been left to the historians of one special racial group which has had no interest in writing about other racial groups. Emphasis was accordingly placed on those facts and interpretations which were creditable to a particular race and section. Unusual progress has been made in the writing and teaching of the natural sciences, and popular traditions have vanished as exact knowledge has increased; but in the writing and teaching of the social sciences popular traditions are allowed to continue unabated.

This situation will not change until Negro students of the social sciences concern themselves with interpretations which are creditable to the Negro people and until the Negro people begin supporting publication so that a market can be furnished for the Negro author. Publication requires a market and is made easier because of it. The publication of the truths of history will lead the public mind to free itself of error and assist in the cessation of the propaganda which is so detrimental to the advance of a submerged group. When these truths become known, a foundation will be raised for a mutual self respect and upon this, the white and the black peoples may proceed to the building of another reconstruction which will be neither white nor black, but will result in a new social order for all irrespective of race or color. (pp. 244-46, 254)

> *Charles H. Wesley, "Propaganda and Historical Writing: The Emancipation of the Historian," in* Opportunity, *Vol. XIII, No. 8, August, 1935, pp. 244-46, 254.*

## Wilson J. Moses

Du Bois's position with respect to Black Nationalism has been described as ambivalent, reflecting his admitted double-consciousness as both a black man and an American, his "two souls, two thoughts, two unreconciled strivings; two warring ideals in one dark body." This often-quoted line registers the double-consciousness manifested in the thought of many Afro-Americans, and, indeed, many Western intellectuals who have attempted to be at once culturally nationalistic, and yet loyal to a more broadly conceived "Western Civilization." Du Bois's early work struggles to fuse two complementary but substantially different mythological traditions. The first of these is "Ethiopianism," a literary-religious tradition common to English-speaking Africans, regardless of nationality. The other is the European tradition of interpretive mythology, transplanted to America by its European colonizers.

The "Ethiopian" tradition sprang organically out of certain shared political and religious experiences of English-speaking Africans during the late eighteenth and early nineteenth centuries. It found expression in the slave narratives, in the exhortations of conspiratorial slave preachers, and in the songs and folklore of the slaves of the Old and the peasants of the New South. On a more literary level, it appeared in the sermons and political tracts of the sophisticated urban elite. The name "Ethiopianism" is assigned to this tradition because early black writers and even some of their white allies often referred to an inspiring Biblical passage, "Princes shall come out of Egypt; Ethiopia shall soon stretch out her hands unto God" (Psalms, 68:31). The verse was seen by some as a prophecy that Africa would "soon" be saved from the darkness of heathenism, and it came to be interpreted as a promise that Africa would "soon" experience a dramatic political, industrial, and economic renaissance. Others have insisted that the real meaning of the scripture is that some day the black man will rule the world. Such a belief is still common among older black folk today.

The "Ethiopian" prophecy seems to have been commonly

known among free black people before the Civil War. In 1858, the African Civilization Society quoted the full verse in its constitution, along with an interpretation by Henry Highland Garnet. According to Garnet Ethiopia would "soon stretch forth her hands,"—"soon" meaning shortly after the work was taken up. The responsibility for seeing to it that the prophecy was fulfilled rested upon the Africans themselves. The signers of the constitution included the leading black nationalists of the day, among them, Daniel Alexander Payne, a bishop of the African Methodist Episcopal Church, and Robert Hamilton, who was later to found *The Anglo-African Magazine.* The quotation appeared in any number of documents published by free Africans in the northern states, and it seems unlikely that many literate free Africans were unfamiliar with it.

At times the verse was directly quoted; at times it was referred to thematically. An early eloquent articulation of the Ethiopian theme was made by Alexander Crummell, an Episcopal priest, who eventually inspired Du Bois. Crummell often used the direct quotation in sermons; but sometimes, as in his 1846 *Eulogium on the Life and Character of Thomas Clarkson,* the reference was indirect:

> Amid the decay of nations a rekindled light starts up in us. Burdens under which others expire, seem to have lost their influence upon us; and while *they* are "driven to the wall" destruction keeps far from us its blasting hand. We live in the region of death, yet seem hardly mortal. We cling to life in the midst of all reverses; and our nerveful grasp thereon cannot easily be relaxed. History reverses its mandates in our behalf—our dotage is in the past. "Time writes not its wrinkles on our brow."

Another example of this indirect "Ethiopianism" was Daniel Alexander Payne's oration "To the Colored People of the United States," delivered in 1862 as the Civil War approached what seemed to Payne a climax of apocalyptic proportions. . . . The theme also appeared in verse, as in Francis Ellen Watkins Harper's "Ethiopia,"

> Yes, Ethiopia yet shall stretch
> Her bleeding hands abroad;
> Her cry of agony shall reach
> Up to the throne of God.

Paul Laurence Dunbar's "Ode to Ethiopia," addressed not to Ethiopia the nation but to the "Mother Race," recounted the past and present struggles of the Afro-Americans and predicted their future triumph:

> Go on and up! Our souls and eyes
> Shall follow thy continuous rise;
> Our ears shall list thy story
> From bards who from thy root shall spring
> And proudly tune their lyres to sing
> Of Ethiopia's glory.

Thus the Rising Africa Theme became a tradition of reinterpreting the Biblical passage to speak to the experiences of the Anglo-African peoples. But "Rising Africa" is only one aspect of "Ethiopianism"; the balancing theme looks to the Decline of the West. The rise in the fortunes of Africa and all her scattered children would be accompanied by God's judgment upon the Europeans. A powerful expression of this belief occurred in *David Walker's Appeal,* published in 1829. In this volume, one of those forgotten American classics nonetheless well known in its time, and a book of importance to the legal and intellectual history of the United States, Walker warned of the impending doom of Western civilization. It would come as a judgment upon Christian sin in enslaving the Africans. "I tell you Americans! that unless you speedily alter your course, *you* and your Country are gone!!!"

"Ethiopianism," with its two thematic components, Rising Africa and Decline of the West, provided one element of Anglo-African literary tradition on which Du Bois' mythmaking is based. Here is a typical example of a poem in the Ethiopian tradition. It was published in the tenth Atlanta University Publication in 1905, over a pseudonym, "The Moon." Probably Du Bois, who edited the Atlanta publications and also edited a periodical called *The Moon* was the author:

> Ethiopia, my little daughter, why hast thou lingered and loitered in the Sun? See thy tall sisters, pale and blue of eye—see thy strong brothers, shrewd and slippery haired—see what they have done! Behold their gardens and their magic, their halls and wonder wheels! Behold their Gold, Gold, Gold!
>
> Flowers, O Mother Earth, I bring flowers, and the echo of a Song's song. Aye and the blue violet Humility, the mystic image flower of Heaven. And Mother, sweet Mother, in these great and misty years, I have seen Sights and heard Voices; Stories and Songs are quick within me—If I have loitered, sun-kissed, O forgive me, Mother yet chide me not bitterly—I too have lived.

The typically "Ethiopian" element of this poem is its assumption that Caucasians and Ethiopians are separate varieties of humanity with distinct destinies competing for honor in the eyes of history and the world. The characters of this poem represent historical forces, not real human beings. The argument is that Africans are a special people with special gifts and that blacks are in some ways superior to whites. To the African genius are attributed such traits as tropical dreaminess, feminine aestheticism, and a childlike love of nature. The Europeans of the first stanza are assigned their own traditional qualities by the use of such words as "pale," "strong," "shrewd," and "slippery."

The dreamy little Ethiopia is a minor avatar of the sleeping titaness who looms in **"The Riddle of the Sphinx"**:

> Dark Daughter of the lotus leaves that watch the Southern Sea!
> Wan spirit of a prisoned soul a-panting to be free!
> The muttered music of thy streams, the whisper of the deep,
> Have kissed each other in God's name and kissed a world to sleep.

This woman is a personification of Africa, a sleeping world, a giantess, raped by pygmies while she sleeps. "The burden of white men bore her back and the white world stifled her sighs." The poet describes the ascendency of the

West, based upon Mediterranean culture, and predicts its eventual going under:

> down
>> down
>>> deep down,
>
> Till the devil's strength be shorn,
> Till some dim, darker David, a-hoeing of his
>     corn,
> And married maiden, mother of God,
> Bid the black Christ be born!

In summary, Ethiopianism may be defined as the effort of the English-speaking Black or African person to view his past enslavement and present cultural dependency in terms of the broader history of civilization. It serves to remind him that this present scientific technological civilization, dominated by Western Europe for a scant four hundred years, will go under certainly—like all the empires of the past. It expresses the belief that the tragic racial experience has profound historical value, that it has endowed the African with moral superiority and made him a seer. Du Bois's poetry, while highly original, is nonetheless a product of this tradition, and therefore traditional. T. S. Eliot's poetry, by way of comparison, works within the European tradition of interpretive mythology although it is clearly innovative.

European interpretive mythology is the second of the two traditions basic to Du Bois's mythmaking. In *The Survival of the Pagan Gods,* a study of classical mythology in the Renaissance, Jean Seznec discusses the medieval practice of examining Greco-Roman mythology with the intention of either discovering within it, or assigning to it, Christian meaning. He discusses the ancient origins of this practice among the pre-Christian Greeks and Romans, who, attempting to understand the meanings of stories that were already very old, developed theories of interpretation in order to render myths intelligible. This tradition, once revived in the Middle Ages, endured throughout the Renaissance, and as Douglas Bush has shown, became a mode functional to English and American poetry.

How can it be known that Du Bois was aware of the tradition of interpretive mythology and that he consciously wrote in this tradition? In Chapter VIII of *The Souls of Black Folk,* in the section titled **"Of the Quest of the Golden Fleece,"** Du Bois demonstrated his awareness of this kind of writing and his desire to experiment with it:

> Have you ever seen a cotton-field white with harvest,—its golden fleece hovering above the black earth like a silvery cloud edged with dark green, its bold white signals waving like foam of billows from Carolina to Texas across that Black and human Sea? I have sometimes half-suspected that here the winged ram Chrysomallus left that Fleece after which Jason and his Argonauts went vaguely wandering into the shadowy East three thousand years ago; and certainly one might frame a pretty and not far-fetched analogy of witchery and dragon's teeth, and blood and armed men, between the ancient and the modern Quest of the Golden Fleece in the Black Sea.

In an earlier chapter of the same book, **"Of the Wings of Atalanta,"** Du Bois had demonstrated his skill at updating mythology and adapting it to the needs of his times. *The Quest of the Silver Fleece,* in 1911, brought to maturity the ideas briefly outlined in the parent essay. In this novel he created a universe in which the ideology of progressive socialism and the traditionalism of Christian black nationalism work harmoniously within the framework of a Greek myth.

*The Quest of the Silver Fleece* is a story of witchcraft and voodoo magic. Zora, the heroine of the tale, makes her first appearance as an elfin child, personifying the supposedly preternatural traits of the primitive mind. "We black folks is got the *spirit,*" she says. White folk may think they rule, but, "We'se lighter and cunninger; we fly right through them; we go and come again just as we wants to." Elspeth, the mother of Zora, is a malevolent black witch, who sows a wondrous cotton crop in a scene reminiscent of Cadmus's planting the dragon's teeth. The cotton crop is first stolen by the aristocratic Cresswell family, then woven into a wedding dress, and perhaps it is the magic of Medea (Elspeth-Zora) that begins to eat away at the vitality of Cresswell's bride. By the end of the story, Zora matures from elf-child to Ethiopian queen, who appears as a haunting "mirage of other days," ensconced in a "setting of rich, barbaric splendor."

A good clue to the meaning of any obscure poetic system may sometimes be found by examining its employment of traditional devices, and this method is useful in dealing with a poet like Du Bois. So typical was Ethiopianism of Du Bois's rhetoric that George Schuyler's satirization of his speaking style, while grotesque, was apt nonetheless. "I want to tell you that our destiny lies in the stars. Ethiopia's fate is in the balance. The Goddess of the Nile weeps bitter tears at the feet of the Sphinx. The lowering clouds gather over the Congo and the lightning flashes o'er Togoland. To your tents, O Israel! The hour is at hand." Among Du Bois's longer and more difficult poems is **"Children of the Moon,"** which blends the Ethiopian and Western mythological traditions. It tells the story of a despairing woman who finds a "highway to the moon," at the end of which lies

> a twilight land,
> Where, hardly-hid, the sun
> Sent softly-saddened rays of
> Red and brown to burn the iron soil
> And bathe the snow-white peaks
> In mighty splendor.

There she discovers a race of black men but no women:

> Black were the men,
> Hard-haired and silent-slow,
> Moving as shadows,
> Bending with face of fear to earthward;
> And women there were none.

Under her guidance the men build a tower which she climbs to "stand beneath the burning shadow of [a] peak, Beneath the whirring of almighty wings," where she hears a voice from "near-far" saying:

> "I am Freedom—
> Who sees my face is free—

He and his."

The god reveals his name, but "who shall look and live?" Not daring, at first, to look, the goddess is persuaded in the end by "the sobbing of small voices—down, down far into the night," to climb:

> Up! Up! to the blazing blackness
> Of one veiled face.
> And endless folding and unfolding,
> Rolling and unrolling of almighty wings.

And then the poem moves to its climax:

> I rose upon the Mountain of the Moon
> I felt the blazing glory of the Sun;
> I heard the Song of Children crying, "Free!"
> I saw the face of Freedom—
> And I died.

The poem calls to mind the Egyptian myth in which Isis, the Nile goddess, ascends the heavens to do battle with Ra, the sun god, to force him to reveal his name.

In order to create the world of **"Children of the Moon,"** Du Bois drew not only upon his knowledge of black Christian nationalism but also upon Greek and Egyptian mythology. The narrator is reminiscent of Isis, the moon goddess, patroness and teacher, Magna Mater of ancient Egypt, and Isis represents the Nilotic Africans whom Du Bois believed to have brought the Egyptians the civilizing arts. She was conceived by Du Bois as a black woman. Born a woman, Isis was later elevated, according to the mythographers, to divine status. The goddess is an appropriate symbol of the spirit of black civilization within Du Bois's poetic system. She becomes the Great Mother of Men in the Moon—black people—as Isis was the nourishing mother of ancient Egypt. "Isis, the mother," said Du Bois, "is still titular goddess, in thought if not in name, of the dark continent."

Du Bois provided one clue to the mythology of **"Children of the Moon"** when he spoke, in a later essay, of Ethiopian history as "the main current of Negro culture, from the Mountains of the Moon to the Mediterranean, blossoming on the lower Nile, but never severed from the Great Lakes of Inner Africa. The Children of the Moon are described as "moving shadows." They live in a twilight land," and they labor beneath the "burning shadow" of a peak. One suspects that this land in which they live is to be associated with Ethiopia, the land of shadows, mentioned in Isaiah and referred to as "Ethiopia, the shadowy," in *The Souls of Black Folk.* Throughout the tradition references to Ethiopia were meant to include all African peoples, of course.

Du Bois's interest in Ethiopian rhetoric made itself felt in much of his writing, as for example, in the herald's oration in the lost pageant *Star of Ethiopia:*

> Hear ye, hear ye! All them that come to know the truth and listen to the tale of the Wisest and Gentlest of the Races of Men whose faces be Black. Hear ye, hear ye! And learn the ancient Glory of Ethiopia, All-Mother of men, whose wonders men forgot. See how beneath the Mountains of the Moon, alike in the Valley of Father Nile and in ancient Negro-land and At-

> lantis the Black Race ruled and strove and fought and sought the Star of Faith and Freedom even as other races did and do. Fathers of Men and Sires of Children golden, black and brown, keep silence and hear this mighty word.

The Mountains of the Moon referred to in the above passage and in **"Children of the Moon"** are a semi-fictitious range, first mentioned in Ptolemy's *Geographica*. Recent scholarship associates them with the Ruwenzori Range. The Children of the Moon are blacks from central Africa, the area of the Nile-Congo watershed. They can be seen either as Congolese or Nilotics, therefore, which makes them symbolic of two of the great branches of African people: not only those who went down the Nile to Egypt but also those who followed the Congo, which "passed and rose red and reeking in the sunlight—thundered to the sea—thundered through the sea in one long line of blood, with tossing limbs and echoing cries of pain." The Children of the Moon symbolized not only the ancient Ethiopians but twentieth-century Afro-Americans as well. And the moon goddess is no more Isis than she is the afflicted womanhood of Harlem.

The tedious tower building in **"Children of the Moon"** parallels the tower building in **"Star of Ethiopia."** "Hear ye, hear ye! All them that dwell by the Rivers of Waters and in the beautiful, the Valley of Shadows, and listen to the ending of this tale. Learn Sisters and Brothers, how above the Fear of God, Labor doth build on Knowledge; how Justice tempers Science and how Beauty shall be crowned in Love beneath the Cross. Listen, O Isles, for all the pageant returns in dance and song to build this Tower of Eternal Light beneath the Star." The Tower of Eternal Light, built in **"Star of Ethiopia,"** like the tower that the Children of the Moon build is reminiscent of Obelisk, which the Egyptians saw as representing a petrified sun's ray. It leads upward towards the sun, for which the Egyptians used the symbol of a winged disk. In 1911, an adaption of the symbol, in which the solar disk is replaced by the face of a black man, was printed on the cover of the *Crisis,* the official organ of the National Association for the Advancement of Colored People, edited by Du Bois. The black face surrounded by wings is, of course, the terrible vision that the goddess finally approaches in **"Children of the Moon."** The wings are the wings of Ethiopia, mentioned by Isaiah in one of Du Bois's favorite Biblical passages:

> Ah! Land of the buzzing wings
> Which lies beyond the rivers of Ethiopia,
> That sends ambassadors by sea,
> In papyrus vessels on the face of the waters:
> To a nation tall and sleek,
> To a nation dreaded near and far,
> To a nation strong and triumphant.

The narrator climbs the Tower up to the sun in much the same way that Isis ascended the heavens, when only a woman, to force the Sun God to unveil his secrets. To lift the veil of Isis is to read the meaning of some obscure riddle. Proclus, the Greek Neoplatonic philosopher, describes a statute of Isis bearing the following inscription: "I am that which is, has been, and shall be. My veil no one has lifted. The fruit I bore was the Sun." What lies behind the veil of this poem? What does the woman see when the wings unveil the face? Perhaps she sees the face of blazing blackness, the eclipse of the West. Perhaps she sees her own reflection, the face of Isis, the African, "Star of Ethiopia, All-Mother of Men, who gave the world the Iron Gift and Gift of Faith, the Pain of Humility and Sorrow Song of Pain, and Freedom, Eternal Freedom, underneath the Star." Du Bois's poetry often unveils the face of a black god as in the story of the King in the land of the Heavy Laden, who summons his only loyal servant, a woman, to go forth in battle against "the heathen." Smiling, the King commands:

> "Go smite me mine enemies, that they cease to do evil in my sight. . . . "
>
> "Oh King," she cried, "I am but a woman."
> And the King answered: "Go, then, Mother of Men."
>
> And the woman said, "Nay, King, but I am still a maid."
>
> Whereat the King cried: "O maid, made Man, thou shalt be Bride of God."
>
> And yet the third time the woman shrank at the thunder in her ears, and whispered: "Dear God, I am black!"
>
> The king spake not, but swept the veiling of his face aside and lifted up the light of his countenance upon her and lo! it was black.
>
> So the woman went forth on the hills of God to do battle for the King, on that drear day in the land of the Heavy Laden, when the heathen raged and imagined a vain thing.

The King is a personification of God, it seems clear; like the "Thing of Wings," he is a veiled godhead. The "Thing of Wings," finally seen as "the blazing blackness / Of one veiled Face," is also a black God. The veil is not only a barrier; it is a symbol of the challenge that this barrier provides. Blackness, or the veil, stands between black folk and the full promise of America, but the veil will be put aside for those who are brave enough to see what lies beyond it. In other words, as Ralph Ellison put it, "Black will make you, or black will un-make you."

The veil is often but not always symbolic of black skin. It represents the limits within which the souls of black folk are confined, but veils also represent the limitations that white folk have placed upon their own vision. Possibly Du Bois borrowed the image from Thomas Jefferson, who spoke of "that immovable veil of black which covers all the emotions of the [black] race." But Du Bois gives things an ironic twist by persistently insisting that the veil is a gift that, like an infant's caul, endows its bearer with second sight.

Du Bois was fascinated by mystic symbolism. As Kelly Miller observed, he was poetic, "his mind being cast in a weird and fantastic mold." He enjoyed ritual, as he tells us himself, in describing his solitary twenty-fifth birthday celebration: "The night before I had heard Schubert's beautiful *Unfinished Symphony,* planned my celebration and written to Grandma and Mabel and had a curious lit-

tle ceremony with candles, Greek wine, oil, and song and prayer." The mysticism of the Sphinx seems to have had real meaning for him as it has had, not only for Garveyites, but for the middle-class Africans and Afro-Americans who have pledged secret societies. Charles Wesley's official *History of Alpha Phi Alpha* recognizes the tendency of middle-class blacks to experiment with the Ethiopian tradition in poetry. . . . Such poetry allows an identification with symbols of stability, permanency, and high culture. English-speaking, middle-class Afro-Americans during the late Victorian and Edwardian periods needed an opportunity to be proud of their Africanness, just as Garveyites would a decade later.

Du Bois's Ethiopianism was really typical of the thinking of black middle-class intellectuals during the first two decades of the twentieth century. Of course, Du Bois was in a position to encourage Ethiopianism by publishing the verse of young poets who were interested in the tradition. Langston Hughes's poem, "The Negro Speaks of Rivers," often reprinted with the dedication, "To W. E. B. Du Bois," first appeared in the *Crisis* of June, 1921, and was possibly inspired by Du Bois's **"The Story of Africa,"** which appeared in that same journal some seven years earlier. The similarities are, in any case, striking.

Thus is it possible to speak of at least one black literary tradition, the "Ethiopian," borrowing a term from Afro-Atlantic political studies and adding it to American literary history. This tradition is manifested in the work of major poets, minor poets, and unsophisticated versifiers. It rested upon a view of history as outlined in Walker's *Appeal* and stated more calmly in such essays as Alexander Crummell's "The Destined Superiority of the Negro." W. E. B. Du Bois is the central figure in this tradition. The most traditional of Afro-American poets, he was yet the most innovative within the tradition. There is a difference in degree of sophistication—but not in sentiment expressed—between Du Bois's **"Riddle of the Sphinx"** and the following lines by Marcus Garvey:

> Out of cold old Europe these white men came,
> From caves, dens and holes, without any fame,
> Eating their dead's flesh and sucking their blood,
> Relics of the Mediterranean flood.

Whether there are other Afro-American literary traditions and what, if any, effects the content of Afro-American literature may have had upon the forms employed must be the subject of future studies.

Can Du Bois the social scientist be reconciled with Du Bois the poet and prophet of race? How could a man so well trained in social science have allowed the Ethiopian tradition, rooted in nineteenth-century *Volksgeist* mythologies, to dominate his thought?

As a youth Du Bois was romantically involved with the idea of social science, which he naively believed might yield a science of racial advancement. He was infatuated, like many other young men of his generation with the notion of a "science of man." But Du Bois's theories of social change were not always consistent. Sociology became relatively less important with the passage of years until by 1910 it was no longer Du Bois's chief concern. Though he was capable of writing perfectly good sociology, it does not appear that he wanted to. He turned—and it would seem with more satisfactory results—to the power of imagination as his chief instrument for changing public morality. He became a crusading journalist, a novelist, and a poet of Ethiopianism, dedicated to embodying his view of history in mythical form. (pp. 411-26)

> *Wilson J. Moses, "The Poetics of Ethiopianism: W. E. B. Du Bois and Literary Black Nationalism," in* American Literature, *Vol. XLVII, No. 3, November, 1975, pp. 411-26.*

### Arnold Rampersad

What Henry James wrote of Nathaniel Hawthorne is equally true of W. E. B. Du Bois: "our author," James wrote, "must accept the awkward as well as the graceful side of his fame; for he has the advantage of pointing a valuable moral." Hawthorne's moral was that "the flower of art blooms only where the soil is deep, that it takes a great deal of history to produce a little literature, that it needs a complex social machinery to set a writer in motion." Du Bois's reputation as a man of literature is surely the "awkward" side of such fame as he possesses, and one meaning of his awkward side is essentially the same as Hawthorne's (as James saw it), with an important difference. The flower of art will bloom only where there is liberty or the memory of liberty. Du Bois understood the need for justice in the growth of the flower of art: "The time has not yet come," he wrote in 1913, "for the great development of American Negro literature. The economic stress is too great and the racial persecution too bitter to allow the leisure and the poise for which literature calls." Or, as James went on in the famous passage about Hawthorne, "American civilization has hitherto had other things to do than to produce flowers. . . ."

The other, more graceful sides of Du Bois's reputation vary with the attitude of each observer but rest somewhere in his pioneering and persisting works of history and sociology and his decades of crusading journalism against neoslavery in the South and in some respects similar oppression in the North. Trained at Fisk, Harvard, and the University of Berlin, he produced essays, monographs, and books of history and sociology that gave him by themselves the most prominent place among black American thinkers, so that the NAACP could write with justification in 1934 that "he created, what never existed before, a Negro intelligentsia, and many who have not read a word of his writings are his spiritual disciples and descendants." Certainly of Afro-American writers and the Afro-American theme one may claim of Du Bois what has been written of the English sociologists Sidney and Beatrice Webb—that every creative writer who has touched on the field of sociology has, directly or indirectly, been influenced by them.

But Du Bois ventured into the field of belles-lettres. And not by accident but as part of the plan of his life. On his twenty-fifth birthnight (1893) he confided solemnly to his journal that "these are my plans: to make a name in science, to make a name in art and thus to raise my race."

A bibliography of his writings runs to some two thousand entries, out of which it is difficult to separate those completely untouched by his love of art. But there are poems enough for a slender volume, a multitude of partly personal, impressionistic essays, some verse drama, autobiographies, five novels—including a trilogy composed near his ninetieth birthday. Great reputations have been made of a smaller volume of writing, but most of this work has contributed little to Du Bois's fame. Indeed, his basic competence as a man of literature has been challenged. An angry Claude McKay, singed by a Du Bois review of his first novel, informed him that "nowhere in your writings do you reveal any comprehension of aesthetics." The poet, novelist, and critic Arna Bontemps thought Du Bois unimaginative in that he leaned toward "the tidy, the well-mannered, the Victorian" in his choice of literature. His first biographer Francis Broderick barely mentioned this belletristic writing and declared that Du Bois wanted "a literature of uplift in the genteel tradition." His second biographer, Elliott M. Rudwick, mentions the creative work not at all. And though Du Bois called his second novel "my favorite book" among the two dozen or more he published, a major historian of the black novel in America dismissed him as a "Philistine."

Du Bois himself did not show great pride in this aspect of his work; he was apologetic on the very few occasions he wrote of his efforts in literature. His first novel was "really an economic study of some merit"—the sum total of his commentary on the work; he was hesitant to write "mere" autobiography; **Dark Princess** was his favorite book but that remark is all he ever ventured about the novel; his poems were "tributes to Beauty, unworthy to stand alone." Nor was he always complimentary about actual achievement in black literature. In 1913 he saw the body as "large and creditable [though] only here and there work that could be called first-class." In 1915 a five-point plan for the future of the race included "a revival of art and literature," presumably moribund. In 1926, surveying the field for the *Encyclopaedia Brittanica* he judged that "all these things are beginnings rather than fulfillments," though they were certainly significant beginnings. In 1933 he mourned that the so-called "Harlem Renaissance" had "never taken real and lasting root" and that "on such an artificial basis no real literature can grow." Somewhere around 1960 one of his fictional characters looked in vain for recent work of major artistic quality: "In the last decade we have not produced a poem or a novel, a history or play of stature—nothing but gamblers, prizefighters and jazz. . . . Once we could hear Shakespeare in Harlem."

But with these splashings of cold water there was an equally cool and lucid sense of the potential of black writing, so that Du Bois could write in April 1920 that "a renaissance of American Negro literature is due," and observe in the decade that followed, almost from the day of his prediction, the accuracy of his insight. Nor is there any lack of evidence that Du Bois was highly regarded as a man of literature, from the early praise of William and Henry James and the reverence in which he was held by black poets such as James Weldon Johnson and Langston Hughes, to the radical socialist magazine *The Messenger,* which in 1919 damned Du Bois with praise of him as "the leading litterateur of the race." But more important than testimonies is a survey of his somewhat motley collection of essays, poems, novels, and other work for the ways in which he helped to shape modern Afro-American writing. For Du Bois, maturing in the most repressive period of black American history, took unto himself the primary responsibility of the would-be mythmaker, applying a luminous imagination and intelligence to "Adam's task, of giving names to things." It is only slight exaggeration to say that wherever the Afro-American subsequently went as a writer, Du Bois had been there before him, anticipating both the most vital ideas of later currency and the very tropes of their expression. Some of these anticipations are slighter than others, but none is trivial to anyone who knows black literature. Collectively they underscore Du Bois's significance and raise challenging questions about the relationship of politics, art, and the individual imagination.

If free verse became the basic medium of black poetry—and it did—Du Bois was, as far as I know, the first black poet publicly to break with rhyme and blank verse in **"A Litany of Atlanta."** The theme of Africa as a proper and necessary object of black celebration was introduced into black verse by Du Bois in his **"Day in Africa."** He was the first to celebrate the beauty of human blackness in his **"Song of the Smoke." "The Burden of Black Women"** is the first published poem to dwell on hatred as the consequence of the white destruction of crucial institutions, particularly marriage and motherhood, in black culture. Du Bois was the first black poet simultaneously to love trees and turn his back on what Nikki Giovanni called "tree poems"—the first, in other words, to resist the concept of poetry as escape from social and political reality. If *Native Son* dramatized the black capacity for violent protest and in so doing, as Irving Howe claimed, changed American culture "forever," Du Bois's John Jones in 1903 and Matthew Towns in 1928 had struck earlier blows against white Americans long before Bigger rebelled. Arthur P. Davis has noted that in **The Quest of the Silver Fleece** Du Bois ended the poisonous reign of near-white heroines in black fiction with his characterization of Zora; the novel is the first *Bildungsroman* in Afro-American fiction, as Addison Gayle points out, and the first black novel to present and analyze economics as a significant factor in American culture in the significant manner of Cable, Dreiser, and Dos Passos. In its portrait of the manipulative Carolyn Wynn Du Bois published in 1911 the first truly psychological study of a character in black fiction—not, as Robert Bone argues, the hero of Johnson's *The Autobiography of an Ex-Colored Man* (1912). **Dark Princess** (1928) is the first work of art, as far as I know, to identify and promulgate the doctrine of the third world.

And when Du Bois wrote in the *Atlantic Monthly* in 1897 of the "Strivings of the Negro People" and declared the irrevocable twoness of the black American, he laid the foundation of all future literary renditions of the subject. True to his gift he both analyzed and simultaneously provided the metaphor appropriate to his analysis. The metaphor was the Veil, anticipatory of the central image of Ellison's *Invisible Man,* for "the Negro is a sort of seventh son, born with a veil, and gifted with second sight in this American world—a world which yields him no true self-consciousness, but only lets him see himself through the revelation of the other world." The crucial analysis followed: "It is a peculiar sensation, this double-consciousness, this sense of always looking at one's self through the eyes of others, of measuring one's soul by the tape of a world that looks on in amused contempt and pity. One ever feels his twoness,—an American, a Negro; two souls, two thoughts, two unreconciled strivings; two warring ideals in one dark body, whose dogged strength alone keeps it from being torn asunder."

If one excludes from consideration a personal desire for fame, there are perhaps four important aspects to Du Bois's enormous concern with the development of black literature in America—and his own part in it (he understood by the middle of his teenage years that—as he told Barrett Wendell at Harvard in 1890,—he had "something to say to the world" and was determined to prepare himself "in order to say it well"). First, Du Bois believed that the production of a body of great literature and other art was the necessary basis for the entrance of Afro-America into the polity of civilized peoples, a notion based on the concept of distinct racial "gifts" then accepted by a host of scientists and social observers attempting to understand the meaning of race. He argued in 1926 that "until the art of the black folk compels recognition they will not be rated as human" (he might have argued instead that until they were rated as human, their art would not be appreciated). He believed, following the line of the more liberal sociologists and anthropologists (but using, nevertheless, the concepts of the same highly suspect racial science) that "the Negro is primarily an artist," though he knew that "the usual way of putting this is to speak disdainfully of his sensuous nature."

Secondly, Du Bois unquestionably saw the art of literature as important in the almost one-sided war of propaganda waged against the black at the turn of the century in books such as Charles Carroll's *The Negro a Beast* (1900), Shufeldt's *The Negro: A Menace to American Civilization* (1907), and Thomas Dixon, Jr.'s *The Leopard's Spots* (1902) and *The Clansman* (1905), the latter filmed eventually by D. W. Griffith as *Birth of a Nation.* But if he declared in 1926 that "all art is propaganda and ever must be, despite the wailing of the purists," he also repeatedly defended the need for candor and artistic freedom. Any mention of black life in America, he noted, had caused for a hundred years "an ugly picture, a dirty allusion, a nasty comment or a pessimistic forecast. The result is that the Negro today," he wrote in 1924 in defence of Eugene O'Neill, "fears any attempt of the artist to paint Negroes. He is not satisfied unless everything is perfect and proper and beautiful and joyful and hopeful . . . lest his human foibles and shortcomings be seized by his enemies for the purposes of the ancient and hateful propaganda." Du Bois knew of black folk, as he wrote two years later, that "we can afford the Truth. White folk today cannot." The black should be set before the world, he wrote in 1915, "as both a creative artist and a strong subject for artistic treatment." But it is important to insist that Du Bois was no part of the clamor by certain middle-class and aristocratic members of the black intelligentsia for a literature set in the middle-class, to show whites that some blacks, at least, were capable of refinement—although it was a call in which his sometime (1919-1926) literary editor on *The Crisis,* Jessie Fauset, was partly complicitous, and with which he appeared to some observers to be in agreement.

Thirdly, Du Bois sought out the power of art because of an increasing sense of the limitation of empirical social science and academic historiography. In 1896 he could congratulate himself on complying with "the general principles laid down in German universities" when he prepared his first book, on the African slave trade; in *The Philadelphia Negro* (1899) he intoned that the social scientist "must ever tremble lest some personal bias, some moral conviction or some unconscious trend of thought due to previous training, has to a degree distorted the picture in his view." But under the pressure of grave social forces he had already begun to doubt—as he stated in 1898—that empirical research into society would "eventually lead to a systematic body of knowledge deserving the name of science." In 1903 he deplored the tendency of inferior sociology to lapse into "bad metaphysics and false psychology"; the next year he declared that sociologists were "still only groping after a science." The goals of social research, and his methods and approaches, became less scholarly, more political, more imaginative. A volume of social study published by him in 1906 did not seek "definite conclusions. Its object is rather to blaze the way and point out a few general truths."

And fourthly, Du Bois's turn toward art was empowered by perhaps the central factor of his overall career—his perception of the need for action, not subservience or contemplation, in the face of American racism. The growth of Du Bois's practice of art coincided with the growth of his political activism, beginning with his return to the South as an adult in 1897 and reaching its first decisive point with his 1903 challenge to the authority of Booker T. Washington, the most powerful black leader of the age. From this step eventually came Du Bois's founding of the radical Niagara Movement (radical in its demands of civil rights and other basic freedoms), and his leadership of the movement in the years between 1905 and 1910, when he felt professionally the weight of Booker T. Washington's antagonism. This period ended with his departure from the university for the fledgling NAACP in 1910, to become editor of its crusading monthly magazine *The Crisis.* His turn to art in the course of these thirteen or so years was not for relief from the hurly-burly of political action but was an aspect of political action itself. And such achievements in form and theme as he accomplished are testimony, in the context of black American literature, to the acuteness of Lukács's observation that "new styles, new ways of representing reality, though always linked to old forms and styles, never arise from any immanent dialectic within artistic forms. Every new style is socially and historically determined and is the product of a social development."

For it is clear that Du Bois showed no great potential for achievement in art much beyond skilled mediocrity and imitativeness until he experienced the goad of Southern racism. He showed very little interest in the discussion of theoretical issues pertaining to art and the process of imagination and literary creation. His pronouncements on literature are generally negligible in depth and scope; one must recover, from observation of his literary practice, the factors that pertained to his performance as a man of literature. And what empowered Du Bois as an Afro-American mythmaker and distinguished him from more superficially gifted and involved artists was a combination of great intellect, greater energy, and—above all—a capacity for feeling the political experience so intensely that its purposes were subsumed, as it were, into every fibre of his intellectual being at least as intensely as the famous poet contemplating the sparrow in the gravel; and allowing that intensity to inspire art and scholarship out of imitation and mediocrity and into the world of action.

Du Bois himself dated the time of his turn toward action. The year was 1897. With his doctoral thesis published as the first volume in the Harvard Historical Studies and the research completed for perhaps his greatest work of scholarship, *The Philadelphia Negro,* he set out to create the mechanism for a one-hundred-year empirical study of black life divided into ten great subjects, each subject the focus of study for one year, every ten years the cycle repeating itself. His base was the classroom and his study at Atlanta University. Du Bois recollected how he came to change the basic course of his life:

> At the very time when my studies were most successful, there cut across this plan which I had as a scientist, a red ray which could not be ignored. I remember when it first, as it were, startled me to my feet: a poor Negro in central Georgia, Sam Hose, had killed his landlord's wife. I wrote out a careful and reasoned statement concerning the evident facts and started down to the Atlanta *Constitution* office, carrying in my pocket a letter of introduction to Joel Chandler Harris. I did not get there. On the way news met me: Sam Hose had been lynched, and they said that his knuckles were on exhibition at a grocery store farther down on Mitchell Street, along which I was walking. I turned back to the University. I began to turn aside from my work. I did not meet Joel Chandler Harris nor the editor of the *Constitution.*

The impact on his art of this heightened degree of Du Bois's understanding of the meaning of action, power, and the political was firm and accruing, but also gradual and sometimes wayward. For he embarked on this radical passage without any congeries of beliefs that might be called ideology in any strict sense of the term; indeed, he proceeded with two biases that on one level appeared to contradict each other as well as ideology itself, but which were, on another, more functional level, its surrogates. First, he retained his respect for empirical sociology and academic historiography; secondly, he deepened his racial or nationalistic commitment to the black folk of America, laying the foundation and developing the basic dialectical superstructure for all subsequent black nationalist pleading. Simultaneously he suppressed the socialist methodology he had learned as a student in Germany, though by the end of the first decade of the century he would identify himself as a quasi-socialist, and then briefly join the American Socialist Party. Socialist analysis—socialist fervor—was resisted both by scholarship as he understood its demands and by the exclusive tendencies of black nationalism. But Du Bois's black nationalism was further tempered by the fact that the essence of his politics was his demand for the *integration* of blacks into American society, a demand that took precedence as an idea and as a shaper of myth and image over the insistent nationalism that formed the basis of his argument that blacks should enjoy all the rights of the typical American citizen.

The absence of an ideologically consistent core of beliefs—the presence of this noble confusion—encouraged Du Bois to develop, especially in his essays between 1897 and 1903 (when *The Souls of Black Folk* appeared) a dazzling variety of metaphoric, ironic, pietistic, and sentimental rhetorical strategies appropriate to liberal intellection and liberal discourse. Much later in life, essentially a communist without a party card, Du Bois regretted that too much sentiment and moralizing, too little Marx and Freud, had informed his early work. The evidence is there, though, that he was aware of a problem even as he wrote. In 1904, writing about *The Souls of Black Folk,* he innocently admitted that "the style and workmanship" of his book did not make its meaning altogether clear, that the collection conveyed "a clear message" but that around this center floated "a penumbra" of subjectivity, vagueness, and half-veiled allusions. "In its larger aspects," he said, groping to understand what he had wrought, "the style is tropical—African."

The aching ideological contradictions—in other words, the *charm* of these moving and important early essays—gave way to more rigid ideas and forms. The next collection of essays, *Darkwater: Voices from Within the Veil* (1920), would draw the wish from one reviewer, a long-time acquaintance of Du Bois, that the author would walk "more in the manner of the Nazarene." Here and in *The Negro* (1915), a survey of the African peoples on the continent and elsewhere, there is a disjunction between analysis and art, as there is in the many dramatized editorials that gave bite to the *Crisis* magazine. Du Bois had consciously become, as he admitted, a propagandist. While it is partly true that with the publication of *The Negro* Du Bois became, as Wilson Moses put it, "a poet of Ethiopianism, dedicated to embodying his view of history in mythical form," no significant formal poetry emerged from this aspect of his writing; he essentially preserved the approach to historiography of writers like Macaulay and Carlyle, for whom the writing of history was a dramatic art. In Du Bois's grand study of the postbellum South, *Black Reconstruction in America* (1935), most of the "artistic" passages can be excised from the text without the slightest modification of the argument and spirit of the work. As a historian Du Bois was showing a certain imaginative and stylistic range; as a poet, however, despite the clear passion he brought to both tasks, he seems to have been relatively uninspired.

The poetry and fiction that Du Bois wrote during his first years of radical commitment are another matter. The bulk of his significant poetry was composed during his leadership of the Niagara Movement, after his decision to join the radical ranks and before the NAACP rescued him from the wilderness of deepening alienation and confusion. The art of this period—1905 to 1910—reflects an intellectual and spiritual turmoil distinctly different from that of *The Souls of Black Folk.* The emblem of this period might well show Du Bois in anguish on a train returning to Atlanta in the last week of September 1906, uncertain of the fate of his wife and daughter, as well as of his work and the university, in the worst race riot in the South in the first decade of the century. On this train journey Du Bois wrote **"A Litany of Atlanta."**

> We raise our shackled hands and charge thee,
> God
> by the bones of our stolen fathers, by the tears
> of our dead mothers, by the very blood of Thy
> crucified Christ: What meaneth this? Tell us the
> plan; give us the sign!

"Surely," the poet asks, "thou, too, art not white, O Lord, a pale, bloodless, heartless thing!" Or is God dead? But the poet recoils from "these wild, blasphemous words":

> Thou art still the God of our black fathers and
> in
> Thy Soul's Soul sit some soft darkenings, some
> shadowing of the velvet night.
> But whisper—speak—call, great God, for Thy
> silence is white terror to our heart! The way, O
> God, show us the way and point us the path!

The thou's and thy's and art's should not obscure the importance of the poem, or its power, for in the fire of the political moment so replete with personal meaning Du Bois severed the ancient link between black poetry and rhyme or blank verse, as well as to the three dominant modes of Afro-American verse of the age—the poetry of social uplift by writers such as Frances E. W. Harper, the Afro-Georgian lyricism of Braithwaite, Dunbar, and others, and the immensely popular dialect tradition, with its poles of maudlin pathos, on one hand, and low comedy, on the other—"the range between appetite and emotion, with certain lifts far beyond and above it," that William Dean Howells told us is the range of the black race.

With **"A Litany of Atlanta"** Du Bois opened the way for a black poetry of secularism, scepticism, and cultural authenticity, a poetry that surfaced swiftly and importantly again in his own works with **"Song of the Smoke,"** where for the first time an Afro-American poet unambiguously praised blackness of skin and the potential of the race compared to the white overlords:

> I will be black as blackness can—
> The blacker the mantle, the mightier the man!
> For blackness was ancient ere whiteness began.

And in **"The Burden of Black Women,"** later retitled **"The Riddle of the Sphinx,"** the hatred authentic to the black experience of life in America but anathema to the tropes of liberal discourse surfaced for the first time in published verse:

> The white world's vermin and filth:
> All the dirt of London,
> All the scum of New York

Valiant spoilers of women
. . . . . . . .
Bearing the white man's burden
Of Liquor and Lust and Lies.

. . . . . . . .
I hate them, Oh!
I hate them well,
I hate them, Christ!
As I hate Hell,
If I were God
I'd sound their knell
This day!

Not all the verse of this period, no matter how politically charged the theme, marked a significant achievement in Du Bois's efforts to poeticize the black experience and predicament. **"A Day in Africa"** introduces a new element into black poetical consciousness—Africa as an object of veneration for black Americans—but its ideas are confused and its language reflects this confusion:

I leaped and danced, and found
My breakfast poised aloft,
All served in living gold.
In purple flowered fields I wandered
Wreathed in crimson, blue and green.
My noon-tide meal did fawn about my feet
In striped sleekness.
I kissed it ere I killed it.

A "wild new creature" threatens the persona, who poises his spear in defiance. But the black warrior sees fear in the eyes of the animal (the white interloper in Africa) and refuses to kill it. Africa is color, freedom, sensual ease, courage, mercy. Yet the poem is an almost total failure; its form is overburdened by Du Bois's nearly absolute ignorance of his subject, Africa, whose history he had just begun to study after being awakened to its complexity by Franz Boas in 1906, when the anthropologist spoke at Atlanta University. Du Bois would not see Africa until 1923. Unlike the other three quoted poems, **"A Day in Africa"** is comparatively unmotivated except in the most abstract of ways. One is reminded again, first, that the apprehension of the need for action is hardly in itself ideology, and that still less is it automatically art when applied to the forms of art. The process and the difficulty of art are not abbreviated by the call to action. The firing of the radical imagination only further complicates the task of persuasion that the radical literateur undertakes. The problem of accommodating political thought within the scope of the imagination is still further subsumed into the creative writer's ultimate problem, at once commonplace and yet urgent—the problem of rhetoric.

Unable to achieve a consistent and credible equipoise between ideology and form, Du Bois found his final achievement as a poet in his position as pioneer, as bridge between often inspired imitation and later poetical authenticity in black literature. One clue to Du Bois's problems of equipoise lies in the fact that the dominant formal referent in his poetry is religion—and Du Bois, once his Congregationalist faith died, was never born again. A list of some of his titles shows his concern: A Litany of Atlanta, The Prayer of the Bantu, The Prayers of God, Hymn to the Peoples, Christ of the Andes; in addition to which he wrote parables featuring a black Christ and in other ways relied on religious constructs for intellectual deliverance. Religion in Du Bois's work has distinctly earthly correspondences; "the impenetrable meaning of human suffering matches the inscrutability of God; Christ is the incarnation of all human hope; Heaven is the world beyond the Veil; and life is Hell." And yet the use of religion is symptomatic of the poet's problems in representing ideas often in conflict with each other but striving for integration. The justification for the use of religion in this way did not come from the place of religion in Du Bois's life, or in the culture of the black folk, but from the historic role of religion in white culture. Thus Du Bois was attempting to fuse political passion within the traditional vehicles of a white spirituality whose effectiveness, indeed, whose very existence he was simultaneously calling into question. The use of the traditional vehicles gives a superficial monumentality to the tenor of his message, but a full union is not possible.

The change in Du Bois's art between the earlier essays of *The Souls of Black Folk* and the poems is reflected significantly in the distance between Du Bois's first important piece of published fiction, the short story **"Of the Coming of John"** in *Souls* and the later novels—but especially so in the case of his first novel *The Quest of the Silver Fleece.* In the short story a young black man leaves his small Southern town and becomes educated—and alienated from his fellow blacks, the whites, and himself; he returns home, is ostracized as a remote and possibly radical man, reacts blindly when he finds his sister struggling with a playful would-be white seducer, kills the man, and then possibly kills himself as a lynch mob closes in. In *The Quest of the Silver Fleece* a young black man discovers education, goes North to work and becomes involved in politics, almost succumbs to corruption, but returns home to rally his people in their struggle for education and a better life, prepared at the end to fight physically for their rights. In *Dark Princess* a young black man, embittered by racism, goes to Europe and becomes involved in a plot for an uprising of the darker people against white colonialism. He returns to the United States to report on the state of black culture, becomes involved in politics, almost succumbs to corruption, but is rescued in time; he atones for his sins by hard work and at the end of the novel is a changed man, dedicated to duty and willing to fight for his beliefs. In the *Black Flame* trilogy (1957, 1959, 1961) a young black man embarks on a life of service to his race as a teacher. Intellectually ungifted but patient and honorable, he is shaped in his life and career by the major events of black American history and by the culture of the South, where he lives almost all his life. He dies in the 1950's in his eighty-eighth year, witness to the first cracks in the wall of segregation but tragically uncertain of the value of his life of service. The trilogy also consistently dramatizes the major personalities and passages of his lifetime—Southern, national, international—with capitalism as the formidable villain of this complementary story, and rising socialism as its struggling hero.

The ideological shifting in the works and its effect upon form are noteworthy. In the first story, **"Of the Coming of John,"** the central drama is the struggle between the divided souls of the young black aspirant to culture in a racist world; and in spite of the violence of murder and possible suicide, pathos—not tragedy—marks the dramatic depth of the tale. The black folk is defined by its ignorance, the white folk by its reaction. The drama takes place in a world of political stasis that immobilizes time and history; society is essentially indecipherable, and the logical inference is an encompassing pessimism. The warring souls of the black, the story seems to say, must forever war, the contradictions therein are both endemic and permanent. Black alienation follows directly from education in racist America, and is worse than inevitable or pathological—black alienation is useless. The only way out of the gloom is perhaps through the wisdom and humanity of the narrator, a nameless professor at the college attended by John; but he or she, who might well be white, is baffled and quite concerned, but impotent. The black man must endure; the world prevails.

This depiction presented Du Bois with few formal problems. But he was never again to make pathos the focus of his art or to accept pessimism as the resolution of a black fiction—not because the situation of blacks never seemed rather hopeless to him or because blacks themselves were never pessimistic, but because he developed a different sense of the functioning of the world and history and a different sense of the potential of blacks and humanity in general. From this sense derived a different sense of the moral and political function of art and a different attitude toward form. The heroes of *Quest of the Silver Fleece* and *Dark Princess* are at first baffled and confused, as John was in the first story; but the burden of their stories is the resolution of bafflement and confusion, with the end of the stories presenting morally and politically earnest heroes and heroines preparing to swim boldly in a world that is still deep but now fathomable. The process shifts from one work to another but the basic pattern is the same. The baffled, divided hero is, in a sense, *reborn* into psychological monism or harmony, which is tantamount to moral and political zeal. This rebirth comes through education both from learned books and from manual labor, reuniting body and mind, intellect and muscle, as the souls are reunited. The hero discovers the way and atones for his sins, accepting duty and work as first principles of life, with love as its crowning glory. The immoral stasis of the world in **"Of the Coming of John"** gives way to the exposition of culture as process, and history and the world as both scrutable and stimulant to optimism. And the formal simplicity of the short story gives way to a formal complication that Du Bois strove with only limited success to manage.

Writing in *The World and Africa* just after World War II about the decline of western culture in the late nineteenth century, Du Bois deplored the fact that "art, in building, painting and literature, became cynical and decadent. Literature became realistic and therefore pessimistic." Though this was written when he was very close to communism, it is consistent with his attitudes toward fiction during the greater part of his life, or once he had become politically alert and committed to action. Art and pessimism were, for him, incompatible if art were to succeed. All art, he said in 1926, attacking the "art for art's sake" movement among certain black writers, is propaganda—

and black art must be propaganda "for gaining the right of black folk to love and enjoy." But his purpose was broader than is apparent in such a crude statement. It was "the bounden duty of black America" to create, preserve, and realize "Beauty" for America, for the aim of art and political struggle was not black power in isolation but a philosophically reconstructed universe. The tools in the creation of beauty had always been and must be, he said, truth—"the highest hand-maid of imagination . . . the one great vehicle of universal understanding"; and goodness, "in all its aspects of justice, honor and right—not for sake of an ethical sanction but as the one true method of gaining sympathy and human interest." Thus, Du Bois went on, "the apostle of Beauty . . . becomes the apostle of Truth and Right not by choice but by inner and outer compulsion."

These terms such as Truth and Beauty and Right are vague enough for us to miss the order of the process Du Bois is describing, but they are significant; indeed, they also suggest quaint ways in which he would, as a practicing writer, oppose realism. In both *Quest of the Silver Fleece* and *Dark Princess* (but *not* in *The Black Flame* decades after) the most terribly stilted language surfaces during decisive emotional or philosophical moments, and appears in the midst of otherwise conventionally mimetic dialogue and narration that show Du Bois to have some definite ability—not mere potential—as a novelist. But the failings of his work are there; though one finds depth of characterization in both novels, many more of the performers are types of humanity rather than creations credible outside of their ideological burden in the particular piece. There is, too, a fair amount of what one must regard as melodramatic and unsatisfying effects, notably in the end of *Dark Princess,* where a typical masque-like scene, replete with symbolism, supplants the otherwise sober auditing of the account. Such effects represent Du Bois's conscious choices as an artist, and it would be a mistake to consider them other than bad choices. They were, however, generated by his philosophy of art and by the fact that there was but one genre into which his story could fit. That genre was not finally the novel, which is what he called *Quest of the Silver Fleece,* or the romance, which is the way he identified *Dark Princess,* but the epic.

Epic in more than one sense—but literally so, in that the mature Du Bois fiction is the gravely serious story, recited in at times too lofty a tone and language, of a young (black) man of quality embarking on the most perilous of journeys within a grand landscape, on the success of which depends the future salvation of his race or nation—salvation on a relatively small scale in *Quest of the Silver Fleece,* on a worldwide scale in *Dark Princess.* What drove Du Bois to the epic form was that ecstatic optimism with which both novels end, an optimism that was the richest dividend of his awakened political consciousness. Applied to his writing, this optimism was compounded by his nostalgia for a vanished innocence within both a mythic Africa and humanity as a whole, by his sense of the potential of Africans and all humanity, and finally by his sense of the history of the world as the history of process. This sense enabled Du Bois to share vicariously in the intellectual and social homogeneity out of which the epic first sprang.

The realism to which Du Bois objected was close to that of such writers as Zola, the earlier Dreiser, and Frank Norris—and the difference between his sense of the epic and theirs is considerable. Their pessimism is formally exemplified in their worship of the fact, the detail, the superficial information of "that harsh, blunt, colorless tool called realism," as Norris himself put it in attempting to transcend its limitations. Du Bois had not turned his back on statistical sociology in order to create art based on accepting the surface as the substance of things; his politics did not allow him to be pessimistic; and his understanding of history and society diverted him—though not always—from those fallacies of naturalism and supernaturalism by which other writers complicated their art but betrayed their philosophical helplessness. Nor could he develop a highly symbolic art which would reflect a contemplative attitude to a mysterious universe and thus deflect the epic thrust of his socially centered narrative. There are two looming symbols in his first novel—cotton (the silver fleece of the title) and a great swamp. The swamp stands for the immoral past of the preliterate black; the best cotton grows where the swamp has been cleared, a task that requires unity and character on the part of the black folk. Thus literally one symbol is a transcendence of the other, and because the cotton is stripped of its monetary and inhuman significance and reidentified with human work and thought and character, it carries within itself as a symbol the force of its own self-transcendence, since its power as a symbol derives from its part in the world of human action.

The major formal tension in Du Bois's fiction, and the source of its major shortcomings, arises from the crucial relationship of the narration to history on one hand and to the particular, chosen moment on the other; between the depiction of historical process and the depiction of its immediate product; between—if you will—life, and the chosen slice of life. Characters fail as art when they take their total essence from history; they tend to succeed when they take their essence more from the historical moment, which is itself governed—but distantly—by history. In **The Black Flame,** hastily written as Du Bois neared death, Du Bois tried to show his understanding at last of this division. The trilogy tells two stories—the epic of history, and the counterepic or antiepic of the black hero as epiphenomenon; counterepic, because the black hero no longer triumphs in his own lifetime, but ends his life apparently inconclusively. The great achievement of this flawed work comes from the ironic interplay between the march of dialectic, crudely related, and the crawling and stumbling of humans defined by their failures as well as their modest virtues.

Du Bois claimed that his life had its significance only because he was part of the great problem of race, and that he had done little to change his day. Perhaps. Within black America, though, his achievement was incomparable. Though he never attained competence as a great poet or novelist, his efforts in those roles combine with his other works to extend our understanding of the history and

character of his people and, indeed, of humanism itself. In spite of his failures as a formal artist there lingers about him more than a trace of what Lukács found in a far greater nineteenth-century writer—glimpses still of "the gloomy magnificence of primary accumulation in the field of culture." (pp. 50-68)

*Arnold Rampersad, "W. E. B. Du Bois as a Man of Literature," in* American Literature, *Vol. 51, No. 1, March, 1979, pp. 50-68.*

### Darwin T. Turner

During the past twenty years many black artists and critics began to insist that work by Afro-Americans must be created and evaluated according to a Black Aesthetic. That is, the work must be appropriate to Afro-American culture and people, and its excellence must be defined according to black people's concepts of beauty. In *The Crisis of the Negro Intellectual,* Harold Cruse pointed to the need for a Black Aesthetic when he castigated Negro critics for failing to establish an appropriate perspective of the relationship of Negro art to Negro culture. Cruse accused critics of rejecting their own folk culture in order to adopt models and ideas devised and approved by whites. Thus, Cruse charged, most Negro critics ignored what should have been their major responsibility: to encourage and to determine standards for original ideas, methods, materials and styles derived from the unique character of black American culture. In even sharper tones, such critics as Imamu Amiri Baraka, Larry Neal, Don L. Lee, Hoyt Fuller, and Addison Gayle, Jr.—to name only a few of the most prominent—insist that black artists must seek subjects, themes and styles within the culture of black folk, that they must use these materials for the benefits of black Americans, and that the resulting art must be evaluated according to criteria determined by black people.

Of course it is not new for a nation, race, or ethnic group to devise an individual aesthetic. To the contrary, a cursory view of the history of European, English, and American literature reveals such a kaleidoscope that one wonders how anyone could argue that only one aesthetic can exist or could deny that any group has a right to define its own aesthetic. An aesthetic, after all, is merely a judgment of what is beautiful according to the tastes of the judge. After determining what kinds of drama were preferred by cultivated Greeks, Aristotle propounded a standard for drama. If William Shakespeare had followed that aesthetic, he might have written excellent imitations of Greek drama, but he would not have created the melodramatic shatterings of unity that dismayed Augustan critics and delighted the Romantics. . . . Equally diversified standards of beauty could be revealed in a history of painting, music, philosophy, or any of the humanistic pursuits. The fact is, any group of people which feels its identity as a group shapes and defines it own aesthetic, which it is free to change in a subsequent generation or century.

It should not be surprising, therefore, that black Americans should insist upon a need of a Black Aesthetic; for, if their African ancestry has not always bound them together, they have nevertheless found identity as a group in their exclusion from certain prerogatives of American citizenship. What is surprising then is not the concept of a Black Aesthetic in literature but that, even before the Harlem "Renaissance," it was articulated distinctly by W. E. B. Du Bois, who has been identified disparagingly with the conservative literary practices of The Genteel Tradition and with the efforts of Negroes to become assimilated by separating themselves from the folk culture. Nevertheless, before the New Negro movement had been labeled, years before Langston Hughes insisted upon the right of new artists to express their individual dark-skinned selves without caring whether they pleased white or black audiences, W. E. B. Du Bois proposed a Black Aesthetic or—as I prefer to designate it in relation to Du Bois—a theory of art from the perspective of black Americans.

Du Bois did not clearly define or delimit his theory. Despite his sustained interest in art, Du Bois was a social scientist and a political leader who considered art—especially literature—to be a vehicle for enunciating and effecting social, political, and economic ideas. Therefore, he sketched literary theory rather than constructing it with the total concentration characteristic of one whose major concern is the art itself. Moreover, like other theorists, Du Bois sometimes experienced difficulty with the practical applications of his theories. For instance, although he first urged black writers to present life exactly as they saw it, he later feared that the writers were overemphasizing lurid aspects. Consequently, to correct what he considered an imbalance, he began to urge more conservative pictures of Negro life. One must admit also that Du Bois, unlike Wordsworth or T. S. Eliot, never created in his fiction, drama, and poetry the great work which would both illustrate and justify his literary theory.

Despite whatever weaknesses he may have revealed in definition or application, there is value in examining Du Bois's theory of black art—not only because it was of extreme importance to his efforts to create a strong and respected black population, but also because he was able to pronounce it from a prominent public platform during the Harlem "Renaissance," a significant moment in the development of literature by Afro-Americans. . . . [This essay is] an examination of Du Bois's theory of black art as he shaped it and applied it as editor of *The Crisis* through the height of the Renaissance to the mid-Depression moment at which his insistence on the importance of independent black institutions became one of the wedges to separate him from the National Association for the Advancement of Colored People.

In 1921, the dawning of a literary Renaissance might have been viewed in the historical research of Carter G. Woodson and the cultural history of Benjamin Brawley. Its rays may have been glimpsed in the popularity of the musical *Shuffle Along,* written by Miller, Lyles, Sissle and Blake, or in the interest in black people displayed by such white writers as Ridgely Torrence and Eugene O'Neill.

By 1921, however, W. E. B. Du Bois had been working for many years as editor of *The Crisis* to promote literary activity and to foster racial pride through literature. As early as 1912, he had solicited manuscripts from and had published work by such previously unknown writers as

Georgia Johnson, Fenton Johnson, and Jessie Fauset. In an editorial in 1920, he had recited his pride in the accomplishments of *The Crisis* and the need for a "renaissance of American Negro literature":

> Since its founding, THE CRISIS has been eager to discover ability among Negroes, especially in literature and art. It remembers with no little pride its covers by Richard Brown, William Scott, William Farrow, and Laura Wheeler; and its cartoons by Lorenzo Harris and Albert Smith; it helped to discover the poetry of Roscoe Jamison, Georgia Johnson, Fenton Johnson, Lucian Watkins, and Otto Bohanan; and the prose of Jessie Fauset and Mary Effie Lee. Indeed, THE CRISIS has always preferred the strong matter of unknown names, to the platitudes of well-known writers; and by its Education and Children numbers, it has shown faith in the young.

> One colored writer, Claude McKay, asserts that we rejected one of his poems and then quoted it from Pearson's; and intimates that colored editors, in general, defer to white editors' opinions. This is, of course, arrogant nonsense. But it does call our attention to the need of encouraging Negro writers. We have today all too few, for the reason that there is small market for their ideas among whites, and their energies are being called to other and more lucrative ways of earning a living. Nevertheless, we have literary ability and the race needs it. A renaissance of American Negro literature is due; the material about us in the strange, heartrending race tangle is rich beyond dream and only we can tell the tale and sing the song from the heart.

By 1921, Du Bois was inculcating pride in Afro-American children through his publication of *The Brownies' Book,* in which—writing as "The Crow"—he taught respect for the blackness of the crow.

In a more characteristic manner, writing with the confidence which Alain Locke later identified with the "New Negro," Du Bois admonished Negroes to accept artistic presentations of the truth of Negro life. In **"Criteria for Negro Art,"** he wrote:

> We are so used to seeing the truth distorted to our despite, that whenever we are portrayed on canvas, in story or on the stage, as simple humans with human frailties, we rebel. We want everything said about us to tell of the best and highest and noblest in us. We insist that our Art and Propaganda be one.

> This is wrong and the end is harmful. We have a right, in our effort to get just treatment, to insist that we produce something of the best in human character and that it is unfair to judge us by our criminals and prostitutes. This is justifiable propaganda.

> On the other hand we face the truth of Art. We have criminals and prostitutes, ignorant and debased elements, just as all folks have. When the artist paints us he has a right to paint us whole and not ignore everything which is not as perfect as we would wish it to be. The black Shakespeare

must portray his black Iago as well as his white Othello.

> We shrink from this. We fear that evil in us will be called racial, while in others it is viewed as individual. We fear that our shortcomings are not merely human but foreshadowing and threatenings of disaster and failure. The more highly trained we become the less we can laugh at Negro comedy—we will have it all tragedy and the triumph of dark Right over pale Villainy.

> The results are not merely negative—they are positively bad. With a vast wealth of human material about us, our own writers and artists fear to paint the truth lest they criticize their own and be in turn criticized for it. They fail to see the Eternal Beauty that shines through all Truth, and try to portray a world of stilted artificial black folk such as never were on land or sea.

> Thus, the white artist, looking in on the colored world, if he be wise and discerning, may often see the beauty, tragedy and comedy more truly than we dare.

Admitting that some white writers, such as Thomas Dixon, might see only exaggerated evil in Negroes, Du Bois nevertheless insisted that blacks would survive any honest treatment of Afro-American life:

> We stand today secure enough in our accomplishment and self-confidence to lend the whole stern human truth about ourselves to the transforming hand and seeing eye of the Artist, white and black, and Sheldon, Torrence and O'Neill are our great benefactors—forerunners of artists who will yet arise in Ethiopia of the Outstretched Arm.

Within the next two years the Renaissance of the New Negro produced its first literary works: *Shuffle Along* (1921) was enthusiastically received by a Broadway audience; Claude McKay and Jean Toomer created *Harlem Shadows* (1922) and *Cane* (1923); Willis Richardson's *The Chip Woman's Fortune* (1923) became the first serious play by an Afro-American to be staged on Broadway. Even during these early triumphs, however, Du Bois worried about a barrier which might obstruct the creation of honest black art—the prejudice of American audiences, who expected blacks to be "*bizarre* and unusual and funny for whites."

In the same essay, written for a predominantly white audience rather than the more mixed audience of *The Crisis,* Du Bois's exploration of the possibilities for Negroes in the contemporary theater led him to more optimistic conclusions. If they could escape from the prejudiced expectations of white audiences, they could create strong Negro drama by emphasizing their blackness.

As evidence, Du Bois cited The Ethiopian Art Theatre's successful performances of *Salome, The Chip Woman's Fortune,* and *The Comedy of Errors a la Jazz.* Published statements by the company explained that Director Raymond O'Neill restrained the black performers from attempting to imitate the more inhibited white actors. Instead, he encouraged them "to develop their peculiar racial characteristics—the freshness and vigor of their emotional responses, their spontaneity and intensity of mood, their freedom from intellectual and artistic obsession."

Du Bois was even more pleased by the Ethiopian Players' selection of black subjects. Unintentionally paraphrasing William Dean Howell's earliest praise of Paul Laurence Dunbar, Du Bois insisted that blacks could make a distinctive contribution to American drama by interpreting black subjects. He did not oppose black actors who wished to demonstrate their ability to perform "white" roles for white audiences. Nor did he deny the usefulness of expanding the cultural awareness of black audiences by staging "white" plays for them. Of greatest importance, however, was the opportunity for black actors and writers to examine "their own terrible history of experience."

Black writers, he admitted, would develop slowly. The race needed to gain "something of that leisure and detachment for artistic work which every artist must have." As evidence that serious black dramatists were emerging despite their lack of leisure, he called attention to his own ***The Star of Ethiopia,*** a pageant commemorating blackness.

Wise men believe, Du Bois concluded, "that the great gift of the Negro to the world is going to be a gift to Art." The Ethiopian Players were significantly promoting awareness of this talent by beginning to peel from drama critics "the scales that blinded them for years to the beauty of Negro folk songs, that make them still deaf to the song of Negro singers and but half-alive to the growing Negro drama and the ringing Negro actor."

Even in less laudatory reviews, Du Bois thrilled to Negro writers who truthfully and seriously probed into problems of Afro-American life. Although he complained that Jean Toomer weakened *Cane* by too little knowledge of Georgia, excessive striving for artistic effect, dearth of feeling, and "much that is difficult or even impossible to understand," Du Bois boasted,

> The world of black folk will some day arise and point to Jean Toomer as a writer who first dared to emancipate the colored world from the conventions of sex. It is quite impossible for most Americans to realize how straight-laced and conventional thought is within the Negro World, despite the very unconventional acts of the group. Yet this contradiction is true. And Jean Toomer is the first of our writers to hurl his pen across the very face of our sex conventionality. . . . [His women are] painted with a frankness that is going to make his black readers shrink and criticize; and yet they are done with a certain splendid, careless truth.

In 1925, writing for a predominantly white audience, Du Bois became the first significant critic to probe issues which remain not fully resolved today, even though they are fundamental to the establishment of a Black Aesthetic: what is the difference between art by a Negro and Negro art? Or, what are the unique characteristics of Negro art?

Although he praised Henry O. Tanner, Charles W. Chesnutt, and William Stanley Braithwaite as artists, Du Bois denied that they had contributed significantly to American Negro art. American Negro art, he explained, was a group expression consisting of biographies written by slaves and by free blacks who had achieved

> . . . poetry portraying Negro life and aspirations, and activities, of essays on the "Negro Problem" and novels about the "Color Line" . . . pictures and sculptures meant to portray Negro features and characteristics, plays to dramatize the tremendous situation of the Negro in America, and, of course, . . . music

American Negro art "was built on the sorrow and strain inherent in American slavery, on the difficulties that sprang from Emancipation, on the feelings of revenge, despair, aspirations, and hatred which arose as the Negro struggled and fought his way upward."

Whenever a mass of millions having such common memories and experiences are granted intellectual freedom and economic wealth, Du Bois explained, they will establish a school of art which, whether using new methods of art, will inevitably bring new content—a truth which is different from anything else in the world: "If this truth . . . is beautifully expressed and transformed from sordid fact into art it becomes, from its very origin, new, unusual, splendid."

The uniqueness of Afro-American artistic expression had been revealed and discovered in "new music, new rhythm, new melody and poignant, even terrible, expressions of joy, sorrow, and despair." This new music, Du Bois argued, was earning respect. Next to win recognition would be Negro literature, which presented "new phrases, new uses of words, experiences unthought of and unknown to the average white person." Creating "a distinct norm and a new set of human problems," the new writers were impeded only by white readers' inability to understand the work and by black readers' stubborn demands for favorable propaganda. As the new artists matured, they would improve in thought and style. In the process of maturing, they would move from the wild music, laughter, and dancing of slavery into a more deliberate, purposeful, restrained, but true artistic expression.

The conclusion of Du Bois's magnificent effort to define Afro-American art betrays a weakness which gives a curious ambivalence to his criticism. He could identify the substance of that art but not the spirit. Whenever the spirit manifested itself in an exuberance which offended his temperament—his personal preference for decorum—Du Bois, wincing, felt compelled to excuse or denounce the work. Because he did not believe such wildness to be a characteristic inherent in the Afro-American psyche, he identified it, if genuine, as evidence of the manner in which slavery had distorted or repressed the psychological development of blacks. Just as often, he feared that the wildness was not a sincere expression of the artist but an effort to attract popularity from white critics by repeating the clichés about the character of black people. Unable to resolve this dilemma, which he failed to perceive as a dilemma, Du Bois at times seems a genteel anachronism as a critic during an era characterized by wildness of whites, as well as blacks. This was the gay Jazz Age of sheiks and flappers, raccoon coats and skirts that bared the knees, boot-

leg gin and speakeasies where one Charlestoned in shooting distance of well-known racketeers, "new" morality and trial marriages, free love and lurid front page headlines about the latest love-nest scandal. It was an era of youth, in which many whites, Freuding themselves from their Puritan inhibitions, enviously projected upon blacks the image of the primitive untroubled by the inhibitions of society. In such an era, it is not surprising that even a relatively sedate but young Countee Cullen atavistically boasted that his heart was "pagan-mad" and that the blood of blacks was hotter than that of whites. Not so for New-England-born, Harvard-trained W. E. B. Du Bois, who was fifty-seven-years old before Cullen published his first volume of poems. Quite simply, Du Bois knew that he was not pagan-mad; but he was Negro. Therefore, Negroes were not inherently pagan-mad. Therefore such wildness was not essential to, or desirable in, Negro life and art.

Instead one sought Beauty and Truth. In *The Crisis* of May 1925, Du Bois proclaimed a new editorial policy:

> We shall stress Beauty—all Beauty, but especially the beauty of Negro life and character; its music, its dancing, its drawing and painting and the new birth of its literature. This growth which *The Crisis* long since predicted is sprouting and coming to flower. We shall encourage it in every way . . . keeping the while a high standard of merit and never stooping to cheap flattery and misspent kindliness.

At the same time, Du Bois continued his demands that black readers accept realistic portraits. (pp. 9-17)

As early as 1926, however, Du Bois's statements reveal the ambivalent sentiments or the inherent contradictions which have deceived critics who unsuspectingly have fixed Du Bois at one or another of his positions. In a complimentary review of *The New Negro* (1925), Du Bois wrote:

> With one point alone do I differ. . . . Mr. Locke has newly been seized with the idea that Beauty rather than Propaganda should be the object of Negro literature and art. His book proves the falseness of this thesis. This is a book filled and bursting with propaganda, but it is a propaganda for the most part beautiful and painstakingly done. . . .
>
> . . . If Mr. Locke's thesis is insisted upon too much it is going to turn the Negro Renaissance into decadence. It is the fight for Life and Liberty that is giving birth to Negro literature and art today and when, turning from this fight or ignoring it, the young Negro tries to do pretty things or things that catch the passing fancy of the really unimportant critics and publishers about him he will find that he has killed the soul of Beauty in art.

In the same issue of *The Crisis,* Du Bois, announcing the second annual Krigwa awards competition in literature and art, emphasized both his belief that Negro art must act as propaganda and his willingness to accept reflections of all avenues of Afro-American life:

> We want especially to stress the fact that while

we believe in Negro art we do not believe in any art simply for art's sake. . . . We want Negro writers to produce beautiful things but we stress the things rather than the beauty. It is Life and Truth that are important and Beauty comes to make their importance visible and tolerable. . . .

Write then about things as you know them. . . . In *The Crisis,* at least, you do not have to confine your writings to portrayal of beggars, scoundrels and prostitutes; you can write about ordinary decent colored people if you want. On the other hand do not fear the Truth. . . . If you want to paint Crime and Destitution and Evil paint it. . . . Use propaganda if you want. Discard it and laugh if you will. But be true, be sincere, be thorough, and do a beautiful job.

Undoubtedly, Du Bois remembered the dictum of John Keats that Beauty is Truth and Truth is Beauty. With whatever license is granted to a poet, however, Keats ignored any responsibility for explaining his meaning. More lucidity is generally required of a literary critic.

If one extracts the essence of Du Bois's instruction to black readers, his rebuttal of Locke's doctrine, and his exhortation to prospective contestants, one recognizes a general pronouncement that literature by blacks must be unflinchingly true to Afro-American life even in its pictures of the ugly and the unheroic. It also must be didactic and beautiful. Even viewed superficially, the proposition seems difficult to use as a touchstone for any single work of art.

The critical process is further complicated by Du Bois's failure to clarify his abstractions. Although he occasionally perceived the need, he never successfully defined Beauty in relation to material, thought, or method—perhaps because he presumed his taste to be characteristic of all people. In **"Criteria of Negro Art,"** a speech prepared for the 1926 Chicago Conference of the NAACP, Du Bois made his most detailed effort to resolve the question of the relation of beauty to Afro-American art; yet, in his initial premise, he reflected his assumption that his standards were the standards for all blacks—at least for all cultivated blacks. "Pushed aside as we have been in America," he wrote, "there has come to us not only a certain distaste for the tawdry and flamboyant but a vision of what the world could be if it were really a beautiful world." Du Bois continued:

After all, who shall describe Beauty? What is it? I remember tonight four beautiful things: The Cathedral at Cologne, a forest in stone, set in light and changing shadow, echoing with sunlight and solemn song; a village of the Veys in West Africa, a little thing of mauve and purple, quiet, lying content and shining in the sun; a black and velvet room where on a throne rests, in old and yellowing marble, the broken curves of the Venus of Milo; a single phrase of music in the Southern South—utter melody, haunting and appealing, suddenly arising out of night and eternity, beneath the moon.

Du Bois's rhetoric is persuasive. His emphasis is upon apparent catholicity of taste. Yet a question obtrudes. Does the beauty of the scene at Cologne depend upon the viewer's reaction to a particular style of architecture and a particular quality of song? Would Du Bois's sense of ultimate beauty in the scene have been marred if the music had not been "solemn song" but jazz?

Even if Du Bois had resolved questions about Beauty, he still would have failed to appreciate the complexity of Pilate's question. Du Bois perceived a difference between a black man's and a white man's awareness of the Truth of Negro life. But he failed to comprehend that black men themselves may differ in their visions of the Truth of Afro-American life. In consequence, whereas he rejected obviously idealized portraits as untrue, he often admitted bewilderment that young authors never wrote about the decent, hard-working Negroes in their own families. Moreover, although he graciously urged young writers to describe the sordid if they wished, he soon suspected them of rejecting authentic pictures of low black life in favor of derogatory stereotypes.

I do not intend to demean Du Bois by suggesting that his definitions, criteria, and perceptions are inferior to those of other artists and critics still esteemed by many literary scholars. To the contrary, compared with others of his century—or any century—he fares well. His concept of Beauty certainly is as valid and as meaningful as Edgar Allan Poe's definition of poetry. Du Bois's assumption that his visions of Beauty and Truth were universally accepted is no more arrogant than Matthew Arnold's presumption that, from his preferences in poetry, he had acquired touchstones with which to measure the excellence of the poetry of any country. Instead of wishing to demean Du Bois, I merely suggest that, because he based his critical judgment on abstractions which were concrete to him but not necessarily to all other black contemporaries, the application of his theory to particular works of black writers sometimes resulted in appraisals significantly different from those of younger black artists, who shared their own perceptions of Beauty and Truth.

Significantly, although his interest in Beauty and Truth suggests a concern for "universal" values—a concept too often used to minimize the work of a black writer on a theme of black life, Du Bois's discussions of Beauty and Truth in literature always led him to a position strikingly comparable in spirit, if not always in detail, to that adopted by many current exponents of Black Arts: literature must serve a function for the good of black people, and its worth must be judged by black people.

He concluded his discussion of Beauty in **"Criteria of Negro Art":**

Thus it is the bounden duty of black America to begin this great work of the creation of Beauty, of the preservation of Beauty, of the realization of Beauty, and we must use in this work all the methods that men have used before. And what have been the tools of the artist in times gone by? First of all, he has used the Truth—not for the sake of truth, not as a scientist seeking truth, but as one upon whom Truth eternally thrusts itself as the highest handmaid of imagination, as the one great vehicle of universal understanding. Again artists have used Goodness—goodness in all its aspects of justice, honor and right—not for sake of an ethical sanction but as the one true method of gaining sympathy and human interest.

The apostle of Beauty thus becomes the apostle of Truth and Right not by choice but by inner and outer compulsion. Free he is but his freedom is ever bounded by Truth and Justice; and slavery only dogs him when he is denied the right to tell the Truth or recognize an ideal of Justice.

Thus all Art is propaganda and ever must be, despite the wailing of the purists. I stand in utter shamelessness and say that whatever art I have for writing has been used always for propaganda for gaining the right of black folk to love and enjoy. I do not care a damn for any art that is not used for propaganda.

And in rhetoric prophetic of a Black Aesthetic, he surged to a climax:

. . . the young and slowly growing black public still wants its prophets almost equally unfree. We are bound by all sorts of customs that have come down as second-hand soul clothes of white patrons. We are ashamed of sex and we lower our eyes when people will talk of it. Our religion holds us in superstition. Our worst side has been so shamelessly emphasized that we are denying we have or ever had a worst side. In all sorts of ways we are hemmed in and our new young artists have got to fight their way to freedom.

The ultimate judge has got to be you and you have got to build yourselves up into that wide judgment, that catholicity of temper which is going to enable the artist to have his widest chance for freedom. We can afford the Truth. White folk today cannot. As it is now we are handing everything over to a white jury. If a colored man wants to publish a book, he has got to get a white publisher and a white newspaper to say it is great; and then you and I say so. We must come to a place where the work of art when it appears is reviewed and acclaimed by our own free and unfettered judgment.

Du Bois argued that young black writers were being diverted from their artistic responsibilities especially by the popularity of Carl Van Vechten's *Nigger Heaven,* which he denounced as "an affront to the hospitality of black folk (who admitted Van Vechten to their circles) and to the intelligence of white." In Du Bois's opinion the book was pernicious, not only because its commercial success persuaded blacks to pander to white stereotypes of their life but also because it destroyed both Beauty and Truth:

It is a caricature. It is worse than untruth because it is a mass of half-truths. . . . [To Van Vechten] the black cabaret is Harlem; around it all his characters gravitate. . . . Such a theory of Harlem is nonsense. The overwhelming majority of black folk there never go to cabarets. . . .

Something they have which is racial, something distinctly Negroid can be found; but it is expressed by subtle, almost delicate nuance, and

not by the wildly, [sic] barbaric drunken orgy in whose details Van Vechten revels. . . .

Van Vechten is not the great artist who with remorseless scalpel probes the awful depths of life. To him there are no depths. It is the surface mud he slops in. . . . Life to him is just one damned orgy after another, with hate, hurt, gin and sadism.

Both Langston Hughes and Carl Van Vechten know Harlem cabarets; but it is Hughes who whispers,

"One said he heard the jazz band sob

When the little dawn was grey."

Van Vechten never heard a sob in a cabaret. All he hears is noise and brawling.

Earlier Du Bois had lamented the limitations of Du Bose Heyward's *Porgy* because, by excluding educated Afro-American Charlestonians, it implied that the waterfront world was a total picture of black life in that city. Nevertheless, Du Bois now insisted that Porgy himself had a human and interesting quality absent from Van Vechten's characters.

How does one determine that a writer has created characters who are human as well as interesting? Can any reader truly determine whether an author has delineated degraded characters with compassion or has exploited them?

Du Bois could not find answers to these questions. Perhaps his orientation to scientific research persuaded him that sincerity can be measured. Or perhaps, more concerned with other matters, he did not even consider the questions fully; the theory was clear to him at least. A black should write honestly about the Afro-Americans he knew. So created, a work would sparkle with Truth and Beauty. It would be useful black literature. If, however, the writer seemed excessively absorbed with cabaret life, Du Bois was prepared to impale him with the pen reserved for those who dished up black humanity piping hot to a slobbering white public.

Even if he did not fully examine questions needed to clarify his own criteria of art, Du Bois nevertheless quickly sensed a possible weakness in his efforts to propagandize for the race by encouraging young blacks to write about themselves. What if, for the sake of publication, they all began to imitate Van Vechten?

Earlier in 1926, Du Bois had initiated a symposium on "The Negro in Art." He asked various authors and publishers to consider several questions:

Are writers under obligations or limitations as to the kinds of characters they portray? Should authors be criticized for painting the best or the worst characters of a group? Can publishers be criticized for failing to publish works about educated Negroes? What can Negroes do if they are continually painted at their worst? Should Negroes be portrayed sincerely and sympathetically? Isn't the literary emphasis upon sordid, foolish and criminal Negroes persuading readers that this is the truth and preventing authors from writing otherwise? Is there danger that young colored writers will follow the popular trend?

The overlapping questions reveal Du Bois's basic concern: is the literary world conspiring to typify Negroes by sordid, foolish, and criminal characters? And if so, what can be done to prevent that?

Some of the responses by whites must have confirmed Du Bois's worst fears. Carl Van Vechten bluntly stated that the squalor and vice of Negro life *would* be overdone "for a very excellent reason." Such squalor and vice offer "a wealth of novel, exotic, picturesque material." He discounted pictures of wealthy, cultured Negroes as uninteresting because they were virtually identical with those of whites, a pronouncement which validates Du Bois's convictions about Van Vechten's superficiality. The only thing for the black writer to do, Van Vechten concluded, was to exploit the vice and squalor before the white authors did.

Henry Mencken chided blacks for failing to see the humor in the derogatory caricatures created by Octavus Cohen. Instead of applying scientific criteria to art, he added, blacks should write works ridiculing whites. Mencken did not explain who would publish the caricatures of whites.

Another white author, John Farrar, shrugged off the stories of Octavus Cohen with the admission that they amused him immensely and seemed not to libel Negroes. In contrast, although he confessed scant knowledge of the South, he thought Walter White's novel *The Fire in the Flint* "a trifle onesided." William Lyons Phelps mildly admonished Negroes to correct false impressions by setting good examples in their lives. Having no answers but more questions, Sinclair Lewis proposed a conference to consider the issues. He also suggested establishing a club for blacks—at a small hotel in Paris.

Sherwood Anderson reminded *The Crisis* that he had lived among Negro laborers, whom he had found to be "about the sweetest people I know," as he had said sometimes in his books. In short, he wrote, Negroes were worrying too much and being too sensitive; they had no more reason to complain about their portraits in literature than whites would have. Julia Peterkin asserted that Irish and Jewish people were not offended by caricatures, so Negroes should not be. She used the occasion to praise the "Black Negro Mammy" and to chastise Negroes for protesting against a proposal in Congress to erect a monument to the Mammy.

Such responses probably did not surprise Du Bois, but they strengthened his conviction that black writers must fight for their race. Even the sympathetic white writers revealed flaws. For example, Paul Green's Pulitzer Prize winning play, *In Abraham's Bosom,* impressed Du Bois as an example of "the defeatist genre of Negro art which is so common. . . . The more honestly and sincerely a white artist looks at the situation of the Negro in America the less is he able to consider it in any way bearable and therefore his stories and plays must end in lynching, suicide or degeneracy." Du Bois added that, even if such a writer learned differently by observing black people's refusal to accept failure, the publisher or producer would prohibit a portrayal of triumphant blacks. Pathetic, inevitable defeat or exotic degeneracy—these would be the dominant images of black life unless black writers corrected the images.

In April, 1927, while announcing the annual competition in literature and art, Du Bois reminded his readers of the impressive black heritage revealed in the fine arts of Ethiopia, Egypt, and the rest of Africa. In contemporary America, he insisted, that heritage must be continued in the art of spoken and written word. It must not be restrained by the white person's desire for silly and lewd entertainment; it must not be blocked by the black person's revulsion from unfavorable images. "The Negro artist must have freedom to wander where he will, portray what he will, interpret whatever he may see according to the great canons of beauty which the world through long experience has laid down." Du Bois was beginning to sound like his future son-in-law Countee Cullen. He would now accept anything black writers wanted to do if only they did it beautifully, but he was no more specific about his concept of Beauty.

When James Weldon Johnson published *God's Trombones* (1927), Du Bois rejoiced at Johnson's preservation of the Negro idiom in art, Johnson's beautiful poetry, and Aaron Douglass's wild, beautiful, unconventional, daring drawings, which were stylized to emphasize Negroid rather than Caucasian features of the black figures.

But works by whites continued to disappoint him even when they were sufficiently good to be recommended to readers. His praise of *Congaree Sketches* by E. C. L. Adams was dampened by what he felt to be a significant omission:

> even to the lowest black swamp peasant there are the three worlds ever present to his imagination: his own, the world of the risen black man and the world of white folks. No current folk lore can omit any one of these and be true, complete and, therefore . . . artistic.

In the entire collection, Du Bois complained, he found not one allusion to the rising black man characterized by ambition, education, and aspiration to better earthly things.

In 1928, black writers provided Du Bois with examples which he used to illustrate his concept of the difference between praiseworthy black literature and atrocious black literature. He hailed Nella Larsen's *Quicksand* as a "fine, thoughtful and courageous novel," the best by any black writer since Chesnutt. Subtly comprehending the curious cross currents swirling about black Americans, the author, he felt, created an interesting character, fitted her into a close plot, and rejected both an improbable happy ending and the defeatist theme: "Helga Crane sinks at last still master of her whimsical, unsatisfied soul. In the end she will be beaten down even to death but she never will utterly surrender to hypocricy [sic] and convention."

In contrast, Du Bois stated that Claude McKay's *Home to Harlem* was a shameful novel, redeemed only by the fact that the author was "too great a poet to make any complete failure in writing." Du Bois noted virtues in the work: the beautiful, fascinating changes on themes of the beauty of colored skins; McKay's emphasis upon the fact that Negroes are physically and emotionally attracted to other Negroes rather than to whites; and the creation of Jake and Ray, interesting and appealing characters. Despite these commendably perceptive insights into black life, Du Bois argued, *Home to Harlem* pandered to white people's enjoyment of Negroes portrayed in

> that utter licentiousness which conventional civilization holds white folk back from enjoying—if enjoyment it can be called. That which a certain decadent section of the white American world, centered particularly in New York, longs for with fierce and unrestrained passions, it wants to see written out in black and white and saddled on black Harlem. . . . [McKay] has used every art and emphasis to paint drunkenness, fighting, lascivious sexual promiscuity and utter absence of restraint in as bold and as bright colors as he can. . . . Whole chapters . . . are inserted with no connection to the main plot, except that they are on the same dirty subject. As a picture of Harlem life or of Negro life anywhere, it is, of course, nonsense. Untrue, not so much on account of its facts but on account of its emphasis and glaring colors.

Between the levels of *Quicksand* and *Home to Harlem,* Du Bois placed Rudolph Fisher's *The Walls of Jericho.* Fearful that casual readers would draw from it only echoes of Van Vechten and McKay, Du Bois stressed the psychological validity of the two working-class black people who are the focus of the major plot. The book's weaknesses were the excessive sophistication and unreality of the background and such minor characters as Jinx and Bubber, who speak authentically but do not seem as human as the major figures. But, Du Bois continued in bewilderment, Fisher "has not depicted Negroes like his mother, his sister, his wife, his real Harlem friends. He has not even depicted his own soul. The glimpses of better class Negroes are ineffective make-believes." Why, Du Bois asked. Hearing no answer, he concluded with the hope that Fisher's novel was an indication of black novelists' movement upward from Van Vechten and McKay.

Despite his frequent attacks upon white authors' distortions of black life and black people, Du Bois did not contend that white Americans could never portray blacks successfully. Exceptions occurred: Paul Green wrote sincerely even though he belabored the defeatist theme; the E. C. L. Adams book, *Nigger to Nigger,* was a sincere attempt to collect and present the philosophy of black peasants. Nevertheless, such exceptions did not relieve his skepticism:

> I assume that the white stranger cannot write about black people. In nine cases out of ten I am right. In the tenth case, and Du Bose Heywood [sic] is the tenth case, the stranger can write about the colored people whom he knows; but those very people whom he knows are sometimes so strange to me, that I cannot for the life of me make them authentic.

In the waning moments of the Renaissance, Du Bois seemed increasingly reluctant to castigate an Afro-

American writer except when that writer rejected his blackness. For example, although he had previously objected to Wallace Thurman for glib, superficial comments on black life and culture, Du Bois, when reviewing *The Blacker the Berry,* merely remonstrated with Thurman for not believing his thesis:

> The story of Emma Lou calls for genius to develop it. It needs deep psychological knowledge and pulsing sympathy. And above all, the author must believe in black folk, and in the beauty of black as a color of human skin. I may be wrong, but it does not seem to me that this is true of Wallace Thurman. He seems to me himself to deride blackness. . . .
>
> It seems that this inner self-despising of the very thing he is defending, makes the author's defense less complete and sincere.

(pp. 17-25)

In the early years of the 1930s, while America floundered in an economic depression, it was clear that night had fallen on the heyday of the Harlem Renaissance. If Afro-Americans—intelligentsia, artists, and workers alike—were not cast out, they were at least ignored by a huge republic trying to pull itself erect. As Du Bois re-examined the position of blacks in America during those troubled times, he re-evaluated his own ideas about the appropriate course for his people. For a decade, from a platform within an integrated and prointegrationist NAACP, he had argued that black writers must do things for black people and must be judged by black people. Now he extended that concept of black independence and black control to the entire spectrum of black existence in America: black people must develop and control strong black institutions for the good of black people. Coming as it did from the pages of the voice of NAACP, and from a man whom white supremacists had vilified as the chief advocate of integration, the idea probably was even more startling when Du Bois expressed it in the 1930s than when, a quarter of a century later, Stokely Carmichael re-introduced it tersely as "Black Power."

Although Du Bois seemed unable to convert those who immediately attacked his position, he tried repeatedly to explain the logic which guided him to a seemingly inescapable conclusion. Personally, he still believed the best society to be an integrated one—a fact which should be obvious to anyone who remembered that, for more than twenty-five years, he had dedicated himself to effecting the full integration of blacks into American society. Despite his private desires, however, he was compelled to admit a bitter truth:

> . . . that we are segregated, apart, hammered into a separate unity by spiritual intolerance and legal sanction backed by mob law, . . . that this separation is growing in strength and fixation; that it is worse today than a half-century ago and that no character, address, culture, or desert is going to change it in one day or for centuries to come.

In such a deplorable circumstance, it is futile to pretend that one is simply an American: one must recognize that he is a Negro. It is pointless to argue that there is no such creature as an American Negro when twelve million human beings are identified and treated as Negroes. It is senseless to continue to debate whether or not segregation is desirable; segregation is a fact. In such a circumstance, the only matter for American Negroes to debate is what they can do to prevent their genocide. The solution, he explained, was to "carefully plan and guide our segregated life, organize in industry and politics to protect it and expand it and above all to give it unhampered spiritual expression in art and literature."

A step which blacks could take immediately was to make their institutions more serviceable by concentrating on their true purpose. That is, as one could no longer deny the fact of being Negro, so it was absurd to pretend that a Negro college was just another American college. It must be recognized as a Negro institution. (pp. 26-7)

Beginning with such a premise, he explained, the Negro university would expand from the examination of black life, history, social development, science, and humanities into a study of all life and matter in the universe. The study must begin with a focus on black people, and it must continue from the perspective of black people. This is not merely the best route; it is the only route to universality.

In the antithesis of this theory, Du Bois found reasons for his failure to bring about the kind of literary Renaissance of which he had dreamed—one in which honest, artistic literary works about blacks by blacks would be bought and read by blacks. Such a Renaissance never took root, he now argued; the so-called "Renaissance" failed

> because it was a transplanted and exotic thing. It was a literature written for the benefit of white people and at the behest of white readers, and starting out privately from the white point of view. It never had a real Negro constituency and it did not grow out of the inmost heart and frank experience of Negroes; on such an artificial basis no real literature can grow.

By the time he published **Dusk of Dawn** seven years later, Du Bois had practiced his theory. After severing connections with the NAACP, Du Bois had returned to Atlanta University to help develop a strong black institution. Although he was less interested in explaining artistic theory than he had been earlier, his brief summation in **Dusk of Dawn** roots him firmly in a Black Aesthetic and identifies him, more clearly than any previous statement, as a progenitor of a Black Arts movement. Creative art, he stated, was essential to the development and transmission of new ideas among blacks:

> The communalism of the African clan can be transferred to the Negro American group. . . . The emotional wealth of the American Negro, the nascent art in song, dance and drama can all be applied, not to amuse the white audience, but to inspire and direct the acting Negro group itself. I can conceive no more magnificent or promising crusade in modern times.

To achieve this end, black people must be re-educated in educational institutions oriented to black people:

> There has been a larger movement on the part of the Negro intelligentsia toward racial grouping for the advancement of art and literature. There has been a distinct plan for reviving ancient African art through an American Negro art movement, and more specially a thought to use the extremely rich and colorful life of the Negro in America and elsewhere as a basis for painting, sculpture, and literature. This has been partly nullified by the fact that if these new artists expect support for their art from the Negro group itself, that group must be deliberately trained and schooled in art appreciation and in willingness to accept new canons of art and in refusal to follow the herd instinct of the nation.

In two decades of conscious and unconscious questing for a Black Aesthetic, W. E. B. Du Bois experienced many difficulties in shaping and applying an idea which, he sensed, was sound. Some of the difficulties resulted from his personal limitations: his failure to clarify criteria, his dependence upon undefined abstractions, his inability to harmonize his awareness of the utilitarian value of literature for a specific group with his concern for the creation of Truth and Beauty, his fallacious assumption that his aesthetic was necessarily the aesthetic of most black people. Perhaps the major reason for his lack of success, however, is that, with this idea as with many others, Du Bois was twenty-five to fifty years ahead of those twelve million blacks he wanted to lead from self-respect to pride to achievement. (pp. 27-8)

> *Darwin T. Turner, "W. E. B. Du Bois and the Theory of a Black Aesthetic," in* The Harlem Renaissance Re-examined, *edited by Victor A. Kramer, AMS Press, 1987, pp. 9-30.*

## Arnold Rampersad

W. E. B. Du Bois's **The Souls of Black Folk** was a controversial book when it appeared in 1903, but few readers opposed to it could deny its originality and beauty as a portrait of the Afro-American people. In the succeeding years, the collection of essays lost little of its power, so that it remains acknowledged today as a masterpiece of black American writing. In 1918, the literary historian Benjamin Brawley still could feel in Du Bois's book "the passion of a mighty heart" when he hailed it as the most important work "in classic English" published to that time by a black writer. About thirty years after its appearance, the poet, novelist, and NAACP leader James Weldon Johnson judged that Du Bois's work had produced "a greater effect upon and within the Negro race in America than any other single book published in this country since *Uncle Tom's Cabin*." With admiration bordering on reverence for the book, Langston Hughes recalled that "my earliest memories of written words are those of Du Bois and the Bible." In the 1960s, the astute literary critic J. Saunders Redding weighed the impact of **Souls of Black Folk** on a variety of black intellectuals and leaders and pronounced it "more history-making than historical." In 1973, Herbert Aptheker, the leading Du Bois editor and scholar, hailed the text as "one of the classics in the English language."

These are fervent claims for a book of thirteen essays and a short story written by an academic who had been rigidly trained in history and sociology (especially at Harvard and the University of Berlin, where Du Bois did extensive doctoral work), and whose previous books had been an austere dissertation in history, *The Suppression of the African Slave-Trade to the United States,* and an empirical sociological study of urban blacks, *The Philadelphia Negro.* Clearly, however, *The Souls of Black Folk* was something other than academic history and sociology. If white academics and intellectuals mainly ignored its existence (although Henry James called it "the only Southern book of distinction published in many a year"), its impression was marked on the class of black Americans who provided the leadership of their race. Among black intellectuals, above all, *The Souls of Black Folk* became a kind of sacred book, the central text for the interpretation of the Afro-American experience and the most trustworthy guide into the grim future that seemed to loom before their race in America.

The main cause of the controversy surrounding *The Souls of Black Folk* was its devastating attack on Booker T. Washington. The head of the Tuskegee Institute in Alabama was already a famous man when his autobiography *Up from Slavery* was published in 1901. His epochal compromise speech at the Atlanta Exposition in 1895 had catapulted him to the position of leading spokesman for his race before the white world, a friend of rich industrialists like Andrew Carnegie and a dinner guest in the White House of Theodore Roosevelt. Nevertheless, *Up from Slavery* reinforced Washington's authority to a significant extent. Above all, he has used the skeleton of the slave narrative form (that is, the story of a life that progresses from a state of legal bondage to a state of freedom and a substantial degree of self-realization) not only to describe his rise in the world but also to dramatize the heart of the Tuskegee argument that the salvation of Afro-America lay in self-reliance, conciliation of the reactionary white South, a surrender of the right to vote and the right to social equality, dependence on thrift and industriousness, and an emphasis on vocational training rather than the liberal arts in the education of the young. To these ideas, Du Bois and *The Souls of Black Folk* was unalterably opposed.

I wish to suggest here that perhaps the most important element in the making of Du Bois's book, which drew on his previously published material but also on fresh work, derived in significant degree from his full awareness of *Up from Slavery.* While this could hardly be an altogether novel suggestion—given Du Bois's attack on Washington in his book—the crucial area of difference between them has not been adequately recognized. I would argue that this crucial element involved Du Bois's acute sensitivity to slavery both as an institution in American history and as an idea, along with his distaste for Washington's treatment of the subject in *Up from Slavery.* To some extent Du Bois's book functions, in spite of its only partial status as an autobiography, as a direct, parodic challenge to certain forms and assumptions of the slave narrative (in all their variety) which had so aided Booker T. Washington's arguments. While it does so mainly to refute the major ideas in Washington's influential text, at the same time its con-

trariness of form is made obligatory by Du Bois's peculiar attitudes toward slavery.

The resulting book can be seen as marking Du Bois's sense (and that of the many writers and intellectuals influenced by him) of the obsolescence of the slave narrative as a paradigm for Afro-American experience, as well as the beginning of a reflexive paradigm, allied to the slave narrative, that leads the reader—and the race described in the book—into the modern Afro-American world. William L. Andrews has pointed out . . . in his essay on slavery and the rise of Afro-American literary realism, that postbellum slave narratives de-emphasized the hellishly destructive nature of slavery and offered it instead as a crucible in which future black manhood was formed. Du Bois's approach, I would argue, is in part a revival of the earlier, antebellum spirit of black autobiography and the slave narrative, but in more significant part also differs from that earlier spirit. In both the earlier and the later slave narratives there is progress for the black as he or she moves away from slavery. Du Bois's central point, as we shall see, is different.

For Booker T. Washington in *Up from Slavery,* slavery was not an institution to be defended overtly. Nevertheless, its evils had been much overstated, as he saw them, and its blessings were real. The evils, insofar as they existed, were to be acknowledged briefly and then forgotten. While this approach in some senses is to be expected of an autobiography by a man born only seven years before emancipation, it also underscores Washington's public attitude to American slavery in particular and to history in general. In Washington's considered view, neither slavery nor history is of great consequence—or, at the very least, of daunting consequence to any black man of sound character who properly trains himself for the demands of the modern world. In *Up from Slavery,* Washington writes flatly of "the cruelty and moral wrong of slavery," and he remarks conclusively about the former slaves that "I have never seen one who did not want to be free, or one who would return to slavery." "I condemn it as an institution," he adds. Tellingly, however, this condemnation springs from a need to clarify the major message about slavery in his chapter on his slave years, "A Slave among Slaves." The need itself springs from the patent ambiguity of Washington's view of slavery.

Whatever he intends to do, Washington stresses the fundamentally innocuous, almost innocent, nature of the institution. Of his white father (said to be a prosperous neighbor, who refused to acknowledge him) and of his poor, black mother (who sometimes stole chickens in order to feed herself and her children), Washington's judgment is the same. In lacking the courage or generosity to acknowledge his son, his father "was simply another unfortunate victim of the institution which the Nation unhappily had engrafted upon it at the time." In her thievery, his mother "was simply a victim of the system of slavery." Moreover, Washington's lack of hostility to his father allegedly reflected the complacent attitudes of other blacks to whites. There was no "bitter feeling toward the white people on the part of my race" about the fact that many whites were fighting as soldiers in the Confederate army to preserve slavery; where slaves had been treated "with anything like decency," they showed love and tenderness to their masters, even those in the military. The chapter "A Slave among Slaves" ends with a striking tableau of the day of emancipation. Whites are sad not because of the loss of valuable property but "because of parting with those whom they had reared and who were in many ways very close to them." Blacks are initially ecstatic, but the older freedmen, "stealthily at first," return later to the "big house" to consult their former masters about their future.

Doubtless sincere in his expressions of antipathy to slavery, Washington nevertheless emphasizes the benefits gained by blacks through the institution. "Notwithstanding the cruel wrongs inflicted upon us," he asserts, "the black man got nearly as much out of slavery as the white man did." With Afro-Americans comprising the most advanced community of blacks in the world (as Washington claimed), slavery was indisputably a fortunate act. Indeed, it was further proof of the notion that "Providence so often uses men and institutions to accomplish a purpose." Through all difficulties, Washington continues to derive faith in the future of black Americans by dwelling on "the wilderness through which and out of which, a good Providence has already led us."

For Washington, the acknowledgment of Providence piously marks his negation of the consequences of forces such as those of history, psychology, economics, and philosophy at play in the field of slavery. (Providence does not perform a more positive function in his scheme, in which there is little room for religious enthusiasm or spiritual complexity. Of religion and spirituality in *Up from Slavery* he writes: "While a great deal of stress is laid upon the industrial side of the work at Tuskegee, we do not neglect or overlook in any degree the religious and spiritual side. The school is strictly undenominational, but it is thoroughly Christian, and the spiritual training of the students is not neglected.") Willing to share in the belief that economic competition and greed had been at the root of slavery, and that slavery itself was ultimately the cause of the Civil War, he pushes no further into causes and effects even as he everywhere, as a champion of pragmatism, lauds the value of "facts" and the "need to look facts in the face." In his scheme, the mental legacy of slavery to the black freedman is not conflict, but a blank, a kind of tabula rasa on which is to be inscribed those values and skills that would serve the freedman best in the new age. Although he offers a critical view of the past of his people, "who had spent generations in slavery, and before that generations in the darkest heathenism," Washington in fact invites a vision of the Afro-American as black Adam. This Adam is, in a way, both prelapsarian and postlapsarian. He is an Adam in the Eden of the South, with the world before him. He is also Adam who has fallen. The fall was slavery itself. Slavery, as seen in this context, is a "fortunate fall"—the fall by which Africans gained the skills and the knowledge needed for the modern world. But who is responsible for the fall? Who has sinned? The answer surely must be the black slave himself, since *Up from Slavery* places no blame on the white world. The failure to investigate the origins, the nature, and the consequences of slavery has led Washington to a subtle and yet far-reaching defamation of the African and Afro-American peoples.

The black American Adam, in his prelapsarian guise, and in the simplicity of his capabilities, must be protected from the fruit that would destroy him—in this case, knowledge in the form of classical learning. Otherwise, the black man may become a kind of Satan, excessively proud. Washington denounces the idea, apparently embraced eagerly by many blacks in the aftermath of the Civil War, "that a knowledge, however little, of the Greek and Latin languages would make one a very superior human being, something bordering almost on the supernatural." Inveighing against false black pride, he dismisses passionate black claims to the right to vote. The secret of progress appears to be regression. Deploring the mass black migration to the cities, he often wishes "that by some power of magic I might remove the great bulk of these people into the country districts and plant them upon the soil, upon the solid and never deceptive foundation of Mother Nature, where all nations and races that have ever succeeded have gotten their start." His garden is a priceless source of resuscitation. There, "I feel that I am coming into contact with something that is giving me strength for the many duties and hard places that await me out in the big world. I pity the man or woman who has never learned to enjoy nature and to get strength and inspiration out of it."

This refusal to confront slavery (or even the understandable association in the minds of many blacks of agricultural work with the terms of slavery) and this black variation on the myth of an American Adam make *Up from Slavery* an odd slave narrative according to either the antebellum or the postbellum model. Nevertheless, the hero moves from slavery to freedom and into his future as from darkness to light. Holding the story together is the distinction Washington quietly makes between himself and the other ex-slaves in general. He is the hero of a slave narrative. He sheds the dead skin of slavery, seeks an education, builds on it, and emerges as a powerful, fully realized human being, confident, almost invincible (within the bounds of discretion). This is seen as a possibility also for Washington's disciples, as the graduates of Tuskegee are represented. "Wherever our graduates go," he writes near the end of his book, "the changes which soon begin to appear in the buying of land, improving homes, saving money, in education, and in high moral character are remarkable. Whole communities are fast being revolutionized through the instrumentality of these men and women." The same cannot be said of the masses of blacks who have not been to Tuskegee or who have not come under the Tuskegee influence in some other way. In *Up from Slavery,* they remain blanks. This was hardly the first slave narrative in which the central character saw great distance between himself and other blacks. In Du Bois's *The Souls of Black Folk,* however, that distance would shrink dramatically.

When *The Souls of Black Folk* appeared in 1903, slavery had been officially dead in the United States for forty years. Du Bois himself, thirty-five years of age in 1903, had not been born a slave. Indeed, he had been born on free soil, in Great Barrington, Massachusetts, in a family that had lived there for several generations. One ancestor had even been a revolutionary soldier. Nevertheless, the shadow of slavery hangs powerfully over *The Souls of Black Folk.* Thus Du Bois acknowledged the fact that his book is about a people whose number included many who had been born slaves, and a vast majority who were immediately descended from slaves. On this central point, *The Souls of Black Folk* is a stark contrast to *Up from Slavery.*

In July 1901, shortly after the latter appeared, Du Bois reviewed it in *Dial* magazine. This was his first open criticism of Washington. In 1895, he had saluted Washington's compromising Atlanta Exposition speech as "a word fitly spoken." In the following years, however, he had watched with increasing dismay as the head of Tuskegee propagated his doctrine of compromise and silenced much of his opposition through his manipulation of elements of the black press and other sources of power. Du Bois's attack on him in *Dial* was decisive. The *Dial* review, followed by *The Souls of Black Folk* (where the review again appeared, in adapted form), created "a split of the race into two contending camps," as James Weldon Johnson later noted astutely. Cryptically noting that Washington had given "but glimpses of the real struggle which he has had for leadership," Du Bois accused him of peddling a "Lie." Surveying the various modes of black response to white power from the earliest days in America, he concluded that the vaunted Tuskegee philosophy for black self-improvement was little more than "the old [black] attitude of adjustment to environment, emphasizing the economic phase."

In *The Souls of Black Folk,* unable to fashion an autobiography to match Washington's, young Du Bois nevertheless infused a powerful autobiographical spirit and presence into his essays. From about three dozen of his published articles on aspects of black history and sociology, he selected eight for adaptation or reprinting as nine chapters in *The Souls of Black Folk.* The brief fifth chapter, **"Of the Wings of Atalanta,"** about commercialism and the city of Atlanta, was new, as were the last four chapters: **"Of the Passing of the First-Born,"** Du Bois's prose elegy on the death of his only son, Burghardt; **"Of Alexander Crummell,"** his tribute to an exceptional black man; **"Of the Coming of John,"** a short story; and **"Of the Sorrow Songs,"** an essay on spirituals. Holding these various efforts together is the central figure of Du Bois, who presents himself as a scholar and historian but more dramatically as an artist and a visionary who would not only depict the present state of black culture but also try to prophesy something about its future and the future of the nation.

Du Bois understood clearly that the representation of slavery was central to the entire task. Unlike Washington in *Up from Slavery,* he believed that slavery had been a force of extraordinary—and mainly destructive—potency. Destructive as it had been, however, slavery had not destroyed every major aspect of the African character and psychology (topics on which Washington had been silent); the African core had survived. But so had slavery. Where Washington saw opportunity on every hand for the black, if the right course was followed, Du Bois proclaimed that American slavery was not dead. In one guise or another,

it still persisted, with its power scarcely diminished. The act of emancipation had been both a fact (such as Washington loved to fasten on) and a mirage: "Years have passed since then—ten, twenty, forty; forty years of national life, forty years of renewal and development, and yet the swarthy spectre sits in its accustomed seat at the Nation's feast. . . . The Nation has not yet found peace from its sins; the freedman has not yet found in freedom his promised land."

Although there were elements of agreement between Washington and Du Bois on the nature of slavery, *The Souls of Black Folk* portrays the institution in terms essentially opposite to those in *Up from Slavery.* Du Bois does not deny that slavery had its benign side, but in almost every instance his conclusion about its effects is radical when compared with Washington's. American slavery had not been the "worst slavery in the world," and had known something of "kindliness, fidelity, and happiness"; nevertheless, it "classed the black man and the ox together." Less equivocally, and more typical of Du Bois's view of slavery, black men were "emasculated" by the institution. Emancipation brought them "suddenly, violently . . . into a new birthright." The white southern universities had been contaminated by "the foul breath of slavery." Instead of the providential view of slavery espoused by Washington, for Du Bois the institution had amounted to "two hundred and fifty years of assiduous education in submission, carelessness, and stealing."

Du Bois's emphasis on slavery as a social evil is only one part of the scheme by which he measures the Afro-American and American reality. Central to his argument is his belief in the persistence of the power of slavery beyond emancipation. Many current ills had their start in slavery. The widespread tendency of white businessmen and industrialists to see human beings as property, or "among the material resources of a land to be trained with an eye single to future dividend," was "born of slavery." The "plague-spot in sexual relations" among blacks—easy marriage and easy separation—"is the plain heritage from slavery." Many whites in the South live "haunted by the ghost of an untrue dream." "Slavery and race-prejudice are potent if not sufficient causes of the Negro's position" today. Du Bois does not pretend, in the manner of a demogogue, that slavery and neo-slavery are absolutely identical. He sometimes proposes a new slavery as only a distinct possibility. The power of the ballot, downplayed by Booker T. Washington, is absolutely needed—"else what shall save us from a second slavery?" And yet, if the black man is not actually a slave, he is actually not free. "Despite compromise, war, and struggle," Du Bois insists, "the Negro is not free" and is in danger "of being reduced to semi-slavery." Repeatedly he invokes the central symbol of enslavement to portray the status of the modern black. Today, blacks are "shackled men."

In the final analysis, black Americans live in neo-slavery. The race passed from formal slavery through an interim illusion of emancipation ("after the first flush of freedom wore off ") into a new version of slavery that in many respects continues the old. The law courts were used by the white South as the first means of "reenslaving the blacks."

Examining estates that once were slave plantations, Du Bois marvels at how the design and disposition of the black cabins are "the same as in slavery days." While for Booker T. Washington the Tuskegee education eradicates the vestiges of slavery from students at the institute, Du Bois sees the legacy of slavery as inescapable: "No people a generation removed from slavery can escape a certain unpleasant rawness and *gaucherie,* despite the best of training." Even the Tuskegee philosophy, as has been pointed out, reflects for Du Bois, in its spirit of compromise, the timidity forced on blacks by slavery.

It is vital to recognize that, far from being the result of distorting bitterness or propaganda, Du Bois's position on neo-slavery at the turn of the century, which he amply documents with vivid examples (many drawn from his personal experience), is fully supported by a wide range of leading historians. Central to their analysis were not simply the repressive local laws but the even more confining decisions of the Supreme Court in *Plessy* v. *Ferguson* in 1896, which held that "separate but equal" facilities were constitutionally valid, and in *Williams* v. *Mississippi* in 1898, which endorsed that state's plan to strip blacks of the franchise given them after the Civil War. Rayford W. Logan dubbed the period before the end of the century the "Nadir" of the Afro-American experience. "When complete," C. Vann Woodward wrote of these segregationist laws, "the new codes of White Supremacy were vastly more complex than the ante-bellum slave codes or the Black Codes of 1865-66, and, if anything, they were stronger and more rigidly enforced."

Du Bois's attitude toward slavery, the black present, and the black future is heavily dependent on his attitude toward the preslavery situation of blacks—that is, to Africa. In *The Souls of Black Folk* he does not dwell on the historical evidence of African civilization before slavery that twelve years later would form virtually the main subject of his Pan-Africanist volume, *The Negro* (1915). But where Washington writes only of heathenistic darkness in *Up from Slavery,* Du Bois concedes heathenism but also attributes to the slave a complex, dignified, and usable past. "He was brought from a definite social environment," Du Bois explains,"—the polygamous clan life under the headship of the chief and the potent influence of the priest. His religion was nature-worship, with profound belief in invisible surrounding influences, good and bad, and his worship was through incantation and sacrifice." In other words, the African lived in a stable, consistent, complex social order, complemented by strong and formal religious beliefs. Far from being a blank, the mind of the black, both in Africa and as a slave brought to the New World, was a remarkable instrument. And because of this background, the slave's natural reaction to slavery was not passivity—which was learned later—but revolt. "Endowed with a rich tropical imagination," Du Bois asserts, "and a keen, delicate appreciation of Nature, the transplanted African lived in a world animate with gods and devils, elves and witches; full of strange influences,— of Good to be implored, of Evil to be propitiated. Slavery, then, was to him the dark triumph of Evil over him. All the fateful powers of the Underworld were striving against him, and a spirit of revolt and revenge filled his heart."

In ascribing to the black in Africa and in the New World a mind that in its own way is as powerful as that of any other race in the world, Du Bois does more than merely try to boost his race's reputation. He shifts the terms of the debate toward the question of the black mind and character, and introduces questions of history, psychology, myth, and art. He also introduces into his scheme at least two other elements severely downplayed by Washington in *Up from Slavery.* One is the role of imagination; the other, that of memory. Otherwise derogatory of blacks, many white racial "scientists," including the Count de Gobineau, the author of the influential *Essay on the Inequality of Human Races,* had often credited them with remarkable imaginative and artistic faculties (the "rich tropical imagination" Du Bois ascribed to the transplanted African). Du Bois allows this credit to influence not only what he wrote about blacks but also how he wrote it.

Booker T. Washington, finding little that is useful in the African and the slave past, seems in *Up from Slavery* to harbor a deep suspicion of the black imagination, or even to be unaware that it exists. Indeed, his entire attitude toward the imagination contrasts with Du Bois's. While he reads books, or advocates the reading of books, he mentions no novels or poems. He is proud of the fact that his keenest pleasures are in the practical world. "Few things are more satisfactory to me than a high-grade Berkshire or Poland China pig," he writes. "Games I care little for." Du Bois is different. From early in his life, he tells us, he has seen the development of his imagination as one possible key to simultaneous self-realization and the leadership of his race against the whites. "Just how I would do it I could never decide," he writes of his youthful dreams of racial and personal victory; "by reading law, by healing the sick, by telling the wonderful tales that swam in my head,—some way."

In fact, Du Bois's greatest cultural claims for blacks are in the areas of art and imagination. In these claims, slaves play the decisive role. He lauds them as musicians, especially when music is blended with spirituality in the "sorrow songs." In a nation where "vigor and ingenuity" are prized, rather than beauty, "the Negro folk-song—the rhythmic cry of the slave—stands to-day not simply as the sole American music, but as the most beautiful expression of human experience born this side the seas." Of the three gifts from blacks to American culture, the first is "a gift of story and song—soft, stirring melody in an ill-harmonized and unmelodious land." (The other gifts are toil and "a gift of the Spirit.")

Recognizing imagination as a source of black strength, and confirming the power of the imagination in Africa, slavery, and thereafter, also freed Du Bois as a thinker and a writer. In his previous book, *The Philadelphia Negro,* he had warned fastidiously that the scholar "must ever tremble lest some personal bias, some moral conviction or some unconscious trend of thought due to previous training, has to a degree distorted the picture in his view." This timidity is abandoned in *The Souls of Black Folk,* which is full of impressionistic writing, including occasionally startling descriptions of people and places, and clearly subjective judgments. Du Bois based the book on his scholarly knowledge of history and sociology, but the eye and mind of the artist are given almost free play.

He was well aware of the possible price of indulging the imagination and even believed that he had paid a part of that price. A year after the book appeared, in a note about it published in the *Independent,* Du Bois conceded that "the style and workmanship" of *The Souls of Black Folk* did not make its meaning "altogether clear." He was sure that the book presented a "clear central message," but also that around this core floated what he called a shadowy "penumbra" of vagueness and partly obscured allusions. Similarly, in his preface, **"The Forethought,"** Du Bois was restrained in outlining his plans. He will sketch, "in vague, uncertain outline," the spiritual world in which the ten million black Americans live." In both pieces, Du Bois is acknowledging the "tropic imagination" of blacks, of which he is one. His elite, formal, Western education has curbed this tropic imagination for too long; now it is free.

A crucial factor here is the connection thus proclaimed between the author of *The Souls of Black Folk* and the masses of American blacks, the despised slaves they had been or were descended from, and the Africans beyond the seas. Du Bois made this connection for all to see when he said of his book, in the note in the *Independent* just cited, that "in its larger aspects the style is tropical—African." In his "Forethought," too, he had linked himself to other blacks, and to slaves: "Need I add that I who speak here am bone of the bone and flesh of the flesh of them that live within the Veil?"

By indulging his imagination, Du Bois gains for his book much of its distinction. Where Booker T. Washington stresses cold facts, and avoids metaphors and similes, imagination leads Du Bois to the invocation of keen images to represent black reality, and to major insights. Chief among the images is that of "the Veil," which hangs between the black and white races, an apparently harmless fabric but one that the rest of the book shows to be in some respects an almost impregnable wall, and the prime source of misery. In one place he even links his image of the veil to the symbol of an ongoing slavery; at one and the same time, he records "the wail of prisoned souls within the veil, and the mounting fury of shackled men. Linked to the image of the veil, but going beyond it, and inscribed in the very title of the book, is the idea of black American "double consciousness." Taking the basic idea of double consciousness as a feature or a capability of the human brain from the reflections of leading psychologists of the time, such as his former professor William James, Du Bois applied the notion with telling force to the mental consequences of the social, political, and cultural conflicts that came with being Afro-American. Perhaps no more challenging single statement about the nature of the black American mind, about the psychological consequences of slavery and racism, has ever been offered. Both the notion of black invisibility and of innately conflicted Afro-American consciousness would be reflected powerfully in future black poetry and fiction.

The "souls" of the title is a play on words. It alludes to the "twoness" of the black American that Du Bois initially suggests in his first chapter. America, a predominantly white country, yields the black "no true self-consciousness, but only lets him see himself through the revelation of the other world." The result is "a peculiar sensation, this double-consciousness, this sense of always looking at one's self through the eyes of others, of measuring one's soul by the tape of a world that looks on in amused contempt and pity. One ever feels his twoness,—an American, a Negro; two souls, two thoughts, two unreconciled strivings; two warring ideals in one dark body, whose dogged strength alone keeps it from being torn asunder." "Such a double life," Du Bois writes later, in his chapter on religion, "with double thoughts, double duties, and double social classes, must give rise to double words and double ideals, and tempt the mind to pretence or revolt, to hypocrisy or radicalism." Another way of seeing these two souls surely is as a contest between memory and its opposite, amnesia. American culture demands of its blacks amnesia concerning slavery and Africa, just as it encourages amnesia of a different kind in whites. For Du Bois, blacks may not be able to remember Africa but they should remember slavery, since it has hardly ended.

"In the days of bondage," he writes of the slaves, stressing their imagination, "they thought to see in one divine event the end of all doubt and disappointment; few men ever worshipped Freedom with half such unquestioning faith as did the American Negro for two centuries. . . . In song and exhortation swelled one refrain—Liberty; in his tears and curses the God he implored had Freedom in his right hand. At last it came,—suddenly, fearfully, like a dream." The first decade after the war "was merely a prolongation of the vain search for freedom, the boon that seemed ever barely to elude their grasp,—like a tantalizing will-o'-the-wisp, maddening and misleading the helpless host." Freedom never came, but something else did, very faintly, that "changed the child of Emancipation to the youth with dawning self-consciousness, self-realization, self-respect."

The fundamental progression of the Afro-American in history, as seen by Du Bois, is from a simple bondage to a more complex bondage slightly ameliorated by this "dawning" of "self-consciousness, self-realization, self-respect." "In those sombre forests of his striving, his own soul rose before him, and he saw himself,—darkly as through a veil; and yet he saw in himself some faint revelation of his power, of his mission." This realization, although "faint," facilitates Du Bois's shift toward what one might call cultural nationalism in the black: "He began to have a dim feeling that, to attain his place in the world, he must be himself, and not another." Cultural nationalism does not mean anti-intellectualism: "For the first time he sought to analyze the burden he bore upon his back, that deadweight of social degradation partially masked behind a half-named Negro problem."

The diminution of the myth of freedom, the elevation of the power of slavery, allows Du Bois to establish a continuum of African and Afro-American psychology. Times change and the nature and amount of data change, but the black mind remains more or less constant, for Du Bois sees it as irrevocably linked to its African origins. If that constancy is anywhere observable, it is for Du Bois in black Christian religion, which in the main is a product of slavery. For him, "the frenzy of a Negro revival in the untouched backwoods of the South" re-creates tellingly "the religious feeling of the slave." The full meaning of slavery "to the African savage" is unknown to Du Bois, but he believes that the answer is to be found only in "a study of Negro religion as a development" from heathenism to the institutionalized urban churches of the North. The black church is the key to knowing "the inner ethical life of the people who compose it." Then follows a venture in analysis that may be taken as the foundation of Du Bois's sense of the Afro-American mind, or soul.

By the 1750s, after the initial impulse to revolt had been crushed by white power, "the black slave had sunk, with hushed murmurs, to his place at the bottom of a new economic system, and was unconsciously ripe for a new philosophy of life." The Christian doctrine of passive submission facilitated this shift in which "courtesy became humility, moral strength degenerated into submission, and the exquisite native appreciation of the beautiful became an infinite capacity for dumb suffering." A century later, black religion had transformed itself once again, this time around the cry for abolition, which became a "religion to the black world. Thus, when Emancipation finally came, it seemed to the freedman a literal Coming of the Lord. His fervid imagination was stirred as never before, by the tramp of armies, the blood and dust of battle, and the wail and whirl of social upheaval." Forty years later, with the world changing swiftly, Du Bois sees "a time of intense ethical ferment, of religious heart-searching and intellectual unrest." This leads him, looking backward and forward, into history and into the future. "From the double life every American Negro must live, as a Negro and as an American, as swept on by the current of the nineteenth while yet struggling in the eddies of the fifteenth century,—from this must arise a painful self-consciousness, an almost morbid sense of personality and a moral hesitancy which is fatal to self-confidence." These are the secondary, but almost equally binding, shackles of neo-slavery.

The authenticity of slavery as metaphor for the black experience is firmly underscored in the most "creative," or imaginative, areas of *The Souls of Black Folk.* These are the autobiographical passages of the book; the biographical chapter, on Alexander Crummell; and the short story, **"Of the Coming of John."** The sharpest focus of the autobiographical element occurs in **"Of the Passing of the First-Born,"** about the death of Du Bois's son (who died of dysentery in Atlanta). In certain respects this is an almost classical elegy, in impassioned and yet formal language. But it is one in which the central mourner, as a black, can find no consolation. Thus it is in truth anti-Christian, a bitter parody of the Christian elegy such as Milton's *Lycidas.* For Du Bois, unable to believe in Booker T. Washington's Providence, doubt completely infects his vision of his son's future: "If still he be, and he be There, and there be a There, let him be happy, O Fate!." Perhaps one day the veil will be lifted and the imprisoned blacks set free, but not in Du Bois's time: "Not for me,—I shall die in my bonds." The metaphor of black life as slavery preempts the annealing possibilities of the elegy.

This chapter underscores the memorable autobiographical impressions left by the first few pages of the book, in which Du Bois discusses his first, youthful encounter with racism: "Then it dawned upon me with a certain suddenness that I was different from the others [his white classmates]; or like, mayhap, in heart and life and longing, but shut out from their world by a vast veil." Taking refuge in fierce competitiveness, he wins small victories but understands at last that "the worlds I longed for, and all their dazzling opportunities, were theirs, not mine." Many of his black friends deteriorate into sycophancy or into hatred and distrust of whites. Du Bois does not, but "the shades of the prison-house closed round about us all; walls strait and stubborn to the whitest, but relentlessly narrow, tall, and unscalable to sons of night."

Thus, just as the acceptance of the idea of neo-slavery forbids Du Bois the writing of classical elegy, with its formal consolation, so does that acceptance also forbid Du Bois the writing of anything that resembles either the "classical" slave narrative—the account of a life that has passed from bondage to freedom, from darkness to light—or its white American counterpart, the rags-to-riches autobiographical tale built on the materialist base of the American Dream. Indeed, if one isolates Du Bois as the hero of *The Souls of Black Folk,* one sees the reverse pattern. He goes from light into darkness, from the freedom of infancy and childhood into the bondage of maturity. Each modern black American, he argues implicitly, re-creates this regressive journey. So too has the black race, in its New World experience, enacted a historical regression. Preslavery African manhood and womanhood have deteriorated into passivity, moral hesitancy, cynicism, and rage.

Du Bois does not see all blacks as succumbing to pressure, but in any event those who resist have no hope of a lasting triumph. The most honored single figure in *The Souls of Black Folk* is Alexander Crummell (1819-1898), who struggled against tremendous odds but succeeded in being ordained as a priest in the almost entirely white Protestant Episcopal Church, earned a degree from Cambridge University, then went on to years of diligent service in Africa and the United States. Crummell also helped to found the American Negro Academy, in which Du Bois himself was involved. Clearly he stands as Du Bois's idea of the highest achievement among black Americans. Pointedly, Crummell was born when "the slave-ship still groaned across the Atlantic." His life is one of trial and tribulation, but also of resistance to doubt, hatred, and despair. He decides early to live for his people: "He heard the hateful clank of their chains; he felt them cringe and grovel, and there rose within him a protest and a prophesy." But no great triumph followed. For all his service and achievement, Crummell's name is now barely known. "And herein lies the tragedy of the age: not that men are poor,—all men know something of poverty; not that men are wicked,—who is good? not that men are ignorant,—what is Truth? Nay, but that men know so little of men." Again, the consolation of faith is impossible: "I wonder where he is today?"

The short story **"Of the Coming of John"** (in a sense, one of "the wonderful tales that swam in my head" to which

Du Bois alludes early in the book) further underscores the destructive force of neo-slavery. Black John, a simple country boy, comes to "Wells Institute" to be educated. But education cannot save him from racism, and his spirit deteriorates: "A tinge of sarcasm crept into his speech, and a vague bitterness into his life." Education alienates him from his own people; he returns home only to be struck by the "sordidness and narrowness" of what he had left behind. Unwittingly he tramples on the religious beliefs of the local blacks, and he preaches democracy in the black school although it is under the control of a reactionary white judge. Dismissed from his job there, he wanders in a daze until he sees his sister tussling with a white man he had known as a boy. He kills the man. John tells his mother he is going away—"I'm going to be free." Not understanding, she asks if he is going north again. "Yes, mammy," John replies, "I'm going,—North." He is soon lynched by revengeful whites. Going north and freedom are meaningless for John and for blacks in America. Freedom does not exist, except in death.

Education is only one of the forces that, subverted by racism and neo-slavery, betray John when he should have been elevated by them. For a person of Du Bois's complicated and elite schooling, this must have been a particularly poignant aspect to the condition he describes. Education should lead to light and truth. Booker T. Washington rearranged the chronology of his life in *Up from Slavery* to end his book close to the dizzying personal height of a Harvard honorary degree awarded in 1896 to the former illiterate slave. With the invitation in hand, "tears came into my eyes." But education for John leads to darkness and death. The fate of Alexander Crummell and of the author of **The Souls of Black Folk** is not much more exalted.

**The Souls of Black Folk** offers no transcendent confidence in the future. Du Bois's essay on religion, **"Of the Faith of the Fathers,"** ends with an assertion of the existence of "the deep religious feeling of the real Negro heart, the stirring, unguided might of powerful human souls who have lost the guiding star of the past and seek in the great night a new religious ideal." Only in concluding the book does Du Bois appeal to the longest possible historical view. The assumption of whites that certain races cannot be "saved" is "the arrogance of people irreverent toward Time and ignorant of the deeds of men. A thousand years ago such an assumption, easily possible, would have made it difficult for the Teuton to prove his right to life." As powerful as it was, American slavery thus becomes for him, in the end, only an episode in the African people's history, not the history itself.

Before this point, however, he has engaged slavery valiantly in his text. His point of view is clear. Admitting and exploring the reality of slavery is necessarily painful for a black American, but only by doing so can he or she begin to understand himself or herself and American and Afro-American culture in general. The normal price of the evasion of the fact of slavery is intellectual and spiritual death. Only by grappling with the meaning and legacy of slavery can the imagination, recognizing finally the temporality of the institution, begin to transcend it. (pp. 104-23)

*Arnold Rampersad, "Slavery and the Literary Imagination: Du Bois's 'The Souls of Black Folk',"* in Slavery and the Literary Imagination, *edited by Deborah E. McDowell and Arnold Rampersad, The Johns Hopkins University Press, 1989, pp. 104-24.*

---

### FURTHER READING

Aptheker, Herbert. *Annotated Bibliography of the Published Writings of W. E. B. Du Bois.* Millwood, N.Y.: Kraus-Thomson Organization Limited, 1973, 626 p.
  Comprehensive bibliography of Du Bois's published writings, prepared by Aptheker at Du Bois's request.

———. *The Literary Legacy of W. E. B. Du Bois.* White Plains, N.Y.: Kraus International Publications, 1989, 371 p.
  Collection of introductory essays on Du Bois's works.

Broderick, Francis L. *W. E. B. Du Bois: Negro Leader in a Time of Crisis.* Stanford: Stanford University Press, 1959, 259 p.
  The first book-length biography of Du Bois. Broderick made use of Du Bois's private papers at the University of Massachusetts until Du Bois closed them to the public after his 1951 indictment as an unregistered agent of a foreign power.

Brodwin, Stanley. "The Veil Transcended: Form and Meaning in W. E. B. Du Bois's 'The Souls of Black Folk'." *Journal of Black Studies* 2, No. 3 (March 1972): 303-21.
  Analyzes the essays in *The Souls of Black Folk.*

Clarke, John Henrik; Jackson, Esther; Kaiser, Ernest; and O'Dell, J. H., eds. *Black Titan: W. E. B. Du Bois.* Boston: Beacon Press, 1970, 333 p.
  Anthology by the editors of *Freedomways.* Includes tributes to Du Bois by Kwame Nkrumah, Langston Hughes, and Paul Robeson, among others; critical essays on Du Bois; and selected essays and poems by Du Bois.

DeMarco, Joseph P. *The Social Thought of W. E. B. Du Bois.* Lanham, Md.: University Press of America, 1983, 203 p.
  Traces the evolution of Du Bois's social thought throughout his lifetime.

Diggs, Irene. Introduction to *Dusk of Dawn: An Essay Toward an Autobiography of a Race Concept,* by W. E. B. Du Bois, pp. vii-xxvi. New Brunswick, N.J.: Transaction Books, 1984.
  Brief biography of Du Bois by his former student and assistant.

Du Bois, Shirley Graham. *His Day Is Marching On: A Memoir of W. E. B. Du Bois.* Philadelphia: J. B. Lippincott Company, 1971, 384 p.
  Biography and personal memoir by Du Bois's second wife.

Elder, Arlene A. "Swamp Versus Plantation: Symbolic Structure in W. E. B. Du Bois' *The Quest of the Silver Fleece.*" *Phylon* XXXIV, No. 4 (December 1973): 358-67.

Examines symbolism in *The Quest of the Silver Fleece.*

Finkelstein, Sidney. "W. E. B. Du Bois's Trilogy: A Literary Triumph." *Mainstream* 14, No. 10 (October 1961): 6-17.
  Examines Du Bois's *Black Flame* trilogy, determining "there can be no doubt of the fact that it is a work that could only have been produced by a man of genius."

Hackett, Francis. "The Negro Speaks." *The New Republic* XXII, No. 279 (7 April 1920): 189-90.
  Reviews *Darkwater: Voices from Within the Veil,* arguing that it "must be reckoned among those [books] that add not only to the wisdom but to the exaltation and glory of man."

Kostelanetz, Richard. "W. E. B. Du Bois: Perhaps the Most Important Black in American Intellectual History." *Commonweal* LXXXIX, No. 5 (1 November 1968): 161-62.
  Reviews Du Bois's third autobiography, a work informed "by the American theme of personal possibility and disciplined accomplishment in spite of racial prejudice and social disadvantage."

Review of *The Quest of the Silver Fleece,* by W. E. B. Du Bois. *The Literary Digest* XLIII, No. 21 (18 November 1911): 926.
  Favorable review of Du Bois's first novel.

Logan, Rayford W., ed. *W. E. B. Du Bois: A Profile.* New York: Hill and Wang, 1971, 324 p.
  Collection of critical essays about Du Bois's life and works.

Moore, Jack B. *W. E. B. Du Bois.* Boston: Twayne Publishers, 1981, 185 p.
  Biography concentrating on Du Bois's life and works and deemphasizing his conflicts with opponents.

Rampersad, Arnold. *The Art and Imagination of W. E. B. Du Bois.* Cambridge, Mass.: Harvard University Press, 1976, 325 p.

Evaluation of Du Bois's intellectual influences and changing thought.

Stepto, Robert B. "The Quest of the Weary Traveler: W. E. B. Du Bois's *The Souls of Black Folk.*" In his *From behind the Veil: A Study of Afro-American Narrative,* pp. 52-91. Urbana: University of Illinois Press, 1979.
  Examines the structure of *The Souls of Black Folk.*

Stillman, Clara Gruening. "Tracing the Color Line." *New York Herald Tribune Books* (25 June 1939): 12.
  Praises *Black Folk Then and Now: An Essay on the History and Sociology of the Negro Race.*

Stone, William B. "Idiolect and Ideology: Some Stylistic Aspects of Norris, James, and Du Bois." *Style* 10, No. 4 (Fall 1976): 405-25.
  Explores style and politics in Frank Norris's *The Pit,* Henry James's *The Ambassadors,* and Du Bois's *The Souls of Black Folk,* all published in 1903.

Taylor, A. A. Review of *Black Reconstruction: An Essay Toward a History of the Part Which Black Folk Played in the Attempt to Reconstruct Democracy in America, 1860-1880,* by W. E. B. Du Bois. *The New England Quarterly* 8, No. 4 (December 1935): 608-12.
  Praises *Black Reconstruction,* maintaining that it is a work written from the "enlightened point of view" that a black person is an average and ordinary human being and not a "distinctly inferior creation."

Tuttle, William M., Jr., ed. *W. E. B. Du Bois.* Englewood Cliffs, N.J.: Prentice-Hall, Inc., 1973, 186 p.
  Brief biography featuring essays by Du Bois, reactions from his contemporaries, and essays by scholars August Meier and Francis Broderick.

Wesley, Charles H. "W. E. B. Du Bois the Historian." *Freedomways* 5, No. 1 (First Quarter 1965): 59-72.
  Overview of Du Bois's career as a historian.

# Steve Erickson

## 1950-

(Full name Stephen Michael Erickson) American novelist, editor, and journalist.

Through haunting images, Erickson's novels explore malevolence and alienation in the twentieth century, often blending fantasy with such actual occurrences as environmental crises and political campaigns. Avoiding simple plot structures, Erickson embeds stories within stories to present disorienting, dreamlike scenarios. His lyrical, experimental prose often evokes apocalyptic, surreal landscapes plagued by natural disasters. Although occasionally faulted for incoherence, Erickson is lauded for his allegorical treatments of complex subjects. Reviewers frequently recognize the theme of relativity in such works as *Tours of the Black Clock,* which examines the essence of a modern, post-Einsteinian world in which such phenomena as time, space, and good and evil, have no absolute definition. Thomas Pynchon stated: "Erickson has that rare and luminous gift for reporting back from the nocturnal side of reality, along with an engagingly romantic attitude and the fierce imaginative energy of a born storyteller."

As a student at the University of California, Los Angeles, Erickson majored in film and journalism. Critics occasionally allude to Erickson's film background when discussing his first novel, *Days between Stations,* which reflects such cinematic techniques as fades, cross-cuts, and vivid imagery. A bleak, futuristic landscape mirrors the alienation of the three main characters, each of whom is desperately searching for identity, love or recognition. A victim of amnesia, Michel seeks the missing reel of an epic French film directed by his grandfather, certain that clues to his past are in the movie. His lover, Lauren, leaves her husband in Los Angeles to accompany him to Paris on his quest for identity. They are pursued by Lauren's husband, a cyclist who dreams of winning an Olympic gold medal. Although some reviewers found Erickson's use of cinematic conventions confusing, many considered his conception of a world overwhelmed by natural disaster, from sandstorms in Los Angeles to dried canals in Venice, the most compelling element of *Days between Stations.* Frederika Randall stated: "The hapless and often witless characters in this richly convoluted story finally prove far less interesting than the vision of a world where cultural memory has dried up and there is nothing left but a series of powerful, disconnected celluloid images."

Like *Days between Stations,* the surrealist form of *Rubicon Beach* relies more on imagery than plot, and Erickson's dreamlike impressions have been compared to those of Jorge Luis Borges and Gabriel García Márquez. Time and place become blurred as the narrative shifts radically through three distinct stories and such disparate locations as South American jungles, contemporary Hollywood, the moors of England, and Depression-era Chicago. The characters' identities also fluctuate; a character named Cale

mysteriously transforms into a man named Jack Mick Lake toward the novel's conclusion, when the three sections, connected by dreams, begin to merge. Some critics charged that the lyrical prose of *Rubicon Beach* reveals that Erickson emphasizes style rather than substance or insight. Others maintained, however, that the narrative is unified, engaging readers with the sense of drifting within the writer's imagination.

Although similar in style to his previous works, Erickson's *Tours of the Black Clock* is regarded by many critics as thematically and technically superior. The narrator of this work is Banning Jainlight, the illegitimate son of a Pennsylvania farmer. When he realizes that the family's half-Native American domestic servant—who has been repeatedly raped by his father and half-brothers—is his mother, Jainlight retaliates by murdering one sibling, injuring the other as well as his father, and burning down the house. Unremorseful, Jainlight travels to Vienna, where he is employed as a pornography writer for Hitler. The two men become bound by mutual obsession: Hitler for his young niece Geli, and Jainlight for a 15-year-old girl named Dania. Many critics viewed the relationship between Jainlight and Hitler, both murderers, as a device for examining

136

the relative nature of evil in the twentieth century. Caryn James observed: "It is a great part of Mr. Erickson's achievement that he shows his readers the humanity of evil—a force all the more chilling because it cannot be dismissed as a monstrous act of fate—yet allows hope and compassion to struggle through."

Written in the form of a journal, *Leap Year* chronicles the events of the 1988 presidential campaign. Accompanying Erickson on his journey through twenty-three states is the ghost of Sally Hemings, Thomas Jefferson's slave and mistress who declined an opportunity for freedom, choosing to remain with her master. Sally's voice is interspersed with Erickson's narrative, which often contemplates America's lost idealism. The novel's lyrical and experimental approach to typically dry political reportage intrigued numerous critics. Charles Bowden asserted: "[I] kept being sucked in by the risk of it all, kind of like watching those old tapes of [comedian] Lenny Bruce in action as his manic raps spun off into space with no safe destination." Many asserted that *Leap Year* utilizes the personalities and events of the 1988 election to explore the nature of life in contemporary America. Mirroring the subjective reality of previous novels, Erickson portrays a campaign in which it is impossible to determine the true message of a candidate in the midst of a deluge of distorted media images.

(See also *Contemporary Authors,* Vol. 129.)

## PRINCIPAL WORKS

NOVELS

*Days between Stations*   1985
*Rubicon Beach*   1986
*Tours of the Black Clock*   1989
*Leap Year*   1989

---

### Kirkus Reviews

[Steve Erickson's **Days between Stations** is an] impressionistic, self-dissolving, and often unbearably jejune first novel. Comprising the murky triangle here are: a young woman from Kansas named Lauren; her bicycle-racer husband Jason; and her lover [Michel], who manages a Los Angeles club aptly named The Blue Isosceles—but whose main energies go into his Paris attempts to recover the lost cinema masterpiece of his grandfather Adolphe Saar (clearly based on Abel Gance and his *Napoleon* of the Twenties). Michel, however, also suffers from amnesia—a malady that serves as a sort of general anesthetic over the shreds of plot: Lauren briefly flees the turmoil of an admitted infidelity by Jason; her baby dies of crib death; she flees once more, to Paris, where she again meets up with Michel—and where she's also pursued by amends-making Jason. But all this movement seems to be little more than

an excuse for Erickson to unroll swatches of his gauzy prose:

> Neither of them should have known these things except that now there was nothing left to survey, or touch, or hear outside, nothing to feel but the things that neither could know of the other; and therefore they felt everything. Not the details or the definitive traumas but the resulting carnage by which each had been ravaged.

And Erickson's attempts at adapting cinematic conventions—fades and cuts—to fiction are equally entangling and ineffectual. (A scene in which Michel makes love to Lauren, who's buried under sand inside an office when a sandstorm in Los Angeles suddenly blows up, is unintentionally hilarious.) An unimpressive debut.

> *A review of "Days between Stations," in* Kirkus Reviews, *Vol. LIII, No. 4, February 15, 1985, p. 149.*

### Publishers Weekly

[In Erickson's **Days between Stations**] Michel Sarasan awakens one morning in Paris plagued with amnesia. Certain only of the scanty facts on his passport, Michel travels home to Los Angeles, a place beset by sandstorms and blackouts. He soon plunges into an affair with Lauren, a woman exasperated by her marriage. To prod Michel's memory, he and Lauren go to Paris, where freezing citizens burn down buildings for warmth. Nothing about Michel's identity emerges until he learns that Fletcher Grahame, who is restoring a silent film directed by Michel's grandfather, Adolphe, now seeks that film's missing final reel. When Michel somehow brings Grahame that finale, he receives in turn a movie he himself made about his mother. . . . While Michel feverishly scrutinizes his film for clues to his past, a new crisis distracts him: Lauren's husband wants her back. A plot rampant with ambiguities and bizarre harbingers of doomsday in a futuristic world, and the author's surrealistic style make this first novel impenetrable. Only the section dealing with Adolphe's career as a director (he is a thinly disguised version of Abel Gance) is both vibrant and easily comprehended. (pp. 85-6)

> *A review of "Days between Stations," in* Publishers Weekly, *Vol. 227, No. 10, March 8, 1985, pp. 85-6.*

### Dennis Pendleton

A blend of the surreal and the real, this novel of filmic images [Erickson's **Days between Stations**] is also *about* film. It is set in the near future when nature has gone out of control. The plot deals with the searchings of three people: Lauren's for meaning and love in her life; her husband Jason's, for the Olympic gold; and her lover Michel's, for his past. There is a long account of the making of an epic 30-hour film by Michel's grandfather, which was never shown and whose parts were scattered. Michel believes the answers to his past lie in this film and that by reassembling it he will find the truth. None of this has much significance, and the characters are nonentities, but some individual scenes are oddly compelling.

*Dennis Pendleton, in a review of "Days between Stations," in* Library Journal, *Vol. 110, No. 8, May 1, 1985, p. 76.*

## Frederika Randall

Sometime in the not too distant future, the planet Earth is rapidly going to the dogs. Los Angeles is swept by sandstorms that darken the sky and send dunes crawling up the buildings. A pall of smoke hangs over Paris, where the lights have gone out and bonfires burn out of control. The canals of Venice have inexplicably dried up, and the streets, smelling of garbage, are periodically plunged into deep fog. The landscape is fabulous, bleak; the lovers who travel through it, Michel and Lauren, are just the opposite—romantically alienated and drunk on their own eroticism. There is a healthy dose of cinematic surrealism in the Los Angeles writer Steve Erickson's moody first novel [*Days between Stations*], along with a decidedly unhealthy dose of overwrought "Fleurs du Mal" bad dreams. Lauren, wife of a Vietnam veteran and world-class cyclist named Jason, stumbles into an adventure with the estranged, degenerate Michel (or Adrien—a victim of amnesia, he isn't sure which). Tortured by the past he cannot remember, with only a reel of film for a clue, he makes a voyage via flashbacks to Paris of the 1920's, where his grandfather is filming an epic of the death of Marat. With the magical ease of a movie that floats back and forth in space and time, the author at one point sets Lauren adrift on a houseboat from the Seine out onto the Atlantic, through the straits of Gibraltar to meet Jason in the desiccated Venice. She arrives wearing a large gold ring on her ankle; she doesn't remember why. The hapless and often witless characters in this richly convoluted story finally prove far less interesting than the vision of a world where cultural memory has dried up and there is nothing left but a series of powerful, disconnected celluloid images.

*Frederika Randall, in a review of "Days between Stations," in* The New York Times Book Review, *May 12, 1985, p. 18.*

## Paul Auster

In his second novel, **Rubicon Beach,** Steve Erickson has shunned the strictures of realistic fiction to create a highly imaginative work whose true subject is the imagination itself. This is a book that draws heavily on the stuff of movies and other books, and it mixes a number of genres and influences with varying degrees of success. Part science fiction, part surrealist love story, part political fable, **Rubicon Beach** combines all these elements into something whose overall impact is curiously close to that of opera. The strong passages attain a stirring lyrical intensity; the weak passages are by turns leaden and bombastic. One is inclined to forgive Mr. Erickson for his lapses, however, since he has taken on some ambitious themes, and such boldness can often lead a writer into dangerous waters.

That he has largely managed to keep himself afloat is very much to his credit.

The book is divided into three distinct parts, each with its own set of spatial and temporal boundaries. These boundaries ultimately prove to be unstable, with events from one arena intersecting with the others, and by the end the three episodes have merged into a single story. There is something arbitrary about this arrangement, but at the same time it seems plausible enough. For we know from the beginning that we are in the land of make-believe, an anarchic place governed only by the logic of dreams.

The story opens in a postapocalyptic Los Angeles, an ominous city of canals and singing buildings. From there the narrative shifts abruptly to the jungles of South America, moves northward through Mexico and winds up in the streets of contemporary Hollywood. In the final section, we find ourselves in Chicago during the Depression, travel to the moors of southern England in the 1950's and then sail back into the mythological heart of America. Characters vanish from one world and reappear in another; names and identities slide. The hero of the first section, Cale, strangely metamorphoses into someone called Lake in the third (the names are nearly anagrams of each other), but then the two men meet and temporarily join forces to recapture their lost destinies.

A nightmare murder—a young woman decapitating a man with a long, glinting knife—is witnessed several times by the same person until the witness understands that he, in fact, is the victim. A manuscript of poems written by a crazed screenwriter about the beauty of this woman's face is found in a library archive somewhere in the darkness of the future—a time referred to enigmatically as America Two. This woman can sleep and dream with her eyes open; her eyes can blaze like beacons through the murkiest fog; merely to look at her can drive a man to the brink of delirium. An island sails across the ocean; a train station is located inside an enormous tree; a man spends several years scribbling mathematical equations on the walls of his house, then into the earth itself.

> Soon the moors where he lived were filled with arithmetic; he then took to adding and subtracting on the roads leaving Penzance, down on his knees with his back to the end of the island, adding and subtracting himself into a corner of Cornwall. . . . Months passed, and when the spring gave way to summer, and the summer to autumn and winter, and when the year gave way to the next, Lake was still writing equations, new ones in the spaces between the old.

Imagery is far more important in this novel than plot, and Mr. Erickson is at his best when he allows his images to speak for themselves. Water dominates the action of **Rubicon Beach,** as though we were meant to be immersed in the depths of the writer's unconscious, and as the references to canals and rivers and oceans accumulate, the events take on an almost Jungian tonality, an inwardness of archetypes and half-remembered dreams. As the story begins to crystalize at the end, one understands that this book is in some sense intended as a warning to those who lack the courage to cross the Rubicon of their imaginations—a warning that applies equally to individuals and to countries (in this case America).

> He made a mistake once. I don't know if he knows it. He was standing on the banks of a river listening to something from the other side, something he had never heard but had always *known*. And instead of crossing the river, he listened for as long as he could stand it and then turned his back and returned the way he had come. And he's never heard it again. He should have crossed that river.

*Rubicon Beach* owes a strong literary debt to such writers as Borges and Gabriel Garcia Marquez—not to speak of Rod Serling and other American fabulists—but Mr. Erickson has learned his lessons well, and he writes with vigor and assurance. There are moments when his energies outstrip his ideas—the political subtext of the novel is vague and unconvincing, for example, more willed than truly imagined—but he moves the action swiftly from scene to scene, and the narrative maintains its momentum throughout. If the book does not always resonate as fully as he would have liked, it is consistently entertaining, and one does not think twice about following him down the labyrinthine paths of his bizarre and striking tale. *Rubicon Beach* represents a considerable advance over Mr. Erickson's first novel, *Days between Stations,* which was published only last year. There is no question that he is a young writer to be watched.

> Paul Auster, "Across the River and into the Twilight Zone," in The New York Times Book Review, *September 21, 1986, p. 14.*

## Art Gardner

I'm not the type of person who remembers his dreams, and perhaps that's why I enjoy those works which try to recapture that elusive experience. *Rubicon Beach* is both dream and reality. In his second novel author Steve Erickson has fashioned a simple and complex tale of imagery and character. Like all dreams, the novel's setting is a mixture. The reader finds himself captivated in an environment that flourishes in imagination and yet has foundations in reality.

Because of this, the novel doesn't lend itself to an easy summary. Divided into three parts, the story traces the lives of three characters. Cale, a prisoner of guilt, finds himself lost in a Los Angeles that only vaguely reflects the city we know. Jack, a captive of vision, tries to abandon the truth he's discovered. And Catherine, a victim of beauty, is the woman who passes between dream and reality. These three lives cross and entwine in a carefully woven fabric that stretches across both time and space.

Using reoccuring images and variations of themes the author builds layer upon layer. This blending is what gives the work its dream quality. At times, however, you feel that Erickson's reach has extended his grasp. Some of the passages seem strained or contrived, as in his continual reference to Bobby Kennedy as "the man who quoted poetry." And yet, others will linger in the mind long after the reader is finished. Ultimately, *Rubicon Beach* may be

more style than substance. It is a personal work that may not be completely understood by those who read it. But, if one can relax in the rhythm of its words, this is a book which will flow through the mind's eye like a silk covered dream.

> Art Gardner, in a review of "Rubicon Beach," in West Coast Review of Books, *Vol. 12, No. 4, November-December, 1986, p. 36.*

## Caryn James

As the 20th century bleeds into the 21st, herds of silver buffalo stampede across the plains of the American West. On a small island, bodies of the dead hang ritually in trees until they call out their names, a sign that they can rest peacefully in graves. And the white-haired young man who runs the ferry to that island always reaches a blind spot on the river where landmarks vanish in the fog. At that moment "there might as well have been no sun in the sky or anything that called itself a country," Steve Erickson writes at the start of his magnificent, haunting third novel, *Tours of the Black Clock.*

Banning Jainlight dies an old man on this island, and his ghostly voice takes over to narrate much of the novel as he recalls his peculiar life's journey. A "big redheaded American galoot" from Pennsylvania, he crushes his half-brother's skull between his hands when the brother almost dupes the adolescent Jainlight into sleeping with his own mother. Fleeing the crime, for which he feels no remorse, Jainlight turns up in Vienna in 1936, where he writes personalized pornographic stories for Hitler—fictions that we never read but that alter the shape of history. Jainlight, who wonders vaguely about his missing conscience, embodies Mr. Erickson's subject, the 20th century itself.

Viewing history from the unmoored perspective of that blind spot on the river, Mr. Erickson reinvents "a century when time and space have liberated themselves of all reference points," and perhaps good and evil have done the same. The novel's structure reflects that fluidity, as it cuts back and forth through 100 years of time, "the black clock of the century." Here is a Borgesian labyrinth where characters invent each other through their imaginations, where there are glancing references to history as we know it but no stable foothold from which we can observe that *this* is real and *that* invented.

At first Jainlight lives in a historically precise context. The man whom military intermediaries identify only as Client X—the propaganda minister with a telltale limp—is clearly Goebbels. When these employers pass Jainlight on to Client Z, the pornographer knows he is now creating fantasies of mastery and submission for "the most evil man in the world."

As fantasy and history become more tangled in the novel, so do the identities of Hitler and Jainlight. Recalling Hitler's youth in Austria, Jainlight thinks, "When I see the vagabonds of Vienna I see two men in each of them: one is the Leader, and the other is me." Soon after, Hitler's "blackboot boys" are "beating an old Jew outside a candleshop" when Jainlight looks up and sees a woman in a window. That night, she comes to his room in a vision and they make love. He puts her in his next story, where Hitler instantly knows her as Geli Raubal, his niece and the great passion of his life.

About Geli Raubal's identity the novel is historically accurate. She was shot in 1931, and though her death was ruled a suicide, it seemed suspiciously convenient, both for Hitler's enemies and for supporters who feared that the relationship was distracting him from his mission. And just as Mr. Erickson's imagination taps into history, Jainlight's taps into Hitler's obsession for his dead lover. The resurrected Geli so absorbs Hitler that the invasion of Russia never begins; but eventually he turns west, conquering England and Mexico in a war that persists at least into the 1970's.

Geli is no simply defined ghost, though. Her identity blends with that of the woman above the candleshop. Named Dania, she may or may not have been imagined by Jainlight, but she has a history, will and physical power of her own. She is capable of being "at once in three separate moments": in the Sudan, where she was born to Russian refugees; in Vienna, where Jainlight finds her; and on the mythic island where she spends her last years and where Jainlight dies at her feet asking forgiveness.

*Tours of the Black Clock* has an emotional depth missing from Mr. Erickson's previous novels, which also contain ambitious dreamlike scenarios *Days between Stations* is overwhelmed by the cross-cutting technique used so lucidly here. And even *Rubicon Beach,* a rich, accomplished journey into America's future, is sometimes too cold in its artificial blend of fantasy and realism.

But in *Tours of the Black Clock* we see the Nazis try to push a 4-year-old out a window; her mother jumps through the window carrying her daughter along, so the child "won't be so utterly lonely, out there in the black Vienna night." The sexual encounters between Jainlight and the visionary Dania/Geli have as much physicality as any realistic novel. And we are brought so close to Jainlight that we almost sympathize with him but never lose sight of his hideous moral blindness. The novel has a few touches too blunt to overlook. A blueprint of a house is, in fact, the map of the 20th century; the room containing its conscience is hidden. Yet this is a rare and original novel, written in controlled prose that balances the resonance of the dark river with the flash of the silver buffalo.

Though Mr. Erickson leaves us with a surprising redemptive ending that Dania wills into being, he is too honest to deny his relativistic view of history. Jainlight takes Hitler, now "an old weak sick man," through Mexico bent on keeping him alive for a revenge more terrible than death. When anti-Nazi guerrillas see him beating a frail white-haired man, Jainlight almost tells them who that man is. But he stops himself, for if the guerrillas see this senile Hitler, "the pure righteous wrath of their fight would have to accommodate the humanity of his evil. They're fighting for an age in which the heart and consciousness have not been stripped of the reference points that have become denied to time and space."

It is a great part of Mr. Erickson's achievement that he shows his readers the humanity of evil—a force all the more chilling because it cannot be dismissed as a monstrous act of fate—yet allows hope and compassion to struggle through.

*Caryn James, "The Missing Conscience of the 20th Century," in* The New York Times, *January 7, 1989, p. 17.*

### Tom Clark

"I build my own house that defies architecture," declares Steve Erickson's monster-hero at one point in *Tours of the Black Clock.* "I've compelled the landscape of history to readjust to my visions."

Big claims. But does the construction live up to that confident billing?

In his third novel, following on critical successes with *Days between Stations* and *Rubicon Beach,* Los Angeles writer Erickson offers a challenging, provocative, maddeningly flawed fractured-funhouse-mirror edifice of language, a wild Gaudi-esque structure of phantasmagoric glitter and glass blown from the debris of this century's history.

His creative mortar is the nightmarish imagination of that rough beast of a protagonist-narrator, whose psychic projections—violent and sexually obsessive—have the power to alter world events, distorting reality intensely enough to actually (it says here) tip the course of history.

Historical cornerstone of this precarious fantasy structure is a passage from William Shirer's *The Rise and Fall of the Third Reich,* quoted by the novelist in an extended epigraph. From Shirer's allusion to Adolf Hitler's alleged only true love, his young niece Geli Raubal (a mysterious suicide in 1931), this chaotic, symbol-laden tale of fratricide, sexual compulsion, revenge, and redemption through love is built.

The Frankensteinian manifestation at the center of things is one Banning Jainlight, hulking illegitimate son of a Pennsylvania farmer and a half-breed domestic. After witnessing the rape of his mother, murdering one of his half-brothers, tossing his father out a window and burning down the family homestead (no wonder he has a few fantasies!), Jainlight flees to New York City, where he picks up work as a pornographer, churning out customized sex dreams by the page for the titillation of an anonymous foreign client.

Early in 1937, a step ahead of lawmen pursuing him for his crimes back home, our hero escapes to Vienna. There he discovers the identity of his mystery client—none other than the Führer himself. It turns out that Jainlight's masturbatory erotic prose has enabled Hitler to revive his lost love for his niece. The young ogre has meanwhile become powerfully enamored of an elusive 15-year-old Russian girl he has seen only once, and that through her window. In his zonked-out imagination, however, time and space are no obstacles, and he quickly closes the gap.

Hitler's voyeurism and Jainlight's deranged preoccupation with the girl in the window bind the two men in a sort of fateful symbiosis that lasts until Hitler dies—not in that Berlin bunker in 1945, but, by the Jainlight/Erickson revision of history, 25 years later in a seedy New York City detective's office.

Working the same experimental terrain as John Hawkes, Thomas Pynchon and William Burroughs, Erickson attempts to subvert daylight normalcy. The disturbing nighttime dreamscapes of compulsive alienation that he proposes as his alternative do hold a certain fascination. He effectively creates a brooding, self-enclosed world of driven sensuality. His effort to engage history on a cosmic scale, though, is affected negatively by a serious case of overreaching. While over the myth dimension, this book may indeed provide billboard outlines for a profound parable of man's fall, that ambitious bid for profundity becomes itself a terrible burden for the novelist, and of its weight, *Tours* too often slides off the deep end into the bathetic and the ridiculous.

> Tom Clark, "A Fantastic View of the Third Reich," in Los Angeles Times Book Review, January 29, 1989, p. 3.

## Kathy Acker

Imagine a *film noir* about Hitler. "Geli was twenty, with flowing blond hair, handsome features, a pleasant voice." So begins Steve Erickson's third novel [*Tours of the Black Clock*], or, rather, so begins the quotation from William L. Shirer's *Rise and Fall of the Third Reich* at the commencement of Mr. Erickson's meditation on Hitler's obsession with his niece Geli Raubal. No *film noir* ever had it better.

Mr. Erickson's own sentences, like verbal mirrors of *film noir* images, lapse into ambiguity, disappear and reappear in the ocean of sense and meaning, just like the landscapes he describes.

The first landscape is an island, Davenhall Island, which keeps disappearing in the fog. So do its inhabitants. The boatman of the only ferry to and from this island is insane. He is also the only white person in Davenhall's population. What world is this? The population of Davenhall is Chinese, and Davenhall isn't in China.

In Mr. Erickson's work, everything is strange and, at the same time, recognizable—which makes sense. Dreams lie alongside of, even define, actual histories; this multiplication of dream, fantasy and history results in myth. The sentences that form Mr. Erickson's myth are often ambiguous, for they can never decide between dream and historical actuality.

The boatman asks a question, "Where in the universe am I?" The answer comes 15 years later, when the boatman has become really mad. He hears the voice of the principal narrator of the novel, Banning Jainlight, who destroyed his own family and became Hitler's pornographer.

Right before the boatman hears this voice, he glimpses a girl in a blue dress who disappears. Love for this girl drives him to the house of his mother, whom he hasn't seen for years. Finally, at the center of the family, he hears the voice of the man who is both his father and Hitler's pornographer and, through the father's voice, he hears that of Hitler.

Here is myth. . . .

"It's 1925 and I'm eight." So begins Banning Jainlight's, the pornographer's, story. Daddy's a tyrannical rancher in western Pennsylvania who's especially mean to Indians; mommy's not worth talking about. When Jainlight is 16 years old, his brothers bring him to an Indian woman who Jainlight believes is a whore until he sees that his brothers are forcibly holding her down so that he can have her. He intuits that this woman is his mother. So he slaughters one brother, badly hurts the other, returns home, breaks the back of the tyrant and sets their home, the whole American family structure, on fire.

Jainlight's story, even its beginnings, is not only personal. Memories of the brutalities inflicted on the American Indians and of the early patriarchal and, thus, sexist foundations of American civilization rise up, like a bad smell, through the details Mr. Erickson provides about Jainlight. One of the author's literary predecessors is Faulkner.

But Mr. Erickson's not above a bad joke, in the tradition of the Marx Brothers and even of Abbott and Costello. His *film noir* often descends or ascends, depending upon your sense of humor, into black, if not bad, humor. After Jainlight has set his family house on fire, Mr. Erickson adds, "God had nothing to do with it."

By the end of *Tours of the Black Clock,* this statement has become more than a black, bad joke. For Mr. Erickson's story, as it proceeds, is more than a story: it becomes a meditation on evil, on "the most evil man in the world." Since the narrator of this meditation is himself a murderer, hardly free of the taint of evil, the *absolute* quality of evil is being questioned. Mr. Erickson's formal ambiguity is also a metaphysical one.

Hitler, the human representation of evil, is depicted as a man obsessed by love or passion for his niece. He may or may not have, out of jealousy, caused his niece's death. His sexual obsession seems to be one of the causes of his political evil. Why? Mr. Erickson seems to be saying that since no actual incident could penetrate Hitler's obsession, Hitler didn't know time, human living time. In his blindness he destroyed time and so created the black clock of Mr. Erickson's 20th century. Where there is no time, there are only absolutes.

But Mr. Erickson is not simplistic. In *Tours of the Black Clock,* there are two 20th centuries. The first is that of Hitler, who destroyed time because of sexual obsession. Hitler's century is "the rule of evil" and its "collapse." Here, in this world, is pure good and pure evil. The second is that of Albert Einstein. In this universe there are no absolutes; relativity or time defines all phenomena.

*Tours of the Black Clock* is, above all, a gorgeous argument against a culture of absolutes and for a way of life based on questioning.

Whereas Jainlight is the narrator, partly even the writer, of Hitler's world, the other world, the relative one, is seen through the eyes of Dania, a dancer who kills men by dancing. Dania is both actual and fantastic: she is the real Geli Raubal. And both good and evil: she is the one who transforms the evil aspect of sexual obsession, through the act of giving birth, into that which is at the heart of the world, that is, good. Transformation is the landscape of relativity.

If, formally, past and future tenses keep interrupting the story's continuing narrative, they do so because, for Mr. Erickson, time must exist.

Mr. Erickson is not telling a story; he is telling a myth. A myth is history that does not exclude the realms of imagination, dreaming, desiring. A myth is history that comes from those humans who have not severed heart from brain. Mr. Erickson is a gambler, a dealer in myths, who, if he can rid himself of some slight sentimentality or sentences whose gorgeousness sometimes slips into easiness, will be one of the fabulous mythmakers who are needed in these times of the deprivation of the imagination.

> *Kathy Acker, "I Was Hitler's Pornographer,"*
> *in* The New York Times Book Review, *March 5, 1989, p. 29.*

## Paul Kincaid

This is the century, we learn in an aside in Steve Erickson's latest novel, *Tours of the Black Clock,* in which Einstein removed all referents from time. The Black Clock, therefore, stripped of numbers and even of hands, is the twentieth century, and for all the vivid characters who people these pages, it is the century itself in various guises that is the protagonist of this remarkable book.

Our confused and confusing age also lies at the heart of Erickson's first novel, *Days between Stations,* where he surveys the century through the eyes of Adolphe de Sarre. Traumatized by the First World War, Adolphe enters the fledgling world of the cinema and makes one acclaimed masterpiece which transcends the normal boundaries of silent film; but his obsessions and weaknesses prevent his ever finishing the work, and its ramifications have a chilling effect on later generations. Both his grandson Michel and Michel's lover Lauren are haunted by odd blanks within their lives that memory cannot fill. Their quest for certainty in an emphatically uncertain world is set against a Ballardian landscape in which surreal natural catastrophes mirror their alienation. . . .

Erickson's second novel, *Rubicon Beach,* reflects many of the same obsessions and concerns. Superficially a narrower book with a more controlled structure, it contains three apparently separate stories. Cale, released from prison, lives in a strangely altered Los Angeles, and is haunted by visions of a girl cutting the head off a man who might be him. Catherine, a girl from the jungles of South America, finds herself an object of strange desires in Hollywood. And Jack Mick Lake is a mathematical genius who finds a number for everything, and discovers that there is an unknown number between nine and ten. Yet these stories are linked by dreams, as one character reflects: "Life didn't

belong to him anymore but rather to his dreams, which had been repossessed by age."

The concern with time and the disorienting effects of relativity, the part nature plays in imitating the disorders of the mind, the strength of the dreams of which his characters must partake, and underlying it all the threads of faith and treachery that bind them, come together also to provide the structure of his latest novel. The earlier books held out the promise of a writer who could produce something genuinely new, and *Tours of the Black Clock* comes close to fulfilling that promise. Here the literary skills are more finely tuned, and the reader more readily accepts each new strangeness.

Erickson follows the same structural practice of embedding one story within another to provide unusual resonances, but in this book one narrative might have its own framing device embedded in it. The result, when successful, can be dazzling, but when unsuccessful can create a bleak confusion. In the space of one short chapter, for instance—and none of the chapters is long—he shifts the time-frame from 1948 to 1951 to 2007 to 2004 to 1917 to 1923. Dates and duration are obsessively recorded throughout the book, but more to free it from time than to tie it to any strict ordering of events. An added complication has the century bifurcated so that we end up sailing simultaneously down two different streams. It is a measure of Erickson's ability that, by and large, he carries us with him throughout.

His human characters are, as ever, followers rather than leaders. They pursue a logic which is perverse but inexorable. Banning Jainlight lives in Vienna and writes pornography for Hitler, which prompts Hitler to abandon his invasion of Russia and instead invade Britain; in 1967 the two meet again in a basement beneath a flooded Venice while war continues in the world above them.

The heroine of Jainlight's dreams, and of his fiction, is Dania, a woman he glimpsed only once but who continues to be the subject of spectral erotic encounters. Yet Dania lives in a world whose history we recognize. She carries with her a blueprint of the century, in which her father obsessively searched for the secret room which contains the century's conscience. She retreats to a remote, fogenshrouded island where she bears a white-haired son who may be the child of a ghostly Hitler from a different branch of time. The boy grows up to operate the ferry between the island and the shore, and on each journey there is a point where neither bank is visible, a symbolic moment that echoes through the book as our place in the age of the featureless clock.

> *Paul Kincaid, "Removing the Referents," in* The Times Literary Supplement, *No. 4504, July 28, 1989, p. 830.*

## Charles Bowden

Steve Erickson, a surrealistic novelist based in Los Angeles, traveled 7,000 miles by train and auto in 23 states tracking the 1988 presidential election [in his novel *Leap Year*].

He was in Atlanta for the Democratic convention, but mainly bagged the event by television in his hotel room. He was in New Orleans for the Republican Convention, but split before it began in order to take in the music and bars of Austin, Tex., as well as a UFO belt in the Panhandle. He was periodically hounded by Sen. Albert Gore and his wife Tipper—they kept showing up either wasted or demented as Erickson hallucinated his way across the landscape of the United States. This was not a surprising event in Erickson's world. After all, a frequent companion in his travels was Sally Hemings, the late Thomas Jefferson's black slave and, for almost two centuries, the whispered companion of Jefferson's nights and mother of his children.

Hardly Teddy White's *Making of the President?* Well, no. But considering the boredom of the '88 campaign, and the barrenness of the making-of-the-President-style of coverage in the hands of White's journalistic descendants, dumping this structure is not much of a loss.

The fundamental problem with the genre of campaign books is that we haven't cared much about recent presidential races. Erickson solves this problem by using the election and its players as props in his discussion of what's gone wrong with this country. And his novelist's feel for language is a relief from either the dead newspaper prose or poli-sci jargon that lurks in election books. He takes a gamble, and sometimes he wins, and sometimes he loses, but it is fun watching him play his cards. This is not gonzo journalism—there are no Hunter Thompson-style interviews with real presidential candidates in the men's room. In fact, it's not journalism at all. Erickson does not report, he imagines what it all means.

*Leap Year* (the title plays with the calendar fact of 1988) insists on some distinctions and ideas Erickson has hatched. One is the big difference between the United States, a clattering heap of people, government and shopping malls, and America, the idea behind the physical reality of the country.

"I'm not looking for America," he announces early on. "It's not that. Enough people over the years have done that, they looked as far as the sun illuminated their line of vision, until they couldn't follow that light any further. I'm going against the light." But of course he is looking for America, since he finds it far more interesting than the artifact-strewn presence of the United States.

Another idea that fascinates Erickson is "the nuclear imagination," a state of mind he finds exemplified by Gary Hart and Pat Robertson. Einstein was probably the first person afflicted with this perspective. "By nuclear imagination," Erickson explains,

> I mean that poetry that Einstein conceived and compelled us to accept in the face of empiricism. . . . People with nuclear imagination not only conceive of the abyss and confront it, but are liberated by it; everything they do is infused with the blood of an Armageddon with no god, a judgment day in which the guilty and the innocent are damned with equal cosmic merriment.
>
> (p. 3)

In short, people with the nuclear imagination are turned on by the sense of ice cracking beneath their feet, and say pretty much whatever they want to say as a way of mocking the gods, since, of course, everything might go to ruin at any second.

A lot of this book consists of just such musings; how a reader reacts to them depends on one's appetites and expectations. For my money, I think Erickson misses as much as he hits, but I kept being sucked in by the risk of it all, kind of like watching those old tapes of Lenny Bruce in action as his manic raps spun off into space with no safe destination.

Just how do we react to the fact that this deathless black woman has been traveling around our country with a knife, slashing Americans for more than a century and a half while searching for her lost lover? Whenever Sally's thoughts appear they are in italics and presented in a severe English that rings like the judgments of God and whose meaning is often biblical in its vagueness. When she locates Jefferson in 1988, he is living in the pueblo of Walpi on the Hopi Reservation. ". . . I decide," Sally reflects,

> I'll pretend to be asleep . . . I'll pretend not so to fool him, since there's no more fooling him; I'm not sure who I'm fooling, who I'm pretending for. It may be myself. As the hour before daylight has almost passed, in the last moment before daylight when I believe I've finally fooled them all, I have a vision.

Like all good ghosts, Sally Hemings never quite spells out this vision. But then Erickson never quite does either. Amid the debris of his road trips, the problems back at home with his family and cats, the random insights gained in topless bars, the asides on rock 'n' roll, various candidates, and, of course, the autopsy of the United States' Darth Vader, Ronald Reagan, Erickson does not so much wrap up the election and the nation in a nice tidy bundle of theses as keep probing where it all went wrong.

"There I am left," he decides, "with the dreadful crushed fact which is that it isn't the United States that I love, it's America."

Don't we all. Just ask Sally Hemings who lived as a slave but still can't shake her passion for the idea behind the word. (p. 7)

*Charles Bowden, "The Ghosts of the 1988 Presidential Campaign," in* Los Angeles Times Book Review, *October 15, 1989, pp. 3, 7.*

### G. Michael O'Toole

This journal of the most recent presidential election by the extraordinarily gifted L.A.-based novelist is not your standard "Making-of-the-President"-type fare. [In *Leap Year*] Erickson uses the election as a vehicle to muse on the "myth of America," a myth in conflict with the "reality of the United States." The author is accompanied sporadically on this part-geographical (7000 miles and 23 states), part-surreal journey by the ghost of Sally Hemings, Thomas Jefferson's mulatto mistress who, by remaining with her master in Paris in 1789 instead of setting herself free, may well have forever altered the course of American history.

Searching for her lost lover, Sally is Erickson's link to the mythical America that might have been. Her flight, he contends, may well have led the slaveowner Jefferson ("The greatest and guiltiest American who ever lived") to implement his ideals about human rights more forcefully, thus absolving the bonds of slavery and sexism much earlier on.

Erickson structures his journal by interweaving and contrasting the Jeffersonian vision with scathing commentary on the contemporary political scene. Of the previous office holder, he states that "Reagan is the Rorschach that answers the question: We haven't cared much about being a good people; we're not into it. We prefer the memory of a rich people or a safe people"—definitely not what one hears on the network news. Nor is this: "Let's not pretend we didn't elect him in spite of his contradictions and hypocrisies: we chose him for them."

In evaluating Reagan's would-be successors, Erickson is especially attuned to the plight of Gary Hart and his all-too-human failing in the arms of Donna Rice ("I personally distruct anyone who thinks straight in such circumstances . . . "). Hart is the embodiment of a mindset that the author calls the "nuclear imagination . . . (not) simply the heightened awareness of doom, it's the relationship that one establishes with the doom. People with nuclear imagination not only conceive of the abyss and confront it, but are liberated by it." Not that such an imagination is necessarily correct morally: "Gandhi had it, but so did Hitler."

And, says Erickson, so does Pat Robertson, the former television evangelist who, "if (he) actually believed in God he wouldn't exploit God so recklessly." The author's examination of Robertson and his constituency, the Christian Right, and their frightening concept for democracy, is exemplary. He also exposes the essence of Jesse Jackson: "For all of Jackson's moving language about how far it would mean he has come to become vice-president, he remains one of the few people whom the job is beneath."

But this "summer God laughs at America's faith" ultimately pits George Bush ("a glorified office boy . . . who never believed in anything") and his dubious, if inevitable, protege ("This is undoubtedly the sweet revenge of those who most hate my generation. Dan Quayle is an older person's ideal of a younger person.") against the hapless Michael Dukakis, who, by the second presidential debate is already regarded " . . . as the man who once lost a presidential election that hadn't happened yet."

Erickson concludes with the end of Sally's search for Thomas Jefferson at an ancient Hopi reservation. Despite the hit-and-miss effect of this imagery, he has by now succeeded in making his point—his is a most mercilessly, unsentimentally honest and courageous discourse on the sorry state of the body politic circa 1988.

*G. Michael O'Toole, in a review of "Leap Year," in* West Coast Review of Books, *Vol. 15, No. 2, November-December, 1989, p. 41.*

## Greg Tate

Steve Erickson's writings belong to a venerable and arcane tradition in American letters that could be called Gothic Fabulism. This canon would accommodate the morbid forefathers of our literature of the fantastic, Poe, Hawthorne, and Melville. The tradition they began was brought into this century by Faulkner, and carried forward by Raymond Chandler, Richard Wright, Ralph Ellison, Ishmael Reed, Cynthia Ozick, Toni Morrison, Louise Erdrich, John Edgar Wideman, and Don DeLillo. Central to Gothic Fabulist doctrine is the idea that the novel has enough authority to pass judgment on the sins of entire civilizations—to subject everything from ethics to eating habits to a retentive scrutiny bent on scraping clean a culture's moral crevices.

More often than not, GF books deflate the vainglorious puffery of manly rites of passage while celebrating the exacting ceremonies of such acts. In our homegrown existentialist library, the protagonist not only recounts nightmares out of American history (often through parables), but re-enacts the more tortuous nightmare of personal remembering—a passage of no small aching, not least because the typical hero has made the horrors of civilization his own drive-in monster movie, usually as a means to reckon with some private scar of shame. The Gothic Fabulists tend to see the novel as a handy place to go shedding buckets of cultural blood guilt.

So it isn't surprising that this is the one American literary lineage—apart from slave narratives and the testimonials of Native Americans—that persists in upping the spiritual costs to white American manhood of its genocidal history. (p. 75)

Erickson is the baby of this bunch. For my money, he is the only heavyweight contender around among American novelists under 40, excluding genre-specialist William Gibson. Erickson's three novels—*Days between Stations, Rubicon Beach,* and *Tours of the Black Clock*—are at once illuminating and irritating, deeply moving and deeply unsatisfying. The irritation and dissatisfaction generally derive from the fact that Erickson, like all Gothic Fabulists, is an unrepentant allegorist who, unlike the luminaries of his breed, has so far lacked the patience to create a strong sense of place, that necessary evil his forebears and contemporary betters have carried over from the 19th-century social novel. In Erickson's case, this seems a result not of bad research but a lack of imagination—specifically the paced, structural imagination of a more-or-less linear novel. It may also have something to do with a sense of cultural displacement as a white American liberal in the '80s. But we'll pick up on that theme a little later (don't you worry).

Erickson is good at getting your juices going over his alternative-world stories; he always leaves me feeling like his books didn't happen to me, I dreamed them. Erickson's novels always come out of the gate like Ben Johnson on steroids. Unfortunately, he usually finishes the race with as much kick as a Dali stopwatch. But if Erickson comes up short on the wind needed to be a long-distance narrative runner, he is, in the clutch, a dogged archeologist of his characters' secrets:

> One day out on the water, right before the sun fainted into dark, her father picked her up to gaze over the side of the boat. There, for the first time, she saw her own face. She thought that it was a strange and marvelous watercreature, like the roots of trees with pink mouths off the coast of England or the fish that dead men watched in the dirt. Had her father looked over the side of the boat with her, she might have understood it was her face.

My man's last and most critically celebrated novel, ***Tours of the Black Clock,*** is also his least distinguished. Up until its midpoint, the book seems bent on elevating the horrific moral codes of Jim Thompson pulp to higher literature; then alas, it settles in for an excruciating execution of a premise as hokey as anything ever devised by another Gothic Fabulist, Roger Corman. Set in the '30s and '40s, ***Tours of the Black Clock*** presents the tale of an adolescent midwestern farmboy turned fratricidal psycho-killer and fugitive. While on the lam he makes a Dantean descent from bouncer (for a New York gangster) to pulp fiction writer to, at last, Hitler's pornographer.

The farm-belt chapters are as engrossing as dime-novel fiction ever gets, so full of language, mystery, and verve that they sustain our interest through the flagging Chicago midsection. The Third Reich windup is a total bust, primarily because Erickson seems to expect the reverberations of Nazi evil to invigorate his flaccid storytelling and his main character's mounting banality. Along the way, some of the most promising material of the early chapters is scrapped—particularly the psychoanalytic breakthrough latent in having Erickson's protagonist murder and maim his family, not for greed, lust, or kicks, but for racial revenge. Having discovered that his family's old half-Native-American servant, whom his two elder brothers had been raping for years, was in fact his mother, and this discovery coming when his brothers try to goad him into having a go at her, he cold loses it. After killing one brother, crippling another, and maiming his father, the narrator burns the house down and hits the road.

Is this Oedipus meets Cochise in search of Neal Cassady, or what? Never mind the turnabout on that American stereotype, the untrustworthy half-breed: Erickson lost a metanovelistic opportunity to expose America's toilet morals by exposing the conventions of two of its toilet genres, the Western and the porn novel. To understand how maddening I found this misfire, imagine what a crock *Mumbo-Jumbo* would have been had Ishmael Reed decided midway that Papa La Bas, instead of being the last word on 7000 years of space and time, would live out the rest of the novel as Warren G. Harding's amanuensis. As sad-ass satire such a narrative derailment might have a chance, but Erickson is too somber for such transparent tomfoolery.

In one sense, his books read like brooding boys-own adventures, the Hardys gone upriver to become lords of the flies. The voice in them is what Muddy Waters once described as Mannish Boy. Its bumbling combination of giddy muscle and emotional immaturity speaks to such a sense of exile in the world of adult responsibilities that you wonder if it isn't the author's own.

***Leap Year,*** Erickson's most recent book, is a New Journalese essay about the 1988 presidential campaign. Here we find Erickson fighting back another form of adolescent regression: he doesn't want to be overwhelmed by cynicism and disillusionment in the face of American electoral politics. For the close-to-the-bone tone alone it is Erickson's most melancholic work, a *Mr. Smith Goes to Washington* for the '90s. ***Leap Year*** portrays the crumbling idealism of a young intellectual comer who believes in his country more than his country believes in itself.

Erickson finds it hard to admit, during a year of dogging the campaign trail, that he's learned not to trust his homeland. Though the reflexive, reflective, casually moralizing tone of ***Leap Year*** evokes Norman Mailer's campaign epics, Erickson is both more naïve and less optimistic about his nation's regenerative powers than Mailer could ever be. No way he would have written a book so innocently outraged at the quadrennial political spectacle staged by our Big Daddies. Nor would Mailer, who knows how much vitality and resistance runs underground, keep looking for redemption among the most high rather than the most low.

Only after swimming, with much textual pleasure, through Erickson's earnest investigation of the notion that our fate depends on which gringo becomes president did I understand why his fiction so often goes awry. The writer I'd mistaken for a Gothic Fabulist is not, in fact, an anatomist of the nations' nihilistic soul—he's really a Jeffersonian Democrat who believes, against every last grain of American history, that individual liberties and manifest destiny can be reconciled, that somehow populism and capitalism are twains that can meet. Erickson and other liberals realize that the systematic denial of democracy to the government's victims at home and abroad did more to bring fragmentation and chaos onto the American scene than anything since the Civil War. Unfortunately, they also believe that assuaging their blood-guilt through sensitivity is tantamount to agitating for change.

But the admission of hypocrisy doesn't get it. In ***Leap Year,*** Erickson breaks up his reportage with italicized sections rendered in the voice of Sally Hemings, the slave whom Jefferson is alleged to have raped when she was 15 and who became his lover later in life. Hemings's voice is symbolic of all those locked out of Jefferson's vision of democracy by his ofay will to power. Hemings's voice is also adoring and power-struck—she wants a chance to get out of the cotton-picking sun and into the big house. But as Erickson circles in on her consciousness, what she's really after is a place somewhere between Jefferson's vision of a nation of yeomen with the wind at their backs and his alienation from their unlettered aspirations to be fruitful and multiply. She wants, in other words, to be not just any slave, a slave of the office and what it represents, in order to secure a future for her children.

This astute observation dovetails nicely with Erickson's

reading of Jesse Jackson's humbled and self-aggrandizing performance at the last convention:

> The reason many blacks weren't happy with Jackson's speech was that he chose to speak not to his dissatisfactions, and therefore theirs, but rather to his redemption. . . . Jackson didn't just repent, he asked forgiveness, and the masterstroke of the convention was the line "Be patient, God is not finished with me yet." None of us could quite believe what we'd heard. Jackson finessed his dilemma by saying that he was an instrument of God, and that God had been less than hasty in the matter of making Jesse Jackson perfect. If everyone would just give Him a little more time, God would get it right, eventually. . . . Who was going to turn down an appeal to give God a little more time? By begging the crowd to stick with him, Jackson had asked us to stick with God.

Gary Hart was Erickson's man. He liked the fine madness of Hart's vision, which he saw as capable of reconstructing the American character by making it look at uncomfortable aspects of itself. I buy this about as much as I did the argument that a Reagan presidency would produce political clarity, perhaps even inspire revolt among the wretched of the earth. This is where Erickson loses me—he apparently believes that the nation's moral salvation depends on white men overcoming their dark nights of the soul. Burdened by this supremacist folly, Erickson's books wade into deep waters only to wash out with all the weight of a fish gone belly-up. (pp. 75-6)

*Greg Tate, "You Look Fabulist," in* The Village Voice, *Vol. XXXV, No. 14, April 3, 1990, pp. 75-6.*

# Jules Feiffer

## 1929-

(Full name Jules Ralph Feiffer) American cartoonist, playwright, novelist, scriptwriter, illustrator, and editor.

Best known for his satirical cartoons and plays, Feiffer addresses themes of political corruption, random violence, sex, personal relationships, and anxiety in the American middle class. Often compared to humorist James Thurber, Feiffer frequently employs a sparse background, against which he sets an individual character coming to terms with personal crises and the apparent meaninglessness of life. Peter Eckersley observed: "No one since Thurber has sounded so well the chasms of mistrust, misunderstanding, and unholy panic between men and women unsure of their identities and sexual roles." Some critics have commented that Feiffer's style of social satire so successful in his cartoons is ineffective on stage. Most of his plays, however, have received generous praise, and Feiffer is often cited as one of the most important contemporary satirical dramatists. Feiffer is also credited with having significantly influenced the style of a younger generation of political cartoonists.

Feiffer was born and raised in the Bronx, New York, and by age six he was determined to be a cartoonist. He began his career in 1946 as a ghost writer for Will Eisner's comic book, *The Spirit,* and began drawing his own syndicated cartoon, *Clifford,* in 1949. *Clifford,* which follows the adventures of a young boy, filled a void that Feiffer found in other comics of the time that often used children as characters, but never presented the child's viewpoint. In 1956 Feiffer began contributing his cartoons, simply titled *Feiffer,* to the *Village Voice* and quickly gained a reputation for his modest line drawings and incisive captions. Most of his cartoons present either two characters in conversation or one speaking directly to the reader. Their expressions change little from frame to frame, and the cartoon's emphasis lies in a powerful final line, in which the characters lower their guard to reveal frank emotional statements. Many critics have noted that the strength of *Feiffer* lies in its statements rather than in its illustrations. Francis King noted: "[Feiffer] will certainly enjoy no immortality as a draughtsman. His people are no more than so many sticks, indistinguishable except for their gender, to which he attaches the balloons of his brilliant conversation." In 1960 Feiffer adapted an earlier story, a satire of military life, into the animated cartoon *Munro.* The title character, a four-year-old boy, is drafted into the army and cannot convince anyone that he is a child. Feiffer won an Academy Award for *Munro* in 1961. He has also written several plays, including *Feiffer's People* and *Hold Me!,* based on his cartoons.

*Little Murders,* probably Feiffer's best-known play, takes place in the New York apartment of the Newquist family. The Newquists live in a world where muggings, obscene phone calls, blackouts, and murders are accepted as ordi-

nary daily occurrences. Patty, the Newquists' daughter, is the only family member who retains an optimistic outlook despite the horrors she sees in the city. When she is killed by a sniper's bullet on her wedding day, the Newquists decide to fight back, randomly shooting passersby from their apartment window. Although the violence and strong language of *Little Murders* initially appalled American audiences, the play was well-received in England, where it won the London Critics Award for best play of 1969. *Little Murders'* later success in an off-Broadway revival was attributed by many to the increase of violence in America. Feiffer stated that *Little Murders* was a straightforward reflection of the frustration and senselessness felt by city dwellers at the time it was written; however, many critics contended that while *Little Murders* accurately depicted urban violence and anxiety, its brutal honesty blunted the play's humor. *Little Murders* won an Obie Award and an Outer Circle Award in 1969, and was later adapted for film.

Feiffer's screenplay for the 1971 film *Carnal Knowledge,* later adapted for the stage, recounts the changing attitudes of two men, Sandy and Jonathan, toward their relationships with women. *Carnal Knowledge* generated controversy when it was banned from a theater for obscenity by the Georgia Supreme Court. The United States Supreme Court later overturned the decision, but negative criticism, mainly from feminists, continued to beset the film. Sandy and Jonathan, who feel obligated to compete for women, are ultimately unable to sustain meaningful relationships. Many critics charged that the movie is a misogynist representation of women from the perspective of the two men. Some, however, defended Feiffer's negative portrayal as a statement about the general misunderstandings between the sexes, not as a direct attack on women. Stephen J. Whitfield wrote: "Feiffer, as a satirist, hardly exempts women from the humanity he habitually prosecutes. The misogyny of the characters makes them quite unsympathetic, and should not obscure the misanthropy of their creator, since the film has no affirmative images of humans of either gender."

Feiffer's next major play, *The White House Murder Case,* which won the 1970 Outer Circle Critics Award, deals with deception and the abuse of power. The play alternates scenes between the site of a war in Brazil, where the United States Army has accidentally killed many of its own men, and the White House, where the first lady has been murdered by one of the president's cabinet members. Contrasting darkly humorous, morbid scenes of suffering soldiers and serious scenes in which the president attempts to uncover his wife's murderer, *The White House Murder Case* presents the president's cabinet as a government entity with sufficient power to suppress both scandals. While critics applauded Feiffer for so aptly satirizing the war in Vietnam and the Nixon presidency, most commentators agreed that the transition between scenes was awkward and that the black humor of the war scenes was too terrifying to be funny. Defending his dramatic style, Feiffer explained: "To me satire is an attempt to get at the root of a situation, and expose it to the extension of logic. Taking logic to the point where it becomes ridiculous; revealing certain truths about situations that otherwise might not be evident."

Turning away from the political subject matter with which he had been associated, Feiffer next wrote *Knock Knock,* a comical farce about two men, Abe and Cohn, who have lived together for twenty years. Cohn, a realist, and Abe, a dreamer who believes in miracles, conduct an ongoing philosophical debate that becomes the central theme of the play. When Joan of Arc visits their secluded home, claiming that the sky has disappeared and they must accompany her to heaven with a message for the emperor, the men's roles are reversed; this time Cohn is the believer and Abe the skeptic. *Knock Knock* won overwhelming acclaim. Comparing the play to Feiffer's cartoons, Howard Kessel wrote: "[Many] Feiffer cartoons take certain logical premises and pursue them ruthlessly until they end in paradox. This is the technique of *Knock Knock,* where common verbal absurdities are suddenly translated into literal stage terms and pushed to their furthest limits."

Two of Feiffer's subsequent dramas, *Grown Ups* and *Elliot Loves,* although generally considered successful, garnered mixed reviews. Many critics agreed that Feiffer's depiction of a family's members' animosity and aggressions toward

each other was unoriginal and that *Elliot Loves,* which examines miscommunication between men and women, was strongly reminiscent of *Carnal Knowledge.* David Patrick Stearns observed: "Told in Feiffer's digressive style, [*Elliot Loves*] sometimes makes you want to run for the nearest exit. But when it's over you applaud Feiffer's courage to verbalize truths many of us are afraid to think."

(See also *CLC,* Vols. 2, 8; *Contemporary Authors,* Vols. 17-20, rev. ed.; *Contemporary Authors New Revision Series,* Vol. 30; *Dictionary of Literary Biography,* Vols. 7, 44; and *Something about the Author,* Vol. 8.)

## PRINCIPAL WORKS

### PLAYS

*Crawling Arnold*  1961
*Little Murders*  1967
*Feiffer's People*  1968
*God Bless*  1968
*Dick and Jane,* in *Oh! Calcutta!*  1969
*The White House Murder Case*  1970
*Munro*  1971
*Knock Knock*  1976
*Hold Me!*  1977
*Grown Ups*  1981
*Anthony Rose*  1989
*Elliot Loves*  1990

### SCREENPLAYS

*Carnal Knowledge*  1971
*Little Murders*  1971
*Popeye*  1980

### NOVELS

*Harry, the Rat with Women*  1963
*Ackroyd*  1977
*Tantrum*  1979

### OTHER

*Munro* (animated cartoon) 1961; adapted for the stage, 1971
*The Great Comic Book Heroes* (editor) 1965

---

### Walter Kerr

*Little Murders* begins with an innocent bounce and a coldhearted breeziness that augor well—quite, quite well. Mr. Feiffer has listened to New York City and heard things. He's heard ordinary, sensible people turning on their air conditioners in February in order to drown out the roar of helicopters. He's heard rifle fire—sources unknown at 97th Street and Amsterdam Avenue, telephone calls from a faceless menace who simply breathes hard at girls who answer, fingers pawing at the apartment-door peephole, buildings rumbling, sirens sobbing. . . . .

Mr. Feiffer, with the alert ears and eyes of a leprechaun on LSD, has also imagined a happy response to the noises that regale us by night and to the ever-ready switchblades that seek our ribs by day. [Patsy Newquist], the lemon-meringue daughter of a family man who hates his name (Carol) and a mother who gobbles lovingly at her children (one of whom is in training to become a homosexual), brings home a fiancé.

Her young man [Alfred] has worked out an entirely satisfactory technique of survival. He is rather tall, rather strong. He is aware that "there are lots of little people who like to hit big people." And so, when the punks come after him on the better-lit street corners, he simply stands there, humming to himself while being hurt. He *does* get hurt—he has bandages to show for it the minute we see him—but the hurt hurts less when you let it roll over you. Attackers get baffled, and sometimes stop. [Alfred] is not, let it be said, a pacifist. He is an apathist.

The author's rumpled tilt of mind, somewhere between a sudden impulse to sass everybody, caroms gently off the characters—gently and grotesquely—while [Alfred] is being shown snapshots of a son shot down by a sniper, while all and sundry are failing to get another son out of the bathroom, while resisting windows are being raised to let some more Manhattan air and mayhem in, while a minister is being sought to perform a wedding ceremony that will not have the word "God" in it.

The felicitously funny passages are all set pieces, to be sure, and you frequently wonder what the next, or the last, amusing monologue has to do with any Significant Situation that may be developing. . . . .

[Alfred] is droll indeed as he explains, over dinner, how he was once a much sought-after photographer until he unaccountably began to "lose people," leaving only inanimate objects of various sorts on his negatives. [Patsy] describes her working day—a matter of bodies hurtling at her on subway and in elevator—with a controlled fury that might have been used to cook the dinner, father [Carol] pours a wispy thunder over all those about him, and mother [Marjorie] purrs and pouts as her nearest and dearest refuse to confide in her. All are adroit at ducking whenever stray bullets whine in at the windows from across designer Ming Cho Lee's yellow-gray courtyard.

Then the comedy comes to a point when it can no longer keep a grin on its face, not even a twisted one. Mr. Feiffer gives over the business of suggesting serious comment from inside a lazy, lunatic stance and, like a too successfully reformed gag man, goes straight. Suddenly [Patsy] must see her lover's inertia as something to sob about, banging her pretty head against the scenery like an unheeded prophet. Suddenly [Alfred] must see the whole disintegrating into those infinite, infinitesimal dots that go to make up a newspaper photograph. Suddenly somebody is killed—and all our clowns are reaching for rifles, equipped with telescopic sights, of their own.

In the process, the jape sours . . . . The souring doesn't

come from the image of irrational violence Mr. Feiffer would like us to recognize as universal: that's been there all the time. It comes from a droop at the mouth and a glaze at the eyes. We stop seeing it through the distorting lenses of agreeably far-out humor and stare at it head-on, in the dull, symbolic shades of a canned Sunday sermon.

A pity, because the ground plan, and the early grimaces are so pleasantly preposterous.

> *Walter Kerr, "Feiffer's 'Little Murders'," in*
> The New York Times, *April 26, 1967, p. 38.*

## Jack Kroll

In his classic early cartoons Jules Feiffer carried on the tradition of James Thurber and William Steig in their rueful dissection of middle-brow idealism. At the same time he was the link between the burgeoning idea of "popular culture" and writers like Bellow, Malamud and Roth. In his later plays and movies—***Little Murders, God Bless, Carnal Knowledge***—Feiffer moved closer to these writers while keeping his comic's license. You could say that Feiffer is the comic muse of the urban Jewish artist-intellectual.

His charming, mournfully hilarious play, ***Knock Knock,*** is a very personal work. Using the same velvet scalpel that soothes as it draws blood in his cartoons, Feiffer depicts two middle-aged dropouts from our pre-apocalyptic state. His shambling, seedy heroes, called Abe and Cohn, have retired to a little house in the country, from which they haven't moved in twenty years. These superannuated babes in the wood are slowly simmering to a crust on the back burner of existence. Copies of *Partisan Review* and *New Republic* fleck the house like intellectual dandruff, and the walls are plastered with the icons of humanism—Tolstoy, Beethoven, Gandhi, Toscanini, Gershwin and Joe Louis.

Abe is a retired stockbroker and Cohn a long-unemployed musician, but they're really one character split into two dialectical poles—the two sides of Feiffer's own spirit. Ironically, Cohn, the musician, is the realist, believing only in things he can touch. Abe is the romantic, hedging his bets "just in case" there's a prince inside the frog of reality. Their life together is an unvicious circle of silly arguments about food and philosophy, punctuated by occasional single taps on a typewriter keyboard—the symbol of their confounded creativity.

In one of their spats Cohn wishes for a new roommate and his wish is promptly granted in the form of a mad magus named Wiseman who is a mixture of Mephistopheles and Groucho. This leads to another invader, none other than Joan of Arc, who calls Abe and Cohn to join her in a pilgrimage to Heaven before the coming holocaust. This cute kid from the realms of sainthood causes Abe and Cohn to switch credos—Abe becoming the skeptical realist and Cohn the true believer. All of which allows Feiffer to create some tenderly sardonic comedy about idealism and the female as male fantasy. When it turns out that Joan is also Cinderella, Cohn comments: "On the one hand Shaw wrote about you; on the other hand, Walt Disney."

The territory between Shaw and Disney is Feifferland, which is where this tender and brainy farce takes place. *Knock Knock* is a laughing elegy for the gently demoralized humanist spirit represented by Feiffer himself. He sketches this screwed-up but still hopeful spirit in a mad mélange of echoes from Pinteresque colloquies to Grouchoid semantics to Shakespeare's Lear.

> *Jack Kroll, "Feifferland," in* Newsweek, *Vol. LXXXVII, No. 5, February 2, 1976, p. 68.*

## Robin Brantley

[Feiffer's] work from the second half of the 60's—his plays *Little Murders, God Bless* and *The White House Murder Case* and many of his cartoons—has an insistent political focus. His more recent work—the script for the 1971 movie *Carnal Knowledge, Knock Knock,* an unproduced play, a new novel—deals with more personal themes. It's an interesting reflection of the shift in focus between the 60's and the 70's and brings to mind the epithet "human litmus paper," which a friend used to describe Feiffer's ability to smell out the emotions of the people he knows.

It's this litmus-paper quality that allows so many people to see themselves in Feiffer's work, to make the phrase "I felt like a character in a Feiffer cartoon" almost a standard of urban conversation. Perhaps more than any other contemporary cartoonist, Feiffer has captured the anxieties of middle-class, liberal, city people—sex, the bomb, the duplicity of politicians, any of various neuroses that come up on the analyst's couch. These anxieties are reflected in the words his cartoon figures speak and they show up in the creased brows, crossed legs and hunched backs that flow from his pen. And, if the characters in his plays and novel have often been less than fully developed, still the themes—random violence, war, corruption in high office, the liberal sellout and, more recently, the necessity for hope and change—strike sympathetic chords.

The theme of *Knock Knock*—the necessity for hope and change—reflects changes both in Feiffer and in United States society, as he has observed it. After feeling the need to attack society in the 60's, to point out its ills, Feiffer is interested now in coming to terms with, if not the society itself, the despair it creates and, at the same time, after a decade of confusion about his roles as husband, parent and artist, in coming to terms with himself. . . . . He says *Knock Knock* is about affirmation, about "living out your life with some hope, despite the fact that it doesn't seem to exist, reinventing it if necessary." Feiffer's change in outlook may best be illustrated by the different endings of *Little Murders* and *Knock Knock.* As a friend of his pointed out, in *Little Murders* everyone retires into the house; in *Knock Knock* everyone gets out of the house.

More prosaically, *Knock Knock* is about two middle-aged men—a realist named Cohn and a dreamer named Abe—who live in the woods and what happens when Cohn is granted three wishes. The play is filled with puns, comedy routines from old radio shows, falling scenery and just plain bad jokes. Three of the worst jokes are the source for the title of the play. They are delivered by Joan of Arc when she arrives halfway through the first act. Example:

Two knocks are heard at the door. "Who's there?" "Joan." "Joan who?" "Joan ask me no questions and I'll tell you no lies." Atrocious. But funny on the stage, gauging from audience reaction. (pp. 44-5)

> *Robin Brantley, " 'Knock Knock,' 'Who's There?': 'Feiffer'," in* The New York Times Magazine, *May 16, 1976, pp. 44-6, 48-50, 54, 56, 59-60.*

## Ross Wetzsteon

Imagine the Marx Brothers in a play by Beckett, or Cain and Abel as a Catskills comedy team, or the Odd Couple in Wonderland. In the phantasmagoric world of Jules Feiffer's *Knock Knock* God is not dead but on a bender. Or rather, in this hilarious philosophical vaudeville, in which our most cherished beliefs are mercilessly mocked as nothing but childish fairy tales, Feiffer goes beyond even Dostoevsky: 'If Goldilocks is dead, anything is possible'.

Anything, one could even say, is *probable*—if it's preposterous enough. For in the world of this play, everything we take for granted, not just the fairy tales we live by, but even the laws of nature, and especially the laws of perception, everything is suddenly problematic—as if sunlight were to shine down from the stars, as if gravity were to make things fall upward, as if leaves were to bud brown in the fall.

Feiffer is asking the most fundamental questions—what can we really know? what can we really believe in with any degree of certainty?—so the apparent formlessness of his play, its lack of a 'realistic' narrative line, its absence of 'meaningful' continuity, its seemingly gratuitous leaps and bounds from madness to the magical to the mundane, all reinforce his answer; nothing, dahling, nothing. Except possibly punch lines; What is the question to which 9W is the answer? Do you spell your name with a V, Herr Wagner?

When even cause and effect become a practical joke, when any effort to reason becomes a parody of sanity, when every attempt at logic becomes a burlesque of truth, how can man confront the apocalypse with anything but a pratfall? All I need tell you is that two old bachelors have been living alone in the woods for years, arguing over faith and scepticism, when suddenly Joan of Arc—or is it Cinderella?—comes knocking at their door. Scepticism and faith become opposite sides of the same coin—which turns out to be a slug. But how can you despair when the joke's so funny? Even the knock-knock joke takes on metaphysical dimension—for in the world of this play, as in the world of the knock-knock joke, the questions are direct and straight-forward, the answers oblique and preposterously lucid.

'How long?' one of Feiffer's characters asks in a truncated invocation of Shaw's Saint Joan, and there's Feiffer's Joan, hanging from the ceiling in a slapstick ascension. 'How long?' 'So long'. (pp. 40-1)

> *Ross Wetzsteon, in a review of "Knock*

*Knock," in* Plays and Players, *Vol. 23, No. 10, July, 1976, pp. 40-1.*

## Clive Barnes

As a cartoonist Jules Feiffer has always been a playwright, and as a playwright Mr. Feiffer has always been a cartoonist. Now the two suddenly come together and, happily, the whole is larger than the sum of the parts—if that makes any more sense than it used to. But Mr. Feiffer makes a lot of sense. . . . .

[Feiffer's show] is entitled *Hold Me!* and that just about sums it up. "Look Back in Angst" might also serve, or even "My Mother, the Doctor."

What Mr. Feiffer is exploring is urban paranoia or New York rot. Remember when Harold Pinter, once asked to explain what his plays were about, suggested "the weasel under the cocktail cabinet."? Mr. Feiffer writes about the cockroach under the sink, the daffodil under the heel and the analysis under the heel and the analysis under the couch. He is lovely and irreplaceable.

Although all these pieces are, in fact, cartoon sub-titles, illuminated and occasionally enlarged, this is, in strange fact, more of a play than a series of sketches.

For years Mr. Feiffer has produced a cartoon strip that is a "Peanuts" for the disturbed classes. And rather like Charles Schulz's "Peanuts" strip, Mr. Feiffer maintains an even tone and a constant cast of characters. In Mr. Feiffer's case the characters appear to be Bernard (who seems a lot like Mr. Feiffer himself), the enemy, and Mr. Feiffer's memories of his mother.

When one character announces to existence that "getting out of bed in the morning is an act of false confidence" we know that we are in the magically peculiar and peculiarly magical world of Feiffer: a world full of the perils of rejection, the dangers of acceptance, the wild and perpetual struggles of ego for id, the dire discomfort of parenthood, the unceasing wars between men and women, nature and art and Bernard and the rest. It is a jungle out there, and here is a neatly annotated route map.

It is 20 years since Mr. Feiffer started his weekly cartoons for the Village Voice. It does not seem 20 years, but then I have never ever met a 20 years that seemed like it. The double decade always creeps up on one like yesterday. This show takes some of the best of those cartoons and puts them in living, vivid, talking—and often breathing—three-dimensional stage form.

The jokes remain funny because Mr. Feiffer never makes jokes. He muses on urban man cesspool of urban man's mind, the beauty of his neuroses, and the inevitability of his wilting disappointment. With a subject like that you cannot go wrong for, after all, it is just plain folks. . . . .

I have always appreciated that strange, wayward phrase by Gertrude Stein: "Bitterness was entertained by all." Few people can entertain so much bitterness, or be so bitterly entertaining about it as Jules Feiffer. How much does a man have to suffer to be as funny as that? And then think of his mother!

*Clive Barnes, "Jules Feiffer's 'Hold Me!' Is a Look Back in Angst," in* The New York Times, *January 24, 1977.*

## William Kennedy

[Jules Feiffer's] *Ackroyd,* is a novel by designation, but really an argument, a psychoanalytical case history, a 349-page cartoon which is comic without being funny, and tantalizing in a tedious way. It is an intelligent work that may intrigue those whose interest in the novel is lofty but uncritical.

There is no agreement on what constitutes a novel, nor should there be, but a writer of fiction leaves out certain traditional elements of the form at his peril. Gertrude Stein advised us that remarks aren't literature, and she might have added that neither is analysis. Feiffer provides his characters with enough psychologically aberrational chitchat to keep four psychiatrists solvent, but he forces them to work out their destinies in much the same way that his cartoon characters move through their epiphanies—with repetition, and with voices that usually sound like Feiffer's, even if they are ballerinas. As these epiphanies in the cartoons take place in a spatial vacuum—in front of a blank wall, in midair, in a living room furnished with only a television set—so it is with *Ackroyd.*

Much of the action in the second half of the book takes place in Washington, and yet Feiffer makes no use whatever of the city. His scenes in the Vietnam war take place chiefly in one room with filing cabinets. Manhattan is evoked through the name-dropping of people and places. A room's objects may have a symbolic meaning but never a narrative one. He has almost, but not quite, negative interest in setting a scene, diagramming action, or creating atmosphere. All important to him is the psychological stitching of the story.

Having said this, let me say further that in the stitching lies the mystery which is the lone strength of the book.

*Ackroyd* is an abstract detective story, a parallel to Agatha Christie's 1926 mystery, *The Murder of Roger Ackroyd.* The theme of Feiffer's novel is doubling, or tripling—people cloning new personalities for themselves by emulative behavior.

Ackroyd is a pseudonym for the youthful first-person narrator who, as a private detective, takes on a client named Oscar (Rags) Plante, a sports columnist, novelist, and Johnny Carson show regular. When Plante hires Ackroyd, he follows the pattern of a Chandler or Hammett client by immediately feeding the detective misleading clues. The association nevertheless leads to a long, ambivalent relationship in which Ackroyd proves his worth by finding one of Plante's stolen notebooks and then tracks down the meaning of the code words Plante had written to himself in the notebook, and then, presumably, forgotten.

The tracking unveils Plante's life story—how he grew from a nobody in Saratoga High School to become a famous writer. In the tracking, which becomes obsessional, Ackroyd murders his own pseudonymous self, resumes his own name, and becomes a hero of the political left, a la Daniel Ellsberg.

As Plante imitated a schoolboy football hero who was his friend, so Ackroyd imitates Plante, even to living with Plante's wife and son, consorting with his mistress, and taking over his apartment and his profession by becoming a writer.

Feiffer's prose is sparse and often biting ("She is dressed in self-hate") but undistinguished. His dialogue reads passingly well but everybody talks like Ackroyd except Plante, who speaks in sentences with proliferating and pretentious subordinate clauses.

The appeal of the novel lurks, then, not in the writing but in the repeated explosion of the false or incomplete clues or theories about Plante's motives and personality. And while this never leads to any firm conclusions, but only to further theorizing, the perpetuated sense of mystery saves the book.

This is the first novel in memory which would have been improved by cartoons to accompany the text. Feiffer with pen and ink is a maestro of the incisive nuance. Feiffer at the typewriter is not.

> William Kennedy, "Prose Cartoons," in Book World—The Washington Post, *June 19, 1977, p. K3.*

### Francis King

Just as, by now, one tends to associate Osbert Lancaster's cartoons with the tough, toothy aristocracy of Belgravia and the Shires, so one tends to associate Jules Feiffer's with the tormented intelligentsia, usually Jewish, of New York. Governments rise and fall, fashions come and go; but the typical Lancaster or Feiffer characters, so far from undergoing any profound psychological change, do not even age.

Both cartoonists are literary but Feiffer is the more literary of the two. A hundred years hence Lancaster's jests may seem as pointless as du Maurier's or Charles Keane's do today; but it is probable that he will still be admired for the piquancy of his line. Feiffer, on the other hand, will certainly enjoy no immortality as a draughtsman. His people are no more than so many sticks, indistinguishable except for their gender, to which he attaches the balloons of his brilliant conversation. When he achieves the sudden, startling revelation of some moment of intellectual or emotional sleight-of-hand, self-deception or vacuity, the means are wholly verbal. It is, essentially, a writer's, not an artist's, torch that he flashes into a room cluttered with ideas, aspirations and motives on which the dust lies thick, to make the reader gasp: 'My God, I'd no idea it was really like that!' But when, as in *Ackroyd,* the flashes of the torch of his genius are joined together to make a continual illumination, the result is less satisfactory.

This novel is full of typical Feiffer characters. These are the sort of people who do not merely know something (that would be too simple) but either, in their usual state of doubt, think that they know something or, in their rare

moments of certainty, know that they know something. The driving-force of their lives is a craving to establish the reality, not merely of the people and things around them, but of themselves. Any sort of communication or even self-communion is almost always bound to get fouled up. At one point, the hero-narrator says of a night spent with a woman: 'We exchange stares in the darkness; it's like glaring in braille.' When not glaring in braille at each other, Feiffer's characters are glaring in braille at their own reflections.

At the start of the novel the hero-narrator has just put up his shingle as a private-eye of the Philip Marlowe type. It is typical that he should use, not his own name, but one borrowed from Agatha Christie, 'Roger Ackroyd', since this is a book in which everyone is perpetually concealing or changing identity. In a mild parody of the usual Chandler interview between hard-boiled detective and distressed women client, Ackroyd finds himself faced with Annabelle Plante—'her features . . . spread very wide apart, so that it's more like looking at a face on a movie screen than a face in person'—to whom, inevitably, he is attracted. She has an improbable story of a series of pet parakeets stolen from her nine-year-old son, Josh, and blames her estranged husband, Oscar 'Rags' Plante, a famous sports-writer turned best-selling novelist, for the theft. Ackroyd solves the mystery of the disappearing parakeets with as much ease as the reader—the boy has himself been stealing them, while his mother keeps replacing one with another—but, while doing so, he is approached by the suspected father (himself masquerading under a name not his own) with the request that he keep under surveillance his 'wife' (in fact his mistress), whom he pretends to believe to be two-timing him.

The rest of the novel, which covers the years 1964-71, is taken up with various, equally abortive assignments undertaken by Ackroyd on behalf of Plante. Plante hires him to trace a missing notebook, containing the essential jottings for his next novel; to escort Josh between mother and father; to discover why he is no longer invited to smart parties; to find out who are the people responsible for spreading malicious rumours about him . . . But all these tasks are really pretexts. What Plante is really saying to Ackroyd, as to a psychiatrist, is 'Tell me who I am'; and, like a patient with a psychiatrist, he is as prone to cover up his tracks as to reveal them. For Ackroyd, in turn, the search for the essential Plante becomes, without his intending it, a search for the essential Ackroyd. Each is a hollow man, who can only believe in his own existence if others assure him of it.

No one in the book is precisely the person whom others think him to be; no one is precisely the person whom he thinks himself to be. In revealing these endless series of deceptions and self-deceptions, Mr. Feiffer has produced some splendid passages of dialogue. In contrast with the enervation of style so common in English novels, there is hardly a page that does not crackle with electricity. 'His eyes appear to be the only part of him not under sedation.' 'She wears enough rings to cut a man to pieces.' 'That machismo that gives a good name to impotence.'

When a book yields up such pleasures; it is baffling to have to admit that its total effect is one of pointlessness and even tedium. The probable reason for this is that, once the reader is aware that each character is no more than a series of lantern-slides projected on to totally blank cut-out, the processes, however ingenious, by which each blank cut-out will eventually be revealed cease to be of very much moment. (p. 23)

> *Francis King, "Hollow Men," in* The Spectator, *Vol. 240, No. 7810, March 11, 1978, pp. 23-4.*

## Morris B. Parluff

As has often been noted, the gifted professional writer may convey a depth of understanding of psychology that the professional psychologist may be less able, or unwilling, to provide. When Feiffer intimates [in *Tantrum*] that adulthood is, in fact, a difficult period, when he has his characters express the wish that there might be something easier for beginners, the reader experiences a sense of relief that his own concerns (or more likely those of his neighbor) have been shared. What makes the exposure of such intimate and dark preoccupations tolerable and perhaps useful is that Feiffer, unlike academic psychologists, has the freedom to provide his readers with glimpses of some truths through the veil of illusion and exaggeration.

Feiffer, like such fellow philosopher-moralists as Sören Kierkegaard, Girolamo Savonarola, and Richard Pryor, tends to regard sorrow as one of the conveniences of life. Sorrow appears to serve as a lingua franca immediately intelligible to all. It is also a universally shared emotion that successfully isolates all people. As a theme, therefore, it has an almost irresistible appeal. Feiffer in treating this subject is no less passionate than his cited colleagues, but somewhat more benign and certainly a better cartoonist-playwright-screenwriter-novelist.

In . . . *Tantrum*, Feiffer extends and deepens his style of earnest humor. His dalliance with the woes of everyday life here takes on an even more startlingly irreverent and relentlessly amusing character. He is in top form. His caricature is sheer genius. However, if you do more than smile, you have probably missed the point.

*Tantrum* may look like a comic book and read like a comic book, but it is, in fact, a cartoon novel. It synthesizes dialogue and cartoon in a most felicitous manner to enhance the action and mood. *Tantrum* is the first all-new Feiffer cartoon book published in about 20 years and is not to be confused with his earlier dozen or so cartoon books, which primarily represent compilations of his previously published cartoons: *Feiffer on Civil Rights* (1967), *Pictures at a Prosecution* (1971), and *Feiffer on Nixon: The Cartoon Presidency* (1974).

Feiffer's satiric gifts and exceptional cartoon artistry have been showcased in the *Village Voice* since 1956, and, somewhat less regularly, in the *London Observer* since 1958. The array of cartoon characters self-consciously omits the extremes of high and low education and refinement, as if in recognition that such groups have fewer and less interesting desires. Instead, Feiffer has elected to por-tray the insatiable restlessness, anxieties, and self-doubts of the pseudoeducated and the pseudosophisticated. (pp. 92-3)

Feiffer romps through the emotions of depression, narcissism, greed, envy, and lust with the detached zeal of a cultural atheist. His outrageous deftness suggests that perhaps all his previous highly successful publications were but rehearsals for this classic characterization of the tyranny of peevishness. His slashing, brilliant insights are not designed to ablate the buffoonery he describes but only to highlight it.

Leo, our non-hero, is a 42-year-old family man who experiences life as a series of unremitting joyless demands. He cannot reconcile himself to the strong evidence that life may be capriciously unfair. He is further discomforted by the premonition that he already has one foot on Charon's ferry. His is the unheroic lonely battle experienced by those who have satisfied their top-priority needs of adequate shelter, food, health, and sex and are then confronted with the compelling needs that lurk just beneath survival. He suffers the subjective stress of "making it" but feeling "unfulfilled." Leo's condition, while comprehensible and familiar, lacks the instant appeal of more congenial causes of despair: poverty, pestilence, famine, war, or even discrimination. Indeed, his discontent is a shade unseemly. After all, he is middle-aged! He has responsibilities and duties! His preoccupation appears self-indulgent.

We are better prepared to be sympathetic to the more agitated thrashing about of the young as they seek quixotically to preserve their errant hope that unalloyed virtue, truth, beauty, and justice exist or could exist for them. We can manage to be wistful and even compassionate at the recurring spectacle of adolescence: new whiners being poured into old battles. The petulance of those who attempt to extend adolescence into middle-age is, however, another matter. In short, Leo is a garden-variety middle-class, middle-aged, successful, depressed individual. He needs help.

It is Leo's unique approach to finding happiness—a solemn business at best—that commends him to our attention. He does not turn to the usual institutionalized resources available to the rest of us. He does not turn to religion, nor does he seek out any of the formal therapies—psychological or pharmacological. He apparently lacks the energy to pursue the obligatory middle-aged affair, and he does not seek solace from the currently fashionable sophistries of itinerant ballroom philosophers wearing V-neck sweaters. Leo, instead, seeks and achieves transformation, not by enlightenment but by the magical and surly trick of willing himself to regress physically to the age of two. He successfully usurps the power that inheres in self-evident helplessness. He becomes an infant, indistinguishable from other infants except that he retains the intellectual cunning and singlemindedness of a 42-year-old man who devotes his energies to gaining the gratifications and indulgences that he postulates are the automatic due-due of the infant. He seeks freedom from any and all responsibilities.

Despairing of finding a relationship in adulthood that, despite his limitations, will provide love, respect, and admiration, he resolves to return to an age during which, he presumes (but does not recall), he was loved without demand, purely for himself, and primarily for his engaging limitations. The story traces the adventures of Leo as he attempts figuratively to get his family off his back and literally to get onto theirs. He hopes to relive his life, this time with the benefit of proper advice and counsel. The new, two-year-old Leo wants: "Paid companions. Tutors. Experts in different fields. This time when I age I want decent influences."

One aspect of Feiffer's genius rests in his ability to create a character who can speak in the pseudosophisticated adult patois of our day and then, without missing a beat, shift suddenly to the frank and self-indulgent demands of an infant. The infant Leo indignantly addresses his distraught adolescent children: "It's time you children faced the real world, unblinking. I, your father, have reverted to two. That happens to be my private and personal choice. I will love and support you every bit as strongly as when I was middle-aged. That's all that matters as far as you're concerned. My age is *my* business, not yours. Now carry me piggy back."

Leo makes repeated efforts to return to the bosom of his parental family, but finds that his mother is no longer willing to blithely undertake the responsibility of caring for a child, particularly one she fails to recognize or acknowledge. Over the years, she has learned that the cost of freedom from eternal responsibility for her children is eternal vigilance. Her security against loneliness now demands that she preserve her life with her husband. She sincerely believes that this requires that she protect her husband from the intrusions of the world, and of course from the danger that he might wish to reenter it. She has become the gatekeeper. Leo, the "born again" infant, finds neither cajolery nor threats effective against his mother's panicked determination. He ponders the irony that at the age of 18, he broke out of the parental home in order to gain independence. "What's the good of independence," he rails, "if you're not free to go back?"

He continues his hegira, and in the process of searching for unconditional love and attention without reciprocal demands or responsibilities he turns first to family and then to mother surrogates. The worldly brother whom he envies (oblivious to the fact that his brother is a most unenviable character) is too preoccupied even to recognize Leo's metamorphosis: "Leo! Good to see ya! Lookin' good. Lost weight. Got a hairpiece. Fabulous!" His three sisters, on the other hand, are all too eager to take care of him and to press to their collective bosoms the humiliation of his change: "The worst thing that's happened in the history of our family. We won't talk about it." They are all too eager to seize upon his "condition" to provide the vehicle for their aspiration to martyrdom—finally a solid reason for living. Leo refuses to assume either the guilt or the responsibility.

Ultimately, he leaves off begging from statues—his unresponsive family—and turns for comfort to the statuesque. Infantile sexuality raises its tousled, lascivious head. All of this is told in high style and good humor. The blatant

Freudian underpinnings require no interpretation nor serious amendment. Feiffer is, however, no follower of Freud. It was Freud's thesis that the ego dethrones the pleasure principle and substitutes the reality principle, which can promise greater security and success. Feiffer offers precisely the opposite.

There are several elements of the extended trope that are more troublesome. Without divulging the details of the more surprising elements of the fable, it is necessary to allude briefly to the incident in which Leo is taken by ambulance to join "the others." The others, we are told, are an ever-increasing band of pseudobabies like himself, created by their own willfulness. They are united in their wish to have their own way. They are members of the "me degeneration." Leo is deeply offended by their very existence, for it demeans his sense of uniqueness. He rejects them. He hates them, but he cannot abide the hatred he evokes in them. He cannot assume responsibility for his actions.

But who, then, are the self-indulgent, willful babies whose tribe doth multiply and daily increase? Is the ambulance a clue? Surely there lurks here no oblique reference either to the mentally disordered or to a hypothesized group who secretly aspire to the role of the emotionally crippled (regressed back to infancy). The expectation that being assigned the "sick" role would qualify one for relief from onerous social obligations, personal responsibilities, and the burdens of daily living can no longer be certain. Feiffer is aware that the initiation rites for admission to the public institutions have become strict and the period of hospitalization breathtakingly brief. Such institutions appear to have accepted the slogan of "better living through chemistry." The enforced diaspora of the medicated patient from the hospital to the community hardly provides the opportunity for the patient to long enjoy surcease from responsibility. The mental hospital has long ago, and for many reasons, ceased to be an "asylum." It is unlikely that the growing horde of "recovered" patients who now exist in the ill-prepared community are being caricatured by Feiffer as the disaffected "others." No, we must seek elsewhere.

One thinks of the trek by overaged adolescents to encounter groups or sensory-awareness training or transcendental meditation or Zen, but the humanistic heyday may be over; that children's crusade has slowed perceptibly. The teaching that simply "being" is sufficient to assure one's right to love and human regard has now become less fashionable. In its stead, the philosophical guidance of practitioners of est, actualizations, and life-spring is being sought by large numbers. Here we find an almost total emphasis on taking responsibility rather than assigning responsibility to others. We are now told to assume responsibility for everything that happens to us, or more precisely, everything that we experience as happening to us. The rediscovered cant is that we must preserve the illusion of having the freedom to choose. The recent tolerance of rampant narcissism seems to be receding as the recession deepens and the highest priority needs listed in Maslow's hierarchy reassert themselves.

Then who *are* the "others"? It is, of course, a metaphor. And what is a metaphor? A slight paraphrase of the old pun suggests that Feiffer has provided us with a place broad enough for all of us who are cowed to graze in. Perhaps he is offering a vision of the future rather than an observation of the present, or perhaps he is merely practicing a lively sophistry.

Feiffer is again revealed in this short volume as a wise, perceptive, and enormously witty man. Yet his wit is barely enough to temper his passionate caring. He is not content to be an observer. He complains, but he has trouble dealing with his cynicism. I do not refer here to the advice he has Leo give to a real child—a child characterized by a run-of-the-mill selfishness and lack of nobility: "Never be rational if you want to have your way. Ignore logic. Don't mature! Mature people do the shit work!" This advice seems to me to be sound advice. What I have in mind is *echt* cynicism, which is revealed when he teasingly holds out the pathological hope of a brighter future. The main character does not appear to have gained any profundity through his metamorphosis. He denies everything and affirms nothing. This is not an escapist tale, nor one of rebellion, but merely one of evasion. It is truly a tale of our times. But funny! (pp. 93-4, 97)

*Morris B. Parloff, "The Me Degeneration," in* Psychology Today, *Vol. 13, No. 7, December, 1979, pp. 92-4, 97.*

**Frank Rich**

*Grown Ups* is a new play by Jules Feiffer, and, yes, it is funny—savagely funny. That's Mr. Feiffer's way. But the laughter has a different ring this time—about halfway up the throat it turns into a gasp.

This is no exaggeration. No matter how inured you may be to Mr. Feiffer's style, you still may not be quite prepared for [this] ferocious comedy. . . . In *Grown Ups*, Mr. Feiffer has narrowed his focus from the social fabric of modern America to the psychological fabric of one Jewish-American family. And by turning inward, he has written his most moving and provocative work. Mr. Feiffer is out for blood in *Grown Ups*, and he won't quit until he gets it. Indeed, this play soon becomes one long piercing cry of rage.

The embodiment of that rage is Jake, a *New York Times* reporter. . . . *Grown Ups* unfolds over a year in which he prods his seemingly happy life until it falls apart. What does Jake have to complain about? On the surface, not much. He has a fine wife, a precocious 9-year-old daughter, an immaculate Upper West Side apartment and parents who dote on his every word. His career is in high gear: he's just begun his magnum opus, a book about "the moral and ethical disintegration of the American dream."

When we first meet Jake, he is right in the center of that dream. Mr. Feiffer's Act I is set in the New Rochelle kitchen of the hero's sister—a sunny, spic-and-span picture of suburban bliss. Jake's family has gathered for a party, and his parents, Helen and Jack, can't get enough of their middle-aged son and his accomplishments. When Jake announces that he is not only writing a book but is

also interviewing Henry Kissinger for Esquire, his grasping mother and Willy Loman of a father swoon with joy.

Yet something *is* wrong, and Jake knows it. No matter how successful he may be, he can never satisfy his parents. When his mother recovers from her swoon, she immediately starts to look forward to the day when "Henry Kissinger will interview *Jake.*" And, as *Grown Ups* gathers force, we see that the American dream is not just disintegrating in the world beyond—but within Mr. Feiffer's protagonist. Jake hates himself for having lived by his parents' values—like Helen and Jack, he has pursued success because it is easier to achieve than love.

But what can be done? As the hero half-jokingly tells his sister, he can't escape his parents' legacy by killing them: that's a "short-range solution." Nor can he talk to them; they hear him only when he has a new accomplishment to recite.

As *Grown Ups* moves from New Rochelle to Jake's apartment, the hero decides instead to sever every bond in his life. What follows are two grueling battles in which Jake lashes out at his wife, Louise, and then at his parents. By the end, Jake's storms have kindled a full conflagration: Three generations of a family are locked in an unstoppable round-robin of emotional mayhem—spewing out the previously unarticulated hostilities of five lifetimes at a Sunday brunch.

Mr. Feiffer's Freudian stance is not new, of course: in every miserable grown-up like Jake, there is still the miserable child he can't escape. Nor is the Jewish family of *Grown Ups* particularly novel. While the playwright has his own bitter variations, Helen and Jack—products of their own legacy from "the old country"—are of a piece with the fearsome parents in the novels of Philip Roth and Joseph Heller.

What gives *Grown Ups* its force is its author's ability to construct his exit-less maze of emptiness and guilt in precise, theatrically daring terms. With Strindbergian verve, he strips away exposition and other debris of the conventional well-made play to achieve emotional verisimilitude. There are no scenes of "plot" or "character development." Instead of tidying up and explaining his protagonist's crisis, Mr. Feiffer plunges into it—demanding that the audience follow, kicking and questioning if need be, behind him.

When his characters fight, the battles are triggered not by story twists but by trivial incidents, as happens in life. It's when Louise gets impatient with a Miss Marple mystery or when Helen gives her granddaughter the wrong Dr. Seuss book that Acts II and III explode. And again as in life, the battles don't build to satisfying climaxes. Even threats of suicide and divorce—or, for that matter, declarations of love—can't resolve a circular argument in which Jake finds it impossible to separate his feelings about his wife from those about his mother. All he can do is scream "Stop! Stop! Stop!"

In the calmer Act I, Mr. Feiffer makes us listen to the same innocuous anecdote—about a misbegotten dinner party—three times. Why? By changing the storyteller and the listeners each time as the characters drift in and out of the kitchen, he elliptically lays out the emotional geography of the entire family.

So keen is Mr. Feiffer's sense of language that he can create much of his drama by indirection. Characters are often defined by their use of English—or by the manner in which they correct each other's usage—and they rarely say what they really mean. Mr. Feiffer takes the most familiar tribal greetings—"So what's new?" or "When am I going to see my granddaughter?"—and forces us to see the resentments and hurts that fester underneath. It's when we see the gap that separates such lines from the truth that our laughter curdles.

*Frank Rich, " 'Grown Ups' By Feiffer at Lyceum," in* The New York Times, *December 11, 1981.*

## John Simon

[*Grown Ups*] is an amusing tale of infighting in a typical Jewish family; of how the sins of the fathers and mothers tend to be visited on the children and grandchildren as family life locks people into the reiteration of destructive patterns, even in the process of trying to break them; of how hard if not impossible it is to grow up.

The trouble is that the play intends to be both a comedy, which it certainly is (sometimes with wonderful giddiness), and also something very serious, at which, however, it fails. Comparison with a much greater play may be unfair, but it is enlightening: *A Long Day's Journey Into Night* deals with similar family warfare, but its emotional range is infinitely greater. O'Neill goes from comic exasperation through searing hatred to compassion and forgiveness; Feiffer's span is only from the first of these to the second, and even that halfhearted. When parent and child or husband and wife batter each other most stubbornly and woundingly, they still function as caricatures, as cute Jewish jokes, as people we can feel superior to however much we recognize bits of them in us, as losers who remain unthreatening. Yet this comedy wishes to become drama: The exacerbation and indignation increase, but they never rise above the level of a whine. The author tries to be fair by making husband and wife seem to be equally deluded, but when there should be pity for each, all he can manage is equal self-pity.

And even that isn't followed through. With the parents, self-deludedness exceeds all bounds. Their love is clearly self-love, their pride in their son (and ignoring of their less successful daughter) is pure self-affirmation. Yet even at their worst moments they are still funny-pathetic, which is not the same as pitiable, and the relentless jokiness is primarily at their expense. Which means that Feiffer is still writing as a resentful, embittered son trying to laugh things off; he still isn't a grown-up, even though the vaguely autobiographical hero does seem to assert his emancipation from the family rut by leaving both his wife and the New York *Times,* two moves that knock the desolated parents right out of the ball game.

Yet this ending itself presents unpleasant and insuperable problems. It could be read as the son's ultimate lunacy, but I don't think Feiffer intends it that way. Jake, after all, is a successful writer; has some good notions about child rearing; does not have nervous collapses like his wife, Louise; can read books, which she can't, or barely; can correct her faulty English. So it looks as if the rejection of Louise and the *Times* is, at least in comic terms, an apotheosis; yet there is no indication that Jake can do better elsewhere either in marriage or in career. That, however, makes him a fool against his author's wishes and awareness, and makes the author himself look foolish and delinquent.

Add to this that there is no outer world in this play, not one offstage character who comes to life, no one not caught up in these moils and broils. The implication, then, is that this is all: This family is all families. But that is not earned by them because of the skimpiness of their emotional repertoires, because of jokes that refuse to become more than jokes. . . . [Always] there is the whine under the laughter, polluting the fun without opening up other avenues: genuine compassion, genuine despair, or even genuine scathing misanthropy. (p. 81)

*John Simon, "Look Back in Rancor," in* New York *Magazine, Vol. 14, No. 50, December 21, 1981, pp. 81-2.*

## Noel Perrin

Jules Feiffer has always been an anomaly in the comic-strip world. Comic-strip characters smile. In fact, they smile in special, highly ritualized ways. Attractive women . . . smile with their mouths well open, upper lip straight, lower lip v-shaped, so that what you have is a sort of inverted triangle with a lot of white space where most people have teeth. Men tend to smile more like the faces on smile-buttons. Animals smile with little perpendicular lines at the ends of their mouths.

Mr. Feiffer, on the other hand, [in ***Feiffer: Jules Feiffer's America from Eisenhower to Reagan***] specializes in the bemused look, the glare, the frown and occasionally the idiot smirk.

Cartoon characters are generally frozen in time—which, of course, is one of their great appeals. They are stability in a changing world, a reassurance to the general public in somewhat the way that the buildings on the Princeton campus are to an old grad back for reunion. Dennis doesn't age, or Charlie Brown or even Michael Doonesbury. But one of Mr. Feiffer's specialties is the single strip in which a woman ages from 30 to 60 or a lean-jawed baseball player gets old before your eyes, so that the full tragicomedy of human existence can be seen in a single set of sketches.

Comic-strip characters even use a special kind of punctuation when they talk, quite different from the kind other people use. More primitive. I once counted 86 straight days on which every character in "Mary Worth" spoke continuously with exclamation points except when actually asking questions. In calmer moments, a sentence will end with three dots or with nothing at all—but never, as if there were a rule all cartoonists had to obey, with a period. Mr. Feiffer's characters use periods all the time, and might get in one exclamation point every five strips.

Mr. Feiffer's difference from all other cartoonists (except, in recent years, his growing army of imitators) is well known to his peers. If you look him up in *The World Encyclopedia of Comics,* you read that his universe "is the blackest and most depressing ever to be found in a comic strip." The account rises to real outrage as it describes his "neurotic and poisonous women," his "spineless and craven men," and winds up hurling a fistful of adjectives at the strip itself: atrocious, terrible, bitter.

All this, of course, is what people who don't see the world as a smile-face love him for—though they may love him even more for his sheer intelligence. One of Mr. Feiffer's several innovations in the comic-strip world was the introduction of adult awareness. He was the first (in that world) to make humor out of complexity rather than out of simplicity.

The appearance of a Feiffer retrospective—nearly 500 strips dating from 1956 to 1982—is therefore a matter of celebration. Here, at the rate of two strips a page, is a social, sexual and political history of the last quarter-century as it could be gotten in no other way. The middle-aged can relive their youthful hopes and frustrations; the young can get an education. Both can get two rueful laughs a page.

Mr. Feiffer and his editor, Steven Heller, an art director for *The New York Times,* have put it all together by Presidencies: a chapter each for Presidents Eisenhower, Kennedy, Johnson, Nixon, Ford, Carter and Reagan. . . . A third of each chapter is, on the average, about politics. . . .

The other two-thirds of each chapter belongs to Bernard Mergendeiler, his sexually frustrated hero, to the Dancer in her black leotard and to an even wider variety of radicals, liberals, bigots and victims than I had remembered. Mr. Feiffer perhaps didn't actually invent radical chic, but he certainly gave it currency. And even as he promoted it, he mocked it more savagely and funnily than Tom Wolfe ever dreamed of.

A retrospective asks for judgment. As is often the case when you see a career laid out, there is bad news and there is good news. The bad news is that recent Feiffer strips are not as good as early Feiffer strips. There are exceptions, such as the Youth's monologue on Israel in Lebanon, three pages from the end of the book. That's as good as anything Mr. Feiffer has ever drawn. But like the Dancer, he has gotten a little tired, and sometimes he repeats last year's dance with slightly lower leaps.

The good news is that Mr. Feiffer doesn't need cartoons anymore. All he needs are words. Each chapter begins with a little essay, and some of these are stunning. The one with which he introduces the Carter chapter says more about what was wrong with that basically good man than any cartoon, including a Feiffer, possibly could—and more than I recall seeing in any other short essay.

The other good news doesn't come from this book but from looking on the editorial page of almost any American paper that prints political cartoons. Jules Feiffer himself

may have gotten a little tired, but a whole new generation of cartoonists has learned his lessons and maybe even improved on his technique. As any Feiffer reader ought to know, time does that sort of thing.

*Noel Perrin, "Seven Presidents and Bernard Mergendeiler," in* The New York Times Book Review, *December 19, 1982, p. 8.*

## Larry E. Grimes

There can be no doubt about the fact that "subjectivity" reigns triumphant in Jules Feiffer's **Ackroyd,** for the novel is presented as a series of diary entries that recount the activities of one Robert Hollister, a.k.a. Roger Ackroyd. Feiffer makes effective use of this form, letting it function as a detective's log, a novelist's notebook, a psychiatrist's casebook, and a personal dairy.

The novel records Hollister-Ackroyd's quest for personal identity, hence the subtitle—*A Mystery of Identity.* It amplifies . . . the subjectivity inherent in the hard-boiled formula with which Ackroyd identifies. Ackroyd admits that he "went into business to be Sam Spade." Later, pretty partner in tow, he plays Nick and Nora Charles as he is led from Holiday Inn to Holiday Inn by Oscar Plante, the chief subject of his investigation, his constant antagonist, and his client. Ackroyd is not, however, a simple 1960s version of the hard-boiled detective. In fact, he takes issue with the hard-boiled tradition: "Philip Marlowe does not take divorce cases. Well, I will. It isn't my business to impose judgments on clients."

This departure from the formula is, of course, a major one. Ackroyd's refusal to "impose judgments on clients" is a refusal to exert his will, a refusal to cease being just a detective and to become judge and jury. Ackroyd refuses to assume the ethical attributes essential to the hard-boiled hero. He refuses because (1) he must find himself before he can assert himself and because (2) the only self attainable in the world he inhabits must, of necessity, exist in such a fragile shape as to preclude hard-boiled moral assertion. The novel is the proof and elaboration of this claim.

In the first instance, there is never any doubt in the narrative but that Ackroyd is a self in flux. He states at the outset that he has deliberately become another self, "changing names, going into the detective business." As a detective, he finds that professional duty requires him to assume yet other identities. And finally he leaves the detective business, becomes an army officer and then a speaker and writer who retrieves his real name, Robert Hollister—if we dare to believe him. His ever-changing identity is paralleled in the book by the protean shape of Plante, a.k.a. Logan Jessup. As Ackroyd's alter ego and father substitute, as well as his client and antagonist, Plante affords the younger Ackroyd a model of how one adapts to life as a shifting self.

As the novel moves from absurdist mystery (the case of the missing parakeet) to more complicated investigations centering around missing notebooks and Byzantine relationships, it becomes apparent that Ackroyd must have a clue, a model, or a guide capable of making known to him the secret of how to live in a world of flux. Plante, as said above, provides that model, but not immediately. First Ackroyd must become part of the life-fiction of Oscar Plante and run the risk of self-loss. The matter of parakeets and notebooks brings him into Plante's world and under Plante's influence. By midbook Ackroyd is aware of the magnetism of Plante's life-fiction and resolves to release himself from its pull. At this point, his detection becomes completely subjective. He plans to release himself by

> taking [himself] as a client. My assignment is to build a dossier of the authentic Plante, check out his past and his present with friends, enemies, and, eventually, if I think I am up to it, the subject himself. Once I have a book on the flesh and blood Plante there is a very good chance that the Plante in my head will not be able to stand up to it. It will be like daylight in a haunted head—I meant to write "house," but let it stand.

Ackroyd becomes more forceful, more self-assured, as a result of this decision. Shortly after he has made this decision, he reclaims his old name and tells himself,

> I am confident for the first time that there is an enormous difference between Roger Ackroyd and Robert Hollister; I am not making it up. Ackroyd served his purpose as a transitional figure but, thank God, he's dead and buried and Plante's insideous influence is buried with him.

Of course, life in the world of flux is not that simple. Plante's influence is not so easily put behind. Ackroyd-Hollister soon finds himself in need of Plante. Plante is a successful sports writer and novelist. Hollister, after his break with Ackroyd and as a result of his tour of duty in the army, has become an antiwar celebrity. As a celebrity, he is expected to put his Vietnam experience into book form. This he has difficulty doing. Enter Plante. Plante begins to revise the book and slowly takes it (Hollister-Ackroyd's autobiographical work) over. As Ackroyd puts it, Plante becomes his "ghost."

That being the case, there is nothing left for Ackroyd to do but to attempt to exorcise the spirit. But, as he notes, his detective's license has expired. He must, then, try to get to the heart of the mystery without benefit of a bona fide private eye. (It would seem that one can't even trust oneself with a case anymore.) Ackroyd proceeds as he had planned earlier in the adventure. He goes back to Plante's boyhood home and tries to reconstruct the truth about Plante's life. What Ackroyd finally unravels is the mystery of identity in modern America. He discovers that "[Plante] invented himself from scratch. . . . that's the wonderous part of it, the psychic embodiment of the American Dream—he didn't merely raise himself by his bootstraps, he materialized himself from nonexistence. Small wonder he haunts my soul."

The mystery of Plante revealed, Ackroyd is able to come to grips with the mystery of his own identity. He is free, as he puts it, to "come up with a clue to what . . . to make myself."

In *Ackroyd,* Feiffer has so revised the formula as to "un-

boil" the hard-boiled detective. Ackroyd drops the defining and insular code of the hard-boiled self in favor of fictive life. In *Ackroyd,* theme (the successful self as the fictive self) becomes form: Ackroyd's diary is the novel we are reading. Living becomes synonymous with storytelling, and the only meaningful mode of detection open to Ackroyd at the end of the book does not require a license. For the whole diary is not case record but autobiography—self-detection, the pursuit of the ever-changing mystery of identity. (pp. 537-39)

> *Larry E. Grimes, "Stepsons of Sam: Re-visions of the Hard-boiled Detective Formula in Recent American Fiction," in* Modern Fiction Studies, *Vol. 29, No. 3, Autumn, 1983, pp. 535-44.*

### Stephen J. Whitfield

As cartoonist and dramatist, [Jules Feiffer] has sought to press the language and logic of his characters so far that both the shock of recognition and the release of laughter are effected. He is still in mid-passage in both careers, but he can already be identified as an important and representative figure in the history of Jewish-American drama and in the social context of the popular arts. (p. 168)

Feiffer's faces generally undergo very minute changes of expression; his art calibrates only slight shifts of gesture and emotion. For he gets his effects less as a draftsman than as a dramatist. Through their spoken and private idiom and their rituals of self-deception, his characters betray themselves and indicate the meaning of their own identities. It is as though the comic-strip characters on which he grew up had been rendered vulnerable to the psychologizing of others, though the armor of their own self-delusion is rarely pierced. *Feiffer's Marriage Manual* (1967) for example, is truly adult entertainment, the sophisticate's *Blondie;* and indeed in one series the husband turns into Dagwood Bumstead. In *Feiffer's Album* a woman whom Superman saves from a mugging evaluates with such devastating effect his compulsive derring-do, his exhibitionism, and his flair for prancing about in "skintight, effeminate leotards" that Superman suffers an anxiety attack, his omnicompetence diminishing and Krafft-Ebing. Feiffer's characters are, as the title of another collection aptly labels them, explainers—to each other but mostly to themselves. They are not, to be precise, conversationalists, since they tend to talk past, rather than to, one another.

[Critic Kenneth] Tynam, among others, recognized the primacy of Feiffer's ear—"an odd tribute to pay to a cartoonist." Others, too, stressed the acuteness of Feiffer's dialogue, though one of his readers, Vladimir Nabokov, voiced a minority opinion: "Too many words." (Given the compressed force of Feiffer's language when he needs to be and the fidelity with which he has recorded the loopiness of the vernacular, the novelist's objection is unconvincing, especially since the narrator of *Lolita* asserts that for the pain of existence there is only "the melancholy and very local palliative of articulate art.") As the apolitical concern with "interpersonal relations" in the 1950s yielded to the open conflicts and range of the 1960s, Feiffer's art increasingly focused on the duplicity of official speech and the rhetorical camouflage of reality. In a decade in which "pacification" did not mean peace and racism required code-words, Feiffer became increasingly devoted to exposing the corruption of language. (p. 170)

It was inevitable that his plays would be accused of resembling cartoons, and that he would be dismissed in some quarters as not fundamentally a writer for the theater at all. It is hard to resist the suspicion that his dramaturgical credentials would not have been questioned had he spent formative years in sailors' dives and before the mast. To Feiffer himself such criticism has meant only "that there's a continuity [with the cartoons], that I write like me." His plea of *nolo contendere* means, in effect, that Feiffer writes like no one else. In some instances the continuity has been deliberate. An early cartoon strip about fallout shelters and rioting at the United Nations was expanded into *Crawling Arnold,* and the revue *Hold Me!* was also transferred in part from strips to skits. Such transitions are so feasible because Feiffer conceives his cartoons in such dramatic terms, and he has claimed to enjoy the challenge of working within the limitations imposed in each medium—whether of space or time. His targets have been similar, and the characters in his cartoons have long been on the verge of going to pieces before he put them *in* pieces for audiences to laugh at so anxiously.

On both page and stage, Feiffer is a miniaturist, relying on economy of means for his effects. He writes about a very limited number of characters in a landscape devoid of detail. There is little upholstery, or incorporation of a wider world. Only the psychological states are thick with implication, as the characters try desperately to convey impulses they themselves may not understand and to pick up the signals of others. Since there is nothing monumental or ambitious about his plays, they are not obliged to be brilliant but, as was once said of early Hemingway, "merely perfect." Though Feiffer's lines have the snap of comic authority, he is not notably original in theme or technique; and his debts to the anti-naturalism and the antic terror of the theater of the absurd are obvious. He has left large assertions about the human estate to other playwrights, however. Instead Feiffer has been satisfied to comment upon subtle changes in the atmospherics of American life. With the weird exception of Joan of Arc and her voices (in *Knock Knock* ), all of the characters in his plays have been contemporary Americans.

The scale of his work, which emerges naturally from his experience as a cartoonist, has rendered his dramatic enterprises especially suitable for small or cabaret theater. That is also why there is something unsatisfactory about his two movies. The grisly humor of *Little Murders* depends upon the claustrophobia and paranoia packed within the walls of the Newquist family's apartment. Little is gained by moving the camera into the streets, where the menace is somewhat abated when the imagination of the audience has less work of its own to do. The apparent clarity and precision of the cinema's powers of observation diminish the terror by distorting the pressure of the violence inflicted upon the beleaguered New Yorkers. The problem

with *Carnal Knowledge* is somewhat different. Despite the standard length of the film and its frequent close-ups, the characters are so one-dimensional and reductive that they lack credibility and verisimilitude. The two male characters are more illustrations of an idea (like depersonalization), rather than recognizable types who assume a life of their own independent of the thesis they are supposed to embody. Jonathan and Sandy are conceived so exclusively in terms of their sexual attitudes that the camera is restrained from showing anything else in their lives—neither money nor politics . . . , nor work or family feeling or sports. The film's characters, Pauline Kael complained, lack "even eroticism, even simple warmth." . . . At such close range and with such relentless immediacy, the camera simply demands more than Feiffer's characterizations managed to provide.

Within the limitations he has imposed on himself, he has chosen to record the ruling obsessions and fashions of his time. Having noted the ambiguity of the triumph of "psychological man" in the 1950s, he depicted the political and social turmoil of the 1960s from an independently radical perspective and then, in the 1970s, reflected the receding importance of public conflict. He works within the groove of history in order to comment upon it. For all his sensitivity to the *Zeitgeist,* a corrosively skeptical temperament has kept him disenthralled, detached, and nonpartisan. His plays have little to affirm and usually no message to communicate. If they are united by a common theme, it is a familiar one: truth must be distinguished from fantasy, rationalization, mendacity, and delusion. Buried within the mockery of modern conventions, the deflation of language, the surreal leaps of logic, and the quick stabs of wit is a warning about the treachery of social reality—and, perhaps, an invitation as old as the Delphic injunction.

*Crawling Arnold* documents the transition from the age of private anxieties to the political preoccupations of the 1960s. Its cast of characters includes Barry and Grace Enterprise, who descend into the family fallout shelter and cower before authority as much as they fear the bomb itself; Millie, the maid, who spends part of her time denouncing "white imperialism" before the U.N.: and Miss Sympathy, a social worker who whispers to Millie her support of "the aspirations of your people." But the central character, the Enterprises' 35-year-old son Arnold, engages in apolitical protest: he regresses. Like the protagonist of Joseph Heller's *Something Happened* (1974), who announced, "When I grow up I want to be a little boy." Arnold has chosen to repudiate the responsibilities of adulthood. Growing up in *Crawling Arnold* means acceptance of the normality of atomic terror, submission to irrational authority, conformity to the pieties of middle-class liberalism, the suppression of natural emotions in favor of the banalities of social convention, and commitment to the stability of the nuclear family (the pun is unavoidable). The imperatives of satire have, therefore, stacked the deck in favor of Arnold, whose withdrawal represents a deeper kind of sanity (though not necessarily of wisdom).

Arnold's parents cannot accommodate themselves to his apparent perversity and irrationality, though their own grasp of reality is far from perfect. What that really consists of, beneath the surface of "togetherness" and submissiveness, makes *Crawling Arnold* the farcical analogue of Freud's *Civilization and Its Discontents*. For Arnold has smashed the sound system that will announce that the civil defense drill is over; and he is about to extract sexual favors from Miss Sympathy, who reveals to him that he falls "into my spectrum of attractiveness." The play thus hints at the aggressive and libidinal forces lurking in the subterranean recesses of society. Since the play is a farce, no genuine evil is evoked or analyzed. Arnold describes his own destructiveness as "naughty" behavior; and his conflict with social convention is snap, crackle and pop, not *Sturm und Drang*. The protagonist's escapism may be viewed as a wacky extension of Feiffer's own experience of maturation. Having worked in the comic-book "shlock houses" of Manhattan during World War II, he came to realize that his bosses, "who had been in charge of our childhood fantasies, had become archetypes of the grown-ups who made us need to have fantasies in the first place."

Disenchantment has deepened with his next—and still best—play, *Little Murders.* Staged in 1968, it was written against the backdrop of violence that is likely to be long associated with the 1960s. Within a five-year period, the assassinated had included a President and his brother, civil rights leaders Medger Evers and Martin Luther King, and Malcolm X (murdered during National Brotherhood Week). The national murder rate doubled between 1963 and 1971. (pp. 171-73)

The extravagance and grotesquerie of American violence threatened to outstrip the most gallant efforts of black humorists to imagine something more nightmarish. Feiffer's response was to chart the decomposition of the bourgeois family amid relentless beatings and random snipings on city streets. The Newquists are "an Andy Hardy family" that has already lost one son to an unknown assassin before Act One. The father tries to get through each day "in planned segments"—mornings without getting shot, afternoon without a knife in the ribs, a return home without finding the apartment burglarized or the rest of his family slain. At the end of the day, he can report to the other Newquists, "It's murder out there." . . . The daughter, Patty, is described by Feiffer as "an All-American girl, Doris Day of ten years ago." Through strength of will she hopes to prevail over the madness and mayhem around her. Though her previous boyfriends were homosexuals, she finally latches onto Alfred Chamberlain, a self-proclaimed "apathist." With his paralyzed energies, Alfred is the stock Feiffer cartoon figure of the 1950s, suddenly dropped into the turmoil of the 1960s. (p. 174)

The surreal dimensions of *Little Murders* are ghoulish extensions of the apprehensions of the audience. Feiffer has heightened such fears by punctuating his play with the introduction of characters whose lapsed authority testifies to the utter helplessness of the middle class. A magistrate, Judge Stern, garrulously reminisces about the immigrants' pursuit of the American Dream; but such earnest expectations of improvement, which are daily undermined by the evidence of urban anarchy, turn Alfred off entirely. (Alfred's intimacy with his own father was so minimal that he never called him Dad, or any other name: "The occa-

sion never came up.") The minister who marries Alfred and Patty, Reverend Dupas of the First Existential Church, is no spiritual leader at all but a hip, mindless defender of every form of behavior and belief. He embodies the anomie and moral inadequacy of institutions that once compelled allegiance, and the monologue he delivers—with its short-circuiting of sense and its loopy flights of self-delusion—is the funniest episode in the play. Finally there is Lieutenant Practice, a police officer who maniacally concludes that all the violence must reflect a vast conspiracy to extinguish authority. Paranoids can have enemies too, and the policeman . . . is shot down by the surviving Newquist child as an arbitrary act of vengeance for Patty's death. Rev. Dupas has already been slain, and there is every sign that the slaughter will continue. Contemporary fears have thus been pushed almost to their logical limits, with the playwright combining merriment and dread in equally effective doses.

*The White House Murder Case* was staged a year before the publication of the Pentagon Papers. Both document the discrepancy between the official explanation and the actual justification, between the public pronouncement and the private motive. In Feiffer's play, the war in Vietnam is history; the United States is currently fighting guerrillas in Brazil. Instead of "Charlie," the enemy is "Chico." The Pentagon's Operation Total Win has failed. When American counter-insurgency forces are accidentally killed by their own illegal nerve gas, the administration of President Hale decides that "The American people must be told the truth." That means it will lie, and blame the Brazilians themselves for the American deaths. The President's wife, a peacenik opposed to her husband's policies, threatens to leak the actual facts to the *New York Times,* whereupon she is stabbed to death with a sign pleading, "Make Love Not War." Eventually the assassin confesses: it is the Postmaster General, a political operator concerned about the forthcoming election. That truth also cannot be revealed, so her death is blamed on food poisoning.

Though part of the action takes place in Brazil, *The White House Murder Case* is not strictly speaking an anti-war play. Feiffer's real subject is duplicity—the political definition of truth as whatever is most useful and convenient, whatever "works." That definition undermines the very basis of classical democratic theory, which requires a citizenry enlightened enough to judge the policies of its elected representatives. Our first president supposedly could not tell a lie; less than two hundred years later we found ourselves with a president who apparently could not tell the truth. But Feiffer's play made no attempt to account for the mendacity of Nixon and others or to present the causes and consequences of widespread and willful deceit. Evelyn Hale decries the insertion of advertising values into democratic politics, but this clue is undeveloped and unrelated to the possible vulnerability of the political process to manipulation and deception. Instead the play shrinks the motives of politicians to the crassest sort of self-interest, cloaked in lies. Henry Adams once wrote of President Monroe that his character "was transparent; no one could mistake his motives, except by supposing them to be complex." That, however, is the theatrical problem with Feiffer's comedy, at least once the melodramatic shock of Mrs. Hale's impalement is assimilated. All the characters are replicates of Adams's image of Monroe, which means that they are too reductive, too lacking in nuance, too illustrative of a single insight to sustain dramatic interest. (pp. 174-75)

Instead of silencing or repeating himself, [Feiffer] chose to explore sexual politics [in *Carnal Knowledge*]. . . .

There are indeed cinematic problems with *Carnal Knowledge,* arising largely from the obsessiveness enforced on Sandy and especially Jonathan. They are prisoners of sex, spending much of their life sentence in what amounts to solitary confinement, because of a failure to integrate sexuality with the rest of experience. In the summation of the philosopher Ernest Becker, both the sensualist . . . and the romantic . . . are "pitifully immersed in the blind groping of the human condition." The cruelty and hollowness of their attitudes toward women have resulted in disillusionment and emptiness; but the bleak moral of the film—its implacable seriousness—was lost on feminist critics in particular, who accused Feiffer and Nichols of sharing the very attitudes that *Carnal Knowledge* seemed to mock. "No contemporary film," Joan Mellen claimed, "offers as vicious a portrait of female sexuality. . . . All the women in this film are shallow, crass or stupid." She added that Feiffer and Nichols' "tone and the absence from their film of women at least as articulate as the men amounts to a smug assent, a silent endorsement." Although Molly Haskell found "one intelligent-romantic woman of that film, . . . [she] cannot be envisioned beyond the moment she outlives her romantic usefulness to the men, and so disappears from the movie." (p. 176)

What these criticisms miss is that Feiffer, as a satirist, hardly exempts women from the humanity he habitually prosecutes. The misogyny of the characters makes them quite unsympathetic, and should not obscure the misanthropy of their creator, since the film has no affirmative images of humans of either gender. *Carnal Knowledge* comprises the fullest statement Feiffer has presented of the sexual comedy of self-deception and disenchantment, a subject that he has treated in the entire course of his career as a cartoonist as well. The opening bull session between Jonathan and Sandy, on whether it is better to love or be loved (a dialogue as old as Plato's *Phaedrus*), is the echo of countless panels depicting the uncertainties and ambivalences linked with desire. In transferring such cartoons to the screen, Feiffer and Nichols failed to produce an unqualified artistic success. But they touched an important nerve in a generation whose conscientious objection to the ongoing war between the sexes still reverberates.

After *Carnal Knowledge* the author apparently realized that his pessimism was at wit's end. He professed to be "worn out by evangelizing," with rounding up the usual suspects. The point was "to start working out ways of living a life." His writing had always vibrated with intelligence—but not with whatever consolations and satisfactions the world might surrender. So Feiffer's next play [*Knock Knock*] marked a new phase—if not quite from alienation to accommodation, then at least toward allowing room for fantasy rather than requiring reason of

human beings. As with [*Carnal Knowledge*], the primary characters are two men. But its subject, as Feiffer once explained, is "the absolute collapse of logic. . . . how two particular people deal with the irrationality of order and, finally, the collapse of order."

The two people are Abe, a former broker, and Cohn, an unemployed musician, who have been living in a cabin in the woods. Abe is willing to grant some powers to the imagination; Cohn trusts only his senses. Havoc enters their lives with the arrival of Joan of Arc, who is seeking a sort of Noah's ark that will soon ascend to heaven. She offers the only glimmer of affirmation in a Feiffer play that is not meant to be risible, telling Abe and Cohn that they "should be self-sufficient, but not alienated, not despairing, not sneering, not cynical, not clinical, not dead unless you are dead, and even then make the most of it." Her plea for the avoidance of extremes is as bromidic as Judge Stern's paean to the American Dream in *Little Murders,* but this time some credence is to be placed amid the absurdity. (p. 177)

In praising [*Knock Knock*], *Time*'s reviewer located it within the context of Jewish humor—"skeptical, self-deprecating, fatalistic and with an underlying sadness that suggests that all the mirth is a self-protective mask hiding imminent lamentation." Those terms may stretch *Knock Knock* a little beyond recognition, but it would be hard to deny that there is a Jewish dimension to Feiffer's interpretation of life. There is admittedly little in his topics or his language that betrays ethnic consciousness. Given the satiric possibilities inherent in North American Jewish life, which Roth, Richler, Markfield, Heller, and others have exploited with fiendish delight, it is noteworthy that Feiffer has avoided this topic. Occasionally he creates characters who are clearly Jewish, like Abe and Cohn [in *Knock Knock*] and Judge Stern [in *Little Murders*], and he uses Yiddish words (like *schlepp*) that have entered the American idiom. The cartoons have occasionally included Jewish mothers, smothering with love and aggression, as well as a figure named Bernard Mergendeiler, the sort of victim who might be called a *schlemiel* if that term had not replaced Christ-figure as the most overused term in the critical lexicon. But otherwise there is not much else overt and explicit for the student of Jewish-American expression to identify.

The only exception is *Grown Ups,* a three-act play that Feiffer first wrote in 1974 and which, with revisions, opened at the American Repertory Theatre at Harvard in 1981. The word "Jew" does not appear in it. All the characters are members of one family—the parents, sister, wife, and daughter of a *New York Times* reporter named Jake; and all are manifestly Jewish. All these relatives make demands upon Jake that he finds exorbitant. All his problems stem from his failure to function like an autonomous adult when he is in the bosom of his family which, according to one estimate, is about a 42D. When Jake's sister Marilyn, who shares his frustration and helplessness, has the inspired notion that they should kill their parents, he dismisses the proposal as "a short-range solution." Set in Marilyn's New Rochelle kitchen and in Jake's Manhattan apartment, *Grown Ups* shifts rather jerkily from tense satire of suburban banality to the acrid atmosphere of generational and marital warfare; and the play lacks the formal resolution found in its antecedents, the Jewish domestic dramas of the 1930s and 1940s. But not only does **Grown Ups** offer welcome moments of comic insight, it also shows a remorseless flair for picking at the scabs of familial resentment and indignities that is compelling in its urgency and even its savagery.

To assert that Feiffer lacks the ethnic involvement of, say, Odets or even Neil Simon is not to dismiss the pertinence of Jewishness entirely. Feiffer's life—from the East Bronx to the *Village Voice* and the theater—has been spent primarily in settings and institutions in which the presence of other Jews has been noticeable. By 1930 a popular history textbook was informing public school children that the Jews were "conspicuously successful in the various forms of theatrical enterprise." The creators of the first of the great comic-book heroes, Superman, were, like the three founders of the *Voice* itself, Jews. They were among those who shaped the institutions and values within which an artist like Feiffer operated, and therefore, must have exerted some influence on his vision of the Americans who populate his cartoons and plays. True, it is possible to exaggerate the importance of locale to an author's development. . . . But it would be impossible to divorce Feiffer's stance and style from his lifelong residence in New York, from the pungent wit, nervous energy, open anxieties, quickness and rancor that so many other New Yorkers have defined as sophistication. The city's inhabitants accepted the thrusts of psychoanalysis more easily than the Viennese or Middle Americans have, and this appropriation of the Freudian vocabulary in daily life is also reflected in Feiffer's work. The ambience that he has absorbed has been largely devoid of deliberate incorporation of Jewish religious culture and themes, and is entirely secular in orientation. Nevertheless, the flavor and spirit of that ambience has been heavily and unmistakably Jewish, as though amplifying the jocular definition of an assimilationist as one who only associates with Jews who refuse to associate with Jews. (pp. 178-79)

From the status of outsiders, from the distancing or maginality, many Jews have indeed developed a combative stance toward the rest of society, even after allegiance to Judaism itself has evaporated. "To the degree that there is anti-Semitism in the world, I acknowledge being Jewish," David Levine has proclaimed. "In the same sense, when cartooning is ridiculed, I confess to being a cartoonist." Feiffer's actual relationship to his ethnic origins may not be much more positive than that; but his satiric animus, his leftist perspective, his urban irony, and his psychoanalytic spirit help give his work a Jewish component in the sense that a Jew is most likely to have created it.

Whether that work is of enduring significance is, of course, another question. Satire, in George S. Kaufman's *bon mot,* "is what closes Saturday night"; and posterity rarely revises such quick and devastating judgments. The targets of satire may suffer from familiarity, given the constancy of human affairs; and its humor may leave audiences wondering whether it seemed funny at the time. Feiffer may have realized these dangers and may be trying to get be-

yond satire. Yet to do so may be too subversive of his own talent, which has been to serve as a touchstone of the fashions and follies of his time. It is true that his plays tend to be subjugated to a thesis, which may limit their appeal, even as delusiveness, political chicanery, and sexual stereotyping persist. It is true that Feiffer's capacity for breathing the semblance of life into his characters is undeveloped; but if that were the test of mature art, Damon Runyon would be considered a better writer than Samuel Beckett. It is also true that Feiffer's range is restricted, for he cannot find quite as much dignity and value in life as others have managed to do. As the narrator of his novel **Ackroyd** puts it, "I see like a cop; I see prejudicially; I collect evidence; what can't be included as evidence is not seen; doesn't exist." What Feiffer has seen, however, has been reported with gem-cutting precision; and the requirement to be uplifting as well is demeaning and antagonistic to the imperatives of art, Feiffer's included.

It might also be recalled that what helps make life bearable is the exposition of its incongruities in comic modes. Few of Feiffer's contemporaries have been as unerring and as unsparing in the representation of folly. Few have shown such clarity in the perforation of the confusions, the rationalizations, the deceptions behind which we hide. Few contemporary artists have drawn healthier laughter from pumping irony into the solitude and sadness that may be intrinsic to life. (pp. 179-80)

> *Stephen J. Whitfield, "Jules Feiffer and the Comedy of Disenchantment," in* From Hester Street to Hollywood: The Jewish-American Stage and Screen, *edited by Sarah Blacher Cohen, Indiana University Press, 1983, pp. 167-82.*

## John Simon

Unlike the Caricaturist—Daumier, for instance—who speaks through his art, the cartoonist—say, Jules Feiffer—speaks mostly through the balloons that issue from his characters. The drawing merely sugarcoats the message, makes the consumer feel that he is bypassing the stodgy, old medium of print for the liberated, indeed anarchic, medium of the comic strip. It is very much as a cartoonist, then, that Feiffer turned to the theater in 1967 with his first full-length play, **Little Murders.** His characters, like his cartoon figures, mainly stand there, changing their expressions only minimally, while their tongues send up trial balloons that condemn the world mostly through themselves: their disconnectedness, their dementia, their stupidity. The play rode in on the shirttails of the theater of the absurd, which had just run its course from France and England to America, where all movements come to expire, and, by George—or Sam, or Eugene, or Harold—it worked.

It is the story of Patsy Newquist, a young woman so strong as to eat up her boyfriends, limp-souled creatures like her father, who rages at his effeminate given name, Carol, or limp-wristed wraiths like her brother, Kenny, who spends most of his time on the toilet when not dressing up in Patsy's clothes. Her mother, Marjorie, is one of those quietly tyrannical martyrs whose self-pity is razor-sharp with the edge turned outward. Alfred, Patsy's new swain and husband-to-be, is strong enough to resist being made over by Patsy: an "apathist" who doesn't defend himself when, quite regularly, mugged by weaker men. "Getting your face beat in doesn't hurt?" queries Carol. "Not if you daydream. Muggers tend to get very depressed if you hum all the while." He is also impervious to Patsy's romanticizing zeal, and lives for his work (wildly successful photographs of excrement) and sleep. "What about sex?" asks the despairing Patsy. Answer: "It helps to sleep better." She confesses defeat: How can she mold Alfred into what she wants "if you're not even there when I want to mold you"?

Meanwhile, New York City is going to hell, what with people being shot at from sidewalks and windows if they so much as dare go out grocery-shopping. It is not just benign mugging and robbery; it is universal viciousness that views other people as an invitation to pleasurable target practice. The city is littered with, among other things, the contents of bullet-riddled shopping bags and the victims of unsolved murders. The police force is as corrupt as it is inept; the citizens are arming and barricading themselves. Through the window comes the lethal calling card of the sniper; on the phone, repeatedly, the call of the breather. How funny this was on Broadway in 1967, and, again, off Broadway in 1969. But in between came 1968, and the world started coming unhinged. *Little Murders* stopped being funny hyperbole and was well on its way to becoming dismaying truth. . . .

Jokes about rampaging transvestism, atheistic hippie ministers, ubiquitous governmental prying into privacy, murder for the sheer fun of it are no longer in good taste—no longer even jokes. (p. 108)

John Simon, "Draw Me a Drama," in New York *Magazine, Vol. 20, No. 21, May 25, 1987, pp. 108, 110.*

## Gerald Weales

[In *Anthony Rose,* Feiffer] is once again enmeshed in the parents-and-children concatenation that last engrossed him on stage in *Grown Ups* (1981).

This time, his protagonist is a father and a successful Broadway playwright. Anthony Rose turns up in Kansas City, where a revival of a twenty-five-year-old play of his, *The Parent Lesson,* is in rehearsal, and proceeds to rewrite it, making the father, who long ago abandoned his children, into a sympathetic character, and the grown sons, his victims, into his cruel accusers. He also drives away the actor signed to play the father and takes over the role himself; he reduces the director to the stuttering boy who could never face his own disapproving father; and wins the woman whom the original script assigned to one of the sons.

As one would expect, Feiffer's play is knowledgeably amusing about the ways of actors and writers, the process of creating and staging plays, but its primary concern is with the family as inevitable trap. In the next-to-last scene,

Rose reveals that he has abandoned his own (ungrateful?) family and has tried with no success to find a substitute for them in theater after theater across the country. Now he announces to the assembled players, "you are my family," and, as the director takes us stammeringly into the rehearsal, we see that a new disaster is aborning. It is a very effective moment, a fine open-ended ending that leaves what is coming to the audience's imagination.

Unfortunately, the play does not end there. In a final scene, set three years later in a television studio in Hollywood, we meet most of the principals again, learn specifically and unnecessarily what actually happened, and get satirical comment on the mock-seriousness of concerned TV that begins to pull us toward the political Feiffer. Up to this point, Feiffer's comedy has fed his serious theme; in the last scene, that theme—although still visible—is obscured by a fairly obvious guying of television. If, like Anthony Rose, Feiffer decides to rewrite, I hope he drops the final scene.

Gerald Weales, "Faulty Families," in Commonweal, *Vol. CXVI, No. 21, December 1, 1989, p. 676.*

## Clive Barnes

Nearly 20 years ago (19 if someone is still counting) the cartoonist/writer Jules Feiffer and the director Mike Nichols collaborated on a much-praised movie that cast a shrill, acerbic and misogynistic eye on the Battle of the Sexes—American style—and called it *Carnal Knowledge.*

That eye now seems a little less shrill, a little less acerbic and certainly less misogynistic. Feiffer and Nichols have not simply aged with the years—they have mellowed. But the eye remains a little cock-eyed in its view, still staring bloodshot through jaundice-colored glasses.

In their latest venture—an altogether less ambitious view of sexual skirmishing called *Elliot Loves*—among Feiffer's many amusing aphorisms about sex in the '90s is the firmly, if jokingly, stated "sex without guilt has no moral dimension," which seems to be just what one was supposed to have learned from their *Carnal Knowledge.*

Feiffer's Elliot, an amiable, slightly prissy wimp, opens . . . with a monologue, addressed directly to us, explaining how and why he has fallen in love with Joanna, a woman with style, a barracuda chuckle, two divorces and two children.

The play is the story of their wooing—or rather a report from the trenches of an incident in their wooing.

It is the night Joanna has been invited to meet Elliot's three great High School buddies. They have been asked to dinner by the only one still married—Bobby and his wife Vera. Present at the party are Phil a prickly recovering alcoholic, and Larry an agreeable slob whose main claim to fame appears to be that he pushed his former wife's car off a cliff in a rather drastic form of divorce settlement.

At first Joanna balks with stage fright in the apartment lobby, refusing to accompany Elliot up. Later, unexpectedly relenting; she arrives after dinner, when the men are alone, contemplating the past, and—Phil apart—drinking up a storm.

Joanna and Elliot quarrel, part—and the episode, and for that matter the play, ends with their late-night phone call.

The play is not so much a slice of life as a slice of character, or characters, and the slicing is neat and painless. And hits you straight on the funny bone.

Feiffer is perhaps at his best, most telling and most insightful when he is trying to be least profound. He has very properly moved from the cartoon-like incisiveness of his first play, *Little Murders* , to a broader, more humanistic approach, which unfortunately first resulted in such heavy-handed inquiries into American middle-class angst as *Grown Ups* and *Hold Me!*

*Elliot Loves* presents an altogether clearer, sharper and less pretentious, while still satirical and knowing, image

of the way we are, and in its comparatively modest sketch-like way it seems totally successful, not to mention hilarious.

Feiffer is beautiful when he is worming out the lies and deceptions we tell ourselves—by exaggerating truth, he finds the essential in the caricature. . . .

Somehow—and this represents my reservation about it—the play never quite offers the insights it clearly thinks it is delivering. [*Elliot Loves*] has a certain smugness where its pain should be, and both Feiffer and Nichols, just as they did years ago in *Carnal Knowledge,* appear to be standing back with the satisfied manner of conjurors having revealed an illusion, rather than artists having shown a truth.

*Clive Barnes, "Feiffer Eyes Sex in the '90s," in*
New York Post, *June 8, 1990.*

# Sylvia Fraser

## 1935-

(Born Sylvia Meyers) Canadian novelist, journalist, and autobiographer.

In her novels, Fraser candidly portrays the emotional trauma caused by antagonistic relationships between the sexes. Her fiction commonly depicts characters who feel encumbered by their social positions but eventually reexamine them and realize their ability to change. Although her novels often address acts of violence and sexual abuse, the ever-present possibility for change ultimately renders her work optimistic. The prevalence of cruelty in Fraser's work has autobiographical basis. She was sexually molested by her father for nearly fifteen years. To distance herself from these violations, Fraser developed a split personality and suppressed memories of these events until she was forty-eight years old. Fraser believes that the abuse she suffered and her subsequent uncontrollable temper as a child strongly influenced her five novels, resulting in scenes of severe brutality. She commented: "I wasn't deliberately setting out to write books full of sexual violence, but that's the way it would end up."

Fraser worked for eleven years as a journalist for the *Toronto Star Weekly* before turning to fiction. Her first novel, *Pandora,* an autobiographical work, was lauded as an insightful look into the mind of a child. Growing up during World War II, the title character witnesses social injustice and cruelty, but retains her positive outlook on life. One of the novel's main themes is the development of sexual roles: as boys become more aggressive, girls form cliques, mimicking the patterns of their parents and teachers. Pandora disrupts this seemingly fatalistic pattern by defying both her father and male schoolmates. A similar defiance of gender roles pervades Fraser's next novel, *The Candy Factory.* The narrator, Mary Moon, creates "everyday miracles" in the lives of people in the candy factory where she lives, enabling them to escape such roles as "wife," "chauvinist," and "boss." Condemning the materialism and superficiality epitomized by candy, Fraser emphasizes the individual's capacity to evolve. Many critics thought that the author's self-conscious style distanced Fraser's readers from her characters. Similar criticism followed Fraser's next novel, *A Casual Affair: A Modern Fairytale,* which chronicles the relationship of a nameless man and woman. Allegorical elements and stilted language in this work make it similar to a children's fairytale.

Fraser's historical novels, *The Emperor's Virgin* and *Berlin Solstice,* turn away from the plight of modern relationships, focusing instead on the decline of society. The scenes of rape and molestation in Fraser's earlier works are also found in *The Emperor's Virgin;* however, the explicit sexual violence in this novel was considered gratuitous by many critics. Barbara Campbell wrote: "Sylvia Fraser focuses so intensely on sordid sexuality and brutal violence that her story never gets off the ground. . . . De-

scriptions of shocking brutality, promiscuity and homosexual abuse continually interrupt the story." Set in first-century Rome, *The Emperor's Virgin* is the tale of a vestal virgin deflowered by the Emperor Domitian, then condemned and buried alive. *Berlin Solstice* chronicles the rise of Nazism and addresses similar atrocities in the personage of Kurt Schmidt. Swept up in the enthusiasm of the National Socialist Movement, Schmidt becomes an SS officer responsible for eliminating "undesirables," including his own retarded son and homosexual brother-in-law. Fraser's detailed descriptions of World War II-era Germany were admired for their assiduity.

*My Father's House: A Memoir of Incest and Healing* is Fraser's autobiographical account of her incestuous relationship with her father that subsequently affected her adult interactions with men and indirectly colored her fiction. At a young age the author developed a second personality, "the Girl Who Knows," who took over her consciousness whenever she was molested; this personality provides a second voice in the autobiography. Fraser divides the narrative between the block print account of her life and italicized passages of memories and dreams only recently recovered. Critics hailed *My Father's House* as an important addition to literature on child abuse, and praised Fraser for her frankness on a sensitive topic.

(See also *Contemporary Authors,* Vols. 45-48 and *Contemporary Authors New Revision Series,* Vols. 1, 16.)

## PRINCIPAL WORKS

NOVELS

*Pandora*   1972
*The Candy Factory*   1975
*A Casual Affair: A Modern Fairytale*   1978
*The Emperor's Virgin*   1980
*Berlin Solstice*   1985

OTHER

*My Father's House: A Memoir of Incest and Healing* 1988

---

### Rae McCarthy

*Pandora* is about the growth of one small girl, Pandora Gothic, from July, 1937, when she is still a pre-schooler, to the spring of 1944 when she leaves the second grade. Pandora is a passionate, sometimes violent, little girl, daughter of a lower middle-class family, going to public school during the years of World War II; the war, though never of direct interest, tinges the atmosphere of the novel with black shadows and creates an underlying sense of strain and fatigue that is as effective as it is muted. Pandora's mother is an anxious, martyred woman whose life seems to consist in drab household economics, a religion that teaches acceptance, and a healthy terror of her husband. The father is a one-handed butcher who spends his evenings playing monopoly with imaginary financial giants, bullies his wife and children, envies his brother and is pathetic in his frustrated rage.

One of the most singular features of *Pandora* is its point of view. Many of the observations and impressions are the little girl's own; Fraser has created an imaginatively direct, concrete and vivid language to support this device. . . . Extending beyond the central core of Pandora's consciousness, yet merging smoothly with it, is the voice of the narrator who sees and re-creates a world around Pandora while recording the child's reactions to it.

This multiple viewpoint results in several layers of matter and meaning. There is Pandora's personal story, full of her growing awareness, her sensual notation of objects, people, and experiences as she makes friends, plays around the neighbourhood, goes to a birthday party, visits her grandmothers, and so on. Though much of this story is told in the innocent manner of Pandora's own thought, Fraser blends into it such a richness of authorial humour and insight that almost every reader will recognize some of his own experiences in those of Pandora.

Then there is the matter that goes beyond Pandora and

scans the environment in which she is placed. Fraser's observations of society sometimes recall the gentle irony of a Leacock recording the foibles, laughable, but not unlikeable, of his people. . . . At other times, the tone darkens to a grim objectivity that bespeaks an underlying rage against the wrongs of society; occasionally, this objectivity assumes the pose of a dispassionate and analytical sociologist. . . .

Fraser is adept at brushing obliquely across nerves, across pain and ugliness, without invoking them directly. The effect is to build up a kind of tingling suspense and an acute consciousness of the forms that mask our evils. Perhaps the one weakness of *Pandora* is that this type of social satire in places ceases to be oblique and gains a prominence that becomes a trifle heavy handed. For instance, when Fraser names the triumvirate of school boys who are beating up a Jewish classmate Jessie Christie, Horace Ghostie, and Godfrey Trumps, the allusion to the Trinity seems to me to add very little to the novel, and the chief impression is of a too-contrived device. Though Fraser is concerned with the sense of guilt with which our society burdens the natural child, the same point could have been made without the rather awkward religious symbolism.

However, the great strength of Fraser's novel, the quality that redeems its flaws, is its larger awareness. Fraser has taken *Pandora* beyond mere notation and anecdote and beyond social comment and made it, ultimately, a compassionate expression of her understanding of man's existence. As the little girl gropes painfully between social compromise and some truer self, as she learns to hide her instinctive fear of her peers in a show of bravado, as she grapples with what she feels and what she is told she should feel, as she meets the devastating fact of death, she becomes the representative of mankind. Pandora is not only an appropriate name for this particular tempestuous child; it is Fraser's word for man's whole troubled condition. The final section of the novel is entitled "Love", and love, as Fraser sees it, is man's only hope. Pandora's parents, themselves the deformed children of mankind's mistakes, in an inarticulate spirit of loving sacrifice, decide to try to give Pandora "Another Sort of Life". In the context of the novel this gesture becomes the sign of our hope for the future. And finally, it is the quality of love in Fraser's presentation of her people that raises this novel above the merely skilful. (pp. 701, 703-04)

> *Rae McCarthy, in a review of "Pandora," in* The Dalhousie Review, *Vol. 52, No. 4, Winter, 1972-73, pp. 701, 703-04.*

### Pat Barclay

*Pandora* is deceptive. Although at first glance it appears to be little more than a brilliantly-written description of a war-time Ontario childhood, in reality it is as packed with abstractions as the mythical Pandora's Box. In fact, the book is really an allegory, making it closer akin to *Lord of the Flies* than to *Anne of Green Gables.*

Unlike William Golding, however, Ms. Fraser does not explore the concept of original sin. The evils of Pandora's world, while equally as brutalizing as those on Ralph's island, are present simply as a fact of life, and coexist with that other abstraction which the original Pandora discovered at the bottom of the Box: Hope.

Virtually all of the young Pandora's immediate surroundings demonstrate a divided reality. She has twin sisters who do not like her but will not "tell on" her, and who are addicted to the exasperating practice of reading aloud, "sentences turnabouts". Her mother is pious and self-effacing; her father, a butcher, is a sadistic brute with a steel hook for a left hand. Grannie Cragg is an illiterate but likeable witch with a camomile lawn; Other Grandma, who makes lace and lies in wait for death amid decaying splendour, once danced with Neville Chamberlain. Even Pandora, with her princess-golden curls, has a "double-crown, where the Devil touched her and her hair won't lie flat." And Charlie, her adored cat, came from a garbage-can and has fleas.

In the outside world it is the same. The nice breadman lets her drive his horses and then molests her. The unholy trinity of classroom bad boys bears the names Jessie Christie, Howard Ghostie, and Godfrey Trumps. Rosie, Pandora's giddy glamour-girl aunt who rides a red bicycle and works in the munitions factory, attempts suicide. And Ruth-Ann Baltimore, her anxious-to-be-diplomatic best friend, succeeds in being "mean" to every girl in the class, causing Pandora to ponder the question, "How come the NICE people miss seeing so much?"

Mercilessly, Ms. Fraser introduces the horrors expected of war into life in Pandora's small ken. When the school principal (Col. Burns) makes a scapegoat of an innocent Jewish child, when Jessie Christie tortures a cat, when we squirm at the mindless violence of Pandora's own father, we are brought to the realization that life can be evil anywhere. "Open your eyes, nice people of the world," says Ms. Fraser in effect, "you have nothing to lose but your scales."

Poor Pandora, who is imaginative and sensitive as well as brave, independent, pretty and clever, has a hard time comprehending it all. In her dreams and when, as a punishment, she is shoved into the basement winter storage vault, her mind teams with the grisly stories she has heard her elders repeat. The divided reality becomes one, and the wrong one:

> Pandora smells mothballs. Blue gas rises in a cloud. . . . Her green eyes bleed, then pop, first the right, then the left. Her lungs sear, expand, explode. She claws the gas chamber with the bloody stumps of her paws. . . .

In the end, however, Pandora triumphs. She finds a way to defeat Jessie Christie; now she is strong, too. (pp. 109-10)

. . . *Pandora's* prose style is original and impressive. Its pages sparkle with metaphor and divert us with carefully-researched 1940's detail, from Pandora's Sisman scampers to the uncomfortable hickory bench at the bank. Dozens of quiet jokes reward the attentive reader. (The heroine's full name, for example, is Pandora Gothic.)

Apart from an occasional lapse into sociological jargon,

only the final pages of the novel mar Ms. Fraser's *tour de force:* Other Grandma leaves a small legacy, and Pandora's parents decide to save it to help finance their daughter's future education. Pandora is to have "Another Sort of Life".

Presumably this device is our insurance that Good, or at least Hope, will continue to fight the forces of Evil. Although, allegorically speaking, it is sound enough, on the realistic level it is less successful. In addition to our difficulty in believing in the generosity of either Other Grandma or Pandora's father, there is the matter of Education as the Answer. Perhaps Rationality is what Ms. Fraser really had in mind. (p. 110)

> Pat Barclay, "Rationality in Mind," in Canadian Literature, No. 60, Spring, 1974, pp. 109-10.

### Rae McCarthy MacDonald

*The Candy Factory* is clearly related to *Pandora* in its central vision—the power of compassionate love to work everyday or "human" miracles. The novel is set, as the title suggests, in a candy factory where concern with profits, packaging, advertising, and candy coatings represents the qualities Fraser is intent on exposing—materialism, superficiality, cynicism, and hypocrisy. The first chapter introduces Mary Moon, an antique and virginal employee of the factory who lives in its attic. So bland a nonentity is she that the other employees scarcely know when they have last seen her, though her presence is always marked by the strong scent of powdered roses. Mary Moon, on the other hand, on her nightly patrol of the candy factory, sees and notes everything, especially clues to the unhappy lives of her fellow employees. The second chapter introduces the depraved one-eyed tramp who inhabits the sewers of the factory. Mary Moon, apparently titillated by danger, invites him to her attic where he rapes, and is about to kill, her when she proposes a partnership in the manufacture of "human" miracles, the very commodity in which the tramp has lost all faith. The tramp, amused at the idea, pauses a second, and the chapter ends with the reader unsure of Mary Moon's fate. Each of the following chapters describes one or two of the candy factory employees in whom Mary Moon has taken an interest and tells of the everyday miracles that happen to transform their lives—always accompanied by the unexplained scent of powdered roses in the air. (p. 559)

To repeat, the connection of *The Candy Factory* with *Pandora* is plain. Both are conservatively optimistic about man and offer a vision of redemption, however limited, through love. But *The Candy Factory* fails to fulfil *Pandora's* promise. There is a disappointing plastic quality about the second novel. Characters lack dimension, are stock figures—the society wife, the glamorous, but frustrated, rich man, the career woman, the flower child. Equally facile psychoanalyses of these characters are offered: the key to the rich man's real heart is a reminder of an aborted fetus that a past mistress had viciously presented him as his own; the tramp is the animal he is because he spent his boyhood in war-time France where he lived by selling the dismembered bodies of the dead to their relatives. This kind of subject has a certain shock value, but it is not sufficient to make the reader believe in Fraser's characters. However, that Fraser is not afraid to attempt such effects is, perhaps, to her credit, and her daring is sometimes rewarded. There are several ugly, but intense and effective, sexual encounters; a more timid writer would have avoided them. Several comic scenes, which could well have turned out cliche or unbelievable, are the best element of the novel. . . . At its best . . . the plasticity of the characters and their contrived situations is funny and works as a parody of candy factory society. Unfortunately, this same quality more often creates an impression of glibness and undermines the depth of the novel's vision of the power of love. A tendency to excess that started Gothic echoes in *Pandora* has become pop art in *The Candy Factory,* and the exchange, on the whole, is unprofitable. (p. 60)

> *Rae McCarthy MacDonald, in a review of "The Candy Factory," in* The Dalhousie Review, *Vol. 55, No. 3, Autumn, 1975, pp. 558-60.*

### Francis Mansbridge

Candy factories can be ambivalent places. The manufacture of candies can be as mundane and pointless as the process in any factory—even more so as their product is useless from a practical point of view. Yet this uselessness allows for the possibility of play. Who could devote his entire life to producing a better hard centre? So in Sylvia Fraser's [*The Candy Factory*] the candy factory becomes a suitable metaphor for our contemporary society. Pointless work alternates with other activity which acquires various levels of meaning as the characters struggle to achieve or maintain an uneasy truce with the world around them.

. . . Eleven different characters are explored in depth, while a number of others revolve on the fringes. This scope helps create a rich texture to the novel, although the tendency is for the characters to become stereotyped, each representing a different type of person in society. Fraser tries to avoid this through a detailed exploration of the background of each character, but even at their best they do not stick in the imagination. (p. 104)

All the characters are crippled in their understanding of life, but not hopelessly so. The book is suffused with hope that the narrowness of each character can be broadened. In the opening chapters Mary Moon, the eternal optimist, confronts a Tramp, the ultimate cynic. Optimism wins out. As Mary Moon says:

> "Look in my Special Accounts Book! I have it all worked out—a program of modest miracles, *human* miracles, the very thing you have soured on!"

Human miracles, as the book demonstrates, are at least conceivable.

Ms. Fraser's prose style is as vivid as in *Pandora,* her first novel, although there are parts, especially in her description of the Tramp, which are over-written. The repetitive rhythm and occasionally the phrasing appear to owe something to early Beckett. At its best her style has the stark penetration of Beckett's work, although too often she becomes involved in long sociological dissertations, at best mildly interesting, and at worst boring.

In spite of its readability, the novel is less successful than *Pandora.* The brilliant style often threatens to overwhelm the characters. What is lacking is the impression that her work is as deeply felt as it is keenly perceived. In *The Candy Factory* the novelist is too much the manipulator of the action, and not sufficiently the creator of a convincing fictional world. (p. 105)

> *Francis Mansbridge, "A Better Hard Centre,"*
> *in* Canadian Literature, *No. 71, Winter, 1976,*
> *pp. 104-05.*

### Michael Taylor

[Sylvia Fraser's] *The Candy Factory,* exhibits determination to be original, clever and witty using language in a forceful and often startling manner. She yokes disparate conceits together with considerable verve, so that the constructions of her prose often seem closer to those of the seventeenth-century Metaphysical poets than to those of most contemporary novelists. Her revelling in the rich confectionary of language includes Shakespearean techniques, such as the fusing of the vividly specific with the abstract:

> "Oh, they gave me Thomas Aquinas to help trace my nail of apple cores back to the Garden, but anyone that far out on the forked tongue of disbelief can never do any thing but hiss and quibble on his belly through the tares and thistles of sincere regrets"

Apart from the odd couplings, the "forked tongue of disbelief" and the "tares and thistles of sincere regrets," the self-advertising cleverness of "to help trace my trail of apple cores back to the Garden," and the oddity of "quibble" (with its homonymic suggestion of "quiver") in association with "hiss" and "belly" mark Sylvia Fraser's use of language as self-conscious in the extreme.

Linguistically, then, *The Candy Factory* may offer too clotted a diet for many readers: the candies are rather gooey in their centres. Or perhaps the factory should have operated on a shorter work week. Beau Whitehead's self-analysis, quoted above, is no isolated phenomenon from a stylistic point of view. Its heavy decoration can't really be ascribed to its speaker's character, although there is an attempt throughout the novel to vary somewhat the literary quality of the style to match the consciousness of each chapter's protagonist. Sam Ryan, for example, speaks and thinks in a speedier, more idiomatic version of literary English:

> Sam braked himself. The baby blue image of Laurie Temple kept freezing into that of another "cool" broad who hadn't cracked under the heat of Sammy's passion. Linda the Lady—ice cream clear through, from the frosted strawberry smile right down to the frozen cherry at the bottom.

Matching the coagulations of language are excursions by the book's characters into realms of quasi-mystical and symbolic happenings: the only "clear" chapter dealing with the straight-forward love-affair between Danny, desperately afraid of revealing his need for dependancy, and Daphne, reluctantly in love with a man who alternates between affection and contempt, heavily laced with self-contempt.

Each chapter of *The Candy Factory* deals with one or a couple of the factory's employees or employers. The book begins with Mary Moon, a forgotten employee living a semi-literary life in the factory's dusty loft, who is raped and, I think, murdered by the artist-tramp who lives in the sewers of the basement. We then progress through the various echelons of the company until we reach its president, Charles X. Hunter, and his wife, Celeste. As one might expect, both are shown to be living the ultimate "candied" existence, unfulfilled, artificial, devoted to keeping up the appearance of the efficient, humane executive and the gracious hostess. Their story climaxes the novel's concern with appearance and reality, with the tug of opposites and contraries in the minds of human beings. . . . Charles X. Hunter performs the ultimate act of dispossession by divesting himself of the candy factory, making it over to his newly energized wife, and, with heavy structural symbolism, mounts the stairs to Mary Moon's loft to experience, one imagines, death at the hands of the manic tramp, disguised as Mary Moon. This, no doubt, completes the allegorical scheme of the factory as a representation of life in our decadent, candy civilization.

A peculiar feature of the novel's excessive literary style is its use in exploring what seem to me to be rather revolting acts of sex, excretion and violence. *The Candy Factory* clearly asks us to gorge ourselves to the point of sickness and nausea, but I, for one, prefer plainer, more homely fare. (pp. 112-13)

> *Michael Taylor, in a review of "The Candy Factory," in* The Fiddlehead, *No. 108, Winter, 1976, pp. 112-13.*

## E. L. Bobak

The subtitle of *A Casual Affair* is "a modern fairytale", and predictably, the book is a fairytale in reverse. The prince does rescue the princess, but only by accident; they do not live happily ever after. The prince does not slay the dragon, but tries to slay the princess, etc. The reader may derive some light entertainment from playing this game, or he may be bored with the ease with which he learns the rules. The book stays lightweight with or without this baggage. Its main title describes it well enough.

Scattered throughout the main narrative are eight parables which supply authorial commentary on it. "The Unhappy Prince", for example, elucidates the male protagonist's oedipal relationship with his mother. The parables are heavily ironic and seem like more baggage, as the narrative is clear enough without them. However, hunting down the parallels between main plot and interspersed tales provides more light entertainment for the reader.

The modern fairytale is about a "tall, elegant" man with "pewter hair" (the prince) who drives a white Lincoln, and who has a casual affair with a "slender woman with pale blonde hair" (the princess) who lives in a Glass Tower and drives a Rolls Royce Silver Shadow. They are never named. The princess is bored with her husband and believes they are both "imprisoned" by their marriage. She wants the prince to supply a "miracle" for her, that is, make the break-up of her marriage "count for something". The prince, when confronted with this request, laughs "without mirth". Who wouldn't? She plans to supply a miracle too: she is going to believe in him enough so that he will learn to believe in himself. "For you, that would be the miracle", she remarks. The prince is attracted to her, and though he does not believe in her "life-saving course", he signs up. Any relationship based on these tired old premises is doomed from the beginning, and theirs culminates in attempted murder and suicide. However, while the princess is recovering in the hospital, she learns "to listen to her body from the inside", and envisages yet another miracle, this one based on the integration of eastern and western traditions of thought, that is, according to Fraser, the intuitive and the rational: "She believed that the integration of East and West would bring about an evolution of homo sapiens to a new plateau: Part of the continuing evolution from animal consciousness to human consciousness to cosmic consciousness". In a concession to her view of reality, the prince presents her with a pair of white jade earrings he had purchased for her at the beginning of the affair, but had never been able to bring himself to give her. We have already been supplied with the information that green jade is for wisdom and white jade for truth. The casual affair has proven to the princess that the old codes are emotionally and spiritually bankrupt, and on the strength of her belief in the new miracle, she rows off on a lake alone at night. A secure belief in solitary risk-taking is the current cliché.

That our basic sympathy should be with the princess is undeniable, but Fraser fails to make us believe that a woman given to lengthy and self-righteous psychological dissections of other people (even if they are emotionally hollow men) can ever merit it. . . . Author and heroine share the same shortcoming: they perceive without understanding. A commitment to both character and writer would be easier to drum up if they were the sort that merited green jade earrings.

The author preaches as well as the princess. Fraser sacrifices consistency of tone and atmosphere to insert a feminist statement in the text: "The seventies were a good period in which to be single. The two-by-two society was breaking down. . . . She especially treasured her female friends. . . . " One must reassure oneself that this is indeed the same book that begins, "He parked his white Lincoln in the No Parking zone in front of The Glass Tower. . . . "

Dialogue is wooden and embarrassing. When the prince remarks that he won't be able to see the princess more often than he does, she replies, "That's okay. When two people touch as completely as we have, there's a long, slow afterglow". These barely credible conversational exchanges are enlivened by one-liners like "You're not a bastard. You're a moralist in bastard's drag". But the throwaway line is designed for effect and works best when it is an independent entity. Placed next to the heavy weight of "Until you square your actions with your inner code, you'll always be like Kafka's K . . . ", the wit loses its force. Occasionally it works, when the tone is light, for example, in the car coming back from London when the princess remarks that there's nothing worse than a moralist who doesn't smoke your brand. But most of the time dialogue that should be fluid is laboured and lacks authenticity. (pp. 370-72)

> *E. L. Bobak, in a review of "A Casual Affair: A Modern Fairytale," in* The Dalhousie Review, *Vol. 58, No. 2, Summer, 1978, pp. 370-72.*

## Susan Wood

Sylvia Fraser's third novel, *A Casual Affair,* claims attention for what it hopes to do—but not for what it actually does. Subtitled "a modern fairytale," it pretends to offer both the simplicity and the universality of the traditional fairy tale. As Michael Hornyansky says in his essay "The Truth of Fables," the classic fairy tales "are in fact not children's stories at all but folktales from the half-conscious wisdom of the race, expressing in mythic form certain enduring human truths." You don't have to be a neo-Freudian like Bruno Bettleheim, author of *The Uses of Enchantment,* to recognize that "The Sleeping Beauty," "The Princess on the Glass Hill" and "Beauty and the Beast" do embody universal patterns: the individual released into the adult world, the maimed soul made whole and beautiful by love. Fraser's story embodies elements (and ironic inversions) of these and other tales, and is, moreover, punctuated with fables about princes and princesses, unicorns and doomed white cats. However, the unconvincing affair between young She and old He doesn't offer much insight into "enduring human truth." (p. 130)

The characters are—He and She. In fairy tales, as Max Luthi points out in *Once Upon a Time: On the Nature of Fairy Tales,* the characters "are not personally delineated; the fairy tale is not concerned with individual destinies." In a long modern novel, however, such abstraction is only affectation, especially combined with innumerable realistic details about white jade earrings, Bloody Marys, and the furnishings of various bedrooms. (p. 131)

The woman's situation I find plausible enough; indeed, it has great potential power. Sheltered, passive, wanting someone else to rescue her from a dead marriage, She falls in love with the *idea* of the affair, and believes, must fiercely believe, that she loves the man she casts as the rescuer—despite the fact that she barely knows him, and discovers only crudity, cruelty, and lies. . . . Yet the complexities of this all-too-common projection aren't explored. What She wants to see in him is clear enough. But what does He, casually moving from bed to bed, see in her after the first dismal weekend? Does he want to be "saved"? We don't know; and we soon stop caring. There's no psychological depth to this tale, only psychobabble.

The scattered fairytales, while rather more interesting than the novel, are not really satisfying. They're too obviously comments on the text (which is obtrusively symbolic to begin with) and too arch. In the first one, "How the Scullery Maid Came to the Glass Tower," for instance, the scullery maid is humiliated when she claims to be a princess; in fact, she's raped by a snake. (This is a modern fairy tale.) She's rescued by the miller's son, and their need for each other ennobles them so that "they lived happily ever after—for at least ten years." Exit fairy tale, enter self-conscious irony.

Fairy tales aren't "modern." They're timeless. One of Fraser's problems, as I've indicated, may simply be her form: the gap between the simple, highly resonant fairy tale and the complex novel, between "psychic shorthand" and surface-of-life accumulation of detail. Moreover, as Eric Rabkin argues in *The Fantastic in Literature,* "Fantasy represents a basic mode of human knowing; its polar opposite is Reality," the here-and-now. Perhaps the two forms are not compatible. Certainly Fraser does not manage to sustain her allegory convincingly on both the literal and symbolic levels, but moves jarringly between both. He enters the penthouse just as She pricks her finger on a white rose; many pages later the white cat, symbol of her former protected life, is brutally pulped by rush-hour traffic, the "monster" of the real world. In both cases the blood is so overtly symbolic that it isn't real.

The style of fairy tales is simple; yet here the style is both self-conscious and littered with detail, both pretentious and banal. (p. 133)

> *Susan Wood, "The Fairy Tale Affair," in* Essays on Canadian Writing, *No. 11, Summer, 1978, pp. 130-34.*

## I. M. Owen

The setting [of *The Emperor's Virgin*] is imperial Rome in the last year of Domitian's reign, A.D. 95-96. Domitian reigned for 15 years, for the first half of which he seemed to be well-meaning according to his not very bright lights. Then a rebellion of the troops in upper Germany under Antonius Saturninus seemed to transform him, and he became an insane tyrant on the pattern of Caligula and Nero. After he had put to death his cousin Flavius Clemens and banished Clemen's wife on suspicion of being soft on Christianity, Domitian was murdered by a freedman of Clemens.

What makes the historical novel an especially demanding form is that it must aim at two quite separate kinds of excellence: to be a good novel in its own right; and to be historically convincing. On the first count, *The Emperor's Virgin* fails easily. The central character, Maximus Marcus (not, I think, a possible Roman name), has all the personality of a cigar-store Indian and the plot is a string on which hang a series of anatomically detailed copulation scenes of various kinds but uniform dreariness, the big set-piece being the emperor's defloration of the chief vestal virgin. . . .

In a historical novel, some deliberate alterations of fact for the sake of the plot may sometimes be justified—as here, perhaps, the moving of the rebellion of Saturninus from the middle to near the end of the reign. Cross historical errors are another thing, especially if they are going to be so obvious to readers without special knowledge as to destroy all possibility of illusion. A Jewish ambassador complains to Domitian that his soldiers are desecrating the Temple—which, of course, had been destroyed by Domitian's big brother Titus one quarter of a century before. And (a classic howler this) a statue of Domitian is inscribed "Born: October 24, 51 A.D." (Even the Christians hadn't invented the numbering of the years of the Christian era yet.)

But above all the author should be able to imagine what it was like to live in a period when many of the assumptions that were taken for granted were quite different from our own. For example, Tacitus, a contemporary of Domitian, remarks in his account of Titus's Jewish War: "Various portents had occurred at this time, but so sunk in superstition are the Jews and so opposed to all religious practices that they think it wicked to avert the threatened evil by sacrifices." Such clear statements of the enormous differences between then and now are inevitably rare: the author must imagine them, in a way that convinces us. So unaware is Sylvia Fraser of this necessity that she has a Roman, complaining of the numerous nationalities in Rome, say: "We've become a city of mongrels." Now, quite apart from the fact that Rome had been cosmopolitan for a very long time, what she has done here is to impute to a first-century Roman a post-Darwinian notion of racial purity that would never have crossed a Roman mind. Sylvia Fraser would have done better to stick to 20th-century Toronto.

> *I. M. Owen, "Where Have All Deflowerers Gone?" in* Books in Canada, *Vol. 9, No. 4, April, 1980, p. 16.*

## Lois Gottlieb

The irony which pervades [*A Casual Affair: A Modern Fairytale*] results from Fraser's manipulation of three techniques. By using the clichés of pulp romances, Fraser emphasizes the grotesque features of modern mating rituals and de-sentimentalizes the subject. By loosely weaving through the novel the motif of the brave knight rescuing the beautiful princess and the two living happily ever after, Fraser holds up the perfect world of Romance to the modern world, and measures the decay of both. Finally, by alternating the story of love in this "real" world of cliché and exhausted myth with original fairy tales and folk tales, Fraser recasts the lovers' problems in a more simple, often more humorous light. Through these techniques Fraser has tried, unsuccessfully, to impose complexity and significance on her story. But what starts out as a banal relationship between the heel with a heart of brass and the loving woman who waits, in vain, for his reform, remains banal through the end of the novel. (p. 261)

In the context of this novel, . . . exorcism of the romantic fairy tale proves too easy. The modern Knight as chauvinist and the modern Princess as independent woman have not been evenly matched, despite the effort of the objective narrative style to convince us otherwise. According to Fraser's story, love is impossible because the woman is too unafraid, too loving, too ready for risks. By contrast, the man is fearful, ambivalent, and imprisoned by the old rules of the game. He is attracted to the new creature, but he is also terrified by her. Their first attempt at lovemaking is a flop because he becomes impotent after she whispers, "I love you." He redeems himself on his second attempt by carrying out what Fraser portrays as a near rape in a parked car. Clearly, the Knight has to bear the social failures of decades of sex-role stereotyping, since he has also enjoyed his unjust triumphs, but Fraser buries him under a mountain of idiosyncratic defects. When the Princess announces, "The reason love has such a tough time is that the sex that controls it is the one that values it the least," the reader makes a more specific interpretation: this man is too old, too cynical, too harried, too hostile towards women, too satisfied with his glamourous rut.

The novel stacks the deck against fairy tales, against love and happiness emerging from any new style of coupling; it also stacks the deck against the old style of coupling by making conventional marriage—portrayed at one point as a gigantic, voracious snake—a symbol of emotional abuse and social oppression. By forcing the failure of female-male relations, Fraser's novel joins the ranks of other novels by women, both Canadian and American, which explore the same realms and offer the same conclusion: the modern woman is alone.

There is compensation for the woman who rejects the fairy tale and escapes the clutches of the *True Confessions* cliché, as long as she is prepared to take risks. There is adventure, there is knowledge, and there is, for Fraser's woman, a healing immersion in the rough but fruitful sea of life. Unfortunately, Fraser has been so insistent about the abstractness of her characters that it is impossible to be concerned with their fates. The woman who rows herself away from the Yacht Club harbour, in the final scene, and dangerously heads on the dark, glistening waters towards the open seas, is no more substantial than the man who recedes into the polished anonymity of the Club's cocktail party.

What damages the novel far more than stacking the deck and abstracting the life out of the characters, however, is Fraser's choice of tone and style. Parody and mockery are used with an irritating archness and self-consciousness. Further, the bothersome tone of the journalist, kept well in control in *Pandora,* and heard somewhat more often in *The Candy Factory,* is everywhere in evidence in *A Casual Affair*: the perspective which sweeps the 70s and summarizes its impact on men and women in a paragraph has only a superficial ring of truth; the selection of the significant detail (the contents of a medicine cabinet) to interpret the whole (in this case, the history of the marriage of the Knight and his vile wife) is clever but dispensable; the capsule profile of people and events is glib and unconvincing.

The journalist's style, ephemeral and often trivial, conflicts with the artist's aims. And Fraser's aims are, after all, both current and timeless. What can heal the split between mind and body, between what we need and what the world allows? Certainly technology, concern with status and image, hypocrisy, the power of an oppressive past, all widen the split. And while there may have been the possibility, once upon a literary time, that the union of a woman and a man could bring everything back together again, our age, as viewed through Fraser's skeptical eyes, must rid itself of that old lie. But to reject the fairy tale version of integration in favour of some instant attachment to a trendy label, such as the Spiritual Revolution, casts doubt on the integrity of Fraser's argument. (pp. 262-63)

*Lois Gottlieb, "And They Lived Separately Ever After," in* Journal of Canadian Fiction, *Nos. 31/32, 1981, pp. 261-63.*

## Lorna Irvine

A pastiche of traditional popular formulas, [the stories in **The Candy Factory**] slightly alter established codes in order to incorporate contemporary fashions in sexual roles. In toto, the novel is a ghost story, replete with gothic overtones; its chief ghost, Mary Moon, is presented as the author of each story. However, this format seems but a convenient artifice for allowing Mary Moon freedom to interfere with the endings of the seven central stories and to elucidate, in the two framing stories, her reasons for changing the anticipated endings. Yet in spite of certain alterations, she assimilates change without revoking the basic formulas she uses. The novel does not cancel formulaic myths, as it would if its aim were chiefly parodic, but rather reshapes them.

What reshaping occurs? The novel offers as *topos* a contemporary urban world, commercial, mass-producing, faceless. Like the candy produced in the factory of the novel, the characters . . . do fit into confined moulds. On one level, these moulds are their stories, on another their representation as characters within these stories. Essentially, the character moulds, or codes, divide into masculine and feminine; thus, the sexual dynamics of each story are crucial to its development. By no means is this focussing on sexual roles arbitrary but signifies a major assumption in popular fiction: that is, pornography, hard-boiled detective fiction, love story, melodrama (all of which are present in **The Candy Factory**) commonly describe a sexually divided world in which the term 'masculine' denotes activity, aggresiveness, sadism; the term 'feminine' passivity, introversion, masochism. Because these antithetical terms frequently function as nouns instead of adjectives (masculine=man; feminine=woman), the battle between the sexes becomes a major ingredient in formulaic plots. With varying degrees of success, Mary Moon endeavours to reshape this battle both by diminishing the gender specificity of the terms masculine and feminine, and by minimizing their opposition. Thus, although **The Candy Factory** uses and even exaggerates popular fictional roles for its male and female characters, it does so in order to dramatize their frequent absurdities and to suggest their inadequacies in reflecting today's world.

Before they are altered, the seven central stories read like a compilation of contemporary popular fiction. The first,

the story of the tramp, is pornography, a revelation of historical and individual acts of sadism. The tramp emerges from the bowels of the candy factory, the basement of its hierarchical structure, to comment on various struggles for power. But in this story, the power struggle becomes increasingly limited; we are told of the tramp's attacking a woman, an attack that culminates in sexual violation and possible murder. . . . The opposition between the sexes is total. As the female character in this story, Mary Moon figuratively presents herself without a face, the necessary prop for fantasized seduction and rape; she waits, lights candles, stares into a mirror, is "swaddled in a flimsy white gown of antique lineage, slashed low to reveal milky white shoulders and a slender neck." Her masochism invites the tramp's brutality. Images of female helplessness and entrapment increase the sexual tension: "The woman, her hands over her face, began to pray"; she is "like a frightened moth caught in a storm." Thus, the codes of pornography reinforce the dichotomy between men and women that underlies those of the following stories.

The tone of the next story abruptly changes. Conscientiously saccharine, the story of Danny and Daphne depicts the age-old struggle between man's yearning for independence and woman's for protection, the stuff of countless jokes. . . . Their actions seem unreal; Danny performs as if he were "in one of those schmaltzy slow-motion commercials." Significantly, their rigidity results from their efforts to comply with established sexual roles, Danny's that of assertive masculinity, Daphne's of affiliative femininity. An essential conflict is thus programmed into their roles. Represented here as elsewhere in the novel by actual battle imagery, this conflict, this battle between the sexes, dominates the plot. . . . Controlled by the omnipresent advertising of sexual codes, these characters unwittingly expend their energy in protecting themselves from attack rather than in loving each other.

In the next story, Mary Moon shifts to the world of the hard-boiled detective, Sam Ryan, a loner "like Mike Hammer, like Sam Spade." The phallic connotations of these last two names stress the sexual specificity in this genre. For, confined in his behaviour by a limited definition of masculinity (aggressive, tough), the Op has a correspondingly limited understanding of femininity. Like the detectives with whom he associates himself, Sam fluctuates between defining women as sexually frigid or sexually promiscuous. . . . His dehumanization of women is further emphasized in his use of the slang characteristic of this genre—"cool babes," "dames," "whores," "pussycats," "broads"—and in the macho image he attempts to create by plastering his walls with *Playboy* cartoons and photographs. Because his relationships with women are struggles for proof of his masculinity, sexuality again becomes a battle. (pp. 45-7)

Up to this point in **The Candy Factory,** Mary Moon has used three fictional genres in which antagonism between male and female characters is a traditionally accepted necessity of plot development. She turns now to two stories that illustrate more ambiguous kinds of sexual stereotyping. The first, the story of Beau and Morgan, although less formulaic than the previous stories, nonetheless makes use of popular clichés about relationships between men. Its major clichés address homosexuality. Beau is presented as ethereal, sensitive, masochistic; Morgan as physical, tough, sadistic. Both men have had neurotic relationships with their mothers. On one side of the Freudian dilemma, Beau's mother attempts to compensate for an unhappy marriage by enslaving her son. The result is that Beau has spent his adult years attempting to escape from "the sexual feelings" that his mother has aroused in him. In his office, he keeps a replica of Michelangelo's *Pietà,* an image that symbolizes both his passivity and his attitude to women; he can empathize only with the virgin/mother. On the other side, Morgan's black Mama actually commits incest with her son. And this union dominates Morgan's life. . . . Apart from being actors in a suggested formula for gay fiction, the white Beau and the black Morgan illustrate from a different perspective the preserved dichotomy between masculinity and femininity that inevitably results in struggle.

If the story of Beau and Morgan is based on the codes of gay fiction, that of Eve and Brigitte is based on the popularized codes of women's liberation. It too is filled with clichés about women's relationships with each other. Eve, "surer of her shorthand than of her femininity," certainly despises men: "She had had quite enough, this last year, of lovers with burnt-out fuses crawling to her in their tattered Superman suits." Masculine and tough, she is presented as a threatening bitch. But, if she cannot form close relationships with men, neither can she with women. Thus, her struggle with the feminine, passive Brigitte demonstrates yet again a stereotyped sexual antagonism. Although the story presents other hackneyed examples of women's liberation . . . , what it predominantly illustrates is the inability of individual women to cooperate with each other. When Eve and Brigitte come to blows, their physical struggle makes concrete the often abstract tensions that initiate conflict between women in much popular literature.

The sixth and seventh stories are melodramas, the first told from the perspective of the wife, Celeste, the second from that of her husband, Charles. Celeste's character is an amalgam of fantasy (the fairy-tale princess) and middle-class ethics (the self-denying wife and mother). Like Ibsen's Nora, she seems a puppet, manipulated originally by her father and now by her husband. Her doll-filled room with its obsessively frilly decorations stresses her immaturity. . . . Narcissistic and masochistic, Celeste suffers the fate of the passive woman; she has no identity and therefore cannot maintain a mature relationship with her husband. Furthermore, her passivity forces her husband to assume a dictatorial control of the family. Once again, traditionally feminine qualities are pitted against masculine ones so that the battle between the sexes necessarily becomes the major conflict of the plot.

Celeste's melodrama prepares us for Charles'. As the president of the candy factory, he has power and wealth. Both represent his masculinity. But like Celeste, he too has been manipulated; the sexual mores of his ancestral past hang heavily over the present. In his office, a grandfather clock that has belonged to his grandfather, his father, and now

himself loudly reminds him of the patriarchal family with its stress on masculine dominance. But from the wall, his mother's portrait reminds him only of "how she used to call him twenty times a day to see if she should put on her rubbers." Inevitably, the roles are repeated in his own marriage. . . . These domestic stereotypes, Celeste and Charles, thus play out a drama that has been written long before they were born, a drama of discordant family life, a drama in which women and men cannot coexist.

If *The Candy Factory* were merely a compilation of typical popular fictions, the sexual roles of its various characters would now be reasonably clear. But, when we return to the opening story, "The Legend of Mary Moon," we discover directives that encourage us to criticize and reformulate with Mary Moon the conflicts of the characters. Here, she explains to us that all the stories arise from "the mistakes and disappointments of her own life." Moreover, they are "in a spooky way a whole book of characters in a timeless dance with lost possibilities of her own life." Apparently she has written these stories to fulfil certain of her wishes. But how do they do so? As she observes the lives of the people around her, she sees the same sexual conflicts that have dominated her life—formulaic stories with formulaic endings. The material in her Special Accounts Book reveals only her own mistakes and disappointments; the characters always fall short of what she can see to be their potential. Thus, she interferes. Instead of preserving the impasse arrived at in each story, an impasse that results from role playing, Mary Moon chooses to alter the endings. By forcing the characters to confront their pasts, she offers to each the possibility of exorcising that past. And thus, to the hand moulds "dating from the time old Xavier presided over the Production Line," she attempts to give new shapes.

Although the plots remain formulaic, her proposed endings alter the conflict. What she attempts to make manifest is a latent content not dominated by a character's gender. For, as she observes "the small gestures that indicate what a person really thinks and feels apart from what he says he thinks and feels," she realizes that stock sexist responses and gestures are only superficial signs of more profound conflicts. The genres she uses certainly require struggle; but they do not require that struggle to be a sexist one. Thus, she shows that both male and female characters need to be released from the outmoded battle between the sexes. Instead of their measuring each character against a sexual opposite, she suggests that writers should find alternative ways of dramatizing destruction and growth. For that struggle discussed by Beau between the Death Wish and the Life Wish is common to male and female characters alike and need not be typified by sex. By thus shifting her focus, Mary undertakes to assimilate changes in value to popular fictional constructs. Contemporary social awareness of sexism necessitates a changed presentation of fictional characters.

Not surprisingly, the endings that Mary offers extend character codes. Before she interferes, her stories demonstrate traditional conflicts; trapped by their fictional roles, the masculine characters disavow gentleness, the feminine characters aggression. Each story threatens to end with a stalemate. But her experiences with the tramp have shown Mary how to break the stalemates. The tramp's story is therefore a catalyst for the following stories, and for this reason, Mary herself is the female character in it. Her past has typed her as a woman, just as the pasts of each of her characters have sexually typed them. If she is to show that characters need not be so typed, she must undergo an experience that extends her own character. Thus, she turns to that other artist, the tramp. In this story, she seeks to combine the brutality of the tramp's limited sight (he has only one eye) with her own equally limited vision of benevolence. By allowing the tramp to pierce her anonymity, to give her a face, she accepts a changed role in her own story. Furthermore, along with her alter-ego, the tramp, she acknowledges that "nature seldom needs to be altered *or* interpreted . . . *except, of course, human nature.*" In the following stories, the alterations result from her desire to cancel the sexual division between activity and passivity, masculinity and femininity.

Thus she is able to reformulate the codes of the love story. As long as Danny experiences "his vulnerability . . . as loss of power. His tenderness . . . as loss of control," he remains trapped—the man of steel. Until Daphne can enact her realization that "she should have established herself from the start as a person with tastes and needs of her own," she remains faceless. In order to make them realize how arbitrary are the boundaries within which they believe they can act, Mary creates a situation that forces both of them to change their typical responses. Danny's plunge into the water to save Daphne from her apparent imminent drowning corrodes his steel-like armour. This baptism, a symbol Mary uses in various ways in each story, gives Danny a new perspective on his life. Because he can now acknowledge his need of affiliation, Daphne can respond to the change in his character by acknowledging hers for independence. Able to concentrate on the sharing of gentleness and assertiveness, they can begin to use creatively the energy they have wasted in barricading themselves from each other.

Read in terms of its ending, the portrait of Sam Ryan reveals the self-destructiveness of the hard-boiled detective's macho image. Throughout, Mary emphasizes his sexual conflicts; plagued by doubts about his masculinity, he encounters repeated situations that exacerbate his anxiety. . . . Unable to fit human beings into the sexual moulds he thinks that he understands, Sam feels as if he were disappearing. This feeling is astute; the Op traditionally defines himself in opposition to women. But why should he have to define himself in this way? In order to exaggerate the archaism of restrictive sexual stereotyping in this genre, Mary translates Sam's latent fears into actual situations. . . . With his sexual anxieties thus graphically realized, Sam must passively listen as the ghostly voice constructs for him a different role: "Why do you think you have to steal love? . . . Why not just a man who's sometimes mean, sometimes meek and often lonely?" If he can learn to define himself by humane values rather than specifically sexist ones, he may also learn how to solve the crimes he has so badly misconstrued.

In each of these stories, the pervasive images of faceless-

ness seem to suggest not only the absence of idiosyncratic features in stereotyped characters but also the dehumanizing effects of our sexist mythologies. Male and female characters waste their energy in battling against each other; their roles are antagonistic. In the story of Beau and Morgan, Mary illustrates the profound psychic split experienced by the individual because of the established dichotomy between masculine and feminine characteristics. Beau recognizes the problem: "I am becoming a man without a body, incapable of rational action, while you are becoming a man without a mind, incapable of rational thought." Here is the disastrous splitting of what should be a unified personality. At the conclusion of this story, Mary thus offers her vision of the male character: a blend of activity and passivity, of aggression and gentleness. Beau must act to save Morgan from dying while Morgan must accept his intervention. . . . Morgan's tears and Beau's physical interference unite the two men. Symbolically, their union verifies the feminine and masculine polarities of the personality, and emphasizes bisexuality. Without recognition of both poles, the human personality cannot be complete.

The complementary story of Eve and Brigitte dramatizes a similar splitting, presented here from the perspective of women. Eve's aggressiveness and Brigitte's passivity are polarized. Furthermore, stereotyped role playing occurs throughout, underlined by the frequent use of game imagery. But with Mary Moon's help, both women are forced to analyze the destructive rules by which they have played their lives. . . .

Mary alters the ending of this story by allowing Eve and Brigitte to become friends. Removed from the stultifying sexist competition, they can now pursue their individual growth.

Nonetheless, Mary does not imply that new definitions of male and female characters will be easily developed, nor new roles easily assumed. Speaking succinctly to Celeste Hunter, the ghostly voice informs her that "the old games have broken down . . . and you don't know what the new ones are." This observation applies not only to melodrama but to each of the stories in **The Candy Factory.** The novel seems, then, to make two major assertions: the old sexual codes are now inadequate; new codes exist but have not yet been satisfactorily incorporated into popular fiction. Its focus is primarily on the destruction of the old—thus, the various representations of death—although it tentatively offers directions for the new. While suggesting that popular culture is a mirror, it implies that the present mirror is not spacious enough. Consequently, Celeste's melodrama emphasizes the necessary breaking of conventional characterizations: Celeste "saw her vanity mirror and plunged through it in a splatter of splintered quick-silver." Again, references to facelessness evoke stereotyping. After breaking her doll's face, Celeste finds herself the defendant in an absurd trial "to save face," a trial that concludes by having her own face replaced with that of a donkey. In the melodrama of her life, her role has established and limited her character: "You were the longest, wettest soap-opera in town. That was your *theatre,* and how you *gloried* in it . . . you always took your parts from the scripts your husband brought home." But Celeste's story, too, has a hopeful ending. Mary shows her that the battle she has waged with Charles—the battle between the sexes—is in fact a sham battle. She should have been fighting for her "own life and dignity." Thus, although a new script for her life has not yet been clearly printed, it will be determined by her ability rather than her sex.

Faceless portraits, traps, games, mirrors—all suggest the limitations of the characters and imply sexual determinism. So too do the images of machines and robots that dominate Charles' story. In an earlier description of Charles, Sam Ryan imagines him "not human! He was humanoid! *a robot.*" Throughout most of his story, Charles does perform like a robot, spewing out memorized speeches, divorced from his emotions, trapped in a predetermined, masculine role. But Mary's interference with the ending of Celeste's story correspondingly affects the ending of Charles'. When, with her eyes open, Celeste leaves home in "that silly melodramatic way," Charles no longer has a rationale for his actions. Now he has to look at the "bloody human problems" he has always avoided. Furthermore, because Celeste establishes a new role for herself by replacing him as the chairperson of the board of directors of the candy factory, Charles need maintain no longer the equation between masculinity and power. Mary presents his release positively. He escapes from the industrial hierarchy that he has always hated and from the battle with his wife that has sapped his energy. His epiphany is perhaps the most striking of all. Catapulting himself through his window (another example of breaking glass), Charles at last takes his feet off the ground and becomes for a moment a space traveller. He has been freed from his "corporate identity" and from his conventional masculine role.

In the final chapter of the novel, Mary makes some effort to tie up loose ends; yet she fittingly allows it to conclude with an ellipsis. She does not attempt to develop her altered formulas perhaps because she cannot rid herself completely of the old ones. We recall the endless struggle of her parents who relive "every mortification of their married life" while they watch the wrestling matches on television. Parental images are not easy to erase. Nonetheless, Mary understands that elucidation of the past must precede the assimilation of new values. In each story, the characters recall their parents and analyze their relationships with them. Mary thus encourages them to exorcise the past so that their futures will be more various. Charles' vision of the future seems also Mary's: "Soon, with the blindfold of daylight removed, he would be able to see Infinite Time and Infinite Space . . . light beamed forth billions of years ago; galaxies hurtling through the universe—the discus game of the gods." Here is an old/new topos, borrowed from science fiction and applicable to all the stories she has written. With the removal of sexist blindfolds, each character's space will be extended. Games will continue, but the battle between the sexes will not be one of them. (pp. 47-54)

Up to a point, the stories of *The Candy Factory* use static formulaic structures. At the same time, however, they offer wider limits and suggest certain upsettings of estab-lished fictional worlds. The novel therefore seems kinetic; even without complex character development and with the ghostly, artificial interferences of their creator, the stories attempt to reactivate prototypes. Perhaps, as John Moss suggests, the factory of the novel has "no higher meaning—it is simply a representative family-run capitalist monolith, emblematic of our society in general." But if not a higher meaning, the workers in that factory do have an alternative one. Both emblem and potential, they portray the dangers of preserving the dichotomy between masculine and feminine and of encouraging the struggle between men and women. Through her narrator, Mary Moon, Sylvia Fraser seems therefore to imply that sexist stereotypes no longer mirror our society. Popular culture must reflect the changes. (p. 54)

> *Lorna Irvine, "Assembly Line Stories: Pastiche in Sylvia Fraser's 'The Candy Factory',"* in Ca-*nadian Literature, No. 89, Summer, 1981, pp. 45-55.*

## Lorna Irvine

The story of a young girl's growing up, from her birth until she is almost eight, Sylvia Fraser's **Pandora** (1972) dramatically illustrates, within a working-class family, . . . a politicizing of the private. . . . Taking full advantage of the potential of the female *bildungsroman* genre. . . . Fraser interweaves her story of a young girl's development with numerous cultural observations, just as she brings history and psychology into the picture by way of the book's epigraph, a quotation from Bullfinch's rendition of the myth of Pandora.

Perhaps better than any other, this myth reflects attitudes toward female development from a masculine perspective. It is a myth in which individual and cultural development are combined, a myth that has traditionally been used to explain idiosyncratic psychology as well as to characterize women as a group. Categorized as the first woman, Pandora, like Eve, was the creation of man and, among other characteristics such as curiosity, she most significantly epitomized sexual temptation. By opening the forbidden box, she altered the face of the earth, creating trouble, interfering with man's peace of mind and, as far as medieval monks were concerned, obstructing their spiritual duties. Although the myth also illustrates hope, most renditions stress Pandora's rebellion and her sexuality. Thus, as well as being a full-scale attack on modes of production and on woman's role in the family, Fraser's novel is also an attack on a cultural history that makes women accountable for mankind's suffering.

More specifically, when read from such an ideological perspective, **Pandora** becomes a political novel, presenting sexual politics as the training ground for massive, fullscale destruction, a novel that contains, beneath a series of metaphoric games—the most notable of which is *Monopoly*—a radical criticism of sexual dichotomies. Indeed, the world in which Pandora moves toward maturity is consistently differentiated: mothers and fathers are presented as different kinds of people, not merely different persons. In his introduction to the novel, David Staines observes that

*Pandora* has been related to the tradition "of such novels as Richard Hughes's *A High Wind in Jamaica* and William Golding's *Lord of the Flies,* novels which expose the potential cruelty and evil of children." Yet if at one time or another, all the children of the novel behave in calculating, and often cruel, ways, a more gender-directed reading reveals that the novel concentrates on exposing the cruelty of young boys who grow up to be men, and shows some of the effects of this cruelty on the female psyche. Even more radically, the novel methodically anatomizes social structures that encourage the development of political theories such as Naziism. (p. 224)

Fraser sees change dominating familial structures. Thus, although a number of the female characters presented in *Pandora* lead unsatisfactory lives, and seem oblivious to their frequent powerlessness, the major character movingly functions as a revision of the myth of womanhood. Furthermore, based on material that has traditionally been devalued—the female body—and told in a language that has traditionaly been ignored—women's language—*Pandora* proposes "another sort of life." This refrain which ends the novel, and Pandora's repeated chanting of these words, thus serves as an interpretive aid, implying the coming change that the novel's narrator foretells in the lives of girls and women.

Within the ironically named "Gothic" family, the representative family of the novel, the struggle between a father's rage and a mother's forbearance dominates the early action and suggests ways in which gender patterns are reproduced. . . . [The] Gothic family also reveals particular economic tensions that make more absolute the division of labor within the family and that insist on the father's overt dominance. Yet this novel also reflects a more universal familial organization. The passive, quiet twins, Ada and Adel, obey authority and, because they are female, emulate their mother's secondary role in the hierarchical patriarchal structure where the father's authority, no matter how bizarre, is accepted.

*Pandora* thus presents the family as the ground in which certain sexual tensions first blossom, the place where civilization establishes and develops its discontents. Pandora's father's rage early defines him, while her mother's hymn singing defines her. Metonymies multiply as sexual dichotomies assume increasingly complicated meanings. Lyle Gothic's machine-like impersonality is suggested by the steel hook which replaces one of his arms and by his "steel-rimmed" eyes, interpreted by Pandora as narrow windows of rage. Against him, his wife's incorporeality is no fit adversary; Pandora imagines her mother leaving her body behind, floating off on the notes of the hymns she constantly sings.

Marital tension fills the house. Lyle Gothic sits in the living room, shouting for his wife—who is slavishly sifting ashes in the basement—to bring him a drink, while Pandora watches. She sees her mother run to her father, observes her sisters as they flatter him with quiet attention. She watches and she learns, for indeed she knows something about plagues. With Nietzschean insight, she recognizes in this patriarchal family the presence of barely controlled violence. Her father states: "*When* have I ever struck any-

one in this house? When have I ever done *any*thing to *any* of you, but work my ass off for you?" Lyle Gothic's bewilderment is real; overwhelmed by his mother, and by the houseful of women he has to support, he hardly knows himself why he is constantly furious or why he is unable to discuss his feelings. Caught in the gender battle, he seems doomed to play out a foreordained part. Thus, when Pandora questions male authority, she infuriates him. He threatens to throw her naked into the street, stripped of all the signs of his protection and his name, a father's response to a daughter's subversiveness.

Why does Pandora rebel? Partly, her narrative function is to question the daughter's role in a father-dominated family. But Fraser has also provided us with certain psychological determinants. Pandora is highly intelligent, periodically reckless, questioning. As the youngest member of the family, she has benefited from the chance to observe her sisters' and mother's status. Like her author, she seems more interested in women than in men—her maternnal grandmother, her teacher, Miss Macintosh. Even her birth suggests a female creation of the world, in "flesh-heave, mountain-burst, joy-throe, pain-spasm, silt, seaweed, dinosaur dung, lost continents, blood, mucus". Against this female genesis, the religion of the fathers seems stultifying, even deadly. Pandora angrily defies it: "*'In the Beginning God made this lovely world. God who is Good, and who Always was.'* . . . It was my father. He laid the World, and he killed the Easter Bunny, and he *choked* Baby Victor!" This perverse catechism haunts the novel throughout. Men and boys repeatedly use aggression in their efforts to make the world fit their desires so that the *mise en scene* of the family in this novel is precisely that posited by Freud in *Beyond the Pleasure Principle,* the cosmic battle between life and death. Because the tensions evoked are universal, and increasingly deadly, the intelligent and willful Pandora, the new woman, needs to find a new space and new rules.

Sexual perversion also becomes a social metaphor. The contracted Eden that is the neighborhood Paradise Park harbors a male "snake" who exposes himself to Pandora and her girlfriend. Even the breadman, thought by Pandora to be her friend, sexually accosts her. The experience frightens her and creates a physical revulsion that extends to all the men and boys she knows. It extends too to her own body, embarrassing her so that "fear and shame gorge like buzzards on her burden of guilty knowledge, leaving only a few twisted bones". In this way, Fraser presents Freud's seduction fantasy, finally interpreted by him as not actual, an hysterical symptom, an "expression of the typical Oedipus complex in women." In *Pandora,* real occurrences structure the female psyche in ways that lead to subversion, not hysteria. By thus presenting a profoundly alienating sexual experience that is inevitably associated with the aggressive father, the narrator suggests a less phallocentric interpretation of female development. Pandora learns to value her own femininity precisely because she finds the masculine world so unappealing. Freudian theory narrates male, not female, desire, whereas here much of society reflects a perverted masculinity. (pp. 225-26)

When Pandora moves outward, she further discovers that male aggression dominates society. Bigotry controls the very institutions that might be expected to escape it— church and school. Class dictates some of the school's practices. . . . Racial, religious and sexual strife controls the politics of the schoolyard. Against a forming female society, the boys sadistically effect disruption. In fact, their sadism is also practiced against members of their own sex who draw attention to themselves by their powerlessness or their difference. Dirty Danny is cruelly beaten because he is a "Wop." Japanese children are unmercifully teased. The newspaper with its repeated atrocities seems to lend authority to their actions. Jessie Christie and other of the boys get pleasure out of tormenting girls, not necessarily by physical prowess (Jessie wears glasses), but by belittling sexual innuendo that humiliates them. A young Jewish boy, the same boy whom Pandora's Christian mother has labeled "an Hebrew," someone who "doesn't accept Jesus Christ" and who would therefore be an unsuitable husband for her daughter, becomes the butt of pranks that rapidly turn into acts of war. When the community makes Jason the scapegoat for allegedly tampering with the church's sacrament, this small, conservative corner of Ontario participates in the fascist philosophy dominating Europe during Pandora's growing years.

Yet the patriarchal law that is evoked during this sacrilegious episode proves wrong. When the police come to Laura Secord school, to check up on this crime so "awful that only a BOY could think of it," Pandora feels suffocated. Just as her father does, the policemen fill up all her space. When they unite with the principal and the priest to condemn Jason, they connect themselves with an unholy trinity of father, son and holy ghost: Godfrey Trumps, Jessie Christie and Horace Ghostie. Against such fascism, Pandora's favorite teacher, Miss Macintosh, stands out alone, only to lose her job. Pandora has received a pragamatic lesson in subversion: *"Can school, church and state ALL be wrong?"* Fittingly, this lesson comes from a woman: "People *do* make mistakes. Even people with titles and uniforms. *Especially* people with titles and uniforms because sometimes they think they can't go wrong." (pp. 227-28)

Pandora's introduction to the law is therefore not a step on the road to maturity but rather a cautionary lesson about the fallibility of the patriarchy. Furthermore, she also learns that women have a moral responsibility to object to injustice. (p. 228)

*Pandora* appears . . . to be a fairly radical novel, one that deconstructs patriarchal establishments and practices. Its style contributes to this subversive perspective. Specific rhetorical devices insist on the reader's constant attention and reflect the narrator's interest in the tensions she describes. For example, repeated split, hyphenated words ("flesh-heave, mountain-burst, joy-throe, pain-spasm") illustrate a split and doubled narration, emphasized also in the reader's conflicting views of what is happening. Such ambiguity needs fluid language, language that is not reified. The notion of a specifically female language is certainly a controversial one. Nonetheless, as Jane Gallop points out, many current French feminist critics "see 'neu-

tral language' as itself an 'area of oppression'," and want "to use the fluid, the inconsistent, the unfinished to undermine the oppressive 'phallic seriousness of meaning'." Although Fraser does not attempt a radical linguistic exposé in the manner of the French-Canadian writer, Nicole Brossard, the style of *Pandora* certainly encourages the reader to question traditional grammatical forms and, more important, traditional meaning.

Indeed, the narrator of this novel wants the reader to laugh at language. To this end, the text is filled with puns that often undermine rigid meanings. She has fun with words, does not take them quite seriously, refuses them authority. At the same time, she never loses sight of the atrocities committed through language: "The Nasty Vowels grab Pandora's golden curls. The Nazi Vowels shave her head. The Vowel Nazis drag her *bump! bump! bump!* down the attic steps, and *hup! hup! hup!* out into the snow. The Foul Nazis strip off her nightie, with their black germ-hands." As well, alliteration, assonance, onomatopoeia, all privilege sound. To be sure, in the early world of Pandora, sound does dominate sense. She cannot read. But such playing with sound also reminds us of language's oral roots. Echoes of northern sagas appear here and there, recalling societies where old and powerful women like Grannie Cragg exercised power. In fact, when Pandora tries to teach her grandmother to read. Grannie Cragg assures her that the vowels, those Nazi vowels, "wouldn'ta helped me where I been, Chickee, and they aren't going to help me where I'm going." (p. 228-29)

In this novel, the use of an outspoken narrator . . . has political implications. The narrative voice is peculiarly domineering, inserting itself into the narrative, not just to give more information about the characters and events, but also to instruct the reader. Our experience of *Pandora* thus seems heavily controlled, even manipulated. Certainly, the abrupt division of narrative perspective, for example that between Pandora's and the narrator's, emphasizes structurally various psychic splits. But I also suggest that this narrator obliges the reader to take seriously the sexual divisions of the plot, to be aware that the gender of a novel's central character determines certain of the ways novels are read, and even to acknowledge that the sex of the writer may influence perception. (pp. 229-30)

The attack on the patriarchy that dominates this novel continues to the end. Its implications become increasingly terrifying. Men have been associated with war throughout. When Lyle Gothic prophesies the future, as the novel draws to a close, he sees the second of the wars to end all war smoothly shifting its focus. . . . As we now know, that psychological "switch" ["from The Rocket to The Bomb"] means the possible extermination of the human race. This vision reflects Freud's "fateful question" at the conclusion of *Civilization and Its Discontents*, the question about "whether and to what extent" human beings "will succeed in mastering the disturbance of their communal life by the human instinct of aggression and self-destruction. . . . Men have gained control over the forces of nature to such an extent that with their help they would have no difficulty in exterminating one another to the last man." The *Monopoly* game that Lyle Gothic plays against various imagined opponents—Howard Hughes, J. Paul Getty—becomes an economic correlative for the violence that he sees all around him.

Yet just as the myth of Pandora also balances possible destruction with a more hopeful prophecy, so in the final section of the novel, Pandora tentatively becomes the inheritor of her grandmother's money and therefore of a "different sort of life." Certainly, this different life suggests her removal from the economic restrictions of Oriental Avenue. Pandora knows that her father, as well as her mother, has agreed to give up his share of his mother's legacy in order to invest in his daughter's future, a gesture that helps to release her from some of her fear of her father's power. . . . (pp. 230-31)

On a cultural level, moreover, the ending functions as a metaphor for contemporary women's extrication of themselves from hampering social structures. In Fraser's novel, the world creatively opens up and hope dominates, suggesting an alternate destiny. Female sexuality at last blossoms, as the matrons of Oriental Avenue are subsumed in a different vision of femininity. Pandora and her friend Arlene "haul themselves onto their island. They sink back into its poachy contours. They embrace, trailing strands of albumen. They feel each other's beating hearts. They press their bodies in mutual exploration. . . . Lips, their juice and flexibility. Cheeks, their comfort and contour. Chests, their budded mystery. Bellies, their warmth. Hands, their infinite variety. Thighs, their power. Genitals, their vulnerability." After Pandora's squalid baptism in the mud in her father's ruined victory garden where she makes "angels in the *uck-guck* iodine muck" and feels "the rats fall out of her ears," this rebirth seems remarkably positive. Remaking history, she and Arlene become the first women, "wallowing in primordial stew." (pp. 231-32)

> Lorna Irvine, "Politicizing the Private: Sylvia Fraser's 'Pandora'," in Mosaic: A Journal for the Interdisciplinary Study of Literature, *Vol. XVII, No. 2, Spring, 1984, pp. 223-33.*

### R. B. Hatch

With **Berlin Solstice** . . . Fraser establishes a reputation as a historical novelist, creating a brilliant inside account of the rise and fall of the Third Reich, one which develops both psychological and historical reasons for Germany's fall into barbarism. Indeed her use of form to create historical understanding counterpoints much of the recent theoretical debate on the writing of history. . . . (p. 134)

As the title indicates . . . most of the novel takes place in the old capital, Berlin, during Germany's winter solstice, the period from the 1920's to the end of World War Two. So frequently do her characters traverse the city from east to west and back again that by the novel's end the reader feels he knows Berlin almost as well as his own city. Painstaking accumulation of detail does more than supply a geographical location: the well-known Berlin names—Hardenberg Strasse, the Zoo, the Tiergarten, Cafe des Westens—present a grid on which the actual events of the Third Reich can be firmly grounded.

Particularization of detail also allows Fraser to flesh out convincingly some of the more famous figures from the Nazi party. Since the novel focuses on actors and drama, Goebbels, the Minister of Art and Propaganda, appears often. The Reich's second-in-command, Goering, has a brief walk-on part, dressed in his green forester's garb. At several points, the Fuhrer himself strides to centre stage. . . . Of all the leaders in the Nazi high command, Fraser devotes her most extended portrait to the "Blonde Beast," Reinhard Heydrich, the leading architect of the Nazi "Final Solution" for the Jews. She shows his development from the son of a Dresden music teacher to the Head of the Reich Main Security Office. While never denying Heydrich's cold, cruel side, she draws so close to his personal life, allowing his character to shine forth from behind his own eyes, that for long moments we are even led to sympathize with him.

The idea of "sympathizing" with such a monster must seem anathema to many, of course, but Fraser grasps an essential point in the art of history: to gain an understanding of how one of the world's great civilizations fell into barbarism, we need to be able to imagine the aspirations of the criminals and to comprehend the intersection of their private and public lives. To this end she develops a narrative stance which employs indirect quotation so extensively that the reader remains continually within the psyche of her characters. Consequently the fictional world presents a repeated echo of the characters' thoughts and rationalizations, Fraser wisely declining to intervene with editorializing comment.

Yet as Georg Lukacs observed, the historical novelist obtains his greatest success in interpreting history, not with major historical figures, but with his own fictional creations who, while highly individualized, can also represent classes and trends. For this purpose Fraser presents a number of fictional characters who illuminate the pressures at work on the German population, two of the most successful being Ilse Schmidt and her husband Kurt. A simple country girl from the south, Ilse is ideal for showing the attractions of national Socialism to the "Volk." As the Head Nurse in the *Lebensborn* clinic in Mullhorig, Ilse throws herself into the job of finding "biological mates" for unmarried German women, and then provides loving care to the babies produced by this mating. Under Fraser's skilful hand we watch this idealistic and compassionate young woman struggle to retain her belief in the Lebensborn's ideal of race even as she confronts moral dilemmas in the program. The first opposition comes from her Roman Catholic parents who object to the enterprise on religious grounds. Yet their abstract considerations mean nothing compared to what she faces when the doctors inform her that Aryan philosophy demands the death of all deformed Lebensborn children. So deeply is Ilse involved with the Lebensborn ideal and so loving is her personality, that for several years she does not even recognize her own son's mental slowness, or that her husband will not be promoted until his family is "purified." In the character of Ilse, Fraser depicts the powerful attraction of the National Socialist ideals of purity and perfection, and how these conflict with compassion and love, weakening the very fibre of both individual and political well-being.

A similar sort of clash between idealism and practice appears in Ilse's husband Kurt, only here with much more far-reaching consequences, since Kurt's loyalty as an SS officer eventually wins him the trust of his superiors for one of their most difficult and secret tasks—eliminating the mentally ill, the Jews, and other "subhumans." Step by step we watch Kurt travel deeper and deeper into the mire of Nazi practice, all the while attempting to hold pure his oath of loyalty to the Fuhrer. Unlike Ilse, who manages to keep heart and head apart, Kurt finally faces himself, recognizing the extent to which his many compromises undermined his idealism, turning it into greed for self-gain.

While Fraser undoubtedly gives a superb account of the attractions and consequences of Nazi ideology, she proves not nearly so successful in portraying the other side, the Resistance. Her two principal resistance figures, Count Wolfgang von Friedrich and Carmel Kohl, are not convincingly drawn, and since their stories form a large part of the novel's centre, the novel contains a serious flaw. Yet the flaw reveals an interesting aspect of Fraser's historical conception and narrative point of view. For her resistance Fraser chooses people from the theatrical community. In the early parts of the novel both the Count and Carmel vacillate between accepting and rejecting the Nazi ideology. Fraser's intention is to show how the artistic world, with its emphasis on different roles and its mirroring of what lies outside, allows the individual to remain uncommitted to any particular doctrine. In Fraser's handling, the characters appear almost whimsical, with no central core of moral being. Thus, when they both decide to oppose the Nazis, the decision appears unmotivated and arbitrary. Fraser was obviously aware that this leap creates problems because she gives Carmel and the Count a winter love scene in the Harz mountains. But this becomes little more than a cheap scene from a *Liebesroman* and does little to advance either the plot or our understanding of the characters.

That a resistance, however small, developed in Germany is well documented, and although Fraser mentions in an end-note that she did not base her fictional characters on real people, the stories of historical resistance fighters were available to her. For the Count it seems likely that she drew in some small part on von Stauffenberg, the principal conspirator in the assassination attempt on Hitler on 20 July 1944. Carmel may well have been modelled on Zarah Leander, a famous singer and actress. Yet in a society in which Hitler could boast that there was no crime atrocious enough to cause the people to rebel, a portrait of resistance will require substantial psychological underpinnings of the sort that may well not be commensurate with Fraser's omniscient narrative.

Fraser's difficulties in presenting credible resistance figures assumes an even more interesting dimension in the last chapters when she repeatedly uses the term "bourgeois" to describe the degeneration of the Nazi ideal of purity into a fascination with self and the accumulation of wealth. In fact she ends the novel on a darkly cynical but powerful note when Colonel Kurt Schmidt, the typical Nazi, remains with Hitler in his Bunker until his suicide,

and then buys his way out of Russian-held Berlin to escape into the bombed Underground on his way to freedom in the West. While Fraser offers no hint as to his eventual success, the novel leaves the impression that our own "bourgeois" society continues to harbour his spirit, even to create it anew. The winter solstice, the cold war, remains. (pp. 134-36)

> *R. B. Hatch, "Cold War," in* Canadian Literature, *No. 107, Winter, 1985, pp. 134-36.*

### Janet Hamilton

"My life was structured on the uncovering of a mystery," Fraser explains, and it is this view of her life that determines the manner of telling in *My Father's House.* What Fraser offers are dramatized scenes from her past, including scenes of abuse, linked by passages that explain her development in the terms provided by the mystery of incest uncovered. This is autobiography in the confessional mode and, as confession, gains by the intensity of its author's purpose: to cast the most personal of events and feelings in the light of an achieved understanding. At the same time, because of this purposefulness, the author of a confession is pressed to an unusual degree to convince the reader of the soundness of his or her understanding, the legitimacy of the meaning he or she imposes on past events. Central to the best confessions is the capacity to inspire such confidence, which their authors achieve through some combination of frankness, sensitivity, and breadth of vision.

There is an intensity to Fraser's account that does compel. As with her novels, the energy of the prose and an eye for telling detail propel the reader along; her signature descriptions of places and people deftly suggest a child's felt world. In talking of her father's "reverence for things that once were and can never be again", she defines a sensibility, if not a personality. And there is the ring of good sense in some of her discrete wisdoms: about her husband, for instance, "who practiced the truth of good manners—formalized compassion".

The strength of *My Father's House* thus lies in its evocation of a past; its weakness lies in the terms the author provides for making sense of that past—in her achieved understanding. The source of the sense Fraser makes is based on the lifting of the "amnesia", three years ago, about the incidents of sexual abuse. At several points in the book, she elaborates on the nature of this amnesia. For instance, "I as a child created a secret accomplice for my daddy: by splitting my personality in two. Thus somewhere after the age of six, I acquired another self with memories and experiences separate from mine, whose existence was unknown to me." In adolescence, Fraser contends, she creates a third self, her task now "to keep my personalities separate".

The use of the term "amnesia" here and the theory about self-induced splitting are perplexing, perhaps inaccurate. One imagines some process of repression and dissociation, and certainly this process, as described, is useful to the literary needs of the project: unravelling the mystery of sexual identity now fascinates as unravelling the mystery of birthright once did. Yet, the inexactness of Fraser's explanation for both the forgetting and the remembering leaves one uneasy about the judgement operating here. What form of repression could have Fraser disavowing incidents that recurred over the first 17 years of her life, while leaving her to function as well as she did? How are we to understand the status of her memories?

The author offers some terms of understanding where plausibility is not a question: the need to forgive, to take responsibility, to eschew self-absorption. But they do not allay the reader's uneasiness, which is only intensified by other of the book's approaches to analysis. Understandably, the child identifies herself with the princesses of fairy stories, but it is somewhat alarming to find the adult, her amnesia lifted and resolution in sight, believing that "like Sleeping Beauty I was both cursed and blessed at birth." The child identifies with movie heroines, but even the adult, in reliving incidents of sexual abuse, recalls "the child Regan in the movie The Exorcist, riding her bed like a brass bronco". Indeed, between the amnesia and the three selves, the book too often calls to mind some amalgam of The Seventh Veil, Random Harvest, and The Three Faces of Eve.

Other explanatory cannons simply misfire. The author more than once mistakes the sequence of events by which Eve comes to be ashamed of her nakedness; she refers to Dr Frankenstein's monster as Frankenstein; she introduces literary allusions to ill effect: "For whom the bell tolls? It tolls for me."

The critic Julian Symons, writing about confessional autobiography, concludes that "nobody exposes himself entire." The problem here is not, then, the selectivity of Fraser's memories, nor is it her confessional drive to explain them. It is the unconvincing application of the terms of analysis to the subject of her sexual identity—along with the inaccuracies—that undermine the reader's confidence in "the truth as Fraser now understands it".

*Janet Hamilton, "Repressing Abuse: The Crime against Sylvia," in* Quill and Quire, *Vol. 53, No. 8, August, 1987, p. 33.*

## Jane O'Grady

*My Father's House* is in some ways the familiar story of the gifted small-town boy or girl destined to become a writer, but running parallel is the subterranean world of the sexually-abused child.

Sylvia Fraser continually juxtaposes the self-images of blonde, fairytale princess and cobwebbed Miss Haversham, as she describes how, at the age of seven, the unendurable guilt and revulsion of incest caused her to split into two personalities. "Another little girl" was created to do the shameful things for which her father threatened and bribed her, while her outwardly normal self forgot all previous and subsequent sexual abuse.

Fraser does not make Sybil-type claims for her two personalities. They were not watertight, and her alter ego "leaked emotions" to her ordinary self. Her precocious,

popular school-days, success in college and career, blissful courtship and happy marriage were poisoned by incest, for as a child she had inexplicable epileptic-type fits, as well as internal seizures of fear when entering her father's house or encountering physical affection from others. And later her compulsive affair with the philandering father of an old schoolfriend destroyed her marriage. When, three years ago, at the age of 48, Fraser recovered these buried memories through hypnosis, she felt she at last understood her self-sabotage, and why her novels always turned out to be full of sexual violence which "seemed to be coming from somewhere very deep".

Even at the outset of *My Father's House,* when everything seems as respectable as the hear-no-evil, see-no-evil, speak-no-evil monkeys in the well-dusted parlour, interspersed italicised passages convey a child's-eye or adult-nightmare view of incest. These passages, Fraser explains, may be the recently recovered experiences, thoughts and feelings of her alter ego, or dreams occurring at any stage of her life—an explanation which exhibits the cavalier psychoanalytic attitude to the distinction between reality and fantasy: what is important is how it feels. But her task is to *convey* feeling, and, after their initial impact, the incest passages soon become melodramatic and belaboured. Words such as "guilt", "fear" "love" and "hate" placed in unpunctuated strings, in alternating or repeated succession, obliterate the feeling they are supposed to produce.

And Fraser's images are unsatisfyingly imprecise, both in the way they are expressed and in only marginally applying to her (any old nightmare will do). The reader, given once again what may be a dream, thought, or metaphor, of a screaming and or blood-stained Miss Haversham, Rapunzel, cartoon-witch from Disney's Snow White, or heroine from Andersen's Red Shoes, is finally alienated and immune.

Like many people involved in therapy, Fraser is so entranced by the potential to create an intriguing web of cross-references and themes that she neglects what they originally applied to, thus losing their significance. Fraser makes a rigid division between the conscious and unconscious, and fails to unravel the connections between the causes and the consequences of her psychological disturbance. While understandably blaming her depression, anxiety, and the irrational affair on her childhood experience, she treats this like a causal laxative. Its outcome is clear, but the way it works obscure.

However insistently Fraser brandishes incest as the missing link both in her past and present writings, it remains artistically unassimilated. Like congealed psychoanalytic symbols, the dredgings of her unconscious are too self-indulgently personal, yet too sloppily generalised. Even her terrible experiences with her father often emerge as if they were secondhand, because they are wrapped in layers of literary allusion and processed through melodrama.

*Jane O'Grady, "My Heartache Belongs to Daddy," in* The Sunday Times, *London, February 26, 1989, p. G13.*

# Nikki Giovanni

## 1943-

(Born Yolande Cornelia Giovanni) American poet, essayist, editor, and author of children's books.

Giovanni gained widespread popularity during the 1960s for her revolutionary poems in *Black Feeling, Black Talk* and *Black Judgement,* two works that feature rhythmic, often angry verse. She made her poems accessible to a multi-generational and international audience through public readings at universities and best-selling recordings accompanied by gospel music. Concentrating on themes of family, blackness, womanhood, and sex, Giovanni's poetry is conversational and strongly influenced by rhythm and blues music. Although many early admirers faulted her for later taking a more domestic and personal stance toward societal change, Giovanni contends that the evolution of her ideas reflects the changing attitudes of herself and the world she observes. In much of her work, Giovanni focuses on the individual's search for love and acceptance, reflecting what she considers a general struggle in the black American community. John W. Conner commented: "[Giovanni] sees her world as an extension of herself, she sees problems in the world as an extension of her problems, she sees herself existing amidst tensions, heartache, and marvelous expressions of love. But the tensions, heartaches, and expression of love do not overwhelm the poet. She controls her environment—sometimes with her mind, often with her heart."

Giovanni was born in Knoxville, Tennessee, but her family soon moved to Lincoln Heights, Ohio, a predominantly black community. Her happy childhood, spent partly with her grandparents in Tennessee, became a major theme of Giovanni's poetry. The author received her bachelor's degree in history from Fisk University, where she was strongly influenced by a creative writing workshop taught by novelist John Oliver Killens. While at Fisk, Giovanni rejected her formerly conservative views in favor of the radicalism she encountered in fellow classmates. *Black Feeling, Black Talk* and *Black Judgement,* her first two volumes of poetry, reflect the anger and enthusiasm of the 1960s community of writers and political activists with whom Giovanni became involved. This group included such poets as LeRoi Jones (Amiri Baraka), H. Rap Brown, and Don L. Lee (Haki R. Madhubuti). One of Giovanni's best known poems, "The True Import of the Present Dialogue, Black vs. Negro," from *Black Feeling, Black Talk,* is a call to black Americans to destroy both the whites who oppress them and the blacks whose passivity and compliance contribute to their own oppression. Adopting this revolutionary stance, Giovanni advocates open violence and expresses her impatience for change. "Nikki Rosa," from *Black Judgement,* which recounts Giovanni's contented childhood, is often considered the author's signature poem. Speaking affectionately of her supportive family, the poet asserts that happiness is dependent on love, not material possessions, and this love is the

staple of unity within the black community. *Black Feeling, Black Talk* and *Black Judgement* were well received, and Giovanni quickly gained recognition as a prominent contemporary poet.

Giovanni maintained the personal perspective of "Nikki Rosa" in her next volume, *Re:Creation,* and in the essay collection *Gemini: An Extended Autobiographical Statement on My First Twenty-five Years of Being a Black Poet.* The birth of her son in 1969 and her increasing passion for rhythm and blues music influenced these pieces, which are less angry than Giovanni's previous work. Here, the poet views the black revolution as a personal rather than a collective movement. Both volumes received negative appraisals from formerly enthusiastic critics such as Ruth Rambo McClain, who stated: "[Regrettably], Nikki Giovanni, my sparkling gnat throwing huge fiery sun poems into the Black Heavens, [has been] transformed (re:created?) into an almost declawed, tamed Panther with bad teeth." Critics also believed that the author manipulated the language in *Re:Creation* to conform to song-like rhythms at the expense of the poems' content. Overall, however, commentators praised Giovanni for verse that appealed to an audience that had previously been alienated by militant black poetry and that gave a personal approach to uplifting black America. In her 1972 collection, *My House,* Giovanni depicted personal and public lives as complementary forces working toward change. Divided into two sections, "The Rooms Inside" and "The Rooms Outside," the volume received mixed reviews. While some critics felt the dichotomy between public and private in *My House* was forced, most commentators agreed that Giovanni successfully demonstrated the mutual influences of the individual and society. *The Women and the Men,* Giovanni's following volume, contains poems from *Re:Creation* and *Black Judgement,* as well as new works.

In *Cotton Candy on a Rainy Day,* Giovanni's most somber collection, the poet breaks from her theme of interaction between the individual and society and addresses isolation and loneliness. Many critics claimed that this volume reflects the poet's disappointment with the loss of the idealism of the 1960s. Paula Giddings noted: "Giovanni has evolved to be that creature which often finds itself estranged from the history which created it." After her initial disillusionment, however, the author ultimately reaffirms her belief in the possibility of change, and she closes *Cotton Candy on a Rainy Day* with poems about friendship and love. Despite thematic variations throughout Giovanni's career, the poet's work is unified by her consistently personal and often revealing voice. William J. Harris observed: "On the whole what is most striking about Giovanni's poetry is that she has created the charming persona of 'Nikki Giovanni.' This persona is honest, searching, complex, lusty, and, above all, individualistic and charmingly egoistical."

(See also *CLC,* Vols. 2, 4, 19; *Contemporary Authors,* Vols. 29-32, rev. ed.; *Contemporary Authors New Revision Series,* Vol. 18; *Contemporary Authors Autobiography Series,* Vol. 6; *Black Writers; Children's Literature Review,* Vol. 6; *Dictionary of Literary Biography,* Vols. 5, 41.)

## PRINCIPAL WORKS

POETRY

*Black Feeling, Black Talk*   1968
*Black Judgement*   1968
*Re:Creation*   1970
*My House*   1972
*The Women and the Men*   1975
*Cotton Candy on a Rainy Day*   1978
*Those Who Ride the Night Winds*   1983

CHILDREN'S BOOKS

*Spin a Soft Black Song: Poems for Children*   1971
*Ego Tripping and Other Poems for Children*   1971
*Vacation Time: Poems for Children*   1980

OTHER

*Night Comes Softly: An Anthology of Black Female Voices* (editor)   1970
*Gemini: An Extended Autobiographical Statement on My First Twenty-five Years of Being a Black Poet*   1971
*A Dialogue: James Baldwin and Nikki Giovanni* 1973

*A Poetic Equation: Conversations between Nikki Giovanni and Margaret Walker*   1974
*Sacred Cows . . . and Other Edibles*   (essays)   1988

---

## Don L. Lee

Nikki Giovanni has published two thin volumes of poetry, ***Black Feeling, Black Talk*** and ***Black Judgement,*** which reflect her awareness of the values of Black culture as well as her commitment to the revolution. In **"The True Import of Present Dialogue"** she asks the Black male/warriors to "kill the nigger" in themselves, to let their "nigger mind die," to free their black hands and "learn to be Black men." Like many of us, Miss Giovanni is concerned that Black men have been sent out of the United States to kill other "colored" peoples of the world when the real enemy is here. She expresses this same concern in **"Of Liberation,"** where she points out that there is an international bond between all peoples of color. Stress is placed on unity, the need to work together for mutual progress.

**"Poem (No Name No. 3")** mentions leaders of the Black revolution who have been either silenced permanently or at least hampered seriously in their efforts to increase the awareness and involvement of our people and help them to effect a means to cast off the chains. Cautioning, warning the apathetic, Miss Giovanni states: "if the Black Revolution passes you bye its for damned sure / the white reaction to it won't."

In the autobiographical **"My Poem,"** the poet tells us that she has been robbed, that because of her involvement in the movement she expects at any time a deliberate, planned attack on her very person. In spite of harrassment and personal danger, however, she expresses her conviction that the killing/silencing of one revolutionary will not stop the onward movement of our people. . . . (p. 68)

Nikki writes about the familiar: what she knows, sees, experiences. It is clear why she conveys such urgency in expressing the need for Black awareness, unity, solidarity. She knows how it was. She knows how it is. She knows also that a change can be affected. (p. 70)

Traditionally, most people think of poetry as writing that has certain prescribed forms and that revolves around a "poetic," light theme. This point of view is concomitant with the "art-for-art's-sake" concept Nikki rejects. In **"For Sandra,"** she lets us know why her subject and form are what they are. She says that she

> . . . wanted to write
> a poem
> that rhymes
> but revolution doesn't lend
> itself to be-bopping

She then thought of writing a "tree" poem, but couldn't find a model to view in order to make a fit description, for "no trees grow in manhattan"—only asphalt. Then she thought to write "a big blue sky poem / but all the clouds have winged / low since no-Dick was elected."

> so i thought again
> and it occurred to me
> maybe i shouldn't write
> at all
> but clean my gun
> and check my kerosene supply
>
> perhaps these are not poetic
> times

These are hard lines that force thought. These are the lines that suggest the writer has a real, serious commitment to her people and to the institutions that are working toward the liberation of Black people.

Her sharpness shines through like the sheen of a sister's greased-up dark limbs. Yet, she has serious problems with many of her longer "militant" poems, such as **"Of Liberation".** . . .

[Some lines] read like a first outline of a college freshman's essay. What is perhaps more important is that when the Black poet chooses to serve as political seer, he must display a keen sophistication. Sometimes Nikki oversimplifies and therefore sounds rather naive politically. For example, are brothers like Imamu Baraka and Larry Neal to be excluded from black revolutionary leadership because they have "white degrees?" (Or Nikki herself, for that matter!)

In some cases she has used contradictory mis-information, as in **"Ugly Honkies, or The Election Game and How to Win It."**

The lines

> the obvious need is a new liberal white party
> to organize liberal and radical honkies

are contradicted seven lines later with

> the worst junkie or black businessman is more
>     humane
> than the best honkie.

If the last statement is true, why organize whites? The emphasis on organization should be aimed at the weaker Blacks. The poem is a street corner rap, not a poem. The poet's longer works often look like first or second drafts needed to fill up the pages.

Nikki is at her best in the short, personal poem. She is definitely growing as a poet. Her effectiveness is in the area of the "fast rap." She says the right things at the right time. Orally this is cool, but it doesn't come across as printed poetry. (pp. 72-4)

> *Don L. Lee, "Nikki Giovanni," in his* Dynamite Voices, *Broadside Press, 1971, pp. 68-74.*

**June Jordan**

Well, this "extended autobiographical statement" by Nikki Giovanni is not an autobiography . . . If you read through the 13 separate essays [in *Gemini: An Extended Autobiographical Statement on My First Twenty-five Years of Being a Black Poet*] you can conclude that Nikki Giovanni came from a middle-class background: Both parents were college graduates and pursued professional careers. She grew up in Knoxville, Tenn. She took her own undergraduate degree at Fisk University. She loved her grandmother, and her mother, especially, loves her son, Thomas, loves her sister, Gary, and liked to fight for her, from when she was 4 years old. Her family has long regarded Miss Giovanni as a genius, and she has long regarded herself as a genius. More than that, of an autobiographical nature, her fans will not learn—not here.

The reader never hears of any real trouble in her life; she must have had some. There are no Giovanni word-dealings with personal pain, or anguish. And where are the men who have figured in her life? (Even her father and grandfather receive comparatively incidental mention, before disappearing from the page.) And who are the people who have helped her with her career? And who are her friends? And so forth.

That's enough about what's missing. What you do have is a collection of essays with titles such as **"Spiritual View of Lena Horne," "On Being Asked What It's Like to Be Black,"** and **"Don't Have a Baby Till You Read This."** Compared to the autobiographical writings of Maya Angelou, or of Alice Walker in "To Hell With Dying," or of Julius Lester, in "Search for the New Land," this is light stuff. Still, it is an entertaining collection of mostly high-spirited raps. Its interest is guaranteed by Miss Giovanni's status as a leading black poet and celebrity.

All the essays are first person, "I"—writings. Some of them are enjoyable—jive pieces of pure jive. Witness **"Revolutionary Tale,"** where the reader is promised the story of how and why Miss Giovanni arrived "late," to join "The Movement." Instead, the reader is taken on a float among the laughing bubbles of a really tall tale.

Over-all, the style of the book poses some difficulty; paragraphs slide about and loosely switch tracks on the reader. But, now and then, she can make you laugh. And two of the essays are unusual for their serious, held focus and for their clarity. These two, **"The Beginning Is Zero"** and **"Black Poems, *Poseurs* and Power,"** stand apart from the rest; they do not blur and drift.

**"The Beginning Is Zero"** gives us a grateful look at Charles Chesnutt, 19th-century black novelist. Guided by Miss Giovanni, we consider the man, his influence and his revolt. We come to understand how he has remained important to white and black literature. We learn, for example, that "Chestnutt [sic], by making the Black man innocent and the white man his executioner, introduced Jesus as a Black man into the American context." This is a useful piece of scholarship and tribute.

**"Black Poems, *Poseurs* and Power"** offers the reader an engaging piece of self-criticism, in the sense that it questions where we, black folks, are heading, how we are handling the trip, and why. Miss Giovanni believes: "There is a tendency to look at the Black experience too narrowly." This can lead to a blacker-than-thou kind of non-think: Black may discriminate against black, for instance, if the brother or the sister is not wearing the "right" the

"Black" clothing of the moment. Or, such non-think may lead to the Last Poets performing "Die Nigga," which as Miss Giovanni points out, is negative and "just not the same concept as 'kill.'" In short, she wants to call off the asinine sanctimony that sets black against black and lets the real enemies rest, laughing, at the sidelines.

From this, she proceeds to condemn the "latent militarism of the [black] artistic community" as "despicable." She remembers the abundance of black artists, equipped with military "guard," who appeared at the 1968 Black Power Conference at Philadelphia. ("Even the guards had guards.") Here the non-think resulted in black becoming the enemy of black. Miss Giovanni comments, "It's a sick syndrome with, again, the Black community being the loser."

One more essay must be mentioned, her last: **"Gemini—A Prolonged Autobiographical Statement on Why."** This will prove particularly interesting to everyone familiar with the author's poems. When you compare the poetry with the ambivalence and wants expressed in this essay, it becomes clear that a transition is taking place inside the artist.

She has written in one poem: "Nigger / Can you kill. . . . Can we learn to kill WHITE for BLACK / Learn to kill niggers / Learn to be Black men." Now, in this final essay she is a woman writing: "I don't want my son to be a warrior. . . . I don't want my son to be a George or a Jonathan Jackson. . . . I didn't have a baby to see him be cannon fodder." Whatever the depth of the transition, the uncertainties are real and plainly spoken: "Perhaps Black people don't want Revolution at all. That too must be considered. I used to think the world needs what I need. But perhaps it doesn't." And, the final, two lines of the book: "I really like to think a Black, beautiful, loving world is possible. I really do, I think."

To be sure, that is a puzzling conclusion. Is it the black part, or the beautiful, or the "loving world" part, that leaves her unsure—or all of them? Maybe that was the goal, to raise more questions about herself, at the age of 27, than she would or could answer. At 27, that might seem fair enough, and a lot less surprising than an honest-to-God autobiography. (pp. 6, 26)

> *June Jordan, in a review of "Gemini: An Extended Autobiographical Statement on My First Twenty-five Years of Being a Black Poet," in* The New York Times Book Review, *February 13, 1972, pp. 6, 26.*

## Donez Xiques

*Gemini,* the first book of prose by a talented young poet, Nikki Giovanni, is a collection of thirteen essays subtitled "An Extended Autobiographical Statement on My First Twenty-Five Years of Being a Black Poet." For many readers these essays will serve as an introduction to an intellectually astute, witty and persuasive writer who once referred to herself as a "revolutionary poet in a pre-revolutionary world."

In an interview Nikki Giovanni remarked, "If you have a population where there is suffering, you are all suffering." In this collection of essays she wields prose in an endeavor to probe the reader. She asks, ". . . is there such a thing as normal in an abnormal world run by subnormal people?" The negative reply explains why she can say, "Nobody's trying to make the system Black; we're trying to make a system that's human so Black folks can live in it."

Her essays are concerned with change and challenge needed to affect the system. She believes that "the state of the world we live in is so depressing. And this is not because of the reality of the men who run it but because it doesn't have to be that way. The possibilities of life are so great and beautiful that to see less wears the spirit down." Four chapters in this book are devoted to those who are involved with articulating the vision for change—artists, writers, musicians. Here she explores blackness as a cultural entity and discusses the role of the artist in relationship to the community at large.

Despite Nikki Giovanni's considerable talent, in the final analysis, *Gemini* struck me as a book that did not need to be written. It has all been said before—more incisively, more humorously, more poignantly. This is not to imply, however, that the book is worthless. But there are real stylistic weaknesses in it. The author is uneven and inconsistent.

At times, what purports to be the voice of black awareness emerges as downright silliness. The reader finds it impossible to take her seriously when she writes passages such as the following one: "Why would Dostoevski need to write *Crime and Punishment?* For the same reason Shakespeare needed to write—not to pass information but to pass time. There are no great honkies—anything that excludes our existence is not great."

One is uneasy, too, about the contradictory statements in *Gemini.* When Nikki Giovanni points simultaneously in two different directions, the result is only confusion. One cannot follow her, nor can one be confident of her leadership. She writes: "Most of us accept responsibility of / for living. It's very worrisome when we find black people committing suicide by dope, self-hatred and the actual taking of life. It means we have gotten away from our roots. This is when the poet must call." In another passage, however, we read: "We need to get rid of whitey. I mean, if we can't kill a whitey, how can we ever justify killing a brother? . . . We can only justify offing a brother if we have already offed twenty whiteys—that's the ratio, I told him, for offing a brother."

And, finally, when a black writer admonishes the black community to beware of wearing *"wigs"* and to get their own thing together, then I, for one, cannot understand why the revolutionary writer, Nikki Giovanni, entrusted *Gemini* to a white publishing company. (pp. 186-87)

> *Donez Xiques, in a review of "Gemini," in* America, *Vol. 126, No. 7, February 19, 1972, pp. 186-87.*

## Suzanne Juhasz

[Nikki Giovanni] comes to her art knowing that she is as female as she is black and that somehow she must, in her own life and art, express how these aspects of herself come together and define her. She has always defined herself as a black woman, seeing Women's Liberation as a white woman's movement; seeing black women as different from both white women and black men: "But white women and Black men are both niggers and both respond as such. He runs to the white man to explain his 'rights' and she runs to us. And I think that's where they are both coming from. . . . We Black women are the single group in the West intact." But her ideas about the black woman's role in the movement have changed over the past several years, I think, moving from a more traditional view (black womanhood comes second to black revolution) to one that is stronger and more individualistic. . . . (p. 155)

As a woman, as a black, as a black woman, Giovanni defines herself in terms of two primary factors, which she sees as related: power and love. . . .

Power and love are what are at issue in Nikki Giovanni's poetry and life. In her earlier poems (1968-1970), these issues are for the most part separate. She writes of personal love in poems of private life; of black power and a public love in political poems. She won her fame with the latter. (p. 157)

In poems such as [**"The True Import of the Present Dialogue, Black vs. Negro"**], Giovanni speaks for her people in their own language of the social issues that concern them. Her role is that of spokeswoman for others with whom she is kin except for the fact that she possesses the gift of poetry: "i wanted to be / a sweet inspiration in my dreams / of my people . . . " (**"The Wonder Woman"**). The quotation is from a later poem in which she is questioning that very role. But as she gains her fame, the concept of poet as "manifesting our collective historical needs" is very much present.

In defining poetry as "the culture of a people," Giovanni, in [a] statement from **Gemini,** uses "musician" and "preacher" as synonyms for "poet." All speak for the culture; all *speak,* with the emphasis on the sound they make. Making poems from black English is more than using idioms and grammatical idiosyncrasies; the very form of black English, and certainly its power, is derived from its tradition and preeminent usage as an oral language. So in Giovanni's poems both theme and structure rely on sound patterns for significance.

> i wanta say just gotta say something
> bout those beautiful beautiful beautiful outasight
> black men
> with they afros
> walking down the street
> is the same ol danger
> but a brand new pleasure

In the opening stanza of **"Beautiful Black Men (with compliments and apologies to all not mentioned by name),"** the idiom ("outasight") is present, so is the special syntax ("they afros"), but more centrally are the rhythms of speech employed to organize the poetic statement. The

statement is political, because the poem, like many of hers from this period, is meant to praise blackness: in praising, to foster, to incite. For the proper pride in and achievement of blackness is revolutionary. The poem is not a treatise, however; it is an emotionally charged utterance that, as it develops, creates through its own form the excitement about which it is speaking. In the first stanza, the repetitions, the emphases that the pause at line breaks creates, the accelerations within lines because of lack of pauses, all achieve the tenor of the speaking voice. As the poem progresses, the excitement that the speaker feels as she describes her subject is communicated by her voice on the page. . . . (pp. 157-58)

A sense of humor is never lacking in Giovanni's poetry—serious purpose does not negate the ability to laugh! [In **"Beautiful Black Men (with compliments and apologies to all not mentioned by name)"**], she mocks with affection the black male's love of splendor as it accompanies his dislike of cleanliness. What comes through in her tone is love as well as clear-sightedness, both qualities giving her the right to appreciate "beautiful, beautiful, beautiful black men." From wanting to say, having to say, something about beautiful black men, the poem moves, gathering speed and intensity as it goes, to a scream, a stamp and a shout that impel the person reading to likewise shout, likewise praise—to *feel* as the speaker feels. . . . (p. 159)

[Giovanni's] love poems are private and describe the woman enacting rather than criticizing the socially prescribed female role. They speak for Giovanni only and are not meant to incite anybody to any kind of revolution. Such a private / public dichotomy in her work may be neat, but it contains too great a degree of ambivalence for a woman poet like Giovanni to feel comfortable with it or to maintain it for long. How can the woman who sees herself as a sweet inspiration of her people and the woman who has been trained not only to sit and wait but also to need and to value interpersonal, private relationships be the same poet? In **"Adulthood"** (*Black Feeling, Black Talk/Black Judgement*)**,** she writes about going to college and learning that "just because everything i was was unreal / i could be real"—not from "withdrawal / into emotional crosshairs or colored bourgeois / intellectual pretensions," "But from involvement with things approaching reality / i could possibly have a life." What about not merely black reality, but her own reality? And what is the relation between them? Especially as through her poetry she becomes a genuine public personality, she needs to ask these questions. And what about the revolution?

A poet may be musician, preacher, articulator of a culture, but she or he is also a dreamer. In a series of poems about herself as dreamer, Giovanni explores the conflicting and confusing relations between her roles as poet, woman, and black.

In **"Dreams"** (*Black Feeling, Black Talk/Black Judgement*)**,** she describes her younger years—"before i learned / black people aren't / supposed to dream." She wanted, she says, to be a musician, a singer, a Raelet or maybe Marjorie Hendricks, grinding up against the mike screaming "baaaaaby nightandday." But then she "became more sensible":

and decided i would
settle down
and just become
a sweet inspiration

(The significance of the black singer—the musician as articulating the culture—appears throughout her work, as in **"Revolutionary Music"**: "you've just got to dig sly / and the family stone / damn the words / you gonna be dancing to the music" . . . "we be digging all / our revolutionary music consciously or un / cause sam cooke said 'a change is gonna come.' ")

A few years later, in **"The Wonder Woman"** (*My House*), she must deal with the fact of having become that sweet inspiration. "Dreams have a way / of tossing and turning themselves / around," she observes; also that "the times / make requirements that we dream / real dreams." She may have once dreamed of becoming a sweet inspiration of her people:

> . . . but the times
> require that i give
> myself willingly and become
> a wonder woman.

The wonder woman is a totally public personage who cannot—must not—integrate her personal needs and experiences into that role if they do not coincide. Giovanni makes this clear in poems about female stars, like Aretha Franklin, and in poems about herself, such as **"Categories"** (*My House*). . . . (pp. 165-66)

**"Categories"** [questions] black/white divisions (political and public), if they can—and they do—at times violate personal reality, describing in its second stanza an old white woman "who maybe you'd really care about" except that, being a young black woman, one's "job" is to "kill maim or seriously / make her question / the validity of her existence."

The poem ends by questioning the fact and function of categories themselves . . . , but, in doing so, it is raising the more profound matter of the relations between society and self. The earlier **"Poem for Aretha,"** 1970 (*Re: Creation*), begins with a clear sense of the separation between public and private selves:

> cause nobody deals with Aretha—a mother with
>    four
> children—having to hit the road
> they always say "after she comes
> home" . . .

Again Giovanni explains the significance of the musician/artist to society: "she is undoubtedly the one person who puts everyone on / notice," but about Aretha she also says, "she's more important than her music—if they must be / separated." (It is significant that the form of both these poems is closer to thought than speech. No answers here, only questions, problems.)

One means of bridging the gap between public and private is suggested in **"Revolutionary Dreams,"** 1970 (*Re: Creation*). . . . "Militant" and "radical" are poised against "natural" here, as they were in **"Categories."** But this poem makes the connection to gender: the "natural

dreams," of a "natural woman" who does what a woman does "when she's natural." The result of this juxtaposition is "true revolution." Somehow the black woman must be true to herself as she *is* to be both a poet and a revolutionary, for the nature of the revolution itself is in question. Revolutions are not only in the streets, where niggers must be asked if they can kill. Revolutions do not occur only in male terms, as Giovanni had begun to understand, humorously, in **"Seduction"** (*Black Feeling, Black Talk/Black Judgement*), in which the male keeps talking politics . . . while she is resting his hand on her stomach, licking his arm, unbuckling his pants, taking his shorts off. The poem is, however, set in some hypothetical future: "one day." It concludes with that future:

> then you'll notice
> your state of undress
> and knowing you you'll just say
> "Nikki,
> isn't this counterrevolutionary . . . ?"

The implicit reply is no, but it is not until her 1972 volume, *My House,* that Giovanni can make this answer with self-confidence. In the poems of *Black Feeling, Black Talk/Black Judgement* and of *Re: Creation,* the doubts are present, and possibilities for solution occur and disappear. However, *My House* as a book, not only the individual poems in it, makes a new statement about the revolution, about the very nature of political poetry, when the poet is a black woman.

Earlier, in **"My Poem"** (*Black Feeling, Black Talk/Black Judgement*), she had written:

> the revolution
> is in the streets
> and if i stay on
> the 5th floor
> it will go on
> and if i never do
> anything
> it will go on

Perhaps, but it will not be the same revolution, she has realized; and she has also come to understand that it will take place, as well, on the fifth floor.

In "On the Issue of Roles," Toni Cade, editor of one of the first collections of essays about being black and female, *The Black Woman,* makes a comment that seems to me to be a valuable gloss to the statement of Giovanni's *My House.*

> If your house ain't in order, you ain't in order.
> It is so much easier to be out there than right
> here. The revolution ain't out there. Yet. But it
> is here. Should be. And arguing that instant-
> coffee-ten-minutes-to-midnight alibi to justify
> hasty-headed dealings with your mate is shit.
> Ain't no such animal as an instant gorilla.

Ida Lewis points with a different vocabulary to the same phenomenon: "A most interesting aspect of her [Giovanni's] work is the poet's belief in individualism at a time when the trend in the Black community is away from the individual and towards the mass." In *My House,* Giovanni is trying to be a natural woman doing what a woman does when she's natural—in doing so, dreaming natural dreams, having a revolution. She is integrating private and public; in doing so, politicizing the private, personalizing the public. This action is occurring in poetry.

*My House* is divided into two sections, "The Rooms Inside" and "The Rooms Outside." The inside rooms hold personal poems about grandmothers, mothers, friends, lovers—all in their own way love poems. **"Legacies,"** in which the poet describes the relationship between grandmother and granddaughter, is a very political poem. . . . Black heritage is explained in personal terms. The little girl in the poem recognizes an impulse to be independent, but the speaker recognizes as well the importance of the old woman, of her love, to the grandchild in achieving her own adulthood. Although the poem ends by observing that "neither of them ever / said what they meant / and i guess nobody ever does," it is the poem itself that provides that meaning through its understanding.

Overtly political are poems like **"Categories"** or **"The Wonder Woman,"** but also political are the gentle love poems (**"The Butterfly," "When I Nap"**), and indeed all the poems that are about Giovanni as private person. . . . (pp. 166-170)

The poems of the rooms outside are not calls to action from the public platform; they are dreams, some funny, some apocalyptic, of old worlds and new. In each of these poems, *My House*'s equivalent to the earlier poems of black feeling and black judgment, the poet stresses the element of personal vision. . . . (p. 170)

This artist has begun to learn—through a process of coming to terms with herself as black woman, black poet, that art can create as well as reflect reality, as revolutions do.

It is fitting to the purpose of *My House* that its final poem, which is in "The Rooms Outside," is **"My House."** . . .

The first stanza follows Giovanni's familiar oral structure. Phrases stand against one another without the imaginative extensions of figurative language: word against word, repeating, altering, pointing. A love poem, to one particular lover. It starts in a tone reminiscent of both **"Beautiful Black Men"** and **"All I Gotta Do"**—the woman is there to adore her man: "i only want to / be there to kiss you"; "as you want"; "as you need." But although the gentle tone persists, an extraordinary change is rung with a firm emphasis on the personal and the possessive in the last three lines: "where i want to kiss you," "my house," "i plan." She is suiting his needs to hers as well as vice versa. . . . (p. 171)

Nonetheless, she makes it clear that she is still very much of a woman, using the traditionally female vocabulary of cooking and kitchens to underscore her message. But this woman is active, not passive: she means, wants, bakes, calls, runs. She orders experience and controls it. The element of control asserts itself not only through direct statement—"cause i run the kitchen"—but through vocabulary itself: "i mean"; "[i] call them yams" (in the latter phrase asserting blackness itself through control of language: "yams" and not "sweet potatoes"). She controls

not only through need and desire but through strength, ability: "i can stand the heat." . . .

The house and its elements . . . assume symbolic proportions, surely emphasized by the fact that the poem [continually calls] attention to its existence as a poem. The house is a world; it is reality. . . . (p. 172)

I am making a message, both poet and poem are insisting; and now they explain how messages work. "Trying to speak through" language rather than speaking it means that word and thing are not identical: that words are not yams, and thus language frees the poet to create realities (dreams) and not just to copy them. So that somehow this not-very-silly poem is carrying out a revolution. . . . (p. 173)

The act of naming, of using language creatively, becomes the most powerful action of all—saying, calling. Calling fudge love, calling smiling at old men revolution is creative (rather than derivative) action that expresses more than her own powers as woman and poet. In **"Seduction"** there was a significant gap between language (rhetoric) and action, between male and female. In that fable, men and words were allied and were seen by the woman poet as impotent. The woman was allied with action (love), but she was, in the poem, mute. The man calls her action "counterrevolutionary." Now, in **"My House,"** the woman's action, love (an overt expression of the personal, private sphere), is allied to language. Giovanni brings her power bases together in this poem, her dominion over kitchens, love, and words. No longer passive in any way, she makes the food, the love, the poem, and the revolution. She brings together things and words through her own vision (dream, poem) of them, seeing that language (naming) is action, because it makes things happen. Once fudge has been named love, touching one's lips to it becomes an act of love; smiling at old men becomes revolution "cause what's real / is really real." Real = dream + experience. To make all this happen, most of all there must exist a sense of self on the part of the maker, which is why the overriding tone of the poem is the sense of an "i" who in giving need feel no impotence from the act of taking (both become aspects of the same event). Thus this is *her* house and he makes her happy, thus and only thus—"cause" abounds in this poem, too: this, her poem, can be his poem. Not silly at all.

In bringing together her private and public roles and thereby validating her sense of self as black woman poet, Giovanni is on her way towards achieving in art that for which she was trained: emotionally, to love; intellectually and spiritually, to be in power; "to learn and act upon necessary emotions which will grant me more control over my life," as she writes in *Gemini*. Through interrelating love and power, to achieve a revolution—to be free . . . (pp. 173-74)

*Suzanne Juhasz, " 'A Sweet Inspiration . . . of My People': The Poetry of Gwendolyn Brooks and Nikki Giovanni," in her Naked and Fiery Forms: Modern American Poetry by Women, A New Tradition, Harper Colophon Books, 1976, pp. 144-76.*

## Michele Wallace

Nikki Giovanni, a kind of nationalistic Rod McKuen, was the reigning poetess of the Black Movement during the sixties. Most of us remember her best for poems like ["The True Import of Present Dialogue: Black vs. Negro"] written in 1968. . . . (p. 235)

She attached herself to a black poets' movement in New York that had been started by LeRoi Jones [Amiri Baraka]. The poems generally exhorted blacks to return to their roots and to partake in revolutionary action like killing honkies. There were a great many men and very few women involved; Giovanni was one of the few that lasted.

She had a remarkable facility for riding the tide of public opinion. When it became obvious that (1) the black male poets were going to shut her out and that (2) she could not depend upon a black female audience as long as her poems advocated outright violence, she began to speak positively of the church and to focus more on having babies and loving the black man. Her albums sold quite well. She herself had a baby and refused to disclose the name of the father. Early in the seventies she told young black women to become mothers because they needed something to love. She also told young black people that school was useless and a waste of time—despite her own years of education at Fisk University. Soon after, she backed away from these positions, amending her original statement about having babies to you-should-only-have-one-if-you-could-afford-to-take-care-of-it-like-she-could, and actually encouraging blacks to go back to school. Concomitantly, she began to make a lot of money on the college lecture circuit. She received an award for her work with youth from the *Ladies' Home Journal*. It was presented by Lynda Bird Johnson on national television.

Both [Angela] Davis and Giovanni represented the very best black women had to offer, or were allowed to offer, during the Black Movement. They carved out two paths for women who wished to be active. Davis's was Do-it-for-your-man. Giovanni's was Have-a-baby. Neither seemed to have any trouble confining herself to her narrow universe.

Unfortunately, and I believe unintentionally, Davis set a precedent for black female revolutionary action as action that could never be self-generated. When I visited Riker's Island several years ago, I met a few female revolutionaries suffering the consequences of that example. The run-of-the-mill female prisoner was there because of her man—her pimp, her dope supplier, or the man she had accompanied on a stickup. The political women were there for the same reason.

But only the most adventurous were ready to follow Angela Davis's lead. The majority took Nikki Giovanni much more seriously. She was the guiding light for those who had been left behind in the flurry and chaos of the revolution. No doubt she prompted many by word and deed to have babies so that they could have "something to love." By the time she advised them later to first make sure they had enough income to support the child, a lot of women were already on welfare. (pp. 236-38)

Although she rarely chose to reflect it in her work, Giovanni did realize the black woman's dilemma to some extent. A line from one of her later poems ["All I Gotta Do"] is unfortunately more typical: "what i need to do / is sit and wait / cause i'm a woman . . . " (p. 239)

> *Michele Wallace, "Chapter 3," in her* Black Macho and the Myth of the Superwoman, *Warner Books, 1978.*

## Nikki Giovanni [interview with Claudia Tate]

[Tate]: *Your earlier works,* **Black Feeling, Black Talk, Black Judgment** *and* **Re: Creation,** *seem very extroverted, militant, arrogant. The later work,* **The Women and the Men** *and* **Cotton Candy on a Rainy Day,** *seem very introverted, private, lonely, withdrawn. Does this shift in perspective, tone, and thematic focus reflect a conscious transition?*

[Giovanni]: I'll tell you what's wrong with that question. The assumption inherent in that question is that the self is not a part of the body politic. There's no separation.

I'm not a critic of my own work. It's not what I'm supposed to be about. I think literary analysis gives academics something to do. Books are generally amusement parks for readers. They will ultimately make a decision about which book to ride. But as for critics, they have to write a book as interesting as the one they're criticizing or the criticism is without validity. If they succeed, then the book they're writing about is only their subject; it is not in itself necessary. The critics could have written about anything. And after all, they've got to have something to do. It's Friday and it's raining, so they write a critique of Nikki Giovanni. It's not serious. And I'm not denigrating myself; it's just that it's no more serious than that.

*Is there a black aesthetic? If so, can you define it?*

It's not that I can't define the term, but I am not interested in defining it. I don't trust people who do. Melvin Tolson said you only define a culture in its decline; you never define a culture in its ascendancy. There's no question about that. You only define anything when it's on its way down. How high did it go? As long as it's traveling, you're only guessing. So too with the black aesthetic.

As the black-aesthetic criticism went, you were told that if you were a black writer or a black critic, you were told *this* is what you should do. That kind of prescription cuts off the question by defining parameters. I object to prescriptions of all kinds. In this case the prescription was a capsulized militant stance. What are we going to do with a stance? Literature is only as useful as it reflects reality. I talk about this in **Gemini;** I also say it's very difficult to gauge what we have done as a people when we have been systematically subjected to the whims of other people. (pp. 62-3)

*Is there validity to* For Colored Girls Who Have Considered Suicide When the Rainbow Is Enuf *and* Black Macho and the Myth of the Superwoman, *and the subsequent criticism these works incite?*

Evidently there is or it wouldn't fly. You're essentially

asking does it have a motor? It's got to have a motor or it wouldn't fly. Otherwise it'd just sit out on the runway. I have problems with this man–woman thing because I'm stuck on a word. The word's "boring." (p. 66)

I wrote a poem about a black man, and Don Lee wrote the most asinine thing I've ever read. His criticism was that Nikki Giovanni's problem is that she's had difficulty with a man. *Kirkus Review's* critical response to *The Women and the Men* was "Oh she's just in love." My life is not bound in anything that sells for $5.95. And it will never be. No matter what you're seeing, it's not me. If I'm not bigger than my books, I have a problem. I have a serious problem. I don't take my books personally because they're not personal. They reflect what I have seen, and I stand behind them because they are about reality, truth. I'm not America's greatest writer, but I'm credible.

The truth I'm trying to express is not about my life. This is not an autobiography we're talking about. *Gemini* is barely one, and it comes close. It was what I said it was, an autobiographical essay, which is very different from autobiography. Even autobiographies are not real because we only remember what we remember. And the truth has to be bigger than that, and if it isn't there's something wrong with your life. What we remember is only a ripple in a pond. It really is. And where does the last ripple go and who sees it? You never see the end of your own life. We put too much emphasis in the wrong places. And what we do to writers, particularly, is we try to get away from what is being said. We brand them. Of course, I'm back to the critics again.

The point of the writer is to remind us that nuclear energy, for example, is not just some technical, scientific thing, not that Pluto is the last planet and it's freezing, but that such things are comprehensible to the human mind.

We've got to live in the real world. If we don't like the world we're living in, change it. And if we can't change it, we change ourselves. We can do something. If in 1956 I didn't like the way the world was, it was incumbent upon me to at least join a picket line. I didn't have to join a picket line happily. I didn't have to join it with full knowledge of what this could mean to me. None of that was required of me. It was only required that I try to make a change so that ten years later I'll be able to go to Knoxville, Tennessee, and I'll be able to walk down Gay Street without having to move aside for some cracker. And in ten years we did. That was a limited goal, but I won. All I'm trying to say is, okay, if you can't win today, you can win tomorrow. That's all. My obligation is to win, but winning is transitory. What you win today, you start from ground zero on the next plateau tomorrow. That's what people don't want to deal with.

You're only as good as your last book. And that's what writers have a problem with. You say you wrote a book twelve years ago. Hey, I'm real glad, but I want to know what you are doing now. I complained about [Ralph] Ellison in *Gemini* in this regard. And I think it's a valid complaint. God wrote one book. The rest of us are forced to do a little better. You can't live forever on that one book. No matter how interesting, or how great, or how whatev-

er, you are forced to continue, to take a chance. Maybe your next book won't be as good as your last. Who knows?

A lot of people refuse to do things because they don't want to go naked, don't want to go without guarantee. But that's what's got to happen. You go naked until you die. That's the way it goes down. If you don't want to play, you're not forced to. You can always quit. But if you're not going to quit, play. You've got to do one or the other. And it's got to be your choice. You've got to make up your own mind. I made up my mind. If you're going to play, play *all* the way. You're going to sweat, and you're going to get hit, and you're going to fall down. And you're going to be *wrong*. Probably nine times out of ten you're going to be wrong, but it's the tenth time that counts. Because when you come up right, you come up right beautifully. But after that you have to start again. We as black people, we as people, we as the human species have got to get used to the fact we're not going to be right most of the time, not even when our intentions are good. We've got to go naked and see what happens. (pp. 67-9)

*What makes a poet different from a John Doe who's cleaning gutters?*

The fact that I write poetry and do it well makes me different. I dare say I probably wouldn't clean gutters nearly as well. Though if it came to cleaning gutters, I could do it. If I am a better poet, it's because I'm not afraid. If artists are different from ordinary people, that's because we are confident about what we are doing. That's the difference between what I would consider to be a serious artist and those who are in it for the fun. A lot of people are always into thinking they can become famous. Kids are always asking how one becomes famous. Well, I don't know. You know if you're talking fame, you're not a serious person. (p. 72)

You know people write me and say, "I want to be a writer. What should I write about?" How the hell should I know what one should write about?

Nobody's going to tell me what to write about because it's about me dancing naked on that floor. And if I'm going to be cold, it's going to be because I decided to dance there. And if you don't like to dance, go home. It's that simple. So the artistic attitude is that you take your work seriously. However, we writers would all be better off if we didn't deceive ourselves so frequently by thinking everything we create is important or good. It's not. When you reread something you need to be able to say, "Gee, that wasn't so hot. I thought it was really great ten years ago." But sometimes you can say, "Hey, it's not so bad."

*What about the prose?*

I don't reread my prose because I'm kind of afraid. I suppose one day I will. At least I would like to think so. But I'm very much afraid to be trapped by what I've said. I don't think life is inherently coherent. I think what Emerson said about consistency being the hobgoblin of little minds is true. The more you reread your prose the more likely you're going to try to justify what you've said. I don't really object to being an asshole. I don't take it personally.

If I never contradict myself then I'm either not thinking or I'm conciliating positions and, therefore, not growing. There has to be a contradiction. There would be no point to having me go three-fourths of the way around the world if I couldn't create an inconsistency, if I hadn't learned anything. If I ever get to the moon, it would be absolutely pointless to have gone to the moon and come back with the same position.

That's been a quarrel I've had with my fellow writers of the sixties. If you didn't learn anything what was the point of going through a decade? If I'm going to be the same at thirty-eight as I was at twenty-eight, what justifies the ten years to myself? And I feel that's who I've got to justify it to—ME.

Though I don't reread my prose, I do reread my poetry. After all that's how I earn my living.

*How do you polish the poems?*

A poem is a way of capturing a moment. I don't do a lot of revisions because I think if you have to do that then you've got problems with the poem. Rather than polish the words, I take the time to polish the poem. If that means I start at the top a dozen times, that's what I do. A poem's got to be a single stroke, and I make it the best I can because it's going to live. I feel if only one thing of mine is to survive, it's at least got to be an accurate picture of what I saw. I want my camera and film to record what my eye and my heart saw. It's that simple. And I keep working until I have the best reflection I can get. Universality has dimension in that moment.

*Do you have a particular writing method—a special place, a special time for writing?*

One thing for sure I can say about me is that if my book is going to bust, it's going to bust in public. It is either going to be so bad or so good. That's true of most of my books. Nothing is ever half way with me. It's shit or it's great. That's my attitude. I think that's the only way to go. Now other people are much more cautious. They'll do the safe thing and handle it right. Jean Noble put twelve years into *Beautiful Are the Souls of My Black Sisters.* Jean's book is beautiful, and I'm glad she did. Alex put twelve years in *Roots.* I couldn't be happier he did. I'm glad for Alex; I'm glad for me because I've got galleys. But I could no more put twelve years into anything. Nothing is worth twelve years to me. I can't grow a garden. I can't see waiting that long just for some vegetables. Some people can do it; I'm not one of them. I believe in accepting the limits of my competency.

That's a weakness. Yeah, I'll admit it. I just don't get a thrill out of seeing tomatoes grow. I do get a thrill seeing my poems, and I will take the time for them. But if after a year I was working on a poem, not a book but a poem, I would say something's wrong with either the poem or me. That's probably not the best way to be a writer. I wouldn't even want to consider myself an example. I'm essentially undisciplined. I do a lot of thinking, a lot of reading, but I wouldn't recommend my writing method. On the other hand I can't be like Hemingway and get up at six o'clock every morning and write for two hours. He had a wife who got up and cooked his breakfasts. I don't have time to sit there and write for two hours whether I have something to say or not. I write when it's compelling.

I'm not good at moving. I understand why Andrew Wyeth felt that if he left Brandywine he wouldn't be able to paint. It's very difficult for an artist to move. Richard Wright moved to Paris, and people said his work suffered. He didn't live long enough to reestablish his connection with his new place. I think people really overlook this. I never knew Wright, but I'm sure there was a lack of connection. It was very difficult for me to move from Cincinnati to New York. And it was equally difficult for me to move from New York back to Cincinnati. I have to feel at home in order to write. No matter what kind of little shack home is; I have to be at home. I'm very territorial.

*How do you regard your audience?*

I have always assumed that whoever is listening to a reading of mine, whether it be from my first book [*Black Feeling, Black Talk*] to the most recent, whether a kid or a senior citizen, deserves to hear my best. I think a lot of writers make the assumption that the people in the audience are not generally very bright. So they don't give them their best because they think they won't understand it. I also think there ought to be improvement in every subsequent piece of work.

We were talking about my writing habits. If my next book isn't at least an emotional improvement over my last book, I would never submit it to a publisher. I like to think there's growth. If there's no growth, there's no reason to publish. But I think the people who read me are intelligent. That's one reason I continue to be read because I do make this assumption: if you're reading me, you've got something going for yourself. That's arrogant. Writers are arrogant.

I would really feel badly if somebody said, "Well, I read you in '69 and I'm glad to say, you haven't changed." That would *ruin my day.* That would send me into a glass of something, and I don't drink. I'd have to say who are you and what have you read because I think I've changed. (pp. 72-5)

I have a heavy foot. And the advantage of that is not necessarily that I speed. It's that I will go in the wrong direction fast enough to recognize it and turn around and still beat you. We're going to make mistakes. It's not what so-and-so says that defines a mistake. It's what I decide is an error: that was wrong; that was dumb; that was insensitive; that was stupid. . . . But I've got to go on and try again. That's the only thing we really have to learn.

I'd like to beat the winners. That's the only fun. I wouldn't want to be the only black poet in America. It's not even interesting. I want to be among the best. And it's going to take a lot of poets because we don't even have enough to make a comparison. I'm looking for a golden age, and I would very much like to be a part of it. But there's no race now. In twelve years I produced fifteen books. That's not bad. I would like to have a little more attention.

I'm looking for a golden age, and the only way that's going to happen is for a lot of people to have a lot of different ideas. We don't need just one idea. That's my basic quarrel with some writers, and it remains. We don't need somebody telling us what to think. We need somebody to encourage us to think what we want to think. That was the problem with the black aesthetic. That's why *Negro Digest* went out of business—because it was boring.

On this level your critics do bear responsibility. I'm going to be very clear about this. You critics really praise what you understand. The fact that you understand it is almost suspect. Because once you get the critics all saying, "Well, that's really good," then you have to know something's wrong. If the ideas and concepts of a work are all that comprehensible, then the work hasn't broken any new ground. There has to be something new. (p. 78)

> *Nikki Giovanni and Claudia Tate, in an interview in* Black Women Writers at Work, *edited by Claudia Tate, Continuum, 1983, pp. 60-78.*

## Paula Giddings

It was the publication of ***Black Feeling, Black Talk, Black Judgement*** (1968, 1970) that began [Giovanni's] rise to national prominence. She captured the fighting spirit of the times with such lines as "Nigger can you kill?" (in **"The True Import of Present Dialogue, Black vs. Negro"**) and "a negro needs to kill / something" (**"Records"**). These poems were distinguished more by the contrast between the words and the image of their author than by anything else. Also in the volume were a number of personal poems, including gentle satires on sexual politics, and introspective, autobiographical ones, such as **"Nikki-Rosa,"** still one of her best. It talked about growing up, the value of a loving childhood and challenged the stereotype of the angry militant: " . . . they'll / probably talk about my hard childhood / and never understand that / all the while I was quite happy," she wrote.

From the beginning, the personal, feeling poems were juxtaposed against those of violent militancy. But in subsequent books she spurned the latter completely. Her vision in ***Black Feeling*** which saw "our day of Presence / When Stokely is in / The Black House" (**"A Historical Footnote to Consider Only When All Else Fails"**) narrowed, in her autobiographical essays *Gemini* (1971), to the conclusion that "Black men refuse to do in a concerted way what must be done to control White men." In any case, as she wrote in *My House* (1972), "touching" was the "true revolution" (**"When I Die"**).

But Giovanni's books after ***Black Feeling*** did more than repudiate violence. As critic Eugene Redmond pointed out, they offered her views from a new perspective: that of the rite of passage toward womanhood. The growing-up motif is a common one in literature, especially among women writers. It has provided some of their most memorable work and, in Giovanni's case, a unifying theme in her work.

In *Gemini,* she is the feisty woman-child who, to the consternation of her mother, defies middle-class convention and gets suspended from Fisk. She traces her relationship with her older sister, that evolves from shameless idolatry to the realization that love "requires a safe distance." In these essays we are introduced to other members of her family, including a wise and warm grandmother and a newly born son, who reappear in later books.

As the title suggests, ***My House*** continues this theme, and Giovanni explores the legacies passed from generation to generation; and the lighthearted pleasures of love and mischief. Sex sans politics does allow more playfulness; in the book's title poem, she writes about kissing you "where I want to kiss you / cause it's my house / and i plan to live in it."

The evolvement away from the political poems had a significant impact on her career. Her work became distinguished from that of others in her generation at a time when it was propitious to stand out from the rest. By the early seventies, the Black movement was in disarray, factionalized, and largely reduced to internecine bickering. Giovanni, however, could still maintain an appeal across ideological lines. (pp. 212-13)

Pursuing the rite-of-passage theme eventually leads to becoming a woman; an adult, graced or burdened with the responsibilities of maturity. ***The Women and the Men*** recognized a coming of age. For the first time, the figure of the woman-child is virtually absent. In "The Woman" section, the dominant theme is the search for identity, for place, in the community of Black women. In the poem **"The Life I Led,"** whose title is already suggestive, the poet even envisions her physical aging process: "i know my arms will grow flabby / it's true / of all the women in my family." The free-spirited love poems are grounded in the concern that "my shoulder finds a head that needs nestling." Although there are fewer poems in this volume that get a rise from an audience, the collection is clear and definite in its tone. It is as if the search for identity and womanhood had come to fruition. In place of the nervous, mercurial relationships of youth, there is a relaxation evident. Now the poet is capable of "lazily throwing my legs / across the moon" (**"I Want to Sing"**).

In each of Giovanni's books, there is a poem or two which signals the direction of a subsequent book. In ***The Women and the Men,*** **"Something to Be Said for Silence"** contains the lines "somewhere something is missing / . . . maybe i'm just tired"; and in **"December of My Springs,"** another poem, Giovanni looks forward to being "free from children and dinners / and people i have grown stale with."

The next book, ***Cotton Candy on a Rainy Day*** (1978), recognizes the completion of a cycle. " . . . Now I don't fit beneath the rose bushes anymore," she writes, "anyway they're gone." (**"The Rose Bush"**.) The lines are indicative of the mood of this book, which talks about a sense of emotional dislocation of trying "to put a three-dimensional picture on a one-dimensional frame," as she wrote in the title poem. She has evolved to be that creature which often finds itself estranged from the history which created it: a bright Black female in a white mediocre world, she notes in **"Forced Retirement."** The consequences are an emotional compromise to a bleak reality, for compromise is necessary to forestall inevitable abandonment. Although the men in her life "refused to / be a man," Giovanni writes in **"Woman,"** she decided it was "all / right." The book is immersed in world-weary cynicism, as the lines, "she had lived long and completely enough / not to be chained to the truth" suggest (**"Introspection"**).

*Cotton Candy* does have its upbeat poems, but it is the rain dampening the spirit of another time which prevails. There is an emotional as well as a physical fatigue in the "always wanting / needing a good night's rest" (**Introspection"**).

The same mood dominates . . . ***Those Who Ride the Night Winds*** (1983), but in a different way. Frankly, this collection is so hollow, the thinking so fractious, that it makes a reader ask new questions about the author. One of the needling problems in Giovanni's books, particularly those published after 1975, is that as her persona matured, her language, craft, and perceptions did not. Although lyricism, and profundity were never her forte, the simplistic, witty vocabulary in her earlier work were appropriate for the observations of the woman-child. But more is needed from a fortyish woman who contemplates the meaning—or meaninglessness—of life. The symptoms which appeared sporadically in earlier books, of a poet losing control of her theme, completely engulf *Night Winds.* Perhaps it is because even greater resources are needed to pass through the life stage of introspection to commenting on the world around her.

From the first of the book we know that Giovanni will take on such subjects as art and the human condition. In the preface she tells us: "The first poem . . . ever written . . . was probably carved . . . on / a cold damp cave . . . by a physically unendowed cave man / . . . who wanted to make a good impression . . . on a physically endowed / . . . cave woman. . . . " Already it is evident that she is in over her head. The poem **"Love: Is a Human Condition"** is typical of the quality of thought in this book—which often borders on the incoherent. It begins, "An amoeba is lucky it's so small . . . else its narcissism would lead / to war . . . since self-love seems so frequently to lead to self-righteousness. . . . " What does size have to do with narcissism? And isn't self-righteousness often a function of the lack of genuine self-love? Of course the fundamental question is what an amoeba has to do with the poem's title in the first place. One must ask, she says, "if the ability to reproduce oneself efficiently has / anything to do with love. . . . "

Unfortunately, in terms of imagery and craft, similes like this one are all too common: "Lips . . . like brownish gray gulls infested by contact with / polluted waters circling a new jersey garbage heap . . . flap in / anticipation . . . " (**"Mirrors"**). In search for some philosophical meaning of her life (one assumes), the poet subjects her readers to lines like "My father . . . you must understand . . . was Human . . . My mother / . . . a larva . . . and while I concede most Celestial Beings . . . have / taken the bodies of the majority . . . I chose differently . . . No / one understands me . . . " (**"A Word for Me . . . Also"**). Little wonder. Although the poet concedes confusion in the succeeding stanza, Giovanni doesn't seem to understand that even "non-sense" poems must have some internal logic and meaning to justify their existence.

Even the love poems, which were once entertaining, are flat and uninspiring in this book. The same concepts, words, and even phrases which once described the gleam-in-the-eye flirtations are superimposed on what seems to be more meaningful relationships. The result is an overwhelming sense of triviality.

We look for relief in the poems written in the names of the artist Charles White, the playwright-activist Lorraine Hansberry, and the slave poet Phillis Wheatley. What more fertile subjects for a politically conscious poet? But there is no relief from the lack of substance, the lack of structural and aesthetic power, the trite philosophizing.

Underlying the problems in *Night Winds* may be Giovanni's own philosophy of writing. It was conceived at a time when we were generous, some could call us loose, in our definition of poetry. Seduced by the content of the writings of many young Turks, we bestowed the label of "poet" as a reward. Few demanded that poetry weave emotion and creative imagination with the mastery of language. Few exhorted that the use of "free verse" required even greater skill than more traditional forms. Then, the message, not the medium, was important.

In *Gemini,* written at a time when many believed that intellectualism eroded the spirit, Giovanni wrote: "I couldn't see anywhere to go intellectually and thought I'd take a chance on feeling." Convinced that too many Black writers had been stymied by the self-conscious quest for perfection, she said in *Poetic Equation:* "I am perfectly willing to expose a great deal of foolishness [in my work] because I don't think infallibility is anything to be proud of." The point, she continued, was to learn from mistakes and go on. It is a philosophy which has made her a highly prolific writer. It is also one which allowed her to touch the rapid, irregular pulse of an earlier time. The appeal of the early Giovanni, as a poet and a media personality, was her highly individual way of thinking and feeling, her maverick attitude toward respectability, her concern for the elderly, her "silly" love poems, and a confessed fallibility in the face of humorless ideological dictates. Her lack of concern with craft and technique—even in literary circles—was not unappealing when the prevailing ethos was protest, whether in the form of political or personal rebellion. But as times and her own focus changed, Giovanni's lack of growth combined with a diminution of creative energy and spirit has made her latest book a sad parody of earlier ones.

Looking over her entire career, Nikki Giovanni's achievements are many. Not the least of them is chronicling the life passages of a young Black woman imbued with the sensibilities of the sixties. But her greatest challenge, as a poet, lies ahead in the eighties. One hopes that she will be able to fulfill an earlier promise. (pp. 214-17)

*Paula Giddings, "Nikki Giovanni: Taking a Chance on Feeling," in* Black Women Writers (1950-1980): A Critical Evaluation, *edited by Mari Evans, Anchor Press/Doubleday, 1984, pp. 211-17.*

## William J. Harris

Even though Nikki Giovanni has a large popular audience, she has not gained the respect of the critics. Michele Wallace calls her "a kind of nationalistic Rod McKuen"; Eugene Redmond claims her poetry "lacks lyricism and imagery"; Haki Madhubuti (Don L. Lee) insists she lacks the sophistication of thought demanded of one with pretensions of a "political seer" and finally, Amiri Baraka and Saunders Redding, united on no other issue, declare in their different styles that she is simply an opportunist. These critics illustrate the problem of evaluating Nikki Giovanni dispassionately. Her limitations notwithstanding, there is a curious tendency of normally perceptive critics to undervalue her, to condescend to her rather than to criticize her.

When Michele Wallace compares Giovanni to McKuen, she is suggesting that both are popular poets. This is true enough, but still there is a crucial difference between them: McKuen is a bad popular poet; Giovanni is a good one. He is a bad popular poet because he presents conventional sentiments in a shamelessly sloppy form. His retellings of conventional stories in conventional ways, without a trace of thought or feeling, have won him a ready audience. In essence, he is the genius of the unexamined life; he is the opposite of a serious artist who is dedicated to the exploration of his life. The serious artist deals in fresh discoveries; McKuen in clichés. Giovanni, on the other hand, is a popular poet but also a serious artist because she tries to examine her life honestly. (p. 218)

Giovanni is a good popular poet: she is honest, she writes well-crafted poems, and, unlike McKuen, she pushes against the barriers of the conventional; in other words, she responds to the complexities of the contemporary world as a complex individual, not as a stock character in anybody's movie about Anyplace, U.S.A. In fact, much of Giovanni's value as a poet derives from her insistence on being herself; she refuses to go along with anybody's orthodoxy. Since she is always reacting to her multifarious environment, it is not surprising that her career has already gone through three distinct stages: first, the black militant; then the domestic lover; and now the disappointed lover. Therefore, it is clear that her move from Black militant poet to domestic woman poet is not a contradiction, as some critics maintain, but only a response to her times: the seventies and eighties call for different responses than did the sixties. Unlike Madhubuti she is not doctrinaire; she does not have a system to plug all her experiences into. She examines her time and place and comes to the conclusions she must for that time and place.

Giovanni does have weaknesses. At times she does not seem to think things through with sufficient care. Furthermore, she often does not bother to finish her poems; consequently, there are many unrealized poems in her oeuvre. Finally, not unlike a movie star, she is possibly too dependent on her public personality. In other words, she can be self-indulgent and irresponsible. Paradoxically, her shortcomings do grow out of the same soil as her strengths, that is, out of her independence of mind, her individuality, and her natural charm.

Since her first book in 1968, Nikki Giovanni has published a number of volumes of poetry, . . . and even though her attitudes have changed over the years, the books are unified by her personality. Like many poets of the period she is autobiographical and her personal stamp is on all her work. There is also a consistency of style, even though there is a change of mood: the poetry is always direct, conversational, and grounded in the rhythms of Black music and speech. Her poems are also unified in that they are written from the perspective of a Black woman. Moreover, her themes remain constant: dreams, love, Blackness, womanhood, mothers, children, fathers, family, stardom, fame, and sex. (pp. 219-20)

In Giovanni's first stage she wrote several classic sixties poems expressing the extreme militancy of the period. These include **"The True Import of Present Dialogue, Black vs. Negro,"** and **"For Saundra."** In 1968 Giovanni spits out:

> Nigger
> Can you kill
> Can you kill
> Can a nigger kill
> Can a nigger kill a honkie

The poem these lines are taken from, **"The True Import of the Present Dialogue, Black vs. Negro,"** is intended to incite violence by asking for the literal death of white America. It captures the spirit of the sixties, that feeling that Armageddon, the final battle between good and evil, is imminent. It is informed by the example of Frantz Fanon, the Black revolutionary author of *The Wretched of the Earth,* whose book Eldridge Cleaver called "the Bible" of the Black liberation movement. In it, Fanon declares: "National liberation, national renaissance, the restoration of nationhood of the people, commonwealth: whatever may be the headings used or the new formulas introduced, decolonisation is always a violent phenomenon." Cleaver correctly claims that Fanon's book "legitimize[s] the revolutionary impulse to violence." No matter how romantic that moment now seems, there was then a sincere feeling that it was a time of revolution; and Giovanni, along with Madhubuti, Baraka and others, expressed these revolutionary ideas in their poems. Furthermore, Giovanni's poem **"The True Import of Present Dialogue, Black vs. Negro"** embodies more than the literal demand for the killing of whites: it also expresses a symbolic need on the part of Blacks to kill their own white values:

> Can you kill the nigger
> in you
> Can you make your nigger mind
> die

Eliot has said that poetry should not deviate too far from common speech; these Black revolutionary poets—in a sense Eliot's heirs—demonstrate that they have absorbed the subtleties of their language. For example, in the above poem Giovanni exploits the complex connotations of the term "nigger"; she uses it in this stanza to suggest the consciousness that wants to conform to white standards; consequently, to kill the "nigger" is to transform consciousness. In more general terms, the entire poem is cast in the form of a street chant: the rhythm is intended to drive the reader into the street, ready to fight. In fact, the source of much of the form utilized in the 1960s Black Arts Movement is street language and folk forms such as the chant and the dozens, a form of ritualized insult.

Giovanni's **"For Saundra"** provides the rationale for the New Black Poetry:

> i wanted to write
> a poem
> that rhymes
> but revolution doesn't lend
> itself to be-bopping
>
> . . .
>
> maybe i shouldn't write
> at all
> but clean my gun

In short, Giovanni is saying that the times will not allow for poems which are not political in nature, which do not promote revolution. In the 1960s art had to subordinate itself to revolution. Ron Karenga insisted: "All art must reflect and support the Black Revolution."

Even though such revolutionary figures as Karenga and Baraka stressed collective over individual values, Giovanni remains an individual, implicitly questioning the call for revolutionary hatred in the very titles of such poems as **"Letter to a Bourgeois Friend Whom Once I Loved (and Maybe Still Do If Love Is Valid)."** She feels the tension between personal and revolutionary needs—a tension that runs throughout her work in the revolutionary period. Baraka demands: "Let there be no love poems written / until love can exist freely and cleanly." Giovanni understands that there are times of hate but also realizes that to subordinate all feeling to revolutionary hate is too abstract and inhuman.

Yet Giovanni's independence can be irresponsible. At times she seems a little too eager to gratify human desires at the expense of the revolution. She confides in **"Detroit Conference of Unity and Art"** (dedicated to former SNCC leader H. Rap Brown):

> No doubt many important
> Resolutions
> Were passed
> As we climbed Malcolm's ladder
> But the most
> Valid of them
> All was that
> Rap chose me

Even a nonrevolutionary reader would question the political commitment of the above lines. If one is going to set herself up as a serious poet-prophet—and Giovanni has—one had better be concerned about the revolutionary business at a meeting, not one's love life. This is the sort of frivolousness that Giovanni's critics, such as Madhubuti and Wallace, rightfully attack. However, at other times, Giovanni's frivolousness was refreshing in those tense and serious days of revolt. **"Seduction"** delightfully points out that the revolution cannot be conducted twenty-four hours a day. The poem centers around a brother so earnestly involved in the revolution that he does not notice

that the poet has stripped both of them. The poem concludes:

> then you'll notice
> your state of undress
> and knowing you you'll just say
> "Nikki,
> isn't this counterrevolutionary . . . ?"

Part of Giovanni's attractiveness stems from her realization that for sanity, there must be sex and humor, even in revolutionary times.

When the revolution failed her, Giovanni turned to love and began writing a more personal poetry, signaling the onset of the second stage of her career. The literature of the seventies was quite unlike those of the hot and hopeful sixties. . . . For Giovanni idealism of the sixties had been replaced by the despair of the seventies. . . . The sixties stood for endless possibility; the seventies for hopelessness and frustration. However, in *My House* she seeks an alternative to public commitment and finds one in domestic love. Giovanni is not the only Black figure to seek new alternatives in the seventies: Cleaver found God; Baraka found Marxism; Julian Bond shifted allegiances from the activist organization SNCC to the staid NAACP. (pp. 220-23)

Giovanni has exchanged the role of revolutionary Mother Courage, sending her Black troops into battle, for the role of domestic Black woman, making fudge for her Black man. While the poem may make the reader uncomfortable—has it set the feminist movement back fifty years?—one can sympathize with Giovanni's desire to retreat into domestic comforts in the face of a disappointing world. In **"My House"** she declares her domesticity loudly, militantly, perhaps to give herself confidence in her new role. Later she will celebrate the domestic more quietly and convincingly. . . .

[In **"Winter"** from *Cotton Candy*], Giovanni gathers supplies to retreat from the cold world; however, it is only for a season. And unlike **"My House,"** this poem creates a snug place one would want to retire to; Giovanni has become more comfortably at home in the domestic world of **"Winter"** than in the brash **"My House."**

If she implicitly questioned "pure" revolution earlier, in the seventies she questions all ideologies that try to define or categorize her. . . .

It is not surprising that this maverick does not want to be fenced in by anybody—friend or foe. She will not go along with anybody's orthodoxy.

By the third stage of her career, love, too, has failed Giovanni. In the title poem from *Cotton Candy on a Rainy Day* (1978), she notes:

> what this decade will be
> known for
> There is no doubt it is
> loneliness

and in the same poem she continues:

> If loneliness were a grape
> the wine would be vintage

If it were a wood
the furniture would be mahogany
But since it is life it is
Cotton Candy
on a rainy day
The sweet soft essence
of possibility
Never quite maturing

. . .

I am cotton candy on a rainy day
the unrealized dream of an idea unborn

*Cotton Candy* is Giovanni's bleakest book and reflects the failure of both revolution and love in the late seventies. Possibility has become stillborn.

*Cotton Candy's* bleak title poem provides a good example of the problems the reader faces in trying to evaluate Giovanni. Even though the poem is not a total success, it is better than it appears on casual reading. At first the title seems totally sentimental: "cotton candy" conjures up images of sticky, sappy love—it seems to catapult us into the world of Rod McKuen. . . . Despite the poem's sometimes vague language which suggests the conventional popular poem, **"Cotton Candy"** has serious moments which save it from the world of pop songs and greeting cards. When we look closely at the cotton candy image we see it refers to a world of failed possibility; and the language, at least for a few lines, is stately and expressive of a generation. . . . (pp. 223-26)

A curious aspect of Giovanni's appeal has little to do with her language per se but with the sensibility she creates on the page. It isn't that she does not use words effectively. In fact, she does. Not only did she use Black forms effectively during the sixties; in the seventies she mastered a quieter, less ethnic, free verse mode. However, on the whole what is most striking about Giovanni's poetry is that she has created the charming persona of "Nikki Giovanni." This persona is honest, searching, complex, lusty, and, above all, individualistic and charmingly egoistical. This is a verbal achievement having less to do with the surface of language than with the creation of a character, that is, more a novelistic achievement than a lyric one.

Giovanni's lust is comedic (see **"Seduction"**) and healthy; it permeates her vision of the world. . . . A source of her unabashed lustiness could be the tough, blues-woman tradition. She could be following in the footsteps of Aretha Franklin's "Dr. Feelgood." The following Giovanni poem explicitly exploits and updates the blues/soul tradition:

its wednesday night baby
and i'm all alone
wednesday night baby
and i'm all alone

. . .

but i'm a modern woman baby
ain't gonna let this get me down
i'm a modern woman
ain't gonna let this get me down
gonna take my master charge
and get everything in town

This poem combines the classic blues attitude about love—defiance in the face of loss—with references to contemporary antidotes to pain: charge cards.

The poem **"Ego Tripping,"** one of her best poems, grounded in the vital Black vernacular, features her delightful egotism. The poem is a toast, a Black form where the hero establishes his virtues by boasting about them. Her wonderfully healthy egotism, which is expressed succinctly in these witty lines: "show me some one not full of herself / and i'll show you a hungry person" abounds in **"Ego Tripping."** . . . In a way **"Ego Tripping"** is an updating of Hughes' "The Negro Speaks of Rivers" from a woman's perspective. Hughes' poem is a celebration of the collective Black experience from the primordial time to the present. Giovanni's poem creates a giant mythic Black woman who embodies and celebrates the race across time. The poem doesn't only claim that Giovanni is Black and proud: it creates a magnificent Black woman whose mere gaze can burn out a Sahara Desert and whose casual blowing of her nose can provide oil for the entire Arab world. In a word, she is "bad!" Since it is not Giovanni speaking personally but collectively, it is not a personal boast but a racial jubilee.

Giovanni is a frustrating poet. I can sympathize with her detractors, no matter what the motives for their discontent. She clearly has talent that she refuses to discipline. She just doesn't seem to try hard enough. In **"Habits"** she coyly declares:

i sit writing
a poem
about my habits
which while it's not
a great poem
is mine

It isn't enough that the poem is hers; personality isn't enough, isn't a substitute for fully realized poems. Even though she has created a compelling persona on the page, she has been too dependent on it. Her ego has backfired. She has written a number of lively, sometimes humorous, sometimes tragic, often perceptive poems about the contemporary world. The best poems in her three strongest books, **Black Feeling, Black Talk, Black Judgement, Re:Creation,** and **Cotton Candy,** demonstrate that she can be a very good poet. However, her work also contains dross: too much unrealized abstraction (flabby abstraction at that!), too much "poetic" fantasy posing as poetry and too many moments verging on sentimentality. . . . Giovanni must keep her charm and overcome her self-indulgence. She has the talent to create good, perhaps important, poetry, if only she has the will to discipline her craft. (pp. 226-28)

*William J. Harris, "Sweet Soft Essence of Possibility: The Poetry of Nikki Giovanni," in* Black Women Writers (1950-1980): A Critical Evaluation, *edited by Mari Evans, Anchor Books, 1984, pp. 218-28.*

**Marita Golden**

In *Sacred Cows and Other Edibles,* Nikki Giovanni—

poet, personality, social critic, iconoclast and raconteur—exhibits the best and the worst uses of the essay as a vehicle for expression, verbal performance and exploration of the mundane and the special. . . . The topics Giovanni submits to her unique brand of analysis are as different as the stances she assumes. Tennis, termites, game shows, black political leaders, literary politics, the profession of writing, odes to fellow writers and the proper celebration of national holidays are some of the subjects Giovanni explores with humor that is street and worldly wise, and with occasional insights that, in the best Giovanni style, turn a neat phrase too.

The problem with *Sacred Cows and Other Edibles,* however, is that it falls short precisely because Giovanni's glib, wise-cracking overly conversational style (which has made her poetry so popular) is ill-suited to the intellectual requirements of the essay. These pieces mildly entertain more than they probe; more often than not, the reader is merely reminded of what is obvious rather than introduced to another way of seeing things.

Giovanni is at her best in the selection titled **"Reflections on My Profession"** and **"Four Introductions"**—pieces dedicated to writers, among them Paule Marshall and Mari Evans. In **"An Answer to Some Questions on How I Write"** Giovanni asserts, "I don't have a lifestyle. I have a life," which made me want to cheer this hearty refutation of categories and oversimplification of the human equation. And puncturing the vague pomposity of the current hot cliché, the "role model," Giovanni says: "When people do not want to do what history requires, they say they have no role models. I'm glad Phillis Wheatley did not know she had no role model and wrote her poetry anyway." And she sums up the job of the writer with a feisty confidence saying, "We write because we believe that the human spirit cannot be tamed and should not be trained." This is Giovanni at her best—sparkling *and* thoughtful.

But the overall quality of this collection is marred by the author's penchant for digression. Several pieces cry out loudly for editing. In one essay ostensibly on the writer's profession, Giovanni wanders over an unruly terrain that detours to a discussion of Vanessa Williams, the Miss America Pageant, Bob Guccione, her son Tom and her dog Bruno. She apologizes for the "tendency to digress" without much conviction, blaming it on having passed her 40th birthday. The longer the essay, the more Giovanni seems to glory in her ability to free-form associate a host of incompatible ideas and examples so that it becomes like reading a conversation with someone who has 100 opinions on a single topic.

Politically, Giovanni adopts a neo-black conservatism—knocking special privileges, and racial and sexual quotas. I've no problem with her political views, but whatever Giovanni's political beliefs or how long they last, they deserve stronger justification than "Life seems so unfair lately to those of us who are ordinary."

Black conspicuous consumption, buppies and materially successful blacks come in for special praise. Giovanni long ago decided she was a winner and so she has spun gold in most of her career endeavors, exhibiting little patience with those too busy complaining to hustle up some luck. She criticizes black political and social leaders for promoting a perception of the black community as weak, fragmented and hopelessly mired in despair, all she asserts quite convincingly, for the sake of their corporate and foundation-supported bread and butter.

*Sacred Cows and Other Edibles* is quintessential Nikki Giovanni—sometimes funny, nervy and unnerving with flashes of wisdom. But this collection will be appreciated most by those already among the converted, rather than those searching for someone to follow.

*Marita Golden, "Tennis, Termites, Game Shows and the Art of Writing," in* Book World—The Washington Post, *February 14, 1988, p. 3.*

# Doris Grumbach

## 1918-

(Born Doris Isaac Grumbach) American novelist, critic, and biographer.

Drawing upon historical, biographical, and autobiographical elements, Grumbach's novels involve a process of constant reflection and reinterpretation of facts, paralleled by characters who frequently reflect upon their own lives and professions. Often placed in academic environments, these characters are intelligent but unable to use their knowledge to lead satisfying lives or enjoy fulfilling relationships.

Grumbach was a teacher and a literary critic before she wrote her first novel, *The Spoil of the Flowers.* Set in a boarding school, this work condemns inhumanity among privileged and powerful people. Although critically respected for its sensitive character portrayal, *The Spoil of the Flowers* remains Grumbach's least known novel. *The Short Throat, the Tender Mouth,* her next work, is a semi-autobiographical account of a group of New York University students during three politically heated months in 1939. These bright undergraduates are enthusiastic about their futures, but ultimately fail to realize their potential. While some critics thought that inadequate character development resulted in the creation of stereotypes in *The Short Throat, the Tender Mouth,* most praised this novel for capturing the excitement of the time period.

After her second novel, Grumbach took a hiatus from writing fiction and concentrated on *The Company She Kept,* a literary biography of Mary McCarthy. This work caused a public controversy concerning Grumbach's use of private information and her melange of fact and fiction. McCarthy objected to the use of tapes and letters she had sent her biographer, claiming that they had been for Grumbach's personal enlightenment, and not for print. McCarthy was successful in suppressing material from the biography. *The Company She Kept* hinges upon Grumbach's assertion that only a faint distinction exists between McCarthy's life and her fiction. Grumbach uses events in McCarthy's novels to illuminate occurrences in the author's life. Many critics objected to this method of research, which they considered extremely hypothetical and claimed that Grumbach relied too heavily on other critics' interpretations of McCarthy's works.

Ten years after the publication of *The Company She Kept,* Grumbach published a well-received novel, *Chamber Music,* based on the lives of composer Edward MacDowell and his wife, Marian. The main characters, Robert and Caroline, have a dispassionate marriage, marked by the revelation of Robert's incestuous relationship with his mother and his homosexual affair with a student. After Robert's death from syphilis, which Grumbach describes in clinical detail, Caroline finds happiness with her lesbian lover, Anna. Although *Chamber Music* often deals with shocking material, the novel possesses a reserved, Victori-

an style that critics admired. Victoria Glendinning wrote: "What gives the main part of this book its polish and flavor is the contrast between matter and manner." Some commentators, however, contended that Grumbach's use of Caroline as narrator restricts her ability to adequately examine the novel's characters and their motives. Similar criticism befell Grumbach's next novel, *The Missing Person.* The protagonist, Franny Fuller, is a Hollywood starlet modeled after Marilyn Monroe. The simple narrative style of this novel reflects Franny's superficial personality.

Grumbach again fictionalizes historical figures in *The Ladies,* retelling the story of two eighteenth-century women, Lady Eleanor Butler and Sarah Ponsonby, who elope to the secluded Welsh village of Llangollen. Echoing opinions of Grumbach's previous historical novels, Valerie Miner observed: "This book feels as if the writer put tracing paper over history, elaborating here and there, but essentially following a predetermined course." Others argued that *The Ladies* is an admirable departure from many pessimistic lesbian novels, such as Radclyffe Hall's *The Well of Loneliness,* which recount tales of loss and unrequited love. By contrast, Sarah and Lady Eleanor lead blissful lives, tending to their elaborate estate and receiving Sir Walter Scott, Edmund Burke, and the Duke of Wellington as occasional guests. Sandra M. Gilbert expounded: "[If] there is anything problematic about *The Ladies,* it is that all seems to go almost too well for Lady Eleanor and her beloved." *The Magician's Girl,* which follows the lives of three college friends, presents a much more dismal picture of life than does *The Ladies:* one woman commits suicide at an early age, another is tragically killed in an auto accident just when she believes she has found happiness, and the third achieves fame by photographing freaks.

(See also *CLC,* Vols. 13, 22; *Contemporary Authors,* Vols. 5-8, rev. ed.; *Contemporary Authors New Revision Series,* Vol. 9; and *Contemporary Authors Autobiography Series,* Vol. 2.)

## PRINCIPAL WORKS

NOVELS

*The Spoil of the Flowers*   1962
*The Short Throat, the Tender Mouth*   1964
*Chamber Music*   1979
*The Missing Person*   1981
*The Ladies*   1985
*The Magician's Daughter*   1987

OTHER

*The Company She Kept*   (biography)   1967

---

**John Muggeridge**

*The Missing Person* is one of those frequent novels written for adults who block their ears. Written in flat *Redbook* cover-story prose, it depicts scenes from the life and sexploitation of Franny Fuller (whose marriages—first to an amiable jock, and then to a Jewish New York playwright—make her an obvious preincarnation of Marilyn Monroe) interleaved with Marxist-feminist musings of the sort that Grumbach's school of journalists indulge in as reflexively as breathing. Even Franny, dumb, lost blonde that she is, identifies with the powder-puff proletariat. Her fellow aspirants to stardom she calls "sisters in passivity . . . who could never resolve anything for themselves because they had never been told it was possible"; in Franny's view being a man meant being able to think things up for yourself and make them happen; all women were, like her, "waiting for the Great Something they dreamed about all their lives to happen to them." No wonder, then, that the two wholly sympathetic male characters in *The Missing Person* are Eddie Puritan, Franny's homosexual agent, the only person capable of making her feel complete, and Ira Rorie, a girlishly named new-class Negro forced by segregated housing to inhabit his Cadillac, with whom she exchanges life stories and enjoys her only reciprocally satisfying sexual encounter.

In the end, however, melancholy lyricism triumphs over ideology. There is in *The Missing Person* more of *Photo-*

*play* than of *Socialist Woman.* A damp-eyed whimsicality afflicts all but the sternest-souled writers on Hollywood, and Grumbach catches such a heavy dose of it that finally she is reduced to incoherence. (p. 27)

> *John Muggeridge, in a review of "The Missing Person" in* The American Spectator, *Vol. 15, No. 1, January, 1982, p. 27.*

**Valerie Miner**

The Ladies of Llangollen are real figures, and Doris Grumbach has tried to convert their marvelous adventure into a novel [*The Ladies*]. . . . The story, itself, is a whopping good one, but Grumbach's writing raises serious concerns about the distinction between historical narrative and fiction.

Eleanor Butler is an independent young woman who enjoys athletic activity and vigorous reading. Sarah Ponsonby, delicate and sensitive, is sent off to finishing school to escape her uncle's lecherous intentions. Eleanor and Sarah meet and form an unlikely friendship. "After a fortnight of walking the grounds and exploring the nearby town, reading and listening, talking before the fire and in their beds, smiling at each other surreptitiously across the silent supper table and laughing together during their private breakfasts at the prospect of spending the day ahead alone together, Sarah knew she loved Eleanor."

For years the two correspond and visit and then decide to elope. The first escape is disastrous, with Sarah almost dying of pneumonia. They are caught and made to return home. Their families surrender at their second attempt, baffled but relieved to be free of these peculiar women. Eventually after many miles and much hardship, they come upon the pretty village of Llangollen and fall in love with a house that they name "Plas Newydd," New Place.

Their life is full of passion, risk, humor and originality. But Grumbach's treatment is curiously distant and cool. She says she has "changed names, switched facts about, changed and abridged the chronology, inferred, interpreted, denied, imagined. I have 'made them up' as I imagine they might have been." Like her previous "novel" about the MacDowell family, *Chamber Music,* this book elicits caveats about the practice and quality of such non-fiction fiction.

Good fiction is a process of discovery for both the author and the reader, creating an imaginative world of its own. This book feels as if the writer put tracing paper over history, elaborating here and there, but essentially following a predetermined course. It is more of an intellectual study of renowned figures than an intuitive creation of vital characters.

Grumbach's writing is carried by external details rather than by insights about the ladies' feelings or consciousness. By the end, the narrative degenerates into catalogues about visitors and gifts, leaving many gaps about Eleanor and Sarah as people.

What, one wonders, was it like to be Irish in Wales in the late 18th and early 19th Century? How did they really feel about the villagers and vice-versa? Why was their maid so loyal when she wasn't being paid? Neither Eleanor nor Sarah emerges as very sympathetic. Beyond their eccentric daring, they seem stiff and almost trivial.

The affected Victorian narrator is at once stuffy, amused and judgmental. "English stages were commodious. Ten persons shared their interior, rather more on top, and six horses moved the vehicle. The Ladies were assessed for every 30 miles of their trip because their luggage was so heavy. To this cost Eleanor raised aristocratic objections, but the drivers were adamant and collected the tax."

An academic epilogue outlining subsequent inhabitants of Plas Newydd bears no narrative tie to the previous material, intensifying the book's self-conscious, critical tone. Ultimately Grumbach reveals the same weary resistance any scholar might feel about a subject studied too long. Did she begin the project before she realized she disliked the ladies? Did the classic competition arise between author and subjects or does she just bear a generally misanthropic nature?

Grumbach's best work is on the intellectual connection between Eleanor and Sarah and on their lesbianism. Their literary taste is fascinating, ranging from Plutarch to Fielding. They often search their books for references to women like themselves and by the end of their lives they have met a few other lesbians. They enjoy Madame de Sevigne's letters, partly because Eleanor decides Madame is in love with her daughter. And Sarah dismisses the novels of Jane Austen: " 'They are all about marriage, and mothers and daughters,' she told Eleanor. 'Neither subject is of especial interest to us.' "

As the years pass, their devotion increases. Eleanor supports Sarah through her spells of madness, while Sarah sees Eleanor through migraines, aching teeth, cataracts and blindness. Eleanor becomes interested in magic and Sarah turns to Methodism, one of their few divergencies. They continue quietly, happily, confirmed in the choice of this rich, iconoclastic life.

The ladies spun a fine story, but *The Ladies* lacks engaging drama, character development and suspense of the spirit. (pp. 3, 13)

> *Valerie Miner, in a review of "The Ladies," in* Los Angeles Times Book Review, *November 11, 1984, pp. 3, 13.*

## Sandra M. Gilbert

Famous eccentrics in their own time, and thought as late as 1936 to haunt the Welsh valley where they spent most of their lives, the "ladies" were Eleanor Butler and Sarah Ponsonby, two Anglo-Irish aristocrats who eloped together in 1778 and settled just outside a Welsh village, whence they became known as "the Ladies of Llangollen." [In *The Ladies*], frankly revising and rearranging some of the facts of their strange and poignant love affair, Doris Grumbach has recounted their story with grace and wit.

Sixteen years older than Miss Sarah Ponsonby, Grumbach's Lady Eleanor Butler is a sort of 18th-century ver-

sion of Stephen Gordon, the heroine of Radclyffe Hall's controversial 1928 novel, *The Well of Loneliness.* Like Stephen, Eleanor is raised as a boy by a disappointed father who had yearned for a son, and, like Stephen, she is so good at "boyish" things that she almost believes she is a boy, dressing in breeches, roaming her family's ancestral grounds like an upper-class female Huck Finn, and taunting her effete citybred tutor with his "weak nervous system." Unlike Hall's Stephen Gordon, however, Grumbach's Lady Eleanor is the hero of a plot that has a happy ending. Where Stephen Gordon was forced by the medical and cultural conventions of her time (and Hall's) to acknowledge that she was an "invert" and surrender the woman she loved to a male rival, Lady Eleanor woos and wins the fragile school girl Sarah Ponsonby, the "beloved" with whom she finds a life of "sweet repose."

To be sure, Grumbach demonstrates that the road to reposeful Llangollen is strewn with obstacles for the runaway ladies. Though the 39-year-old Eleanor dons male attire and rides 15 miles to spirit the 23-year-old Sarah away from the genteel country house where she is being sexually harassed by her guardian—"fat, proud, lascivious, gouted Sir William Fownes"—the couple's first attempt at escape is foiled when Sarah falls ill and the fleeing lovers are overtaken by irate relatives. Even after Eleanor and Sarah do contrive their getaway, moreover, they spend a hapless *Wanderjahr,* plagued by money troubles and uncertain about where to settle. Nevertheless, all ends well once the weary travelers arrive in friendship's vale, just outside Llangollen, where their odd pastoral idyll really begins.

Indeed, if there is anything problematic about *The Ladies,* it is that all seems to go almost too well for Lady Eleanor and her beloved. One would not, of course, wish Doris Grumbach to have written a new *Well of Loneliness* about the love and friendship between these notable women, but as it stands, *The Ladies,* like Grumbach's earlier *Chamber Music,* seems here and there to flirt with the conventions of an increasingly popular new genre: the Happy Lesbian novel. In such works, two women who have entered upon what the critic Lillian Faderman calls "romantic friendship" and moved from there to a more sexually explicit romantic love, stand alone against a world of brutish heterosexual men and uncomprehending heterosexual women. Invariably kind, even noble to each other—the exemplary female lovers in these novels rarely fight and never break up—these heroines may well be the latest angels in the house of fiction. Certainly Grumbach occasionally hints at such a characterization; at one point, for instance, she writes about the escaping Eleanor and Sarah that "like orphaned strays, like fairytale children . . . they lay together . . . two runaway women of quality in an abandoned barn, escaped from the protection of great houses and powerful men into a singular enterprise."

What ultimately redeems *The Ladies* from trendy sentimentality, however, is the sureness with which Grumbach accumulates small details about the lives of her protagonists and the tough but loving irony with which she portrays their idiosyncracies. Top-hatted, short-haired, and dressed in severe riding habits, her sexually rebellious aristocrats are never political radicals; on the contrary, they always remember that they are "women of quality," so that Eleanor, "the more conscious prose stylist" of the two, reacts to the French Revolution with a comically conservative pronouncement: "Fatally spreads the pestilential taint of insubordinate principles." Spending days "of strict retirement, sentiment, and delight," the pair nevertheless manage to encounter a dancing bear along with the assorted aristocrats and literati who come to call, and they take deliciously funny pleasure in the Italian mottoes—for instance, "Ecco! Caro Albergo!"—that decorate their trees.

Finally, then, despite a few lapses into a not quite convincing utopianism, Grumbach does create a half-sardonic, half-serious utopia for her ladies of Llangollen, a fantasia about 18th-century deviance that compares in many ways with such earlier feminist fantasies as Virginia Woolf's *Orlando* or Charlotte Perkins Gilman's *Herland.* Eleanor and Sarah, she declares, "seemed to each other to be divine survivors, well beyond the confines of social rules, two inhabitants of an ideal society . . . They had uncovered a lost continent on which they could live, in harmony, quite alone and together."

Even while it makes us smile, though, Grumbach's story of that "lost continent" is bittersweet, for, as she shows, the isolation of her "fair recluses" was profound. Though many admired their eccentricity, many, like Madame de Genlis, deplored it. Thus, though Eleanor and Sarah were together, they were alone, in a society that was prepared to admire their friendship but not yet ready to liberate their love.

> Sandra M. Gilbert, "A Passionate Friendship," in Book World—The Washington Post, September 30, 1984, p. 7.

## Catharine R. Stimpson

In [*The Ladies*], Doris Grumbach compellingly recreates the lives of two women who so defied convention and so baffled their contemporaries that they became celebrities.

In *Chamber Music,* Miss Grumbach loosely based her three major characters on real people—the composer Edward MacDowell, for one. Yet she said she was writing "fiction, not biography." In *The Ladies,* she has even more audaciously blurred biography and fiction, "garbled, changed, or rearranged" facts others have assembled and myths still others have disseminated.

As Miss Grumbach tells the story, Lady Eleanor Butler and Sarah Ponsonby belonged to 18th-century Irish families of better breeding than behavior. Sixteen years older than Miss Ponsonby, Lady Eleanor had lost her family's love at birth because she was not a son. Dressed in male clothing, she grew up to think of herself as masculine. In her mid-30's, Lady Eleanor met Sarah, an orphan stranded with a kindly cousin and her lecherous husband, Sir William Fownes. Sarah quickly became the "missing person" of Lady Eleanor's heart. For the next six years, their attachment made existence manageable.

Finally, however, neither could bear Sir William's sexual harassment of Sarah or the Butler family's plans to dispatch Lady Eleanor to a convent. In 1778 the two women ran away together. Their families caught and separated them, uncertain if they were dealing with "romantic friendship" gone wild or monstrosity. Willful, smart Lady Eleanor escaped from house arrest to turn up again, miles away, in Sarah's bedroom. Thwarted in their attempts to thwart passion, the families permitted the two women to go to England—if Lady Eleanor left Ireland forever.

Banished, the ladies were free. They used their precarious liberty to enter into a lifelong pact of fidelity to each other, to them deeper and more sacramental than marriage. Without known models to follow, they became modern inventors of their own identity, one rooted in romantic rebellion and mutual feelings of love and delight.

After two years of wandering, the women settled, with Mary-Caryll, their formidable servant, in the Welsh town of Llangollen. They rented a stone cottage and four acres and significantly named it Plas Newydd, or New Place. Crusoes who had chosen their island, they built a practical yet exotic world—with animals and gazebos, vegetables and picturesque stones from local ruins, a brewery and a library of hand-bound books. Lady Eleanor designed an androgynous costume for them both—beaver hats, men's shirts and stocks, outer garments modeled on women's riding habit. They cut and powdered their hair. They grew stout.

All gaped. Some laughed. Lady Eleanor and Sarah marveled at their love and honored their pact. Eventually they permitted the titled and the famous to visit them in their "retirement"—Edmund Burke, the Duke of Wellington, Sir Walter Scott. After one meeting, they turned William Wordsworth away.

Although Lady Eleanor and Sarah transformed themselves into "heroines" of their self-scripted drama, Miss Grumbach's imagination also reaches out to describe their renunciation, deprivation and loss. Even as they make a world for themselves, her Lady Eleanor and Sarah partially disintegrate. As their financial worries lessen, they become greedier. As notoriety becomes fame, they construe themselves as victims. Cold-mannered, hot-tempered, Lady Eleanor ages into a more benign version of her reactionary, choleric, blind, drunken father.

Lady Eleanor died in 1829, at the age of 90. Until she died two years later, at 76, Miss Grumbach's Sarah, given to visions and hallucinations, acted as if Eleanor were still there. As they wished, they shared a grave with Mary-Caryll.

The singular "Ladies of Llangollen" attracted attention for many reasons—their flagrant independence and solitude; their bluestocking pursuits; their titled families, whose codes they both violated and retained; their ingenious house and gardens. Yet perhaps what most baffled, shocked and titillated observers was their sexuality. This female couple defied heterosexual norms but radiated sexual signals. The women were hard to interpret but impossible to ignore. Given the challenge, some people toiled to bowdlerize the more perturbing aspects of their lives.

In 1847, for example, a John Hinklin compiled a historically minded travel guide: *The Ladies of Llangollen As Sketched By Many Hands,* dedicated to the two women who next lived in Plas Newydd. Lady Eleanor and Miss Sarah, he declared, came to Llangollen "impelled by a desire to lead a secluded life of celibacy." Others asserted the women were together only because men had so disappointed them. Miss Grumbach will have none of this twaddle. Her ladies are lovers, together because they wish to be. Unhappily, the language of **The Ladies** is occasionally thin when Miss Grumbach describes sexuality, falsely archaic, even fey, when she describes passion. In part this happens because she has two conflicting ambitions—to restore a past romantic sensibility and to display a contemporary awareness of the ironic complexities and inevitable comedies of that romantic sensibility.

Despite this, **The Ladies** is boldly imagined, subtly crafted. Miss Grumbach has a serious purpose. Her Lady Eleanor and Sarah poignantly feel themselves to be alone. A guilty sense of strangeness haunts Sarah's pleasures. As the two women read, they search for "some mention of existence like their own." **The Ladies** eloquently documents the existence of women who lived as they wished to, instead of as society expected them to.

> Catharine R. Stimpson, "The Lovers of New Place," in The New York Times Book Review, *September 30, 1984, p. 12.*

### Anita Brookner

From the quotation from Flaubert with which it is prefaced—"Everything one invents is true, you may be sure"—it could be conjectured that there are elements of biography in [*The Magician's Girl*], Doris Grumbach's story of three women growing up in America in the years between 1920 and 1970. This has become something of a formula in recent years and may reflect women's curiosity about themselves and the way that early beginnings mature into not very much, for despite the achievements that come with age, a sense of disillusion persists in all these stories, however formulaic, and brings to mind another quotation, from Stendhal, one not used by Doris Grumbach: "Is that all?"

**The Magician's Girl** is a title that might be applied to all three of the women in the present story, for each is perceived as singular. Minna and Liz grow up in New York City, Maud in the tiny Hudson River village of New Baltimore. Minna is the pretty, timorous daughter of comfortable parents, Liz the daughter of gentle Jewish Greenwich Village radicals. Maud, the third of the trio, is the most obviously monstrous, a fat and frankly ugly girl who rapidly achieves true singularity as a poet. She is not the only gifted one, for Liz finds her vocation as a photographer, and here a whisper of discomfort enters this apparently seamless chronicle, for Liz likes to photograph freaks of all kinds and is clearly based on Diane Arbus, down to her excursions to flophouses and Hubert's penny arcade. They all become roommates at Barnard and keep in touch in an episodic way, as is the custom for women in novels of this kind. Maud attracts a man noted for his looks but not for

his staying power, and is the first to marry and give birth—to twins, whom she neglects and discards. Second whisper of discomfort: these twins speak to each other in their own incomprehensible language and seem to be based on the famous British twins whose curious involution and crimes came to the attention of English doctors and lawyers in recent times.

Maud, the daughter of a nurse and an army sergeant, marries her Leo but soon tires of him, having expended her store of human love on her brother, Spencer. Her every waking moment is spent on composition, and her poems, of which she sends copies to Minna, are usually consigned to the oven in which, in due course, she decides to lay her head. The chapter describing her obsessional and fairly disgusting day is horrifying, with a sense of madness overtaking life and life itself retreating. Liz keeps a cool head on her shoulders as she photographs her giants, her cripples, and her mental defectives. Liz's partner is a woman, Helene, with whom she lives in passionate friendship until the latter's death from cancer. She rises to heights of fame with her terrible chronicles and has exhibitions of her work in small but noted galleries.

Minna, the most discreet and delicate of the three, marries a doctor, has a son, and pursues an honorable career as a history professor. Minna's story, with which the book starts, also features at the end. She takes a long sabbatical from her husband and home and goes to Iowa on an assignment to research into the lives of five female employees in a shirtwaist factory. In Iowa she has an extraordinary adventure. At the age of 60 she falls in love with a boy of 22. They enjoy a very happy love affair, which is cut short only when Minna is run over by a car on a snowy road. In the end only Liz is left, but Maud lives posthumously through those copies of her poems which she has given to Minna and which Minna has saved for publication.

In a sense readers have grown very used to these stories of women (there are usually three of them), and it is a genre which provides much information over and above the story it purports to tell. Women long to know the truth about each other and have been encouraged to review their lives as part of 20th-century history. And history, or rather History, does come into these stories, but in an anecdotal and rather facile manner. The Depression is interesting only as an explanation of a family's indigence, the emigration from Eastern Europe as an explanation for the eating habits of a grandmother. The war in Vietnam accounts for the death of a son. None of this is exactly the equivalent of *War and Peace* or *The Red and the Black.* The effect is to reduce women to chroniclers of their emotional lives and thus to reinforce their sense of sisterhood.

But on the other hand these are not mere fireside tales, as they might have been in the days before women went out into the world and worked for a living. The drama of a woman's attempts to combine her desire to remain at home and her ventures into a wider life has not yet been played out: at times it seems as if it has yet to be properly explored. Women derive some excitement from this dichotomy, some terror, and much fatigue. In viewing her three women as isolates, Doris Grumbach deprives her story of a certain amount of reality, removes, as it were, its fibrous content. The true essence of working life is the boredom of repetition. Yet Minna, Liz, and Maud know only heights and depths, ecstasy or suicide. This is not the whole story.

The time to romanticize a life comes when all the hard work has been done, and this is what Doris Grumbach has chosen to examine. Yet she is as romantic as any of her characters and every bit as wistful. There is a sense of loss here which has more to do with advancing age than with retreating prospects of hope and happiness. Only in Minna's case do the two refuse to go together, for Minna, golden-haired at 60, and against all ascertainable evidence, remains both hopeful and lucky in her late love. Her story is a fairy story for all women of 60 and over. It is Liz, the survivor, living precariously with a dying partner, who seems to have found a realistic answer to the problems of existence, although her immersion in the world of ugliness would seem to have promised her the suicide the author has visited on Maud. Words, on the whole, tend to preserve their practitioner, and Maud's suicide can be seen to be premature, particularly when viewed in the light of her earlier persistence.

Freud's question—"What do women want?"—has still not been answered. Perhaps stories such as this can be seen as an honorable attempt to find an answer, yet how quickly they have hardened into a formula which does more in the way of digging up curiosities than in seeking a solution. Perhaps the questions are in the end more important than the answers. Certainly that is the effect that Doris Grumbach's novel has on the reader. There is one important observation to be made of *The Magician's Girl:* it is blessedly free of ideology, of didactic feminism. It is also a beautifully easy read, discreet and beguiling, and attractively low-key. It is an honorable addition to the annals of women's reading and takes its place effortlessly beside many much noisier counterparts.

> *Anita Brookner, "Story of Late Love and Sisterhood," in* Book World—The Washington Post, *January 4, 1987, pp. 3, 13.*

### David Holahan

His cameo appearance in Doris Grumbach's seventh novel is so fleeting that he isn't even assigned a name. Still, his lot, summed up in less than a page, typifies both the tone and the direction of *The Magician's Girl.* He is an author, a young and successful one, whose very achievement is his undoing: "the frightened, lonely writer" withdraws into "the diminishir ̣ oxygen of a garment bag to avoid his second novel."

This sad, wonderfully written book is awash in such flotsam of human lives, battered on the cruel reefs of existence, distorted by bitter disappointments and mean ironies—that is, when not snuffed out by plain bad luck. The three heroines, who come from divergent backgrounds, are united as roommates at Barnard College in the late 1930s. Their careers are followed into the 1970s. . . .

To be sure, this is not a cheery trio. The supporting cast is even less so. Indeed, matters become so dismal that it is easy to anticipate the sorrowful denouements. Near the end, Minna, now 60, is blissfully in love with a 22-year-old student ("normal" relationships are scarce in this opus). The joyful union rejuvenates the main character, cleansing her psyche of a lifetime of trepidations. Is it too good to last? Well, of course it is. Minna herself foresees that the good times will stop rolling: "It's an illusion, I'm sure. Like the girl who is sawed in two by the magician on stage."

The human circus that Grumbach has fashioned is overdrawn. She is saying that we are all deformed in some fashion; that, in essence, all humans are freaks of a sort—in spirit, if not in body. Her accounts of individual examples are vivid, moving and believable. What isn't is the preponderance of such sorry characters in her pages. The suicidal novelist whom she touches on briefly is an example. Fortunately, Grumbach's superb insights and captivating prose engross the reader in spite of her gloomy vision. She herself has just completed her seventh opus and is alive and well, if a bit pessimistic.

> *David Holahan, "In Doris Grumbach's Novel, to Be Human Is to Be a Freak," in* Chicago Tribune—Books, *January 18, 1987, p. 6.*

### Paula Deitz

A line from Sylvia Plath's poem "The Bee Meeting"—"I am the magician's girl who does not flinch"—provides the title as well as the epigraph of Doris Grumbach's new novel. And since one of her three main characters, the poet Maud Noon, is more than loosely based on Sylvia Plath (in the morning she "opened the oven door and lit the gas," and at midnight placed "her head, like a penitential offering, into the red-hot purifying fumes of the gas oven"), the reader knows that his own knowledge of certain literary figures and events may be called upon as part of the evidentiary process of biography the omniscient narrator alludes to in the introductory paragraph.

Since not even diaries and letters can be counted on to reveal the mysterious truth about the self, Ms. Grumbach turns to a kind of truth by invention as the basis for her fiction. Although the theme is not an unusual one—the story of three Barnard College roommates in the late 1930's, their childhoods and adult lives—*The Magician's Girl* is most disturbing, and therefore at its best, in its acute awareness of the pains endured unflinchingly by the young.

Maud herself, raised in a Hudson River town upstate, becomes fascinated early on by words like "post" and "leave," associated with her Regular Army father. Her imagination intensifies as she is forced to play outside alone in the cold, locked out of the house while her mother sleeps off night duty at the hospital. Though Ms. Grumbach's prose has a matter-of-fact plainness, it shocks with its simple, quirky revelations, as when Maud feels her ungainly ugliness the more keenly for her mother's attraction to the Miss America Pageant, which she attends annually in Atlantic City. Of the three heroines as girls, she comes through the best.

Minna Grant has a more refined, Upper West Side background, being raised at the hands of an overprotective mother fearful even that one might fall through flat sidewalk cellar doors. And again Ms. Grumbach sounds a true note with Minna's youthful ambition to swim like the Channel crosser Gertrude Ederle (whose father here is the Grants' butcher). The Lindbergh kidnapping is a kind of undertow during Minna's years at Hunter College High School. And, finally, Elizabeth Becker, who lives in Greenwich Village with Communist sympathizer parents who have lost their teaching jobs, sees the world from the El, in images framed by upper-story windows, on her excursions to uptown galleries, where one day she discovers the urban photographs of Berenice Abbott.

These are all rich images, informed with the magic conveyed by the small details that reveal the forming of these lives. But, alas, the promise of Part One goes unfulfilled as the three develop into stock figures amid a series of clichéd events that mar the freshness of their inner selves. Minna, who is, we are told, "destined to be an anxious young woman," shows not the least sign of neurotic behavior as a lithe, self-assured blonde at Barnard, or as a successful history professor in a loveless marriage that she finishes off with great aplomb—going on from there to find happiness in an affair at the age of 60 with a much younger man.

Maud Noon predictably drowns herself in poetry and depression, without the insights attributed to her as a young girl, rejecting all, husband and children, except her mentor, the eccentric Barnard poet-professor Otto Mile. Mile, who resembles Ezra Pound (the story here becomes a little like Steve Allen's anachronistic televised dinner parties for famous people of all times), is incarcerated in St. Elizabeths Hospital for the criminally insane in Washington after publishing anti-Semitic poems and being tried for wartime anti-American diatribes. After Maud's death, copies of her poems are resurrected by Liz and Minna and handed over to James Laughlin (who is the publisher, in fact, of New Directions) for a book called *Poems Returned From Saint Elizabeth's*. From then on, both Minna and Liz are sought after by the Noon biography mill. To complete the scene, Liz Becker becomes a Diane Arbus-style photographer of freaks.

The book could have been satire, but it is not; and though all fiction must by definition be contrived, one hopes that the combination of people and events will release an original illumination. Something may shine through at the end when Minna escapes her Central Park West marriage forever for the University of Iowa and her course "Woman and Labor in the Nineteenth Century." One day before her daily workout at the pool (though, we are told earlier, she had a "culminative phobia" about swimming that canceled out this pleasure), she announces to a new acquaintance: "I'm in love . . . . It's an illusion, I'm sure. Like the girl who is sawed in two by a magician on-stage." "Even if it is an illusion," her companion responds, "some valuable things are invented by belief." What the story may finally be about is the illusion of free will in the face of determinism.

*Paula Deitz, "Truth by Invention," in* The New York Times Book Review, *February 1, 1987, p. 22.*

### Merle Rubin

Compressed—magically?—within the limits of Doris Grumbach's short novel [*The Magician's Girl*] are the lives of three women who grow up in the 1920s, meet at Barnard College in the late 1930s, and—still keeping in touch—go their separate ways.

Trim, blond Minna Grant is brought up within the apparent security of an Upper West Side Manhattan neighborhood, but also within the very real web of fears transmitted by her over-anxious mother. Downtown, in Greenwich Village, independent Liz Becker becomes entranced with the odd glimpses of other people's lives that catch her eye as she rides the city's El. And upstate, in a small village, Maud Mary Noon, ungainly, fat, myopic, begins crafting a world of sounds, images, and words from the meager materials at hand.

By the novel's end, it is 1978. Two of the women are dead: one by suicide years earlier, the other in a recent accident. What sticks in the mind is a series of pictures, each so freshly and strikingly rendered as to defuse any questions about whether or not these tableaux may be contrived, clichéd, improbable, or all too typical: There is little Maud, feeling safe just knowing her older brother is in the next room, even though he's closed the door for privacy. And Maud's mother, haunting the Miss America pageants, reporting back on "perfect beauty" to her conspicuously plain daughter. And Maud, writing poems, oblivious of her surroundings. There's Liz, obsessed with recording through the camera's "objective" eye the predicaments of people whose freakish exteriors give them no place to hide. And a younger Liz, visiting with her beloved grandmother on a strip of benches between the uptown and downtown traffic on Broadway. And Minna, herself a grandmother, beginning a new life in Iowa City, embarking on an improbable, sexually explicit, yet lyrically portrayed, love affair with a man young enough to be her grandson.

Just as Liz's Arbus-style photographs capture cross sections of lives in a temporal instant that fixes a spatial impression, so Grumbach's luminously transparent narrative seems to "fix" the duration of a lifetime—three lifetimes—within its synoptic overview. What is most poignant about this novel is that its special aura of serenity tinged with sadness comes not from the pains and losses the characters endure, although there are many of these, but from the conviction it conveys that life, for all its sorrows, is so rich with possibilities as to make any one life—however long—much too short.

*Merle Rubin, in a review of "The Magician's Girl," in* The Christian Science Monitor, *February 26, 1987, p. 22.*

## Stacey D'Erasmo

In *The Magician's Girl,* Doris Grumbach has cleverly packed an allegory of the woman artist and her relationship to fate and culture inside a fictional frame that should have a name but doesn't: the collective coming-of-age story of women who meet at an Eastern all-women's college (in this case, Barnard in the late 1930s), become friends, and in their various adventures with sex, love, and ambition, play out the options available to women of their era and class. There is often an odd, voyeuristic elitism in such novels—*The Group,* for instance, or Alice Adams's *Superior Women*—a genteelly ghoulish display of the triage inflicted by culture on the Best and Brightest Women of Our Generation. The nice ones usually don't make it out alive, and they die slow.

In this novel, the "group" is three: Minna Grant, blond, beautiful, and anxious, who becomes a professor of history; Liz Becker, daughter of New York radicals, who becomes a photographer and is also the book's token lesbian; and Maud Noon, the poet, hugely fat, myopic, brilliant, and suicidal. Real women such as Diane Arbus, Sylvia Plath, Anne Sexton, and Zelda Fitzgerald hover over the text like sad angels, their biographies trailing through the characters as both artistic subconscious and warnings about the price women have traditionally paid for artistic license. Their influence is composite: Becker's work resembles Arbus's, but it is Noon who absorbs most of the Arbus biography. Noon's death alludes directly to Sylvia Plath, but her poetry sounds more like Sexton's. Ezra Pound makes an appearance in the figure of Otto Mile, famous poet, Noon's mentor, and eventually her correspondent from his exile at St. Elizabeth's in Washington, D.C., where he studies anti-Semitism and the curious animal droppings in the corner of his room.

Lovers, parents, friends, and children all die in *The Magician's Girl*—at the end only Liz remains—but the suicide of Maud Noon is lingered over and probed. Noon is a walking anthology of women poets, but Grumbach has made a subversive mélange of their respective elements. Obese, recalcitrant, and unrepentant, Noon has the will of Emily Dickinson in the girth of Amy Lowell—a combination designed to give English departments everywhere nightmares. No matter what happens to her, she writes, but she slips downward at the same time, starving for the artistic encouragement and recognition that is, typically, bestowed in spades after her death. The final blow comes when, abandoned by her pretty, shallow husband and separated from her children, she shuffles out of her cold apartment to her mailbox on Christmas Day in search of magazine acceptances and finds that Otto Mile, that joker, has sent her a letter consisting of a blank sheet of paper. At this last word from him, she gives up for good and puts her head in the oven. Soon after, she becomes quite famous, partly by way of her friend Liz, who saves Noon's work and gets it published. Although the melodrama is high here, the writing is strong and pointed. Maud's ritual wait for the mailman who only brings her work back to her, the endless mornings of toast and margarine as she tries to write, and her degrading hopelessness are laid out with a glaring exactness of detail. In her portrayal of

Maud, Grumbach aims a good, hard blow at the myth of the wilting, agoraphobic female poet and, through Maud's relationship to Mile, at the patriarchy that writes the poetic canon.

Maud dies in the middle of the novel; the rest buries her vitality in tired myths about art and life. Although their friendship is the symbolic and narrative foundation for the collective plot, Liz, Minna, and Maud do not have many scenes together, and when they do the dialogue is tinny and stiff. Once their number has been reduced to two, Liz and Minna flounder in an epistolary relationship that is not illuminating. Liz, although treated well by the other characters (and by history) as the artist who survives, barely exists as a personality. Once she meets Helene, her lover for life, at a bar named the Old Colony (a lot like the old, actual Sea Colony), Liz pretty much settles down and disappears. The last we hear of her is that Helene is dying of breast cancer.

Minna Grant's fate takes up most of the last section of the book, a May Sartonesque tale of love in old age as Minna, now past 60, embarks on an affair with an undergraduate. Grumbach does a nice turn on the Amor and Psyche myth in this part, with the aging Minna as the lover who appears by night to the youth; but it seems cruel, if not inadvertently comic, that poor Minna gets run down by a car. In episodes like these, Grumbach's allegorizing runs away with her good sense, and the effect is morbid. The elegance and neatness that characterize magic and myth do not mesh well with female carnage, unless you conflate art, fate, and death—and leave the novel's politics safely up in the air.

Stacey D'Erasmo, "Group Dynamics," in The Village Voice, *Vol. XXXII, No. 12, March 24, 1987, p. 46.*

## Marianne Wiggins

Few readers want to see a writer writing, as if the text were a rehearsal for a talent contest. When that text is at times both luminous and unselfconscious, then the effect of having come close to something that could have been brilliant compounds embarassment with disappointment. Such is the effect of Doris Grumbach's *The Magician's Girl.*

The reader floats through pages of events in a New York City unlocated in time, until a signpost advises, "for those who were adolescents in the early thirties the high tor of drama was the kidnapping of the Lindbergh baby". Yet Grumbach's description of the city leaves us without a sense of period—an effect which is doubly disconcerting in a Grumbach novel because, at her best, she can draw the single line which holds the full suggestion of expanded form; she is a master of the quick sketch. When her narrative shifts to describing the specific, it soars.

The "magician's girl" of the title is never realized with any such specificity in this uneven, frustrating book. The reader is presented with an epigraph from Sylvia Plath—"I am the magician's girl who does not flinch"—and dedications to Flaubert and William Kennedy, both of whom have drawn their deadly portraits of the self-destructive woman. It comes as no surprise, then, that one of the three heroines is, indeed, an under-appreciated poet and does, in fact, stick her head in a gas oven one fine frigid morning.

Only one of the three survives Grumbach's contrivance to the end. This is the lesbian photographer Liz, whom Grumbach shamelessly models on the real-life Diane Arbus. Liz, it seems, is "the magician's girl who does not flinch" because she is the ultimate voyeur, one who achieves her own place in life by immortalizing human beings as grotesques. It's a pity that the novel leaves us certain that any one of Liz's pictures would be worth a thousand of Grumbach's words.

*Marianne Wiggins, "Deadly Portraits," in* The Times Literary Supplement, *No. 4394, June 19, 1987, p. 669.*

# Ken Kesey

## 1935-

(Full name Ken Elton Kesey) American novelist, short story writer, and scriptwriter.

The following entry presents criticism on Kesey's novel *One Flew over the Cuckoo's Nest*. For discussions of his complete career, see *CLC*, Vols. 1, 3, 6, 11, and 46.

A transitional figure linking the Beat generation of the 1950s with the counterculture movement of the 1960s, Kesey is best known for his first novel, *One Flew over the Cuckoo's Nest*. Like most of Kesey's fiction, this book focuses on alienated and nonconformist individuals who attempt through love, hope, rebellion, and humor to overcome their limitations and to retain their sanity and self-respect. *One Flew over the Cuckoo's Nest* is considered an important work of contemporary American literature for its disjointed, colloquial prose style, its parabolic commentary on modern social ills, and its inventive symbolism and archetypal characters. R. L. Sassoon commented: "With great originality the author has succeeded in achieving, almost throughout the novel, a subtle balance and correspondence between the social burden of mirroring purposefully place and time and the personal art of creating fiction with the immediacy, the completeness in itself, of myth or parable."

Kesey received his bachelor's degree from the University of Oregon and later attended creative writing classes at Stanford University during the 1950s. He began writing *One Flew over the Cuckoo's Nest* while working as a night attendant in the psychiatric ward of the Veterans Administration Hospital in Menlo Park, California, where he was simultaneously captivated and revolted by the institutionalized treatment of mental illness. At the hospital, Kesey volunteered for a series of government-sponsored experiments involving such hallucinogenic drugs as LSD-25, psilocybin, and mescaline, a drug derived from the peyote or mescal cactus. Kesey used peyote while writing sections of *One Flew over the Cuckoo's Nest*. Set in a mental facility in the northwestern United States, the novel is narrated from the perspective of Chief Bromden, a huge schizophrenic of mixed white and native American heritage from the Columbia River region. Bromden feigns being deaf and dumb to avoid being "worked on" by the hospital staff and other enforcers of what he calls the "Combine," a term for a machine that threshes and levels crops as well as Bromden's own word for a brutal agency of normative control designed to alter or "correct" deviant or undesirable behavior. As the novel opens, Bromden views existence on the ward as a humorless cartoon laden with human misery. His observations of the real world are initially rendered in paranoid terms; his acute awareness of the staff's desire to control all aspects of the men's lives, for example, leads him to fantasize that the staff manipulates patients mechanically via electronic circuitry concealed behind the hospital's walls.

Bromden's views are challenged by the arrival of Randle Patrick McMurphy, a swaggering ex-marine, gambler, and braggart, who describes himself as a "good old red, white, and blue hundred-percent American con man." He is immediately identified as a nonconformist by the patients on the ward, including Harding, an effeminate intellectual who feels emasculated by his spiteful wife, and Billy Bibbit, an adolescent whose self-image depends on the approval of his dominating mother. McMurphy explains to the men that after authorities erroneously labeled him a psychotic, he submitted to psychological therapy to avoid a sentence of hard labor at a state work farm. By demonstrating to the ward the value of laughter as a source of sanity and a weapon against repression, McMurphy becomes involved in a comic power struggle with "Big Nurse" Ratched, a cold, efficient administrator of conformity who demeans and manipulates patients into attacking one another under the guise of "therapy" to maintain her control. McMurphy is later angered to discover that his term, unlike those of other patients who volunteered for therapy, is of an unspecified duration and his release is dependent on Nurse Ratched's approval. After a brief period of attempting to live by the rules of the ward, McMurphy organizes an unapproved fishing expedition and, later, a wild party in the ward at which Bibbit loses his virginity to a prostitute. The next morning, McMurphy attempts unsuccessfully to escape, and Nurse Ratched threatens to inform Bibbit's mother of his promiscuity. When Bibbit commits suicide, unable to bear the thought of his mother's disapproval, McMurphy is finally driven to attack Nurse Ratched. He is subsequently lobotomized to demonstrate to the ward the futility of resistance. Bromden smothers McMurphy in order to deny the Big Nurse her victory and to accept responsibility for the role he and the other patients played in contributing to McMurphy's downfall. Bromden then escapes to Canada as a sane individual.

*One Flew over the Cuckoo's Nest* garnered moderate critical attention following its initial publication in 1962. Malcolm Cowley, one of Kesey's teachers at Stanford University and a highly respected chronicler of the "lost generation" of the 1920s, commented in a letter to Kesey that the book's rough draft contained "some of the most brilliant scenes I have ever read." Most reviewers were also positive, concurring with the opinion of William Peden: "[Mr. Kesey's] storytelling is so effective, his style so impetuous, his grasp of his characters so certain that the reader is swept along in McMurphy's boisterous wake. . . . Mr. Kesey, in short, has created a world that is convincing, alive, and glowing within its own boundaries and in terms of his own ground rules. His is a large, robust talent, and he has written a large, robust book." Kesey's novel, however, received scant scholarly attention until the 1970s, when its anti-establishment bias attracted a diverse audience of readers and its previously unacknowledged complexity elicited a wide variety of interpretations. Since that time, *One Flew over the Cuckoo's Nest* has been perceived as, among other things, a biblical parable, a Western romance in the American tradition, and a boy's book about freedom from institutionalized repression.

Adherents of the view that McMurphy functions as a Christ figure in *One Flew over the Cuckoo's Nest* often note the scene in which he is forced by the Big Nurse to undergo electroshock treatment on a cross-shaped table, his resistance to Nurse Ratched for the benefit of the other patients, and his sacrificial death via lobotomy following Bibbit's suicide, which is often viewed as an act of betrayal against McMurphy's endorsement of the rebellious life. According to Ronald Wallace, the novel "does reflect the kind of affirmation and hope symbolized by the life, death, and resurrection of Christ, and it does argue for individual freedom and action." Some critics, characterizing Kesey's book as a contemporary Western, cite the archetypal relationship between Bromden and McMurphy as analogous to the Western novel's typical alliance between the white male and native American, through which civilized, matriarchal values are rejected in favor of the unrestricted freedom of natural instinct and other traits common to masculine ideals of frontier life. Supporting this thesis is the fact that McMurphy is often related explicitly by Kesey to the western film and comic book character, the Lone Ranger; with the assistance of his Indian sidekick, McMurphy combats the matriarchal and mechanized fig-ure of the Big Nurse in the comic-book fashion of the Western dime novel.

Perhaps the most frequently debated issues regarding *One Flew over the Cuckoo's Nest* surrounds the book's alleged immorality, sexism, and racism. Some critics fault McMurphy's affected belief in liberation through sexual freedom as simplistic or unconvincing, identifying his brash language and behavior as immoral and unheroic. Similarly, his attack on Nurse Ratched is often interpreted as a refutation of his own humanity and status as hero. Kesey is recurrently reproached for his negative portrayals of women and blacks; Nurse Ratched is described by Bromden as having enormous, constricted breasts and a face "like an expensive baby doll," and the chief refers to the sadistic black nurse's aides as "black boys" and "niggers." Those who fault McMurphy as a childish whoremonger and misogynist frequently cite his tendency to regard women as either emasculating "ball-cutters" or golden-hearted prostitutes. In a letter to the *New York Times,* Marcia L. Falk objected to Dale Wasserman's stage adaptation of *One Flew over the Cuckoo's Nest*: "With a pseudo-radical posture, [the work] swallows whole hog all the worst attitudes toward women prevalent in our society and delivers the pig right back to us, suitably decorated and made righteous."

Many critics assert that the issue of racism and sexism depends largely on the question of who is the novel's protagonist. Although some identify McMurphy as the tragic hero who resists oppression and rejects Nurse Ratched's asexuality and false propriety through his belief in "fighting and fucking," most concur that *One Flew over the Cuckoo's Nest* is a comic novel featuring Bromden as its unbalanced protagonist and dominant perspective. Scarred by his experiences in World War II and by his white mother's psychological destruction of his Indian father, Bromden is often interpreted as a victim of racism whose own sexist and racist assumptions serve as a metaphor for cruelty and insanity. Despite Bromden's inferred enthusiasm for McMurphy's attitudes, several reviewers note that he subtly indicates to the reader the juvenile nature of McMurphy's behavior when, for example, he compares his friend to a mischievous schoolboy and describes his revelry with a prostitute as "more like two tired little kids than a grown man and a grown woman in bed together to make love." Despite the racist or sexist assumptions implied in *One Flew over the Cuckoo's Nest,* many concur that the book implicitly conveys the views of its narrator, Chief Bromden, whose disturbed judgment functions as a distorted reaction to dehumanizing social realities. Janet Sutherland, defending Kesey against a ban imposed on his book in the Bellevue Public Schools in Washington, asserted: "Ken Kesey's *One Flew over the Cuckoo's Nest* is not obscene, racist, or immoral, although it does contain language and scenes which by common taste would be so considered. Like all great literature, the book attempts to give an accurate picture of some part of the human condition, which is less than perfect."

(See also *Contemporary Authors,* Vols. 1-4; *Contemporary Authors New Revision Series,* Vol. 22; *Dictionary of Liter-*

*ary Biography,* Vols. 2, 16; and *Concise Dictionary of American Literary Biography,* 1968-1987.)

## PRINCIPAL WORKS

NOVELS

*One Flew over the Cuckoo's Nest*    1962
*Sometimes a Great Notion*    1964

OTHER

*\*Ken Kesey's Garage Sale* [editor and contributor]    1973
*The Day after Superman Died*    (commemorative short
    story)    1980
*Demon Box*    (stories and articles)    1986

\*This work contains reviews, articles, interviews, and Kesey's un-
    produced screenplay *Over the Border.*

---

### Time

The world of this brilliant first novel [*One Flew over the Cuckoo's Nest*] is Inside—inside a mental hospital and in-side the blocked minds of its inmates. Sordid sights and sounds abound, but Novelist Kesey has not descended to mere shock treatment or isolation-ward documentary. His book is a strong, warm story about the nature of human good and evil, despite its macabre setting. For as the boardinghouse provided a stock slice-of-life locale for an-other generation of writers, the sanitarium seems to appeal to many modern writers as a comparable microcosm of the times.

The narrator is a giant of a man, the half-breed son of an Indian chief. Scarred by World War II and his white mother's destruction of his proud father, he opts out of things so completely that for years the staff of the mental hospital have believed him to be deaf and dumb. His skewed observation of the ward-world is well managed; the reader has a vivid sense both of "the Chief 's" sick per-ceptions and of the reality behind them.

The ward has two kinds of citizens: the Chronics (the Walkers, the Wheelers and the Vegetables) and the Acutes, who have hope of being fixed up and sent back Outside, where, the Chief is convinced, everything is run by "the Combine." Chief representative of the Combine in the hospital is a purse-mouthed Sataness known as Big Nurse. Big Nurse is a specialist in control; she controls ev-eryone—the patients and the doctors and the "black boys" who clean up the ward and push the Chronics around.

> She wields a sure power that extends in all direc-
> tions on hairlike wires too small for anybody's
> eye but mine; I see her sit in the center of this
> web of wires like a watchful robot, tend her net-
> work with mechanical insect skill, know every
> second which wire runs where and just what cur-
> rent to send up to get the results she wants.

Savior of the ward—and especially the Chief—from the

organized inhumanity of Big Nurse is a patient named Randle Patrick McMurphy. A laughing, brawling, gam-bling man of the world, McMurphy begins his duel with Big Nurse in sheer human exuberance and ends it in a grim, heroic struggle to the death.

Author Kesey, 26, who worked as a nursing assistant in the mental wards of two California hospitals while he was writing his novel, has used his empathy with the Insider's view of the Outsider's world to tilt the reader's comfort-able assumption about the nice normalities, has made his book a roar of protest against middlebrow society's Rules and the invisible Rulers who enforce them. But Kesey's lunatics and his story are full of gaiety too—including a wild ward party complete with wine, women and song. As the Chief says admiringly of Randle P. McMurphy: "He won't let the pain blot out the humor no more'n he'll let the humor blot out the pain."

> *"Life in a Loony Bin," in* Time, *New York,*
> *Vol. LXXIX, No. 7, February 16, 1962, p. 90.*

### Rose Feld

Undoubtedly there will be controversy over some of the material in Ken Kesey's novel [*One Flew Over the Cuck-oo's Nest*], but there can be none about his talent. His is a powerful book about a mental institution, written with sustained vitality and force which hold the reader until the final word.

There are four major characters in *One Flew Over the Cuckoo's Nest.* First among them is Miss Ratched, the nurse, a fifty-year-old woman who, over a score of years, has been in control of a ward now made up of forty men, half of them chronic cases, half acute. Second is the Chief, the giant half-Indian chronic, one-time football hero who, to escape the world of reality, has retreated into a fog of deaf and dumb silence. The third is Harding, the self-committed, highly articulate intellectual, ashamed and afraid of being different. Fourth is the latest arrival in the ward of misfits, Randle P. McMurphy.

Like a whirlwind, McMurphy comes charging into the room filled with hopeless men. A red-haired Irishman, tall, broad, with enormous hands and shoulders, he takes over as "the bull goose loony" from the word go. Swagger-ing, clowning, rowdy and bawdy, he explains himself. In his own words he is no "nut." He is a tramp, a gambler, a disturber of the peace.

With four more months of prison sentence to serve, he got into "a couple of hassles" at the work farm and to his amazement and delight was ruled as a psychopath by the court. It couldn't be better, as he saw it. No more work, three good meals a day and the chance to roll dice, make bets and gamble at cards.

To the inmates of the ward McMurphy represents every-thing they are not, a man who is strong, confident, fearless, arrogantly male. To the nurse, however, he becomes a mounting threat to her authority and power. Senior to the doctors in age and years of service, she has ruled the ward with relentless discipline. Under the cloak of therapy, she has had offenders punished with increasing severity of treatment, large doses of tranquilizers, shock treatments and, for the most difficult, lobotomies.

With growing intensity, the battle is waged between the rebellious Irishman who takes every opportunity to diminish her size with laughter, obscenity and ridicule, and the woman, grimly sadistic under her fixed smile, who knows that she holds the winning card. Before she can play it, however, several of her charges, among them the half-Indian who has lived in fear of the Combine which makes the fog, have had a taste of manhood and courage. How the final victory is snatched from Miss Ratched makes the unforgettable ending of the book.

Exception will probably be made by institution experts to several incidents in the novel which, while possible, seem highly improbable. But as a work of fiction, for background, for story, for strong writing that holds harsh humor, anger and compassion, and, most of all, for the creation of Randle P. McMurphy, this is a first novel of special worth.

*Rose Feld, "War Inside the Walls," in* Books, *New York, February 25, 1962, p. 4.*

## William Peden

Although mental illness has fascinated the creative imagination since the golden age of Greek drama, it was not until the middle decades of our own century that fiction writers, including William Maxwell in America and Anna Kavan in England, attempted to explore with knowledge, understanding, and integrity the borderland between "sanity" and "madness." This gray region provides setting and subject for three very different new American novels, Ken Kesey's *One Flew Over the Cuckoo's Nest,* Michael Rumaker's *The Butterfly,* and Garet Rogers's *The Jumping Off Place.*

*One Flew Over the Cuckoo's Nest* is an extremely impressive novel. . . . Set in a mental hospital in Oregon, it centers around the struggle between a new inmate, McMurphy, and Big Nurse, who dominates her ward and its inhabitants. McMurphy is a bigger-than-life American folk-hero type, a brawling, lusty, and warmhearted life-giving force. Big Nurse is authoritarian and matriarchal. Beneath the voluptuous-appearing body that so intrigues the inmates, she is a frigid emasculator bent on destroying the men entrusted to her care.

The struggle between these two contrasting forces (one of several similar contrasts around which the novel is built) begins the moment McMurphy swaggers into Big Nurse's ward, and each instinctively recognizes the Enemy the other represents. It gains in intensity as McMurphy brings laughter, courage, and hope to the men whom Big Nurse has cowed into submission, and it rises to a literally screaming climax involving McMurphy, Big Nurse, and all the other people whom the author has created so effectively: Chief Broom, who serves as Mr. Kesey's narrator, a gigantic Indian who has gradually retreated into simulated deaf-and-dumbness; the highly literate, Harding-like McMurphy, aware that "we are the victims of a matriarchy here, my friend"; Dr. Spivey, whose authority Big

Nurse has painstakingly usurped, and Big Nurse's orderlies, who prowl through the ward like black panthers.

Beneath the suspense-charged action, above and beyond the rhetoric and the violence and the horseplay and the exaggeration and the comedy (McMurphy's fishing expedition is a great tall-tale in itself ), the author presents a continuous life-and-death struggle, a finally declared warfare between good and evil, tyranny and freedom, love and hate. His storytelling is so effective, his style so impetuous, his grasp of his characters so certain that the reader is swept along in McMurphy's boisterous wake. In spite of contrivance and caricature, the reader is likely to agree with Chief Broom that "it's the truth even if it didn't happen." Mr. Kesey, in short, has created a world that is convincing, alive, and glowing within its own boundaries and in terms of his own ground rules. His is a large, robust talent, and he has written a large, robust book. (p. 49)

*William Peden, "Gray Regions of the Mind," in* Saturday Review, *Vol. XLV, No. 15, April 14, 1962, pp. 49-50.*

## Irving Malin

New American Gothic disrupts our "rational" world view or pictures our unreal concerns; it gives us violent juxtapositions, distorted vision, even prophecy, without becoming completely private. When it seeks to present a "social" situation, to proclaim Truth, it lacks authority.

What are the irrational forces Gothic presents? It is primarily concerned with love, knowing that—as Leslie Fiedler has said—"there can be no terror without the hope for love and love's defeat." The typical hero is a weakling. The only way he can escape from the anxiety which plagues him is through a compulsive design. He "loves" this plan, and he compels others to fit into it. His concern for them is not benevolent; it is narcissistic. Narcissism, compulsion, cruel abstractionism—these are found in *Other Voices, Other Rooms, Reflections in a Golden Eye, The Cannibal, Malcolm,* and *The Violent Bear It Away.*

New American Gothic usually deals with a microcosm because the "buried life" does not need a large area of society in which to reveal itself. We have in the novels listed above: Skulley's Landing, an army post in peacetime, a rooming house in Germany, a Chateau, and the backwoods. The private world, however, displays the "big" tensions of contemporary America: "unnatural" self-love and disintegration of order.

New American Gothic is "poetic," using a great deal of imagery. Three images are especially important: haunted houses (imprisonment), violent journeys, and distorted reflections. Because Gothic deals with a narrow view of personality and a microcosm, it creates an intensive, vertical world—one best created in the story or short novel. (p. 81)

*One Flew over the Cuckoo's Nest* by Ken Kesey is a Gothic novel. It employs the themes and images already mentioned, but it does so in a new way. It is not simply imitative. The important theme is, again, the compulsive design. The "Big Nurse"—as the narrator calls her—is an authoritarian, middle-aged woman who tries to impose her will upon her lunatics—she must make them fear and respect her so that she can feel superior. She exerts power not to help others but to help herself: her compulsive design cannot stop—except through violence—because it is all she has.

The "Big Nurse" is no longer a woman—she has become a Frankenstein monster. All of her gestures, commands, feelings, and possessions are mechanized: "there's no compact or lipstick or woman stuff, she's got that bag full of a thousand parts she aims to use in her duties today—wheels and gears, cogs polished to a hard glitter, tiny pills that gleam like porcelain, needles, forceps. . . . " She is "precise, automatic." But God has played a trick on her: the Big Nurse cannot flee from nature. Although she is monstrous, she is still partially female—and the more she tries to exert her "will to power," the more she desperately wants (unconsciously) sex—some kind of affection. She is torn between two worlds.

Obviously, Mr. Kesey must offer us others who combat the design of Big Nurse (and her helpers). There are two. The narrator, an inmate of the asylum, lives in a kind of fog, but he is able to recognize that the authoritarian ruler is more insane than he—after all, he has some kind of affection for his "papa," an Indian chief, who used to take him hunting. He has pity for himself and the other "Acutes" and "Chronics." The narrator senses the faults of the "Combine"—that whole rigid routine, of which Big Nurse is only one cog. Although he always thinks of plots, fiendish motives—a paranoid pattern, in fact—the narrator is praised by Kesey. The insane do *see*; they are less innocent than the slaves of the Combine—such people as silly Red Cross helpers, corrupt government officials, TV viewers. In the upside-down world, the "cuckoo's nest," "insane" and "sane" are meaningless words—words the Combine imposes. Thus the absurd scene in which the hospital staff debates whether an inmate is "negatively Oedipal," or "psychopathic," or "schizophrenic," neglecting that fact that he is *human*.

The narrator cannot resurrect himself; he cannot triumph over Big Nurse. He seeks a guide in the new inmate, Mc-Murphy. This con-man enters laughing: "You boys don't look so crazy to me." Soon McMurphy begins to see that he must assert his will if he is to remain a happy man, and not become a machine. He *plays* with Big Nurse, irritating her smooth order by breaking a window, by not doing his appointed job, by asking for outrageous things. His play inspires the other inmates, especially the narrator, who regain some of their laughing, fighting vitality. But the Combine finally squeezes McMurphy: it makes him a *thing* by performing a lobotomy on him (after he tries to kill Big Nurse). The narrator cannot bear this transformation; mercifully he kills McMurphy and then runs away from the institution.

Mr. Kesey is less concerned with ideas than he should be. There are the "good guys" and the "bad guys." The Combine is dismissed quickly, but we wonder whether it is enough to proclaim the insanity of the system—after all, there are some "rational" adults who realize its falseness and still function in it. Nature—the woods, the streams, sex, the family—is praised without philosophical probing.

What if we don't fish? Can we still be human? Of course, Mr. Kesey is not "simple-minded"—he does show us that life contains many terrifying ambiguities. Big Nurse tries to fool the Acutes into thinking McMurphy is a charlatan, who cares less about them than *she* does. For a moment we believe that the benevolent "father" may be a fake. Black and white change to grey.

Mr. Kesey impressively uses imagery—he is a poet, not a philosopher. He employs a consistent range of images to express his almost manic condemnation of the system—we accept these more easily than his "message." And the images *are* the real meaning of his novel.

Several images represent the values of the Combine: imprisonment, mechanization, unreality. On the very first page we see that people are locked-up—in the institution and in the inhumanity of designs. The narrator refers to the henchmen of Big Nurse—their "eyes glittering out of the black faces like the hard glitter of radio tubes out of the back of an old radio." The image brilliantly arranges the scene: not only does this tell us that the narrator is slightly "mad"—it prepares us for the compulsive, automatic actions of the attendants, which help to make them unreal. Here are some other Combine-images: Big Nurse is "precision-made, like an expensive baby doll. . . . " She has made herself into a product, an almost "perfect work." . . . Mr. Kesey is so adept at stating these images that he needs only to *describe*, not to *explain*. Thus when McMurphy returns after his operation, the narrator says: "There's nothin' in the face. Just like one of those store dummies. . . . " We remember the Nurse as doll, the henchmen as "cartoon figures."

Opposed to these images of the Combine are natural images—free movement, warmth, pastoral. McMurphy is presented this way: "He stands looking at us, rocking back in his boots, and he laughs and laughs." He does not feel trapped; he shakes with humanity. Play is crucial. His carnival idea, his card games, his fishing expedition, his "marriage" of the whore and Billy—all these demonstrate that his capricious spirit is not mechanized. But Mr. Kesey realizes that such "openness" is never completely achieved in the Combine-world. McMurphy *can only be natural by violence*. He has to smash windows, break through imprisonment. The narrator remembers the woods, but he thinks: the "bird breaks, feathers springing, jumps out of the cedar into the birdshot from Papa's gun." The movement must be cataclysmic, after being inhibited for such a long time. Also the body cannot be "romantically" soft, constantly threatened as it is by automation. McMurphy's hand contains carbon, scars and cuts; the narrator sees himself at first as deaf-and-dumb. (He joins the mutes in *The Heart Is a Lonely Hunter* and "Raise High the Roof Beam, Carpenters.") Mr. Kesey maintains that the Combine and nature interact—we have horrifying oppositions.

But this dialectic also produces humor: "you have to laugh at the things that hurt you just to keep yourself in balance, just to keep the world from running you plumb crazy." "Humor blots out the pain." Mr. Kesey gives us many amusing scenes which are "black"—Big Nurse for example, informs Billy, the whore's betrothed, that she is going to tell his mother!—but he knows that if we can laugh at the unreality around us, we retain our humanity. Gothic and comedy are Janus-faced. *One Flew Over the Cuckoo's Nest* is an honest, claustrophobic, stylistically brilliant first novel which makes us shiver as we laugh—paradoxically, it keeps us "in balance" by revealing our madness. (pp. 82-4)

> Irving Malin, "Ken Kesey: 'One Flew Over the Cuckoo's Nest'," in Critique: Studies in Modern Fiction, *Vol. V, No. 2, Fall, 1962, pp. 81-4.*

## R. L. Sassoon

A vision of Hell . . . An ironical view of American society . . . intimations of an ideal of fun and self-realization in community . . . all these develop out of Mr. Kesey's semi-fantasial, semi-realistic treatment of a mental institution, the setting of [*One Flew over the Cuckoo's Nest*]. It tells a story at once horrific and humorous: an appalling nightmare that has its sources in the most ordinary, recognizable reality and issues continually into the delightful farce of only daydream. If at the extremes beyond credibility the narrative and point of view are sometimes frankly infantile—so also, the author implies, is the world with which he deals, not only the mental institution but its explanatory context, America. With great originality the author has succeeded in achieving, almost throughout the novel, a subtle balance and correspondence between the social burden of mirroring purposefully place and time and the personal art of creating fiction with the immediacy, the completeness in itself, of myth or parable.

The story is told us by a half-Indian inmate of the hospital, whose long-standing pretense to being both deaf and dumb makes it possible for him to hear (literally and imaginatively—"But it's the truth even if it didn't happen") all that goes on, day and night, in the wards. The hospital is a place, essentially, for the rejects of a matriarchal, increasingly technocratic and fanatically collective society. Through the narrator's naive but vividly mythopoetic (and/or mythomaniac) mind is conveyed a vision of humanity reduced to "controlled" machinery "installed" and adjusted in living bodies by the agents (the hospital staff) of a super-institution he calls the "Combine." While we laugh both with and at the absurdity of it, we are also uncomfortably chilled by this infernal revelation that we may all of us be electronic puppets functioning, well or poorly (that is, on the "outside" or in the hospital), according to some panoramic design which absolutely negates the possibilities of freedom and individuation: such that we may have become categorically without privilege or responsibility. (p. 116)

At night Bromden sees the floor of the dorm sink away from the walls, dropping him and his ward-mates into a science-fictional hell of machinery and radio tubes and transformers; robot devil-mechanics approach a patient and tear him open and go to work on his insides . . . "Right and left there are other things happening just as bad—crazy, horrible things too goofy and outlandish to cry about and too much true to laugh about—but the fog is getting thick enough I don't have to watch." The "fog," which swamps the ward from time to time, is protective;

but it also serves, by isolating man from man, to keep the patients in a state of cooperative docility. If all this is nightmare, and in its way comic too, Bromden also knows and speaks about such grim realities as shock therapy and, worse, the frontal lobotomy. Moreover, the daily routine of the ward is sordid and humiliating in every detail; the patients are degraded, wretched and resigned.

Into this world where men are either reduced to animals or turned into automatons, there enters a rough-and-tumble, logging and gambling man, whose relative freedom and invulnerability, his male wildness and woodsy common sense and humor, all convince the narrator—it is pathetic as much as comic—that this one must be "controlled" by some *anti-Combine*. The new-comer, McMurphy, who has feigned psychopathy because a mental hospital seems more pleasant to him than the state farm to which he has been sentenced for a few months, comes immediately into open conflict with the hospital staff. At first for kicks, but ultimately out of concern for his too easily cowed ward-mates, he engages in a battle to the finish—hilarious in its maneuvers but sombre in its presages of a sacrificial martyrdom—for the souls of these men.

His rival and enemy is "Big Nurse," a tyrannical, sadistic woman whose authority over the ward is almost total. Her gelid inhumanity is symbolized, with poignant irony, by nothing better than her preposterously huge breasts tightly packed behind ever clean and stiffly starched hospital-white: they are a bastion, not the sign of flesh of womanhood. McMurphy is a threat to her "control" over herself as well as over the ward. A genuine therapist, he commences at once to teach the patients to laugh—"Because he knows you have to laugh at things that hurt you just to keep yourself in balance, just to keep the world from running you plumb crazy. He knows there's a painful side . . . but he won't let the pain blot out the humor no more'n he'll let the humor blot out the pain." Worse, he influences them to try to accept themselves, even to assert themselves. And all the while Big Nurse and her flunkies are waiting for the chance to make him bow bloody or else to annihilate him—and that chance comes.

Before the appalling denoument, however, some of the ward have known the thrills of camaraderie of a wild, free-wheeling fishing trip, the delights of liquor, marijuana and sex—in short, have experienced (howsoever childishly, yet therapeutically) their own urges toward freedom and self-expression. Enough that some, who are voluntary patients, elect to leave the institution; and Bromden, who is committed, finds means and courage to escape.

The great power of the Combine is, after all, that it is believed in—whether explicitly, as by Bromden, or implicitly, as by (the author suggests) most of this society. It is a kind of corrosive religion, wrongly terrifying and wrongly consoling; its victims are not only those who have failed to be "adjusted to surroundings" but also those who have succeeded—for in doing so they have surrendered their capacities to *respond,* either to their own inner natures or to the world about them. The vicious circle of not being able to feel and not being able to make oneself felt—reflected in the impotence of the patients, but also in the cold sterility of the world from which they have run away—is guaranteed by what Bromden calls the Combine in its imposition of an ideal of non-humanity. The uniqueness and value of McMurphy is his aliveness, his uninhibited responsiveness to things and to people—which ultimately develops into a *responsibility for* Bromden and the other patients, such that he sacrifices himself so they, too, may choose to know the fullness of life, its joys and its pains.

When Bromden, after years of total isolation as a supposed deaf-mute, feels the greater necessity of using his voice to speak to McMurphy, he begins to recall his life before he entered the mental institution and those occasions that led him unconsciously to seek an escape from any human intercourse. He remembers a critical instance in his childhood, and his peculiar (and yet only too apt) understanding of it, when having spoken quite purposefully to three strangers who are looking for his father, he is ignored by them, because what he has to say does not communicate to them (that is, they prefer not to hear him)—

> I get the funniest feeling that the sun is turned up brighter than before on the three of them. Everything else looks like it usually does—the chickens fussing around in the grass on top of the 'dobe houses, the grasshoppers batting from bush to bush, the flies being stirred into black clouds around the fish racks by the little kids with sage flails, just like every other summer day. Except the sun, on these strangers, is all of a sudden way the hell brighter than usual and I can see the . . . *seams* where they're put together. And, almost, see the apparatus inside them take the words I just said and try to fit the words in here and there, this place and that, and when they find the words don't have any place ready-made where they'll fit, the machinery disposes of the words like they weren't even spoken.

In the wonderfully unembarrassed and naive, yet rather dignified, language of his narrator, Kesey continually focuses on the equal absurdity and pathos of man's inability and unwillingness *to listen* (whether to the urgent speech of one's own body and heart and spirit, or to those occasional essays at communication from outside), an abdication which can only make him increasingly a stranger both in the natural world (which anyway he is rapidly marring beyond recognition) and amongst his fellows. Bromden's half-stoical, half-childish flight into a bizarre, purely interior life is exactly correlate to a panicked society's determination to "control" human nature, reducing expression and activity to certain common-denominational patterns of predictably mechanical performance. It is taken for granted that this mass dehumanization serves a communal, quasi-sacred purpose, just as Bromden quite matter-of-factly, submissively, accumulates his real and imaginary evidences of an all-powerful, all-controlling Combine. Not until his encounter with McMurphy does he recover any sense of human realities and, simultaneously, the will and courage to return to real life.

Mr. Kesey's personal vision, while relating to universal problems of existence, springs from and reflects parabolically the individual's struggle for wholeness and survival in the specific context of American life today. For the most part he has made his perceptions and criticisms of this context implicit in the depiction of his characters and the development of the story. Unnecessary, therefore, and a dilution seem to me those passages where the author tends, in my opinion, to step outside of his fiction, as it were, in order to present a sort of more "objective," or explanatory, assessment of the social situation or to emphasize certain why's and wherefore's of his characters' actions and mental processes. For instance, it is out of Kesey's way in this novel, I think—and certainly out of his narrator's—to make so much of a point as he does of "exposing" the matriarchal aspects of our society or of "explaining" Bromden's and other characters' flights into neurosis with reference to bad, castrating mothers and/or wives, social pressures to tow the line, and so on. There is little originality of style or matter in the sections of the novel conceived for such ends and they are written unconvincingly; they may serve for some readers as a justification of the major portion of the novel and of the author's unique approach to reality by offering some sort of recognizable social and psychological matrix from which to interpret the characters' motivations and the author's purpose. As such, however, they may be misleading; this novel strikes me as much more of a myth or parable than a direct journalistic commentary on the times, and the intrusions of the latter, perhaps only because they are too close to being clichéd, do not always mix. Moreover, while Kesey has imagined his characters vividly and presented them with depth of understanding, his consciousness of the actual social ills of our times is comparatively superficial, focused as it is on symptoms rather than essential factors. If I belabor the point, it is because I think it would be a mistake, and a diminishment of the work, to view this novel as primarily a social "protest" or "evaluation." Rather, I see it as an intensely imaginative conception of the personal tragi-comedy of awakening to selfhood in a world largely held together through a utilitarian, artificial programming of human nature. While the setting and conditions are appropriately contemporary, properly judged and found wanting, the concern is for the timeless individual: his battle against and for himself, against and for those around him—that harsh struggle for personal values and self-fulfillment.

Mr. Kesey writes with both anger and compassion, with severe irony and broad, congenial humor. Following him with the involvement his style demands, one cannot but experience a vision that is truly authoritative and original. (pp. 117-20)

> *R. L. Sassoon, in a review of "One Flew Over the Cuckoo's Nest," in* Northwest Review, *Vol. 6, No. 2, Spring, 1963, pp. 116-20.*

**Robert Boyers**

There is no lack of conviction in Ken Kesey's *One Flew over the Cuckoo's Nest,* but neither is there an attempt to deal with human sexuality as a complex phenomenon. Kesey's novel is wholly successful as an indictment of modern society, and as an exploration into the kind of subtly repressive mechanisms we help to build into the fabric of our daily lives. Kesey's solution to our common problem is the opening of floodgates, the releasing of energies which have too long lain unused or forgotten. Chief among these are the twin resources of laughter and uninhibited sexuality, the linkage between which Kesey manages to clarify in the course of his novel.

The novel is set in a mental institution which is, in many respects, a microcosm of the society-at-large. It is to Kesey's credit that he never strains to maintain the parallel at any cost—it is a suggested parallel at most, and, where it suits his novelistic purposes, Kesey lets it go completely. His protagonist is one Randle Patrick McMurphy, pronounced psychopathic by virtue of being "overzealous in [his] sexual relations." His purpose in the institution, as in life apparently, is both to have a hell of a good time, and to defy "ball cutters," defined by McMurphy himself as "people who try to make you weak so they can get you to toe the line, to follow their rules, to live like they want you to." McMurphy is a truly monumental character—a gambler, a braggart, a fantastic lover, and a gadfly who insults and goads those who resist his charismatic injunctions. While he is something of a sensualist who dwells regularly on the ecstasies of sexual transport, and even goes so far as to bring his whores into the hospital to restore the vitality of his moribund fellow-psychopaths, McMurphy feels himself and his comrades the victims of women, not their lords and masters as his rhetoric would have it. His techniques of resistance and defiance are mostly pathetic, as they can achieve what are at best pyrrhic victories. One is never tempted to question the validity, the nobility, or even the necessity of McMurphy's defiance, but no mature reader will be convinced that his techniques can realistically accomplish what Kesey claims for them at the novel's end—the reclamation of numerous human beings who had grown passive and torpid before McMurphy's arrival.

At one point, McMurphy characterizes the inmates of the hospital as "victims of a matriarchy." In Kesey's view, modern society is a reflection of womanish values—archetypically responsible, cautious, repressive, deceitful, and solemn. One must look to the spirit of the whore if one would know what is best in women, and what can best bring out what is vital in men. There is no doubt that Kesey labors under a most reactionary myth, involving the mystique of male sexuality, which sees men as intrinsically better than women in terms of the dynamism and strength they can impart to the universe. Unable rationally to account for the disparity between such a projection and the puny reality of our male lives, Kesey waxes fatalistic, though never submissive, and sees "ball cutters" everywhere. It is a kind of paranoid, conspiratorial view of things, not without its measure of accuracy, but it somehow evades the crucial issues which Kesey and others have raised.

At the heart of Kesey's notion of what is possible for modern liberated man is a phenomenon which one may call porno-politics. It is a phenomenon which resides primarily in the imagination of a few thousand people, most of them young and bright, and which is occasionally manifested in the hysterical behavior of certain radical partisans of unpopular causes, a behavior which, by the way,

many would call resolutely antipolitical, for all its pretensions to the contrary. Advocates of porno-politics are usually utopian socialists who lack the vision and patience to realize their goals politically: that is, they are youthful dreamers who are frustrated by the customary routines through which men achieve power or influence in order to alter the political relations which obtain in their society. Frequently, the retreat into varieties of porno-politics results from people relying too heavily on the flexibility of a given political system, and on the sheer magnetism of their own sincerity, which they and their associates had always considered irresistible. When the erstwhile utopian realizes how restrictive and closed the political structure of his society is, despite its aggressive disclaimers, and when he is made aware of the basic indifference to his ideals and to his attractiveness among the masses of people, he is suffused by a kind of anger and dread. As the society affords him virtually no outlet for these feelings, which rarely become specific enough to fix legitimate targets anyway, the befuddled utopian permits his vision of the possible to undergo a remarkable transformation. Unable to affect masses of men or to move political and social institutions, he transfers the burden of realizing a perfectly harmonious society to sex.

In Kesey's novel, we have what seemingly amounts to a *reductio ad absurdum* of familiar Freudian propositions. It is repressed sexuality which ostensibly lies behind every psychosis, and which is responsible for the acquiescence of all men in the confining conventions of Western society. It is in the spirit of random and thoroughly abandoned sexuality that Kesey's McMurphy would remake men, and subsequently the world. What is a little frightening in a novel like this, though, is that such a projection does not at all operate on a metaphorical level. Sex is not here a mere metaphor for passion, nor for any positive engagement with one's fellow human beings. There is a literalism in Kesey's suggestions of sexual apocalypse, with its unavoidable ramifications into a political and social context, which cannot be lightly taken. Other talented people are caught up in such projections, and are delivering gospels of sexual salvation with a hysterical dogmatism that is, for many of us, laughable and pathetic. This is so particularly for those who have observed the failure of libertarian sexual experimentation and random coupling to affect substantially the pettiness and self-absorption even of those who are most easily committed to libertarian modes and who have no need perpetually to justify such commitments ideologically. How futile it is for intelligent people seriously to expect their sexual programs and practices to have a liberating effect on masses of men, when what these people want is to be left alone to enjoy what they have. What porno-politics essentially amounts to is a form of entertainment for a middle-class audience, which alternatively writhes and applauds before the late-night news, and welcomes the opportunity to indulge and express postures it considers intrinsic to its worth as modern men: tolerance and righteous indignation.

Kesey's brilliance is evidenced by his ability to be seduced by porno-political utopianism, and yet not to yield to it entirely. What save him are his sense of the ridiculous and his understanding of men as fundamentally dishonest and irresolute. Kesey wants to believe that the source of all terror and passivity is somehow sexual, that the liberation of sexual energies in the form of primal fantasies will enable men to conceive of themselves as more passionate and autonomous individuals. But his intelligence forces him, as it were, against his will, to tell a truth which is more complex and disheartening. He recounts a group therapy session which had taken place in the institution some years before McMurphy's arrival. Unlike the usual dispirited proceedings, this particular session stood out for the violent release of confessions that it evoked from the habitually desultory and tight-lipped inmates. Once the momentum is established, the inmates begin shouting confessions: "I lied about trying. I did take my sister!" / "So did I! So did I!" / "And me! And me!"

At first, all of this seems satisfying, at least from a conventionally clinical point of view: repressed memories are rising to the surface, where they can be handled therapeutically. But, almost immediately, we are shown that not only did such events never occur in the lives of these men; they do not even represent their fantasy lives. Such "confessions" have nothing at all to do with the wish-fulfillment that is a strong component of compulsive fantasies. What the inmates have done is simply to exploit certain readily available clichés issuing from standard interpretations of modern man as the perennial victim of sexual repression. The inmates are victims of something much more embracing and diversified than simple sexual guilt or repression, though the sexual element may be particularly significant in the case of two or three inmates among many. What is sickening is their desire to please the therapists by revealing what they are supposed to, rather than what is really inside them. Finally, they are shamed by the resounding announcement of hopeless old Pete: "I'm tired," he shouts—a confession so simple and true that it puts an abrupt end to the rampant dishonesty of the others. Kesey loves McMurphy, and identifies with his aspirations—he wants men to be free, to laugh the authorities down, to refuse to be manipulated. He wants, moreover, to go along with McMurphy's sexual orientation, and to be as optimistic as McMurphy about the effects of sexual liberation on the reigning political and social atmosphere. But McMurphy is not a mask for Kesey, nor is any single character in the novel. In fact, as much as Kesey admires McMurphy's stratagems for outwitting the matriarch *par excellence* who goes under the title Big Nurse, we are never quite certain whether to laugh at McMurphy as well as with him. Big Nurse, as the personification of "the system" at its most callow, repressive, yet ostensibly enlightened, represents a tendency toward antiseptic desexualization which is abhorrent. We want McMurphy to bewilder her, to kill her with his charming nonchalance and boyish exuberance, and to parade his own aggressive sexuality before her. We want her to be teased and tempted so that she will be provoked to try to castrate McMurphy, if not actually, then symbolically, as she has successfully whipped the other inmates. We want to see McMurphy put to the test of the vitality and resilience he proudly proclaims, as if he could redeem us from any misgivings we might have about our own potency.

And yet, throughout this novel, we know that nothing McMurphy does, or encourages his comrades to do, will make any substantive difference to the system that we all despise. McMurphy, through an ideological predisposition, which in his case is more instinctive than learned, attributes to sex what even he knows it cannot accomplish. His is a heroic endeavor in every way, but McMurphy is at bottom a little lost boy who gets into the big muddy way up over his head. The picture of him, in bed with his whore at last, almost at the end of the novel, is utterly revealing: " . . . more like two tired little kids than a grown man and a grown woman in bed together to make love." McMurphy can behave as brashly as he likes, and speak with utter abandon of sex, but for him it has still an element of mystery, of vows exchanged, even if only for a brief duration. His libertarian apocalyptism is sincere, but in McMurphy's own character we can see that a libertarian sexual orientation ultimately has little to do with making men free as political and social beings. McMurphy needs no sexual swagger to be free, though, in his case, it is a believable accouterment of his personality. What is indispensable in McMurphy's character is his propensity to laugh, in his lucid moments to see himself as something of a spectacle, not wholly detached nor different from the other inmates who have failed to retain their resilience. When he loses his laugh, he grows desperate, and places upon sex that burden of hope for transcendence which the reality of sexual experience must frustrate. When, at the very conclusion of the book, McMurphy rips open Big Nurse's hospital uniform, revealing, for all to see, her prodigious breasts, we see where McMurphy's porno-political vision has led him. Unable to affect a world that victimizes him, a civilization which, in the words of the British psychoanalyst R. D. Laing " . . . represses not only 'the instincts,' not only sexuality, but any form of transcendence," McMurphy is driven to rape the reality incarnated in Big Nurse. In his fear and frustration, he does not see what, of all things, should be most obvious to him: that he cannot make another human being aware of his humanity by destroying or suppressing those elements of his own humanity that have made McMurphy a beautiful person. By his action, he demonstrates the original futility of his project, the necessary brutalization of his sexual ethic, and the dehumanization implicit in the act of invoking an *Eros* which is imperfectly understood and crudely employed. (pp. 44-7)

> Robert Boyers, *"Attitudes Toward Sex in American 'High Culture'," in* The Annals of the American Academy of Political and Social Science, *Vol. 376, March, 1968, pp. 36-52.*

## Leslie A. Fiedler

[*The excerpt below derives from the concluding volume of* The Return of the Vanishing American, *a three-volume study in "literary anthropology" in which Fiedler attempts "to define the myths which give a special character to art and life in America." The essay from which the following excerpt was taken focuses upon the mythical treatment of the native American in various works of contemporary American literature.*]

Primitivism is the large generic name for the Higher Masculine Sentimentality, a passionate commitment to inverting Christian-Humanist values, out of a conviction that the Indian's way of life is preferable. From this follows the belief that if one is an Indian he ought, despite missionaries and school boards, to remain Indian; and if one is White, he should do his best, despite all pressures of the historical past, to go Native. Ever since the oft-quoted observation of Crèvecoeur that there must be something superior in Indian society since "thousands of Europeans are Indians, and we have no example of even one of those aborigines having from choice become Europeans . . . ," White men in America have continued to echo that primitivist hyperbole, whose truth cannot be diminished merely by disproving Crèvecoeur's facts. (p. 169)

[In *One Flew Over the Cuckoo's Nest,* Kesey retells] the old, old fable of the White outcast and the noble Red Man joined together against home and mother, against the female world of civilization. . . . [The novel's setting is] at once present and archaic—a setting which Ken Kesey discovered in the madhouse: *our* kind of madhouse, which is to say, one located in the American West, so that the Indian can make his reappearance in its midst with some probability, as well as real authenticity.

Perhaps it was necessary for Kesey to come himself out of Oregon, one of our last actual Wests (just as it was necessary for him to have been involved with one of the first experiments with the controlled use of LSD), since for most Americans after Mark Twain, the legendary colored companion of the white fugitive had been turned from Red to Black. Even on the most naive levels, the Negro has replaced the Indian as the natural enemy of Woman. . . . (p. 177)

[*One Flew Over the Cuckoo's Nest*] opens with an obviously psychotic "I" reflecting on his guards, one of whom identifies him almost immediately, speaking in a Negro voice: "Here's the Chief. The *soo*-pah Chief, fellas. Ol' Chief Broom. Here you go, Chief Broom. . . . " Chief Bromden is his real name, this immense schizophrenic, pretending he is deaf-and-dumb to baffle "the Combine," which he believes controls the world: "Look at him: a giant janitor. There's your Vanishing American, a six-foot-six sweeping machine, scared of its own shadow. . . . " Or rather Bromden is the name he has inherited from his white mother, who subdued the full-blooded Chief who sired him and was called "The-Pine-That-Stands-Tallest-on-the-Mountain." "He fought it a long time," the half-breed son comments at one point, "till my mother made him too little to fight any more and he gave up."

Chief Bromden believes he is little, too, what was left in him of fight and stature subdued by a second mother, who presides over the ward in which he is confined ("She may be a mother, but she's big as a damn barn and tough as knife metal . . . ") and, at one point, had given him two hundred successive shock treatments. Not only is Mother II big, however, especially in the breasts; she is even more essentially *white*: "Her face is smooth, calculated, and precision-made, like an expensive baby doll, skin like flesh-colored enamel, blend of white and cream and baby-blue eyes . . . " and her opulent body is bound tight in a

starched white uniform. To understand her in her full mythological significance, we must recall [*The Myth of the White Woman with a Tomahawk,* the autobiographical account of] that seventeenth century first White Mother of Us All Hannah Duston, and her struggle against the Indians who tried to master her.

Hannah has represented from the start those forces in the American community—soon identified chiefly with the female and maternal—which resist all incursions of savagery, no matter what their course. But only in the full twentieth century is the nature of Hannah's assault made quite clear, first in Freudian terms and then in psychedelic ones. "No, buddy," Kesey's white hero, Randle Patrick McMurphy, comments on the Big Nurse. "She ain't pecking at your *eyes*. That's not what she's peckin' at." And when someone, who really knows but wants to hear spoken aloud what he is too castrated to say, asks at *what,* then, R. P. McMurphy answers, "At your balls, buddy, at your everlovin' *balls*." Yet toward the close of the book, McMurphy has to be told by the very man who questioned him earlier the meaning of his own impending lobotomy at the hands of Big Nurse ("Yes, chopping away the brain. Frontal-lobe castration. I guess if she can't cut below the belt she'll do it above the eyes"), though by this time he understands why he, as well as the Indian (only victim of the original Hannah's blade), has become the enemy of the White Woman.

In his own view, McMurphy may be a swinger, and in the eyes of his Indian buddy an ultimate Westerner, the New American Man:

> He walked with long steps, too long, and he had his thumbs hooked in his pockets again. The iron in his boot heels cracked lightning out of the tile. He was the logger again, the swaggering gambler . . . the cowboy out of the TV set walking down the middle of the street to meet a dare.

But to Big Nurse—and the whole staff of the asylum whom, White or Black, male or female, she has cowed—he is only a "psychopath," not less sick for having chosen the nuthouse in which he finds himself to the work-farm to which his society had sentenced him. And she sees the purpose of the asylum as being precisely to persuade men like him to accept and function in the world of rewards and punishments which he has rejected and fled.

To do this, however, she must persuade him like the rest that he is only a "bad boy," *her* bad boy, quite like, say, Huckleberry Finn. But where Huck's substitute mothers demanded that he give up smoking, wear shoes, go to school, she asks (it is the last desperate version of "sivilisation") that he be sane: "All he has to do is *admit* he was wrong, to indicate, *demonstrate* rational contact and the treatment would be cancelled this time."

The choice is simple: either sanity abjectly accepted, or sanity imposed by tranquilizers, shock treatments, finally lobotomy itself. But McMurphy chooses instead if not madness, at least aggravated psychopathy and an alliance with his half-erased, totally schizophrenic Indian comrade—an alliance with all that his world calls unreason. . . . And this time, the alliance is not merely explicitly, but quite overtly directed against the White Woman, which is to say, Hannah Duston fallen out of her own legend into that of Henry and Wawatam.

For a while, the result seems utter disaster, since McMurphy, driven to attempt the rape of his tormentor, is hauled off her and duly lobotomized, left little more than a vegetable with "a face milk-white except for the heavy purple bruises around the eyes." Whiter than the White Woman who undid him, white as mother's milk: this is McMurphy at the end, except that Chief Bromden will not let it be the end, will not let

> something like that sit there in the day room with his name tacked on it for twenty or thirty years so the Big Nurse could use it as an example of what can happen if you buck the system. . . .

Therefore, in the hush of the first night after the lobotomy, he creeps into the bed of his friend for what turns out to be an embrace—for only in a caricature of the act of love can he manage to kill him:

> The big, hard body had a tough grip on life. . . . I finally had to lie full length on top of it and scissor the kicking legs with mine. . . . I lay there on top of the body for what seemed like days. . . . Until it was still a while and had shuddered once and was still again.

It is the first real *Liebestod* in our long literature of love between white men and colored, and the first time, surely, that the Indian partner in such a pair has outlived his White brother. Typically [as in Mark Twain's *Huckleberry Finn* and William Faulkner's "The Bear"], . . . Huck had been younger than Jim, Ike than Sam Fathers. Everyone who has lived at the heart of our dearest myth knows that it is the white boy-man who survives, as the old Indian, addressing the Great Spirit, prepares to vanish. Even so recent a novel as Berger's *Little Big Man* has continued to play it straight, closing on the traditional dying fall, as Old Lodge Skins subsides after a final prayer, and his white foster son says:

> He laid down then on the damp rocks and died right away. I descended to the treeline, fetched back some poles, and built him a scaffold. Wrapped him in the red blanket and laid him thereon. Then after a while I started down the mountain in the fading light.

But on the last page of *One Flew Over the Cuckoo's Nest,* Chief Bromden is on his way back to the remnants of his tribe who "have took to building their old ramshackle wood scaffolding all over the big million-dollar . . . spillway." And his very last words are: "I been away a long time."

It is, then, the "Indian" in Kesey himself, the undischarged refugee from a madhouse, the AWOL Savage, who is left to boast: *And I only am escaped alone to tell thee.* But the "Indian" does not write books; and insofar as Kesey's fable can be read as telling the truth about himself as well as about all of us, it prophesies silence for him, a silence into which he has, in fact, lapsed, though not until he had tried one more Gutenberg-trip in *Sometimes A Great Notion.*

It is a book which seems to me not so much a second novel as a first novel written (or, perhaps, only published) second: a more literary, conventionally ambitious, and therefore *strained* effort—for all its occasional successes, somehow an error. *One Flew Over the Cuckoo's Nest* works better to the degree that it is dreamed or hallucinated rather than merely written—which is to say, to the degree that it, like its great prototype *The Leatherstocking Tales,* is Pop Art rather than *belles lettres*—the dream once dreamed in the woods, and now redreamed on pot and acid.

Its very sentimentality, good-guys bad-guys melodrama, occasional obviousness and thinness of texture, I find—like the analogous things in Cooper—not incidental flaws, but part of the essential method of its madness. There is a phrase which reflects on Kesey's own style quite early in the book, defining it aptly, though it pretends only to represent Chief Bromden's vision of the world around him:

> Like a cartoon world, where the figures are flat and outlined in black, jerking through some kind of goofy story that might be real funny if it weren't for the cartoon figures being real guys. . . .

Everywhere in Kesey, as a matter of fact, the influence of comics and, especially, comic books is clearly perceptible, in the mythology as well as in the style; for like those of many younger writers of the moment, the images and archetypal stories which underlie his fables are not the legends of Greece and Rome, not the fairy tales of Grimm, but the adventures of Captain Marvel and Captain Marvel, Jr., those new-style Supermen who, sometime just after World War II, took over the fantasy of the young. What Western elements persist in Kesey are, as it were, first translated back into comic-strip form, then turned once more into words on the conventional book page. One might, indeed, have imagined Kesey ending up as a comic book writer, but since the false second start of *Sometimes A Great Notion,* he has preferred to live his comic strip rather than write or even draw it.

The adventures of Psychedelic Superman as Kesey had dreamed and acted them, however—his negotiations with Hell's Angels, his being busted for the possession of marijuana, his consequent experiences in court and, as a refugee from the law, in Mexico—all this, like the yellow bus in which he used to move up and down the land taking an endless, formless movie, belongs to hearsay and journalism rather than to literary criticism, challenging conventional approaches to literature even as it challenges literature itself. But *One Flew Over the Cuckoo's Nest* survives the experiments and rejections which followed it; and looking back five years after its initial appearance, it seems clear that in it for the first time the New West was clearly defined: the West of Here and Now, rather than There and Then—the West of Madness. (pp. 179-85)

It is only a step from thinking of the West as madness to regarding madness as the true West, but it took the long years between the end of the fifteenth century and the middle of the twentieth to learn to take that step. There is scarcely a New Western among those I have discussed which does not in some way flirt with the notion of madness as essential to the New World; but only in [*Beautiful Losers* by] Leonard Cohen (though Thomas Berger comes close) and in Kesey is the final identification made, and in Kesey at last combined with the archetype of the love that binds the lonely white man to his Indian comrade—to his *mad* Indian comrade, perhaps even to the *madness* of his Indian comrade, as Kesey amends the old tale. (p. 185)

> *Leslie A. Fiedler, "The Higher Sentimentality," in his* The Return of the Vanishing American, *Stein and Day Publishers, 1968, pp. 169-87.*

## Terry G. Sherwood

[*A small portion of the essay excerpted below was published previously in CLC, Vol. 1.*]

Although first published in 1962, Ken Kesey's **One Flew Over the Cuckoo's Nest** still enjoys a wide readership. Kesey's "hippy" reputation and the book's unusual expression of anti-Establishment themes, ranging from rebellion against conformity to pastoral retreat, would explain its current popular appeal. The critics' response to the book is less understandable. A warm reception by reviewers has been followed by relatively little critical interest. The book deserves more attention as an imaginative expression of a moral position congenial to an important segment of the American population and as a noteworthy use of Popular culture in a serious novel. This essay will demonstrate the central importance of the nexus between Kesey's aesthetic, informed by comic strip principles, and his moral vision, embodying simple, elemental truths. Kesey's references to comic strip materials are not just casual grace notes but clear indications of his artistic stance. Significantly, the importance of the comic strip to Kesey has been confirmed by Leslie Fiedler [see excerpt dated 1968], the one major critic discussing the novel at length, although he neither affirms such a high degree of artistic consciousness in Kesey nor examines certain essential details.

The climactic ward party ends with reference to the comic strip hero, the Lone Ranger. Harding asks to be awakened for McMurphy's escape. "I'd like to stand there at the window with a silver bullet in my hand and ask 'Who wawz that'er masked man?' as you ride—." The insightful Harding clearly recognizes that McMurphy, like the comic strip savior, whose silver bullet annihilates Evil, has freed the inmates from the clutches of the monster Big Nurse. The Lone Ranger reference underlines an aesthetic set out clearly in the novel. Briefly, Kesey's method embodies that of the caricaturist, the cartoonist, the folk artist, the allegorist. Characterization and delineation of incident are inked in bold, simple, exaggerated patterns for obvious but compelling statement. As in the comic strip, action in Kesey's novel turns on the mythic confrontation between Good and Evil: an exemplary he-man versus a machine-tooled, castrating matriarch ever denied our sympathies. Both are bigger than life; both are symbolic exaggerations of qualities; neither is "realistic." Bromden's description of the inmates' and ward attendants'

stylized behavior is instructive. "Like a cartoon world, where the figures are flat and outlined in black, jerking through some kind of goofy story that might be real funny if it weren't for the cartoon figures being real guys." Characters and incidents are types, bound by set characteristics, before they are uniquely individual. In demonstrating the centrality of such comic strip elements, I will indicate first how they are reinforced by other materials from Popular culture sharing similar techniques, then more explicitly how they shape character and incident, and finally how Kesey's failure to heed the dangers of his mode is symptomatic of the book's moral flaws and central to critical evaluation.

Kesey draws from one form of Popular culture, the folk song, in his initial characterization of McMurphy. We hear lines from "The Roving Gambler" and "The Wagoner's Lad" in McMurphy's exuberant solo on his first morning in the asylum. Both songs treat a typical opposition between the wanderer and society in terms of romantic love. With characteristic bravado the gambler McMurphy sings, "She took me to her parlor, and coo-oo-ooled me with her fan"—I can hear the whack as he slaps his bare belly—"whispered low in her mamma's ear, I luh-uhvv that gamblin' man." The town-bred girl is inevitably drawn to the rover living by the uncertainties of the card game, not the genteel, stability and sexual constriction of the matriarchal parlor. Despite McMurphy's resonating exuberance, the second song is more darkly intoned, with the harshness of farewell and the settled community's stony resistance, thereby predicting McMurphy's unalterable battle with Big Nurse. The lad's poverty and way of life ensure parental disapproval. "Oh, your parents don't like me, they say I'm too po-o-or; they say I'm not worthy to enter your door—Hard livin's my pleasure, my money's my o-o-wn, an' them that don't like me, they can leave me alone." Like the comic strip, a method of the folk song is presentation of simple, typical behavioral patterns, while eschewing introspection and highly subtle characterization. Simple details express typical patterns. The town girl's fan cools the heat of the wanderer's movement, and the wagoner's lad expresses proud opposition to economic bigotry by refusing the girl's offer of hay for his horses. Murphy's brief medley is self-characterization—footloose virility, uncompromised independence, gambler's whim, acceptance of harsh physical effort, and resistance to society worked out within the easily understood boundaries of folk art.

Kesey further mines Popular culture in frequent references to McMurphy as the cowboy hero. When McMurphy approaches to break the nurses' window, Bromden says, "He was the logger again, the swaggering gambler, the big red-headed brawling Irishman, the cowboy out of the TV set walking down the middle of the street to meet a dare." Elsewhere, McMurphy speaks in his "drawling cowboy actor's voice." The television "western" intersects the Lone Ranger and folk song references to emphasize frontier values. Kesey uses the stereotyped cowboy hero for precisely the reasons he is often attacked: unrelenting selfhood and independence articulated with verbal calmness and defended by physical valor and ready defiance of opposition. Stock "western" formulae constitute a convenient reservoir of popular literary associations for depicting McMurphy in easily definable terms.

Kesey's mode of simplification voices a moral vision rooted in clearcut opposition between Good and Evil, between natural man and society, between an older mode of existence honoring masculine physical life and a modern day machine culture inimical to it, between the Indian fishing village and the hydroelectric dam. Modern society standardizes men and straitjackets its misfits; it causes the illness which it quarantines. The spiritual residue of the American Old West opposes the machine culture; but the West, as such, is doomed like McMurphy. For Kesey, Popular culture's hardened simplicity of detail expresses continuing American values and problems, etched deeply in the American consciousness. Modern machine culture is the most recent manifestation of society's threat to the individual, perhaps the most threatening.

Thus, Kesey turns to the comic strip, a more recent aspect of Popular culture, for his literary materials. Here he finds the method of exaggeration basic to his aesthetic. In *The Electric Kool-Aid Acid Test* Tom Wolfe delineates Kesey's attention to comic strips. For Kesey, the comic book superheroes (Captain Marvel, Superman, Plastic Man, the Flash, *et al.*) were the true mythic heroes of his contemporary adolescent generation. Kesey was interested significantly in this comic strip world during his Stanford University, Perry Lane days, the gestation period of *One Flew Over the Cuckoo's Nest.* He realized this interest most spectacularly later in Merry Prankster days by affecting the superhero's costume to image transcendant human possibility (witness his Flash Gordon-like garb at a Viet Nam teach-in in 1965 and his cape and leotards at the LSD graduation in 1966). The longevity of his interest, antedating his first novel and lasting after his Mexican exile, affirms its personal significance. Wolfe's book colors in the authorial consciousness behind the Lone Ranger reference and Bromden's belief that McMurphy, despite his wardmates' fear of his self-aggrandizement, was a "giant come out of the sky to save us from the Combine." The Lone Ranger's mask mysteriously separates him from other men, his origin is uncertain, and his silver bullet has supernatural powers; that is, he has divine characteristics. Bromden's vision of McMurphy as a saving giant recalls airborne superheroes like Superman and Captain Marvel, miraculously aiding others in one fell swoop; also, we are hereby conditioned for the depiction of McMurphy as Christ, sacrificed on the cross-shaped electroshock table on behalf of the ward. (pp. 96-100)

The comic strip also inspires the characterization of Big Nurse. The Combine, a machine culture which harvests and packages men, is modern Evil; and Big Nurse, its powerful agent. She shares the comic strip villain's control over modern technology; her glass enveloped nurses' cubicle is the ward's electronic nerve center, and she punishes on the electroshock table. She is Miss Ratched—the ratchet—essential cog in ward machinery (also the ratchet wrench, adjusting malfunctioning inmates?). Her giantism is expressed in her nickname, Big Nurse, and frequently in descriptions of her. "She's like a Jap statue. There's no moving her and no help against her." "Her nostrils flare

open, and every breath she draws she gets bigger, as big and tough-looking's I seen her get over a patient since Taber was here—I can smell the hot oil and magneto spark when she goes past, and every step hits the floor she blows up a size bigger, blowing and puffing, roll down anything in her path." Kesey scales her to match the giant of the sky, McMurphy. Like the comic strip villain, she never enjoys our sympathies, even when rendered voiceless and physically weak by McMurphy's uncavalier assault following Billy Bibbit's suicide.

Our lack of sympathy is tied to her static nature as a principle, not a human being. The comic strip is essentially a pictorial representation of stereotyped moral and psychological truths for unsophisticated readers. The Lone Ranger's mask, the image of his mysterious separateness, and Freddy Freeman's crutch, the image of his mortal half, pictorially express constants in their natures. Kesey's characterizations of McMurphy and Big Nurse emphasize similar repeated details. In McMurphy's motorcyclist's cap we see the stereotyped anti-social belligerence of cycle gangs; in his scarred fists, his ready valor and worker's energy; in his red hair, the Irishman's volatility; in the scar on his nose, an emblem of wounds bravely received in aggressive assertion of self; in his white whale underpants, his untamed and socially destructive natural vitality. A hard shell of plastic, starch, and enamel incase Big Nurse's humanity. The impenetrable surface of her "doll's face and doll's smile" iconographically represents her stunted feelings. The militaristic, stiff nurse's uniform constrains the sexual and maternal potential of her admirable bosom. She is part of a machine attempting to level even sexual differences. The stable lines in Kesey's characterization of the two antagonists stress their essential natures.

Imaginative variations of comic strip principles show Kesey's sophisticated manipulation of his mode, as in Bromden's metamorphosis through McMurphy's influence. Bromden's rejuvenation is the gauge of McMurphy's savior's power and is Kesey's promise of hope. Bromden escapes, not McMurphy. The modern world cannot accommodate the free-wheeling Irishman. The freedom of the Old West is gone; its spirit resides only in myth; the Irish minority has been assimilated. McMurphy is hounded into a prison farm and, despite delusions of freely choosing the asylum, drawn fatalistically into the showdown with Big Nurse. . . . He cannot remain in a conformist world in which men no longer share the ecstasy of violence and the gambler's defiance of fate; but, by sacrificing himself, he can infuse the spirit of rebellion and selfhood into those able to combine it with other strengths. His diminishing strength transfers to Bromden. McMurphy cannot lift the tub room control panel, but, possessing the "secret" power of "blowin' a man back up to full size," can empower Bromden to make the symbolic gesture of throwing the panel through the asylum wall, of turning the machine upon itself. The doomed giant can create another giant. Shazam. The six foot, eight inch "Vanishing American," the first man in the ward, has been deflated by a racist society which bulldozes its Indian villages and, after using the tribesmen to fight crippling wars, incarcerates them in asylums to clean floors for white inmates. Kesey looks to dormant Indian values, represented *in po-*

*tentia* by Bromden's size, for answers to problems of modern culture. Residual Indian pastoralism and regard for physical life, plus a yet strong sense of community, represent a possibility for life in defiance of the Combine; but these values need inspiration, inflation by McMurphy's Spirit. Kesey's central image is the superhero's metamorphosis from mortal weakness to supernatural strength.

The relationship between the white McMurphy and the Indian Bromden is further delineated in Kesey's strategic Lone Ranger reference. Bromden is McMurphy's Tonto, the silent but loyal Indian companion under auspices of his white spiritual guide. Equation of McMurphy and the "masked man" not only stresses McMurphy's savior role in "western" terms, but also sums up the previous relationship between McMurphy and Bromden in order to overturn the traditional expectation of Indian subservience. The Lone Ranger and Tonto become, respectively, the sacrificial Christ and his independent disciple, a writer of Holy Scripture carrying Good News composed of both men's values. Only Tonto leaves the asylum: Bromden's Indian values imbued with McMurphy's Spirit are Kesey's final answer to the questions asked by the book. Strategic use of the Lone Ranger, just before McMurphy's demise and Bromden's complete metamorphosis, crystalizes the book's pivotal racial relationship before redefining it. Again, a skillful hand adapts the comic strip materials.

Different kinds of comic strips serve the author's purpose. Although the showdown with Big Nurse most obviously expresses modern man's resistance against a crippling society, she expresses only locally a general condition delineated in part by strokes of Kesey's animal cartoonist's pen. As noted earlier, Kesey borrows frequently from other forms of Popular culture, using techniques similar to the comic strip's. He modulates between forms with considerable finesse. Appalled by the predatory group therapy, McMurphy discusses this "peckin' party" with the ineffectual Harding. The discussion takes its cue from McMurphy's homespun metaphor. Despite his fastidious complaint about McMurphy's metaphorical mixture ("bitch," "ballcutter," "chicken") Harding spins out variations on the animal imagery to articulate his latent antagonism against Big Nurse. Initial denial that she is a "giant monster of the poultry clan, bent on sadistically pecking out our eyes" yields to his own categorization of her as wolf and the men as rabbits. "All of us here are rabbits of varying ages and degrees, hippity-hopping through our Walt Disney world." Animal metaphors depicting static human traits, a common device in folk literature, are frequent in the novel, *e.g.,* Williams, the black attendant, "crawls" to Big Nurse "like a dog to a whipping." To invoke Disney is to translate the animal metaphors into modern cartoon terms especially appropriate to a modern standardized world. (pp. 100-03)

Bromden's first extended description of the conformist ward weds the cartoon to similar literary forms. After depicting the ward inmates and attendants as cartoon figures "flat and outlined in black" locked irrevocably into set behavior and speaking "cartoon comedy speech," he shifts to a similar mode. "The technicians go trotting off, pushing the man on the Gurney, like cartoon men—or like puppets, mechanical puppets in one of those Punch and Judy acts where it's supposed to be funny to see the puppet beat up by the Devil and swallowed headfirst by a smiling alligator." The puppet show reaches out with one hand through the alligator image to Kesey's animal metaphors and with the other to the "dreamy doll faces of the workmen" in Bromden's hallucination and the doll faces of Billy Bibbit and Big Nurse. (The standardized world includes even Big Nurse, who in her stunted emotional development, is victim as well as victimizer.) Kesey deftly shifts from the cartoon to the puppet show to toys, changing terms within his aesthetic frame without altering it.

The same principle governs in a less obvious way McMurphy's white whale underpants, a gift, he tells us, from a co-ed "Literary major" who thought him a "symbol." This is one of the few times when Kesey goes beyond popular culture *per se,* but Melville is readily adaptable for his purpose. We are reminded that McMurphy is not a "realistic" character, but a representation of certain qualities shared by Moby Dick—natural vitality, strength, immortality, anti-social destructiveness. However, this is a caricature white whale, emblazoned on the Irishman's black underpants to emphasize his sexually intoned vitality, and bearing a devilish red eye linked to McMurphy's red hair and volatile Irish nature. This is a cartoon Moby Dick, minus the cosmic horror and mystery, precise in its suggestions and domesticated for Kesey's purposes.

Designating McMurphy a "symbol" is a clear statement of Kesey's aesthetic, as are the "flat and outlined" cartoon men. But to demonstrate the presence of this aesthetic, as done hereto, is not to elucidate its ultimate moral significance for Kesey. In this regard, Harding is absolutely central for through him Kesey guides our response to important elements in the novel. Harding has concealed his homosexuality, at least bisexuality, behind insincere sexual bravado and, more importantly, behind his considerable learning. He is the modern intellectual avoiding simple realities. Unlike the co-ed, who could appreciate McMurphy's vitality and sexuality while labeling him with terms from her academic vocabulary, Harding initially rejects McMurphy's homely "analogy" of the "peckin' party," clouding the truth with modern psychological cant. Yet, besides Bromden, he is the most aware character and not prevented by snobbish scorn of McMurphy's "TV-cowboy stoicism" from seeing in McMurphy's deliberate affectation of cowboy drawl an affirmation of "western" values. McMurphy instructs him, not *vice versa,* and his identification of McMurphy and the Lone Ranger is a final measure of new knowledge, expressed significantly in Popular cultural terms. No longer "Perfessor Harding" defeated in the symbolic blackjack game by another queen, he has the vision of wisdom to see Big Nurse as Evil Monster.

Harding is closest to the intended reader, college educated and uprooted from moral values of Popular culture by academic prejudices. Like the reader, he can recognize the comic strip aesthetic but is unwilling to admit its moral truths. The novel offers simple truths in a simplified mode, taunting the reader for his literary condescension and related moral weakness. Like McMurphy we must turn to our "cartoon magazine" and television "westerns" for a rudimentary vision of human values, and away from a specious notion of moral complexity in the modern world. Kesey encourages anti-intellectualism, at least anti-academicism. Significantly, Harding is not cured of homosexual impulses, just his fear of admitting them; far removed from the springs of fully realized physical existence, the intellectual can learn self-consciously from those who drink directly. Harding's change is paradigmatic for the intended effect on the educated reader aware of the nature of Kesey's aesthetic, but lacking the moral perception lying behind it.

Of course, given that moral problems tend toward more complexity and not less, this necessary link between moral vision and literary mode causes us uneasiness. The book lures us in the wrong direction. Even the reader recognizing the self-indulgence in exaggerating the modern world's complexity may deny that moral problems are simple or that a frontier defiance dependent upon physical courage and raw individuality can solve them. McMurphy lacks the introspective self-irony and spiritual wisdom which could enrich and humanize his readiness to act in a physical world. In my judgement the book's major weakness lies partially in a wavering treatment of McMurphy as "symbol." Kesey rejects the profounder symbolism of Melville, frightening in its incomprehensible mysteriousness, for the delimited symbolism of the comic strip superhero. Our sympathy with these "unrealistic" and superhuman heroes is always reserved. We cannot expect psychological fullness from them. Kesey wishes to shorten partially this aesthetic distance to increase our sympathy with McMurphy, the human opposite to the plastic monstrosity Big Nurse. Kesey risks the simplification of his statement. Unfortunately, he does not manage to have it both ways: as he rounds out the character McMurphy, we rightly expect a fuller range of human response than necessary for a "symbolic" representation of masculine physical vitality. But our expectations remain unsatisfied. The rebel McMurphy resembles the prankish schoolboy against the schoolmarm or the naughty boy against the mother. Although the book recommends laughter as necessary therapy against absurdity, there is a euphoric tone of boyish escapism and wish-fulfillment to McMurphy's humor too often reminiscent of the bathroom or locker room. The euphoria at times embarrasses, as in the maudlin, communal warmth of the fishing boat trip and the ward party. In sum, the novel too often shares the wish-fulfillment of the comic strip without preserving the hard lines of its mythic representation.

Admittedly, other attempts to humanize McMurphy also reveal Kesey's awareness of the problems posed by his "symbolic" characterization, however unsuccessful his solutions. The brawler McMurphy uncharacteristically paints pictures and writes letters in a "beautiful flowing hand." His upset caused by a return letter suggests an emotional softness complementary to more typical behavior, as does his sensitivity to the personal loss necessitated by his savior's responsibilities. The visit to McMurphy's old home emphasizes his fatigue and "frantic" anticipation of that loss. The dress flapping in the tree commemorates his first act of love, freely given by the nine-year-old "little whore," and thereby keynotes his loving but defi-

antly anti-Social relationships with his prostitute lovers. We are asked to believe that the sensitive and anguished letter writer, the energetic lover, and the tavern warrior are at bottom the same character apotheosized in his savior's role; his "psychopathic" sexuality and violence are really the human feeling and zest for life in which his Calling is grounded. As the Lone Ranger acting outside Society on behalf of humanity, he protects those qualities from extinction in others. Accordingly, his self-sacrifice is consistent with the lesson in gratuitous love taught by his childhood lover. Despite these attempts to fill in the simple comic strip outline of McMurphy's character, such details are too incidental, too hastily appended, to modify substantially our more limited version of him.

Kesey's handling of sex suffers from a failure to consider all implications of his materials, comic strip included. According to Leslie Fiedler, the love between McMurphy and Bromden expresses mythically an escape from the values of a white civilization ruled by women; but Fiedler overlooks the inadvertent blurring of Kesey's mythology caused by the unclear status of sex, both before and after McMurphy's death. The "symbolic" McMurphy is the blatantly sexual doctor of "whambam" seeing the inmates' sexual inadequacies as important expressions of psychological debility. Bringing prostitutes into the asylum is saving therapy which, contrary to Kesey's intents, fails to save. Neither of the Irishman's two principal disciples, Harding and Bromden, is fully heterosexual. Sefelt's prodigious sexual powers are merely adjunct to his epilepsy and Billy Bibbit's sexual initiation brings suicide. Despite McMurphy's joking estimate of Bromden's sexual potential, the Indian is asexual; he embraces only the lobotomized body of McMurphy in defense of the Spirit; this murderous act of love could even be seen as homosexual in nature if it were not for the book's overt heterosexuality. Bromden's sexuality simply is not restored with his physical power. McMurphy's Spiritual influence is unsexed further by its comic strip ties: the superhero lives in a boys' escape world in which sexuality is released in muscular athleticism or violence; the Lone Ranger and Tonto are above sexuality, if not innocently homosexual; likewise the TV cowboy is rarely sexual. The meaning of McMurphy's physical assault on Big Nurse, a public exposure of inherent femininity in a figurative rape of machine morality, is eroded by Kesey's failure to free McMurphy from such inadvertent implications of asexuality in the comic strip characterization, and by the failure to provide a convincing heterosexual disciple for McMurphy. The book seems at times an unwitting requiem for heterosexuality, most ironically sounded in the innocent child's embrace of McMurphy and the prostitute Sandy after the ward party. However, we must conclude only that Kesey fails to harness the potential allusiveness of his materials.

We are left with a somewhat sentimentalized over-simplification of moral problems. Admittedly, Kesey's opposition of Good and Evil is less bald and the victory of Good less clear than might seem. The superhero McMurphy is sacrificed to the machine culture and Big Nurse remains in the ward. There is little hope that the Combine can be defeated. Only limited defiance is possible, for Harding by accepting his homosexual inclinations, for Bromden by escaping from the asylum. . . . Perhaps Bromden's story is like the comic strip, a world only as it ought to be. After all, McMurphy must die and Bromden's interpretation of his future is euphoric, without convincing evidence of further satisfaction. Whether he finds his fellow tribesmen (perhaps drunk or widely disseminated) or fishes atop the hydrolectric dam (that others do so is only hearsay) or flees to Canada (also Combine territory?), he must remain outside Combine society. Perhaps the only escape from modern life is the tenuousness of hallucination. Kesey's irony compromises the victory of Good, suggesting that things may be more difficult than they seem. [In a footnote, the critic adds: "Fiedler contends that the frontier in the 'New Western' is the mind itself, that Bromden's schizophrenia symbolizes the new reality, and that McMurphy is attracted to Bromden because of his madness. However, the book itself will not bear the weight of such an argument, since McMurphy strives to save Bromden from his schizophrenia, not enter into it himself. Fiedler's argument could have been strengthened had he recognized the ambiguity of Bromden's whereabouts at the book's end and asserted that *all* events in the book are hallucinations."]

However, these notes in a minor key do not really discolor the euphoric ending. The book's beginning is too easily forgotten and we are pushed along by Bromden's optimism. We are to hope, not despair, and, more importantly, not define the line between. Kesey believes in the comic strip world in spite of himself. This is the moral ground on which critical faultfinding must begin. Kesey has not avoided the dangers of a simplistic aesthetic despite his attempts to complicate it. He forgets that the comic strip world is not an answer to life, but an escape from it. The reader finds Kesey entering that world too uncritically in defense of the Good. (pp. 103-09)

> *Terry G. Sherwood, "'One Flew Over the Cuckoo's Nest' and the Comic Strip," in* Critique: Studies in Modern Fiction, *Vol. 13, No. 1, 1970, pp. 96-109.*

## Marcia L. Falk

[*An instructor of literature and writing at Stanford University, Falk is primarily concerned with the relationship between art and the attitudes it reflects and engenders in society. In the letter below, originally published in* The New York Times *on December 5, 1971, Falk objects to sexist notions conveyed in Dale Wasserman's stage adaptation of Kesey's* One Flew over the Cuckoo's Nest.]

To the Editor:

In response to Walter Kerr's belated review of **One Flew Over the Cuckoo's Nest**: I too saw the show after it had been running for quite a while, in San Francisco. I was shocked at what I saw (though I should have known better, having read the book) because, in the long time the play had been running, never once had I read a review which warned me of the blatant sexism I was to witness onstage, or even asked some of the most obvious questions about the political statements of the play.

Kerr finally raised the key question: Why is Nurse Ratched, the omnipotent, omni-malevolent villain of the play, a woman? Kerr didn't speculate why, but he did note parenthetically that "There are other such women in the background of the play." The truth is that *every* woman in the background is such a demonic figure, and the play is full of false yet dangerous clichés about their power over men.

The most striking example is Chief Bromden's mother: she has made his father small, she has grown to twice his size. It is largely because of her power to threaten male virility that the Chief is now in a mental institution. Of course, she is *only a symbol*; as a white woman married to an Indian man, her emasculation of her husband only *represents* the White Man's brutal destruction of all cultures other than his own.

Why is white racism depicted in these terms? It should be remembered that this white woman's singular unforgivable act was her refusal to take on her husband's name! Somehow, in the confused vision of the author and playwright, the refusal of women, an oppressed class, to utterly submit to male-oriented social structures is identified with the attack of white men, the oppressor class, on peoples of color.

The whole play is constructed from such a muddled vision. It pretends to challenge all the reactionary institutions in our society—prisons, mental hospitals and the Federal Government itself, which has destroyed the Indian reservations. But it never once challenges the completely inhuman sexist structure of society, nor does it make any attempt to overthrow sexist or racist stereotypes. The only blacks in the play are stupid and malicious hospital orderlies. And the only right-on women in the play are mindless whores. In fact, in this play, if a woman is *not* totally mindless, she is a direct threat to (male) life.

Thus the play offers us this basic sexist dichotomy: women are either dumb and silly (like the quivering young nurse, terrified of McMurphy; like the squealing, wiggling prostitutes who come to build up the men's egos) or they are shrewd, conniving, and malicious (castrating wives, dominating mothers, and a super-powerful domineering nurse). Every man in the play has been psychologically mutilated by a woman, from the guilt-ridden Billy Bibbit, whom his mother and Nurse Ratched are in cahoots to destroy, to the cynical Harding, whose "wife's ample bosom at times gives him a feeling of inferiority."

It goes without saying that, just as there are no positive, fully human female figures to identify with, there are likewise no strong, healthy male figures. Of course, we are *supposed* to believe in McMurphy, the super-male macho hero who equates strength with sexual parts and whose solution to every problem is sex. We laugh and cheer as McMurphy humiliates the young nurse by sticking a banana up her skirt, manhandles his girlfriends as he passes them around (confident of his masculinity, he can afford to be generous), and generally bullies everyone in his social sphere.

If *that* represents the healthy exercise of the human spirit, then the White Man too was healthy as he stole from the

Indians everything they had, raping their culture and treating them as objects not worthy of human respect.

Kerr points out that *Cuckoo's Nest* is a play about conditioning in this society, and that young people identify with it because it exposes that threat to human freedom. This play is not *about* conditioning nearly so much as it *is* a dangerous piece of conditioning itself. With a pseudo-radical posture, it swallows whole hog all the worst attitudes toward women prevalent in our society and delivers the pig right back to us, suitably decorated and made righteous.

If you do not perceive exactly how destructive this work is, imagine for a moment the effect it must have on a girl child watching it. Who, in this play, can *she* grow up to be? Where is *her* place in the struggle for human freedom? At best she can mature into a good sex object, equipped to build the egos of emotionally crippled men by offering a "liberated" attitude toward sex! Above all, she learns from viewing this play that any aggressiveness, intelligence, strength, or potency on the part of the female is always dangerous, evil, and ugly. She learns to hate women who dare to try to be as powerful as men. She learns to squelch her own potential for strength, or she learns to hate herself. She is, after all, destined to become a woman, and women are hateful and fearful things.

The answer to Kerr's question seems to be that Nurse Ratched is a woman because Ken Kesey hates and fears women. And apparently Dale Wasserman, along with everyone else who helped adapt Kesey's novel and engineer it into a piece of theater, are so thoroughly conditioned by the basic sexist assumptions of our society that they never even noticed, or cared to question, the psychic disease out of which the book's vision was born. (pp. 450-53)

(Ms. Falk has requested that her original wording be noted here. In paragraph 7, lines 5 and 6, "balls" should be substituted for "sexual parts" and "to get a good fuck" for "sex." Likewise, in the penultimate paragraph, line 5, "sex object" originally read "piece of ass.") (p. 453)

> *Marcia L. Falk, in a letter to the Editor of The New York Times on December 5, 1971, in* One Flew Over the Cuckoo's Nest: Text and Criticism *by Ken Kesey, edited by John Clark Pratt, Viking Press, 1973, pp. 450-53.*

## Janet R. Sutherland

In the judgment of one recent patron of the Bellevue Public Schools, Ken Kesey's *One Flew Over the Cuckoo's Nest* is not a decent book for students to read or teachers to teach. While literary critics might be able to dismiss such pronouncements as simply untutored, public school people have to deal with them frequently and take them seriously, in the interest of preserving their right of access to literature and the student's right to read. It is in this context that I offer a defense of Kesey's novel against the charge that it is an improper and even evil book, fit only "to be burned."

Ken Kesey's *One Flew Over the Cuckoo's Nest* is not obscene, racist, or immoral, although it does contain language and scenes which by common taste would be so considered. Like all great literature, the book attempts to give an accurate picture of some part of the human condition, which is less than perfect. Kesey's book is set in a mental hospital; the language, attitudes, and habits of the inmates are typical of disturbed men whose already distorted world is being further systematically dehumanized by the ward nurse. The story is told in the first person through the eyes of an Indian whose health is gradually restored to him and to others through interaction with the robust new inmate McMurphy, a picaresque figure who is transformed into a tragic hero as he struggles to help the inmates regain control of their lives. To charge that the book is obscene, racist, or immoral because it gives a realistic picture of the world of the insane is to demonstrate a lack of the minimum competency in understanding literature we expect of high school students. The charge also ignores the extent to which this novel does conform to the standards outlined in the guidelines for selection of instructional materials in the Bellevue schools.

Our students are taught that to understand the general meaning of a book, the reader has to take all the details into consideration. The theme emerges from a complex combination of scenes, characters, and action, often in conflict and often contradictory. To judge a book simply on a few passages which contain unconventional language or fantasies is missing the point. In the case of the Indian narrator, we are seeing and hearing at times the hallucinations typical of schizophrenia. Chief Bromden has been systematically ignored and abused all his life to the point of madness. It is no wonder that his consciousness is filled with horrors, obscene and otherwise. What Kesey is telling us, beyond giving us a realistic idea of the actual language of the asylum, is that what is being done to these people is an obscenity. When McMurphy comes upon the scene, it is as if his outrageous speech and action are the only possible answer to the vicious way in which the men's privacy and smallest efforts of will are being pried into and exploited and diminished. His profanity is a verbal manifestation of the indecencies they suffer, the only appropriate response to it, a foil which helps us to see its actual nature, and a means by which the scene is transformed into a world in which some tenderness and love are possible. Big Nurse speaks properly but does unspeakable things. McMurphy's speech is outrageous; he fights the profane with the super profane and moves beyond profanity to help the men create a new respect for themselves. He restores Harding's ability to face reality, gives Billy a sense of his manhood, and convinces Chief Bromden that he is indeed his actual six foot six, not a withered deaf mute.

If the reader is really sensitive to the specific language of the book, he will see how Kesey uses its subtle changes to signal changes in the Chief's state of mind. The fogged-in scenes are characterized by confusion and some description of the grossness of the asylum's inmates and black help. As Chief Bromden recovers his powers of perception, including his sad past and the scenes of white racism and war which has produced his state of alienation, the sentence structure and word choice change markedly. So also the emphasis on McMurphy's outward grossness shifts in the Chief's eyes to an apprehension of what he is suffering inwardly, to his deeds of kindness to the men, his complicated and puzzling deals, and his final decision to protect another man though he knows it means his doom. The Chief sees beyond McMurphy's outward geniality to the marks of anguish on his secret face.

To understand the book, then, is to experience through this unique point of view the emergence of at least three themes which the book has in common with other major works of literature. First, there is the idea that we must look beyond appearances to judge reality. Just as the reader has to look beyond the typically racist language of the inmates to find in the book as a whole a document of witness against the dehumanizing, sick effects of racism in our society, so Bromden has to look beyond the perception of the world which limits his concept of self. When the perception changes, he begins to see the reality of his growth. Chief Bromden is sick from racism and is made whole again when he learns to laugh in spite of it and to realize his identity as an American Indian. Second, there is the idea that fools and madmen have wisdom. Writers from Shakespeare to Kesey have suggested that the world is sometimes so out of joint that it can only be seen from some perspective so different that it cuts through illusion to truth. Lear and Hamlet both experience a kind of madness for this reason, madness in which it might be added, they too abandon propriety of speech. (Polite language has hardly ever been associated with madness in literature.) And through this madness, in Kesey's book, the third theme emerges: the idea that the bumbling fool may be transformed into a worker of good deeds. McMurphy assumes almost the stature of the typical quest hero at his death. The circumstances of his life have required him to rise above the "lowness" of his original station to become a deliverer, to give up his life for his friend. The idea is that each human soul is worthy, and it is the genius of heroism to work transforming deeds which discover the worthiness both in themselves and in other humble men.

The book, then, works through the eyes and action of madmen to go from a vision of the world where all things are profane to a vision of the world where all human things are potentially sacred. Certainly teaching the book compels a discussion of obscenity, for it is impossible to understand it fully without realizing that what people do to each other in cruelty is the true obscenity, not shadow words. The book does not teach profanity; it teaches that the world of the insane is full of profanity. It does not teach racism; it clearly connects racism with cruelty and insanity. It does not teach immorality; it suggests that the fantasies of an unbalanced person are sensitive to a disruption of ordinary morality.

Frankly, the charge that the book teaches immorality puzzles me a little. Certainly Big Nurse's cruel manipulation of the men is immoral, but the young are hardly likely to identify with her and want to emulate her. Are Chief Bromden's fantasies immoral? Or are we to assume that because McMurphy is by common standards immoral that students are going out to copy him wholesale? Probably not any more than they would be inclined to copy Hamlet the murderer, Macbeth the assassin, or Oedipus the mother-lover, attractive though these tragic figures

are. McMurphy, after all, winds up with a prefrontal lobotomy, experiencing a psychic death as final as the physical death his friend Bromden later provides.

The policies of the Bellevue Public Schools provide a set of guidelines for text selection. I have tried to show how the use of this book would "enrich and support the curriculum" in English and "help the pupil improve his power of discrimination and his quality of choices" by showing that it is a piece of literature rich in design and details, and that its thematic material stands well within the tradition of great literature. As such, it clearly relates to our expectation that the student achieve minimum competency in dealing with the structure and texture of a book.

Second, within the context of that program for increasing competency in understanding literature, I have also shown how the book can be considered appropriate. More essentially, because here is where the charges against the book seem to lie, I have established a distinction through my reading of the book between the common taste which might object to the use of a four-letter word in the book, and what I consider "good taste," which will place that word in context and see its relationship to the book as a whole. I think I have established a clear sense of the difference between this book and a dirty joke. It does not comment on human experience to leave the reader with a guilty snicker of complicity in the disregard of human frailty for the sake of a cheap sensation. It deals with human weakness, eccentricity, and suffering to increase the reader's respect for the transforming power of love, which teaches us to overcome weakness, to tolerate eccentricity, and to endure suffering.

I think the book admirably fulfills the requirements of the fourth principle of the guidelines, that it "contribute to the pupil's growing understandings and appreciations of his culture and other cultures so that he can live compassionately and reasonably with his fellow men." Most students know very little about either the world of the mentally ill or the alienated condition of the American Indian. The detail of the book richly provides this information. The weaving of these details into this particular story moves the reader to deep sympathy with the Indian and much compassion for the inmates of his asylum. I think it is a profoundly humanizing book.

Fourth, and last, but not least, I would like to consider the student's freedom to read, "an inherent right and a necessity in a democratic society." I think our schools and our curriculum have to be defined vigorously against the naive reader who reacts out of a Victorian sense of propriety and out of vague fears of the magic power of the written word to want to condemn everything in literature which seems to him unconventional or strange. Attitudes such as these toward literature are a real danger to the student, in that if we yield to them we simultaneously seek to reduce the student's right to entertain ideas and teach the validity of these attitudes in the degree to which we acknowledge they have any power. We teach the student to fear ideas, or we teach the student that we fear ideas, any time we kill a book, which is, after all, as Milton told us, "The lifeblood of a master spirit."

Kesey is a valid part of the world of American literature. His books, if not available in the library at our high school, would easily be found in any bookstore or book rack. The attempt to "protect" the students from his view of the world is in the first place futile: they like *One Flew Over the Cuckoo's Nest* and will read it anyway. Second, such an attempt would be stupid. Why neglect the opportunity to provide a framework of reason in which such an admittedly difficult book can be read, discussed, and understood—unless we want to garner the doubtful honors attributable to playing the role of Big Nurse of education, and further alienate the young people we are attempting to communicate with?

I conclude with the description of one remarkable scene in Kesey's book: Patients are allowed to vote in weekly group meetings about policies which concern their welfare and entertainment. McMurphy has requested that though the regular TV watching time is in the evening, patients be allowed access to the TV during the daytime while the World Series is being played. Big Nurse does not like this assertation of individual will which will upset the daily routine, so she opposes McMurphy and then overrules the patients' affirmative vote on a technicality. In spite of her ruling McMurphy puts down his tasks and pulls his chair in front of the TV as the game broadcast begins. It is a battle of wills, and the patients watch to see who will win. Big Nurse pulls the great lever and cuts off the power. But McMurphy remains solidly there, in front of the TV, watching the empty screen. One by one the others join him, and soon they're all sitting there, "watching the gray screen just like we could see the baseball game clear as day," and Big Nurse is "ranting and screaming" behind them. (pp. 28-31)

It is unfortunate that the patron who has lodged the objection to this book was so distracted by its alleged obscenity, racism, and immorality that he couldn't appreciate this scene. It has something to say about the need for authority to establish itself through reasonable, not arbitrary action. It also illustrates the utter futility of ever trying to get between a human being and anything he holds as dear as baseball. (p. 31)

> Janet R. Sutherland, "A Defense of Ken Kesey's 'One Flew Over the Cuckoo's Nest'," in English Journal, *Vol. 61, No. 1, January, 1972, pp. 28-31.*

## Ronald Wallace

Although Ken Kesey's *One Flew Over the Cuckoo's Nest* has been a highly successful first novel, a popular school textbook, an off-Broadway play, and a celebrated film, it has met with some rather strong criticism. The book has been charged with harboring "sexist" assumptions, portraying women as malignant "ball-cutters" or shallow "twitches," in a world gone wrong as a result of men having lost their "machismo." Marcia L. Falk, for example, assuming that the theme of the novel is the restoration of traditional male values to modern society, complains of "the psychic disease out of which the book's vision was born," insisting that the book, which purports to oppose

conditioning, is "a dangerous piece of conditioning itself. With a pseudo-radical posture, it swallows whole hog all the worst attitudes toward women prevalent in our society and delivers the pig right back to us, suitably decorated and made righteous [see letter above dated 1971]. Similarly, at least one high-school board of education banned the book from the classroom on the grounds that it was racist, depicting blacks as rather ugly caricatures of evil.

Such charges are not altogether misdirected; the book does treat most of its characters as caricatures, and women and blacks are cast in consistently negative roles. Raymond M. Olderman, in his excellent study of the recent American novel [see excerpt in *CLC,* Vol. 3], reflects such misgivings about Kesey's method of simplification. According to Olderman, Kesey's "flat portrayal of women and of blacks is more stereotypic and uncomfortable than funny or fitting with his cartoon character pattern. It borders too much on the simplistic."

Further, critics have not only questioned the book's treatment of women and blacks; they have also been dissatisfied with the hero, McMurphy, and with the "solution" he seems to offer to the horrors of modern life. Bruce E. Wallis, for example, argues that "the doctrine he formulated in theory cannot be effected in practice. . . . One is not bound . . . to suppose that such self-indulgence will have in reality the same meritorious outcome that it can be manipulated to achieve in art." Indeed, McMurphy's "program" of fighting and fucking, of violence and sex, is as potentially manipulative as Big Nurse's shock therapy and lobotomy. The dictums to "enjoy" and "be free" can be as repressive and constricting as the dictum to conform. If mandatory muscle and wholehearted whoring is Kesey's plan for survival, then it is admittedly too simplistic, as well as utterly impracticable in real life.

Such criticisms of the novel, however, are based on two faulty assumptions: first, that the novel is a romance, and second, that McMurphy is its hero, fully embodying its values. It is important to recognize that the book is not a romance; it is a comedy. Also, McMurphy does not ultimately embody the book's comic values; Chief Bromden does.

It is perhaps not surprising that most critics read the novel as a romance. It is, after all, structured on the typical romantic antitheses: the self versus society, the human versus the mechanical, emotion versus reason, primitive versus civilized, freedom versus control, heart versus mind. McMurphy, a fascinating character, is seemingly the embodiment of Good in opposition to the Big Nurse's Evil. The plot focuses on the conflict between the Nurse's fixed pattern, unbreakable routine, and submission of the individual will to mechanical, humorless control, and McMurphy's freedom, self-reliance, and Dionysian revelry. In the course of the novel, Good finally subdues Evil, and although McMurphy loses his life, most of the inmates in the asylum go free, their health and vitality restored.

The novel, then, is structured on the kind of oppositions present in romance, and the final triumph of McMurphy over the Big Nurse seems that of nature over civilization, man over machine, emotion over reason. But the book's structural devices are finally more typical of comedy than of romance. The struggle between McMurphy and the Big Nurse is consistently portrayed in comic terms, and the final wisdom of the book is that of high comedy.

The most obvious comic devices in the novel are the reversal of expectation and the inversion of values, and the most obvious reversal is that of the human and the mechanical. According to Henri Bergson, comedy results when the mechanical is encrusted on the living; this happens throughout Kesey's novel. From the outset, people become things, and things take on a malevolent life of their own. The Big Nurse is described as made of plastic and enamel, her fingernails glowing like soldering irons. The black orderlies, her hand-picked extensions, are constantly seen in mechanical terms. According to Chief Bromden, the book's narrator, "they got special sensitive equipment detects my fear and they all look up, all three at once, eyes glittering out of the black faces like the hard glitter of radio tubes out of the back of an old radio." (pp. 90-2)

The reversal of people and machines is, however, but one of several comic reversals that structure the book. Male and female roles are comically reversed. If men have traditionally oppressed women, now the women oppress the men. In the asylum, the weak, ineffectual men are controlled by strong, domineering women, rendering the sexual roles themselves comic. Indeed, Kesey takes the worst male stereotype available—that of over-weening power, control, force, manipulation—and imposes it on the women in the book, and the worst female stereotype—pettiness, bitchiness, lack of self-confidence, anxiousness to serve—and imposes it on the men. Thus, thirty-one-year-old Billy Bibbit remains his mother's weak, effeminate child; Harding, embarrassed by his lovely hands, is rendered impotent by his sexually demanding wife; and Chief Bromden's father "shrinks" when his wife muscles him out of his land and his heritage. (p. 92)

Just as the traditional male-female roles are reversed, so are the traditional black-white roles. Whereas the blacks were traditionally the slaves of white masters, now the whites are the slaves of black masters, and Washington, named for the father and capital of our free country, is their leader.

To fault Kesey for his treatment of women and blacks is to miss the comedy of a device that has informed comic art from Aristophanes to Erica Jong, the reversal of traditional roles. In our day the traditional roles have themselves become grotesquely comic; their reversal compounds the comedy.

The reversal of human and mechanical, and of traditional male-female and black-white roles, is a comic indication that the world is out of joint. The motive force behind all these reversals is, according to Bromden, the Combine, the social structure that threshes and levels individuals, turning them into caricatures. The microcosm of this malign social structure is the institution, and Nurse Ratched's ward in particular. Indeed, the discrepancy between the institution's official image and its actual practice provides some of the blackest comedy in the book. The PR man who pops up periodically best articulates the institution's view of itself. Himself a figure of fun . . . , PR rhapsodizes on the progress made by his institution. "Oh, when I think back on the old days, on the filth, the bad food, even, yes, brutality, oh, I realize, ladies, that we have come a long way in our campaign!" PR's catalogue of horrors fairly accurately, if unintentionally, describes his own institution. . . . [Although] the orderlies are prevented from disciplining the patients with socks filled with buckshot as they would prefer, they are taught equally effective methods by the Big Nurse. Her methods culminate in such humanitarian techniques as shock treatments and lobotomies, which result in cures like Ruckley's, his eyes "all smoked up and gray and deserted inside like blown fuses," and Taber's, who goes "wandering round in a simple, happy dream. A success." For all the institution's claims, it is obvious that the methods employed to "help" the patients do more to keep them maladjusted, or adjusted so well that they cease to be human. (pp. 92-3)

It becomes increasingly apparent in the course of the novel that the inmates, who are supposed to be sick, are really healthy, and the Combine, which is supposed to be healthy, is really sick. . . . The reversal of sanity and insanity is, then, a final comic device structuring the novel and exposing the humorous society.

Kesey's metaphor for this society is the institution, and the emblem of the institution is the Big Nurse. As representative of the humorously mechanical society, Nurse Ratched resembles the archetypal comic villain. Like the typical villain of traditional comedy, the Big Nurse is a boastful impostor and self-deceived pedant who pretends to know more than she does. She is the obsessed antagonist who tries to force the plot of the novel into compliance with her own comic delusions and who, in the end, must be defeated or expelled if the comic values of life and continuity are to be celebrated. She recalls the comic doctors of Molière and the pedants of Fielding and Pope, but she more closely resembles the villains of recent comic fiction. Like Nabokov's Clare Quilty, Hawkes's Miranda and Tremlow, and Coover's Horace Zifferblatt, for example, she is an extreme personification of her humorous society, her very excesses rendering her comic. Disturbed by the "permissive philosophy" of modern mental hospitals, the Nurse manages to maintain the old brutalities in modern disguise. Substituting subtle psychological cruelties for physical punishment, she succeeds in debilitating the men mentally and spiritually, in persuading them of their inadequacy. (p. 94)

Like the comic villains mentioned above, the Big Nurse is powerful and destructive, but she is also finally unable to destroy the comic values and assumptions implicit in the novel. By treating the Nurse as a caricature of evil, Kesey controls and tempers her power, allowing Chief Bromden and several other inmates to escape, healthy and intact, from the control of the Combine. In the course of the novel, as in most comedy, her obsessions turn back on her. Although she destroys McMurphy's body, she is unable to destroy his spirit or meaning, and, at the end, she is exhausted and depleted.

Her very name is a joke, qualifying her omnipotence. McMurphy punningly calls her Miss Rat-shed; her name also rather neatly suggests both her nature and her fate: wretched. Further, like a ratchet wrench she keeps her patients "adjusted," but like a ratchet, a gear in the Combine, she is herself mechanically enmeshed. Personifying the Combine, she is responsible for the very mechanical symbols that ultimately render her comic. (pp. 94-5)

If, as is typical of the comic *alazon,* the Nurse helps to defeat herself, the machine turning on its creator, McMurphy is significantly responsible for her defeat, and he adopts several roles in an effort to unplug or short-circuit her. One of the Nurse's main weaknesses is her lack of a sense of humor, her inability to see what the Chief refers to as the "funny side to things." This is perhaps the most significant thematic distinction between McMurphy and the Nurse. While the Nurse's smile is chiseled or painted on her plastic face, McMurphy's laughter is genuine and all-encompassing. Laughter is McMurphy's most effective weapon, and in his role as laughter he resembles Meredith's comic spirit or the traditional comic *eiron.*

The first thing McMurphy notices when he appears on the ward as a new admission is the absence of laughter. Although the men often "snicker in their fists, . . . nobody ever dares let loose and laugh." According to the Chief, the institution itself prevents it: "The air is pressed in by the walls, too tight for laughing." Indeed, the whole book is in some ways a vision of a world without laughter, and it is McMurphy's job to restore laughter, and thus health, to this sterile, humorless world. McMurphy explains, "I haven't heard a real laugh since I came through that door, do you know that? Man, when you lose your laugh you lose your *footing.*" . . . When McMurphy laughs, "dials twitch in the control panel at the sound of it," indicating, early in the novel, that the Combine is beatable and that the appropriate weapon is laughter.

Teaching the men to laugh is no easy problem, however, for it involves making them see their own inherent comedy; they must learn to laugh at themselves as well as at their situation. In a world without laughter, the inmates are suspicious of McMurphy, whose "big wide-open laugh" makes everyone uneasy. Initially unable to appreciate McMurphy's sense of humor, the patients label him a boastful impostor, a manipulator. Harding dismisses him as "cowboy bluster," and "sideshow swagger," calling him "a backwoods braggart." Indeed, McMurphy is partly in the tradition of the boaster and braggart, the backwoods teller of tall tales common in nineteenth-century American humor. Brash con man and swaggering gambler, he descends upon the ward as if he, and not the Nurse, owned it. But it's soon clear to the patients and the reader that McMurphy's boasting is, unlike the Nurse's, a consciously adopted comic pose, indicating his perception of the comedy of things. Whereas the Nurse always takes herself very solemnly, McMurphy rarely fails to see his own human comedy. In his first conversation with Harding, he boasts that he has been a bull goose catskinner, gambler, and pea weeder, and now "if I'm bound to be a loony, then I'm bound to be a stompdown dadgum good one." Parodying his own role of cowboy hero, McMurphy tells Harding that the ward isn't big enough for both of them and that Harding must either meet him

"man to man or he's a yaller skunk and better be outta town by sunset." (pp. 95-7)

The typical comic plot, as I have noted, is structured as a conflict of two archetypal characters, the *alazon* and the *eiron.* If the Nurse is the boastful impostor and self-deceived fool, McMurphy becomes the witty self-deprecator who pretends ignorance in an effort to defeat his opponent, to bring her to confusion. Although McMurphy's natural tendency is to use violence or virility to subdue people, his profession as con man has admirably prepared him for the role of *eiron.* As a "good old red, white, and blue hundred-per-cent American con man" McMurphy knows the virtue of pretending ignorance to take people in. Thus he pretends to lose card games at low stakes so that he can entice others to lose at higher stakes. It is this kind of strategy that proves ultimately most successful against the Big Nurse. Perceiving that the Big Nurse is literally impregnable and that her technology will always be stronger than his own physical prowess, McMurphy bets the inmates that he will be able to defeat the Nurse by adopting the *eiron's* pose. The Chief explains McMurphy's strategy. "A couple of times some stupid rule gets him mad, but he just makes himself act more polite and mannerly than ever till he begins to see how funny the whole thing is—the rules, the disapproving looks they use to enforce the rules, the ways of talking to you like you're nothing but a three-year-old—and when he sees how funny it is he goes to laughing, and this aggravates them no end. He's safe as long as he can laugh, he thinks, and it works pretty fair." Pretending to be unaffected by the Nurse's manipulations, McMurphy effectively short-circuits them.

The teeth-brushing episode is McMurphy's first victory over the Nurse. When McMurphy questions the ward policy of locking up the toothpaste and unlocking it at a specific time only, the black attendant absurdly insists, "What you s'pose it'd be like if *evahbody* was to brush their teeth whenever they took a notion to brush? . . . My *gaw,* don't you see?" Instead of reacting hostilely, McMurphy enthusiastically agrees, his very agreement ridiculing the rule and the attendant. "Yes, now, I do. You're saying people'd be brushin' their teeth whenever the spirit moved them. . . . And, lordy, can you imagine? Teeth bein' brushed at six-thirty, six-twenty—who can tell? maybe even six o'clock. Yeah, I can see your point." Prepared for a fight, the attendant doesn't know how to respond to McMurphy's agreement and retreats.

McMurphy then uses a similar strategy on the Nurse. When she approaches, "her lips are parted, and her smile's going out before her like a radiator grill . . . and every step hits the floor she blows up a size bigger." But McMurphy, apparently dressed only in his cap and a towel, is as polite as can be, pretending ignorance and full cooperation. When she asks him where his clothes are, he sadly replies in all innocence that they were stolen. The Nurse is confused until she realizes that "that outfit was *supposed* to be picked up" and McMurphy should be wearing his hospital "greens," not a towel. McMurphy apologizes and obligingly begins to remove the towel, flustering the Nurse into commanding him to leave it on. McMurphy pretends confusion and redirects the Nurse's anger against the attendant, an extension of herself, by insisting that he neglected to issue McMurphy a uniform. McMurphy crowns his victory by casually removing the towel to reveal his black-with-white-whales undershorts, ridiculing the Nurse's fear that he was naked underneath. Using the *eiron's* methods of pretended ignorance and self-deprecation, McMurphy defeats the *alazon,* turning the Nurse's humorlessness against her. (p. 97-8)

McMurphy's first strategy for helping the patients is that of the comic *eiron:* pretended ignorance and wise laughter. But McMurphy eventually moves beyond humor to myth, reflecting the primitive origins of comedy itself. Most scholars now agree that comedy is an outgrowth of certain ancient rituals and fertility rites. *One Flew Over the Cuckoo's Nest* is virtually structured on the four elements of the fertility ritual F. M. Cornford describes in *The Origin of Attic Comedy:* the carrying out of death and the subsequent renewal of life; the fight of summer and winter, a seasonal antagonism that must end in the victory of summer over the sterility of winter; the struggle between the young king and the old; and death and resurrection, which are often imaged in the dismemberment and rebirth of a god. In the novel, the Chief and the other inmates suffer a ritual death, witness the fight between the cold, white Big Nurse and the warm, redheaded Irishman, and are finally freed to new life through McMurphy's symbolic dismemberment and the Nurse's symbolic death. Wylie Sypher notes that "from the earliest time the comic ritual has been presided over by a Lord of Misrule, and the improvisations of comedy have the aspect of a Feast of Unreason, a Revel of Fools." In his effort to restore humor to the men's lives, McMurphy adopts this role of Lord of Misrule, bringing the festivity and revelry of ancient ritual to the ward.

The first element of revelry McMurphy brings to the ward is, of course, laughter. For the Lord of Misrule, laughter is aggressive, a substitute for actual physical attack. As Sypher notes, the Greeks used laughter "to express a disdain roused by seeing someone's mischance, deformity, or ugliness. . . . To be laughed at by the ancients was to be defiled." . . . But McMurphy's laughter seems to have another function as well, a function that is perhaps best stated in Freudian terms. For Freudians, laughter is an upsurge from the unconscious, releasing powerful archaic impulses. Laughter celebrates and frees the irrational as a means of countering the repressive demands of the superego. In *One Flew Over the Cuckoo's Nest,* laughter releases repressed energies in the patients, helping them to recover a portion of their atrophied instinctual lives. . . . [Bromden, for example, suddenly] notices, for the first time, the institutional smells with which he lives. Later he rediscovers the smells of nature. Having refused to take his tranquilizers one evening, he sneaks out of bed and gazes into the moonlight.

> The wire was cold and sharp, and I rolled my head against it from side to side to feel it with my cheeks, and I smelled the breeze. It's fall coming, I thought, I can smell that sour-molasses smell of silage, clanging the air like a bell—smell somebody's been burning oak leaves,

> left them to smolder overnight because they're too green.

> It's fall coming, I kept thinking, fall coming; just like that was the strangest thing ever happened. Fall. Right outside here it was spring a while back, then it was summer, and now it's fall—that's sure a curious idea.

Having recovered his instinctual life, Bromden recalls the ritual change of seasons, winter inevitably giving way to spring. (pp. 99-100)

But McMurphy does not use jokes and laughter alone to restore instinctual life to the ward. According to Freud, alcohol and sex are even more effective restoratives, and McMurphy is quite prepared to oblige. On the fishing trip the Chief drinks four cans of beer, "shorting out dozens of control leads down inside me." The very presence of Candy, a prostitute, on the ward is enough to short-circuit it. Bromden notes that "apparatus burned out all over the ward trying to adjust to her come busting in like she did—took electronic readings on her and calculated they weren't built to handle something like this on the ward, and just burned out, like machines committing suicide." The idea of machines taking on enough life to commit suicide is itself, of course, comic. Finally, McMurphy's singing, like his laughter, his booze, and his sexuality, is capable of "joggling the wiring in all the walls."

As a Dionysian Lord of Misrule, McMurphy thus presides over a comic fertility ritual, restoring instinctual life to the patients. Wylie Sypher remarks that "if the authentic comic action is a sacrifice and a feast, debate and passion, it is by the same token a Saturnalia, an orgy, an assertion of the unruliness of the flesh and its vitality." The final orgy in the book represents a culmination of the sexuality, drunkenness, vitality, and laughter represented by McMurphy. Mixing wine and cough syrup, and thus using the Combine's own resources as part of the revelry, the men get drunk; Billy Bibbit and Candy participate in a mock wedding ceremony, celebrating the loss of Billy's virginity. . . . Finally, when the Big Nurse appears on the scene, the men retain their ability to laugh. "Every laugh was being forced right down her throat till it looked as if any minute she'd blow up like a bladder." "The men were immune to her poison. Their eyes met hers; their grins mocked the old confident smile she had lost."

Thus McMurphy adopts two comic roles in battling the Nurse: the *eiron's* pretended ignorance and comic perspective and the Lord of Misrule's laughter and revelry. But his commitment to the men ultimately precludes the kind of detachment necessary for a true *eiron* or Lord of Misrule, and his participation in an ancient comic ritual necessitates his sacrifice. Even in his third role, that of sacrificial redeemer, however, he remains deeply comic.

As Wylie Sypher suggests, the story of Christ, sometimes mistaken for a tragedy, is really a comedy. "The drama of the struggle, death, and rising—Gethsemane, Calvary, and Easter—actually belongs in the comic rather than the tragic domain. The figure of Christ as god-man is surely the archetypal hero-victim." In his role as Christ figure, McMurphy thus parodies a comedy, the Christian drama inherent in the plot rendering the novel at once more comic and more serious. If McMurphy is a parody of Christ, he nonetheless reflects Christ's meaning and values.

Although allusions to the Christian story occur throughout the novel, the three episodes that most clearly reflect parallels are the fishing trip, the shock therapy, and the orgy. Midway in the book, McMurphy manages to persuade ten patients, along with Candy and Doc Spivey, to accompany him on a salmon-fishing trip. The symbolism is overt. First, Ellis, the Chronic nailed to the wall, pulls his hands down for a moment and advises Billy Bibbit to be a "fisher of men." Then Chief Bromden notes with appropriately biblical intonation, "McMurphy led the twelve of us toward the ocean." Finally, the fish, an obvious symbol of fertility, is also the traditional symbol of Christianity.

On board the fishing boat, the men drink and cavort, and even catch fish. But the single most important consequence of the trip is the restoration of the men's sense of humor. If McMurphy can't walk on water like his predecessor, his laughter can, and it's laughter that ultimately saves the men. The Chief describes McMurphy "spreading his laugh out across the water," laughing "because he knows you have to laugh at the things that hurt you just to keep yourself in balance, just to keep the world from running you plumb crazy. He knows there's a painful side; he knows my thumb smarts and his girl friend has a bruised breast and the doctor is losing his glasses, but he won't let the pain blot out the humor no more'n he'll let the humor blot out the pain." When the men begin to laugh, it's no longer just amusement at McMurphy's antics, it's laughter "at their own selves as well as at the rest of us." Seeing their own weaknesses and failures in a comic perspective, they are practically cured.

If the fishing excursion invigorates the men, it depletes McMurphy, who begins to appear like the man of sorrows. Obviously suffering from the strain of infusing his own life into others, McMurphy is "beat and worn out," "dreadfully tired and strained and *frantic,* like there wasn't enough time left for something he had to do. . . ." What he has to do, of course, is complete the role of redeemer by dying for the men, and the shock treatments he subsequently receives comically parallel the crucifixion. Early in the book, Harding describes the shock treatments: "You are strapped to a table, shaped, ironically, like a cross, with a crown of electric sparks in place of thorns." Once inside the shock shop, McMurphy himself humorously perceives his role. "Anointest my head with conductant," he intones. "Do I get a crown of thorns?" Another patient adopts the role of Pilate, insisting, "I wash my hands of the whole deal," but it is finally the Big Nurse who completes that role, offering McMurphy the same deal Pilate offered Christ. If he will recant, if he will "*admit* he was wrong," then the "treatment would be canceled." McMurphy characteristically refuses, and the mock crucifixion continues.

The mock crucifixion does not, however, prevent McMurphy from participating in the prearranged orgy, a kind of Last Supper, complete with wine, prayer, and betrayal. Drunkenly blessing the union of Billy Bibbit and Candy, Harding intones, "Most merciful God, accept these two poor sinners into your arms. And keep the doors ajar for the coming of the rest of us, because you are witnessing the end." The end comes the morning after the orgy when the Big Nurse uses her powerful weapon of guilt on Billy Bibbit, forcing him, like Judas, to betray his savior and commit suicide. Faced with the inevitable, McMurphy, like Christ, "gave a cry. . . . he let himself cry out: A sound of cornered-animal fear and hate . . . when he finally doesn't care any more about anything but himself and his dying." Ultimately McMurphy is crucified on the lobotomy table.. . . . At the end, Bromden participates in a comic communion, partaking of McMurphy's body by killing it. The Chief escapes to become McMurphy's biographer, and, as the participants in the orgiastic Last Supper would all agree, "it's every word gospel."

The Christian parallels have led one critic to claim that "the novel is expressly formulated as nothing less than the bible for a twentieth-century religion of self-assertive action, with a message of salvation modulated to the needs of repressed individuals in a constrictively conformist society." If the novel is something less than that, it does reflect the kind of affirmation and hope symbolized by the life, death, and resurrection of Christ, and it does argue for individual freedom and action. At the end, the Nurse and the repressive institution she symbolizes are shrunken and impotent, and the inmates, with a renewed sense of the funny side of things, have released themselves from the asylum.

But the novel is not quite so simple. The conflict is not so clearly one between pure good and pure evil. McMurphy is not merely a hero, he is a comic hero, and like other comic heroes, he reveals a decided ambivalence. As I noted at the outset, readers have criticized McMurphy (and Kesey) for his attitude toward women and blacks, for his aggressive sexuality, and for his conviction that the irrational, the chaotic, the Dionysian, must triumph over the rational, the ordered, the Apollonian. Assuming that Kesey intended McMurphy as an ideal model of healthy manhood, these readers have found Kesey's vision to be disappointing, his solution to the problems of the contemporary world impracticable and simplistic. But it is possible that Kesey himself was aware of McMurphy's shortcomings and that he intended them as a means of undercutting McMurphy, ultimately directing reader attention away from McMurphy to the more adequate embodiment of the book's comic philosophy, Chief Bromden, the author of the novel. Perhaps when a critic like Robert Boyers complains that "we are never quite certain whether to laugh at McMurphy as well as with him" [see excerpt above dated 1968], he has discovered an intentional complexity in the novel, and in McMurphy's character.

If McMurphy exposes his humorous society, he also exposes himself, both consciously and unconsciously. Like the Big Nurse, her attendants, Doc Spivey, and PR, McMurphy is deflated through caricature. If he is often depicted as a parody of Christ, he is as often described as a kind of cartoon cowboy or comic-book superhero. The inmates see him in these simplistic terms, making him "hitch up his black shorts like they were horsehide chaps, and push back his cap with one finger like it was a ten-gallon Stetson." . . . Indeed, McMurphy clearly resembles the typical comic-book superhero who uses his secret powers and physical strength to defeat the evil, scientific villain.

The comparison of McMurphy to TV cowboys and comic-book superheroes in part adds to the pain and tragedy of McMurphy's role, since, unlike his make-believe counterparts, he can be hurt both emotionally and physically; it also in part elevates McMurphy, since he often consciously caricatures himself, thus revealing his comic perspective. But the comparison also serves to expose McMurphy's deficiencies. For instance, most superheroes have rather unsatisfactory sex lives, exerting their energy to protect their secret identities from prying females. Although McMurphy seems to believe that free sexuality and libidinous zest are the best answers to psychic repression, his actual sexual experiences are comically discrepant with his immodest claims. McMurphy's only sexual experience actually described in the book is one with a nine-year-old girl, who is the aggressor. Later, at the orgy, when McMurphy and Sandy fall into bed, they are "more like two tired little kids than a grown man and a grown woman in bed together to make love." McMurphy's infantile sexuality is at odds with his avowed potency. (pp. 101-06)

McMurphy's program for liberating the men is not an unqualified success. In the course of the battle with the Big Nurse, both Cheswick and Billy Bibbit, unprepared for McMurphy's tactics, commit suicide. Even more significantly, McMurphy himself loses his comic perspective at the end and becomes evil to fight evil, using his old methods of violence and virility against the Big Nurse. Robert Boyers puts it succinctly: "In his fear and frustration, he does not see what, of all things, should be most obvious to him: that he cannot make another human being aware of his humanity by destroying or suppressing those elements of his own humanity that have made McMurphy a beautiful person." Indeed, McMurphy's initials, RPM, may suggest his power, but they may also suggest his futility, going around in circles, being played on the Combine's machine.

Like the typical comic hero, McMurphy exposes himself as well as his humorous society. Unlike the typical comic hero, he dies for his mistakes. At the end, trying to fight the Combine with its own dehumanizing weapons, McMurphy becomes almost a tragic figure, prompting critics like Ruth H. Brady to conclude that the novel is "anything but hopeful." Indeed, if McMurphy were the only hero of the novel, alone embodying its values, the novel would be a tragedy or, perhaps, a melodrama. But McMurphy is not ultimately the hero of the book—Chief Bromden is.

It is important to remember that the ostensible author of **One Flew Over the Cuckoo's Nest** is not Ken Kesey, but Chief Bromden, a schizophrenic Indian. . . . Thus it is Bromden, and not necessarily Kesey, who is ultimately responsible for the creation of McMurphy. McMurphy is Bromden's romantic vision of what a hero should be like, his action and motives existing only insofar as Bromden

imagines them. McMurphy becomes in part a metaphor for Bromden's own development, and the central focus of the novel is on Bromden's growth toward health and a comic understanding of himself and his society.

Chief Bromden is, after all, the only fully developed character in the book. While McMurphy, Big Nurse, and the minor characters surrounding them remain, for the most part, rather flat caricatures, Bromden, at first a caricature, changes, grows, and develops in the course of the novel, emerging at the end as a complete and strong individual. He is the only character with a past. Although we do see fragments of McMurphy's childhood, Bromden's Indian heritage and his childhood experiences are integrally related to his adult existence. In the course of the novel Bromden flashes back to various childhood memories, the most important being his encounter with the government officials, the experience that resulted in his deaf and dumb act. Not finding Bromden's father home, the government officials calmly and openly discuss their plans to steal his heritage, as if young Bromden were not even there. Bromden comments, "I remembered one thing: it wasn't me that started acting deaf; it was people that first started acting like I was too dumb to hear or see or say anything at all." His experience with the government officials persuades Bromden that the only way to survive in a hostile white world is to play deaf and dumb. The strategy enables him to see and hear things he otherwise couldn't. The Big Nurse and her attendants freely expose their villainy to him since they perceive him to be no threat.

A related event from the Chief's past that has significance for the book as a whole is the conflict between his mother and father. Mrs. Bromden was a domineering woman who cared little for her husband's Indian heritage and was instrumental in selling his land to the government. As the Chief tells McMurphy, "my mother made him too little to fight any more and he gave up." The Chief's childhood experience here closely parallels the plot of the novel. Just as the Chief's mother worked on his father to make him small, so the Big Nurse works on the Chief and McMurphy. Just as the government officials failed to hear or see Bromden, so the medical staff labels him deaf and dumb. In some ways the Chief's novel is a fictionalized account of his childhood experience. Thus McMurphy and the Big Nurse are not "real" characters at all, but rather the Chief's metaphors for his own "real" experience. (pp. 106-08)

From the outset, the Chief is a comic figure, the discrepancy between his paranoid delusions and the reader's view of reality accounting for much of the humor early in the book. The Chief is firmly convinced, for example, that the mythical Combine controls everything "on hair-like wires too small for anybody's eyes but mine." The Chief literally sees microphones in the broom handles, wires in the walls, pernicious devices in the electric shavers, clocks that accelerate and decelerate at will. . . . Taken literally, the Chief's vision of things on the ward is outrageously comic.

If the Chief's image of the ward is comic, so is his self-image. Although he is actually six-foot-eight, he thinks of himself as little. He tells McMurphy, "I'm way too little.

I used to be big, but not no more. You're twice the size of me." Harding describes him as "a giant janitor. There's your Vanishing American, a six-foot-eight sweeping machine, scared of its own shadow." The discrepancy between the Chief's self-image and his actual size can be added to the comic reversals mentioned earlier: sane and insane, male and female, people and machines, black and white. (p. 108)

Bromden is an Indian, and consequently a victim of race prejudice, who is himself prejudiced. The blacks are "niggers" to the Chief, forces of pure evil, malevolent machines. "If you brush against their hair," he confides solemnly, "it rasps the hide right off you." If his prejudice is based on some painful firsthand experience, Bromden is nevertheless comic in the manner of Joseph Heller's Chief White Half Oat in *Catch-22*. "Racial prejudice," says that chief, "is a terrible thing, Yossarian. It really is. It's a terrible thing to treat a decent, loyal Indian like a nigger, kike, wop or spic." . . .

Chief Bromden is thus a comic figure, the discrepancy between his vision and the reader's and the reversal of literary conventions assuring his comedy. But if the Chief is comic, he is also a hero. Since Bromden has written the novel, it is Bromden himself who exposes his own comedy. The plot traces Bromden's growth toward the kind of comic perspective that enables him to write such a novel. When he can turn the Combine into comedy, he has defeated it. (p. 109)

Bromden's development toward a comic understanding parallels McMurphy's development from *eiron* to Lord of Misrule to sacrificial redeemer. When McMurphy begins to ply the *eiron's* strategy of pretended ignorance against the Nurse and her staff, winning the battle over the teeth brushing, Bromden recalls his father's use of a similar strategy against the government officials. When the officials originally approached Bromden's father about selling his land, he pretended not to understand, speaking instead in a parody of Indian dialect [until they began to comprehend that they were being ridiculed]. . . . Remembering what laughter can do, Bromden begins to see the comedy of his situation. When McMurphy organizes the fishing expedition, Bromden wants to go, but is afraid to expose his deaf and dumb act.

> I kept getting this notion that I wanted to sign the list. And the more he talked about fishing for Chinook salmon the more I wanted to go. I knew it was a fool thing to want; if I signed up it'd be the same as coming right out and telling everybody I wasn't deaf. If I'd been hearing all this talk about boats and fishing it'd show I'd been hearing everything else that'd been said in confidence around me for the past ten years. And if the Big Nurse found out about that, that I'd heard all the scheming and treachery that had gone on when she didn't think anybody was listening, she'd hunt me down with an electric saw, fix me where she *knew* I was deaf and dumb. Bad as I wanted to go, it still made me smile a little to think about it: I had to keep on acting deaf if I wanted to hear at all.

That night Bromden's comic sense develops further. Mc-

Murphy discovers the collection of chewing gum stuck underneath the Chief's bed and begins to sing the comic song, "does the Spearmint lose its flavor on the bedpost o-ver niiiite?" Although the Chief is initially angry with McMurphy for making fun of him, he soon begins to perceive his own comedy.

> But the more I thought about it the funnier it seemed to me. I tried to stop it but I could feel I was about to laugh—not at McMurphy's singing, but at my own self.

The Chief must regain his laugh before he can regain his speech, and his first words to McMurphy when he has stopped laughing are "thank you." Having recovered his comic sense, Bromden recovers his health.

But it is not until the fishing expedition that Bromden fully appreciates the comedy of existence. On the boat, when all of the men collapse together in laughter, Bromden joins their human community, both involved and detached at the same time, in the true spirit of high comedy. . . . Participating in the cosmic comedy, Bromden learns that if laughter cannot ultimately defeat death and failure, that fact need not prevent one from acting. At the close, during the orgy, Bromden can even laugh in the very heart of the Combine.

The final result of the Chief's new knowledge is the novel itself. Bromden learns to perceive his life as a comic fiction and to transform that fiction into art. Laughing at himself and his society, he writes a novel that makes the reader laugh, thus perpetuating his own comic vision. Form and content merge as Bromden writes a book in praise of laughter that itself induces laughter. (pp. 110-12)

It is finally the Chief, then, and not McMurphy, who embodies the novel's comic values. McMurphy dies; the Chief lives on as a distinct individual, not merely as a reincarnation of McMurphy as some critics have suggested. The Chief, for example, never adopts McMurphy's attitude toward violence and sex, nor does he reflect the machismo values of his hero. Bromden creates in McMurphy an extremity of total freedom as a balance to the nurse's extremity of total control, in an effort to locate the mean. He renders both characters comic in order to expose the flaws inherent in both approaches to human existence.

Faced with two extreme choices—the sterility, total control, and deadly order of the Combine, or the obsessive sexuality, total freedom, and chaos of McMurphy—the Chief resists both. If Bromden has learned anything from his experience, it's to be himself, to refuse to let others remake him in their image. . . . At the end, Chief Bromden has recreated himself in his own best image: strong, independent, sensitive, sympathetic, and loving, with a comic perspective on his human limitations. As an artist Bromden manages to combine the vitality, spontaneity, and freedom of McMurphy with the control and form of art. Freedom without form results in McMurphy's destruction. Form without freedom results in the horrors of the Combine. Writing a novel that combines both freedom and form, fictionalizing experience to give it meaning, maintaining the proper comic perspective on self and society, Bromden represents Kesey's hope for the future:

> The Good Guys will win. The consciousness now being forged will hang, tempered and true, in the utility closet alongside old and faithful tools like Mercy and Equality and Will Rogers.

It's what laughter can do. (pp. 112-13)

> *Ronald Wallace, "What Laughter Can Do: Ken Kesey's 'One Flew Over the Cuckoo's Nest'," in his* The Last Laugh: Form and Affirmation in the Contemporary American Comic Novel, *University of Missouri Press, 1979, pp. 90-114.*

## Jack Hicks

> I been silent so long now it's gonna roar out of me like floodwaters and you think the guy telling this is ranting and raving my *God;* you think this is too horrible to have really happened, this is too awful to be the truth! But, please. It's still hard for me to have a clear mind thinking on it. But it's the truth even if it didn't happen.
>
> —Ken Kesey

Along with Norman Mailer and Allen Ginsberg, Ken Kesey represents the familiar unsettling artistic type. For all three of these men, the once comforting borders separating the artist's work from his life are thoroughly dissolved. Mailer's prominence as a public figure, as the personal existential eye of the American hurricane, has dominated our attentions and his as well, and his work has surely suffered for it. But Ginsberg and Kesey are younger breeds and knottier figures: each has sought to transcend the category of poet or novelist by making his life a larger poem or fiction. Both Ginsberg and Kesey have become powerful cultural figures over the last decade, exemplars and proponents of a countercultural life-style, modes of being attractive to millions of young Americans. In the case of Kesey, especially, biographical concerns have overshadowed the writing, a fact demonstrated by the mere existence of Tom Wolfe's pop biography, *The Electric Kool-Aid Acid Test.* (pp. 161-62)

Kesey attended the University of Oregon and graduated in 1958. During his years in Eugene, he was a minor campus celebrity, an athlete, and an accomplished actor. In that time span, Kesey also came under the influence of the first of a series of prominent writer-teachers, James B. Hall. By 1958, when he entered Stanford University as a writing student, Kesey had completed a decent body of writing: short stories, one-act plays, poetry, and an unpublished novel about college athletics, *End of Autumn.* The years following (1959-60) were a natural watershed for Kesey. (p. 162)

Another unpublished novel, *Zoo* (1960), about San Francisco's North Beach, grew from Stanford's writing seminars, but an unlikely extracurricular experience as a medical volunteer was of far greater import to Kesey's life and writing. By this time Kesey had married and fathered a child and, like the classic graduate student, found his debts exceeding his income. Heeding a friend's tip that a government medical experiment paid human guinea pigs at the rate of seventy-five dollars a day, Kesey presented himself at Menlo Park Veterans Hospital, volunteering for experiments with "psychomimetic" drugs. Between spring of 1960 and spring of 1961, fully two years prior to psychologists Timothy Leary and Richard Alpert and their infamous experiments at Harvard, Kesey ingested a wide variety of psychedelic (mind-altering) drugs: LSD-25, psilocybin, mescaline, peyote, morning glory seeds, IT-290 (a meta-amphetamine)—the list swells to a small pharmacopoeia. Kesey extended the experiments beyond the hospital. Although the singular effects of his drug experiences would have been quite powerful enough, Kesey took a job as night attendant on a psychiatric ward at Menlo Park Hospital to supplement his income. As he recounts vividly in *One Flew Over the Cuckoo's Nest* and later in *Kesey's Garage Sale,* he was fascinated and disgusted by life on the ward; and he often raised his perceptions to a higher power with on-the-job doses of peyote. Out of this experience grew his first and most successful novel, *One Flew Over the Cuckoo's Nest* (1962), and an entire life-style, neither of which the American public will soon forget. (pp. 162-63)

Ken Kesey's overriding passion in the last eighteen years, both personally and artistically, has been the qualities and possibilities of human consciousness and particularly the modes of literary rendering of every sort of mental state. . . . Frankly, one can learn as much in the turnings and tracings of his life as in his fiction, for we can read in the scattered lees of his past a cultural history of underground America in the 1960s. But my main interest here is in the particular artistic uses of those experiences in his single major fiction to date, *One Flew Over the Cuckoo's Nest.* More exactly, I wish to consider the novel as one of the few successful literary treatments of the alteration or expansion of human consciousness.

That the novel was warmly greeted seems indisputable. Critic Malcolm Cowley, teaching at Stanford during Kesey's stay, saw the promise in a rough, semifinished manuscript. He advised Kesey in a letter that the book contained "some of the most brilliant scenes I have ever read" and "passion like I've not seen in you young writers before." Thirteen years later, Cowley seemed to have renewed his estimate by including *One Flew Over the Cuckoo's Nest* in his Viking Critical Library series. Cowley's early appraisals strike me as correct: the novel is vividly and powerfully realized and, though Kesey remembers long scenes as coming "more easily to my hand than anything before or since," it was doggedly written and revised.

His account of the novel's origin is an apocryphal variant among modern underground novelists. Much of Malcolm Lowry's *Under the Volcano* issued from the author's alcoholic deliriums; William Burroughs attributes the surreal qualities of *Naked Lunch* to his use of marijuana; his friend Jack Kerouac wrote much of his fiction—*On the Road* and *Dr. Sax,* for example—with the aid of benzedrine. Kesey's version differs only in detail, the drug of his choice being peyote, "because it was after choking down eight of the little cactus plants that I wrote the first three pages." Actually, before his experiences with peyote, Kesey had been fumbling through the book, mainly because of problems with point of view. With the aid of Wallace Stegner at Stanford, he worked toward a resolution. A letter to Kesey's friend Ken Babbs recalls: "I am beginning to agree with Stegner, that it is truely [sic] the most important problem in writing. The book I have been doing on the lane is a third person work, but something was lacking, I was not free to impose my perception and bizarre eye on the god-author who is supposed to be viewing the scene. . . . I am swinging around to an idea that I objected strongly to at first; that the novelist to be at last true and free must be a diarist."

So, at Stegner's suggestion, he shifted to a first-person narrative and, under the unsubtle pressures of peyote, [began writing his novel]: . . .

> The big ward door is a funnel's bottom. We keep it locked so all the backlog won't come pouring in on us and suffocate us like ants in the bottom of an hour glass. When the big nurse comes through she close it quick behind her because they're out their pincing at her ass. She locks it with a sigh and swings a load of clanking bottles off her shoulder; she always keep them their in a fresh laundried pillow case and is inclined and grab one out at the tiniest provokation and administer to you right where you stand. For that reason I try to be on the good side of her and let the mop push me back to the wall as she goes by. "Home at last," I hear her say as she drags past and tosses her pillowcase into a corner where it crashes, mixing everything. "What a night, what a night." She wipes her face and eyes like she dipping her hands in cold water. "What a relief to get back home," is what she say near me, because I don't talk.
>
> Then she sight the colored boys. Wheoo, that's something different! She goes into a croach and advances on them where they huddled at the end of the corridor. My god, she gonna tear them black limb from limb! She swole till her back splitting out the white uniform, she let her arms get long enough to wrap around them five six times, like hairy tentacles. I hide behind the mop and think My god, this time they're gonna tear each other clean apart and leave us alone. But just she starts mashing them and they start ripping at her belly with mop handles all the patients come pouring out of the dorms to check on the hullabaloo and the colored boys fall in line behind the nurse, and smiling, they herd the patients down to shave. I hide in the mop closet and listen to the shriek and grind of shaver as it tears the hide off one then another; I hide there, but after a while one colored boy just opens out his nostrils like the big black ends of two funnells and snuffs me right into his belly. There he hold me wrapped in black guts while two other black bastards in white in white go at my face with one of the murder combines. I scream when they touch my temples. I can control the screaming until they get to the temples and start screwing the electrodes in, then I always scream and the last thing I hear that morning is the big nurse whooping a laughing and scuttling up the hall

> while she crash patients out of her way with the pillowcase of broken glass and pills. They hold me down while she jams pillowcase and all into my mouth and shoves it down with a mop-handle.

Self-disordered states of consciousness may be initially helpful for a writer, but some sort of refining and revision is always necessary. In this case, revisions brought the style and structure of the novel into focus. Comparing the early and final manuscripts, we can note several changes. Primarily, the difference is one of telling and showing. Note that Kesey places emphasis in the original on Chief Bromden's *narration* of events, on the oral qualities of his tale. Kesey is more concerned here with capturing the semiliterate qualities of Bromden's speech, with creating an idiolect replete with intentionally awkward and agrammatical constructions, phonetic spellings, and dropped verbs. His speech is clanging and oddly awkward to the ear, but it is also more metaphorical than the final version ("The big ward door is a funnel's bottom"); this is yet another narrative detail placing the narrator squarely between events and the reader. The early manuscript is generally unfocused: it lacks the detail allowing us to see characters, observe action, overhear dialogue.

By contrast, the final manuscript is more sharply focused and more thoroughly dramatized. Emphasis is properly placed on establishing vividly differentiated characters in a concrete situation. Although the black attendants are phantasms in the pervasive fog of Bromden's tale in the early version, revision focuses them on the stage of the narrator's consciousness. They are described more trenchantly, their actions made specific, they are given idiomatic dialogue: "Here's the Chief, the *soo*-pah Chief, fellas. Ol' Chief Broom. . . . Haw, you look at 'im shag it? Big enough to eat apples off my head an' he mine me like a baby." Because the drama of Bromden's consciousness is Kesey's main interest, he reshapes his narrator into a less obviously mediating character. Much dialect is dropped and metaphor diminished in favor of a more fully dramatized narrative. The final focus early in the novel is on Chief Bromden's acutely heightened but passive *state of consciousness;* his narrative is a distorted, detailed film on which a menacing world leaves its grain and shadow. "They're out there" is buried in the second page of Kesey's first draft. This phrase opens the completed novel, establishing the major emphasis on Bromden as pure receiver: mute for twenty years, he can only receive the world and have it impinge upon his consciousness, and his only weapons are scrambling devices. Hallucinations, nightmares, and fantasies heighten characters and scenes that press on his mind, and his last retreat is into the fog that descends regularly to seal him deeper in his own insanity.

The state of Chief Bromden's consciousness is clinically termed paranoid schizophrenia. He is insane. He can perceive the world only in fragments that happen to him, fragments that assume menacing cartoon shapes from which unconsciousness is the only refuge. Terry G. Sherwood accurately reads *One Flew Over the Cuckoo's Nest* as a kind of comic strip, the aesthetic of which is "that of the caricaturist, the cartoonist, the folk artist, the allegorist. Characterization and delineation of incident are inked in bold, simple, exaggerated patterns" [see excerpt dated 1971]. But this is a recurring mode of perception limited to Bromden's early consciousness. Things are unreal for him, "like a cartoon world, where the figures are flat and outlined in black, jerking through some kind of goofy story that might be really funny if it weren't for the cartoon figures being real guys." Thus the world of the asylum, rendered through Bromden's schizoid mind, is a black and white world, one in which people are dehumanized, represent or embody qualities, or exist as static states. The Chief's hallucinations and nightmares further define the specific threat of each character. Our first glimpse of Big Nurse, for example, occurs when she enters the ward to find the black attendants loafing:

> I can see she's clean out of control She's going to tear the black bastards limb from limb, she's so furious. She's swelling up, swells till her back's splitting out the white uniform and she's let her arms section out long enough to wrap around the three of them five, six times. . . . So she really lets herself go and her painted smile twists, stretches to an open snarl, and she blows up bigger and bigger, big as a tractor, so big I can smell the machinery inside the way you smell a motor carrying too big a load. I hold my breath and figure, My God this time they're gonna do it! This time they gonna let the hate build up too high and overloaded and they're gonna tear one another to pieces before they realize what they're doing!
>
> But just as she starts crooking those sectioned arms around the black boys and they go ripping at her underside with the mop handles, all the patients start coming out of the dorms to check on what's the hullabaloo, and she has to change back before she's caught in the shape of her hideous real self.

Bromden's nightmares caricature truth even more. On the evening of the "vegetable" Blastic's death, he has a terrible premonitory vision. As he enters sleep, he has a vision of the entire ward being lowered into a deep, hellish chamber: "a whole wall slides up, reveals a huge room of endless machines stretching clear out of sight, swarming with sweating, shirtless men running up and down catwalks, faces blank and dreamy in firelight thrown from a hundred blast furnaces. . . . Huge brass tubes disappear upward in the dark. Wires run to transformers out of sight. Grease and cinders catch on everything, straining the couplings and motors and dynamos red and coal black." Out of this inferno, a gigantic worker swings a hook toward Blastic, the man's face:

> so handsome and brutal and waxy like a mask, wanting nothing. I've seen a million faces like it.
>
> He goes to the bed and with one hand grabs the old Vegetable Blastic by the heel and lifts him straight up like Blastic don't weigh more'n a few pounds; with the other hand the worker drives the hook through the tendon back of the heel, and the old guy's hanging there upside down, his moldy face blown up big, scared, the eyes scummed with mute fear. He keeps flapping

> both arms and the free leg till his pajama top falls around his head. . . . The worker takes the scapel and slices up the front of Old Blastic with a clean swing and the old man stops thrashing around. I expect to be sick, but there's no blood or innards falling out like I was looking to see— just a shower of rust and ashes, and now and again a piece of wire or glass.

Chief Bromden's aberrations are a form of peculiarly heightened truth. He *does* foresee Blastic's death accurately. His paranoid vision of Big Nurse, recurringly depicted as a mechanical, domineering figure entombed in ice or glass, is likewise accurate in its symbolism. She oversees this world from a raised glass booth, a doubly threatening figure who is obviously in control and thoroughly shut off from the human consequences of her power: "What she dreams of there in the center of those wires is a world of precision efficiency and tidiness like a pocket watch with a glass back."

When the knowledge of what goes on around him is too intense for his consciousness to transfigure by distortion, the fog descends. The device is effective under Kesey's hand and works in several ways. Because Bromden is both paranoid and passive, he imagines that Big Nurse regularly turns on the fog machine to hide her machinations. And it is here that she is caught up in the web of institutions impinging upon and blinding Bromden's consciousness. The army, Department of Interior, his Anglo mother, Big Nurse—all are aspects of "The Combine," "a huge organization that aims to adjust the Outside as well as she has the Inside." The fog is a paranoid metaphor, a concrete figure of fear and secrecy, of the threat that "they" are systematically deceiving you. But the fog is also a grotesque comfort representing unconsciousness for Bromden. As he recalls his army days, "You had a choice: you could either strain and look at things that appeared in front of you in the fog, painful as it might be, or you could relax and lose yourself."

Briefly then, this is the state of the Chief's consciousness before Randle McMurphy arrives on the ward. Bromden, who was born a half-blooded Columbian Indian of immense stature, has been worn down by life. Evidently, he has been deaf and dumb for the last twenty years, consigned to sweep the floors of this microcosmic ward and unable to perceive people humanly or to leave his imprint on the world. But inmate McMurphy's appearance alters much of this.

Bromden's first impression of Randle McMurphy is that of a vital, protean figure. He strikes the diminished narrator as being like his lost, disgraced father, a full-blooded Columbian Indian chief. But, more than a surrogate father, McMurphy is a cartooned, holy con man: "The way he talks, his wink, his loud talk, his swagger all remind me of a car salesman or a stock auctioneer—or one of those pitchmen you see on a sideshow stage, out there in front of his flapping banners, standing there in a striped shirt with yellow buttons, drawing the faces off the sawdust like a magnet." Like the best American con men, McMurphy finally sells himself. He does not offer a product but evokes and embodies a way of life to ponder and desire.

His effect on the patients is electric. They are collectively dominated by Big Nurse and her staff, but he very quickly sets off human responses in them; his impulse runs precisely counter to Big Nurse's. He runs toward vitality, spontaneity, friendship, and warmth—the accumulated detritus that makes a human life and a person. By the midpoint of *One Flew Over the Cuckoo's Nest,* he has propelled his fellow patients into a major act of resistance. Randle Patrick McMurphy (*R*evolutions *P*er *M*inute) is exuberant; through his efforts near the end of a group therapy session, the fog parts for Bromden, and he recognizes that his fellows are also fogged in: "Maybe Billy's hid himself in the fog too. Maybe all the guys finally and forever crowded back into the fog." Billy Bibbit and Colonel Matterson, Old Pete and his own wrecked alcoholic father, their "faces blow past in the fog like confetti."

Bromden has a sudden, insightful hallucination of "that big red hand of McMurphy's . . . reaching out into the fog and dropping down and dragging the men up by their hands, dragging them blinking into the open. First one, then another, then the next. Right on down the line of Acutes, dragging them out of the fog till there they stand, all twenty of them, raising not just for watching TV, but against the Big Nurse, against her trying to send McMurphy to Disturbed, against the way she's talked and acted and beat them down for years." In those hands and faces, Bromden sees a fused image of all that has systematically driven him into the fog. For the first time in twenty years, he can act. With Bromden casting the deciding vote, the ward rebels and turns on the television to watch the World Series (one of the stranger acts of rebellion for our time). They see, appropriately, a cartoon: "A picture swirls into the screen of a parrot out on the field singing razor blade songs." Enraged, Big Nurse turns the set off, "and we're sitting there line-up in front of that blanked-out TV set, watching the gray screen just like we could see the baseball game clear as day, and she's ranting and screaming behind us." As the first part of the novel ends, the group is self-conscious for the first time, watching a small blank screen out of which each man has been dragged into the world, white and shining, by Randle McMurphy.

As their first handshake telegraphs to Bromden, McMurphy's function is to feed his consciousness, to aid in psychic recovery: "My hand commenced to feel peculiar and went to swelling up out there on my stick of an arm, like he was transmitting his own blood into it. It rang with blood and power." Paramount among his influences on Bromden is the recovery of memory. In *One Flew Over the Cuckoo's Nest,* Kesey suggests repeatedly that memory, knowing one's individual and collective pasts, is a key to any sense of present or future. For patients like Ruckly, "memory whispers somewhere in that jumbled machinery." Significantly, the recovery of memory for Bromden is a process of reimagining the sources of his own pain and paralysis. McMurphy triggers him and, as the novel progresses, Bromden experiences vital parts of his past in flashbacks. Flashbacks are a familiar technique for the first-person novelist. They permit him to offer the reader a past for his characters, a sequence of motivation. But in addition, each time Bromden experiences these dreams of key moments in his past, he retrieves a part of himself from

the fog and becomes more conscious. His flashbacks are poignant and often painful. They involve reenacting the oppression and destruction of his father by his mother, the wasting of his tribe by various U.S. government agencies, and his own paralysis and emasculation.

Very gradually, as Bromden reclaims his past, his sense of himself and of things beyond himself evolves. He perceives differently. For one thing, he is conscious of himself in relation to a larger world: "I realized I still had my eyes shut. . . . I was scared to look outside. Now I had to open them. I looked out the window and saw for the first time how the hospital was out in the country." For another, he sees a more humanized existence around him. People are no longer cartoons: "For the first time in years I was seeing people with none of that black outline they used to have." In fact, Bromden has almost ceased to see the world as a stream of aberrated and unrelated phenomena. He can form associations; in this context, the purely associative cognition demonstrated by Matterson suddenly becomes sensible: " 'Mexico is . . . the walnut'. . . . I want to yell out to him Yes, I see: Mexico *is* like the walnut; it's brown and hard and you feel it with your eye and it *feels* like the walnut! You're making sense, old man, a sense of your own. You're not crazy the way they think. Yes, I see." He can relate events in the present with his own past. At the ward windows, for instance, Bromden sees that "the stars up close to the moon were pale; they got brighter and braver the farther they got out of the circle of light ruled by the giant moon. It called to mind how I noticed the exact same thing when I was off on a hunt with Papa."

So Randle McMurphy serves as an energy source and an inspiration to Bromden and his fellows. They become less lethargic and more interested in their own sexuality and physical existence. But mainly, they become able and willing to struggle for life. Through McMurphy's prodding and coaxing, they venture into the world outside, the occasion being a deep-sea fishing expedition. By this time, McMurphy has become aware of the paradox of his existence in the asylum. The inmates are voluntary admissions but lack the psychic abilities to sign themselves out; he is *committed* but can be released only on Big Nurse's judgment. What follows is a sequence establishing McMurphy as a kind of holy con man who "sells himself" by giving up his life for the patients on the ward. For if Kesey's protagonist is the true American hero, the confidence man, he is also an avatar, a Christ—the healer, literally a fisher of men. A pattern of Christ-like suffering is carefully wrought in the background of *One Flew Over the Cuckoo's Nest.* Early in his tenure on the ward, while examining the electroshock table, McMurphy is told: "You are strapped to a table, shaped, ironically, like a cross, with a crown of electric thorns." Later, as he is about to receive his first shock treatment on that very table, he regards the graphite conductant: " 'Anointest my head with conductant. Do I get a crown of thorns? . . . They put those things like headphones, crown of silver thorns over the graphite at his temples'."

The fishing scene is an extended figure of Christ and his disciples, an instance of McMurphy as fisher of men. Here we see that McMurphy is Kesey's laughing Christ—profane, spontaneous, and above all loving, leading men not to immortality but back into this physical world. After a series of trials, the men are safely at sea on an old fishing craft. They repeatedly request McMurphy's aid in handling the boat and landing fish, but he laughingly refuses them. Imperiled by hostile men, seas, weather, and fish, they survive and flourish as a community. By the end of the trip, Bromden notices that the men have been energized by the trip, but the robust McMurphy looks "beat and worn out." His men are physically cannibalizing him. Slightly later, the Chief notes "the windshield reflected an expression that was allowed only because he figured it'd be too dark for anybody in the car to see, dreadfully tired and strained and *frantic,* like there wasn't enough time left for something he had to do." And finally, part 4 of the novel concludes as directly as possible: "his relaxed, good-natured voice doled out his life for us to live, a rollicking past full of kid fun and drinking buddies and loving women and barroom battles over meager honors—for all of us to dream ourselves into."

Near the end of the novel, after McMurphy has been quieted by repeated electroshocks and is about to be lobotomized, his purpose has become even clearer to Chief Bromden. By this time the Chief is fully conscious, able to articulate the peculiar insistence that his friend feels to defy Big Nurse and go the full route of consciousness reduction by lobotomy:

> We couldn't stop him because we were the ones making him do it. It wasn't the nurse that was forcing him, it was our need that was making him push himself slowly up from sitting, his big hands driving down on the leather chair arms, pushing him up, rising and standing like one of those moving-picture zombies, obeying orders beamed at him from forty masters. It was us that had been making him go on for weeks, keeping him standing long after his feet and legs had given out, weeks of making him wink and grin and laugh and go on with his act long after his humor had been parched dry between two electrodes.

At this point, Bromden and the entire ward have changed radically. Following McMurphy's attack on Big Nurse and his subsequent lobotomy, many of the Acutes have signed themselves out or otherwise taken control of their lives. Big Nurse's domain is toppled, and Randall McMurphy's mind must be dimmed, extracted as fealty. Bromden performs a final action, the mercy-killing of the burned-out husk that remains of McMurphy. He quickly assimilates his master through a series of ritual actions. Like McMurphy, he becomes protean, a water force that breaks through walls of glass or ice. In a repetition of McMurphy's earlier actions, Bromden seizes the control panel and hurls it through the window—one of the many ritual cleansings and baptisms in the novel: "The glass splashed out in the moon, like a bright cold water baptizing the sleeping earth." Bromden escapes northward, now a con man and storyteller himself, but we recognize at the novel's conclusion that the only certitude is Bromden's new consciousness. What lies ahead is at best tentative,

but it is certain that Bromden has come through whole and sound. . . . (pp. 164-76)

> *Jack Hicks, "Fiction from the Counterculture: Marge Piercy, Richard Brautigan, Ken Kesey," in his* In the Singer's Temple: Prose Fictions of Barthelme, Gaines, Brautigan, Piercy, Kesey and Kosinski, *University of North Carolina Press, 1981, pp. 138-76.*

**William C. Baurecht**

Ken Kesey's *One Flew Over the Cuckoo's Nest* (1962) portrays sexual mythology as a primary motif in the individual's struggle for consciousness and to become free from institutional oppression in contemporary America. The use of a "schizophrenic episode" as a central stylistic and thematic device illustrates Kesey's idealized perception of modern heroism. Kesey portrays our national ideology of virile heroism in a story of democracy's triumph in true brotherhood. Two men, Chief Bromden and Randle Patrick McMurphy, come to love each other profoundly. Herein is the novel's radical departure from tradition. In our culture the portrayal of real love between men, not typical comradeship or male bonding, is difficult, if not nearly impossible, to achieve artistically and believably, because male affection is suspect.

The novel dramatizes a resurrection ritual through the narrator's *schizophrenic episode.* Kesey's central consciousness, Broom, is first of all a victim of racism. He is rescued by McMurphy, a messiah who shows him and the men in the ward the "way home." Chief Bromden repeatedly creates his own womb when he withdraws into his fog, wherein he is finally purified by the love of his messiah. Haunted by an image of his "giant" father, Broom must learn to accept his father as chief and refuse to replicate his father's dissipation from that "giant" into the racist culture's expected image of an alcoholic Indian. Broom's centering episode is in his discovery of true and unrestrained love for another male. At the novel's end Broom pursues an American pastoral ideal by fleeing north to Canada rather than remaining on the battleground that is mundane society. Broom rejects victimhood in a heroic male mode. He smothers the corpse-like martyr, McMurphy, in a lover-like embrace, smashes his way out of the asylum, and dashes north to open country. Some day Broom may return to the mundane world of America, without a woman, and become responsible for his brothers' welfare. If he returns he will be forced by history to engage in unromantic political activism rather than in revolutionary, messianic, warrior-like activism. Sitting behind a desk with a pen is, after all, not the romantic image of heroism manning the barricades or leading the charge of comrades, illustrated so vividly by McMurphy's heroism. If Broom ever becomes a political activist, which he implies he may become, ending the novel with such a commitment would not structurally resolve, with literary tightness, the McMurphy-Broom love, nor would such an ending, although required by political realism, correspond to the mythology of male independent action. But the novel does end with a strong emphasis upon the central motif of male love. Finally, evil is located in clearly-defined external sources of oppression, rituals, and ideologies in American culture that are collectively called the Combine, the grim reaper of prevailing linear consciousness, in Kesey's transcendental world view.

*One Flew Over the Cuckoo's Nest* is a distinctly American novel because it is clear that no other culture could have produced it, given the novel's distinct mythology and ethos derived from the Western. Ken Kesey's work graphically portrays American masculinity snared in its myth of individual possibility, i.e. rugged individualism. Myth is a multifaceted cultural and psychic phenomenon. In this essay I use "myth" both to mean a fiction or half-truth which so captivates one's emotions that it becomes a religious verity and (in Richard Slotkin's words) an "intelligible mask of that enigma called the 'national character.'" The American democratic dream renders one equal *in potentia* to all others. Accordingly, *One Flew Over the Cuckoo's Nest* is a tragic portrayal of a working-class hero's moral ascension and the implications for contemporary American males of that messianic encounter with society's limitations upon personal freedom. Ken Kesey endows his hero, Randle Patrick McMurphy, with mythic stature, using exclusively American literary allusions and associations drawn from the Western novel and film, and from American folklore. As Dixon Wecter, in *The Hero in America* (1941), argues, the authentic American hero must be a man of the people and not one who sets himself up as above the people. (pp. 279-81)

Randle Patrick McMurphy is such a democratic hero, but he is not a *macho* archetype embodying the American male's capacity for violence and misogyny as most critics who have written about the novel contend. Rather, McMurphy is something quite different, revealing both the dominant American male literary myth of "the territory ahead" and a repressed homoeroticism that exceeds in emotional intensity Leslie Fiedler's provocative, but accurate, thesis that male bonding in American literature (especially between a white protagonist and an ethnic minority campanion) reveals a cultural denial of mature loving male relationships in which American men can engage. McMurphy does represent certain sexist and violent tendencies, which upon close scrutiny, however, are transcended by his symbolic heroism and his humanity. If this were not true, then it would be easy to categorize McMurphy as a reprehensible American male fantasy, a stereotype from out of that unique American creation, the Western.

On the other hand, McMurphy is an outlaw. It is understandable that American male mythology so admires and is so compelled by the ethos of the outlaw as hero because the United States is a nation founded by European outlaws and renegades, malcontents, and uncommonly stubborn and idealistic deviants who demanded something more than European institutions provided them (especially in the nineteenth century), who pursued their idealism, and who insisted that their wills were primary determinants of behavior. America, consequently, became the "City upon a hill," the *garden* in mythology, the retreat of plenty in a festering and hopelessly fallen world. The outlaw lives on the open road and thrives outside society's prevailing bourgeois institutions. Chief Bromden is also an outlaw, and when he escapes the ward, his "territory ahead" becomes Canada, because in the American male myth there must always be a place *outside* to escape to as man seeks freedom, self-integrity, and self-respect. The West is no longer a journey *outward,* a direction toward a frontier of sparcely inhabited space, it is a journey *inward* for Kesey, but also a journey above the forty-ninth parallel, where the garden *may* exist in myth because the people whom one will meet there are not absorbed in all of the same oppressive cultural assumptions and because there is much sparcely populated land with abundant timber, lakes, mountains, and wildlife.

Love, not power, glory, *machismo,* or the masculine imperial will, is the key to the meaning of *One Flew Over the Cuckoo's Nest* as an expression of a national male mythology. Climaxing in McMurphy's attack on Big Nurse, he totally forgets himself in his act of love for the men in the ward. His momentary insanity, in the vain attempt to exact revenge for Billy Bibbit's death, underscores the prevalence of injustice in society's dictation of behavioral norms and in man's helplessness to stand alone against those norms. No greater love hath any man than to give his life for his comrade or comrades. This is the key to Broom's "schizophrenic episode" and to the remission of his culturally prescribed insanity. Because Ken Kesey does not directly reveal McMurphy's thoughts and motives, one must examine the implications of what he does, and everything he does is in relation to Chief Bromden.

In the oral tradition of the tall tale, Chief Bromden tells us the story of McMurphy as he observes it. Its authenticity is established by his peripheral presence on the scene. He speaks to no one through most of the story except to McMurphy and, at the end, to the men. The tale filters through the Chief's schizophrenic consciousness. Unlike the tall tale which begins ex post facto, we have the feeling that Broom is telling us most of the story as it takes place; therefore we are more intimately drawn in. The tale is a resurrection myth whose central incident is a rescue, a typical motif of the tall tale. As a disciple, Broom, in a sense, recites the gospel of McMurphy according to Chief Bromden, or St. Bromden, if we are to assume that through his resurrection Bromden's salvation leads him to become a teacher of the gospel. (pp. 281-83)

In lighting upon Bromden as a narrator, Kesey brilliantly created a tightly structured novel in which form and content are inseparable. The Chief as narrative consciousness accounts for the novel's understatement and for the universal suggestiveness regarding masculinity in American culture. Kesey believes that the Chief is a creation of Indian consciousness, a spiritual source with which Kesey had communed while writing the novel. Because Kesey had never known an Indian, he had no living model to imitate as he wrote the book. Kesey states that at first he credited Broom's creation to the mind altering, transcendental influences of peyote which he had used while writing. Later Kesey changed his mind, explaining that the Chief's spirit exists, and that he merely relayed the spirit's consciousness. Kesey thinks of himself as a *transmitter* rather than as a creator; this is in accordance with his transcendental consciousness.

> After years of getting off behind being prognosticator of what seemed to me a stroke of genius, if not a masterstroke, I was notified that a certain spirit was getting a little peeved at the telegraph operator for being so presumptuous as to take credit for messages coming in, as though the receiver were sending the signal.

What Kesey means here is that Chief Bromden was not a personal creation but a spirit of the Indian within American culture speaking through Kesey. The message he finally received from the spirit was:

> I . . . am the entity that spoke through your words. It was my task to acquaint your people with this particular transgression upon the human soul. You availed yourself of the transmission. If you need something of which to be proud, be proud of this availability.

I do not cite this to be accused of the intentional fallacy. The point is this, the metaphor (while, for Kesey, the spirit is probably *real*) excellently depicts the psychic consciousness of the artist. Kesey received the resonance of the male dilemma diffused throughout American culture from the consciousness (he calls it *a spirit*) which created Broom. The fact that Broom is an Indian adds dimension to the male dilemma, but, as in high art, Broom is more *everyman* than specifically Indian. The implications and motifs become universal. . . . Bromden's point of view gives thematic dimension as well as credence to the story.

What adds further dimension to the mythic interpretation of the novel are the parallels between a *schizophrenic episode* and a *mythic hero journey*. Because of these parallels we can rely upon Broom's authenticity and the clarity of his truth, even though he is classified a schizophrenic by society. Joseph Campbell describes the parallels between the two phenomena in which the imagery is identical. He breaks the schizophrenic episode into five stages of imagery. The first stage is a "break away or departure from the local social order and context." The second stage is "a long, deep retreat inward and backward, as it were, in time, and inward, deep into the psyche." Third, a series of "darkly terrifying" encounters within the depths of one's private inner world follow. Fourth, for those who will spontaneously reemerge from their schizophrenic episode, "encounters of a centering kind, fulfilling, harmonizing, giving new courage," reintegrate the personality. Fifth, and finally, a rebirth journey into a new life integrated into reality ends the episode. These are the stages through which Broom has passed in the novel, and McMurphy is his centering force and his guide. The universal formula of a mythological hero journey is described by Campbell as separation, initiation, and return [Joseph Campbell, in *Myths To Live By,* 1973]. Again, Broom takes this journey through McMurphy's tutelage, a role a psychotherapist frequently plays, or, in a primitive culture, a role played by a shaman.

As a prelude to Broom's rebirth as a man, he again begins to love another and himself. The simple act of receiving a package of chewing gum from McMurphy causes Broom to desist in his strategy of bizarre behavior that society labels schizophrenia. A simple act reveals McMurphy's loving and sensitive nature. He conquers Broom's fifteen years of silence. Broom's mask is lowered as he says "thank you." Brotherhood is what Broom most desperately needs to feel. McMurphy's act is a combination of *philia* (friendship, brotherly love) and *agape* ("love which is devoted to the welfare of the other"). Although one could argue that the underlying mythology in the novel is the traditional flight from women expressed in American literature and popular culture, the book graphically portrays as well the emotional withdrawal of men from themselves that they are encouraged to adopt. (pp. 283-86)

Broom immediately realizes the kindness, openness, and unselfishness of McMurphy's interest in him. Broom is so moved that he wants to say that he loves McMurphy, but society's restrictions upon the expression of homoeroticism is so relentless, intransigent, and punitive that Broom is unable to tell his friend the significance of receiving the package of gum. Broom tried to think of something to say to McMurphy, but the only thought which occurred "was the kind of thing one man can't say to another because it sounds wrong in words." Broom then explosively confesses his history, explaining the destruction and death of his "giant" father through alcoholism after society stole his way of life and denied the validity of what he was. This self-revelation fatigues Broom, who momentarily feels embarrassed and defensive. He tries to pass off what he has said as crazy. McMurphy ironically agrees that it *is* crazy, but says that it *does* make sense. Racism and economics make Broom's father's experience seem crazy.

Broom's bizarre behavior is a survival strategy that, like all behavior labeled *schizophrenia,* is invented in order to endure an intolerable situation. Psychiatrist R. D. Laing explains that the schizophrenic "cannot make a move, or make no move, without being beset by contradictory and paradoxical pressures and demands, pushes and pulls, both internally from himself, and externally from those around him. He is, as it were, in a position of checkmate." Temporarily, Broom publically steps out of his adopted, protective role of schizophrenia. He realizes the truth of McMurphy's assurance that he is not actually crazy, that to the contrary, he is a victim.

Broom's blighted spirit then blooms with *philia* and *agape,* no longer is he defined only as a simple tool he constantly pushes to sweep clean the ward. He is elated and wishes to touch his new friend, but again taboo inhibits him from responding as his spirit urges. Broom wonders if he is homosexual but knows that it is a lie. He thinks, "That's one fear hiding behind another." The fear of latent homosexuality lurks behind the fear of wanting to embrace his friend as an expression of love, in order to show his appreciation and vulnerability, and to allow affection to pass between them physically. The root of this fear is the primary terror of males to express vulnerability, softness, and the need to be comforted. Men may lose face among other men if they display such human frailty. The male child is cast out, condemned under Medusa's gaze to maintain physical inviolability vis-á-vis other males. This taboo denies Broom the fullness of thanking his friend. "I just want to touch him because he's who he is." Therefore, one level of Mc-Murphy as myth represents male love, *philia* and *agape*. He is the ideal friend, as well as a messiah, teacher, and democratic saint.

McMurphy is a fabulous character of mythic, heroic stature. Thus far critics have failed to comment upon the fact that **One Flew Over the Cuckoo's Nest** is an elaboration of a *fable*. The novel's title derives from a counting-out rhyme, partially quoted as the book's epigraph, in which a girl (significantly, because boys are not supposed to be helpless and need rescuing) is trapped in a cuckoo's nest and is plucked out by a goose. McMurphy, of course, is the "bull goose loony" who plucks the men (victims) out. As a title the rhyme works because the obvious colloquial definition of cuckoo is "crazy," and the nest is the asylum. But the rhyme's apt use is far more sophisticated and subtle. One must reconcile the nursery rhyme with the novel's meanings because not only is part of the rhyme used by Kesey in the title and epigraph, but . . . it is also quoted completely by Chief Bromden who lies in an isolation room after his last EST treatment, the only shock treatment he emerges from of his own volition. Because Broom, in this scene, recalls the rhyme and then never again reenters the fog of schizophrenia, the rhyme is a key to the myth in Broom's resurrection ritual. Broom tells us that he has always liked, even as a child, the goose who flies over the nest. The rhyme is a pleasant childhood memory of his grandmother and his native culture, and it is recalled when his mind is released from reality to freely associate. Myth intertwines with Broom's realistic memories, and the rhyme is most significant because it connects Broom with what he is, an Indian, with his dead grandmother whom he loves, with her culture, and with McMurphy. In the rhyme a mysterious girl, paradoxically a "fisher*man*" (Broom's heritage because his ancestors were fishermen), is in need of a savior. A victim or merely an innocent, she is saved by the goose who swoops down and plucks her out. Just so, Broom and the acutes on the ward are saved by their messiah, McMurphy, the American confidence man out of P. T. Barnum.

The rhyme, then, is a miniature fable. A fable is a story that satirically criticizes human folly, most frequently acted out by animals (but not exclusively) pointing out a moral. Not only does the child's rhyme suggest that **One Flew Over the Cuckoo's Nest** is fabulous, but also Kesey's careful use of animal imagery throughout supports this analysis. McMurphy is the "bull goose loony" as messiah. The men are rabbits and "dirty chickens" pecking each other to death. Finally, the rhyme is also significant because in a schizophrenic episode the mad journey often takes the schizophrenic deeply within himself into a cosmic realm where the person experiences ego loss within animal form, a phenomenon that parallels Joseph Campbell's description of the mythic hero journey.

In the beginning, Broom has taken refuge in "caginess," the ethos of rabbithood, and his psychic defense, which defines him as a schizophrenic, is the fog. Broom reasons that in modern society a man must be cagey in order to defend himself against violation and defeat, that fighting is pointless, perhaps suicidal. The cause of Broom's fog

was an incident in World War II involving a helpless comrade. The war is the trauma, following upon racism that Broom suffered in the land of his ancestors, which pushes him over the edge. At Anzio, Broom as a warrior was compelled to listen to the death screams of another warrior who was tied to a tree in the blazing sun, but Broom was absolutely helpless because to attempt rescue was suicidal. The enemy lay waiting in ambush in a farmhouse near by. This traumatic horror creates the fog. Broom's spirit is crushed by guilt and impotence when he is trapped in the ultimate "double-bind," choosing death or choosing life at the expense of a fellow warrior's death. Broom's psychosis continually fogs him in; the fog is his troubled mind's creation, a symbolic equivalent of a shroud which protects him in self-isolation. The fog preserves his sense of freedom and integrity while it simultaneously buffers him from feelings of guilt for abrogating his responsibility to commune with other men and to be his brother's keeper. (pp. 286-90)

The Chief's repeated withdrawals into the fog become both less terrifying and less comforting because McMurphy is working his magic as Broom's messiah. Love, *philia* and *agape*, draws Broom voluntarily out of his fog; this is his centering experience, which finally reintegrates his shattered ego and gives him new courage. As with schizophrenics who thus "heal," as it were, Bromden reemerges from the fog by choice. His last shock treatment was administered after he chose to join McMurphy in defense of George, the cleanliness fanatic. This act was Bromden's first willful decision to return permanently to the community of men. At this point, he is no longer concerned with threats to his ego and with self-exposure.

Joining his master, Broom emerges to fight in defense of his brothers. George is only his first public attempt to fight back. At the novel's end Broom seeks out his Indian brothers (no women are mentioned) in his village before fleeing to Canada. The male bond here is exclusive because in male mythology it is the warrior's bond in combat. Broom returns to society and his people as a warrior, a role still as important and respected in many Indian cultures in America as it is in the masculine mystique. Another minority male, "a Mexican guy," aids Broom without hesitation in his escape, lending him ten dollars and a jacket. Broom's new-found faith in his manhood and brotherhood is expressed in his intention to repay the man's hardearned money. Through the coupling of love and communal responsibility, Broom is reborn a man and a warrior, after a prolonged schizophrenic episode. In pointed contrast, Cheswick, a suicide, is a victim of despair. Cheswick is disillusioned when he believes that McMurphy is only a self-interested confidence man. When a man is convinced that all are dreadfully alone and compete only for self-aggrandizement, the resulting despair, in Kesey's world view, may be fatal. McMurphy is a messiah because his ritual death lifts the acutes from their despair, and they return to the "sane" world of American society.

As the novel ends, the Combine still controls society through coercive, paternal cultural patterns. Broom's father was weakened and then destroyed by the intransigence of the Combine's racism. Consequently, Broom's father failed not only his people as their chief but also, and as importantly, his son in his collapse as protector and spiritual guide. Before his death McMurphy had replaced Bromden's lost father. In Bromden's lengthy schizophrenic episode he acts out his quest to know, honor, and love his father as himself and to experience brotherhood. By exorcizing the ghost of his withered father, Broom emerges healed; he becomes capable of assuming both the paternal role of an activist "chief" and the fraternal role of a caring comrade.

Romantic male myth (reflected in the novel's ideology and mythology) places man's "natural" home outside the settlement of civilization. Although McMurphy is Kesey's hero, Bromden is a survivor with the potential for heroism as he emerges from the asylum with a healthy, rebellious understanding of himself as a man and his society. Chief Bromden and McMurphy portray what is generally missing in the writing of American men, a genuine, profound male love that transcends friendship, male bonding, and comradeship in arms. This is Kesey's radical departure from American tradition. But, finally, one must admit that these men live without women, suggesting that the underlying mythic fear of woman remains.

Separation, initiation, and return: Kesey's narrator self-defensively drifts off into his schizophrenic fog in order to preserve his fragile "sanity"; he centers in the "darkly terrifying" space of the human mind, and he ultimately emerges a potential hero, profoundly changed but willing and able to lead other men, possibly his people. (pp. 290-92)

*William C. Baurecht, "Separation, Initiation, and Return: Schizophrenic Episode in 'One Flew Over the Cuckoo's Nest'," in The Midwest Quarterly, Vol. XXIII, No. 3, Spring, 1982, pp. 279-93.*

## Thomas H. Fick

Nathanael West's *The Day of the Locust* (1939) is the classic portrayal of emptiness and despair erupting into violence on what was once the frontier, the California toward which Jack Burden drives, in Robert Penn Warren's *All the King's Men* (1946), feeling that he is "drowning in West," in a motionless "ooze of History." Five years later, J. D. Salinger's Holden Caulfield (*The Catcher in the Rye*, 1951) dreams of fleeing to a rustic cabin to live a sequestered life with his girl. Yet when he goes West it is not to freedom but to recover his shattered nerves in the relative restriction of a Hollywood sanitorium. But if, as these novels suggest, the West provides no ready-made opportunities for escape, there is another intangible and portable frontier which can be maintained by constantly calling attention to the defining extremes of freedom and restriction. The modern frontiersman invests his energy in disruption rather than flight: he must be a fighter, not for the sake of violence or of winning permanent victories but for the clearer distinctions and hence greater freedom that conflict engenders. Yet this investment in a conflict from which there is no easy flight often demands an emphasis

on personal inviolability—on the public to the exclusion of the private man—which can be a condition of defeat.

Ken Kesey's *One Flew Over the Cuckoo's Nest* (1962) concerns just such a man, one whose successes and failures can help us to understand the special demands of the psychic frontier. *Cuckoo's Nest* takes place in an Oregon insane asylum—a version of Holden's sanitorium. In *The Closed Frontier* Harold Simonson remarks that "one way of escaping nineteenth-century conventions was to go west, another way was to go 'beyond'." Randle Patrick McMurphy, the protagonist of *Cuckoo's Nest,* does both. A footloose westerner, he ostentatiously transgresses the limits of society, much like Kesey himself, whose destination—Furthur [sic]—was emblazoned on the Pranksters' bus. McMurphy teaches the inmates of the insane asylum to create their own truths and identities, but to do so he must share himself and inevitably compromise his own.

Committed to the asylum as a psychopath, McMurphy is a down-home hipster who vitalizes the sterile ward with the energy of his language. "Some thief in the night boosted my clothes," he explains to Nurse Ratched when he appears the first morning wrapped in a towel (with his white whale undershorts beneath). The Nurse's confusion inspires McMurphy to more elaborate jive, a burst of verbal energy that cuts through the inert institutional vocabulary: "'Pinched. Jobbed. Swiped. Stole,' he says happily. 'You know, man, like somebody boosted my threads.' Saying this tickles him so he goes into a little barefooted dance before her." And McMurphy makes his presence felt with fancy footwork as well as fancy talk, on his first day dancing away from the aides with all the grace and savvy of a street fighter and politician: "One of the black boys circles him with the thermometer, but he's too quick for them; he slips in among the Acutes and starts moving around shaking hands before the black boy can take good aim." His beautifully choreographed entry—the physical counterpart of his verbal maneuvers—confirms the source of his strength: reaction, not just motion. His physical vitality expresses a love of struggle, of the conflict from which his identity as hipster takes form. Later, when he has become the acknowledged bull goose loony, Chief Bromden (chin jerking with emotion) accuses him of "always *winning* things," to which McMurphy wearily responds, "Winning, for Christsakes. . . . Hoo boy, winning." Of course he *does* win, and shamelessly, but the pot is the excuse for the process, the joyous feints and games.

The centrality of process rather than goal can be seen in the relative weakness of the fishing expedition and final party, scenes that offer a telling contrast with the dominant narrative rhythm of parry and thrust. Both belie the energy of conflict because they seem to promise not temporary respites but permanent victory. Under McMurphy's tutelage, the fishing trip begins with the Acutes' invigorating and self-promoting confrontation with two predatory service station attendants, and McMurphy successfully outmaneuvers the captain of the boat, who refuses to take the group out without proper authorization. But the fishing scenes drag, for all their consistent good humor, prize flounders, bruised nipples, and brotherhood. The fish are no Moby Dicks (as big Nurse seems to be) and offer only dumb resistance. The ward party at the end of the novel is unsatisfactory for similar reasons: no idyll of strife, the celebration consists of dull stories, flabby fun, and saccharine brotherhood. Though ill at ease outside the intense but narrow range of ecstatic battle, in these episodes Kesey nevertheless makes a gesture toward static joy, perhaps from a lingering respect for the unhip notion of success. The celebrations are not without merit; there *are* moments of rest in even the most driven of lives. Such consummations, however, are important as the beginning of a new cycle, not the completion of an old. We see McMurphy perfectly at rest only when marshaling his energy for the final, stylized assault on Big Nurse. . . . (pp. 19-21)

McMurphy most clearly reveals his dedication to process through his stories, which stand equally opposed to institutional stasis and to private revelations. In his stories and scarcely-believable brags—his self-conscious construction of a public self—McMurphy exemplifies the therapeutic aggression that affirms personal integrity by claiming absolute possession of personal materials. Soon after McMurphy arrives, one of the inmates calls him a "backwoods braggart." Although the remark is intended to be cutting, it contains much truth: like his frontiersmen ancestors, "McMurphy" is as much a fiction as a fact. Unlike the mute, stuttering, or squeaky-voiced inmates, McMurphy knows that how big you are depends in part on how big you sound: Chief Bromden, six-foot-eight and silent for the last twenty years, is a pigmy. In conformity with this conviction, McMurphy's therapy for the inmates consists as much of talk as of action; he teaches them to replace an imposed identity with an imagined identity of their own creation. As Billy Bibbit grins and blushes, McMurphy invents him a personal history worthy of a salacious Mike Fink:

> Billy 'Club' Bibbit, he was known as in them days. Those girls were about to take off when one looked at him and says "Are you *the* renowned Billy Club Bibbit? Of the famous fourteen inches?" . . . And I remember, when we got them up to the hotel, there was this woman's voice from over near Billy's bed, says, "Mister Bibbit, I'm disappointed in you; I heard that you had four—four—for goodness *sakes!*"

Later, on the way to the fishing excursion, McMurphy helps the inmates capitalize on what they had always thought a weakness. When two service station attendants try to take advantage of them, the inmates (with McMurphy's help) affirm their manhood by posing as criminally insane. "You see that freckle-faced kid there?" McMurphy says.

> Now he might look like he's right off a *Saturday Evening Post* cover, but he's an insane knife artist that killed three men. The man beside him is known as the Bull Goose Loony, unpredictable as a wild hog. You see that big guy? He's an Indian and he beat six white men to death with a pick handle when they tried to cheat him trading muskrat hides.

The Acutes learn, as Harding puts it, that "mental illness [can] have the aspect of power, *power,*" or, more generally,

that one should have confidence in the self one chooses to invent. McMurphy's lies reveal hypocrisy even as they assert independence. He is the antithesis of those passive victims—suburbanite or institutional drudge—who are no more than blank screens for the receipt of others' projected desires and expectations. This crucial difference is made clear when McMurphy refuses to let Nurse Ratched thwart his plan to watch the World Series: "It didn't make any difference that the power was shut off in the Nurses' Station and we couldn't see a thing on that blank gray screen, because McMurphy'd entertain us for hours, sit and talk and tell all kinds of stories . . . ."

"Bull sessions" led by the bull goose loony provide an antidote to the "Therapeutic Community" (an intensified version of the outside world) which is ostensibly intended to help the inmates adjust to normal society but is actually devoted to destroying personal integrity by defining the individual as common property. The philosophy of this community, as Bromden understands it, is "Talk . . . discuss, confess. . . . Help yourself and your friends probe into the secrets of the subconscious. There should be no need for secrets among friends." The result of such talk, however, is the "pecking party" that thoroughly unmans Harding, already the least confident of the group. McMurphy's entertaining gab is diametrically opposed to the generic "honesty" of institutional therapy, which can blur personal boundaries and leave one vulnerable to assimilation by repressive organizations like Bromden's "Combine." If McMurphy sometimes seems two-dimensional—a cartoon cowboy—it is neither because Bromden sees him as a superhuman savior, nor because of a weakness in Kesey's powers of characterization, but because McMurphy stands resolutely opposed to any violation of the inner man. In particular, he humorously but firmly rejects Big Nurse's cold, relentless probing, her insistence that the private self is community property, and that as such, it should be reduced to "phrenic this or pathic that," the simultaneously impersonal and cheaply revelatory language of psychiatry. McMurphy's lack of conventional psychological complexity, his insistent exteriority, is in fact a defense rather than a denial of the private individual.

Candy's presence in the novel raises an issue that grows from the peculiar demands of McMurphy's character. Robert Boyers accuses Kesey of "porno-politics"; the substitution of a sexual paradise for a difficult-to-achieve political vision [see excerpt dated 1962]. For all the talk, however, adult sexuality, like politics, is conspicuously absent from the novel. If, as Terence Martin has noted, the primary motive of female tyranny is to make men into little boys, it is even more centrally the men's motive to remain boys on their own terms. Like so many American classics, *Cuckoo's Nest* is a boy's book, and paradise is surprisingly asexual, if not strictly bachelor as in many other American novels. McMurphy's women are appropriately boys' companions; although Candy and Sandy are physically robust and sexual women, in every other way they are good bad *girls,* hardly more substantial than promiscuous versions of Cooper's chaste and often infantile blond heroines. The paradoxical climax of the final party is not Billy Bibbit's deflowering or Sefelt's astonishing epileptic orgasm, but the transformation of Sandy and Mc-Murphy from adult lovers into "two tired little kids." Despite all his whoring, McMurphy has in this case much in common with the chaste Natty Bumppo, for his virility too (as Leslie Fiedler says of Natty) is ultimately "not genital but heroic" (*Love and Death*). It is true that Nurse Ratched, Billy Bibbit's mother, and Vera Harding embody the dual threats of regimented society and family and are the focus of a conventionally ghoulish misogyny. Yet women can also serve the cause of freedom, at least when they do not demand the commitments of adult relationships or marriage. The two types of women embody the polarities of Hip and Square, spiritual frontier and confinement, upon which the world of *Cuckoo's Nest* is predicated. *Cuckoo's Nest* effectively draws upon the energy of opposition by presenting sex not as orgiastic but as offering the opportunity for both aggressive confrontation and strategic retreat.

McMurphy's sexuality complements a personal consistency that obliterates the distinction between past and present. Returning from the fishing trip, for example, he stops by his childhood house and tells the men of his own sexual initiation. Seduced at ten by a prepubescent whore, in retrospect McMurphy marvels at how little difference there is between girls and women, between his boyhood and adulthood: " 'Jesus, nine years old' he said, reached over and pinched Candy's nose, 'and knew a lot more than a good many pros'." At ten he was already a little McMurphy and his woman a whore in a child's body, just as Candy (no more proficient for all her professional experience) is a child playing prostitute. We should be prepared, as McMurphy is, to accept the rag flying above the house as a remnant of the same dress (a token of his conquest) that he threw out the window years before. Past and present merge for the seamless man.

Although McMurphy's apparently inexhaustible vitality accounts for a great deal of the novel's appeal, *Cuckoo's Nest* is concerned with depletion as well as renewal, the second term in the hipster's equation and one horizon of the spiritual frontier. It soon becomes clear that McMurphy's commitment to telling stories for others, as well as for himself, is a dangerous undertaking. As the inmates drive home from the fishing trip, Chief Bromden remarks that McMurphy's "relaxed, good-natured voice doled out his life for us to live, a rollicking past full of kid fun and drinking buddies and loving women and barroom battles over meager honors—for all of us to dream ourselves into." One does not, however, dole out one's life—and especially one's fictional public life—with impunity. Unlike the others, Bromden notices that the relaxed voice comes from a man who is "dreadfully tired and strained."

McMurphy, who comes in bigger than life and restores the inmates' power, ends as a clockwork version of his former self, his defeat the fitting—even affirmative—conclusion to a life lived consistently on the very edge of experience. Only superficially predicated upon an orgiastic vision, *Cuckoo's Nest* stresses a perpetual search rather than the definitive climax—a vision, finally, of strife rather than of fulfillment or mechanical immortality. And while McMurphy's extraordinary physical presence is undeniable,

his legacy is to be found as much in Harding's effort to make his thin voice "sound like McMurphy's auctioneer bellow" as in the chief's successful attempt to throw a control panel through the asylum's barred window and escape. The language of the "backwoods braggart" is an intentional violation of taste and credibility; and because opposition rather than truth is its goal, such language can end, like the braggart himself, only in total collapse. (pp. 21-4)

McMurphy's defeat is the result of an engagement that for all its emphasis on parry and thrust is predicated upon a monolithic heroism, upon a stable identity or *point d'appui* from which physical and verbal sorties can be made, and part of Kesey's strategy is to play this integrity off against another more conflicted version of heroism frequently associated with the frontier. McMurphy is among the "negative heroes" whose function, Terence Martin writes, "is to measure the world in which we live by the worlds in which they are unable to live" ("Negative Character"). Yet not all negative heroes are so depleted, even when, like Nathan Slaughter (in Robert Montgomery Bird's *Nick of the Woods,* 1837) or Natty Bumppo in Cooper's Leatherstocking Tales, they devote themselves as required by convention to their genteel charges. Of course neither Natty nor Nathan had to survive on the psychological frontier of modern American life; their wilderness offered possibilities for escape that McMurphy, in a madhouse backed up to the very western edge of the continent, does not have. But there is a more fundamental difference between these two types of hero: unlike McMurphy, Nathan and Natty find power in division, their doubleness conserving and purifying a strength otherwise dissipated in commitment to others. Nathan is both a violent Indian killer (the mysterious "Jibbenainosay") and a pious Quaker so solemn that he is a source of amusement to the rough frontiersmen. His blood-curdling psychopathic hipness depends upon the opportunities for evasion provided by his social persona. And Natty has the Great Serpent to assume part of the burden of violence. But McMurphy has only himself.

The double hero exemplified by Natty and Nathan—men who may have both their public spectacles *and* their private lives—defines a tradition of American heroism to which McMurphy offers an alternative, with its own rewards and dangers. The contemporary version of the divided man is the comic book superhero (e.g., Superman, Batman, The Incredible Hulk) whose doubleness is a way of re-creating the moral equivalent of the wilderness by concentrating social constraints in one identity while leaving the other free to act out dreams of force in a world purified of human commitments. The conflicting pulls toward community and self that ultimately drain McMurphy's energy are distributed between the two selves of the double hero; like Nathan Slaughter, the modern superhero can alternate between the spectacularly public (Superman) and entirely private (Clark Kent), and so preserve his powers without compromising his self. One may describe the typical comic book superhero as both square and hip at the same time: transformation rather than sustained force is the key to the superhero, who radically cons the world each time he changes from pipsqueak to savior.

In *Cuckoo's Nest* Kesey makes use of the divided hero in order to define by contrast the special qualities of his integral and undivided man. The influence of the comic book on Kesey's art has been discussed many times, but it is important to note that McMurphy is only half of a "superhero." Unlike Superman or Captain Marvel (Kesey's favorite), McMurphy is an undivided man, and his engagement cannot be interrupted with a SHAZAM! The centrality of this energetic wholeness is confirmed rather than undermined by the relative weakness of Bromden's efforts to convey a sense of his hero's private self. At times, Bromden remarks, McMurphy would do things

> that didn't fit with his face or hands, things like painting a picture at OT with real paints on a blank paper with no lines or numbers anywhere on it to tell him where to paint, or like writing letters to somebody in a beautiful flowing hand. How could a man who looked like him paint pictures or write letters to people, or be upset and worried like I saw him once when he got a letter back?

One answers that he must not, a response demanded by the categorical nature of Bromden's praise: "He's what he is, that's it. Maybe that makes him strong enough, being what he is." The sudden revelation of McMurphy's painting, anonymous correspondence, and flowing penmanship rounds off an angular—even abrasive—personality, substituting arts and crafts for craftiness. It is a rare evocation of McMurphy's carefully concealed private identity, significant in its very implausibility. And while McMurphy does become more frantic as his commitment to the inmates increases, it is only because he cannot draw upon this other side. Without the saving options of flight to the frontier or refuge in an anonymous private identity, his single self can only snap.

McMurphy's death is a direct consequence of his successful efforts to establish a community of men, a success demanding forms of personal commitment in conflict with his essentially public nature. When McMurphy wins his first major bet with the inmates by cracking Big Nurse's icy facade, he is given an important but unrecognized lesson. As he sits before the blank television screen, Nurse Ratched screams, "You're committed, you realize. . . . Under jurisdiction and *control* . . . ." One by one, the inmates drop their work and join him to listen to his stories. The nurse means that he cannot voluntarily leave the asylum, as most of the other inmates can. And indeed, the prospect of this "commitment" is what first causes McMurphy temporarily to knuckle under to the nurse's authority. But the other form of commitment—to *others*—that this scene strongly evokes is more dangerous, and is finally McMurphy's triumphant undoing. As John Wilson Foster points out [see Further Reading], McMurphy and Big Nurse are from the same world and play by the same rules. Incarceration can be circumvented. But McMurphy's growing commitment to replenish the imagination and the self-confidence of those who join him in front of the TV set cannot.

McMurphy's revolution succeeds. But by turning rabbits into men he thereby negates the very terms of his freedom. McMurphy is destroyed not by the Combine but by the united needs of the inmates—a "combine" of a very different sort. (pp. 25-7)

The last pages of the novel are spent dismantling the web of concerted action strand by strand. The inmates rapidly disband: only half a sentence is given to the departure of Sefelt, Fredrickson, and three others. Anything but occasions, these departures stand in telling contrast to the massive presence of the two celebrations, as well as to the jarring sentimentality of Sandy's and Turkel's earlier escape across the "wet, sun-sparkled grass." Picked up by his bitchy wife, Harding is concerned above all with the *style* of his departure, just as McMurphy had earlier put himself wholly into the style of his entrance. As Harding explains, "I want to do it on my own, by myself, right out that front door, with all the traditional red tape and complications. I want my wife to be here in a car at a certain time to pick me up. I want them to know I was *able* to do it that way." Harding does not deny the possibility of more substantive confrontations, but for the moment he means only to construct a public self to shield his private integrity. He engages the rituals of society without yielding to them, like the chief's uncle who becomes a lawyer, Bromden remarks, "purely to prove he could." This might be McMurphy's motto. To prove, without thought of past or future, of reputation or permanent gain—*purely* to prove—is to find a force beyond the power of society to cast human energy in the form of mechanism or to reduce the private man to public formulae. Bromden learns from McMurphy that freedom can be achieved only through renewed gestures of mastery, and that energy must not be enshrined as a *fait accompli*. McMurphy is a savior without being a saint.

Despite his obvious physical courage, McMurphy's gestures of mastery are primarily verbal; fittingly, the major legacy of McMurphy's death is the chief's transformation from mute to storyteller. After the lobotomy, McMurphy lies with his eyes "open and undreaming," emptied not just by the operation but by the transmission of imaginative energy, a gradual process whose effects the chief noticed on the way back from the fishing expedition. The chief is the primary recipient of this transmission; he is so full of his story that it seems about to roar out of him "like floodwaters," and he can say, with a true artist's sensibility, that "it's the truth even if it didn't happen." Like McMurphy himself, the chief has learned to distinguish between the facts that lie and the lies that save. It is important to keep in mind that Chief Bromden's story, like one of McMurphy's extravagant boasts, is a tall tale; he recreates both McMurphy and his own madness from a position of recovered sanity and creative energy. The chief seldom portrays his past psychosis in convincing clinical terms; he consistently veers toward the extravagant. When Bromden describes his hallucinations and fears, the dominant impression is not of madness but of art. . . . (pp. 27-8)

The necessary complement of the chief's newly acquired imaginative freedom is the possibility of perpetually renewed flight, of feints and strategic retreats in the interest not of winning for good, but of winning the freedom to enter the fight once again. Bromden's exuberant escape (after smothering his shorted-out savior) is a fitting counterpart to McMurphy's evasive entrance: "I remember I was taking huge strides as I ran, seeming to step and float a long ways before my next foot struck the earth. I felt like I was flying. Free." In flight, Bromden joins those American heroes who typically achieve their stature on the run. . . . As a professional wrestler, the identity McMurphy tentatively suggested to him earlier, Bromden hitchhikes north. McMurphy has not only made Bromden big again, he has shown him how to tell a story. Bromden survives.

Yet in some ways the novel turns away from the opportunity to clinch the value of those acts of imaginative aggression—tall tale and brag—that confirm personal integrity. Before McMurphy drew him from the fog, Bromden would sometimes imagine himself into the painting of a tranquil mountain landscape (a gift of the man known as "Public Relations") from which he could look back at a safely contained ward: "It's a real nice place to stretch your legs and take it easy." The last paragraphs of the novel provide a similar frame, PR for a primitive isolation at odds with the predominant values of sophisticated struggle on the hipster's new frontier:

> I might go to Canada eventually, but I think I'll stop along the Columbia on the way. I'd like to check around Portland and Hood River and The Dalles to see if there's any of the guys I used to know back in the village who haven't drunk themselves goofy. I'd like to see what they've been doing since the government tried to buy their right to be Indians. I've even heard that some of the tribe have took to building their old ramshackle wood scaffolding all over that big million-dollar hydroelectric dam, and are spearing salmon in the spillway. I'd give something to see that. Mostly, I'd just like to look over the country around the gorge again, just to bring some of it clear in my mind again.
>
> I been away a long time.

This vision of extraordinary innocence seeks to rehabilitate the individual by diminishing the value of conflict. The language does emphasize possibility ("I might . . . I think . . . I'd like . . . I'd like"), and the boys indeed seem victorious. The battles with Big Nurse, however, did not make the opposition less threatening but more a force to be engaged even at the expense of one's life. Indeed, McMurphy warned the Acutes against those who, like Big Nurse, want to win by making others weaker rather than making themselves stronger. Yet the last paragraphs do precisely this; the Combine is reduced to a humming shell, and while the Indians' laid-back rebellion has a certain miniature charm, it evokes none of the aggressive excess that defines McMurphy's hipper brags and stories, and, certainly, none of the comic horror that characterizes Bromden's inspired and self-liberating tales of the Combine. Indeed, Bromden's final words—I been away a long time—not only resurrect family (albeit bachelor and native) but imply that victory waits complete in a sentimental past, a product of nostalgia rather than invention. By de-emphasizing the language (if not the fact) of conflict Kesey replaces the hipster with the noble savage, and

evokes a dusty vision of the western hero to which McMurphy has thus far offered a modern alternative. (pp. 28-30)

[In] the modern American novel failure can be as much a sign of grace as success: it substantiates the threat of repression and legitimizes the quest for purity. In *Cuckoo's Nest* McMurphy pays the steep but unavoidable price of monolithic heroism on the modern frontier: he chooses to share himself and in the end must pay with his life. *Cuckoo's Nest* is a powerful novel which effectively translates into contemporary terms the enduring American concern with a freedom found only in—or between—irreconcilable oppositions. (p. 30)

> *Thomas H. Fick, "The Hipster, the Hero, and the Psychic Frontier in 'One Flew Over the Cuckoo's Nest'," in* Rocky Mountain Review of Language and Literature, *Vol. 43, Nos. 1-2, 1989, pp. 19-32.*

---

## FURTHER READING

Adams, Michael Vannoy. "Sex as Metaphor, Fantasy as Reality: An Imaginal Re-Encounter with Ken Kesey and the Counter-Culture." *Indian Journal of American Studies* 15, No. 2 (Summer 1985): 83-96.

> Rejects Robert Boyer's interpretation of Kesey's *One Flew over the Cuckoo's Nest* as an example of "pornopolitical utopianism" (see excerpt dated 1968) and re-evaluates prevailing attitudes of the 1960s counter-culture through retrospective analysis of the novel.

Barsness, John A. "Ken Kesey: The Hero in Modern Dress." *Bulletin of the Rocky Mountain Modern Language Association* XXIII, No. 1 (March 1969): 27-33.

> Contends that the protagonists of Kesey's novels *One Flew over the Cuckoo's Nest* and *Sometimes a Great Notion* exemplify the Western American hero more common to literature of the nineteenth century than to that of the twentieth.

Boardman, Michael M. "*One Flew over the Cuckoo's Nest:* Rhetoric and Vision." *The Journal of Narrative Technique* 9, No. 3 (Fall 1979): 171-83.

> Identifying Kesey's book as a tragedy, Boardman analyzes problems the author may have encountered in confronting the widely accepted view that tragedy in the modern age is impossible due to significant differences between the viewpoints of author and reader.

Bryant, Jerry H. "Novels of Ambiguity and Affirmation: The Drama of Consciousness." In his *The Open Decision: The Contemporary American Novel and Its Intellectual Background,* pp. 236-82. New York: Free Press, 1970.

> Relates *One Flew over the Cuckoo's Nest* to Bryant's concept of the "open decision," in which the good of the individual emerges as he or she attains self-awareness.

Carnes, Bruce. *Ken Kesey.* Boise, Idaho: Boise State University, 1974, 50 p.

General critical and biographical overview of Kesey's life and career. Includes a selected bibliography.

Foster, John Wilson. "Hustling to Some Purpose: Kesey's *One Flew over the Cuckoo's Nest.*" *Western American Literature* 9, No. 2 (Summer 1974): 115-29.
Identifying the novel as "a combination of gamesmanship and inspired lyricism," Foster contends that the book "can be regarded as either an elaborate game or the unravelling of a vision—or both at once."

Handy, William J. "Chief Bromden: Kesey's Existentialist Hero." *North Dakota Quarterly* 48, No. 4 (Autumn 1980): 72-82.
Examination of the narrator of *One Flew over the Cuckoo's Nest,* in which Kesey's orientation is identified as "that of the existentialist writer rather than that of the realist or naturalist writer."

Heatherington, Madelon E. "Romance without Women: The Sterile Fiction of the American West." *The Georgia Review* XXXIII, No. 3 (Fall 1979): 643-56.
Survey in which Heatherington argues that the stereotypical characterizations of women in *One Flew Over the Cuckoo's Nest* and other novels set in the American West tend to negate the inherent romantic element of the Western and to restrict the genre's potential as a serious narrative form.

Kunz, Don R. "Mechanistic and Totemistic Symbolization in Kesey's *One Flew over the Cuckoo's Nest.*" *Studies in American Fiction* 3, No. 1 (Spring 1975): 65-82.
Analysis of Kesey's creation of meaningful symbols in his novel.

Larson, Janet. "Stories Sacred and Profane: Narrative in *One Flew over the Cuckoo's Nest.*" *Religion and Literature* 16, No. 2 (Summer 1984): 25-42.
Explores the narrative structure and dialectic of myth and parable in Kesey's novel as these elements relate to the theme of transcendence.

Leeds, Barry H. *Ken Kesey.* New York: Frederick Ungar Publishing Co., 1981, 134 p.
Biographical and critical overview of Kesey's life and works. Includes commentary on *One Flew over the Cuckoo's Nest* as well as on the stage and screen adaptations of the novel.

Madden, Fred. "Sanity and Responsibility: Big Chief as Narrator and Executioner." *Modern Fiction Studies* 32, No. 2 (Summer 1986): 203-17.
Rejects the common identification of *One Flew over the Cuckoo's Nest* as McMurphy's story and identifies Chief Bromden as the novel's protagonist, attributing the novel's racist and sexist observations to his unbalanced perception.

Martin, Terence. "*One Flew over the Cuckoo's Nest* and the High Cost of Living." *Modern Fiction Studies* 19, No. 1 (Spring 1973): 43-55.
Identifies as heroic McMurphy's act of self-sacrifice and

willingness to compete with Nurse Ratched for the psychological benefit of the other inmates.

McMahan, Elizabeth E. "The Big Nurse as Ratchet: Sexism in Kesey's *Cuckoo's Nest.*" *The CEA Critic* 37, No. 4 (May 1975): 25-7.
While affirming the value, popular interest, and teachability of Kesey's book, McMahan urges "that colleagues should present the novel in a way that will disclose its concealed sexist bias."

Porter, M. Gilbert. *The Art of Grit: Ken Kesey's Fiction.* Columbia: University of Missouri Press, 1982, 102 p.
Brief biographical and critical study covering *One Flew over the Cuckoo's Nest, Sometimes a Great Notion,* and *Demon Box* (see excerpt in *CLC,* Vol. 46).

Pratt, John C., ed. *One Flew over the Cuckoo's Nest: Text and Criticism.* New York: Penguin Books, 1973, 567 p.
Incorporates the text of the novel with a rough draft of the book's opening scene, published articles by Kesey, and criticism by James E. Miller, Jr., Joseph J. Waldmeir, Dale Wasserman, and others.

Tanner, Stephen L. "Salvation through Laughter: Ken Kesey and the Cuckoo's Nest." *Southwest Review* LVIII, No. 2 (Spring 1973): 125-37.
Analysis of themes and images in Kesey's novel. Tanner asserts that although he utilizes literary conventions such as myth, imagery, and a dramatic plot, "Kesey has created a novel which in terms of the social or cultural tradition is highly unconventional."

————. *Ken Kesey.* Edited by Warren French. Boston: Twayne Publishers, 1983, 159 p.
Biographical and critical study covering Kesey's works prior to *Demon Box.* Includes a selected bibliography.

Wallis, Bruce E. "Christ in the Cuckoo's Nest; or, The Gospel According to Ken Kesey." *Cithara* 12 (November 1972): 52-8.
Evaluation of Kesey's use of allegorical Christian elements. Wallis contends that *One Flew over the Cuckoo's Nest* "is expressly formulated as nothing less than the bible for a twentieth-century religion of self-assertive action."

Ware, Elaine. "The Vanishing American: Identity Crisis in Ken Kesey's *One Flew over the Cuckoo's Nest.*" *MELUS* 13, Nos. 3 and 4 (Fall-Winter 1986): 95-101.
Investigates the origins of Chief Bromden's psychosis by examining circumstances in his childhood and youth that led to his hospitalization.

Weixlmann, Joseph. "Ken Kesey: A Bibliography." *Western American Literature* 10, No. 3 (November 1975): 219-31.
Nine-part survey listing primary and secondary materials, published letters to Kesey, and numerous bibliographical sources.

# Hanif Kureishi

## 1954-

English scriptwriter, playwright, and novelist.

Set in contemporary England, Kureishi's works explore interracial relationships, immigrant assimilation, homosexuality, and sexual discrimination. The necessity for the English to recognize ethnic groups as compatriots, a conviction strongly influenced by James Baldwin's writings on American society, is a prevalent theme in Kureishi's acclaimed screenplays, *My Beautiful Laundrette* and *Sammy and Rosie Get Laid*, and his novel, *The Buddha of Suburbia*. Like Baldwin's, Kureishi's characters come from diverse racial and economic backgrounds. Although Kureishi does not consider himself a spokesperson for any particular social group, he has received some disapproval from the Pakistani and Indian communities for what they consider unrealistic and negative characterizations of Asians as homosexuals, promiscuous women, and criminals. Many critics, however, believe that Kureishi's portrayal of individual desires and weaknesses render his characters more human and believable.

Born of mixed Pakistani and English parentage, Kureishi was raised in a London suburb. His early plays often feature white characters whose faith in the optimism of the 1960s gradually turns into disillusionment as they encounter unemployment and poverty in 1980s London. In one of these early plays, *The King and Me*, a young housewife's obsession with Elvis Presley blinds her to family and social matters. Kureishi deals more specifically with racial issues in *Borderline*, which examines the concerns of Asian immigrants in England. Based on weeks of interviews conducted by Kureishi with Pakistanis and Indians in Southall, the play focuses on conflicts between a young girl, Amina, and her parents, who plan to send her to Pakistan for an arranged marriage. However, like Kureishi himself, Amina comes to realize that she is English and cannot conform to her parents' expectations. On a visit to Asia in 1985, Kureishi was shocked by the racial discrimination he suffered in India and felt alienated by what he considered a corrupted Pakistani society. Estranged from his father's homeland, Kureishi reaffirmed his ties to England. His encounters on this trip aided him in understanding the Pakistani emigrant's experiences in London and influenced his screenplay *My Beautiful Laundrette*.

Kureishi's early themes of disillusionment and conflict between immigrants recur in *My Beautiful Laundrette*. The protagonist, Omar, comes from a Pakistani family and is trying to overcome the racial prejudice he experienced growing up in the 1960s, represented by politician Enoch Powell's "Paki-bashing" demonstrations. Despite growing hatred and violence between Pakistani businessmen and unemployed white youths, Omar goes into business with his lover and childhood friend, a hoodlum named Johnny. Although some Indian and Pakistani groups were outraged at the film, claiming that Omar's homosexuality

and the promiscuity of his female cousin were false representations of their communities, most critics praised the screenplay as an honest and unromanticized portrayal of London's immigrant population. Ian Jack observed: "Here at last is a story about immigrants which shows them neither as victims nor tradition-bound aliens. They're comprehensible, modern people with an eye to the main chance, no better or worse than the rest of us." The title characters of Kureishi's next screenplay, *Sammy and Rosie Get Laid*, are a Pakistani man and a white woman who live in a racially mixed neighborhood, where riots erupt. Sammy's father is a corrupt political figure who fled Pakistan to live with his son. Shocked by the hatred he finds in London, disappointed with his son, and overcome with guilt for his past, Sammy's father ultimately kills himself. Although some commentators claimed that *Sammy and Rosie Get Laid* contained an overabundance of sex and that the depiction of public demonstrations was unrealistic, Kureishi was lauded for his adept treatment of interracial marriages and relationships.

Kureishi's first novel, *The Buddha of Suburbia,* is a loosely based autobiographical account of the author's experiences growing up in England. Filled with references to

Kureishi's own musical and literary influences, the book follows the hero, Karim Amir, from the home of his English mother and Indian father to the sexually open world of London theater. Karim leaves his suburban family to become an actor and enters a heterogenous circle of artists, ultimately learning to appreciate his Indian father and gaining faith in his own future. *The Buddha of Suburbia* presents several issues of social inequality; for example, Karim is rejected by a lover because of his heritage, and his cousin, a lesbian, is compelled to enter an arranged marriage. Some critics dubbed *The Buddha of Suburbia* an overambitious first novel, claiming Kureishi raises many controversial topics without thoroughly exploring them. Most commentators, however, praised Kureishi for his intimate account of a racially mixed family and a young man's experiences in contemporary British society. Harriett Gilbert wrote: "[It's the] combination of real, impatient curiosity with what I can only describe as critical tolerance that gives [*The Buddha of Suburbia*] force, not only as a novel, but as a political signpost: an indication of how we might break through our racial smugness, misunderstandings and anger."

## PRINCIPAL WORKS

PLAYS

*Borderline*    1981
*Birds of Passage*    1983
*Outskirts, The King and Me, Tomorrow—Today!*    1983

SCREENPLAYS

*My Beautiful Laundrette and The Rainbow Sign*    1986
*Sammy and Rosie Get Laid: The Script and the Diary*    1988

OTHER

*Mother Courage*    (adaptation of a play by Bertolt Brecht)    1984
*The Buddha of Suburbia*    (novel)    1988

---

## Rowena Goldman

*The King and Me,* written by Hanif Kureishi, seems concerned not purely with a bored young mother's obsession with her idol, Elvis Presley, but with the nature of obsession itself. Living in a dingy, high-rise flat, Marie idles her life away mooning over pictures of the 'King' and dancing dreamily to his records. Her one chance of sanity remains in the hope that her luckless husband, Bill, will win an Elvis impersonation contest which will then despatch them on a lightning tour of Elvis's home town. There are some good lines which indicate Marie's desperation and her bitterness at being a mother. My eyes have 'jumped out of their sockets waiting for those kids to grow up'. Bill loses the competition under a barragè of cynical leg-pulling by a seedy compere and goes home to destroy the mountains of *memorabilia* surrounding Marie. Whether the removal of these external trappings can free Marie

from the inner confines of her hero-worship is a question left unanswered.

> *Rowena Goldman, in a review of "The King and Me," in* Drama, *London, No. 136, April, 1980, p. 60.*

## Judy Meewezen

[*Outskirts,* by Hanif Kureishi,] is a series of pictures of the lives of Bob and Del, schoolfriends bound by the secret of a past crime, now leading separate and different lives. Del is a teacher and Bob, upon whom the twelve scenes concentrate, is unemployed. The barrenness of Bob's life is illustrated in arrogant adolescence and in his present state of stubborn helplessness, when it is given an extra dimension through his wife's secret decision to have an abortion. Kureishi's play deals with the themes of prejudice, unemployment and the breakdown of family life in a style that is passionate and yet unsentimental and objective—it is up to the reader/spectator to make judgements. Despite the acute realism *Outskirts* is underpinned by careful composition based upon flashbacks and the responses of Bob's mother. The fine structure does not have the effect of intruding on the realism, but of heightening it.

Two shorter plays **Tomorrow-Today** and **The King and Me . . .** accompany **Outskirts** in this volume. Here the characters make vain attempts to evade the emptiness of their existence through crime and fantasy.

For readers who don't seek a hint of real optimism, these pictures of urban tragedy, of those who exist on the outskirts of social, moral and material prosperity, are tense and fascinating. They are very firmly stage plays, that is they are written with great awareness of the actor's art and as such demand that readers contribute forcefully to the creative process. This is an excellent quality in a dramatic talent, that, in its maturity, could be forbidding.

> *Judy Meewezen, in a review of Outskirts, The King and Me, and Tomorrow-Today, in* British Book News, *February, 1984, p. 115.*

## Alan Brien

I was never prepared for the audacity, the sheer kick-in-the-guts shock, incorporated in such a contemporary tale [*My Beautiful Laundrette*].

Could such a portrait of Pakistanis in Britain have been screened without protests and pickets if its author had been a known white racist? I am certain no gentile, of whatever colour, would succeed in bringing an equivalent panorama of a Jewish dynasty to the screen. Would a Jew be willing to show his own relatives conforming to parallel anti-Semitic stereotypes? And if not, how can Hanif Kureishi do so with his family look-alikes?

Part of the answer must be that he has had the *chutzpah* to strike while the irony is hot. We can all handle "A Modest Proposal" or "A Short Way with Dissenters" now it has had a long pause to cool off. *My Beautiful Laundrette* is a rare example of genuinely painful satire, masquerading as fanciful comedy-thriller, that deserves mention in the same breath, though more Defoe-esque than Swiftian. One of several disturbing demands it thrusts upon us is this: so these Pakistani landlords are callous, businessmen semi-crooked, husbands spendthrift and unfaithful, wives superstitious, journalists incontinent and alcoholic, heirs mercenary and gay — does this make 'Pakis' more, or less, like us?

In the essay, **"The Rainbow Sign"**, which is included with the script, Kureishi analyses and illustrates the points which are somewhat hidden under the meringue of entertainment in the film. It is a vivid, witty and penetrating piece. Particularly worthwhile is his insistence that Orwell's England of mild, tolerant, knobbly-faced workers, where rubber truncheons and Jew-baiting were unimaginable, has gone forever.

> *Alan Brien, "All the People Like Us," in* New Statesman, *Vol. 111, No. 2865, February 21, 1986, p. 27.*

### Ian Jack

Neither the white nor the brown race emerges with much credit from *My Beautiful Laundrette*. . . . The whites in the film are mainly racist youths with skin the colour of uncooked pastry, weighed down by big boots and their own stupidity. The Pakistanis are altogether lighter people, sharper, quicker on their feet. They make money and jokes, they have the best lines. One keeps a traditional Muslim wife at home and has it away with a white mistress in the office. Another imports heroin. "In this damn country which we hate and love, you can get anything you want", says the first. "It's all spread out and available. That's why I believe in England. You just have to know how to squeeze the tits of the system."

I suspect—sheer conjecture; no evidence—that this racial portrayal partly explains the film's success with British audiences. Here at last is a story about immigrants which shows them neither as victims nor tradition-bound aliens. They're comprehensible, modern people with an eye to the main chance, no better or worse than the rest of us. True, we, the white British, don't come off so well; but then the British in the film are skinheads, aren't they, and therefore have little to do with *us*. We identify instead with the two boy heroes, one white, one brown, who become lovers and open their beautiful laundrette despite the opposition of the white yobs and the brown cynics. The last frame has them splashing each other with water over a sink, delightfully individual individuals who, through love, have made a nonsense of racial antipathy.

Subtract the fashionable elements of homosexuality, heroin-smuggling, violence and fantasy, and *My Beautiful Laundrette* could be an updated version of *Guess Who's Coming to Dinner*. There is nothing wrong with that, perhaps, but it is not the message Hanif Kureishi is concerned to put across in his thirty-page essay, **"The Rainbow Sign"**, which accompanies his filmscript. . . . Perhaps we have misread the film. Kureishi's essay entirely lacks the comforting (some might say complacent) humanism which flows from the film's ending.

The essay is autobiographical and finely told. Kureishi, the son of a well-to-do Pakistani father and English mother, grew up in the London suburbs longing to be white and fearful of the word "Paki". Then Powellism came and changed him. He tore down his posters of the Beatles and put the Black Panthers on his bedroom wall. He became cold and distant and began to feel "very violent", though he could never accept the black militant view that white meant evil; his mother, after all, was that colour. Later he visited Pakistan under its military régime, grew impatient with the illiberalism and lack of opportunity he found there, and came "home" to a country with which he has never wanted to identify himself.

The white British take a great deal of punishment: Kureishi attacks them for their ignorance, their complacency and their inability to conduct a reasoned argument. Orwell's notion that "decency" is an eternal strain in English society may be no more than "blind social patriotism . . . vanity . . . self-congratulation". It crumbled with the Paki-bashers, went up in flames with Asian homes in east London.

He has a solution. The white British must make the adjustment and find a new and broader way of defining themselves, otherwise Britain faces "insularity, schism, bitterness and catastrophe". He is probably right, though whether the adjustment can be achieved through making the whites feel guilty is more questionable; poor British whites already feel put-upon and have made more "adjustments" to the bewildering changes in their economic and social life over the past twenty years than any other social class in western Europe. The answer may yet lie in the quieter humanist voice of *My Beautiful Laundrette.*

> *Ian Jack, "Brutish Way of Life," in* The Times Literary Supplement, *No. 4335, May 2, 1986, p. 470.*

### Michael Gorra

"From the start I tried to deny my Pakistani self," writes the half English, half Pakistani playwright Hanif Kureishi at the start of **"The Rainbow Sign,"** the rich autobiographical essay published here with his script for *My Beautiful Laundrette.* "It was a curse and I wanted to be rid of it. I wanted to be like everyone else"—particularly when, he says, he saw his school friends joining the marches of Enoch Powell's "Paki-bashing" National Front in the late 1960's. **"The Rainbow Sign"** describes the process through which Mr. Kureishi learned that he could never be like everyone else, in his mother's England, where he was born, or Pakistan from which his father had emigrated. "We are Pakistanis," he's told on a visit to his father's family in Karachi, "but you, you will always be a Paki."

Mr. Kureishi's master in this essay is James Baldwin, whose epigraph to *The Fire Next Time* ("God gave Noah the rainbow sign, / No more water, the fire next time!") he has borrowed as his own. For as Mr. Baldwin, in that 1963 volume, considered the separatism of the Black Muslim leader Elijah Muhammad, but rejected it to affirm his own American identity, however painful, so Mr. Kureishi describes his consideration, and final rejection, of the possibility of a return to Pakistan. He does, he admits, find much in Pakistan attractive and tempting, particularly the closeness and importance of family relations, so different from what he calls the "false intimacy and forced friendship" of his life in London. But family, he learns there for the first time, can also be stifling. He learns too that Pakistan's Islamic theocracy has no place for a playwright.

But above all, he writes, he learns in Pakistan that in the end he considers England his homeland. The problem, he argues, is that the England to which he inevitably belongs does not want him. And from the rage that perception provokes comes both the warning in the epigraph he takes from Mr. Baldwin, and the demand that "the white British . . . learn that being British isn't what it was." They must, rather, make the recognition he has had to make for himself, a recognition that parallels the one Mr. Baldwin demanded of America. Britain and Pakistan (or, one might add, Britain and any of its former imperial possessions) "have been part of each other for years. . . . Their futures will be intermixed," as Mr. Kureishi's own blood is intermixed.

What that future will include is one of the things his script for *My Beautiful Laundrette* suggests; indeed, the very existence of a hit movie about Pakistani entrepreneurs in London is itself suggestive. In **"The Rainbow Sign"** Mr. Kureishi does not quite have Mr. Baldwin's control of tone. When, for example, he sums up his Anglicized relatives' dislike of Pakistan's theocracy, it is not always clear whether he has aimed his irony at the dislike, at the theocracy itself or at both. But he has no such problems in the screenplay. There he remains aloof from all his characters, and develops his sense of their position in England out of the juxtaposition of their voices. And there he steps out from under the tutelage of Mr. Baldwin and displays a confident mastery of his own voice, his own world.

Mr. Kureishi's England is a "silly little island" gone soft and lazy, one whose riches are "spread out and available" for anyone with the energy to pick them up. So the Pakistanis have become the slumlords and businessmen of South London, and talk of making Margaret Thatcher happy by "keeping this damn country in the black," while the white slum toughs around them add racial prejudice against their new masters to their class hatred of their old ones.

Mr. Kureishi's presentation of Pakistani businessmen has some of the same satiric vigor and sting that characterized the early Philip Roth in his treatments of American Jews; one can imagine it provoking the same hostile response from its subject. "That country has been sodomized by religion," his character Nasser says, in explaining why he can't return to Pakistan. "It is beginning to interfere with the making of money." But Mr. Kureishi balances that statement with the anger of the drug-peddling Salim's claim that in England "We're nothing . . . without money." Taken together, **"The Rainbow Sign"** and *My Beautiful Laundrette* not only describe the pain of living in a country where that might be so, but suggest that with writers like Mr. Kureishi, Pakistanis have invigorated more than just the British economy.

Michael Gorra, "He Could Never Be Like Everyone Else," in The New York Times Book Review, *May 4, 1986, p. 26.*

## Jill Forbes

*Sammy and Rosie* is a writer's and actors' film. Hanif Kureishi's charm and talent lie in his penchant for a romanticised street life in combination with unusual relationships. This is what happily saves him from earnestness. Here the eponymous couple are thoroughly modern, or so it would seem, semi-detached but still best friends and wondering if after all they ought to have a child but finding themselves on the whole unable to take the plunge. Rosie is a professional carer while Sammy makes a profession of irresponsibility, and between them, as a set-piece party scene suggests, they contrive to befriend examples of most of the well-documented types that frequent the city streets.

But Sammy and Rosie, who may get laid but not by each other, are acted off the screen and out of mind by relations or friends who have a firmer idea of what life is about. Sammy's father . . . comes back to England after all these years making money and helping to run a military dictatorship in the sub-continent. He is a hard man who late in life repents of the way he treated the son he abandoned in England and wants to give him some money. He also wants to look up Alice, a landlady he had loved many years ago; but hers is quite another England, to be found somewhere leafy and suburban, the sort of place that successful Asian businessmen aspire to and successful East End crooks send their mothers: driveways, mock wattle-and-daub and isolation. Totteridge, for example. Alice has harboured a passion all these years and intends to indulge it now she is a widow. (p. 65)

Finally, there is Danny, a benign, black Mephistopheles, whose enigmatic smile haunts the screen. He contrives to be present at every significant event, when the police raid the house of the woman who had minded him as a child, when the speculative bulldozers, directed by one of Alice's sons, move in and clear the site under the motorway. He alone has the *savoir vivre* which derives from patience in the face of transience. His home is a caravan underneath the arches, the spiritual centre of the film towards which all the characters gravitate, and which is destroyed.

Kureishi, to my mind, has been praised for all the wrong reasons: he is not a realist nor does he have a multicultural message, but he does invent extravagant situations which border on the farcical (witness his liking for making characters shin down drainpipes). (pp. 65-6)

On the other hand, *Sammy and Rosie* falls into the trap that lies in wait for farce. Towards the end it gets so seriously out of hand that the bemused viewer would willingly have allowed a few loose ends in return for being spared the pain of so much freneticism—which, incidentally, rather undermines the serenity and experience that had made Rafi and Alice such an attractive contrast to Sammy and Rosie. Too much is happening on the streets and it is too picturesque. Kureishi might yet write the British *West Side Story*; he has certainly initiated a genre which can probably be explored for some films to come. (p. 66)

*Jill Forbes, "Underneath the Arches," in* Sight and Sound, *Vol. 57, No. 1, Winter, 1987-88, pp. 65-6.*

## Peter Porter

*Sammy and Rosie Get Laid* is a strange film to come from the makers of *My Beautiful Laundrette.* Where that was psychologically intimate and personal — a piece of cinematic chamber music — *Sammy and Rosie* is inflated and hectoring, a small-budget *Sardanapalus*. Its sense of hysteria is emphasized ironically by a rather threadbare representation of public violence: you have to work on a scale like Delacroix's to turn Brixton riots and Ladbroke Grove evictions into properly demonic tableaux. Here they are certainly meant to be set-pieces against which the individual fates of the characters are revealed. Instead, they look like inserts from a television serial, attempts to galvanize the lives of the dramatis personae.

In Hanif Kureishi's diary of the making of the film, [*Sammy and Rosie Get Laid: The Script and The Diary*] which covers the period from the first delivery of his script to Stephen Frears, its director, through vicissitudes of conferences, casting, shooting and plot-altering to final cutting, we get a clear enough picture of his intentions. His people are embodiments of the residual idealism and prevailing sourness of the hollow 1980s, as felt by a consciousness nurtured by the hopeful 1960s. The trouble with Kureishi's portrayal and Frear's realization of them is that they appear drugged with self-satisfaction, zombies of moral smugness. Seldom has a movie had so much sex and so little feeling. The moral pivot is one night of changed partnerships, what Kureishi in his diary calls the "fuck night", in which the pairings-off, though invested in the plot with ethical significance, seem to the viewer more the product of indigenous narcissism.

Kureishi's diary is an interesting and honest document. He recognizes that there is a gap between the celebrated filmmaker—he writes about promoting *Laundrette* in Italy and America, and of his nomination for a scriptwriting Oscar, all while *Sammy and Rosie* is being made—and the causes he wants to work for. One diary entry reads "the social issue . . . is that of . . . dissenting middle class people, who own and control and have access to the media and to money, using minority and working-class material to entertain other middle-class people". He goes on to wonder if "what we're doing is a kind of social voyeurism". But it is not voyeurism the film is guilty of, but replacing living people with stereotypes. The result is that, since they are on film, they are, by the nature of the cinema, glamorous. This is as unswervable a box-office rule for alternative film-makers as for Hollywood.

Kureishi and Frears are right to show Britain as a vicious and self-divided society. Their picture of nastiness, if only sketched in, is concentrated in the right places—property developers, the police, a long-held-back national vindic-tiveness. But, in the foreground, they put a troupe of sleepwalkers hardly seeming to notice the misery around them.

*Peter Porter, "Polemical Pairings," in* The Times Literary Supplement, *No. 4425, January 22, 1988, p. 87.*

## Gilbert Adair

The project of *The Buddha of Suburbia* is summarised, item by item, in its first three sentences:

"My name is Karim Amir, and I am an Englishman born and bred, almost. I am often considered to be a funny kind of Englishman, a new breed as it were, having emerged from two old histories. But I don't care—Englishman I am (though not proud of it), from the South London suburbs and going somewhere."

There, pithily encapsulated, is the contract signed by Kureishi with his reader . . . which the novel respects to the letter. No one can complain of disagreeable surprises (or agreeable ones, for that matter) lurking dormant and unheeded in its small print. There *is* no small print: what you pay for is what you get.

There too, alas, is what's wrong with this droll, digressive *Bildungsroman*, since a tenet not merely of modernism (or post-modernism) maintains that fiction of real and enduring value should always be in breach of contract with its own project. I enjoyed quite a lot of *The Buddha of Suburbia.* I enjoyed its raunchily graceful, giggle-inducing similes (Karim, dolling up for some decorous debauchery in Hampstead, describes his talc-powdered testicles as being "as fragrantly dusted and tasty as Turkish Delight") and the exultant relish with which it demythifies a few of the sacred *culturata* of the metropolis. But Kureishi's *curriculum vitae* . . . , not to mention his current high visibility on the English cultural scene, led me to expect a novel that would be rather more than a programmatic recap of his gifts; more than, in classic first-novel fashion, "promising".

Aside from adumbrating Karim's picaresque progress through a dreary but also—as in his two films—carnivalesque London, his initiation into the splendours and miseries of (bi)sexuality and his seriocomic endeavours to make his way in the world of fringe theatre, those prefatory sentences give the game away in a second respect. They sound exactly like the voice-over narration of a film—a film, in fact, by Stephen Frears.

Much of *The Buddha of Suburbia* (a real misnomer of a title, as the god in question, Karim's amateur guru of a father, becomes marginal to the narrative after a handful of chapters) reads like an extended movie treatment. Its rambling apology for a plotline is charted mostly through some very speakable dialogue. It has, as did *Sammy and Rosie,* a wonderfully vivid and vocal supporting cast of suburban social-climbers, forlorn Indian immigrants, theatrical poseurs and gamey leftist radicals. And its "soundtrack", so to speak, is threaded through with rock standards which function as the instantaneously legible signifiers of its period (the early seventies). It might have made a good film, and it really ought to have.

But it does possess one virtue that operates with greater force on the printed page than it could ever have done on any screen. *The Buddha of Suburbia* is an utterly, unself-consciously multiracial artefact. Karim himself, sexy, dusky and game for anything, is the offspring of a racially mixed marriage, and what lends his story its consistent energy and ebullience is the fact that none of the races in Kureishi's beige-y spectrum is accorded narrative supremacy over any other. Here at least, from surface to psyche, the equality is absolute. If such a strategy works more effectively in a literary context, it's simply because, the characters' racial origins not being infallibly determinable by either their names or their behaviour, one gradually finds oneself forgetting just which are white and which are not. This is an exploit impossible, for an obvious reason, in the cinema. For that, much may be excused.

> *Gilbert Adair, "The Skin Game," in* New Statesman & Society, *Vol. 3, No. 94, March 30, 1990, p. 34.*

## Neil Berry

Karim Amir, the narrator and protagonist of Hanif Kureishi's first novel [*The Buddha of Suburbia*], is the son of an Indian father by an English mother, and a creature of the late 1960s with a dizzying story to tell. When the novel opens, Karim is a teenager growing up on the fringes of South London, avid for progressive rock music and a rapt spectator of his father's carryings-on. "Daddio", a reluctant civil servant by day, has taken up with another (English) woman, the flamboyant Eva, at whose arty parties he is establishing himself as a modish guru. All too familiar with local fathers who never stop twittering about DIY and double glazing, Karim is not especially embarrassed when his own father emerges as a suburban Buddha, speaking of higher things.

Like Kureishi's screenplays for the films *My Beautiful Laundrette* and *Sammy and Rosie Get Laid, The Buddha of Suburbia* mixes "ethnic" vignettes with whimsy and a vast amount of concupiscence. Regretting the separation of his parents, Karim finds distraction in Eva's son Charlie—a cool Adonis, destined, with the arrival of punk, to become a Johnny Rotten-style star. But he is turned on by girls, too, and is learning that choosing between the sexes can be as "heart-breaking as deciding between the Beatles and the Stones". Karim reserves some of his heterosexual energy for his cousin, the streetwise, feminist, anti-racist Jamila. She also has a lot of lust to slake—though in Karim's uncle Anwar, Jamila is faced with an obdurate Muslim father, bent on lining up an arranged marriage for her.

In a novel thronged with excessive, incontinent characters, Jamila's husband, Changez—a fat, balding, priapic *ingénu* from Bombay—proves outstanding. Changez—who insists that his dowry include the works of Conan Doyle—envisages Britain as a "sexual goldmine", and arrives in an excitable state. He can get no satisfaction from Jamila, however: she has married him for pragmatic reasons, and for sex looks elsewhere—coupling still, under Changez's very nose, with the obliging Karim, whom she

nicknames "Creamy", and causing Changez to seek the services of a Japanese concubine. From Karim and Jamila, Changez receives patronizing affection. But to his father-in-law, he is a crushing disappointment—useless as he turns out to be both at procreation and at helping out in Anwar's shop. Changez, meanwhile, refers to Anwar as an old "fucker", whose aim is to "ruin my erection". Relations between the pair deteriorate until (in an episode set down with distinct levity) Anwar is incapacitated trying to strike Changez down, and shortly after, dies.

All this might well seem to justify claims that Hanif Kureishi trades in facile caricatures of Asians. But his quality as an observer of Asian mores becomes a less obtrusive issue when the narrative shifts from the suburbs to London itself, providing Karim with ampler scope and turning the second half of the *Buddha of Suburbia* into what often feels like a separate novel. Thrilled when Eva and Dad swap stultifying Chislehurst for a pad in West Kensington, Karim loses no time in joining them, and strikes out as an ambitious young metropolitan actor. Interlarded with youthful paeans to living in London, much of the remainder of the story is concerned with Karim's progress through thespian bohemia—and a characteristically tumescent progress it contrives to be.

Karim falls in love with an actress, stunning, well-born Eleanor; and from his doomed relationship with her he learns the painful lesson that the rich are different. At the same time, Karim's acting skills draw the attention of the glamorous and influential London theatre director, Matthew Pyke. As he grooms Karim for success on the stage, the consummately liberated Pyke adopts an approach to his protégé (and to Eleanor) that is nothing if not physical. By way of saluting the young man's contribution, the director even puts his wife at Karim's disposal—while vouchsafing some not altogether welcome intimacies of his own. At one get-together, everybody appears to become locked in sexual congress with everybody else, and the narrative dissolves into an orgiastic blur—like a speeded-up film. Whether all this springs from an itch to outrage residual pruderies, or from authorial nostalgia for sexier times, the result is monumentally overblown.

When Karim conquers London (in a dramatic role modelled on Changez), we might be reading a lewd new version of Dick Whittington. A febrile season in New York ensues, during which Karim chums up once again with old flame Charlie—now a brutalized, expatriate megastar, with a ripe contempt for James Callaghan's Britain. On the other side of the Atlantic, the "Winter of Discontent" impends. While not about to dispute Charlie's assertion that Britain is clapped out, Karim becomes increasingly homesick and returns to London. Jamila, it emerges—a mother by this stage, living in a commune, with Changez still at hand—has come out as a lesbian; Karim's hapless mum has found a boyfriend; and Dad and Eva, conquerors of the capital on their own account, are meditating marriage. What a mess everything has been, muses Karim—in the same breath desperately affirming his faith in the future.

With echoes of Kerouac and the Colin MacInnes of *Absolute Beginners, The Buddha of Suburbia* does not lack zest. It is full of youthful fervour, but it is also chaotic, littered with over-the-top incidents and wasted themes. In an essay that prefaces the text of *My Beautiful Laundrette,* Kureishi wrote with elliptical brilliance about being at once English and Asian, and about the bankruptcy of Britain's traditional self-images. Such challenging topics bob tantalizingly into view in *The Buddha of Suburbia*—and as quickly vanish. The novel began as a droll short story. . . . Much expanded, it has finished up an over-egged, barely-digestible pudding.

> *Neil Berry, "Conquerors of the Capital," in The Times Literary Supplement, No. 4539, March 30, 1990, p. 339.*

## Harriett Gilbert

Hanif Kureishi has written two screenplays: for one of the best and for one of the most disappointing films of the Eighties. Mercifully, with his first novel, he's abandoned the gothic, indulgent polemic of *Sammy and Rosie Get Laid* and created a work that rivals *My Beautiful Laundrette* for unsettling charm. Attractive, immediately likeable, *The Buddha of Suburbia* is also a switchback of questions and idiosyncratic perceptions important to anyone living in this multi-racial society.

Its hero-narrator is Karim Amir, the British-born son of an English mother (working-class) and an Indian father whose Bombay childhood included a tennis court and servants. A self-declared 'new breed' of Englishman, Karim is largely indifferent to race, except in so far as it adds to his problems at school, on the streets and in the playground. Seventeen when the novel opens, his main desire is to dig his way out of suburbia and arrive where there's 'trouble, any kind of movement, action and sexual interest': in other words, in London.

He achieves this wish when his father, who has whimsically become a Buddhist teacher, walks out on his mother to live with one of his students: an ambitious, 'artistic' and passionate middle-class woman from Beckenham High Street who's determined to sweep both herself and her lover-guru away to celebrity. When she whisks Amir senior to Barons Court, Karim clings tight to their shirt-tails, leaving his younger brother and mother to cope as best they can in the sticks.

Discovered and cast as Mowgli in an expressionist production of *The Jungle Book,* Karim begins to discover the trouble and movement for which he was looking: confronting, with wide-open mouth, eyes and flies, an infinite variety of prejudice, greed, self-righteousness and devious lust. There are moments, especially towards the beginning of the story, when Kureishi indulges in an imitation Holden Caulfield striptease: tweaking aside the precocity and street-wise toughness of his hero to reveal the vulnerable, muddled boy underneath. But for the most part, Karim is the author's own invention: bi-racial, bi-sexual, omnivorously greedy, yet generous almost in spite of himself, intelligent, ignorant, honest, deceitful and graced by the way in which he repeatedly offers racists, snobs and poseurs the benefit of the doubt.

The setting of the novel, too, is indisputably Kureishi's. Both town and suburbs are kaleidoscopic with wealth and poverty, sweetness and violence, cultures slithering around one another, much polymorphous perversity. And, as with a kaleidoscope, there is little sense of perspective. All is shifting colour and shape as we follow Karim from the home where his mother sits sighing and drawing in a sketch book, to Anwar and Jeeta's corner shop, to his father's mistress's West London flat, to pubs, rehearsal halls, left-wing communes and the rooms where his childhood companion, Jamila, lives in resolute celibacy among books by Angela Davis, Germaine Greer, Kate Millet and Malcolm X, with her fat 'arranged' husband Changez.

The major respect in which this world is different from that of Kureishi's screenplays is that, instead of occurring in some almost-but-not-quite present, it's held very firmly in history. In effect, it's contained by the 1970s: beginning with *Steptoe and Son* on the telly, the Rolling Stones, Pink Floyd and flares, moving through punk and the heyday of subsidised theatre, ending as Callaghan falls and the Yuppies start rising. This allows for some easy nostalgia but really the time span is arbitrary: there's no obvious way in which Karim's development parallels, or is paralleled by, the national political development.

This looseness, however, is appropriate; Kureishi isn't interested in tying up neat little packages. On the contrary, in pursuit of the meanings of racial identity and racism, of culture clash and post-imperial adjustment—and of the ways in which these things may honestly, usefully, be written about—he's willing to open up every parcel in sight. Left-wing political activism; Muslim cultural traditionalism; the intricate, hidden colonialism of liberal, white intellectuals: these and more get unwrapped and examined with beady, respectful eyes. And it's this combination of real, impatient curiosity with what I can only describe as critical tolerance that gives the book force, not only as a novel, but as a political signpost: an indication of how we might break through our racial smugness, misunderstandings and anger.

> *Harriett Gilbert, "Concrete Jungle Book," in The Listener Vol. 123, No. 3159, April 5, 1990, p. 22.*

## David D. Kim

Like his screenplays for *My Beautiful Laundrette* and *Sammy and Rosie Get Laid,* Hanif Kureishi's [*The Buddha of Suburbia*] is packed full of all the good stuff—sex, class conflict, racial tension. Once again, Kureishi depicts a bleak South London in a spare, unsentimental style. This time, however, he's gone back to the '60s and '70s, during which we find Karim Amir growing up in a depressed working-class suburb amid flared pants and platform shoes. A study in unfocused ambition, Karim is young, horny, and confused.

*The Buddha of Suburbia* opens as Karim's father, Haroon, goes around town, Karim in tow, holding seminars on pseudo-Buddhist philosophy, preaching enlightenment to other frustrated suburbanites. Eva, a free spirit with an infectious can-do attitude, organizes Haroon's "appearances" and unleashes repressed desires in both father and son. Haroon gets divorced and shacks up with Eva; Karim follows.

In typical Kureishi fashion, family and cultural ties are pitted against ambition and sexual desire. Karim is a microcosm of all these divided loyalties: half-Indian, half-English, bisexual, ambivalent about work. For the moment, his decision to live with dad and Eva sits easily with his desire to flee South London and be near Eva's son, Charlie, "a boy upon whom nature had breathed such beauty . . . that people were afraid to approach him, and he was often alone."

Startlingly seductive, annoyingly elusive—Charlie is a familiar creature. Like most of the characters in *Buddha,* he reflects an aspect of Karim's personality that's either absent or not yet fully formed. It is the *idea* of Charlie and the ambition he personifies that entice Karim. The physical Charlie is little more than a trend barometer: pretty schoolboy, hippie, Johnny Rotten clone. Following the star of this blond love object, Karim is able to wend his way through *Buddha's* maze of characters without getting too bogged down.

While Karim cavorts about London, Kureishi makes sure to remind us that England isn't always an easy place to live, especially if you're Indian. But the violent racial turmoil of *Laundrette* is overshadowed by more pervasive questions of cultural identity, especially as they afflict Karim's cousin Jamila, a no-nonsense radical who diligently reads Angela Davis. One of the few people Karim truly respects, she's both his political conscience and the most problematic link to their Indian roots. Jamila resists her father's pressure to accept an arranged marriage; only after papa Anwar nearly starves himself to death does she grudgingly agree to marry Changez, a slightly befuddled roly-poly from the old country. She sees Anwar's obstinacy as "old-fashioned, extreme and narrow-minded," but she also gives in.

Her adjustment to married life is quick. She simply ignores Changez as he gets used to his new home by, among other things, witnessing Jamila and Karim, his only friend, fucking in her camp bed. Changez is devastated, though Karim has no great regrets. His indifference toward Changez suggests the selfish cruelty of stepbrother Charlie. In fact, Karim seems consciously to emulate Charlie's voraciousness. . . .

Karim adopts his stepbrother's cunning methods and takes up acting. A token role in *The Jungle Book* requires him to smudge mud-colored makeup on his body, "so that [he] resembled a turd in a bikini-bottom." Karim survives Kipling, then joins a bigger production that takes him to New York, where the ever mutable Charlie thrives as a punk-rock icon.

Their reunion is a culmination of sorts, a final reckoning for Karim's unsettled emotions. He moves in with Charlie, but by now Karim's sexual longing has lost its goal, dispersed among the various layers of fame and fortune that shroud his stepbrother. The erotic vitality they once shared has degenerated into passive nihilism. . . .

Karim packs up and goes back to London, immediately making the rounds of friends and family, who welcome their wayward hero. The journey is metaphorical, but *Buddha* never gets preachy or sentimental about the sanctity of home. Though he chooses an extended family to personify the elements necessary to Karim's maturation, Kureishi isn't out to exalt traditional values. His choice says more about the importance of cultural context than blood ties; Karim, like many of Kureishi's characters, constructs his identity from people around him. As with any fiction, it's not always clear what elements are autobiographical. But if his characters are any indication, Hanif Kureishi never forgets where he came from.

> *David D. Kim, in a review of "The Buddha of Suburbia," in* Voice Literary Supplement, *No. 86, June, 1990, p. 5.*

### Félix Jiménez

[In *The Buddha of Suburbia*, Hanif Kureishi] has crowded into less than 300 pages what might be called a novel but is rather a constant, furious, streaming 1970s circle-jerk that takes in Pakistanis, Indians, Englishmen and Americans as well. The initial cast of characters includes Charlie (Karim's squeezing partner and a rock-superstar wannabe) and Charlie's mother, Eva Kay, who doubles as Haroon's lover. Both couples make love in the first seventeen pages—Haroon and Eva on a public bench, Karim and Charlie in a bed—and then father and son go back home, complicitous, to poor old Mum; Margaret, who won't sleep with a man "stinking of sick and puking all night."

That's South London in this novel, a place where flesh is king and Buddha: Everybody yields and everybody knows. The day after the opening trysts, Karim finds his mother's sketchbook, a kind of minimalist diary where everything is summarily recorded. She knows. She even knows about Eva's most intimate secret (her one-breasted chest) and has detachedly inked her view of it for posterity, along with her husband's tragic, paunchy figure:

> Standing next to him, slightly taller, was Eva, also naked, complete with one large breast. They were holding hands like frightened children, and faced us without vanity or embellishment, as if to say: This is all that we are, these are our bodies. They looked like John Lennon and Yoko Ono. How could Mum be so objective?

But objectivity, it seems, leads to dead-end streets in South London, where only the pragmatic and the adulterous prevail. By the end of part one, "In the Suburbs," the marriage has crumbled, Haroon and Eva continue with their carnal rampage and mystical entertaining (nights spent discussing the secrets of Confucianism, Sufism, all isms, with friends) and poor Margaret is left to her soap-opera self. "You both left me," she pines to Karim as he prepares to follow Charlie to London.

Part two, "In the City," picks up three years later, when Karim is 20 and planted in London, with Dad and Eva and a few desires: "parties where girls and boys you didn't know took you upstairs and fucked you . . . all the drugs you could use. You see, I didn't ask much of life; this was the extent of my longing. But at least my goals were clear and I knew what I wanted." One-track mind? Well, the problem with the novel is not Karim's unbearable fascination with phallic phantoms but the fact that he's been listening to Cat Stevens too much. Although musical references pop up throughout the book—everything from Nat King Cole to the Rolling Stones to Pete Townshend—the only song that really comes to one's mind is Stevens's syrupy "Father and Son": *Look at me, I am old but I'm happy.* Karim's politics are every bit as suburban as his father's, he just punks it out differently. When Haroon—*a k a* Daddio, God or Harry—ends his marriage, wanders around and stays up late, Karim takes notes. He'll surely repeat the feat, make it better, less boring. And he won't wait for his middle-age crisis. Karim becomes the artsy sexual samurai his world seems to be waiting for. Ever eager, against his better judgment, he discovers the cheap thrills of possession ("I was being kissed a lot lately: I needed the affection, I can tell you," he tells us); and in awe of Charlie's musical triumphs with his Mustn't Grumble band, Karim tries his hand at acting, which is what he has done all his life, more or less. Then the novel becomes a tad more philosophical, if you will. Karim has all the reasons for his likes and dislikes but, alas, can't quite thread them together. Actually, he admits he's fallen in love with Charlie because, like his father, he insists on standing apart. "I liked the power that they had and the attention they received. I liked the way people admired and indulged them." By then, he's a lost case.

The heightened sense of wanderlust that drowns Karim is reminiscent of—if not totally akin to—that of Sammy and Rosie, the successful, oversexed protagonists of the bittersweet Kureishi film that bears their names. But here, as opposed to the author's screenplay heroes, Karim, Charlie and the gang seem to be transacting in silence against their worst primary fear: boredom. Nothing, not even society's decay and possible demise, is more atrocious to these characters than a moment without excitement.

This is where Kureishi parts ways with his literary influences—particularly the Salman Rushdie of *Shame* and *Midnight's Children*—whose social concerns he has abandoned in search of a more yuppified style. Kureishi's characters do not seduce with ideas, as does Saleem Sinai of *Midnight's Children;* they seduce with seduction, crassly and harshly, as they fiercely explore the empty possibilities of the dominant leisure class. When they think, they wander; when they don't, they lust.

Our redefined Oedipus doesn't really do much. Kureishi has given Karim such a narrow, albeit real, scope of interests that the only thing he can do is follow his travails and quote his friends: Louise Lawrence the onetime masseuse (who discovered socialism "in a forest of pricks and pond of semen," realizing that "nothing human was alien to me"), Richard (who "talked about wanting to fuck only black men") and Eleanor (who "worked with a woman performance artist who persuaded her to extract the texts of poems—'Cows' teeth like snowdrops bite the garlic grass'—from her vagina before reading them"). Naturally, Karim is taken by Eleanor for a while. He needs her exoti-

cism, still believes he's nothing without a hot, adventuresome, experienced nobody by his side.

Aimlessness and glands rule the novel so powerfully that near the end, when Kureishi strives to make sense of the whole indulgent mess, the only possible recourse is the tried-and-true device of a sojourn abroad, return ticket included. Karim the actor has finally made it to New York—he'd said he would—where he meets Charlie the superstar again, and they move together to the East Village. Charlie has turned into a joyless, materialistic pig; Karim has fits of depression and self-hatred. He's nothing but Successful Charlie's mental yardstick: "I was a full-length mirror, but a mirror that could remember." He does—the good times, the illusions, the corners he turned in search of Charlie, the heartbreak and the accumulation of events both senseless and sensual. What's left? Predictably, the return to London, Pop's marriage proposal to Eva, a new beginning. The end.

Funny, but Kureishi is an intelligent writer—all too intelligent—to end the book with such nirvanistic complacency after a nonstop wandering hell. Something somewhere tells us that there's a sequel to the novel, which has already been optioned off for a movie. Then again, we could join with Karim in singing The Smiths' ode to nothingness: *Sixteen, clumsy and shy / I went to London and. . . .* Or perhaps we should remember Eva's lament at the beginning of the novel: "The cruellest thing you can do to Kerouac is reread him at 38." I felt a bit cruel reading Kureishi at 30. (pp. 63-4)

> *Félix Jiménez, "Gland Illusion," in* The Nation, *New York, Vol. 251, No. 2, July 9, 1990, pp. 63-4.*

## Ian Buruma

[The theme of ***The Buddha of Suburbia***] is essentially the same as the one that has exercised the minds of English novelists, and indeed the English people, for what seems like forever: the long and arduous climb up the slippery slope of society. In short, getting on. (Karim even does what English boys are all alleged to do in the better schools of the land: he falls in love with his best friend and jacks him off in his bedroom, under the no doubt approving eyes of the rock stars on the wall.)

The most valued arrow in the quiver of the successful British social climber is charm. Karim, who is of Kureishi's own age and background—Pakistani, suburban, lower-middle-class—has, as they used to say in Huxley's time, bags of charm: "Dad taught me to flirt with everyone I met, girls and boys alike, and I came to see charm, rather than courtesy or honesty, or even decency, as the primary social grace. And I even came to like people who were callous or vicious provided they were interesting." The "interesting people," with interesting radical opinions, are the ones who get the blow jobs. Not the least of Kureishi's charms is his propensity to satirize his own predilections.

There is a mythical quality to Kureishi's South London suburbs; they are both a hell to escape from into the exciting anarchy of the city, and a source of eternal comfort and inspiration, indeed much like the mythical school that horrified and inspired previous generations of British writers. The shadow of Bromley hangs over Kureishi's work in the way that Eton hung over the work of Cyril Connolly. School and suburb seem to be gilded prisons from which there is no ultimate escape, not on the Riviera, or in the deserts of Arabia, or in Manhattan, or even in Notting Hill Gate. The English writer, it seems, is more frequently a hostage to his adolescence than his counterparts abroad. (I say his, for fewer women appear to share this predicament.) The English literary dandy is so often an eternal schoolboy, playing over and over again the fantasies bred in the oppressive hothouse of the school dormitory or the suburban parlor.

Kureishi is rather good, not surprisingly, on suburban parlors. His view of his native suburb is unlike the affectionate satire of, say, John Walters on Baltimore; it is, instead, an odd mixture of hatred and sentimentality, snobbery and high comedy. Anybody who has ever spent a Sunday afternoon in the sepulchral greenery of Bromley, Beckenham, or Penge can understand the hatred. But the snobbish division of everybody into interesting people (gays, punks radicals, non-whites) or ghastly suburbanites makes for some cardboard characters, who behave much as one would expect them to do in a comic book for freaks in the 1960s. The "straights" are relentlessly straight, and, of course, racist—that is, until they are turned on by one of the freaks, through drugs, or, as is more often the case in Kureishi's tales, sex.

In a diary kept by Kureishi during the filming of *Sammy and Rosie Get Laid* and published together with the script [*Sammy and Rosie Get Laid: The Script and the Diary*], Kureishi announces his personal philosophy: "I saw the '60s on TV and was formed by what I missed out on." And so he continues to think "in that now old way, in terms of the 'straight' world and the rest. . . . I still think of businessmen as semi-criminals; I'm suspicious of anyone in a suit." And so on and so forth. As I say, adolescence is hard to shake for the gilded youth of England.

Still, Kureishi has created some memorable characters who do not conform to stereotypes—quite the contrary, in fact. He is particularly good on Indians and Pakistanis, like the young Asian-English boy in *My Beautiful Laundrette* who falls in love with the white punk. His homosexuality was not what made him interesting; but the fact that he was Asian, straight-looking, and gay was a departure from the norm. If he had been white and camp, the effect would not have been nearly so fresh. As far as this novel is concerned, the funniest character is Dad, the Buddha of Suburbia himself, who leads the natives by the nose in hilarious meditation sessions. There is some great comedy in this, but it is somewhat undercut by the impression that Kureishi himself takes Dad's Zen sessions a little too seriously. When Dad tells Karim that "I want to help others contemplate the deeper wisdom of themselves which is often concealed in the rush of everyday life," Karim answers: "It's the best thing I've heard you say." Karim, too, must have watched the '60s on TV.

Kureishi has some good sport with Karim, when he drifts into a theater troupe in the city as the first step up the so-cial ladder. Karim, the nice boy from Beckenham, "an Englishman born and bred, almost," is asked to perform as Kipling's Mowgli, and is instructed to learn how to speak with a stage Indian accent. He is humiliated, of course, but it is the price that he must pay for the company of interesting people. Despite these comic interludes, however, the inner-city half of the book is less good than the suburban part. There is too much worrying about career, too much melancholy thought and universe-carrying. This includes much agonizing about the ultimate emptiness of success and the shallowness of human relationships. And these agonies are set (where else?) in New York, that soulless, wicked capital of capitalist anomie. And so, in the end, Karim returns to (where else?) home sweet home.

What makes Kureishi's novel and screenplays different from the average fare is the race factor. It is new to see young Indian-Englishmen snog with punks behind the washing machine. And it is to Kureishi's credit that he treats "race relations" with a large dollop of humor. But there is an irritating tendency, not uncommon among middle-class fantasists, to romanticize what French intellectuals call, with evident relish, *les marginaux:* blacks, gays, freaks, militants. It is part of Kureishi's inner-city vision to lump these together. As in Auden's famous remark about New Yorkers, Kureishi's characters are not British, they are Londoners: white Londoners, blacks, gays, straights, Pakis, punks, dykes, all screwing in one big heap. All you need is love. I can dig that.

But there is another point as well. "One plus of the repressive '80s has been cultural interest in marginalized and excluded groups," writes Kureishi in his diary. Well, yes; but the best writing on "marginals" is done by people who don't regard them as such, by people who, temporarily or permanently, live among them, who are part of them. And despite his subcontinental ancestry, Kureishi is hardly marginal. You feel that he looks at the marginals much as Jack Kerouac did, or Norman Mailer, or Mick Jagger. They are types to admire, to imitate, to be titillated by, before retreating into another dining room, to regale one's friends with tales of the mean streets. One is also reminded of Auden and Isherwood's camp proletarianism, with their hanging out with rough trade and smoking Woodbines. Isherwood remarked that if homosexuality had not existed, he would have invented it. Anything to lash out and shock the booboisie of England.

Kureishi's world is not unlike that of Jagger and the Stones. They, too, are products of the London suburbs, having their inner-city dreams, mimicking black blues, strutting as though they were raised in the heat of the ghetto, faking badass cockney accents. They, too, are imaginary street fighting men. But at least Jagger doesn't take himself seriously. His politics are rock 'n roll fantasy. What is mildly amusing in a three-minute rock song becomes very tiresome, however, in a feature-length film or novel. It is silly to compare, as Kureishi does in his script for *Sammy and Rosie Get Laid,* a London housing estate to Soweto, or to liken a bunch of kids leaving a squatter area to "the PLO leaving Beirut." It is irresponsible to say in a radio program that the anti-poll tax riots in London were "terrific."

The constant hyperbole about "oppression" under the Thatcher government blunts the real criticism to be aimed at her policies. The result is a kind of "Weimarization" of politics: the fantasy of oppression becomes so pervasive that any amount of extremism against the status quo is welcomed, almost for aesthetic reasons. As with the satirists of Weimar, and indeed many of the interesting people in London, social snobbery often lies at the root of Kureishi's politics. This phenomenon is especially marked in a society that does not value its intellectuals: snobbery is their last recourse. When Harold Pinter, the dean of interesting people, disembarks from his Mercedes Benz to sneer at the greedy new rich of Thatcherism, you know where he stands: businessmen are semi-criminals, they are boring men in suits who are not entitled to have what Pinter has, they should know their place. When the squatters in *Sammy and Rosie* must move on, it is because "the government's encouraging fat white men with bad haircuts to put money into the area." Note the fat, note the white, note (above all) the bad haircuts. These are definitely not interesting people.

The thing about Britain is that the interesting people are not taken very seriously here. They never have been. British philistinism sees to that. And yet it is not always easy to decide which is more annoying: the indifference of the suburbanites or the frivolousness of those who rebel against them. (pp. 34-6)

> *Ian Buruma, "The English Novel Gets Laid,"*
> *in* The New Republic, *Vol. 203, Nos. 8 & 9,*
> *August 20 & 27, 1990, pp. 34-6.*

# Philip Larkin

## 1922-1985

(Full name Philip Arthur Larkin) English poet, critic, and novelist.

The following entry presents criticism on Larkin's *Collected Poems* (1988). For an overview of Larkin's entire career, see *CLC,* Vols. 3, 5, 8, 9, 13, 18, 33, and 39.

A major English poet of the post-World War II era, Larkin wrote verse that appeals to traditionalists as well as to casual readers of poetry, evinced by the widespread critical and popular interest in his posthumously published *Collected Poems,* a best-seller in Great Britain. Crafted in strict metrical patterns that capture the cadences of everyday speech, Larkin's poems project a distinct voice, variously self-deprecating, sharply cynical, pensive, humorous, or quietly celebratory. "The voice was unmistakable," observed Clive James. "It made misery beautiful."

Larkin frequently focused on death and the bleakness of contemporary existence, exposing sham and hypocrisy in human behavior, religion, and urban values, and consistently expressing pessimism and futility about human endeavors. Larkin's misanthropy, his sparse poetic output, and his secluded lifestyle as a bachelor and librarian in the northeastern town of Hull, from which he rarely ventured, contributed to his reputation as a poet of gloom and was reinforced by statements he made about art and life. Concerning poetic inspiration, for example, Larkin observed: "Deprivation is for me what daffodils were for Wordsworth." However, many critics note that Larkin's greatest works balance grimness with a sense of hope and beauty and suggest that he views art as a means for discovering and communicating these qualities. Edward Mendelson commented: "[Larkin] created an official self-portrait of the artist as bitter, disillusioned, lonely, resentful of any energy and happiness enjoyed by others—even while he insisted that their energy was doomed and their happiness an illusion. . . . [But] the alternative truth spoken quietly by his poems was a shy, persistent vision of freedom and exaltation."

Setting exacting standards for his work, Larkin desired to be represented by eighty-five poems published in three slim, carefully arranged volumes—*The Less Deceived, The Whitsun Weddings,* and *High Windows*—plus a late piece, "Aubade," one of only a few poems Larkin wrote during the last decade of his life. He considered his first collection, *The North Ship,* immature because of rhetorical excesses, and two pamphlets, *XX Poems* and *The Fantasy Poets No. 21: Philip Larkin,* contain many pieces that were reworked and collected in the three major publications. *Collected Poems,* edited by Anthony Thwaite, features poems from these volumes as well as pieces Larkin chose not to release during his lifetime. While critics debated the appropriateness of Thwaite's inclusion of poems Larkin himself considered inferior, they used the chronological

arrangement of the collection to comment on the poet's development.

Larkin's earliest poems, written mostly during the 1930s, are influenced by the style and social concerns of W. H. Auden, and the lyrics steeped with metaphorical language and lush imagery in *The North Ship* indicate his interest in the work of W. B. Yeats. Larkin credited his reading of Thomas Hardy's verse for inspiring him to write with greater austerity and to link experiences and emotions with detailed settings. This breakthrough into a "mature" style, as Larkin termed it, is exemplified in what critics refer to as "the Larkin line"—a taut pentameter arrangement in which various emotional tones and effects are achieved through concentrated phrasing that features common language, subtle rhymes, compound adjectives, and concrete images. According to Derek Walcott, Larkin's great achievement was having explored "the possibility of [the pentameter's] defiant consistency, until technical mastery became freshness."

Larkin's first mature poems were printed in *The Less Deceived,* which won critical acclaim and contributed to a 1950s literary trend in England known as The Movement. Writers associated with The Movement, including Kingsley Amis, John Wain, and Elizabeth Jennings, wrote fiction and poetry about ordinary experience with attention to realism and rationalism, consciously avoiding idealistic principles of romanticism and the literary experiments of modernist writers. Recurring themes in Larkin's work—the prospect and inevitability of aging and death, solitude versus community and marriage, the encroachment of urbanization, and issues pertaining to religion and social rituals—are examined in *The Less Deceived,* the title of which reflects Larkin's insistence on the need for exposing and surmounting illusions and false ideals. "Going," usually considered the first of his mature poems, and "Aubade," Larkin's last great work, both present unequivocal statements of his fear of death. "Church Going," in which a cyclist on a journey stops to enter a deserted church, is one of several poems exploring religion. The speaker in the poem admits to feeling spiritually empty and mocks the institution of religion. The tone of the poem gradually transforms into serious reflections, however, simultaneously dismissing delusions of religion while recognizing the inner needs it serves ("And that much can never be obsolete, / Since someone will forever be surprising / A hunger in himself to be more serious"), a balance that critics find in many of Larkin's works. "At Grass," for example, which concerns two retired racehorses in a pasture, laments the passing of vitality while evoking a sense of beauty in the beasts and their surroundings. Elements of harmonious natural beauty and youthful vigor are counterposed with impending mortality as well in "Wedding-Wind," one of many Larkin poems addressing the topic of marriage. Some of Larkin's marriage poems are celebratory, while others discuss the hardships and compromises of matrimony or, as in "Dockery and Son," address the circumstances of the poet's bachelorhood and his devotion to art.

The title poem of *The Whitsun Weddings* is typical of Larkin's work, as the speaker undertakes a short journey and offers pointed observations on landscapes and people. Traveling by train to London during a traditional time for spring weddings in Great Britain, the speaker remarks with detached amusement on the spoiled landscape or the disagreeable fashions and character types he views at several wedding receptions, but eventually expresses feelings of affirmation for the young couples. "The Whitsun Weddings" concludes with forceful imagery that augments feelings developed throughout the piece, a practice that also occurs in the title poem of *High Windows.* This verse begins with observations on sexual freedom among young people, which the speaker compares with the liberation from religious restrictions he experienced when he was young, and concludes with images suggesting contemplations of eternity. Other famous Larkin poems detail features of suburban landscapes, including playgrounds and hospitals, and several, including "Mr. Bleaney" and "Vers de Société," satirize social behavior and expectations. While unusually celebratory, "Show Saturday," which concerns an annual fair, is considered by many as representative of Larkin's aesthetics. Elizabeth Spires commented: "Like so many of Larkin's poems, 'Show Saturday' attempts to make spiritual sense of the world not through a dogmatic religious framework but through poetic vision, the poet perceiving the excellence of creation

in the 'single supreme versions' (human, animal, vegetable) gathered for Show Saturday. This vision, recognizing as it does the linkages and correspondences of the material world but detached from any belief system, constitutes the underpinnings of the poet's faith."

(See also *Contemporary Authors,* Vols. 5-8, rev. ed., and 117; *Contemporary Authors New Revision Series,* Vol. 24; and *Dictionary of Literary Biography* Vol. 27.)

## PRINCIPAL WORKS

### POETRY

*The North Ship*   1945
*XX Poems*   1951
*The Fantasy Poets No. 21: Philip Larkin*   1954
*The Less Deceived*   1955
*The Whitsun Weddings*   1964
*High Windows*   1974
*Collected Poems*   1988

### NOVELS

*Jill*   1946
*A Girl in Winter*   1947

### NONFICTION

*\*All What Jazz: A Record Diary, 1961-1968*   1975
*Required Writing: Miscellaneous Pieces, 1955-1982*   1983

\*Updated, 1985 edition covers the years 1961-1971.

---

### Seamus Heaney

Philip Larkin was uniquely cherished, and not just in England, largely because of his gift for winning the respect of two kinds of readers: those scrupulously concerned about literary standards and those other non-specialist listeners-in to what is generally available. This means that his ***Collected Poems*** is already a classic, with a guaranteed life on the market and in the memory.

The volume contains more than might have been expected. The six previous volumes, including ***XX Poems*** printed in Belfast in 1951 and the Fantasy Press pamphlet of 1954 [***The Fantasy Poets: Philip Larkin***], naturally constitute the bulk of the book. But [editor] Anthony Thwaite has chosen to include a number of 'unfinished' poems that Larkin had preserved in typescript, as well as 'a substantial selection from his earlier poems, from 1938 until the end of 1945.' This means that altogether 83 poems appear in print here for the first time, 61 of which were written between February 1946 and the poet's death in December 1985.

The 1946 date marks a starting point because in that year Larkin wrote **"Going,"** 'the first poem of his maturity which he chose to preserve'. Entitled in manuscript "Dying Day," it reveals Larkin's imagination shedding its tentativeness:

There is an evening coming in
Across the fields, one never seen before,
That lights no lamps.

Much that is admirable in the best of his work is felt here: firmness and delicacy of cadence, a definite geography, a mutually fortifying congruence between what the language means to say and what it musically embodies. Verbal felicity, intellectual sureness and formal inviolability have all come together; the force of a personality gets concentrated in a melody. In fact, Larkin's power to convince could be described in terms that he once applied to W. H. Auden, 'the talent for finding images, rhythms and phrases that completely win the reader's confidence.'

Put like that, it sounds simple; but one has only to turn to the poems written before 1946 (and sensibly relegated by the editor to the final section of the book) to appreciate the long effort Larkin expended upon the work of finding his true voice. As an enormously gifted schoolboy versifier, he had written lines that showed no aspiration to modernity and little perviousness to the ordinariness of life which would eventually engross him. Keats, Shakespeare and Tennyson play their notes, pathos and inversions abound, and at this stage the melody is almost altogether in the mimicry: 'Now night perfumes lie upon the air, / As rests the blossom on the loaded bough.' At Oxford, something more up-to-date did begin to make its presence felt, as Auden-speak. He wrote devotedly, constantly and ambitiously in an idiom and in forms which were almost entirely ventriloquistic:

Tired of a landscape known too well when
   young:
The deliberate shallow hills, the boring birds
Flying past rocks.

There followed, of course, that phase of 'Celtic fever' when Yeats's influence was supreme and Larkin wrote the poems included in his first volume, *The North Ship,* which was published to less than Yeatsian *eclat* in 1945. There he was capable of dramatising himself as 'a sack of meal upon two sticks' and of asking that 'a snow-white unicorn . . . put into my hand its golden horn.' It was his inevitable embarrassment at slips and excesses of this kind that led him to seek the antidote of Thomas Hardy and to promulgate his virtues, for it was famously Hardy who taught him to restring the lyric instrument so that it spoke in his proper register at last.

At that point, certain richly rewarding technical considerations begin to preoccupy him, such as the handling of the short two-stress line, or the invention of compound adjectives ('source-encrusting doubt'), or the minting of phrases like 'deep gardenfuls of air', which achieve a similar surprise, concentration and outreach.

But it is in the deployment of rhyme, especially of the feminine variety, that the new emotional expressiveness is best discerned. By May 1949, he has got the taste for it, in **"On Being Twenty-Six,"** where he offers the hinged chimes of doubt / drought, flag / slag, trash / ash, and (best) world / pearled. By the following October, in **"No Road"** he has half-rhymed 'ailment' with 'fulfilment' and a rhetorical device has become a vehicle of sensibility. We are then well on our way to the climactic desolations of **"Aubade"** and its exquisite pairing of impairing concepts—think with / link with, vision / indecision, brave / grave, sun / done.

If there is a doubt about the book, it concerns the rightness of putting so much juvenilia and bottom-drawer stuff on display. One argument in favour of this, of course, is that it adds to the record poems which extend Larkin's readers' affection for him without necessarily altering their sense of the dimensions of his achievement. Anthony Thwaite names his candidates for the new equal opportunity list, and they all do have their claims, especially **"An April Sunday"**, **"Far Out"**—a perfectly turned dialogue with Robert Frost's poem, "Neither Far Out Nor In Deep"—and **"When first we faced."** And, yes, also the long unfinished **"The Dance,"** an unresolved but compelling orchestration of themes like those in **"Reasons for Attendance,"** and **"Vers de Societe,"** skilfully self-dramatising and hurtfully self-revealing. I would want to add **"Autumn"** and **"A slight relax of air where cold was"** and hum and haw with pleasurable uncertainty about what to think of many others.

Still, one recognises in all of it what one had presumed anyhow: a gift for strict self-criticism. Many beautiful and true lines were denied their place in the canon because they came in poems which were not successful as whole things. And, inevitably, in these hitherto unpublished poems there are echoes and premonitions of lines and rhythms which have become part of the common poetic ear. 'Uncontradicting solitude' (the subject of **"Best Society"**) will call up a much later and far more desperate apostrophe to **"Unresting death,"** as well as that munificent threshing of 'unresting castles' in **"The Trees."** Everywhere there are similar promptings and resonances, particularly on the recurring subjects of deprivation, age and hospitals. . . .

Most of the poems newly published here come from notebooks and homemade booklets which the poet carefully retained. There are seven typed-up compilations representing work done between 1939 and 1942, and then, more importantly, eight folio notebooks full of drafts and dated final versions, which Larkin kept between October 1944 and November 1980. Obviously, the professional librarian in him was conscious of the assistance this would provide for archivists in the future but it is also a powerful indication of how seriously, purposefully and hopefully Philip Larkin embraced the vocation of poetry. His masquerade as a 9-to-5 man who occasionally hit one off is called into question by this evidence of a path followed over a lifetime in silence and in discipline.

It is unfortunate, therefore, that he did not testify more forthrightly to the necessity of this vulnerable inner journey. He kept it all under social wraps, conniving happily and decisively with a prevalent philistine streak in English cultural attitudes. Mocking the notion of reading foreign poets, exalting his taste for low-brow reading, all that was a sort of punitive haughtiness, a protective colouring of Lucky Jim-ism which came close to selling the imaginative past. He refused, in other words, to accept any responsibility to play an educative role; Yeats might make a scarecrow of himself among schoolchildren, but not Larkin.

Seamus Heaney, "Unresting Death," in The Observer, October 9, 1988, p. 44.

## Ian Hamilton

Philip Larkin, we are told, left instructions in his will that certain of his writings had to be destroyed, unread. His executors obeyed: the word is that several of the poet's notebooks, or journals, are now ashes. Did Larkin expect to be so obeyed? Or did he imagine that perhaps someone, somehow, might take a peek at the material before it reached the flames? And if such a thought did cross his mind, why didn't he destroy the stuff himself? He must have known that, by not doing so, he was bequeathing at least the possibility of a dilemma. But then some of his most moving poems contrive a subtle, unsettlable dispute between revelation and concealment. There is a wanting-to-be-known that can desolate or undermine our self-sufficiency.

And now, it seems, there are things about Philip Larkin that we'll never know. So what? Well, put it like this, the loss can be made to sound not at all what Larkin, as we know him from the poems, would have wholly wished. But then again, who knows? After all, those now-incinerated notebooks might have been full of household accounts or noughts and crosses: the instruction to destroy them a librarian's last, bleakest joke. Throw these away and you are doomed to imagine that my life was not really as boring as I always used to say it was. Having something to hide is generally reckoned to be better than having nothing to show, he might have thought.

There are no explicit instructions in Larkin's will concerning the publication or re-publication of his poems. He seems not to have minded the idea of having his most early work exhumed. Nor did he leave any advice about what ought to happen to the various unfinished pieces he would leave behind. We can assume, therefore, that he must have envisaged a *Collected Poems* rather like the one we've now been given: a volume that adds something like eighty poems to his lifetime's known tally. This is a hefty addition, since the poems we already know him by and most admire total a mere 85. I'm thinking here of the poems collected in *The Less Deceived, The Whitsun Weddings* and *High Windows.* So his 'output' has been almost doubled. (I say 'almost' because *The North Ship,* reprinted 'with considerable hesitation' in 1966 and offered more as a curiosity than to be admired, adds another 30 titles to the list.) What it all boils down to, or up to, is that Larkin the thrifty now has a *Collected Poems* of substantial bulk.

Ought we to think, though, as he generally did not, that adding means increase? Kilograms aside, the plumpened Larkin oeuvre does not carry a great deal of extra weight. On the contrary, a poet whom we value for his sparingness, for not out-putting work that he wasn't 'pretty sure' amounted to the best that he could do, is now to be seen as somewhat cluttered with botch-ups, immaturities and fragments. It's as if this most bachelor of poets had suddenly acquired a slightly messy family life.

Apparently, it could have been messier. Anthony Thwaite has decided not to include various squibs and limericks (these will appear later on in Larkin's *Letters*), and has also ruled against certain of Larkin's unfinished pieces. . . .

Was there not a case, in Larkin's case, for two *Collected* volumes: the first a one-volume reprint of the three grown-up, finished books plus the handful of poems he completed after publishing *High Windows* (these, of course, would include the marvellous **"Aubade"**); the second, a mop-up of juvenilia, fragments, occasional light verse, even limericks and squibs? Thwaite's edition does divide itself in two, with mature Larkin at the front of the book and learner Larkin at the rear, but it makes no other formal separation between the poems Larkin passed for press and those which, for one reason or another, he hadn't wished to see in print.

I find this a bit disconcerting. The beauty of Larkin's three grown-up books, or one of their beauties, is that you can open them at any page and find something that only Larkin could have written. And even his most lightweight pieces are consummately 'finished'—there is nothing slovenly or make-weight or derivative. With this *Collected Poems,* there is an almost fifty-fifty chance that 'any page' will reveal lines which you'd swear could not possibly have sprung from Larkin's pen.

> I declare
> Two lineages electrify the air
> That will like pennons from a mast
> Fly over sleep and life and death
> Till sun is powerless to decoy
> A single seed above the earth:
> Lineage of sorrow; lineage of joy . . .

The next line does not, alas, read: 'Going well so far, eh?' In fact, there are about fifty similarly exalted lines to go before the thing finally deflates:

> Joy has no cause
> Though cut to pieces with a knife,
> Cannot keep silence. What else could magnetise
> Our drudging, hypocritical, ecstatic life?

This poem, entitled **"Many famous feet have trod,"** was written in October 1946, and thus earns its place among the 'mature' work. 1946 is the year in which Anthony Thwaite believes Larkin's 'distinctive voice' can first be heard. So it can, in the poems **"Going"** and **"Wedding Wind,"** which we already know. In the other 1946 poems printed here, we have to strain to pick it up, in odd lines, now and then; and in **"Many famous feet . . . "** I'm afraid I can hear no trace of it at all. Larkin used to chuckle that he of all people had once written a never-published volume called *In the Grip of Light.* I'm inclined to think that the chuckle was intended to cover those 'pennons from a mast', that 'lineage of joy'.

1946 was in fact the year in which Larkin read Thomas Hardy's "Thoughts of Phena" and experienced a literary conversion, 'complete and permanent'. Hardy rescued him from Yeats, just as Yeats—three years earlier—had captured him from Auden. Under the Hardy regime, he was indeed able to find his own distinctive voice, but the

Yeats and Auden periods offer almost nothing in the way of even potential Larkinesque. To peruse the eighty or so pages of juvenilia that are reprinted here is to discover scant line-by-line poetic 'promise'. Anthony Thwaite finds Larkin's Auden poems 'astonishing and precocious' and they are, to be sure, pretty good going for a kid of 17. But they are also fairly stiff and dull, and, because of their enslavement to the icy Master, we have no way of guessing what their author might or might not do should he ever manage to break free: it could be everything or nothing. . . .

The sheer bulk of Larkin's juvenilia might seem irksome when presented as part of a **Collected Poems,** but biographically the bulk does matter quite a lot. This juvenilia period, 1938-46, would be later looked back on as a lost idyll of aliveness and fertility. By the age of 24, Larkin had written two books of poems—*The North Ship* and *In the Grip of Light*—and two novels—*Jill* and *A Girl in Winter.* Three of these books were published, but none of them had made much of a splash. In 1947 and 1948 he seems to have written almost nothing, and when the poetry does start up again in 1949 it is a poetry of failure, loss, rejection. In **"On Being 26,"** the poet regrets the flagging of his 'pristine drive', the withdrawal of 'Talent, felicity', and is bitter about having now to settle for something 'dingier' and 'second best'. . . . Thus burnt-out, and 'clay-thick with misery', the poet falls silent yet again. There is nothing between May 1949 and January 1950. In this month, Larkin's first really spectacular development takes place. In **"At Grass"** the theme is still to do with 'what has pleased and passed', but the subject is thoroughly *out there:* retired racehorses perhaps plagued by memories of erstwhile triumphs. In the next few months, we have **"If, My Darling," "Wants," "No Road,"** and **"Absences."** Within a year, the clay-thick self-pity of 1949 has become lighter, wiser, more sardonic:

> Always too eager for the future, we
> Pick up bad habits of expectancy.
> Something is always approaching; every day
> *Till then* we say.

It's an extraordinary falling-into-place, and the month-by-month dating of the poems gives the whole business a certain narrative excitement: although we will have to wait for Andrew Motion's biography to tell us what happened, or didn't happen, in 1947-8. (p. 3)

Although I have grumbled about Thwaite not separating the unfinished pieces from the finished, there is undeniably a drama in observing that straight after finishing the expansive **"Dockery and Son"** (just in time, one guesses, for it to be included in the **Whitsun Weddings** book), Larkin spent over a year grappling with a longish narrative poem, to be called **"The Dance."** The wish, evidently, was to build on the **"Dockery"** model, to combine narrative relaxation with verse-strictness, but Larkin seems to have discovered that relaxation, for him, usually means a drift towards light verse, or over-surly self-parody—not at all what he wanted for this essentially angry and distressed love poem. . . .

The very awkwardness [of **"The Dance"**] reminds us how many of Larkin's best effects depend upon him sounding both superior *and* vulnerable, unloving and in need of love. It's a difficult balancing-act, breathtaking when it works; when it doesn't, he can veer uneasily between the boorish and the sentimental. **"The Dance"** was, it seems, en route to failure, and Larkin was probably right not to persist with it, but there is a memorable painfulness in watching him trying to wrench this exposed and ambitious poem into shape.

Since **"Aubade"** in 1977, Larkin published only four poems—two rather charming birthday poems (one for Gavin Ewart, the other for Charles Causley), a poem about a dead hedgehog, and a couple of stanzas specially written for a *Poetry Review* special number on poetry and drink. After his death in 1985, a handful of unpublished poems was found. The strongest of these are desperately miserable, indeed inconsolable, as if Larkin had grown weary of trying to fathom 'whatever it is that is doing the damage'. The last poem of any weight was written in 1979 and it isn't easy to read, if you care at all about what happened to this awesome yet companionable poet. But unhappily it does help to explain the six-year silence:

> Love again: wanking at ten past three
> (Surely he's taken her home by now),
> The bedroom hot as a bakery,
> The drink gone dead, without showing how
> To meet tomorrow, and afterwards,
> And the usual pain, like dysentery.
> Someone else feeling her breasts and cunt,
> Someone else drowned in that lash-wide stare,
> And me supposed to be ignorant,
> Or find it funny, or not to care,
> Even . . . but why put it into words?
> Isolate rather this element
>
> That spreads through other lives like a tree
> And sways them on in a sort of sense
> And say why it never worked for me.
> Something to do with violence
> A long way back, and wrong rewards,
> And arrogant eternity.
>
> (pp. 3, 5)

*Ian Hamilton, "Phil the Lark," in* London Review of Books, *Vol. 10, No. 18, October 13, 1988, pp. 3, 5.*

## Blake Morrison

The first surprise of [**Collected Poems**] is that there should be so many poems in it. Though Larkin claimed to like about Hardy what other people dislike—that "he wrote so much"—his own mature output over three volumes was fewer than a hundred poems, and he denied that there were more hiding away ("I hardly ever finish a poem that I don't publish"). Perhaps he never realized how much there was. For though it's true that over fifty of the new poems here must rank as juvenilia, that still leaves nearly eighty new poems, gathered from fugitive publications or appearing for the first time, written after **The North Ship.** It is an unexpectedly full harvest.

Anthony Thwaite has arranged the book chronologically, uncollected work mingling with collected and dates of completion printed under each poem. There are many revelations as a result—one sees how productive certain years were, how certain themes cluster together, and how certain images from abandoned poems were rescued later on—the "lean old leather case" from a poem of 1953, for example, turning up in **"Livings"** eighteen years later. More controversially, Thwaite begins the *Collected* in 1946, with the first "mature" poem **"Going"**, originally called, we now discover, "Dying Day" (a more explicit and diminishing title). All the work up until 1946, including *The North Ship,* is left to the end in a section (again chronologically arranged) called "Early Poems". Some may balk at this but Larkin himself didn't consider *The North Ship* a mature work, and though he allowed it to be reprinted (with a disowning introduction) in 1966 might well, for a *Collected,* have done without this section altogether. It's offered as a sort of scholarly appendix, of interest not in itself but for its prefigurings, its influence markers, and to make you grateful for how miraculously better Larkin was as a poet after 1946.

In the event, the juvenilia prove a good deal more interesting and complicated than that. For one thing, they show Larkin not "developing" but going backwards. After the first few schoolboy poems, routinely Keatsian seasonal evocations identifiably Larkinesque only in their lugubriousness, he hits his stride as early as 1940, at seventeen. There's a scornful little poem called **"Schoolmaster"**, for instance, a sort of "Toads Pre-visited", about a young man happily accepting a life of conformity, the years "stretching like aisles of stone / Before him". And as a more irreverent companionpiece, there's his own farewell to school, **"Last Will and Testament"**, written with Noel Hughes, donating their remains to the Science Sixth "for minute dissection".

Larkin the schoolboy often acts his age: his first shots at imitating Auden remind you that he is fifteen years younger and has a lot to learn. In other poems, though, he achieves a tough, modern, Audenesque tone that seems only, say, five years behind the master. We enter the landscapes of the 1930s—docks, factories, soldiers, strangers, frontiers, permits, "evening like a derelict lorry", "allotments fresh spaded", "the red clubhouse flag", "boring birds / Flying past rocks", "the brilliant freshman with his subtle thought", "the muffled boy, with his compelling badge, / On his serious errand riding to the gorge". The tone and metre seem extraordinarily authoritative, even if the authority is Auden's:

one Spring day his land was violated;
A bunch of horsemen curtly asked his name,
Their leader in a different dialect stated
A war was on for which he was to blame . . .

"Interesting, but futile," said his diary . . .

Only in books the flat and final happens . . .

By the end of 1940, in a poem inspired by the Coventry air-raids, we have moved on a decade. An embittered and self-pitying imagery of war starts up, along with a subject-matter of partings, meetings, lovers waiting on deserted station platforms: a bit more in this vein and Larkin might have begun to sound like Alun Lewis. Of particular interest from this home front period is **"A Stone Church Dam-**

**aged by a Bomb"**, the earliest of Larkin's poems to prefigure one of his major later pieces:

Planted deeper than roots,
This chiselled, flung-up faith
Runs and leaps against the sky . . .

A Dylan Thomas-like rhetoric runs and leaps away with this poem thereafter, but many of its features survive to re-emerge in **"Church Going"** eleven years later: the dead that "lie" around the church, "shapeless in the shapeless earth"; the building's "scatter[ed] magnificence"; above all the image of the church as a "shell"—here "that whispering shell", in 1954 "this special shell", but either way a place hollowed out of (and now hollow of) religious faith.

After 1942 Larkin begins to write the poems that will make up *The North Ship,* frailer, more inward, Yeatsian pieces. You can see why, for a time, he felt pleased by them: there's a consistency of tone which the uncollected work of this period lacks. All the same, it's impossible to read through the seventy poems of 1938-45 without feeling that he could have put together a much stronger volume by keeping half a dozen of the more successful efforts in *The North Ship* and adding to them his Audenesque forays into "the ego's country". Instead, Larkin allowed himself to be what he called "the circumstances' tennisball", batted back and forth between Yeats and Dylan Thomas, as if, in 1945, the neo-Romantic game were the only one worth playing. His first book was a lot more voguishly immature than it need have been.

So, too, the next five years were unhappier—and less productive than they would have been had Larkin had the right kind of publishing encouragement at the start, not the encouragement of R. A. Caton at the Fortune Press. These were the years of *In the Grip of Light,* a "portentous" title, so he said, for a book of poems he was later thankful had been turned down by several publishers. Now that we can at last look at these poems, they seem less portentous than Larkin suggested, if not much better. Between 1946 and January 1950 he wrote just twenty. If he was in the grip of anything, it was darkness: the mood is depressed, and it's not hard to see why. For someone who had two novels and at least seventy poems behind him by the time he was twenty-four, and who might reasonably have looked forward to these next five years as the high-point of his creative life, the lack of productivity and rejection of what productions there were brought about an acute sense of failure; Anthony Thwaite is persuasive when he claims in his introduction that it was fear of a similar rejection, and of dilution of his reputation, that made Larkin wary thereafter of allowing into print any "inferior" piece.

The low-point seems to have been May 1949, when he wrote three different poems on the subject of his depression: a twenty-sixth birthday dirge, which describes how the deftness and talent he once had have disappeared, to be replaced by "ash", "trash", "blackened pride", "second-best" achievement; another, more allegorical piece which finds the ghostly, death-like figure of failure installed "at my elbow like a bore"; and a third, which speaks of "Horror of life", "elbowing vacancy". The death of his father the previous year must have had much to do with this depression: Larkin commemorates him in a minor masterpiece of these years, the simple, moving, **"An April Sunday"**, about his father's prodigious jam-making:

> Five loads—a hundred pounds or more—
> More than enough for all next summer's teas,
>
> Which now you will not sit and eat.
> Behind the glass, under the cellophane, . . .
>
> Remains your final summer—sweet
> And meaningless and not to come again.

The mature Larkin was to re-employ such cadences, but he was too dispirited at this point to recognize that he had struck his true note. Images of disturbance and even derangement proliferate. In March 1950, he testily addresses Kafka after reading some complaint of his about suffering five months' writer's block:

> My dear Kafka,
> When you've had five years of it, not five
>       months,
> Five years of an irresistible force meeting an
> immoveable object right in your belly,
> Then you'll know about depression.

Yet by the time he wrote this Larkin was already coming out of the wilderness. **"If, My Darling"**, written two months later, is a sort of private health warning, a way of saying "my mind's not right", but doing so with humour and grace. It's the first poem in which Larkin shows signs of dramatizing himself: the persona of the mature work—awkward, lonely, bored, fucked up—puts in a fleeting appearance. Once he could wear his defeat like an overcoat, not hide beneath it, Larkin was away.

1950 was his *annus mirabilis*. On the third of January he completed **"At Grass"** and over the next twelve months wrote **"Deceptions"**, **"Coming"**, **"Two Portraits of Sex"**, **"Spring"**, **"If, My Darling"**, **"Wants"**, **"No Road"**, **"Wires"**, and **"Absences"**, as well as ten more poems not collected in *The Less Deceived*. His move to Belfast that year accelerated his development, as **"The Importance of Elsewhere"**, written at the end of his term there, happily concedes. Not that the place itself gets much of a look in: the only other direct description of Belfast occurs in **"The March Past"**, an embryonic example of Larkin-ceremonials in which a "bullying"—Orange?—march provokes "a blind / Astonishing remorse for things now ended". But Belfast did underwrite his existence to the extent of destroying the old (over-writing) poetic persona: from here on there was a new "salt rebuff " to his speech.

1950 is such a decisive turning-point that Anthony Thwaite might have been forgiven for starting the *Collected* there, rather than in 1946. None the less, and though it's the sort of comforting thought Larkin would never have allowed himself, it may be that the *Light* years of 1946-9 were the key ones for his subsequent development: the very abortiveness of the poems leads one to suspect that deeper and more complex feelings are being explored. They also show the inadequacy of Larkin's always suspiciously easy account of his exchange of Yeats for Hardy in 1946; the "Celtic fever", we now see, raged on long after. Larkin's version of his development was, roughly,

that the early poems had nothing to say and were saying it, whereas the later poems leave nothing to be said. But the poem he used to exemplify the transition, **"Waiting for Breakfast"**, is a great deal stranger and messier than his account suggests, as are many of the poems that follow it. This isn't to make the case for Larkin as *symboliste* in pieces like **"Age"** and **"Absences"** so much as to point to those plain-ruminative poems (**"Arrivals, Departures"**, **"Latest Face"** and **"Whatever Happened?"**) that don't, after all, yield up their meaning.

But one thing the new material in the *Collected Poems* does help to establish is how often the knots and blockages in Larkin's work have to do with sex, not always distinguishable in his mind from death. (In one unfinished poem, he portrays death as a rent-collector who, when he reaches the attic where the speaker is cowering, turns out to be a desirable woman instead.) A recurrent figure in the poems is that of the violated girl, who first turns up (appropriately enough) in **"Mythological Introduction"** (1943); from the same period come "a girl dragged by the wrists / Across a dazzling field of snow", lovers "dissolving in the acid of their sex", "the eatings of slight love", "carrion kisses" and a girl in a blizzard who wants to wind her lovers in her hair; a little later (1946) comes a golden-skinned woman "lying on a leaf " who berates her lover for "denying the downlands", for refusing her his body "when all I meant / Was to make it bright, that it might stand / Burnished before my tent".

These images of dazed innocence on the one hand and corrosive sensuality on the other look forward to the violations of **"Deceptions"** and **"Sunny Prestatyn"**. More importantly, they suggest how far an obsessive guilt and fear governed Larkin's attitude to sex, and how, for all the comfortable and confident and often very funny positions he was able eventually to take up, he remained tormented by sex, seeing it as something enclosing and destructive and hostile to artistic ambition. . . .

**"Marriages"** (1951) is characteristically acerbic: while a privileged few, it suggests, marry equally attractive partners, the remainder are "frogmarched by old need": skin-disease shacks up with "soft horror of living", "Adder-faced singularity / Espouses a nailed-up childhood", and so on. From the same year, **"To My Wife"** (truth-telling in all but its title) sees marriage as the closing up of "that peacock fan / The future was" in exchange for something stark, choiceless, verbless: "No future now. I and you now, alone." Four years later there's **"Counting"**, which adds up to fewer than fifty words but needs no more to explain what marriage takes away:

> Thinking in terms of one
> Is easily done—
> One room, one bed, one chair,
> One person there,
> Makes perfect sense; one set
> Of wishes can be met,
> One coffin filled.
>
> But counting up to two
> Is harder to do;
> For one must be denied
> Before it's tried.

Throughout the 1950s this same struggle continues: work, solitude and freedom in conflict with love, sex and marriage—the last a word, along with "wedding", which rings out again and again.

Reasons for the Larkin persona's nonattendance at the altar are legion: he is selfish and would make a bad mate; he hasn't met the person he loves; he seems to be operating in the wrong league, where all the women he meets are too ugly, or principled, or stubborn, or shy; art in any case should come first. The only good couple, he seems to be saying at his gloomiest, is a dead couple, like the earl and countess in **"An Arundel Tomb"**, just as the only real love poems he is able to write are when (as in **"Broadcast"**) the woman is altogether elsewhere. Less crudely, one could say that for Larkin as for Eliot there persisted always "a sense of life lived according to love", "still promising to solve, and satisfy / And set unchangeably in order", and making it impossible for him to settle for anything less than the dreamed-of ideal. The solitudinous alternative to marriage—"the gas and grate, the old cold sour grey bed": words not from **"Mr Bleaney"** but from an unpublished poem of 1962—can't be said to be attractive either, but it has at least a monkish purity, "an integrity of self-hatred".

All this accords well enough with the image we already have of Larkin the undeceived bachelor. What's less expected is the extent to which his poems are only about marriage, as if his chief debt to Hardy were not a tone of voice but a conviction derived from the "Poems of 1912-13" that marriage is *the* poetic subject. Larkin's diverse reflections on marriage seem to blend into one continuous choice poem, or "come and choose wrong" poem, the speaker either dissecting his fear of having made the wrong decision or callowly boasting of how he's got it right. The choice-poem sometimes merges with the comparison-poem, in which Larkin takes an imaginative leap into the lives of the lonely, the uxorious or the ladykilling ("Think of being them!"), measures his own life against theirs, and in the process finds a way to think about himself and his unmarried state. Other, larger matters of freedom, selfishness and destiny come into such self-interrogation but the force of Larkin's obsession is to make you doubt that these matters are other or larger.

It seems surprising that more of these witty and phrase-making pieces weren't ever collected. But it's true also that Larkin was a shrewd critic of himself, and knew when a poem was saying only what another had said better, or, more rarely, when it hadn't yet come to fruition. When **"Vers de Société"** appeared in *High Windows* in 1974, it was taken by some to be a poem about the burdens of high office, the confession of a scowling public man. The foetal version, **"Best Society"** (1951), reveals its origin in an older and deeper quarrel:

> Much better stay in company!
> To love you must have someone else,
> Giving requires a legatee,
> Good neighbours need whole parishfuls
> Of folk to do it on—in short
> Our virtues are all social; if,
> Deprived of solitude, you chafe,
> It's clear you're not the virtuous sort.

> Viciously, then, I lock my door.
> The gas-fire breathes. The wind outside
> Ushers in evening rain. Once more
> Uncontradicting solitude
> Supports me on its giant palm;
> And like a sea-anemone
> Or simple snail, there cautiously
> Unfolds, emerges, what I am.

However locked up inside this particular argument about selfishness, Larkin was sharp enough to see how "phoney" the ending was. Snails and sea anemones? "In a pig's arse, friend." But the poem didn't deserve total abandonment and twenty years later he knew to keep the gas fire and *"Virtue is social"* while also introducing Warlock-Williams and his crowd of craps.

Another poem that didn't deserve abandonment, but suffered it, was **"The Dance"**, worked at for nearly twelve months in 1963-4. "Drink, sex and jazz", it begins, not a bad headline-encapsulation of Larkin's abiding concerns, and until abruptly petering out after twelve stanzas the poem looks set to be one of his major pieces. The elaborately rhymed eleven-line stanzas; the wonderfully snarling humour, visited on everything and everyone from "the faint thudding stridency [of] / some band we have been 'fortunate to secure' " to the "weed from Plant psychology" with his "crazy scheme . . . for making wine from beetroot"—all this is familiar enough. What's more telling and vulnerable is his description of the woman who has brought him out of his shell—her arms bare, her body on the dance-floor suggestive of "A whole consenting language"—and of his own "tense elation" at dancing with her. In the final stanza he stares into her eyes ("hazel, half-shut") and "Something in me starts toppling". But Larkin evidently didn't topple, not enough to resolve the emotional situation which underlies the text and which, resolved, might have allowed him to complete the poem itself. None of the couples in Larkin's poems comes quite so close to coming good.

**"Love Again"** is one of a handful of poems completed after **"Aubade"** in 1977, and it begins with an echo of that majestic poem's second line: rather than "waking at four to soundless dark" the speaker is "wanking at ten past three / (Surely he's taken her home by now?)", tormented not by thoughts of death but by sexual jealousy:

> Someone else feeling her breasts and cunt,
> Someone else drowned in that lash-wide stare,
> And me supposed to be ignorant,
> Or find it funny, or not to care,
> Even . . . but why put it into words?
> Isolate rather this element

> That spreads through other lives like a tree
> And sways them on in a sort of sense
> And say why it never worked for me.
> Something to do with violence
> A long way back, and wrong rewards,
> And arrogant eternity.

No poem of Larkin's displays such fierce sexual possessiveness—fierce enough to make everything in the poem but the brutal clarity of the jealousy itself seem mystifying and even incoherent: what violence? which wrong rewards? whose arrogant eternity? A long way back, thirty years, in fact, stands the corpsefaced undergrad maddened by tits and knickers. His successor has not acquired any greater equanimity, though he has acquired a completely authentic voice and here it speaks with shocking candour. It is Larkin's last great poem and reminds us that he always felt his poems to be much more naive and emotional—"embarrassingly so"—than he was given credit for: the awful way his poems laid him open just never seemed to strike his critics, but he had a proper sense of exposure himself and knew how much he could get away with. He would certainly have felt that he hadn't got away with it here: showing himself to be lonely was one thing, owning up to masturbation quite another. Late Larkin would not have wanted to veer back to late Yeats and crazy old, dirty old man stuff. Silence was preferable.

Unsurprisingly, there are fewer new poems from this last period, post-***High Windows,*** than from the 1950s and 60s. As early as 1971 Larkin had begun to present himself as a burnt-out case, someone who had little else to look forward to: "All that's left to happen / is some deaths (my own included)." His giving up poetry, or (as he preferred to put it) its giving up him, made the years only bleaker, though bleaker still (truly appalling, in fact) was the thought that even the poetry he had written was futile, since the ideas and feelings it expressed "applied only to one man once / And that one dying". The few poems that did get written are never bad, but they usually—as with two delicate love poems written in six weeks between December 1975 and February 1976—give rise to an interest which only biography will satisfy, not literary criticism. Nor do those poems teach us much we didn't know already about Larkin's love of booze and jazz, and that sense of responsibility which made him willing, for all his writer's block, to compose an ode to the Humber Bridge or turn out dutiful birthday tributes to friends. "Smiles are for youth. For old age come / Death's terror and delirium", he writes of **"Heads in the Women's Ward"**, a poem which reminds us how Larkin is, among other things, our great poet of hospitals, recognizing them as the place where you can't pretend any more, where life most cruelly falls short of its ideal. There are hospitals throughout Larkin's work, but too many of them towards the end, as well as aches no medicine can cure. "We should be careful / Of each other, we should be kind / While there is still time", he ends one tender, Roy Fuller-like poem about jamming a hedgehog in his mower. But there isn't much kindness in the late work, and there wasn't much time.

Anthony Thwaite's edition of the poems is fine and scrupulous, but less comprehensive than it might have been: we shall need, soon enough, a scholarly edition of the Complete Poems, not just with notes and variants, but with the squibs, fragments and manuscript poems he has excluded. All the same, what we have should be enough to ensure that Larkin will never again be patronized as a dried-up toad squatting on modernism, but be seen as an original, obsessive, deep-feeling poet who consistently refused the consolations of conventional belief. It is the best kind of posthumous protection a poet could have.

*Blake Morrison, "In the Grip of Darkness," in* The Times Literary Supplement, *No. 4463, October 14-20, 1988, p. 1151.*

**Stephen Spender**

With a poet who was such a discriminating selector of his own best work, the reader may fear that to publish all the poems [in ***Collected Poems***] may lead to a dilution of the effect made by the best. This does not happen with Larkin because the contrast between his successes and his failures is self-evident. The failures simply fall away, leaving the successes clear. Among the successes are some poems which remained unpublished because they were unfinished. Outstanding among these is **"The Dance,"** describing the poet going to a dance because a girl he fancied was also going there: and the embarrassments, interruptions, 'indecisions and revisions' of that evening. It is a poem with curious parallels (presumably conscious) with Eliot's "Prufrock."

> Suddenly it strikes me you are acting more
> Than ever you would put in words: I feel
> The impact, open, raw,
> Of a tremendous answer banging back
>
> As if I'd asked a question.

Taken as a whole the ***Collected Poems*** adds up to a self-portrait of the artist—done in the Dutch manner—of Larkin in an interior surrounded by books and notebooks and with a window in the wall behind him through which can be seen a seascape with ships and wharfs outside. HULL! I seem to remember a photograph of Larkin (was it on television?) with his back to the camera so that the viewer could not see his face. Certain of the poems suggest that, turned away from the reader, he is looking at himself and his surroundings in a concealed mirror. He sees his own image in cold tones, with little colour, and in negative terms (what he isn't, what he doesn't do, where he doesn't live, the wife he doesn't marry)—not without a certain self-disparaging narcissism, (Auden: 'Narcissus doesn't fall in love with his reflection because it is beautiful but because it is his'), a touch of self-congratulation that he is not as his contemporaries are (his immediate contemporaries—in his poems he is very conscious of being of his own generation.)

In **"Dockery and Son"** the poet distinguishes his own life sharply from that of Dockery, his scarcely-acquainted-with near-contemporary of college days 20 years before, who, as he learns, married at the age of 19 and now has a son going to the same college:

> Dockery, now:
> Only nineteen he must have taken stock
> Of what he wanted, and been capable
> Of . . . No, that's not the difference: rather, how
>
> Convinced he was he should be added to!
> Why did he think adding meant increase?
> To me it was dilution.

There are two angles from which the reader may view Larkin's self-portrait—those from which, also, he seems to view himself. From one angle, he is seen as a neurotic failure in terms of 'life' and personal success: lonely, sexually inhibited, without family or acquisitions, consoling himself with the thought that other men's worldly values and achievements are delusions, the truth being that

Life is first boredom, then fear
Whether or not we use it, it goes.
And leaves what something hidden from us
    chose,
And age, and then the only end of age.

From the second angle, the poet is seen as choosing to be solitary, not harbouring the 'innate assumptions' about life of which Dockery's fathering a son at the age of 19 is an example. The subject of this second self-portrait observes others with a freshness and truth of a vision recalling Tolstoy's *Childhood, Boyhood and Youth.* He assembles and orders these observations in poems so architecturally constructed that they seem like homes, nests, outposts of solitude he inhabits: satisfactory to himself; and from whose one or two bare bookish rooms, he looks quite triumphantly down at the little comedies of other lives, sometimes mocking, . . . sometimes sniggering. . . . (p. 40)

Yet Larkin, the outsider among his contemporaries and the inhabiter of his vocation, is not, as he well might be, an aesthete, regarding his art as proof of his superiority to others who are not artists. Poetry is not for him an ivory tower from which he excludes others. It is, rather, those others, the 'seekers after happiness' who exclude the poet from their world of much-advertised values. There is in his work the frustrated sense of a community in which the values of poetry could be shared. Sometimes this bursts through as a lived vision: for example of the marriages, in **"The Whitsun Weddings"**:

Free at last,
And loaded with the sum of all they saw,
We hurried towards London, shuffling gouts of
    steam.
Now fields were building-plots, and poplars cast
Long shadows over major roads, and for
Some fifty minutes, that in time would seem
Just long enough to settle hats and say *I nearly
    died,*

A dozen marriages got under way.

And in **"Show Saturday,"** a description of some kind of fair or meet in the countryside where dogs, ponies, wrestlers, people selling things and children are seen in a setting of tents and beer-marquees, exhilaration takes over in a public exaltation of living. The poem ends with the poet's approval of this traditional parade as communal life surviving from the past.

something they share
That breaks ancestrally each year into
Regenerate union. Let it always be there.

The poet and his success-seeking contemporaries cannot escape having in common the prospect of death and the need for love; though the poet characteristically experiences love as his feelings about the girl who marries someone else. He finds evidence of love surviving from the past into our present time in the stone tomb of an earl and his countess in a church in Arundel where 'One sees, with a sharp tender shock, / His hand withdrawn holding her hand.' The poem concludes, wryly but movingly:

Time has transfigured them into

Untruth. The stone fidelity
They hardly meant has come to be
Their final blazon, and to prove
Our almost-instinct almost true:
What will survive of us is love.

Larkin's self-portrait is of the poet who finds himself the isolated heir to a tradition and a vocation eroded by the circumstances of modern life. Earlier in the present century, in a similar situation, Rainer Maria Rilke invented in the *Duino Elegies* what was, in effect, a private religion of the poetic imagination with its machinery of angels towering over an industrial landscape and transforming materialist conditions into spiritual values. In similar circumstances, Eliot and Auden bolstered up their poetry with the theology of the Anglican Church. Larkin does not accept any such system of beliefs external to his poetry, or put there for the purpose of providing it with a theology or philosophy.

In certain poems—his best ones—Larkin's genius is to extract from places the quintessential characteristics belonging to the past that make them numinous and to realise them in language that is idiomatically modern, shifting often from the conversational to the deeply serious. **"Church Going,"** rightly considered his masterpiece, brings together, almost as a single identity, the poet as a touristic visitor to the church, 'bored, uninformed, knowing the ghostly silt / Dispersed', and the reader, but locates and intensifies for the reader feelings of which he is only vaguely conscious. The word 'representative' seems here significant. As poet, Larkin, totally dedicated though he is—and contemptuous of today's 'seekers after happiness'—is nevertheless not the superior aesthete or intellectual. He is the 'representative of those bored and uninformed,' who vaguely feel what he piercingly identifies.

A serious house on serious earth it is
In whose blent air all our compulsions meet,
Are recognised and robed as destinies.

The sadness pervading many of the poems derives from the poet's sense that the past monuments and the English countryside are spiritual capital running out, overwhelmed physically by the spread of the modern urban world and, spiritually, by everything that can be summed up by the word 'advertising'. A question lingers in the mind after one has read them. Does not Larkin underestimate the value of living, being alive, of life itself? There is a widely shared opinion among many people—including some of the greatest poets of the present century, most notably Yeats—that even if it is tragic, poetry should not be depressive. It should 'show an affirming flame' (Auden).

In a few poems (some of which are love poems) Larkin does this, but they are exceptional sorties into happiness. It is the self-portrait—Larkin himself in his poems—which conveys the depressiveness (much as happens in the case of Thomas Hardy.)

In a wonderful unpublished poem about the sun, called **"Solar,"** and in the concluding stanza of **"High Windows,"** Larkin seems to look beyond the earth and the earth's atmosphere to outer space, uninhabited by God or man, for exhilaration:

Rather than words comes the thought of high
  windows:
The sun-comprehending glass,
And beyond it, the deep blue air, that shows
Nothing, and is nowhere, and is endless.

(pp. 40-1)

*Stephen Spender, "Self-Portrait in the Dutch
Manner," in* The Spectator, *Vol. 261, No.
8366, November 12, 1988, pp. 40-1.*

## Robert Richman

The *Collected Poems* of Philip Larkin brings together
what may be the most important body of poetry written
in the post-World War II period. The size of the volume
comes as something of a surprise, however. Larkin, who
died in 1985 at the age of sixty-three, published four slender books in his lifetime (the longest was forty-eight
pages). . . . Anthony Thwaite, the editor of the *Collected
Poems* and one of the executors of Larkin's estate, has
brought forth a volume containing 242 poems—172 in a
first section ("Poems 1946-83") containing all of what
Thwaite considers Larkin's mature work (omitting, aston-
ishingly, *The North Ship*) and seventy poems in a second
section ("Early Poems 1938-45"). This latter section contains, in addition to *The North Ship,* twenty-two previously unpublished poems; the book's first section, meanwhile,
contains sixty-one poems in print for the first time. Both
sections have poems from *In the Grip of Light,* a volume
Larkin tried, and failed, to publish in 1947. All of the
"new" poems—which have been retrieved from Larkin's notebooks and typescripts—have been arranged
chronologically in the book's two sections along with the
previously published material, both collected and uncollected. As it turns out, these added poems do not really
enhance what one might legitimately refer to as Larkin's
real oeuvre. Most of the rejected poems—and this is what
they must be called, as Larkin considered them unfit to
publish or collect in his lifetime—should really have been
consigned to an appendix.

Not everything about Thwaite's edition is so muddled, of
course. Dates of composition have been provided; these,
along with the chronological arrangement of the poems,
permit the reader to follow more closely the ups and
downs of Larkin's career. Thus, we can see how the brilliant **"At Grass,"** which was completed on January 3,
1950, emerged phoenix-like from a long period of uncertainty, and seemed to be the catalyst for a quick succession
of marvels, all written in the following year: **"Deceptions," "Coming," "If, My Darling," "Wants," "Absences," "Spring," "No Road,"** and a number of others.
From the perspective afforded by this book, good poems
often seem to be the greatest inspiration for more good
poems. Any biographer of Larkin who would locate the
sources of poetic inspiration primarily in external events
might bear this in mind.

Thwaite's additions also confirm the prevailing view of
Larkin as our late Prince of Despair. The new poems are
like versions of the Larkin we all know. Though less interesting and often less technically accomplished, they show
us that the poet's description of himself from a 1979 inter-

view—"Deprivation is for me what daffodils were for
Wordsworth"—was no exaggeration. (pp. 5-6)

Not the least interesting thing about Larkin's poetry is
how many different forms his bleakness took. He wrote of
solitude: "the dining-room declares / A larger loneliness"
(**"Friday Night in the Royal Station Hotel"**). Existential
dread was a favorite theme: "the solving emptiness / That
lies just under all we do" (**"Ambulances"**). Old age was an
obsession: "Why aren't they screaming?" the poet asks of
**"The Old Fools."** He also wrote about his own mortality:
"Unresting death / One whole day nearer now" (**"Aubade"**), as well as about the death of others ("All know
they are going to die. / Not yet, perhaps not here, but in
the end, / And somewhere like this" (**"The Building"**).
There is the anguish of calamities (in **"The Explosion,"**
about a mining disaster); rape (**"Deceptions"**); and work
(**"Toads"**). Even nature is perceived to be full of woe:
"[t]heir greenness," Larkin writes about **"The Trees,"** "is
a kind of grief." His verse teems with the bitterness of false
hope. In **"Home is So Sad,"** Larkin complains how home
began as "A joyous shot at how things ought to be, / Long
fallen wide"; in **"A Study of Reading Habits,"** literature
is exposed as humbug. In **"I Remember, I Remember,"**
nostalgia itself is revealed to be nothing more than a nostalgic lie.

There was much that made Larkin despondent in the
world of middle-class England as well: he was a magnet
to the iron filings of vulgarity in contemporary life. In
**"Going, Going,"** for example, he deplores "the bleak high-
risers," "[m]ore houses . . . more parking," and grimly
predicts that "All that remains / For us will be concrete
and tyres." In **"The Whitsun Weddings,"** the poet's eye is
drawn to the "fathers with broad belts under their
suits . . . mothers loud and fat; / An uncle shouting
smut." In **"Here,"** Larkin takes note of the "cut-price
crowd," and in **"Arrivals, Departures,"** Larkin's "traveller"—unlike the one, for example, in William Blake's
"Ah! Sun-flower"—carries a sample case.

It was perhaps inevitable that Larkin's ardent pursuit of
despair should lead to himself. In **"Dockery and Son,"** a
poignant account of a visit to his old college, Larkin learns
from the Dean that Dockery, who was at school with the
poet, has a son enrolled there. Dockery was "[c]onvinced
he . . . should be added to!" and this startles the bachelor
poet. "Why did he think adding meant increase? / To me
it was dilution." This is a confession not just of Larkin's
reluctance to make the requisite sacrifices for family life—
*There's not enough of me to go around*—but of his insecurity as well: *I think so little of myself, why should I create
more littleness?*

**"Dockery and Son"** may not fully persuade us of Larkin's
uncertain self-esteem; but about his distaste for modernity
there can be no doubt. Even skeptics of psychology will
have difficulty disputing the notion that much of Larkin's
querulousness about the modern world—its people, its
ways, its art—stemmed from an uneasiness about his own
place in it. This characterization is not meant to deprecate
Larkin as a man or artist: far from it. But it can't be denied
that there was much discontent in the poet's character.
His often expressed distaste for cheap suits, highways,

"perms," the libidinous, ignorant younger generation, and marriage and children provides ample evidence. Larkin once remarked in an interview that "children are very horrible, aren't they? Selfish, noisy, cruel, vulgar little brutes"—as if this were all there was to it.

Larkin's inclination to disparagement can also be seen in **"Self 's the Man."** This poem begins with an affirmation of the big-heartedness of a married man named "Arnold," but quickly shifts to become a revelation of the subject's essential selfishness. (pp. 6-7)

Some critics have attempted to disarm Larkin's bleakness by attributing it to an invented persona. A recent example is Grey Gowrie's review of Larkin's **Collected Poems** in the October 15, 1988 edition of the *Weekend Telegraph.*

> Larkin himself was not the bored, uninformed, emblematically cycleclipped representative of a provincial culture," wrote Gowrie. The "role . . . [is a] literary creation. . . . Indeed, the making of fictions and the use of fictional techniques are insufficiently considered by critics of poetry, too quick to assume poems strip bare where novels dress up.

In the case of certain poets, questioning the validity of a poem's "I" is sound critical practice. With Larkin, however, it's a mistake. Obviously, it's impossible to say precisely how disaffected Larkin was. Yet, speaking as someone who believes that poetry often traffics in fictional scenarios, I have to think that Larkin himself possessed the powerful tendency for discontentment that is expressed in his poetry. The proof is in the prose writings, interviews, and Larkin's own statement that he always tried "to avoid [a] false relation between art and life. . . . I think that one of the great criticisms of poets of the past is that they said one thing and did another. . . . "

It is important to highlight the authenticity of this disaffected self, because doing so makes Larkin's heroic attempts to overcome his hardheartedness that much more affecting. Dismissing Larkin's irascible side has another negative effect: it divests his poetry of the element that constitutes its greatest appeal. When Larkin aired his misanthropy, it struck a chord in those of us for whom the easiest response to a confusing world is to assail it. Larkin's embodiment of the pandemic impulse to speak and act out of fear and weakness, rather than from confidence and strength, is one reason why his poetry has achieved such a remarkable popularity. It is also one of the reasons why his verse is probably more fully representative of the postwar era than that of any other poet.

One of Larkin's chief aims as a poet, certainly, was to render his bleak outlook as plainly as possible. To this end, he purged many of his lines of imagery. The idea was that no aesthetic cushion (except humor, of which there is a good amount in Larkin) should ease the pain. This pictorial stinginess, and its accompanying gloomy realism, are the chief traits of the English poetic group known as the Movement, which emerged in the Fifties and of which Larkin was considered to be a leading member. In the introduction to the first Movement anthology, *New Lines* (1956), Robert Conquest, the book's editor, wrote that George Orwell was the most decisive influence on the

poets in this group. These included Donald Davie, John Wain, D. J. Enright, Thom Gunn, and Elizabeth Jennings. Claiming a novelist, critic, and political commentator as a poetic inspiration cast the Movement poets in an unpoetic light from the very start. But this was their wish: to deal with ordinary experience in "new lines" of prosaic language untainted by idealism and mysticism (qualities they associated with the romantic rhetoric of Dylan Thomas), allusion and ambiguity (techniques they rejected in Eliot and Pound), or most forms of poetic lyricism. Blake Morrison, the Movement's historian [see *The Movement: English Poetry and Fiction of the 1950s*], has written that its writers were devoted to the principles of "rationalism, realism, and empiricism."

Empiricism is the key word in considering the Movement poets. The term is linked to the philosophical school of logical positivism, which in its simplest definition—from *Webster's Ninth Collegiate Dictionary*—holds that "all meaningful statements are either analytic or conclusively verifiable or at least confirmable by observation and experiment and that metaphysical theories are therefore strictly meaningless." This describes, to a large degree, the philosophical position of the Movement poets.

A form of the word "empirical" turns up once in Larkin's oeuvre. In **"Lines on a Young Lady's Photograph Album,"** from *The Less Deceived,* the poet wrote:

> But o, photography! as no art is,
> Faithful and disappointing! that records
> Dull days as dull, and hold-it smiles as frauds,
> And will not censor blemishes
> Like washing-lines, and Hall's-Distemper
>     boards,
>
> But shows the cat as disinclined, and shades
> A chin as doubled when it is, what grace
> Your candor thus confers upon her face!
> How overwhelmingly persuades
> That this is a real girl in a real place,
>
> In every sense empirically true!

"In every sense empirically true!" does characterize a good deal of Larkin's best verse. One thinks, for example, of **"Aubade,"** a marvelous late poem in which the poet wondered, with a fervently logical and empirical completeness, "how / And where and when I shall myself die." Yet in **"Lines on a Young Lady's Photograph Album,"** Larkin claims that photography, not poetry, is the "[f]aithful and disappointing" art. This seems to suggest that poetry is capable of something more than the unrevised rendering of reality found in a typical photograph, or in an ordinary Movement poem.

The equivocal attitude toward the Movement aesthetic implied in **"Lines on a Young Lady's Photograph Album"** was not unprecedented. Earlier in his career, Larkin had written a more metaphorically lavish and openly hopeful kind of poetry than the bulk of what he produced during his Movement phase. Larkin's first book, *The North Ship,* published in 1945, when the poet was just twenty-three, showed the influence of Yeats, whom Larkin later spurned. The second of the book's thirty-two poems started off like this:

This was your place of birth, this daytime
   palace,
This miracle of glass, whose every hall
The light as music fills, and on your face
Shines petal-soft; sunbeams are prodigal
To show you pausing at a picture's edge. . . .

To focus on a face flattered by "petal-soft" beams of light and not—as in the typical poem of Larkin's maturity—on a scene distorted by the ugly lights of a hotel corridor; to write of a palace rather than of fish docks or dirty canals; to honor one's place of birth rather than attend to scenes of death; to celebrate a miracle, rather than bemoan a disaster—this was the youthful, pre-Movement Larkin. In the poems of **The North Ship,** the poet improved the drab hues of reality instead of mirroring them, and the results were remarkably good.

A few years later, however, Larkin radically altered his views, or so it seemed. In **"Deceptions,"** from **The Less Deceived** (the book that followed **The North Ship**), Larkin claimed to be no longer fooled by illusions, poetic and otherwise, and derided those who sought "fulfilment's desolate attic." When **The North Ship** was reissued in 1966, Larkin affirmed in the introduction that his youthful "Celtic fever" had long since abated and the Romantic in him was "sleeping soundly." What repudiated his early poetry most, though, were the lines of conclusively verifiable statements, untouched by any glimmer of transcendence.

The truth is, even during his Movement stage, Larkin was writing poems that went very much against the grain of Movement verse. Nevertheless, it was the Movement side of Larkin that caught the attention of readers and critics in England and America. Indeed, when Larkin started getting the attention of the major literary periodicals in the United States during the late Fifties and early Sixties, he was presented by critics such as A. Alvarez and M. L. Rosenthal as a dejected confessional poet—someone, that is, very much in the mold of Robert Lowell, who was then the commanding presence on the poetry scene. To be sure, the Movement-Larkin and the confessional writers did share a predilection for gloominess and the honest baring of it in poetry. But too many of Larkin's poems overstepped the narrow boundaries of both Movement and confessional verse for him to be comfortably placed in either group.

It should be noted, in any case, that the poems that do adhere more or less to Movement aesthetic principles are much better than most of those by other Movement poets. There are phrases and lines in Larkin that are unimaginable in, say, Kingsley Amis or Elizabeth Jennings. . . . ["Dockery and Son"] is composed entirely of standard Movement materials: anti-metaphorical language, bleak subject matter, and a distrust of any redeeming metaphysics. Yet in its overall effect the poem escapes these narrow aesthetic confines. Little in postwar English poetry is as memorable as Larkin's middle-aged ruminations on bachelorhood. . . . (pp. 7-9)

Clearly, no miracle or transcendent flash saved the poet from his fate; hence the Movement virtue of Orwellian realism is perfectly realized. The detached, empirical assessment in **"Dockery and Son"** is just right for the poet's emotion—an emotion Larkin remarked as having arisen from "one of those tremendous jolts life gives you sometimes, when you see what's been happening to you, and how powerless you are to do anything about it."

Even the poetry of the Movement phase that does not reach such heights is distinguished by a perceptive mastery and by vibrant language and metrical interest. Indeed, Larkin integrated metrical form and contemporary speech more successfully than any other poet of our time. So much of Larkin's poetry seems on first reading to be ordinary speech duly transcribed; yet there is scarcely a line that doesn't scan: "Not quite your class, I'd say, dear, on the whole"; "Canals with floatings of industrial froth"; "Approached with acres of dismantled cars"; "Naturally the Foundation Will Bear Your Expenses." What these lines show is that contemporary speech and time-honored poetic forms need not diverge. Not the least important aspect of Larkin's achievement was his sifting through the slag-heap of postwar English for such lines that merge successfully the past and the present. One can imagine Larkin pacing the floor of his Hull flat, hitting on one of these gems, eyes aglow, smiling slightly, muttering to himself (in perfect iambic tetrameter): "Mm. Well. Eureka, I suppose."

As beautifully written and on the mark as many of Larkin's Movement poems were, however, there were some experiences they could not do justice to. Larkin knew this, and willingly abandoned the Movement attitude when it no longer suited his material. Thus, in a few poems, he evoked transcendent emotions with images that Seamus Heaney has referred to as "visionary" [see Heaney's essay, "The Main of Light," in *Larkin at Sixty,* edited by Anthony Thwaite; Faber and Faber, 1982]. In these poems—Heaney cites **"Livings," "Water,"** and **"Solar"**—the poet can be seen, in Heaney's words, "repining for a more crystalline reality" beyond the mundane rationality that governed Larkin's customary outlook. Heaney believes—and this runs contrary to what many of Larkin's critics have claimed—that the poet never entirely disowned the Symbolist and Yeatsian aesthetic of **The North Ship.**

What's interesting about **"Solar"** is that its Symbolist-inspired language is used to invoke the kind of hopefulness we do not normally associate with Larkin. . . . (pp. 9-10)

[The] evocation of the sun is totally devoid of the corrosive irony Larkin usually reserved for such objects, and thus illustrates how intent the poet was in rummaging around in "fulfilment's desolate attic." **"Solar"** suggests something else, too. To place the poem next to **"Self's the Man"** is to see how uninterested Larkin was in reconciling the oppositions within his poetry, and in himself. This was no failing; it is a testimony to his courage. Resolving these antagonisms would have meant the denial of an important aspect of Larkin's complex spirit. Larkin's reluctance to temper his clashing experiences for the sake of aesthetic conformity is one more reason his poetry will survive.

Some poems take this division of feeling as their subject. In **"Days,"** for instance, the question posed by the childishly naïve, empirical-Larkin in the first stanza ("Where can we live but days?") is answered by the disturbing image in the second stanza. This image seems to come straight from the dream side of life—a side of life the speaker of the first stanza, one senses, can't comprehend:

> What are days for?
> Days are where we live.
> They come, they wake us
> Time and time over.
> They are to be happy in:
> Where can we live but days?
>
> Ah, solving that question
> Brings the priest and the doctor
> In their long coats
> Running over the fields.

**"High Windows,"** the title poem of Larkin's last book, also has a divided feeling. The first three of the poem's four stanzas consist of the caustic observations of the hidebound Larkin regarding the sexual freedom of the young. Larkin noted with dismay that the "[b]onds and gestures" that inhibited him when he was young have been callously "pushed to one side / Like an outdated combine harvester." However, in the last stanza, there is a mammoth shift in perspective. An entirely different Larkin—one who obviously doesn't believe, as the empiricists do, that meaningful statements must be conclusively verifiable—declares that

> Rather than words comes the thought of high
>   windows:
> The sun-comprehending glass,
> And beyond it, the deep blue air, that shows
> Nothing, and is nowhere, and is endless.

The high windows one assumed, before reading the poem, to be metaphors for an older, better world, turn out to be portals to a void that makes discussions of taste and sexual habits seem beside the point. Embracing both the trivially mundane and the spiritually momentous, **"High Windows"** provides a fuller and more comprehensive image of Larkin's shifting, provisional self. (pp. 10-11)

A similar division of emotion is found in what have been referred to as the advertising poems in *The Whitsun Weddings.* **"Sunny Prestatyn,"** about a travel poster defaced by a vandal; **"Essential Beauty,"** a condemnation of billboards that "cover slums with praise / Of motor-oil and cuts of salmon"; and **"The Large Cool Store,"** a criticism of how our "young unreal wishes" are heartlessly exploited by a store's clothing displays, have been viewed by many critics as further evidence of Larkin's desire to malign anything that attempts to propose, as he wrote in **"Essential Beauty,"** "how life should be." The fact is, however, that there is nothing in them to sully the cause of illusions in these poems. Few of us, after all, are taken in by advertising; so how effective is Larkin's use of it as a metaphor to attack illusion? Not very, I suspect.

Although **"Solar," "Days,"** and the advertising poems ameliorate the image of an unrelentingly disillusioned Larkin, none of them is among Larkin's finest poems. (p. 11)

The struggle that raged in the poet between his hopeful and unhopeful selves had been better examined in three earlier poems. **"Church Going," "The Whitsun Weddings,"** and **"At Grass":** for me, these are the three greatest poems of Larkin's career. What distinguishes them from an excellent but somewhat lesser poem like **"High Windows"** is the more modulated and tentative shift from one realm of feeling to another. It was the kind of subtle shift Larkin evidently grew less and less capable of in his later years.

The voice with which **"Church Going"** begins is that of the bored atheist, to whom the empty church he visits is a baffling, rather absurd monument. . . . (p. 12)

Yet five stanzas later, at the end of the poem, Larkin acknowledges an acceptance not of religious faith but of the stirrings of spiritual seriousness in him that his excursions to the church induced:

> For, though I've no idea
> What this accoutred frowsty barn is worth,
> It pleases me to stand in silence here;
>
> A serious house on serious earth it is,
> In whose blent air all our compulsions meet,
> Are recognised, and robed as destinies.
> And that much never can be obsolete,
> Since someone will forever be surprising
> A hunger in himself to be more serious,
> And gravitating with it to this ground,
> Which, he once heard, was proper to grow wise
>   in,
> If only that so many dead lie round.

This isn't the kind of explosive affirmation we find in **"Solar";** yet in its very guardedness there is a greater emotional force. Larkin's language mirrors the poem's shift in view. The two metaphors—the "hunger . . . to be more serious" and the feeling of "gravitating" to the ground of the Church—reflect Larkin's new approval of forces and motivations beyond the area of rational choice. And the astonishing line, "In whose blent air all our compulsions meet"—unlike anything preceding it in Larkin's poetry up to this point—suggests, in its luminousness, the new imaginative terrain Larkin was beginning to explore in this final stanza of **"Church Going."**

In **"The Whitsun Weddings,"** the cautious move to generosity from despair is also prompted by an unexpected event: a wedding. This poem begins with the poet observing a suburban landscape from a train, focusing, typically, on the countryside's ugliest features: "the backs of houses," a "nondescript" town, and "acres of dismantled cars."

When a wedding party comes into view, it is the "girls / In parodies of fashion" Larkin first sees. However, by poem's end, he has learned to appreciate, even share, the emotions of the wedding party. Thus, **"The Whitsun Weddings"** re-enacts metaphorically the drama played out in **"Church Going"** and **"High Windows."** In the latter poem, Larkin's contemplation of the infinite emerged from the most mundane concerns. In **"Church Going,"** a form of faith arose from the worst sort of spiritual passivity. In **"The Whitsun Weddings,"** an emotional involvement in the wedding springs from the poet's bachelorhood. What all these poems seem to suggest is, beware of certainty, which itself may be an illusion.

Actually, **"The Whitsun Weddings"** deals with two weddings: the one between bride and groom, and the one between the poet and the event. Each had its own offspring: in the case of the marriage, children; in the case of Larkin, the poem. Each act is seen to represent a diminution of the miracle-denying empiricist. The poem's two weddings are a coincidence, perhaps. But the image of a fertile rain at the poem's end certainly is no chance event. . . . (pp. 12-13)

The "arrow-shower" of imaginative strength, "sent out of sight"—i.e., beyond the empiricist's view—is portrayed as vigorous enough to pull free of the evertightening "brakes" of the poet's intelligence.

At first glance, **"At Grass"**—which takes as its subject the former glory of two retired race horses—appears to be an occasion for another typically bleak Larkinesque meditation on the ravages of time. But the sense of gloom and decay with which the poem opens gives way to its opposite. (p. 13)

As in **"Church Going"** and **"The Whitsun Weddings,"** it seems as if the poet woke up that day yearning for something to confirm his despair; once again, he was surprised by hope. The line "They gallop for what must be joy" is another statement of faith in the possibility of joy; but also an expression of self-criticism and humility.

Interestingly, Larkin's Movement outlook is presented here, as in **"The Whitsun Weddings,"** as a threat. The bridles that the groom and groom's boy bring out in the final stanza—is this a metaphor for the empirical-Larkin's desire to censor all hope? I believe it is. In beautifully depicting Larkin's internal struggle, and in acknowledging the possibility of secular faith in a godless world, **"At Grass"** may be Larkin's single greatest poem. (pp. 13-14)

Larkin's best poems suggest that despair may contain the seeds of hope, and that even the bleakest landscape may contain something worth praising. To overlook this central point of Larkin's verse is to make him merely the despairing spokesman for a dreary age. His work attains its distinction, in part, by resisting the idea that the human spirit can be explained purely by means of logical analysis and facts—and, by extension, psychological, historical, and sociological models. In showing the poetic imagination's ability to resist these powerful adversaries, Larkin left an important poetic legacy.

To locate this legacy the reader will have to learn to read through the many failed poems (in Larkin's eyes as well as ours) that encumber the *Collected Poems.* Yet even in a partly bungled edition it is hard not to come to the conclusion that Larkin's poetic achievement may very well be the greatest of our time. (p. 14)

> Robert Richman, "The 'Collected' Philip Larkin," in The New Criterion, *Vol. VII, No. 8, April, 1989, pp. 5-14.*

**Howard Nemerov**

Since first coming to know Philip Larkin's work, I have wished there might be more of it—how few poets there are of whom one could wish that—and now [in *Collected Poems*], by the affectionately devoted and studious editorship of his friend and executor, the poet Anthony Thwaite, there is more of it, abundantly more, almost doubling what the poet published in about a book a decade during his productive and too short life.

The books were *The North Ship* (1945), *The Less Deceived* (1955), *The Whitsun Weddings* (1964), and *High Windows* (1974). They include a very fair share of the finest and most moving poems of this age and, indeed, former ages. For a short list of my favorites: **"Deceptions," "Church Going," "Sunny Prestatyn," "High Windows," "The Old Fools,"** and, for me best of all, if a choice must be made, **"Vers de Société."**

The last named may be idiosyncratic to myself, the others being included in most everyone's short list; but it deals decisively and at an elegant distance with one of the big themes, the debate between ourselves as social and sociable beings and each self as a prisoner in his solitude. The speaker of the poem has just got an invitation to a party, a party of the sort that Shakespeare's Apemantus characterized definitively before the cocktail party came: "Such a serving-forth of becks and jutting-out of bums." The speaker offers an interpretive reading of what the invitation said and what it meant. It goes:

> My wife and I have asked a crowd of craps
> To come and waste their time and ours; perhaps
> You'd care to join us?

to which the immediate response is: "In a pig's arse, friend."

But outside the window night is falling, time is passing, old age is coming on within; and solitude (good) is becoming loneliness (bad), so that after some stanzas of debate the new response will likely be: *"Dear Warlock-Williams: Why, of course—"* Warlock-Williams being not only the name of the host but also one of those oddly right inventions, British as could be, that so characterize Larkin's fastidious and acerb manner. (pp. 1, 11)

Larkin is the poet of failure, unhappiness, even despair. Doubtless all poets, life and the world being what they are, might be thought to be so, but by no means in Larkin's degree. If Auden gave a title to the Age of Anxiety, Larkin may be thought to have defined the Age of Disappointment. The scene of his work, both the old and the newly accessible, is a generally unrelieved landscape of hopeless futility, and it is one of the last mysteries of art that while thus acknowledging, and even rubbing our noses in, the misery of our human situation between the this and the that, a poet can convey to us so strong a sense of humor, charm, and delight. And this Larkin does, giving to the common disappointment of our lives its lonely voice. As another poet has said of him:

> *He was our modern; in his attitude,*
> And not in all that crap about free verse.
> He understood us, not as we would be

Understood in smartass critical remarks,
But as we are when we stand in our shoes and
    say.

(p. 11)

*Howard Nemerov, "Philip Larkin: Facing Life without Illusions," in* Book World—The Washington Post, *May 7, 1989, pp. 1, 11.*

## Derek Walcott

The average face, the average voice, the average life—that is, the life most of us lead, apart from film stars and dictators—had never been defined so precisely in English poetry until Philip Larkin. He invented a muse: her name was Mediocrity. She was the muse of the diurnal, of habit, of repetition. She lived in life itself, not as a figure beyond it, a phantom of yearning, but as the plain, transparent companion of a confirmed benedict.

"Benedict" seems better than "bachelor" when we think of Larkin because of the word's monkish associations, suggesting his medieval patience in waiting for the right phrase to come, as well as what seemed to his readers to be a willful self-immolation as a librarian in Hull—since nothing sounds more ordinary, more mediocre than that. Increasingly silent as his last years passed, he seemed pleased to encourage this image of himself—Larkin the librarian, a bookworm smothering itself in a silken silence. Obviously, if Hull was all there was to life, if work was a cold toad that squatted on his heart, and if excitement and enthusiasm were dismissed as suspicious spasms, we were not to expect anything more radiant than this poem, as brief and frighteningly funny in its Keystone Cop ending as its topic:

> What are days for?
> Days are where we live.
> They come, they wake us
> Time and time over.
> They are to be happy in.

"They are to be happy in." God as a nanny, God as a schoolmaster, a parson, a constable:

> Where can we live but days?
>
> Ah, solving that question
> Brings the priest and the doctor
> In their long coats
> Running over the fields.
>
>                     **("Days")**

And this:

> For nations vague as weed,
> For nomads among stones,
> Small-statured cross-faced tribes
> And cobble-close families
> In mill-towns on dark mornings
> Life is slow dying.
>
>            **("Nothing To Be Said")**

A shudder and a nod from the reader. Is this catharsis? Spiritual redemption? You mean that's it?

If so, then what is it in Larkin that has made his [*Collected Poems*] a best seller in Great Britain? Thirty-five thousand copies two months after publication last autumn. As the shade of a popular hermit, Larkin might say, bemused by the irony that nothing sells writing better than the writer's death, that there is a small fortune to be made in conspicuous isolation, that books may be "a load of crap," but they keep being read, borrowed, stolen, indexed, and bought. The fate he seemed to prefer, that of being remaindered and neglected because for him there was "nothing to be said," has been resoundingly contradicted by the size of his following, which numerically must be the equivalent of an audience at a rock concert. Even *The Whitsun Weddings* and the last short book, *High Windows,* had a large audience.

But has that fate been contradicted or confirmed? If his large readership consists mostly of average persons leading average lives, this is not because Larkin pitched his tone to accommodate them, the way that other popular poets, like Kipling, Frost, Betjeman, or Stevie Smith, did. His life, on the surface, was not exemplary. There was nothing to be envied in it. Partly it is patriotism that makes Larkin popular. Not a jingoistic bitterness lamenting the loss of England's power, not even his mockery of that power, but something gentle and piercingly sweet that tells the sad truths of ordinariness, as the poems of one of his models, Edward Thomas, do. An unread predecessor often opens the way to popularity for his apprentice. So Larkin's popularity is not only his, but owes much to Thomas. This is Thomas's "Aspens":

> All day and night, save winter, every weather,
> Above the inn, the smithy, and the shop,
> The aspens at the cross-roads talk together
> Of rain, until their last leaves fall from the top.

And here is early Larkin:

> On shallow slates the pigeons shift together,
> Backing against a thin rain from the west
> Blown across each sunk head and settled
>     feather,
> Huddling round the warm stack suits them best.
>
>                   **("Pigeons")**

There is in Larkin, in poems like **"The Whitsun Weddings,"** a Georgian decency that is aware of England's smallness, and keeps the poem no wider than the rail-lines of the meter in his many poems of departure. But departure for what? Never abroad, always England, an England that is quietly loved, just as it is in Thomas, and in a way beyond the architectural nostalgia of Betjeman. . . . (p. 37)

I have no idea how many times I have read the poems in *The Whitsun Weddings, High Windows,* and, although not as often, *The Less Deceived.* On my small bookshelf my fingers scuttle past Frost, Eliot, Pound, Yeats to pluck the thin Larkin volumes almost hidden among them. One has to prepare one's intellect for the great moderns. Often reading Yeats first thing in the morning is like being awakened to the boom of a reverberating gong. Reading Stevens is like having chocolate for breakfast. With Larkin, the tone is matutinal or crepuscular as with most poems, but it is also the tone of ordinary day. His first lines are immediate, and intimate, as if they were resuming an interrupted conversation:

Sometimes you hear, fifth-hand,
As epitaph:
He chucked up everything
And just cleared off.
                    **("Poetry of Departures")**

Why should I let the toad work
Squat on my life?
                              **("Toads")**

No, I have never found
The place where I could say
This is my proper ground,
Here I shall stay.
                    **("Places, Loved Ones")**

This was Mr. Bleaney's room . . .
                         **("Mr. Bleaney")**

About twenty years ago
Two girls came in where I worked—
A bosomy English rose
And her friend in specs I could talk to.
                         **("Wild Oats")**

When I see a couple of kids
And I guess he's fucking her and she's
Taking pills or wearing a diaphragm . . .
                      **("High Windows")**

Groping back to bed after a piss.
                            **("Sad Steps")**

This is not only poetry, it is exchange. No other poet I know of makes the reader an intimate listener as well as Larkin does. The poems are not confessional, they are shared with the reader, with the joke always turning on Larkin. He would never write:

I have measured out my life in coffee spoons.

The Eliot line is too heraldically plangent. Larkin would describe the spoon. When he eats "an awful pie" at a railway station, the pie is not a symbol—a tacky epiphany. He will continue to eat more pies. "I have measured out my life in awful pies" would be closer to his experience. The railway platforms go on; the awful pies are eaten. The poet does not separate himself from the others in the cheap restaurant. Often the poet, for Larkin, is

. . . the shit in the shuttered château
Who does his five hundred words
Then parts out the rest of the day
Between bathing and booze and birds . . .
                    **("The Life with a Hole in It")**

And yet he can startle with this, from **"Aubade,"** the way Marvell suddenly darkens:

Man hands on misery to man,
It deepens like a coastal shelf.
Get out as early as you can
And don't have any kids yourself.

And, of death:

Most things may never happen: this one will.
                            **("Aubade")**

In verse, tone is one thing, but in pitch lies the seismographic accuracy of the individual voice, the shadings as personal as a thumb-print. Larkin's voice, in the late

books *The Whitsun Weddings* and *High Windows,* was accurately set not only in its middle-class timbre, but, even more finely, by the use of cliché and aside, and a vocabulary frayed by repetition, perfectly in its milieu, the chat of a librarian or a don, of someone who "also writes verse." The muted pitch is that of a man in a suit, after work, having an ale and a sandwich in a better-than-average pub, as well as that of a guest at an upper-middle-class party, holding a bell glass of tolerable sherry, nearly dazed with boredom but making small talk. The references in **"Naturally The Foundation will Bear Your Expenses"** are as swift and compact as shoptalk, and must be difficult not only for some American readers, but even for those English readers who may not get the cynical, slightly self-lacerating business of cashing in on the lecture and highbrow radio racket:

Hurrying to catch my Comet
One dark November day,
Which soon would snatch me from it
To the sunshine of Bombay,
I pondered pages Berkeley
Not three weeks since had heard,
Perceiving Chatto darkly
Through the mirror of the Third.

Crowds, colourless and careworn,
Had made my taxi late,
Yet not till I was airborne
Did I recall the date—
That day when Queen and Minister
And Band of Guards and all
Still act their solemn-sinister
Wreath-rubbish in Whitehall.

It used to make me throw up,
These mawkish nursery games:
O when will England grow up?
—But I outsoar the Thames,
And dwindle off down Auster
To greet Professor Lal
(He once met Morgan Forster),
My contact and my pal.

The poem's humor lies in its being written, tonally, in dialect, that is in the argot of chaps who write things, brilliantly mediocre chaps of course, with the conceited casualness of talking only to their peers or compatriots, regardless of whether those outside the circle get the references or not. The poem is set in self-parodic stanzas, again like something from Kipling or a hymn book, making a personal anthem with literature as its subject. And how shockingly accurate it is, precisely because of its pitch! Even a deliberately forced and desperate rhyme like Auster/Forster (simultaneously mocking itself and saying to those outside the circle: "Christ, you know who Auster is, it's the North Wind for God's sake") pins and immolates the character, an academic ponce.

On the Comet, Britain's pride of the air, he revises a lecture he's given at Berkeley in California (good American bucks for an English accent), then lifts his head from the lecture to look through the jet's window, and sees (as through a glass darkly) the publication of the talk by Chatto and Windus over the Third Programme, the English channel devoted to almost nauseating expertise.

Then, in the middle stanza, ceremony is mocked. The speaker escapes the gray, self-pumping parade of Remembrance Day, toward the sunshine of India. The smugness of the character is so perfectly adaptable that even the sunshine of Bombay will be exploited, for there he will meet Professor Lal, "my contact and my pal," who once met the author of *A Passage to India.*

> But I outsoar the Thames . . .

He's bigger than all that, he's left behind the Thames of Spenser, even of Eliot, the lecture in the briefcase.

> And dwindle off down Auster

—the jet is getting smaller, and, with it, his sense of responsibility, lost for the career. There is not a more acid portrait of English academic hypocrisy.

Even oral composition is mental writing. Poetry is speech, but it is also writing. Words have shapes. It is composition in verse before it is anything else. Meter precedes breath, shape foreshadows content. Melody indicates meaning. The rest comes afterward. But in most free verse speech is supposed to shape form.

Development, for Larkin, lay not in metrical experiment, or in varieties of stanzaic design, not in Pound's frenzied and very American injunction to "make it new," since Larkin despised the avantgarde, but in concentration on the shifts and pauses possible within the pentameter. Pound had written: "to break the pentameter, that was the first heave," but for Larkin the great achievement was not to betray the pulse or the breath of the pentameter by abandoning it or condemning its melody as archaic, but in exploring the possibility of its defiant consistency, until technical mastery became freshness. The patience and subtlety with which he succeeded in writing "the Larkin line" were not achieved by tricks. There are tricks in modulation as well as tricks of bombast.

Larkin continued to rely on the given beat of the pentametrical line throughout his career. He shadowed it with hesitations, coarsened it with casual expletives, and compacted it with hyphens—when the hyphenated image had always been considered a mark of desperate inertia—to the point where a hyphenated image, with its aural-visual fusion, was powerful enough to contain a minipoem in itself:

> Some lonely rain-ceased summer's evening . . .
> That vast moth-eaten musical brocade . . .
> time's rolling smithy-smoke . . .
> dark, shining-leaved cabbages . . .
> sun-comprehending glass . . .
> Beside grain-scattered streets, barge-crowded
>     water.

The tension of the right-hand margin, the cliff or frontier that the casual, ambulatory breath approached as it neared the edge of the pentameter, pushed description to fall back on the hyphen; but the two paces backward from the threat of collapse, from the banal enjambment of running the description into an extra half-line and an epigrammatic caesura, was resisted with patient honesty. The compression that ensued out of an absolute devotion to the rhythm produced, in its microcosmic clarity, like a lens or a dew-bead, a world that is whole.

The hyphenated image is not colloquial, but Larkin's achievement is to make it sound as if it were, as if such phrasing could slip into talk, into apparently diffident but actually heraldic observation, as casually as "in a pig's arse, friend." And accepting this, we hear a unified conversational drone, which at the crest of its shared rhythm flashes with illuminating asides, and which flatters us, as Auden often does, into believing that we too are capable of such compressions. After years of sticking to the beat, a devotion that Larkin praised in classic jazz and made him reject Charlie Parker as sneeringly as in painting and in theater he sneered at Picasso and Beckett, he achieved a clear tone in the instrument, as with the clarinet of Sydney Bechet, while the wire brushes supply the background. The heartbeat is the bass, the wire brushes whirr and lift the rhythm, and the improvisations, the stops and riffles of the clear clarinet, may appear to leave the meter, but they return to it, and it is the return that supplies the delight.

One of the most flattering experiences I have had was when Larkin included me in his *Oxford Book of Modern Verse* of 1973. I mention this not only from the pride of being recognized by a poet for whose work I had great affection and whose severity of judgment I feared, but also because it contradicts, self-contradicts, the image of a beleaguered provinciality that Larkin offered his readers. This image, continually repeated, was of a weary, sneering recluse who "never read foreign poetry," for whom China was a good place to travel to, if one could get back on the same day, who despised "the myth-kitty" into which poets rummage to pluck classical fragments from the sawdust of the Greco-Roman bran tub, and for whom books were "a load of crap." (pp. 37-8)

At the expense of Oxford, Larkin seemed to be again taking the mickey out of the literary establishment, to play the conservative when they must have expected daring. By then, however, the Angry Young Men and the redbrick rebels had continued their mugging, like Lucky Jim making faces, until the mugging had reached the rictus of a conservative mask. But we were always that, Kingsley Amis, one of Larkin's close friends, argued, as did John Osborne. What we mocked were the false postures, the old farts' pomposities, the dead mind of Oxbridge. We loved England behind all the face making and the satire, and the England we loved was one of traditional simplicities. This was the general tone of Larkin's *Oxford Book of English Verse,* which found merit in decently industrious verse, as if its editor were the J. C. Squire of our time. If he found only those values in my own work, that was okay by me.

Because behind Larkin's cultivated philistinism, one of the penalties of playing the recluse, there was also that perception which, in his own phrase, "loneliness clarifies." But he maintained the mask, physically that of a bespectacled egghead who was a librarian and hated literature, a waxworks dummy who loved jazz and wrote a column about it for *The Daily Telegraph,* an antipatriot who loved rural England, and who could mock it as he did in **"Naturally** the Foundation . . ." and still accept a medal from the Queen:

> That day when Queen and Minister
> And Band of Guards and all
> Still act their solemn-sinister
> Wreath-rubbish in Whitehall.
>
> It used to make me throw up,
> These mawkish nursery games:
> O when will England grow up?
> —But I outsoar the Thames.

But he also wrote the lines that follow, not with the prosaic concern of a conservationist, but with a love as old as Spenser's, and more deeply frightened by highways and "MI cafés" than any lines of Betjeman's:

> I thought it would last my time—
> The sense that, beyond the town,
> There would always be fields and farms,
> Where the village louts could climb
> Such trees as were not cut down;
> I knew there'd be false alarms . . .
>
> And that will be England gone,
> The shadows, the meadows, the lanes,
> The guildhalls, the carved choirs.
> There'll be books; it will linger on
> In galleries; but all that remains
> For us will be concrete and tyres.
>
> **("Going, Going")**

"And that will be England gone." Who is this? The Rupert Brooke of the Thatcher government celebrating boating, tea, and Granchester? Kipling in the day of the dole? Which Larkin is honest? The one accepting a medal from the very hand it has tried to bite, since there is no real difference between being handed a medal and being draped with a wreath (in fact, some might see both gestures as the handshake of death, as Browning mocked Tennyson for "leaving us for a handful of silver")? Or the other Larkin, the tender elegist pierced by the last light of calendar country? And without irony or ambiguity, the answer is both. Light, with Larkin, is a religious experience. Whether one believes in it or not, as he writes, it goes out, or goes on.

> There is an evening coming in
> Across the fields, one never seen before,
> That lights no lamps.
>
> **("Going")**
>
> On longer evenings,
> Light, chill and yellow,
> Bathes the serene
> Foreheads of houses.
> A thrush sings,
> Laurel-surrounded . . .
>
> **("Coming")**

The tenderness, the prayerlike, sacred translucence of those lines are in the same spirit as a poem by Edward Thomas, a spirit that appears fragile because of its precision, but that really increases our love for the poet, and not only for his poetry but for the personality behind the poetry.

Eliot avoids us, like a man who can't bear being touched, except by the finger of God. He wrote, with his customary humble vanity, that poetry was a turning away from personality, and that only those who had personality would understand this. That it was not a turning loose of emotion, but a turning away from it. By paradox, no poet, if to judge only by features, looks more apersonal than Larkin, and yet few other contemporary poets, even those classified as "confessional," are as intimate and open as that average, antiromantic, bespectacled visage whose personality is stamped on every line, either as observer or sufferer. We love Larkin, and that is it, simply. And we must be careful to make a distinction between love and popularity. There are minor poets whom we love clearly and cleanly, mainly because they are not posing for their busts. We can discern the edges of hardening marble, the immortalized lineaments when poets turn into bards, can see the seamed toga casually tossed over one shoulder, and eventually we are at a distance from them. As their lines become marmoreal, poets hear their own echo as oracles.

This happened to Eliot with *The Four Quartets,* to Stevens in the plummy vacancies of his later work, to Pound as he began to screech, even to Williams once he felt the laurel tightening on his forehead. Poetry is a narrow spring, the mountain cold brook of Helicon, and it is not its narrowness that matters but the crystalline, tongue-numbing cold of its freshness, which, in the largest works, still glitters like an unpolluted spring. Larkin is of that stream, and he makes a lot of "great" modern poetry sound like noise. This modesty is saintly, even more than it is hermetic or, amid the roar and grayness of our cities, reclusive. A great poet like Joyce never lost the narrow, clear, refreshing temperature of that mountain spring, huge as his ambition was, and if there is one great poet who would recognize his kinship with Mr. Bleaney, it would be the one who created Leopold Bloom.

I have tried to distinguish love of a poet from his popularity. I would dislike it, for selfish reasons, if Edward Thomas were popular. But I feel happy that Larkin is being so widely read. One of the reasons for his popularity is its accurate placing of the temper of a shrinking Britain. There may even be a general, and even genial, self-mockery in the acceptance of England as tacky and moth-eaten, a place as narrow as its lanes and alleys, jammed with "colourless and careworn" crowds. Larkin's verse is as narrow as this, but it too is packed with gray-faced people whose predecessors managed an immense empire.

And, in a sense, Larkin's popularity may be of the same sort as Kipling's, if instead of Victoria we now have Margaret Thatcher. Here he is on the old business of sending troops abroad and having to bring them back:

> Next year we are to bring the soldiers home
> For lack of money, and it is all right.
> Places they guarded, or kept orderly,
> Must guard themselves, and keep themselves orderly.
> We want the money for ourselves at home
> Instead of working. And this is all right.
>
> **("Homage to a Government")**

—all right, when compared with Kipling's

> Far called our navies melt away

On dune and headland sinks the fire.
And all our pomp of yesterday
Is one with Nineveh and Tyre . . .
("Recessional")

Behind Kipling's prophetic posture there is a boast, one that is contained in Byron's "the glory that was Greece / And the grandeur that was Rome." (pp. 38-9)

The opposite is so in Larkin's abrupt, epigrammatic sanity. And yet this has appealed to the very thousands who would have recited Kipling and Tennyson at the peak of the empire's glory and grandeur. If there is one great thing that Larkin's poetry, however temporarily, may have done, it is to make stained glass plain, to clarify, by its transparency, the true ordinariness of postempire Britain, by supplying his readers with what he calls "a furious, devout drench," without the twilight trumpets and the doom. (p. 39)

Larkin's is a poetry of clichés. But the clichés inspire him to pursue them carefully toward some cryptic or sometimes illuminating resolution. Bleaney alone in his room; an admirer turning the pages of a photograph album; spring in the park with its prams and nurses; sticking to one's job while daydreaming of adventure; parking a bicycle outside a church and removing cycle clips; trains, windows, streets. It is like LaForgue, in its urban geography, its elegiac domesticity, the sadness of the professional traveler encountering the glitter of set cutlery in provincial hotels, and clichés need a language of cliché.

Herein lies Larkin's astounding courage. Poets with similar themes, like MacNeice, or the early Eliot and the early Auden, wrote of cities and isolation, but never that relentlessly, never with the varied repetitiveness that Larkin takes to be the meter of life.

To reinforce his craft he chose models whose subjects were first of all ordinary, banal: Betjeman, the novelist Barbara Pym, Stevie Smith. The process of the spirit was through the rubbed, worn-out familiarity of the common to something that would shine from that friction, as it does at the end of **"The Whitsun Weddings":**

. . . and what it held
Stood ready to be loosed with all the power
That being changed can give. We slowed again,
And as the tightened brakes took hold, there
    swelled
A sense of falling, like an arrow-shower
Sent out of sight, somewhere becoming rain.

and in the blazing epiphany at the end of his celebration of some imaginary minor master, with its wonderful, leaping assonances of crusted logs aflame and the hiss of spit into the flames in **"The Card-Players":**

Rain, wind and fire! The secret, bestial peace!

Once, the delight was underlined by the fact that there was so little of Larkin's poetry, that its scale refreshed its rarity, and that what little there was was perfect, so useful and private that the poems felt as familiar as a bunch of keys. One picked them up as casually; they were small, shining, and slipped easily into the pocket of memory. Now, of course, another Larkin joke has been played on us. The

*Collected Poems* is not an immense block of a book, but it is large, containing several dozen previously unpublished poems, and its very prolixity is a contradiction of the parsimonious writer we believed Larkin to be. He said late in his life that he had not abandoned poetry, but that it had abandoned him. We waited for years for the next Larkin poem, patient, because we anticipated its metrical perfection. In the meantime, we could always go back to those volumes we were beginning to know by heart from rereading. Now this proof of Larkin as a fecund, if not voluminous, poet is both startling and amusing. It means that he once wrote as hard and as often as any other poet of his time, and how does the ample Larkin compare with the almost anorexic slenderness of his last book, *High Windows*? (pp. 39-40)

The thin Larkin managed to get out of the fat one mainly because of the severity of his judgment, even if all the poems in the collected volume were publishable, and it makes us admire him even more that he could have found so many excellent poems unsatisfactory enough to have kept them from print. The choices had nothing to do with career, or with being a perfectionist. What it had to do with was his belief in breathing, in the poem's life. Thus the lovely poems that he remarkably excluded from his narrow books fail only in the sense that they best belong not to his reputation but to poetry. Larkin is a moral poet, an honest one, who hated grandeur and the posing that encourages experiment. This is not conservatism, it is, purely, devotion. And this is why poets will continue to cherish him beyond his current popularity—for that crisp dismissal of "what's not good enough," or what "has nothing to say," that if applied to so many of his contemporaries would reduce them to a few lines of poetry enough, in his view, for any lifetime. (p. 40)

*Derek Walcott, "The Master of the Ordinary," in* The New York Review of Books, *Vol. XXXVI, No. 9, June 1, 1989, pp. 37-40.*

## Edward Mendelson

The worst disservice Philip Larkin's readers did to him was believing what he told them. A writer, like a government, speaks with two voices, an official one and an unofficial one. Only the second is truthful. In a government, the two voices are easily distinguished. The official spokesman stands behind a lectern and reads a prepared statement saying that everything is under control and progress is assured on all fronts. The unofficial spokesman cups his hand over a telephone in the back room and quietly tells a reporter that all hell has broken loose.

A writer's two voices are equally distinct, although readers have a natural tendency to conflate them. The official voice speaks smoothly and consistently through interviews, lectures, and essays. The unofficial one argues with itself in novels, plays, and poems. The official voice either has all the answers or at least knows how to clarify and contain the question. The unofficial voice has nothing but questions.

In most writers the official voice is the voice of clarity and optimism, while the unofficial voice points to the dilemmas and darknesses that the official voice ignores. In Larkin, this pattern was reversed. His official voice spoke in essays and interviews about permanently lowered expectations, and adopted a comically aggressive tone of provincial disgust with everything in the contemporary world, including Larkin himself. His critics (with the honorable exceptions of Barbara Everett, Andrew Motion, and Seamus Heaney), finding the same disgust and constraint in the poetry, tended to assume that Larkin's official voice was an adequate spokesman for the unofficial one.

By the time Larkin died in 1985, at the age of 63, he had created an official self-portrait of the artist as bitter, disillusioned, lonely, resentful of any energy and happiness enjoyed by others—even while he insisted that their energy was doomed and their happiness an illusion. But this partial portrait was no more truthful than any other official one. Larkin suffered all the bitterness of his official prose, but the alternative truth spoken quietly by his poems was a shy, persistent vision of freedom and exaltation.

Larkin seems to have been embarrassed by his own vision, and did his best to help readers ignore it. Most of the reviewers of his *Collected Poems* have been too busy quoting his famously caustic aphorisms to look for anything else, and it is hard to blame them. His deceptively unreflective style, the formal perfection of his rhymed and rhythmical stanzas, served as an effective camouflage for Larkin's vortices of feeling. More than any other British writer of his time, he seemed to transform the material bleakness of the austere 1940s and 1950s, and then the moral bleakness of the moneyed 1960s and 1970s, into an inescapable statement of the bleakness of almost everything.

In Larkin's official version of the human condition, life started badly and ended worse. From the moment you were born it was already too late to change for the better, because "They fuck you up, your mum and dad." And the poem that opened with this line closed with the advice that logically followed: "And don't have any kids yourself." If you try to think of art as a compensation for life's failures (as the unofficial Larkin in fact believed), the official Larkin offered the disillusion of long experience: "Get stewed: / Books are a load of crap." And if you dared to look toward something better, Larkin brought you down to earth in one poem after another that looked with unrelieved horror toward "the whole hideous inverted childhood" of old age—"and then the only end of age." The building most likely to appear in a Larkin poem is the hospital, imagined repeatedly as a cliff lowering over the hopes of anyone still living. (p. 29)

Larkin dwelled from the start on losses that were absolute and pervasive. And his sense of loss was less a satiric protest against the condition of the universe than an explicit sense that he was lost or divided from something—something that was desirable, calm, lovely, unalterable, and utterly inaccessible.

Even in the rare moments when Larkin modulated his bitterness to turn briefly sentimental over the possibility of happiness, the happiness he imagined lay somewhere over the horizon, outside the life he could perceive. The erotic energies of the couples on the train to London after the Whitsun weddings swell "Like an arrowshower / Sent out of sight, somewhere becoming rain." In **"Sad Steps"** the "strength and pain / Of being young" is lost for Larkin but "is for others undiminished somewhere." The direction marker always points somewhere else.

Larkin's lost or distant treasure came into clearer focus as it grew more distant. In his early poems it took the vague form of an elusive and imaginary lover whose absence Larkin found more moving than the presence of any living woman could be. In his later poems, it transformed itself into a vivid intensity beyond understanding, a celestial emptiness more compelling than anything earthly and tangible. Whatever form it took, it was always exempt from time and death.

In an unsettling and exhilarating poem, written when he was 29 and first printed in this collection, Larkin begins the poem in a mood of gothic horror as he waits for death to climb the stairs and open the door. But the poem ends with the arrival of death's opposite:

> Light cringed. The door swung inwards. Over the threshold
>
> Nothing like death stepped, nothing like death paused,
> Nothing like death has such hair, arms so raised.
> Why are your feet bare? Was not death to come?
> Why is he not here? What summer have you broken from?

The emotional force of this poem depends on its refusal to identify itself as either a wishful fantasy or a grateful recollection. Larkin pointedly titled it **"Unfinished Poem"**—he could never describe the satisfactions that might have followed its final stanza. When an alternative to death arrived in his later poems, it never arrived in so human a form.

In **"The Large Cool Store,"** ten years after **"Unfinished Poem,"** the contrast of daytime's sensible clothes and night's ruffled and fantastic lingerie propels Larkin, in a course of a few lines, from his initial fantasy of the separateness and unearthliness of women to the recognition that it is not women but his unreal wishes that escape the bounds of earth. The mere juxtaposition of two kinds of cheap clothing shows

> How separate and unearthly love is,
> Or women are, or what they do,
> Or in our young unreal wishes
> Seem to be: synthetic, new,
> And natureless in ecstasies.

In the world of matter and the flesh, the only possible objects of an unreal wish are synthetic, natureless, and inevitably disappointing. A few years later Larkin discovered that the real object of his wish was not an object at all, but a bright emptiness entirely beyond the changes of nature and the heaviness of matter.

Like any more explicit mystic, Larkin could name that emptiness only in terms of what it was not. A poem with the laconic title **"Here"** called it "unfenced existence . . .

untalkative, out of reach"—silent and beyond the grasp of words. The title poem of Larkin's last book of poems, *High Windows,* begins in his characteristic official mixture of sexual jealousy and compensatory disgust, but the poem ends far beyond it. Envying in four-letter detail the sexual freedom of the young, he guesses that, when he was young, he was envied in the same way for his freedom from religious dread. Then, as he senses through generations of envy the vanity of human wishes, words suddenly give way to vision:

> immediately
> Rather than words
> comes the thought of
> high windows:
> The sun-comprehending glass,
> And beyond it, the deep blue air, that shows
> Nothing, and is nowhere, and is endless.

Larkin's revelation following rage aligns him with earlier poets whose visionary sense was more explicit. Yeats among schoolchildren, "thinking of that fit of grief and rage" that turned a childish day to tragedy, suddenly saw a vision in human form:

> Thereupon my heart is driven wild:
> She stands before me as a little child.

And George Herbert—a miniaturist, like Larkin, who looked out from narrow places to the infinite—felt the same visionary transformation as a personal appeal:

> But as I rav'd and grew more fierce and wilde
> At every word
> Me thoughts I heard one calling, *Child!*
> And I reply'd *My Lord.*

Larkin's consoling vision could not share the personal drama of theirs, partly because Larkin wore the protective reticence that is the 20th century's vulgar tongue. (Wandering into a church, he is careful to remember that he is out of place; "Hatless, I take off / My cycle-clips in awkward reverence.") But it is not simply the fault of his century that his consolations never speak inviting words or wear a human face. Once or twice, the ideal and the human coincide, as in **"Unfinished Poem,"** or in a late unpublished love poem four lines long that ends "there was one constant good: / she did not change." (The poem is a rare glimpse into Larkin's real private life that was apparently far less bleak than the life portrayed in his poems.) But in his darker moods he believed that

> Only one ship is seeking us, a black-
> Sailed unfamiliar, towing at her back
> A huge and birdless silence. In her wake
> No waters breed or break.

In his poems Larkin often responds to death's invitation by knocking back a stiff drink and wisecracking about the indifferent universe. But he also knew that he was isolated most of all by his own persistent refusal of a world that might have asked for his company had he been willing to listen. (pp. 30-1)

Larkin thought himself uniquely disbarred from that wild glad surrender that others somehow managed to partake in. His last substantial poem, **"Love Again"** (as in many poems throughout his career, love for someone who is certainly in bed with someone else), interrupts its own envious complaint in the same way **"High Windows"** does, but this poem turns away from words toward a private emptiness, not an infinite one:

> why put it into words?
> Isolate rather this element
> That spreads through other lives like a tree
> And sways them on a sort of sense
> And say why it never worked for me.
> Something to do with violence
> A long way back, and wrong rewards,
> And arrogant eternity.

"Violence / A long way back." At the end of his life, Larkin's voice suddenly speaks as if from the analyst's couch to reveal private truths that his official plain-speaking voice never permitted itself to say.

Whatever that violence was, its heritage was the "wrong rewards" of an isolation Larkin only pretended to accept. Watching young couples dancing, in **"Reasons for Attendance,"** he first insists that his lonely satisfaction in art is richer than their joint satisfaction in sex, and then cancels that insistence in the final line:

> Therefore I stay outside
> Believing this; and they maul to and fro,
> Believing that; and both are satisfied,
> If no one has misjudged himself. Or lied.

The irony cuts both ways. Larkin can only half convince himself that, when compared with those who burst into fulfillment's desolate attic, he is the less deceived.

Balanced against his loneliness, the "unfenced existence: / Facing the sun" that Larkin saw through high windows was both nothing and everything. His moments of illumination could not keep his envies from recurring, but nothing else could silence those envies when they returned. And consistently, through all the ironies and bitterness of his poems, shines Larkin's pleasure in their own making. In his most adult and accomplished poems he often retains an adolescent's gawky air of self-discovery and self-forgetfulness. In longer poems he often rolls self-defining phrases over his tongue:

> Yet stop I did: in fact I often do,
> And always end much at a loss like this . . .
>                         **"Church Going"**

> Strange to it now, I watch
> the cloudless scene:
> The same clear water
> over smoothed pebbles . . .
>                         **"To the Sea"**

And he has an adolescent's delight in closing his poems with bright sentential hopes, sometimes carefully scuffed lest a more cynical part of himself snicker at them. The stone couple on **"An Arundel Tomb"**

> prove
> Our almost-instinct almost true:
> What will survive of us is love

And the Show Saturday out in farm country gives its visitors something that deserves the same kind of permanence,

> something they share
> That breaks ancestrally each year into
> Regenerate union. Let it always be there.

Larkin is always too reticent for loud displays of technical bravura, but he reveals more quietly his sly pleasure in his own skill. His rhymes are often hidden among the unemphasized lowlands of his sentences, so that it is possible to read one of his fully rhymed poems without noticing that it is rhymed at all. His transitions from one phrase to the next often sound solidly reasonable, until you trace the logic in detail and discover that the poem made a daring associative leap while you were blinking. "It's unhappiness that provokes a poem," he told an interviewer, but his poems console the grief that provokes them. "Do you feel terribly pleased when you've written one?" the interviewer asked. He answered, "Yes, as if I've laid an egg." (pp. 31-2)

> Edward Mendelson, "Larkin's Eggs," in The New Republic, *Vol. 200, No. 23, June 5, 1989, pp. 29-33.*

## Clive James

At first glance, the publication in the United States of Philip Larkin's *Collected Poems* looks like a long shot. While he lived, Larkin never crossed the Atlantic, and, unlike some other British poets, he was genuinely indifferent to his American reputation. His bailiwick was England. Larkin was so English that he didn't even care much about Britain, and he rarely mentioned it. Even within England, he travelled little. He spent most of his adult life at the University of Hull, as its chief librarian. A trip to London was an event. When he was there, he resolutely declined to promote his reputation. He guarded it but would permit no hype.

Though Larkin's diffidence was partly a pose, his reticence was authentic. At no point did he announce that he had built a better mousetrap. The world had to prove it by beating a path to his door. The process took time, but was inexorable, and by now, only three years after his death, at the age of sixty-three, his renown has reached a kind of apotheosis. On the British best-seller lists, Larkin's *Collected Poems* was up there for months at a stretch, along with Stephen Hawking's *A Brief History of Time* and Salman Rushdie's *The Satanic Verses*. In Larkin's case, this extraordinary level of attention was reached without either general relativity's having to be reconciled with quantum mechanics or Ayatollah Khomeini's having to pronounce anathema. The evidence suggests that Larkin's poetry, from a standing start, gets to everyone capable of being got to. One's tender concern that it should survive the perilous journey across the sea is therefore perhaps misplaced. A mission like this might have no more need of a fighter escort than pollen on the wind.

The size of the volume is misleading. Its meticulous editor, Anthony Thwaite—himself a poet of high reputation— has included poems that Larkin finished but did not publish, and poems that he did not even finish. Though tactfully carried out, this editorial inclusiveness is not beyond cavil. What was elliptically concentrated has become more

fully understandable, but whether Larkin benefits from being more fully understood is questionable. Eugenio Montale, in many ways a comparable figure, was, it might be recalled, properly afraid of what he called "too much light."

During his lifetime, Larkin published only three mature collections of verse, and they were all as thin as blades. *The Less Deceived* (1955), *The Whitsun Weddings* (1964), and *High Windows* (1974) combined to a thickness barely half that of the *Collected Poems.* Larkin also published, in 1966, a new edition of his early, immature collection, *The North Ship,* which had first come out in 1945. He took care, by supplying the reissue with a deprecatory introduction, to keep it clearly separate from the poems that he regarded as being written in his own voice.

The voice was unmistakable. It made misery beautiful. One of Larkin's few even halfway carefree poems is **"For Sydney Bechet,"** from *The Whitsun Weddings.* Yet the impact that Larkin said Bechet made on him was exactly the impact that Larkin made on readers coming to him for the first time:

> On me your voice falls as they say love should,
> Like an enormous yes.

What made the paradox delicious was the scrupulousness of its expression. There could be no doubt that Larkin's outlook on life added up to an enormous no, but pessimism had been given a saving grace. Larkin described an England changing in ways he didn't like. He described himself aging in ways he didn't like. The empire had shrunk to a few islands, his personal history to a set of missed opportunities. Yet his desperate position, which ought logically to have been a license for incoherence, was expressed with such linguistic fastidiousness, on the one hand, and such lyrical enchantment, on the other, that the question arose of whether he had not at least partly cultivated that view in order to get those results. Larkin once told an interviewer, "Deprivation for me is what daffodils were for Wordsworth."

In the three essential volumes, the balanced triad of Larkin's achievement, all the poems are poised vibrantly in the force field of tension between his profound personal hopelessness and the assured command of their carrying out. Perfectly designed, tightly integrated, transforming a psychological falling apart into an aesthetic fitting together, they release, from their compressed but always strictly parsable syntax, sudden phrases of ravishing beauty, as the river in Dante's Paradise, by giving off sparks, suggests that light is what it is made of.

These irresistible fragments are everyone's way into Larkin's work. They are the first satisfaction his poetry offers. There are other and deeper satisfactions, but it was his quotability that gave Larkin the biggest cultural impact on the British reading public since Auden—and over a greater social range. Lines by Larkin are the common property of everyone in Britain who reads seriously at all—a state of affairs which has not obtained since the time of Tennyson. Phrases, whole lines, and sometimes whole stanzas can be heard at the dinner table.

There is an evening coming in
Across the fields, one never seen before,
That lights no lamps . . .

Only one ship is seeking us, a black-
Sailed unfamiliar, towing at her back
A huge and birdless silence. In her wake
No waters breed or break . . .

Now, helpless in the hollow of
An unarmorial age, a trough
Of smoke in slow suspended skeins
Above their scrap of history,
Only an attitude remains . . .

And as the tightened brakes took hold, there
    swelled
A sense of falling, like an arrow-shower
Sent out of sight, somewhere becoming rain . . .

How distant, the departure of young men
Down valleys, or watching
The green shore past the salt-white cordage
Rising and falling . . .

Steep beach, blue water, towels, red bathing
    caps,
The small hushed waves' repeated fresh collapse
Up the warm yellow sand, and further off
A white steamer stuck in the afternoon . . .

Later, the square is empty: a big sky
Drains down the estuary like the bed
Of a gold river . . .

At death, you break up: the bits that were you
Start speeding away from each other for ever
With no one to see . . .

Rather than words comes the thought of high
    windows:
The sun-comprehending glass,
And beyond it, the deep blue air, that shows
Nothing, and is nowhere, and is endless.

Drawn in by the subtle gravity beam of such bewitchment, the reader becomes involved for the rest of his life in Larkin's doomed but unfailingly dignified struggle to reconcile the golden light in the high windows with the endlessness it comes from. His sense of inadequacy, his fear of death are in every poem. His poems could not be more personal. But, equally, they could not be more universal. Seeing the world as the hungry and thirsty see food and drink, he describes it for the benefit of those who are at home in it, their senses dulled by satiation. The reader asks, How can a man who feels like this bear to live at all?

Life is first boredom, then fear.
Whether or not we use it, it goes,
And leaves what something hidden from us
    chose,
And age, and then the only end of age.

But the reader gets an answer: there are duties that annul nihilism, satisfactions beyond dissatisfaction, and, above all, the miracle of continuity. Larkin's own question about what life is worth if we have to lose it he answers with the contrary question, about what life would amount to if it didn't go on without us. Awkward at the seaside, ordinary people know better in their bones than the poet among his books:

The white steamer has gone. Like breathed-on
    glass
The sunlight has turned milky. If the worst
Of flawless weather is our falling short,
It may be that through habit these do best,
Coming to water clumsily undressed
Yearly; teaching their children by a sort
Of clowning; helping the old, too, as they ought.

Just as Larkin's resolutely prosaic organization of a poem is its passport to the poetic, so his insight into himself is his window on the world. He is the least solipsistic of artists. Unfortunately, this has now become less clear. Too much light has been shed. Of the poems previously unpublished in book form, a few are among his greatest achievements, many more one would not now want to be without, and all are good to have. But all the poems he didn't publish have been put in chronological order of composition along with those he did publish, instead of being given a separate section of their own. There is plenty of editorial apparatus to tell you how the original slim volumes were made up, but the strategic economy of their initial design has been lost.

All three of the original volumes start and end with the clean, dramatic decisiveness of a curtain going up and coming down again. The cast is not loitering in the auditorium before hand. Nor is it to be found hanging out in the car park afterward. *The Less Deceived* starts with **"Lines on a Young Lady's Photograph Album,"** which laments a lost love but with no confessions of the poet's personal inadequacy. It ends with **"At Grass,"** which is not about him but about horses: a bugle call at sunset.

Only the groom, and the groom's boy,
With bridles in the evening come.

Similarly, *The Whitsun Weddings* starts and ends without a mention of the author. The first poem, **"Here,"** is an induction into "the surprise of a large town" that sounds as if it might be Hull. No one who sounds as if he might be Larkin puts in an appearance. Instead, other people do, whose "removed lives / loneliness clarifies." The last poem in the book, **"An Arundel Tomb,"** is an elegy written in a church crypt which is as sonorous as Gray's written in a churchyard, and no more petulant: that things pass is a fact made majestic, if not welcome.

As for *High Windows,* the last collection published while he was alive, it may contain, in **"The Building,"** his single most terror-stricken—and, indeed, terrifying—personal outcry against the intractable fact of death, but it begins and ends with the author well in the background. **"To the Sea,"** the opening poem, the one in which the white steamer so transfixingly gets stuck in the afternoon, is his most thoroughgoing celebration of the element that he said he would incorporate into his religion if he only had one: water. **"The Explosion"** closes the book with a heroic vision of dead coal miners which could be called a hymn to immortality if it did not come from a pen that devoted so much effort to pointing out that mortality really does mean what it says.

These two poems, **"To the Sea"** and **"The Explosion,"** which in *High Windows* are separated by the whole length of a short but weighty book, can be taken together as a case in point, because, as the chronological arrangement of the *Collected Poems* now reveals, they were written together, or almost. The first is dated October, 1969, and the second is dated January 5, 1970. Between them in *High Windows* come poems dated anything from five years earlier to three years later. This is only one instance, unusually striking but typical rather than exceptional, of how Larkin moved poems around through compositional time so that they would make in emotional space the kind of sense he wanted, and not another kind. Though there were poems he left out of *The Less Deceived* and put into *The Whitsun Weddings,* it would be overbold to assume that any poem, no matter how fully achieved, that he wrote before *High Windows* but did not publish in it would have found a context later. Anthony Thwaite [editor of *Collected Poems*] goes some way toward assuming exactly that— or, at any rate, suggesting it—when he says that Larkin had been stung by early refusals and had later on repressed excellent poems even when his friends urged him to publish them. Some of these poems, as we now see, were indeed excellent, but if a man is so careful to arrange his works in a certain order it is probably wiser to assume that when he subtracts something he is adding to the arrangement.

Toward the end of his life, in the years after *High Windows,* Larkin famously dried up. Poems came seldom. Some of those that did come equalled his best, and **"Aubade"** was among his greatest. Larkin himself thought highly enough of it to send it out in pamphlet form to his friends and acquaintances, and they were quickly on the telephone to one another quoting phrases and lines from it. Soon it was stanzas, and in London there is at least one illustrious playwright who won't go home from a dinner party before he has found an excuse to recite the whole thing.

> This is a special way of being afraid
> No trick dispels. Religion used to try,
> That vast moth-eaten musical brocade
> Created to pretend we never die,
> And specious stuff that says *No rational being
> Can fear a thing it will not feel,* not seeing
> That this is what we fear—no sight, no sound,
> No touch or taste or smell, nothing to think
>     with,

> Nothing to love or link with,
> The anaesthetic from which none come
>     round . . .

Had Larkin lived longer, there would eventually have had to be one more slim volume, even if slimmer than slim. But that any of the earlier suppressed poems would have gone into it seems very unlikely. The better they are, the better must have been his reasons for holding them back. Admittedly, the fact that he did not destroy them is some evidence that he was not averse to their being published after his death. As a seasoned campaigner for the preservation of British holograph manuscripts—he operated on the principle that papers bought by American universities were lost to civilization—he obviously thought that his own archive should be kept safe. But the question of *how* the suppressed poems should be published has now been answered: some other way than this. Arguments for how good they are miss the point, because it is not their weakness that is inimical to his total effect; it is their strength. There are hemistiches as riveting as anything he ever made public:

> Dead leaves desert in thousands . . .

He wrote that in 1953 and sat on it for more than thirty years. What other poet would not have got it into print somehow? The first two lines of a short poem called **"Pigeons,"** written in 1957, are a paradigm distillation of his characteristic urban pastoralism:

> On shallow slates the pigeons shift together,
> Backing against a thin rain from the west . . .

Even more remarkable, there were whole big poems so close to being fully realized that to call them unfinished sounds like effrontery. Not only would Larkin never let a flawed poem through for the sake of its strong phrasing; he would sideline a strong poem because of a single flaw. But **"Letter to a Friend About Girls,"** written in 1959, has nothing frail about it except his final indecision about whether Horatio is writing to Hamlet or Hamlet to Horatio. The writer complains that the addressee gets all the best girls without having to think about it, while he, the writer, gets, if any, only the ones he doesn't really want, and that after a long struggle.

> After comparing lives with you for years
> I see how I've been losing: all the while
> I've met a different gauge of girl from yours . . .

A brilliantly witty extended conceit, full of the scatological moral observation that Larkin and his friend Kingsley Amis jointly brought back from conversation into the literature from which it had been banished, the poem has already become incorporated into the Larkin canon that people quote to one another. So have parts of **"The Dance,"** one of his longest single poems, even though unfinished. The story of an awkward, put-upon, recognizably Larkin-like lonely man failing to get together with a beautiful woman even though she seems to be welcoming his attentions, the poem could logically have been completed only by becoming Larkin's third novel, to set beside his other two, *Jill* and *A Girl in Winter.* (Actually, the novel had already been written, by Kingsley Amis, and was called *Lucky Jim.*)

But there might have been a better reason for abandoning the poem. Like the Horatio poem and many of the other poems that were held back, **"The Dance"** is decisive about what Larkin otherwise preferred to leave indeterminate. **"Love Again,"** written in 1979, at the beginning of the arid last phase in which the poems that came to him seem more like bouts of fever than like showers of rain, states the theme with painful clarity.

> Love again: wanking at ten past three
> (Surely he's taken her home by now?),
> The bedroom hot as a bakery . . .

What hurts, though, isn't the vocabulary. When Larkin speaks of "Someone else feeling her breasts and cunt," he isn't speaking with untypical bluntness: though unfalteringly well judged, his tonal range always leaves room for foul language—shock effects are among his favorites. The pain at this point comes from the fact that it is so obviously Larkin talking. This time, the voice isn't coming through a persona: it's the man himself, only at his least complex, and therefore least individual. In his oeuvre, as selected and arranged by himself, there is a dialogue going on, a balancing of forces between perfection of the life and of the work—a classic conflict for which Larkin offers us a resolution second in its richness only to the later poems of Yeats. In much of the previously suppressed poetry, the dialogue collapses into a monologue. The man who has, at least in part, chosen his despair, or who, at any rate, strives to convince himself that he has, is usurped by the man who has no choice. The second man might well be thought of as the real man, but one of the effects of Larkin's work is to make us realize that beyond the supposed bedrock reality of individual happiness or unhappiness there is a social reality of creative fulfillment, or, failing that, of public duties faithfully carried out.

Larkin, in his unchecked personal despair, is a sacrificial goat with the sexual outlook of a stud bull. He thinks, and sometimes speaks, like a Robert Crumb character who has never recovered from being beaten up by a girl in the third grade. The best guess, and the least patronizing as well, is that Larkin held these poems back because he thought them self-indulgent—too private to be proportionate. One of the consolations that Larkin's work offers us is that we can be unhappy without giving in, without letting our wish to be off the hook ("Beneath it all, desire of oblivion runs") wipe out our lives ("the million-petalled flower / Of being here"). The ordering of the individual volumes was clearly meant to preserve this balance, which the inclusion of even a few more of the suppressed poems would have tipped.

In the *Collected Poems,* that hard-fought-for poise is quite gone. Larkin now speaks a good deal less for us all, and a good deal more for himself, than was his plain wish. That the self, the sad, dithering personal condition from which all his triumphantly assured work sprang, is now more comprehensively on view is not really a full compensation, except, perhaps, to those who aren't comfortable with an idol unless its head is made from the same clay as its feet.

On the other hand, to be given, in whatever order, all these marvellous poems that were for so long unseen is a bonus for which only a dolt would be ungrateful. Schnabel said that Beethoven's late piano sonatas were music better than could be played. Larkin's best poems are poetry better than can be said, but sayability they sumptuously offer. Larkin demands to be read aloud. His big, intricately formed stanzas, often bridging from one to the next, defeat the single breath but always invite it. As you read, the ideal human voice speaks in your head. It isn't his: as his gramophone records prove, he sounded like someone who expects to be interrupted. It isn't yours, either. It's ours. Larkin had the gift of reuniting poetry at its most artful with ordinary speech at its most unstudied—at its least literary. Though a scholar to the roots, he was not being perverse when he posed as a simple man. He thought that art should be self-sufficient. He was disturbed by the way literary studies had crowded out literature. But none of this means that he was simplistic. Though superficially a reactionary crusader against modernism, a sort of latter-day, one-man Council of Trent, he knew exactly when to leave something unexplained.

The process of explaining him will be hard to stop now that this book is available. It is, even so, a tremendous book, and, finally, despite all the candor it apparently offers, the mystery will be preserved for any reader acute enough to sense the depth under the clarity. Pushkin said that everything was on his agenda, even the disasters. Larkin knew about himself. In private hours of anguish, he commiserated with himself. But he was an artist, and that meant he was everyone; and what made him a genius was the effort and the resource he brought to bear in order to meet his superior responsibility.

Larkin went to hell, but not in a handcart. From his desolation he built masterpieces, and he was increasingly disinclined to settle for anything less. About twenty years ago in Britain, it became fashionable to say that all the poetic excitement was in America. Though things look less that way now, there is no need to be just as silly in the opposite direction. The English-speaking world is a unity. Britain and the United States might have difficulty absorbing each other's poetry, but most people have difficulty with poetry anyway. In Britain, Larkin shortened the distance between the people and poetry by doing nothing for his career and everything to compose artifacts that would have an independent, memorable life apart from himself. There is no inherent reason that the American reader, or any other English-speaking reader, should not be able to appreciate the results.

Art, if it knows how to wait, wins out. Larkin had patience. For him, poetry was a life sentence. He set happiness aside to make room for it. And if it turns out that he had no control over where his misery came from, doesn't that mean that he had even more control than we had thought over where it went to? Art is no less real for being artifice. The moment of truth must be prepared for. "Nothing to love or link with," wrote Larkin when he was fifty-five. "Nothing to catch or claim," he wrote when he was twenty-four, in a poem that only now sees the light. It was as if the death he feared to the end he had embraced at the start, just to raise the stakes. (pp. 89-92)

*Clive James, "Somewhere Becoming Rain," in*

The New Yorker, *Vol. LXV, No. 22, July 17, 1989, pp. 88-92.*

## Elizabeth Spires

[*Collected Poems* is] a surprisingly thick book when compared with the four individual volumes—running from 42 to 48 pages—that preceded it. To the 117 poems that Larkin himself chose to preserve, Anthony Thwaite, the editor of the present volume, has added 125 unpublished or uncollected poems, thus more than doubling Larkin's available body of work. There are at least a dozen, and perhaps as many as eighteen, previously uncollected poems that serious readers will be very happy to have. These include **"New Year Poem," "Mythological Introduction," "A Stone Church Damaged by a Bomb," "Deep Analysis," "Come then to Prayers," "And the wave sings because it is moving,"** and part I, **"Oils,"** of **"Two Portraits of Sex."** Almost all of the previously uncollected work of literary merit was written before 1950, some of it included in a typewritten manuscript put together in 1947, *In the Grip of Light,* a book for which Larkin could not find a publisher. Much of the rest, however, is not up to the impossibly high standards that Larkin usually imposed on himself. Although Larkin had instructed in his will that his manuscripts and unpublished poems be destroyed, a contradictory clause permitted his trustees to decide what uncollected work should be published. They have probably allowed us to see too much, although it could be argued that anything written by Larkin is of intrinsic interest, if not to the general reader, then to the critic.

The real problem, however, is not one of quantity but of arrangement. [Editor Anthony] Thwaite has chosen to arrange the poems in the strict chronological order of their composition, thus violating Larkin's own brilliant ordering of the four individual books. This is a great loss for the reader coming to Larkin for the first time who must wade through the dazzling, the very good, and the not-so-good and attempt to make sense of it all. A preferable alternative to the present chronological jumble would have been to present the four individual books intact, with previously uncollected work arranged chronologically in a separate section in the back of the book. It is depressing to think that Larkin's future readers will never know that, besides being a superb poet, he was also his own best editor, taking into account sophisticated thematic, tonal, and dramatic considerations when ordering each book.

Although the *Collected Poems* will certainly increase Larkin's general readership, as it should, it will not make a critical reappraisal necessary. Larkin's reputation is assured. He stands, unassailed, as one of England's two or three finest twentieth-century poets although we can never, I think, place Larkin in the same pantheon as Yeats or Eliot, both of whom, in their greatest poems, set out to work in a transcendent mode, to capture the inhuman, timeless moment. "We are not suited to the long perspectives," wrote Larkin in **"Reference Back,"** consciously and deliberately choosing to be a poet of the here and now, to faithfully record his earthly finitude.

Larkin's poems are, on one level, almost immediately accessible. He said in one interview, "there's not much to say about my work. When you've read a poem, that's it, it's all quite clear what it means" [*Required Writing*]. Well, not quite. Not all of the poems are as "easy" as Larkin makes out, though, in general, they can be characterized as small, lucid, and beautifully realized, speaking to us with force and passion on his two great subjects, love and nature. He undertook no large-scale poetic projects and made no attempt to connect, culturally or intellectually, to anything outside or beyond England. In fact, he rejected the notion of an overshadowing classical "tradition," as espoused by Eliot. Writing in D. J. Enright's *Poets of the Nineteen-Fifties,* Larkin declared, "As a guiding principle I believe that every poem must be its own sole freshly created universe, and therefore have no belief in 'tradition' or a common myth-kitty. . . . To me the whole of the ancient world, the whole of classical and biblical mythology means very little, and I think that using them today not only fills poems full of dead spots, but dodges the writer's duty to be original." As a result of this attitude, his poems suffer at times from a peculiar English insularity and can be maddeningly self-centered. In these respects, in esthetics as well as actual practice, Larkin is a minor poet. If such a standard is employed, however, it should be added that there are very few poets writing in England or America today who can meet the standard that Larkin set and consistently maintained in his mature work. (p. 5)

The kinds of poems he wrote and chose to preserve fall, with some exceptions, into three general categories:

1) Violently mechanical "verse," heavily rhymed and metered, characterized by a savage wit and egocentric stance. The tone ranges from the humorous and ironic (**"Toads," "Toads Revisited," "Money"**) to something more bitter and, at times, frighteningly crude and misanthropic (**"Self's the Man," "This Be the Verse," "Annus Mirabilis," "Vers de Société"**); 2) Short lyric poems, less overtly personal, often pastoral in nature. Rhyme and meter, when used, are more muted, the tone quieter; in general, intellectual and emotional affects are more layered and complex (**"Cut Grass," "Water," "Forget What Did," "How Distant," "Born Yesterday," "Wedding Wind"**; some poems, like **"Sad Steps"** and **"High Windows,"** seem tonal "cross overs," belonging to both the first and second categories); and 3) Longer-lined meditations, usually two or three pages, in which the poet proceeds at a measured or leisurely pace; closely akin in tone to the poems in the second category but more narrative and descriptive (**"Church Going," "The Whitsun Weddings," "To the Sea," "The Building," "Show Saturday"**).

Larkin's "verse" poems often take the form of scathing social commentary (particularly on marriage, modern family life, the propagation of the human species), reversing Eliot's famous dictum that poetry is "an escape from personality." Larkin, in a poem like **"This Be the Verse,"** seems helplessly and hopelessly mired in personality and prejudice:

> They fuck you up, your mum and dad,
> They may not mean to, but they do.
> They fill you with the faults they had

And add some extra, just for you.

But they were fucked up in their turn
By fools in old-style hats and coats,
Who half the time were soppy-stern
And half at one another's throats.

Man hands on misery to man.
It deepens like a coastal shelf.
Get out as early as you can,
And don't have any kids yourself.

Hidden under the surface irony, the "music-hall" tone, a deep anger fuels the poem, an anger reinforced by the intentionally crude word choice and metronome-like quality of the meter. The poem alludes to undisclosed wrongs that can never be made right. It, and others in the same vein, are the protest of a man who has spent too much time recovering from early omissions and woundings, from childhood neglect, religious domination, sexual guilt. The poet is shown *in extremis,* in unhappy isolation, protesting his forced membership in the human race. One wonders where Larkin can go from such an extreme position of "intelligent rancour, an integrity of self-hatred" (**"Marriages"**).

Fortunately, the dark alter ego present in the "verse" poems appears only occasionally, at carefully spaced-out intervals, in Larkin's four individual books (but, unfortunately, with a much more alarming frequency in the all-inclusive **Collected Poems**). Strangely, or perhaps not so strangely, these angry poems are some of his best known and most widely quoted work, accounted for, one supposes, by intense reader identification with their unmistakable and unambiguous message. But although we may, in our most pessimistic moments, identify with the sentiments, the "verse" poems do not, to employ Larkin's own criteria, help us to "enjoy or endure."

More often than not, however, Larkin transcends the small, petty human dimension, the entrapments of personality, to write a more generous, expansive poetry. Although he was never, in the strict sense, religious, many of his greatest poems are concerned with the spiritual and communal aspects of human experience, the world often presented as a stage for the intersection of the sacred with the secular. What may be commonplace occurrences for the ordinary man—a stop by a bicyclist at a country church, a holiday at the seaside, a visit to a county fair—are, for Larkin, days of praise and discovery, of ritual and ceremony.

One of his first mature poems where this spiritual curiosity is evident is **"Church Going."** As the poem opens, the attitude of the speaker is one of approach and avoidance: "Once I am sure there's nothing going on / I step inside, letting the door thud shut." But although the bicyclist professes to be "much at a loss . . . wondering what to look for . . .," the poem, as it progresses, mourns the passing of an age of faith, concluding:

For, though I've no idea
What this accoutred frowsty barn is worth,
It pleases me to stand in silence here;

A serious house on serious earth it is,
In whose blent air all our compulsions meet,

Are recognised, and robed as destinies.
And that much never can be obsolete,
Since someone will forever be surprising
A hunger in himself to be more serious,
And gravitating with it to this ground,
Which, he once heard, was proper to grow wise
    in,
If only that so many dead lie round.

Larkin's "frowsty barn" is a house for the spirit, the poet acknowledging the possibility of a Grand Order ("compulsions . . . robed as destinities"), the sanctity of the dead. Although the word is never used, and perhaps deliberately avoided, it is clear that the speaker stands on *holy* ground. Despite the speaker's agnostic pose, he recognizes a spiritual impulse, "A hunger in himself to be more serious," the poem concluding, appropriately, with a moment of silent meditation.

In **"Water,"** first collected in *The Whitsun Weddings,* Larkin half-seriously, half-playfully proposes a new-style religion:

*If I were called in*
To construct a religion
I should make use of water.

Going to church
Would entail a fording
To dry, different clothes.

My liturgy would employ
Images of sousing,
A furious devout drench.

And I should raise in the east
A glass of water
Where any-angled light
Would congregate endlessly.

The man who in **"Sympathy in White Major"** raises a glass of gin here plays priest to the secular in raising a simple glass of water. His "religion," is minimal, pared to the extreme, although it does incorporate one or two traditional elements, such as baptism and purification. His imagined religion is non-exclusionary, a place where the "any-angled light" of human individuality can join itself to a larger unity continuing into eternity. In celebrating the consecration of water, Larkin celebrates the ordination of one of the most commonplace yet essential substances necessary for life. It is a religion without inward division, whose only "creed" is tolerance and communality.

The sacramental also comes into play in **"The Whitsun Weddings"** which immediately follows **"Water"** in Larkin's original ordering (but does not, alas, in the *Collected Poems,* one of the many losses in terms of thematic and dramatic juxtaposition and linkage). The poem is set in June, on the seventh Sunday after Easter when the Holy Ghost descended upon the apostles in tongues of flame. The speaker, riding alone, is on a train bound for London, filling at each stop with newly married couples from the lower and middle classes. Although Larkin is often savage toward such types, here he describes a cross-section of humanity with good-natured tolerance and regard. . . .

[There is an implicit interest] in life happening, valuable

no matter how tawdry or tasteless. The train ride spans, metaphorically, an entire lifetime:

> Some fifty minutes, that in time would seem
>
> Just long enough to settle hats and say
> I nearly died,
> A dozen marriages got under way.

Fifty minutes or fifty years, the poet presents life, precious life, as passing in the blink of an eye. As the train approaches London

> . . . walls of blackened moss
> Come close and it was nearly done, this frail
> Travelling coincidence; and what it held
> Stood ready to be loosed with all the power
> That being changed can give. We slowed again,
> And as the tightened brakes took hold, there swelled
> A sense of falling, like an arrow shower
> Sent out of sight, somewhere becoming rain.

The transformation of pentecostal tongues of fire into falling rain is an ambiguous image, suggesting both a human falling off or failing as well as a shower of spiritual grace. The poem succeeds in suggesting the full ambiguity and mystery inherent in marriage, part ordeal, part sacrament, in which the newly married are propelled with frightening speed toward an overcast and possibly anticlimactic future. And yet, whatever the outcome, they are *changed,* the secular world charged, as Larkin sees it, with mystic significance.

In subsequent poems, Larkin continues to see daily life in terms of rite and ritual, often making use of the image of sacramental water. In **"To the Sea,"** the poet captures "the miniature gaiety of seasides" but takes as his hidden subject the human congregation, the same cross-section of humanity, dressed in different clothes, that appears in **"The Whitsun Weddings."** The tone and attitude of the poem betray a tenderness toward life:

> Still going on, all of it, still going!
> To lie, eat, sleep in hearing of the surf
> (Ears to transistors, that sound tame enough
> Under the sky), or gently up and down
> Lead the uncertain children, frilled in white
> And grasping at enormous air, or wheel
> The rigid old along for them to feel
> A final summer, plainly still occurs
> As half an annual pleasure, half a rite . . .

For Larkin, holidays *are* holy days, occasions of communality and celebration resonant with meaning and memory. The poem ends with an image of baptism. . . . [There is a longing] for human fellowship and relatedness, a belief that "our falling short" can be mitigated by a sense of charity and duty toward others, basic Christian precepts. Larkin, who once said he tried to make "every day and every year exactly the same" (*Required Writing*), represents life's repetitions, daily, yearly, generational, as being of supreme value.

Larkin shifts from the expansive, all-embracing tone and attitude of **"To the Sea"** to something harder-edged and angrier in **"High Windows"** as he half-skeptically, half-longingly muses on the sexual revolution of the sixties:

> When I see a couple of kids
> And guess he's fucking her and she's
> Taking pills or wearing a diaphragm,
> I know this is paradise
>
> Everyone old has dreamed of all their lives—
> Bonds and gestures pushed to one side
> Like an outdated combine harvester,
> And everyone young going down the long slide
>
> To happiness, endlessly. I wonder if
> Anyone looked at me, forty years back,
> And thought, That'll be the life;
> No God any more, or sweating in the dark
>
> About hell and that, or having to hide
> What you think of the priest. He
> And his lot will all go down the long slide
> Like free bloody birds. *And immediately*
>
> Rather than words comes the thought of high windows:
> The sun-comprehending glass,
> And beyond it, the deep blue air, that shows
> Nothing, and is nowhere, and is endless.

The glass of water raised in the east in **"Water"** is here transformed into "the sun-comprehending glass" of the poet's own soul or inner being, his "high windows" flat (Larkin lived most of his adult life in top floor flats) a perfect vantage point to contemplate eternity. Or oblivion. The poem exists in a state of suspension between traditional and modern values, the past presented as guilt-ridden and sexually repressed, the present pleasureable but lacking in commitment or consequence. Individual freedom, in this case sexual freedom, is pictured as an uncontrolled descent where all "will go down the long slide / Like free bloody birds." The struggle between what the "I" wants and what society demands and imposes almost breaks the poem apart at the end of the fourth stanza, the tone and idiom shifting dramatically from the crude language of the street to more elevated poetic statement. Juxtaposed to the frightening image of slaughter are Larkin's high windows, wordless and ineffable, reminiscent of George Herbert's divine windows (to which Larkin's poem may owe a debt), in which life's mysteries are contained but not articulated.

Although Larkin's paradise is not, as he mockingly asserts, the paradise of unfettered sexuality in **"High Windows,"** it *is* to be found here on earth in occasions such as **"Show Saturday,"** possibly his greatest poem. Sacred as any Sunday is Show Saturday, where young and old come together not to worship a Supreme Creator but to celebrate the richness and variety of human creation. . . . (pp. 5-9)

The lines, packed with dense description, spill over, running to as many as fourteen syllables, as if to signify the wealth of earthly abundance. Much of the imagery, so seemingly "realistic," is, in fact, symbolic or allusive: the human talent of "growing and making" allusive to the biblical story of the talents; the rustic tables in the "long high tent" where leeks sit "like church candles" reminiscent of altars in a church. Like so many of Larkin's poems, **"Show Saturday"** attempts to make spiritual sense of the world not through a dogmatic religious framework but through poetic vision, the poet perceiving the excellence of creation in the "single supreme versions" (human, animal, vegetable) gathered for Show Saturday. This vision, recognizing as it does the linkages and correspondences of the material world but detached from any belief system, constitutes the underpinnings of the poet's faith.

The poem closes with an invocation as the show is dismantled for another year:

> Let it stay hidden there like strength, below
> Sale-bills and swindling; something people do,
> Not noticing how time's rolling smithy-smoke
> Shadows much greater gestures; something they
>     share
> That breaks ancestrally each year into
> Regenerate union. Let it always be there.

The tone is reverent, the poem ending not with a wish or imperative but with supplication. One could say, in fact, that Larkin is *praying*. Certainly **"Show Saturday"** is his most spiritual poem where, despite the example of his own single, solitary life, he desires "regenerate union." Paradise is *here*, or could be, Larkin suggests, here in the on-going daily life of earth, the poem echoing the beautifully naive sentiment of an early poem, **"Days,"** that days "are to be happy in."

**"Show Saturday,"** dated December 3, 1973, was the last poem to be finished and subsequently included in *High Windows,* published in 1974. Although it could have easily concluded the book, in Larkin's ordering it does not. Instead, *High Windows* ends on a more apocalyptic note with **"The Explosion"** (again, the dramatic effectiveness of the book's closure is lost in the chronological reordering of the *Collected Poems*). The first half of the poem presents [miners] advancing, carefree and unaware, toward their impending death. . . . The second half of the poem takes a surprising turn:

> At noon, there came a tremor; cows
> Stopped chewing for a second; sun,
> Scarfed as in a heat-haze, dimmed.
>
> The dead go on before us, they
> Are sitting in God's house in comfort,
> We shall see them face to face—
>
> Plain as lettering in the chapels
> It was said, and for a second
> Wives saw men of the explosion
>
> Larger than in life they managed—
> Gold as on a coin, or walking
> Somehow from the sun towards them,
>
> One showing the eggs unbroken.

The attitude toward death and Christian belief is very different here from, say, **"Aubade"** where the poet flatly asserts that religion is "That vast moth-eaten musical brocade / Created to pretend we never die." Not only are the dead in **"The Explosion"** shown as momentarily radiant and transfigured, the possibility is offered in the highlighted sixth stanza that an afterlife awaits them. Death is presented in the context of both light *and* life, in the symbolic, regenerative images of the sun and unbroken eggs (the sun, for Larkin, always perceived as a source of life, as when he writes in **"Solar,"** "The eye sees you / Simplified

by distance / Into an origin . . ."). In the open-endedness of **"The Explosion,"** and in its placement as the last poem in *High Windows,* Larkin's artistic instincts prevail over whatever doubt and fear the subject of death held for the man.

Obviously, it is possible to misrepresent Larkin by focusing too exclusively on his poems of faith and slighting, by omission, those more reflective of his personal unhappiness and pessimism. In harsh counterpoint to Larkin's desire for "regenerate union" are the terrified sentiments of other late poems. In **"The Old Fools,"** the hard fact of his own mortality shadows whatever hope poems like **"Show Saturday"** and **"The Explosion"** may hold out for the reader. He writes:

> At death, you break up: the bits that were you
> Start speeding away from each other for ever
> With no one to see. It's only oblivion, true . . .

And in much the same vein, he pictures death in **"Aubade"** as

> . . . total emptiness for ever,
> The sure extinction that we travel to
> And shall be lost in always. Not to be here,
> Not to be anywhere,
> And soon; nothing more terrible, nothing more
>     true.

Often, it seems, in the "I-centered" poems (where we would identify the person speaking as Larkin the man), the poet denies himself the consolation and reassurances so forthcoming in his less overtly personal poems. While disquieting, this is not so much a tragedy for the reader as it is, in its implications, for Larkin.

In the end, there is no way to reconcile the wild oscillation in the poems between vision and faith on the one hand, and doubt and despair on the other. We must simply accept the fact that the two sides of the poet uneasily co-exist, recognizing that the poems' often contradictory attitudes do not so much lessen the art as humanize the man. In reading Larkin, it may be helpful to go full circle, back to **"New Year Poem,"** written in 1940, in which the voices of the living direct the poet on his course:

> 'It is to us that you should turn your straying at-
>     tention;
> Us who need you, and are affected by your for-
>     tune;
> Us you should love and to whom you should
>     give your word.'

In his greatest poems, Larkin did precisely that. The poems of Larkin that help us to "enjoy and endure" and that will be read and admired by future generations are not the poems of personal cavil against the universe's great game of existence but the poems that attend to the living, that perceive the pattern, that count each day a sacred day. (pp. 9-10)

*Elizabeth Spires, "Sacred Days: The Collected Poems of Philip Larkin," in* The American Poetry Review, *Vol. 19, No. 3, May-June, 1990, pp. 5-10.*

## FURTHER READING

### Bibliographies

Bloomfield, B. C. *Philip Larkin: A Bibliography.* London: Faber, 1982, 187 p.

Dyson, Brian *et al,* editors. *Philip Larkin: His Life and Work.* Hull: Brynmor Jones Library, 1986.

Tierce, Mike. "Philip Larkin: Secondary Sources. 1950-1984." *Bulletin Of Bibliography.* Vol. 43, No. 2 (June 1986): 67-75.

### Reviews of *Collected Poems*

Ash, John. "A Poet in Spite of His Fans: Philip Larkin's Great Depression." *The Village Voice* XXXIV, No. 31 (8 August 1989): 56.
> Praises *Collected Poems* but admonishes "Larkinism" and "Larkinites"—those who herald Larkin as a champion of traditional, anti-modernist values in art and society.

Brookhiser, Richard. Review of *Collected Poems. The American Spectator* 22, No. 10 (October 1989): 46-8.
> General discussion of Larkin's poetic language and subject matter in which the critic characterizes Larkin as a love poet.

Dunn, Douglas. "Larkin's Golden Treasury." *Punch* 296 (21 October 1988): 35, 38.
> Positive assessment of the previously unpublished pieces in *Collected Poems,* which the critic calls "the publishing event of the year."

Filkins, Peter. "The Collected Larkin: 'But why put it into words?'" *The Iowa Review* 20, No. 2 (Spring-Summer 1990): 166-181.
> Overview of Larkin's work with emphasis on the poet's development. The critic relies on the chronological arrangement of *Collected Poems* to trace relationships between previously published and unpublished pieces.

Flamm, Matthew. "The Bard of Deprivation." *The Nation* 249, No. 3 (17 July 1989): 93-4.
> Discusses Larkin's poems in relation to his experiences.

Fleming, Thomas. "Testaments of the Age." *National Review* XLI, No. 10 (2 June 1989): 58, 60.
> General commentary on Larkin's poetic concerns and achievement. The critic expresses disappointment that most of the previously unpublished pieces in *Collected Poems* are inferior to Larkin's best known work.

Forbes, Peter. "Choice Cuts." *The Listener* 120, No. 3084 (13 October 1988): 33.
> General discussion of abiding concerns in Larkin's verse, concentrating on previously unpublished pieces.

Lucas, John. "The Unofficial Laureate." *New Statesman & Society* 1, No. 19 (14 October 1988): 32-3.
> Brief discussion of Larkin's provincialism and xenophobia.

McClatchy, J. D. "Songs of a Curmudgeon." *The New York Times Book Review* (21 May 1989): 24-5.
> Discusses poems from various phases of Larkin's career. The critic views *Collected Poems* as "a fascinating and indispensable text."

Skinner, John. "Philip Larkin by Philip Larkin." *Ariel* 20, No. 1 (January 1989): 77-95.
> Combines interpretation of Larkin's poems with his commentary on his life and poetics to trace autobiographical elements in his work.

Wiltshire, John. "Philip Larkin: The Life with a Hole in it." *The Cambridge Quarterly* XIX, No. 3: 255-65.
> Discussion of Larkin's life and work, drawing upon *Collected Poems,* Jean Hartley's reminiscences of her relationship with Larkin in *Philip Larkin, the Marvell Press and me,* and the essays collected in *Philip Larkin: The Man and his Work,* edited by Dale Salwak.

Wojahn, David. "Four from Prospero." *The Georgia Review* XLIII, No. 3 (Fall 1989): 589-601.
> Review of *Collected Poems* focusing on Larkin's approach to grim realities of existence.

Wood, Michael. "Dismantling the Larkin Myth." *Parnassus: Poetry in Review* 16, No. 1: 165-73.
> The critic challenges the "myth" that Larkin's breakthrough and lasting importance as a poet resulted from his renunciation of the verse of W. H. Auden and W. B. Yeats that had influenced his early work. According to Wood, Larkin avoided risk and challenge in order to propogate his reputation as a poet of gloom.

### Books on Larkin: 1980-1991

Chambers, Harry. *An Enormous Yes. In Memoriam: Philip Larkin, 1922-1985.* Calstock: Peterloo Poets, 1986, 67 p.
> Melange of poems and tributes to Larkin and his works; includes illustrations as well as a number of poems and prose pieces by Larkin.

Harvey, Geoffrey. *The Romantic Tradition in Modern English Poetry: Rhetoric and Experience.* Basingstoke: MacMillan, 1986, 134 p.
> Places Larkin in a Romantic tradition that includes William Wordsworth, Thomas Hardy, and John Betjeman, writers united by their view of the poet as one who recognizes a "complex set of relations existing in a state of tension."

Hoffpauir, Richard. *English Poetry from Hardy to Larkin.* London: Associated University Presses, 1991, 332 p.
> Survey that focuses particularly on poets whose works value restraint and order.

Latre, Guido. *Locking Earth to Sky: A Structuralist Approach to Philip Larkin's Poetry.* New York: P. Lang, 1985, 470 p.
> Draws upon structuralist methodologies of such critics as Roman Jakobson and David Lodge to interpret Larkin's work.

Morrison, Blake. *The Movement: British Poetry and Fiction of the 1950s.* London: Oxford University Press, 1980, 326 p.
> A history of the development and concerns of writers associated with The Movement, a trend in English literature during the 1950s with which Larkin is often linked.

Petch, Simon. *The Art of Philip Larkin.* Sydney: Sydney University press, 1981, 108 p.

Explores the poet-reader relationship developed in Larkin's work, with attention to Larkin's strategies for manipulating particular responses. Also addresses the poet's outlook on moral and social issues, provides a psychological profile of the poet's persona, and explores satirical elements in Larkin's work.

Rossen, Janice. *Philip Larkin: His Life's Work.* Iowa City: University of Iowa Press, 1989, 156 p.

Explores a variety of issues pertaining to Larkin's work, including his use of the lyric form to express personal feelings and social commentary; communal and national interests represented in his verse; his mysogyny; and reasons for the writer's block that affected Larkin during various phases of his career.

Salwak, Dale, editor. *Philip Larkin: The Man and his Work.* Basingstoke: MacMillan, 1988, 184 p.

Collection of essays by several critics focusing on various traits in Larkin's verse.

Thwaite, Anthony, editor. *Larkin at Sixty.* London: Faber, 1982, 148 p.

Collection of anecdotes, tributes, and criticism by twenty noted literary figures on the occasion of Larkin's sixtieth birthday.

Whalen, Terry. *Philip Larkin and English Poetry.* Basingstoke: MacMillan, 1986, 164 p.

Links Larkin's work to that of various poets and poetic traditions, including those the poet expressed distaste towards—D. H. Lawrence and Ezra Pound, Imagism and modernism.

# Craig Lucas

## 19??-

American playwright and scriptwriter.

In his plays, Lucas often creates a disorienting effect by merging past with present, and fantasy with reality. Through comic dialogue, he exposes human pretensions, frailties, and potential strengths. While generally praising the witty language in his plays, critics are divided regarding his use of absurdist techniques. Some berate his plays as devoid of logical character development and coherent plot structure, while others interpret Lucas's disjointed plots as metaphors for contemporary social and political conditions.

In *Blue Window,* winner of the Los Angeles Drama Critics' Award, Lucas satirizes affected, narcissistic behavior in modern society. At a Sunday evening dinner party in New York, guests of varying backgrounds and occupations discuss their work and ideas, often simultaneously, while the hostess, Libby, bustles to and from the kitchen trying to conceal her missing teeth. While some reviewers found the superimposed action confusing, others praised the play's insightful dialogue. Edith Oliver observed: "Mr. Lucas has a fine ear for a particular kind of New York social chatter, especially among people who don't know one another, and for the hints of fear and unhappiness and loneliness that break through amusing lines." *Three Postcards,* a musical written in collaboration with composer and lyricist Craig Carnelia, also explores the volatile emotions behind seemingly placid situations. In this play, three women gather for a reunion in a fashionable restaurant. Although old friends, they are unable to communicate honestly, and their true feelings of dissatisfaction are revealed through daydreams and individual memories occurring throughout the meal. Many critics enjoyed the play's comic dialogue, and were intrigued by the hypnotic effect of overlapping past events upon the present.

Lucas's next work, *Reckless,* has been described as cartoon-like because of its surreal elements. The performance begins with the main character, Rachel, in bed with her husband on Christmas Eve, chattering gleefully about the holiday and her children. Her euphoric state is disrupted, however, when her husband announces that he has hired someone to kill her, and that she has only moments to escape. The subsequent plot presents Rachel's bizarre journey with a compassionate physical therapist and his deaf-mute wife, both of whom conceal their true identities. While many reviewers found the plot structure confusing, others considered the play to be an examination of the unexplainable forces that control humanity and the difficulties of escaping the "reckless" events of the past. Several critics viewed the play as an intensely political comment on American society, with Rachel's daft personality representing the false "American Dream" in the face of widespread social discord. Social commentary is also apparent in *Prelude to a Kiss,* in which a young bride trapped within a dying man's body serves as a reflection of the heartbreak and frustration associated with the AIDS epidemic. Occasionally categorized as an inverted fairy tale, *Prelude to a Kiss* revolves around the trauma experienced at the wedding ceremony of the main characters, Peter and Rita. When a sickly old man, unknown to all the guests, kisses Rita, she takes on his personality. Subsequent events concern the problem of maintaining love in the face of Rita's undesirable transformation and her impending mortality. Frank Rich wrote: "[This play celebrates] the redemptive power of unselfish love that never dies, of true love that survives transient flesh." The winner of a 1990 Obie Award—off-Broadway theater's highest honor—*Prelude to a Kiss* is regarded as Lucas's most successful and satisfying play to date.

In addition to plays, Lucas has also written the acclaimed film, *Longtime Companion.* Generally considered the first mainstream theatrical work to confront the AIDS epidemic, this film chronicles eight years of painful illnesses, deaths, and broken friendships experienced by a group of homosexual New Yorkers coping with AIDS. Lucas has been praised for promoting awareness of the fatal disease in a sober, accurate, and unsentimental tone.

## PRINCIPAL WORKS

### PLAYS

*Blue Window*   1984
*Three Postcards*   [with Craig Carnelia]   1987
*Reckless*   1988
*Prelude to a Kiss*   1990

### SCREENPLAYS

*Longtime Companion*   1990

---

### John Simon

Craig Lucas, the author of ***Blue Window,*** is a canny manipulator of words, has a good ear for the bourgeois and bohemian languages of New York, and perceives the interplay of incongruous characters with the eye of an enterprising satirist. "You lay down with a psychiatrist (I assume the solecism is deliberate)," someone says, "and you wake up with flaws." A family therapist explains her calling: "We try to look at the dynamics of the family and see if we can't blame someone else for it." A neurotic young woman addresses a sympathetic male: "Oh, Norbert . . . you're so sweet, and you have such a stupid name!"

Much of the dialogue of this play that comprises a pre-party, a party, and a post-party sequence involving several singles and couples (one lesbian pair) is superimposed like the talk in a Robert Altman film, even as the characters co-exist in a kind of simultaneous three-ring circus. It all sounds like the captions of *New Yorker* cartoons impishly strung together and can get frightfully confusing, though with method, perhaps even a trifle too much of it, in the confusion. Sometimes a sudden, single, nakedly exposed statement subsumes all the characters in several different, embarrassing senses, and symbols, notably the blue window of the title, echo through the play with cunningly shifty meanings. But all this ingenuity does not shake down into a shapely action, a dramatic experience, a palpable play. And when, in the end, comic pain aspires to tragic suffering, the fabric rips. . . .

[Still, you] may sink in the quicksands of *Blue Window,* but you'll sink unbored.

> *John Simon, in a review of "Blue Window," in* New York *Magazine, Vol. 17, No. 30, July 30, 1984, p. 53.*

## Edith Oliver

[The setting for *Blue Window*] is an abstract living room, with vignettes of other rooms appearing here and there as required. The backdrop, a large abstract painting on a scrim, is a clue, for Craig Lucas's play—an engaging comedy with a sad strain running through it—is itself an abstract, a mosaic of overlapping episodes and conversations. *Blue Window* is about a dinner party whose hostess and guests are of assorted backgrounds and assorted sexes. The place is an apartment in this city; the time is a Sunday evening. In the first scene—pre-party—the characters wander in, busy with their own concerns and unaware of one another—the action is simultaneous—but they soon sort themselves out. The hostess, whose name is Libby, mixes punch in a large bowl, making sporadic telephone calls to her young man, one Griever, who has promised to come early and help her with the food. But he is too pre-occupied with his reflection in a mirror, as he dresses and blow-dries his hair, to make any effort. A psychiatrist called Boo practices Italian with her lover, a writer named Alice, whose new novel is the occasion for the party; they are about to go to Europe. Tom, a musician and a former lover of Libby's, plays a composition of his own to his girl Emily, a secretary. The final character is Norbert, a sky diver. Just before the scene ends, Libby faces the audience and smiles, to reveal a gap of missing teeth.

The second scene is the party. The guests discuss their work and ideas, and writers and books, as the hostess, scurrying to and from the kitchen, tries to conceal the gap in her face. "Her lip itches" is Alice's conclusion. Mr. Lucas has a fine ear for a particular kind of New York social chatter, especially among people who don't know one another, and for the hints of fear and unhappiness and loneliness that break through amusing lines. His tone always seems exactly right. In the kitchen, Libby explains to Griever that she broke the caps off her teeth opening a jar of caviar. Suddenly, Emily stands and then, wander-

ing around, sings a charming, plaintive song, "The Same Thing . . . ". (p. 78)

The third scene is post-party. The guests have gone home—only Norbert remains with the hostess. This time, it is Griever, alone, who makes the calls to her and then sadly gives up. Boo and Alice, having had too much to drink, pick on each other and irritably discuss their affair. Emily and Tom watch television with the sound off. In a long monologue, Libby tells Norbert a terrible story that explains her panic and insecurity (and loose teeth). The words "blue window" occur in several speeches, but their symbolic value, whatever it may be, seems forced and out of key. (pp. 78, 80)

> *Edith Oliver, in a review of "Blue Window," in* The New Yorker, *Vol. LX, No. 29, September 3, 1984, pp. 78, 80.*

## Clive Barnes

There are lots of things you can write home about on *Three Postcards*—the musical play by Craig Lucas and Craig Carnelia . . . and many of them are unflattering.

You might call the show pretentious, irritatingly difficult to follow or annoyingly cute. And I think you would be right.

You might decide to lay into Carnelia's skitteringly inconsequential, sub-Sondheimian score—and you would have a point.

Or you might find fault with the consistently inconsistent strain of anarchy that runs through the show—the willful breaking of sense, time and character rules, the sense of an inside joke not quite turned inside out.

But then I look at my own postcard of the show and find—rather terrifyingly—that I have written, almost without thinking: "Having a Great Time! Wish I Were Here!!" Now, what on earth did I mean by that? Wish I were *there?* I was there, wasn't I?

You see, it is a show that raises almost as many doubts as enthusiasms. In a defensive way I very much enjoyed it, but I'm going to have a hard time convincing you how.

The setting is a cafe—more of a chic restaurant, I suppose. Two men are drinking coffee. They get up. One says something like: "I've decided." Then he goes to the piano at the back of the set.

He's the pianist. The other man puts on a funny colored tux. He's the waiter. His tux has a sort of salad design on it.

There is only one table. Just as well. There are only three customers—three women, meeting, it seems, after an absence of some time, although time proves an uneven marker in this piece.

One woman, Big Jane, is simply a mess, and the other two periodically do their best about it. The second is hyperactive and given to fantasy; the third appears to be rich and neurotic.

All three of them are pretty neurotic, if it comes to that. So is the show.

But I found myself succumbing to it because of its simply its all-embracing atmosphere, its sudden intimacy. Its extraordinary virtues creep up on your boredom, unannounced, unexpected. It is like an unpromising stranger at a cocktail party who suddenly starts to talk disquieting sense.

A story is told of a '40s photograph of a wedding party—the people, the car, the frozen clouds, the atmosphere—that sums up the whole impact of nostalgia, the transience of life and time.

The evening is full of such baby depth-charges, as it dizzily charts its characters' strange emotional lives. We are sucked into its odd ambiance and, almost hypnotized, we are entranced even while essentially unenlightened. At least I was—and, after all, this is my postcard.

> *Clive Barnes, " 'Postcards': Had a Wonderful Time," in* New York Post, *May 15, 1987.*

## Mel Gussow

In ***Three Postcards,*** a new musical play by Craig Lucas and Craig Carnelia, one character is obsessed by a newspaper article about the self-transforming power of subatomic particles. They change shape as scientists watch them. Presumably this is meant to be a metaphor for the show. . . .

Though we think we are overhearing a desultory conversation at the table next to us in a trendy restaurant, actually the characters are supposed to be describing the essence of their sad lives. The truth, however, is that the play consists of particles—unchanging and ultimately unrewarding. The ordinary sometimes descends to the banal.

***Three Postcards*** begins with a waiter and a pianist (Mr. Carnelia, who is also the composer and lyricist) finishing their own dinner, having a whistling competition and then seguing into table service. Enter three women, gathered as if for a reunion. Their conversation is filled with breathless phrases that end before they arrive at a period. Occasionally they suggest that the stories have been told before—and some of them should never have been told in the first place.

The time span is confusing, as the dialogue ambles from childhood to prospective future, stopping for a long period in the recent past, when a character identified as Big Jane lingered for almost five years in Martinique and refused to see her friends . . . The talk is often as revealing as the postcards remembered by the women ("You'd love this hotel. The water's blue").

In the background, Mr. Carnelia plays music of his own composition, always amiable but seldom rising above sub-Sondheim. On cue, the cast sings. All are in good voice, but the words do not sound so very different from the conversations. One ballad simply dispenses with poetic invention and uses dummy lyrics ("This song should say . . . ").

In brief, strange interludes, the characters speak the unspoken. . . . "I hate you," [the waiter] says offhandedly to Little Jane—and she does a quick doubletake, as if her ears misled her. . . .

The show is periodically enlivened by [the waiter's] dry recitation of specials not on the menu, lavishly described concoctions from soup (cream of fennel) to sorbet (lime, made on the premises). The specials remind one that the play itself offers little nourishment.

> *Mel Gussow, "The Stage: 'Postcards'," in* The New York Times, *May 15, 1987, p. C3.*

## William A. Henry III

***Three Postcards*** is outwardly a work of serene, minimalist simplicity. Three women, no longer girls and not yet matrons, meet for a meal at a trendy restaurant. Some of their talk is about how much they matter to one another, but they do not communicate. Only in daydreams and memories (enacted in scenes interspersed with their meal) do they reveal much of what they are really feeling. Then a casual question makes plain that the woman who seems the most contented is in fact coping with cruel domestic tragedy and that her friends' seeming triviality amounts to a benign conspiracy of silence to allow her a few moments of escape.

This poignant material is told obliquely and often with a fey nuttiness. The audience begins to understand that it has stepped outside the literal world when the most neurotically self-absorbed of the women confides to one of her companions that the waiter hates her, and a few moments later, he does indeed turn and say, deadpan, "I hate you."

> *William A. Henry III, in a review of "Three Postcards," in* Time, New York, *Vol. 129, No. 21, May 25, 1987, p. 71.*

## Jerry Tallmer

[Craig Lucas's ***Reckless***] is a drama about, among a dozen other things, one woman who never stops talking and another woman—younger, a paraplegic, in a wheelchair—who pretends to be unable to talk or hear. In a way, though playwright Lucas might think me daft, these two are a little like Hamm and Clov of Beckett's *Endgame*—Hamm, who cannot walk, Clov, who cannot sit.

The woman with the logorrhea . . . is Rachel Mary Ellen Sissle Fitzimmons, whom we meet on Christmas morning in the middle of "one of my euphoria attacks." Her husband kisses her, and through his tears tonelessly announces: "I took a contract out on your life." As the hired killer comes busting in at the bay windows downstairs, repentant hubby hustles Rachel out into the snow in bathrobe and slippers to make the best getaway she can.

She makes it to a phone booth at a gas station, which is where she meets Lloyd, who is searching for gas. He gives her a lift as, indomitably optimistic, she chatters away—a lift at first to nowhere, then to his house, which is where we meet woman No. 2.

For about a half-hour we, like Rachel, watch Lloyd tenderly wheeling his young wife Pooty around the premises and communicating with her in sign language, which Rachel amusingly struggles to absorb. I was just connecting all this to that spastic girlchild in the wheelchair in the heartbreaking *Joe Egg,* when suddenly, with Lloyd out of the room, Pooty starts to talk, shocking the hell out of Rachel and us. Her muteness is a ruse to keep Lloyd's love.

From there, **Reckless** gathers force, burlesque turns, TV game-show parodies—irresistible to the playwright, but perhaps a mistake—psychiatric parodies, absurdities of violence, shootings, poisonings, deaths, regenerations, and the long arm of coincidence stretched a bit too far.

If this sounds negative, it isn't meant that way. And if John Guare walked barefoot in his blue leaves over the ground of **Reckless** many years ago, well, so be it. One source feeds the other, as long as the other is worthwhile. **Reckless** is very worthwhile.

> *Jerry Tallmer, " 'Reckless': Killingly Funny Start to Season," in* New York Post, *September 26, 1988.*

## Frank Rich

"I'll be home for Christmas," sings Bing Crosby, "if only in my dreams."

With that soothing lyric lingering in our ears, the lights go up on Craig Lucas's anything-but-comforting **Reckless**. . . . It's Christmas, all right—in more ways than one. With **Reckless,** a revision of a play briefly seen Off Off Broadway in 1983, Mr. Lucas has given us a bittersweet Christmas fable for our time: *It's a Wonderful Life* as it might be reimagined for a bruising contemporary America in which homelessness may be a pervasive spiritual condition rather than a sociological crisis. (p. C19)

While **Reckless** finally has a simple emotional pull akin to that of a Crosby ballad born of the lonely World War II home front, it yanks us through every conceivable absurdist hoop, fracturing narrative, language and characterization on the way to its rending destination.

**Reckless** begins as a cheerful contemporary fairy tale. Rachel, a contented mother of two young boys, sits up in bed with her husband and counts her Yuletide blessings. Rachel is having a "euphoria attack"; she's convinced she is "going to be terminally happy." Even the snowstorm swirling outside the bedroom window is benign—a "monster" perhaps, but a sweet one that will "carry us away into a dream."

Only moments later, however, a panic-stricken Rachel finds herself leaping through her window in her housecoat and slippers, beginning a bizarre odyssey that may or may not be a dream. Among other adventures, she becomes the unofficial adoptive child of a physical therapist and his deaf paraplegic wife, serves as a contestant on the game show "Your Mother or Your Wife?" and witnesses a double murder engineered by an embezzling employee of a nonprofit humanitarian foundation called Hands Across the Sea. As Rachel leaves her own children farther and

farther behind, Christmas follows Christmas, and town follows town, each of them named Springfield. "I don't even know what state we're in," says the heroine by the middle of Act II.

Neither do we. Rachel's fantastic journey induces a state of dreamy disorientation in the audience, as if it, too, were tumbling through existence in a perpetual free fall. But Mr. Lucas isn't idly spinning out a shaggy dog story; a pattern emerges from the screwball riffs. Like Rachel, almost everyone she meets proves to be using an assumed name and running guiltily away from a past life. We learn that the play's most selfless characters have accidental manslaughters in their past, that the most paternal men and maternal women have deserted their children. "Do you think we ever really know people?" asks Rachel early on. Mr. Lucas's implicit answer is no. The only hope for the people in **Reckless** is that they truly know themselves.

Although the process by which Rachel and the others achieve that self-knowledge is sometimes spelled out in clinical terms (especially in the stridently Oedipal game show), Mr. Lucas at his best dramatizes his characters' breakthroughs with striking originality. After intermission, the comic dreaminess of **Reckless** curdles and darkens until finally we realize that clichéd Freudian landmarks (from the journey through the birth canal to the loss of parents) have been re-enacted elliptically in the crazy-quilt narrative, to traumatic effect. "The past is irrelevant; it's something we wake up from," is Rachel's Pollyanna view of life in the first act. By Act II, she and we come to appreciate, as other lines have it, that "things happen for a reason" and that "the past is the nightmare you wake up to every day."

While this realization dawns, Mr. Lucas ingeniously merges his characters' pasts and presents, their real lives and their dream lives. . . . [A] psychiatrist in **Reckless** reminds us dreams are also anagrams—of our wishes and fears. Mr. Lucas's play is an anagram in which all the quirky character and plot details of Act I are rearranged into a new and revealing pattern in Act II. Eventually that pattern takes shape as a hallucinatory maze of transference: the evening's haunting final scene can be read—with equal validity and equal pathos—as a first session between a therapist and her new patient or as an unexpected Dickensian reunion between a mother and a long-lost son. Either way, loving hands reach across the sea: The characters have at last come home for Christmas, if only in their dreams.

**Reckless** is not flawless. Mr. Lucas can be carried away by his own cleverness; there are cloying gags and self-indulgent repetitions. But the writer's compassion, so redolent at times of Anne Tyler's *Dinner at the Homesick Restaurant,* usually rescues his play from its precious excesses. "Life's been reckless with these people," we're told of the homeless people inhabiting a shelter. Mr. Lucas feels for all victims of life's recklessness—from those psychotic homeless who "carry no identification whatsoever" to the ordinary rest of us whose own intimations of homelessness and death must arrive sooner or later with one hurtful form or another of parental abandonment. (pp. C19, C22)

There have been merrier Christmases than Mr. Lucas's, but how many of them have been so true? (p. C22)

*Frank Rich, "A Christmas Fable of People Who Learn to Know Themselves," in* The New York Times, *September 26, 1988, pp. C19, C22.*

### John Simon

What is Craig Lucas's *Reckless* about? As a doctor running a shelter for the homeless states, "Life's been reckless with these people," and it is certainly reckless with everyone in the play, though the recklessness seems reciprocal. The past with its torments may be something we wake up from or, more likely, keep waking up into. Life may be a dream, but our worst dreams may turn out to be our life. It's rather a tall order for a play, but the absurdist mode may make it easier for the playwright.

Easier, that is, if he knows what he's doing. But does he? Rachel, the sweetly sappy heroine, is in bed with her husband, Tom, on the night before her beloved Christmas, when he tells her that the killer he has hired to off her is due any minute and she must escape through the window in nightgown, robe, and slippers. She finds this rather mean but complies, and is picked up in a phone booth by a kindly therapist, Lloyd, who takes her home with him to Springfield, Massachusetts, where he lives with his paraplegic and deaf-mute wife, Pooty. Only, as Pooty later confesses to Rachel, she's not a deaf-mute; the additional affliction was to get her extra attention at the rehabilitation center and her therapist to marry her. Since Lloyd did this in part out of love for her honesty, she's doomed to live her lie forever.

Soon Rachel, still in her nightgown (is the whole play a dream? Perhaps, perhaps not), gets a secretarial job at the center, assisting a grimly taciturn woman whom she eventually discovers to be an embezzler and placidly accepts as such. Meanwhile, Lloyd confesses to having escaped from his first wife after running over someone with his snowplow and taking the $35,000 set aside for his children's education. To pay them back (why now? Don't ask!), he, Rachel, and Pooty go on a crazy TV game show as man, wife, and mother, respectively, and win $100,000 while revealing scrumptiously Freudian complexes. It is Christmas again, and Tom, who has seen her on TV, comes to reclaim Rachel for himself and their children. An anonymous gift of champagne found on the doorstep proves to be poison when Tom and Pooty drink from it and drop dead. Afraid of being thought the murderers, Rachel and Lloyd escape to Springfield, Ohio, and start a new nonlife.

Lloyd has become an alcoholic (champagne only) and refuses to take off his Santa suit from the fatal Christmas party; he also stops talking, as Christmas after Christmas and Springfield after Springfield roll by (there's one in every state, and the pair keeps moving). Now the story gets absurd in good and earnest, forfeiting whatever slight initial interest it generated. Absurdism needs theatrical poetry and breakneck humor to sustain it; Lucas, however, quickly runs out of these. What is even more necessary,

and what he lacks in the first place, is some solid conviction, without which absurdity remains trivial—some profound belief, moral value, existential urgency that the playwright firmly espouses but chooses to approach obliquely via the absurd.

As *Reckless* meanders and maunders all over the blurry map, it understandably offers no answers but inexcusably doesn't ask the necessary questions, either. Why, to start with, would Tom take out a contract on Rachel? And, further, is Rachel a lovable fool, a plain fool, a wise person playing the fool, or none of the above? Ambiguities are all very well, but a patchwork quilt of them—nothing but them—will not hold us for an evening.

Alternatively, *Reckless* may be viewed as camp from start to finish. The crazy coincidences, the seeming (or real) non sequiturs, the detachment from feeling—except perhaps at the very end—would suggest such a sensibility. But then we really must laugh more, much more: Unfunny camp is a true monstrosity. (p. 75)

*John Simon, "A Funny Thing Happened on the Way to Springfields," in* New York Magazine, *Vol. 21, No. 40, October 10, 1988, pp. 75, 78.*

### Mimi Kramer

*Reckless,* a new play by Craig Lucas, . . . tries to package its own inadequacies as a statement about contemporary life. Mr. Lucas is the author of *Blue Window,* which won the L.A. Drama Critics' Award (among others), and *Three Postcards,* a musical on which he collaborated with the composer-lyricist Craig Carnelia. I never saw *Blue Window,* much to my regret, but I remember *Three Postcards* as a sweetly hip and unpretentious interlude. *Reckless* begins promisingly, with a husband and wife bedded down for the night in their suburban home on Christmas Eve. The wife, Rachel, is waxing eloquent about Christmas, family, and well-being, while the husband, Tom, sits silent, watching a flickering television screen. Just as we feel we can stand no more of the wife's effusions, the husband tells her that he has taken out a contract on her life. A hit man is due to arrive at any moment, he explains, and bundles her out into the snow. Why Tom has changed his mind and decided to spare Rachel is not clear, but we're jovially willing to accept a plot device that we hope will set Rachel on a journey of discovery as refreshing as the opening scene.

At the local filling station, Rachel hooks up with Lloyd, a mysterious physiotherapist, who takes her home to his deaf-mute, paraplegic wife, Pooty, and the three set up house together. Lloyd turns out to be living bigamously under an assumed name, having deserted a previous family consisting of a wife afflicted with multiple sclerosis and two children, one of whom, owing to Lloyd's unfortunate handling of a snowblower while inebriated, is permanently brain-damaged. Pooty turns out to be only feigning deafness in order to secure her husband's love and attention; in their relationship with Rachel there is enough of zany interest to engage the mind for perhaps the next ten or fifteen minutes. But, in a scene guaranteed to insult the intelligence of any self-respecting audience, Rachel consults a psychiatrist—the first in a long line—and we get not only a recap of the plot but a spoon-feeding exegetical statement on how dreamlike it has all been. From this point on, **Reckless** becomes increasingly studied in its perversity and incoherence, and it ends by falling apart completely. Rachel takes a job at a humanitarian organization staffed by two sinister types. There is an extended game-show sequence, a double murder involving some poisoned champagne, a suicide (also involving champagne), a talk-show sequence, and yet another murder. The penultimate sequence finds Rachel catatonic in a halfway-house shelter for the homeless.

By this time, Mr. Lucas's play has become mired in its own pretensions. . . . **Reckless** is ultimately mute; and style without substance is glib. It's possible to feel, indignantly, that when Mr. Lucas begins raising issues like mental illness and homelessness he is touching on subjects he has not earned the right to broach. You could graft any number of interpretations onto his play—that we're all escaping from something, that we all forge identities for ourselves, that the wrongs and traumas that we visit on our children are not our responsibility, only something that in turn was visited on us—but if you did you'd be putting more work into the enterprise than the playwright was willing to; all he has done is to cock a few bottles of champagne at us. . . .

I wish someone would declare a ban on plays with extended game-show sequences. I'd like to think audiences are above them. Prize-winning playwrights certainly should be.

*Mimi Kramer, in a review of "Reckless," in* The New Yorker, *Vol. LXIV, No. 34, October 10, 1988, p. 85.*

## Robert Brustein

This decade was preparing to close without an identifying mark other than a mindless smirk plastered across a simpering yuppie face. Suddenly, there are signs of social definition. You won't often find these in American movies, where, reflecting the illusory optimism of Reaganism, the typical motif is wish fulfillment through supernatural agencies—altering family destiny (*Back to the Future*), extricating old people from unpleasant situations with extraterrestrial help (*Cocoon 1* and *2, Batteries Not Included*), accelerating the age of children (*Big*), exchanging the identities of adults and kids (*18 Again* plus a half-dozen movies whose names I've blocked). But if Hollywood continues to be in thrall to fantasy, the American stage is once again assuming a traditional obligation to measure and challenge the form and pressure of the time.

In recent months, Howard Korder's *Boy's Life* anatomized the weightless malaise of affectless young studs; David Mamet's *Speed-the-Plow* tested the limits of friendship as the last refuge of decent conduct; and now Craig Lucas's **Reckless** is analyzing the disintegrating boundaries of human relationships. **Reckless** is the most radical of the three. . . .

**Reckless** begins with a couple in bed watching TV ("It's just the news—it's not real") while Bing Crosby sings "I'll Be Home for Christmas." Babbling contentedly under her flowered comforter, Rachel tells her husband, Tom, of her unspeakable happiness ("I'm having one of my euphoria attacks"). He responds by announcing he's taken out a contract on her life; in five minutes, he says morosely, an assassin will stage her "accidental" death. Feeling belated remorse, he helps her escape, in bathrobe and slippers, through the bay window into the falling snow. And thus begins her strange odyssey through a dimension where every day is Christmas and every town is named Springfield. Rachel, attended by six female psychiatrists who invariably think her story a dream, is plunged into a series of phantasmagoric experiences—alien encounters that parallel the conditions of a totally mad country.

Rachel takes refuge in the home of Lloyd and his wife Pooty, a paraplegic who also pretends to be deaf. In love with the needy, Lloyd works in a benevolent organization called "Hands Across the Sea." Like everyone in the play, Lloyd has a shameful history—he abandoned his first wife and stole $35,000. Rachel tells him, "The past is irrelevant—it's something we wake up from," but for him, "It's the nightmare you wake up to every day." In order to repay the theft and obliterate this Joycean nightmare, all three appear on a TV game show called "Your Mother or Your Wife"—Pooty pretending to be Lloyd's mother, Rachel his wife. And to the accompaniment of earsplitting studio audience screams, he wins $100,000 by correctly guessing how the women answered such questions as "If Lloyd were a salad dressing, what flavor would he be?"

During another Christmas celebration, one year later, Pooty and Rachel's returned husband, Tom, die drinking champagne, poisoned by a disgruntled employee in Lloyd's organization. Rachel and Lloyd escape. Lloyd, still wearing his Santa costume, turns catatonic, breaking his silence to tell the gabby Rachel to "shut the fuck up." Capable only of watching TV and sipping champagne, he dies of anorexia. Rachel lands in a madhouse, also bereft of speech. Her analyst takes Rachel to a TV interview show, partly to relieve her delusion that someone is trying to shoot her. Someone is—though the bullet intended for Rachel lodges in the forehead of the guest personality. In the final scene, Rachel has also become an analyst—in snowy Alaska, where it's always Christmas. The patient she treats is her own son. He doesn't recognize her, and she doesn't reveal her identity.

Determinedly disjointed and disorienting, the play contains its own crafty logic. . . . Rachel is the embodiment of misplaced American optimism. The contrast between her Pollyanna cheerfulness and the catastrophic world she encounters is reminiscent of the jarring views of life represented in the movie *Blue Velvet,* where artificial images of serenity were also juxtaposed against scenes of brutality, sudden death, and sexual corruption. Rachel is a daytime spirit in a night-town of the soul, her conventional notions of happy suburban life and healthy family values continuously undercut by greed, mayhem, murder, inane media displays, and a therapeutic discipline grown insensitive to the implacable darkness hidden within the folds of existence. In its illogical plotting and lobotomized atmosphere, **Reckless** is a deeply political play, possibly the most fundamental criticism we are likely to get of the American Dream as marketed by the ad agencies and the mass media, and, incidentally, of the contemptible jingoism being peddled by the Bush campaign. (p. 28)

> Robert Brustein, "The Voice of the '80s," in The New Republic, *Vol. 199, No. 18, October 31, 1988, pp. 28-9.*

## Gerald Weales

[Craig Lucas's] **Reckless** is something of a problem for me. . . . I have the impression that audiences are responding only to the funny surface of the play. What's more, I am reluctant to go beneath that surface for fear I will founder in a morass of contemporary platitudes about the difficulties of surviving in an accidental universe. (p. 687)

Aside from the ludicrous calamities that befall the central characters ("Life's been reckless with these people," says a doctor in the shelter scene), Lucas offers television parody and psychiatrist jokes. He may intend the roles that Rachel and her friends assume in the game show to parallel shifting identities in the play as a whole and to make some point about on-screen/off-screen realities (Rachel comforts a crying Tom, "It's just the news, come on, it's not real"). But the TV scenes are as obvious as the kind of parody television does of itself. The string of therapists—none of whom can help Rachel, of course—derives its substance only from its place in the long line of comic analysts who have appeared in American plays and movies since the 1920s.

In the second act, Rachel loses her often reiterated belief that there is purpose in the events she has been a part of and concludes, "Things just happen!" In the scene that follows, Lloyd dies and she goes silent. In the last scene, which is played in a very different tone from the rest of the play, she is speaking again, as a therapist herself now, and her patient is Tom, Jr., whom she has not seen since her precipitous exit into the snow. Now grown, haunted by the disappearance of his mother, the death of his father, his brother's apparent madness, he needs help at Christmas (most of the violent events in the play take place at Christmas) and he finds it in this doctor who somehow reminds him of his mother. "I'm sorry I kept you waiting," she says as he exits. She speaks as the doctor, apologizing to the patient for his having had to sit a while in the waiting room, but the line belongs to the mother who has made the son wait twenty years. What are we to make of that last line? A sentimental coda to a farcical horror story? A last joke in a play in which therapy is useless and Rachel's gestures of amiable succor regularly lead to disaster? Neither reading is quite satisfactory.

On the surface, Lucas's play suggests the work of playwrights as different as [Christopher] Durang, Albert Innaurato, and John Guare, all of whom write farces that deal glancingly with the dark side of contemporary life. For me, however, their work seems not to go through laughter to pain but to become a defense against it, revelation as denial. They do not play games at graveside, as Samuel Beckett does; they just play games. **Reckless** seemed to do much the same thing. I laughed at it (perhaps with it) and admired Lucas's talent for oblique dialogue, and I found myself wondering if it might be played so that all those allusions to identity, self-knowledge, rationality would seem neither gratuitous nor portentous by letting the characters escape caricature. Even so, there might be trouble with that last scene. I doubt that Rachel could ever be a Camus/Sartre existentialist, accepting the absurdity of existence, and choosing to create herself despite that frightening knowledge. I prefer an uglier last scene. If we have been given glimpses of the chaos beneath the comic horrors and Rachel's Pollyanna gloss on them, the final scene could be played with great force as a positive scene that does not recognize that it confirms the negation. (pp. 687-88)

> Gerald Weales, "Laughing on the Outside: Craig Lucas's 'Reckless'," in Commonweal, *Vol. CXV, No. 22, December 16, 1988, pp. 687-88.*

## Howard Kissel

[You might imagine Craig Lucas's **Prelude to a Kiss** to be a] poetic play about memory, dreams or woeful loss. Instead, as you might expect from the author of **Reckless,** it is a play about nothing.

For much of the first act it appears to be about yuppies in love, though the male seems bizarrely innocent and the female extremely bizarre. At their wedding, an old geezer whom neither knows gives the bride an especially intense kiss.

In doing so, we learn, he has managed to switch bodies with her. Does he know he has the power to do this? If so, why has he decided to enter the body of a young woman? Is this something he has wanted to do for a long time?

We learn nothing about his motivation. Nor does the switch reveal anything interesting about such subjects as age or gender. Nor, needless to say, does it yield much in the way of mirth.

The play ambles along haphazardly, its strongest scenes those that satirize, quite conventionally, the bride's wealthy parents. . . .

Lucas' gift—though it may be that of his polished director [and frequent collaborator] Norman René—is an ability to make what is utterly vapid seem portentous, as if some meaning really were buried in the carefully timed pauses and actors' asides.

At one time this might have passed for absurdism. Now it just seems like TV writing with added pretensions (a line directed at someone in the first row, some banal political humor). . . .

[The] play hinges on coy surprises rather than any genuine understanding of character.

*Howard Kissel, "Lucas' 'Kiss' of Death," in* Daily News, *New York, March 15, 1990.*

## Clive Barnes

The quality—and pungent charm—of Craig Lucas' new play *Prelude to a Kiss* is so elusive yet so pervasive (so, already, does the title, as it sounds like stale copy for a perfume ad!) that it might first be as well to make some Polonious-like stab at defining its genre.

Why not call it a contemporary screwball romantic comedy of fairy tale transmogrification with a few shrewd platitudes about mortality added for intellectual ballast? Why not?

The important thing about *Prelude to a Kiss* is that it is funny, touching, involving, romantic, sexy, and has a satisfyingly happy ending—in which absolutely everything is as clear and merry as a wedding bell.

Well, almost everything is almost as merry—admittedly one of the three central characters shuffles off to shuffle off his mortal coils succumbing to a double whammy of lung cancer and cirrhosis of the liver. But he was old, he did smoke and drink too much, and also he was—almost unwittingly, perhaps—a sort of a villain.

Lucas' story is an inverted fairy tale. You have all heard of the princess who kisses the toad who turns into a prince. Well, here is a prince (called Peter) who kisses, and marries, a princess (called Rita) who promptly turns into a very old toad (called Julius Becker).

Of course the mechanics of the plot are somewhat difficult—even you might say fanciful. But you only need the same degree of suspension of disbelief that you brought to, say, the Gary Ross and Anne Spielberg screenplay for the movie, *Big.*

Peter and Rita meet in the prelude to a marriage made in heaven. The physical attraction is intense—and they even drink the same kind of beer.

Then comes the marriage—and a strange incident with an Old Man. Then the honeymoon. And the horror. The Rita Peter married is not the Rita Peter wooed. Women change. Men change. But does anyone change as much as Rita changed?

She always had a bad memory, but now, although a professional bartender, she can't recall the recipe for Long Island Iced Tea. Why, she can't even remember whether she has any brothers or sisters.

It is Lucas' skill that we as an audience feel so romantically indignant our hero being thus short-changed and true love being so defiled, that we are rooting for Peter to get to the bottom of this odd case of mis-identification.

And so he does. It is all a case of mistaken transmigration—some kind of involuntary transmogrification, an awkward instance of soulful transference.

The solution is as unlikely as the problem. No matter. We cheer with the knee-jerk happiness of children seeing the slipper fit Cinderella's foot. Peter and Rita are together again. Until death—or another accident of time and occasion—puts them apart.

*Prelude to a Kiss* is unquestionably Lucas' most successful, tightly organized and best written play to date.

*Clive Barnes, "Fairy Tale Gone Wrong," in* New York Post, *March 15, 1990.*

## Frank Rich

Peter, the ingenuous hero in *Prelude to a Kiss,* loves the sign at the roller coaster: "Ride at Your Own Risk." It promises a journey into "the wild blue" in which anything can happen. The same sign could be posted at *Prelude to a Kiss,* for Craig Lucas, the author of *Reckless* and *Blue Window,* has again written a play that propels the audience through hairpin emotional turns, some soaring heavenward and others plummeting toward earth, until one is deposited at the final curtain in a winded and teary yet exhilarating state of disorientation.

I loved this play. . . . But as the man says, ride at your own risk. *Prelude to a Kiss* takes a most familiar genre, romantic comedy, in directions that are idiosyncratic and challenging. The play's title comes from the Duke Ellington song sung by Ella Fitzgerald that perfumes the evening, and Mr. Lucas follows its prescription that "just a simple melody with nothing fancy, nothing much" can blossom into "a symphony, a Schubert tune with a Gershwin touch." The playwright also takes a cue from his characters' favorite book, *The White Hotel,* because *Prelude to a Kiss,* though only a prelude compared with D. M. Thomas's novel, is also a psychoanalytic fairy tale that rises from a maze of transference into a cathartic conflict between sex and death.

Mr. Lucas is not pretentious, and his play is as airily composed and, at first, as funny as the old-time Hollywood confections it sometimes paraphrases. Peter, a microfiche specialist at a scientific publishing concern, and Rita, a bartender aspiring to be a graphic designer, meet at a Manhattan party, fall under the spell of love and are married at the bride's family home in Englewood Cliffs, N.J. It is a fine romance, with lots of storybook kisses. . . . (p. C15)

The romance consummated, the trouble begins. . . . Through a magical plot device that could happen only in a movie—and frequently does—Rita's soul seems to have migrated to another body. The body is that of an old, bespectacled, pot-bellied man, played by Barnard Hughes, who is dying of lung cancer.

"I'm not equipped for this!" Peter cries. While he had sworn to Rita that he would love her even more in old age, when her teeth had yellowed and her breasts had sagged, he had not expected to be put to so blunt a test so soon. Can he love a woman who now looks like an old, decrepit man? What makes *Prelude to a Kiss* a powerful, genuine fairy tale rather than merely a farcical exploitation of the form's narrative devices is that Mr. Lucas insists on playing out Peter's outrageous predicament for keeps. . . .

It is not difficult to figure out the genesis of *Prelude to a*

*Kiss.* Mr. Lucas is also the author of **Longtime Companion,** a much more conventionally written feature film about AIDS, and this play can be taken as an indirect treatment of the same subject. The epidemic is to Mr. Lucas what Babi-Yar was to D. M. Thomas, and Peter's fidelity to his true love's soul, even as that soul is trapped in a dying male body, is a transparent metaphor. Yet Mr. Lucas never betrays his play's fantastical tone or sense of humor; its setting is a unspecifically "precarious" New York, and AIDS is never mentioned. The result is a work whose anguish excludes no one. The questions that Mr. Lucas addresses are 'timeless ones about the powers of compassion and empathy in a brutal universe where everyone is inevitably abandoned by parents, children and lovers and where the only reward for that suffering is to disappear to "no one knows where." (p. C15, C18)

[It] is Mr. Lucas's gift that he makes life's sacrifices seem its affirmation, not its burden, even as he by no means underestimates the courage required to make the leap. The leap is not merely figurative. Like **Blue Window** and **Reckless, Prelude to a Kiss** is dominated by the image of a window. Mr. Lucas often demands that his characters jump through it, leaving home for the unknown of a starry night and the arduous prospect of selfless love, just as he demands that audiences take the leap out of a literal reality and into the imaginative realm of an adult fable.

The amazing part is that if you can go the esthetic distance with this playwright, you may find yourself inspired to take the other, more intimate, much more dangerous leap, too. Though **Prelude to a Kiss** is never more than a heartbeat away from the fearful nightmare of death that inspired it, the experience of seeing it is anything but defeating. Mr. Lucas opens the window on love—true love, not fairy-tale love—so wide that, even in this cynical time, it seems a redemptive act of faith to take a free fall into the wild blue. (p. C18)

> Frank Rich, " 'Prelude to a Kiss': a Fairy Tale of Souls in Love and in Flight," in The New York Times, *March 15, 1990, p. C15, C18.*

### John Simon

When, in the opening party scene of a play, the middle-aged host and hostess copulate on the floor and no one pays the slightest attention, we know that reality is not where it's at. When the heroine is almost always needlessly barefoot in Act I, and always shod in Act II, we know that some sort of fancy stylization (perhaps directorial) is afoot. But when throughout no one drinks just beer but always only Molson's, and, furthermore—in a bar, at home, anywhere—never out of a glass but straight from the bottle, we suspend our belief, not our disbelief.

Craig Lucas's **Prelude to a Kiss** is a fantasy, which is fine (think of *Peter Pan,* for example), but it is a mendacious, meretricious fantasy, which is bad. Even the title lies: The play is the postlude to a kiss, but that would not jibe with what Ella Fitzgerald is singing in the background. . . . If the play were an honest fantasy, I wouldn't divulge certain plot points—you'd never learn from me whether Tinker Bell lives or dies—but when the author counts on gentle-

manly silence from the critics to get away with his unscrupulousness, I say the hell with that.

In **Prelude,** a sick old man with only months to live stumbles onto a suburban wedding, kisses the bride, and forthwith exchanges inner identities with her. Much to the bewilderment of Peter, the groom, Rita, the bride, behaves queerly during their Jamaican honeymoon; back in New York, through a number of slips, Rita betrays her true identity: She is the Old Man in Rita's body—he wanted to enjoy youth and passion once more before dying. Eventually, the real Rita, in the Old Man's shape, moves in with Peter, and they have a pretty nice marriage going, but—as is protested a bit too coyly—no sex. There's more, but this is quite enough.

The Old Man, though it is never stated, is homosexual, else he would become Peter, so as to enjoy Rita's lovemaking. (Note, by the way, that "Rita" and "Peteah" rhyme, so as to enhance the confusion of genders). Instead, he/she goes on a honeymoon with handsome Peter, buys herself expensive trinkets charged to Rita's father, and proves only too willing to give up his/her job as a bartender and let Peter bring home the bacon. (But why would the educated, comfortably middle-class Rita have worked as a barkeep in the first place?) The fake Rita self-betrayingly refers to her dentist father as a surgeon; why, having boned up on the real Rita's diaries, would she make such mistakes? The answer here, as elsewhere, is that this is a logicless play for an MTV audience that never connects the dots between dotty moments.

A hokey charade, then, whose chief purposes are to mock heterosexual relationships and to satisfy cravings for the unobtainable heterosexual male, without concern for minimal structural consistency. Thus Peter says to Rita (who now inhabits the Old Man's body) that he misses her "little white feet"; whereupon the Old Man (i.e., Rita) holds up his and inquires cutely, "What? You don't like these?" Yet if that seeming Old Man were really Rita, she/he would say something like "So do I." But Lucas has no intention to be anything but cutely mischievous all the way, without even making fantasy-sense. Again, would the fake Rita (if there were no hidden agenda) give "herself" away by discussing with Peter how she prefers the term "hole" to "crack," adding that she really likes "hole and dick," then consider his suggestion, "slit," only to exclaim, after some reflection, *"Tool* I like"? . . .

[The author has Peter] incessantly addressing the spectators—sometimes in the middle of a speech to another character—a hoary device that has been milked to death in recent dramaturgy; it serves mostly to help lazy playwrights over scenes that would take real ability to dramatize properly. (p. 87)

The climactic piece of dental-dramatic advice is the Old Man's Parthian shot: "The next time, floss!" Indeed, flossiness is all, and if you enjoy two and a half hours of smart-ass chatter and campy subversion—e.g., the honeymoon lament "It's a real busman's holiday with you around: You could f— up a wet dream!" this may be your cup of . . . whatever. What is fantasy for? Presumably to fulfill some innocent universal yearnings: to fly like the other

Peter and never grow old, to be fabulously wealthy and work philanthropic wonders with your money, to live on a desert island in harmony with a loved one. But what kind of wholesome longings does *Prelude to a Kiss* satisfy? (p. 88)

> *John Simon, "Bodying Forth," in* New York Magazine, *Vol. 23, No. 12, March 26, 1990, pp. 87-8.*

## Edith Oliver

*Prelude to a Kiss* is a modern comedy with a difference. Once upon a time, at what appears to be a cocktail party, Peter meets Rita, and they fall in love immediately. Peter's job, he says, is to take "little tiny transparent photographs." Rita is an insomniac who claims that she hasn't slept since she was fourteen . . . ; by avocation, she's a bartender. "We can go to my place," she says, and he jubilantly replies, "Everything worked out great for everybody!"

Not quite. At the party, the Freudian novel *The White Hotel* is mentioned; he summarizes it, and she cites various cases of Freud's. The whole play, for that matter, has a Freudian tinge, which I noted and then forgot. There is a wedding at her parents' house, and an old man, unknown to all present, gives the bride a long, tender kiss. On the subsequent honeymoon, Peter . . . notices that Rita has changed in some mysterious way, and when he runs into the old man he realizes that during that wedding kiss the old man absorbed her spirit. No more story; I've told you too much already, and no synopsis, no matter how skillful, could do justice to the richness of this play, to its characters and their quirks and often startling conversation, and, above all, to its humor. *Prelude to a Kiss* is consistently entertaining, though never at the expense of feeling. "Enchanting," "charming," "mysterious"— those are the adjectives, and if "whimsical" weren't such a blight, that would do, too. A wise friend of mine once said, "A truly light touch is a priceless gift" . . . *Prelude to a Kiss* is a fragile play, which in the wrong hands could easily collapse.

> *Edith Oliver, "Aftermath of a Kiss," in* The New Yorker, *Vol. LXVI, No. 6, March 26, 1990, p. 74.*

## Clive Barnes

[Craig Lucas's *Prelude to a Kiss*] is a dazzling yet gently charming play that seems even better on a second viewing than on first acquaintance. First of all it is enormous fun, and its evasive, nutty poetry has a magic that is all of its own. Rarely, if ever, can the classic boy-meets-girl-loses-etc. story have been more imaginatively or more wittily treated. It is simply bewitching.

For one thing, in what other version does marriage make the girl involuntarily turn into a toad? But I get before myself. Peter meets Rita and they fall dizzily in love. At their wedding reception an old stranger turns up, kisses her rather personally, and before you can say "dybbuk" or

even "incubus," he has taken over her sweet young body, and left her, mind, soul and heart, marooned in his own doomed carcass, wracked with lung cancer and cirrhosis.

The luckless Peter goes off merrily to his honeymoon with this singularly unpleasant old man, totally unaware of the switch, because it is packaged in the body and health of his sometime beloved.

Slowly what has happened dawns on him—and the tension of the play is largely contained in Peter's realization (just a step or two behind the audience itself ) of the truth and whether, or at least how, right can be put to right, and the souls put back in their proper containers.

I'm not sure about the mechanics of the whole process—in fairness we have had a number of movies of late, such as *Big* or *All of Me,* where quite similar fantasies placed no lesser strain on credibility—but in the theater it works gloriously.

It also raises very serious and even profound questions about the nature of love. Do we love the package or the packaging, does "for better or for worse" really mean what it says, and what really is love's chemistry?

> *Clive Barnes, "Good Move for 'Kiss'," in* New York Post, *May 2, 1990.*

## Frank Rich

"The world's a really terrible place—it's too precarious," says Rita, the young heroine of *Prelude to a Kiss,* the Craig Lucas play newly arrived on Broadway. Rita, a bartender aspiring to be a graphics designer, lives in a modern city whose ills are all too depressingly recognizable. Crack dealers approach first graders, unspeakable diseases consume the bodies of the young and old, and there is never any escape from "the constant fear of being blown up." As Rita warns Peter, the young man with whom she has found love at first sight, the world is so rotten she couldn't even think of bringing children into it.

Yet two hours of stage time later, Rita has reversed her perspective entirely, and not because the world has changed. In this wonderful play, a comic and affecting fairy-tale for and about adults, Mr. Lucas acknowledges much that is defeating about civilization as we now know it, then heroically insists on finding a reason to go on living anyway.

Mr. Lucas's reason—that "the miracle of another human being" is "never to be squandered"—may sound sentimental, but as dramatized it is not. There's nothing treacly about *Prelude to a Kiss,* a play that acknowledges even those modern terrors it leaves unmentioned, like AIDS, by forcing its young lovers to test their bond against the threat of imminent physical decay and death. "My love is a prelude that never dies," sings Ella Fitzgerald in the Duke Ellington song whose nocturnal blues haunts the evening. What this play celebrates, and it's as rare as the moonlight in Ellington's music, is the redemptive power of unselfish love that never dies, of true love that survives transient flesh.

As in any classic fairy tale, Rita and Peter must overcome

such terrifying obstacles to seal their union and live happily ever after that their hard-won hope and elation at the final curtain is contagious. It's hard to recall a recent play so suffused with sorrow that sends one home so high; the heady feeling of disorientation that lingers at the denouement, a heightened sensitivity to love and death alike, recalls not only the Grimms but also D. M. Thomas's psychoanalytic fable about the Holocaust, *The White Hotel,* that is pointedly Rita and Peter's shared reading. . . .

While Act I recounts the courtship, marriage and Caribbean honeymoon of Peter and Rita in the hip terms of contemporary, Manhattan-dry romantic comedy, the laughs never deflate the passion of lovers who are not joking when they exchange sentiments like "I would really, really like to see you with all your clothes off and stuff like that." Meanwhile, the baroque storyteller's diction of Peter's narration—"That night everything was miraculously restored," goes one typical line—helps prepare the audience for its own leap into fantastical plot twists that are no less enchanting for taking place in such prosaic settings as Englewood Cliffs, N.J., and are no less moving for involving such surreal events as a chaste heterosexual love affair between two men.

By the time the laughter subsides, at least temporarily, in Act II, *Prelude to a Kiss* has deftly locked its audience with its characters into what Peter describes as "one of those dreams in which you keep telling yourself 'Hang on!' " because you know that sooner or later you will have to wake up. And so you do. But Mr. Lucas's revivifying dream of love, as beautiful as it is miraculous in these precarious nights, hangs on.

*Frank Rich, "Providing a Reason to Keep on Living in a Terrible World," in* The New York Times, *May 2, 1990, p. C15.*

### John Simon

I have already voiced my distaste for this insalubrious fantasy [see Simon's previous excerpt], and, little if anything having been changed, need not repeat myself now. . . . [Craig Lucas's *Prelude to a Kiss*] concerns the psychological disjunctions occasioned by a sick old man's wandering into the wedding of two bright young things, Peter and Rita, kissing the bride, and so exchanging souls with her— enough to give soul kissing a bad name. Antinaturalism is used here to provide the audience with frissons not unlike those from a horror movie, with a rather unholy secret agenda under the seemingly harmlessly eerie surface. Will this *fin de siècle* go down as the age of David Lynch and Craig Lucas?

Lucas, the author of *Prelude,* is trying to write, besides a fantasy, a sophisticated New York comedy, for which he isn't sophisticated enough. Thus he thinks that "spaetzle" has a plural, "spaetzles," which (worse yet) he thinks is pronounced so as to rhyme with "schnitzels"; his semantics (e.g. "inappreciative" for unappreciative) is as bad as his syntax (*passim*), and he considers references to Freud and *The White Hotel* an earnest of culture. Meeting Rita for the second time at the joint where she tends bar, Peter tells her about the Thomas novel:

PETER. It's very depressing, the book.

RITA. Uh-huh.

PETER. This lovely, very neurotic woman goes into therapy with Freud himself—

RITA. Right.

PETER. And he sort of cures her so that she can go on to live for a few years before being killed by the Nazis in a lime pit. Happy. Happy stuff.

RITA. So why were you in Europe for ten years?

PETER. How did you know I was in Europe?

RITA. Word gets around.

PETER. You asked Taylor about me? You were asking around about me? Let's get married.

RITA. Okay.

This is modeled on similar scenes jumping from mundane chatter to declarations of passion, in Noël Coward (e.g., *Private Lives, Shadow Play*)—where, however, there is more logic, more savoir faire, and much more wit.

Here is a relevant moment from *Private Lives*. Amanda and Elyot, divorced but still in love, meet on the moonlit terrace of a hotel on the Riviera, where they are lovelessly honeymooning with new spouses. To evade their true feelings, they chat about travel.

AMANDA. Did you eat sharks' fins, and take your shoes off, and use chopsticks and everything?

ELYOT. Practically everything.

AMANDA. And India, the burning Ghars, or Ghats, or whatever they are, and the Taj Mahal. How was the Taj Mahal?

ELYOT. (*Looking at her*): Unbelievable, a sort of a dream. . . .

AMANDA. And it didn't look like a biscuit box, did it? I've always felt that it might.

ELYOT. (*Quietly*): Darling, darling, I love you so.

AMANDA. And I do hope you met a sacred elephant. They're lint white, I believe, and very, very sweet.

ELYOT. I've never loved anyone else for an instant.

There you have it: non sequiturs erupting into no longer repressible passion, the essential gotten at obliquely and deviously, even foreign travel to establish sophistication. Only instead of *The White Hotel,* it's sacred white elephants, which is much better. Coward's high camp turns medium high in Lucas, which, as camp goes, is rather worse than low. By the way, some readers defending *Prelude* against my critique, pointed out an error: The scene where Rita and Peter rattle off vulgar terms for sexual organs to turn each other on—which I questioned as a heterosexual gambit—occurs before, not after, Rita is changed into the Old Man. That merely strengthens my point: The still unchanged Rita is behaving in bed like a man. This play is not what it purports to be. (pp. 125-26)

*John Simon, in a review of "Prelude to a Kiss,"
in* New York *Magazine, Vol. 23, No. 19, May
14, 1990, pp. 125-26.*

---

## FURTHER READING

Canby, Vincent. "What's Art All About? Truth, Beauty, Unruliness." *The New York Times* (24 June 1990): H1.
Discusses Lucas's *Prelude to a Kiss* as a metaphor for the AIDS epidemic, and finds the play artistically superior to *Longtime Companion*.

# Peter Matthiessen

## 1927-

American novelist, nonfiction writer, short story writer, and editor.

Described by William Styron as "a writer of phenomenal scope and versatility," Matthiessen is a novelist and naturalist who writes with compassion and conviction about vanishing cultures, oppressed peoples, and exotic wildlife and locales. Although he has written several highly acclaimed novels, including *At Play in the Fields of the Lord* and *Far Tortuga,* Matthiessen is probably best known for his nonfiction, in which he combines objective scientific observation with lyrical and learned explication of such concerns as the impact of modern civilization on the natural world and the consequences of environmental destruction. Conrad Silvert commented: "[Matthiessen is] a rhapsodist who writes with wisdom and warmth as he applies scientific knowledge to the peoples and places he investigates. Works of lasting literary value and moral import have resulted."

Born in New York City to a prosperous family, Matthiessen served in the United States Navy from 1945 to 1947. He attended the Sorbonne at the University of Paris from 1948 to 1949 prior to enrolling at Yale University, where he received his bachelor's degree in 1950. In ensuing years, Matthiessen joined a group of expatriate writers in Paris whose members included William Styron, Richard Wright, George Plimpton, James Baldwin, and Terry Southern. While in Paris, Matthiessen and Harold L. Humes cofounded *The Paris Review,* an influential literary magazine on which Matthiessen continues to serve as an editor. His early novels, which are generally considered conventional coming-of-age stories, include *Race Rock,* in which he traces the rivalries, friendships, and love relationships between a group of friends to their respective childhood emotions and conflicts; *Partisans,* about an American journalist who risks his career to vindicate an aging Communist who has been betrayed by members of his own party; and *Raditzer,* in which a young liberal aboard a naval vessel during World War II finds himself defending an abusive sailor against the ship's crew. Although some reviewers considered Matthiessen's early novels lacking in focus and his characterizations unconvincing, many acknowledged his gradual improvement and lyrical use of theme and language.

During the mid-1950s, Matthiessen set out to visit every wildlife refuge in the United States. His first nonfiction work, *Wildlife in America,* is an encyclopedic survey of America's fauna complete with lists of rare, declining, and extinct species and an extensive bibliography. In the late 1950s, Matthiessen began traveling to the exotic locales that influenced his later fiction and nature writings. *The Cloud Forest: A Chronicle of the South American Wilderness* reflects his experience in remote parts of the South

American continent, while *Under the Mountain Wall: A Chronicle of Two Seasons of the Stone Age* relates his participation in an expedition into central New Guinea during which Matthiessen and his friends became the first white explorers to make close contact and live amongst the Kurelu, a primitive society situated in the Baliem Valley. Matthiessen's concern for traditional cultures, natural ecologies, and the destructive nature of civilization informs his next novel, *At Play in the Fields of the Lord.* Set in the remote jungles of South America, this surrealistic work describes the corruption and impending destruction of the Niaruna, a primitive tribal society, by civilized forces represented by a small group of missionaries, a pair of opportunistic mercenaries, and a corrupt South American military dictator. The tribe's destruction is ultimately secured by Martin Quarrier, a missionary who is unwittingly manipulated by secular powers, and Lewis Moon, a Native American mercenary who attempts to unite the Niaruna militarily. Although Matthiessen later described the book as "ornate, full of 'fine writing,' " but "essentially an old-fashioned novel," *At Play in the Fields of the Lord* has garnered accolades from many prominent writers and critics and is widely considered one of his most accomplished works of fiction.

During the decade following the publication of *At Play in the Fields of the Lord,* Matthiessen wrote several acclaimed works of nonfiction. *Sal Si Puedes: Cesar Chavez and the New American Revolution* chronicles the efforts of Cesar Chavez to organize farm workers in California in the interests of improving wages and living conditions for migrant laborers. While some critics contended that Matthiessen expresses too much uncritical regard for Chavez, others concurred with Peter Nabokov, who called *Sal Si Puedes* "a superbly conceived and written chronicle of Cesar Chavez' self-discovery as an organizer." *Blue Meridian: The Search for the Great White Shark* recounts Matthiessen's experience as a member of a film crew led by diving expert Peter Gimbel, who successfully located and filmed underwater the world's largest ocean predator, the great white shark. Gimbel's footage appears in his film *Blue Water, White Death. The Tree Where Man Was Born,* a journal of Matthiessen's travels in East Africa, was published with the companion volume *The African Experience,* a collection of photographs by Eliot Porter. Incorporating information derived from such formal disciplines as anthropology, zoology, and geology, Matthiessen provides a lyrical portrait of the region's people, flora, and fauna while inquiring as to the origins of *homo sapiens.* According to a critic for *Saturday Review, The Tree Where Man Was Born* "ranks with Isak Dinesen's . . . 1937 classic *Out of Africa.* Matthiessen combines three elements in his writing: a gift for acute observation of both wildlife and men, a sense of African tribal history and myth, and a vividly personal account of his own encounter with Africa."

In his experimental novel *Far Tortuga,* Matthiessen employs a lean, objective prose style to delineate the tensions that contribute to the demise of the crew of the *Lillias Eden,* a turtle-fishing boat in the Caribbean. Favoring realistic physical description over authorial commentary, Matthiessen uses experimental typography and pictographic symbols, such as a smudge to denote the death of a crew member and stretches of white space "to achieve resonance, to make the reader receive things intuitively." By contrasting the viewpoint of Speedy, a man who has adapted to modern realities, with that of Captain Raib, an authoritarian man who is trapped in the past, Matthiessen chronicles the collapse of a traditional way of life resulting from such pressures as American politics and tourism. In the manner of Captain Ahab in Herman Melville's *Moby-Dick,* Raib endangers his crew by recklessly seeking to find the uncharted and conceivably mythical island of the title. Although response to *Far Tortuga* ranged from Terrence des Pres's assessment of the book as "an outright masterpiece" to Bruce Allen's estimation of it as "an adventurous failure . . . lacking a harmonious whole," *Far Tortuga* is generally considered Matthiessen's most complex work of fiction.

Matthiessen received both a National Book Award and an American Book Award for *The Snow Leopard,* a nonfiction account of his 1973 trip to remote upper regions of Nepal. In addition to recounting his search with biologist George Schaller for Himalayan blue sheep and for a rare species of snow leopard, Matthiessen attempts through meditation and Zen Buddhism to resolve feelings of loneliness and sorrow occasioned by the death of his second wife, Deborah Love Matthiessen. *Sand Rivers* records Matthiessen's trek into the Selous Game Reserve in Southern Tanzania, one of Africa's largest remaining wild areas, with former warden Brian Nicholson and photographer Hugo van Lawick. His next two works, *In the Spirit of Crazy Horse* and *Indian Country,* address political conflicts and legal issues surrounding modern Native Americans. *In the Spirit of Crazy Horse* concerns Leonard Peltier, a member of the radical national American Indian Movement (AIM) who was convicted under suspect circumstances of the murder of two agents of the Federal Bureau of Investigation in 1975. The publication of *In the Spirit of Crazy Horse* led to libel suits by former FBI agent David Price and by former South Dakota governor William J. Janklow, who accused Matthiessen of presenting his personal opinions as well as those of AIM members as objective fact. The Federal Court of Appeals acquitted Matthiessen of Price's accusation on the grounds that his statements were clearly presented as opinion and therefore protected under the First Amendment. *Indian Country* centers on the struggles of Native Americans to defend their land and culture against damaging incursions, particularly those of corporations who have resorted to poisoning reservation land and water to obtain mineral and uranium rights on the Western reservations.

*Nine-Headed Dragon River: Zen Journals, 1969-1982* incorporates Matthiessen's notes from a series of meditation exercises in the Rinzai school of Zen in the early 1970s with early excerpts from his previous book, *The Snow Leopard,* and a highly personal account of his 1977 Soto Zen sessions in Los Angeles that culminated in a trip to Japan with his teacher in 1981. *Men's Lives: The Surfmen and Baymen of the South Fork* draws upon Matthiessen's experience during the 1950s as a commercial fisherman on Long Island, where he still resides. This book chronicles from an insider's perspective the vanishing lifestyle of the island's native fishermen, who are able to trace their ancestry back to the region's early settlers. Taking his title from a line in a Walter Scott novel, "It's no fish ye're buyin', it's men's lives," Matthiessen records how the fishermen have been economically weakened by sports fishing lobbies that forbid them to catch or sell the striped bass, a staple fish, and how many have been forced to sell their land due to the incursion of wealthy individuals who have caused property to be valued and taxed at exorbitant rates.

Beginning with the short story collection *On the River Styx, and Other Stories,* Matthiessen stated that he hoped henceforth to concentrate solely on writing fiction. The stories in this volume, some of which had been published earlier in *Midnight Turning Gray,* include "Travelin Man," in which an escaped black convict turns the tables on a white game-poacher who is hunting him on an uninhabited island off the Carolina coast, and "On the River Styx," in which an environmental lawyer from Washington, D.C., takes his wife fishing at a secluded Florida coastal village only to encounter hostility from local residents who suspect he is investigating their involvement in drug trafficking and racial segregation. Paul W. Rea asserted: "*On the River Styx* showcases Peter Matthiessen as one of the finest stylists and social commentators writing today. Despite their disturbing subjects, these stories virtually read themselves; the man knows how to tell a moral tale." In his recent novel *Killing Mr. Watson*, Matthiessen explores the death of Edgar Watson, a contemptible but charismatic man who was murdered in 1890 by the residents of a village in the Ten Thousand Islands region off Florida's southwest coast. Relating the homicide from the conflicting perspectives of the individuals involved, Matthiessen creates an ambiguous story that reflects the indeterminacy of the original case. Tim McNulty commented: "Like Faulkner's powerful tale *The Bear*, [*Killing Mr. Watson*] is a deeply historic narrative that touches the very roots of our culture's attitudes toward the land, the native people who dwelled there, and the rich tapestry of life that once graced it. Peter Matthiessen has returned to what may prove his most powerful genre, but if this historic snapshot of our national character is fiction, it is a fiction that, a century later, still troubles our world."

(See also *CLC*, Vols. 5, 7, 11, 32; *Contemporary Authors*, Vols. 9-12, rev. ed.; *Contemporary Authors New Revision Series*, Vol. 21; *Dictionary of Literary Biography*, Vol. 6; and *Something about the Author*, Vol. 27.)

## PRINCIPAL WORKS

NOVELS

*Race Rock*    1954
*Partisans*    1955
*Raditzer*    1961
*At Play in the Fields of the Lord*    1965
*Far Tortuga*    1975
*Killing Mr. Watson*    1990

SHORT FICTION COLLECTIONS

*Midnight Turning Gray*    1984
*On the River Styx, and Other Stories*    1989

NONFICTION

*Wildlife in America*    1959
*The Cloud Forest: A Chronicle of the South American Wilderness*    1961
*Under the Mountain Wall: A Chronicle of Two Seasons of the Stone Age*    1962
*Oomingmak: The Expedition to the Musk Ox Island in the Bering Sea*    1967
*The Shorebirds of North America* [with Ralph S. Palmer and Robert Verity Clem] 1967
*Sal Si Puedes: Cesar Chavez and the New American Revolution*    1969
*Blue Meridian: The Search for the Great White Shark*    1971
*Everglades: Selections from the Writings of Peter Matthiessen*    1971
*The Tree Where Man Was Born*    1972
*The Snow Leopard*    1978
*Sand Rivers* [with photographer Hugo van Lawick] 1981
*In the Spirit of Crazy Horse*    1983
*Indian Country*    1984
*Men's Lives: The Surfmen and Baymen of the South Fork*    1986

*Nine-Headed Dragon River: Zen Journals, 1969-1982*    1986

OTHER

*Seal Pool*    1972; also published as *The Great Auk Escape*, 1974    (juvenile novel)

---

## Thomas Curley

[The setting of *At Play in the Fields of the Lord* ] is the Amazon jungle in, I think, Peru, the fields of the Lord in which Mr. Matthiessen has let his characters loose to play; the time, the recent past. The light and death chosen ages before, came to the Niaruna Indian in the person of four white missionaries (two couples), a Catholic priest and a pair of soldiers of fortune down on their luck, one of whom, an American Indian named Lewis Moon, attempts to save the Niaruna from the particular light and death represented by Christianity and Western civilization. But before Moon begins his attempt, we are treated to more than a hundred pages of comic richness as the newly arrived Protestant couple meet in turn their co-religionists, Padre Xantes, the rowdy, drunken soldiers of fortune and the natives of Madre de Dios. What a name, one of the missionaries thinks. Just "suppose some Catholic had come along and changed the name of Chippewa Flats to Mother of God, North Dakota?" But Madre de Dios is a dirty, lecherous spot and Matthiessen has a lot of fun embarrassing the fundamentalists. Without our knowing it, the game has already begun in the fields of the Lord.

Lewis Moon is the main actor, since it is he who undertakes to foil the "Christers" and the government but at times one of the missionaries, Martin Quarrier, almost upstages him. Quarrier's steady, stupid honesty, at first ridiculous, becomes exasperating and then, despite oneself, so admirable, that when he loses his son to the jungle, suffers defeat and then death, one is forced to remember that it is Lewis Moon we are asked to keep our eyes on. I don't know whether Matthiessen intended this, and it doesn't much matter, since it contributes to the richness of the novel in the sense that it makes an otherwise virtuoso parody of missionaries and do-gooders a serious and ambiguous achievement.

Moon, a half-breed himself, hates the white man's culture with its hypocrisy and stupid, dull religiosity. Matthiessen even has the priest deliver a short sermon on what "we" might learn from the Indian.

> . . . . they do not seek for meaning: they *are*. They are not *heavy* the way we are, they are light as the air; their being is a mere particle of the universe, like a leaf or wing of dragonfly or wisp of cloud. Unlike ourselves, they are eternal.

Yes, yes, Padre, but it is the heaviest man of all, Martin Quarrier, who stands against Moon and forces us to question the latter's romanticism.

I don't know where Matthiessen stands (I suspect with Moon) but only bad critics nag at that question. To my mind, Moon, who survives and who at the end is, to himself, ". . . neither white nor Indian, man nor animal, but some mute, naked strand of protoplasm" is less memorable than the thick, clumsy Quarrier who dies under a "Christian" Indian's machete. In the fields of the Lord, Quarrier's work is "play for mortal stakes," as Frost has it, whereas Lewis Moon is only a minor deity in the Romantic pantheon.

I have emphasized what I think is the dramatic core of the novel, but there is much more to it than that. Matthiessen seems to know his Indians and their culture at first hand; he has also created a character in Wolfie, Moon's companion, who speaks fair to middlin' Stengelese. It's been a long while since I've read a new novel I enjoyed as much. (pp. 413-14)

> Thomas Curley, in a review of "At Play in the Fields of the Lord," in Commonweal, Vol. LXXXIII, No. 13, January 7, 1966, pp. 413-14.

## Stanley Trachtenberg

In *At Play in the Fields of the Lord,* Peter Matthiessen invokes the romantic tradition of primitive nobility corrupted by civilization. It is a view that goes back in American fiction at least as far as *Typee,* but where Melville recognized the necessity of leaving paradise, Matthiessen feels the need only for a deeper, more individual Eden. His spokesman for this return in time is Lewis Moon, part white, part Cheyenne, an outlaw from both cultures, who is inducted into the savage Niaruna tribe as a semi-divinity when he parachutes into the Amazon jungle. Moon's identification with the Niaruna is opposed by the evangelist Martin Quarrier, who couples the desire to love with an obligation to proselytize, but who sacrifices both his son's life and his wife's sanity to his conviction. Resulting from a limited vision of possibility, the sacrifice proves futile as well as obsessive. Unaware, as is the more sophisticated Dominican Father Xantes, that true conversion must be preceded by total disorientation, Quarrier is equally unable to recognize the dignity and beauty which the ecological balance sustains.

Even Moon, however, fails to find in the savage culture more than a provisional identity. "We are naked and have nothing," he is told by one of the fiercest of the tribesmen, "Therefore we must decorate ourselves, for if we did not, how are we to be told from the animals." Like the white man's religion, the savages' paint constitutes a separation from nature beyond which Moon must pass. Unlike the contemporary hero, Moon is not puzzled by a problematic universe; his search is merely for his place in an archetypally established order. As he discovers more about his true situation, however, this quest broadens from a social to a teleological one. Eventually beyond ideology, it leads to a desire for unity with God. Only when Moon passes through his real initiation of exposure, submitting himself directly to elemental hazards, does he find his true inheritance as a human, thereby reestablishing the continuity of

individual vision with a sense of a continuing past. As such the resolution of the novel avoids the tentative accommodation of Elliott and Espey, but in doing so Matthiessen exceeds the value judgment which Moon can justifiably sustain by attributing his superiority to his independence. This superiority establishes an artificial conflict with humanity which must then, either by force or by love, subdue him and thereby vindicate its own dependence. This judgment, reminiscent of the appraisal of the ultra right-wing Hollingsworth in *Barbary Shore* is, however, not as in Mailer's novel, that of a nympholeptic madwoman. It is uttered here by the wise fool and validated by the sensitive ingenue; thus presumably it is the judgment of the novel. Like Hollingsworth's, however, Moon's independence is, in fact, illusory. Depending on his rejection of any environment, it is exposed by his frantic search for a congenial one. Moon's rebirth, finally, like that of Mailer's Mike Lovett, is to a new freedom which celebrates itself without comprehension and consequently conviction of its own worth. (pp. 447-48)

> Stanley Trachtenberg, "Accommodation and Protest," in The Yale Review, Vol. LV, No. 3, March, 1966, pp. 444-50.

## Steven V. Roberts

"Sal si puedes," Spanish for "escape if you can," is the self-mocking name that Mexican-Americans call the *barrio* in San Jose where Cesar Chavez spent part of his childhood. [As Matthiessen relates in *Sal Si Puedes: Cesar Chavez and the New American Revolution;* the] rest of those years were spent tramping the back roads and fields of California's verdant San Joaquin Valley, a member of the faceless, nomadic army who pick the fruits and vegetables most Americans seem to think appear by magic in their supermarkets. What made Cesar Chavez different was that he accepted the challenge of "sal si puedes." He has tried to escape, and take his people with him.

Chavez is the head of the United Farm Workers Organizing Committee, the most recent in a long series of unions that have tried, with little success, to organize the poverty-ridden farm workers. For more than four years the United Farm Workers Organizing Committee has been striking the growers of California table grapes, and for almost two years it has been promoting a nationwide boycott against the fruit.

In the process, the union has attracted support ranging from the labor establishment to the Black Panthers. Housewives have traded bridge clubs for picket lines; Charlotte Ford and George Plimpton have raised money at chic cocktail parties; clergymen of all faiths have preached that not eating a grape is a holy act. Since the death of Martin Luther King, Cesar Chavez has become the nation's favorite radical.

What is the source of the union's strength? What lies behind the mystique of Cesar Chavez? In his excellent new account of Chavez and his movement, Peter Matthiessen offers this perceptive explanation:

> Chavez is the only leader in the nation who has

gained the fierce allegiance of the New Left without appeasing it. The students and the black militants are not drawn to Chavez the Revolutionary or Iconoclast or Political Innovator or even Radical Intellectual—he is none of these. In an ever more polluted and dehumanized world, they are drawn to him, apparently, because he is a true leader, not a politician: because his speech is free of the flatulent rhetoric and cant on which younger voters have gagged: because in a time starved for simplicity he is, simply, a man.

Matthiessen is not a political writer but a novelist (his last novel was *At Play in the Fields of the Lord* ) and a naturalist. (Some of the book's most eloquent sections describe the despoliation of California by irrigation and pesticides.) He focuses on Chavez as a personality, and that is an important part of the story. For Chavez is a truly humble man, a man of the land and the people who are close to it. When he refuses to wear a tie, when he accepts only $5 a week in expense money, when his tastes for luxury extend to Diet-Rite soda and matzos, it is not merely for the effect. That is the way he is.

He has been accused in recent years of a nascent messiah complex, and he does wear a Jewish mezuzah because he thinks Christ wore one. ("He certainly didn't wear a cross," Chavez explains.) But when he looks at his family and says, "Beautiful! Three generations of poverty!" there is more pride than bitterness in his words. (He is also a man of great gaiety. Matthiessen remembers leaving Chavez at the headquarters of the San Francisco archdiocese. Moments later the author heard a rapping sound and there was Chavez, silhouetted in a window high above the street, dancing and clowning for his friend below.)

Chavez is more than a humble man. He is an exceptionally shrewd organizer. He opposes *chicanos* who glorify *la raza,* the Mexican race, when he sniffs even a hint of racism. At a time when white liberals have been ousted from the civil-rights movement, he has not only recognized their good intentions but given them something concrete to do. And at a time when violence seems to have become a fact of public life, Chavez has maintained the principles of nonviolence. A deep admirer of Gandhi, he rejects the current notion that a group's militancy should be equated with the number of guns it has stashed away. "We are as militant as anybody," he once told me, and he is right.

For the real importance of Chavez lies in what is happening to the membership of the union. While others talked about participatory democracy, the farm workers were practicing it. "He wanted the people who did the work to make the decision," said Dolores Huerta, Chavez's able chief lieutenant. "He wanted the workers to participate, and he still does, because without that the Union has no real strength. This is why he would never accept outside money until the strike began: he wanted the workers to see that they could pay for their own union." . . .

Learning to do things for themselves has changed the farm workers. People with little formal schooling are organizing successful boycotts across the country. Moreover, they are losing the sense of shame society hammered into them for so long. Today they are proud to be *chicanos,* though

five years ago, as Chavez remarked, "They wanted to be anything *but chicanos.*"

They are demanding equality and dignity in communities where the growers have ruled them like feudal lords, and they are gaining a new sense of their own potential. "It's so great when people participate," enthused Chavez when he saw the art work in the union's new headquarters. "It's only a very small revolution, but we see this art beginning to come forth. When people begin to discover themselves like this, they begin to appreciate some of the other things in life."

One of the criticisms of Chavez, however, is that he has not thought enough about the "other things in life." While working to improve the life of the farm worker, he has not done much to help some of the young people leave the farms and get the education they are clearly capable of absorbing.

At times, success seems very far away. The boycott has made an impact, but the growers have shown little sign of giving in, and the Nixon Administration offers no prospect of outside help. The Defense Department even dramatically increased its quota of grapes for the troops in Vietnam. Many workers, moreover, are still too poor and insecure to join a union. Yet the struggle goes on. "We can't go back," Chavez's cousin once said: "We got nothing to go back to."

                    *Steven V. Roberts, "Sal Si Puedes," in* The
                    New York Times Book Review, *February 1,
                    1970, p. 8.*

**Peter Nabokov**

Peter Matthiessen's *Sal Si Puedes* [is] a superbly conceived and written chronicle of Cesar Chavez' self-discovery as an organizer and his triumphant organizing of Mexican-American field workers in California. . . . But we are most definitely not looking at a manifestation of *La Raza* or *machismo* (*chicano* manliness) consciousness. In Matthiessen's estimation, these are felt by Chavez to be drags on his mission, the fulfillment of a humanistic vision of meaningful living which transcends color and culture.

Through a novelist's ability to sweep us into *processes* of human development, Matthiessen pursues the elusive Chavez, his life story, and his organizing techniques. He is not disappointed. In the profile which emerges from Matthiessen's relaxed discussions, impressions, skillful interviewing, and quietly worked descriptions, an earthy, aloof, spiritual, immediate subject takes shape. This is Cesar Chavez, a man responsible for his actions. Matthiessen seems to make us privy to Chavez' ability to step through the painstaking details necessary to the organizer's trade, which must actually be a life rather than a profession, for it draws on total intuition and commitment and, as Matthiessen says, a sharing of "this astonishing hope of an evolution in human values."

The narrative is also an original piece of consciously ecological reportage. Matthiessen can paint the soft nightmare of the remade, defoliated, poisoned California earthscape with surrealistic force. The interconnectedness of work, environment, and sustenance are ever present: The farm worker toils in chemical-infested earth beneath hot, glaring clouds of dust, steam, and pesticide vapor, picking contaminated fruits which will be doctored by more laboratory substances to make them appear delicious. The back-breaking work, the relationships with frustrated against-the-wall growers, the sense of an America thrown away to the lords of money, asphalt, and confrontation, is relieved only by the serene power of Matthiessen's central figure, Chavez, and his courageous movement towards, as the Matthiessen subtitle reads, "The New American Revolution." Matthiessen has been criticized for idolizing Chavez, but I consider the criticism irrelevant. (p. 41)

*Peter Nabokov, "Taking the Lid Off," in* The Progressive, *Vol. 34, No. 7, July, 1970, pp. 40-1.*

### Edward Weeks

Like many of our young independent novelists . . . Peter Matthiessen has had to supplement the income from his fiction, and for some time he did this as a commercial fisherman and captain of a charter boat out of Montauk. When his reputation as a naturalist became better known, he was signed on as the writing member of expeditions to the Amazon, New Guinea, and Alaska, and in this capacity, in 1968, he joined the film team led by Peter Gimbel to find and photograph underwater the Great White Shark, the most dangerous creature in the sea, known as the "white death" in waters where it is usually to be found.

[As Matthiessen relates in **Blue Meridian: The Search for the Great White Shark,** the] Gimbel team would begin their search off the coast of South Africa, photographing from aluminum cages, 6 by 6 by 3.5 feet, with air tanks, steel fittings, 110 pounds of lead ballast, and a flotation chamber holding compressed air in the center of the roof so that the buoyancy of the cage could be adjusted to the desired level, or brought swiftly to the surface. Peter Gimbel had been diving for twenty years; it was he who took the first pictures of the *Andrea Doria,* 225 feet down in the dark currents off Nantucket; he has the coolness and caution of a professional, and is an admirable teacher. In the Bahamas, where he first rehearsed the equipment and crew, he gave Matthiessen his baptism in the cage: then together they explored the Blue Hole, leaving the cage to swim into a cave in its wall so narrow that the divers had to enter single file. Matthiessen's weights were too light, and his scuba tank kept clanging on the cavern roof; Gimbel handled the beam, and both were shocked when it illuminated the caudal fin of a large shark which they had trapped by accident and which was circling to avoid them. They made it back to the cage, and with air almost gone, went up to the surface. "A nurse shark," Gimbel told the men on deck. "Eleven or twelve feet—the biggest I've ever seen." No harm done but a foretaste of what was to come.

This was the plan for South Africa: on a chartered whale-catcher, the *Terrier VIII,* the Gimbel team would follow the Norwegian-manned fleet in its hunt for the big sperm whales. With spotter planes and sonar, the whales would be tracked down and killed, and as the blood spread, the sharks, hopefully a Great White among them, would come in to ravage the carcass—and the cameras would begin. Underwater there were to be four performers, Gimbel and Stan Waterman, the producer and associate producer, who would double as divers and cameramen, and Ron and Valerie Taylor, the most skilled and intrepid husband-and-wife team in Southern waters. The Taylors would operate the cages, and Ron would be an alternate cameraman when needed. (pp. 109-10)

Matthiessen, in his strong graphic prose, tells the story, writing down his dislike of South Africa, of the callous competence with which the whales were blasted, and his anger at such unrestricted extermination. On deck he watched the business of the birds, the wandering albatross, the sooty shearwaters, and storm petrels, and when he is dubbed into one of the cages, he watches, with a trepidation the reader shares, as shark after shark attacks the dead whales. Whitetips, blues, duskies, and tiger sharks, they come and go. One ten-foot blue nosed so insistently at the cage that Peter kicked it in the side and it slid away. Gimbel remarks, "If you *really hurt* one, he'll go find something easier to eat." The contrast between the savagery of the sharks, "doomed to keep swimming, open-mouthed, from birth to death," and the intimacy of the divers is striking.

Good film depended on water clarity, on wind, waves, sensitive equipment, and sensitive people, whose health and tempers were strained as the search led from Durban to the Indian Ocean and thence to Ceylon, with the main character, the Great White, never coming into focus. . . . [Off the coast of South Australia], chumming with large gobs of a dead horse, they brought the Great White up from the depths, and now it was the sharks who patrolled the men. They bit the skiff, bit the propeller, mouthed the metal cages with such violence that their teeth went spinning from their jaws. As Matthiessen wrote: "They do not attack boats; they attack *anything.*" The largest that could be measured with any accuracy was sixteen feet, and with a predator of that size, no diver was swimming in the clear, as they had been with the lesser breeds.

For its natural history, for its persistent courage, and for its terrifying portrait of White Death, this book, along with its dramatic illustrations, will live in the memory of all who read it. (p. 110)

*Edward Weeks, "The Peripatetic Reviewer," in* The Atlantic Monthly, *Vol. 227, No. 3, March, 1971, pp. 109-10.*

### Christopher Lehmann-Haupt

In June, 1964, a boat out of Montauk, L. I., that specialized in sport fishing for sharks caught a great white shark 17½-feet long and more than 4,000 pounds in weight. As Peter Matthiessen, the nature writer and novelist, writes in **Blue Meridian,**

> This monster was towed ashore and hauled out on the docks of Montauk, and as I lived not far

away I went down one day to see it. Though white sharks vary in color, or lack of it—some are gray-white or brown or even a bruised blue—then tend to pale as they grow older, and this one was a dirty grayish white, like a cadaver. Its length was awesome, and so was its vast maw, but most appalling was its girth, its massiveness: one saw immediately how such a beast could take a seal in a single dreadful gulp.

Or a large part of a man, he might have added, for the "white death," as the fish is also called, is a man-eater of legendary stature.

Peter Gimbel saw the Montauk shark, too, and he brooded over it. Peter Gimbel is the scion of the department-store family and a former investment banker, who now makes underwater films and is considered to be among the best scuba divers in the world. . . .

He brooded over the great white shark, and decided to see if he could photograph it from up close—make a movie in which the huge fish would star. So he set to work to devising an underwater-cage affair to shoot pictures from, sold a treatment of his film idea to the Columbia Broadcasting System, organized a crew of crack diving photographers, and in 1969 set out for the east coast of Africa to put his system to the test. . . .

*Blue Meridian* is the result, constructed from Mr. Matthiessen's direct observations while he could spend time on the project, from letters written to him by Gimbel when he could not, and from diaries kept by members of the film crew. While the book is basically an advertisement for Gimbel's film (*Blue Water, White Death,* it is called) it is a very high-class advertisement, filled with strong descriptive writing, interesting lore about diving and undersea life, high-tension scenes involving the relationships of the crew and the fluctuating fortunes of the adventure, and some of the most spectacular color photographs I have ever seen.

One of the most curious problems of the project—on the solution to which depended the success of the movie, the book, and Gimbel's future as a filmmaker—was to find a climax. The crew had had great success in the waters off Durban, South Africa, by suspending the underwater cages from commercially killed whales waiting to be towed ashore, and photographing the sharks that gathered to feed off the carcasses. . . . But no great white sharks had shown up, and the more good footage the crew got, the more close-ups of the white death seemed a natural climax.

One wonders as one reads along just how the discovery of the monsters will provide that climax—especially to Mr. Matthiessen's verbal report. Mr. Matthiessen himself solves this problem somewhat artificially—first, by making it ominously clear that the photographers were to keep their cameras going no matter what was happening to their mates (as if something catastrophic was in the offing); and second, by ranging back in time as the moment of truth approaches to record eyewitness accounts of famous attacks by white sharks on men. These devices of building drama are not without effect: "It's shock that kills most people in a shark attack," one of the divers ob-

serves; I want to tell you that shock made it difficult for this reader to survive even descriptions of shark attacks, not to mention the color photograph of one unfortunate diver lying on the operating table shortly after being bitten by a shark.

But when the crew finally located their "prey" off the southern coast of Australia, nothing very serious happened: Gimbel got his climactic visual scenes, but Mr. Matthiessen's prose account is a little anticlimactic. And the reader is left to wonder just why Gimbel found it necessary to undertake all this, to expose himself and his colleagues to such incredible danger. (The question is put to Gimbel several times, but his answers are never satisfactory—a lot of Hemingweming nonsense about response to danger and testing the limits blah.) One also wonders why the great white shark must become extinct, as Mr. Matthiessen assures us it will become, along with the whales whose commercial destruction he reports in the powerful opening passages of *Blue Meridian.* One senses a connection between the two questions—between the thrill of danger and the relentlessness of human scavaging—and one senses that Mr. Matthiessen senses it too. Which may explain the subtle ambivalence he seems to have brought to the writing of this book.

Still, I admit I can't wait to see the film.

*Christopher Lehmann-Haupt, "White Monsters of the Deep," in* The New York Times, *April 23, 1971, p. 35.*

### Anatole Broyard

[In] *The Tree Where Man Was Born,* the text of this dual volume [work that also includes Eliot Porter's photographs collected under the title *The African Experience*]— Peter Matthiessen describes the African as he stands puzzled between past and future. One is already destroyed, the other not yet created—and the present is a void. The much romanticized Masai is still one of the handsomest of men, but he is succumbing to venereal disease and infertility. He has kept his famous pride, his stubborn refusal to change, but it has reduced him to hawking his second-best spear or knife to tourists. In fact, like the animals in the game parks, his life has little meaning beyond being a tourist attraction.

Large animals, Mr. Matthiessen tells us, are so scarce that only one out of 12 East Africans has seen a lion in his lifetime. They can be seen, for the most part, only in the parks, and to go there one must first have a car. In any case, the average African of today has little use for wild animals. They no longer represent a challenge, a chance to prove himself. They are no longer guards or spirits of the bush, speaking to each tribe in a chanted mythology, but footpads of the night, something like muggers, or despoilers of crops.

Capable of eating 600 pounds of grass or browse in one day; fond of knocking down trees, the elephant is turning the woodlands to dust. The lion, once secure in his power, is now on the brink of starvation because in the days of plenty he never learned to hunt with the guile of the wild dog or the implacability of the hyena. Human beings are fencing in all the water holes, putting up houses around them.

Experts argue ecology without agreeing. Zoologists contradict the hunters and wardens, who have spent their whole lives in the bush. But though scientists are looking at Africa through microscopes and cameras instead of gunsights, they still haven't been able to do anything about the tsetse fly, the greatest impediment to progress on the continent. To swim in Africa's lovely rock-bound pool is to risk bilharziasis, a painful and persistent disease.

The African, who was once so resourceful on his own, has been stunned into something resembling a trained animal, suitable only for the simplest task on safari or in the household, according to the author. Those who are educated to fill the proud posts of civilization are often found wandering the town's streets, looking for that civilization amid the poverty, the politics, the revolutions and the rhetoric of great powers competing for influence. The whole continent resembles a mired elephant photographed by Mr. Porter, all its immense strength useless because it cannot get hold of anything that doesn't give beneath its weight.

Mr. Matthiessen has a number of adventures, but they are almost all in the company of scientists, who risk their lives not to dance around and feast for a week on an elephant, but to chart its habits. Some of these scientists seem to suffer from a sort of hysteria as they go about their work, as if they too were baffled and infuriated by the new Africa. We no longer read the magnificent passages of a Burton or a Doughty: this is not even the Africa of Evelyn Waugh or Graham Greene. What was once a country of mystery, myth and ritual, of art that influenced Picasso, Modigliani and many others, has now become a "problem."

If anyone could have found the color, the lost romance of Africa, it would have been Mr. Matthiessen. His novel of South America—*At Play in the Fields of the Lord*—caught all the incongruities of the primitive confronting the civilized and vice versa. In just one tribe, one jungle town, he found enough melancholy ironies to furnish forth a convention of social scientists. But even his extraordinary talents as a novelist, naturalist and travel writer are hard-pressed to squeeze any real juice out of *The Tree Where Man Was Born.*

The book is fascinating in its way for the splendor of Mr. Porter's photographs and for Mr. Matthiessen's prose, but the story we are all awaiting, the *feel* of emergent Africa, is still as shrouded in mist as the crests of its fabled mountains. Already, the quotations from African mythology that serve as epigraphs for the chapters have a remote and quaint sound that tells us they no longer have the conviction and immediacy that can come only from a still vital culture.

> *Anatole Broyard, "The Elephant in the Mire,"* in The New York Times, *October 17, 1972, p. 39.*

## Saturday Review

In what must be one of the most stunning books of this or any year, Peter Matthiessen, the novelist and naturalist [and photographer Eliot Porter] . . . have put in tandem their passions and their impressive talents to evoke the human and natural history of East Africa—one of the world's last splendors and the greatest wildlife spectacle in the world. The conception of [*The Tree Where Man Was Born/The African Experience*] is the publisher's, and it is one of those ideas that really works. The volume is produced in oversize format to display to best advantage Porter's gorgeous and breath-taking color photographs. Matthiessen's 100,000-word text, which could be a book in itself (and was recently excerpted in three parts in *The New Yorker*), is both informative and intensely moving. As a picture-and-text portrait of East Africa, it reminds one only of Peter Beard's beautiful *The End of the Game* (1965); as text alone, it ranks with Isak Dinesen's (the Baroness Karen von Blixen) 1937 classic *Out of Africa*. Matthiessen combines three elements in his writing: a gift for acute observation of both wildlife and men, a sense of African tribal history and myth, and a vividly personal account of his own encounter with Africa. He traveled primarily in Kenya and Tanzania (mostly by Land Rover), sometimes alone, sometimes in the company of such other wildlife experts as George B. Schaller, who had come to the great Serengeti game preserve in 1966 to study predator-prey relations, and Iain Douglas-Hamilton, a scientist oblivious of risk and bent on identifying every elephant in the area by photographing it head on (to record ear nicks)—i.e., as it charged. Matthiessen's travels take him to remote and isolated tribes—there are hunters and cultivators, and some caught in between—and he writes of them with utmost awe and empathy—their primitive ways of life and sophisticated beliefs, and their tenuous relation to a modern Africa, embarrased at their existence. He writes also of the ever-present game, the extraordinary landscape, the endless skies. Like this rare and powerful book, the Africa he and Porter evoke is finally timeless, majestic, throbbing with life, indivisible. (pp. 78-9)

> *Review of "The Tree Where Man Was Born/The African Experience," in* Saturday Review, *Vol. LV, No. 44, October 28, 1972, pp. 78-9.*

## Peter Matthiessen with George A. Plimpton

[Plimpton]: *James Dickey feels that* **Far Tortuga** *is a turning point in the evolution of the novel, that you are "creating our new vision." Would you say something about this book's development?*

[Matthiessen]: *Far Tortuga* is based on a sea turtle fishing voyage off Nicaragua: *tortuga* is the Spanish word for sea turtle, and sometimes refers to a cay where green turtles are found. I started work on the book in 1966, and since then, it's been put aside many times, but I never tired of it. I was moved by the stark quality of that voyage, everything worn bare by wind and sea—the reefs, the faded schooner, the turtle men themselves—everything so pared down and so simple that metaphors, stream-of-consciousness, even such ordinary conventions of the novel as "he said" or "he thought," seemed intrusive, even offensive, and a great impediment, besides. So from the start I was feeling my way toward a spare form, with more air around the words, more space: I wanted the descriptions to be very clear and flat, to find such poetry as they might attain in their very directness and simplicity. In fact, I can only recall one simile in the whole book. And eventually, I attempted using white space to achieve resonance, to make the reader receive things intuitively, hear the silence in the wind, for instance, that is a constant presence in the book.

In Japanese *sumi* painting, in a drawing of a bamboo stalk, the brush moves upward, leaving a white space between strokes to suggest the nodes of the bamboo that separate sections of the stem; it's the emptiness that brings the rest to life. Similarly, the emptiness and silence represented by white spaces set up reverberations in what is written. (pp. 79-80)

*Has your study of Zen affected this book?*

Perhaps it has contributed to a need for spareness, the presentation of a coffee cup, a cockroach, with a minimum of literary adornment. Zen training helps one to see in a fresh way, to dissolve the screens that build up from early childhood and obscure one's perceptions, and I suppose I am trying to present things directly, let objects and actions speak for themselves, so that the reader will not have to perceive things through the screens in the minds of the characters.

*How does your editor feel about this experimental novel?*

Well, I guess he was pretty suspicious at first, assured me it wouldn't sell, of course, but after he'd spent some time with it, it began to get to him. Some readers may be wary—certain critics, too—of the strange type set-up on the page: they'll say, "Oh-oh! An *experiment!*" But actually, the experiment, if that is what it is, is very simple, no tricks or word games at all, and once the reader gets the feel of the new form, the book is quite straightforward. In the beginning, since you don't know the crew, it doesn't really matter much that you're not always sure which man is speaking: by the time you do care, you will recognize each man, not only by the idiosyncrasies of speech but by his small obsessions. There's a ship's manifest with each crewman's name, kin, and particulars, and a deck plan of the vessel which serves as a sort of stage set, and an end paper map for following her course off Nicaragua—all these help.

*Do you recognize other influences?*

I mentioned *sumi* painting, and an admiration of *haiku* poetry may well have influenced the brief descriptive passages. But leaving space experiments aside, the basic physical format derives from the screenplay, even though the person speaking is not identified directly, and the camera directions are replaced by descriptive writing. The dialogue is realistic, but toward the end, I recognized that I had put an element of folksong in it, naturally enhanced by the power and simple beauty of the turtle men's speech. And of course a turtle boat is a good situation for the sort of experiment I was trying—a small isolated world, a confined stage which nobody could leave, and men who sing the refrains of their bewilderment over and over.

*Could the form you have developed be adapted to other types of novels?*

I hope so, since I'd like to try again; next time, I'll carry it further, perhaps, if I can do so without loss of clarity and feeling.

*What was that one simile, and why did you leave it in the book?*

I guess I didn't want to take it out. It comes when the *Eden*'s men first see Far Tortuga on the horizon, and refers to an island, "like a memory in the ocean emptiness." The image seemed to me mysterious, nostalgic, suggesting that the turtlers were returning to a mythical childhood place, perhaps even that, unknown to themselves, they were already dead and had entered another world. In any case, the image occurred naturally, and I didn't want to take it out just to be consistent. (pp. 80-2)

> *Peter Matthiessen and George A. Plimpton, in an interview in* The Paris Review, *Vol. 15, No. 60, Winter 1974, pp. 79-82.*

### Francine du Plessix Gray

Upon reading Peter Matthiessen's **The Snow Leopard** I sent the author the following letter:

Peter.

I have just read your last book and feel beckoned to write the kind of letter I only write once or twice in a decade.

Let me begin this way: It has, to use the same words with which you describe a Nepalese family eating by a fire, "the pace and dignity of a sacrament."

When I finished it yesterday evening, at an hour when I habitually wouldn't think of doing anything else but begin reading something else, there was only one thing I could do: I went into a solitary room and shut out all light and lay flat on my back for a long while, partaking in some kind of sacramental substance issued forth by your book.

The whole business of reading **The Snow Leopard** was a form of spiritual exercise for me. What purity, what uncompromisingness, above all what *rigor,* as there must be in all genuine spiritual quest or work of art. And how hard to read anything else afterwards. (p. 791)

One needs to descend very slowly from **The Snow Leopard,** the way you probably need to descend slowly from the heights of your mountain tops or the silence of your zendos.

Thank you for this Exercise. Thank you for the breadth and spareness and luminosity of it. (Your language is at its peak in this work, unsurpassed in precision and rightness.) Thank you for buttressing our deep need to let go, accumulate less, live more simply, know ourselves a little better. Thank you for the candor of your tears, and for those I shed in response. Thank you for the unabashedness of your sentiments, a freedom I obviously partake of in this letter but which may be easier for me, being of a profoundly Slavic nature, than for one raised, as you were, in the crucible of Anglo-Saxon reticence. Thank you for what may be (only time can tell us that) a very great book.

With admiration and gratitude,

Francine G.
(p. 792)

*Francine du Plessix Gray, in a review of "The Snow Leopard," in* Commonweal, *Vol. CV, No. 24, December 8, 1978, pp. 791-92.*

## Jeffrey Carroll

There is certainly no one in American letters who occupies the same bench Peter Matthiessen does. Unique in his considerable skills with both fiction and non-fiction forms, Matthiessen is nearly thirty years beyond his first book, and his work continues to improve and change. He has had a critical following for years; Lillian Hellman, William Styron, Thomas Pynchon, Roger Tory Peterson, Gerald Durrell, W. S. Merwin, Jim Harrison and James Dickey are among those who have praised him in print—but only with *Far Tortuga* in 1975 did he begin to carry a larger public with him on his literary journeys.

Two other writers should be mentioned to place Matthiessen in the context of the contemporary American literary traveler, a tradition begun with Thoreau but which has lately grown increasingly exclusive. Edward Abbey, in *Desert Solitaire* and *The Journey Home,* eulogizes the American West, and Edward Hoagland's vantage, particularly in *The Courage of Turtles* and *Walking the Dead Diamond River,* is a tender melancholic New England one. There are other great naturalists—most prominently Peterson and Edwin Way Teale—working still in the old tradition, but even Abbey and Hoagland, their spiritual inheritors, have forsaken the poetry of wonder in their early books for either anger, in Abbey's case, or bemused observation, in Hoagland's.

When *The Snow Leopard* was awarded the National Book Award in 1979, it was for "Contemporary Thought," a curious but understandable categorizing of a book that blends memoir, poetry, zoology and the best elements of adventure fiction with a careful explication of Zen Buddhism; Matthiessen reached for something evidently beyond the grasp of his contemporaries. *The Snow Leopard* succeeds in its interconnectedness and thought arising out of a confrontation between the self and the unknown.

Physical journey is nothing new to Matthiessen. It has formed the core motif for almost all his published work, from the first novel, *Race Rock* (1954), through the geographically organized *Wildlife in America* (1959), the novel *Raditzer* (1961), the surreal journeys of the novel *At Play in the Fields of the Lord* (1965), through the anthropological trio of *The Cloud Forest* (1961), *Under the Mountain Wall* (1962) and *Blue Meridian* (1971), the impressionistic *The Tree Where Man Was Born* (1972) to *Far Tortuga* (1975). Though this last novel is memorable for its poetry, tone and dialect, it lacks a cohesive narration; its beauty is in its white spaces. *The Snow Leopard* engages the strangest journey of his life and fuses it with

Eastern philosophy, the encompassing Buddhist illumination which he discovers as the path and goal of his journey:

> We climb onward, toward the sky, and with every step my spirits rise. As I walk along, my stave striking the ground, I leave the tragic sense of things behind; I begin to smile, infused with a sense of my own foolishness, with an acceptance of my failures of this journey as well as of its wonders, acceptance of all that I might meet upon my path. I know that this transcendence will be fleeting, but while it lasts, I spring along the path as if set free.

It is a lesson hard-learned in this 85-day hike into the Himalayas; the journey's excitement has been tempered by tragedy, his wife's death a year earlier. Tension exists between bodily escape through wilderness, and the genuine but static visionary wonder of the temples and snows, the "frozen atmospheres" of the mountains; in this tension Matthiessen discovers, first, "I have failed. I will perform the motions of parenthood, my work, my friendships, my Zen practice, but all hopes, acts, and travels have been blighted. I look forward to nothing."

And then, through the alchemical powers of nature Matthiessen repeatedly enjoys and suffers, "along the water-courses . . . against time, in the weary light of dying summer," he experiences the *"now"* that is the answer, or reward, for the "not-looking-forward, the without hope-ness." Of all his tasks, expected and unexpected, Matthiessen is most at pains to "explain" Zen Buddhism, fully aware of the wise reluctance of those schooled in Zen thought to attempt to explain its essence in words.

There are no lessons without tasks of learning. The journey is ostensibly a scientific one, for the purpose of finding, with biologist George Schaller, the *Bharal,* or Himalayan blue sheep; it is a grand excuse, however, for Matthiessen's own journey:

> Red leaves drift on the still lake; a B'on-po coughs. High above this campsite in the silver birches, on a meadow near the sky, blue sheep are grazing.

From this level of poetic observation Matthiessen ascends into the atmospheres of his being, physical danger and mental anguish—and the snow leopard, a sudden symbol of goals, is never seen:

> Have you seen the snow leopard?

> No! Isn't that wonderful?

He has created, finally, a journey of standing still, and found for himself the freedom of "traveling light" in mind or mountains, within burdens of memory or expectation. The magic of the snow mountains is, in part, their permanence, against which the author must admit his transience, and by so doing live in the moment without anxiety. Time drops away.

The despair of Matthiessen's return to Kathmandu and all the cares he thought he could leave behind—but which haunted him for nearly three months—is tempered by the glimpse he has gotten of the sharp-edged temple of the now. The glimpse is purely inward; the triumph he achieves is in standing still and knowing he is a part of his soul's movement. *The Snow Leopard* is that glimpse reflected in the crystal of the written word. Matthiessen, for us, has married motion and contemplation as well as anyone has; in effect, Western act and Eastern thought become reconciled. (pp. 183-85)

*Jeffrey Carroll, in a review of "The Snow Leopard," in* Hawaii Review, *Vol. 10, Spring–Fall, 1980, pp. 183-85.*

## Joseph Kastner

Peter Matthiessen's last book, *The Snow Leopard,* was less an account of his trip into the Himalayas looking for a legendary mountain animal than an exploration of himself, seeking some meaning in his troubled life. Now in *Sand Rivers,* he has cleared himself of introspection and written an extroverted account of a trek into one of the last primeval places in Africa, the Selous. He gives us all the expected bits of safari lore—the unwary animals, the close calls, the naive native carriers, the sardonic old Africa hand who greets the American writer sceptically and ends up respectful and friendly. Of course, since it is Matthiessen who is telling all this, *Sand Rivers* has—as his books always do—a special grace of perception and an understanding of nature made up in equal parts of love and learning.

The Selous Game Reserve in Tanzania is 22,000 square miles of wilderness, four times the size of the famous Serengeti preserve, as big as Maryland. Poachers get in around the edges, taking elephant ivory or rhino tusks (to be made into aphrodisiacs for the Chinas or, dagger handles for OPEC princes). The Selous water holes are jammed with hippopotamus, the grasslands dotted with antelope, the trees and skies full of tinker birds, boubous, griffons and hammerkops. The air sounds with the "tinny notes of the trumpeter hornbill," "the deep tearing coughs of a restless leopard," the chirping of millions of frogs "that hurl their voices at the stars in a bug-eyed cosmic ecstacy." The streams are bedded with a white quartzite, hence sand rivers.

Matthiessen and photographer Hugo van Lawick went to Selous as publicity agents (of a kind) to call attention to a last unspoiled piece of Africa and save it from neglect or the fate of the game parks, tamed by Land Rovers and Minibusses, where animals accept men because they are accustomed to them. In the Selous animals accept men because they have not known them.

Their book is an evenly told story, without sermonizing or any real climax—and it eloquently accomplishes their goal. . . .

At a waterhole where hippos were staying under water "cooling the cumbersome machinery of their brains, . . . two pink eyed gladiators" emerged "with a quake and rumbling . . . reared up on their hind legs, mouths wide and ivory clacking; their huge heads locked." The party stumbles head on into a rhinocerous with her calf: "The immense and ancient animal remains motionless . . . I am in pure breathless awe of their protean life form, six hun-

dred thousand centuries on earth, the ugliest and most beautiful life imaginable." But the rhino simply twitches an ear and "settles backward inelegantly on her hind quarters." The moment of purest excitement seems to come when the expedition leader takes Matthiessen into a hidden clearing and tells him "you're the only white man besides myself ever to see it."

The leader, a tall and sometimes truculent man named Brian Nicholson had been warden of the Selous until the hard-pressed government could no longer afford proper care. In his day he had shot rampaging elephants at point-blank range and killed 20 man-eating lions. He seems at first a colonial throwback, as scornful of imported scientists—"boffins with their great pulsating brains selecting facts to fit their precious theories"—as of the native Africans. But he himself turns out to have done pioneering research on elephants and for all his prejudices feels, like other old hands, that civilization is turning first-rate Africans into third-rate Europeans. The Selous is "the only place on earth where I feel I belong" and he aches to save it.

Hugo van Lawick's photographs are lovely and revealing and, though they show familiar animals, are never perfunctory. They serve the book best when they evoke the innocence of the Selous—elephants ambling through a blue-white shallows, antelope skittering into a golden haze, water bucks placid in a violet dusk. Matthiessen's text itself is touched with a photographic immediacy: harrier hawks "with bare vulturine lemon-yellow faces" that go off in "a strange weary flight through the bony trees"; baboons that "descended stiffly from a tamarind and moved off like old men"; zebras "fleeing like striped spirits through the trees."

A famous photographer once remarked that, for him, the ideal camera would be a lens screwed into his forehead and focused by his brain so that he could take pictures without any intervention. In a sense, Matthiessen, the writer, is equipped with that ideal camera. The things he sees are captured with the click of a thought on his mind and later fixed and printed by a prose rich with specific and poetic imagery.

*Joseph Kastner, "Safari to Save the Selous," in* Book World—The Washington Post, *Vol. XI, No. 16, April 19, 1981, p. 4.*

## Martha Gellhorn

Successful safaris in East Africa are like successful love affairs. Every moment is significant, delicious and fascinating to the participants; onlookers may well feel benevolent but a bit bored. *Sand Rivers* is the almost total recall of a month on safari in the Selous, a remote game reserve about the size of Wales in south-eastern Tanzania. . . . Brian Nicholson, who had been Warden in the Selous for twenty years until 1973, was the authority on local lore and the leader.

Peter Matthiessen was apparently awed by the Warden like a new boy at school wanting to get on with the Captain of the House. He repeats Nicholson's talk and anecdotes verbatim. They sound all right but standard for the profession in that part of the world, no pearls of wisdom and certainly not a barrel of laughs. Matthiessen's reverence is puzzling, since his own papers as a hardship traveller and naturalist are in perfect order.

Fascinating day follows fascinating day: every visible animal, bird, reptile, insect, tree, flower, stone is noted by its correct name and described. The roll-call of birds will fill bird-watchers and ornithologists with envy. Opening the book at random and quoting a random paragraph gives a fair impression of the whole.

> That night or early the next day, the elephant sagged down and died against the green grass bank between the plain and the white sand of the river, and a day later, more than three hundred vultures had assembled, including one huge lappet-face and a few white-headed vultures which we had not seen before in the Selous, and even two beautiful palm-nut vultures, which may have joined the madding throng for social purposes since they are not known to consume carrion. The first to arrive shared the carcass with hyena and lion, but perhaps these animals were already well-fed, for as the hordes of dark birds circled down out of the sky the carnivores withdrew, and the elephant disappeared beneath a flopping mass of vultures that stained the river sands all around a dark grey-green.

The last, best seventy pages of *Sand Rivers* reports a foot safari, the planned climax of the larger outing. The Warden, Matthiessen and eight novice African porters set out to walk through deep bush, where the only tracks were laid down by passing elephant, without a compass but with an elephant-gun and a shot-gun. Close and sometimes alarming encounters with large dangerous animals were expected and enjoyed; otherwise those days (it is not clear how many) would have been merely proof of impressive stamina. The heat in the Selous is a curse. After four days of it in February 1970 I longed never to return. Matthiessen, who is offhand about tsetse flies, makes nothing of the heat; and the Warden must be impervious since he lived happily for twenty years in that suffocating climate. The man of the wilderness and the man of the world were equals on that trek and became friends.

A piece of sickening information: Matthiessen says that the cause of growing wholesale destruction of rhinoceros is a new fashion among rich Arabs for daggers with rhino horn handles. This is far worse than the idiot oriental notion that powdered rhino horn is an aphrodisiac which has boosted the price of rhino horn in Hong Kong higher than the price of pure gold. At the present rate of massacre, that strange, enormous beast, which long preceded us on this planet and has never harmed us, will be extinct in ten years.

Half-way through this static, curiously earnest book, I stopped to read again Peter Matthiessen's unforgettable novel *At Play In The Fields Of The Lord.* After an extraordinary South American journey and when the experience had settled, where it belongs in the mind's compost heap, he brought out a work of imagination which is fiercely alive, full of terrors, truths, surprises and mad hi-

larity. My hope is that Matthiessen will use his scrupulous record of the Selous as compost for an Africa novel to rival *At Play In The Fields Of The Lord.*

*Martha Gellhorn, "Scouring the Selous," in* The Times Literary Supplement, *No. 4099, October 23, 1981, p. 1227.*

## Richard F. Patteson

The relationship between man and nature . . . has always been an object of human contemplation. But a "holistic and 'organic' view of nature"—forced upon us by quantum mechanics and relativity theory and expressed politically in the environmental movement—is a comparatively new development, and it has found its most striking literary articulation in the work of Peter Matthiessen. Matthiessen's position as both naturalist and novelist makes him an ideal exponent of the ecological awareness that is gradually shaping our consciousness, and his novel *Far Tortuga* (1975) is his most ambitious attempt to cast the holistic vision in a fictional narrative.

The casual reader opening *Far Tortuga* for the first time can readily see that the novel contains certain eccentricities: snatches of dialogue without the usual narrative transitions; brief, stark descriptive passages, again with a minimum degree of authorial presence; and white spaces—many of them—lying between dialogue and description. These formal elements are crucial to the book's meaning and effect, but their function can be understood only in relation to deeper, less obvious structural patterns. The plot involves a series of dualities or oppositions grounded largely in conflict between a presumably idyllic past and an unacceptable present. The cast of characters—Caribbean turtlemen—divides along these lines; some long for "de back time," while others are content to dwell in the present or look forward to a more promising future. The turtlers' concerns are personal and political. They talk incessantly about days when turtle fishing was better, before tourism and American economic hegemony made turtling a vanishing way of life.

But Matthiessen's own viewpoint is broader than this, and the novel is more than an indictment of human and environmental waste. Not until we look at the greater oppositions in the novel—those scarcely articulated by the characters themselves—do we see what Matthiessen is really about. The island of Far Tortuga, which may or may not have existed (*tortuga* in Spanish means "turtle"), comes to be identified with the Edenic past that figures so prominently in American literature. For Matthiessen, however, the significant event in the Eden story is not original sin so much as expulsion from the garden: man's separation from nature. The ultimate "back time" is the time when man was a part of his world, not a stranger in it. Matthiessen is only one of a growing number of contemporary writers and critics who postulate an organically interconnected reality—"the unified nature of existence," as Matthiessen calls it in *The Snow Leopard.* That ecological outlook is also fundamentally oriental. Only in the west have man and nature been seen as separate entities. The east Asian, whether Hindu, Buddhist, or Taoist, vividly senses the relatedness of all things. In *Far Tortuga* Matthiessen, a student of Zen, transforms the turtlemen's various struggles with each other, with "modern time," and above all, with nature into a vision of unity that the novel's style and typography play a large part in expressing.

Matthiessen's absorption with oriental thought shapes *Far Tortuga* in a number of important ways. Commenting on the novel's technical peculiarities [see interview with George A. Plimpton above], Matthiessen says:

> I was feeling my way toward a spare form, with more air around the words, more space: I wanted the descriptions to be very clear and flat, to find such poetry as they might attain in their very directness and simplicity. In fact, I can only recall one simile in the whole book. And eventually, I attempted using white spaces to achieve resonance, to make the reader receive things intuitively, to hear the silence in the wind, for instance, that is a constant presence in the book.

Matthiessen adds that Zen training "helps one to see in a fresh way, to dissolve the screens that build up from early childhood and obscure one's perceptions." The art forms that Matthiessen specifically cites as influences on his techniques are sumi painting and the haiku. The sumi painting of the Sung dynasty (960-1279) is characterized by a landscape of stark simplicity and vast empty spaces. When a human figure appears in these pictures, it is small; the human does not dominate. One has only to compare this style with European art of the same period to see how widely the two cultures diverge in their views of the cosmos and man's place in it. (pp. 70-2)

Matthiessen's debt to oriental thought as a way of apprehending experience directly, intuitively, has much to do with his deliberate avoidance of metaphor in *Far Tortuga.* He wants to present the world in a manner freed from the diachronic thought patterns that are so closely bound up with the linear structure of occidental languages. Curiously, the reluctance to use metaphor seems to place Matthiessen in the same camp as the "new novelists," but he does not really belong there. Richard Wasson points out that writers of the past, against whom Robbe-Grillet and other new novelists reacted, "did not accept the difference and distance between the subject and the Other, so they continually tried to overcome discontinuities, to suggest through a reconciling metaphor a link between things." This is clearly a dualist's attempt to conquer dualism. Robbe-Grillet rejected it because, in his view, the attempt is dishonest. Reconciliation can never be effected. Matthiessen, on the other hand, declines to use metaphor because it is *unnecessary.* From the perspective of Zen (and most other eastern thought) the universe *is* whole; man and the world *are* one—we need not strive (through metaphor) to make it so.

This notion of wholeness lies at the heart of oriental philosophy and informs, on the deepest levels, *Far Tortuga.* Alan Watts observes that "Taoism, Confucianism, and Zen are expressions of a mentality which feels completely at home in this universe, and which sees man as an integral part of his environment. Human intelligence is not an imprisoned spirit from afar but an aspect of the whole intri-

cately balanced organism of the natural world." From this point of view, as Watts goes on to say, conflict is superficial and oppositions are fundamentally harmonious because they are seen as relational, part of the whole.

The plot of *Far Tortuga* is far from harmonious. Captain Raib Avers, a veteran turtler from the Cayman Islands, assembles a crew of eight and sets out, too late in the season, toward the Miskito Cays off the coast of Nicaragua. The eight on board include Raib's inexperienced, scholarly son Buddy; another kinsman, Vemon Evers, who has a weakness for alcohol; the superstitious stowaway Wodie Greaves; a mysterious engineer known as Brown; the chronically discontent Athens Ebanks; and three more or less competent hands—Byrum Watler, Will Parchment, and Junior "Speedy" Bodden. During the voyage a number of conflicts break out between Raib and the members of his crew. Eventually three of them (Athens, Vemon, and Brown) abandon the enterprise. Raib, with more than a trace of the monomania that seems to afflict ship captains in literature, insists on continuing, even though the vessel is in bad condition, the fishing poor, and the weather is turning ominous. By the end of the novel five of the remaining six, including the captain, are dead, and their ship, the *Lillias Eden,* has been claimed by a stormy sea.

At no point during the voyage do the men stop talking and arguing, and it is their talk that contains most of the novel's major conflicts. The weather is bad because the season is late, as an experienced turtler tells one of the crew members at the outset of the expedition: "You sailin late, Byrum! Get more wind den turtle in de May time!" Yet one of the legendary figures in the novel, Captain Steadman Bodden, who clearly represents "de back time" when things were right for turtlers, perished in bad weather. Matthiessen's point is plain: a return to a simpler, unspoiled past is no solution, although Captain Raib, throughout the novel, certainly thinks it is.

A number of other oppositions develop during the course of the voyage, and most of them hinge on Raib's insistence that there was a time when things (the weather, the fishing, life in general) were better. Sailing ships themselves, for instance, are "a thing of de past," as one character remarks early in the novel. Good sailors are also hard to find. (pp. 72-4)

Good turtlers are difficult to find for much the same reason that turtlers are becoming scarce. Tourism, American economic imperialism, the race to get rich have all contributed both to environmental damage and to a decline in traditional ways of life in the Caribbean. Ships once were built of Cayman mahogany, one of "dem good old woods dat used to grow right in de island" but no longer does. Not only the good timber, but the ships themselves, and the turtles, are disappearing: "De schooners all gone," the captain complains, "and de green turtle goin. I got to set back and watch dem ones grow big on de Yankee tourist trade dat would not have amounted to a pile of hen shit in times gone back." And many of the men who would have been turtlers "all abondinin dere home, dey livin up dere in Tampa and Miami." The American dollar has had a negative effect on the area, but the crew members are aware of more direct interference as well. Speaking of an unscrupulous relative of Captain Raib, Speedy says,

> De people of Caymans should have de sense to know dat dat mon never followed de truth! He go around yellin about progress, about bringin in oil bunkerin stations and gamblin, to make poor people rich; but it does Yankees dat pay him off—*dey* de ones dat gone get rich! And de home people gone get frigged! And we don't like dat, de Yankees gone find out we all commonists, and dey gone take over, mon—dat be dere little way! Oh, mon. I done a couple hitches on a United Fruit vessel, and I seen just how dey done in de small countries!

Talk of Cuba and the Bay of Pigs is frequent. The men of the Eden seem to feel that if Yankee imperialism does not ruin the Caribbean in one way, it will in another. The back time is slipping further and further into a legendary past.

Conflicts between characters also grow out of the past/present opposition. Raib repeatedly criticizes both Athens and Vemon for not measuring up to the standards of the past. Raib says to Speedy and Byrum, "Course it very hard to find good men today. You two fellas is very good, and den Will—I speakin about de work on deck now. You fellas is about as good as you will find today. But it not like it used to be in the old days." (pp. 74-5)

By far the most important conflicts between characters in *Far Tortuga* are those involving Raib, Brown, and Speedy. While Raib virtually lives in the past, Brown seems at first to have no past. Eventually, elements of his history begin to surface, but the details are fragmentary and tentative. As Speedy observes, "Plenty like Brown down along de Sponnish shores, don't come from no place—more and more, like, seem to me." He appears to be Colombian (his real name, he claims, is Miguel Moreno Smith), but all he will admit freely is that he fought with Che in Guatemala. As a revolutionary, Brown has been an opponent of tradition. His climactic struggle with Raib Avers occurs after Captain Andrew Avers's death. Captain Andrew has been transferred to the Eden after a tense encounter with Desmond's ship, the *Davy Jones,* and when the old man dies, his knife disappears. The Eden meets a band of wild, somewhat hostile Jamaicans, and Brown—suddenly brandishing Captain Andrew's knife—jumps ship to join them. Raib, already enraged that his father has turned against him, is far from willing to let the upstart Brown get away with Andrew's knife. The knife is for Raib a symbol of tradition, of the old ways. To Brown, the theft of the knife is a natural act—a way of showing his contempt for the very traditions that Raib reveres. In the end Raib's crew (what is left of it at this point) persuades the captain not to pursue Brown, and another link with the past is severed.

Raib's relationship with Speedy is more problematic. Speedy, although Raib's most competent crew member, is also the one who, whenever Raib laments the passing of the old ways, always replies, "Modern time, mon." Speedy's phrase is a leitmotif that echoes throughout the novel. He alone of all the crew is truly comfortable in the present. He does, however, have a past. "Well," he recalls,

"my father he left my mother and den she went down to the copra plantation. When I were six; I were de oldest one. So I learn to cook: call dat school days, mon." Speedy is willing—far more willing than Brown—to discuss his past. But unlike Raib, he is not obsessed with it. For Speedy, the past is something that happened, just as the present is happening; there is no real conflict between the two. He rejects neither past nor present, but understands, intuitively, that they are parts of the same whole. Speedy recognizes that conditions change, yet he also recognizes that attempting to live in the past is no way to experience the present. Speedy regrets the loss of tradition and the ruin of the Caribbean as much as Raib does. The difference between them is that Speedy is adept at finding ways to live in "modern time," while Raib is not.

Because of his talent for living in the admittedly debased present, Speedy also has a future. Raib's future is largely a matter of fantasy and wishful thinking. Speedy is concrete, specific, and quite practical: "I gots fifty-five acres in Roaton, mon. In de Bay Islands. And I got three cows. A mon dat got cows, he got it made." Throughout the novel, as Raib rages about the old days, Speedy keeps his mind set on a future that is not divorced from the present because both are part of the totality of experience. Near the end, after several of the crew have perished in the storm and the Eden has sunk, Speedy says, "I goin home mon. Dat land in Roatan waitin for Speedy, fifty-five acres, mon, and cows. I take anybody with me dat don't get in my way. If Wodie die, den I am sorry. If Byrum die, den I am sorry. But Speedy goin home." After this speech, it hardly comes as a surprise that Speedy alone, of the men who remained with Raib, survives.

These various conflicts between man and man, man and nature, past and present, tradition and "progress" are put into perspective (if not solved) by the novel's larger, mythic oppositions. The key is Far Tortuga itself and what it means to Captain Raib. The island, as Matthiessen helpfully informs the reader in a prefatory note, is "a remote cay on the outer banks of Nicaragua that is not to be found on modern charts; Far Tortuga may have been worn away in a hurricane, leaving only submerged reef, but it seems more likely that this cay was a mere dream and legend of the turtle men." To Raib it is a dream. Late in the novel, when all else has failed, he decides that his last chance at a large catch is to strike out for the dangerous Misteriosa Reefs. "I got the theory," he explains, "dat green turtles makes dere nests at Far Tortuga, and dat would mean dat quite a few could be driftin out dat way already." The cay is more than just a place to catch turtles, however. Raib goes on to insist that the old-timers purposely kept the secret of Far Tortuga to themselves. "Dat island," he muses, "is a very nice place. A *very* nice place. And dere good shelter in de lee, cause it high enough so it got trees—grape trees and jennifer trees, and den logwood and mongrove: got a little water dere if you know how to dig for it. Plenty birds. I thinkin one day I might build a little shack out dere on Far Tortuga. Dass my dream." Raib is of course describing a place he has never seen except with his mind's eye. Speedy, alive with the concrete, with the fulfillment of present time, can only reply, "Got no dream, mon. I got fifty-five acres, mon, and cows. I go along every day, do what I got to do, and den I lays down to rest." This distinction is important because Speedy, more than any of the novel's other characters, lives life as it is. "The courage-to-be right here and now and nowhere else," Matthiessen writes "is precisely what Zen, at least, demands: eat when you eat, sleep when you sleep!" Speedy is "at rest in the present" and at home in the world.

*Far Tortuga* assumes a further mythic dimension when it is seen as a variation on the Eden story. Raib's ship, a broken-down remnant of "de back time," is the *Lillias Eden.* Eden is a family name, but the only character in the novel who uses it is Captain Desmond Eden, Raib's opportunistic half brother. The connection of the name with a character associated so strongly with "modern time" hints that the conventional way of perceiving the Eden myth is not the correct one, at least not in this novel. Other signs in the book point to the same conclusion. The *Eden* does sink; Far Tortuga may not even exist. Matthiessen appears to bring up Eden only to deny it. What he really denies, however, is a welter of traditional associations. He finds in the myth, beneath usual Judeo-Christian interpretations, a universal significance.

*Far Tortuga* is not a moral allegory in the conventional sense; sin is not the issue. Even more importantly, the reader should not make the mistake of identifying Eden with a legendary past when everything was better. To do so would be to surrender to the same dualistic frame of mind that prevents Captain Raib from fully experiencing the present. Instead of conceiving Eden (and Far Tortuga itself ) in historical terms, one should think of it as a condition always available in the present but never available if pushed into the past. . . . "Eden" is a state in which man is at peace with himself and one with nature; the fall is a state in which man has separated himself from nature and consequently, from his fellow human beings. All the conflicts in the novel grow out of this primal one. The concept of Eden—the time when man was one with the rest of the universe—as the original "back time" is erroneous only because it depends on a separation of past from present. The fall, in Matthiessen's view, has not *happened;* it *happens.*

One of the aims of Zen is the attainment of satori, a state of enlightenment or insight into the true nature of reality. That reality is said to lie beyond the sway of oppositions and dualities. . . . People who have experienced satori write about the disappearance of distinctions between past and present and between self and world. Man is no longer "a small, selfish ego, but rather he is open and transparent, united to all, in unity." *Far Tortuga* attempts to present both the striving, the conflicts, that most of us endure, and at least a suggestion of the vision of unity and harmony that Zen and other oriental religions offer. The novel, as we have seen, is shaped by oppositions, but its final effect is peaceful, even as death claims most of its characters.

The last and most dramatic conflict in the book is explicitly between man and nature. The storm rages; the men struggle against it. Most of them are destroyed, but the impression left upon the reader is not one of heroic, self-asserting battle followed by defeat, but of reconciliation. The novel begins and ends, after all, with descriptions of nature. Only gradually do characters emerge as individual personalities, and just as gradually, they disappear. This is not inconsistent with Zen teaching, which holds that human individuality is only temporary, never "true" or "real." The disappearance of man, or his reception into a totality greater than himself, is foreshadowed early in the novel: "On the bottom, the flayed skin of an angelfish is yellow-gray, shaped like a face. Through a faint rainbow of petroleum, the white sand is scattered with cans and bottles in welt-colored crusts of coralline algae, and sand-shrouded old conchs, each with a hole knocked in the whorl, and white coral skeletons poxed with red hydrozoans." Man and his waste fade into insignificance when seen against the immensity of nature. And even Raib, possessed as he is by conflict and struggle, realizes that there is a reality more permanent than the vain striving of the individual. Speaking to his son Buddy, he looks at the north star and says, "It were watchin on de night dat you were borned, and it be watchin when day night comes dat you die."

When the novel's conflicts and tensions are seen in this light, it becomes more apparent why Matthiessen has chosen such a peculiar narrative format. The decentralization of man's position in the universe is the point; man, whether through Zen or by some other means, must understand that he is a part of nature and that to damage any segment of it, including himself, is to damage the whole. Throughout the book, short chunks of dialogue alternate with short chunks of description, almost as if Matthiessen were trying to equalize man and nature or to restore a balance. This is not to say that Matthiessen denigrates or trivializes the struggles of his characters. On the contrary, their concerns are meant to be ours as well. But he invites us to see them as part of something greater—a universal harmony that can, perhaps, only be occasionally glimpsed. Matthiessen's method of presenting a character's death is consistent with this goal. When one of the men dies, his name appears at the bottom of a page that is blank except for a smudge, like a splash. The technique mimics the dropping overboard of a body, but it also conveys, rather like sumi art, the littleness of the individual and the vastness of the universe that receives his remains. More specifically, the water into which these bodies fall suggests their inevitable acquiescence into something beyond the individual, something eternal. It is like Matthiessen's explanation of prajna in Hinduism—"a profound vision of . . . identity with universal life, past, present, and future."

In the *Tao Te Ching,* water is associated with the Tao itself—the way or process of the universe, the reality that underlies and flows through all things, the indivisible whole: "Highest good is like water. Because water excels in benefiting the myriad creatures without contending with them and settles where none would like to be, it comes close to the way." And in Buddhism, as Matthiessen himself remarks, individual minds are seen as part of a "Universal Mind . . . in the way of waves; the waves do not derive from water, they *are* water, in fleeting forms that are not the same and yet not different from the whole." But such a vision of wholeness is difficult to experience and still more difficult to sustain. Gregory Bateson laments that we "have lost that sense of unity of biosphere and humanity which would bind and reassure us all with an affirmation of beauty. Most of us do not today believe that whatever the ups and downs of detail within our limited experience, the larger whole is primarily beautiful." Matthiessen's achievement in **Far Tortuga** is a reaffirmation of that beauty through the restoration of a sense of relationship between man and his world. (pp. 75-81)

> *Richard F. Patteson, "Holistic Vision and Fictional Form in Peter Matthiessen's 'Far Tortuga',"* in Rocky Mountain Review of Language and Literature, *Vol. 37, Nos. 1-2, 1983, pp. 70-81.*

## Julian C. Rice

In **Indian Country,** Peter Matthiessen uses the skills of a polished fiction writer to present the saga of the present-day Indian Wars. We are introduced to "traditional" Indians who are quiet, humble men, more truly in the spirit of Crazy Horse as he is consistently remembered than the urbanized militants of Matthiessen's preceding book [**In the Spirit of Crazy Horse**]. The spiritual life of these Indian people continues to be assaulted by aggressive missionaries as well as by purveyors of various kinds of junk, new and old—television, pollution, drugs, booze, etc. Traditional Indians are desperately fighting for their lands, and for the Indian identity which is inseparable from that land, in their own communities, in their schools, and in the federal courts. Many Americans will be shocked to learn about the ruthless policies which their government continues to force on Indian people, but Matthiessen's selection of urgent and little-known environmental battles will alarm the majority of readers (and voters) into complete attention.

In Northern Arizona and New Mexico the Navajo people and their land have been criminally battered by Kerr-McGee, who, "attracted by cheap, defenseless labor" and inadequate safety regulations, employed Indian miners who "perhaps because they had no concept of radiation" were given neither masks nor drinking water. They often drank from the puddles of "hot" water on the mine floor. A few years after the mine closed, more than half of these had died or were dying of lung cancer, dust poisoning, pulmonary fibrosis and other "ravages." Kerr-McGee left behind seventy-one acres of "spent uranium that is estimated to retain up to eighty-five percent of the original radiation." Throughout the western states the piles of "tailings" have been washed or may still be washed into rivers used for drinking water. The ash from the tailings also travels by wind and in towns like Durango, Colorado it has affected many children with severe respiratory ailments. On July 16, 1979, a dam at a United Nuclear Corporation tailings mill near Church Rock broke, "releasing ninety-five million gallons of radioactive water" into the Rio Puerco River. Several of these Three Mile Island-like episodes have not been publicized because "most of the victims have been Indians," because about seventy-five percent of known uranium reserves in the United States is controlled by the seven major oil corporations, and because the "great energy consortiums are looting the

Southwest (and the Great Plains) under the red-white-and-blue banner of 'energy independence' for America." But if the monster can be identified, he can be stopped. Recently, after many legal setbacks, Indian and non-Indian environmentalists prevented the U.S. Forest Service from turning a sacred mountain of the Karuk and Yurok people of Oregon into "Doctor Rock Recreation Area, Zone 7-11A Recreation Area, Primitive Experience." Matthiessen realizes that the beast's language radiates his essence, and he has put him squarely in our sights. (pp. 59-60)

> *Julian C. Rice, in a review of "Indian Country,"* in Western American Literature, *Vol. XX, No. 1, May, 1985, pp. 59-60.*

## Mark Abley

"In the language of my people", a Cherokee spokesman told the United States Congress in 1978, "there is a word for land: Eloheh. This same word also means history, culture, and religion. We cannot separate our place on earth from our lives on the earth nor from our vision nor our meaning as a people." Jimmie Durham, who was testifying against the construction of a dam that would flood the ancient towns and burial-grounds of his people, is but one among dozens of eloquent voices that Peter Matthiessen quotes in **Indian Country.** So passionate is his catalogue of destruction that it reads, in places, like a requiem for America.

At the book's heart is Matthiessen's vision of the holiness of the land itself. "One cannot love the Creator", he points out, "and desecrate Creation." Or as Durham informed the baffled politicians, "When we speak of land, we are not speaking of property, territory, or even a piece of ground upon which our houses sit and our crops are grown. We are speaking of something truly sacred." **Indian Country** is a selection of Matthiessen's recent essays describing the struggles of American Indians (in Florida, Tennessee, New York, South Dakota, and five south-western states) to retain that sacredness against an onslaught of dams and power-plants, mines and chain-saws, American services and beliefs. In so far as Matthiessen's audience lies in the dominant culture, the essays amount to a polemical appeal for a change of heart.

And in so far as Matthiessen is a realist, he knows that **Indian Country** is unlikely to have much effect. The forces against his ideals are the strongest in the nation: the US government, the US army, big corporations and labour unions—not to mention the power-structure within many Indian bands. His outrage has several foundations: moral and political anger against the continuing maltreatment of Indians; spiritual rage at the loss of their ancient, holistic values; and ecological horror at the mutilation of America's wild spaces.

Though he claims in a brief foreword that "**Indian Country** is essentially a journal of travels and encounters with Indian people", it is also a book of history. White Americans have often spoken nobly of their predecessors on the continent; Thomas Jefferson suggested in 1793 that "the Indians have the full, undivided, and independent sovereignty as long as they choose to keep it, and . . . this may be forever". Their behaviour tells a different story: that Indian country remains intact only until its resources of water, trees, minerals, or arable soil are suddenly found to be "necessary". One of Matthiessen's most melancholy chapters describes the remnant Pit River bands of northern California—a state which reduced its Indian population from about 125,000 to less than 20,000 in the thirty years after the United States bought it from Mexico. Sometimes the genocide was overt. . . . More commonly, though, the injustice wore a cloak of legality. The Pit River nation lost its land to settlers, Matthiessen observes, by its failure

> to send a delegation for eight hundred miles on foot across unknown country to an unimaginable place to make marks on a "talking leaf " in unknown language in order to claim title to ancestral lands that they did not know were threatened and had never conceived of "owning" in the first place.

The heroes of *Indian Country* are those few scattered women and men, and those fewer communities, that remain on the land and that allow little compromise with a consumer culture. Their lives are a far cry, in faith as well as in time, from the slave-owning Christian merchant by the name of John Ross whose political adroitness gained him a position of leadership within the Cherokee nation even though he was only one-eighth Cherokee by blood. Ross's letters and private papers—assembled by the indefatigable Gary E. Moulton—are full of grovelling rhetoric. "We should be wanting in liberal and charitable feelings were we to doubt the virtue and magnanimity of the People of Georgia", he wrote in 1829, a few years before the people of Georgia and the US army evicted the Cherokee at gunpoint from their homeland and sent most of them on a forced march westward into unsettled territory. More than four thousand died on the "Trail of Tears". To his credit, Ross was resolute in his opposition to the Removal Act. But even in the strange land beyond the Mississippi, he continued to prosper. The second volume of his *Papers* includes a bill-of-sale from 1854 recording his exchange of a young black man for a mulatto woman of eighteen and her son of five.

Ross, like his successors among Indian politicians up to the present, fully accepted the white man's notions of property. The traditionalists whom Matthiessen so admires have a separate understanding of the use and ownership of land. Some half a century after the Cherokee migration, Senator Henry Dawes of Massachusetts visited their new reservation and came to an interesting conclusion: "There was not a pauper in that nation, and the nation did not owe a dollar. . . . Yet the defect of the system was apparent. They have got as far as they can go, because they own their land in common. . . . There is no selfishness, which is at the bottom of civilization." To civilize the Indian nations, Senator Dawes introduced a bill which eliminated their communal ownership of property in favour of individual land-title: apportioning, in other words, land which the people already owned. So successful was the Dawes Act that within a few years, Indian

country across the United States had shrunk from 138 million to 52 million acres.

What remains is under constant threat. Matthiessen devotes a couple of bitter chapters to the plight of the Hopi and Navajo peoples of the Arizona desert, the site of "the ugliest ecological disaster of our time". (He is not given, incidentally, to loose superlatives.) At Black Mesa, a mountain that the Hopi hold particularly sacred, the Peabody Coal Company has built what is probably the world's largest strip mine on land so arid that it can never be reclaimed. Even the visible pollution, however, may be less serious than Peabody's invisible depletion and poisoning of the underground water, on which the Hopi and Navajo depend for what is left of their traditional life.

In his efforts to write a cool, factual prose, Matthiessen occasionally buries too much of his artistic talent which was so evident in *Far Tortuga,* one of the loveliest American novels of the past twenty years, and in *The Snow Leopard,* his classic Asian travel-book and spiritual autobiography. As a journalist and essayist he is articulate, brave, but (at moments) unsure. *Indian Country* suffers a little from his personal ambivalence towards the radical tactics of the American Indian Movement (AIM). Apparently he supports the idea that native peoples in the United States should argue their case before the United Nations or the International Court of Justice, though a nation that denies the jurisdiction of the World Court over its policies in Central America is unlikely to accept outside intervention when it comes to "American" land.

Jimmie Durham lost his battle, by the way. The local farmers were evicted, the valley of the Little Tennessee was drowned and the Cherokee burial-grounds were destroyed. Tellico Lake, which washes over them, has failed to attract industry to its haunted banks. The government may soon make it a dump for toxic chemicals. Meanwhile, a new board-game called *Custer's Revenge* has appeared. "Victory was achieved", Matthiessen tells us, "when a naked white man caught and 'ravished' an Indian woman." Such is the fate, in the land of the free, of those whom Columbus called *una gente in Dios*—a people in God.

*Mark Abley, "Custer's Revenges," in* The Times Literary Supplement, *No. 4329, March 21, 1986, p. 299.*

## Victoria Scott

The first Buddhist masters to come to America at the turn of the century did so because they felt that Zen had entered a period of decline in Japan; although monasteries remained open to all, those who applied were interested in the logistics of running the family temple more than in attaining enlightenment. Whether these teachers' faith in American practitioners is justified is the most important question raised by [*Nine-Headed Dragon River: Zen Journals, 1969-1982,* the] latest of Peter Matthiessen's books.

The Nine-Headed Dragon River runs beside the Temple of Eternal Peace, the monastery of Dogen (1200-1253), the founder of the Soto school of Zen. Like the river, Matthiessen runs beside the eternal peace he seeks, glimpsing it once in a while—just often enough to keep running. He knows he has but to recognize that "all of reality is in the *is*—the *now* of every moment," but this is a challenging peak to scale even for a veteran explorer like Matthiessen.

The first part of **Nine-Headed Dragon River** is frank, fascinating, almost confessional, consisting of Matthiessen's notes from a series of Rinzai Zen *sesshins* (weeklong meditation intensives punctuated by private interviews with the Zen master). This is the most interesting part of the book, precisely because it is the most personal, revealing many of the incentives and pitfalls that await an ardent traveler on the Zen path. For example, Matthiessen really does work to see through the "I" that wants enlightenment so badly; in the process, he naturally becomes more aware (sometimes painfully so) of just how persistent his writer/father/husband self is.

The second part of **Dragon River** is excerpted from Matthiessen's immensely successful **Snow Leopard** (an account of his 1973 pilgrimage to the Himalayas). The excerpts provide a choppy transition between the Rinzai *sesshins* and the Soto Zen studies that Matthiessen began in Los Angeles in 1977. (Soto is distinguished from Rinzai in that it traditionally emphasizes "just sitting" over the study of *koans*—i.e., riddles that the student must ponder and answer to the satisfaction of the Zen master.) But this section does let Matthiessen show that, although his Rinzai teacher has advised him to "expect nothing," he persists in clinging to the ambition of spiritual attainment itself.

Chastened but still interested, Matthiessen discovers and comes to a sort of peace with Soto Zen. This last part of the book is a fairly impersonal travel diary of Matthiessen's 1981 trip to Japan with his Soto Zen teacher, a young mathematician from Los Angeles, and is interspersed with a detailed history of the Soto and Rinzai schools.

In **Dragon River,** Matthiessen attempts to tackle the subject that eluded him in **Snow Leopard**—namely, what an enlightened state of mind is and how to attain it. But enlightenment defies him once again. Despite wanting desperately to follow the Buddhist path to its conclusion, he acknowledges (much to his credit) that "after years of Zen practice, I am still woefully deficient in that simplicity of spirit, that transparency of heart, that is evident in many people who have never heard of Zen at all."

Matthiessen is torn between his desire for enlightenment and his recognition that he is not yet there. He even admits that his American Zen teacher—one of the handful who learn the language of their Asian teachers and serve as translators and mentors for the next generation of American Buddhists—"inevitably was more steeped in Japanese Zen tradition than I would ever be, *or felt like being.*" This statement says much about the ambiguities and difficulties of transplanting Buddhism to American soil.

**Dragon River** is an ambitious work but an incomplete one. It does not misrepresent Zen, and it certainly provides important insights into the process of seeking enlightenment as a 20th-Century American. But it is not compellingly

written, except in the first (and rawest) section, and for all its accuracy, it appears to have been put together piecemeal. Thus it is a prime example of the growing pains of a uniquely American form of Buddhism.

> *Victoria Scott,* in a review of *"Nine-Headed Dragon River,"* in Los Angeles Times Book Review, *May 18, 1986, p. 11.*

## Jonathan Raban

In March 1961 a northeasterly gale tore through the beach resorts and summer homes of the Hamptons on eastern Long Island. The wind blew whole sand dunes back into the sea, exposing a surface of rutted peat on which were printed the cart tracks and the hoofmarks of the oxen of the first colonial settlers. The fishermen and farmers were just one wild morning away from the 20th century. It's tempting to see a message in the gale—that history is at once tenaciously near at hand and very easily dispersed. In [**Men's Lives: The Surfmen and Baymen of the South Fork,** a] magnificent and somber portrait of the fishing community of the South Fork, Peter Matthiessen shows a stubbornly surviving culture being carelessly exterminated. **Men's Lives** is fired, as Mr. Matthiessen's best work always is, by love and indignation in equal parts. (His text is complemented by scores of historical and contemporary photographs.)

The remaining fishermen of the Hamptons can put names to the owners of the 17th-century oxcarts. The Millers and Lesters gossip with Mr. Matthiessen about their ancestors' dealings with the Montauk and Shinnecock Indians as if they were talking about grandma and grandpa, with all the "great-great-greats" left out. They have been clam dredging, lobster potting, launching dories into the surf, setting traps and nets and lines, in an unbroken family chain that reaches all the way back to the original Dutch and English colonization of the island. The Dorset accent of the locals around Accabonac Creek in what is now East Hampton (the Bonackers) is still tinctured with Elizabethan usages; their dangerous, uncertain but blessedly independent livelihood "on the water" continues to demand of them those ancient American virtues, like self-reliance and solitude, that have elsewhere come to mean only the titles of unread or half-read essays by Emerson. The Long Island fishermen still—just—live as if Governor Winthrop were the leading political light in their territory.

For more than 30 years, Peter Matthiessen has been living among the Bonackers. They are his close friends and colleagues. In the 1950's he worked as a professional fisherman with his own rigs, the Merlin and the Vop-Vop, and Mr. Matthiessen's life is an important strand in **Men's Lives** (the title comes from Walter Scott—"It's no fish ye're buying, it's men's lives"). He writes as a trusted intimate of the men and women of Accabonac, and it is the intimacy of this story that makes the book. The people talk to Mr. Matthiessen as they would never talk to an inquisitive outsider, in a language rich in local allusion and technical detail. For his part, Mr. Matthiessen himself, on the colors of the sea, on laying a seine, on catching the right wave on which to beach your dory, is a tough and knowledgeable craftsman who, by a stroke of readers' luck so improbable as to seem somewhat improper, also happens to be a very fine and equally professional writer. The experience and understanding that shine through every page of the narrative make it all the harder to bear the steadily sinking graph of its unfolding.

When Mr. Matthiessen apprenticed himself to the Bonackers in the early 50's, the fishing community was still fully intact. No one made very much money, but there were few legal restrictions, land prices were low, and there was plenty of fish. In a typically exact and vivid passage, Mr. Matthiessen describes a blowfish catch:

> The haus seine sometimes came ashore like a drowned dirigible. The panicked fish filled themselves with air and sand, packing the bag tight with white squeaky bellies and chafing the twine with their abrasive skin, and the crew had to attack the bag with icepicks to deflate it enough to winch the haul ashore.

Flush times—but there were warnings of the gale to come. The Matthiessens' black cleaning woman complained that her social status was being endangered by the low company kept by Mr. Matthiessen when he went fishing. The "resort economy" of Sag Harbor and similar places was beginning to boom. The increasing number of anglers who fished for striped bass with rod and line had begun to lobby the State Legislature at Albany for the passing of a "bass bill" designed to prohibit commercial fishermen from netting this valuable fish. The sports, as the anglers were wryly labeled by the Bonackers, used conservation as their fashionable flag of convenience—although, as Mr. Matthiessen argues here briskly and persuasively, there is precious little evidence to suggest that seining/netting is an important factor in the mysterious annual fluctuations of the bass shoals. Nevertheless, there were many more anglers than Bonackers and thus many more votes to be won by the main-chance politicians who took on the anglers' dubious cause.

It is at this stage of the story, with the siege lines drawn up and the 300-year-old culture of Accabonac marked out for liquidation, that Mr. Matthiessen transforms a village chronicle into a classic case study of—"genocide" is too strong a word, but it is not *far* too strong a word for the systematic destruction of a community, a way of life, a proud history. People with a lot more money than the Bonackers and a great deal more political clout wanted the Bonackers' land, the Bonackers' fish, the beaches from which the Bonackers launched their rigs with unpicturesque trucks. For the Hamptons to blossom, the Bonackers had to be got out of the way.

Licenses and taxes were slapped on every conspicuous bit of the fishermens' gear. As land prices went rocketing up in the 60's, the fishermen found their homes were being valued out of all proportion to their means. In 1983 the sports at last got their bass bill through the New York State Senate. The Republican Senator Owen Johnson said cheerfully that any fishermen put out of work by the bill could easily find work "changing sheets in motel rooms." (pp. 1, 30)

As the seine crews broke up, men forced by circumstances into loneliness embraced their condition with that spiky defiance that victimized people habitually employ to flaunt their stigma. One seiner turned trapper told Mr. Matthiessen: "The only individuals I have to deal with are the gulls, and I don't understand them, and they don't understand me, and we get along fine." "Everybody on the beach is nervous," said a doryman, "Guess we don't know what's to become of us." Marriages cracked; tempers frayed; there was a streak of acid in every casual social encounter.

This is the way a culture ends, not with a bang but a series of angry whimpers. There are still fishermen working out of the South Fork, but every year more of them are taking literally the old fisherman's saying that goes "I'm going to put this oar over my shoulder and head west, and when somebody asks me what it is, that's where I'll stick it in the ground and settle."

*Men's Lives* ends, as it must, with a funeral—the burial of Lindy Havens, which is also the symbolic burial of the community to which he belonged. As Mr. Matthiessen and Milt Miller leave the Oakwood Cemetery, Mr. Miller puts his arm round Mr. Matthiessen's shoulder and says, "Well, I don't guess *none* of us are goin to get away with it, now are we, Pete? Try as we might." The remark stands as an exact statement of the fate of the surfmen and baymen of the South Fork. They're not going to get away with it, try as they will.

It is hard to see how it could have been otherwise. The economic logic that is even now arguing them out of existence is impeccable in its way; it reflects something fundamentally pitiless in the basic fabric of things. Nor, alas, is Peter Matthiessen's book simply an unhappy tale of Long Island. I have been reviewing his book in the cabin of a small boat galebound in a harbor on the English Channel, 3,500 miles or so from the South Fork. Change the Indian place names to Norman ones, substitute a few different species of fish, and *Men's Lives* becomes a heartbreakingly precise analysis of what is going on outside my own porthole. The highest compliment I can pay to his remarkable book is to acknowledge, not without some writerly grudges, that Mr. Matthiessen understands the man in the woolly hat whom I am now squinting at through the glass far more intimately than I ever can myself. (p. 31)

> *Jonathan Raban, "This is the Way a World Ends," in* The New York Times Book Review, *June 22, 1986, pp. 1, 30-1.*

### Duncan Spencer

Matthiessen is a writer with a great deal of confidence. Who else can bring out a book from either side of the world examining two states of art in the same year?

*Nine-Headed Dragon River* is a book about Zen. Zen, which is short for Zen Buddhism and short, too, for *"zazen"* which means sitting meditation, and which is the most familiar expression of it to us Westerners, did not die with the '60s. It just dropped out of sight, where it is probably a good deal more comfortable.

*Men's Lives* is a book about the indigenous fishermen of the far eastern tip of Long Island, a part of the world now dominated by the superwealthy of New York. The remaining fishermen and clammers are the area's white trash, not to quibble about it; their natural prey is the white-fleshed striped bass.

Crude-spoken, sometimes offensive, sometimes anti-Semitic, always disreputable (to the increasingly upscale inhabitants who have claimed this New England-oriented part of Long Island), the fishermen, known as "Poseys" and "Bonakers" among themselves, depending on their relations and birthplace, are the salt of the earth to Matthiessen, who himself fished professionally—and later as a sideline—during the early '50s.

Both of these books are remarkable, memorable nonfiction. They are what nonfiction can be when the author lets his subject speak, and when he has gained enough knowledge to write with confidence about subjects which are not well known. Matthiessen's prose is as strong and pure as ever.

Take Zen. *Dragon River* is a Zen book, as the author warns, "A Zen book composed against the best instincts of its author, who has no business writing upon a subject so incompletely understood—far less a subject such as Zen which is fundamentally impossible to write *about.*" However, Matthiessen reports in the next sentence, he has practiced this intellectual's religion for 15 years; these are his journals, the diary of an amateur enthusiast and more than that, and he was introduced to Zen through the shared experience of the death of his wife Deborah Love from cancer. That death was tormented, as such things are in this country by lies, chemicals, radiation, drugs. ("I could not clear my nostrils of the stink of flowers in the cancer ward, the floor shine on that corridor of death," he writes.) Yet he and she were sustained by Zen. . . .

His is the enthusiasm of the West for the East. He believes; he plunges into the lore; he longs for a great experience; he meditates, learning the painful *"zazen"* discipline of sitting absolutely still for hours; he tries to subdue his old weaknesses ("greed, anger and folly"), and for a time achieves a state of grace:

> In the midmorning sittings, I become a sapling pine, warmed by the sun, swaying in the wind, inhaling wind, water, minerals, exhaling warm, fragrant amber resin. Tough roots budge subterranean rock, the trunk expands, sinewy limbs gather in sunlight far above, new needles shining in new sun, new wind, until the great pine is immovable, yet flexible and live, the taproot boring ever deeper into the earth. Then the tree evaporates and there is nothing, and nothing missing, only emptiness and light.

To many, Zen will always be an annoying import. They are truly foreign to the Western mind, these "nonlinear Eastern perceptions." These endless, sententious Haiku (three lines, 17 syllables) poems and veiled pronunciamentos: "All are nothing but flowers/In a flowering universe."

Luckily, we have the profoundly Western mind of Matthiessen emptying out his notebooks in beautiful sentences,

or else this book might be far more than anyone ever wanted to know about Zen. The link, and the theme which joins *Nine-Headed Dragon River* to *Men's Lives,* is the idea of personal discipline.

The thought that work, the digging of flowerbeds, say, or the hauling of nets through the surf, is valuable in itself, and not just as a means to get something (flowers, fish) is what Matthiessen is really talking about in both books. With Zen, he is attempting to learn a discipline; with the disappearing fishermen of Long Island, he is celebrating a discipline now almost lost.

No one knows when the first nets were laid off the windy tip of Long Island or along that vast beach which stretches from Montauk to the end of the New York City subway line at Coney Island; but all that is left now is a small community of fishermen at Montauk, Amagansett, Springs, and Three-mile Harbor, all just east of East Hampton. Matthiessen is their memorialist and advocate.

What's going on in that part of the world is that it has been "discovered." The glitter people have "discovered" the dunes, hardwoods, ponds, etc., and have bought them, leaving little room for the fishermen who have lived there, and their families before, for generations, since about 1660 when the place was settled by a band from the Massachusetts Bay colony. Matthiessen is a queer hybrid, a native to the place himself, yet certainly in any accounting would be considered a rare catch for dinner at one of the Hamptons' summer palaces.

What separates Matthiessen from the chorus of tree-huggers and whale-huggers and literary log-rollers now bewailing everything at the shoreline is that he has spent three years as a commercial fisherman (in the mid-'50s) and has lived the life. The result is that he knows the work, knows the people, and tells the story from their point of view. What gives this story edge is that the netters are considered almost outlaws by "sportsmen" who prefer to use rod and line to catch their "stripers." To the shallow view of summer people and the new squires of Long Island, the sportsmen are in the right, the "commercials" are despoilers.

Matthiessen is one of the American prose poets. He writes with apparent ease the most beautiful, flexible and simple descriptive passages. He is as good at description in his American way as D. H. Lawrence was in his English way. He uses language in its musical realm, and he never gets it wrong when he's talking about the ocean. When he discovers a whale skull in early December it is so:

> The beautiful form, crouched like some ancient armored creature in the wash, seemed to await me. No one else was on the beach, which was clean of tracks. There was only the last cold fire of dusk, the white birds fleeing toward the darkness, the frosty foam whirling around the skull, seeking to regather it into the deeps.

But besides beauty, Matthiessen has something important to say. The fishermen he chronicles, like the Zen monks, are men in tune with nature, men who submit to its discipline, men to whom money is less important, and position almost incomprehensible; yet they have secrets—they are somehow blessed in their lives of hardship, their unceasing routines dictated by nature or custom. They are real, their work is real while we, perhaps, have lost our way. The monks of Zen are obscure, the fishermen are members of an unimportant underclass soon to be pushed aside by designers, architects, decorators and their clients, the important upper middle-class people who own things.

This is Matthiessen's hidden program, to celebrate the people from what he called in *Far Tortuga,* the "back time." They are the experts: the South Fork fishermen, for instance, who probably know more than the ecologists and scientists who study (and are baffled by) the striped bass, the Zen scholars who are seeking enlightenment in the dark before dawn.

> *Duncan Spencer, "Zen and the Art of Fishing," in* Book World—The Washington Post, *June 29, 1986, p. 5.*

## Rick Fields

Peter Matthiessen does not live in a Zen monastery or community. He comes and goes. He sits *sesshin*—extended week-long periods of sitting meditation—but he also sits at home and, on the road, in hotel rooms and tents and, occasionally, on mountain tops. He pursues his family life and his work as a writer interested in social issues as well as in fiction. In this sense he is emblematic if not typical of most American Zen students, and his Zen journals [collected in *Nine-Headed Dragon River: Zen Journals, 1969-1982*], which span some fifteen years, in many ways sum up the history of American Zen so far.

Matthiessen is not a professional Zen man. Rather he is an inspired amateur in the best sense of the word. And it is just as the record of such a student that his account will have value for so many of his fellow and future companions on the path.

He encounters his first *roshis* (Zen masters) by chance in the driveway of his home in Sagaponack, Long Island. They happen to be there visiting his wife, Deborah. He has appeared unannounced after a seven-month journey in Africa. Curious, he tries sitting *zazen* (Zen meditation) and decides that this is not for him: "I swore that this barbaric experience would never be repeated; in addition to all that pain, it had been so *boring!*"

But, then, "that winter, to my own astonishment, I found myself sitting *zazen* everyday, not only in my Australian hotel room but on shipboard." His practice is deepened, tragically, when his wife begins to die of cancer, and her teacher Eido-roshi, as well as her fellow students, care for her with compassion and strength. The account of this period is piercing and spare, and the experience of impermanence and suffering—central elements in Buddhist teachings—runs like a thread through the book.

Though Matthiessen gives clear and useful accounts of the philosophical rationale for *zazen* and Buddhist practice, it is not as philosopher or scholar that he comes most alive to the reader. Nor is it in the descriptions (abandoned halfway through the book) of his own meditation experiences. Rather, it is as a naturalist, an observer and participant in the world of nature, that he comes closest to expressing the fundamentally inexpressible experience of Zen. In this, of course, he follows many of the Chinese and Japanese Zen adepts, who like the haiku poet Basho found Zen revealed or embodied in the everyday world of nature—from the grandeur of Mount Fuji to the wonder of a frog, or of fleas and lice, for that matter.

Like his Asian predecessors, Matthiessen finds shining transcendence in the creatures and plants around him—in a Spring Peeper sitting in the dark *zendo,* in a white moth alighting on his aching knee, in a beaver slapping its tail to mark territory in Beecher Lake at Dai Bosatsu Monastery in the Catskills. This is a sensibility—a naturalist's sensibility—to which American Buddhists, or American spiritual seekers of any tradition, might well pay closer attention. Matthiessen's grounding in the natural world, and the precision of an eye trained by both *zazen* and a naturalist's exactness, gives rise to what might be called a prose style of Zen realism. Aside from its own virtues and delights, such an eye might serve as a useful corrective to the lofty flights of metaphysical kite-flying that "spiritual" people seem so prone to. Matthiessen's powers of observation keep our feet on the ground—a good place to begin from.

But there is yet another, even more engaging sense in which Matthiessen might be called a naturalist of Zen. In the early days of his *zazen* practice, we learn from these journals, he takes support and delight in imagining or becoming—somewhat hesitantly, for this is not, as it were, by the book—various creatures he has observed. He sits, at dawn, as "a deer in the early woods," or he becomes "an eagle on a mountain ridge, entirely alert and full of its own eagleness . . . gold eye fixed on the first streak of dawn. . . . " Here the Zen naturalist approaches the realm or at least the technique of the shaman—he takes on the power and clarity of the natural world. Not much is made of this—it's presented as his own little trick, which "will fall away like armatures, like scaffolding"—but it is nevertheless all the more charming and convincing for being presented so modestly, as nothing more than what it is.

The journals are divided into three periods: The Rinzai Journals cover the early days of Zen, when *sesshins* were full of "tears, laughter, and small miracles" and the headlong pursuit of *kensho* (seeing into one's true nature) was paramount. The most memorable figure sketched in this section is that of Soen Nakagawa-roshi, the now legendary Zen master who died in 1984. Intent on puncturing his American Zen students' "self-conscious spirituality, 'the stink of Zen,' " Soen once

> put a large pumpkin on the roshi's cushion, then hid behind the door, snickering wildly as earnest students prostrated themselves before the pumpkin, only to hear the laughter of the bell that ended their "confrontation with the roshi" and sent them packing back down stairs to their black cushions.

The second section is made up of excerpts from the Himalayan Journals of *The Snow Leopard,* which won the National Book Award in 1979. This material, which will be familiar to readers of the earlier book, gains rather than diminishes by its placement in this new setting. (pp. 113-14, 116)

In the last section of the book, the Soto Journals, the Zen student finds himself a close student and dharma heir apparent of Bernard Tetsugen Glassman-sensei, a Brooklyn-born former aeronautical engineer ten years his junior, whom he accompanies on a pilgrimage to Japan. It is here that the themes of the earlier sections of the book are woven, ever so subtly, into a quieter, more orderly pattern. The Zen student is no longer so impressed with the tears and laughter of his earlier days, and the figure of Dogen, the thirteenth-century founder of Soto Zen and the master of "just sitting," comes to the fore. The pilgrimage traces both Glassman-sensei's lineages and the career of Dogen, and the author's journey is now interwoven with the history and settings of those who have, in the course of time, become his Zen ancestors.

In the first sections of the journals, visits to his wife's grave in the meadow of Dai Bosatsu and to his home on Long Island punctuate and mark the years. Later the pilgrimage brings him to the memorials and shrines of Dogen and other great Zen masters of the past. A golden autumnal hue, a tone—the continuity of impermanence again—softly lights the way.

The living Zen masters encountered are deftly drawn in all their humanity, drinking sake and whiskey past midnight, and then rising for *zazen* before dawn. (Some students "want to dehumanize the teacher so that he reflects some personal deity of their own," Tetsugen reflects. "We try to improve a little, but we are who we are.") (pp. 116, 118)

[Ever] the spiritual and naturalist seeker, Matthiessen searches for the source of an elusive and haunting bird's song. All the Zen masters he meets tell him it is the nightingale, but the naturalist knows that the nightingale is not found in Japan. Finally, he does spot it, as he did not, quite, spot that other elusive quarry of the spiritual search, the snow leopard, in the Himalayas of the earlier book.

> A fresh wind down off Fuji-san . . . and the one sound strong enough to carry over wind and river was the light, sweet song of that unseen bird, lost in the leaves of a maple overhead. A moment later I laid eyes on it at last. The bird had none of the magical colors with which I had painted it in my imagination, "nothing special." It was small and plain and brown, the *uguisu* or bush warbler. . . .
>
> (pp. 118-19)

*Rick Fields, in a review of "Nine-Headed Dragon River: Zen Journals, 1969-1982," in Parabola, Vol. XI, No. 4, November, 1986, pp. 113-14, 116, 118-19.*

**Thomas R. Edwards**

Most of the people who admire Peter Matthiessen's novels and books on travel and nature don't know him as a writer of short fiction. In his introduction to **On the River Styx**

he explains that in his younger days he wrote some 30 stories, few of which now satisfy him; "perhaps a dozen" found print, and he moved away to other forms. Seven were collected in 1984 as a chapbook, **Midnight Turning Gray;** to these the present volume adds two new stories and another old one, the whole arranged in chronological order and with a certain modesty: "It's still fun to write short stories, I discover, and of course one hopes that in close to forty years there has been a little bit of progress." There has indeed, but the light the book casts on the progress of a career may matter as much as the quality of its contents.

In the earliest stories a talented young writer gets started. The best one, "Sadie" (1951), uses the business of training and selling hunting dogs in rural Georgia to gradually disclose a drama of male rivalry and violence. Every young would-be writer of Mr. Matthiessen's generation—he graduated from Yale in 1950—dreamed of writing such a story, whose skill with imagery, point of view, characterization by speech and deferred revelation seems born for the New Critical analysis that occupied literary classrooms and journals then. But its technical elegance is fairly tested by its inelegant materials and idioms, which creative writing courses didn't teach you; if "Sadie" sounds a little like a collaboration between William Faulkner and Henry James, it's still a fine story.

The other three tales from the early 1950's are also formally accomplished, but less demanding in substance. Here he uses what could have become a mandarin style to explore the vulnerabilities of a mandarin world: in "The Fifth Day," a rich college boy learns something shaming about what tough working-class talk conceals; in "The Centerpiece," a similar young man remembers a domestic crisis, with larger implications, during Christmas dinner at his German-born grandmother's country house in 1941; in "Late in the Season," a young wife has to recognize the brutality of her pretentiously elegant husband when they find a huge snapping turtle stranded near their summer place. Small and gracious social areas are penetrated by disruptions from outside, but the governing sensibility of the stories remains inside, and its ironies seem theoretical and a little wistful.

Then the range begins to expand, socially, geographically and imaginatively. "Travelin Man" (1957) is an almost mythic tale of an escaped black convict's duel to the death with a white game-poacher for possession of an uninhabited island off the Carolina coast. "The Wolves of Aguila" (1958), even more mythic, follows a professional wolf hunter, a Navajo who can "think like an animal," into the deserts of Sonora, where he learns something surprising about what animals really are. "Horse Latitudes" (1959)—perhaps a finger exercise, in a remote key, for the superb novel **At Play in the Fields of the Lord** (1965)—makes rather unfocused comedy of a feud between a Baptist missionary and a Lebanese merchant aboard a freighter bound for the Amazon. "Midnight Turning Gray" (1963) stays closer to home geographically, but not culturally, in its account of an inmates' riot at a New England mental hospital.

None of these stories try for the finish of the earlier ones;

rather, they show an impulse for formal departure that mirrors the actual departures, to South America, the Caribbean, New Guinea, the Arctic, central Asia, American Indian country and elsewhere, that have marked Mr. Matthiessen's career as novelist and literary naturalist. One travels, of course, not just to but also away from somewhere, and in the stories he seems to be leaving behind him the writer he might otherwise have become, one more chronicler of privileged people to whom life gives everything but what they most deeply desire.

The two recent stories, American in setting and longer, denser and more complex in mood, express not departure but the shock of return. In **"On the River Styx"** (1985) Burkett, an environmental lawyer, comes with his wife from Washington to a secluded fishing village on the Gulf Coast of Florida. The motel, the food and the mosquitoes are almost as awful as the sullen white locals, who assume that a Government man must secretly have his eye on the drug trafficking that is the town's real business. Even Dickie, their black fishing guide, rebuffs Burkett's efforts to get to know him.

When Dickie does unbend, he goes too far, stealing the couple's rum and their tape player, and despite their attempts to mitigate redneck justice, everything collapses in a tragicomic nightmare of racism, bullying, humiliation and rage. The conclusion—when Dickie refuses to shake hands and mutters, "You leavin here. Leavin us stuck wit it," and poor Burkett thinks, "I'm stuck with it, too"—acknowledges that changes of place don't get you very far in the end.

The book's last, longest and best story, **"Lumumba Lives"** (1988), deals even more intricately with being in the wrong place. Here the place is the town of Arcadia, in the Hudson Valley, to which Henry Harkness returns after years in Africa with the Foreign Service, or more accurately the C.I.A. His wealthy family's estate, on the river south of Tarrytown, has been sold and given over to new houses, paddle-tennis courts and other amenities for today's diminished rich; but Henry buys the old gardener's cottage, planning to redo it "with English wallpapers, old walnut furniture, big thick towels and linen sheets, crystal and porcelain, such as his parents might have left him."

Might have, but mostly didn't—his stern father, an Assistant Secretary of State of the old school, outraged by his son's role in subverting the Lumumba regime in the Congo, refused even to *sell* him the family house. Henry's service *pro bono publico* has alienated him from his family, his class (watching his neighbors at play, he reflects, "I have lost my life while soft and sheltered men like these dance at their tennis") and even his inferiors, like the chummy real-estate agent whom he snubs by insulting the wine the man serves him at dinner.

His dream of regaining his lost life, among Purdy shotguns and silver brandy flasks and his grandmother's painting, a minor example of the Hudson River School, finally fails when he attempts a sacramental duck hunt. He kills his bird (*"Not a difficult shot,"* he imagines his father commenting), but while trying to retrieve it from the river he

encounters some black fishermen, whose amiable jiving turns ugly when they see that he thinks they mean to steal his gun. . . . At the end, humiliated and terrified, he waits in ambush for a dark pursuer who never comes, "in the autumn garden, cooling his forehead on the night-blue metal, in the haunted sunlight, in the dread of home."

The sunlight is haunted, I suppose, both by personal ghosts, the forebears Henry will never live up to, and by a national ghost. Even the elitist, the closet racist, feels a baffled yearning for what once seemed promised to everyone here, that vision of a more humanly receptive land that ugliness and incivility haven't yet quite erased:

> For a long time, by the riverside, he sits on a drift log worn smooth by the flood, withdrawn into the dream of Henry Hudson's clear blue river, of that old America off to the north toward the primeval mountains, off to the west under the shining sky.

It remains hard to feel at home in America, and even the most substantial acts of settlement, like the Harkness estate, don't appease the suspicion that the *right* place for us, the true Arcadia, lies to the north, or west, or somewhere. It's interesting to know that the fictional Harkness property occupies the site of a very similar real place called Matthiessen Park, and tempting to wonder if in this flawless story Peter Matthiessen isn't obliquely exploring a small area of his sense of America after his own, far more worthy, absences. In any event, this book of departures and ambiguous returns fascinatingly suggests some of the history of a splendid writer's imagination. (pp. 11-12)

> *Thomas R. Edwards, "Failed Journeys to the Wrong Place," in* The New York Times Book Review, *May 14, 1989, pp. 11-12.*

## Andre Dubus

In the introduction to his debut collection of short stories *On the River Styx,* Peter Matthiessen, naturalist and explorer, National Book Award winner and author of five novels and 13 works of non-fiction, states, "It's still fun to write short stories, I discover, and of course one hopes that in close to forty years there has been a little bit of progress." Matthiessen can rest assured there has been more than a little bit of progress, as this fine collection reveals; he is one of those rare writers who hit the ground running.

His first published story, **"Sadie,"** which appeared in *The Atlantic Monthly,* in 1951, is a polished gem. It is lean and compressed, the imagery clear, but what is most impressive about the then-college-senior author is his easy command of voice and his expert writing of dialogue:

> "I was over in Cady last February to see about their dogs, which they say is the best in Georgia. I was told to see this Mister Pentland, and if he weren't there, a feller name of Dewey Floyd."
>
> ". . . He your boss?"
>
> "Yessuh."
>
> "How about Mister Floyd?"

"Yessuh. Bofe 'em. Leastways, de Yankee man's de boss o' de outfit, an' ah kinda wuks fo' him, but mos'ly ah wuks wid Mistuh Dewey Floyd. It's him dat got me de job. Ah's de spottah. When a dawg is p'intin, ah hollers, an' when a dawg is los', ah fines him."

Ten stories make up this collection. They are arranged chronologically according to the years they were written. The first seven were composed in the 1950's, the eighth in 1963 and the last two in 1985 and 1988 respectively. One of the longer stories, **"Travelin Man,"** a riveting tale of an escaped convict who is being hunted down on a wilderness island and so must become the predator to save himself, reveals Matthiessen's stylistic strength: his descriptions of nature:

> Ocean Island is long and large, spreading down some four miles from the delta, southwest toward Cape Romaine. The true land is a narrow spine supporting red cedar, cypress, yaupon, live oak, and the old-field pine, and here and there a scattering of small palmettos. There are low ridges and open groves and clearings, and a core of semi-tropic woods. Its south flank is salt marsh and ocean beach, and to the north, diked years ago above the tide, lies a vast brackish swamp.

There is a wide thematic and textural range to these stories. In **"The Fifth Day,"** we spend an afternoon with the young, well-bred Dave Winton in a rowboat on a bay as he and the older "tough Brooklyn guinea" Joe Robitelli throw dragging hooks over the side in search of a drowned vacationer. Joe would rather sit back in the boat, drink beer and let others drag hooks. Dave feels compassion for the bereaved family on shore and contempt for Joe. The tension between these two men is not so much resolved as it is honored by the author. The final scene back on shore with the body and the family is a wise, profound stroke of subtlety by Matthiessen.

In **"The Centerpiece,"** we are taken to Christmas in a small American town in 1941. Our unnamed protagonist and his family have traditionally gathered at Grandmother Hartlingen's (called "Madrina" by the family) for a German Christmas. Though Madrina was born in New York City,

> a heritage of Christmas in Bavaria was imprinted in the first pages of her mind, not only of the Hartlingen gathering itself but of the beauty of this tradition to all Germans, at home or abroad. . . . No shell threatened the household of habit her universe had become, and although she crocheted for the soldiers, and was offended by the Red Cross refusal of her offer for blood—good German blood, she assured them—she saw no grounds whatsoever for renouncing her German Christmas.

Fifteen-year-old, fiercely patriotic Millicent does not agree and stays outside in the family car, refusing to step into the house. Matthiessen's deft hand resolves this story in a moving and believable fashion. (p. 383)

Of these stories, **"The Wolves of Anguila,"** though weak, still shows considerable versatility. The protagonist, Will Miller, a hunter who contracts his skills out to government agencies and ranchers, finds himself confined more to the extermination of coyotes and bobcats than to that animal he considers most worthy of his attention: the great gray wolf or *canis lupus*. We are introduced to Miller at a significant time in his life's work:

> The southerly withdrawal of the gray wolf into the brown, dust-misted mountains of Chiuahua and Sonora had come to Will Miller as a loss, a reaction he had never anticipated. He was uneasily aware that persecution of the wolf was no longer justified, that each random kill he now effected contributed to the death of a wild place and a way of life that he knew was all he had.

Nevertheless, with mixed feelings of elation and penitence, he would travel to the scene of the last raid. It is to this spiritually ambiguous last raid that the story takes us. But due to the younger Matthiessen's overreliance on symbol and metaphor, he sidetracks himself, and this story of such rich possibilities never seems fully realized.

The title story alone is worth the price of this volume. Written in 1985, it is one of the most sophisticated in structure and scope, and purely focused in style. It resonates. In **"On the River Styx,"** we follow Burkett, a Washington, D.C., lawyer for the Interior Department, and his wife Alice on a fishing sojourn to the Gulf Coast of Florida where they encounter a modern-day dose of good-ole-boy racism. Here is a glimpse of the story's opening image:

> On his sculling pole, leaning out over the stern, as far away from the white people as possible, the bony figure—the shadowed face under the straw hat, the tattered shoulder of his faded shirt, the unnameable odor—swung in arcs on the hot white sky, back and forth and forth and back against the wild green walls. The water, browned by mangrove tannin, turned gray when the sun clouded over, and the dark islets spread way, parted, regathered, always surrounding. With their silent boatman, his wife had said, it was like traveling the River Styx.

Matthiessen strikes an oppressive chord right from the outset. When the Burkett's portable radio and a bottle of rum show up missing, and when Dickie, a black man, becomes the primary suspect and the Burketts argue about whether to pursue the matter or not, the story takes off into potentially explosive and unpredictable territory.

This comfortable professional couple, Matthiessen masterfully shows us, who marched in civil-rights demonstrations and want to do the right thing about Dickie's alleged thievery, are perhaps more protected than they know, not so much from the New World silence as from Old World noise. Peter Matthiessen seems to know a great deal about both and, in 40 years at his craft, is capable of casting light and life on all the ports of call in between. (pp. 383-85)

*Andre Dubus, in a review of "On the River Styx," in* America, *Vol. 161, No. 16, November 25, 1989, pp. 383-85.*

**Paul W. Rea**

[The ten stories collected in *On The River Styx*] span Matthiessen's writing career from 1950 to 1988. Though they range widely, each presents its natural setting vividly; Matthiessen has long exhibited an uncanny talent for evoking places. Thematic threads interweave these stories: death, violence, or threats of both, particularly when occasioned by racial conflict. As the jacket notes suggest, Matthiessen forces readers to face "the brutality of nature, and the surpassing brutality of man, its desecrator."

The collection opens with **"Sadie,"** an early effort published in *The Atlantic* while he was still a senior at Yale. Written imagistically by attaching earthy details to each character—somewhat like Faulkner's "Barn Burning"—the story tracks the self-destructive tendencies of a poacher who squints coldly out from under his hat after he has killed both his favorite dog and his best friend. Here Matthiessen exhibits his extraordinary ability to evoke animals and landscapes, possibly even at the risk of more sketchy characterizations.

**"The Fifth Day"** is a macabre tale of two men who, using a rowboat, drag the ocean bottom for a man who drowned five days before. They bicker in the heat, making half-hearted efforts to hook the body. In the end, when the drowned man finally surfaces and his family appears, the blasé boatman finally reacts when confronted by the dead man's family. Matthiessen's early stories often end surprisingly, as great short stories so often do. Subtle hints typically prepare us for the surprise, but in this story the motivations for the boatman's change of heart remain obscure.

**"The Centerpiece"** is recounted through the eyes of a fourteen-year old boy who enjoyed a traditional German Christmas at the house of his immigrant grandmother. Everyone gathers for the festivities except "Silly Milly," his teenage cousin who refuses to leave the car. It is 1941, and she will not attend a *German* Christmas. Even in this indoor setting, Matthiessen's awareness of nature comes through:

> The wreathed light from the windows gave body to the darkness . . . It gave the house a snug, enchanted air, like some magic sanctuary of childhood deep in a wood.

Here—and in the descriptions of the candles and chandeliers, the benedictions and toasts—one hears echoes of James Joyce's famous Christmas story, "The Dead." During the banquet, a candle sets the centerpiece afire, charring Santa in his sleigh. Despite this negative note, this may well be the most affirmative of the stories.

In contrast, another dinner story, **"Late in the Season,"** presents a couple whose antagonisms become aggravated by an odd catalyst: a snapping turtle they bring home. On one level, Matthiessen probes attitudes toward wildlife. He tells the story from the wife's viewpoint, using interior monologue. Noting how her husband is afraid of the turtle yet also fascinated, she muses that this

> is the very way he behaves with me . . . as though I were some slightly disgusting animal,

and yet he prides himself on his technique, which doesn't include having children.

With the beast scratching suggestively, the husband and wife bicker at the table, echoing the unpleasantries of one of Hemingway's couples.

**"Travelin Man"** is extraordinary. It rivets the reader to the inner life of a black convict who escapes to a remote barrier island—only to find it inhabited by a white poacher. Matthiessen's ear for dialect rings true, with blues and spirituals providing background music. And Matthiessen's understanding of the psychological workings of racism evokes James Baldwin. Moreover, because the convict hides and hunts in the wilds, Matthiessen's awareness of nature invigorates every page; plants and animals become minor characters. Using interior monologue, Matthiessen builds this encounter to heights of intensity, at times invoking the tragic flight of Joe Christmas in Faulkner's *Light in August.* Kurt Vonnegut told Matthiessen that this is the best story he'd ever read.

**"The Wolves of Aguila"** is an unusual item. Except for its fine evocation of animals and landscape, it seems as much a character sketch as a short story. When a wolf strikes livestock in southern Arizona, the government hires an Indian who wants out of trapping.

> When the wolf lay inert at his feet, a hush seemed to fall in the mesquite and paloverde, as if the bright early-morning desert had died with the shot . . . In the carcass, already shrunken, lay the death of this land as it once was, and in the vast silence a reproach.

The Indian crosses into Mexico, sets out on the Sonoran Desert, and meets two boys whom he associates with hostile wolves. The hunter feels hunted; the Gran Desierto prevails.

Reflecting Matthiessen's experience with ships in the Caribbean—experience that paid off richly in his *Far Tortuga* (1984)—**"Horse Latitudes"** is a study of characters in conflict. Here, as told by a sly co-passenger who resembles the author, a freighter is carrying an American Baptist missionary with a pink snap-on bow tie plus a Lebanese merchant who shrugs compulsively and pulls his hair out. These eccentrics are conflict junkies. The narrator notes wryly that "their claws were set so deep into each other that if they pulled apart, they would soon bleed to death." This is the most satiric story in the collection.

**"Midnight Turning Gray"** exhibits the moral outrage that has characterized Matthiessen's recent nonfiction. Written in the early sixties, when Ken Kesey was writing *One Flew Over the Cuckoo's Nest* and Frederick Wiseman was filming *Titticut Follies,* this story similarly protests conditions at a New England mental institution. The central characters, a young nurse and a patient with a head wound, find themselves pitted against the established figures on the staff. The young nurse sees the institution as "a great crushed anthill"; some of the staff refer to it as a "monkey house." The new inmate realizes that "if people ain't nuts when they come into this place, they sure as hell must be by the time they get out." This story, however, becomes predictable: the staff characters are too explicitly described, rather than revealed through action, dialogue, and detail; the good nurse's disillusionment seems inevitable; and the ending does not surprise. Despite these limitations, though, **"Midnight Turning Gray"** is a powerful moral and political indictment.

The last two stories, written in the eighties and running nearly forty pages each, also deal with racial conflicts. Set on the remote Ten Thousand Islands coast of Florida, **"On the River Styx"** evokes its setting tactilely. A well meaning government lawyer and his wife incite racial tensions in an area where the local whites have two reasons to resent outsiders, especially those from Washington: they wish to continue segregation, and they are running drugs. But when a tape deck belonging to these liberal tourists shows up missing, it is the racist town potentate who pursues the thief. The result is that the black servants absorb the punishment and resent the outsiders: "You leavin' here. Leavin' us stuck with it." Obviously, this story could be read as an allegory of freedom riding or other liberal incursions into Southern status quo.

**"Lumumba Lives"** is at once a homecoming, a parable of lost American innocence, a meditation on change, and a commentary on contemporary racial tensions. After years of working for the U.S. in Africa, a government agent returns to his boyhood home in Westchester County. He is shocked by "the dirtied brick and fire bruises of the abandoned factory, the unbeloved dogs, the emptiness." Repulsed by the siege mentality of the suburbanites who now inhabit his old neighborhood, he broods along the Hudson, where he runs into ironic conflicts with African-Americans. This story is technically experimental and thematically complex, relating American foreign policy to domestic unrest.

*On the River Styx* showcases Peter Matthiessen as one of the finest stylists and social commentators writing today. Despite their disturbing subjects, these stories virtually read themselves; the man knows how to tell a moral tale. (pp. 22-3)

> *Paul W. Rea, in a review of "On the River Styx and Other Stories," in* The Bloomsbury Review, *Vol. 10, No. 3, May-June, 1990, pp. 22-3.*

## Marianne Wiggins

When I finished reading Peter Matthiessen's last novel, *Far Tortuga,* 15 years ago, I felt the need to re-read *Moby Dick.* This was not because *Far Tortuga,* like *Moby Dick,* is a seafaring moral-and-philosophical epic about survival and the myth of heroism, confined, as such tales have to be, to an all-male cast of seafaring characters; but because, like *Moby Dick, Far Tortuga* was a novel so singular, so riffy in its many strains of individual human blues, so beautiful and original that it stood alone as something unlike anything I'd ever read.

What it had in common with Melville's classic was its incomparability to other works of fiction. What it had in common with the other novels of its decade—*Executioner's Song, Rabbit Redux, Good as Gold, The*

*Ghost Writer, Gravity's Rainbow*—was, to borrow a minimalist's phrase, less than zero.

*Far Tortuga's* gifts were lasting. On the surface, it's the tale of the doomed schooner *Eden* casting for sea turtles in the Cayman Islands and manned by nine doomed men, only one of whom survives the expedition. At *Eden's* helm is one Capt. Raib Avers, an anti-Ahab figure in his decrepitude and dereliction, but a leader whose visionary mission takes them, nevertheless, to their destruction.

That is, more or less, the plot. But what took one's breath away was Matthiessen's command of rhythm and of language. "I wish I could speak good," he had one of his sailors say: "De things I *feelin*. . . . "

It is that particular evocation, what Matthew Arnold called "the amount of felt life," that is the hallmark and the genius of all of Matthiessen's books. Whether he is writing fiction or nonfiction, what is at the center of his prose is a richness of experience, a kinesthetic sensitivity to how the world is lived in by all living things, not merely men and women. He evokes The World, its mysteries and histories, and makes it felt.

In the decade-and-a-half since *Far Tortuga,* he has written (to name a few) *The Snow Leopard, In the Spirit of Crazy Horse, Indian Country* and, most recently, *Men's Lives*—all of them nonfiction and each one of them contributing to his reputation as a world-class man of conscience, adventurer, peacemaker, conservationist, Zen Buddhist.

Now comes his long-awaited return to fiction, a new novel called *Killing Mister Watson.*

The book opens in the wake of a catastrophe, the great Florida hurricane of 1910, which devastated that part of its western coast known as the Ten Thousand Islands. On the morning of 24 October, 1910, a man is cleaning out dead chickens from the fish fuddle, petrified furred things and driftwood and wreckage that came to lodge beneath his house during the gale. Working at ground level, he can see the feet and legs of his neighbors walking past his house toward the beach as a motor launch approaches. In the motorboat is Mister Watson, a man they've known for years. Minutes after Watson comes ashore, they kill him.

Matthiessen describes the scene—the potent symbol of a man tidying the subterranean structure of his house from which he witnesses the return and execution of the object of communal fear—in nine swift pages. Then he spends the next 400 pages taking us inside that act of violence from every point of view. He, the writer, adopts the voice of law. He asks the reader to become the dead man's, and the killers', jury.

At the center of this exercise of judgment, this novel-as-a-dead-man's trial, is an actual event in history.

Even before the Florida press sensationalized his murder, Edgar ("E. J.") Watson was a legend in the land. It was known that he'd been born 11 November, 1855, but every other fact about his life was open to debate. It was widely believed that he'd killed at least one man before arriving on the Florida coast—and it was broadly rumored that he'd been the man who'd pulled the trigger on the Queen of Outlaws, Maybelle (Belle) Shirley Starr, on her own birthday in February, '89. He'd had at least three known wives and Lordy knows how many bastards.

His was an outsized life, violent and contemptible, punctuated by the dastardly but characterized by a personal charisma that seemed to charm the pants off everyone—that is, until they killed him. "Watson talked his way into the clear again," Matthiessen has somebody say about him, "just like he done so many times before. That feller was a borned politician, probably could of got hisself elected president." Another character remarks, "Seemed like Watson was about all us local people talked about in them days."

It is through the voices of those "local people" that the novel is narrated. With the exception of the first chapter, which is called "October 24, 1910," the day Watson is killed, each succeeding chapter takes its name from one or another of the witnesses to Mister Watson's life and death. There are a dozen different witnesses in all, "speaking" to the reader in a loosely chronological order leading up to the day of the murder, sometimes repeating themselves, more often than not contradicting what someone else has testified to. (pp. 1, 5)

It takes daring in a novelist to front-load the mechanism of dramatic tension the way that Matthiessen has done in *Killing Mister Watson.* Simply reading the title tells the reader all. It is an extremely difficult structure to sustain, and unfortunately the book suffers from being somewhat overlong. Watson is, in fact, killed twice—once at the beginning and again 50 pages from the novel's end. Those final 50 pages seem superfluous. Once the central character is really truly dead, the local people seem not to have a thing to talk about that really interests them.

And mercy do they talk. If for no other reason, *Killing Mister Watson* should be read for the simple beauty of its can't-confuse-it-with-nothin-else-on-earth Florida cracker's life and talk. To a person, Matthiessen has entered the minds and souls of his many narrators.

In a preface to the novel, he acknowledges the descendants of those characters in the novel whom he interviewed, three of whom had actual childhood memories of Watson. But it is one thing to interview people living in the modern Florida, and quite another to extrapolate from their childhood memories a completely felt life. Few of us can know what living in the Ten Thousand Islands was like at the beginning of this century, but *Killing Mister Watson* evokes an unforgettable experience of regional Americana.

In a historical sense, this novel stands with the best that our nation has produced as literature. Specificity has always been the hallmark of our better writers. And by that I don't mean the "new realism" as heralded by Tom Wolfe. What I mean is something more in the vein of what Eudora Welty was alluding to when she was asked what she thought of William Faulkner's work. She answered that it was like having a mountain in the neighborhood.

If we could draw that kind of map, then somewhere around Los Angeles there is Mount Nathanael West. Else-

where, we know where, there is Mount Flannery O'Connor; a range called Hemingway. Mount Matthiessen, it seems to me, is that place on the map where men and women go and speak in the specific language of their region about the moral implications of irrevocable, nearly always violent, acts. "It wasn't justice they was after," one of the local people in the novel reasons about Watson's murder: "It wasn't justice they was after, but a good night's sleep. . . . Folks just got tired of him, I guess."

In his own way, Watson was the mountain in the local people's neighborhood—a volcanic one. But unlike the despicable central character in *Paris Trout,* for example, Matthiessen has meticulously assembled a character who is both likable and lethal. Everyone loves looking at volcanoes from a distance. The Japanese revere Mount Fujiyama—and not in the least because they hope it is reliably "dead."

As a philosophical study of the duality of human—and all—nature, *Killing Mister Watson* is first-rate. As a political allegory, it is stunning. Throughout the book, the "local people" refer to Watson's qualities as a born leader, to his presidential-size charisma. Several other minor villains in the book, average desperadoes, are referred to as "bad actors."

That, and other subtle references to the time we live in, lard the book. Those references, and a whole lot else about the novel, guarantee, in my opinion, its author's place, and the place of the novel, in our evolving sense of who we are and what we struggle to attain through literature. (p. 5)

*Marianne Wiggins, "Of Justice and a Good Night's Sleep," in* Los Angeles Times Book Review, *July 8, 1990, pp. 1, 5.*

### Tim McNulty

Throughout his career Matthiessen has paid particular attention to that dynamic terrain where nature, human culture, and political pressures intersect. This has led to books on the tribal peoples of New Guinea and East Africa, as well as to two books that explore the history and politics that fuel contemporary American Indian issues. At the same time Matthiessen's enduring interest in Zen Buddhism helped inspire *The Snow Leopard* (1987), a poetic account of a journey to the Tibetan Plateau which won the National Book Award in 1978, and more recently *Nine-Headed Dragon River* (1987), his journal of a pilgrimage to Japan with his teacher Tesugen-zenji. In 1982 *Sand Rivers* received the John Burroughs Medal for nature writing, and two years later the Philadelphia Academy of Science awarded Matthiessen its gold medal for his outstanding contributions in nature writing.

Understandably, it came as a surprise to many when Matthiessen revealed in an interview in 1988 (*Words from the Land,* Peregrine Smith) that he was leaving nonfiction behind, possibly for good. "I've always thought of nonfiction as a livelihood," he explained to Stephen Trimble, "my way of making a living so I could write fiction." Nonfiction "comes from outside, not from within." He said he was ready to return to fiction and hoped to stay there.

Last year's publication of **On the River Styx, and Other Stories** (1990) heralded that return. In this startling and somewhat haunting collection, Matthiessen explores the chafed and darkened side of human endeavors, often propelling his characters toward a knife-edge of discovery and oblivion. Many of the stories are set amid the poverty and racial tensions of the rural South. The title story, perhaps the most powerful in the collection, takes place in a backwater fishing village along southwest Florida's Gulf Coast.

That same maze-like jumble of islands, mangrove thickets, and dark tidal waterways that border the Everglades provides the setting for Matthiessen's remarkable new novel, **Killing Mr. Watson.** His first in fifteen years, it brings together, in a vivid and compelling way, the very best elements of his unique vision.

At the turn of the century, Florida's southwestern coast was a wilderness outpost sparsely inhabited by the Mixed-blood descendants of Indians, runaway slaves, transients, fugitives, and a few homesteaders eking a meager subsistence out of the swamplands. Enter Edgar J. Watson, an affable, mannered farmer and family man, known for his Island Pride cane syrup and his generosity to his neighbors. But Watson—who was a historical character on the Florida coast—possessed another, darker side. He did nothing to counter rumors that he was wanted for killings upstate and in the West, and he was known to have slit at least one citizen's throat in an argument over a land claim. While his political connections kept him out of jail—"No decent American is going to believe that a man who pays his bills is a common criminal," he confides to his hired man—fear and mistrust grow into terror around the settlements as Watson's drinking takes a serious turn, and people working on his plantation begin to disappear.

As the novel opens, in the wake of the worst hurricane to hit the Gulf Coast in memory, Watson is murdered at the hands of his fellow townsmen. That event—well documented in the historical record—becomes the focal point from which Matthiessen launches his story.

In an innovative twist reminiscent of **Far Tortuga,** Matthiessen structures this novel as an overlapping series of first-person monologues. The voices are of those historical principals and their descendants associated with the Watson legend. Based on Matthiessen's own interviews with the families of those involved, and interspersed with commentary by a fictional historian, the narrators soon begin to grow into discreet and individual characters, each with their own particular slant on events.

In the manner of Durrell's *Alexandria Quartet* (1982), conflicting accounts begin to meld into a complex and multifaceted portrait. We see Watson as a well-connected businessman, entrepreneur, devoted husband, and father, yet, at the same time as a shrewd, unpredictable, treacherous, and cold man. The Watson that emerges from Matthiessen's fiction is utterly more believable than the Watson of the various "historical" accounts. And his portrait of avarice, greed, and brutality is one that has become emblematic of the frontier outposts of American commerce.

Like the Brazilian rainforest that formed the setting for *At Play in the Fields of the Lord,* Matthiessen's Everglades are a pristine wilderness on the verge of the rapid and ravenous impact of commercial exploitation. Throughout these narratives we are given glimpses of the wasting of egret and heron rookeries for plumes, the wholesale slaughter of alligators for hides, and the initial dredging operations that would turn the clear grass and gravel-bottom streams of the coastal Everglades into muddy sloughs. Part and parcel to his unspoken crime is the commercial boosterism espoused by Edgar J. Watson and his associates.

Ultimately, **Killing Mr. Watson** goes far beyond the "reimagined life" that Matthiessen alludes to in his author's note. Like Faulkner's powerful tale *The Bear,* it is a deeply historic narrative that touches the very roots of our culture's attitudes toward the land, the native people who dwelled there, and the rich tapestry of life that once graced it. Peter Matthiessen has returned to what may prove his most powerful genre, but if this historic snapshot of our national character is fiction, it is a fiction that, a century later, still troubles our world. (pp. 22, 24)

> *Tim McNulty, "A Life Reimagined," in* The Bloomsbury Review, *Vol. 10, No. 5, September-October, 1990, pp. 22, 24.*

## Verlyn Klinkenborg

Peter Matthiessen writes, as we all do, in an ironic age when moralists who love their morals are generally repugnant. But Matthiessen, who understands that uneasy moralists appeal to ironic minds, has grounded his career on a sense of responsibility, whether to individuals, to cultures, or to nature at large, which we may as well call morality. His early novels are filled with figures who unwillingly assume responsibility of one kind or another for people they might easily and reasonably disavow. The reader notices a repeated question in Matthiessen's fiction, a question that I think is ultimately the same one that led him into the strong vein of naturalist nonfiction—if that is the phrase for a body of work, almost a separate career, that includes **The Snow Leopard** and **Men's Lives**—that has coexisted with and at times eclipsed his fiction. The question is this: Am I my brother's keeper? It has a corollary: How am I to know my brother?

In his early novels, Matthiessen's protagonists keep their brothers despite themselves. In **Race Rock** (1954) George McConville, heir to moneyed ineffectuality, assumes responsibility for his relations with two disturbing figures from his boyhood, Daniel Barleyfield, a half-breed Indian, and Cady Shipman, a tough case George simultaneously envies and hates. In **Partisans** (1955) Barney Sand, an American journalist, risks his neck for an expelled Communist named Jacobi—himself at risk in defense of his principles—with whom he had only a brief encounter as a child. In **Raditzer** (1961) Charlie Stark protects the novel's eponymous anti-hero, a weasel of a man who inspires distaste in everyone including Stark, whose revulsion somehow turns into responsibility. As Raditzer teeters toward his suicide before a troop of fellow soldiers, only Stark is able to say, as Peter after Gethsemane couldn't, "I know him." These characters do not love the responsibility they have taken, and yet they have taken it. There is nothing priggish in them or their actions; the morality they exercise seems to arise from the preconditions of human existence.

In *At Play in the Fields of the Lord* (1965) Matthiessen first brought to his fiction a glimpse of the difficult terrain he often explores in his nonfiction, where he is an unparalleled traveler and adventurer. (Though he is never just that: an adventurer's motives are too blurred, his purposes too sybaritic even at the extremes of discomfort. Matthiessen's writings in the absurdly masculine literature of adventure are nearly always marked by a richer and more meditative consciousness than one usually finds there.) *At Play in the Fields of the Lord* pits two men against each other in the South American jungle. One, Martin Quarrier (names are everything in this novel), is a raw-boned Protestant missionary out to save the Niaruna Indians; the other, Lewis Moon, part Cheyenne, is a renegade so ironic as to be totally disengaged from life. Quarrier dies having lost faith in his own ability to convert the Niaruna; Moon is reborn as a primitive among them.

In answering the question, am I my brother's keeper?, one normally draws the boundaries of moral kinship as narrowly as is conscionable and as widely as is practicable. But in *At Play in the Fields of the Lord,* Matthiessen implies that we have no way of defining limits to our responsibility for each other because we are bound together—individuals, cultures, species—in an interdependent whole. Responsibility in Matthiessen's sense is not the white man's burden, the paternalist task of lifting an individual or a race into useful servitude, but the burden of preservation, of non-violation, the ecological imperative: a morality based on identity but also on respect for otherness. It is a hard morality to bear, for it tends to convert the converted, turning missionaries into anthropologists, moralists into ironists (and sometimes vice versa). (pp. 43-4)

Superficially, *Killing Mr. Watson,* Matthiessen's new novel and his first in fifteen years, is a Western set on the edge of the Everglades. Edgar J. Watson, a man with great personal force and a mysterious past, comes to town one day in the early 1890s—town in this case being the forbidding Ten Thousand Islands region in southwestern Florida, where dry land is scarce and the primary vocation is egret-plume hunting for the fashion trade. Watson prospers far beyond his neighbors. Word of his past, rumored to contain several murders, gets out, and in the subsequent uncertainty caused by the fact that "you didn't ask a man hard questions, not in the Ten Thousand Islands, not in them days," his reputation becomes greatly exaggerated (or does it?). After a hurricane devastates the coast, Watson returns to the town of Chokoloskee, where his wife and children have waited out the storm. There he is gunned down by nearly all of Chokoloskee's men acting in concert (we learn this in the novel's first ten pages). Their provocation was the discovery of the murder of a man and woman at Watson's homestead. But as Sheriff Frank Tippins remarks of the vigilantes, "It wasn't justice they was after but a good night's sleep."

As in *Far Tortuga,* Matthiessen depicts almost off-

handedly (which is the tone his characters use) the complex relations that exist between humans and their environment, both social and natural. He shows us the steady degradation of nature, the inroads on a wilderness as first one species then another is shot out, fished out, or driven away. Those who do the shooting, fishing, and driving reveal a wry awareness of environmental decay that gradually deepens into sadness as time passes. "Used to call this place God's country," Bill House says, "and we still do, cause nobody but God would want no part of it." This is a fitting spot for Watson, who imagines himself a developer, someone who will drain the Everglades and put all that useless swampland to the plow.

Matthiessen creates one memorable voice after another, until the reader ends up enjoying the texture of speech in this novel most of all. In the local accent, broadened by racial confusion, Matthiessen delivers the stern flatness of experience found in a near-wilderness, where men and women are too much alone with their thoughts. He conveys the occasional poetry (and humor) of ordinary people without overbuilding its significance or making his characters sound like a lost colony of bards. Their stories loop and spin and digress with an easy disregard for consequence, without vitiating the novel's narrative tension. Because the denouement opens the book, there is no tension, only a steadily thickening atmosphere, a slowly worsening tropical depression.

At the heart of *Killing Mr. Watson* lies a surprising emptiness, surprising most of all because of the moral intensity of Matthiessen's previous novels. *Killing Mr. Watson* stands apart from the rest of Matthiessen's fiction by the amorality of the world it depicts, by the absence from it of a point of judgment, a position from which ethical issues might become clear. The men who shoot Watson do so because they are certain, as the narrator of the prologue—who disappears for good three pages later—says, that "if no one is innocent, none can be guilty." Their motive is cowardice, not respect for law; what offends them about Watson is not his reputation but the way his cold eyes make them kowtow in public. Their stand is no more dignified and ultimately less principled than what Faulkner in *Absalom, Absalom!* (another novel about a mysterious stranger with a suspicious past) calls "meddling interference arising out of the disapprobation of all communities of men toward any situation which they do not understand." At its best, their communal act—killing Mr. Watson—is an ironic, degraded form of the responsibility Matthiessen's earlier characters take upon themselves.

Among those who knew him there is an attempt of sorts to invest Watson with mythic proportions, to justify his fate. A French ornithologue says of him, "He is—accursed." Mamie Smallwood remarks, "Say what you like about Mister Watson, he looked and acted like our idea of a hero." Onc night, after Watson has nearly been caught in a sugarcane fire, he makes a sort of confession to a young man who is barely competent to understand much less assess his words. He explains how he came to the Ten Thousand Islands, but he admits to no crimes. Instead, he offers this precept: "Here's the lesson I learned, Henry, and I learned it well, and it's stood me in good stead all my life: No decent American is going to believe that a man who pays his bills is a common criminal, no matter what!" We come no closer to Watson than this piece of ambiguity, the credo of any white-collar swindler. We never learn whether he is guilty of the crimes that have fallen at his doorstep, and so we never know whether or not to justify the vigilantes. By the end of this novel, some readers will have joined the posse that shoots Watson down, some won't: "If no one is innocent, none can be guilty."

It may have been part of Matthiessen's purpose in **Killing Mr. Watson** to force the reader into this quandary, to make us confront the specter of frontier justice that rests only on a belief that no one has the courage to verify. Or it may be that this quandary arises through a flaw in the novel itself. As Matthiessen states in his author's note, there is a "fact" to the Watson story: such a man lived and died on the southwest coast of Florida, and out of the fragments of his life the local inhabitants created a lurid myth. Matthiessen has chosen to cast his narrative in the manner of nonfiction, to make it read like a series of depositions. In a sense, he has been truer to his voices than to his larger tale. The reader is distanced from Watson by a kind of cracker humor, a backwoods irony that works against revelation and judgment. Much as the reader delights in these voices, there is no consensus, and the divisions that exist among them do not clarify the matters of guilt or justice at all. The voice the reader yearns to hear, Watson's own, never speaks at length. (A diary of Watson's is mentioned at one point but never quoted.) The narrator we hope to find—one who understands the truth buried in this muddle, one we would like to associate with Matthiessen—does not exist. The reader is left to seek evidence of Watson's guilt or innocence only among the stuff from which his guilt was fabricated by the men who murdered him—a tissue of gossip and rumor.

Because of this ambiguity, the nerve leaks out of the novel, and the tragedy, always threatening, filters away. The reader is left with the sense that when the book is done, when Mr. Watson has been buried in a sandbar and the town of Chokoloskee has begun to soothe its guilty righteousness, every question raised by the appearance of this man and by his killing remains unanswered. Not every dark story is a tragedy. Tragedy requires consciousness and inevitability, sensing one's fate without being able to avert it, the quality that leads one to ask what mistake it was that brought down the whole of one's ambition. There is no consciousness to spare among the characters in this book. Watson's utmost ambition is to outlive his past, which no one ever does. To the last he believes that he is stronger, quicker, and smarter than the men who gather at the Chokoloskee landing to unload their rifles and shotguns into him. In the end, Bill House, one of the men who murdered Watson, says, "His death weren't no tragedy!" He is right. The tale of those men, and the part they played

in killing Mr. Watson, is no tragedy either, just a good, dark story. (pp. 44-5)

*Verlyn Klinkenborg, "Moral Swamp," in* The New Republic, *Vol. 203, No. 19, November 5, 1990, pp. 43-5.*

---

## FURTHER READING

Bawer, Bruce. "Nature Boy: The Novels of Peter Matthiessen." *The New Criterion* 6, No. 10 (June 1988): 32-40.

Addresses the change in subject matter and scope in Matthiessen's novels beginning with *At Play in the Fields of the Lord.*

Bender, Bert. "*Far Tortuga* and American Sea Fiction Since *Moby-Dick.*" *American Literature* 56, No. 2 (May 1984): 227-48.

Analyzes Matthiessen's contribution to the American tradition of the sea novel. According to Bender, *Far Tortuga* "should rank second only to *Moby-Dick* among America's great sea novels."

Bishop, Peter. "The Geography of Hope and Despair: Peter Matthiessen's *The Snow Leopard.*" *Critique* XXVI, No. 4 (Summer 1985): 203-16.

Classifying *The Snow Leopard* as "a modern classic of travel writing," Bishop commends Matthiessen's effective use of personal and philosophical commentary.

Grove, James P. "Pastoralism and Anti-Pastoralism in Peter Matthiessen's *Far Tortuga.*" *Critique* XXI, No. 2 (1979): 15-38.

Explores Matthiessen's unsentimental treatment of nature and modern civilization. Contains a bibliography of criticism on Matthiessen's individual works of fiction and nonfiction.

Patteson, Richard F. "*At Play in the Fields of the Lord:* The Imperialist Idea and the Discovery of the Self." *Critique* XXI, No. 2 (1979): 5-14.

According to Patteson, the "richness and complexity of the book result from Matthiessen's success in uniting two literary traditions—the solitary American hero's search for himself and the imperialist-explorer's search for savage worlds to civilize and possess."

Schnitzer, Deborah. " 'Ocular Realism': The Impressionistic Effects of an 'Innocent Eye'." In her *The Pictorial in Modernist Fiction from Stephen Crane to Ernest Hemingway,* pp. 7-62. Ann Arbor, Mich.: UMI Research Press, 1988.

Explores Matthiessen's use of Impressionism in creating pictorial figures and images in *Far Tortuga* and relates the novel to works by various authors and artists.

# Vladimir Nabokov

## 1899-1977

(Full name Vladimir Vladimirovich Nabokov; also wrote under the pseudonym V. Sirin) Russian-born American novelist, poet, short story writer, essayist, playwright, critic, translator, biographer, autobiographer, and scriptwriter.

The following entry presents criticism on Nabokov's novel *Lolita* (1955). For an overview of Nabokov's complete career, see *CLC,* Vols. 1, 2, 3, 6, 8, 11, 15, 23, 44, 46.

Nabokov is widely recognized as one of the outstanding literary stylists of the twentieth century. His intricate, self-conscious fiction often investigates the illusory nature of reality and the artist's relationship to his craft. Nabokov maintained that "art at its greatest is fantastically deceitful and complex"; by emphasizing stylistic considerations above notions of moral or social significance, he championed the primacy of the imagination, through which he believed a more meaningful reality might be perceived. Viewing words as significant objects as well as vehicles for meaning, Nabokov made use of intellectual games involving wordplay, acrostics, anagrams, and multilingual puns to create complex, labyrinthine narratives. Although some critics fault Nabokov for his refusal to address social and political issues, many maintain that beneath his passion for "composing riddles with elegant solutions," as he himself stated, his fiction conveys a poignant regard for human feelings and morality. Arthur Mizener, a colleague from Cornell University, described Nabokov's writing as "a joke within a joke within a joke, an enormously complicated and subtle joke which is deadly serious."

Nabokov was born into an aristocratic family in St. Petersburg, Russia. His father, one of the founders of the Constitutional Democratic Party, instilled in the Nabokov children the importance of education and liberal thinking. Although numerous critics express astonishment at Nabokov's adroit mastery of English, he actually learned the language before comprehending his native tongue. When Nabokov was seventeen, his favorite uncle died and left him two million dollars and a country estate. The year, however, was 1916, and Russia was undergoing vast political and social change. The Nabokovs fled the country during the Bolshevik Revolution, ultimately settling in London. Nabokov began studying Russian and French literature at Cambridge University on a scholarship awarded for "political tribulation." After graduating in 1922, Nabokov traveled to Berlin to work with his father on a Russian refugee newspaper. That year his father was killed at a political rally of Russian exiles while trying to shield the lecturer from right-wing assassins. The murder deeply affected Nabokov, and elements of the experience would recur throughout his writing. He remained in Berlin for several years, marrying in 1925 and writing poetry, fiction, and translations to earn a living. His wife's Jewish ancestry necessitated their relocation to France in 1937

and to the United States in 1940 to escape Nazi persecution. In 1948, Nabokov accepted a post at Cornell University as a professor of Russian literature. During his tenure there, he wrote *Lolita,* the work that brought him notoriety and popular success as a novelist and allowed him to concentrate solely on his writing career until his death in 1977.

The story of a middle-aged man's obsessive and disastrous lust for a twelve-year-old schoolgirl, *Lolita* is widely considered one of the most controversial novels of the twentieth century. Rejected by four American publishers because of its pedophiliac subject matter, the book was finally published by Olympia Press, a Parisian firm that specialized in pornography and erotica. *Lolita* attracted a wide underground readership, and tourists began transporting copies of the work abroad. While United States Customs permitted this action, the British government pressured the French legislature to confiscate the remaining copies of the book and forbid further sales. However, English author Graham Greene located a copy and, in a pivotal *London Times* article, focused on the novel's language rather than its content and designated *Lolita* as one of the ten best books of 1955. Public curiosity and controversy merely fueled the book's popularity, and in 1958 it was published in the United States. Within five weeks, *Lolita* was the most celebrated novel in the nation, and remained on the *New York Times* best-seller list for over a year. Initial reviews were varied; while several critics expressed shock and distaste, the majority believed the "pornography" charges to be erroneous. Praising Nabokov's lively style, dry wit, and deft characterizations, many reviewers concurred with Granville Hicks, who called the novel "a brilliant *tour de force.*" Beat novelist Jack Kerouac described *Lolita* as "a classic old love story," and Charles Rolo asserted: "*Lolita* seems to me an assertion of the power of the comic spirit to wrest delight and truth from the most outlandish materials. It is one of the funniest serious novels I have ever read; and the vision of its abominable hero, who never deludes or excuses himself, brings into grotesque relief the cant, the vulgarity, and the hypocritical conventions that pervade the human comedy."

The origin of *Lolita* has been traced to Nabokov's 1939 novella *Volshebnik (The Enchanter)*. Discovered among Nabokov's papers after his death and translated by his son Dmitri, *The Enchanter* is a cautionary moral tale in which a pedophiliac is destroyed by his desire to consummate his love for an adolescent girl. The novel *Lolita* is purported to be the confessions of "Humbert Humbert," a pedophile in prison awaiting trial for murder. Actually an urbane European gentleman, Humbert begins his story by explaining that he has chosen his pseudonym "because it expresses the nastiness best," and then describes his childhood. At the age of thirteen, he fell deeply in love with a young girl named Annabel Leigh. Of the numerous literary allusions woven throughout the story, Humbert's childhood love, named after the adolescent heroine of Edgar Allan Poe's poem "Annabel Lee," is one of the most conspicuous. Humbert explains that their affair remained unconsummated due to ill-timed circumstances and Annabel's death several months after their meeting. Because of this, he remains susceptible to the charms of pubescent girls, whom he refers to as "nymphets." When asked what inspired him to write about such an unconventional subject, Nabokov told numerous reporters the same anecdote. In 1939, he read a newspaper article about a scientist's attempts to persuade an ape to draw. After several months, the animal finally produced a sketch of the bars of his cage. "My point," Nabokov stated, "is that in a sense the book, which is kind of a memoir, represents the grating of Humbert's personality, which he tries to break through." Throughout his writing, Humbert is well aware of the indecency of his obsessions, but remains seemingly powerless to change.

After an inheritance provides Humbert with enough money to travel, he moves to the United States and seeks inexpensive room and board in Ramsdale, a quaint New Hampshire village. When Mrs. Charlotte Haze shows the prospective lodger an available room in her home, Humbert is unimpressed until he catches a glimpse of her twelve-year-old daughter, Dolores, and becomes immediately obsessed with her. He dubs Dolores "Lolita" and continually refers to her as "my own creation." Critics have commented that, with this phrase, Nabokov estab-

lishes Humbert's inability to view Lolita as a person. Humbert devises various schemes to get close to the young girl, including marrying her widowed mother, whom he abhors, so that he may become Lolita's stepfather. Conveniently, and with Nabokov's characteristic irony, an accident soon eliminates Humbert's overbearing wife. After finding her husband's diary and reading his true feelings concerning herself and her daughter, Charlotte runs into the street to mail a letter that will expose his immorality, but is killed by an oncoming car. Playing the role of the grieving husband for the gawking crowd, Humbert quietly pockets the letter and escapes with his reputation untarnished.

Humbert drives to the summer camp Lolita has been attending to break the news of her mother's death. Desiring Lolita sexually and not wanting to upset her, he tells her only that her mother is sick. Humbert's craving for sexual intercourse is soon fulfilled, but he is somewhat chagrined to discover, on their first night together, that Lolita is not only experienced, but a more experienced lover than he. Serving as Lolita's guardian, Humbert psychologically controls Lolita and smothers her with gratuitous affection and attention. It is this aspect of imprisonment that first prompted *Lolita* to be branded as an immoral work. Several commentators maintained that the accusations of pornography stemmed from Nabokov's lack of authorial judgment regarding Humbert's actions, and some argued that the true crime of the novel is not the murder Humbert commits but his curtailment of Lolita's childhood. Lolita is not entirely blameless, however, for at twelve she is already sexually experienced, and, despite Humbert's extravagant designs, it is *she* who first seduces him. As Lolita begins to realize her power over Humbert, she gradually becomes manipulative. Lolita's portrait, as well as other characterizations in the novel, have won Nabokov consistent, unified praise for his ability to evoke both repugnance and sympathy in the reader. For example, it is generally agreed that Lolita has a highly unattractive personality, yet her unhappy life inspires compassion. Humbert is a pedophile and murderer but wins the reader's admiration for his humor and brutal honesty, while Charlotte is depicted as both a piranha and a pawn.

Much of the remainder of the novel chronicles Humbert and Lolita's affair during a two-year cross-country road trip through America. This highly acclaimed sequence has been regarded as an ingenious metaphorical comparison between young, unsophisticated America and old, cultured Europe. The jarring contrasts between Humbert's cultivated speech and Lolita's 1950s-era teenage slang, and her preference for movie magazines and candy to his enlightened positions concerning culture and the beauty of the countryside are examples of their differing values. Despite growing callousness toward Lolita, Humbert becomes anxious, jealous, and possessive, chiefly because of her long disappearances and vagueness concerning her whereabouts. In Waco, Texas, Lolita finally escapes and proves virtually impossible to track down. However, several years later, Humbert receives a letter from a Mrs. Richard Schiller, who proves to be Lolita. Certain that Schiller is the man for whom Lolita left him, Humbert packs a gun and travels to the man's home, intent on revenge. Upon his arrival, he finds Lolita pregnant, "hopelessly worn at seventeen," and learns that it was not Schiller who prompted Lolita's departure, but Clare Quilty, a famous playwright she had met at her summer camp. Humbert carefully plots Quilty's murder and elaborately stages his death scene for the reader. Quilty struggles valiantly, both physically and verbally, but ultimately proves no match for Humbert. After the slaying, Humbert is stopped by police for driving on the wrong side of the road, and is subsequently arrested for the murder. While in jail, he realizes that his efforts to "fix once and for all the perilous magic of nymphets" by eternalizing Lolita on paper is impossible. To Humbert, Lolita's enchanting quality was her innocence, which, in reality, was never there. Once possessed, she, by definition, will no longer be the nymphet he desired.

Throughout *Lolita,* Nabokov engages the reader in a battle of wits. The novel's foreword, written by "John Ray, Jr., Ph.D.," a bogus Freudian psychiatrist, introduces Humbert's confession through obtuse psychological jargon, which Nabokov deplored. Unwary readers believe the foreword is sincere, especially because of *Lolita*'s controversial subject matter. Nabokov's myriad uses of anagrams, acrostics, and puns provide clues and red herrings concerning Lolita's mysterious lover; Humbert learns of Quilty's existence late in the novel, but notes that astute readers should have realized this sooner. Nabokov also parodies numerous styles of literature in *Lolita;* it is variously viewed as a satire of the confessional novel, the detective novel, the romance novel, and, most frequently, as an allegory of the artistic process. As the novel's controversy diminishes over the decades since its initial publication, critics continue to acclaim *Lolita* as a masterful work of art.

(See also *Contemporary Authors,* Vols. 5-8, rev. ed., Vols. 69-72 [obituary]; *Contemporary Authors New Revision Series,* Vol. 20; *Dictionary of Literary Biography,* Vol. 2; *Dictionary of Literary Biography Documentary Series,* Vol. 3; *Dictionary of Literary Biography Yearbook: 1980;* and *Concise Dictionary of American Literary Biography: The New Consciousness, 1941-1968.*)

## PRINCIPAL WORKS

NOVELS

*Mashenka*   1926
   [*Mary,* 1970]
*Korol', dama, valet*   1928
   [*King, Queen, Knave,* 1968]
*Soglyadatay*   1930
   [*The Eye,* 1965]
*Zashchita luzhina*   1930
   [*The Defense,* 1964]
*Kamera obskura*   1932
   [*Laughter in the Dark,* 1938]
*Podvig*   1932
   [*Glory,* 1971]
*Otchayanie*   1934
*Despair*   1937
*Dar*   1938

   [*The Gift,* 1963]
*Priglashenie na kazn'*   1938
   [*Invitation to a Beheading,* 1959]
*Volshebnik*   1939
   [*The Enchanter,* 1986]
*The Real Life of Sebastian Knight*   1941
*Bend Sinister*   1947
*Lolita*   1955; published in the United States, 1958
*Pnin*   1957
*Pale Fire*   1962
*Ada*   1969
*Transparent Things*   1972
*Look at the Harlequins!*   1974

SHORT STORY COLLECTIONS

*Vozurashchenie chorba*   1930
*Soglydatay*   1938
*Nine Stories*   1947
*Vesna v Fialte i drugie rasskazy*   1956
*Nabokov's Dozen*   1958
*Nabokov's Quartet*   1966
*A Russian Beauty*   1975
*Tyrants Destroyed and Other Stories*   1975

POETRY

*The Empyrean Path*   1923
*Poems: 1929-1951*   1952
*Poems*   1959

OTHER

*Izobretenie val'sa*   (play)   1938
   [*The Waltz Invention,* 1966]
*Nikolai Gogol*   (criticism)   1944
*Conclusive Evidence*   (autobiography)   1951
   [*Drugie berega,* 1954]
*Speak Memory: An Autobiography Revisited*   (autobiography)   1966
*Strong Opinions*   (essays)   1973
*Lolita: A Screenplay*   (play)   1974

---

**Granville Hicks**

The problem presented by Vladimir Nabokov's *Lolita* is literary not moral. The moral issue has, of course, been raised, and it will be raised again and again in the weeks to come. It would have been raised if *Lolita* had had no previous history, but the novel is borne to us on a tide of scandal. Rejected by four American publishers, it was published in 1955 by the Olympia Press of Paris. The French government, however, forbade export of the book, and immediately there was an uproar. Articles about *Lolita* have appeared in a dozen American periodicals in the past year or two, and the debate was on long before Putnam announced that it would publish the novel.

The moral issue is simple. A little while ago I had a letter from a woman who objected to the fact that I had praised John Cheever's *The Wapshot Chronicle,* which was, she charged, an immoral work. To substantiate her charge, she listed the improper words that, she said, Cheever employed. I think she included at least one that isn't in the novel at all—she admitted that she had burned her copy and couldn't check—but the important thing is that the words were all words with which my correspondent was familiar and which she could bring herself to put down on paper. Whatever she regarded as corrupting in the novel couldn't, she made clear, corrupt her.

This is the old story. The roster of novels that have created scandals is long: Flaubert's *Madame Bovary,* Zola's *Nana,* Hardy's *Tess* and *Jude,* Dreiser's *Sister Carrie,* Joyce's *Ulysses,* and Lawrence's *Lady Chatterley's Lover*—to name but a few. The persons who have suppressed or tried to suppress these books have never argued that they themselves had been unaware of the existence of the supposedly objectionable kinds of behavior the books portrayed; on the contrary, the self-appointed censors have usually shown a comprehensive knowledge of vice. The argument is always that it is somehow injurious to the public morality to have these matters, whatever they may be, brought into the open. If we go on pretending that they do not exist, the argument runs, in essence, all will be well.

The case for the defense is also in essence always the same: there is no such thing as an inherently unsuitable subject for literary treatment; everything depends on what the writer does with it. And over the years the defense has had the better of the argument. Unworthy books have doubtless been defended, but they have quickly been forgotten and no harm done. The worthy books, on the other hand, such as those I have mentioned, survive, and in time they make the whole debate seem irrelevant. What they are grows more and more evident, and what they are "about" matters less and less.

What *Lolita* is "about" is by now pretty well known. It is about a man who is sexually attracted to girls of twelve or so, or at least to certain girls of that age, the type he calls "nymphets." The book purports to be the confessions of this man, Humbert Humbert, written while he is awaiting trial for murder, and, although there are some preliminary scenes in his native Europe, most of it portrays his relations with an American girl, Dolores Haze, known to him as Lolita. At first Humbert marries Mrs. Haze, a widow, in order to be near Lolita, but he is delivered from the marriage—and from the temptation to commit murder—by his wife's death, and he and the girl embark upon a transcontinental pilgrimage during which he yields himself fully to his obsession. After some time, however, he loses Lolita to another man of the same tastes, and he spends some years in tracking down his rival, whom in the end he kills. (p. 12)

[It] is astonishing how readily Nabokov persuades the reader to identify himself with this obsessed man. We don't like him, but we cannot comfort ourselves with the thought that he is wholly alien to us.

At the same time no one can say that Nabokov has made vice attractive, has encouraged us to regard Humbert's aberration as a trivial matter. On the contrary, we never forget that he is condemned by his obsession to a bleak and terrible existence. This is human bondage in its most extreme form. The transcontinental trip, although there are episodes of pure comedy and although Humbert looks back with longing on his moments of ecstasy, is in its total effect the kind of nightmare that one would pray to be spared.

Nor are we allowed to ignore the fact that the experience is hell for Lolita as well as for Humbert. Lolita is such an unattractive little girl that, after the first sense of horror at the abnormality of the relationship wears off, we are likely to feel that what happens to her doesn't matter. It is Humbert, in one of his more analytical moods, who reminds us that it does. "Nothing," he reflects at the end,

> could make Lolita forget the foul lust I had inflicted upon her. Unless it can be proven to me—to me as I am now, today, with my heart and my beard, and my putrefaction—that in the infinite run it does not matter a jot that a North American girl-child named Dolores Haze had been deprived of her childhood by a maniac, unless this can be proven (and if it can, then life is a joke), I see nothing for the treatment of my misery but the melancholy and very local palliative of articulate art.

But if horror is the book's dominant note, it is far from being the only note that is struck. Although Nabokov was born in Russia and had written a dozen books in Russian before he attempted to write in English, he is a stylist of the greatest virtuosity. Hard as it may be to believe this, *Lolita* is in large part an extremely funny book, and the humor is of many kinds. For one thing, Humbert's obsession repeatedly forces him to become an impostor, and he is always aware of the comic aspects of the roles he plays. For another, he is erudite, and Nabokov permits him to indulge in Joycean games with words. Then there is a broad vein of satire, particularly in the description of the tourist's America. Nabokov's humor takes astonishing forms: Humbert's slaying of his rival, for instance, is portrayed in such fantastic terms that the scene becomes slapstick comedy of the most macabre kind.

Humor is the last quality one would expect to find in a book on *Lolita*'s theme, but, finding it, one might suppose that Nabokov was simply kidding, that Humbert's obsession wasn't taken seriously and didn't really count. Not at all. The scenes in which Humbert's passion is made explicit, although restrained in language, are fully and horribly convincing. This is the core of the book, and make no mistake about it. (pp. 12, 38)

*Lolita* is a brilliant *tour de force.* Is it also a novel of enduring importance? Nabokov's admirers are convinced that it is, but I cannot feel that they have succeeded in saying why. I am not sure that the book won't come to be regarded primarily as a literary curiosity, so skilfully done that it is vastly more interesting than the average run of fiction and yet not one of the memorable novels.

I remind myself that some such judgment of *Ulysses* was formed by many early readers who were impressed by the brilliance of Joyce's stylistic achievement. Perhaps the future will be as interested in Humbert Humbert and Dolores Haze as we are in Leopold Bloom and Stephen Dedalus. Whether that happens or not—and my guess is that it won't—I am sure that the future will exonerate *Lolita* from the charge of pornography as completely as we have exonerated *Ulysses*. (p. 38)

Granville Hicks, "'Lolita' and Her Problems," in The Saturday Review, *New York, Vol. XLI, No. 33, August 16, 1958, pp. 12, 38.*

## Gene Baro

[Nabokov's *Lolita*] is a sad comedy of vice. In the form of a confession, it tells the story of pseudonymous Humbert Humbert, the son of a well-to-do European hotel owner, who, during his early adolescence, falls rapturously in love with the young daughter of a family that rents a villa near his father's hotel. Whether it was because of the frustration of his first affair or for another reason, Humbert finds himself thereafter particularly susceptible to the inchoate charms of "girl-children," between the ages of nine and fourteen, "nymphets" of a certain rough, passionate, yet delicate demeanor.

But this is no chronicle of a debauchee. Humbert Humbert is a man of sensibility, a scholarly intellectual, fully aware and self-analytical. Though he can invoke Dante's Beatrice or Poe's Virginia, or enumerate the societies where the union of adult males with female children is sanctioned, it is he himself who provides the sharpest consciousness that his desires are vice. For many years, he struggles against his obsession, pursuing it painfully only in imagination; he marries without relish and divorces without pleasure. A bequest from an uncle takes him to America. In fact, his vital energies are too much involved in the mere maintenance of an apparent balance; his promise is frittered away, and he becomes at length the victim of periodic breakdowns.

It is after one of these breakdowns that Humbert Humbert goes to live in the New England town where he meets the child Lolita. He marries Lolita's mother in order to be near the girl; an accident removes the mother, and Lolita is left in his possession. To his astonishment, Humbert discovers that she is tainted by experience. The story of their life together as they cross and recross America, as they try to settle down and fail, the story of Lolita's flight and Humbert's pursuit is sordid, comic, pathetic and tender.

Mr. Nabokov does not make vice attractive. His hero is an idealist, by turns cynical and sentimental, made conscious by the falsity of his own life of the falsity of the lives and values around him. He is a man who will prefer to face his doom if he cannot have relief from his torment. The mood of this novel is a kind of grisly picaresque. Humbert Humbert's narrative is rich in word play, fantastic conceits, homey images. The writing is always alive, the characterizations firm, the social insights wryly intelligent. If the world of the obsession never quite takes the place of the more ample world of common reality, it has at least a notable consistency and artistic force. But then, in this novel everything is lightly spoofed but human suffering and the consolatory nature of art.

According to Mr. Nabokov, "*Lolita* has no moral in tow"; but even a novel developed from aesthetic principles implies moral choice. Humbert Humbert knew that one's destiny depends in great part upon one's vision of the beautiful.

Gene Baro, "Wry Comedy of One Man's Sad Obsession," in New York Herald Tribune Book Review, *August 17, 1958, p. 5.*

## Charles Rolo

Here it is at last, Vladimir Nabokov's *Lolita*—first issued in 1955 by an unorthodox Paris press after being rejected by a string of American publishers; banned by the French government, presumably out of solicitude for immature English-speaking readers (the ban was later quashed by the French High Court); pronounced unobjectionable by that blue-nosed body, the U.S. Customs Office; and heralded by ovations from writers, professors, and critics on both sides of the Atlantic.

The novel's scandal-tinted history and its subject—the affair between a middle-aged sexual pervert and a twelve-year-old girl—inevitably conjure up expectations of pornography. But there is not a single obscene term in *Lolita,* and *aficionados* of erotica are likely to find it a dud. *Lolita* blazes, however, with a perversity of a most original kind. For Mr. Nabokov has distilled from his shocking material hundred-proof intellectual farce. His book is slightly reminiscent of Thomas Mann's *Confessions of Felix Krull;* but *Lolita* has a stronger charge of comic genius and is more brilliantly written. Mr. Nabokov, a Russian *émigré* now working in his second tongue, has few living equals as a virtuoso in the handling of the English language.

A mock sententious foreword explains that the manuscript which follows is the confession of one Humbert Humbert, who died in captivity in 1952 just before his trial was due to start. Humbert introduces himself as a European of mixed stock who, at the age of twelve "in a princedom by the sea," loved and lost a *petite fille fatale* named Annabel Leigh, and has thereafter remained in sexual bondage to "the perilous magic" of subteen sirens—he calls them "nymphets." There follows a sketch of his tortured career up to the time when, in his late thirties, he settles in a quiet New England town (an American uncle has left him a legacy, and he dabbles in scholarship) under the same roof as a fatally seductive nymphet, Dolores Haze—a mixture of "tender dreamy childishness and eerie vulgarity." This "Lolita" is the daughter of his landlady, whom he marries with murderous intent. But an accident eliminates Mrs. Haze, and Humbert the Nympholept finds himself the guardian of his darling, who, on their first night together, turns out to be utterly depraved and plays the role of seducer. Their weird affair—which carries them on a frenzied motel-hopping trek around the American continent—is climaxed by Lolita's escape with a playwright and Humbert's eventual revenge on his rival.

What is one to make of *Lolita*? In a prickly postscript to the novel, Mr. Nabokov dismisses this question as a problem dreamed up by "Teachers of Literature": he rejects the satiric interpretations which critics have put upon *Lolita* and asserts, in effect, that it is simply a story he had to get off his chest. That all of this is too ingenuous by half is evident from the parodic style in which *Lolita* is written: a combination of pastiches of well-known styles, spoofing pedantry, analysis of passion *à la française,* Joycean word games, puns, and all kinds of verbal play. Wild, fantastic, wonderfully imaginative, it is a style which parodies everything it touches. It surely justifies, at least in part, those critics who have seen in *Lolita* a satire of the romantic novel, of "Old Europe" in contact with "Young America," or of "chronic American adolescence and shabby materialism." But above all *Lolita* seems to me an assertion of the power of the comic spirit to wrest delight and truth from the most outlandish materials. It is one of the funniest serious novels I have ever read; and the vision of its abominable hero, who never deludes or excuses himself, brings into grotesque relief the cant, the vulgarity, and the hypocritical conventions that pervade the human comedy.

> *Charles Rolo, in a review of "Lolita," in* The Atlantic Monthly, *Vol. 202, No. 3, September, 1958, p. 78.*

## The Catholic World

*Lolita* is a novel which has had a somewhat sensational career; the original English edition was banned in France. Its very subject matter makes it a book to which grave objection must be raised. Mr. Nabokov meets this objection in a postscript, in the following manner:

> That my novel does contain various allusions to the physiological urges of a pervert is quite true. But after all we are not children, not illiterate juvenile delinquents, not English public school boys who after a night of homosexual romps have to endure the paradox of reading the Ancients in expurgated versions.

*Lolita* is a romp. It is the record of the relationship between a middle-aged man and a young girl, a child of twelve he calls a "nymphet." As a study of an unnatural infatuation, of a man and mind obsessed, it might be said to have a certain clinical authority. But the aura of evil, the implications of a decadence universally accepted and shared—this is a romp which does not amuse.

> *A review of "Lolita," in* The Catholic World, *Vol. 188, No. 1123, October, 1958, p. 72.*

## Thomas Molnar

There may yet develop, in literary and legal circles, a "*Lolita* case," as there has been a case of *Ulysses* and of *Lady Chatterley's Lover.* This does not mean that Nabokov's book reminds me of either; if similarities are to be searched for, I would think of the eighteenth-century *Les liaisons dangereuses* by Choderlos de Laclos, and, nearer to us, Thomas Mann's *Confessions of Felix Krull.*

*Lolita* is a confession too, although certainly not of a penitent. It is far less matter-of-fact than Laclos' novel which is, like *Lolita,* the narrative of two systematically planned seductions by an older man, one of his victims being a sixteen-year-old girl, conquered under the eyes of her young fiancé.

*Lolita*'s originality is that it speaks of the unspeakable in such a manner that it becomes credible, understandable, almost normal. As Lionel Trilling says, the reader simply cannot work up sufficient indignation; instead, he remains an amused observer, a sophisticated peeping Tom. Austere censors may, of course, warn him of the sensuous atmosphere in which the story is immersed, the quasi-incestuous relationship between Humbert Humbert, a scholarly, analytical-minded, very good looking "big hunk of a man," and his twelve-year-old stepdaughter, the boyish-girlish "nymphet," Lolita. The censor's case is even better when he points out that this rapport borders on the horrifying since Humbert marries Lolita's mother in order to be closer to the child, and becomes the involuntary cause of his wife's death which gives him access to the nymphet's—no longer innocent—bed.

More than one bed, many beds. The last two-thirds of the novel is a fantastic journey through the forty-eight States, through motels, hotels, lodges, and rented homes, the dreary, uniform scenes of desperate love-makings and furtive side-glances at suspicious innkeepers, hotel guests, and chambermaids. . . .

Humbert is a feather-weight intellectual, with his point of gravity situated below the belt; but he becomes a tragic—although at the same time comic—character in his pursuit of an impossible happiness for the morsels of which he pays an ever higher price of self-debasement, humiliation, and remorse. The depth of his personal inferno is aptly measured by two episodes: the moment when Lolita, still unaware of her mother's death, finds her new stepfather in her own bed, intent like a lover, fearful and humble like a dog waiting to be patted; then that other moment, this time one of painful reminiscence, when Humbert recalls the picture of himself, having just possessed Lolita and now adoring in her the suffering, debauched child, but with lust again rising in him, imperious, demanding submission.

The central question the reader ought to ask of himself is whether he feels pity for the girl. Our ethical ideal would require that we look at Lolita as a sacrificial lamb, that we become, in imagination, her knight-protector. Yet this is impossible for two reasons. One is very simple: before yielding to Humbert, the girl had had a nasty little affair with a nasty little thirteen-year-old in an expensive summer camp. Besides, she is a spoiled sub-teenager with a foul mouth, a self-offered target for lechers, movie-magazine editors, and corrupt classmates. The second reason is that throughout their not-quite-sentimental journey, Lolita remains as unknown to us as to Humbert himself, seen only in bed or in the car, existing only through the lustful gaze of her stepfather. She remains an object, perhaps even to herself, and only at the very end, as a teenage mother, married to a simpleton and comically serious in her vulgarity, does she become human, no longer a corrupt little animal, and no longer a nymphet.

Yet both she and Humbert, her mother and friends, the many people we pass by in the lust-and-anguish-driven car, form a fantastic, wonderful cavalcade of humanity, described, analyzed, judged with incomparable virtuosity. It has been said that this book has a high literary value;

it has much more; a style, an individuality, a brilliance which may yet create a tradition in American letters.

This is because Nabokov's writing has the rare quality of dominating the reader, body and mind, his curiosity and fears, his capacity for pity, amusement, tears and laughter. The author rides with him up-hill and down-vale, enmeshes him in the marvels of a description, or entertains him, as a veritable mental juggler, with the urbane tricks of a cultured conversationalist.

Mr. Nabokov complains in the epilogue that he had to abandon his wonderfully rich, flexible and docile Russian for an English in which he can be no better than second rate. Never have I heard of such false, although likable, modesty! Mr. Nabokov's English is beautiful and immensely suggestive, espousing with the greatest ease the mood of men, the color of landscapes, the ambiance of motels, girls' schools, and small towns. It is an ocean of a language, now calm, limpid, transparent, then turning into a roar, with waves upon waves of scintillating metaphors, images, innovations, allusions. The author swims in this ocean like a smooth-bodied fish, leaving the pursuer-reader amidst a thousand delights.

*Thomas Molnar, "Matter-of-Fact Confession of a Non-Penitent," in* The Commonweal, *Vol. LXIX, No. 4, October 24, 1958, p. 102.*

### Donald Malcolm

A gift for comedy seldom comes to a writer unaccompanied. Usually it attaches to some less endearing quality, such as a tendency to preach and moralize. Sometimes, as in parody, it is coupled with the flinty disposition of the critic. Sometimes, as in satire, it is joined to a spirit of ferocious indignation. But of all such pairings the oddest by far is the conjunction of a sense of humor with a sense of horror. The result of this union is satire of a very special kind, in which vice or folly is regarded not so much with scorn as with profound dismay and a measure of tragic sympathy. Literature is not rich in examples of such work, but certain of Mark Twain's writings come to mind, as does Nikolai Gogol's *Dead Souls.* And to this abbreviated list we may now add Vladimir Nabokov's **Lolita.**

It is the horrific rather than the comic aspect of the novel that has captured critical attention. This is not surprising, since Mr. Nabokov has coolly prodded one of the few remaining raw nerves of the twentieth century. Accustomed as the modern reader may be to scanning, with perfect composure, those clumps of naughty monosyllables that make up the ordinary "powerful" novel of sexual deviation, he is apt to find himself wholly disconcerted by Mr. Nabokov's restrained and witty chronicle of the lust of a man for a child. Such a lust, it must be admitted, is monstrous. But it must also be understood that the monsters Mr. Nabokov has created belong to mythology or poetry, not to naturalism. They have about them a queer surcharge of meaning, as if they were enormous similes for the insoluble predicaments of life. And while the details of their surroundings—an America of filling stations, motels, and roller rinks—are conjured up with the preternatural clarity of a view through binoculars, the very intensity of this vision admits of no possibility that we are looking at an ordinary world.

The novel purports to be the manuscript of a man who is awaiting trial for murder, and who chooses to crouch behind the pseudonym Humbert Humbert because that name, he feels, "expresses the nastiness best." His tone, however, is not the characteristic whine of the penitent but an artful modulation of lyricism and jocularity that quickly seduces the reader into something very like willing complicity. He was born in France, of mixed European parentage, Humbert begins, and typically adds, "I am going to pass around in a minute some lovely, glossy-blue picture-postcards." His father owned a luxurious hotel on the Riviera, and it was there, when he was thirteen, that Humbert met a little girl his own age, named Annabel, and the two fell agonizingly, shamelessly, and clumsily in love. Only their inexperience and the surveillance of their elders prevented the immediate consummation of this romance, but one day—the last of Annabel's stay—they managed to slip away to a desolate portion of the beach for a brief session of caresses. "I was on my knees, and on the point of possessing my darling, when two bearded bathers, the old man of the sea and his brother, came out of the sea with exclamations of ribald encouragement, and four months later she died of typhus in Corfu."

Although he takes a sardonic view of psychoanalysis and all its works, Humbert is inclined to believe that his blighted romance in that kingdom by the sea has given him a permanent sexual bias toward little girls between the ages of nine and fourteen who exhibit a special fey grace and insidious charm that link them to Annabel, and whom he designates "nymphets." As for grown women:

> The human females I was allowed to wield were but palliative agents. I am ready to believe that the sensations I derived from natural fornication were much the same as those known to normal big males consorting with their normal big mates in that routine rhythm which shakes the world. The trouble was that those gentlemen had not, and I *had,* caught glimpses of an incomparably more poignant bliss.

Since society employs a sterner word for this rapture, Humbert Humbert lives a thoroughly miserable life, in which periods of excruciating temptation alternate with residency in the better madhouses of Europe and, eventually, of America. But at last, in a New England town, Humbert comes upon a little girl who seems an absolute incarnation of his lost love, at the sight of whom the intervening twenty-five years of his life "tapered to a palpitating point, and vanished." Her name is Dolores Haze, called Lolita or Lo. Her age is twelve. In a desperate extremity of desire, Humbert marries Lolita's mother, solely to have access to the child during the brief period of her nymphancy. This heroic sacrifice is promptly and abundantly rewarded by the fates, who arrange that the mother should be struck down and killed by an automobile. Humbert's most polluted dream has finally come true.

Not altogether a beast, in spite of his grotesque passion, Humbert determines to dose the child with sleeping pills and achieve his transport by indirection, out of a scrupulous regard for her purity. To his consternation and delight, however, it is Lolita who boldly, directly seduces him. Poor Humbert, it seems, is not even her first lover, for she has been learning about sex at her summer camp, and so assiduously has she studied that she finds her eager stepfather somewhat maladroit. With this demonic orphan in tow, a giddy Humbert sets off at once on an aimless tour of America, stopping at every garish resort, Corn Palace, or zoo that promises to keep the nymphet amused and compliant. But Lolita's appetite is no match for Humbert's:

> There she would be, a typical kid picking her nose while engrossed in the lighter sections of a newspaper, as indifferent to my ecstasy as if it were something she had sat upon, a shoe, a doll, the handle of a tennis racket, and was too indolent to remove.

Inevitably there are quarrels, and inevitably Humbert wins them, for reasons that are made clear in a quietly horrible passage that echoes through the book: "At the hotel we had separate rooms, but in the middle of the night she came sobbing into mine, and we made it up very gently. You see, she had absolutely nowhere else to go."

Ultimately, Lolita does find somewhere else to go. She accepts the protection of Clare Quilty, a playwright and pervert with whom she has been conducting a secret flirtation. And so dexterously does Quilty whisk her from sight that several years elapse before Humbert is able to locate his wayward nymphet and learn the name of her seducer, whom he has determined to kill. By then, Lolita is no longer a nymphet, being all of seventeen. And she is married, though not to the perverse playwright, who threw her out when she refused to indulge his taste for sexual fancywork, but to a deaf and earnest young veteran by whom she is hugely pregnant. Yet in spite of "her ruined looks and her adult, rope-veined narrow hands and her goose-flesh white arms," Humbert knows "as clearly as I know I am to die, that I loved her more than anything I had ever seen or imagined on earth, or hoped for anywhere else." For her own part, Lolita remembers her bestial stepfather without rancor, but she is politely incredulous at his proposal that she leave her husband for him: "In her washed-out gray eyes, strangely spectacled, our poor romance was for a moment reflected, pondered upon, and dismissed like a dull party." And now the real horror of their previous relationship, which Mr. Nabokov has kept in solution, so to speak, by skillful comedy, is at last permitted to crystallize. Humbert realizes that the most miserable of family lives would have been preferable to "the parody of incest, which . . . was the best I could offer the waif."

On his way to assassinate the playwright, he reflects that

> Unless it can be proven to me—to me as I am now, today, with my heart and my beard, and my putrefaction—that in the infinite run it does not matter a jot that a North American girl-child named Dolores Haze had been deprived of her childhood by a maniac, unless this can be proven (and if it can, then life is a joke), I see nothing for the treatment of my misery but the melancholy and very local palliative of articulate art.

But the art that palliates Humbert's misery has not notably relieved the distress of reviewers, most of whom have felt obliged to ask themselves, "Why has the author done this horrid thing?" Some have concluded, rather desperately, that he hasn't done it at all. According to one interpretation, Mr. Nabokov has merely written an allegory of a European intellectual who falls in love with America and discovers, to his gentle sorrow, that the country is still a trifle immature. Aside from the difficulty of assigning roles (who plays New Jersey?), the fact that Mr. Nabokov is obviously capable of writing such a story without the aid of a nympholeptic allegory throws considerable doubt on the argument. It has also been suggested, ingeniously, that Mr. Nabokov *really* wanted to write a tale of romantic passion in the grand, or nineteenth-century, manner, and found that the only way to make such a passion interesting to the contemporary reader was to disguise it as psychopathology. If this interpretation is correct, one can only say that Mr. Nabokov has beautifully concealed his disappointment at having to portray his heroine as a child.

In view of the great amount of thought that has been devoted to the question, it doubtless would seem light-headed to suggest that the author wrote the story merely because he found it fascinating. But perhaps one might plausibly suggest that the artistic (as distinct from the clinical) interest of the novel is all the justification its story requires. For the bizarre relationship of Humbert and Lolita lies at the very heart of the complex and pervasive irony of the book. Sometimes it is an explicit term in the satiric equation, as when Humbert, in a macabre effort to be a good father to his diminutive paramour, immerses himself in wholesome and thoroughly American books on child care. But sometimes the relationship functions invisibly, like one of those strange lamps that scientists and outdoor advertisers delight to use—the kind that gives off no light of its own but kindles a lurid glow in certain pigments. For example, there is a conversation, between Humbert and the headmistress of a girls' school, in which Mr. Nabokov enjoys himself at the expense of progressive education. A mildly satirical point is made by the woman's cheerful prattle about educating Lolita for adjustment to a group life of malts, movies, and hair-fixing parties. But the total effect of the passage depends upon the reader's awareness of Lolita's actual circumstances and Humbert's melancholy account of her "sobs in the night—every night, every night—the moment I feigned sleep." Having previously imparted this knowledge, Mr. Nabokov is able to imply, pleasantly, that the modern educator's sanitary notion of "adjustment to life" leaves the tragedy of life quite out of the calculation, and he is able to do this with the same stroke of the pen by which he indicates the vast distance that separates Lolita from happier children.

Instances of this compound irony might be multiplied indefinitely, for the story of Humbert's journey across America is no more a simple chronicle of a wandering madman than is the tale of Chichikov's journey across the Russia of *Dead Souls* merely an account of a roving swindler. A great many aspects of the national life are thrown into high and ludicrous relief at the approach of Humbert and Lolita, and the relationship of the miserable couple is set off sharply by this background of normal American life. The reciprocal flow of irony gives to both the characters and their surroundings the peculiar intensity of significance that attends the highest art. The special class of satire to which *Lolita* belongs is small but select, and Mr. Nabokov has produced one of its finest examples. (pp. 195-96, 199-201)

Donald Malcolm, "Lo, the Poor Nymphet," in The New Yorker, *Vol. XXXIV, No. 38, November 8, 1958, pp. 195-96, 199-201.*

## Mathew Winston

In *Lolita* Vladimir Nabokov plays a very serious game with the relations between a work of art, the experiences that underlie it, and the effects it may have upon its readers. The book's protagonist, narrator, and supposed author, Humbert Humbert, continually forces us to maintain a double perspective by calling on us to pass moral and legal judgment upon him as a man and aesthetic judgment upon him as an artist. "You can always count on a murderer for a fancy prose style," Humbert informs us in the book's third paragraph, and from that point on the murderer, madman, and pedophile is balanced against the artistic creator, stylist, lover of language, and master of literary allusion. Although Humbert sometimes tries to separate his Jekyll and Hyde aspects, as when he assures us that "the gentle and dreamy regions through which I crept were the patrimonies of poets—*not* crime's prowling ground," his own book proves that the same habits of mind guide both writer and criminal.

Humbert tells us that he thought at one time of using his notes for his defense in the forthcoming trial. But the main impulses of his imaginative recreation are artistic and celebratory. The artist wants "to fix once for all the perilous magic of nymphets." The lover wants to write a history which will glorify his beloved for future generations (it is to be published only after both of them are dead). In his final words, "this is the only immortality you and I may share, my Lolita," Humbert appears as Renaissance sonneteer, boasting that he will make his love immortal in his writing, while ruefully admitting that such permanence is no adequate substitute for possessing the lady, or, as Humbert expresses it, "Oh, my Lolita, I have only words to play with!"

Humbert's desire for the literary immortality of his book reflects his need to stop the passage of time in his life or at least to pretend it does not exist. His actions, as we shall see, are designed toward this end, and his language is consistent with his actions. Twice in a single paragraph he mentions that his interrupted sexual liaison with Lolita's predecessor took place on an "immortal day." He says that his ultimate quest is for "the eternal Lolita." Even when he is on the verge of his final separation from Lolita, Humbert still pleadingly holds out the hope that "we shall live happily ever after."

*Lolita,* then, is Humbert's bid for the immortal future of which he and his nymphet are personally incapable. But the book is also a memorial of the past, a "souvenir" of Humbert's travels, a record of events that have already happened. Humbert is preoccupied with memory, that

dead thing which was once living experience, now resurrected and transmuted by the imagination. He is "a murderer with a sensational but incomplete and unorthodox memory," the author of essays on "Mimir and Memory" and "The Proustian theme in a letter from Keats to Benjamin Bailey," and the possessor of a powerful nostalgia for his Mediterranean past. He is obsessed by his memory of Annabel Leigh to the point that his entire life becomes an attempt to make his "immortal" moment with her in the past eternally present, to possess her forever. He fails to perpetuate Annabel through Lolita, who effaces her, and he cannot make his liaison with Lolita permanent, but he does succeed by writing his "memoir." (pp. 421-22)

The experiences of a lifetime undergo the selective distortions of memory and of artistic shaping and become a book. So far so good. But the process does not stop there, for a work of art affects its readers or spectators in turn. As Humbert knows, any art form consists of a set of conventions and so it tends to develop conventional expectations in its participants. Dolores Haze is partially molded by the promises of advertisements and the advice of movie magazines. Charlotte Haze has her perceptions and her "mode of expression" shaped by "soap operas, psychoanalysis and cheap novelettes." Humbert is familiar with the patterned experiences and clichéd phraseology of these forms and is able to use his knowledge to deceive Charlotte. He is similarly aware of "the rules of the movies" and tellingly describes the stereotyped plots of "musicals, underworlders, westerners." As a writer, Humbert shows his mastery of such literary forms as the detective novel, the confessional autobiography, and the Gothic romance; he parodies them at will. (pp. 422-23)

Yet Humbert is curiously trapped by his own predilection for seeing his life through a veil of literature. To begin with, he tends to view himself as a character in a work of fiction. He first perceives Lolita in the context of a fairy tale and in the same framework later enters Pavor Manor to murder Quilty. He elaborately stages his opportunity to masturbate against Lolita ("Main character: Humbert the Hummer. Time: Sunday morning in June. Place: sunlit living room. Props: . . . "), and he plots his subsequent seduction of her, part of which he compares to "a cinematographic scene," with equal care. He "rehearses" the death of Richard Schiller when he thinks that unfortunate man is Lolita's abductor. He executes Clare Quilty in a singularly literal version of "poetical justice" and then comments to himself, "This . . . was the end of the ingenious play staged for me by Quilty." When Charlotte discovers his diary, Humbert thinks to excuse himself by claiming that its entries are "fragments of a novel," which, in a manner of speaking, they are indeed. Later, he invents a film on which he is supposed to work as an excuse to withdraw Lolita from Beardsley School.

While writing *Lolita* and living through the experiences it relates, Humbert repeatedly imagines literary parallels to whatever situation he finds himself in. His references, allusions, and quotations reveal that Lolita suggests to him Petrarch's Laura at one moment, Proust's Albertine at another, and Mérimée's Carmen at regular intervals. One of the most important equations he makes is between his childhood love, Annabel Leigh, and the heroine of Edgar Allan Poe's poem "Annabel Lee." The name and early death of the former seem to suggest the parallel to Humbert, although it is probable that Annabel Leigh's name, like Humbert's own, is his creation. In any case, once he has made the association, Humbert continues to see himself as a version of Poe in many other circumstances as well. Such a fusion of life and art may be merely the harmless game of a literary mind, but it is an exercise which must necessarily distort the narrator's memory of events as they happened and which, insofar as it shapes his perceptions and understanding, influences his actions as well.

The most serious danger of subjugating life to literature in this way is that one may begin to regard the people one knows as literary characters and to treat them accordingly. Humbert reflects on this process in a passing comment about John Farlow:

> I have often noticed that we are inclined to endow our friends with the stability of type that literary characters acquire in the reader's mind. No matter how many times we reopen *King Lear,* never shall we find the good king banging his tankard in high revelry, all woes forgotten, at a jolly reunion with all three daughters and their lapdogs. . . . Whatever evolution this or that popular character has gone through between the book covers, his fate is fixed in our minds, and, similarly, we expect our friends to follow this or that logical and conventional pattern we have fixed for them. Thus . . . Y will never commit murder. Under no circumstances can Z ever betray us. We have it all arranged in our minds, and the less often we see a particular person the more satisfying it is to check how obediently he conforms to our notion of him every time we hear of him. Any deviation in the fates we have ordained would strike us as not only anomalous but unethical.

Humbert's casual remark about what *we* are inclined to do accurately describes a limitation of his own perceptions and a consequent tendency of his actions. He sees his first wife, Valeria, as a "comedy wife" and so treats her as a "brainless *baba*"; he is overwhelmed when she acts "quite out of keeping with the stock character she was supposed to impersonate" by breaking out of her assigned role and deserting him for a taxi driver. Since Humbert needs to impose upon his life the fixity of a literary work, he later attempts to force Lolita into the invariable pattern of a literary character, and therein lies his crime and his sin.

Who is Lolita? "She was Lo, plain Lo, in the morning, standing four feet ten in one sock. She was Lola in slacks. She was Dolly at school. She was Dolores on the dotted line. But in my arms she was always Lolita." Humbert wishes to negate Lo, Lola, Dolly, and Dolores and, just as he wants her always in his arms, he wants her to be always and only Lolita. "*My* Lolita," he keeps insisting, "my own creation." Humbert's solipsistic imagination refuses to acknowledge the individuality of the girls he loves or to allow them freedom to shape their own lives. First, his unorthodox memory converts his childhood love into a Poetic Annabel Lee. Then, he tell us, "I broke her spell by

incarnating her in another." He reincarnates Annabel in Dolores Haze, whom he makes into a creation he names Lolita. "It was the same child," he claims, "Annabel Haze, alias Dolores Lee, alias Loleeta."

Humbert recreates Annabel Leigh only in his memory and imagination, but he directly interferes with the life of Dolores Haze when he imposes on her the stability of type of a literary character called Lolita, a creature "not human, but nymphic." He wants to turn his life with Lolita into a revision of "Annabel Lee" with a happy ending in which she will be immutably young and forever his and they will live happily ever after. Humbert desperately and pitiably attempts to stop the movement of time, which presents to him the threat of his enchanting nymphet metamorphosing into an ordinary woman. Of course he cannot succeed, for people stubbornly persist in changing and even, as John Ray's foreword reminds us, in dying. "The past was the past" insists Lolita after she has managed to escape from Humbert and to redefine herself as Clare Quilty's mistress and then as Mrs. Richard F. Schiller. But Humbert must ignore the passage of time as best he can: "I could have filmed her! I would have had her now with me." He needs the stability of type that equates Lolita with Annabel Leigh and through time in his imagination to an eventual Lolita the Third who will merrily cavort with Grandfather Humbert.

Eventually Humbert begins to acknowledge the evil and the futility of the web of multiple entrapment he has spun about Lolita and the cruelty of keeping her from a life in which, as she puts it in Nabokov's screenplay of the novel, "everything was so—oh, I don't know—normal." He gradually learns that he knew nothing about her thoughts or feelings and, in fact, carefully avoided any recognition of her personality which might interfere with the satisfaction of his own physical and psychological needs. He is able to feel for the first time the full pathos of "her sobs in the night—every night, every night." He discovers, in short, that Dolores Haze is a person and not a character.

Separated from Lolita, alone in a psychopathic ward and then in prison, afflicted by his heart in more ways than one, Humbert turns to "the melancholy and very local palliative of articulate art. To quote an old poet: 'The moral sense in mortals is the duty / We have to pay on mortal sense of beauty'." In his supposed quotation Humbert plays moral values against aesthetic ones. Humbert has been a monster, as he himself confesses. He has tried to "fix" Dolores Haze within the unchanging boundaries of a literary character he has created. Repentant and remorseful, he glorifies her and compensates himself by writing a book about his love for her. The corollary of this process, of course, is that both of them are converted into the literary characters we encounter in ***Lolita,*** a book which, as we have seen, endeavors "to fix once for all the perilous magic of nymphets." Humbert's greatness as a writer lies in his success at "fixing" Lolita within the pages of a book, but the identical process in his life constitutes his greatest crime as a human being.

The novel ***Lolita*** makes its readers question the possibility of valid judgment and the ambiguity of value. Our questioning begins with John Ray's condescending foreword, which treats the book as a case history, as a work of art, and as an ethical treatise. It is continued by Humbert's frequent attacks against and defenses of himself. Humbert sees and presents himself in different lights—as a degenerate, as a faunlet trapped in an aging body, as a father and a lover, as a poet and a madman. Sometimes he claims he is innocent, or at least "as naïve as only a pervert can be." He begins with good intentions and is initially determined to preserve what he thinks is Lolita's purity, although it turns out that she seduces him. (Ironically, his admirable intent may only prove that he is no longer a faunlet, since he made no such attempt to keep Annabel chaste.) At other times, and increasingly as the book progresses, he condemns himself as guilty. It is possible to take either perspective, as is shown in Humbert's climactic encounter with Quilty:

> "Concentrate," I said, "on the thought of Dolly Haze whom you kidnapped—"
>
> "I did not!" he cried. "You're all wet. I saved her from a beastly pervert."

Who is the protective guardian and who the selfish sex fiend? Handy-dandy, which is the justice, which is the thief?

The ultimate judgment on Humbert is up to us. In order to help us arrive at it (or perhaps to further hinder us), we are presented with various kinds of evidence: numbered exhibits one and two, a reconstructed diary, a few letters, a class list, a diagram of an automobile accident, some poems. We are also given examples of famous writers who loved young girls and statistics about the sexual maturation of females in different parts of the world. Comparative sexual customs and the varying attitudes and laws at different times, in several countries, and even in separate states of the United States emphasize the point that there is no single standard of judgment and no trustworthy norm either for Humbert or for us to be guided by. Is Humbert innocent or guilty? And of what? Can we determine whether he is sane or mad? Is he the creator of a splendid character or the despoiler of a young girl's life?

We are made into Humbert's judge and jury and are accordingly addressed as "your honor" and as "ladies and gentlemen of the jury," for Humbert presents his legal and moral case to us. Beyond that, we are also "the astute reader" who is called upon to appreciate Humbert's artistry. Although Humbert asks his "learned readers" to view his history with "impartial sympathy," he also wants us to recognize how much we have in common with him: "Reader! *Bruder!*" Our dilemma is that we simultaneously have to evaluate a man's life and criticize his artistic creation. Our identities as judges and as readers come together when Humbert implores us, "Human beings, attend!"

A further complication in the reader's situation emerges when Humbert invokes our aid: "please, reader," he begs, "imagine me; I shall not exist if you do not imagine me." By reading the book we bring Humbert and Lolita back to life. We transform the past incidents of Humbert's life into the present as they take place anew for us. We also help to provide Humbert the literary immortality he hopes for from the future. As past and future merge within the reader's consciousness, we enable the lovers to transcend time and achieve the timeless present which Humbert so ardently desires. But we do so at the cost of trapping them eternally within an unchangeable pattern. Each time we read the book we participate in the seduction at The Enchanted Hunters, in Lolita's desertion of Humbert, and in Humbert's grotesque murder of Clare Quilty by reenacting these events in our minds. Just as King Lear will never be merrily reunited with all his daughters, so Humbert and Lolita will never live together happily ever after.

If we do not read the book, then Humbert and Lolita are "dead" and forgotten, even nonexistent. But if we do, we compel them to repeat the identical events, and so we fix them as literary characters. The reader relives the experience of Humbert as writer, which in turn recapitulates the manner in which Humbert has led his life. And far off in time and space, Vladimir Nabokov grins, assumes his alias of Aubrey McFate, and makes it all happen. (pp. 423-27)

> *Mathew Winston, " 'Lolita' and the Dangers of Fiction," in* Twentieth Century Literature, *Vol. 21, No. 4, December, 1975, pp. 421-27.*

## Robert T. Levine

Lolita the Nymphet dwells on an enchanted island whose boundaries are not spatial but temporal: the age limits of nine and fourteen. Humbert Humbert aspires to live out his days on that island. He anticipates a perpetual ecstasy that will make amends for the soiled, wasted days of his youth. But he cannot live there. No adults allowed. In his desperate effort to climb onto the island, he pulls Lolita off it and into the unenchanted ocean of adulthood too soon. This essay will examine the various expressions in *Lolita* of Dolores Haze's departure from that childhood isle and the various ironies resulting from Humbert's part in her departure.

Humbert, in the first chapter of his memoir, informs us that Lolita did indeed have a precursor: the maiden Annabel Leigh. By the time we have reached the final chapter, we may realize that there was another precursor to Lolita: the prostitute Monique. Of course, she is a less prominent character than Annabel, who is echoed throughout the novel. Yet Monique is important thematically because the effect Humbert has on her foreshadows his effect on Lolita. He has been attracted to Monique by her "curiously immature body" and her childish mannerisms. On the day after their first transaction, he observes that "she seemed to have grown less juvenile, more of a woman overnight."

On the day after the "honeymoon" night of Humbert and Lolita, as they are riding away from The Enchanted Hunters hotel, Lo says: "Let us stop at the next gas station . . . . I want to go to the washroom." A few moments later, "she started complaining of pains, said she could not sit, said I had torn something inside her." What has actually happened is that Lo has experienced her menarche. This scene has been prepared for earlier in the novel when Humbert wonders: "Has she already been initiated by mother nature to the Mystery of the Menarche?" At their next stop after the gas station, Humbert buys Lo among other items "a box of sanitary pads." So on the day following her first sexual intercourse with Humbert, Lolita—suddenly aging like her precursor Monique—biologically leaves her childhood by beginning the cycle of menstruation.

Has Humbert torn anything physical inside Lolita? Probably not. Although we have been told that "she was not quite prepared for certain discrepancies between a kid's life and mine. Pride alone prevented her from giving up," Lolita's accusation may indicate merely that she doesn't recognize the phenomenon of menstruation. Her ignorance, as well as her precocity, is stressed by Humbert: "What adults did for purposes of procreation was no business of hers." Yet, whether or not Humbert has torn anything physical inside her, we may be certain that he has torn something spiritual in her. He has destroyed her joy for living; he has induced in her a cynicism alien to the world of childhood, where magic and hope should prevail. In the course of describing Lo's tennis game, Humbert refers to his tearing of her spirit:

> She preferred acting to swimming and swimming to tennis; yet I insist that *had not something within her been broken by me*—not that I realized it then!—she would have had on the top of her perfect form the will to win, and would have become a real girl champion. (my italics)

Because of the adult cynicism induced in her by Humbert, Lolita cannot take seriously "the will to win." She senses that in the end there will always be defeat. When on one occasion Humbert promises her some childish delight (like going to a roller rink) in return for her sexual cooperation, but then reneges on the promise, her drained spirit is hauntingly expressed in her face. . . . (pp. 471-73)

Soon after beginning his story, Humbert exclaims: "Ah, leave me alone in my pubescent park, in my mossy garden. Let them [nymphets] play around me forever. Never grow up." But they do grow up. McFate forces them to grow up. And Humbert, entirely against his intentions, aids McFate. By the end of the novel, H. H. has fully recognized his crime, has seen that he is clearly guilty, has executed the offending part of himself—Clare Quilty. Humbert makes his crime evident to the reader when he recounts the epiphany he had on a Colorado mountain slope while listening to the voices of children welling up from the mining town in the valley:

> I stood listening to that musical vibration from my lofty slope, to those flashes of separate cries with a kind of demure murmur for background, and then I knew that the hopelessly poignant thing was not Lolita's absence from my side, but the absence of her voice from that concord.

This passage, cited by Nabokov as one of the novel's "subliminal coordinates" and frequently commented on by critics, asserts that Lolita still belongs in the world of childhood, where both sex and tennis can be dealt with simply. In that concord, Lolita can experiment behind the bushes with Charlie Holmes and see "the stark act merely as part of a youngster's furtive world, unknown to adults." She can enjoy herself playing tennis even if the game is "formless pat ball" and even if she and her girl opponent

"rush out after every ball, and retrieve none." The reader may, retrospectively, appreciate the irony in Lo's frivolous account of the activities at Camp Q (she is mimicking the Camp Q advertising brochure): "We loved the sings around the fire in the big stone fireplace or under the darned stars, where every girl *merged her own spirit of happiness with the voice of the group*" (my italics). For all its phoniness, Camp Q did provide a setting for the concord of children and Lo's voice was part of the concord. (pp. 473-74)

But some readers have felt that Humbert is not to blame for Lolita's leaving the enchanted land of childhood. They argue that Lolita lost her childhood and innocence when she lost her virginity with Charlie Holmes at Camp Q. They argue that it is Lolita who seduces Humbert at The Enchanted Hunters hotel. Lionel Trilling, for example, writes about Humbert: "Perhaps his depravity is the easier to accept when we learn that he deals with a Lolita who is not innocent, and who seems to have very few emotions to be violated" [see Further Reading list]. Such arguments are, in my opinion, misguided. They confuse virginity with innocence. . . . Before cohabiting with H. H. at The Enchanted Hunters, Lolita—however precocious, however cynical in her teeny-bopper way—is still just a kid, dwelling in a "youngster's furtive world." Her state immediately after leaving Camp Q, as she rides with Humbert toward The Enchanted Hunters, is neatly depicted in the following exchange:

> "It's a sketch, you know. When did you fall for my mummy?"

> "Some day, Lo, you will understand many emotions and situations, such as for example the harmony, the beauty of spiritual relationship."

> "Bah!" said the cynical nymphet.

She is not yet a nymph, still a nymphet. Copulation in the forest with Charlie Holmes will not destroy the perilous magic of nymphets, but that magic will surely be destroyed by congress with a pentapod monster. (pp. 474-75)

[An expression of Lolita's childhood] occurs in the town of Wace, where Lo and Hum attend a play by Clare Quilty and Vivian Darkbloom. The only feature of the play that pleases Hum is "a garland of seven little graces . . . seven bemused pubescent girls in colored gauze." In the play, each girl represents one of the seven visible colors of the rainbow. Taken together, these visible colors may be seen as representing childhood. A few lines later, H. H. refers to Lo as "my own ultraviolet darling." Why "ultraviolet"? Well, she is of course deeply tanned from the sun's ultraviolet rays. And she does go beyond the ordinary children-colors in her beauty and charm. But also . . . there is the sense that she has left childhood. As her voice is no longer present in the musical scale of children's shouts, so has she lost her proper place in the visible spectrum of children. How appropriate that Nabokov, a confessed synesthete, should mark in both auditory and visual terms Lolita's passage from childhood.

In removing Lolita from that concord and spectrum, Humbert is caught up in the Sophoclean irony of being an agent against his happiness and of being ignorant when he thinks he is wise. He seems to know his world:

> I knew I had fallen in love with Lolita forever; but I also knew she would not be forever Lolita. She would be thirteen on January 1. In two years or so she would cease being a nymphet and would turn into a "young girl," and then, into a "college girl"—that horror of horrors.

And then (if we may continue the series by adding H. H.'s words from elsewhere) into "that sorry and dull thing: a handsome woman." He knows, but he does not know. Does not know what he will do to her life. *"Lolita, qu'ai-je fait de ta vie?"* He may be "a great big handsome hunk of movieland manhood," but his adulthood is not a disguise. He is no faunlet. Woolly-chested Professor Humbert will deprive his favorite North American girl-child of her childhood.

A further irony in Humbert's behavior stems from his presenting himself to the reader as a champion of individual freedom. In his disquisition on nymphets, he complains about society's restrictions: "I found myself maturing amid a civilization which allows a man of twenty-five to court a girl of sixteen but not a girl of twelve." He frequently laments the intellectual imprisonment imposed upon Americans by the clichés of Madison Avenue and Hollywood. Yet the major act of his life has been to take away the freedom of Dolly Haze, the freedom necessary to nymphetage.

Humbert views Charlotte Haze as a prime threat to his freedom. Nevertheless, he intrudes into Lolita's life in the same way that Charlotte has intruded into his. He has despised Charlotte for wanting to pry into his present and past so that she can own him, so that she can render him entirely Our Hum, to stand on the shelf with her other possessions—Our Great Little Town, Our Christian God, Our Glass Lake, Our Beach, Our Doctor. Charlotte insists on learning all about Hum's prior lovers. She makes big plans concerning Monsieur Humbert without consulting him: "In the fall we two are going to England." She burgles his desk to invade his diary, whose "microscopic script" can be deciphered only by a prying and loving wife. (Lolita, who does not love Humbert, cannot decipher the diary's "nightmare curlicues").

Now consider Humbert's behavior toward Lolita. Hum is to Lo as Charlotte has been to Hum. Humbert tries to imprison Lo in every way. He must know all about her sexual history. . . . He tries each day to map out her life. In the tradition of Charlotte, he burgles her room. He opens her mail. For all his European breeding and sensitivity, he wants to make of her an *objet d'art* for his own shelf. Is his goal of My Lolita any less selfish, any less smothering, than Charlotte's goal of Our Hum? He is shocked at Lolita's indifference to his love: "Never did she vibrate under my touch." He can scarcely accept that he "had never counted," that "in her washed-out gray eyes, strangely spectacled, our poor romance was . . . dismissed like a dull party, like a rainy picnic to which only the dullest bores had come, like a humdrum exercise, like a bit of dry mud caking her childhood."

He urges the reader to recognize kinship with the despicable Humbert: "Reader! *Bruder!*" Yet Humbert, too, must recognize kinship with people whose tendencies he has despised: Quilty and Charlotte. To understand Lolita's feelings about him, he need only recall that, rather than "sit for a while on the piazza" with Charlotte, he preferred to "nurse that tooth." Humbert must disperse the fog of solipsism and lust so that he can get a clear view of himself. The many mirrors of Pavor Manor seem to provide that view at last. From the final enlightened perspective of his narration, when he can look back on events and see clear guilt, he acknowledges his cursed intrusion into Lolita's life: "children under 12 free, Lo a young captive."

The captivity of Dolores Haze was taken so seriously by certain unimaginative segments of the reading public, when *Lolita* first appeared, that the novel was branded as immoral, degenerate. Humbert's sensitivity and moral growth were not fairly weighed. But the critical counterreaction to this early Philistine assessment of the novel may have led to a complementary distortion. It seems to me, judging from recent criticism, that now Lolita's plight is not taken seriously enough. And one can understand how, even without the provocation of Philistines, Lolita's side may be slighted. After all, the novel narrated by so fascinating a figure as witty, sensitive, artistic, unpredictable Humbert Humbert centers—despite its worship of Lolita—on H. H. Our narrator, toward the end of his memoir, admits:

> It struck me . . . that I simply did not know a thing about my darling's mind and that quite possibly, behind the awful juvenile clichés, there was in her a garden and a twilight, and a palace gate—dim and adorable regions which happened to be lucidly and absolutely forbidden to me, in my polluted rags and miserable convulsions.

If the reader is to get closer to those "dim and adorable regions" of Lolita's mind, he must at times sift the information H. H. gives from the misleading interpretation which H. H., befogged by lust, imposes on that information. Previously, this essay has discussed the reluctance of some readers to appreciate Lolita's innocence. Such readers are too much influenced by H. H.'s notion of a "nymphean evil." . . . Humbert and a number of his readers are slow to recognize Lolita's intelligence; for some time, H. H. believes that her I.Q. of 121 is too high. Her sensitivity, also, is not always appreciated. One critic, for instance, has recently written that "the poignancy of this loss [Lolita's loss of her childhood] afflicts only Humbert" and that Lolita "is quite as indifferent to the injury he supposes he has done her as she is indifferent to his love of her." But how can the reader ever forget "her sobs in the night—every night, every night—the moment I feigned sleep"?

Humbert yearns for the timeless world. He wants to dwell with his Lolita in places of fantasy like the Hotel Mirana and Our Glass Lake. He wants to keep a hermetic seal around room 342 of The Enchanted Hunters. He, however, is the one who breaks the seal of Lolita's childhood, making the grains of sand fall even faster in the hourglass. His plan to live with Lolita in the magic world of nymphets is as "out of reach" as the anonymous nymphet seemingly seen undressing at "a lighted window across the street" whose "tender pattern of nudity" is abruptly "transformed into the disgusting lamp-lit bare arm of a man in his underclothes reading his paper by the open window in the hot, damp, hopeless summer night." Only in art can Humbert have his way. In the world of the imagination, Lolita can stay on the enchanted island. She can be spoken of eternally in the present tense: "that intangible island of entranced time where Lolita plays with her likes."

Yet art is not life for Humbert. Art is not a cure, just a "very local palliative." He is driven to seek that "incomparably more poignant bliss" of nymphet love not in the world of imagination but in the real world of "lovely, trustful" America, where his cumbersome presence fatally dissolves the magical mist of Dolly Haze. (pp. 475-79)

> *Robert T. Levine, " 'My Ultraviolet Darling':*
> *The Loss of Lolita's Childhood," in* Modern
> Fiction Studies, *Vol. 25, No. 3, Autumn, 1979,*
> *pp. 471-79.*

## Brenda Megerle

Is *Lolita* a pornographic novel? The consensus of *Lolita* criticism is that the novel is "about" art, not sex. As Alfred J. Appel, editor of *The Annotated Lolita* and *Lolita*'s most prolific critic, puts it, "*Lolita* is not merely about sexual perversion, but rather about love and the search for ineffable beauty, and as such . . . ultimately 'about' its own creation" [see Appel's "*Lolita*: The Springboard of Parody" in the Further Reading list]. But charges of obscenity and "moral leprosy" continue to haunt the criticism of the novel, primarily because critics who explicate *Lolita* in terms of art do not account for why a tale of sexual aberration is not only included in but made the very *modus operandi* of a book about an aesthetic quest. What, if anything, does the eroticism of Part I contribute to a novel "about art"?

An analysis of how eroticism functions within *Lolita* should shed light on the novel as a whole, on Nabokov's larger purposes, as well as on specific parts of the work. Any pornographic fiction is designed to affect the reader in a specific way, but critics tend to avoid detailed discussion of the erotic effect of Part I and address themselves to other affective aspects of *Lolita.* These, I believe, have more in common with the eroticism of the novel than has yet been proclaimed. [In *Escape into Aesthetics: The Art of Vladimir Nabokov*] Page Stegner finds that *Lolita* "moves us to a compassionate understanding of the suffering produced by an idealistic obsession with the never-to-be-had," but I believe that compassion falls far short of the complex medley of emotions evoked by *Lolita.* Any compassion the reader feels is experienced because he himself is participating in the very emotions which evoke his "compassion." The eroticism of Part I of *Lolita* is one way Nabokov ensures the reader's direct emotional involvement with the novel. Nor do I believe that the book's effect can be contained by metaphysical conclusions. Appel argues that the games and parodies filling the novel's pages

constantly frustrate the reader's expectations and therefore show the reader the superficiality of his own assumptions. The reader should thus experience a "change of consciousness," since Nabokov has suggested through parody that "reality" is itself a fiction. . . . [He attempts] to reduce the experience the novel imparts to a matter of reality versus imagination, but the aesthetic experience as it is evoked by the author of *Lolita* embodies many more polarities within its matrix: pleasure and pain, the spiritual and the physical, the "beastly and the beautiful," and the "little given" and "the great promised." I believe that *Lolita* is about tantalization, specifically the tantalization which Nabokov finds in the aesthetic experience, and that the erotic emotions the book inspires are the supreme analogue of the artist's desire to "possess" the aesthetic object. Nabokov is, I think, able to impart this experience to his readers because the matter and the manner of his novel are one and the same. *Lolita* is indeed allegorical of itself, but in a special and specific way that has not been sounded by previous criticism of the novel.

If we posit that the subject as well as the technique of *Lolita* is tantalization, our focus on the novel may be sharpened considerably. The reader is morally, sensually, and mentally teased, even as he reads a novel about the moral, physical, and cerebral tantalization inherent in the artist's experience. Nabokov must have written the novel with its page-by-page effect on the reader in mind; whether the reader experiences the correct qualities of tantalization directly affects his ability to apprehend the subject of the book—the consequences of tantalization for art and the artist. I trust that this emphasis on affect is correct, for such a perspective seems to explain best all the elements of the novel and their functions relative to each other—even the Foreword by John Ray, Jr.

Hindsight discovers a frustrating combination of accuracies and ironies in Ray's introduction, but as the first clue the reader has to the story of Lolita, this preface simply leads the reader to entertain expectations of a "general lesson" of "ethical impact." However, the very first words of the novel proper are Humbert's "Lolita, light of my life, fire of my loins." This line certainly carries an impact, but it is hardly an "ethical" one. Nabokov is continuing in the tradition of Defoe, another novelist who claimed moral enlightenment as his justification for publishing scandalous "memoirs." Humorously adopting Defoe's ruse, Nabokov pretends to "justify" essentially aesthetic attempt with an ostensibly moral purpose. While Defoe's artistic purpose apparently was to imitate a real autobiography, to make *Moll Flanders* seem like a "real" story and have his readers experience it as such, Nabokov's is, I believe, to lead his readers through the emotions attendant on intense artistic endeavor. In each case, the foreword teases the reader into believing that a moral judgment will be made about the events and characters of the narrative, but there is no authorial judgment or even an authorial voice apparent in these supposedly autobiographical memoirs. Humbert's repeated appeals to his readers as his "jury" echo Ray's suggestion that we should be able to judge Humbert, but every progressing paragraph of Humbert's diary makes that judgment more and more difficult for us. We see Humbert's dilemma from his own point of view, and Nabokov is careful to show us that Humbert is never as culpable as he might be. He cannot murder Charlotte, he shows a fatherly concern over Lolita's education, his perversion is diminished by comparison with that of Quilty, etc. (pp. 338-40)

The question of immorality . . . hovers about *Lolita,* in part because the novel offers no authorial judgment of Humbert Humbert's actions, and in part because Part I *is* pornographic in effect. It teases our moral sense and our physical senses as well. In Part I Nabokov deliberately titillates the reader with Humbert's prolonged approach to the consummation he so devoutly desires, but *Lolita* criticism has not accounted for *why* this section of the novel is erotic. Time and again critics turn with apparent relief to Humbert's own disclaimer of the relevance of erotic feelings to his story: "I am not concerned with so-called 'sex' at all. Anybody can imagine those elements of animality. A greater endeavor lures me on: to fix once for all the perilous magic of nymphets." Here, say the critics, is evidence that the book is "really" about art, about capturing some sort of magic. The artistic experience is indeed the underlying subject of the novel, and it is true that the passage serves as an abrupt reminder to the reader that the book holds much more between its covers than pornography, but it is just as importantly a joke at the reader's expense. Humbert chooses to announce that he is unconcerned with sex just as the reader is anticipating a recital of how Lolita "initiates" Humbert into the wonders of sexual intercourse. Aroused by the erotica of the preceding twenty-eight chapters, the reader does not wish only to imagine the elements of animality in Humbert's possession of Lolita and is frustrated that they are not presented in detail. In "On a Book Entitled *Lolita*" Nabokov defends himself against charges of pornography, explaining that "pornography" connotes "mediocrity, commercialism, and certain strict rules of narration. . . . Old rigid rules must be followed by the pornographer in order to have his patient feel . . . security of satisfaction. . . ." Certainly *Lolita* differs from traditional pornography, for Nabokov takes great care that his readers will experience no such security. Chapter 29, which deals with Humbert's suspenseful and agonizing first night in bed with a not-completely-drugged Lolita, is the dramatically appropriate place for Nabokov to tease the reader about his prurient interest in what he has been reading: "However, I shall not bore my learned readers with a detailed account of Lolita's [sexual] presumption." The learned reader would, of course, be anything but bored, and he must know that his leg is being pulled when Humbert pleads, "Please reader: no matter your exasperation with the tenderhearted, morbidly sensitive, infinitely circumspect hero of my book, do not skip these essential pages." Without its affective value for the reader, who is not about to skip the pages which promise to satisfy the desire aroused by all the preceding chapters, this would be a throwaway line.

With such reader-directed comments, Nabokov ensures that the manner and the matter of *Lolita* remain at one. The subject of the novel is titillation (necessarily followed by frustration) in that Humbert is always motivated by a maddening desire to possess in a final and ultimate way a thing that will no longer be itself if it is ever so

possessed. . . . Like the "gaudy moth or butterfly still alive, safely pinned to the wall," a "fixed," sexually possessed Lolita can no longer possess the childish innocence and blithe freedom that were at the core of her attractiveness. Thus Humbert's ideal is unattainable by definition. Sexual desire is an excellent metaphor for this craving for unattainable beauty; as Humbert himself puts it, "sex is but the ancilla of art." Indeed, Nabokov makes sex the handmaiden of *his* art as the reader is moved through sexual tantalization to share Humbert's passion for an ideal (Humbert's complete and explicit possession of Lolita, the aesthetic object) which proves just as unattainable for the reader in his narrative experience as it does for Humbert in his emotional life. The details of Lolita's sexual presumption that Humbert maddeningly withholds are the affective analogue of what is withheld from Humbert himself, what makes his possession of Lolita incomplete. The jokes of chapter 29 thus affectively imitate the tantalizing quality of the aesthetic experience that Nabokov wishes us to apprehend, for they at once excite the reader's desire, while warning that frustration will be the outcome. Placed as they are near the end of Part I, their hints that no satisfaction of the reader's desire for explicit sexual details will be forthcoming aid Humbert in gently grading his story into the expression in Part II of the "continuous risk and dread" that poisoned his bliss.

As Nabokov notes in **"On a Book Entitled *Lolita*,"** the rising succession of erotic scenes ceases at the end of Part I, and many readers cease at the end of Part I, too. What happens to the method of titillation in Part II of *Lolita*? Although there is an emotional falling off from the anticipation which characterizes Part I, Nabokov does not dismiss the eroticism of *Lolita* as he develops Part II, nor do I dismiss it from my discussion of the novel's tantalization. The eroticism of Humbert's love for Lolita, the teasing promise of an approaching fulfillment, is always in Humbert's mind and in the reader's consciousness as a reminder of what is inexorably receding farther and farther from our grasp as Part II progresses. Unsettled by the ominous tone of the opening pages of Part II, we seek to recapture the magic of Part I and seek the source of the gathering gloom, asking ourselves what its components are and why it cannot be dispersed. Thus Humbert's quest and our own become cerebral in nature as our intellects are teased by such questions.

The shift from sensual to cerebral tantalization is the affective counterpart of the thematic shifts between Parts I and II. Part I of *Lolita* seems to be a story about a desire that can be consummated, while Part II is more clearly about a desire that cannot be. Humbert's pleasurable lust for an attainable object becomes his despairing love for an object which is mysteriously unattainable. If the sexual desire so vividly portrayed in Part I is an apt metaphor for the yearning for ineffable beauty, then a "nymphet" is the appropriate symbol for that tantalizingly unattainable goal. In fact, one guesses that Nabokov did not so much choose to write a novel of sexual perversion as a symbolically consistent work that happened to require a young girl as one of its terms. Humbert craves a nymphet, an unmetamorphosed butterfly, a not-quite woman, because her allure is in her very unripeness, in the teasing promise of future fulfillment. Thus Humbert represents the artist whose creative imagination fills in "the gap between the little given and the great promised—the great rosegray never-to-be-had."

In Part II of the novel Humbert's earlier effort to "fix" Lolita in a sexual sense becomes his effort to fix or capture her on an artistic or imaginative plane: the imagination Humbert exercised in Part I in filling the gap between the given and the promised must be extended in Part II to keeping Lolita solipsized, seemingly frozen in her twelve-year-old beauty, and to blotting out the physical traces of time and experience. Again the aptness of the pubescent girl as aesthetic object becomes apparent, for such a one is especially vulnerable to time and change and therefore constantly challenges the preserving faculties of Humbert's imagination.

Humbert is usually successful in overlapping and encasing the real Dolores with his own "fanciful Lolita"; nevertheless, Humbert's envisioned Lolita remains dependent for her existence on the real Dolores. Humbert's Lolita floats between him and Dolores, for Dolores is the screen on which Humbert must project his vision. Humbert's ideal Lolita is sexually passive, "emprisoned in her crystal sleep" like Poe's Annabel Lee, but the enchanted sleep of both Annabel Lee and the Annabel Leigh of Humbert's boyhood is that of death. Dolores is alive, and her very liveliness threatens Humbert's vision of sexual passivity. As Part II begins, Humbert and Lolita begin the journey across America which is intended to keep Lolita isolated from anyone who could interrupt and so destroy Humbert's dream by removing the real Dolores on whom the imagined Lolita depends. But Lolita begins threatening to become unsolipsized even as the journey begins, and much of Part II is taken up with Humbert's and the sympathetic reader's being teased and baited by this possibility.

Specifically, Humbert is teased by jealousy; he perceives the primary threat to his dream world in young men who seem attracted to Dolores and who might take her (and therefore Lolita) away from him. Thus Humbert's suspicious eyes transform ordinary teenage males into "gangling, golden-haired high school uglies, all muscles and gonorrhea." That Humbert's vision of Lolita is most threatened by a Lolita with straying sexual interests is strongly suggested by the scene at Beardsley in which the possibility of another lover momentarily destroys the barriers erected by Humbert's preserving imagination. . . . Fearing that Dolores is clandestinely meeting another male and lying to him about it, Humbert spirits her away on a second cross-country tour. By this time, his paranoia has so escalated that he takes a gun with him, obscurely feeling himself being enmeshed in some threatening "pattern of fate." The threat Humbert perceives is, of course, Dolores's giving herself to another man and so taking Lolita away from him: "I ripped her shirt off. I unzipped the rest of her. I tore off her sandals. Wildly, I pursued the shadow of her infidelity; but the scent I travelled upon was so slight as to be practically undistinguishable from a madman's fancy."

The reader is also teased by the shadow of Dolores's infidelity. We too hear that she misses her piano lessons, that she gives an unconvincing explanation of where she was while truant, and we see her wild dash out to a telephone booth on a stormy night after Humbert makes his suspicions known to her. We see her hastily hang up the telephone when Humbert approaches and emerge from the booth in an oddly sunny and loving disposition, begging to leave Beardsley on another long trip, this time to the places *she* wants to visit. Tantalized with such suspicious behavior, the reader wants to know what—if—anything—Dolores is up to. We want to know now more than ever what is taking place in *her* mind, what her reactions to her present situation are, and what her plans for the future might be. But as aesthetic object, Dolores Haze must remain frustratingly inscrutable or "hazy" for the reader as well as for Humbert. The door of her consciousness is never opened to us; we always view her from the outside. The underlying theme of the artist's experience demands that she remain wholly other, for inherent in the artist's quest as Nabokov seems to define it, is the foredoomed attempt to assimilate and even possess in some ultimate way a beauty or reality that lies beyond the artist himself. Thus Humbert enacts the role of artist as his "Frigid Princess" shuts her mind as well as her heart to him and so guarantees in two dimensions the frustration of his quest to possess her. That Dolores's thoughts remain opaque to the reader ensures the affective reproduction of the aesthetic experience in *Lolita,* for like Humbert we are teased into the desire for greater knowledge of the object than we are allowed to possess.

The general anxiety that Lolita may become unsolipsized is, of course, finally focused in the person of Clare Quilty. The mystery of Dolores's thoughts and intentions and the related mysteries of who takes her away and for what purpose ultimately coalesce in the identity of Quilty. But the tantalization of the mystery is continued and not resolved by Quilty, for he thus embodies both the subject and technique of the novel: "His main trait was his passion for tantalization," writes Humbert. "Goodness, what a tease the poor fellow was! He challenged my scholarship." Appel asserts that these words embody Humbert's and Nabokov's self-criticism, but as I hope the argument of this essay will demonstrate, Nabokov's task in *Lolita* is not to criticize tantalization but to demonstrate affectively its complex effects on the artist and his art. Appel is quite correct in noting that the games and parodies of *Lolita* frustrate the reader's expectations, but he is incorrect in concluding that Nabokov frustrates the reader's desires because he wishes to parody or criticize them. Rather, Nabokov frustrates the reader's desires because the artist's desires are also doomed to frustration. He wishes the reader to understand the nature of the artist's desires, and this is a far more difficult task than mere criticism, for it requires all the evocative powers at the author's command. As in chapter 29, Nabokov rises to this challenge by at once highlighting and joking about the reader's frustration at not receiving the details about Lolita's mysterious disappearance which seem to be promised him. Humbert demands the name of her abductor from a rediscovered Dolly:

> "Do you really want to know who it was? Well, it was—"

And softly, confidentially, arching her thin eyebrows and puckering her parched lips, she emit-
ted a little mockingly, somewhat fastidiously,
not untenderly, in a kind of muted whistle, the
name that the astute reader has guessed long
ago.

Here, the method of tantalization is apparent in Nabokov's very style, in the crescendo of adverbs which describe how Dolly pronounces a name we are not allowed
to hear. As Nabokov knows, most readers have made no
correct guess, and the name of Clare Quilty is withheld for
sixteen more frustrating pages.

But how do Quilty and the much bruited Döppelganger
motif fit into the virtually allegorical scheme which I have
described? It is a commonplace of *Lolita* criticism that
Quilty represents Humbert's guilt and that Humbert judges and exorcises that guilt by killing Quilty. The underlying, allegorical level of the novel requires that Humbert's
guilt be objectified in another character so that the precise
nature of the artist's culpability can be defined and carefully distinguished from all that is "tenderness, kindness,
ecstasy" in the aesthetic experience. Quilty's "appreciation" of Lolita, the aesthetic object, is that of a hedonist;
it is destructive and not integrated with the saving preser-
vative and creative intentions which characterize Humbert's love, the love of the artist. ("And do not pity C. Q.
One had to choose between him and H. H., and one wanted H. H. to exist at least a couple of months longer, so as
to have him make you live in the minds of later generations"). Ironically, Dolores smiles upon the hedonist who
would use and discard her, not upon the artist. That she
does so emphasizes that the aesthetic object more readily
fills the needs of the hedonist, simply because his demands
are more easily met. The hedonist acquiesces to the demands of time and would satisfy the shifting appetites of
the moment, but the artist's appetite is for eternity: he
would immortalize the aesthetic object.

The matter and manner of Part II remain unified through
tantalization on both the narrative and allegorical planes,
for Quilty (Humbert's guilt) teases Humbert and so makes
it impossible for Humbert to keep Lolita "safely solipsized" and to enjoy his concept of her. Following Humbert
and Dolly about the country in the "Aztec Red Convert-
ible" or leaving provocative signatures for Humbert to
find in hotel registers, Quilty teases Humbert into trying
to put his finger on the canker in his bliss, into trying to
define and name the tormentor who appears on the horizon of every day with Lolita and who finally takes her
away altogether. "Queer!" remarks a sadder but wiser
Humbert. "I who was jealous of every male we met—
queer, how I misinterpreted the designations of doom."
On the narrative level, Humbert mistakes Quilty, Lolita's
lover, for a detective hired by some busybody, while on the
allegorical level the artist searches outside himself for an
answer that exists within his own being. The source of the
poison in the artist's experience and the source of his
"doom" lie in what Quilty represents—part of the artist
himself. Humbert's experience of Lolita embraces Quilty's
selfish sensuality as well as other dimensions. Thus the
very proximity of the source of the artist's sorrow at once
tantalizes him and prevents his focusing on it. The artist

has the effect of both Humbert and Quilty put together;
he breaks both the life and the heart of the aesthetic object:
"She [Dolly] groped for words. I supplied them mentally.
('*He* broke my heart. You merely broke my life')." "The
moral sense in mortals is the duty / We have to pay on
mortal sense of beauty," because the artist must in part destroy the object in order to capture it. As Nabokov the
butterfly collector must know, the "gaudy moth or
butterfly . . . safely pinned to the wall" no longer possesses the beauty of its freedom and flight, even though it is
"captured" for all to appreciate. Just so, the aesthetic object "fixed" in art has the life broken out of it, as Lolita's
life is broken by being sexually captured. The death which
concludes both "Annabel" myths proves prophetic. Ironically, Humbert's early desire for a drugged, virtually life-
less Lolita becomes an unattainable desire for a Dolores
full of the life she relinquishes at seventeen. The "art" or
imagination he once exercised in limiting her vitality finally becomes the art he employs to save as much of that life
as he can. In either case art proves woefully inadequate for
the task.

Thus moral tantalization is not the least of the artist's difficulties; it informs the frustration he feels when his work
reveals its necessary imperfection. And the work of art
must be imperfect, because art must destroy to preserve;
in "capturing" the object art destroys part of that object's
original life and beauty. The artist is thus torn between
two alternatives, neither of which is an adequate response
to his original, glowing conception of the aesthetic object
and neither of which is free of some moral taint. He can
attempt to preserve the beauty he perceives in some artistic medium and pay the price of destroying by failing to
preserve a precious quality of that beauty, or he can turn
his back on the object, leaving it whole and free, but thus
allowing time and change to destroy it forever. The artist
confronted with the aesthetic object is teased by a moral
choice as muddied by motivation and circumstance as that
faced by the reader who is teased into believing that he
should and can pass moral judgment on Humbert. In general terms, the artist's moral dilemma is the ultimate
source of the "continuous risk and dread" that poisons his
bliss.

But however tormented and teased, the artist remains enthralled with the "perilous magic" of the aesthetic object,
and this fascination is the source of the exhilaration and
excitement of the aesthetic quest as Nabokov portrays it
in *Lolita.* Invoking the confessional autobiography, the
detective mystery, and the pornographic novel, Nabokov
uses any and every mode that titillates, tantalizes, and
lures us on to seek the unattainable. Yet it was inevitable
that tantalization become both the subject and technique
of *Lolita,* for what is the novel but, in Nabokov's own
words, the record of his "love affair" with the "English
language"? His medium and his subject unite in the language he uses, and if I have read the book rightly, language is Nabokov's Lolita, the tantalizing source and repository of the great promised, the never-to-be-had—the
perfect novel. (pp. 340-47)

*Brenda Megerle, "The Tantalization of 'Lo-
lita'," in* Studies in the Novel, *Vol. XI, No. 3,
Fall, 1979, pp. 338-48.*

## Phillip F. O'Connor

*Lolita* stays like a deep tattoo. Critics tumble over one another racing to publish articles on its twists, myths and artifices. Paperback houses have reprinted it again and again. It is the second most often cited title in *Book Week*'s Poll of Distinguished Fiction, 1945-65. It has been made into a movie, a successful one at that. Sales and critical attention have opened the way for the appearance of many of Nabokov's other novels, particularly his early or Russian novels. Without *Lolita,* Nabokov's rise to literary sainthood might have been delayed beyond his natural years. Indeed, it might never have occurred.

Nabokov's twelfth novel was brought out in 1955 by Maurice Girodias' Olympia Press in Paris when the author was fifty-six years old. It had been rejected by four American publishers on a variety of grounds, all, according to Andrew Field, stemming from "a compound of fright and incomprehension" (*Nabokov, His Life in Art*). Though Girodias had now and then published the works of distinguished writers such as Durrell, Beckett and Genet, he was known mainly for an output of "dirty books." He saw in *Lolita,* some of whose literary values he recognized, mainly a weapon in the fight against moral censorship. Nabokov was soon forced to insist that he would be hurt if his work became a *succes de scandale.* The author needn't have worried; during the year following its publication, *Lolita* was given not a single review and soon became just another book on the Olympia list, not even sufficiently pornographic to compete with some of Girodias' other titles, such as *White Thighs* and *The Sex Life of Robinson Crusoe.*

An early sign of the lastingness of *Lolita* seems to be the unanimity of contempt it aroused in snobs and slobs alike after it did find a public of sorts. Orville Prescott in the daily *New York Times* (August 18, 1958) declared:

> *Lolita,* then, is undeniably news in the world of books. Unfortunately it is bad news. There are two equally serious reasons why it isn't worthy any adult reader's attention. The first is that it is dull, dull, dull in a pretentious, florid and archly fatuous fashion. The second is that it is repulsive.

Prescott shared contempt with "Stockade Clyde" Carr, a barracks-mate of Nabokov's former student and, later, editor, Alfred Appel, Jr. Appel found and purchased the Olympia edition in Paris in 1955 and brought it back to his Army post, where Clyde, recognizing the publisher said, "Hey, lemme read your dirty book, man!" Urged to read it aloud himself, Clyde stumbled through the opening paragraph: "Lo . . . lita, light . . . of my life. Fire of my . . . loins. My sin, my soul. Lo . . . lee . . . ta" then tossed down the book and complained, "It's goddam littachure!" . . . Nabokov seems to have anticipated some of the fads, fashions and contempts of both schools. In the foreword to the novel, Nabokov's alter-ego, or mask, the scholar John Ray, Jr., says " . . . those very scenes one might ineptly accuse of a sensuous existence of their own, are the most strictly functional ones in the development of a tragic tale, tending unswervingly to nothing less than moral apotheosis." Nabokov's works are full of such clues

and warnings, but only sensitive readers pick them up. In fact, *Lolita* remained an underground novel until 1956 when Graham Greene in *The London Times* placed it on his list of the ten best novels published during the previous year. As Field points out:

> Greene's pronouncement aroused great controversy, but also stimulated the interest of many important and respected critics and writers, who, with few exceptions, were quick to recognize the enormous importance and non-pornographic nature of the novel.

By 1959 many literary people had taken and followed Greene's signal (I might say, "*Not until* 1959 . . . "). V. S. Pritchett in *The New Statesman* appreciated the novel and addressed the problem of the so-called pornographic content, no doubt aware that the U.S. Customs Bureau had for a time confiscated copies of *Lolita:*

> I can imagine no book less likely to incite the corruptible reader; the already corrupted would surely be devastated by the author's power of projecting himself into their fantasy-addled minds. As for minors, the nymphets and schoolboys, one hardly sees them toiling through a book written in a difficult style, filled on every page with literary allusions, linguistic experiment and fits of idiosyncrasy.

Such praise seems mild, given what we now know of the general richness of the novel. To one degree or another, for example, critics have demonstrated that *Lolita* is a full-blown psychological novel with roots deep in nineteenth century models; a detective novel with conventions that date back to Poe, perhaps beyond; a confessional novel; a Doppelganger Tale; an extended allegory for the artistic process; a sexual myth more complicated and mysterious than comparable Freudian stereotypes; even a fable with correspondences to the Little Red Riding Hood story. And of course it to some degree parodies these types.

In his final confrontation with Quilty, "the kidnapper," Humbert, "the detective," comically plays his role to the extreme. Then, as if to remind us that popular genres often share both conventions and cliches, Nabokov mixes matters; that is, for moments at least, a scene from a detective novel becomes, as well, a scene from a Western, "detective" becoming "cowboy," etc. Quilty has just knocked Humbert's pistol ("Chum") under a chest of drawers:

> Fussily, busibodily, cunningly, he had risen again while he talked. I groped under the chest trying at the same time to keep an eye on him. All of a sudden I noticed that he had noticed that I did not seem to have noticed Chum protruding from beneath the other corner of the chest. We fell to wrestling again. We rolled all over the floor, in each other's arms, like two huge helpless children. He was naked and goatish under his robe, and I felt suffocated as he rolled over me. I rolled over him. We rolled over me. They rolled over him. We rolled over us.

The final sentences signal exhaustion, not only in the narrator and his opponent but, as importantly, in the author who lurks behind them and the reader who waits ahead.

Yet Nabokov still isn't satisfied; as parodist he has recognized and used the possibilities for exhaustion in the detective/Western, pushing the scene to its sterile limits; now he provides the rewarding twist, presented in Humbert's comment:

> In its published form, this book is being read, I assume in the first years of 2000 A.D. (1935 plus eighty or ninety, live long, my love); and elderly readers will surely recall at this point the obligatory scene in the Westerns of their childhood. Our tussle, however, lacked the ox-stunning fisticuffs, the flying furniture. . . . It was a silent, soft, formless tussle on the part of two literati, one of whom was utterly disorganized by a drug while the other was handicapped by a heart condition with too much gin. When at last I had possessed myself of my precious weapon,—both of us were panting as the cowman and the sheepman never do after their battles.

Heretofore in the scene we've been presented with a mocking of roles and literary genres; but now we find connections between poor detective writing and poor Western film making, specifically in the fight-scene cliche. Not only do genres share cliches; so do modes (fiction and film).

Here, as in many of Nabokov's novels, parody is close to essence. Literature is not the only object of Nabokov's playful pen. Material as unrelated as the author himself (anagramatically called Vivian Darkbloom) and artifacts of the American culture, such as motels, come under the writer's amused eye. That Nabokov's work and its parts are at the same time themselves and imitations of themselves is no surprise to readers of *The Real Life of Sebastian Knight, Laughter in the Dark,* and other of the author's subversive fictions. (pp. 139-41)

Characters imitate literary or historical figures outside the work (Humbert Humbert as Edgar Allan Poe), they imitate characters within the work (Humbert as Claire Quilty) and they imitate themselves (Humbert, the lecherous father and Humbert, the dutiful father). They constantly confront mirrors, adopt disguises or masks, and become, at least in terms of *motif* butterflies, hunters and chess pieces. Word-games abound, particularly those that involve repetitions (Humbert Humbert or John Ray, Jr. J—R J—R) and connotative resonances (like the surname Haze). Punning and similar games which allow a kind of verbal playback appear frequently. Clues, false clues, symbols and allusions are bounced against each other like the white dot in an electronic tennis game, though the author's hand remains steadily, constantly on the controls. And beneath all the trickery and games, as if in concession to realists like Flaubert and Saul Bellow, there lies a more or less traditional, a tragic, love story.

Humbert's comment on the fight, quoted above, also reveals a quality that readers attending Nabokov's parodic vision may easily overlook: a depth of characterization. There are dimensions to Lolita, Quilty, Charlotte and others in the novel. Humbert is extraordinarily complicated: a lover, criminal, detective, cowboy, mocker, serious in each endeavor, even the most foolish. After noting "this mixture in my Lolita of tender dreamy childishness and a kind of eerie vulgarity," Humbert shares the depths of his feelings for her, saying:

> . . . all this gets mixed up with the exquisite stainless tenderness seeping through the musk and the mud, through the dirt and the death, Oh God, oh God. And what is most singular is that she, *this* Lolita, *my* Lolita, has individualized the writer's ancient lust, so that above and over everything there is—Lolita.

The subject here, however, is the novel and its readers: what happened and what might have happened. Consider. Because Lolita survived, as literature, as a popular novel, it prepared the way for subsequent Nabokov works, especially **Pale Fire** and **Ada,** which might otherwise have found no audience of notable size, might not even have been published by a commercial press. In sustaining a reasonably healthy life for itself, *Lolita* also made possible the translation and publication of Nabokov's important early novels, including **Mary, King, Queen, Knave, The Defense** and **The Eye.** Further, it brought invitations for Nabokov's short stories from editors of good-paying magazines who previously had ignored his work. . . . Finally, it provided for the author that glowing credential of a writer's popular success, a movie, which came about largely because of solid paperback sales. A work, then, which at the beginning was completely ignored, then existed as a controversial under-the-counter pornographic novel was finally published by a respectable house (The first Putnam edition appeared in August, 1958, and there were seventeen printings in the following thirteen months.) seemed to catapult its author into daylight. Yet this was decades after he had begun writing. How strange, especially when one recalls that *Lolita* was not discovered by an informed critic making a studied response *or* by an enterprising editor at a commercial publishing house but as the result of the bare mention of it made by another practitioner of Nabokov's lonely craft, a mention that itself might have gone unnoticed had the novel lacked the power to stir and sustain controversy. The oddness of it all might appeal to no one more than to Nabokov himself.

And so it did.

In **"An Afterword to Lolita"** he recalls his experiences with the four American publishers who'd rejected his novel before he sent it to Girodias: He found some of the reactions "very amusing." One reader thought the book would be all right if Lolita were turned into a twelve-year-boy and he was seduced by Humbert, "a farmer, in a barn, amidst gaunt and arid surroundings, all this set forth in short, strong, 'realistic' sentences." Nabokov insists that everybody knows that he detests symbols and allegories,

> . . . an otherwise intelligent reader who flipped through the first part described *Lolita* as "Old Europe debauching young America," while another flipper saw in it "Young American debauching old Europe." Publisher X, whose advisers got so bored with Humbert that they never got beyond page 188, had the naivete to write me that Part Two was too long. Publisher Y, on the other hand, regretted that there were no good people in the book. Publisher Z said if he printed *Lolita,* he and I would go to jail.

The author, after years of absurd neglect, had developed a shell of protection; any response now would amuse him. In jail or an asylum he would surely have laughed, perhaps scribbled out the folly of his fate on the walls of his cell.

I've intended my remarks to be informative and stimulating, not conclusive, and therefore I must warn myself away from the temptation to make something definite of all of this. The best closing is to be found in some of the words Nabokov himself wrote about *Lolita.* They seem to be a gentle phosphorescent light by which trailing fish—critics, teachers, writers, students, publishers and the like—might be guided. When he thinks of the novel, he says:

> . . . I seem always to pick out for special delectation such images as Mr. Taxovich, or that class list of Ramsdale School, or Charlotte saying "waterproof," or Lolita in slow motion advancing toward Humbert's gifts, or the pictures decorating the stylized garret of Gaston Godin, or the Kasbeam barber (who cost me a lot of work), or Lolita playing tennis, or the hospital at Elphinstone, or pale, pregnant, beloved, irretrievable Dolly Schiller dying in the Gray Star (the capital town of the book), or the tinkling sounds of the valley town coming up the mountain trail (on which I caught the first known female of *Lycaeides sublivens* Nabokov).

These parts he calls "the nerves of the novel." They are the "secret points, the subliminal co-ordinates by means of which the book is plotted."

And surely, I dare add, some of the reasons the novel has survived even its own audiences. (pp. 141-43)

> Phillip F. O'Connor, " 'Lolita': A Modern Classic in Spite of Its Readers," in A Question of Quality: Seasoned "Authors" for a New Season, Vol. 2, *edited by Louis Filler, Bowling Green University Popular Press, 1980, pp. 139-43.*

## Thomas R. Frosch

It has been said that *Lolita* is simultaneously "a love story and a parody of love stories" and that its parody and its pathos are "always congruent." In this article I wish to explore what such a condition—that of being both parodic and authentic at the same time—may mean.

First, however, I suggest that we best describe *Lolita* generically not as a love story or a novel of pathos but as a romance. The plot itself is composed of a series of typical romance structures, each one a version of the quest or hunt and each one an embodiment of a specific type of suspense or anxiety. We begin with the pursuit of Lolita, and the anxiety of overcoming sexual obstacles. Next, once Humbert and Lolita are lovers, we have a story of jealousy and possessiveness, as Humbert is beset by fears of rivals and by Lolita's own resistance. Finally, in Humbert's dealings with Quilty, we have a third and fourth type, each with its attendant style and anxiety: the double story and the revenge story. Furthermore, these plot structures are infused with the daimonic (that is, a quality of uncanny

power possessed originally by beings, whether good or evil, midway between gods and people), which is a primary characteristic of romance as a literary mode. Lolita is an inherently unpossessable object; her appeal consists partly in her transiency—she will only be a nymphet for a brief time—and partly in her status as a daimonic visitor to the common world. The quest is thus an impossible one from the outset; it is variously presented as a quest for Arcadia, for the past, for the unattainable itself; it is nympholepsy. Even in the rare moments when Humbert is free from his typical anxieties, he is not totally satisfied. . . . Humbert is a believer in the enchanted and the marvelous. Like Spenser's Red Cross Knight, he rides forth on his quest adorned by the image of his guiding principle, in his case a blue cornflower on the back of his pajamas—the blue cornflower being Novalis' symbol of infinite desire. *Lolita* contains numerous parodic allusions to other literary works, especially to Mérimée's *Carmen* and Poe's "Annabel Lee," but the real anti-text implied by the allusions and parodies together is the romantic sensibility in general from Rousseau to Proust.

But exactly how seriously are we meant to take Humbert and his quest? The book's complexity of tone and the question of Humbert's reliability as a narrator are the first issues in an investigation of the relationship between the parodic and the authentic.

Nabokov takes great delight in rapid and unpredictable changes in tone; we are never permitted to rest for long in the pathetic, the farcical, the rapturous, or the mocking. One of the clearest examples of tonal complexity is the novel's "primal scene," the seaside love scene with Annabel Leigh. After a buildup of high erotic suspense during which the two children are repeatedly frustrated in their sexual attempts, the famous episode concludes as follows: "I was on my knees, and on the point of possessing my darling, when two bearded bathers, the old man of the sea and his brother, came out of the sea with exclamations of ribald encouragement, and four months later she died of typhus in Corfu." We misread this little rollercoaster ride from the impassioned to the hilarious to the poignant if we take any one of its tonalities as definitive. Certainly this is not simply a satire of the romantic; its effect comes rather from the coexistence of its three tonalities in a single moment. In such a passage, we might expect the romantic to go under, partly because of its inherent vulnerability and partly becuase, as the dominant tone of the long buildup, it is apparently punctured by the intrusion of the burlesque. Yet the paragraphs that follow return to a tone of erotic rapture in a scene that is chronologically earlier than the seaside scene. The second scene, describing another frustrated tryst, concludes as follows: "That mimosa grove—the haze of stars, the tingle, the flame, the honeydew, and the ache remained with me, and that little girl with her seaside limbs and ardent tongue haunted me ever since—until at last, twenty-four years later, I broke her spell by incarnating her in another." If Nabokov had intended to puncture Humbert's rhapsody, it would have been more appropriate for him to arrange the two scenes chronologically so that the ribald bathers would appear at the end of the entire sequence, instead of in the middle. As it is, nothing is punctured; if anything, the romantic has found a new energy after the interruption. It is as if, in the following paragraphs, the romantic has been given the bolstering it needs to be able to hold its own with the jocular.

The novel's narrative point of view is as elusive as its tone. Clearly, when Humbert tells us, as he does repeatedly, that he has an essentially gentle nature and that "poets never kill," he is belied by the destruction he wreaks on Charlotte, Quilty, and Lolita. And when Humbert accuses Lolita of "a childish lack of sympathy for other people's whims," because she complains about being forced to caress him while he is spying on schoolchildren, Nabokov is being sarcastic. Humbert also fails to see things that the reader can pick up; for example, he misses the name Quilty ("Qu'il t'y") concealed in a friend's letter to Lolita. Just as clearly, though, Humbert is sometimes Nabokov's champion, as for example in Humbert's satirical comments about psychoanalysis and progressive education. At other points, Nabokov's attitude toward his persona is quite intricate: Humbert says of his relationship with Annabel that "the spiritual and the physical had been blended in us with a perfection that must remain incomprehensible to the matter-of-fact, crude, standard-brained youngsters of today"; and Humbert does serve as a serious critic of modern love from the standpoint of a romantic exuberance of feeling, even if his criticism is undercut by his own divided love, in which what he calls his "tenderness" is always being sabotaged by what he calls his "lust." (pp. 171-73)

Humbert subtitles his story a confession. More accurately, it is a defense. Portraying himself as a man on trial, Humbert repeatedly refers to his readers as his jury. "Oh, winged gentlemen of the jury!" he cries, or, "Frigid gentlewomen of the jury!" But he also frequently addresses us directly as readers; in the middle of a torrid sequence he speculates that the eyebrows of his "learned reader . . . have by now traveled all the way to the back of his bald head." And late in the book, in a parody of Baudelaire's "Au lecteur," he addresses the reader as his double: "Reader! *Bruder* !" The reader is sitting in judgment on Humbert; the purpose of his story is to defend what he calls his "inner essential innocence"; and the rhetoric of the book as a whole, its strategy of defense, is proleptic, an answering of objections in advance. Humbert's self-mockery, for example, has to be understood as a proleptic device, and, indeed, to follow the style of *Lolita* is to track the adventures of a voice as it attempts to clear itself of certain potential charges. As we will see, in many ways the defense is Nabokov's, even more than Humbert's.

At the end of the novel, Humbert sums up his defense by passing judgment on himself; he would give himself "at least thirty-five years for rape" and dismiss the other charges, meaning chiefly the murder of Quilty. But there are further accusations that the novel strives to evade. As a whole, the book defends itself against a utilitarian concept of art. This charge is rather easily evaded by the use of John Ray, who introduces the novel as an object-lesson in the necessity of moral watchfulness on the part of "parents, social workers, educators." Nabokov's obvious satire here is intended to remove the allegation of his having a conventional moral purpose. Other accusations are handled within the text itself. In addition to conventional moralists, Nabokov detests psychiatrists and literary critics, and it is against these types of readers—or these metaphors for the Reader—that Humbert wages constant war. Anti-Freudianism is one of Nabokov's pet themes, and Humbert is a man who, in his periodic vacations in insane asylums, loves nothing more than to take on a psychiatrist in a battle of wits. His chief defense against a psychoanalytic interpretation of *Lolita* is to admit it readily and dismiss it as trite and unhelpful. When he describes his gun, he says, "We must remember that a pistol is the Freudian symbol of the Urfather's central forelimb"; Humbert beats the analysts to the draw and says, in effect, "So what?" At another point, he anticipates a Freudian prediction that he will try to complete his fantasy by having intercourse with Lolita on a beach. Of course he tried, Humbert says; in fact, he went out of his way to look for a suitable beach, not in the grip of unconscious forces but in "rational pursuit of a purely theoretical thrill"; and when he found his beach, it was so damp, stony, and uncomfortable that "for the first time in my life I had as little desire for her as for a manatee."

Ultimately, we have to understand Nabokov's anti-Freudianism in the context of a hatred for allegory and symbolism in general. In *Ada,* Van Veen says of two objects that both "are real, they are not interchangeable, not tokens of something else." Nabokov is against interpretation; an image has no depth, nothing beneath or behind or beyond; it is itself. Discussing Hieronymus Bosch, Van tells us, "I mean I don't give a hoot for the esoteric meaning, for the myth behind the moth, for the masterpiece-baiter who makes Bosch express some bosh of his time, I'm allergic to allegory and am quite sure he was just enjoying himself by crossbreeding casual fancies just for the fun of the contour and color." Another of Nabokov's heroes, Cincinnatus in *Invitation to a Beheading,* is a man whose mortal crime is to be opaque, or inexplicable, while everyone else is transparent. To be inexplicable is to be unrelatable to anything else; Humbert refers to the "standardized symbols" of psychoanalysis, and Hermann, a bad literary critic, points out a resemblance that nobody else can see. Nabokov's hero-villains are often allegorists, like Humbert, who imposes his fantasy of Annabel Leigh on Lolita and turns her into a symbol of his monomania.

Allegory, as Angus Fletcher has shown, is daimonic and compulsive; it is a spell, enchanted discourse. Nabokov, on the contrary, tries to create structures that defy interpretation and transcend the reader's allegorism, Freudian or otherwise; like Mallarmé, he dreams of a literature that will be allegorical only of itself. Thus, Humbert evades our attempts to explain him according to prior codes or assumptions. First of all, he insists that women find his "gloomy good looks" irresistible; therefore, we can't pigeonhole him as someone forced into perversion by his inability to attract adult women. Then, too, Lolita is not "the fragile child of a feminine novel" but a child vamp, who, furthermore, is not a virgin and who, even further, Humbert claims, actually seduces him—a claim that is at least arguable. And finally, when we are forced to compare Humbert to Quilty, a sick, decadent, and cynical man, a man who is immune to enchantment, it becomes impossible simply to categorize Humbert as a pervert like all others. In all these ways, Humbert is not only made to look better than he otherwise would; he is also made difficult to explain and classify, and his uniqueness is a crucial theme of his defense. In *Ada,* Van Veen acclaims the "individual vagaries" without which "no art and no genius would exist." In *Despair,* Hermann the Marxist longs for the "ideal sameness" of a classless society, where one person is replaceable by another, while his rival, the artist Ardalion, believes that "every face is unique." In fact, even Hermann admits that his double resembles him only in sleep or death; vitality is individuation. It is a favorite theme of Nabokov. We are told in *Pnin* that schools of art do not count and that "Genius is non-conformity." The author himself always hates being compared to other writers: "Spiritual affinities have no place in my concept of literary criticism," he has said. In light of this, it is worth noting that the alienation and linguistic eccentricity of a character like Pnin are, in addition to being poignant and comical, the valuable signs of his singularity. Whatever else they are, heroes like Pnin, Humbert, and Kinbote are recognizable; they are rare birds. Humbert tells us that he is even singular physiologically in that he has the faculty of shedding tears during orgasm.

Humbert's chief line of defense is that he is no "brutal scoundrel" but a poet. Nympholepsy is aesthetic as well as sexual; the nymphet in the child is perceived by the mind. Humbert does not wish merely to tell us about sex, which anyone can do; he wants "to fix once for all the perilous magic of nymphets"; he wants to fix the borderline between "the beastly and beautiful" in nymphet love. He calls himself "an artist and a madman, a creature of infinite melancholy"; he is an explorer of that special romantic domain of sensation, the feeling of being in paradise and hell simultaneously; and he is a sentimentalist who revokes the anti-romantic bias of modernism in a sentimental parody of Eliot's "Ash Wednesday." The problem is that in portraying himself as a romantic dreamer and enchanted poet, rather than as a brutal scoundrel, he leaves himself open to another charge: literary banality. He recognizes his position as a spokesman for values that no one takes seriously anymore and says that his judges will regard his lyrical outbursts and rhapsodic interpretations as "mummery," so much hot air to glorify his perversion. His nymphet, on the other hand, is at best bored by his mummery, and the two often operate as a vaudeville team. . . . (pp. 174-77)

Humbert fears Lolita's "accusation of mawkishness," and his madcap and mocking humor defends him against any such accusation by the reader. So too does the presence of Charlotte, a trite sentimentalist whose mode of expression he mocks and against which his own appears unimpeachable. Yet he says, "Oh, let me be mawkish for the nonce. I am so tired of being cynical."

If the book's central rhetorical figure is prolepsis, its central structural figure is displacement, or incongruity. Often cultural or geographical, incongruity appears in such local details as Charlotte's calling her patio a "piazza" and speaking French with an American accent; but more generally it appears in Humbert's old-world, Euro-

pean manner—aristocratic, starchy, and genteel—set in a brassy America of motels and movie magazines, and in his formal, elegant style of speaking posed against Lolita's slang. But Humbert is not only out of place; he is also out of time, since he is still pursuing the ghost of that long-lost summer with Annabel Leigh. The incongruity is also erotic, in the sexual pairing of a child and an adult, and, in the application of romantic rhetoric to child-molesting, it appears as a problematic relation between word and thing. The geographical, linguistic, and temporal aspects of Humbert's dislocation are often related to Nabokov's own exile; but I wish to emphasize here another primal displacement, Humbert's status as a nineteenth-century hero out of his age. In this literary dislocation, a romantic style is placed in a setting in which it must appear alien and incongruous. Humbert's problem is to defend his romanticism in a de-idealizing, debunking, demythologizing time. (pp. 177-78)

Humbert, in his displaced and belated romanticism, must prove that he is not an imitation. Nabokov's use throughout his work of various doubles, mirrors, anti-worlds, and reflections has been much documented and explored. His heroes are typically set in a matrix of doubleness: the condemned man Cincinnatus in *Invitation to a Beheading,* for example, is doubled both by his secret inner self—his freedom or his imagination—and by his executioner. Among its many functions, the double serves as a second-order reality, or parody. The double Quilty parodies Humbert who parodies Edgar Allan Poe. Humbert is referred to many times as an ape, and an ape is not only a beast but an imitator. Nabokov has written that the inspiration of *Lolita* was a story of an ape who, when taught to draw, produced a picture of the bars of his cage. So Humbert, the ape, the parody, gives us a picture of his emotional and moral imprisonment and enchantment. To be free is to be original, not to be a parody.

"I am writing under observation," says the jailed Humbert. Once upon a time, observers walked out of the sea to destroy the best moment of his life; before their arrival, he and Annabel had "somebody's lost pair of sunglasses for only witness." Fear of discovery is Humbert's constant anxiety; he feels that he lives in a "lighted house of glass." The observer, the jury, the brother in the mirror represent the reader and also the self-consciousness of the writer. Robert Alter has pointed out in his excellent study *Partial Magic* that an entire tradition of the "self-conscious novel," stemming from *Don Quixote,* employs a "proliferation of doubles" and mirror-images to present a fiction's awareness of itself as fiction and to speculate on the relation between fiction and reality. *Lolita* certainly participates in this tradition, but the sense of time expressed by its displacements and its literary allusions suggests that we understand its self-consciousness as specifically historical. . . . Humbert's jury is the literary past, which sits in judgment over his story. Humbert is both a mad criminal and a gentleman with an "inherent sense of the *comme il faut*"; self-consciousness figures here as the gentleman in the artist, his taste or critical faculty, his estimation of what he can get away with without being condemned as an imitator, a sentimentalist, or an absurdly displaced romantic.

What is on trial, then, is Humbert's uniqueness and originality, his success in an imaginative enterprise. To what judgment of him does the book force us? Quilty is the embodiment of his limitations and his final failure. He first appears to Humbert in the hotel where the affair is consummated; thus as soon as the affair begins in actuality, Humbert splits in two; and later, practicing to kill Quilty, he uses his own sweater for target practice. Described as the American Maeterlinck, Quilty is a *fin-de-siècle* decadent and thus the final, weak form of Humbert's romanticism; his plays reduce the themes of the novel to the sentimental and the banal: the message of one of them is that "mirage and reality merge in love." Quilty, who is worshipped by Lolita and who couldn't care less about her, incarnates the ironies of Humbert's quest: to possess is to be possessed; to hunt is to be hunted. In addition, to be a parody, as Humbert is of a romantic Quester, is to be defeated by doubleness: Quilty is an ape who calls Humbert an ape.

In relation to Lolita, Humbert accepts complete guilt. The end of the book is filled with outbursts against himself for depriving her of her childhood. A poet and a lover of beauty, he finishes as a destroyer of beauty. At one point, learning how to shoot, Humbert admires the marksmanship of John Farlow, who hits a hummingbird, although "not much of it could be retrieved for proof—only a little iridescent fluff"; the incident aptly characterizes Humbert's actual relationship to his own ideal. At the end, he recognizes that "even the most miserable of family lives was better than the parody of incest, which, in the long run, was the best I could offer the waif." All he can achieve is parody. When he calls himself a poet, the point is not that he's shamming but that he fails. Authenticity eludes him, and he loses out to history. What he accomplishes is solipsism, a destructive caricature of uniqueness and originality, and he succeeds in creating only a renewed sense of loss wherever he turns: of his first voyage across America with Lolita, he says: "We had been everywhere. We had really seen nothing. And I catch myself thinking today that our long journey had only defiled with a sinuous trail of slime the lovely, trustful, dreamy, enormous country. . . . "

Humbert is finally apprehended driving down the wrong side of the road, "that queer mirror side." This is his last dislocation and is symbolic of all of them. We can now address one further form of displacement in Humbert's quest, the displacement of the imagination into reality. The mirror side of the road is fantasy, and Humbert has crossed over. Lolita was a mental image, which Humbert translated into actuality and in so doing destroyed her life and his; but his guilt is to know that she has a reality apart from his fantasy. (pp. 178-80)

[At] the end, Humbert—who was a failed artist early in his career, who tried to translate art into life and again failed, and who then turned a third time to art, now as a refuge, a sad compensation, and a "very local palliative"—sees art as a way to "the only immortality" he and Lolita may share. Having in effect destroyed her, he now wants to make her "live in the minds of later generations." A new idea of art does begin for him in his own imaginative failures. Then, too, he now claims to love Lolita just

as she is, no longer a nymphet and now possessing an identity, dim and gray as it may be, that is separate from his private mythology. (p. 180)

At this point I wish to turn from Humbert's engagement with the parodic and the romantic to Nabokov's, and I will begin with several points about parody in general. Parody is representation of representation, a confrontation with a prior text or type of text. The mood of the confrontation varies with the instance. We can have parody for its own sake; for example, in the *Times Literary Supplement,* Gawain Ewart translated an obscene limerick into two prose passages, one in the style of the *Oxford English Dictionary,* the second in the style of Dr. Johnson's dictionary. Then we can have parody for the purpose of critique—satirical parody. . . . *Lolita* includes examples of both types: for instance, the roster of Lolita's class with its delightful names (Stella Fantazia, Vivian McCrystal, Oleg Sherva, Edgar Talbot, Edwin Talbot . . .) and the Beardsley headmistress' spiel about her progressive school ("We stress the four D's: Dramatics, Dance, Debating and Dating"). But as a whole the novel participates in a third type, parody that seeks its own originality, what Robert Alter would call metaparody: parody that moves through and beyond parody.

When Alter calls parody "the literary mode that fuses creation with critique," he is saying something that is strictly true only of satirical parody. What is common to all three types is that they fuse creation with differentiation. Parodists use a voice different from their own in such a way as to call attention to themselves. Parody is at once an impersonation and an affirmation of identity, both an identification with and a detachment from the other. This sense of displaced recognition, this incongruous simultaneity of closeness and distance, is a primary source of the delight and humor of parody, although it should be noted that parody is not inevitably comic, as in the case of John Fowles's *The French Lieutenant's Woman,* for example. Some parody, such as Stephen's, emphasizes the distance, but we also need to remember John Ashbery's idea of parody to "revitalize some way of expression that might have fallen into disrepute." It may be true that some aggression is inherent in all parody, no matter how loving, but it is an aggression that is more primal than intellectual critique: it is the kind of aggression that says, "This is me. This is mine."

[In his introduction to *The Portable Nabokov*] Page Stegner has said that Nabokov uses parody to get rid of the stock and conventional, and Alfred Appel, Jr., that he uses parody and self-parody to exorcise the trite and "to re-investigate the fundamental problems of his art." I think it is finally more accurate to say that he uses parody to evade the accusation of triteness and to elude the literary past in the hope of achieving singularity. Nabokov's parodism is an attempt to control literary relations, a way of telling his jury that he already knows how his book is related to prior work. More than that, it is a way of taking possession of the literary past, of internalizing it. Nabokov has repeatedly noted and critics . . . have often stressed the idea that he writes in a borrowed language. But in his difficult condition of personal and linguistic exile, Nabokov also points to another, more general kind of displacement. Irving Massey has suggested [in *The Gaping Pig: Literature and Metamorphosis*] that many works of literature deal with the problem that "*parole* is never ours," that we all speak a borrowed idiom in expressing ourselves in the public medium of language. It is also relevant that a writer inevitably speaks in the borrowed language of literary convention. Like so many other writers of the nineteenth and twentieth centuries, Nabokov dreams of detaching his representation from the history of representations, of creating a *parole* that transcends *langue*.

In relation to romance, parody acts in *Lolita* in a defensive and proleptic way. It doesn't criticize the romance mode, although it criticizes Humbert; it renders romance acceptable by anticipating our mockery and beating us to the draw. . . . [I am suggesting] that *Lolita* can only be a love story through being a parody of love stories. The most valuable insight about *Lolita* that I know is John Hollander's idea of the book [in his "The Perilous Magic of Nymphets"] as a "record of Mr. Nabokov's love-affair with the romantic novel, a today-unattainable literary object as short-lived of beauty as it is long of memory." I would add that parody is Nabokov's way of getting as close to the romantic novel as possible and, more, that he actually does succeed in re-creating it in a new form, one that is contemporary and original, not anachronistic and imitative. Further, it is the book's triumph that it avoids simply re-creating the romantic novel in its old form; for Nabokov to do so would be to lose his own personal, twentieth-century identity. (pp. 181-82)

We might say that Nabokov must kill off a bad romantic and a bad artist in Humbert in order for his own brand of enchantment to exist. Nabokov's recurrent fascinations are romantic ones; he writes about passion, Arcadia, memory, individualism, the ephemeral, the enchanted, imagination, and the power of art. Indeed, his problem in *Lolita* is essentially the same as Humbert's: first, to be a romantic and still be original, and, second, to get away with being a romantic. *Lolita* has been taken as a critique of romanticism, and I am not arguing that it should be read as a romantic work. Rather, in its final form it is a work of complex relationship to romanticism, a dialectic of identification and differentiation. Like Byron in *Don Juan*, Nabokov in *Lolita* is divided against himself, although in a different way: Byron is a poet struggling against his own romantic temperament, while in Nabokov we see a romantic temperament trying to achieve a perilous balance in an unfriendly setting. But the results do illuminate each other: in *Don Juan* a romantic lyricism and melancholy are achieved through mocking parody and farce; in somewhat similar fashion, Nabokov uses the energies of his style—its parody, its centering of language, its flamboyant self-consciousness—first against the spirit of romance and then in behalf of it. This, then, is the status of style in *Lolita*, and this is why style is elevated to such prominence; perhaps this is even why it must be a comic style: it functions as a defensive strategy both against the romanticism of the material and against the anti-romanticism of the "jury." (p. 184)

*Thomas R. Frosch, "Parody and Authenticity in 'Lolita'," in* Nabokov's Fifth Arc: Nabokov

and Others on His Life's Work, *edited by J. E. Rivers and Charles Nicol, University of Texas Press, 1982, pp. 171-87.*

## Margaret Morganroth Gullette

Pedophilia is a curious phenomenon of twentieth-century fiction. . . . Writers use the subject as an indirect but powerful way of dealing with anxieties about the life course. Pedophilia represents in an extreme form a normal problem of human development, the transition from latency to accepting adult sexuality and therefore aging. Behind every story of pedophilia is a drama of normal human regret at growing older in the body, distorted by the protagonist's illusory attempt to circumvent his aging in *this* particular way, by trying to possess youth vicariously through the bodies of the young.

These stories of adult sexual longing for children—and the inevitable punishment it entails—are the darkest of the dark stories that can be written about the life course. These darkest stories tell us that the one unavoidable process that we all undergo—aging—consists simultaneously of a crime and a punishment. Let it be said at once that many midlife fictions take the opposing view: Bildungsromane of the middle years (beginning with the *Odyssey*) continue the progressive ideology of Bildungsromane of youth, promising a future containing increased knowledge, freedom, security, love, or some combination of similar appreciations. Time is on our side. The decline story, on the other hand, shows us a character dreading the future—dreading "the beast in the jungle," in Henry James's metaphor. And the next worst case, along this psychological spectrum of despair, is the story in which the protagonist is shown as idolizing some time in his or her past. Dread of the future depends on adoration of the past. In a decline story, typically, some earlier point in the life course (childhood or youth) is described lyrically; the middle-aged present, harshly, realistically, with detachment that is often ironic.

Both pre-adult stages are viewed with value-laden tones of longing and nostalgia. What adolescence has in common with childhood in this view is that both are fundamentally innocent ages. The decline writer likes to linger over the timid recessive period where affection still stands back from sex and can be approved for doing so. We could call this the idealization of latency. The latency period in a novel like *Brideshead Revisited* does not have the narrow chronological limits Freud set to it. In some inner sense that has nothing to do with technical virginity, characters in decline novels can be latent into their twenties and be praised or envied by their authors for this. No doubt many readers of *Brideshead* would find Freud unforgiving or mistaken in his belief that people need to move forward more rapidly into adulthood. To them, latency is safe, charming, and incorrupt. In twentieth-century fiction, it often remains the "lost paradise" (as Proust explicitly called it) that characters contrast with the misery of the middle years.

Of all post-Rousseau ideas of childhood, the writer who tells a decline story needs above all the belief that children have a special, lovable inner life that adults cannot share. A writer's belief in the sacredness of childhood does not require than an individual child be ideal. Lolita certainty is not. Nevertheless, the secret or profound truth turns out to be the specialness of the child's mind. Borrowing enclosure imagery from Proust, Nabokov provides Humbert Humbert with one of his rare intuitions of Lolita's grave, intense subjective life:

> and it struck me, as my automaton knees went up and down, that I simply did not know a thing about my darling's mind and that quite possibly, behind the awful juvenile clichés, there was in her a garden and a twilight, and a palace gate— dim and adorable regions which happened to be lucidly and absolutely forbidden to me, in my polluted rags and miserable convulsions.

The main point of this passage is that an adult discovers the value of a child at the same time that he discovers how inaccessible the child is. Although the magic inner world has a gate—Nabokov sees children as naturally trusting and confiding—the adult is locked out. Because of the "miserable convulsions" of sexuality, he is polluted. However the decline novelist defines adulthood, the decline story's idea of an adult is of someone irrevocably sundered from the paradise of childhood. (pp. 215-17)

The greatest difference—the one that decline stories rely on—is that between the innocence of children and the wrongness of adult sexuality. It is because children are believed to be "pure" that Humbert speaks understandably of his passion as "foul lust" and "hot poison," why he describes his dreams as "pollutive" even before we know what effect his enactment of his dreams will have on Lolita's life. (pp. 219-20)

No decline story—and, *a fortiori*, no account of pedophilia—is complete unless it includes distasteful physical images of mature, aging bodies. In . . . Nabokov, the middle-aged protagonist looks with disgust at other bodies that show signs of age. . . . [Humbert also] loathes his own body, a loathing which he projects onto adult women. Charlotte Haze, his second wife, takes the brunt of Humbert's disgust as "that sorry and dull thing: a handsome woman," with her "heavy hips, round knees, ripe bust, the coarse pink skin of her neck." In fact, Humbert dislikes all mature women: Jean "was a long-limbed girl in harlequin glasses, with two boxer dogs, two pointed breasts and a big red mouth." It bothers him that he is particularly attractive to such women. To him they are "the coffin of coarse female flesh within which my nymphets are buried alive." Aging is already a kind of death.

The fact that these women are attracted to him is an unpleasant reminder that he is their appropriate partner. . . . In *Lolita,* all manifestations of sexuality on the part of adult women, even the most natural, are repulsive. "When I had done such a simple thing as kiss her, [Charlotte] had awakened at once, as fresh and strong as an octopus (I barely escaped)." This is humorous only as long as we accept Humbert's view that Charlotte is personally repulsive; indeed, the early comedy of his loving nymphets derives in part from the unexpectedness of his response to

normal adult sexuality. At first, this is only strange and funny.

Intercourse with women is grotesque in part because being adult sized is itself a grotesque thing. "I am ready to believe that the sensations I derived from natural fornication were much the same as those known to normal big males consorting with their normal big mates in that routine rhythm which shakes the world," Humbert says when he's trying to sound normal. Although a big man himself, he hates bigness—which is after all what being "grownup" basically means. His "massive nakedness" against "the cool feel of armchair leather" is another unpleasant item in a scene calculated to show him at his most depraved. His sexuality he sees in the same hyperbolic, grotesque way, as an "engorgement." He owns, or is, a "gagged bursting beast." His sexual urge is presented as almost constant, and his insatiability overcoming his tenderness is the sign of his immense cruelty to Lolita, making each intercourse with her a form of rape.

All the signs of post-pubertal development, the pedophile sees as unnatural. Adults smell. When Humbert wants to castigate himself most, he describes himself as a "heavy-limbed, foul-smelling adult," who "had had strenuous intercourse three times that very morning." . . . Hairiness is unpleasant, of course, as a sign of adult sexuality. Humbert describes the adult woman who will satisfy his lust momentarily as "an animated merkin." Himself too he describes derogatorily in terms of hair: "But instead I am lanky, big-boned wooly-chested Humbert Humbert, with thick black eyebrows. . . . " We may not realize how awful his hairiness is to him, as a sign of exile from ideal beauty, until, just before he goes to meet Lolita for the last time, he tells us that he "shaved [his] face and chest." All grownup characteristics—over-sized frame, hairiness, smell—are unnatural to the soul that feels itself to be essentially childlike, punished by being buried in "my adult disguise."

No one until Nabokov, or to my knowledge, since, has fixed this amazing malaise so completely, although many decline stories of a milder type are filled with disgust at the failings of the adult body: rotting teeth are a cliché of the genre. (pp. 221-23)

[Humbert is also] presented as vain, a studied dresser. The decline figure, if female, is often something of a clothes-horse; if male, something of a dandy. Vanity in dress and appearance is the overt sign of resistance to aging, of the adult longing to be not merely attractive, but young and attractive. In a midlife Bildungsroman, this resistance would be a good sign: it would be all that was needed to make the protagonist attractive again. In a decline novel, vanity never succeeds, and never can, because adulthood is inescapably ugly, and sexuality in older people can never charm. Their vanity only underlines their hopeless situation, the innate uncontrollable condition of locating love and beauty only outside the self, in unattainable youth.

Adolescents in these decline stories are physically desirable and basically asexual, beautiful and indifferent. This combination is necessary in all its features: it produces the pedophile's ideal type. . . . [Humbert's Lolita is] slender, delicate, childlike, almost or entirely hairless, and beautiful: the opposite of adult, in short. . . . Humbert's nymphets are all ladlike, hipless: of Lolita, he notices "her bi-iliac garland [is] as brief as a lad's." In playing tennis, she . . . reveals "a pristine armpit." (pp. 223-24)

Unlike forward, heavy-breathing adults, insistent and possessive, the children as shown are self-contained. . . . Far from seeming to seek the embrace of adults, they shun physical contact with them. Although Lolita had intercourse daily in summer camp, her mechanical encounters with Charlie are treated comically, as external events that left her core untouched. Although very early on she had a crush on Humbert, her hard kiss is, he knows, "a bit of back-fisch [sic] foolery in imitation of some simulacrum of fake romance." She is never physically aroused by him; on the contrary. "She had entered my world, umber and black Humberland, with rash curiosity; she surveyed it with a shrug of amused distaste, and it seemed to me now that she was ready to turn away from it with something akin to plain repulsion. Never did she vibrate under my touch, and a strident 'what d'you think you are doing' was all I got for my pains." Lolita "seduces" Humbert Humbert, not out of any vulgar adult desire for intercourse, but out of childish "curiosity."

Although it would seem to be against their interests, pedophiles admire the coolness that adolescents possess by dint of being still in the pre-sexual, narcissistic stage. . . . Lolita's rejection acts as an aphrodisiac on Humbert, as we are reminded perhaps too often. The only mature women whom Humbert can bring himself to desire are those whose situation also makes them indifferent to sex: prostitutes and a kind drunk like Rita, who gives herself "out of sheer chumminess and compassion," not avidity. Miserable about his own adult avidity, the pedophile sees the asexuality of children not as a stage toward adult life, but as a desirable condition in itself. In the Bildungsroman, latency is neither permanent nor idealized. When D. H. Lawrence is most understanding of the character of Miriam in *Sons and Lovers,* for example, he explains her unhappiness with Paul as a lover as a necessary stage in her development, eventually to be superseded by normal desire. Desire, for the pedophile, is yet another curse that comes with adulthood. Humbert says as much in calling his erotic love for Annabel a "premature love, marked by a fierceness that so often destroys adult lives."

Making Humbert a man who is imprisoned in his aging skin was one of Nabokov's most subtle and brilliant inventions in *Lolita.* In representing Humbert's anguished sense of time passing (which might have been more ordinary material), the story of a pedophile offered him dazzling opportunities for hyperbole. Pedophilia, in his version of it, exaggerates the normal dislike of aging, the normal anxicty over the passage of time. Time is a greater enemy for this kind of midlife exile because nymphets pass so quickly out of the magic age. The pedophile—like all decline figures, only more so—never has any hope from the life course or any optimism about time passing. He wants time to stop. Actually, he would prefer to roll it backwards, as children believe they can do: Nabokov dowers Lolita as

a younger child with a happy belief in *reversible* time. " 'Oh look, all the nines are changing into the next thousand,' " she says about the odometer, a nice mechanical symbol of time passing; " 'when I was a little kid,' she continued unexpectedly, 'I used to think they'd stop and go back to nines, if only my mother agreed to put the car in reverse'." Rolling time backwards should seem as silly to Humbert as it does to Lolita. But falling in love with her gives him the psychic illusion, at least momentarily, that he has magically regained his lost past. "The twenty-five years that I had lived since then [since Annabel], tapered to a palpitating point, and vanished." In Humbert's perilous image, the lucky pedophile lives on an island of time. "I would have the reader see 'nine' and 'fourteen' as the boundaries—the mirrory beaches and rosy rocks—of an enchanted island." He has moments of intense fantasy about temporal impossibilities. "Ah, leave me alone in my pubescent park, in my mossy garden. Let them play around me forever. Never grow up."

In teaching us about his "island" early in the novel, the learned lecturer sounds unconcerned about the age limit ("fourteen") that is the end of his happiness. But children do grow up. It is the laws of time and nature that the pedophile tries to tamper with: all the dangers of this attempt gradually darken the story. As Humbert's passion becomes more intense and equivocal, it loses its character as a comic oddity. A normal event in family life—a child's going off to camp, which may be mildly fraught for any parent as a marker of time passing—is for Humbert disastrous. When Charlotte drives Lolita off to camp, he says portentously, "The motion of fate was resumed." He is doomed by time as no one else in literature has been. (pp. 224-26)

To himself, Humbert is a pathetic figure, victim, inevitable loser; to us, at this point, he's a parody as father or lover. Nabokov makes sure we see something vicious as well as ridiculous in Humbert's fear of Lolita's aging: he weighs and measures her so often not as a father would, but because he worries about her getting too tall, too heavy, too muscular. His worry (until he loses her) is pure egotism: he will lose a desirable object. As ex-nymphet, she will be disposable; the only problem he anticipates is having to decide "what to do with my little concubine who was now sixty inches tall and weighed ninety pounds." At his moral nadir, his wit is not meant to be cute. His most implausible fantasy is of using her as a breeder for future Lolitas. The crime that Humbert doesn't yet know he's committing—depriving Lolita of her childhood—he here blithely anticipates committing on two other generations of children who are even more his own. Among other normal emotions that Nabokov counts on in his readers is the sense that all the years of childhood are valuable, not just the years between nine and fourteen, and of course that all these years are valuable in themselves, not for the ways we as adults can exploit them. In case some reader freakishly refuses to recognize this, Nabokov brings in a normal adult at the end, a man who can envelop "his lumpy and large offspring" "with a casual arm." All literature refers in some ways, usually tacit, to assumptions about "normalcy," but *Lolita* hauls these up on every page. The ghost of normal father-daughter relationships—much more than the ghost of mature male-female relationships (*no* example of which is provided in the story)—hovers over the whole novel, to aggravate the reader's sense of discomfort.

It is Humbert's callousness toward the growing child (shown as becoming uglier, pimply), as well as his anger at losing her last precious years because she runs away, that keep latent in readers the idea that he is on trial for having murdered Lolita. (All the students in my 1982 course on "The Literature of the Middle Years of Life" thought she was the likeliest candidate.) Nabokov reminds us that the "three empty years" after she leaves him are dreadful to Humbert because time is passing: "the general impression I desire to convey is of a side door crashing open in life's full flight, and a rush of roaring black time drowning with its whipping wind the cry of lone disaster," he declaims melodramatically. When he gets her letter and wordlessly starts the fourth long trip he has made on her account, Nabokov is still building suspense about his intentions. Humbert has asserted that his plan is to kill her supposed "kidnapper," but we have reason to fear what his reactions might be to an older, married, pregnant woman. References to his revenge in the chapters that describe the years she is gone are carefully ambiguous. "But not for a second did I forget the load of revenge," he boasts. Hints of murder are placed in teasing locations: the lake in front of the Enchanted Hunters motel, where they spent their first night, is described as a "blood bath" in one of Humbert's poems. What Nabokov details in chapters 25 and 26 is supposed to be the despair of love, but love of that kind is not incompatible with revenge. The fact that Humbert gets into his car without comment after the words "Yours expecting," suggests the worst.

For this novel of pedophilia to end properly, Lolita has to be "frankly and hugely pregnant" at the end: she has to be, from the point of view of the true pedophile, an object of revulsion. Pregnancy, of course, is the absolute termination of nymphage. Not only is the perfect body of childhood deformed, but it is deformed by the one unmistakable sign that a female child has moved off the enchanted island of timelessness and into the irreversible time of the life course. Her looks are "ruined." Her head "looked smaller" because her female body with child is so much bigger. She looks "womanish." She is hairy: "her bare shins and arms had lost all their tan, so that the little hairs showed." She is a "couple of inches taller"—the height he had feared her reaching. She wears glasses (a sign, like rotting teeth, of the wear and tear of aging). As late as this, Nabokov maintains suspense: "The death I had kept conjuring up for three years was as simple as a bit of dried wood," Humbert states when he sees her. This death that he had been "conjuring up" he again implies was her murder at his hands, rather than the death of her nymph-childhood. To make our subliminal suspense even greater, Humbert is presented at his most vain and dandified, his most preserved-from-time. Just before this meeting is when he has shaved his face and chest.

> Then, with the stern and romantic care of a gentleman about to fight a duel, I checked the arrangement of my papers, bathed and perfumed my delicate body, shaved my face and chest, se-

lected a silk shirt and clean drawers, pulled on transparent taupe socks, and congratulated myself for having with me in my trunks some very exquisite clothes. . . .

Elegance of this elaborate, female kind is now revealed as a sign not of resistance to aging, but of feeling hopelessly aged: "I sat quite still in my old car, old and frail, at the end of my journey, at my gray goal, *finis*, my friends, *finis*, my friends."

Humbert's meeting with Lolita in these carefully prepared circumstances is the crux of the novel, the recognition scene, the scene of reversal, the scene of cure. Two things simultaneously end: her nymphage and his pedophilia. And they end, to our surprise, but as they must, together.

When Humbert sees her pregnant, he wins his salvation (and earns our forgiveness) by discovering that he loves Lolita despite the violence of time and procreation that she should represent to him, and therefore that he cannot kill her. This is where his story, as a love story, begins. "I could not kill *her*, of course, as some have thought. You see, I loved her. It was love at first sight, at last sight, at ever and ever sight." In the long rhapsodic parataxic passage that follows, he catalogues her physical decay as emphatically and completely and lovingly as he had once catalogued her nubility: "and there she was with her ruined looks and her adult, rope-veined narrow hands and her gooseflesh white arms, and her shallow ears, and her unkempt armpits, there she was (my Lolita!) hopelessly worn at seventeen. . . . " Even the idea of her bearing a child, with its alienating physical consequences ("her lovely young velvety delicate delta . . . tainted and torn") cannot diminish his love. "Even then I would go mad with tenderness at the mere sight of your dear wan face." For the reader, his lyricism here begins to undo all prior grotesque images of female maturity. It also undoes the praise of nympholepsy, as much as one bittersweet rhapsody can undo a whole volume of adoration of latency. On the verbal level, the lyricism of love is the cure for cool wit, melodramatic self-pity, and self-conscious verbal gamesmanship.

So far as we have let ourselves become complicit victims of Humbert's image of female maturity, more is required to rescue us than lyricism about Lolita as an individual woman. The goddess of love, patroness of adult sexuality, has to be transformed into an appealing figure. This change too is mediated by the adult Lolita. "I definitely realized, so hopelessly late in the day, how much she looked—had always looked—like Botticelli's russet Venus, the same soft nose, the same blurred beauty. In my pocket my fingers gently let go and repacked a little at the tip, within the handkerchief it was nested in, my unused weapon." If Nabokov here revives an old hint that Humbert's organ is an instrument of death, he also suggests that Humbert, now relaxed by loving truly (or aged into post-menopausal onanism), relinquishes his fierce sexuality. Humbert transfers the ferocity to Quilty, whom he wishes to see not as a double, (another hairy, horny male seducer of nymphets), but as an opposite, because he represents infidelity to Lolita. Although no longer a pedophile, Humbert is not yet completely cured: he can be considered so when, on the last page, he imaginatively restores Lolita to the childhood chorus from which he had ravished her. When Humbert murders Quilty even though he has relinquished Lolita, we are supposed to recognize Nabokov's idea that adult sexuality, even in its "normal" mode, is dangerous, possessive, and vengeful.

What would earlier seem incompatible images come together in the scene of cure, both verbally and iconically, with redemptive effect. Lolita becomes "my fall nymph." "She was only the faint violet whiff and dead leaf echo of the nymphet I had rolled myself upon . . . but thank God it was not that echo alone that I worshiped." Autumnal imagery belongs to the middle years; by appropriating it for Lolita (somewhat prematurely, we may observe), Humbert makes a little peace with the life course. Nabokov—achieving something almost as hard for him—admits to his text necessary clichés of emotion. "And presently I was driving through the drizzle of the dying day, with the windshield wipers in full action but unable to cope with my tears." A murderer may have a "fancy" prose style, but a lover has a simple and to some extent banal one. So much was hinted earlier, just before the brief chapter in which Humbert orders the printer to fill up a page with her name: "Oh let me be mawkish for the nonce! I am so tired of being cynical." Humbert's habitual voice (the voice that Nabokov treats so often with ironic detachment because it is so dispassionate) is given a context in which it is to be read as a mask. Humbert's more sentimental style (given us, to be sure, only in small doses) is intended to be human, guilt-ridden, and a relief.

Likeness reconciles; unlikeness divides. Lolita, having made Venus attractive, can now redeem the figure of Charlotte too. Humbert's wife is transformed by a little of the mist/cloud imagery that has formerly been reserved for her daughter. When Lolita pregnant smokes, "Gracefully, in a blue mist, Charlotte Haze rose from her grave." This transformation of Charlotte was prepared for in an earlier passage in which mother and daughter are likened to each other: "Behind the brashness of little Haze, and the poise of big Haze, a trickle of shy life ran that tasted the same, that murmured the same." This is only one of a number of hints that Nabokov has placed that Humbert will be cured, and that the narrator of the story is not the same man who perpetrated it: "adult Lotte loved me with a mature, possessive passion that I now deplore and respect more than I care to say." "Oh, my poor Charlotte, do not hate me in your eternal heaven . . . " he has prayed.

After he sees Lolita pregnant, the signs of Humbert's pedophilia fall from him, starting with dandyism. He forgets to change his clothes, bathe, shave. "I became aware of my mud-caked dungarees, my filthy and torn sweater, my bristly chin, my bum's bloodshot eyes." In prison, he grows a beard. And with such final signs of his immersion in the life course, he is able to feel for the first time—most important of all signs of cure—the full weight of his guilt. . . . Cured of lust and resigned to putrefaction, he can belatedly learn what he should have known before (from her tears, every night), but wouldn't recognize, that she too had a public voice ("trite brashness"), which was the cover of her vulnerability and precious innerness ("a garden and a twilight and a palace gate"). In many Bildungsromane, learning comes late in the story. In this novel, learning comes too late to save Humbert from crime and remorse.

*Lolita* is central to a chapter on decline motifs, because—despite Humbert's cure—it expresses . . . those elements (regret for lost childhood, pain at being an adult, discomfort about adult sexuality) that are at the root of decline stories. It proliferates with decline elements—privatives of the desirable human condition—as well. It makes Humbert homeless; it gives him "guilty locomotion." . . . Nevertheless, in permitting Humbert a cure, in killing him the way it does—through textual evasiveness and marginality—*Lolita* softens the decline story. It shies away from depriving Humbert of all value. (pp. 226-30)

Elegy is the mode that expresses lost love, and there's no doubt that the protagonists of . . . stories of pedophilia recognize themselves as intense lovers, however guilty they finally feel. . . .

The particular first-person form of Nabokov's tale is the strongest proof of Nabokov's elegiac intention. Humbert has no one to tell his story to—especially the story of his cure—once he has asked Lolita twice to come with him and she has twice refused. For many reasons, foremost among them his fidelity to her, it is not conceivable that any other, more loving, female will ever listen to it. Humbert's final home is a prison, and his audience finally an anonymous, judgmental multitude, us. Indeed, first-person narratives about others (Lord Jim, Gatsby, Lolita) often convey an air of sadness and failure, as if the best listener—the most understanding—were unobtainable, and we, the readers, were a kind of second best. Perhaps the elegy takes its tone from the author's feeling that the right listener for the tale has been irrecoverably lost. Or perhaps—since neither Lolita nor Gatsby nor Jim can be imagined as understanding the story—there never *was* a perfect listener. The elegy makes do with us, because nonetheless the story must be told: someone was cherished too much to be forgotten. Although Nabokov said that he intended only Lolita's story to be "tear-iridized," Humbert's value increases because he tells the story that exposes him so cruelly. The degree of pity that Nabokov extends to his protagonist . . . [is visible in the treatment of his death]. (p. 230)

Nabokov treats Humbert's disease as . . . an episode that lasted twenty-five years, followed by a cure. The length of the episode testifies obliquely to the power of the original dread. But what is permanent in Humbert is his fidelity to Lolita, despite her change. His death makes infidelity impossible: his *cure* cannot be turned into an episode. We cannot imagine *Lolita* ending with Humbert falling in love with some other mature woman. His wanderings—which in midlife novels often represent sexual restlessness—have to be over; so he says goodbye to another wanderer, his car Melmoth. The Bildungsroman outcome—in which Humbert could find a midlife mate—would have seemed ridiculous and banal to Nabokov. The last words of the novel are addressed directly to Lolita (the listener who cannot hear), in the vocative of ultimate fidelity trying to overcome eternal separation. We are not surprised to learn that Nabokov yearned to write what we are calling elegy. "I think that what I would welcome at the close of a book of mine is a sensation of its world receding in the distance and stopping somewhere there suspended." Humbert contrite gets to write this privileged genre. His self-ascription as a poet turns out to be a true claim.

Humbert's death, accordingly, far from being insisted upon—as strict punishment would demand—occurs quietly, classically, off-stage. In fact, we learn it only deductively, because we are holding the book as we read, "Thus, neither of us is alive when the reader opens this book." John Ray's letter told us immediately that Humbert had died of heart disease, but only as a matter of preliminary fact, which we have to relearn at the end as part of the elegiac decline structure. "Heart disease" is transvalued: it may be that it was not the tiger in Humbert, but the suffering lover that overworked his heart to the point of death. This kind of death is a form of pardon. It would not be appropriate either for a tragic figure or for a true decline figure, but it is perfectly suited to a figure rescued from decline by elegiac expiation. (p. 231)

*Margaret Morganroth Gullette, "The Exile of Adulthood: Pedophilia in the Midlife Novel," in* Novel: A Forum on Fiction, *Vol. 17, No. 3, Spring, 1984, pp. 215-32.*

## Richard H. Bullock

The black and umber world of Humberland begins with the words, "Lolita. Light of my life, fire of my loins. My sin, my soul," and a first reading of the novel suggests that the terms "fire of my loins. My sin" summarize the book. This view, though, which makes of the narrator and protagonist Humbert Humbert a faithful recorder of his own evil acts with an overly complicit adolescent, fails because it ignores the text's rococo entanglements of fact and fiction, reality and fantasy, artist and art. Humbert is the narrator and he narrates his own story, but serious problems exist in verifying the facts of his narrative, due to his solipsistic nature and to the closed, circular nature of the story he tells. Moreover, these problems suggest a view of Humbert as an artist who fails in his attempt to "safely solipsize" Lolita, the object of his desires. That Humbert fails in this attempt is obvious. But the Humbert who fails as an artist of the flesh and imagination must not be confused with the Humbert who narrates the novel; the two Humberts must carefully be distinguished if the problems involving their natures, their roles, and their success or failure are to be solved.

Yet, Humbert himself complicates and confuses the search for answers. As the narrator, Humbert is seemingly only superficially believable, a narrator whose word cannot be trusted, his memory being in his words "sensational but incomplete and unorthodox." As long as the novel is seen as a confession, as Humbert recounting his life as it happened, Humbert's reality as protagonist and the truthfulness of all his statements as narrator remain forever unverifiable and problematic. However, Humbert the narrator of the events of Humbert the character's life must not

be regarded as confessor. Rather, he is an artist engaged in the creation of a work of art centered in his own being but existing outside the realm of fact by its nature as art. In other words, the Humbert who performs the actions of the novel, along with Claire Quilty and Lolita herself, must be read as fictions created by a second Humbert, the narrator and novelist.

Humbert the character lives divided in a divided world. A half-English, half-Swiss European living in America, his heritage and location bespeak a divided self, and this cultural split creates conflicts within him, as when on arriving at the Haze house he must repress his desire to leave because of his "old world politeness." In addition, his emotions are capable of expression in two opposing directions simultaneously. When Valeria departs with her Russian, Humbert feels anger, an intense emotion, and boredom, an extreme affectlessness, at once. Humbert's mind thinks in term of divisions, as the consuming passion of his life, "to fix once for all the perilous magic of nymphets," is a search for that point at which "the beastly and beautiful merged." In a sense, Humbert is man's representative in the great chain of being, caught between spirituality and animality and trying to merge them in his own self. But his obsession with divisions and bifurcations goes far beyond that, leading to a radical division between the the world of physical objects and that of mental events.

In childhood the enamored Humbert talked with his Annabel of solipsism, showing an early interest in exclusively mental events, and much of his preferred world is solely mental, especially his world with Lolita. After masturbating against her leg and rendering her "safely solipsized," Hum speaks constantly of "the hermetic vision of her which I had locked in" and replaces Dolores Haze with another, fantastic, imaginative Lolita. Humbert's hermetically sealed mind affects his life in other ways, too. For one thing, his isolation affects his speech, as Lo points out in saying, "You talk like a book, *Dad.*" In other words, Humbert talks as he would write, replacing in his mind his actual audience with a created, semifictional and somewhat indeterminate audience—his oral language is directed at a fiction, not a genuine other. He wonders if his fantasies will affect the girls he uses as subjects, later in their lives, despite their never knowing it. So he posits a mental world of cause and effect in which by thinking one might influence the thoughts or destinies of others, a power available only to the solipsist for whom everyone else is imaginary. In effect, his disease of depravity might be contagious. This contagion does seemingly happen; Valeria, Charlotte, and Lo all die prematurely after being caught up in his "voluptas," Val and Lo dying in childbirth, as if his influence renders them incapable of surviving fruitful union or of producing possible future nymphets—his prey. In the physical world, the references to mirrors, to Our Glass Lake, and to that room at The Enchanted Hunters, among others, all point to a closed, sealed, inwardly-turned universe, and Hum's efforts while in Beardsley, as well as on the road, to keep Lo from seeing anyone are attempts to "safely solipsize" his relationship with her, to make physical reality a function of his own mind. Even more important to the novel are the treatments of mental isolation as a prison of one sort or another. . . . In a very real way, Humbert is even imprisoned in the words of his text and exists only in their context while demanding another mind's assistance to make his life: "I shall not exist if you do not imagine me."

Time as Humbert conceives it also contributes to his closed universe. After Lo deserts him, he writes a scholarly article in which he postulates "a theory of time based on the circulation of the blood and conceptually depending . . . on the mind's being conscious not only of matter but also of its own self, thus creating a continuous spanning of two points (the storable future and the stored past)." Blood circulates in a closed system, and what activates and drives it is the heart. If Humbert's model is valid for him, the physical and emotional disease of his heart (which we know to be fatal) must affect his perceptions, memories, and the interplay of his past and future. (pp. 187-89)

[In] looking at his past he cannot separate fact from fantasy, and he cannot obtain verification of past events, as when he searches for the news photograph of himself in The Enchanted Hunters to find that it shows only a blurred, unidentifiable shoulder. The blood circulating in its closed system will apparently retain fantasies, while facts lose their veracity; when he declares that he has "fallen in love with Lolita forever," he acknowledges that "she would not be forever Lolita . . . The word 'forever' referred only to my own passion, to eternal Lolita as reflected in my blood." Time goes by, people age, circumstances change, but Humbert's mental construct remains, a mythically circular world in which time is abolished and Lolita is ever as she was, "golden and brown, kneeling, looking up, on that shoddy veranda."

This position, as we shall see, is not the novel's final statement, for Humbert at the close of the novel, just before its rebeginning, affirms a nobler sense of love for Lolita and no longer relies on his constructed world of nymphets. Nevertheless, the novel as Humbert the narrator crafts it follows a circular pattern by relating events leading up to the relating of the events and so participates in a larger sense in a closed, circulatory, and ultimately artistic world. In fact, many aspects of the world of Humbert the narrator have cyclical patterns which reflect their narrator's mind. Annabel, Valeria, Charlotte, and Lolita all die prematurely following relationships of one sort or another with Humbert. In a related pattern, Val and Lo die in childbirth after abandoning Hum for other men, reflecting the pattern of gain and loss Humbert follows with women throughout his life, Rita being the only exception. Moreover, after his long journey across the United States with Lolita, a journey that forms a great circle, Humbert repeats the trip a second time with Lo and then a third with Rita. These cycles, however, are only echoes of the larger, complex cycle that forms the structure of the book itself, centers on the changing relation of Humbert the character's fantasy world to reality, and so demonstrates Humbert's growth as he changes from actor to storyteller.

In the third paragraph of the first chapter, Humbert explains that "there might have been no Lolita at all had I not loved, one summer, a certain initial girl-child." Had there been no Annabel Leigh to bewitch him and take him

out of normal time and normal relationships, neither Lolita the nymphet nor *Lolita* the novel would have been possible. However, Annabel did exist, at least for him, and Humbert did fall in love with her and her kind, leading him to Lolita. Until he meets Lolita, though, his sexual activities are twofold: to relieve his body he frequents prostitutes, and to relieve his mind he frequents park benches, where he can watch nymphets playing while "pretending to be immersed in a trembling book." In these parks filled with nymphets playing in pulsating and melting shadows, Hum watches and fantasizes, never considering interfering with a child's innocence. He repeatedly disavows any criminal intent, insisting that "the gentle and dreamy regions through which I crept were the patrimonies of poets—*not* crime's prowling ground." His physically sexual life and his life of sexual fantasy are at this time completely split, and he is "aware of not one but two sexes, neither of which was mine." When this division of sexual satisfaction into physical and fantastic becomes intolerable to him, he marries Valeria, at first childlike (or -ish) and cute, in an attempt to merge his body's needs and his fantasies, but soon Valeria violates his dream with a vengeance. From "fluffy and frolicsome" she becomes a "large, puffy, short-legged, big-breasted and practically brainless *baba*" and Hum again begins to think of children.

His fantasy world intact and possibly strengthened in its isolation from reality by his experience with fat Valeria, Humbert arrives in the U.S. and eventually meets Lolita. Immediately his fantasies take on a new aspect: no longer does he look at nymphets indiscriminately, glad for a peek at lacy underthings, but now he directs all the power of fantasy toward his image of Dolores Haze. Dolly becomes for Hum Annabel's exact image down to a mole, and time ceases to exist. . . . Lolita becomes the object of all of Humbert's fantasies, and she in turn cooperates with them to a remarkable degree, first passively, allowing Hum to take liberties while removing an object from her eye and while sitting with Hum and Mrs. Haze in the dark, and later initiating small intimacies herself. Then, one Sunday while her mother is in church Humbert nabs "the honey of a spasm" by masturbating against Lo's thigh as she sits passively on his lap. At this point Humbert's fantastic vision of Lolita is most intense, and she is "safely solipsized"; his sexual activities, he believes, are completely divorced from their object ("Blessed be the Lord, she had noticed nothing!") and

> still Lolita was safe—I was safe. What I had madly possessed was not she, but my own creation, another, fanciful Lolita having no will, no consciousness—indeed, no life of her own.

Once Lo's mother is killed and Hum picks up Lo from camp, this internalization is threatened by their proximity and lack of external constraints, and with their first act of intercourse, Hum's mentally-oriented fantasy must change. According to Humbert, Lolita seduces him after a night of agony and failed narcotics, but this momentary merger of fantasy and reality is only the capstone of a night in which the borders between the two realms blur. At one point Lolita frees herself "from the shadow of [Hum's] embrace" and at others Hum "would dream I regained consciousness, dream I lay in wait." Maintaining this blend of reality and unreality could only result in schizophrenia, so beginning with the pair's first coupling, the two realms exist in a contiguous state, rather than an identical, blended one. Upon leaving The Enchanted Hunters that morning, Humbert realizes that "whether or not the realization of a life-long dream had surpassed all expectation, it had, in a sense, overshot its mark—and plunged into a nightmare." More specifically, he begins to feel "an oppressive, hideous constraint as if I were sitting with the small ghost of somebody I had just killed." In the sense of the archaic pun or the Freudian identification of intercourse and dying, he indeed sits with such a ghost, but he analyzes his state correctly in a more important sense: his pure fantasy, killed by its realization, must be replaced by something less pure, less ideal, less exclusively fantastic because it has been made flesh. Instead of owning a shadow to play with in his fantasies, he possesses the object throwing the shadow, too, forcing a deeply ironic twist to his use of the term "ghost"—the ghost of a shadow, it must, in terms of a dualistic universe of mentality and physicality, be corporeal.

Humbert's control over Lolita as another person and not merely as a figment of his imagination must be less than absolute, so he cements his hold on her by revealing her mother's death. This simple fact—that "she had absolutely nowhere else to go"—colors Humbert's intertwined fantasy and reality from now on, as he may now command her to perform sexually with him; her complicity now involves obedience.

At the beginning of Part Two, when the two are on the road, Humbert describes a rented cabin as

> a prison cell of paradise, with yellow window
> shades pulled down to create a morning illusion
> of Venice and sunshine when actually it was
> Pennsylvania and rain.

The prison cell echoes the various themes of prisons and sealed minds running through the book, but it also alludes to Humbert's severely limited options at this point. His fantasy become reality is a young girl, technically an orphan, and far below the age of consent. He must keep her compliant, if not willing, to do his bidding in bed and at the same time he must avoid possible legal ramifications. In an even more direct way, the cabin is a prison for Lolita. . . . At the same time, Hum's use of the window shades to illustrate the illusion, rather than reliance on his powers of imagination, suggests a twofold change in Humbert's imaginative powers: he cannot imagine as well as he could before since objectively he finds Lolita "a disgustingly conventional little girl," but neither does he have to—his dream has come true. Still, she is his nymphet Lolita, his to do with as he pleases *if he can convince her to,* a qualification bespeaking the altered nature of their relationship. At first he relies on threats of isolated farmhouses and reformatories to make her compliant, along with the device of the trip itself, "whose sole *raison d'etre* . . . was to keep my companion in a passable humor from kiss to kiss." These strategems, however, lose efficacy and must be replaced by a system of bribes as her reluctance to be part of Humbert's world grows and he per-

ceives her to be ready "to turn away from it with something akin to plain repulsion."

With the play *The Enchanted Hunters* the figure of Claire Quilty enters overtly, exerting his influence directly as if in answer to Lo's growing distaste for Humbert. At this point, Humbert and Lolita have been drifting apart for many pages, and Humbert's control over her is ebbing fast. As if through a chink in the armor of Hum's solipsistic fantasy world, Quilty steals in and Lolita falls in love with him, her new emotions demonstrated by her sudden change in demeanor: "with a yelp of amorous vernal laughter, she . . . rode back, feet at rest on stopped pedals, posture relaxed, one hand dreaming in her print-flowered lap." Clearly, this behavior is not a reaction to Humbert, who for crawling to Lo on his hands and knees receives for his pains only an " 'Oh no, not again'."

In this new situation, Humbert's fantasy cannot survive intact. On discovering Lo's absence from her piano lessons, he finds her in the living room, and "with a sickening qualm" his nymphet-forming "focal adjustment" disappears and he sees, not Lolita, light of his life, etc., but Dolores Haze. . . . No longer a nymphet, she reminds him instead of a prostitute, and after a fight and her escape from the house, she becomes aware of her ability to control the situation and does so immediately: " '*this* time we'll go wherever *I* want, won't we?'."

As a symbol of her new-found control over Humbert, Lolita demands intercourse while Humbert, having "adjusted" and seeing her again as a nymphet, is now her prisoner. He sheds "torrents of tears," and then they begin a new round of travels, but travels very different from the first, as Quilty now becomes an ever-present force hanging in the background and obviously influencing Lo. Early in the trip she slips away to make a phone call and shortly after that rids herself of Hum for a few hours, apparently to see and possibly to have intercourse with Quilty. When Hum returns, he suspects her infidelity and pursues its "shadow" only to declare that "the scent I travelled upon was so slight as to be practically undistinguishable from a madman's fancy." From creating fantasies almost palpable with reality, Humbert moves to searching futilely for evanescent shadows created by someone else, thereby confessing to a complete breakdown of his ability to control the reality he has created and implying that another figure, Quilty, is at this point a stronger controller of Lolita's reality than he.

With this display of Humbert's impotence, Quilty becomes visible, hanging behind the doomed pair's aging automobile in a car Humbert knows is stronger than his by "many times." Quilty's car seems to be attached to Humbert's by a silken rope reminiscent of the threads Humbert sent through the Haze house in search of Lolita in an earlier, happier time when he was the spider, not the fly. After seeing another of Quilty's plays, Hum and Lo move on to Waco, where Lo gives him the slip as if rehearsing for her big escape to come. Humbert, powerless to stop her, responds not imaginatively, but physically; he slaps her across the face and then dissolves in remorse, for "it was of no avail. Both doomed were we."

Hum's knowledge of his coming fate does not cure him of his delusions, though, and neither does his loss of control. Even after Quilty has entered the scene, after Hum has realized that he must lose Lolita, after he sees his imminent defeat and his powerlessness to defend himself against it, he is still capable of declaring that "despite her advanced age, she was more of a nymphet than ever." He dwells at this time for nearly five pages on her tennis game and finds her yet a true nymphet because her movements, her style, reveal a childlike innocence grounded in her lack of a will to win and a "cheerful indifference" to competition. This lack, though, is not a trait inherent in her, but rather results from Humbert's having broken something in her, making her continued nymphetcy a result of traits imposed on her by Humbert in the realization of his fantasy, to her great expense, and ironically, her adoption of traits formerly only aspects of his fantasy removes these traits from his control. Clearly, too, Quilty is the controller now, daring to appear and play tennis with Lo and then impudent enough to stand in the distance and watch Lo play with a dog in full sight of Humbert. (pp. 189-94)

When, finally, Humbert's two-year romp with Lolita is discontinued by Lolita's escape from the hospital in a town called Elphinstone after a bout with a virus, he begins his painstaking trip, alone and searching for Lolita and her abductor, whose character, if not his name, begins to solidify for Humbert. Essentially, he is a literary tantalizer, a sower of false clues and blind allusions designed to keep Humbert looking but to prevent him from finding. He has, Humbert discovers, strong affinities with Humbert, and the people of Elphinstone insist he is Humbert's brother. (p. 194)

In despair, Humbert eventually gives up the search, destroys or gives away Lolita's things, and commits himself to an institution, bereft not only of Lolita in the flesh, but also of his fantasies of Lo as nymphet. . . . (p. 195)

The borderline between beautiful and beastly, fantastic and physical, has become a vast, impenetrable no-man's land, this separation and renunciation completing the rebound from the total merger Humbert and Lolita experienced so long ago. Hum no longer has an object for his fantasies, and he has no fantasies either. In a gray reality untinted and untainted by his mind, he finds solitude "corrupting" because his depraved sexual tastes remain; but then he finds Rita.

Rita occupies a very special place in Humbert's world and in his book: she is the only woman with whom Hum carries on a genuinely mutual, illusion-free relationship. Hum admits that he needs "company and care," and Rita, "the most soothing, the most comprehending companion that I ever had," gives him that care freely. In return, Humbert devotes two pages of the warmest prose of the novel to her, words honestly and openly affectionate and a little nostalgic: "hi, Rita—wherever you are, drunk or hangoverish, Rita, hi!" While with her, Hum abandons his vengeful search and lives, like the mysterious Jack Humbertson whom the pair find in their hotel room one morning, in the gray present for two years, as a fairly normal, productive scholar. . . . As he learns too late, his fantasies were wonderful precisely because of their impossibility and his

being granted his desire has led, as in tales of genies and fairies too numerous to count, to woes he never expected. His all-too-rich imaginative life has brought him to a complete loss of fantasies and to a new maturity of outlook and behavior, but not before dragging him through a nightmarish underworld, from which he has emerged a wiser, if sadder, man.

But this is the not the end of his story. He receives a letter from Lolita, now the pregnant seventeen-year-old wife of a Mr. Robert Schiller. Leaving Rita and his life with her, he packs "Chum," his revolver, and begins yet another vengeful journey to her and Dick Schiller, who Humbert thinks is his tormenter. (pp. 195-96)

All is gray and sunless when he arrives at the Schiller house, and on talking with the very pregnant Lo he realizes that she sets their "poor romance" at no value whatever, "like a bit of dry mud caking her childhood," and that despite it all, despite her having demonstrably outgrown nymphetcy, he

> knew as clearly as I know I am to die, that I loved her more than anything I had ever seen or imagined on earth, or hoped for anywhere else . . . What I used to pamper among the tangled vines of my heart . . . had dwindled to its essence: sterile and selfish vice, all *that* I cancelled and cursed. . . . I loved my Lolita, *this* Lolita. . . .

He abandons his vice as he later abandons his legacy from dead Charlotte Haze and recognizes in himself mature love for Lolita as she is, as a human being. . . . Hum sees Lo as she is, worn out and hugely pregnant, and loves her. He also notes traces of her former nymphetcy, but "thank[s] God it was not that echo alone that I worshipped." In this new state of consciousness and love, he must ask Lo to come with him or at least to say she someday might, but of course she declines, her refusal a reproof to him of his wretched treatment of her. Her refusal makes "all the difference" because it proves that his perverted past still exerts control and influence on the events of his life. His perversion does matter; hence the death of Quilty, who has assumed the pervert's role after wrenching it away from Humbert during his and Lo's second trip West, is a necessity for Humbert—to exorcise his demons, he must kill this projection of his Frankensteinian fantasies. (p. 196)

Humbert realizes now that his perversion has always controlled him, while his control has always been minimal at best. During "icebergs in paradise," moments akin to those in which he saw Lo as a person instead of a nymphet, he would feel the despair and shame of his acts and be ready to ask forgiveness and repent—but "all at once, ironically, horribly, lust would swell again," and his depravity would take control of him again. (pp. 196-97)

His duty now clear to him, Humbert becomes a new person. His "old world politeness" disappears in his visit to Ramsdale, and he prepares for the death of Quilty by first casing Quilty's house in the darkness of a black, landscapeless night and then returning the next morning dressed in black, the sun "burning like a man." He acknowledges his presence in the monster's lair and his slavery to the perversions that Quilty represents by referring to Quilty as "master," but now Humbert is the "enchanted hunter," the master, and Quilty the prey. Quilty does retain power, for his presence makes Humbert's weapon with its mock-Freudian associations feel "limp and clumsy" in his hand, and Hum feels that his first shot might "trickle out" of the rug after penetrating it. Forcing Quilty to read Hum's poem/death sentence/invocation gives Humbert new strength, though, and he objectifies his adversary as "the person." The distancing renders Quilty powerless—words bounce off, offers of new depravities go unheeded, and after an absurd and mythic number of wounds, Quilty, the repository and personification of Humbert's evil, finally, melodramatically, dies.

Although Hum asserts that "this . . . was the end of the ingenious play staged for me by Quilty," it is not the ending written or planned by Quilty. . . . Instead it is Humbert's ending, his final purgation of his old, evil self—in his victory he becomes the playwright. However, Humbert cannot rest easy, for, as he says, "I see nothing for the treatment of my misery but the melancholy and very local palliative of articulate art." Quilty's death on a physical level is not enough; after Humbert's incarcertion, he writes *Lolita,* for his solace and to give himself and Lolita "the only immortality [she and he] may share." Thus, in its spiralling circuit, the novel moves into and through the realm of art as it moves from ending to rebeginning, and Quilty, along with all the other characters, gains in symbolic significance as the question of his reality as a distinct character is nullified. Whatever he may have been, he is now Humbert's exorcised demon, and the narrative no longer poses as a chronicle of real events, but reveals itself as a fictional construct in which the "reality" of events and characters is no longer troublesome: all is symbol, all is fiction, all is art. (p. 197)

The world of *Lolita* . . . is a world in which the duality of mind and body, creation and creature, ideation and sensation, fantasy and reality merge eternally in the spiralling progress of the narrative, and along its way the novel makes important statements about what art is, what it is not, and what it can do. As Nabokov would wish his perfect novel to end, the book's close "is a sensation of its world receding in the distance and stopping somewhere there suspended." Humbert acknowledges the fragility and tenuousness of this very local and melancholy palliative for life in the world; still, the timelessness and immortality such a palliative offers are worth the effort of doing it, for it is the only "way out." For Nabokov as well as Humbert, the work of art is "the only immorality you and I may share," for both "only have words to play with," and it is with words and their controlling that each artist acts within his world as "precise fate, that synchronizing phantom," abolishing time and creating palpable shadows by creating a timeless world. When we return to the first lines after finishing the novel, then, "Lolita" reverberates with meaning, signifying fact, fantasy, and their magical transformation into art, and "Lolita" is now not only a girl, a fantasy, and a book, it is the constitutive element of all three: a word. The first line now bespeaks not a moldy passion, but rather an expansive, embracing totali-

ty, the outer pair of phrases framing and subsuming the inner: "Lolita. Light of my life . . . my soul." (p. 202)

*Richard H. Bullock, "Humbert the Character, Humbert the Writer: Artifice, Reality, and Art in 'Lolita'," in* Philological Quarterly, Vol. 63, No. 2, Spring, 1984, pp. 187-204.

## Steven H. Butler

For all the raised eyebrows that greeted *Lolita*'s first appearance some thirty years ago, many critics tend to dismiss Humbert's sexual aberration and pornographic writing when discussing the novel's "real" subject (whatever it may be). In typical fashion, Alfred Appel remarks [in *The Annotated Lolita*] that "Nabokov's constant theme [the creative process] is masked, but not obscured, by the novel's ostensible subject, sexual perversion." Similarly, Page Stegner suggests [in *Escape into Aesthetics: The Art of Vladimir Nabokov*] that we must see "[t]hrough the surface of his perversion" to discover Humbert's longing for "an ideal state that nymphets represent, a quality that exists beyond space and time." As a result of this tendency, little attention has been paid to Nabokov's own assertion (through the admittedly dubious voice of John Ray, Jr. in the Foreword) that the novel's "aphrodisiac" scenes are "the most strictly functional ones in the development of a tragic tale tending unswervingly to nothing less than a moral apotheosis." Surprisingly, as parodic as this assertion may be, it also contains a measure of truth. For even though the "aphrodisiac" scenes have nothing to do with a moral apotheosis, they are indeed functional if we view the novel in terms of the modern experience of beauty. (p. 427)

[In] *Lolita,* we shall see that the "aphrodisiac" scenes function in a . . . complex manner. For just as one of the novel's strategies is to demonstrate that Humbert's nympholepsy is again an objective correlative for his experience of beauty, a second strategy is to involve the reader in this experience through the creation of a work of art that is partly but not entirely pornographic.

If we are to perceive how Humbert's nympholepsy functions as an objective correlative for his experience of beauty, we must first consider how he goes about discrediting the greatest obstacle to this perception. The obstacle is, of course, psychoanalysis. Since Humbert admits to being both artist and pervert, it would be possible to view his life story as evidence of the neurotic basis of artistic creation. In the light of Nabokov's well-known hostility to Freud, that such a view is anathema goes without saying. But, for the purposes of the present study, it will still be instructive to review some of the tactics that Humbert employs to discredit the Freudian view of the artist.

Since psychoanalytical studies of art generally attempt to elucidate the relation between an artist's life or creative work and his *unconscious* sexual conflicts (as in the case of Freud's study of Leonardo da Vinci), Humbert's basic tactic is to make clear that he is fully conscious of his "neurosis" and its origin. He begins his Confession by suggesting that his lifelong passion for nymphets (girls between the ages of nine and fourteen) is the result of his unconsummated boyhood romance with an "initial girl-child" Annabel Leigh (in that "princedom by the sea" of the French Riviera), and he insists on his consciousness of reliving the past when he rediscovers Annabel in Lolita some twenty-five years later: "All I want to stress is that my discovery of her was a fatal consequence of that 'princedom by the sea' in my tortured past. Everything between the two events was but a series of gropings and blunders, and false rudiments of joy. Everything they shared made one of them."

Similarly, once Humbert begins his cross-country travels with Lolita (after they have become lovers), he knows that future analysts will expect him to seek a surrogate Riviera to approximate the setting of his romance with Annabel Leigh: "The able psychiatrist who studies my case—and whom by now Dr. Humbert has plunged, I trust, into a state of leporine fascination—is no doubt anxious go have me take my Lolita to the seaside and have me find there, at last, the 'gratification' of a lifetime urge, and release from the 'subconscious' obsession of an incomplete childhood romance with the initial little Miss Lee." By anticipating such an expectation, Humbert can then deflate it all the more effectively: "Well, comrade, let me tell you that I *did* look for a beach, though I also have to confess that by the time we reached its mirage of gray water, so many delights had already been granted me by my traveling companion that the search for a Kingdom by the Sea, a Sublimated Riviera, or whatnot, far from being the impulse of the subconscious, had become the rational pursuit of a purely theoretical thrill." The efficaciousness of this tactic is obvious. Since the analysand is already conscious of his impulse, the analyst is reduced to silence.

To these examples, many more could be added. For, as Page Stegner has remarked, "[i]n one sense *Lolita* might be considered an extensive parody of Freudian myths and Freudian explanations for psychological aberration." As stated before, moreover, this aspect of the novel can be viewed as an expression of the author's own hostility to Freud. But whereas Nabokov's polemic is sometimes weakened by the fact that his "objections to Freud . . . strike one quite often as themselves obsessive," the specific interest of the Freudian parody in *Lolita* is that it relates directly to Humbert's experience of beauty. Therefore, in addition to making clear that he is conscious of his impulses, Humbert's parody is designed to demonstrate that Freudians misperceive the relation between art and sex.

Humbert's objection to the Freudian view is presented forthrightly when he states: "It is not the artistic aptitudes that are secondary sexual characters as some shams and shamans have said; it is the other way around: sex is but the ancilla of art." By viewing nympholepsy as a sexual problem, psychoanalysts can only come to a false understanding of his life. For a true understanding, nympholepsy must be seen as the symptom of an artistic problem. Accordingly, to set the record straight, Humbert pauses at the very moment of the novel's erotic climax (after narrating the scene at the Enchanted Hunters Hotel during which he and Lolita become lovers) to articulate his motivation as a writer: "I am not concerned with so-called 'sex' at all. Anybody can imagine those elements of animality.

A greater endeavor lures me on: to fix once for all the perilous magic of nymphets." (pp. 428-30)

[When] Humbert attempts to describe Lolita's charm as a nymphet, it becomes clear that beauty is no longer associated with purity. Nymphets are twofold in nature. They are both divine and infernal:

> What drives me insane is the twofold nature of this nymphet—of every nymphet, perhaps; this mixture in my Lolita of tender dreamy childishness and a kind of eerie vulgarity, stemming from the snub-nosed cuteness of ads and magazine pictures, from the blurry pinkness of adolescent maidservants in the Old Country (smelling of crushed daisies and sweat); and from very young harlots disguised as children in provincial brothels; and then again, all this gets mixed up with the exquisite stainless tenderness seeping through the musk and the mud, through the dirt and the death, oh God, oh God.

This difference in the conception of beauty necessarily entails a difference in how it is experienced. Since the beauty of nymphets involves all of Humbert's senses and faculties (smell, taste, and touch as well as mind, sight, and hearing), love and lust are inseparable. Instead of spiritual transcendence, Humbert's ideal leads to sensations of heaven and hell:

> Reader must understand that in the possession and thralldom of a nymphet the enchanted traveler stands, as it were, *beyond happiness.* For there is no other bliss on earth comparable to that of fondling a nymphet. It is *hors concours,* that bliss, it belongs to another class, another plane of sensitivity. Despite our tiffs, despite her nastiness, despite all the fuss and faces she made, and the vulgarity, and the danger, and the horrible hopelessness of it all, I still dwelled deep in my elected paradise—a paradise whose skies were the color of hell-flames—but still a paradise.

Humbert's sexual aberrance is thus a fitting objective correlative for his experience of beauty. . . . [Nympholepsy] dramatizes the breakdown of the Platonic distinction between art and eros as well as the guilt and torment that result from this breakdown. In the modern experience of beauty, feelings of elevation are accompanied by feelings of distress. Accordingly, in Humbert's case, his bliss as a nympholept is tempered by bouts with insanity, fears of being betrayed by Lolita, worries that his forbidden love may be discovered, and sensations of being followed by various agents of doom (McFate, Trapp, and Quilty). After being seduced by Lolita, Humbert himself comes to understand that when art and eros cease to be distinct the dream of beauty is likely to turn into a nightmare: "Whether or not the realization of a lifelong dream had surpassed all expectation, it had, in a sense, overshot its mark—and plunged into a nightmare."

It might be objected here that a straightforward reading of Humbert's experience of beauty reduces *Lolita* to the level of "literary banality." This point is made by Thomas Frosch, who observes that the "feeling of being in paradise and hell simultaneously" belongs almost stereotypically to the "romantic domain of sensation" [see Frosch's excerpt above]. In order to protect the novel from the charge of banality, Nabokov must therefore parody Humbert's sensations: "In relation to romance, parody acts in *Lolita* in a defensive and proleptic way. It doesn't criticize the romance mode, although it criticizes Humbert; it renders romance acceptable by anticipating our mockery and beating us to the draw." In fact, for Frosch, it is through the parody of Humbert's romantic sensations that Nabokov achieves originality: "I would add that parody is Nabokov's way of getting as close to the romantic novel as possible and, more, that he actually does succeed in recreating it in a new form, one that is contemporary and original, not anachronistic and imitative."

In contrast, I would argue that our appreciation of *Lolita* does not suffer from a straightforward reading of Humbert's experience. Part of the novel's achievement is simply to make clear that Humbert's sensations of heaven and hell result from the breakdown of the traditional distinction between art and eros in his conception of beauty (rather than from a personal neurosis). And precisely because these sensations are typically romantic, *Lolita* allows us on one level to elucidate—in terms of aesthetic theory—what Mario Praz has called the "romantic agony." Further, while I agree with Frosch that *Lolita* is an original art form, I do not find its originality in the distancing effect of parody. I find it rather in the power of the text to elicit from its readers an affective response that is analogous to Humbert's experience of beauty.

Given Humbert's conception of beauty, we have seen that he is doomed to an infernal paradise ("a paradise whose skies were the color of hell-flames"). Yet to him remains the challenge of celebrating his doom by conveying to his readers his sensations of heaven and hell: "I am trying to describe these things not to relive them in my present boundless misery, but to sort out the portion of hell and the portion of heaven in that strange, awful, maddening world—nymphet love. The beastly and beautiful merged at one point, and it is that borderline I would like to fix, and I feel I fail to do so utterly. Why?"

If we leave aside for the moment Humbert's sense of failure, this challenge brings us to the pornographic aspects of his writing. For, as Gabriel Josipovici has remarked [in *The World and the Book: A Study of Modern Fiction*], Humbert's ultimate goal as a writer is to capture "Lolita's mysterious beauty not through carnal possession but through language." In order to capture Lolita's mysterious beauty through language, Humbert's strategy is to make us share in his sensations. Thus, his writing purposely excites erotic emotions without ever becoming entirely pornographic. Rather, the most characteristic trait of his writing is a constant modulation between the beastly (erotic) and the beautiful (aesthetic) portions of nymphet love.

Typical of these modulations is Humbert's recollection of some moments of tenderness in his love for Lolita. At such times, it seems that lust may ultimately give way to love. But just as we begin to perceive this possibility, we are abruptly brought back to the reality of sexual passion: "I would lull and rock my lone light Lolita in my marble arms, and moan in her warm hair, and caress her at random and mutely ask her blessing, and at the peak of this human agonized selfless tenderness (with my soul actually hanging around her naked body and ready to repent), all at once, ironically, horribly, lust would swell again—and 'oh, no,' Lolita would say with a sigh to heaven, and the next moment the tenderness and the azure—all would be shattered." In contrast, the famous masturbation scene is typical of the reverse modulation from the erotic to the aesthetic. Here, after being explicitly asked by Humbert to identify with him ("I want my learned readers to participate in the scene I am about to replay"), we are first involved in the detailed description of his erotic machinations, and we may even fear for him the possibility of detection. Then, at the moment of orgasm, we experience a corresponding relief that the scene has passed without incident. And, finally, we may even let ourselves be swayed by Humbert's retrospective view of the scene as an artistic triumph: "What I had madly possessed was not she, but my own creation, another fanciful Lolita—perhaps, more real than Lolita; overlapping, encasing her; floating between me and her, and having no will, no consciousness—indeed, no life of her own."

At other times, the modulations are even more rapid. Then, almost imperceptibly, the beastly and the beautiful are fused in Humbert's language and in our minds. For instance, while following his lustful narration of shopping for Lolita's intimate apparel in a department store, we are suddenly and unexpectedly transported back into the aesthetic and mythical setting of the French Riviera: "I sensed strange thoughts form in the minds of the languid ladies that escorted me from counter to counter, from rock ledge to seaweed, and the belts and the bracelets I chose seemed to fall from siren hands into transparent water." Similarly, even at the novel's erotic climax, when Humbert describes his attempts to seduce Lolita, the beastly and the beautiful are fused. In the following passages, the carnal images of Humbert's "burning life" and "tentacles" are juxtaposed against the ethereal image of "nebulous Lolita"; "mountains of longing" are juxtaposed against "mists of tenderness"; and the "haunch" of the "enchanted prey" is juxtaposed against the "soft sand of a remote and fabulous beach":

> And less than six inches from me and my burning life, was nebulous Lolita! After a long stirless vigil, my tentacles moved towards her again, and this time the creak of the mattress did not awake her. My pillow smelled of her hair. I moved toward my glimmering darling, stopping or retreating every time I thought she stirred or was about to stir. A breeze from wonderland had begun to affect my thoughts, and now they seemed couched in italics, as if the surface reflecting them were wrinkled by the phantasm of that breeze. Time and again my consciousness folded the wrong way, my shuffling body entered the sphere of sleep, shuffled out again, and once or twice I caught myself drifting into a melancholy snore. Mists of tenderness enfolded mountains of longing. Now and then it seemed to me that the enchanted prey was about to meet halfway the enchanted hunter, that her haunch was working its way toward me under the soft sand

of a remote and fabulous beach; and then her dimpled dimness would stir, and I would know she was farther away from me than ever.

Finally, when the Confession is viewed in its entirety, there is a modulation from the erotic beckoning of the opening lines ("Lolita, light of my life, fire of my loins. My sin, my soul") to the aesthetic vision of the conclusion: "And do not pity C. Q. [the murdered Clare Quilty]. One had to choose between him and H. H., and one wanted H. H. to exist at least a couple of months longer, so as to have him make you live in the minds of later generations. I am thinking of aurochs and angels, the secret of durable pigments, prophetic sonnets, the refuge of art. And this is the only immortality you and I may share, my Lolita."

The cumulative effect of these modulations is not that Humbert ever transcends his lust." It is rather that our sense of the text is analogous to his sense of Lolita. In both cases, the beastly and the beautiful are combined. Thus, in its exploration of the modern experience of beauty, the originality of *Lolita* is to fuse love and lust through the language of Humbert's confession. . . . [As] a result of the perfect harmony between Humbert's subject and language, we perceive Lolita as he does. Consequently, despite his initial sense of failure, Humbert has actually succeeded in fixing the borderline between the beastly and the beautiful. Through his linguistic fusion of the erotic and the aesthetic, he has rendered his experience of beauty and made it our own. In the end, he can indeed promise lasting life to his nymphet. For, as Nabokov writes in a poem, is it not Lolita who has "set the entire world a-dreaming?" (pp. 431-34)

> *Steven H. Butler, " 'Lolita' and the Modern Experience of Beauty," in* Studies in the Novel, *Vol. XVIII, No. 4, Winter, 1986, pp. 427-37.*

## Erica Jong

"Lolita is famous, not I," Nabokov said to one of the many interviewers who came to interrogate him after the *succès de scandale* of *Lolita.* And like so many Nabokovian utterances, it was both true and the mirror image of true. Lolita's fame made her creator both a "brand-name" author—to use that distressing contemporary locution—and an adjective.

Vladimir Vladimirovich Nabokov, alias V. Sirin (Volodya to his friends), born on Shakespeare's birthday, 1899, became famous in 1958-59, at the fairly ripe age of 60, through the notoriety of his fictive daughter Lolita, Dolly, Lo, Dolores Haze, of the soft brown puppybody and equivalently gamy aroma.

Like most famous literary books, *Lolita* seduced the world for the wrong reasons. It was thought to be dirty. It has this in common with *Ulysses, Miller's Tropics, Lady Chatterley's Lover:* it won its first passionate proponents by being banned. When it came to wide public consciousness, it was reputed to be a scandalous book about a scandalous subject: the passion of an aging roué for a 12-year-old girl.

As one whose literary debut was also steeped in scandal,

I know intimately the ambivalent feelings of an author who gains wide fame and commercial acceptance through a misunderstanding of motives. Much as one wants the acceptance conferred by best-sellerdom, it is bittersweet to win this by being thought a pervert. This alone explains Nabokov's half-mocking reference to *Lolita*'s fame. Nabokov knew that he had been toiling in the vineyards of the muse since adolescence. The public did not. Nabokov knew that he had translated *Alice in Wonderland* into Russian, the public did not. With 11 extraordinary novels, a study of Gogol, an autobiography, numerous short stories, poems and translations behind him, the author of *Lolita* was hardly a literary novice. His identity as a novelist, poet and literary scholar had been honed and polished in three languages since he privately printed his poems in St. Petersburg at the age of 15, and he had endured more traumas than sudden fame. The generous, amused, self-mocking way he reacted to *Lolita*'s stardom contains within it all the paradoxes of a career rich in paradoxes, a career that seems to have the very symmetry, balance and irony of his novels themselves.

It is almost superfluous to introduce *Lolita*—even on her 30th birthday—because Nabokov, who thought an author should control the world in his book with godlike authority, anticipated all the possible front (and rear) matter any reader could wish.

We have the mock-introduction by "John Ray, Jr., Ph.D.," a spoof on scholarly psychobabble and tendentious moralizing, two things Nabokov detested as much as he detested Freudian symbol-mongering in literary criticism. . . .

His impersonation of "John Ray" in the foreword to *Lolita* is one of the most delicious of literary parodies, and his own afterword **"On a Book Entitled *Lolita*"** is, I believe, the last word on the subject of the sensual versus the pornographic. I always wonder why it is not quoted more often in those endless, predictable and anesthetizing debates that go on about the nature of pornography and eroticism (and to which I am inevitably invited).

Here is Nabokov on that dreary subject:

> While it is true that in ancient Europe, and well into the eighteenth century . . . deliberate lewdness was not inconsistent with flashes of comedy, or vigorous satire, or even the verve of a fine poet in a wanton mood, it is also true that in modern times the term 'pornography' connotes mediocrity, commercialism, and certain strict rules of narration. Obscenity must be mated with banality because every kind of aesthetic enjoyment has to be entirely replaced by simple sexual stimulation which demands the traditional word for direct action upon the patient. Old rigid rules must be followed by the pornographer in order to have his patient feel the same security of satisfaction as, for example, fans of detective stories feel—stories where, if you do not watch out, the real murderer may turn out to be artistic originality. . . . Thus, in pornographic novels, action has to be limited to the copulation of cliches. Style, structure, imagery should never distract the reader from his tepid lust.

People who cannot tell the difference between that sort of masturbatory stimulation and imaginative literature deserve, in fact, the garbage they get. . . .

Nabokov thought of *Lolita* as his best novel in English and he had been trying to write it at least since his Berlin days. (Perhaps the literary artist is born like a woman with all her eggs present in their follicles; they have only to ripen and burst forth—and ripeness is all. But sometimes it takes half a lifetime for them to ripen.) Nabokov began what was to become *Lolita* as a novella in Russian called *The Enchanter* (*Volshebnik*), which he composed in the fall of 1939. . . .

In *The Enchanter* all the elements of *Lolita* are present: the Central European lover, the nymphet, the marrying-her-mother theme, but in *The Enchanter* it is the nymphet's unnamed lover (who later becomes Humbert) who is killed by a truck, not the nymphet's mother. Nabokov claimed he destroyed *The Enchanter* soon after moving to America; but his memory apparently lied to him, for the novella turned up in his files and was published in 1986.

One of the many glories of *Lolita* is the evocation of the American landscape, American slang, American teenagers of the 50's—all seen with the freshness only a twice-exiled European would bring. The difference between *The Enchanter* and *Lolita* is the difference between a postcard of Venice and a Turner painting of the same scene—all the difference in the world—and it inheres in the details, the divine details. Even before *The Enchanter* the idea for *Lolita* was present in Nabokov's imagination. In *The Gift* (*Dar*), Nabokov's autobiographical Russian novel (published serially in Berlin in 1937-38, and in its entirety in 1952 in New York), there exists this amazing premonition of *Lolita*:

> Ah, if only I had a tick or two, what a novel I'd whip off! From real life. Imagine this kind of thing: and old dog—but still in his prime, fiery, thirsting for happiness—gets to know a widow, and she has a daughter, still quite a little girl—you know what I mean—when nothing is formed yet, but already she has a way of walking that drives you out of your mind—A slip of a girl, very fair, pale, with blue under the eyes—and of course she doesn't even look at the old goat. What to do? Well, not long thinking, he ups and marries the widow. Okay. They settle down the three of them. Here you can go on indefinitely—the temptation, the eternal torment, the itch, the mad hopes. And the upshot—a miscalculation. Time flies, he gets older, she blossoms out—and not a sausage. Just walks by and scorches you with a look of contempt. Eh? D'you feel here a kind of Dostoevskian tragedy? That story, you see, happened to a great friend of mine, once upon a time in fairyland when Old King Cole was a merry old soul.

The language of *Lolita* is as amazing in its way as the language of *Ulysses* or *A Clockwork Orange*. Nabokov has the same lexicographical itch. *Lolita* teems with loving lexicography, crystalline coinages, lavish list-making—all the symptoms of rapture of the word. "Nymphet" was a coinage of this novel, as were the more obscure "libidream,"

"pederosis," "nymphage" and "puppybodies." (French critics pointed out that Ronsard had used the word "nymphette" to mean little nymph—a fact Nabokov knew—but he used his English term in a different sense.)

*Lolita* is a novel about obsession. The subject was hardly a new one for Nabokov, though the form the obsession takes is new in this novel: nymphage. Luzhin in *The Defense* is obsessed with chess; Sebastian Knight in *The Real Life of Sebastian Knight* with literary immortality; Kinbote in the later novel *Pale Fire* with regaining his Zemblan kingship; Hermann in *Despair* with killing his double; Fyodor in *The Gift* with transcending time through literary creation. (p. 3)

Humbert Humbert is in love with something which by definition cannot last. That prepubescent state he calls nymphage lasts from 9 to 13 at best, a fleeting four years, often less. The honey-hued shoulders, the budbreasts, the brownish fragrance of the bobby-soxed nymphet all are destined to be abolished by the advent of womanhood, which Humbert despises every bit as much as he worships nymphage. Humbert's dilemma puts the dilemma of all obsessional lovers in high relief. What he loves he is doomed never to possess. It cannot be possessed because time rips it away from him even as he possesses it.

The villain here is time. And the dilemma is the dilemma of the mortal human being who foresees his own death. It is not a coincidence that so many of Nabokov's heroes are doomed and so many of his novels are cast in the form of posthumous autobiographies. His subjects are nothing less than mutability and time, Eros and Death, the twin subjects of all muse-poetry.

Humbert Humbert is, like so many Nabokovian narrators, a man obsessed with an irretrievable past. When he rediscovers his nymphet in Ramsdale (even the place names in *Lolita* are full of sexual innuendo and irony), he recognizes at once that he has discovered the reincarnated essence of his Riviera puppy love, who perished of typhus decades earlier:

> It was the same child—the same frail, honey-hued shoulders, the same silky supple bare back, the same chestnut head of hair. A polka-dotted black kerchief tied around her chest hid from my aging ape eyes, but not from the gaze of young memory, the juvenile breasts I had fondled one immortal day. And, as if I were the fairy-tale nurse of some little princess (lost, kidnapped, discovered in gypsy rags through which her nakedness smiled at the king and his hounds), I recognized the tiny dark-brown mole on her side. With awe and delight (the king crying for joy, the trumpets blaring, the nurse drunk) I saw again her lovely indrawn abdomen where my southbound mouth had briefly paused; and those puerile hips on which I had kissed the crenulated imprint left by the band of her shorts—that last mad immortal day behind the 'Roches roses.' The twenty-five years I had lived since then, tapered to a palpitating point, and vanished.

Time is what he seeks to abolish. Time is the enemy of all lovers. Obsession has a life of its own: the object, however irreplaceable and particular it seems, can change, though it is in the nature of obsession not to recognize that.

The obsession of Humbert with Lolita has been compared to many things: the obsession of the artist with the creative process, the butterfly collector with his specimen, the exile with retrieving a lost homeland (a characteristic Nabokovian theme). It is all these things, and more. And yet the book works, above all, because it is so clearly the story of a man maddened by an impossible love, the impossible love for an impossible object: a banal little girl who calls him "kiddo." Are not all impossible, obsessional loves inexplicable to other people? Do our friends *ever* understand what we see in them? Isn't that inexplicability the wonder and the terror of obsessional loves?

The publishing history of *Lolita* is almost as Nabokovian as any of Vladimir Nabokov's creations: it seems almost a case of life imitating art. . . .

It is not surprising that the typescript of *Lolita* was rejected by four major New York publishers (Viking, Simon & Schuster, New Directions and Farrar, Straus & Giroux). Although it contained not one "mural word," *Lolita* was a genuinely new creation and genuinely new creations do not usually fare well with mainstream publishers in any age. It was not only that *Lolita* dealt with forbidden obsessions; *Lolita* was, above all, literary. American puritanism is more comfortable with sex when it stays in the gutter than when it rises to the level of art.

What is even more amazing than the response of the publishers was the early response of Nabokov's friends Edmund and Elena Wilson and Mary McCarthy to this masterpiece, which Nabokov thought "by far my best English work." We are amazed to read in the Nabokov-Wilson letters that Edmund Wilson wrote to Nabokov of *Lolita,* "I like it less than anything of yours I have read," and that Mary McCarthy, who did not finish the manuscript, called the writing "terribly sloppy all through." (p. 46)

Had Edmund Wilson not dubbed the book "repulsive," "unreal" and "too unpleasant to be funny," had he not conveyed these sentiments to his own publisher, the publishing history of *Lolita* might have been different. As it was, fate—which is such an important character in *Lolita*—arranged that *Lolita* would have her first publication in English, in France, in 1955 under the auspices of Maurice Girodias's Olympia Press. . . . The printing was small, perhaps only 5,000 copies, but big enough so that Graham Greene found a copy and pronounced *Lolita* one of the three best novels of 1955 in *The Times* of London. (pp. 46-7)

Graham Greene saw literature and language where others had seen only perversion and pornography. *Lolita*'s eventual triumph can be traced ultimately to his intervention. . . .

It was widely assumed that *Lolita* would provoke legal action in England and the United States (the Olympia Press edition had even been banned at one point in Paris at the request of British authorities) and the novel was debated in the British Cabinet, but the publication proceeded without legal impediment. (A New Zealand ban came later.)

United States publication took place on July 21, 1958 (Putnam), and the book hit No. 1 on the New York Times best-seller list in January 1959, where it was eventually nudged out of place by another child of Russia, *Dr. Zhivago* by Boris Pasternak.

Most of *Lolita*'s reviews paid more attention to "l'Affaire Lolita" than to the book. One exception was Elizabeth Janeway, writing in *The New York Times Book Review,* who understood that the tragi-comedy was Shakespearean in nature:

> Humbert's fate seems to me classically tragic, a most perfectly realized expression of the moral truth that Shakespeare summed up in the sonnet that begins, 'The expense of spirit in a waste of shame / Is lust in action': right down to the detailed working out of Shakespeare's adjectives, 'perjur'd, murderous, bloody, full of blame.' Humbert is the hero with the tragic flaw. Humbert is every man who is driven by desire, wanting his Lolita so badly that it never occurs to him to consider her as a human being, or as anything but a dream-figment made flesh—which is the eternal and universal nature of passion.

The great thing about masterpieces is that they seem always to have existed, unopposed. Outrageous, inevitable, infinitely rereadable, *Lolita* at 30 is as young as she was as a glimmer in her author's eye. She has, in fact, defeated time—her enemy, her inspiration. (p. 47)

> *Erica Jong, "Time Has Been Kind to the Nymphet: 'Lolita' 30 Years Later," in* The New York Times Book Review, *June 5, 1988, pp. 3, 46-7.*

---

## FURTHER READING

Anderson, William. "Time and Memory in Nabokov's *Lolita.*" *Centennial Review* 24, No. 3 (Summer 1980): 360-83.
    Analyzes the importance of time and the unconscious mind in *Lolita.*

Appel, Alfred Jr. "*Lolita:* The Springboard of Parody." In *Nabokov: The Man and His Work,* edited by L. S. Dembo, pp. 106-43. Madison: The University of Wisconsin Press, 1967.
    Critically acclaimed essay explores the strong moral resonance in *Lolita* through Nabokov's use of irony and self-parody.

————. *The Annotated Lolita.* New York: McGraw-Hill, 1970, 441 p.
    Highly praised work designed to illuminate the text for college students. Includes examinations of Nabokov's allusions, principal motifs, and thematic structures.

Bell, Michael. "*Lolita* and Pure Art." *Essays in Criticism* XXIV, No. 2 (April 1974): 169-84.
    Maintains that readers and critics who focus on *Lolita*'s

aesthetic and moral aspects miss the intellectual and psychological insights of the narration.

Butler, Diana. "Lolita Lepidoptera." In *Critical Essays on Vladimir Nabokov,* edited by Phyllis A. Roth, pp. 59-74. Boston: G. K. Hall & Co., 1984.

   Well-regarded article exploring the butterfly motif of *Lolita.*

Clancy, Laurie. "We Lone Voyagers, We Nympholepts: *Lolita.*" In his *The Novels of Vladimir Nabokov,* pp. 101-14. London: The MacMillan Press, Ltd., 1984.

   Asserts that *Lolita* is the "culmination of stylistic and thematic development" of Nabokov's writing and traces the origins of Humbert Humbert's sexual disorder and artistic and human involvement.

Cranston, Maurice. "Obscenity in the Eye of Only Some Beholders—Contradictions in the Case of *Lolita.*" *Manchester Guardian* (14 May 1957): 5.

   Discloses the English government's urging of France to ban *Lolita,* and surveys the humor and farce of the novel.

Dennison, Sally. "Vladimir Nabokov: The Work of Art as a Dirty Book." In her *[Alternative] Literary Publishing,* pp. 159-92. Iowa City: University of Iowa Press, 1984.

   Informative, detailed discussion of the difficulties plaguing *Lolita*'s publication.

*Geste* (*Lolita* Special Issue) 4, No. 5 (March 1959).

   Issue includes essays on numerous aspects of *Lolita* and its controversy.

Grabes, H. "Autobiography as Demonstration of 'Precise Fate': *Lolita.*" In his *Fictitious Biographies: Vladimir Nabokov's English Novels,* pp. 31-45. Paris: Mouton & Co., 1977.

   Analyzes the function of Humbert's retrospective view and the insight it provides.

Iannone, Carol. "From *Lolita* to 'Piss Christ'." *Commentary* 89, No. 1 (January 1990): 52-4.

   Examines the controversy surrounding *Lolita*'s publication.

Lawrenson, Helen. "The Man Who Scandalized the World." *Esquire* 54, No. 2 (August 1960): 70-3.

   Detailed interview providing much information on Nabokov's childhood, family, personality, and his reactions to *Lolita*'s success.

Lee, L. L. *Vladimir Nabokov.* Boston: G. K. Hall & Co., 1976, 168 p.

   Biographical and critical study.

Long, Michael. "The Enchanted Hunter." In his *Marvell, Nabokov: Childhood and Arcadia,* pp. 135-51. Oxford: Clarendon Press, 1984.

   Illuminates the liberated humor of *Lolita.*

Masinton, Charles G. "What *Lolita* is Really About." *New Mexico Humanities Review* 31 (1989): 71-6.

   Contends that *Lolita* mocks realistic fiction and that its subject is the world of literary tradition and art.

"*Lolita* and the Critics." *New Republic* 139, No. 17 (27 October 1958): 3.

   Negative editorial reaction to reviews of *Lolita* that praise Nabokov's wit but fail to consider that "real Lolitas exist in darkness throughout their lives."

Olsen, Lance. "A Janus-Text: Realism, Fantasy, and Nabokov's *Lolita.*" *Modern Fiction Studies* 32, No. 1 (Spring 1986): 115-26.

   Detailed study of the dual existence of reality and fantasy in *Lolita.*

Packman, David. "*Lolita:* Detection and Desire" and "*Lolita:* Scenes of Desire." In his *Vladimir Nabokov: The Structure of Literary Desire,* pp. 23-67. Columbia and London: The University of Missouri Press, 1982.

   Academic intertextual readings of *Lolita* as a detective novel and an erotic work.

Pinnells, James R. "The Speech Ritual as an Element of Structure in Nabokov's *Lolita.*" *Dalhousie Review* 60, No. 4 (Winter 1980-1981): 605-21.

   Examines Nabokov's use of dialogue and monologue in the novel.

Prioleau, Elizabeth. "Humbert Humbert: *Through the Looking Glass.*" *Twentieth Century Literature* 21, No. 4 (December 1975): 428-37.

   Probes Lewis Carroll's influence on Nabokov's writing by juxtaposing *Through the Looking Glass* with *Lolita.*

Rampton, David. "*Lolita.*" In his *Vladimir Nabokov: A Critical Study of the Novels,* pp. 101-21. Cambridge: Cambridge University Press, 1984.

   Reaffirms the new directions of Nabokov criticism by reconsidering the old criticism. Claims *Lolita* is the Nabokov work with "the best chance of becoming a classic" in that its greatness depends on the human situation it portrays.

Scheid, Mark. "Epistemological Structures in *Lolita.*" *Rice University Studies* 61, No. 1 (Winter 1975): 127-40.

   Dialectical, philosophical commentary on the narration and authorial games of the novel.

Schrader, Paul. "*Lolita:* Rapier Innuendos and Roman Ping-Pong," *American Film* XV, No. 1 (October 1989): 18-20, 22.

   Article on the acclaimed narration and dialogue of the film adaptation of *Lolita.*

Smith, Peter Duval. "Vladimir Nabokov on His Life and Work." *The Listener* LXVIII, No. 1756 (22 November 1962): 856-58.

   Transcript of a British Broadcasting Corporation television interview in which Nabokov discusses life in Russia, his hobbies, writing methods, and the success of *Lolita.*

Tamir-Ghez, Nomi. "The Art of Persuasion in Nabokov's *Lolita.*" In *Critical Essays on Vladimir Nabokov,* edited by Phyllis A. Roth, pp. 157-76. Boston: G. K. Hall & Co., 1984.

   Academic treatment of Nabokov's rhetorical devices and the unlimited control of *Lolita*'s narrator.

Tekiner, Christina. "Time in *Lolita.*" *Modern Fiction Studies* 25, No. 3 (Autumn 1979): 463-69.

   Discusses the chronology of Humbert's activities in *Lolita.*

Toker, Leona. " 'Reader! *Bruder!*': Broodings on the Rhetoric of *Lolita.*" In her *Nabokov: The Mystery of Literary Structure,* pp. 198-227. Ithaca, N.Y.: Cornell University Press, 1989.

   Analyzes the method of "reader entrapment" Nabokov employs in the novel's narrative.

Trilling, Lionel. "The Last Lover." *Encounter* XI, No. 10 (October 1958): 9-19.

    Influential early essay examining many of the themes on which later critics would focus, including Nabokov's use of ambiguity and irony, and his portraits of Humbert and the United States.

# Tom Robbins

## 1936-

(Full name Thomas Eugene Robbins) American novelist and short story writer.

Robbins writes wildly inventive novels reflecting his view that "playfulness is a form of wisdom and not of frivolity." While not denying more serious and somber aspects of life, Robbins's novels emphasize an outlook that finds "joy in spite of everything." Robbins communicates this message through the philosophies his characters espouse as well as through his elaborate writing style. Outrageous metaphors, similes, puns, non sequiturs, absurdist humor, and digressions characterize Robbins's narratives. His novels question literary conventions and societal assumptions about the best way to attain human satisfaction. Incorporating alternative ideas from such diverse sources as pantheism, New Physics, and Eastern mystical religions, Robbins explores his major themes of personal freedom and the quest for higher states of being. Mark Siegel remarked: "The goal of Robbins's art is to alert us to the sacred, to get us to see things in a new, intense way—to get us to let go of our own limited perspectives by exciting us into a new awareness of the world."

Critics often link Robbins to such postmodern writers as Thomas Pynchon, John Barth, and Kurt Vonnegut. Like these authors, Robbins acknowledges the absurdity of modern life, rejects conformity in favor of individual expression, and uses elements of metafiction in his writing. He frequently speaks directly to the reader, commenting on the work in progress or appearing as a character in the novel. However, unlike his recent forebears—who often write black comedy and present a bleak prognosis for contemporary society—Robbins's tone is optimistic and his humor usually cheerful.

Robbins's first novel, *Another Roadside Attraction,* was published in 1971 but did not achieve popular success until a paperback edition was issued in 1973. The novel soon attracted a cult following with young members of the counterculture movement, who valued the way Robbins irreverently questioned and satirized those social conventions that fail to increase the level of joy in people's lives. *Another Roadside Attraction* displays the characteristics of Robbins's fiction: a meandering, bizarre plot, unusual characters, and flamboyant, imaginative prose. Narrated by Marx Marvelous, an academic identified by many critics as the author's alter-ego, the novel centers on a group of eccentrics who find the mummified corpse of Jesus Christ. They bring the body to a large hot-dog stand on the West Coast and endeavor to prove that Christianity is fraudulent. However, realizing that this exposé would not change society's attitudes, one of the group's members decides to melt himself and Christ's body with solar radiation. Mark Siegel viewed this act as "[reaffirming] the primacy of the individual, personal adventure over the public mission."

In his second novel, *Even Cowgirls Get the Blues,* Robbins focuses on an attractive heroine, Sissy Hankshaw, a woman with nine-inch thumbs who is an obsessive hitchhiker. Sissy moves between New York City, where she is a model, and a cosmetic health farm in South Dakota called the Rubber Rose Ranch, which has been taken over by a group of alienated feminist cowgirls. There she meets the Chink, a Japanese-American sage who explains to her the symbolic meaning of her outsized thumbs and instructs her to become her own savior. As the narrative chronicles Sissy's adventures, common themes emerge: the need to live with, rather than against, nature; the necessity for individual transformation rather than societal change; and the superiority of a pantheism that advocates feminine receptivity instead of masculine aggression.

Robbins's next novel, *Still Life with Woodpecker: A Sort of Love Story,* is generally regarded by critics as his least successful work. In this fabulous tale of a modern environmentalist princess and her "metaphysical outlaw" lover, Robbins maintains that individual romantic and personal fulfillment are more important than social activism. Some critics did not find *Still Life with Woodpecker* deeply meaningful, while others appreciated Robbins's creative use of language as well as his celebration of the human spirit. *Jitterbug Perfume* contains Robbins's typical varied cast of characters. The plot revolves around their attempts to traverse time and space in order to discover the ultimate perfume, which they believe holds the secret of immortality. *Skinny Legs and All* concerns such subjects as organized religion and the afterlife, art, relationships between men and women, the Middle East, and the meaning of existence. The novel is divided into seven sections that symbolize Salome's Dance of the Seven Veils as recounted in *The Thousand and One Nights*. According to lore, a different "veil" of illusion is destroyed after each layer of clothing falls, until at the end a great mystery of life is disclosed. Robbins concludes that humanity erred when it stopped worshipping the life-affirming Earth goddess Astarte and began following more belligerent male deities.

(See also *CLC*, Vols. 9, 32; *Contemporary Authors*, Vols. 81-84; *Contemporary Authors New Revision Series*, Vol. 29; and *Dictionary of Literary Biography Yearbook: 1980*.)

## PRINCIPAL WORKS

NOVELS

*Another Roadside Attraction*   1971
*Even Cowgirls Get the Blues*   1976
*Still Life with Woodpecker: A Sort of Love Story*   1980
*Jitterbug Perfume*   1984
*Skinny Legs and All*   1990

---

## Mark Siegel

As in *Another Roadside Attraction,* Robbins employs several interrelated plots to create the thematic effects of *Even Cowgirls Get the Blues.* His concerns in his second novel do not repeat those of the first, but they clearly develop out of them. The central characters in *Cowgirls* are somewhat closer to the mainstream of American culture, though not of it. For the most part, they are survivors cast upon the shores of our time.

The plot in *Cowgirls* that is most obviously applicable to contemporary social change involves a group of women who take over a cosmetic health farm and try to turn it into a working ranch. Although these women come from many walks of life, they share a need to invent or reinvent viable self-images and satisfying roles for themselves. The all-woman ranch provides that opportunity, because it is relatively free from male-oppression, particularly from role-restrictions that are implied by the mere presence of males.

Bonanza Jellybean, the prime mover in the takeover of the Rubber Rose Ranch, comes from a fairly common, middle-class background. As a child she was addicted to westerns and, for a time, was indulged by her parents. However, when she reached puberty, she was denied her dream of living out the heroic lifestyle of the American West by a society that had carefully circumscribed the legitimate roles of its individual members.

In her early twenties, Bonanza revolts and heads up to South Dakota to work on a health farm sponsored by a feminine hygiene concern. She can see that the women clients of the Rubber Rose essentially are being trained to blindly fulfill the absurdly tailored, often degrading role of American-Woman-as-Decorative-Object, and she is able to identify this brain-and-body-washing with her own predicament. After first conducting minor raids on the ranch's hygiene seminars, encouraging the women to see how the sterility of these feminine hygiene products is depriving them of their natural selves—their smells, looks, and personal styles are being covered over, sterilized, and standardized—Bonanza leads a fullscale, militant takeover. Her cohorts, particularly the man-hating Delores del Ruby, agree to establish the Rubber Rose as the first all-woman ranch, a free-form experiment in self-actualization.

The takeover occasions only minor resistance from the owner of the Rubber Rose, a good-natured male eunuch named the Countess. However, Siwash Lake, located on the ranch, is a major migratory home for rare whooping cranes, wards of the United States Government. When the whoopers fail to take their seasonal leave of the ranch, the FBI (as usual) steps in.

Robbins's use of the FBI in all his fiction is highly figurative, to the point of being unrealistically one-dimensional. The FBI represents not only authoritarian, sadistic, life-denying repressiveness, but its minions are the real enemy in all of Robbins's fiction: dull, closed minds. We are also told that the enemy is every expert who practices technocratic manipulation, every proponent of standardization, and every victim who is dull, lazy, and weak enough to allow himself to be manipulated and standardized. In *Cowgirls,* the FBI manages to bungle the whooper showdown with the ranch women so badly that it ends in a shootout that kills several people, including Bonanza Jellybean. Many of the agents themselves are killed by a jolly fat man named Billy West who sells goats. He is apparently a Dionysian figure who aids the Cowgirls because they, too, are in the business of affirming life. However, in the meantime Delores learns to accept men as an enhancement to her life, and nearly all the surviving Cowgirls seem to have grown psychologically and emotionally from the experience of managing to live so-called "male" lives on their own. Some stay on at the ranch, while others take the lesson in self-fulfillment back to cities and into other walks of life.

A second major plot centers upon the education and maturation of Sissy Hankshaw. Sissy was born beautiful, but with thumbs the size of bolognas. Sissy doesn't mind her thumbs, but everyone else in stifling, repressive South Richmond seems to. Her early life is a battle to retain her healthy self-image in the face of a society, including her own parents, that ridicules any divergence from normal appearance or behavior. Sissy herself understands that individuals are best off when they make the best use of their differences, and she becomes the greatest hitchhiker in the country. Like the women at the Rubber Rose, Sissy is determined to fulfill her own needs and to find joy in her personal abilities by expanding, or ignoring, existing social standards.

Between hitching trips across the country, Sissy, with her thumbs carefully hidden, models for the Countess's hygiene advertisements. She has the same penchant for experimenting and for nature that all Robbins's heroes and heroines have, and eventually the Countess succeeds in tying her down for modeling in New York by introducing her to a Real American Indian. His name is Julian Gitche. Unfortunately, this Indian, like the Countess himself, is fairly sterile, eviscerated, and effete, a big city watercolor artist who suffers from chronic asthma. Sissy marries him anyway because he is also kind, but she soon tires of being caged in his New York apartment and takes up the Countess's offer to do an advertising layout with the cranes at Siwash Lake.

While Sissy is at the Rubber Rose, she has a brief love affair with Bonanza Jellybean—another one of those role options Society deems perverse—and she meets a Japanese hermit named the Chink. The Chink provides much of the guidance in *Cowgirls,* and like Amanda in ***Another Roadside Attraction,*** he functions as lover and friend as well as teacher.

The Chink's adventures, particularly his time among the Clockpeople, are actually a third plot strand. Basically, he has learned kindness and humility and how to take joy in living. His time with the Clockpeople illustrates that nothing man-made, such as clock or calendar time, has any absolute value, but that some of these things can make life more pleasant. On the one hand, the Clockpeople's time is a measurement of the apparently unpredictable tremors along the San Andreas fault. Their time measures significant action, but cannot be related to our "normal," artificial clocktime. The Chink notes that all values are basically artificial, yet he concludes that some values are worth fighting for, a few are worth dying for, but none is worth killing for. On the other hand, as he dances to the polkas coming over his transistor radio, he castigates the "organic fascists" who refuse to accept the products of their own technology.

Much of *Cowgirls* might be misconstrued as calling for some kind of pastoral regression—the Chink lives in a cave, cities don't seem to have much to offer, and the book is peppered with dialogues between the thumb and the brain accusing each other of removing man from nature and turning him into a neurotic. However, the Chink despises this simple-minded longing for a vanished past.

The Chink has a great deal to teach Sissy and Dr. Robbins, her self-appointed analyst. When Sissy returns from her first visit to the Rubber Rose, she is despondent about living in the asphalt lock-up of New York City and longs to hit the hitching trail. Julian, the perfectly brainwashed middle-American, declares that her revelling in her affliction, instead of accepting it as a disgraceful deviation from normal thumb-size, is a sign of severe neurosis, and so he sends her to a psychiatrist, Dr. Goldman, who shares his views. Goldman thinks that people who are not normal are crazy either by circumstance or by choice, and he finds

Sissy to be crazy by both. He is confronted, however, by young Dr. Robbins, who believes that the compulsion toward "normalcy" is the source of most of the neuroses in our civilization.

When Robbins first asks Sissy why she turned Julian's pet birds loose in New York, where they were not adapted to live, she replies that freedom is the only thing more important than happiness. This point hits home with Dr. Robbins, who, like Tom Robbins and Western pioneers before him, has always placed freedom above every other facet of self-fulfillment. Tom Robbins, in fact, features the whooping cranes in *Cowgirls* as a major symbol of freedom because they seem to have chosen fidelity to their true natures over survival. This suicidal integrity is like that of the Western heroes who became extinct because they couldn't or wouldn't give up their wild individualism, and it is unlike the egotism of most Americans, worshippers of material success.

Paradoxically, Robbins sees material success as self-destructive: "Success must not be considered absolute. It is questionable, for that matter, whether success is an adequate response to life. Success can eliminate as many options as failure." The cranes remind the narrator that "to live fully, one must be free, but to be free one must give up security. Therefore, to live one must be ready to die." Such sentiments are also part of the code of the Western hero.

Dr. Robbins is so impressed by the Chink's teachings that he takes off the rest of the day, and then quits his job entirely, calling in "well." Dr. Robbins is opinionated and intellectually aggressive, but most of all he is desperately interested in finding out the truth about human life. It comes as no surprise when, at the end of the novel, we learn that the young doctor has been our narrator all along. He seems to be an extension of Marx Marvelous, several leagues further along the way to liberation. However, unlike the truly liberated individual, the Chink, Robbins has severe anxiety attacks about the future of the human race:

> It was entirely possible that everything in the universe was perfect; that all that happened, from global warfare to a single case of athlete's foot, happened because it ought to happen; and while from our perspective it would seem that something horrendous had gone wrong in the development of the human species, vis-a-vis its happy potentialities on the blue green sphere, that that was an illusion attributable to myopia, and that, in fact, development was proceeding beautifully, running right as a Tokyo train, and needing only a more cosmic overview in order for its grand perfection to obscure its momentary fits and faults.
>
> . . . On the other hand, if such an approach was, like religion, merely a camouflage system created to modify experience in order to make life more tolerable—another exercise in escapism festooned with mystic crepe—then one had no choice but to conclude that mankind was a royal fuck-up. Despite our awesome potential; despite the presence among us of the most ex-

traordinarily enlightened individuals operating with intelligence, gentleness and style; despite a plethora of achievements that no other living creatures have come within a billion light-years of equaling, we were on the verge of destroying ourselves, internally and externally, and of taking the entire planet with us, crumpled in our tight little fists, as we shoot down the shit-chute to oblivion.

So Dr. Robbins's concerns as well as his function in *Cowgirls* parallel those of Marx in *Another Roadside Attraction.* What he longs to learn through Sissy and eventually through the Chink is an ultimate form of self-therapy, and this search for self-healing leads us back, through Zen liberation, to religion. The Chink's message is that neither Eastern nor Western religion is natural to Americans, neither Oriental mysticism nor Judeo-Christian theology—which, he points out, is also of Eastern origin, due to the hegemony of Greek thought in classical culture and its own origins in Asia Minor. Western man must return to his natural, Pantheistic roots, long persecuted by invading doctrines. Westerners are "spiritually impoverished" because they have denied the "bawdy goat-man who proved rich harvests and bouncy babies," who really would best serve our natures.

Pantheism, the Chink points out, is also a religion that would return women to their rightful role in spirituality.

> If you scratch back past the Christian conquest into your true heritage, you will find women doing wondrous things. Women were not only the principal servants of the Old God, women were his mistresses, the power behind his pumpkin throne. Women controlled the Old Religion. It had few priests, many priestesses. There was no dogma; each priestess interpreted the religion in her own fashion. The Great Mother—creator and destroyer—instructed the Old God, was his mama, his wife, his daughter, his sister, his equal and ecstatic partner in the ongoing fuck.

Robbins has probably drawn these theses at least in part from Robert Graves' *The White Goddess,* a lengthy study of Western Pantheism. Other anthropological sources dispute the matriarchal theory, as Robbins himself points out.

This emphasis on restoring women to their rightful place in the spiritual community is, of course, another tie-in with the Rubber Rose plot.

Dr. Robbins is hooked and wants to rush off to the Chink's cave as soon as possible. Unfortunately, while he is scheming to run off with her, Sissy's melancholy and her anxiety about the safety of Bonanza Jellybean are growing. When the Countess attempts to cow her into betraying the cowgirls, Sissy beats him severely with her thumbs and runs away. She is nearly raped while trying to hitchhike to freedom, again responding with her thumping thumbs, but she eventually cracks. Condemning herself to normalcy in order to escape her violence and horror, she flees back to Richmond to a recently desmocked plastic surgeon, Dr. Dreyfus.

Robbins has apparently chosen this name for his doctor because the surgeon knows that Sissy's thumbs are a wonder and not a crime, but the doctor is willing to betray this knowledge for the sake of his art. Dreyfus has had his license suspended for turning poor Bernie Schwartz's nose-job into an experiment in cubism, "a nose in *totality*" that "manages to suggest motion even when it is static." Like many Westerners confused by Judeo-Christianity, Dreyfus fails to make the distinction between the artificial illusion of motion—as in our clock time—and the actual process and flux of life.

Dreyfus completes the "normalization" of one of Sissy's thumbs, but before he has time to finish the massacre, Bonanza calls Sissy back to the Rubber Rose to take part in the showdown with the FBI. Confused by her affections for the Chink and for Bonanza and by her own position vis-a-vis mainstream society, Sissy gets her first clue about her new situation from the Chink, who claims he likes the "balance" of her large and small thumbs. "Don't confuse symmetry and balance," he says. As in the Oriental art of flower arranging (the Chink was once a gardener), balance or harmony with nature has little to do with the artificial symmetries of contemporary society, which are often merely uniform, "normative," and restrictive.

The different-sized thumbs may also signify that Sissy will find the "balanced" road for which she's searching somewhere between contemporary American civilization and the complete withdrawal from society that Dr. Robbins envisions for her. For, as the novel ends and the characters disperse, we find the good doctor contemplating his procreative future with Sissy, raising a tribe of big-thumbed babies in a rustic pantheistic environment.

Robbins hypothesizes, or at least Dr. Robbins does, that big-thumbed people would not be able to manipulate tools the way that normal humans do, and so would be forced into a less domineering, more communal and participatory relationship with nature. *Even Cowgirls Get the Blues* is spotted with a running debate between the brain and the thumb, each blaming the other for the distortions and dislocations of human beings from the natural universe. Basically, however, the situation is familiar, as is Robbins's advice: humans must gain a new, healthier perspective on their limited role in the cosmos and must learn to live with, rather than against nature.

To summarize, *Cowgirls* posits the abandonment of outworn mainstream social roles that are destructive in their rigidity. American men and women must seek new roles based more clearly on the true Western spiritual tradition, Pantheism, which embraces a feminine receptivity rather than the more masculine will to dominate.

To the extent that it resembles a mere pastoral regression, Dr. Robbins's dream of living in a cave is probably just mental foreplay for Tom Robbins's other ideas, but not just because it doesn't seem sensible or probable. Man is differentiated from the rest of nature by his brain and by his apposable thumbs, and he owes much of his success as a species to them. While success isn't everything to Robbins, he chooses the amoeba, rather than the whooping crane, as the official mascot of *Cowgirls* because the amoeba is a survivor par excellence. For Robbins, revolutionary or pastoral romanticism is just partial vision; at the same time, he rejects the conventional notion of technological progress.

The Chink's rebuttal of "Organic Fascism" embraces the products of technology and suggests that Robbins is essentially trying to fertilize a marriage of compromise. Death, too, eliminates options, and Robbins seems to overstate his case on purpose. The cranes do leave the ranch in order to survive; Sissy's amputated thumb, like her forshortened "normal" life with her husband, Julian, does give her a kind of balance, as the Chink points out. Extremes may be beautiful, they may be art, and, while they may also prevent the individual from achieving harmony, extremes may yet become each other. As Robbins's epigraph from Blake says, "Excess of sorrow laughs. Excess of joy weeps." Delores del Ruby's Third Vision, brought on by a peyote overdose and an epileptic hatred of men, returns her to heterosexuality, or bi-sexuality.

Robbins has in fact *chosen to accept* a good many goals in his game of life, and survival, freedom, and fulfillment seem to be among them. What you choose to value may still be of great significance. Dr. Dreyfus, the brilliant plastic surgeon who is willing to amputate Sissy's thumbs despite his awareness of their significance, is a fairly kind man who has isolated himself morally from the world. He tries to make art from life, but the result is a horrible parody of the real life-in-motion of Sissy's hitching. His willingness to destroy her "real" art and replace it with his "plastic" is the mark of a man who has lost the ability to differentiate between life and art, or perhaps of one who has chosen to "conquer" the brief chaos of life with the permanence of a life-denying art.

Survival, or rather fear of *not* surviving, is the onus of the human species; it produces the insecurities that produce the fear that causes the greed that forecloses on the house that Jack built—or blows it to smithereens. The fear of not surviving paradoxically reduces our chances for survival. Robbins is, at the same time, concerned about the extinction of various endangered species, because he believes that the world is enriched by its diversity. When polymorphous perversity rears its horny heads in these novels, it usually relates back to the demand for an ever-greater range of perspectives and possibilities. The paradox of the fear of not surviving parallels the paradox of the meaning of meaning; by concentrating our narrow, ego-blindered attention on survival, we may eventually make survival impossible.

Robbins's novels teach that man must step out of ego-bound time to gain a broader perspective on his relatedness to the universe—and then he must take what he learns about the universe and make it personal. By recognizing the demands of the ego as arbitrary and by recognizing life as play, man may be able to rediscover some sense of his oneness with the universe—to learn that, in fact, there can be little difference between the universal and the personal in a liberated consciousness. (pp. 21-31)

*Mark Siegel, in his* Tom Robbins, *Boise State University, Western Writers Series, 1980, 52 p.*

## Tom Robbins    (Interview with Larry McCaffery and Sinda Gregory)

[*The following interview was conducted in 1982.*]

[*McCaffery and Gregory*] : *It's surely no coincidence that so many West Coast writers—you, Ursula Le Guin, Gary Snyder, and others—have concerned yourselves with counterculture values and Oriental philosophy and religion. Do you ever think of yourself as a regional writer?*

[Robbins]: Not really. You know the painter Jacques Louis David had a room, a studio, that overlooked the square where the major guillotine was located in Paris before the Revolution. And he would sit up there all day and watch heads being lopped off, blood flooding the cobblestones. Then he would turn to his easel and paint those very sweet portraits of members of the court. Now there was a man who was rejecting his environment. Most artists have a more direct dialogue with their environment than David, and so do I. But while there is a sense of place in my work, and that place is the Northwest, I see myself not as regional but American.

*Wouldn't you agree, though, that people living out here on the West Coast are more likely to be influenced by Oriental ways of thinking and living?*

Well, the Northwest is, after all, perched on the Pacific rim facing the Orient rather than Europe, and that's bound to affect people in all sorts of ways. A lot of my orientations are Asian rather than European—but they were leaning that way before I moved here. Maybe that's one of the reasons *why* I moved here. Somebody suggested that my penchant for writing episodically came from the influence of Kurt Vonnegut, but I never read Vonnegut until after I wrote my first novel. In fact, that abbreviated, episodic style of writing came to me, in part, from the Zen koan, through John Cage. Back in Virginia, I read *Silence,* in which Cage made use of the Zen koan form, and that influenced me in that direction early on. Later, out here, the Tibetan concept of Crazy Wisdom became fairly central to my way of thinking, and so did aspects of Taoism and Tantra. I'd say that anyone who lives out here who *isn't* influenced by the Far East is behaving a bit like David. (pp. 225-26)

*Did growing up in the South have any specific effect on your writing?*

From my perspective today I can see that the *juice* of my fiction comes out of the South, but I felt so repressed in the South that I'm not sure that if I had remained there I would ever have found a way to channel that juice. Virginia, where I spent a lot of time in my youth, is a fairly repressive place.

*You've said elsewhere that even as a kid you had the sense of being an outsider. Was that sense one of the things that helped lay the foundation for the "metaphysics of the outlaw" that you develop in your fiction? I gather that even as a young man you were already something of a rebel.*

I feel completely at home in the world, I like it here, but from the beginning I've insisted that my stay here be on my own terms and not society's. In that sense, I've been more allied with the outlaw than the outsider. I don't know if it helped shape the unbaked cookie dough of my talent. . . . (pp. 226-27)

*You were also an avid reader as a kid, weren't you?*

I read the stuff that most kids read—the kids who read at all—except for an atlas. One of my favorite playthings as a child was a world atlas that I read from cover to cover. I knew the capitals of all the countries until that frenzy of independence in the '60s, when all those new nations in Africa emerged; then I lost track. But I also devoured adventure and mystery stories—the Hardy Boys and all that—and comic books, too. I was always reading as a kid; I taught myself to read when I was five years old because I couldn't wait to get into books. (pp. 227-28)

*You ended up in a school of music, art, and drama—the Richmond Professional Institute. Were you interested in becoming a performing artist or a painter?*

No, I was interested in writing about art. I had earlier spent two years at Washington and Lee University and then I was out of school for four years. I was kicked out of my fraternity for lobbing biscuits at the housemother. Being expelled from a fraternity at Washington and Lee was tantamount to being expelled from the university itself, because it was the epitome of the preppie college and there was hardly a student there who wasn't in a fraternity. So I hitchhiked around the country for a year, landed in the air force for three years, and then I returned to school. While I was in the air force I met some painters, and that was quite a magical thing. Not only had I never seen a real painting, rather than a reproduction, but to actually go into a studio and smell turpentine, actually see people painting pictures for a living—well, this experience blew my mind and I became friends with these wild bohemian artists and grew very interested in art. At college I took mostly theory courses—I didn't learn how to play an instrument or anything, and although I did take a course in play direction and some courses in painting, I didn't really accumulate much in terms of practical technique. I wanted to write about art. I never thought I could create it.

*But you did some painting later on, didn't you?*

Yes, I have painted for years, when I've had the space. I used to write during the day and paint at night because they were such opposite disciplines that I found it very relaxing to paint after a long day at the typewriter. Lately I haven't had enough space to do any painting, so I've worked with rubber stamps. I design many of my own stamps, and recently I've made little rubber-stamp and watercolor collages.

*Just now, when you said that painting and writing were "such opposite disciplines," what did you mean?*

For one thing, they are physically opposite, at least in the way I practice them. I can get very tense at the typewriter—I end up with a sore neck at the end of the day. Writing is harder physical labor than digging ditches, at least for me, because I have rotten typing posture and don't deal well with machines. So to go then and paint and just move that brush around—well, it's a lyrical, fluid, liberat-

ing feeling; it's more like a dance, swinging and lifting and dipping your muse, rather than trying to knead some words out of her.

*Several of my favorite writers—Coover and Barthelme, for example—worked closely with painting while they were developing as writers. Did your experience with painting affect your views about writing?*

Probably. It may have heightened my visual sense, my passion for color and texture and shape in language. Language is alive for me, in my eyes as well as in my ears, and painting must have contributed to my good fortune in this regard. It probably also contributed to my appreciation of objecthood. I'm very interested in inanimate objects and in the mysterious network of connections—in terms of the poetic, psychological, and historical associations they inspire, as well as in terms of the energy fields—by which all objects are joined. I believe that every object leads a secret life of its own, although it isn't necessary to delve into those secrets to appreciate the object. Does this sound kooky? Is Claes Oldenburg kooky? Oldenburg understands the rich, complex life of the common object, and in a less profound way so does Andy Warhol. The pop artists deepened my relationship with objects, but so did the "old-fashioned" still-life painters such as Morandi and Cézanne.

*Were you interested in realistic painting or in nonrepresentational art?*

I consider the art I'm interested in realistic, but then I consider Jackson Pollock a realistic painter and Andrew Wyeth an abstract painter.

*Could you explain?*

Well, Wyeth's paintings are two-dimensional reductions of the three-dimensional world. Thus, they're abstracted from the external world. They are pictures *of* things. Pollock's paintings don't refer to things, they *are* things: independent, intrinsic, internal, holistic, *real*. Now, in a sense, books are abstractions in that they refer to countless things outside themselves. In my books, when I interrupt the narrative flow and call attention to the book itself, it's not cuteness or self-consciousness but an attempt to make the novel less abstract, more of a real thing.

*That's interesting, because I suspected that that strategy of reminding readers that they're reading a book, reminding them that the author is inventing what's going on, was designed, in part, to expose all forms of knowledge as subjective—that is, to remind the reader that mimetic fiction is another illusion, just as scientific and mathematical descriptions are metaphoric.*

I believe that reading is one of the most marvelous experiences a human being can enjoy. Being alone in a room with a book is so intimate, so individualistic, so kaleidoscopically imaginative; it's erotic to me, sacred. What I want to do with my fiction is to create an experience peculiar to reading alone, an experience that could not be duplicated in any other medium, something that can't be done in the movies, can't be done on television, on stage, record, or canvas. What this means, on the one hand, is devaluating plot to a certain extent, because if it's only a story you're after, how much easier it is to switch on TV or go to a film. Reading requires more from an audience than television or film; the audience has to participate more fully. Keeping plot secondary to "bookness" helps to make it a reading experience, a literary experience, an experience that could only be derived from words on a page. I also have wanted to avoid the escapism that frequently results from a mimetic approach. What I've wanted to do was to break into the narrative and say, "Look, this is a book—you're just reading a book. But it's nice, isn't it? It's still entertaining, isn't it? I still have your attention, don't I? Even though I'm popping through the page and pointing my finger at what I'm doing, even though you're not caught up in the belief that you're living on Tara plantation." (pp. 228-30)

*Did you do much fiction writing before you started on* **Another Roadside Attraction?**

No. I was waiting for the right moment to begin.

*You mean* **Another Roadside Attraction** *was actually the first piece of fiction you'd ever started? You had no apprentice pieces at all?*

Oh, I'd been writing stories off and on since I was five years old, but nothing I wanted to show anyone, and I'd never begun a novel or anything like that. I concentrated on nonfiction. I was waiting to find my voice. Once I found it, I was off and running. But I felt that I couldn't start writing fiction before my voice evolved. One of my art teachers was always encouraging me to go out and become another Faulkner, but that was the last thing in the world that appealed to me. By that I don't mean any disrespect toward Faulkner—I simply didn't aspire to *become anybody else.* So I really didn't want to write, and certainly not to publish, until I was certain my own voice had evolved.

*What was it that helped you find that voice? Was there a specific event that helped you crystallize your sense of voice?*

I think that the times—the '60s—had a lot to do with it. I was very much caught up in that whole psychedelic revolution, and I quickly realized that no one was going to write about it in an appropriate way. I could see that writers were going to *describe* it rather than *evoke* it. And as a matter of fact, that's exactly what happened—almost no good novels came out of the '60s dealing with the kinds of things we were experiencing then, because most writers described them in a reportorial, journalistic manner that was inadequate to reproduce the essence of what was going on. But I realized that I could capture this experience from the inside out, partly due to my experience with LSD. I based my first novel, *Another Roadside Attraction,* on a psychedelic model. Some people complained that *ARA* had no structure, but that book was carefully structured, I spent two years structuring it, although it was not structured in any usual way. There had been plenty of previous books that were nonlinear, but not nonlinear in the way that *ARA* is nonlinear. I don't think there has ever been a book quite like *ARA,* either in content or in form. It may not be great, but it is definitely one of a kind.

*When you said that* **ARA's** *form is based on a "psychedelic model," what did you mean?*

Simply that its structure *radiates* in many directions at once, rather than progressing gradually up an inclined plane, like most novels, from minor climax to minor climax to major climax. There are lots of little *flashes* of illumination strung together like beads. Some of these flashes illuminate the plot; others merely illuminate the reader.

*Could you talk a little more about the effects that drugs had on your aesthetic sensibility?*

Mainly, psychedelics left me less rigid, intellectually and emotionally. Certain barriers just melted away. Reality is not a fixed thing, and I learned to move about more freely from one plane of existence to another. The borderlines between so-called reality and so-called fantasy, between dream and wakefulness, animate and inanimate were no longer as distinct, and I made some use of this newfound mobility in my writing. Also, there's a fairly narrow boundary between the silly and the profound, between the clear light and the joke, and it seems to me that on that frontier is the most risky and significant place an artist or philosopher can station himself. Maybe my psychedelic experiences prepared me to straddle that boundary more comfortably than most. Or maybe you'd say that, as a writer, I'm a borderline case.

*Larry and I find that most of our favorite artists share an ability to be serious and funny at the same time.*

Like the universe, you mean?

*What?*

Quantum physics has taught us that the universe is a balance between irrevocable laws and random playfulness. We've learned that part of the evolutionary process is purposeful and part of it is merely an adventure, a game. I don't know why I said "merely." Games are serious, too. And playfulness, when the player's consciousness is fully operative, can be profound. We could define life as the beautiful joke that is always happening—and find support for that definition in advanced science. (pp. 230-32)

*How did you happen to choose the particular subject matter for* **ARA**—*the demythologizing of Christianity?*

The idea of the discovery of the mummified body of Christ had been kicking around in my head for six or seven years. I was fascinated by the fact that Western civilization is based upon the divinity of Christ in a lot of crucial ways. So what would happen if we were to learn conclusively that Christ was *not* divine? What would this say about the future of Western civilization? Could we continue to lead moral and ethical lives if Christ proved to have died and stayed dead? I had that idea in mind for a long time, and I did a lot of research into the life of Jesus and the history of religion. Actually, however, I didn't demythologize Christianity, I *re*mythologized it. As Joseph Campbell has pointed out, a major problem with Christianity is that it interprets its myths historically rather than symbolically.

*Obviously* **ARA** *takes a pretty dim view of organized religion in general and Christianity in particular. Was there* *a special incident that had made you react against your religious upbringing?*

Yep, it was seeing Johnny Weissmuller for the first time. For years I had attended Sunday school. I also was subjected to a lot of Southern Baptist training at home. So I knew that Jesus was supposed to be "the big man," my hero. But then I saw my first Tarzan movie, and after that Jesus just didn't cut the mustard. I continued to like Jesus, and I still admire the myth—he's still a sort of hero of mine. In *ARA* I have a dialogue between Tarzan and Jesus which was an attempt to resolve, I suppose, all those conflicts in my early years when Jesus and Tarzan were competing—Jesus quite unsuccessfully, as it turned out—for being my main man. You know, religion is organized spirituality. But there's an inherent contradiction there, because the moment you try to organize spirituality, you destroy its essence. So religion is spirituality in which the spiritual has been killed. Or at least diminished. Spirituality doesn't lend itself to organization. The whole process is rather like Heisenberg's uncertainty principle. That was one of the messages of *ARA.*

*Your second novel,* **Even Cowgirls Get the Blues,** *also had its spiritual side—the spiritual side of feminism, modern woman's connection to the goddess, and so forth. And in* **Still Life with Woodpecker,** *where you were dealing with romantic love and outlawism . . .*

And objecthood.

*Yes, and objecthood. You managed to find a spiritual side to those things as well. Does* **Jitterbug Perfume** *have a spiritual theme?*

From one perspective, the perspective of subatomic physics, where matter and energy merge and become one, *everything* is spiritual. Including poodles with rhinestone collars. But, yes, *Jitterbug Perfume* concerns itself with immortality, which is the basis of most spirituality and all religion.

*Do you develop a theory of the afterlife?*

Not exactly. Whether there is an afterlife or not, beyond the pure energy level, is something that can't be known unless you die. Meanwhile, a rigid belief in an afterlife can be very harmful. A belief in Heaven can cause Hell. As long as a population can be induced to believe in a Heaven or a Nirvana, it can be controlled and oppressed. People will put up with all sorts of tyranny and poverty and ill treatment if they're convinced they'll eventually escape to a stress-free dude ranch for eternity. And then they're much more willing to risk their lives for their governments. Also, these old men who run our governments, as long as they believe that life is just a trial for eternal life after death, they will be less hesitant about leading us into a nuclear conflict. I'm convinced that, if we want to end war, then we've got to put all thoughts of an afterlife out of our minds. To emphasize the afterlife is to deny life. And denial of life is the only unpardonable sin. Amen.

*I'd like to take you back to something you said a minute ago about objecthood. Could I ask you about the Camel cigarette pack in* **Still Life?** *Did that idea occur to you in the*

*midst of your work, or did you know from the beginning that you wanted to bring it in?*

This is a case where I had something specific in mind early on. At the beginning of that novel my ambition was to write about objects in a way in which they had never been written about in a work of fiction. People had previously used objects symbolically, of course, and had done so very beautifully and very effectively. But I wanted to write about objects *for their own sake,* to write about the object as if it had a life of its own—which I think inanimate objects do have. In order to get this out of the whole broad social context, I decided I wanted to find some way to put one person alone in an empty room with three objects. Well, that didn't quite work out, for reasons that are still pretty unclear to me; so I decided to concentrate on a single object. And it occurred to me that better than some natural object—like a snail's shell, or a pine cone, or a seashell, something that lends itself to poetic interpretations—would be a popular object, because I have an affinity with popular objects. So I decided to take something out of the supermarket and use it, hopefully in a profound way. I began mulling over our common objects, and by far the richest was the Camel pack. There is a whole mythology and lore about the Camel pack that has gradually evolved in this century. Jokes and riddles have been invented by prisoners, by sailors, by men bored and alone. There are far more of these stories than I mention in the book; I just used a fraction of them.

*You must have gone out and researched this area once you figured out you were going to use the Camel pack.*

I did some research, although I knew some of the lore already. When I first thought of the Camel pack, I figured, This has got to be my object, because there is no other package design, no other common object, no other supermarket artifact that has that amount of richness and resonance.

*So you chose the Camel pack and the basic situation and then worked the plot of* **Still Life** *around these things?*

Right. I wanted to use the Camel pack, and I wanted to use the idea of one person locked in a room with the Camel pack, having to relate in a way in which we don't usually relate to inanimate objects.

**ARA** *seemed like a strikingly original novel when it appeared; but there were a number of other experimental works appearing during that same period with which your book shared certain affinities. Were there any writers you were reading during that period who did have some impact on you while you were working on* **ARA?**

Not any fiction writers. During that period I was mostly reading Alan Watts, Gary Snyder, Timothy Leary, Yogananda, people like that. The only fiction writer who spoke to me then was Hermann Hesse, and he certainly didn't influence my style. (pp. 232-35)

*Brautigan's work is also frequently linked to your own. Did his fiction offer you any specific inspiration?*

When I finally got around to reading *Trout Fishing in America,* it encouraged me greatly. It was the first modern novel to successfully do away with plot. By "successfully" I mean it remained accessible and compelling. It's a landmark book. But I was well along with *ARA* before I ever read a word of it. People are always comparing me to Brautigan and Vonnegut and I can't understand it. The only thing I have in common with Brautigan is the use of imaginative, fanciful, outrageous metaphors and similes, but I was using them before he was and I can prove it. I'm not suggesting that he was influenced by me, either, because he wasn't. And Vonnegut, well, we've both employed an episodic structure, and once in a while our ideas dovetail, but I'm obsessed with the poetics of prose and he clearly is not, I'm optimistic and he's pessimistic, I'm complex and he's simple: His sensibility is much more middle aged and middle class. Vonnegut and Brautigan are far more interesting and important than most of those safe and sane ivory-carvers who get all the awards and "serious" acclaim, but anybody who's concerned with my influences had better look elsewhere.

*To where?*

To James Joyce, for openers. Next, to Alfred Jarry and Günter Grass. Then to Blaise Cendrars, Henry Miller, Claes Oldenburg, George Herriman, and the Coconut Monk. (pp. 235-36)

*[Let's] talk some more about comic writing. As I'm sure you know, there are some critics and readers out there who don't take your work seriously because you are so playful and comic; and because, despite your frequent poignancy and the often savage satiric thrust of your books, you seem fundamentally optimistic. How do you respond to this kind of charge?*

I don't feel any need to respond to it at all. I suppose I *ought* to be discouraged. Comic writing is not only more profound than tragedy, it's a hell of a lot more difficult to write. There seems to be almost a conspiracy against exploring joy in this culture; to explore pain is considered not only worthy but heroic, while exploring joy is considered slight. This kind of attitude strikes me as nearly insane. Why is there more value in pain than there is in joy? This is not to say that pain, anger, alienation, and frustration can't inform us or shouldn't be explored, but only to ask why these emotions should be explored while joy is excluded. Part of this is due to a prevailing sensibility, particularly rampant in academic and journalistic circles, that it is simply not hip to be life-affirming or positive. Some critics prefer books that reflect their own neuroses, their own miserable lives. (p. 236)

*Could I ask you something about women? In all of your books you have a main admirable heroine who winds up meeting what is essentially a male mentor. This seems to suggest that men and women have crucial differences that need to be shared with each other, and runs against the idea that men and women are basically the same.*

They *are* different, and *vive la différence!* Men and women are not alike, and blacks and whites are not alike, and French and Germans are not alike, and gays and straights are not alike. One thing I really hate is the tendency today toward homogeneity. These differences among people are important and we're all enriched by them. The fact that a man is different from a woman enriches the life of both the man and the woman in ways that would be lost were we to become truly unisexual. This doesn't mean that either the man or the woman is limited by sexual definition. But to keep the gene pool from dwindling, to keep options open, to keep life bright and free and interesting, it's imperative that we have variety and maintain differences. It's important that the gypsies not be assimilated into the mainstream, and that certain aspects of black culture remain black. This idea of all of us becoming the same is a greater threat to our survival than nuclear warfare—it's a threat to our psychic existence. Every man has a woman in him, just as every woman has a man in her. Every black has many things in common with every white, just as every white has many things in common with every Oriental. These similarities are good, they're connections, they can help us live peacefully with one another. But the differences are more important than the similarities because the differences give life its fizz, its brew. Everything that makes life really challenging and interesting emerges out of these differences. The similarities form a good foundation, create a structure, a glue to hold us all together. But the really important things in life are a result of the tensions that arise from a balance of opposites. (pp. 237-38)

> *Tom Robbins, Larry McCaffery and Sinda Gregory, in an interview in* Alive and Writing: Interviews with American Authors of the 1980's, *edited by Larry McCaffery and Sinda Gregory, University of Illinois Press, 1987, pp. 222-39.*

### Frederick R. Karl

A cult novel, Tom Robbins's *Even Cowgirls Get the Blues* (1976) is a catchall of pastoral, Eden, spatiality, growing up, marginality, resourcefulness. It probes legends, and it recapitulates Thoreau, Kerouac, and early frontier life. Its protagonist, Sissy Hankshaw, has magic wands—abnormally large thumbs, more like baseball bats than fingers. With Sissy's abnormal thumbs, her hitchhiking ability, we have a parody of the American obsession with the road and, at the same time, an exploration of the legend.

The book has several segments about growing up, many of which, ultimately, fail to hold together. First: Sissy Hankshaw, with the big thumbs, which are legendary and which enable her to wield them as baseball bats when necessary. Sissy is the proverbial oddball who adapts to her affliction and turns it to her advantage. After having met and "gone with" Kerouac, she marries a Mohawk Indian, Julian, who becomes part of the establishment, whereas she struggles to remain herself. Second: the Rubber Rose Ranch, out in the Dakotas, a reducing farm now run by cowgirls. Many episodes are given over to the girls' life on the ranch: Delores del Ruby, with her whip; Bonanza Jellybean, with her bursting jeans; others. The ranch and its affairs feed directly into the feminist movement, which ideologically underlies the novel.

Third: off in the mountains the Chink—actually a Japanese named the Chink by the Clock People. Everything connected to the Chink (and beyond him, the Clock People) partakes of the *Whole Earth Catalog* view of life: he lives off yams, speaks of yin and yang, Zen principles, also of American individuality, and although ancient, screws like a rabbit. The Chink is guru, shaman, wizard. He learns from the Clock People about their sense of time, the two thirteen-hour segments that make up their history and that also, through water, keep them tuned in on the San Andreas Fault.

Because of this disdain for the disorderly, poetry and magic have vanished. "At every level. If civilization is ever going to be anything but a grandiose pratfall, anything more than a can of deodorizer in the shithouse of existence, then statesmen are going to have to concern themselves with magic and poetry." This message from the Chink recalls others, from Norman O. Brown or Castaneda's Don Juan: "the smoke is not for those who seek power. It is only for those who crave to see. I learned to become a crow because these birds are the most effective of all." The question is not one of survival, but the manner in which one survives.

Fourth: the workings of nature. After taking Sissy anally, the Chink argues: "Technology shapes psyches as well as environments, and maybe the peoples of the West are too sophisticated, too permanently alienated from Nature to make extensive use of their pagan heritage. However, links can be established. Links *must* be established. To make contact with your past, to re-establish the broken continuity of your spiritual development, is not the same as a romantic, sentimental retreat into simpler, rustic lifestyles."

Fifth: the whooping crane as natural model. The cowgirls at the Rubber Rose Ranch provide a sanctuary for the cranes, jeopardized by civilization—first "stoning" them slightly, and then feeding and taking care of them. It is this act that leads to invasion by enemies of nature, the police and FBI. The whooping crane is an apt model in that its courtship dance indicates an association with joy, and its life patterns suggest it has discovered that mode in nature the Chink espouses—neither a termite existence of survival (Nietzsche's "last man"), nor complete anarchy of self: instead, a balance of elements.

The reasons for the cult success of the novel are evident. It offers a critique of the larger society and technology in Jeffersonian and Emersonian terms without demanding a new society, simply a new person. Remake yourself, not the society: a comforting message for the 1970s, in a way an outgrowth and a repudiation of the previous decade. Foreign, combining sexual potency and balance, the Chink is a familiar figure in recent fiction—Kesey's Bromden, Berger's old Chief, and those other Indian wise men. Sissy is herself a very appealing character, with her deformity, her ability to make her way, her legendary hitchhiking powers. Then the Rubber Rose Ranch provides a feminist society, presented without condescension, with all the right arguments and activities.

Yet Robbins has written several kinds of novel. By far the most attractive sections concern Sissy growing up in South Richmond, Virginia, with those outsized baseball-bat thumbs. Everything connected with the thumbs makes the novel come alive, as part of her destiny, her growth into

an extremely attractive woman who demonstrates feminine hygiene apparatuses. All such parts are worked through. Other elements are not integrated fictionally; they become set or insert pieces, especially the Chink, his teachings, the Clock People. The rest is a novel that seems part fiction, part sermon; and the wit, which is real, is often dissipated in the message. A novel turns into *Zen and the Art of Motorcycle Maintenance,* which is, after all, not a bad fate. (pp. 173-74)

*Frederick R. Karl, "Growing Up in America: The 1940's and Thereafter," in his* American Fictions, 1940/1980: A Comprehensive History and Critical Evaluation, *Harper & Row, Publishers, 1983, pp. 129-75.*

## William Nelson

Sissy Hankshaw is the unlikely heroine of ***Even Cowgirls Get the Blues;*** she has been born with outsized thumbs, which, by the time she is eleven, constitute 4% of her body weight. Otherwise she is a tall slim pretty girl of 'model proportions.' Her childhood consists largely of trying to cope with misguided would-be helpers who see her as handicapped and the consciously and unconsciously cruel who call attention to her thumbs by pointedly ignoring them or by making jokes about them. Sissy, attempting to make the best of what she has, adopts a career of hitchhiking in which the point is not a potential destination but the process itself. Among her other attributes is complete acceptance of her own sexuality and that of everybody else. Sissy is not the American sweetheart, a glorified version of the girl-next-door, or the one who married dear old dad.

As a consequence of her hitch-hiking she is often warned that she may be picked up by an evil man who will take advantage of her. The implication is a world in which evil quite possibly exists so that young women must guard themselves against its occasional manifestation. In her experience, however, every man who picks her up makes some sort of sexual advance. It is hinted that her abnormal thumbs enhance her sexual attractiveness. Sissy permits them to fondle her as they please so long as they keep driving; she simply looks upon it as a fringe benefit of her hitch-hiking hobby. Conventional responses to the situation are inadequate in two regards. They misjudge the sexual nature of the young girl in assuming that she would automatically reject such stimulation and they underestimate the extent of potential child molesters. The result is comic exaggeration, but it also asserts that conventional wisdom fails to understand the true nature of the world. Instead of innocence corrupted by a failure of the norm, there is lack of innocence experiencing the perverse sexuality as a norm and yet refusing to be contaminated by it. Thus Sissy's responses to the circumstances are seen to be more desirable than those of the society which has so far only succeeded in making her virtually an isolate.

Along the way, Sissy meets Julian Gitche, a Mohawk Indian with a Yale degree in Fine Arts; in a comic reversal he is anything but the 'natural' man that he might conventionally be supposed to represent. He has no interest in Indian culture; in fact, he considers it hopelessly archaic even to think about. He also has asthma and is often incapacitated in critical moments by psychosomatic attacks. Their subsequent marriage seems doomed from the start. A trip to the Cowgirls' ranch brings her to a character known as 'The Chink' who is actually a Japanese-American interned during World War II and a continuing refugee from civilized society. Sissy becomes pregnant as a result of a sexual debauch with the Chink and we then learn the symbolism of her gigantic thumbs:

> In a post catastrophic world, your offspring of necessity intermarry, forming in time a tribe. . . . A tribe of Big Thumbs would relate to the environment in very special ways. It could not use weapons or produce sophisticated tools. It would have to rely on its wits and its senses. It would have to live with animals—and plants!—as virtual equals.

Sissy Hankshaw's thumbs provide the key to her destiny as well as to her character and personality. She is forced to find salvation in herself or, as the Chink says: "Be your own master! Be your own Jesus! Be your own flying saucer! Rescue yourself. Be your own valentine!" What this sunny philosophy amounts to in practical application is difficult to say, but the Chink adds, "Each individual must work it out for himself . . . gather about him his integrity, his imagination and his individuality and . . . leap into the dance of experience." Sissy's thumbs have made it necessary for her to do just that or perish. It is characteristic of all of the cowgirls, who stand for the non-conforming cutting edge of the future in the book, that they are outcasts from the present or at least have the courage of their lack of conviction. The novel implies that only those like Sissy who are among the alienated are likely to be redeemed through the enjoyment of polymorphous sexuality and other attributes of a more natural life style. The world which they experience as insensitive and unsupportive is a world of destruction of the environment, of hypocrisy and sexual perversion, of false values, and a general lack of meaningful interpersonal relationships. Sissy and the other cowgirls comprise fictional representatives of the young of the 60s who referred to themselves as 'freaks' in contrast to 'straight' society. (pp. 165-66)

Part of the conclusion to *Even Cowgirls Get the Blues* reads, "I believe in everything; nothing is sacred. I believe in nothing; everything is sacred." This cryptic remark is perhaps more pretentious than profound, but it does suggest a world in which individual perception, however different from any other perception, is all that its inhabitants have to cling to. Only the 'freaks' are attuned to the liberating perception of Reality. (p. 170)

> *William Nelson, "Unlikely Heroes: The Central Figures in 'The World According to Garp', 'Even Cowgirls Get the Blues', and 'A Confederacy of Dunces'," in The Hero in Transition, edited by Ray B. Browne & Marshall W. Fishwick, Bowling Green University Popular Press, 1983, pp. 163-70.*

---

**Tom Robbins on writing fiction:**

A writer's first obligation is not to the many-bellied beast but to the many-tongued beast, not to Society but to Language. Everyone has a stake in the husbandry of Society, but Language is the writer's special charge. A grandiose animal it is, too. If it weren't for Language there wouldn't be Society.

Once writers have established their basic commitment to Language (and are taking the blue-guitar-sized risks that that relationship demands), then they are free to promote social betterment to the extent that their conscience or neurosis might require. But let me tell you this: social action on the political/economic level is wee potatoes.

Our great human adventure is the evolution of consciousness. We are in this life to enlarge the soul and light up the brain.

How many writers of fiction do you think are committed to *that*?

—*Tom Robbins, in an excerpt in fiction international, No. 15:1, 1984, p. 24.*

---

**Jay Cantor**

[*Skinny Legs and All*] is a fizzy drink. One jigger Bible of the Future: "This is the room where your wisest ancestor was born." One part story: the adventures of amiable redneck Boomer and his artist manque wife, Ellen. One part—make that several parts—preachment, meant to greet the return of the Great Mother. Such concoctions are called "specialty drinks," and they come with tiny made-in-Taiwan paper parasols. A little on the sweet side—you have to be in the right mood for them.

Robbins uses all his considerable charm to put you in the mood, with antic doings from the get-go: "It was a bright, defrosted, pussy-willow day . . . and the newlyweds were driving cross-country in a large roast turkey." The traveling bird turns out to be a cunningly decorated Airstream Van that Boomer gussied up to please his bride, artist-to-be Ellen Cherry. (She secretly thinks she'll dump the philistine redneck when her art career reaches liftoff in NYC, but it's Boomer's invention that amuses the decadent New York art world, sending Ellen into a funk of resentment. Can this marriage be saved?)

On their way to New York, still in the honeymoon phase, they stop to recelebrate their union in a roadside cave, and their gusto lovemaking re-awakens from long slumber some mystical objects—a Conch and a magic Stick. These devotees of the goddess Astarte have been hiding out in the American West from the trepidations of the Jerusalem Yawhists, the anti-goddess gang. They're joined by some American side-kicks, a Sock, a Can O'Beans, and a Spoon, and the walking objects make their way back to Jerusalem to await the Goddesses' big comeback. "The . . . Middle East . . . is the vagina of which . . . the new order of humanity must be born." (What rough Can O'Beans is slouching towards Bethlehem to be born?)

Though the Goddess herself doesn't appear in the novel, she does send a stand-in, a Lebanese belly dancer, who has the usual accoutrements of the Feminine Mystique: "a secret knowledge or hidden wisdom: bright creative power and a dark destructive power, neither of which she had to think about, for she didn't think quite so much as she was thought." In touch with those dark currents that move the tides and the menstrual cycles, she don't need no stinking doctorate—well, I hear Robbins say, who does? But it's hard, behind such valentines, not to hear the prison door clang shut. Anyway, skinny legs and all, she does a knock-out "Dance of the Seven Veils" in a restaurant in New York, for the book's big finale. Those who have eyes to see learn more from her than a mega-dose of windowpane LSD might teach (sex is good; all things co-evolve; reality is just something we make up as we go along).

Myself, I don't read Robbins for his friendly preaching, or even the story or the characters (who are somewhat stock, even to their mock-Jewish or redneck accents), but for the fizz and the paper umbrella, the style and the attitude. (Which is something Robbins values highly. "Liberty . . . cannot . . . result from political action . . . but rather evolves out of attitude.") Robbins's World is filled with the ecstasy of happy hyperbole, metaphor at any cost (but who's counting?), and charming fancies.

I suppose fancies like walking objects might indeed push the limits of the envelope, if there was an envelope in Robbins, if there were limits. Rules are probably overrated (though it's hard to have even a minimal game without them), but I think of them as stand-ins for history and its material impingements on our lives, our sad structural limits, our inevitable death. Despite the talk about the Middle East, history—as a constraint on our inventions, or motive for our actions—is mostly AWOL here. Patriarchy versus matriarchy, for example, duke it out here because . . . well, because some people—monotheists, fundamentalists—are kill-joys.

Fecund, shape-shifting Fancy, and not her necklace of skulls, is the aspect of the Great Mother that Robbins likes best, and I feel like a kill-joy myself wanting his usually amusing characters to live in relation to limits. But I would have liked it if the characters' experience had worked within them to help them arrive at their revelations, if those insights had been won rather than whimmed to them by the author. I share his love for those play-Beatles-songs-backwards and get messages from-a-Spoon days, yet I prefer (I guess I *am* a curmudgeon) a more tightly woven tapestry to wrap myself in, some more binding of character to sentiment, experience to outcome, history's happy possibilities to history's difficulties. Still, with all the fizz, the paper unbrellas, the horns and confetti, I did, usually, at least *want* to join Robbins' party. (pp. 1, 9)

*Jay Cantor, "Yet Another Roadside Attraction," in* Book World—The Washington Post, *March 25, 1990, pp. 1, 9.*

## Charles Dickinson

*Skinny Legs and All* shows Robbins again producing some of the cleverest writing in popular fiction, following the two-book slump of *Still Life With Woodpecker* and *Jitterbug Perfume.*

In this new novel he often nails an image so well it calls for an appreciative rereading: Coins go into a pay phone "with a hollow yet musical clink, like a robot passing a kidney stone." Rap music "sounds like somebody feeding a rhyming dictionary to a popcorn popper." A winter passes "as peacefully and leisurely as a python digesting a Valium addict."

And if this abundance of literary riches isn't enough, *Skinny Legs and All* has an agenda, too.

Robbins is fed up with a lot of things about this world and the people in it: Politicians, anything or anyone connected to organized religion, the small-minded, the untalented, the self-indulgent, the posturing *artiste,* the believers in an afterlife. They have no place in Robbins' view of the world. In fact, there are times when it seems the only reason Robbins wrote this novel was to provide a framework for the delineation of his complaints; and that is the sole—but not unimportant—weakness in this book.

Where else but in a Tom Robbins' novel would one find animate and inanimate protagonists? Five of the main characters are a Conch Shell, a Painted Stick, a Spoon, a Dirty Sock and a Can o' Beans. The Stick and the Conch Shell are objects from the ancient Temple of Jerusalem. Capable of locomotion, and of teaching that talent to other inanimate objects, the unlikely quintet set off on a very slow trek across America, heading back to Jerusalem.

Ellen Cherry Charles and Boomer Petway, artist *manqué* and welder respectively, newlyweds crossing the U.S. in an Airstream trailer that Boomer has welded into the shape of a roast turkey, are the animate protagonists of the novel. Ellen is heading for New York to join the community of artists there; Boomer simply wants to be with Ellen. He is, in Ellen's view, limited in his intellectual perspectives, ignorant of art, but fabulous in bed: in short, a boy toy.

They stop to have sex in a desert cave and Ellen begs Boomer to call her "Jezebel." He complies and this ancient name calls back into action the Conch Shell and the Painted Stick, waiting for as long as necessary in the recesses of the cave. The unexpected movement in the darkness spooks the lovers, who leave behind the Can o' Beans, the Spoon and the Dirty Sock in their haste to flee.

That Ellen asked to be called "Jezebel" is at the heart of Robbins' book. It is the engine that drives his agenda.

Robbins contends that Jezebel has long been the definition of a fallen woman simply because she was a devotee of Astarte, a goddess Robbins calls "the Great Mother, the Light of the World, the most ancient and widely revered divinity in human history."

Astarte threatened the male priests and believers of the relatively upstart Yahweh because "her warm feminine intuition was often at odds with cool masculine reason." . . .

The book's modern equivalent of those intimidated men of religion is Buddy Winkler, a Swaggart-like preacher so anxious for the Second Coming that he concocts a plan to hurry it along. He will go to Jerusalem to destroy Islam's Dome of the Rock, thus clearing the ground for the third Temple of Jerusalem. Buddy figures his mad plan will turn the Arab world against Israel. This holy war will, inevitably, draw the United States and Soviet Union into a nuclear cataclysm that will fulfill the Scriptures' prophecy of Armageddon.

So everything in *Skinny Legs and All* moves toward the east, toward New York City, and ultimately Jerusalem.

Ellen and Boomer arrive in New York and—surprise—it is not Ellen with her paintings who captures the imagination of the art world, but Boomer and his roast turkey Airstream trailer. The tenuous bonds of the relationship—primarily a sexual attraction—can't withstand the strain this twist in ambition and reality puts on them. Boomer—now a sculptor, not merely a welder—is swept into the art world Ellen longs to inhabit. Ellen goes to work as a waitress in a restaurant across the street from the United Nations, Isaac & Ishmael's, which is run by an Arab and a Jew, Abu Hadee and Spike Cohen.

All of this is simply an elaborate and entertaining prelude to Robbins' main objective: Salome's Dance of the Seven Veils. Abu Hadee says of the original dance: "A dancer would drop a veil at each of the seven gates of the Temple in Jerusalem. . . . the veils represented layers of illusion. As each veil peeled away, an illusion was destroyed, until finally some great mystery of life was revealed."

The illusion Robbins most enjoys skewering concerns religion and an afterlife. . . .

A modern version of Salome comes to dance at Isaac & Ishmael's. She schedules a performance of the Dance of the Seven Veils at the exact moment for the kickoff of the Super Bowl, in Robbins' view the nearest thing we have to a universal religious holiday, "when . . . Greeks actually sat down next to Turks, Arabs next to Jews."

As the dance proceeds and each veil drops, certain thoughts come into the minds of Ellen Cherry Charles and everyone else watching. These thoughts are why Robbins wrote the novel. They are the expanded versions of opinions he has touched on throughout the book. He gores most of the same oxen and does it magnificently. He reveals that the "great mystery of life" is so obvious that it's surprising no one has packaged it into a religion. But as an end in themselves, the seven veils make a weak climax to the novel.

Robbins wrote in *Another Roadside Attraction* that "It is style that makes us care." In that respect he has succeeded in making us care deeply about the people and ideas in this stylish homage to feminism, art and Astarte.

> Charles Dickinson, *"Playful Absurdities,"* in Chicago Tribune—Books, *April 1, 1990, p. 3.*

**Tom Clark**

In his previous novels, *Even Cowgirls Get the Blues, Another Roadside Attraction, Still Life With Woodpecker* and *Jitterbug Perfume,* Tom Robbins deployed his hyperactive sense of humor to wage a series of comic campaigns in the ongoing Battle of the Sexes. In his latest, *Skinny Legs and All,* he ambitiously expands the action to other fronts across a broad battlefield of history, pitting not only male versus female but Christian against pagan, Arab against Jew.

Entertaining no longer seems to be enough for Robbins. Indeed, in the propositional asides to his reader, which he inserts into his digressive narrative with the leisurely liberty of a Laurence Sterne, claims for a higher creative mode are clearly set out. . . . (p. 1)

The rearranged, fresh-contexted reality here assembled for us by the fictional creator bears little naturalistic resemblance to the world outside his book's covers. As Robbins hints in his authorial prelude, not that world but a distorted chamber of his artistic imagination—where once "Jezebel frescoed her eyelids with history's tragic glitter, Delilah practiced for her beautician's license [and] Salome dropped the seventh veil while dancing the dance of ultimate cognition, skinny legs and all"—supplies the actual setting of his new book. And we are constantly reminded of the novelist's deliberate artifice by the book's structure: *Skinny Legs* is divided into seven parts, each one to represent a different "veil" of illusion.

The heroine, whom he attempts to guide, via a plot as thinly contrived as one of those legendary veils, through the distractions of history's tragic glitter to ultimate cognition, is a contemporary "Jezebel," Ellen Cherry Charles. Perhaps a relative of Leigh-Cheri, the electrifying, oversexed, red-haired cheerleader-princess of *Still Life With Woodpecker,* Ellen Cherry, pert, round-breasted, with "animated rump" and lush "tangle of caramel-colored curls," is a modern woman of avid, independent mind and sexuality.

An unwilling Southern belle, she flees the confines of her Colonial Pines, Va., family home to become a painter in Seattle, and is pursued there by her hometown beau, a brawny welder named Boomer Petway. Boomer is far more taken with Ellen Cherry's anatomy than with her artistic aspirations, but his philistinism is forgiven when she lays eyes on his amazing Airstream trailer adorned with two giant metal drumsticks and a pair of stumpy wings. She abruptly marries him, and they head east in the shiny motorized fowl.

Along the way, the honeymooning couple stops off somewhere in the wilds of Wyoming or Utah to picnic and make out. Unbeknownst to them, the cave they've picked to tryst in already houses two archaic occupants, who are awakened by the proximate amorous activity.

With user-friendly anthropomorphism, Robbins at this point blithely trots out his main secondary "characters," a pair of inanimate objects possessed of the ability to talk and locomote. They are Painted Stick and Conch Shell, "male" and "female" talismans left in the cave in ancient

Roman times by a wandering Phoenician priestess of the Earth Goddess Astarte.

Through these voluble fetishes, the novelist smuggles in canned history of the Middle East over the last 3,000 years, including such highlights as the building of Solomon's and Herod's temples, and the Crusades. Humankind went wrong by abandoning archaic life-affirming Earth Mother cults, suggests the novelist-turned-sage; Salome and Jezebel, wise in the ways of the goddess, have been victims of a historical bum rap, their vital message lost in the shuffle of endless turf battles for supremacy among the followers of misogynist male deities.

Painted Stick and Conch Shell, we soon find, have a mission: to revive the worship of long-neglected Astarte. To this end, they set out for Jerusalem, enlisting in their company three objects inadvertently left behind in the cave in the hasty exodus of the startled human lovers: Dirty Sock, Spoon and Can o' Beans, each with its own personality. Together, this unlikely band of travelers survive a picaresque odyssey that eventually deposits them in the basement of St. Patrick's Cathedral . . . in New York, where they await an opportunity to cross over the ocean to the Holy Land.

Boomer Petway and his new bride are meanwhile gripped by ridiculous trials of their own. A predatory, artificial and large-breasted gallery owner embraces not only Boomer's turkeymobile—which is soon enshrined in the Museum of Modern Art—but the unwitting "artist" himself. Sudden-sensation Boomer, a Li'l Abner in among the art sharks, drops Ellen Cherry for the horrible gallery lady; next we see him he's off to do a sculpture commission in, of all places, Jerusalem.

The jilted Ellen Cherry, her own canvases a washout, resorts to waiting on tables in the Isaac and Ishmael restaurant, across the street from the United Nations. This well-intentioned but shaky enterprise, run by a Russian Jew and an Arab, suffers constant attacks and threats from religious extremists of both camps—most notably from one of Ellen Cherry's holy-rolling redneck relatives, the rapture-hungry Baptist doomsday preacher of Colonial Pines, who teams up with Zionists in a plot to provoke new Mid-East hostilities.

The book's wet firecracker of an intended climax comes in a final marathon Super Bowl Sunday sermon on the world's problems, delivered into the mind of a newly enlightened Ellen Cherry while a Lebanese belly dancer performs "the dance of the seven veils" at Isaac and Ishmael's. Almost all the inanimate objects get to the Holy Land, and the estranged human lovers are reunited, with Robbins' defiance of realism intact right down to his happy ending.

With this book, Robbins once again proves himself an extremely clever writer, but unfortunately also one whose uncertainties of tone and stylistic overreaching affect nearly every page. His prose, often brilliant, seems bound to draw attention to itself in the most demanding of ways; particularly overloaded with startling or cute analogies, it sometimes slips on its own stretched comparisons and falls on its face. (pp. 1, 9)

Robbins' self-conscious delight in his own stylistic sleight of hand, his assiduous straining after effect with extravagant figures, and his whimsical imaginative indulgence in the paradoxical absurdities of history, can carry *Skinny Legs* and its reader only so far. Beyond, into the "ultimate cognition" Robbins preaches—perhaps to be found on the other side of that "thick veil that shields a being from the transformative and tricky light of liberty, from the dizzy incandescence of self-determination"—this whole unwieldy planetary redemption project continually beckons and gestures, but never actually goes. (p. 9)

> Tom Clark, "Through Salome's Veils to Ultimate Cognition," in Los Angeles Times Book Review, *April 15, 1990, pp. 1, 9.*

### Joe Queenan

Although Mr. Robbins made his name in the 1970's with his zany novels *Even Cowgirls Get the Blues* and *Still Life With Woodpecker,* these were very much products of a laid-back, anti-establishment, 1960's mentality. Pastiches of wisecracks masquerading as literature, these gagfests were very funny affairs: flickering signs of gaiety and hope in a doomed culture that was already capitulating to the sinister Ann Beattie and others of an aggressively maudlin disposition.

Mr. Robbins is still a very funny guy, but he—and we—are getting a bit old for comic books. Which is not to say that *Skinny Legs and All* started out as a laugh riot; seemingly Mr. Robbins intended this compendious compendium to address all the major questions of human existence: Religion, Art, the Future of the Middle East, the War Between the Sexes, the Meaning of Life. Sad to say, Mr. Robbins is not yet ready for the big leagues; he has shown that he can hit the fastball, but he still has plenty of trouble with the curve.

Mr. Robbins begins *Skinny Legs and All* with his trademark pyrotechnics—ludicrous similes and rivetingly inane dialogue—and as long as the fireworks keep coming, things are just fine. In the first 25 pages we are introduced to Ellen Cherry Charles, an aspiring artist and waitress who is a member of the Daughters of the Daily Special, whose hair "did its own stunts" and who declares: "Some marriages are made in Heaven. . . . Mine was made in Hong Kong." She is driving across the heartland of America, in a vehicle redesigned to look like a roast turkey, with Boomer Petway, her welder husband, who is a native of Colonial Pines, "a suburb without an urb," and who has a penchant for asking cowboys whether the proper terminology for their line of work is not, in fact, "bovine custodial officers." So far, so good.

However, when he turns from one-liners to the daunting themes of art and religion, Mr. Robbins is seriously outgunned. After Boomer and Ellen arrive in the Big Apple, the welder becomes the darling of the art crowd, with the fowl vehicle fetching a king's ransom at Boomer's first exhibition. Sending up the downtown arts scene is a conceit so shopworn that one wonders what the Seattle-based Tom Robbins was thinking of. (Maybe he was thinking of downtown Seattle.)

In addition to modern art, Mr. Robbins also dislikes organized religion, which he, *mirabile dictu,* has identified as an enemy of wild and crazy guys such as Boomer, Ellen Cherry Charles and himself. This results in a pointless and anachronistic tirade against a bunch of fundamentalist Christians who are plotting to rebuild the Temple in Jerusalem, in the hope of provoking the Messiah into a second—or perhaps it's a third—coming. All of this is tied in with an Arab and a Jew who build a restaurant across from the United Nations, and with a talking can of beans, a talking spoon and a talking sock, which have survived in some form since the time of Solomon and have many controversial theories about biblical events. The tin can, the spoon and the sock are all a good deal less funny than the humans, with the exception of the mysterious New York belly dancer Salome, who is not funny at all. (Of course, neither was her biblical forerunner; just ask St. John the Baptist.)

Mr. Robbins is at his best when he is being snide, witty or downright juvenile, and at his worst when he is being profound. He is clearly on to something when he has Boomer declare, "If God didn't prefer for us to drink at night, he wouldn't have made neon!" And he makes a very valid point, overlooked by many anthropologists, when he notes that the switch from B.C. to A.D. in the time of Jesus Christ must have caused many Israelites to miss their dental appointments.

But when Mr. Robbins gets on his high horse, the results are pure bunkum. "As long as a population can be induced to believe in a supernatural hereafter, it can be oppressed and controlled," he pontificates. "People will put up with all sorts of tyranny, poverty, and painful treatment if they're convinced that they'll eventually escape to some resort in the sky where lifeguards are superfluous and the pool never closes." Oh, hush your tongue, Tommy, this is pure mush, as a look at the Peasants' Rebellion during the Reformation, the life of Oliver Cromwell or the voyage of the Mayflower can attest. What's more, it's not even your mush; it's stolen from Gibbons's *Decline and Fall of the Roman Empire.*

Mr. Robbins should take a tip from Peter De Vries and mass-produce the kind of short, witty books that do not get confused with *Anna Karenina.*

> Joe Queenan, "Then the Spoon Speaks Up," in The New York Times Book Review, *April 15, 1990, p. 12.*

## Sally S. Eckhoff

*Skinny Legs and All* . . . is about naked truth, accent on naked. Naked, and female. She's the deposed Goddess, she's Jezebel, she's a waitress, and she can strip away the illusions that keep the Middle East at war and the rest of us in a state of emotional and sexual bankruptcy. We must get Astarte back into our lives, says Robbins, give organized religion the boot, and quit suppressing our erotic potential. . . .

*Skinny Legs and All* is less a narrative than a choreographed road trip. Waitress/painter Ellen Cherry Charles moves to New York with her oafish husband, Boomer. Meanwhile, a crazy evangelist friend of her mother's is hatching a plot to blow up the Dome of the Rock in Jerusalem. Behind everybody's backs, an assortment of objects (a stick, a shell, a spoon, a sock, and a can of Van De Camp's baked beans) have discovered the secret of locomotion and decide to go to the Holy City, stopping off in Manhattan on the way. There, the owners of a very unusual Middle Eastern restaurant run by an Arab and a Jew hire Ellen Cherry, get mixed up in her uncle Buddy's scheme, have a close encounter with the itinerant objects, and showcase a belly dancer who knows the dance of ultimate cognition that's going to tie up the whole story. As in Robbins's last novel, (the rather more entertaining) *Jitterbug Perfume,* these nomadic humans who lead parallel lives are drawn to each other and led toward an unpredictable conclusion. In the process of getting there they have nifty revelations and Technicolor sex.

They also meander through numerous and sometimes pointless subplots. The little moral tale about Ellen Cherry and her husband taking on the New York art world is refreshing, but it seems to belong somewhere else. The trials of Painted Stick, Can o' Beans, and friends don't help the story either; their characters aren't resonant. Robbins himself doesn't seem to believe they can walk and talk even though he gave them the gift of life.

But what he does well is enough to hold the center of the book together—almost. The epiphany of *Skinny Legs and All* is one of sense and sexuality. Robbins stages it in the Middle Eastern restaurant where the pipe stem-legged belly dancer, who calls herself Salome, has won the devotion of the clientele. She makes them drool into their beer. She can actually do the Dance of the Seven Veils, a dance so hot it makes all her other routines look like a Shriners parade. (Few pop writers are as fun to read on the subject of women's hips as Robbins.) When Salome sheds those gauzy purple scraps, the illusions that have blinded the human race will likewise fall away. But there's a hitch, and it's a lulu. She'll only do it at the precise minute of the Super Bowl kickoff. The men are having a nervous breakdown. With a giant TV set in one room of the bar and the stage in the other, which ritual for them? Habitual Robbins readers know where they'll find their man. When Salome drops her first veil—the *first* one, mind you—and reveals her loins, you're ready to throw confetti.

Fun as it is, this magnificent striptease doesn't have a catalytic effect. It's a great dance, but it's only a dance. The extraneous characters have sapped the story's tension, their peregrinations shaken its focus. And Robbins's favorite literary device, the unlikely but extremely agile simile/metaphor, becomes tiresome. . . . All Robbins's affection, good will, and clever imagery don't alleviate the sensation that this is an awfully long book. There's too much going on and not enough belief in the characters. It's not your imagination that gets strained, but your patience.

> Sally S. Eckhoff, in a review of "Skinny Legs and All," in VLS, *No. 86, June, 1990, p. 6.*

## FURTHER READING

Nelson, William. "The Comic Grotesque in Recent Fiction." *Thalia: Studies in Literary Humor* V, No. 2 (Fall and Winter 1982-1983): 36-40.

> Attempts to explain the popularity of such comic grotesque novels as Robbins' *Even Cowgirls Get the Blues,* John Irving's *The World According to Garp,* and John Kennedy Toole's *A Confederacy of Dunces.*

Strelow, Michael. "Dialogue with Tom Robbins." *Northwest Review* 20, Nos. 2 & 3 (1982): 97-102.

> Interview addressing Robbins' themes, techniques, and beginnings as a writer.

# Iain Crichton Smith

## 1928-

(Gaelic name Iain Mac A'Ghobhainn) Scottish poet, novelist, short story writer, playwright, author of children's books, scriptwriter, essayist, translator, and editor.

One of Scotland's most prolific contemporary writers, Smith is best known for his poetry in both English and Gaelic about his native island of Lewis in the Outer Hebrides. Often compared to his fellow countryman Hugh MacDiarmid, Smith writes analytic verse, avoiding the sentimentality found in much Scottish poetry. His poetry addresses the conflicts found in Lewis's parochial society, which is centered in Calvinist tradition and the Gaelic language, by portraying the history of the Highlands as marked by defeat and mediocrity. In much of his work, Smith laments the rigidity of religious laws and portrays the struggle for inspiration to escape these bonds. Harriet Zinnes noted: "Smith is that rare poet who has the courage to make statements about experience without sacrificing the poet's first responsibility: the verbal play upon that experience."

Smith endured a troubled, lonely childhood, resulting largely from a tuberculosis epidemic that killed his father and three brothers and compounded by the loss of another brother who drowned while serving in the military in World War II. Although Smith left his hometown of Lewis for the University of Aberdeen in 1945, his work has continued to focus on that area, which he regards as a "barren world . . . except in the imagination." In many of his poems, Smith depicts the rural community as incapable of a greater cultural awareness. For example, "A Young Highland Girl Studying Poetry" presents a girl struggling to understand unfamiliar English literature, intimating that she, like those before her, will not know much poetry but will be skilful "at healing children, bringing lambs to birth." Smith spoke Gaelic at home in Lewis, while learning English in school, and he writes in both languages. In his famous poem "Shall Gaelic Die?," Smith endorses the revival of Gaelic as a modern, written language. Some critics, however, have faulted some of Smith's writing—particularly *The Exiles,* a collection of poetry written in English—for sounding as if parts of it had been translated from Gaelic, thereby losing its emphasis in English. David Constantine defended Smith's style: "Sometimes [the voice] sounds foreign—which I think is a virtue—as though it were coming to us out of translation. All poetic language draws on a foreign usage. A man with two native tongues is at an advantage."

Smith often writes about the exile—the Gaelic speaker alienated from English literary tradition—and the social, religious, and political outcast. In *Murdo, and Other Stories,* for instance, the central characters are misfits, defying the order and structure of society though never escaping them. This struggle between personal freedom and submission to rules is for Smith one of the manifestations of

the conflict between grace and law. He commented: "My ideal poem would be one in which Grace is fighting to emerge by a fight with metre, law, boundaries. This in turn associated with community and the misfit, . . . fighting against restrictions of community, limiting yet freeing." This fight is most evident in Smith's poems in *The Law and the Grace* about the Free Church of Scotland, which presides over the predominant Calvinist sect in Lewis.

Smith's fiction, like his poetry, draws from his experiences in the Highlands and as a teacher and a writer. Often written from the first person perspective, his novels and short stories present intimate portraits of individuals whose experiences parallel those of the society in which they live. *Consider the Lilies* examines one woman's tribulations during the Clearances in the eighteenth and nineteenth centuries, in which many Highlanders were displaced from their homes to make way for agricultural and land use reforms. Of this novel, a critic in the *Times Literary Supplement* wrote: "Mr. Crichton Smith has made the most of one of his skills as a poet—the evoking, through violently compressed language, of attitudes pent up by long introspection." The Scottish literary establishment has only grudgingly accepted Smith as an accomplished writer because of his sometimes unfavorable representation of his homeland. Laurence Graham remarked: "Perhaps [Smith] will some day discover the more positive virtues of his islands and his people and with that discovery will come the one vital thing still lacking in his verse, warmth and community."

(See also *Contemporary Authors*, Vol. 21-24 rev. ed., and *Dictionary of Literary Biography*, Vol. 40.)

## PRINCIPAL WORKS

POETRY

*The Long River*  1955
*Deer on the High Hills: A Poem*  1960
*Thistles and Roses*  1961
*The Law and the Grace*  1965
*At Helensburgh*  1968
*From Bourgeois Land*  1970
*Love Poems and Elegies*  1972
*Hamlet in Autumn*  1972
*Orpheus, and Other Poems*  1974
*The Notebooks of Robinson Crusoe, and Other Poems* 1974
*In the Middle*  1977
*Selected Poems 1955-1980*  1982
*The Exiles*  1984
*The Village, and Other Poems*  1990

NOVELS

*Consider the Lilies*  1968; also published as *The Alien Light,* 1969
*The Last Summer*  1969
*My Last Duchess*  1971
*Goodbye, Mr. Dixon*  1974
*An End to Autumn*  1978
*The Search*  1983
*The Tenement*  1985
*The Dream*  1990

SHORT FICTION COLLECTIONS

*The Hermit, and Other Stories*  1977
*Murdo, and Other Stories*  1981
*Mr. Trill in Hades, and Other Stories*  1984

OTHER

*River, River: Poems for Children*  1978

---

**Edwin Morgan**

[*The essay excerpted below originally appeared in* Lines Review *in Summer, 1965.*]

The note of joy is conspicuously absent from Iain Crichton Smith's poetry, but this absence helps to define the values that are present. Joy goes with release and affirmation. Lacking the experience of release and affirmation, a poet will probe and even nourish his natural tensions, or deal with the tensions in the world to which he is most sensi-

tive. This does not necessarily result in a more profound poetry (though the twentieth century has tended to assume so), but it does ensure that the reader who comes in looking in vain for something visionary will go out differently pleased, stirred to consider solutionless problems: of change, of pain, of loneliness, of old age, of failure and success, of death. In a BBC talk on his own poetry Iain Crichton Smith said: 'I have always believed in a poetry which contains fighting tensions and not in a poetry of statement.' He also mentioned some of the tensions relevant to his own case (that of a Lewisman who has lived most of his life in the Highlands): between mind and body, between legalism and openness, between the old Highlands and the new. And the sort of poetry which comes out of such tensions will generally not state, affirm, recommend, or preach so much as hold within itself 'a precarious balance between opposing elements'. How does his poetry appear in relation to these ideas?

Perhaps basic, as a ground of such tensions and balance, is the sense of place, of the Western Highlands, of Lewis and Oban: the sense of this as the inescapable source of his personal experience, yet simultaneously as a stubborn, anomalous, but not unchanging bastion of the past thrust into twentieth-century international and metropolitan values and influences. To the poet this place offers everything—except its encouragement and comprehension! Without these he is on a treadmill within his own mind, a treadmill he will find it hard to escape from, since it turns, after all, the wheels of his art. In the fine **"Poem of Lewis"** he makes this problem explicit.

> Here they have no time for the fine graces
> of poetry, unless it freely grows
> in deep compulsion, like water in the well,
> woven into the texture of the soil
> in a strong pattern. They have no rhymes
> to tailor the material of thought
> and snap the thread quickly on the tooth . . .

He describes how both the people and the place seem inimical to a developed art; and too stoic and harsh for an art of generous feeling. (pp. 222-23)

This theme is repeated, but with more acceptance on Smith's part, in a later poem, **"A Young Highland Girl Studying Poetry"**. The furrowed brows of the girl puzzling over a subject she has no taste for will clear when she finds her natural place as wife and mother in a simple community. . . . Such a poem, one might say, is realistic; perhaps one should have no quarrel with it. Yet it is disappointing because of—to take the poet on his own terms—the absence of tension, the absence of disappointment on the poet's part that a life spent 'healing children, bringing lambs to birth' should have no access to the world of art.

Temporary acceptance of the physical environment, acceptance of its outward beauty, its colours and shapes, is of course natural, though in Smith's poetry there is very little indeed of the 'visitor's Highlands'. . . . There are no raptures, no intimations of immortality. Instead, an ability to focus a 'scene with figures' in which nature is as much the background of man's work as the object of a poet's contemplation. (pp. 223-24)

In other poems, nature may supply moments of an evocative, rather Chekhovian symbolism, as in **"By Ferry to the Island"**, where an afternoon picnic is remembered through three compared whitenesses, the 'pure white' of a seagull, the 'lesser white' of the sand, and the 'cool white' of a girl's dress. (p. 224)

In the long, ambitious, but somewhat confused poem **"Deer on the High Hills"**, which despite some fine passages is one of his less successful works, Smith does his best either to work nature (both animal mineral and vegetable) out of his system or to tell it to keep its proper and decent place (it is not quite clear which). The elegant ghost of Wallace Stevens, arch-tensionist as he was, glides rather too openly through the strangely rough triplets of this meditation on man's place in the earth he has to inhabit. The poem seems loath to come to its conclusion that the deer, however 'noble' they may appear to the symbol-seeking eye as they flash their antlers or bound down the hills, are deer; that the 'starry metaphysical sky' they lie under is physical; and that although we may like to place the seemingly 'noble', 'proud', 'royal' manifestations of nature in a 'halfway kingdom' between earth and heaven—

> There is no metaphor. The stone is stony.
> The deer step out in isolated air.
> We move at random on an innocent journey.

But there is a tension in this poem which everyone must feel, and which at the end is movingly expressed. Man can neither shake off nature, nor communicate with it. There are moments in everyone's life when nature becomes more than a background, yet we have no way of measuring or explaining its suddenly active power—it may be no more than the moon rising over a stubble-field—or of acknowledging it to its face. If there are sermons in stones, they are sermons for other stones. Man can only overhear them, dimly, tantalized, fretting after a sharper deaf-aid than physics or metaphysics can so far provide. (pp. 224-25)

Yet the poet Duncan Ban McIntyre, as Smith reminds us, did not hesitate to shoot deer, and 'the rocks did not weep with sentiment'. Nature means the fact of death, and a poet's attitude towards this fact becomes important. In two poems, **"In Luss Churchyard"** and **"Sunday Morning Walk"**, he speaks of the necessary indifference of life to death. Both poems involve a walk on a hot summer day; in both, the grass and leaves are described as 'raging' in the brief desperate high growth of the season. In the first poem the poet broods over the gravestones and their inscriptions, and despite the raging of the grass and the 'savage' skull-and-bones carvings on some of the stones, his breast seems 'empty with indifference', and he moves out on to the road again and his steps quicken—though perhaps with a sense of escape. In the second poem, death is more immediate: a dead sheep buzzing with flies: and the poet, after vainly considering whether he should take his stick and beat off the dreadful indignity of the flies 'hissing . . . out of the boiling eyes', leaves them to carry on the inevitable processes of organic nature and walks away, turning his back on 'a death of no weeping or mourning'.

But in a third poem where the telltale image of the 'raging grass' reappears (an image which haunts his poetry), Smith is brought more sharply up against the fact of human death, and here the protective indifference is broken open by pity and shame. In **"Old Woman"**, one of his best and most moving poems (though almost spoiled by the awkwardness of the last two lines), he wishes he could have the old epic indifference to anything so commonplace as death—

> . . . Greek or Roman men
> who pushed their bitter spears into a vein
> and would not spend an hour with such decay

—but although the pity he feels as he watches the dying, helpless old woman 'blindly searching the spoon' round her plate makes him feel equally helpless, imprisoned and impotent, this impotence being dissolved in poetry becomes active, and the reader has no sympathy with the 'Greek or Roman men'. The poet, though 'imprisoned' by his feelings and in no sense uttering a protest as such, makes of the poem itself a moral and social act. A tear, as Blake said, is an intellectual thing.

The broadening out of this theme to include the multiple suffering and death of war is a natural but difficult step. Smith has tried to deal with this in three poems of increasing ambitiousness: **"For the Unknown Seamen of the 1939-45 War Buried in Iona Churchyard"**, **"After the War"** (on the drowning of two hundred servicemen near Stornoway in 1919), and *World War I.* The first two are not very successful; the absence of any defined attitude, the tone of uninvolved bafflement, gives the impression of something forced, and this shows equally in the flat phrases of the first ('These things happen and there's no explaining') and in the showy imagery of the second ('agile herring, drove on drove, go hissing / under their Hades of the blinded hound'). Only in *World War I,* a sequence of eight poems arranged in four sections, **"Haig"**, **"The Soldier's Wish"**, **"November, 1961"**, and **"Poppies"**, does the poet begin to dare to use his identificatory imagination, giving some hint of things as they were, and thereby taking those risks of involvement or commitment of which he is normally so sceptical. The risks add a fruitful tenseness to the poem, since this time the bafflement and the memorializing are countered by at least an elementary dialectic of protest. (pp. 226-27)

This very honest, very interesting, not wholly satisfying sequence of poems shows Smith moving halfway towards a position he may never in fact take up. The fascination the war theme has for him indicates that he is not happy about a too complete reliance on local and personal experience; at the same time, the severely unresolved tensions in the poem—to a Lowland mind, indeed, the very 'honesty' seems like a typically Highland evasiveness!—are the limits beyond which his lack of optimism about human nature and its possibilities for change will not take him. (p. 228)

At any rate, I would not be surprised if some of the wider themes proved more profitable than that of the mind-body dualism which Smith put first on his list of tensions. The poems which touch on this subject—particularly the *Love Songs of a Puritan*—contain some striking passages but seem curiously ingrown and static; the recurrent imagery of god and devil, theology and heresy, sermon and saint makes little impact because the context fails to tell us how seriously it is to be taken; and for all the poet's expressed fondness for 'precision', these poems are sometimes vague and muffled in the too constant play of images and wit. (pp. 228-29)

What seems wrong with these poems is that although they are ostensibly 'love songs', no actual human relationship very convincingly emerges from them. But Smith has claimed, 'I tend to be concerned with people', and it is quite true that when he succeeds in writing less subjectively the whole verse appears to open out and begin to speak, and some of his most attractive poems are character studies like **"School Teacher", "The Widow", "For Angus MacLeod"**, and **"For My Mother"**. The tensions of mind and body are not lacking from these poems, but they have been properly distanced into an affectionate clarity. . . .

These poems, like **"Old Woman"** show one of the directions Smith's poetry seems to be taking: a poetry of sympathy and compassion, involving human beings, especially those of his own immediate experience. The other side of his art leads him towards something more abstract: his fascination with ideas of exactness, harmony, order, music, pattern, grace—ideas which tend to be expressed in non-human terms. (p. 229)

A poet who is apt, through his very gifts, to be seduced by a too salient imagery or music (e. g. 'from aloof azures let its ariels go', or 'and from his Minch of sherries mumble laws') may not find it easy to develop the human subject—matter in such a way that the poem helps it to speak for itself, though this is done very beautifully in **"Old Woman"** and **"For My Mother"**. But the root of the 'caring' has been planted, in a sensitive intelligence, and we can expect to see a broadening as well as a deepening of his already marked and individual achievement. (p. 231)

> Edwin Morgan, "The Raging and the Grace: Some Notes on the Poetry of Iain Crichton Smith," in his Essays, Carcanet New Press, 1974, pp. 222-31.

## The Times Literary Supplement

The image that dominates [*Consider the Lilies*] will be hard to forget—the severe old woman, beleaguered among memories in her scrubbed cottage with the sunlit moorlands and fields all around, but no longer hers since she is under threat of eviction. But it is questionable whether Iain Crichton Smith has the novelistic craft to keep this image in dramatic movement. The woman lives in Strathnaver in Sutherland, around 1814, when the Duke was turning the crofters out to clear his ground for sheep. Mr. Crichton Smith has set himself a task almost perversely hard in the context of Scottish tradition—to render the Clearances as almost purely individual experience, with a minimum of period detail. He has even avoided presenting an eviction directly, as though unwilling to trade on the anger and horror that the Clearances still arouse. The book is enclosed in the consciousness of one so old that she can react only with the most painful slowness to any signal

or challenge from outside her years-old routine. . . . Mr. Crichton Smith has made the most of one of his skills as a poet—the evoking, through violently compressed language, of attitudes pent up by long introversion.

But of course the old woman must interact with other people, e. g., the village gossip, Big Betty (good dialogue), the minister (rather colourlessly done), Patrick Sellar himself, the smoother swine John Loch who succeeded Sellar as agent, and the one who defied them, the militant atheist Donald Macleod. . . . In presenting these men, Mr. Crichton Smith's talents for images like raw jewels and phrases of a bitterly terse wit show as insufficiently dramatic. Sellar's speeches and gestures are sometimes uncertainly contrived, e.g., the way he blurts out his own ambitions to the old woman: surely he would have treated her with brutal curtness? Loch is better, suavely trying to correct Sellar's blundering. But Donald Macleod does not emerge as a presence. Some of his remarks could have been made by a university-educated Englishman in the 1960s but not by a crofting stonemason in the Highlands six generations ago. It is true that Mr. Crichton Smith is deliberately anachronistic: there are references to rubber bands, dungarees, fences, and pictures on the lid of a toybox. And he was surely right to avoid the costumery and laborious mimicry that have clogged historical fiction since Scott. But the modernizing method demands a most artful blend of current language with just enough older touches, and Mr. Crichton Smith is too often colourless in an effort to be timeless. It is an extremely worthy novel, but the various constraints of the form and style chosen finally muffle its effect.

> "Lebensraum," in The Times Literary Supplement, No. 3449, April 4, 1968, p. 356.

## Terry Eagleton

Iain Crichton Smith's Robinson Crusoe reads Sartre, Wittgenstein and Ryle, as well as the *Dandy* and the *Rover;* so it's clear that in the fine title-poem of [*The Notebooks of Robinson Crusoe*] we're in the realm of 'myth' rather than 'history', inhabiting some island of the mind rather than placed within the structure of 18th century mercantilist capitalism. Yet Crusoe was always one of the most potent of bourgeois myths, intersecting a specific history with a generalising image; and it thus isn't surprising that it continues to yield poetic capital in a later era of bourgeois society where the 'metaphysical' resonances of the fable (isolation, identity, the man/Nature relationship) seem as relevant as ever.

**"The Notebooks of Robinson Crusoe"** is a long prose-poem, preceded by three sections of shorter pieces; on a rough definition, it's a kind of *Misanthropos* in the mode of *Mercian Hymns*. If it shares an approximate structure of concerns with Gunn's poem (so that Crusoe's interest in Sartre isn't fortuitous), it nonetheless embodies this in a language whose dense, material, crafted compactions recall the tough, burnished diction of Hill:

> Only, my belly hungers for meat. I famish for—
> liver

and kidney, to bring my club down again and—
    again on
the head of the horned goat enduring my to-
    fro—harassments,
splayed to its hinged knees.

Yet one problem around which the poem turns is that of the relationship between this richly present natural world and the stripped, isolated ego which moves within it. It's a problem which offers itself in various guises—in the relation between the material immediacies of labour and the speculative vacancy of a mind thronged mainly with memories and fantasies, between body and soul, the apparent autonomy of Nature and the impulse to shape it into linguistic significance:

This landscape is my diary.
I inscribe the day on it.
I invest it with grammar.
The rack of rocks I compose
in the blowing wind.
I say, 'That apple tree
reminds me of someone'.
I hang my ghosts on it,
hairily entering the sea.'

Crusoe has a 'dream of returning to a green shade'; and that phantasmic Marvellian reduction to pure essence is an ambiguous theme in Crichton Smith's work. On the one hand such eidetic reduction suggests a human parallel to the sufficiency of Nature. . . . Yet at the same time such return-to-self merely enforces the alienation between mind and world, raw data and constructed meanings. . . . The bare simplicity of the island is 'poison', for 'One man cannot warm the world'; yet to re-enter society, with its flashy, purely phenomenal, sensationalist surfaces, is equally poisonous. It's hardly an original dilemma; yet in Crichton Smith's poetry it is fleshed and deepened by a Scottish rather than characteristically English meditation on the relations between essence and accident, necessity and contingency tyrannic absolutism and enervating mediocrity. (pp. 72-3)

> *Terry Eagleton, in a review of "The Notebooks of Robinson Crusoe" in* Stand Magazine, *Vol. 16, No. 4, 1975, pp. 72-4.*

## Douglas Dunn

No matter how much the contemporary imagination strains for order and symmetry, its products—and this does appear to apply to all schools—are strangely broken, able to contain opposites within the one creative temperament. Iain Crichton Smith's *The Notebooks of Robinson Crusoe* is a good example. At one moment his attention appears totally involved with a social poetry of characters and scenes. Yet in his title poem [**"The Notebooks of Robinson Crusoe"**] he is drawn towards a purely imaginative world which, if it has contemporary ramifications, is more a matter of creation than reflection from observable social surfaces.

There are sound critical reasons for wanting to see more poems by Smith that are written from the part of his imagination which finds the a social natural to it. During several years of reviewing poetry . . . my most consistent suggestion has been that more social or even political reflection is needed, and that a little deliberation in these matters might not be as obstructive as is generally thought. But in Smith's case the suggestion must go the other way. That he has bravely encountered the social world with a sense of criticism and acute observation is admirable enough. The trouble is that although in such sequences as **"By the Sea"** his powers of observation are clear and sharp, his critical perspective is not nearly so demanding as the title of an earlier book—*From Bourgeois Land*—would suggest. Something personal gets in the way. There is a tendency to overstate, and this may well be nothing more than facility within a rough and ready practice of verse and metre leading him into a sentimental version of rhetoric. A poem like **"The Workmen"**, for instance, while certainly warm in feeling, caricatures the free creativity of workers on a building site. Social transcendence does appear to have been intended, but the result is too controversial to be from the imagination, unless from that part of the imagination which indulges in wishful thinking more than it generates originality of point of view—

How casual their grace
though you can hear them swearing, see them
    mocking

the spectators down below, appalled by height
admiring for the moment the young boys
in dusty trousers, comic acrobats.

To write in that way does prove benevolent motives in Smith's outlook on the world. It also shows a failure to maintain realism parallel to the maintenance of a kindly attitude and an imaginative response to what is seen. Do building workers sing "like birds"? Are they always "natural comics"? Is their "careless poise" characteristic? *Do* they possess, even momentarily, a "glory in the sun"? The nature of these formulations may display either lack of experience or a consciousness that is too eager to convert what has been seen into the imaginative ideology of the poet.

The plainly visual, the everyday scene of the poem, is overridden for the satisfaction of ulterior motives. So much is made of it that whatever originality was in Smith's conception of the poem at its beginning rapidly undergoes linguistic and sentimental exhaustion.

Smith's lack of precision in socially reflective poems would be more serious than it is were it not for his parallel interest in a writing which encourages imagination rather than social conclusions. His poem **"The Fall"** is about exactly that—

The Art or life? Which is the way to go?
To hear the water breaking on far shores
is an obsession immediacy might end
by the limitations of the common door
and common windows of our common houses.
But always there's the roar of another wind
and hints and rumours of another snow
and seethings beneath ordinary surfaces.

Five more stanzas of similarly controlled writing within a mode more old-fashioned than traditional directs attention to a recognition of tedium instead of artistry. What the poem says is interesting, but phrases like "the common day's unquestioned light", which were brushed behind the door fifty sweepings ago, do nothing to help it. The drama of the poem's argument—that necessity to attend to both the real, observable world and the unknown—is central to Smith's work.

Using both prose and verse, Smith in his title poem dispenses with indignation, conclusions, moral evocations and sociological analyses without shedding his *bona fides* as the sort of poet for whom society is an important subject. Technically, that awkward conciliation between strict numbers and a less demanding practice of metre is tamed and Smith has the opportunity to allow his writing to follow the contours of imagination. In **"Old Woman"**, Smith's obsessive title and subject, he does provide an example of how well he can use standard techniques. (pp. 73-4)

*Douglas Dunn, "Natural Disorders," in* Encounter, *Vol. XLIV, No. 5, May, 1975, pp. 73-6.*

## Edwin Morgan

The distinctive quality of Iain Crichton Smith's short stories [in the collection *The Hermit, and Other Stories*] is unmistakable, but it is hard to define. The writing is plain; sentences are short and of direct construction; few special effects are aimed at. Occasional awkward phrasing or careless repetition will make the reader feel that the whole book needs a final revising pencil. And yet, despite this, the stories distil a powerful presence and many of them remain in the memory, the laconic plainness of style serving to outline—perhaps all the more convincingly—the various brands of unhappiness from vague discontent to violent despair that are the present collection's main subject.

The centrepiece of the book is the title-story [**"The Hermit"**], a novella. It shows the disruptive effect the arrival of a hermit has on a Highland village community. The hermit is an inoffensive fellow with a long coat and a bicycle who moves into an old RAF hut just outside the village, seems contented, doesn't drink, and buys his necessities from the village shop like everyone else. But he refuses to speak to anyone: even in the shop he merely presents a list; and from this small beginning he unwittingly sets in motion a destructive machine of suspicion, deceit, restlessness, fear, and hate, which finally expels him from the community on a trumped-up charge of attacking a young girl. The end of the story is somewhat sketchy and huddled-up, but the main body of it is given depth and interest by two things: that the narrator himself, a widower shaken by lustful thoughts, is a hermit manqué, and that the hermit's silence awakens the narrator's guilty memories of his wife's unplayed violin and lack of Gaelic, the "silent" wasted life of a city girl in a stifling village. The hermit is a catalyst, moving on like the 'Wandering Jew' to trouble some other community.

Similar moments of crisis, sometimes finely understated, sometimes almost luridly illuminated, form the pivots of other stories. A respectable, elderly married man, passing a police poster which reads "Wanted for Murder", feels a nearly irresistible impulse to give himself up, though he has committed no crime (**"The Impulse"**). An elderly widow in, Canada suddenly aware of the uncertainty of her own future, though in no outward sense seeming desperate or even to be failing, goes into a large store, buys a gun, and shoots herself in the rest-room (**"Leaving the Cherries"**). Both these short but excellent stories take it on themselves to explore the unexpectedly explosive power of an accumulated mass of small guilts, ordinary losses, or normal fears suddenly seen from a new angle. The elderly grocer in **"The Impulse"** *had,* in a sense, murdered his wife: subdued her originality, discouraged her intelligence. Yet they are not even unhappy—are they?

Something approaching the supernatural is used in **"The Brothers"** and **"The Exorcism"**. In the former tale, a Gaelic-speaking writer, living in Edinburgh and writing in English is reminded of his betrayed heritage by a ghostly self-moving typewriter which retypes his fiction in Gaelic. In the latter story, which has odd echoes of Hogg's *Justified Sinner,* a professor of theology wrestles with the soul of a Highland divinity student whom a demonic Kierkegaard has "possessed". These pieces, though well worked out, seem less impressive than the near-throwaway, four-page story **"The Incident"**, where a man of fifty is more truly haunted by a childhood memory of fighting with a brother who then tore up the Western he had been reading, and whose story he therefore never got to the end of. "And it was so trivial that it ought not to be memorable". But the trivial, as Chekhov knew, is greater than many engines.

*Edwin Morgan, "Silent Provocation," in* The Times Literary Supplement, *No. 3948, November 25, 1977, p. 1373.*

## John Mole

Iain Crichton Smith is a fascinating story-teller. Many of his settings [in *Murdo, and Other Stories*] are familiar enough—homes, gardens, a fairground, a castle open to the public—but at the centre there is always some oddity which won't lie down. The eponymous Murdo, an engagingly anarchic joker who has left his job as a clerk in order to write and to become a full-time "drunkard of the universe" while his parents–in–law worry about when he intends going back to the office, is merely the most bizarre of Crichton Smith's sympathetic, baffled square pegs who cannot fit into the dark, round hole of their circumstances. In the midst of daily routine his characters are amazed by sudden possibilities: one has "a strong affection for" a bucket—"he thought that some day it would yield him some extraordinary vision"; another, a troubled wife observing herself and her husband in the Hall of Mirrors (**"At The Fair"**), has an extraordinary vision which seems to speak the truth about their relationship.

Throughout these stories, the absurd illuminates, and the source of illumination is often a grotesque incident. There are passages of oblique, comic detachment in which—despite their naturalistic, domestic surroundings—Crichton Smith presents his characters almost as puppets in, a kind of philosophic Toytown: they are given to thinking or speaking in snatches of cryptic wisdom, even—in the chilling little anecdote **"Mr. Heine"**—in rhyme. But there are also whole stretches of intense, lyrical contemplation which explore these same characters' ambitions and illusions. The two approaches balance and complement each other, resolving switchback sequences of fantasy and precise observation into shapely, haunting tales. It's an imagination in which the dovetailing of the real and the surreal succeeds in defining areas of personal crisis from the outside and the inside: what seems profoundly odd is experienced as entirely convincing. And if there's sometimes an air of eccentricity about this method, it's an artful and luminous eccentricity reminiscent of T. F. Powys, whose Mr. Cronch is evidently a forebear of Murdo:

> He would then see a group of people standing beside a house that had fallen to the ground.
> One of the women would say, "My mother and father are in there dead. And what I want to know is, what is the government going to do about it?"
>
> "I am from the government myself," Murdo would say. "And here are two hundred pounds for you."

There is also, of course, more than a touch of the Joyce brigade here as well. At his most outrageously comic, Crichton Smith shares a snug with Flann O'Brien.

The main tension unifying the stories as a collection is that between, on the one hand, a world of order, routine and the enervating constraints of predictable behaviour ("living in one of those clocks with the small Dutch figures") and, on the other, the urge to break out of that world. This urge is expressed most succinctly by the wife in **"At The Fair"** who frustrated by the seemingly insensitive remoteness of her would-be-poet-husband and concerned that their daughter appears to be becoming like him, thinks "God . . . what is happening to us? Maybe I should leave him. Maybe I should take Sheila with me and leave him. Maybe I should take her into the centre of the fair and teach her to dance. Learning to dance for Crichton Smith's characters means becoming open to experience. In **"At The Fair"** after the wife's crisis, the couple end up walking from the car to the house with their daughter running ahead of them—a kind of understanding, and hence a freedom from restraint, has been achieved within the frame of day-to-day living: a dance to the music of time which transcends the fairground music. For Helen, in **"The Visit"**, bored speechless by the carping chatter of her husband, his brother and her sister-in-law, the dance of her liberation is a beautiful but whimsical gesture. She hides with her nephew and niece in a field of daffodils (her private "Daffodil Land") and watches the adults from the enchanted distance of her regression:

> Boo, she shouted at them, boo, boo, boo. And the daffodils pale and tall were about her. She was the queen and they were the black square people coming from their eternal conferences trying to keep the world going till she was old enough to be rich and without care.

In the volume's most spectacular and exotic story, **"The Missionary"**, the cunningly named Reverend Black passes through an extraordinary dark night of the soul in Africa involving lust, terror and complicity in murder before achieving his own kind of moral and spiritual liberation: "'Come' he repeated. 'Everything is natural. Everything is forgiven.'" He, too, freed from the conflict between The Law and Grace which has obsessed him, has found his own way of dancing.

It would be too simple to call Iain Crichton Smith's stories, in this book, parables, Nevertheless, their unusual, acute angle of vision is the mark of their seriousness. It's a narrow, often rather weird, angle but what it measures is unmistakably the real thing.

> *John Mole, "Learning to Dance," in* The Times Literary Supplement, *No. 4082, June 26, 1981, p. 730.*

### Alan Bold

It is axiomatic that environmental factors play some part in shaping the creative development of any poet yet Smith, it seems to me, has created his best poetry entirely through a sustained exploration of the insular world he inhabited until the age of seventeen when, for the first time in October 1945, he left Lewis to study English at Aberdeen University. "Insular" has become a convenient epithet of abuse in criticism; an examination of Smith's work demonstrates the folly of tying constricting labels round the throat of poetry. . . . (p. 215)

Four clear themes emerge in Smith's poetry generally and his individual poems contain thoughtful variations on these basic themes. They have consistently informed his work and made his poetic voice instantly recognizable even when, occasionally and inevitably, he borrows mannerisms from other poets. The greatest influence on Smith's poetry is undoubtedly that of Robert Lowell whose progress from formal perfection to controlled metrical freedom provided a model for Smith. When other influences impinge on Smith's work he still manages to come back to Lewis. For example his collection **In the Middle** reveals a familiarity with the disembodied emotions paraded in Ted Hughes' *Crow.* **"The Scream"** begins:

> The scream rips through the forest
> tearing the trees down.

Whereas Hughes would have carried the image to a catastrophic conclusion, Smith's gentler muse seeks out a more homely resting place:

> It ends up at a cottage
> deep in a secret wood
> searching the pale windows
> for the kind iron face.

Again, in **"The Cry"** the atmosphere of menace dissolves into the familiar landscape of Lewis in summer:

> gazing across the beloved countryside
> where the hay heavy with scent goldens the
>     slopes.

Like all Scottish islands Lewis has suffered from depopulation, from a steady exodus of citizens who have had to find work in the industrial centres of Scotland. Lewis' present population of some 16,000 represents a little society in decline, a community that confronts the outside world as a spectacle for tourists. Smith's early life with his widowed mother (his father died of TB which produced in Smith's mother a morbid fear of illness) reinforced his tendency to accept life as a gift which, once unwrapped, presented the inevitability of death. The first poem in *Thistles and Roses*—the book that did most to consolidate Smith's early reputation as an important poet—was "**Old Woman.**" It is a portrait of a life that has crumbled before the encroachment of age (as cliffs crumble when assaulted by the sea). It is an image of indignity:

> And she, being old, fed from a mashed plate
> as an old mare might droop across a fence
> to the dull pastures of its ignorance.

This reduction of the human being to a specimen of decay is treated by Smith as the supreme tragedy of life; it is the principal theme that has haunted his poetry as well as novels like *Consider the Lilies* which views the Highland Clearances through the consciousness of "an old woman of about seventy."

The Old Woman theme is, then, a starting point for any examination of Smith's work. It is absolutely crucial to it. When I asked Smith about the importance of this theme to him he answered:

> I think this came from my mother, whom I used as a paradigm of many Highland traits. For some reason I think of the old woman as being stronger than the old man. There is a strong will and determination there that attracts me. There is also a pathos which I find very moving for most of the old women I knew had received very little from life, though that did not diminish their grip on it. Many of them too were religious, as my mother was. Not all of the old women are based on my mother directly but the impetus came from her life.

In Smith's *Selected Poems* . . . there are several poems about old women and each of them draws from Smith his deepest emotions and/or his profoundest sympathy. The poem "**For my mother**" is, naturally, full of admiration for a woman who has weathered the storms of seventy years:

> as if her voyage were
> to truthful Lewis rising
> most loved though most bare
> at the end of a rich season.

A second poem bearing the title "**Old Woman**" (and beginning "Your thorned back") presents a less sympathetic character (probably the darker side of his mother), a woman moulded by the narrow religious principles of the Free Church. . . . "**Old Woman with Flowers**" and "**If You Are About to Die Now**" delicately invoke the poet's thoughts on the final moments of his mother whose death is recorded, and life celebrated, in the first part of the collection *Love Poems and Elegies.*

This sequence of poems shows Smith at his most alert so that every sound and sight around him assumes a signifi-

cance which he attributes to the death of his mother. In the fine first poem of the sequence, "**You lived in Glasgow,**" the poet combines sharp observation with visionary meditation as he sits in Glasgow and thinks about her. . . . Here the solemnity of the mood is emphasized by the deliberately formal pattern of the verse: the emphatic reliance on rhyme and the frequent use of iambic pentameter ("A maxi-skirted girl strolls slowly by"). In "**This island formed you**" Smith thinks of Lewis with "its black hatted men / and stony bibles" then he follows that poem with "**The space-ship.**" Here there is an unexpected metamorphosis whereby his mother dying of lack of oxygen becomes "an astronaut lacking air, / dying of lack of it in the depths of space." The final poem in the sequence, "**The earth eats everything,**" suggests the unforgettable impact of this particular death on the poet. . . .

In the Old Woman poems we see Smith's technical practices as well as one major part of his thematic repertoire. His is a poetry of statement heightened by poetic intensity; the statements are supported not by argument but by imagery. (pp. 215-18)

As well as the Old Woman theme, three further subjects are referred to there: the sea, religion, and an historical pessimism. These subjects sometimes appear on their own, sometimes as part of the Old Woman theme. The sea, for an islander like Smith, is an uncertain and treacherous element so there is nothing remotely romantic about his poems on that theme. "**For the Unknown Seamen of the 1939-45 War Buried in Iona Churchyard**" is an elegiac tribute to the dead. Smith is not concerned with great cosmic meanings but in conveying the commonplace quality of the collective, and theologically pointless, death:

> What happened was simply this, bad luck for those
> who have lain here twelve years in a changing pose.

Smith is not a poet of passion so much as a poet obsessed by the denial of passion (an emotional feature that can be traced back to his childhood in Lewis). There is a characteristic reticence about the poem, a prosaic ("One simply doesn't / know enough") inability to fully embrace the subject, that indicates how uneasy Smith is with abstractions. For him there is no clear concept of Death; there is only the particular death. And yet the poem is saved from bathos by Smith's sheer poetic expertise which is best displayed in the final stanza (unobtrusively rhyming *ababb*) with its terminal pararhyme (a device borrowed, appropriately enough in the circumstances, from Wilfred Owen):

> Best not to make much of it and leave these seamen
> in the equally altering acre they now have
> inherited from strangers though yet human.
> They fell from sea to earth, from grave to grave,
> and, griefless now, taught others how to grieve.

Another sea-poem "**By Ferry to the Island**" contrasts the immense surge of the water by juxtaposing it with the essentially trivial pursuits of the visitors: "Someone made coffee, someone played the fool." In the fourteen-poem sequence "**By the Sea**" the sea is again used as a symbol of permanence beside which human activities are squalid.

Smith's concern with religion is a product of his desire to move clear away from the negativity of the Free Church religion so it is a particularized issue, not an abstract consideration of religion as a philosophical discipline. The Free Church of Scotland was formed when, in the Disruption of 1843, a body of Scottish presbyterians seceded from the Established Church of Scotland. As a sect the Free Church has become, in Scotland, associated with the things it is proverbially against: drink, merriment on Sunday, permissive morals. As such it has been frequently caricatured as a naysaying conspiracy of hypocrisies dedicated to a rigid kirkianity rather than to the teachings of Christ. Smith told me "I was brought up in the Free Church and I have felt since that as a religion it is too constricting, dictatorial and lacking in joy." In **"Sunday Morning Walk"** Smith depicts the island of Lewis in the cold grip of a Free Church Sabbath, a bizarre situation involving the islanders' calculated indifference to the glorious summer that surrounds them. . . . Obviously this bleak denial of life, in the name of religion, has disturbed Smith; in the title poem of his collection *The Law and the Grace* he adopts an argumentative attitude to combat those he imagines might condemn his lack of Free Church religion:

> It's law they ask of me and not grace.
> "Conform," they say, "your works are not
>    enough.
> Be what we say you should be," even if
> graceful hypocrisy obscures my face.

This guilty struggle, with the religion he was conditioned to as a child, could have resulted in an obsessive poetry disfigured by the same sort of religious prejudice Smith was so anxious to avoid. However, he wrote his way out of that predicament by proclaiming his own artistic credo in **"I Build an Orange Church"**. In this poem Smith still has something to believe in but he has replaced conventional religion with a colourful commitment to the insights of art:

> I make a ceiling of intensest blue.
> The seats are heliotrope, the bibles pink,
> hymn books are apple green.

The fourth theme in Smith's work is associated with that "pessimism" he mentioned in his essay on his childhood. In Scotland as a whole there is a strong historical consciousness and it habitually dwells on defeat. Smith is not only a Scot; he is a Gael. . . . The most appalling Gaelic catastrophe was the defeat of the clans at Culloden in 1746, a defeat followed by punitive measures that virtually prohibited the Gaelic way of life (speech, music, dress, customs). As if the quasi-genocidal legislation was not enough to destroy Gaeldom the government operated, from the 1790's to the 1850's, a system of Highland Clearances that removed human beings from their homes to make the Highlands fit for sheep—a more profitable commodity than Gaelic-speaking Highlanders. Smith has written extensively in Gaelic (and has provided outstanding poetic translations from the Gaelic originals of Sorley Maclean). . . . In **"Culloden and After,"** from *Thistles and Roses,* Smith alludes to "fuddled Charles"—the Bonnie Prince Charlie of romantic legend who arrogantly led the clans to their destruction—and isolates the feeling of loss in verse whose rhymes seem to spread out from the centre of each stanza:

> There was a sleep. Long fences leaned across
> the vacant croft. The silly cows were heard
> mooing their sorrow and their Gaelic loss.
> The pleasing thrush would branch upon a
>    sword.
> A mind withdrew against its dreamed hoard
> as whelks withdraw or crabs their delicate claws.

In **"Highland Portrait"** . . . the terrible desolation is complemented by Smith's anger at the commercial travesty the Highlands have become, an empty land ridiculed by tawdry trinkets and lorded over by the descendents of the lairds who carried out the Clearances. . . . A more extended treatment of the Gaelic theme is contained in the long poem **"Deer on the High Hills."**

These four themes—the Old Woman, the treacherous sea, religious freedom, the Gaelic tragedy—are the four main cornerstones on which Iain Crichton Smith has erected the admirable monument of his poetry. All his work is not contained in them but all his most original work, I submit, is. (pp. 218-22)

> *Alan Bold, "A Thematic Note on the Poetry of Iain Crichton Smith," in* The Malahat Review, *No. 62, July, 1982, pp. 215-22.*

## Douglas Dunn

In quality, Smith's work [in *Selected Poems 1955-1980*] ranges from the excellent to the indifferent and predictable. That is, I suppose, the risk taken by a poet who is prolific, and who, by his own account, is a fast worker. Yet so much of his poetry is satisfyingly characteristic. His attitude to technique may have changed over the years from the neat fluency of such poems as **"The Widow"**, **"Statement by a Responsible Spinster"** and **"Old Woman"** to the Europeanized free verse of **"In the Middle"** or the **"Old Woman"** with which this *Selected Poems* ends after almost thirty years of writing, but the same balanced appreciation of modernity of imagery and diction persists throughout. In that pattern of development, Smith is like an equally scrupulous writer, his countryman Norman MacCaig. In both cases, the absence of an audibly cultivated verse—considering, that is, their authority in that idiom—amounts to a loss for the reader as well as a gain. On the positive side, space is left for a natural, spoken voice, and for images which can be described plainly instead of coaxed into regular rhythms. But whether that is entirely welcome is a matter of taste. To a poet it may feel like an exercise of his freedom to write as he chooses. A reader, though, may be disappointed by a loss of music and narrative and the lucidity which they can bring to mysterious subjects and perceptions.

Those earlier poems of Smith's have a memorability which otherwise agreeable later poems rarely achieve as finely in the tune of their language, even if they do in the surprise of their ideas and images. Although Smith has not given up entirely on metre and rhyme, it was perhaps inevitable that he would vary and extend his technical range. His themes are obsessive; they recur consistently, and a different mode of writing offers him the virtue of contemplating similar pictures and ideas within different frames. Old women; young girls; the island of Lewis; the "law" of presbyterian expectations as opposed to the "grace" of poetic understanding; the "sense" of handed-down morality and the sensuousness of a more openly comprehensive view of life; the "will" of men of action and the beautiful stasis of the contemplative mind; the natural balance of life on an island like Lewis and intrusions of television and neon-haloed affluence; Gaelic and the threat to it posed by modernity; the fascination of death and the hurts of grief—these themes, most of them antithetical, crop up again and again. Listing them, though, gives the impression that Smith can be pinned down to one subject or another. In fact, he is much more mercurial, more questing, more liable to surrender to the run of his imagination than to the finite possibilities of a subject.

In his book *From Bourgeois Land* . . . Smith did give in to the opposite trait. He applied himself to the simple arithmetic of Bourgeois equals Possible Fascism. It seemed to translate Marcuse's argument from *Negations* into a Scottish context as if in the hope of jolting small-town, local Gauleiters from their notorious complacency. Undoubted anger was toned down by such poems as **"At the Sale."** Finely written and convincing as the poem is, such lines as "How much goes out of fashion and how soon!" suggest that Smith was writing in an English accent, perhaps influenced by Larkin. That "how", the tone of the entire line, doesn't sound particularly Scots. Fine, too, are the last lines of the poem, reached after playing dextrously over the assorted objects of a Scottish country sale:

> O hold me, love, in this appalling place.
> Let your hand stay me by this mattress here
> and this tall ruined glass,
> by this dismembered radio, this queer
> machine that waits and has no history.

Most of the poem is Smith's. Yet several influences appear in it—Larkin, Lowell and, perhaps, in the first of the lines quoted, Ian Hamilton. Indeed, it is possible that Smith is a poet who has been markedly open to receive the work of others throughout his career. . .

[Smith] has refused any of the easy ways out of the Scottish literary predicament—the minority *éclat* of the defiant Gaelic bard, nationalist ideologies or other similarly narrow historical specialisms. His work is contemporary, engaging and interestingly accessible.

> *Douglas Dunn, "Elegies in Gaeldom," in* The Times Literary Supplement, *No. 4141, August 13, 1982, p. 876.*

## David McDuff

Iain Crichton Smith speaks out of a starkly delineated world [in his *Selected Poems 1955-1980*], that of the islands of Western Scotland. . . . This is a world that is isolated both in time and in space, one of violent extremes, where in order to be heard at all, the poet must learn the hard lessons taught by the elements, and by those who live all their lives in close proximity to them. Here 'the great

forgiving spirit of the world' 'like a shot bird / falls from the windy sky' 'and the early daffodil, purer than a soul, / is gathered into the terrible mouth of the gale.' (p. 68)

Although Smith by and large steers clear of evocations of childhood (perhaps these memories are too painful to write about?), his memories of growing up as a young student in Aberdeen have a similarly clear-eyed, unnostalgic quality, and the 'school of life' is very much present:

> Mica glittered from the white stone.
> Town of the pure crystal
> I learnt Latin in your sparkling cage,
> I loved your brilliant streets.
>
> Places that have been good to us we love.
> The rest we are resigned to.
> The fishermen hung shining in their yellow
> among university bells.
>
> **("Aberdeen")**

In this last image the two facets of Smith's world, the rural/natural and the urban/cultural are fused in a manner that is characteristic of his poetic art. Out of his early struggle between a perception of nature as something free and daemonic, and a constricting social-religious framework that is typified in the concept of 'Puritanism' there emerges a poetic speech that in Auden's phrase is 'the speech of a mature mind, fully awake and in control of itself'. Understanding the narrowness of the leaders of the community in which he lives, even admiring the force and passion of their conviction, which stems from a battle with the elements, and also with hardship and oppression, Smith nonetheless condemns their destructiveness and barrenness, which he sees in the end as the result of a moral and existential choice. . . . The puritanism that casts such a shadow over Smith's poetic landscape may, one feels, be interpreted as a symbol of evil in the world. It is an evil that is associated very much with the 'English' element in Scottish culture. Smith's roots are in a very different culture—that of Gaelic language and literature. The *Selected Poems* contain a fascinating selection of translations from Smith's own Gaelic verse, done by himself. In these poems, the larger world coexists with the local world of rock, sea and sky in a way that is unthinkable for the Lowland, Anglo-Scots tradition, with its chauvinism and its middle-class 'respectability':

> Liberal, Labour or Conservative, what business
>     have they with us?

begins one of these translated poems, and it continues:

> . . . what have the red and blue to do with that
>     dark river in which we swim? . . .
>
> **("Poem")**

Hiroshima, the Soviet Union, Malta, Crete, London and Vienna exist side by side with the landscapes of Uist, Stornoway and Harris in a perfectly natural synthesis, a world-picture that comprehends the essence of locality without imposing a philosophy or interpretation of its own. Here are poems about Sigmund Freud, the First World War, Wittgenstein, Plato. The provincialities of the 'English' culture are left far behind. In the Gaelic poem **"Shall Gaelic Die?"** Smith answers his own question: 'What that means is: shall we die?' The conviction of the universalism of Gaelic as a poetic language seems to penetrate the best of Smith's English-language poetry. This is not to say that his English poems read like translations—but rather that in them one can hear the echo of a voice that is utterly un-English, one that speaks from a culture still in touch with the Christian humanism of the middle ages, modified through what Osip Mandelstam called a 'domestic Hellenism.' . . . (pp. 68-9)

*David McDuff, in a review of "Selected Poems 1955-1980," in* Stand Magazine, *Vol. 24, No. 3, 1983, pp. 68-70.*

**Stephen Regan**

**"Poem of Lewis"**, which opens Iain Crichton Smith's *Selected Poems 1955-1980,* explores the notion of poetry as craft and suggests the extent to which the poet's sensibility is determined by a place and the habits of its people:

> Here they have no time for the fine graces
> of poetry, unless it freely grows
> in deep compulsion, like water in the well,
> woven into the texture of the soil
> in a strong pattern. They have no rhymes
> to tailor the material of thought
> and snap the thread quickly on the tooth.

The poem is characteristic of Crichton Smith's early work, its powerful argumentative edge and strength of diction. It conveys a difficult yet confident struggle for expression; it is less a statement than a meeting of tensions which define the scope of his writing and suggest the forboding element which it inhabits—the daffodil, symbol of delicate natural beauty, is 'gathered into the terrible mouth of the gale'. Elsewhere, the poet's breadth of comprehension and sensuous appreciation of form and colour frequently clash with inherited Calvinist precepts. **"A Note on Puritans"** accuses religious fanatics of 'singleness and loss of grace', while a later poem **"Contrasts"**, asserts the beauty of the landscape against a stern theology, alleviating its sombre colours with those of the moorland, the chanting of psalms with the waves of the sea.

Throughout the early poems there are signs of Crichton Smith breaking with his community and its traditional labouring crafts, and of his establishing an independent existence as a writer and teacher. His vision of his mother gutting fish on the quayside is powerful and deeply felt, and produces a disturbing reference to his own commitment to words:

> Angrily I watch you from my guilt
> and sometimes think: The herring in my hand
> bloody and gutted, would be far more solid
> than this more slippery verse, but that cold wind
>
> appals me as a voluntary price to pay,
> the lonely figure in the doubtful light
> with the bloody knife beside the murmuring sea
> waiting for the morning to come right.

These lines are complemented in section three of the book by a moving prose poem, **"To My Mother"** translated from the Gaelic. Both poems examine the dilemma of the sensitive individual whose desire for education seems to threaten a close attachment to the labouring community and its traditions. Similarly, in **"Aberdeen"**, the image of fishermen is juxtaposed with 'university bells'; the world of 'calm grammar' is invaded by 'writhing North Sea fish'. Monologues by a school teacher and a widow consider the isolated aspirations of educated individuals, but the dilemma is regarded most passionately in **"A Highland Girl Studying Poetry"**. The poem draws its images naturally and unobtrusively from the traditional crafts of fishing, ploughing and lambing, and, in lines strongly reminiscent of Wordsworth, upholds the values of simple affection and spontaneity. These early poems demonstrate a lively sympathy and solidarity, always treating the role of the community as a vital concern, and refusing to settle into complacency.

*Deer on the High Hills* (1962) attempts to portray a personal vision of Scotland without resorting to popular sentiments such as that of 'Prince Charles in a gay Highland shawl'. The opening lines of the poem present the deer in familiar, human terms, yet concede that there is something savagely 'inhuman' and unpredictable about the animal: 'He might suddenly open your belly / with his bitter antlers to the barren sky'. Crichton Smith acknowledges the role of the Gaelic bard, Duncan Ban McIntyre, who shot the deer without remorse, believeing that 'Brutality and beauty danced together'. A similar unillusioned view of Scotland is evident in section three of the book, translated from the Gaelic. There is no attempt to idealise the country and its people, or to isolate them from the most disturbing events of modern history. The time-honoured proverbial wisdom of the Hebrides and the Highlands confronts the horrific consequences of Nagasaki and Hiroshima; the gas of a concentration camp is seen 'writhing like the mist of Lewis over cold rocks'. The language of these poems is usually blunt and forceful, but rises at times to a musical lilt, creating a semblance of the original Gaelic. The publication of these Gaelic poems in translation raises a number of perplexing linguistic concerns, especially in the poem **"Shall Gaelic Die?"**—where any attempt to translate the original would seem to undermine the urgency of the title.

**"Return to Lewis"** is a reassessment of the poet's heritage after cart wheels have been displaced by rubber tyres, the bible by television, and Gaelic by English:

> Tinkers subdued to council houses learn
> to live as others do, earn as they earn
> and English growing as the Gaelic dies
> describes these vast and towering island skies.

The poem also measures a number of changes and developments in poetic technique over a period of twenty years. **"Return to Lewis"** is more conversational, more relaxed, but no less serious and engaging than the early poems; it closes appropriately with a long spoken passage in which a local resident recalls his memories of 'the good old days'. (pp. 64-5)

*Stephen Regan, "Strong Patterns," in* Poetry Review, *Vol. 73, No. 1, March, 1983, pp. 64-7.*

## J. H. Alexander

Smith's first volume, *The Long River,* appeared in 1955. It had only nineteen poems, but they were enough to indicate that he was a writer of exceptional promise. The title is drawn from the longest poem in the collection, a somewhat incoherent **"Meditation Addressed to Hugh Mac-Diarmid"**, in which Smith praises 'That masterful persistence of the spirit / that wears like a long river through the stone.' The fact that this poem is addressed to Mac-Diarmid is important, as is its celebration of sustained creative effort, for *The Long River* is a deeply earnest set of poems, beginning with a wider tribute to 'The Dedicated Spirits' whose 'perpendiculars of light / flash sheerly through the polar night / with missionary fire,' and including a roll call of the 'elemental ones', 'Catullus Shelley Burns / Sappho Blake and Clare. ' Like the young Keats, Smith is consciously using his first collection to dedicate his poetic powers, and in the process both his elevated and austere conception of poetry and the extent of those powers become evident.

In *The Long River* poetry is an arduous quest for beauty, which 'has to be earned / in terror lightning and calm' by 'a blind man hunting a key / on a night of terror and storm' and which when found offers 'more grief than gaiety.' Smith's early poetry is on a cosmic scale, seeking, even at the risk of great pain and emotional ferocity, to cast off all insensitivity and boredom and to invest the whole gamut of human experience with the 'subtle radiance' of a high, passionate romantic lyricism.

The devotion to beauty that has terror comes near to being matched by Smith's poetic ability in this first volume. What will immediately impress each reader, along with his technical versatility and fluency, is his extraordinary image-making faculty. . . . It is true that this fondness for highly original images can lead to obscurity and a clotted density which impair the argument, but this is not an unusual failing in a young poet and, along with the fluency, it is here a sign of an exceptionally richly stocked and active imagination. Not all of Smith's imagery is strikingly original, and one finds in his work repeated and varied use of a number of common images derived from the natural environment of the west coast. In the impressive **"Poem of Lewis"** he distinguishes between the 'fine graces / of poetry', to which Lewis folk are in general immune, and the natural splendours of the landscape. . . . It is this landscape—pure, bare, harsh, haunted—which characterises much of Smith's poetry with the hardness of stone, the impersonal cruelty of the gulls, the fitful glory of light and the terrible splendour of lightning, a cold environment surrounding an ardent humanity, and everywhere the infinitely variable sea.

The title of the second collection, . . . *The White Noon,* is taken from its most important and accomplished piece, **"In Luss Churchyard"**. This poem embodies forcefully that visionary and aesthetic ecstasy which is a prominent feature of Smith's early work. In the churchyard the speaker experiences an intense awareness of natural energy 'where living and dead turn on the one hinge / of a noon intensely white, intensely clear'. Smith's poetry is exceptionally full of colours and hues: green, blue, red, yellow, orange, black, and above all white. They are not in general used systematically, but whiteness habitually suggests extreme purity, spirituality, and atemporality, and it is often linked, as here, with the force of light which 'strikes the stone bible like a gong', 'the noon's implacable sea / of hammered light'. This is a meditation of unforgettable intensity and goes a long way towards justifying Smith's emphasis on the supreme importance of the aesthetic in art. In a cooler poem, which shows the influence of Wallace Stevens' mandarin speculations, he calls the 'Beautiful Shadow' of the aesthetic attitude 'beyond the anguish of the ethical / my best follower and my truest friend,' and in five sonnets under the title **"Grace Notes"** which end the collection, he opposes to theological grace a number of secular graces, among them the intuitive vision of the poet which goes beyond the pretty to the truly beautiful. . . . (pp. 189-91)

The major development in [*Thistles and Roses,* Smith's third collection,] is a pronounced movement away from the high aesthetic ecstasies and the tendency to write poems about poetry which were evident in the first two collections. The title . . . does not refer to a specific poem but suggests a general conflict between severity and softness. There are no thistles as such, but there are repeated references to roses. The sonnet **"Luss Village"** begins with one of Smith's most daring and successful collocations:

> Such walls, like honey, and the old are happy
> in morphean air like gold-fish in a bowl.
> Ripe roses trail their margins down a sleepy
> mediaeval treatise on the slumbering soul.

The sleepy geriatric mildness here is innocent of any hint of thistles, but in the striking poem **"Kierkegaard"** the cold northern environment and the philosopher's father pictured as Abraham cutting his son 'to the head and heart' are opposed to the influence of Regine who 'sank her roses into his cold desert' and 'drove his body deeper into art'. . . . Here the rose helps to give birth to an individual tough enough to accept the crucifixion and the paternal knife. No such fusion, however, took place at the Scottish Reformation in **"John Knox"**, with its opposition between 'false French roses' and Knox's ruthless scythe. One result of this is that nowadays **"A Young Highland Girl Studying Poetry"**, coming from an affectionate but unsoulful stock at whose mouth 'The foreign rose abated', experiences poetry as 'an angled plough' which 'drives its lines into her forehead'. Lacking Kierkegaard's healing fusion in her upbringing, the young girl finds poetry a puzzling and harrowing experience. The basic opposition in the collection would thus seem to be between the harshness or bareness of Scotland's Reformed sensibility, impervious to Kierkegaard, and the very diverse softnesses of 'foreign' refinement and the Eventide Home.

A similar conflict appears in this collection's concern with the status of art. Smith finds that the artist is not readily accepted or taken seriously by his society. **"About that Mile"** introduces a theologically and morally earnest interlocutor who talks of the 'shining moral knife', the construction of fences (a recurring symbol for the protection of the ego), and crucifixion, and opposes them to an interlude of relaxation in his own past; he asks 'why two people living in a mile / of perfume and vast leisure failed their task', and when the speaker presses him on this subject he makes his low estimate of poetry clear:

> 'About that mile,' I said, 'about that mile
> you talked of there.' 'Well,' he pursued, 'what
>    then?'
> 'Do you not,' I questioned with a half-smile,
> 'dream of it sometimes, wish it back again?'
> But he with an equal smile said then to me:
> 'I turn to poetry for such foolery.'

The subject is taken up again in two sonnets under the title **"Studies in Power"**. The speaker, attending a meeting and listening to the debate, doubts the value of his own 'dwarf-ish verse' in the face of the violent 'in / black Roman leather' (Roman severity is a frequent image in Smith's work) and the beautiful 'in her deadly silks', But then, in an image which recurs several times in the verse and prose fiction to represent perfection, he has a vision of the integrity and comprehensiveness of art which resolves his doubt for the moment. . . . (pp. 191-93)

In *Thistles and Roses* Smith's visions lose something of their former afflatus, becoming rather harder and barer, and they have more directly to do with harsh reality and common humanity. The celebrated opening poem, **"Old Woman"**, is tightly observed, over-explicit in the middle, but ending with a sea image at once aesthetically perfect and in close keeping with the subject. . . . The humanity which can form part of the aesthetic attitude is evident also in the communal vision of friends in the pure **"By Ferry to the Island"**, in another art in the following poem **"A Blind Negro Singer"**, and in love in **"Three Sonnets"**: all of these poems are full of light and whiteness. In answer to the persistent doubts about the value of art, and in particular the suggestion that it shields one from the searing flames which the puritan confronts directly, Smith can only insist that art is truly graceful, comprehensive rather than single, fertile rather than barren, and that the fragile orange sunshade which 'shield[s] us from the fire' justifies itself by its poise and its beauty.

In the same year which saw the appearance of *Thistles and Roses,* 1961, Smith published in *New Saltire* an ambitious and important poem in fourteen sections called **"Deer on the High Hills—A Meditation"**. . . . The concern of this sequence (which is by no means always easy to follow) is with the fragility of beauty, and the impersonality of the natural world and the extent to which it can play a part in imaginative work. For part of the sequence the deer are made to function as a natural correlative to the force and grace of art, arrogantly aloof, often ignored but dangerous in times of crisis, poised between the mundane and the visionary, between earth and sky. The poet is asked to know the mundane world thoroughly and to use the hard, bare, intractable landscape as the stuff of poetry rather than raiding the myth-kitty, to use Larkin's phrase, so that he may achieve a deer-like grace. . . . The deer is both amoral and completely at home with its own fragility, untroubled by the 'languaged metaphor' of evil or 'The rampant egos of the flat plains' ever clinging to their identities, whether stones or humans. Thoroughly sensuous, graceful, and alert, the deer surveys the world at its feet 'vigilant always like a tiptoe mind / on peaks of sorrow, brave and

scrutinous.' Yet the poem ends with an acknowledgement of the 'otherness' of the natural world, of the falsity inherent in using it metaphorically. The deer itself may be 'a world away, a language distant,' but man in his loneliness must continue to establish imaginative contact with landscape and its inhabitants, while recognising their integrity, and follow the deer's example in his art. . . . (pp. 193-94)

Smith's concern with the nature of grace and his argument with his society are continued in the fourth collection, *The Law and the Grace.* Here there is a limpid title poem ["The Law and the Grace"], in which the poet answers the call to conform to a church and a society where grace has been legalised with a proud defence of his own angels, which

> are free and perfect. They have no design
> on anyone else, but only on my pride
>
> my insufficiency, imperfect works.
> They often leave me but they sometimes come
> to judge me to the core, till I am dumb.
> Is this not law enough, you patriarchs?

In **"Hume"** as fine a short poem as any he has written, Smith examines the additional challenge to this inner law and grace of art which is offered by rationalism. . . . (p. 195)

Smith's low regard for eighteenth-century rationality results from his awareness that beneath rational argument and calm behaviour there is a more profound life of will and passion. Having established his own poetic identity in his earlier poems, he is now moving towards a critique of that bourgeois society of which he is a member, and several poems are devoted to exposing the passion or the anxieties which lie below its apparently calm surface. One of the poet's functions is to tap the dionysiac and loosen the rigid as Burns does for the Covenanters in 'The Cemetery near Burns' Cottage', to be a lone rider, one of 'the careless ones' who are on hand to rescue the plodding settlers 'with their wagons all weighed down / by women's hysteria, furniture, design': the last word there is nicely ambiguous.

In each of the four collections discussed so far, the force of the whole has been somewhat lessened not only by the presence of inferior work but also by the lack of that overall cohesion between the poems which one finds supremely in Yeats. It is true that the same themes and images often recur, but one is still very much aware that most of the poems are occasional pieces. Smith's fifth collection, *From Bourgeois Land,* is a bold attempt to produce a fully coherent set of poems in criticism of bourgeois values. An epigraph for the volume may be found in the thirteenth poem where, in answer to an interlocutor's suggestion that it is inevitable that young rebellion should mature into acceptance, the speaker says:

> Ah, it is difficult. I know it well.
> But surely it is possible to remain
> a spy within the country and to gain
> a hard-won honesty from hollow hell.

As a spy in bourgeois land Smith has come in for some criticism. It has been argued both that his critique is superficial, that . . . it is 'too one-sided to be true at a poet's level of perception', and also that the subject has led him to produce poetry of less density and resonance than formerly. There is some truth in both these accusations. The collection contains several distressingly slick poems, making easy points easily, and the richness of the earlier style is less in evidence, but *From Bourgeois Land* is nevertheless a substantial achievement.

The fundamental point of the volume is made in the first poem: lack of imagination can lead to unquestioning obedience and, in the extreme case, to the tidy administration of genocide. In the exploration of those barely hidden forces in bourgeois Scotland which, in different circumstances, might result in the extreme case Smith covers a remarkably wide variety of topics with a new lucidity and displays his mastery of a formidable arsenal of poetic tones. In appropriately neat stanzas he introduces, for example: grotesque comedy, as the bourgeois 'weeps all day for the minutest error / and snores from tidy pillows like a frog'; poignancy, with an old photograph of a girl, in a Free Church Manse, which is 'almost rusted in this world of grace'; and in one four-line poem a massively Blakean epigram which sees eternity in a grain of sand. . . . It has been objected that Smith offers as an alternative to bourgeois conformity only a slightly self-conscious bohemianism, but he is a poet and his true alternative is the poems themselves; if his audience should fail him then there is love, and in the last two delightful poems there are children.

The new unity of subject matter evident in *From Bourgeois Land* is maintained in *Love Poems and Elegies* (1972). The love poems are mostly very brief and may strike the reader as somewhat inconsequential, but sometimes they can encapsulate in half a dozen lines or less a world of tenderness, anxiousness, fierceness, and terror. . . . The elegies (which come first) were written when Smith's mother died and adopt the broken style of a notebook of deprivation pioneered by Robert Lowell in *Life Studies*. Again, there is a risk that such poems will mean more to the poet than to the reader, but several factors help to make the set of elegies an impressively austere achievement. The great variety of invention in these poems on death is remarkable, yet they are united not only by their subject but by the relentless variations on funeral black, reaching their climax in a bunch of grapes which is seen as a clutch of black stars and a black jar for which one feels that, like Turner, Smith wants a blacker colour than black. Further, the choice of words and images often moves just beyond the ordinary without breaking the self-imposed decorum. . . . Most importantly, many of Smith's favourite images recur with poignant force in the elegies, so that they may be seen as a retrospective survey of his poetic world in the perspective of death: here are the roses, the fences, the daffodils, moon and stars, the stone, deer, the light and lightning, the vase, grace, and the ticking watch. In the year preceding the publication of these poems Smith said: 'everything I have ever done is really eventually coming to this question. What is death? What is a dead person, and in the end what is the value of writing when one is confronted by a dead person?' The attitudes adopted in the face of death are those Smith has developed over the years—a stark honesty, the cultivation of the 'truly human', and acceptance that

Being who we are we must adore the common
copies of perfection, for the grace
of perfect things and angels is too cold.

The retrospective element in the elegies is also evident in *Hamlet in Autumn,* published in the same year. Hamlet had already played a prominent role in *From Bourgeois Land* as the sensitive prisoner of a grotesquely corrupt society which he experienced as a hall of mirrors, distorted reflections in a spoon. The new volume offers an autumnal picture of this society in decline, beginning with meditations on the fierce revealing light of tragedy from classical times to the present and ending with **"Finis not Tragedy"** and a Stoppard-like punning evaporation glancing once more at the mirror:

It was just that I was not looked at.
It was just
an injustice of the glass.

Hamlet himself is seen as being half in love with death: he 'chewed it, fed on it, watched for it in mirrors', as the Chekovian Russians exclaim in their ennui 'Help us, let something happen, even death'. This is a picture of a weary, bored society, distrusting the intellect, aware of the fact 'That the slaves / sustained our libraries', surviving the decay of Empire, under the threat of nuclear annihilation. Idiots bounce balls; Napoleon's 'subtle genius' is defeated by 'the dense ignorance of life itself'; Francis Bacon's figures scream; Chaplin 'pulls / thick cultures down' and 'trudges on / to thriving emptiness'.

The weariness which is the volume's subject matter (and which effectively draws the varied poems together) is unfortunately reflected in the rather tired language and flaccid structure of some of its contents. The most successful poem, **"For Keats"**, is a dense and tightly imagined piece. Keats was a major influence on Smith's early poetry, and now that autumn is a theme he appears openly with allusions to the three great odes, fused with the death of Tom (during whose last illness Keats had felt his identity threatened) and his own visit to Scotland in search of that nobility and objectivity which he eventually achieved in his last ode **"To Autumn"**. This poem gains, as do many others in the collection, from reminiscences of Smith's earlier meditations—the perfect vase opposed to the imperfect bird, the 'helmet' frequently used for the human spirit, and the recognition of the otherness of nature. . . . (pp. 195-99)

***Orpheus, and Other Poems*** . . . is among the least known of Smith's collections but . . . contains his most impressive single poem. Most of the pieces in it are short and not of great importance (**"In the Dark"** is a notable exception) but the title poem **"Orpheus"** is superb. This gravely joyful set of sonnets consists mainly of a dialogue between Orpheus and Pluto in which several of Smith's central concerns are examined lucidly and imaginatively in the most elevated tone. Pluto explains to Orpheus what he has already subconsciously willed, that his love for Eurydice had to come to an end so that now in writing about her his poetry may be 'more clear / barer and purer'. Pluto's own music, played on Orpheus' lyre, is such 'as the zodiac / if made of solid heavy massive chains might make / which yet were banked with elegies and fire', speaking 'in joy / with its own elegance, intense and sparse'. Orpheus experiences a desire to stay in the underworld, so as to avoid the egotism of life on earth, but he is persuaded to return to the upper world and incorporate in his poetry the rich textures of ordinary life. (pp. 199-200)

The influence of **"Orpheus"** is clearly felt in the first part of *The Notebooks of Robinson Crusoe, and Other Poems* (1975). This part contains a group of fine formal poems with the gravity of their predecessor, several of them dealing with the aesthetic potentialities of common city life, and a number of delicate and sensitive treatments of love which maintain the new lucidity. The short second and third parts of the volume have less to offer, but there is one uniquely wry **"Chinese Poem"** full of a rare mandarin wit. This anticipates the 41 short sections of the extraordinary *Notebooks* themselves which make up the final part. One of the aphorisms in the thirtieth section may stand as epigraph: 'The world of one man is different from the world of many men.' Smith's awareness of the double movement in his own poetic personality comes to the surface in the *Notebooks.* Crusoe is repelled by society, seeing it as 'a Hall of Mirrors in which my face like all faces swells like a jester's in a world without sense'; becoming in his imagination

> my own god worshipping my own images, I would not wish to enter, unshaven and hairy, the monotonous climate of the mediocre, but would prefer my extreme pain to their temperate ordinariness.

In his proud isolation he is at once obsessed by and fearful of his own personality, trying unsuccessfully to keep away from the large mirror in which his wolfish face appears at shaving time. In these circumstances he finds that language disintegrates under scrutiny into pointless wordplay and childish babblings (which at times approach concrete poetry). In spite of all his reservations Crusoe is driven back into an acceptance of society, since for better or worse 'Language is other people.' (pp. 200-01)

*In the Middle* continues the ironic tone of the *Notebooks,* and the concern with common life evident in earlier volumes becomes a pity for that human suffering which is distressingly similar in every country. Irony and pity meet in sad amusement at the grotesque comedy of existence. The title may be taken in a number of senses, but the most direct reference is to a poem of the same title which suggests in a somewhat confusing way the busy confusion of life experienced by a middle-aged poet in the midst of a society which is itself betwixt and between. The main sense in the collection is of the continuity of life's processes. . . . The sense of flux is increased by Smith's familiar conviction that western culture is in decline, the culture of a fading élite, where Lycidas is drowned in a pile of supermarket goods and scholars take part in a grotesque charade.

The verse is spare, highly controlled, largely unrhymed. At times the danger of inconsequentiality is not avoided, and an occasional note of cheapness and easiness is disconcerting, but at its best this collection is no less impressive than the dedicatory poems with which Smith's career began. There is less obvious technical virtuosity, and the absence of rhyme from the work of such a fine rhymer is

an impoverishment, but the early obscurity has largely been purged and there is a classical inevitability about much of this work which is the fruit of long discipline. . . . (pp. 201-02)

> *J. H. Alexander, "The English Poetry of Iain Crichton Smith," in* Literature of the North, *edited by David Hewitt and Michael Spiller, Aberdeen University Press, 1983, pp. 189-203.*

## Iain Bamforth

Iain Crichton Smith is a prolific poet, storyteller and playwright, both in English and Gaelic: *Towards the Human* brings together a miscellany of sage, pithy and sometimes rueful critical pieces and comments on contemporary Scottish and Gaelic poets and poetry. Its essential themes are found in a series of deeply pondered essays on the problems and conflicting loyalties of being a writer in both languages while remaining within a community that is on the periphery—geographically, psychologically, linguistically—of the Anglo-Saxon hegemony. The most obviously engaging (and self-revealing) piece is a longish, previously unpublished essay—**"Real People in a Real Place"**—on the sensuous, historically improvident and impoverished domain of the Gael, and the presently dwindling resources of his culture and consciousness. It rails against those who, often unwittingly and with the best intentions, perceive the island experience as quaint, Edenic and at a remove from their own lives, thereby denying the islanders any status beyond that of a subordinate reality. The world of the Gael is full of incestuously bred ironies; merely to write in English is tantamount to treachery and betrayal, precisely because Gaelic does not have the self-confidence to foray into other linguistic domains.

Liberally quoting from the verse of those Gaelic coevals he most admires—a poetry characterized by a clear-sighted valedictory sadness and strong sense of moral indignation—Smith goes on to show why the community and its "instinctive engineering" are so important to the poet: here he has, despite its constraints and conservatism, an incontrovertible sense of place and human worth. As he reminds us, there is no unholy whiff of nostalgia in these poets' work; their clarity is simply that of a people staring into the abyss of a disappearing culture and a disappearing language. And Gaelic will die, slowly but surely, Smith implies, unless the wider community beyond it is capable of acknowledging that the islanders are no more and no less than people trying to cope with their own realities within the limitations of their own language. As he caustically rejoins, "Even Samuel Johnson took a far more intelligent interest in them than anyone does now".

Much of the rest of the book is devoted to a consideration of that tetrad of modern Gaelic poets, George Campbell Hay, Donald MacAulay, Sorley MacLean and Derick Thomson. Poets writing in Scots and English also attract his attention. "Who else", he asks, celebrating the technical and dialectical panegyrics of Robert Garioch, would have found three rhymes for Spagna, and two for Wamphray?" He is generous and accurate in his assessments of the work of George Bruce and Stewart Conn, but it is in the confrontation with that great monolith of twentieth-century Scotish verse, Hugh MacDiarmid—"a man who tried to flog a nation into consciousness"—that Smith is at his most illuminating and stimulating.

Plainly MacDiarmid's fearsome intellect—supremely factitious and inclusive, so exemplary of the Scottish surfeit of logic, intolerance and practicality—is at some variance with Smith's more reticently cautious and intuitive probings, but the argument between the two produces some felicitious insights. While recognizing the hallucinatory power of the early lyrics—assembled from the improbable basic materials of a thistle, a drunk man and moonlight—Smith can be sternly critical of some of MacDiarmid's later poems. For Smith, MacDiarmid's own failure of imagination to recognize the intrinsic worth of *Sangschaw* and *Penny Wheep,* abandoning their feminine vulnerability for the encyclopaedic, the didactic, the empirical, was, at least, a quintessentially Scottish failure.

*In the Middle of the Wood* is, to some extent, a novelistic exploration of the incipient paranoia sometimes associated with the practice of these virtues. More of a dramatic case-history than an actual novel, it charts the fall from grace of Ralph Simmons, a writer living with his wife in a small Scottish village, into an underworld where the distance between the real and the perceived is lethally blurred. Indeed, as the story begins he is already over the edge: he drags his unfortunate wife to a Glasgow hotel for no good reason, escapes from a taxi on the way home, and then tries to kill himself. In the middle section of the book some of the precipitating factors become clear: a nightmarish holiday in Yugoslavia with his wife and mother-in-law's varicosities and inane repetitions; the continuing trial of justifying himself as writer in a world that has room only for the utilitarian. Subsequently, he spends several weeks in a mental hospital where it occurs to him that a madman is "the most rigorously logical of all beings, not at all scatterbrained, but rather remorselessly reasonable". In the end, he saves himself through nothing more than the recognition and understanding of his fellow patients' sufferings and fears; just as if, as a writer, he had never fully acknowledged a reality beyond the limits of his own imagination. *In the Middle of the Wood* is a moving and poignant record of a passage through a shadow-land; it concludes on an unmistakable note of personal transcendence and an almost ineffable sense of joy and grace.

> *Iain Bamforth, "Logic, Not Nostalgic," in* The Times Literary Supplement, *No. 4392, June 5, 1987, p. 611.*

## Brian Morton

A bearded English tutor used to shout at us in despair, 'Hey, come on now, people, let's not play the *about* game.' Well, hell with it: *The Dream* is about language, relentlessly so.

Jacques Lacan—a particular favourite of the selfsame tutor—thought that the unconscious was organised like a language. Iain Crichton Smith is an unusually canny Lacanian. He recognises that the child's unappeasable dream of unity with everything, of words that precisely match

things and feelings, is both the ultimate frustration and pain and also the one redeeming goal of imagination. For Martin, a lecturer in Celtic at (presumably) Glasgow University, language is breaking down. At the beginning of the novel, he is literally, inexplicably, dumb. The silences between him and his wife, Jean, are now more cold than companionable. While he teaches the philological remnants of 'dead' tongues, modern Gaelic is dying in the Highlands and Islands. His dream is to return to Raws, to help preserve and pass on the language.

It is a dream he appears to share with several of the characters—a Highland policeman's widow, watching at a tenement window; drinkers at city *ceilidhs;* a young girl's mother, haunted by violence and drugs, appeased by an image of peace and quiet—but not with Jean, whose childhood on the island was straitened with a guilty illegitimacy opposite to Martin's. Where she has 'lost' the father she never knew, Martin, partly at his wife's behest, has turned his back on his dying mother. Symbolically at least, it leaves his dream of unity forever unattainable.

If he suffers from what a writer friend calls 'the Highlander's disease' of nostalgia, he has it in a curiously unsentimental strain, inoculated with a sense of history. Martin knows that the Celtic past isn't pristine, but a mess; it's a theme Crichton Smith evoked in the 1984 story **"Mr Trill in Hades",** where a dying school-master uncovers the rot underneath Ancient Greece's mythic grandeur. To Martin, Charles Edward Stuart was 'an evil ghost who had drifted into the Highlands, like some kind of vaporous poison', infecting Scotland with a Jacobitical elevation of fantasy over fact.

The novel's first climax is a night-time search through the streets of Glasgow for an errant girl. In point of fact, Sheila encounters nothing but a sort of addled kindness and evinces a self-sufficiency that turns her mother's dreams of a safe pastoral refuge back inwards on to her own bruised self. It's left to the drunken, rejected Morrison to stumble the first lesson: 'The mother. We'll have to abolish her. Before we grow up.'

The second lesson is James Joyce's 'silence, exile and cunning'. Though Martin looks unlikely to acquire the latter component, his island goodness disguises an impressive survivalism that will see him through. It's no coincidence that this lesson is learned at the end of a liquor-logged evening that once again distorts his speech, but which restores him to a woman, not his mother, that he first met in an art gallery, in front of a painting called *The Misanthrope.*

Crichton Smith plays About with sufficient urgency to rescue *The Dream* from school-masterish bathos. His fiction, which he has called 'imagistic', has none of the brittle particularity of his verse, but it has an intrinsic poetry that overcomes its more nervously prosaic elements. *The Dream* is Crichton Smith's 'Prufrock', a convincing coming-to-terms with a crisis that is both sexual (the impotence of language) and linguistic (the articulation of desire). Martin learns to sleep dreamlessly; human voices have wakened him just this side of drowning in an imaginary past.

Brian Morton, "Highland Games," in The Listener, Vol. 123, No. 3157, March 22, 1990, p. 30.

## Glyn Maxwell

In *The Village* we hear the voice of a true island poet issuing into the encircling silence of sea and air words of compassion and protest and, most vital, words preserving what is to be—has to be—valued. The short lines and stanzas of **"The Village"** (the title poem accounts for half the book) seem softly blown across the page, as if a gentle, teasing wind is what both forms and determines the concerns of this delicate work. The poet's ruminations on, and glimpses of, distant times, figures and places—Homer, Lear, Tolstoy; Greece, Rome, Florence—are inspired by rapidly differing weathers and skies; though wide and ramifying, they are framed by the lanes and windows of the village itself. While sanctioning and adorning the poet's freedom to imagine, equally they enisle him in his temporal and spatial remoteness, and in the loneliness of poetry itself, its aloneness on the page:

>     Hang out your washing
>             like paintings
>     in the calm day.
>             Raphael,
>                 Botticelli,
>     each beside the other
>             in a gallery of blue.

Through gently changing states of calm, joy and fear, Crichton Smith's reveries veer from the ancient past to the dangerous modern ("as the ball / sparkled high in the sky / above Japan"), from the huge shadows cast by great artists to the pathos of local smallness ("The little red van / buzzes about the village. / Letters from England, Canada, New Zealand") and most starkly, the image of

Death as ever-near, a regular with a cigarette, in the midst of fertility and daily errands, sometimes explicitly: "Death strides freely across the country-side, / swinging his stick". . . . Crichton Smith, content to receive and respond, will play either Aeolian harp or weathervane. From the rigours of his north, he faces a warm south that is as much the past as it is a place, a past of serene glory. In his novel **The Dream,** however, mainland émigrés look north, back to the islands of their births, some in deluded nostalgia, some in disdain. Between the contradictions of modern Scotland (allowing the Gaelic tongue to expire while milking a spurious "Highland culture"), the seductive insular dream and the common sense that what's gone is gone, the protagonists are bogged down in guilty inertia.

The other poems in *The Village* are least convincing when the airy spontaneity and light touch of the title poem are sacrificed for soldier matters: war, apartheid, the psychological ravages of television. To observe the horrors of the modern world from a distance (physical or spiritual) is not always to perceive them more clearly: distances blur and exaggerate. This poet's best is sudden and impressionistic, while his more direct tone tends to dissipate itself in repetition and earnestness. Whereas his Marx, "the inevitable and determined one / who set out in the most beautiful urban evening / with a sickle in his hand", is memorable, his overheated onslaught against television is not ("Listen, is there time for the poem to grow / in this incessant noise?") "Barer than the mind / is the soil of Lewis": Crichton Smith strikes the truest notes when he is facing into that bareness, his poems in step with the motion of village existence.

Glyn Maxwell, "Island Voices," in The Times Literary Supplement, No. 4545, May 11, 1990, p. 495.

# John Kennedy Toole

## 1937-1969

American novelist.

Toole's works combine irony, pathos, and acerbic wit in their highly personal examinations of cruelty and alienation. Both of his novels feature vividly evoked Southern milieus, vibrant comic characters, and misfit protagonists searching for acceptance and decency in society. In 1969, Toole committed suicide, but achieved posthumous fame when his novel, *A Confederacy of Dunces,* was printed eleven years later. The unusual circumstances of the book's publication contributed to conflict surrounding the later printing of *The Neon Bible,* a novel Toole had originally composed for a literary competition when he was sixteen years old. Although *A Confederacy of Dunces* is generally considered the more mature of the two novels, both reveal Toole's unique perceptions of the culture of the American South and offer glimpses of his extensive literary talents.

Born and raised in New Orleans, Louisiana, Toole was the only child of an invalid father and a formidable, strong-willed mother. He earned a Master's degree from Columbia University in 1959, and eventually taught at several colleges, including the University of Southwestern Louisiana. When he was twenty-four, Toole began writing *A Confederacy of Dunces* while serving with the U.S. Army in Puerto Rico. Upon his return to the United States, Toole attempted to publish the novel; a two-year correspondence with an editor at Simon & Schuster and several revisions of the manuscript ultimately ended in rejection. In March of 1969, two months after quitting his teaching job at Dominican University, he committed suicide by carbon monoxide poisoning in Biloxi, Mississippi. After Toole's death, his mother discovered the manuscript in a drawer, and was determined to have *A Confederacy of Dunces* published. She received several rejections before approaching novelist Walker Percy, who was then teaching at Loyola University, and convinced him to read the manuscript. In his foreword to *A Confederacy of Dunces,* Percy describes his initial resistance to Mrs. Toole's strong-arm tactics and his later surprised delight at the quality of Toole's work. The novel received enthusiastic reviews upon its long-awaited publication, and won the Pulitzer Prize for fiction in 1981. David Evanier asserted: "[*A Confederacy of Dunces*] is no wisp or tentative sprig: it is a full-blown, fully realized comic masterpiece. . . . Toole explodes on the page with absolute control of an inventive, riotous plot, a rich, vivid New Orleans atmosphere, and, above all, an unforgettable comic hero."

*A Confederacy of Dunces* opens with a vivid description of its slothful protagonist, Ignatius J. Reilly: "Full, pursed lips protruded beneath the bushy black moustache and, at their corners, sank into little folds filled with disapproval and potato chip crumbs." Several critics have maintained that the character of Ignatius is among the finest comic

grotesques in American literature, and that his repulsive physique and warped psyche fuel much of the comedy in *A Confederacy of Dunces*. Although he is thirty years old and possesses a Master's degree, Ignatius is completely supported by his mother, whose concern for her tyrannical son often borders on obsession. He spends most of his time in his sordid bedroom working on his literary masterpiece, "a lengthy indictment of our century." A staunch believer that the medieval world was a time of greater "taste and decency," Ignatius constantly lashes out at the values of modern society, attempting to view the contemporary world through a medieval context of reality. However, Ignatius's hypocritical actions make him an untrustworthy reformer of modern times. For example, he steadily consumes hot dogs and bakery cakes, and avidly watches movies and television in the consumer society he loathes.

Ignatius's belief in the superiority of medieval times, coupled with multiple self-delusions, render him virtually incapable of functioning in modern society. Forced by his mother to get a job, Ignatius is hired as a file clerk in a pants factory, where he creates chaos by, among other acts, leading the bemused factory workers on a "Crusade for Moorish Dignity" before being fired. Later, Ignatius works as a hot dog vendor, but eats more than he sells. "Save the World through Degeneracy," his plan for world peace, is an equally unsuccessful venture. Numerous critics viewed *A Confederacy of Dunces* as an allegory similar to medieval works, with Ignatius on a farcical "quest" or "pilgrimage." Toole won praise for his powerful social commentary: through vivid characterizations and authentic use of various New Orleans dialects, he portrays a Southern culture composed of myriad outcasts, illuminating social and racial problems of the 1960s.

The unusual circumstances behind the publication of *A Confederacy of Dunces* were brought to public attention again in 1987, when *The Neon Bible* was published following a lengthy court battle over rights to the novel. The phenomenal financial success of Toole's first work had made *The Neon Bible* manuscript subject to a bitter dispute among Toole's heirs. Written when Toole was a teenager, *The Neon Bible* describes a boy who is alienated by narrow-minded and judgmental residents of a small Southern Baptist town in Mississippi. Like Ignatius, the protagonist of *A Confederacy of Dunces,* the adolescent David is a sexually inexperienced social outcast. However, David recounts his ostracism from society in a romantic, innocent voice, contrasting with Ignatius's self-righteous, cynical outbursts. The first-person narrative chronicles David's loneliness and coming of age. He is raised in poverty by his mother and his Aunt Mae after his father is killed in World War II. When his mother succumbs to mental illness, David finds a sympathetic friend in his aunt. Coming from "somewhere where they have night clubs," strong, sensual Aunt Mae sharply contrasts with David's weak mother. Many critics lauded the vivid character of Aunt Mae, and some considered *The Neon Bible* to be a more finely constructed work than *A Confederacy of Dunces,* although lacking the latter's verbal brilliance. While some reviewers assert that a self-pitying tone pervades the novel, others contend that *The Neon Bible*'s sentimental style accurately reflects the anguish and uncertainty of youth. Mark Childress wrote: "*The Neon Bible* is, yes, the work of a child, a marvelously gifted and doomed child. It has a child's sweetness, and the innocent terror of discovering that the rules of life are unfair. No doubt *Confederacy* will be longer remembered, but *The Neon Bible* proves clearly that John Kennedy Toole, at sixteen, was a more powerful writer than many of the adults who have been cranking out fiction for these past thirty years."

(See also *CLC,* Vol. 19; *Contemporary Authors,* Vol. 104; and *Dictionary of Literary Biography Yearbook: 1981.*)

## PRINCIPAL WORKS

NOVELS

*A Confederacy of Dunces*   1980
*The Neon Bible*   1987

## Richard Brown

All but the most dedicated admirers of comic fantasy will be made wary by their first impressions of [John Kennedy Toole's] *A Confederacy of Dunces.* Its paranoid title, adapted from Swift, promises the kind of literary self-consciousness that can so often become tedious. It carries an off-putting foreword explaining the author's suicide and the discovery of the manuscript by an American college tutor. The central character is a grotesque version of the unemployable, self-indulgent, middle-aged adolescent with a master's degree and a sordid bedroom scattered with the notebook jottings that are one day to become his major indictment of the modern world. We might be excused for thinking that this has been done before—in Anthony Burgess's Enderby novels, for instance, or more commercially by Tom Sharpe.

Nevertheless, **A Confederacy of Dunces** manages to gather a considerable momentum, has its own distinctive voice and is imaginative enough to escape the cliché. It opens with Ignatius Reilly waiting for his mother by a New Orleans department store and immediately involved in a confrontation with the gauche Patrolman Mancuso who first accuses him of loitering and then tries to save face by arresting an innocent onlooker. As it turns out, arrest for Ignatius would have been a more satisfactory result: his favourite book is Boethius's *Consolations of Philosophy* (composed in prison), and in preserving a precarious freedom he is forced to seek employment compatible with his "world-view" and his "value" (the temperamental gastric seat of his creativity).

First he works for a company called Levy Pants, reorganizing the rat-infested filing system and attempting to start a revolution of the black factory workers. Then he becomes a street hot-dog vendor—which leads him into a plan for global peace based on homosexual infiltration of the armed forces. His mother deserts him and allies herself with the patrolman and the arrested by-stander who somehow manage to expose a pornography racket run from the Night of Joy nightclub. They try to get Ignatius committed as insane but he escapes at the last with Myrna Minkoff, an old college flame and do-gooding liberationist with whom he has been conducting a love-hate correspondence.

But the strengths of this novel do not really reside in this wild narrative and the countless absurd situations it generates. It succeeds, where it does succeed, through the clarity of its episodic architecture, its ability to rely effectively on dialogue for the evocation of scene and character, and through some splendid close observation which arises mainly from a determination to work with the peculiarities of a New Orleans setting and language. From the proprietress of the Night of Joy, as she discusses a new striptease gimmick to revive flagging custom, we are given an uncommonly vivid impression of the French quarter of the city. Ignatius's mother and her new friends, with their bowling parties and tastelessness ("honey that's a sweet little Blessed Virgin you got on top that T.V."), give us "tacky" provincial urban American life. And the black population from Mattie's Ramble Inn have their spokesman in Jones whose comedy again comes from his language as much as from his situation:

> Hey! I'm working in modren slavery. If I quit,
> I get report for bein vagran. If I stay, I'm gainfully employ on a salary ain even startin to be a minimal wage.

The dialogue is pointedly American and there is an added pleasure for a cisatlantic audience in having to translate—for instance when the steatopygic Ignatius on a bar stool "looked like an eggplant balanced atop a thumb tack".

The choice of intellectual endeavour and social change as objects of the novel's satire and the fact that it does have a comic nigger (however free of the worst racist characterization he may be) are rather questionable. But the comedy works and has a tragic, hopeless edge. It is indeed a matter of some regret that we will hear no more from the author.

> Richard Brown, "Tacky Vocations," in The Times Literary Supplement, No. 4034, July 18, 1980, p. 821.

## Harold Beaver

"For sheer pleasure", Osbert Lancaster observed, "few methods of progression can compare with the perambulator. The motion is agreeable, the range of vision extensive, and one has always before one's eyes the rewarding spectacle of a grown-up maintaining prolonged physical exertion." Above all, there is the pasha-like power of infants, derived from the mere act of jettisoning a teddy-bear or rattle, that can readily quell any tendency of grown-ups to independence.

Ignatius J. Reilly, of **A Confederacy of Dunces,** is just such an infant, inflated to grotesque dimensions. Like Ignatius, his author too had apparently been still living with his mother at the age of thirty. It was Thelma D. Toole who relentlessly hawked her son's manuscript, which had been unanimously rejected in the 1960s, until she elicited an enthusiastic commendation from Walker Percy. John Kennedy Toole's posthumous fiction was finally published last year by the Louisiana State University Press. To a universal chorus of praise. It is a masterpiece.

Until the mother publishes her own memoir, it will be hopeless to try to disentangle fact from fiction. For what at one point sounds like hilarious satire of American junk culture, at another sounds like self-satire. The loathing shifts, remorselessly to self-loathing. The title derives from Swift: "When a true genius appears in the world, you may know him by this sign, that the dunces are all in confederacy against him." That must have been John Kennedy Toole speaking. . . .

That suppressed "true genius" was his own. Who else is the mock-hero of this fiction? Who else this grotesque pasha, this southern Oblomov wallowing in his flannel nightshirt in a back bedroom in New Orleans? This lumbering, bloated, belching, hypochondriac slob who is literally a weight round his mother's neck? Mercilessly Ignatius J. Reilly tyrannizes over his mother. Relentlessly he

manipulates everyone by his monumental sloth and size. A true southerner of the old school, he rants against the modern world. A royalist and medievalist at heart, he yearns for the luminous age of Abelard and Thomas à Becket. Boethius's *De Consolatione,* Hroswitha and Batman are his guides as he swings up and down—mostly down—the cycles of Fortuna.

This inert blob of domesticated tissue (like the hero of Walker Percy's *The Moviegoer,* 1963) is compulsively drawn to movies, greedily studying the credits for performers, assistant producers, even hair designers that had previously roused his loathing, nauseating himself on close-ups, inspecting smiles for cavities and fillings. A purulent mess, he seeks out his mirror image in the world. His gloating lust is all expended on the movies and TV (that hang-up was all too true of the 1950s and early 60s), while he lashes out at heterosexuals, homosexuals, Protestants, "newspaper reporters, stripteasers, birds, photography, juvenile delinquents. Nazi pornographers". He dreams of terrorizing the white proletariat:

> The Negro terrorizes simply by being himself; I, however, must browbeat a bit in order to achieve the same end. Perhaps I should have been a Negro. I suspect that I would have been a rather large and terrifying one, continually pressing my ample thigh against the withered thighs of old white ladies in public conveyances a great deal and eliciting more than one shriek of panic.

This man-mountain of heaving fat—all lethargy and rancour—is a wholly novel compound: both rabelaisian, with his gargantuan farts, and melancholy as melancholy Jaques, and coyly virginal as Oliver Hardy. Inflated with gastric gas, when his pyloric valve snaps shut, he bumbles and floats into disaster-prone, knockabout regions of pure farce, like another Pyecraft.

But Ignatius is not the only memorable character. There is also a supporting cast of zany patrolmen, bag-ladies, night-club proprietors, hustlers, strippers, queers, Jewish industrialists, black vagrants, hot-dog vendors and female militants crisscrossing the wide sweep of the Crescent City from Canal Street to the suburbs, from the French Quarter to the wharves along the Mississippi. Bourbon, Royal, Chartres, St Peter, Dumaine: all the lovely names of the Quarter resound. All the accents resound: of the black spivs, the flitty queens, "the German and Irish Third Ward". Mark Twain himself might have saluted such an achievement. A spirit of revelry, of Mardi Gras, hovers over all as Ignatius (now a hot-dog vendor), an Italian patrolman, a Negro doorman and a variety of homosexuals wander about the Quarter in festive drag.

The plot itself is explosively inventive. Again and again I burst out laughing. But it must be remembered that something like a twenty year gap divides this text from the 1980s. Like *Sister Carrie,* **A Confederacy of Dunces** has reached us after a long and painful detour. John Kennedy Toole himself died in 1969, a year of revolt and rejuvenation. His novel is still rooted in an earlier decade of snug, sly, cynical seclusion—of verbal sabotage from the dark wombs of cinemas, family bedrooms, bars, bus terminals, rest-rooms, pool-halls and the back rows of seminars.

Twice Ignatius sallies out (bugged by his mother to find work) to be incongruously transformed: first into a rabble-rousing leader of sweat-shop labour; next, into a sexual campaigner. For, in a grand finale, he attempts to organize an international takeover, "Save the World Through Degeneracy". . . .

> None of the pederasts in power, of course, will be practical enough to know about such devices as bombs; these nuclear weapons would lie rotting in their vaults somewhere. From time to time the Chief of Staff, the President, and so on, dressed in sequins and feathers, will entertain the leaders, i.e., the perverts, of all the other countries at balls and parties. Quarrels of any sort could easily be straightened out in the men's room of the redecorated United Nations.

But this Satyricon of disguises and depravities and chance encounters necessarily moves to a comic resolution. The mother remarries; the Jewish proprietor returns to his factory; his psychobabbling wife is worsted; the stripper hits the big time; the vagrant lands a job; the bag-lady is retired; and Ignatius is rescued by his activist college girlfriend. The havoc littering his trail turns out to be wholly beneficial. This costive buffoon on the prowl—this obese onanist—turns out to be the trickster hero of the Carnival City. The anarchy that surrounds him is restorative and mysteriously creative.

> *Harold Beaver, "Appearance of Genius," in The Times Literary Supplement, No. 4080, June 12, 1981, p. 672.*

### David Evanier

The appearance of this astonishing book [*A Confederacy of Dunces*]—recipient of this year's Pulitzer Prize for fiction—11 years after the author's suicide challenges those of us who have felt that in these times a good book will somehow find its way into print in the writer's lifetime. This one did not, and the flavor of the book itself—the feeling of being almost over the edge, as is the bumbling gargantuan hero of the story—suggests that the novel's fate must have played a part in the death of the writer. Mr. Toole's title derives from Swift and points to his own presentiments about his book's future: "When a true genius appears in the world, you may know him by this sign, that the dunces are all in confederacy against him." Had it not been for Toole's determined mother and the generous intercession of a recognized author, Walker Percy, who started it on the rounds of the publishers (nine of whom turned the novel down), *A Confederacy of Dunces* might never have seen print at all.

This first novel is no wisp or tentative sprig: it is a full-blown, fully realized comic masterpiece. There are some overlong passages and less successful caricatures, but in the main Toole explodes on the page with absolute control of an inventive, riotous plot, a rich, vivid New Orleans atmosphere, and, above all, an unforgettable comic hero, Ignatius Reilly. I had not laughed out loud at a book since *Portnoy's Complaint,* and I had never laughed out loud this much at a book.

But Toole is not only adept at characterizations of individuals—Ignatius, his mother, the black janitor Jones, and the octogenarian Miss Trixie. He is brilliant at rendering groups as well (black workers and the gay community) with startling, incisive, heightened dialogue. But Toole is no baiter of minorities. The surreal satiric thrust is directed at everybody. And no one is more a minority than that crazed minority of one, the behemoth Ignatius.

Ignatius, who is thirty and flatulent, is a raging medievalist, lying abed, recording his thoughts in his Big Chief tablets. He wears a green hunting cap with earflaps that stick out on each side, tweed trousers which are "durable and permitted unusually free locomotion," a flannel shirt, and a muffler. His dialogue is what pitches the book into realms of hilarity. Ignatius sounds like a spoiled mama's boy, effete, crazily arrogant, and bombastic. Yet none of these terms nearly defines him. Once we are sucked into his world by the whirlwind of his harangues, we forget about definitions.

Every day, at home with his mother, Ignatius sits eating doughnuts, drinking milk from his Shirley Temple mug, and watching *American Bandstand* on TV:

> "Oh, my God! What an egregious insult to good taste. . . . Do I believe the total perversion that I am witnessing?" Ignatius screamed from the parlor. . . . "The children on that program should all be gassed." . . .
>
> "Oh, my heavens!" a voice shouted from the parlor. "These girls are doubtless prostitutes already. How can they present horrors like this to the public?"

In the afternoons he attends the movies, "his body filling the seat and protruding into the two adjoining ones." He scans the screen, waiting for the heroine he hates most:

> "Oh, my God!" he screamed. "There she is." He put the empty popcorn bag to his full lips, inflated it, and waited, his eyes gleaming with reflected technicolor. A tympany beat, and the soundtrack filled with violins. The heroine and Ignatius opened their mouths simultaneously, hers in song, his in a groan. In the dark two trembling hands met violently. The popcorn bag exploded with a bang.

Ignatius is forced out into the world by his mother. He creates havoc at a pants factory, where he organizes the black workers into a "crusade for Moorish dignity." Ignatius is partly motivated by his fury at his former girlfriend, Myrna Minkoff of the Grand Concourse, a political activist whose "only desire is to aid you in finding your true self-expression and contentment through satisfying, natural orgasm. . . . A good explosive orgasm would cleanse your being and bring you out of the shadows." When Ignatius is fired from that job, he becomes a frankfurter salesman for Paradise vendors. He makes a sign for his weenie wagon: "TWELVE INCHES (12″) OF PARADISE." He tells a customer:

> "I am sorry, I have only a few frankfurters left, and I must save them. Please get out of my way."

. . . "Whatsa matter with you, friend?"

"What's the matter with me? What's the matter with *you*? Are you unnatural enough to want a hot dog this early in the afternoon? My conscience will not let me sell you one. Just look at your loathsome complexion . . ."

(pp. 729-30)

Every piece fits singularly in this black comedy. There is the question of Ignatius's "sealed valve," which occupies a substantial portion of the narrative. There is the black named Jones, whose dialogue has an authenticity seldom granted to blacks in our literature. Jones works as a janitor in a strip joint for $20 a week:

> I turnin into a expert on flos. I think color cats got sweepin and moppin in their blood, it comes natural. It sorta like eatin and breathin now to color peoples. I bet you give some little color baby one-year-old a broom in he hand, he star sweepin his ass off. Whoa!

There are also stereotypical characters—Myrna Minkoff and the Levys (the owner of the pants factory and his do-gooder wife)—but they are done with such verve that in the absurdist context of the book they are right.

Ignatius Reilly is one of the most libidinous, sexually repressed characters in all American fiction. (A neighbor reports the bickering of Myrna and Ignatius: "The things I useta hear through my window! 'Put down that skirt,' and 'Get off my bed,' and 'How dare you? I'm a virgin.' ") He allows himself to fantasize a love affair with a stripper when he thinks she shares his enthusiasm for Boethius's *Consolation of Philosophy*.

The reader is haunted by the awareness of many things in reading this novel. There is the outcome of Toole's own life. There is the sense that Ignatius is close to John Kennedy Toole, as the mother is seemingly a parallel in some ways to Toole's mother. Nevertheless, the book is blastingly funny, and its objectivity, unsentimentality, and control extend to all its auxiliary characters.

*A Confederacy of Dunces* transcends the suffering of life through laughter, but the feeling of intense sadness is pervasive. If it is *about* anything, it is about the stubborn independence of the neurotic soul of Ignatius. Not for a minute do we see Ignatius in any way other than the booming, ridiculous role he plays. Yet we feel deeply for him.

Toole's fiercely individual vision must have made many a publisher uneasy. He tackles every "group" with equal ferocity, and no one more fiercely than Ignatius. We see everything through Ignatius's perspective, and the ultimate effect of the novel is nonjudgmental: the world as a madhouse, seen by a madman.

If you read no other novel this year, read this one. John Kennedy Toole is dead, but he has left behind something supremely alive. Unforgettable. (p. 730)

> *David Evanier, "Behemoth," in* National Review, New York, *Vol. XXXIII, June 26, 1981, pp. 729-30.*

## Jay L. Halio

[Unfortunately] doomed never to have a sequel of any sort, John Kennedy Toole's *A Confederacy of Dunces* is unique in every sense. It recounts the adventures and misadventures of Ignatius J. Reilly, by general acclaim one of the greatest comic grotesques ever to find his way into the pages of literature. The setting is New Orleans peopled by a galaxy of bizarre, colorful, and funny characters with whom Reilly, "slob extraordinary," as Walker Percy calls him (among other epithets) in his forward, comes into contact—or collision. Reilly is an anachronism as well as an aberration in late twentieth-century society, even in a city like New Orleans, which easily tolerates, or cultivates, the unusual in human nature. Quoting Boethius, addicted to television while highly critical of it (and nearly everything else in contemporary civilization), Reilly turns society upside down, exposing in the process hypocrisies, pretense, and corruption that pop open on every side of him, or rather on every side of the wide wake he leaves behind him. The intricacy of the plot is a masterful achievement as well in a modern *Dunciad* that has all of the power with none of the astringency of its eighteenth-century forebears.

It is strange that such a novel should have had difficulty finding its way into print. (pp. 211-12)

> *Jay L. Halio, "Contemplation, Fiction, and the Writer's Sensibility," in* The Southern Review, Louisiana State University, *Vol. 19, No. 1, Winter, 1983, pp. 203-18.*

## David McNeil

Call it "double-edged" satire, or "double-faceted" satire, or whatever you like—but the kind of satire in which the satirist-persona or satirist-character makes his attack and is ironically ridiculed himself is a kind that appears to resurface regularly in American literature. This subgenre is, of course, by no means exclusively American. In *The Power of Satire*, Robert C. Elliott contends that "the theme of the satirist satirized . . . appears (in various guises) with remarkable regularity throughout the history of satirical writing." The Renaissance certainly provides many examples: *Timon of Athens, Troilus and Cressida, Le Misanthrope*, and *The Anatomy of Melancholy*—a fact which perhaps is best explained by Alvin Kernan in his focusing upon the Elizabethan concept of the satyr [in *The Cankered Muse*]:

> The interrelated tensions which are present in varying degrees in all satire are the very essence of the satyr [Elizabethan satirist-character or persona]. He is at once the simple plain man who speaks plain truth, and the heroic Nemesis of vice who uses all the elaborate tools of the baroque rhetorician. He is the savage enemy of all evil, who is himself tainted with the same failings with which he charges others.

Reverse satire may also be an especially appropriate form for expressing the American tradition of the democratic or leveler ideal. We may be quick to rail at human folly and vice, but we seem even quicker to rail at supercilious condemnation. (pp. 33-4)

This dual function of attacking vice or folly and then checking satiric arrogance . . . [appears] in Mark Twain. Richard Boyd Hauck, in *A Cheerful Nihilism,* calls *A Connecticut Yankee in King Arthur's Court* "Twain's masterpiece of the absurd. . . . double-faceted satire," because the initial satire against the chivalric codes of Arthurian legend (from a nineteenth-century American perspective) reverses itself and becomes an indictment of Yankee ingenuity out-of-control. According to Hauck, the novel is ultimately "a satire directed at the very perception process which allows satire." New-world invention only appears better than old-world superstition. Hank Morgan sits and listens to Sir Dinaden's "worm-eaten jokes," heard by Morgan in his youth thirteen hundred years later, and concludes that there is no "such thing as a new joke possible." Man does not progress; he merely changes location.

John Kennedy Toole's *A Confederacy of Dunces* comes about a century after Twain and is further evidence of reverse satire being a distinguishable vein in American literature. In spite of the prosperity which followed colonization and the Civil War, Toole playfully hypothesizes that the dunces have multiplied and may now possess the upper hand. Seeing twentieth-century America as the culminating horror of an abominable degeneration that began with the Renaissance, Ignatius J. Reilly—the novel's comic hero—is a brilliant embodiment of reverse satire because he epitomizes the very perversions against which he rages. Whenever he is not condemning the modern world for its obscene "excess," he fattens his already obese body with a steady diet of hot dogs, Dr. Nut (a soft-drink), and bakery cakes. This paradoxical aspect of Toole's novel, I believe, continues the American tradition of reverse satire as established by such works as [Ebenezer Cook's] "The Sotweed Factor" and *A Connecticut Yankee in King Arthur's Court.*

Toole's comic hero loathes the superficiality of a consumer society, and yet he chooses the "shiny" hot dog cart "with the white sidewall tires." In fact, Ignatius loathes the very fabric of capitalism but this does not prevent him from driving a hard deal for storing "school supplies" (really pornography) in the "well of his wagon." He continues to work as a hot dog vendor only so that he can gorge himself with hot dogs which, despite their suspicious contents ("Rubber, cereal, tripe. Who knows?"), he finds "curiously appealing." In short, as much as Ignatius rages against the modern degeneration of values, he himself is an all-too-farcical product of that same society. His indignation, which is so central to his character, is sincere yet naive. One is reminded of [Jonathan] Swift's truly satiric definition of satire [in *A Tale of a Tub*]: "*SATYR is a sort of Glass, wherein Beholders do generally discover every body's Face but their Own.*"

Similar to the narrator of "The Sotweed Factor," who is "Contemn'd by Fate, to wayward Curse, / Of Friends unkind, and empty Purse," Ignatius is forced by his financially strapped mother to seek a job. Nobody could be more ill-suited for the job market. Fixed on the ideals of the medieval age, Ignatius may mock the "insidious gospel

of 'The Enlightenment' " but he nevertheless believes in sensible clothing. Hence, he wears a green hunting-cap during an interview with an insurance company because the "office was improperly heated." Miraculously, Ignatius is hired by the Levy Pants Company, which he praises on the grounds that the "obviously reliable worker is completely unmolested." Ignatius, of course, is anything but reliable and Levy Pants turns out to practice the most irresponsible management of private capital. Although Ignatius recognizes his utter unsuitability for the system— "Employers sense in me a denial of their values"—his Boethian beliefs tell him that "[t]here was no fighting Fortuna until the cycle was over." This stoicism bases itself on the inherent consolation of a philosophy that holds a cyclical view of history—why despair when one will eventually rise back up? Ignatius even imagines the indirect benefits that might accrue from entering the work force and points to the paradox: "Perhaps the experience can give my writing a new dimension. Being actively engaged in the system which I criticize will be an interesting irony in itself." Ignatius is not just "actively engaged" in it; he is hopelessly part of it.

It may be said that the most ingenious stroke in *A Confederacy of Dunces* is Ignatius' characterization. Before Fortuna begins her downward swing, Ignatius is happily occupied in an ivory tower of medieval meditation. Asked by a policeman whether or not he is employed, Ignatius replies, " 'I am at the moment writing a lengthy indictment against our century. When my brain begins to reel from my literary labors, I make an occasional cheese dip.' " He also enjoys Hollywood films, the pretense of which pitches him into an oddly excited state of shock and perversion: " 'Filth!' Ignatius shouted, spewing wet popcorn over several rows. 'How dare she pretend to be a virgin. Look at her degenerate face. Rape her!' " In Ignatius, Toole expresses how indictment or censure, if strong enough, can easily escalate into violence and even perversion. But, at every turn, Ignatius himself represents the very abominable perversions that he finds so offensive. He ridicules the "ladies' art guild" for being totally void of "taste and decency," but his own female paragon is found in "a pornographic photograph" of a woman holding a copy of Boethius' *The Consolation of Philosophy.* The picture draws Ignatius' only positive comment on popular culture: " 'What brilliance. What taste.' " Ultimately, Ignatius' lofty spiritual world is as debased as Lana Lee's erotica showcase, "that pure Virginny Belle, Miss Harlett O'Hara" (or according to Jones, the black doorman, "Miss Harla O'Horror")—opportunity goddess of the American South. The difference is that Lana Lee is under no illusions; she knows that her business is selling sexual-fantasy entertainment to "septuagenarians." Ignatius, on the other hand, is all the more outrageous for his preposterous self-deception. Meant to be a moment of intensified Jesuit-like prayer, Ignatius' spiritual ecstasy is nothing more than masturbation perversely inspired by a vision of his long-dead pet collie, Rex. As a comic character, however, Ignatius is far more humorous than offensive.

Much of the ambiguity of the novel comes from the fact that Ignatius' indictment of the century is quite understandable and valid. Is he insane for being one of those "poor souls who simply cannot stand lanolin, cellophane, plastic, television and subdivisions?" Of course not, but Ignatius has odd notions on how to cultivate the imagination: "When the suburbanites grow tired of television and Ping-Pong or whatever they do in their little homes, they could chain one another up for a while." Nor is Ignatius alone in his attack upon modern society. It is a fitting paradox that Lana Lee herself remarks on the depravity to which people have sunk and the increasing difficulty of maintaining some sense of morality along with profits: "It used to be the odd Kiwanis types liked to come in and watch a cute girl shake it a little. Now it's gotta be with some kinda animal. You know what's wrong with people today? They're sick. It's hard for a person to earn an honest buck." Part of what makes Ignatius so memorable as a comic character is that, despite the offensiveness, many of his criticisms and anxieties are shared to some degree by the reader.

A reactionary movement is definitely a little sick or mad, particularly in the Jonsonian sense of "humours," when activitists begin equating animosity with intellect. Myrna Minkoff does exactly this in her assessment of a radical singer who despises all establishment groups: "Like he hated them. I mean, this fellow was sharp." Ignatius tries to harness the forces of sheer hate and violence when he plans to engage three pugnacious lesbians as a "ladies' auxiliary" in his underground movement. Violence may only be a means of achieving the desired end, but there is often a Machiavellian element at the point where reverse satire begins to shift. In *A Connecticut Yankee in King Arthur's Court,* Hank Morgan must guard his Americanization project against those who would prefer to return to dark superstition. This conflict leads to civil war and finally ends in a paradoxical defeat-in-victory for Morgan. As a representative of dark superstition, Merlin has the last laugh: "Ye were conquerors; ye are conquered!" Ignatius is not exactly a Machiavellian, yet he does envision a more controlled society: "A firm rule must be imposed upon our nation before it destroys itself. The United States needs some theology and geometry, some taste and decency. I suspect that we are teetering on the edge of the abyss." The difference between Morgan "the Boss" and Ignatius is that Morgan's mania starts out as common sense, whereas Ignatius is blatantly objectionable as soon as he bursts upon the scene.

More accurately, it is the naivety on the part of the reactionary or satirist that marks the shift in reverse satire. Only once has Ignatius ventured beyond New Orleans and that was a quick bus-trip to Baton Rouge during which he "vomited several times." Ignatius thrives on his belief that what is totally absent in the chaos of modern society is a definite center: "I think that perhaps it was the lack of a center of orientation that might have upset me. Speeding along in that bus was like hurtling into the abyss." In this respect, it is worth noting that Ignatius' favorite philosopher, Boethius, conceives of the deity as a fixed center which regulates and controls the movement of the surrounding universe. If naivety is a characteristic of the archetypal hero in American literature (Ishmael, Christopher Newman, and Gatsby) perhaps it is so because the American psyche suffers the disorientation of a move to

a new land, of a shift of centers. Education and culture may not adequately prepare one for a completely different world—as the heroes of reverse satire reveal. Ebenezer Cook is civilized; Hank Morgan understands eclipses and electricity; and Ignatius, a Master of Arts, finds the melody of "Turkey in the Straw . . . a discordant abomination" compared to the music of Scarlatti.

All of Ignatius' schemes for reforming modern society are naively conceived and therefore doomed to meet with hilarious failure. His complete lack of knowledge of the business world accounts for his quick but shortsighted method of clearing up the backlog of filing in the Levy Pants office—he simply tosses the files in the garbage. Later he tries to organize a labor revolt in the factory but has absolutely no idea of the workers' concerns. Still, one cannot argue with certain aspects of his idealism, such as wanting to end all wars, and Santa's realistic dismissal of this ideal—, "he wants peace. . . . That boy's gotta be put away"—strikes its own satiric chord: One can only blame the fragmented nature of man's fallen world, and to blame that is not to hope for something better. . . . Unlike conventional satire, reverse satire does not point to a right while ridiculing the wrong; it points to the human fallibility of naively trusting in right over wrong, or in reformative schemes. One can only trust that human values will clash and change. (pp. 34-40)

Ignatius J. Reilly is undoubtedly "sad," as some tourists believe him to be—even though they erroneously think that his problem is alcoholism. Man is not a poor judge, Toole is saying; he is merely superficial in his analysis, too quick to make assumptions that conform to his preconceived ideas. Much of Ignatius' problem is physical: his obesity, his closing valve, his "merely mechanical" masturbation. These, however, are caricatured deformities; physicality is the fundamental problem of humankind. Ignatius is a grotesque exaggeration of all the ills of an excessive society, and John Kennedy Toole wants us to laugh at the excess. As mortals we may fear death, but few would follow Ignatius and always ride in the back-seat of a car because they happened to read "somewhere that the seat next to the driver was the most dangerous." Toole's comic hero, or satirist-character, represents our worst anxieties gone mad. He may also be a "sad" character, but the humor he generates causes the reader to focus on the "sad" society to which he belongs.

Ostensibly, Toole uses Ignatius to ridicule academic institutions, and he does so with true Swiftian brilliance. The reader never forgets that Ignatius does have, along with his Mickey Mouse watch, a Master's degree. Instead of expanding his appreciation of literature, graduate study makes Ignatius terribly biased and peculiar, especially with respect to his recommended reading list: "Boethius, of course" and "extensively into early Medieval," but "skip the Renaissance and the Enlightenment . . . mostly dangerous propaganda" and "skip the Romantics and the Victorians too"; "as for the contemporary period" Ignatius suggests "Batman especially, for he tends to transcend the abysmal society in which he's found himself." The university breeds eccentricity, and individuals who are warped insofar as education is concerned can lead the humanist away from society. Needless to say, Ignatius' teaching career at college is short-lived. Trained to be opinionated and combative, Ignatius gets into a terrible conflict with his students and defies what he claims is "the abyss of contemporary academia." Like wars, polemical disputes are proof of man's uncompromising plurality. . . . Formal education certainly does not guard against naivety, extremism, or conflict, and it seems that reverse satire delights in exposing the ignorance of sophisticated pretention and presumptuousness.

Ignatius' contempt for the modern world, including academia, is matched only by his enormous ego. When his mother mentions psychiatric help, he retorts, "Do you suppose that some stupid psychiatrist could even attempt to fathom the workings of my psyche?" As an extremely outrageous and offensive misfit, Ignatius is all the more ludicrous for his sneering disdain and loftiness. Along with Myrna Minkoff, he conspires in a low and malicious vendetta against Dr. Talc, who is himself a satire on the tenured English professor. Constantly seducing female students and "unable to remember anything about Lear and Arthur aside from the fact that the former had some children," Dr. Talc of course deserves to be attacked. Ironically Ignatius becomes self-conscious about serving up the same kind of "easily digested generalizations" that Dr. Talc is "renowned for" and writing his indictment in the style of American literary history: "But I am beginning to sound like the Beards and Parringtons." Nevertheless, he imbibes enough academic jargon; "worldview" is his favorite word. The young drop-out, George, correctly guesses Ignatius' background from his speech and regards him as a warning not to remain in the educational system too long: "You could tell by the way that he talked, though, that he had gone to school a long time. That was probably what was wrong with him. George had been wise enough to get out of school as soon as possible. He didn't want to end up like that guy." Ignatius, equipped with his medieval ideals, lords it over everybody he meets, but conversely, Toole's low-life characters, like the street-hustler George, regard Ignatius as an educated anachronism.

*A Confederacy of Dunces* includes other caricatures from academia besides Ignatius and Dr. Talc. Mrs. Levy functions as a satiric portrait of the business behaviorist who simplistically applies psychological theory to management situations. She refuses to let the weary and senile Miss Trixie retire from the Levy Pants Company, because she "must be made to feel wanted and needed and loved"— even if it kills her. Again we have a beautifully constructed paradox. Those who seek to improve the world only do it more harm by their shortsightedness and aggression. Unlike Ignatius who has spent too much time in academia, Mrs. Levy seems to reflect [Alexander] Pope's adage, "A *Little Learning* is a dang'rous Thing; / Drink deep, or taste not the *Pierian* Spring." It is obvious that Mrs. Levy's plan for Miss Trixie is completely self-serving; when theory is misapplied, the social reformer becomes fair game for the satirist.

As sad as Ignatius is, like Mrs. Levy he has the best intentions. . . . A desire to reform and improve often inspires satire and makes it a highly moral genre. Reverse satire, however, mocks the desire to reform as much as it mocks the social target itself. Ignatius prays to St. Zita to help his mother fight her alcoholism, but this seems to be an afterthought to his self-indulgent prayer to "St. Medericus, the Hermit, who is invoked against intestinal disorders." His wish to see world peace is admirable, but once more it is his outrageous scheme for turning the ideal into reality that strikes the reader—to infiltrate the army with "disguised tarts" like "Timmy . . . the sailor":

> The power-crazed leaders of the world would certainly be surprised to find that their military leaders and troops were only masquerading sodomites who were only too eager to meet the masquerading sodomite armies of other nations in order to have dances and balls and learn some foreign dance steps.

The plan's subversive intention, as ridiculous as the plan itself is, symbolizes the ambiguous and often paradoxical nature of reality: war and conflict transformed into peace and harmony. In a sense, Toole's comic hero is a debased caricature of St. Ignatius Loyola, who designated himself Knight of the Blessed Virgin, began the Jesuit Order, and helped wage a backlash against the Reformation. Ignatius, however, fancies himself as the modern day Boethius, unjustly imprisoned:

> The world will someday get me on some ludicrous pretext; I simply await the day that they drag me to some airconditioned dungeon and leave me there beneath the fluorescent lights and sound-proofed ceiling to pay for scorning all that they hold dear within their little latex hearts.

Bitter disillusion strikes Ignatius when he learns the truth about his own female paragon: "Oh, Fortuna, you degenerate wanton!" . . . Rather than question the feasibility of his reformative scheme or the validity of his ideal, the "satirist satirized" . . . tends to attribute his failure to an unfavorable and circumstantial tide of events. Hence, he remains in his madness or folly because he believes that he will rise to success if he can only survive the downward swing.

Ultimately, reverse satire portrays conflicting positions which can be understood within the context of a Hegelian dialectic. The thesis is defined by the antithesis. This model precisely describes the form of Toole's Swiftian epigraph and title: "When a true genius appears in the world, you may know him by this sign, that the dunces are all in confederacy against him." Toole certainly gives us the dunces as his diminutive title suggests, but he is also whimsically playing with the implied presumption and arrogance on the part of the genius. In *The Intelligencer* papers, Swift refers back to his earlier statement and says that the "genius" generally lacks *"Discretion"*; hence, he becomes an object of attack. Ignatius may be fiction's most indiscreet comic railer since Shakespeare's Thersites. The scurrilous satirist only reveals his own objectionable nature when he attacks his target. Furthermore, while allowing Ignatius some basis for his indictment of modern society, the reader also opposes the scurrilous abuse and therefore may feel cast in the "confederacy" role which, by

Swift's amusing definition, makes Ignatius a genius and the reader a dunce. Hmmph.

As a consequence of this dialectical structure, *A Confederacy of Dunces* can be seen as a wonderful *paradoxia epidemica*. For example, Ignatius identifies his own exile with that of the American Negro, farcically represented by Jones: " . . . both exist outside the inner realm of American society." Like Ignatius, Jones must find a job and discovers that America is the land of inopportune circumstances, of fortune's downward swing. He is paid a slave's wage and Lana Lee, his employer, retains him by exploiting his fear of the police. Ignatius, led to the "Night of Joy" to encounter his paragon Miss O'Hara, precipitates the climactic events which cause Jones to be fired, or in this case, liberated. However, Ignatius and Jones approach the American mainstream from opposite banks. The former enjoys his exile, his Miltonic seclusion which he deems is necessary to perfect his "craft of writing," while the latter would like to find a way to enter the system, to grab a shred of the American dream: "Wha you think a color cat can do to stop bein vagran or employ below the minimal wage?" Ignatius' answer is consistent with his philosophy but peculiarly inadequate and hilarious when offered to someone who could use a little "excess" after a life of suppression: "Your value judgments are all wrong. . . . Live contentedly in some hovel. Thank Fortuna that you have no Caucasian parent hounding you. Read Boethius."

The idealist who possesses a conscience must often face the old end-versus-means paradox, and this is what differentiates Ignatius from the more radical Myrna. Ignatius' scheme to bring about world peace produces a "debate between Pragmatism and Morality"; in his Big Chief copybook he writes: "Like two figures in the medieval Morality play, Pragmatism and Morality spar in the boxing ring of my brain. I cannot await the outcome of their furious debate." (pp. 40-5)

The action in *A Confederacy of Dunces* is carefully designed to highlight the ambivalent and contradictory nature of the world. In the opening scene, Ignatius is about to be arrested when Claude Robichaux intervenes on his behalf and rebukes the officer, Mancuso: "The police are all communiss." As Mancuso's attention turns to Robichaux, Ignatius and his mother slip away and ironically the latter's apprehension also focuses on Robichaux: "He's crazy. . . . He might kill us all. Personally, I think he's the communiss." The action takes another twist later when Mancuso befriends Mrs. Reilly and Robichaux actually becomes her boyfriend. Mrs. Reilly's comment to Ignatius at the end of the novel suggests that ignorance and simplistic ideology are not crucial weaknesses as far as human values are concerned: "Claude is dumb . . . all the time worrying me about them communiss. . . . [But] Claude can be nice to a person. . . . You learnt everything Ignatius, except how to be a human being." Good nature can lie just as easily under wrong-headed McCarthyism as perverse nature can under well-intended idealism.

There are no straight characters in *A Confederacy of Dunces,* nobody who represents the *consensus gentium.*

Perhaps this is why Mancuso cannot bring in a "suspicious" person—everybody is a crank so nobody appears particularly "suspicious"; there is no antithesis. When Mancuso lets Ignatius,—whom he describes to his sergeant as a "great big pervert. . . . The biggest I ever saw in my whole life"—get away, we know that he has no chance of ever catching anything suspect. In a carnivalesque world fraught with buffoons and low-life characters, his quest becomes absurd. Like the knights in *A Connecticut Yankee* who do not know where to start looking for the Grail, Mancuso may have a strong sense of cause yet absolutely no idea of how to fulfill it. Because reverse satire is organically cyclical, it derives much of its comic energy from this kind of treadmill quest. Man's dialectical motivation makes a merry-go-round of his existence.

*A Confederacy of Dunces* is truly comic in a positive and celebratory sense. First of all, Ignatius begins his upward swing and escapes New Orleans: "Now that Fortuna had saved him from one cycle, where would she spin him now? The new cycle would be so different from anything he had ever known." Second but more important, the novel is truly comic for no other reason than that it makes us laugh-happy. Yet we laugh nervously, for *A Confederacy of Dunces* is also a satire against humankind, a satire which has us teetering before the abyss of unredeemable pessimism. Paradox can be a terrible beauty, and it is perhaps somewhat melodramatic—but nevertheless curiously fascinating—to see Ignatius' concern for his "notes and jottings" in relation to the author's fate: "There are all of my notes and jottings. We must never let them fall into the hands of my mother. She may make a fortune from them. It would be too ironic." It is almost "too ironic," in an eerie sense, that *A Confederacy of Dunces* has become such a success thanks to the author's mother, who gave the novel to the world ten years after Toole committed suicide. Toole's tragic fate reminds us that the satiric vision can border dangerously on profound and helpless despair. We are led back to Elliott, who associates satire with the ancient curse and the power to cause death. There is something lethal about being an object of derision, especially when a Falstaffian butt can no longer laugh at himself. (pp. 45-7)

Perhaps it can be said that *A Confederacy of Dunces* gives new richness to a distinctively American vein of reverse satire. The naivety of old versus new begins with Ebenezer Cook and his greenhorn narrator. Twain's contrast of Arthurian superstition with Yankee exploitation develops the idea of false progress and reform. Now we have from Toole one of the most outrageous and memorable malcontents in American fiction, Ignatius J. Reilly, medieval idealist and modern pervert. The heritage of reverse satire is very much alive today. Although little is known about Ebenezer Cook, the double-edged comic spirit of "The Sotweed Factor" was recreated in John Barth's fictitious and farcical biography of the same title. Twain may be a century gone, but his condemnation of the damned human race seems contemporary whenever we hear talk of a limited nuclear war. Toole took himself out of this world but left behind a hilarious novel that will make readers ache with laughter for many years to come. We linger over the ending: "How ironic, Ignatius thought." (p. 47)

*David McNeil, " 'A Confederacy of Dunces' as Reverse Satire: The American Subgenre," in* The Mississippi Quarterly, *Vol. XXXVIII, No. 1, Winter, 1984-85, pp. 33-47.*

## Valerie Martin

It's not difficult to find admirers of . . . [John Kennedy] Toole who think his domineering mother was the reason he despaired of life. She liked to recall him as a boy obsessed with pleasing her. The picture she painted of him as a child, dressed in her homemade costumes, playing parts she wrote for him in theatricals she managed, is a sad and stereotypical one. In her memory he was always thinking of her, always deferring to her superior experience, always seeking her opinion and confidence. "He would come to me at night," she says in the film interview, "and sit on my bed and say, 'Mother, I want to show you how much I love you, but I don't know how.' "

There isn't much concrete evidence for this version of Ken Toole's life. If there were it seems certain Thelma Toole would have produced it. He never wrote a letter addressed to his mother alone, though he did write a few to his father. He never showed her, or anyone else, his first novel, though he did send it off to a contest before condemning it to a drawer. Thelma Toole knew nothing about *Neon Bible* until after her son's suicide.

It's hard to guess what Ken Toole was really like or what he would have thought of strangers battling over the rights to his adolescent efforts. The letters he wrote to his parents while he was in Puerto Rico reveal a clever, dutiful, affectionate son. He spoke frankly of his obsession with Marilyn Monroe, his sadness at the news of her suicide. He made light of the trials of military life and he described his hopes for the novel he had begun to write. He wrote,

> You both know that my greatest desire is to be a writer and since I finally feel that I am doing something that is more than barely readable, I am very concerned about a civilian situation which will make completion and revision of this particular work possible. . . . If this thing can be worked upon, I am almost certain that a publisher would accept it and so do one or two others to whom I have shown excerpts. (I must not set my hopes too high.)

The voice on trial in New Orleans is not so different from the voice in these letters. The narrator of *Neon Bible,* a boy named Dave, tells his story simply and clearly in a voice as different from the exaggerated, self-mocking, cynical Ignatius Reilly as Camus is from Dickens. He's an isolated, alienated young man who has grown up in an ugly house on a clay hill somewhere in Mississippi. He's raised by two women: his mother, who is weak and goes mad, and his Aunt Mae, who is strong and goes to Nashville. Both women are rejected by the Southern Baptist townspeople and Dave spends his childhood looking through windows at the respectable world, perfectly resigned to being an outcast.

*Neon Bible* is a terse but strangely passionate story, told by a boy no one will ever love. It's difficult to believe that the author of this cold and unembellished melancholy was sixteen years old. Walker Percy, in a 1984 interview for the [*New Orleans*] *Times-Picayune,* said the book "shows a style that most of us have to work very hard for many years to perfect. For a young writer to show such talents is remarkable." Reading Toole's powerful rendering of a small town morality, it's hard not to see the grim hopelessness of his own future. . . .

In *A Confederacy of Dunces* there is something of a prophecy. As Ignatius Reilly sets out for a new life, his accomplice asks him if he wants to pack anything. "Of course," he replies. "There are all my notes and jottings. We must never let them fall into the hands of my mother. She may make a fortune of them. It would be too ironic." (p. 88)

> *Valerie Martin, "Publish the Perished," in* Saturday Review, *Vol. 12, No. 2, May, 1986, pp. 47-50, 87-8.*

## Elizabeth S. Bell

As Walker Percy reminds us in his introduction, John Kennedy Toole's novel, *A Confederacy of Dunces,* transports the medieval picaresque tradition to modern-day New Orleans. . . . (p. 15)

Indeed, its tie to the medieval world links the novel with a compendium of medieval types—the pilgrimage, the quest, in strange ways the romance, the anatomy—and it does so in the most medieval of ways: the allegory, or more accurately the allegory within an allegory. In creating this double perspective, Toole has drawn from the intellectual and artistic fabric of the Middle Ages to comment on the contemporary world, melding the underpinnings of medieval thought to the contexts of modern reality. Consequently, as Percy notes, in Ignatius Reilly Toole offers us a grotesque anti-hero—indeed a "slob extraordinary"—who speaks to us as a picaro/questor/pilgrim ironically trailing disaster after him in the wrecks he makes of other people's lives and who ultimately must be rescued from his own folly instead of rescuing those in danger. Yet, ironically he sees himself as his own Boethius—in history an inhabitant of two worlds who was "revered as the depository of classical learning and as the educator of the modern world"—and Ignatius, too, strives Boethius-like to fit his own idiosyncratic world view into the context of the late twentieth century, the timeframe to which he is consigned. Overlaying the entirety of Ignatius's perspective and his voice is Toole's own, pronouncing in different terms a consolation of sorts—his version of the only kind of consolation available for the modern age.

The humor in the novel, and it exists in abundance, derives from the panorama of incongruities between action and expectations with which Toole permeates the novel. Toole spotlights the idiosyncratic nature of Ignatius Reilly's perspective on reality and balances it with the equally chronocentric—and culturally idiosyncratic—perspective of the modern reader. Clearly elements of a classical definition of irony, those incongruities arise inevitably from the clash of two mutually-exclusive world views existing concurrently in the novel: Ignatius's chosen and believed medieval world view and the reader's inherited and fondly-held contemporary world view, the two of which converge and diverge throughout the events of the novel.

Indeed, Ignatius's central position in the novel focuses attention on this duality of perspective, for the readers' interpretation of Ignatius—hence our sympathy and empathy for his actions—depends to large extent on whether we read him allegorically as a medievalist might or literally as the contemporary reader is wont to do. By nature, at least to the modern reader, Ignatius is not an easy person to love; hence, he is not a protagonist who easily gains our empathy. He is lazy, abusive, self-centered, and a troublemaker and thus is intensely disliked by his companions; however, he is also the insecure, child-like, desperate dreamer who acts out his dreams and who finds protectors at every twist of his fate. To the medievalist, or at least in allegorical tradition, he is also the questor/picaro, perhaps like most a bit of a rogue, a non-conformist, a rabble rouser. In literary practice, these characters have traditionally been appealing and functional *because* of their roguishness. Thus, Ignatius serves two traditions in the novel: fictionally as representation of real person and metaphorically as allegorical hero. It is on this level, metaphor, that Ignatius becomes more than the parody, more than the picaro-grown-grotesque he is on a more literal level; he becomes the embodiment of the conflict between pragmatic reality as the contemporary world sees it and a more mystic one as the medievalists saw it.

Only with this understanding of Ignatius can we perceive the inner level of allegory, for it is he, within the mythical New Orleans, who creates for us in a collection of Big Chief tablets the analysis of events as he sees them. On this inner level, through his eyes and his words, we as readers follow the goings on in the enchanted forest Ignatius calls his own. Ignatius's world view operates on his understanding of the orderly, hierarchical, mysterious, mythopoeic Middle Ages. . . . Ignatius bemoans the breakup of the medieval mindset, blaming the problems of contemporary life—"death, destruction, anarchy, progress, ambition, and self-improvement"—on the turning of Fortuna's wheel and the snapping of the Great Chain of Being and his own problems on his being born into a "century I loathe." An admirer of Boethius, who was himself born into a time of cultural change and who saw himself as a bridge linking the texts of an earlier age to those of the future, Ignatius sets about recording for posterity his criticisms of the modern world and his reverence for the older one, seeking to find order and meaning on his own terms. He, in short, writes his own allegory, seen partially as *The Journal of a Working Boy*, casting it in the role of *consolatio* and the narrative form and spirit of [William Langland's] *Piers Plowman*. (pp. 15-17)

As he tells us in his Big Chief tablets, Ignatius—part picaro, part questor, part pilgrim—assumes a spiritual relationship with the 14th-century allegorical Everyman, Piers Plowman, who must, because his secure medieval world is disappearing, face a "vicious fate": Piers, as well as Ignatius, is "faced with the perversion of having to GO TO WORK." Ignatius virtually recasts the story of Piers the Plowman to fit his own concerns, but in so doing he

conceptualizes his own life in the allegorical terms of medieval literature. This focal relationship offers the analogy which moves the events of the novel and which explains Ignatius's dilemma: Although he is living in the contemporary world, his life operates as a medieval allegory, and he clearly believes the allegory to be literal.

Thus, in terms of the medieval allegory he sees his life to be, Ignatius defines New Orleans very much as a closed world, a secure garden, surrounded by an abyss of chaos: "Outside of the city limits the heart of darkness, the true wasteland begins." In fact, he tells us, "The only excursion in my life outside of New Orleans took me through the vortex to the whirlpool of despair: Baton Rouge. In some future installment, a flashback, I shall perhaps recount that pilgrimage through the swamps, a journey into the desert from which I returned broken physically, mentally, and spiritually." Meanwhile, in his adventures in "the Crescent City" of New Orleans, adventures frequently associated with The Night of Joy tavern, Ignatius is joined fittingly enough by a ragtag band of characters, "the faire felde of fine folke" that offer aid of varying kinds to Piers. As in the original *Piers,* these characters are, to Ignatius, representatives of the human condition, a mingling of good sorts with bad, and he conceptualizes them predominantly as *types.* True to the allegory's requisites, Ignatius responds to them not as people, for he does not interact with them or communicate with them on any significant level, but as one-dimensional representatives of allegorical issues he must confront, as an example drawn from his Blue Horse looseleaf filler should demonstrate.

In describing his fellow employees at Levy Pants, Ignatius relies on labels—"the collective workers," "the colored races,"—to define people he otherwise refers to as "a rather pleasant folk," but of a sort that belong only in one setting—"the factory and its folk." To Ignatius they have no reality or meaning outside that setting. His sole purpose in mingling with these workers is to question them about the factory in an effort at pseudo-concern for social reform, for unconsciously he has adopted the reformist stance of Myrna Minkoff, the quintessential campus radical of the day and "loud, offensive maiden from the Bronx" with whom he has shared a stormy and platonic relationship. In his record of the factory scene, a scene which by the way the reader has viewed first-hand, as it were, Ignatius fails to understand the events that have occurred or the nature of the responses he has received from the individuals surrounding him. He has perceived only what he has wished to perceive and, while ignoring the remainder, superimposes his version of reality on the partial, distorted particle that remains. He uses his own distorted record to promote his "view of the moment" on one aspect of his daily life—that which is connected in this case to work—and adds it to other commentaries of like nature in his journal which develops as a form of anatomy of stereotypes, representing various elements of Ignatius's portrayal of the world.

Thus while, as is the case with all stereotypes, these "factory folk"—and others like them from other facets of Ignatius's life—move in predictable roles, in Ignatius's schema they also contend with Fortuna's wheel governing the particulars of their destinies. Because the medieval allegory is a closed world, coincidence and chance combine to provide the movement for plot and to draw the characters together in a thematic relationship that results ultimately in Ignatius's confrontation with his own destiny, the tower or the dungeon of *Piers Plowman.* As the novel ends, Ignatius sees himself faced with two possible destinies, with Fortuna deciding which fate will be his. He believes she smiles on him, for he does escape only moments before it will be too late, and heads out of New Orleans with his fair damsel, becoming in his own definition the picaro/questor/pilgrim setting out anew on his journeys.

But Ignatius also lives in the contemporary world, the world of the reader as well as that of John Kennedy Toole, and the pragmatic reality of life in modern New Orleans also operates in his adventures. From the contemporary perspective, more comfortable with the novel than with the allegory, the events and movements of Ignatius's life are open to another interpretation, and he becomes more charlatan than pilgrim. In the contemporary mindset, individuals are more important than types; thus by contemporary standards, Ignatius's assessment of the people he meets more closely resembles bigotry—racial, sexual, educational, societal—than it does metaphor. The trouble he brings to other people derives inevitably from Ignatius's recognizable character flaws: his ill nature, his indifference to them, his ego-centrism, his sloth.

Furthermore, beyond Ignatius's assignment of role to them, the people he collects around himself deviate from the type and act independently of allegorical consideration. In fact, they extricate themselves from the trouble he creates for them by willful actions and conscious decisions, not luck or destiny. Thus, Mr. Levy deliberately decides to let Miss Trixie take the blame for Ignatius's letter because he knows it will make his life, his wife's life, and Miss Trixie's life much better. Jones deliberately identifies the packets of pornographic photographs as originating from The Night of Joy tavern because he recognizes the inhumanity of Lana Lee and George, and thus he is instrumental in bringing justice to these people. Irene, at the urging of her friends, deliberately commits Ignatius to the mental ward because she knows she and he can no longer function as they have been. Their lives must diverge if either is to survive as a person. What resolutions there are in the novel are brought about by the individuals in the novel acting unexpectedly and decisively, sometimes out of character with the roles they have played, but with the reader viewing the decision-making process they have followed, a process to which Ignatius is oblivious. The ending of the novel, by contemporary standards, is problematical at best with Ignatius—stuffed into the back seat of a white Renault—running away from his mother, believing himself to be in legal as well as mental trouble and being totally incapable of dealing with either.

No matter where we look in this novel—Prime Mover, plot, character, implication—the two world views demonstrably present within its pages are diametrically opposed, for the principles which govern each one of them deny the other's "truths." The foundations of one world view exclude absolutely the foundations of the other: Destiny vs free will, chance vs deliberate action, stereotype vs individual. It is only fitting that the conclusion of this novel should bring this conflict into full view.

The final pages of the novel combine all elements of the disparate world views and exemplify the central problem: the world views are ultimately contradictory and, thus, irreconcilable. *Confederacy of Dunces,* then, ends in a cosmic irony: Only by rejecting the allegorical interpretation of life he has held to throughout the novel, admitting that his own world view is false, can Ignatius find escape as a modern-day picaro.

In the final scenes of the novel, in a set-up reminiscent of a medieval joust, Ignatius—knowing that his mother has committed him to a mental ward—climbs into the back seat of Myrna Minkoff's white Renault and, in the darkened street of his New Orleans neighborhood, safely passes the ambulance that is approaching to take him to Charity Hospital. Allegorically the ending should be positive: the picaro on his white charger confronts the evil knight and escapes to new adventures with his lady-love, gratefully pressing her long pigtail to his lips. As they sail along U.S. 11, Ignatius's pyloric valve even opens, symbolizing in terms with which the reader has become very familiar the happy ending Ignatius believes Fortuna has handed him. But it is also the allegory that indicates this cannot be. The "knight" Ignatius faces in the joust represents virtue in the guise of Charity and—if one stretches the point—Hospitality; it is in fact representative of the very Tower for which Piers the pilgrim and Ignatius, his counterpart, search. He and Myrna "escape," leaving New Orleans for adventures elsewhere, but Ignatius has already told us that beyond New Orleans we find only wasteland and the heart of darkness. By his own world view, then, Ignatius has left the secure closed world of medieval allegory for an outer world of torment and chaos. His escape is false salvation.

Only by adopting the contemporary world view does Ignatius find the possibility of a new life or a happy ending. In the world of the contemporary novel, by one interpretation—closely akin to that popularized in [Ken Kesey's] *One Flew Over the Cuckoo's Nest* (1962)—Charity Hospital represents confinement and the stifling of the individual, and Myrna's Renault becomes both literally and metaphorically the vehicle of escape from a form of imprisonment instigated by Ignatius's mother whose motives are suspect. In these terms the ending of the novel provides Ignatius with the possibility of a better life, but only if he abandons his own medieval world view and embraces that of the contemporary reader. Thus the novel hypothesizes the salvation of the individual in an inherently hostile world, but ironically at the cost of Ignatius's concept of reality. Just as the reader cannot escape the assumptions of the modern world, neither can Ignatius, nor does Toole allow him to.

Although he reacts as if there were no problem, as if in fact it were possible for him to have it both ways, neither of these options can exist without contradictions for Ignatius. Within the framework of the two world views of the novel, the only two world views available to Ignatius, the solution he has adopted and embraced cannot be effective or positive because either interpretation ultimately creates an insurmountable incongruity that undercuts the positive elements of it for him. If part of the interpretation is acceptable, it contradicts other elements of it. Ignatius's positive view of this fate, then, cannot be legitimately maintained by the events and conceptions of the novel. This very conflict—to which Ignatius is oblivious—gives substance to the outer level of allegory, for ironically enough, Toole also sees himself as a modern-day Boethius, seeking his own consolation in philosophy, or at least the modern version of it. In so doing, he creates a double perspective for us—the readers—leading us to a far different conclusion than Ignatius's.

Toole has shown the reader an Ignatius who has never been able to function in the real world, who cannot fulfill the responsibilities of even the most menial of jobs, who is hopelessly inept in his personal involvements and relationships with other people, and who constantly denies the magnitude—or even the existence—of his problems. He is, in short, an Ignatius who desperately needs some form of help—in modern parlance, analysis. From this perspective, Ignatius's "escape" in the end of the novel is not salvation but a form of damnation. He runs from the only help or solace the novel suggests, and in so doing, dooms himself to repeat the fiascos and torments of this past life.

In his version of the *consolatio,* Toole—unlike his counterpart Boethius—finds no resolution. His view, far darker that his ancient counterpart's, leaves Ignatius happily, dunce-like, almost innocently, rushing toward disaster. Both world views have failed him, leaving him with either a wasteland or a world to which he is completely unsuited and in which he is unlikely to survive. The ultimate joke—shared perhaps by Toole and his readers—is that Ignatius's expectations are so far removed from his only real possibilities.

This final irony with its cosmic dark laughter provides the novel's framing allegory, the modern-day allegory of Toole's vision: In the modern age, we accept with gratitude our illusions, for they are preferable to the alternatives. Toole's *Consolation of Philosophy,* then, is more the "consolation of illusion," the only comfort he offers to contemporary human beings, those of us he sees as joined together in a confederacy of dunces. Ironically, and tragically, Toole saw himself as inevitably one of the dunces doomed to the deceptions and vagaries of a hostile world. (pp. 17-22)

> *Elizabeth S. Bell, "The Clash of World Views in John Kennedy Toole's 'A Confederacy of Dunces'," in* The Southern Literary Journal, *Vol. XXI, No. 1, Fall, 1988, pp. 15-22.*

## Michael Malone

Most writers would destroy juvenilia like [John Kennedy Toole's] *The Neon Bible,* a slim, undistinguished tale of a sensitive boy coming of age in the Babbitty bigoted South. Or Time would kindly misplace the old yellowed manuscript for them. Or if the author were a major one, who'd left a large body of work behind, scholars might study the fledgling effort as a prologue of the corpus to come. So why are we being told to read John Kennedy Toole's *The Neon Bible* both as an "extraordinary creation" in itself and as fully half of "an amazing testament to a remarkable genius" (the other half being a good, though by no means great, first novel, a vituperative satire called *A Confederacy of Dunces*)? The answer has little to do with literature.

Toole committed suicide in 1969—according to his mother because the publishing world had rejected *A Confederacy of Dunces;* 12 years later, the publishing world hailed *A Confederacy of Dunces* as a masterpiece and gave it the Pulitzer Prize. The two events are not unconnected, and not unlike Hollywood's tearful bestowal of awards on stars like Charlie Chaplin whom it ostracized for years. If the endurance of the old is a sentimental favorite (recall the hoopla about octogenarian Helen Hooven Santmyer's schlock epic, *And Ladies of the Club*), the death of the young, talented, and misunderstood (especially if a violent death, and irresistibly if self-inflicted) is even more popular with fans in search of sensation—think of Shelley, Van Gogh, James Dean, Marilyn Monroe. And so the story of Toole's suicide at 31 became posthumous news, mentioned everywhere—in Walker Percy's introduction to the novel, in *People* magazine's article on the just-discovered neglected dead genius. The real story was the story *behind* the fiction.

Why bring up this flurry of morbid hype eight years later? Because now a novella of minimal literary merit, presumably penned by Toole at 16, is being published with the same extra-literary saga front and center.

Again we hear how a bright southern boy who'd "skipped two grammar school grades" submitted a novel to Simon and Schuster while in the Army and had it rejected. Again we hear how his mother Thelma, while "caring for an invalid husband and enduring an immeasurable share of grief" when "life seemed to stand still, mired in a swamp of despair," finally came upon the manuscript of *Dunces.* Ignatius J. Reilly, the obese hero of that book, a scurrilously anti-social, repulsively self-involved "writer" of 30 living in an Oedipal farce with his mother, imagines his own "shoddy, low-cost" funeral at which the mother, "insane with grief . . . would probably tear my corpse from the coffin." Toole's mother did better than that. She devoted her life to bringing his genius to glory. She persevered through rejections by eight publishers before living to see the triumphant Pulitzer. She even went on the tour circuit, dramatizing scenes from the book, and singing songs like "Sunny Side of the Street" while accompanying herself on the piano. Yet when she eventually found the manuscript to *The Neon Bible,* she spent the rest of her life trying to block its publication, though she believed it another "masterpiece." (She'd learned that, despite her protests to everyone from the governor on down, Louisiana law planned to give half the profits to her husband's family.) After a long, spicy court battle among Toole's heirs, duly noted in the flap copy, her side lost.

Curiously devoid of the zany humor of *Dunces* (despite the promise of a Marjoe-like evangelist, "The Boy Who Has Seen the Light," who preaches against such sins as USO dances), *The Neon Bible* is not without its grace notes. A flat simpleness of style that sounds in places like a Hemingway parody ("And I laid there and the sun was hot and there was dust all over me"), in other places like a teen-aged diary ("This is the first time I've been on a train." "That night is a night I'll never forget") can also have the fresh sensory vitality of a child's painting. Smells sting the nose in an "alley full of old rotting chairs and beer cases where about ten mangy cats lived." Mud is moving with spring life.

David, the gentle boy narrator, grows up poor and perceptive in the rural Mississippi Bible Belt during World War II, in one of those towns where "if you were different . . . you had to get out." (Oddly, a gay teacher who writes poems, "sways his hips," and talks in a sprinkle of italics—"Oh I *do* wish that boy in the third row would stop leering at me"—is immune to this threat because "he knew too much about things like classical music we didn't know.") But the town hurts David, who spends much of his time in tears: "I put my head on my knees and cried and cried." He is bullied, beaten and subjected to the motiveless malignity of a fairy-tale witch of a schoolmarm who locks him in an old musty room: "I'm going to report you to the state authorities, do you hear that? They'll get you, son, they'll get you." His impoverished parents quarrel over money as in a scene from *Jack and the Beanstalk:* "All of the gas station money, Frank? No, no, you couldn't do that, not for seeds that are never going to grow . . . Frank, you fool, you stupid fool."

David's only friend is Aunt Mae, a wandering road-house chanteuse of 60-some, who's shunned for her Jean Harlow walk in indecent outfits. "I forgot to show you my clippings, didn't I? The notices, the notices! They were superb, particularly about that gown." In the flashflood of sudden plot with which the book ends, Mother goes mad because Poppa's been killed in Italy. Mae, after a stint as a war plant supervisor, leaves David to sing on the radio in Nashville. That same day he finds Mother lying in a pool of blood; she melodramatically dies in his arms. As David is about to bury her in the grave he's dug in the yard, the town's moralistic preacher shows up to take her off to the mental institution. David promptly blows him away with a shotgun, then escapes by train to Nashville. I don't doubt Toole was 16, or less, when he wrote it. One's main response is to recall by contrast how inordinately gifted the young Truman Capote was.

*Michael Malone, "John Kennedy Toole: Hype, Hype, Hooray!" in* Book World—The Washington Post, *April 30, 1989, p. 6.*

## Michiko Kakutani

John Kennedy Toole is one of those writers—Malcolm Lowry and Sylvia Plath are others—whose early suicides turned their lives into legends. In Toole's case, the legend both incorporated and galvanized posthumous literary success: in the wake of his death at the age of 31, his devoted mother sends the manuscript of *A Confederacy of Duncies* to several publishers. . . . The book goes on to win critical acclaim and the 1981 Pulitzer Prize for fiction—kudos that have now led to the publication of Toole's only other surviving work of fiction, a novel, written when he was a teen-ager, titled *The Neon Bible.*

Peopled with larger-than-life characters and crammed full of comic incidents, *Dunces* was hailed by many critics as a masterful satire on contemporary civilization. In this writer's opinion, the praise seemed overdone. Though the novel amply demonstrated its author's energy and capacity for narrative invention, it was a wildly uneven work, veering between bitterness and sentimentality, pretentious misanthropy and dime-store-novel histrionics.

Whatever appeal its hero, Ignatius J. Reilly, garnered by virtue of being an eccentric outsider seemed neutralized by his more unpleasant attributes: self-absorption and egotism bordering on paranoia; laziness and superiority (masquerading as intellectual superiority); intolerance and misogyny (directed primarily at his overbearing mother and importunate girlfriend). In addition, Ignatius suffered from a gratuitously nasty obsession with smells and bodily functions, and a taste for belching.

It's possible, of course, for the reader of *Dunces* and *The Neon Bible* to see certain resemblances between their two heroes. Like Ignatius, the youthful hero of *The Neon Bible*—David, by name—sees himself as a misfit, someone set apart from the community at large. Like Ignatius, he's unusually repressed about sex. And like Ignatius, he has a problem with a formidable mother, who dominates his day-to-day life and his long-term fortunes.

There, however, the similarities end. Whereas Ignatius was a cynic, David is that cynic's precursor—an innocent and romantic, as yet unspoiled by the world. Whereas the tone of *Dunces* was farcical and Rabelaisian, that of *The Neon Bible* is lyrical and elegiac. Whereas *Dunces* was animated by anger, *The Neon Bible* seems rooted in melancholy and nostalgia. If less overtly ambitious than the previously published book, *The Neon Bible* also emerges as an altogether more organic and satisfying novel—a novel that works on the reader not through willful manipulation, but through heartfelt emotion, communicated in clean, direct prose.

Written in the flexible form of a first person reminiscence, *The Neon Bible* tells us the story of David's coming of age. The time is the 1940's; the place, a small town in the South. As in so many novels of this sort, the narrator begins by giving us a portrait of his family and the narrow-minded community he grew up in; he ends by leaving this hermetic world for unknown vistas beyond.

When we first meet him, David is a shy 3-year-old, playing with a toy train. He is half in love with his Aunt Mae, a loud, flirtatious woman, who's arrived to stay with his parents. Aunt Mae's flamboyant clothes and blowsy manner make her something of a joke in town; and in observing her treatment at the hands of local puritans, David receives his first lesson in the moralistic nature of life in his hometown.

Although David's family had once lived in a "little white house in town that had a real roof you could sleep under when it rained," his father has since lost his job, forcing them all to move to a tin-roofed shack that sits alone on a hill on the outskirts of town. From there, David has a view of the entire valley: the new homes built by a land developer, the church emblazoned with a neon sign of the Bible, and the house where they used to live. In their backyard, David's father clears away a patch of scraggly pine trees and spends a week's earnings on seeds that will never grow in the unforgiving soil. His mother has a fit over his foolishness and they come to blows.

Time passes quickly in *The Neon Bible.* The pine trees quickly grow back on the barren ground, erasing the dream of a garden, and we see David grow from childhood into adolescence. He somehow survives the humiliations of school, gets a job in the local drugstore, falls for a pretty out-of-town girl and is initiated into the perils of love.

There are other changes in the offing as well. Aunt Mae gets a job as a singer with a local band and falls in love with one of the musicians. David's father goes off to war and is killed somewhere in Europe. And his mother, unable to cope with her husband's death, retreats further and further into madness. David is scared that the local preacher, who's never forgiven his family for failing to pay its church dues, will somehow manage to commit her to a home for the insane.

Though it ends somewhat abruptly in an incongruous outburst of violence and blood, *The Neon Bible* not only stands as a remarkable achievement for a 16-year old writer, but it also serves as a testament (more valid than *Dunces,* in this critic's opinion) to the genuine talents of Toole.

> Michiko Kakutani, "A Novelist's Story of Love, Pain and (Neon) Signs of Life," in The New York Times, *May 12, 1989, p. C29.*

**Kerry Luft**

In 1981 a novel by a previously unpublished author won the Pulitzer Prize. The fact that the author already was dead, a suicide at age 31, added to the excitement. Literati wondered if there would be any more posthumous works from the author of *A Confederacy of Dunces,* John Kennedy Toole. . . .

Toole's mother died in 1984, and a 1987 court ruling cleared the way for the publication of [his] *The Neon Bible.* Readers will not be disappointed, for this earlier book proves that Toole was the real thing.

On second reading, *A Confederacy of Dunces* doesn't stand up well. A mean-spiritedness burbles beneath the hilarious plot lines, manifested in the figure of Ignatius J. Reilly, the book's preposterous antihero, who spouts contempt for everything and everybody. As for the plot, it is mostly chaotic, a series of funny, grotesque episodes that sometimes do, and oftentimes don't, hold together. The book's strength is its humor; it is so funny that one forgets (or doesn't notice) its faults.

By contrast, *The Neon Bible* is a more successful book, but one that probably won't enthrall nearly as many readers. Its story is better constructed, the characters are more believable and the tone is much more nostalgic than that

of *Dunces* and not nearly so cynical. Yet it lacks the brilliance and uniqueness that set *Dunces* apart.

*The Neon Bible* is the story of David, a young boy growing up in a small Southern town before and during World War II. Because his parents are poor, they live in a beat-up house on a hill overlooking the town. At night, David can see a neon bible illuminating the face of the town's church, the church that expelled his family because they couldn't pay the dues. The boy's only friend is Aunt Mae, a 60-ish bleached-blonde floozy who lives with the family and reminisces about her career "on the stage."

David's father, a ne'er-do-well who insists he can grow vegetables in the claylike soil, heads off to war and is killed. At that point, David's mother starts to unravel, starting the family on an irrevocable spiral downward.

Toole's technique in telling all this is shockingly mature. He didn't attempt any sort of lyricism, choosing instead a fine, simple style that is perfectly in tune with a young boy's naivete. The story of David's heartfelt love for a young girl in town shatters the reader's own heart; the agony David feels when Aunt Mae goes away is no less real. Even at 16, Toole knew that the way to write about complex emotions is to express them simply.

One quibbles only with a certain stiffness in Toole's dialogue. Compared to the rest of the novel, the words that David and the other characters say don't seem very real at all. But, then, dialogue may be the most difficult fictional technique to master—and this is a first novel.

Comparisons between *The Neon Bible* and *A Confederacy of Dunces* ought not to persist, for this book is not nearly as ambitious. It is enough to say it is a fine first novel, especially for a teenage author. It affirms Toole's extraordinary ability; and, even more than before, it leaves the reader wondering what might have been.

> Kerry Luft, "The Late John Kennedy Toole's Long-Rumored First Novel," in Chicago Tribune—Books, *June 25, 1989, p. 3.*

**Jonathan Simmons**

> "Then you must begin a reading program immediately so that you may understand the crises of our age," Ignatius said solemnly. "Begin with the late Romans, including Boethius, of course. Then you should dip rather extensively into early Medieval. You may skip the Renaissance and the Enlightenment. That is mostly dangerous propaganda."

In John Kennedy Toole's *A Confederacy of Dunces,* Ignatius Reilly's dismissal of the Renaissance and Enlightenment (illustrated in the passage above) is not without irony, for it is among the very literary models and aesthetic terminology which come out of these eras that we find the most effective tools for illuminating the character of Ignatius. A discussion of the novel and its central character hardly seems possible without mention of such sixteenth-, seventeenth-, and eighteenth-century comedic and satiric creations as Rabelais' *Gargantua and Pantagruel,* Cervantes' *Don Quixote,* Shakespeare's Falstaff in

*Henry IV: Part I,* and Swift's *Gulliver's Travels* and *A Tale of a Tub.* Indeed, a line from Swift's "Thoughts on Various Subjects, Moral and Diverting" serves as both the epigraph to, and the source for the title of Toole's work: "When a true genius appears in the world, you may know him by this sign, that the dunces are all in confederacy against him."

In addition to the inescapability of referring to these literary models, it also hardly seems possible to discuss the novel without utilizing the concept of the "grotesque," one that found its birth in the Renaissance, and perhaps its greatest literary embodiment in the Enlightenment. One is hard pressed to find any scholarly evaluation of Toole's work that does not employ the term "grotesque," or terms closely related to it, in describing the main character. This essay will look in particular at the birth of the term "grotesque," the implications of its embodiment in literature, its application in the Swiftian satires which serve as models for *A Confederacy of Dunces,* and, finally, its embodiment in the character of Ignatius Reilly.

An intimate relationship exists between the grotesque and the paradoxical, which can be described in the following terms: each utilizes an indirect or negative method of signification. The Swiftian epigraph to Toole's novel is an example of just such a method. It asserts that genius is not located as a result of any outstanding quality inherent in itself, but instead, by the lack of any positive quality in those things surrounding it. It is this shared quality of indirectness and negativity that makes both the paradoxical and the grotesque so particularly suited to the strategy of satire. Toole creates in his protagonist a figure who, while he scorns modern society, reflects so many of its excesses in himself that he ultimately comes to symbolize the very object of his scorn. David McNeil explains how Toole's work fits into a long tradition of what he calls "reverse satire," citing Swift's paradoxical definition of satire as an illustration of what he means: "SATYR is a sort of Glass, wherein Beholders do generally discover every body's Face but their Own" [see McNeil's excerpt]. It is by means of the keen double-edged blade of satire wielded in paradoxical fashion by agents of the grotesque that both Swift and Toole achieve poignant critiques of their respective social orders. (pp. 33-4)

Though the mode of perception that the word "grotesque" implies is very difficult to explain, because, as [R. Cotgrave says in his *A Dictionaire of the French and English Tongues*], there seems to be a lack of "anie peculiar sence, or meaning," the history of the word itself is very clear. [In *On the Grotesque: Strategies of Contradiction in Art and Literature,* Geoffrey] Harpham explains how in the last quarter of the fifteenth century, excavation of an enormous structure in the center of Rome began. Though it was not known until many years later, the labyrinthine passageways and the many rooms they connected actually belonged to Nero's Domus Aurea. The remarkably well-preserved frescoes on the walls of these rooms had been executed by "an austere nonentity providentially named Fabullus." The works did not so much exhibit any outstanding qualities in and of themselves as provide the Renaissance artists and thinkers who saw them with a win-

dow opening onto a first-century Roman aesthetic that had been all but lost during the intervening centuries. Those who descended into the subterranean passageways and rooms, which must have seemed like so many tunnels and caves, by torchlight and sometimes suspended by rope, saw figures similar to what Vitruvius had attacked in *De Architectura. . . .* (pp. 34-5)

When artists of the time brought the strange and marvelous designs out of the grottos, and employed the new stylistic vocabulary found in them in decorating (most notably in the Vatican Loggias, under the direction of Raphael) and then later (most notably in Northern Europe) as the focal point of specific works of art, the term "grottesche" came to describe this new facet of Renaissance art. (p. 35)

At this point one might ask the reason for making so much of the Renaissance coining of a word that describes something in which the Medieval world had apparently already accumulated a long and rich tradition. One need only look at one of any number of illuminated books, or the gargoyles and sculptured details on any gothic cathedral to remind oneself that the grotesque was indeed a part of the Medieval world. But the answer to this question lies in the very issue of naming (or the failure of the Medieval world to do so), for it is this that gives us a clue as to the position of the grotesque in this world, one markedly different to that which it assumes in the post-Medieval world. The fact that the Medieval world lacked a term and theory for its grotesques, in addition to the fact of their physical placement on the "borders" of art, attests to the widespread acceptance of the position of the grotesque on the fringes of reality. If the often-used generalization concerning the world view of the period may be enlisted as aid in a further explanation, the Medieval mind, comfortably able to view reality—both the readily explicable and the totally inexplicable—as ordered by an omniscient deity, was largely unconcerned by anomalies and incongruities that appeared in the realms of human expression. The Medieval grotesque was therefore, in the eyes of the Medieval world, not grotesque at all, but something to be taken largely upon faith as existing somehow within the order of things. This is exactly the point that Harpham makes about the always difficult-to-classify Renaissance essayist Montaigne, a point that can also be extended to the Medieval mind:

> Montaigne's sympathy to pied beauty does not compromise the center, but strengthens it, for it admits everything as a possible center, and admits that the true center is beyond our grasp. Faith in "God" is a faith in the hidden order of apparently disorderly things, the hidden meaning of the apparently meaningless. For Montaigne, there was no true grotesque, because no absolute incongruity. And this is the final paradox: really to understand the grotesque is to ccase to regard it as grotesque.

The Renaissance and Enlightenment, and indeed the whole of the modern world, as the product of the two eras, reflected a very different perspective upon the grotesque, for by the Renaissance strict faith in a divine order, however remote to human understanding, had been broken. In its place, to employ another much-used generalization, was a faith in man's ability to understand and, indeed, order his universe. It would not be stretching the point to say that the same confidence that spurred the fifteenth-century humanists' interest in searching out and reediting classical texts, also sent Roman antiquarians, at the end of the century, beneath the city and led to the discovery of what was called the grotesque. Renaissance man was not as able as his Medieval counterpart to accept upon faith the contradictions and inconsistencies that he found in the human experience. Without a framework that explained or at least brought order to the inconsistencies inherent in the human experience, these inconsistencies began to take on lives of their own. It was not so much a case of the grotesque suddenly assuming centrality in art and literature, as it was of there being no longer any indisputable center in man's vision of the universe. Harpham implies this when he uses the term "center" in his discussion of Montaigne, and this concern is at the heart of Ignatius's oft-repeated story of his ill-fated bus trip out of New Orleans:

> that was the only time that I had ever been out of New Orleans in my life. I think that perhaps it was the lack of a center of orientation that might have upset me. Speeding along in that bus was like hurtling into the abyss.

With the Renaissance, the grotesque thus came to have a name and a voice, and it appeared and spoke through such figures as Falstaff, whose very body bespoke the monstrousness of his world view, and Don Quixote, whose dual existence on the two separate planes of the conscious and the subconscious hinted at there being inexplicable areas in man's existence.

The concept of paradox looms large in Harpham's attempt at a definition of what constitutes the grotesque on the level of human perception. What all of his examples have in common is "that something is illegitimately in something else." In terms of language, he argues that paradox, as "a way of turning language against itself by asserting both terms of a contradiction at once," makes for the most apt comparison with the concept of the grotesque.

At this point we might begin to focus on our protagonist, the rotund Ignatius Reilly, approaching him by means of the Swiftian models mentioned above. There is more to the comparison between Toole's novel and Swift's *A Tale of a Tub* than the fact that the former might just as well be referred to by the same title as the latter. One pattern of occurrences that can be followed throughout the novel is that of Ignatius's taking interminably long—if his mother's complaints can be said to hold water—baths in the same sort of tub that the hack in Swift's *A Tale of a Tub* describes as being thrown overboard in order to divert the attention of dangerous Leviathans:

> "Wait a minute. Let me see if he's still in that tub." Mrs. Reilly listened apprehensively to the great liquid thrashings coming from the bathroom. One whalelike snort floated out into the hall through the peeling bathroom door . . .
>
> "You been in that hot water over an hour."

> "It's hardly hot anymore."
>
> "Then get out the tub."
>
> "Why is it so important to you that I leave this tub?"

Swift's hack and Ignatius share a great zeal for projecting (spinning impossible and impracticable plans) and a grave tendency for digressing in both the conception and the implementation of these projects. Each seems to be working on his own grand literary project. In his Preface, the hack hints at his project:

> This is the sole design in publishing the following treatise, which I hope will serve for an interim of some months to employ those unquiet spirits, till the perfecting of that great work, into the secret of which it is reasonable the courteous reader should have some little light.

Ignatius similarly speaks of his great literary project to the policeman who accosts him in the opening scene of the novel: "I am at the moment writing a lengthy indictment against our century. When my brain begins to reel from my literary labors, I make an occasional cheese dip." If the ludicrous nature of his appearance has not already made us skeptical of seriously considering anything that he says, certainly the detail of the "cheese dip" works to erode, by means of its incongruity, any credence we can lend to his lofty literary claims. When we discover that this great work is contained in the form of disorganized notes and musings written on numerous "Big Chief" tablets, scattered throughout the clutter of his bedroom, we begin to feel the force of contradiction as it lends to Ignatius's characterization as a grotesque. (pp. 35-8)

Ignatius and the hack share not only literary aspirations, which prove beyond a doubt to be ludicrously unreal. They both seem to be busily engaged in projects that have no basis in reality. The hack thus announces: "It is intended that a large Academy be erected." He proposes that it include within its walls "a large Paederastic School," "the School of Swearing," "the School of Salivation: The School of Hobby-horses," and a great number of others along the same lines. Ignatius's two projects, the "Crusade for Moorish Dignity" for better working conditions for the black workers in the factory where he is briefly employed, and his efforts to establish a Sodomite Party in order to "Save the World Through Degeneracy," both turn out to be chaotic failures. Moreover, the motivation for each proves to be an unhealthy rivalry with the "woman" in his life. As he plans for the "kickoff rally" with his sodomites, he writes not of world peace but:

> Does M. Minkoff want sex in politics? I shall give her sex in politics—and plenty of it! No doubt she will be too overcome to respond to the originality of my project. At the very least, she will seethe with envy. (That girl must be attended to. Such effrontery cannot go unchecked.)

It is not hard to see in this that one of the forces governing Ignatius's life is a most profound sexual frustration. After his first day as a hotdog vendor, having eaten almost all of the profits himself, in the course of fabricating an explanation for his angry boss, he stumbles upon the thread of an argument that sheds a good bit of light upon his own situation:

> "The human desire for food and sex is relatively equal. If there are armed rapes, why should there not be armed hot dog thefts? I see nothing unusual in the matter."
>
> "You are full of bullshit."
>
> The incident is sociologically valid. The blame rests upon our society. The youth, crazed by suggestive television programs and lascivious periodicals had apparently been consorting with some rather conventional adolescent females who refused to participate in his imaginative sexual program. His unfulfilled physical desires therefore sought sublimation in food.

When we consider Ignatius's immense size and the fact that his progress through the novel seems to be one unending moveable feast, by his own definition, he must be sexually very active or very troubled. We know that in at least one instance the object of sexual fantasy is, oddly enough, his boyhood dog:

> Ignatius manipulated and concentrated. At last a vision appeared, the familiar figure of the large and devoted collie that had been his pet when he was in high school. "Woof!" Ignatius almost heard Rex say once again. "Woof! Woof! Arf!" Rex looked so lifelike. One ear drooped. He panted. The apparition jumped over a fence and chased a stick that somehow landed in the middle of Ignatius's quilt. As the tan and white fur grew closer, Ignatius's eyes dilated, crossed, and closed, and he lay wanly back among his four pillows hoping that he had some Kleenex in his room.

We are reminded of Harpham's definition of the grotesque as something "illegitimately in something else." If we can imagine Ignatius in a Medieval artistic setting, we might see him as occupying the margin of some illuminated book, as a somewhat amusing but equally puzzling comical figure perhaps coupled with some sort of animal. Instead, in the modern setting where he belongs, as the central figure of Toole's novel, Ignatius's actions and fantasies assume the dimensions of the grotesque. Ignatius is a deeply troubled individual and this is reflected boldly in his sexuality. Ignatius's sexual impulses, like everything else in his life, are centered upon himself, and as a result, like any purely solipsistic venture, are ultimately impotent and sterile. The pirate disguise that Ignatius wears as he wheels his Paradise Vendor cart, which is shaped like the long hot dogs that he does not vend but instead consumes himself, is a figure for the larger issue of the self-deception in which his existence is mired. It is significant that he never really recognizes the suggestiveness of the sign that he has attached to the tip of his cart: "12 inches of Paradise." He is aghast to find that George, the delinquent youth whom he blackmails into tending the cart while he attends the cinema, has sketched an erect penis on his sign. Both the cart he wheels, the countless dogs he fails to vend but consumes himself, and his sexual fantasies concerning his dead dog are images of his own fruitless cycle of self-centered behavior.

The only fruit of Ignatius's sublimated sexual desires, and indeed the only true inspiration that he can legitimately claim, is the gas that he belches in steady streams throughout the novel. Here we find another striking resemblance to Swift's hack. Both *A Confederacy of Dunces* and *A Tale of a Tub* are marked by a preponderance of images concerning the anal and oral release of gas. The protagonist in each novel exhibits so great a degree of preoccupation with such functions as to suggest that these functions take the place of other physical processes, such as sex. It is with great dignity and seriousness that the hack discusses the Aeolists, who put bodily gases to the most creative uses: "This, when blown up to its perfection, ought not to be covetously hoarded up, stifled, or hid under a bushel, but freely communicated to mankind. Upon these reasons, and others of equal weight, the wise Aeolists affirm the gift of BELCHING to be the noblest act of a rational creature."

In his discussion of the novel, William Bedford Clark focuses his attention upon the theme of arrested development—the failure of so many of the characters, including Ignatius, to pass successfully into adulthood. He argues convincingly that Ignatius is a "monstrously overgrown child," echoing Lloyd M. Daigrepont's assertion that "in Ignatius the child and the man are grotesquely combined." This leads us to our second Swiftian model, that of *Gulliver's Travels*. This work, like *A Tale of a Tub*, is a veritable catalogue of the grotesque, dealing perhaps more overtly with the issue of perception, as the world surrounding its protagonist shrinks and grows and changes shapes and forms, constantly challenging the expectations and preconceptions that govern his ability to perceive his world. Again, the grotesque element in the novel is the means by which Swift critiques his society and signals a crisis in the modern world. (pp. 38-41)

Part II of *Gulliver's Travels* abounds with examples of the protagonist's inability to place things in their proper perspective. In the above scene, the real grotesqueness is to be found not in the execution itself, but in Gulliver's failure to place such a monstrous event in its proper perspective. This is what might be referred to as the Lilliputian in Gulliver.

It may come as no surprise then that very early in *A Confederacy of Dunces,* Ignatius's house is referred to as Lilliputian: "The address that Patrolman Mancuso was looking for was the tiniest structure on the block, aside from the carports, a Lilliput of the eighties." Here again the presence of the police officer reminds us of the opening arrest scene, and of the theme of arrested growth. Though Ignatius Reilly is a monstrously large figure, he is a Lilliputian every inch. But this is not where the analogy ends, for just as the grotesque aspect of Gulliver's character is reflected indirectly upon by his description of the execution, so is the monstrous aspect of Ignatius ultimately a reflection of the greater grotesqueness of the society that has created him. In the context of Toole's novel, it is society that is the true grotesque in that it is guilty of arresting the growth of its children and stealing opportunity from its minorities.

Perhaps that which most interestingly marks Ignatius as

a grotesque is the pattern of animal and vegetable imagery that is associated with him throughout the novel. Throughout the course of the novel, he appears as a whale, an elephant, a hippo, a moose and a mosquito. His head with the green hunting cap that sits seemingly inseparably upon it is compared to "the tip of a promising watermelon." He is likened to an eggplant: "nestled upon his perch, he looked like an eggplant balanced atop a thumb tack" and a "wallflower." But most often, Ignatius is spoken of in ursine images. His hands are always referred to as paws and in more than one instance specifically as a bear paw. He is described as having "bristles" that grow in the ears, and at one point is even spoken of as "bellowing and baring a fang or two." His tastes in television even run towards ursine matter: "Ignatius thrust a paw onto the oilcloth. 'Well, I have had enough of this. I'm going into the parlor to watch the Yogi Bear program.'" The most suggestive cluster of bear imagery occurs in an exchange with his mother concerning the possibility of having to mortgage the house:

> "No! You will not mortgage this house." He pounded a great paw into the mattress. "The whole sense of security which I have been trying to develop would crumble. I will not have any disinterested party controlling my domicile. I couldn't stand it. Just the thought of it makes my hands break out."
>
> He extended a paw so that his mother could examine the rash.
>
> "That is out of the question," he continued. "It would bring all of my latent anxieties to a head, and the result, I fear, would be very ugly indeed. I would not want you to have to spend the remainder of your life caring for a lunatic locked away somewhere in the attic. We shall not mortgage the house. You must have some funds somewhere."
>
> "I got a hundred fifty in the Hibernia Bank."

The ursine descriptions of Ignatius are significant first of all in that the bear is associated with hibernation (the "Hibernia Bank" reminds us of this). Ignatius lives in a kind of perpetual hibernation; the dependence that he has upon his mother, especially at his age, is unnatural and his life seems to be going nowhere. If there seems to be doubt over whether it is Ignatius that dominates his mother, or visa versa, the pattern of ursine imagery can help clarify this issue also. (pp. 41-3)

Considering the fact that Ignatius's father, having died some years ago, seems to have been almost erased from the picture of Ignatius's development, certainly the mythic/folkloric image of the bear encourages a reading of Ignatius as a youngster who was dominated into almost complete helplessness by his mother.

[In "Batman and Ignatius J. Reilly in *A Confederacy of Dunces*"] Edward Reilly (no relation) reminds us that the single slender strand of modern culture of which Ignatius does deem to approve is that of Batman. Ignatius says that Batman "transcends the abysmal society" and "his morality is rather rigid." With this we descend once again into the caves where the concept of the "grotesque" originated.

We have seen in the satire of Toole, as in that of Swift, that the grotesque, with its seemingly direct access to the darkest depths beneath the surface of modern society, has proven an effective tool in the artistic rendering of the human experience. (p. 43)

> *Jonathan Simmons, "Ignatius Reilly and the Concept of the Grotesque in John Kennedy Toole's 'A Confederacy of Dunces',"* in The Mississippi Quarterly, *Vol. XLIII, No. 1, Winter, 1989-90, pp. 33-43.*

**Mark Childress**

John Kennedy Toole asphyxiated himself in his car near Biloxi, Mississippi, in 1969, at the age of thirty-one, leaving behind two typewritten manuscripts, $8,000 in worldly goods, and a suicide note, which his mother Thelma read once and destroyed.

One of those manuscripts was a snorting, sprawling, picaresque masterpiece, *A Confederacy of Dunces.* The indefatigably determined Thelma Toole struggled for eight years to convince publishers of her son's "geeeenius", finally forcing the pages on the novelist Walker Percy. Percy took a look, and found that the weird old woman was right; the book was remarkable; he arranged for its publication. *A Confederacy of Dunces* sold millions and won the Pulitzer Prize in 1981.

The other manuscript left behind by the peculiar, sloe-eyed Kennedy Toole was a little novel called *The Neon Bible,* dashed off at the age of sixteen as a writing-contest entry. When I met Mrs Toole in 1981, she vowed it would never be published. "It has the smell of an early masterpiece, but it is the work of a child", she pronounced, trilling Rs in her elocution-teacher style. (Then she went to the piano and thumped out a boisterous version of "Who's Sorry Now".) Mrs Toole later changed her mind about *The Neon Bible,* tried to publish it, then fell out with her late husband's heirs over money, and died trying to prevent publication. Louisiana courts overturned her will, and the book was published in the United States last year, to a resounding silence.

This was undeserved. *The Neon Bible* is, yes, the work of a child, a marvellously gifted and doomed child. It has a child's sweetness, and the innocent terror of discovering that the rules of life are unfair. No doubt *Confederacy* will be longer remembered, but *The Neon Bible* proves clearly that John Kennedy Toole, at sixteen, was a more powerful writer than many of the adults who have been cranking out fiction for these past thirty years.

The story begins:

> This is the first time I've been on a train. I've sat in this seat here for about two or three hours now. I can't see what's passing by. . . . The tingling that has been running up and down the inside of my legs is stopping, and my feet feel like they're really there now, and not like two cold things that don't really belong to the rest of my body. I'm not as scared anymore.

The author's voice is at once tentative and bold, naive and

yet wise enough to engage the reader with the language of suspense. Swiftly a time and place are sketched: a small town, the 1940s deep South, a poor boy named David who lives with his parents and his voluptuous, wild-natured Aunt Mae in a caving-in house on the top of a clay hill. Gothic elements are introduced with surprising grace and economy.

Aunt Mae is the most vivid character, suggesting an acquaintance with the early Erskine Caldwell and Tennessee Williams's faded women—"she was heavy but not fat, and about sixty, and came from out of state somewhere where they had nightclubs. I asked Mother why her hair wasn't shiny and yellow like Aunt Mae's, and she said some people were just lucky, and I felt sorry for her." The painfully shy David moves ghost-like through the novel. At times the story feels postmodern in its lack of event: nothing much happens in this town but gossip and poverty and ugly whispering. Aunt Mae and David suffer various humiliations and the whispers of the dried-up Baptists who serve as the town's moral conscience. David's father can't keep a job, goes off to the war, and is killed. David's mother slowly goes crazy, and maybe she's not the only one. . . .

Often the author shows the tenderness of his years in his technique: a teacher, Miss Moore, "was a nice lady that you can't describe too well. There was nothing different about her from anyone else." This sort of thing would be cut by most editors today, but then, isn't this precisely the way children order their memories and grope toward an understanding of adults? David's eventual understanding is bleak: "If you were different from anybody in town, you had to get out. That's why everybody was so much alike. The way they talked, what they did, what they liked, what they hated. If somebody got to hate something and he was the right person, everybody had to hate it too, or people began to hate the ones that didn't hate it." In one effortless, naive paragraph, the boy sums up the hateful side of small-town Southern life before desegregation.

Perhaps this is a book only a writer could love. *The Neon Bible* is loaded with flaws, not least the arbitrary symbol of the title, a glaringly out-of-place neon sign atop the church in the town, which never quite figures as fully as it should. The dialogue is stilted; the melodramatic ending comes out of nowhere, and the author's limited descriptive vocabulary at times makes the book seem longer than it is. But if you approach it as a formative and unschooled work, the work of a gifted child, you are likely to come away in a state of admiration and mourning for the talent that was lost in that car, near the beach in Biloxi.

*Mark Childress, "Sweetness and Terror," in*
The Times Literary Supplement, *No. 4539, March 30, 1990, p. 338.*

**Dennis Formento**

The original neon Bible of John Kennedy Toole's second published novel [*The Neon Bible*] shines from the yellow brick of the Mid-City Baptist Church, on the Orleans Parish stretch of Airline Highway, across the road from the tracks of the Illinois Central Railroad. The church itself, moved from its original location, stands a couple of miles from the part of town that is actually called Mid-City. I used to ride into town daily past that church and its tacky sign on my way to high school. A couple miles down the road further west, Jimmy Swaggart and [a prostitute] met in a cheap Jefferson Parish motel; and an avowed Klansman was elected state representative for the first time since Reconstruction last November in a district just a few blocks north of the church. The tawdriness and bigotry that Toole wrote against are still around.

John Toole and his mother, Thelma Ducoing Toole, had a good laugh about that Bible when, at fifteen and carrying his first driver's license, he took her to see it in his car. They lived clear on the other side of town, in a world dignified by three centuries of continuous settlement, in the back-of-the-Quarter Marigny neighborhood, within earshot of the bells of St. Louis Cathedral and Our Lady of Victory Catholic Church. Colonel Andrew Jackson led his victorious army back into town through Faubourg Marigny, after they defeated General Pakenham's British force in a battle actually fought after the armistice ending the War of 1812 was signed.

New Orleans often seems to be lagging behind the action, complacently slogging through its ninety-five percent humidity and sweltering heat. Louis Armstrong once pointed out that a lot of fellow musicians refused to leave town, calling it "the greatest place in the world," only too into drink and mediocrity. Even some of New Orleans's favorite sons have gone that way. Of the late, great jazz drummer James Black, who returned from a short stay in New York because "New Orleans needs a house drummer," a fellow musician said recently, "He got stuck here and died early."

John Kennedy Toole became a local hero long after his death, when his novel, *A Confederacy of Dunces,* won the Pulitzer Prize. In his humongous erudition, Ignatius J. Reilly, main character of that book, called any place beyond the city "the Heart of Darkness"; this applied not just to the gravel roads and swamps of the area that was to become New Orleans East or the fishing villages of St. Bernard Parish, but to any part of the world that Ignatius had not visited, which was all of it. Dilettantish, egotistical, unable to hold a job while trying to complete a history of civilization that he was writing in pencil in a grammar school notebook, Ignatius finally did escape into that strange world he had seen just once before—when a trip up the road to Baton Rouge nauseated him so much that he blacked out.

Fewer natives leave New Orleans to settle elsewhere than leave any other major metropolitan area in the United States. Mothers are especially powerful figures in this city, where stoop-sitting and neighborhood gossip provide an alternative to the Channel Four news. It isn't unusual for a young man to live with his mother well into his marriageable years, and all the while to be dotingly served by her. When he goes out job-hunting, she drives him to his interview. When his friends come to visit, she doles out the Cokes, listens politely to their conversation for a while, and then retires to her room or to the TV. Mother love and the soporific atmosphere sometimes hold back even the city's most ambitious children.

David, the main character of *The Neon Bible,* escapes his narrow-minded and bigoted valley, but only as a fugitive and at the cost of the almost complete loss of his identity.

Escape seemed to be an important theme to the young Toole, who took his own life at the age of thirty-two. Some people have said that he killed himself to escape the clutches of his mother, yet he was clearly glad to live in New Orleans, and to teach there, while he wrote in almost total secrecy. Thelma Toole gave birth to John, her only son, when she was thirty-seven and thought incapable of conceiving. She was a flamboyant and intelligent woman who ran an informal school, teaching young girls singing and dance, and also elocution. (Proper elocution is an important element in escaping one's origins, especially in a city where the typical white-folks accent sounds more like Spike of Bensonhurst than Rhett Butler.) The sole support of her "darling" (as she called John) and of her invalid husband, she managed to send her son to the best schools; he rewarded her by winning scholarships to both Tulane and Columbia universities. After his death and the subsequent publication of *A Confederacy of Dunces,* she wrote and performed in a series of soirees that featured dramatizations of scenes from the book, as well as a repertoire of standard songs. And at some point in the performance, she always managed to announce dramatically, "I walk in the world for my son." Some people who knew her characterized her, after her death, as "domineering"; one reviewer even claimed that she and her son hated each other.

That seems to take the cat-fighting mother and son of *Dunces* as a literal portrait of Thelma and John. Kenneth Holditch, professor of English at the University of New Orleans, and a friend of Thelma in the last years of her life, calls the idea "ridiculous," and a reading of *The Neon Bible* reveals a completely different picture of the mother and son relationship, in the story of David, the young boy, and his mother and Aunt Mae. A simplistic reading of *Dunces* is contradicted by the new book.

Holditch, who wrote the introduction to *The Neon Bible,* says Toole was outwardly "happy as few people are" to return to New Orleans after two army years in Puerto Rico. He had gotten a job teaching at Dominican College, and had begun to pursue a Ph.D. in English at another school in town. In 1963, Toole submitted the manuscript of *Dunces* to Simon and Schuster, where editor Robert Gottlieb suggested a series of revisions. But Toole became more and more depressed; friends at school noticed that he was becoming paranoid. In January of 1969 he disappeared, and on March 26, on an isolated road near Biloxi, Mississippi, he ran a garden hose from the exhaust pipe of his car to the sealed cabin, and fired up the engine. He left a suicide note, which his mother later read and destroyed. (pp. 16, 26)

*Dunces* is a terrific satire on the ignorance and stubbornness of life in New Orleans in the early sixties, so perversely true that I couldn't finish it when I first picked it up. It was that funny, painful, and true.

*The Neon Bible* is no *Confederacy of Dunces.* Although tender and nostalgic, it lacks the verbal brilliance of the previous book. But it is a remarkable work by a sixteen-year-old author, written for an unknown literary contest. David, the narrator, is as isolated from the other citizens of "the valley," the unnamed Mississippi locality where he lives, as Ignatius Reilly is from the "dunces" of New Orleans. Abandoned by his father, the boy watches his mother sink into depression and then madness, loses his aunt to the lure of the big-time Nashville music scene, and, as the book closes, finds his mother dead of an unknown cause in their house. When the preacher, leader of the narrow-minded populace that has tormented David's family throughout the book, comes to take his mother away, the boy plugs him in the back of the head with a shotgun. With those who raised him dead or gone, and his enemy eliminated, David escapes to a distant city where "people don't ask so many questions like in a place like the valley." He knows he can't go to Nashville to join his aunt, but he is free to embrace an anonymity many adolescents would die for. . . .

*The Neon Bible* is a sentimental book I like despite its sentimentality. To the reader of *A Confederacy of Dunces,* it will show the tender side of Toole's imagination, and a precocious author's view of the South in the fifties, before civil rights and the other movements of the sixties seemed, at least temporarily, to change everything. (p. 26)

> Dennis Formento, "Louisiana—Fugitives," in
> The American Book Review, Vol. 12, No. 1,
> March-April, 1990, pp. 16, 26.

## Peter Matthews

There is something slightly indecent about the manner in which John Kennedy Toole's *The Neon Bible* has been disinterred—salvaged from the effects of the dead author, dragged through the courts, then published against the express wishes of his mother, Thelma Toole. It is no more than the raw foetus of a novel, written in 1954 when Toole was 16. Yet its naked, somewhat queasy vulnerability seems to complete that weird legend already compiled from the sad circumstances of his life, his suicide, and above all perhaps, his relationship with Thelma.

*The Neon Bible* is a book about Momism, in which Toole finds an unexpected beauty. David, growing up poor and miserable in the American Bible Belt, burrows deep inside his mother's ample bosom, loses himself in the sickly fragrance of his Aunt Mae's cheap perfume. Nothing that follows can compete with the rapt intensity of that first love. The big boys, sniffing out his sissification, pummel him mercilessly. But the absence of the men during wartime creates a benign matriarchy in which he enjoys a frail happiness, easily shattered.

Like Toole's major work, *A Confederacy of Dunces,* whose underlying pathos it illuminates, *The Neon Bible* distills the enchanted, dissociated sensibility of the misfit. Like that later work, it evinces a horror of adult sexuality, of the bad things that the older boys do. Yet such is the heartbreaking precocity of the novel that it becomes impossible to sort out the narrator's innocence from the author's. It is the kind of childish romance, composed of tremulous self-pity and need, in which all the bloodiest infantile dreams are realised: a stern father is sent off to war and killed, a hated schoolteacher stumbles and breaks her leg, the local preacher is messily dispatched with a shotgun. In these subliminal, ritual acts of revenge, the novel rings unerringly true.

Toole's southern Gothic hysteria evokes an era of crushed emotion.

*Peter Matthews, "Incomparable Solace," in* The Observer, *April 1, 1990, p. 66.*

## Tom Shone

[In John Kennedy Toole's *The Neon Bible,* our] 16-year-old narrator, David, tells of his claustrophobic childhood in a small Southern town in the 1940s, his mental circumscription symbolised by the bedroom-window view of a neon bible that illuminates the local church. We are given glimpses of a world outside 'the valley': we hear talk of cities, from which come the films David loves, a distant war in which his father gets killed. But even this remains faint: how should you act when your father dies, he wonders?

David's only hopes of connection with the outside world lie with Aunt Mae, an aged floozie who comes to stay, bringing life, sex and illicit knees-ups in the cinema. But when she is finally drawn away again by her singing ambitions, all David's hopes of a normal childhood disappear with her, and he is left with a mother driven mad by grief for her husband, and a preacher eager to get her sent to the local asylum.

The book is a study in the mental anaesthesia of a young mind forced to deal with too much too early. But in the course of the tale, David's problem transforms into the book's problem. Since David is our narrator—and his capacity for the escape-hatch of irony is restricted to pseudo-naive questions about what the grown-ups get up to in the back of the truck—*The Neon Bible* ends up a very withdrawn, tight-lipped book. In the same way that the brilliance of [*A Confederacy of Dunces*] . . . was bound up with the sprawling exuberance of its anti-hero, Ignatius T. Reilly, and his 'peculiar worldview', *The Neon Bible* suf-

fers from the shrivelled horizons of its young narrator, who is too emotionally stunted to have much of a view on anything.

This said, it is difficult for any judgment of the book to avoid reservation, for whatever its faults it is a phenomenal achievement for a 16-year-old. The valley is populated with a nice line in hysterics such as the local preacher, to whom even *Gone with the Wind* is licentious; and David's teacher Mrs Watkins, knuckles permanently white with fury. Add to these the verbal effluence of visiting evangelist Billie Lee, and you can see the beginnings of Toole's Swiftian fascination with hysterical rant, of which the indignant but undignified babbling of Ignatius T. Reilly is the supreme example.

The book's details are often subtle. For example, the flags hung outside households whose men are away at war, the drying shirts which indicate a safe return, or the candles that signal death (not too many in the rich part of town). But alongside this are a lot of rather sentimental evocations of nature, self-consciously poetic star-gazing that leads nowhere.

Where Ignatius was both fascinated and appalled by 'connection' with the world, David sits with sulky, resentful eyes. His mother is mad, his father dead, he loses his girl. The fact that the ending gets even worse further illuminates the overriding sense of self-pity pervading the novel. No doubt it will provide fascinating material for the two biographies being written about Toole, but that doesn't make it a better book.

Where *Confederacy* was a study in mediocrity taken to the point of flamboyant excess, in monumental failure, *The Neon Bible* is a story of mediocrity pure and simple, of failure unalleviated by farce. Large aspirations and claustrophobic surroundings, fine. Giant surroundings and dwarfed aspirations, fine. But small world and small mind make for a stilted book.

*Tom Shone, "Teenage Kicks," in* The Listener, *Vol. 123, No. 3159, April 5, 1990, p. 25.*

# Jeanette Winterson

## 1959-

English novelist and editor.

Often compared to the works of such fabulists as Jorge Luis Borges and Angela Carter, Winterson's novels blend historical events with the mythical elements of fairy tales. Challenging such institutions as marriage, family, and organized religion, Winterson explores alternative interpretations of reality, often projecting a strong feminist perspective while focusing on the search for individual identity and the nature of passion and romantic love. While some critics fault her work as loosely structured, Winterson is regarded as a fresh, innovative literary voice and is often praised for her poised, economical style and sardonic humor. She is viewed as a representative of a new phase in lesbian fiction, expanding upon typical themes of self-affirmation to achieve a deeper examination of the nature of humanity. Michiko Kakutani stated: "Ms. Winterson possesses an ability to dazzle the reader by creating wondrous worlds in which the usual laws of plausibility are suspended. She possesses the ability to combine the biting satire of Swift with the ethereal magic of García Márquez, the ability to reinvent old myths even as she creates new ones of her own."

Adopted as a child by a Pentecostal Evangelical family in Lancashire, England, Winterson was groomed from an early age to become a missionary for the church. She left the church in her teens, however, when the congregation's discovery of her lesbian sexuality led to alienation and public humiliation, including an exorcism performed by church officials. After leaving her family, Winterson was employed in a mental hospital and a funeral parlor before studying English at Oxford University. A job search following her studies proved unsuccessful until an editor, impressed by Winterson's storytelling abilities during an interview, suggested that she write about her experiences. The resulting autobiographical novel, *Oranges Are Not the Only Fruit,* was an immediate popular and critical success, and won England's prestigious Whitbread First Novel Award.

Jeanette, the protagonist of *Oranges Are Not the Only Fruit,* is raised in a working-class, fundamentalist Christian home. Her Evangelical upbringing makes her an outcast at school, and she becomes alienated from her family and the church when her sexual relationship with a young convert named Melanie is discovered. The repercussions of another lesbian affair force Jeanette to finally leave the church. Jonathan Keates observed: "[The] comic detachment with which the narrator beats off the grotesque spiritual predatoriness surrounding her is matter for applause." Reviewers lauded the novel's characterizations, especially that of Jeanette's fanatically religious mother; the relationship between Jeanette and her narrow-minded mother is rendered with deadpan wit. Critics noted that the humorous parables interspersed throughout the narra-

tive enhance the originality of this "coming out" novel. These brief "fairy tales" have been interpreted as reflections of Jeanette's sexual identity crisis and spiritual confusion. Contrasting with Winterson's autobiographical first novel, the plot of her second work, *Boating for Beginners,* largely centers on elements of fantasy. Loosely based on the biblical story of Noah's Ark, Winterson's novel describes Noah as the owner of a pleasure-boat company who invents God out of ice cream and employs a woman named Gloria to collect animals for his "travelling stage epic about the world and how the Unpronounceable made it." While some reviewers maintained that *Boating for Beginners* lacks the thematic focus of Winterson's other works, most considered the novel highly entertaining.

Winterson's next work, *The Passion,* employs a similarly fantastic scenario. Set in nineteenth-century Europe during the Napoleonic wars, this novel is recognized for its skillful fusion of history and the supernatural. Passion in its many forms motivates the lives of the two main characters, Henri and Villanelle. Driven by his boundless admiration and loyalty for Napoleon, Henri, an army cook, endures much suffering in his determination to follow and serve the man. He meets Villanelle, a woman who frequently cross-dresses, after she is sold to army generals as a prostitute. Like Henri, Villanelle also suffers from unrequited love, as her heart has literally been stolen by a former female lover. The characters of *The Passion* express a decidedly human view of historical events, and most critics link the book's themes with the realms of psychology or metaphysics rather than history.

Like *The Passion, Sexing the Cherry* combines magic realism with sensuous detail. Presenting magical and often grotesque characters against the backdrop of such events as the Great Fire of London, the rise of Puritanism, and the introduction of tropical fruits to England, *Sexing the Cherry* chronicles the story of the "Dog Woman" who, although heavier than an elephant, can become weightless and invisible. Her adopted son Jordan wanders through many fantastic lands; his journey has been interpreted as a metaphorical quest for the nature of reality and the self. Reflecting Winterson's characteristic aversion to mundane and conventional views, Jordan encounters a variety of outlooks on romantic love in his travels. In one village, love is outlawed in an attempt to curb the destruction resulting from epidemic outbreaks of passion. Many critics applauded Winterson's injection of feminist beliefs into the traditional form of fairy tales. Her characters live contented lives through their rejection of customary traditions. The "twelve dancing princesses," for example, live "happily ever after"—without their husbands.

## PRINCIPAL WORKS

NOVELS

*Oranges Are Not the Only Fruit*   1985
*Boating for Beginners*   1985
*The Passion*   1987
*Sexing the Cherry*   1989

---

### Roz Kaveney

Some tones of voice are so similar that they can be made to pun on each other, to play jokes like twins in each other's clothing. The narrative voice of Jeanette Winterson's excellent first novel [*Oranges Are Not the Only Fruit* ] is at times that of a child, charming us into a slightly patronizing sympathy by her naïve surprise at the awfulness of family and surroundings; at other times, an almost identical maturity creeps in under the cover of wide-eyed disingenuousness and goes for the kill. This is a steely, dream revenge of a book, rich in malicious strategy. Whether or not what seems unequivocally presented as fiction is literally autobiographical—the shamelessness could be that of photographic veracity or that of audacious invention—the narrator of this novel is out for blood as well as laughs.

Young Jeanette is adopted by her Evangelical mother, and brought up to be a missionary. This is not the first novel about such an upbringing, nor indeed about being poor but respectable in a small Northern town. Winterson ac-

knowledges that we think we know about such things, then tops our knowledge with squalid or pious outrageousness—the teashop waitress whose glasses are broken by dropped frozen beefburgers; the feud of Mother's sect with the Salvation Army over the best carol-singing patch in the High Street; the assumption that Jeanette's adenoid-induced deafness is rapture, a state of grace. The language wittily juxtaposes religiosity—"I am busy with the Lord in Wigan"—with deflating Lancashire common sense. Amid the comedy, this is an idyll; Jeanette lives in a fool's paradise, but one whose odd passionateness almost makes up for its cultural and emotional thinness.

It is also a novel about the loss of paradise, about disappointment. Jeanette converts, then sleeps with, Melanie; she is genuinely surprised to be denounced from the pulpit and starved and exorcized into recantation. The painful comedy of these scenes turns a cliché of the adolescent coming-out novel on its head; the oppressors have brought Jeanette up to know herself as perfect. She knows no guilt and so cannot feel it about being gay; there is a satisfying briskness to her dismissal of family and religion for letting her down. It is perhaps the most charming come-uppance a comic monster on the scale of Mother has ever had.

The child Jeanette has vivid interior fantasies; the novel is interspersed with her fairy-tales. These are characterized by a fully adult sardonic wit—a prince "was also quite pretty though a little petulant at times". At first they seem a self-indulgence, pointless though engaging padding; as the book darkens, their function becomes plainer. In the literal sections, Jeanette cannot afford to forgive, enjoys the unpardonable return from exile as waitress at a congregation member's funeral tea. But her past has made her who she is; tales of wizards and journeys give her the words to acknowledge the fact: "she had tied a thread around my button, to tug when she pleased". The achievement of this novel is to make us squirm with laughter, then make us acknowledge how sheerly sad it is when the needs of self-preservation turn what has been sacred into a joke.

Roz Kaveney, "With the Lord in Wigan," in The Times Literary Supplement, No. 4277, March 22, 1985, p. 326.

### John Clute

There are far more first novels in the world than second novels, and most of them seem to be about characters who have become, or who are destined to become, first novelists unlikely to write second novels. After the ordeal of the childhood of the first novelist has been bared to the reader, along with the traumatic departure from the old home and the old city and the first love, there is often a sense that little more can be said, that the smithy of the soul has forged its last and one more life of mute toil is about to begin in London. Of course for some there will be a stint at the BBC.

'Like most people I lived for a long time with my mother and father,' begins Jeanette Winterson's *Oranges Are Not the Only Fruit,* and except for the wry and succinct wit of the utterance we could fairly anticipate yet another doddering traipse through yet another provincial town in the Midlands of this densely populated island. Indeed, about two-thirds of the way through this fitfully brilliant first novel, there are some utterly routine moments when the protagonist reaches early-middle adolescence, discovers her sexual nature, becomes inevitably estranged from her mother and her mother's grotesque fundamentalism, and begins to look to the big city for escape. But enough momentum has been achieved by this point for the reader to breast any wave of ennui.

The heart of the novel lies in the dense, polychromatic clarity of its rendering of the circumstances in which the protagonist and her exorbitant mother pass their days, pixillated, obsessed with a revivalist God and His fallible Pastors, insanely blinkered but joyful. It could all be a painting by L. S. Lowry. But, as with most first novels, Paradise is described as a prelude to the scene of eviction. For Ms Winterson's protagonist, the serpent, not unusually, is sex. She is attracted only to other girls; she is soon sleeping with them. She is exiled from her wacky sect, her family, her home, her city. She is growing up. She could well write a novel. The brisk, glittering, vengeful accuracy of her eye for detail and character and the taut strength of her handling of material suggest that *Oranges Are Not the Only Fruit* will have successors.

> *John Clute, "Paradise Lost," in* New Statesman, *Vol. 109, No. 2821, April 12, 1985, p. 25.*

## Ann Hornaday

If Flannery O'Connor and Rita Mae Brown had collaborated on the coming-out story of a young British girl in the 1960s, maybe they would have approached the quirky and subtle hilarity of Jeanette Winterson's autobiographical first novel [*Oranges Are Not the Only Fruit*]. With the characteristically deadpan line, "Like most people I lived for a long time with my mother and father," Winterson introduces us to her evangelist mother, ineffectual father, and a gaggle of at once lovable and grotesque Lancashire locals whom most readers will find, if not recognizable, at least resonant. We meet her mother, for whom "the Heathen were a daily household preoccupation." She grooms Jeanette early on for a missionary life, in the footsteps of Pastor Spratt, her own spiritual idol and lustful obsession (he bears a resemblance to Errol Flynn, "but holy"). We meet Testifying Elsie, who has a collage of Noah's Ark with a detachable chimpanzee made out of a Brillo pad, and who, when Jeanette goes temporarily deaf at age seven, is her only friend. And we meet Melanie, a local fishmonger, who thoroughly captivates the author's 14-year-old imagination—not to mention "Unnatural Passions."

Jeanette grows up in a constant state of odd-kid-out. Her evangelist upbringing makes her a misfit in her Anglican grammar school (she does her September needlepoint project entirely in black, spelling the slogan, "THE SUMMER IS ENDED AND WE ARE NOT YET SAVED"). And her emerging lesbian sexuality makes her a pariah at home and in the church (actually, she's a pariah for a relatively short period of time; soon she becomes A Case, Ripe for

Saving). Things come to a head when Jeanette is "caught" in a liaison with her second lover. Withstanding enormous pressure from family and church, she finally refuses to repent and leaves home.

Winterson's portraits are, happily, not executed in broad strokes, and she portrays her characters' idiosyncrasies with clear-eyed truth and quiet affection. Her sensitivity is especially manifest at the end of the novel, when Jeanette *does* go home again. Her mother is still a little crazy, still denigrates her daughter's choices; but she has "gone electronic," and follows the progress of fellow believers by way of transistor, CB, pumping out hymns on an electric organ (complete with samba backbeat). We're left with the hope that she will eventually change in moral latitude as well.

The novel's flaws are minor. The fables that Winterson intertwines with the narrative become a bit too dense; we lose the father entirely (he might be a spineless wimp, but we still want to know what becomes of him); and Winterson's unambiguous indictments of men ("They want to be the destroyer and never the destroyed. That is why they are unfit for romantic love") are disappointing when she so effectively embraces the ambiguity of her characters. At times her prose veers dangerously close to indulgent high school diary entries. . . . (pp. 32-3)

No doubt there are countless novels on the stands about families, separation, and the emotional spaces people create or don't create for one another, but Winterson's voice, with its idiosyncratic wit and sensitivity, is one you've never heard before. (p. 33)

> *Ann Hornaday, in a review of "Oranges Are Not the Only Fruit," in* Ms., *Vol. XIV, No. 4, October, 1985, pp. 32-3.*

## Emma Fisher

A clever girl is brought up by her adopted mother to be a preacher in a charismatic evangelical church, but her lesbian love-affairs lead to her rejection by the church "family" and by her mother. This was the bizarre, funny and sad story—presumably her own—told by Jeanette Winterson in her excellent first novel, *Oranges are Not the Only Fruit,* published earlier this year. One of the nicer characters in the book, Testifying Elsie, used to let the seven-year-old Jeanette play with her collage of Noah's Ark: "The delight was a detachable chimpanzee, made out of a Brillo pad . . . I had all kinds of variations, but usually I drowned it." In her new book, *Boating for Beginners,* the grown-up Jeanette is playing several different games with Noah's Ark. She mocks fundamentalists, takes off romantic novels, slips in sly asides about literature and criticism, and pokes fun at numerous phenomena of modern life such as fashion jargon ("designer chain mail"), the food business and publishing. As in all the best play there is work of importance going on as well: discussion of what to make of gross reality, poetry and fiction once you've stopped believing in the Bible.

That innocent chimpanzee made of a Brillo pad—the incongruous juxtaposition of the modern and the biblical—

has proliferated manically. We are in the era before the Flood. Noah, pleasure-boat owner and religious publicist, has already written *Genesis: or How I Did It,* and is planning to make a film of it and tour with a road show. But Noah is also an inventor, and in a Frankenstein parody he has created God out of Black Forest gâteau and ice-cream. God (or YAHWEH the Unpronounceable, who calls Noah Mother) decides that the flood is really going to happen. Noah will be all right in his fibre-glass Ark, even though he has perhaps unwisely decided to take the romantic novelist, Bunny Mix—an exaggeration of Barbara Cartland, if that were possible—along with him. Gloria, the heroine of the book, finds another way of escaping the Flood: advised by her familiar, the orange demon (who also appeared in the earlier book), she collects together boats and food, and saves her friends, Doris, an organic philosopher and Noah's cleaning woman, Marlene, a man who regretted his sex change and had the vital bit sewn back on, and Desi, one of Noah's daughters-in-law.

Gloria's mental awakening provides the main story, among all the fizzing satirical fireworks. Starting as an unthinking teenager who only reads romantic fiction and women's magazines, she learns to butt in, to lie and to be rude to intellectuals. She reads Northrop Frye, and assumes herself to be in his second stage of language development, where "persons and matter are separate and the inner life (intellectual) assumes ascendancy". She often talks to Doris and Marlene about Life and Art. Gloria and her mother, Mrs Munde, are near relatives of Jeanette and her mother in the first book. There, the relationship between mother and daughter was painful, clearly and severely told; in the second book, there is some lifting of tension through the removal of the mother into allegory. Many of Gloria's comments on Mrs Munde are the kind of thing Jeanette might have said when she got older, for example: "Living with a colossus, however flawed or deranged, is a tiring business."

This is self-consciously a writer's book, full of jokes about style and modern writers, and also containing little homilies on how to write fiction, and apologies for the kind of fiction it is. When Gloria and Marlene are at Bunny Mix's Health Farm, Bees of Paradise, their exchanges suddenly become linked by those absurd avoidances of the words "he said" or "she said" which are so typical of bad fiction: "panicked Marlene", "marvelled Gloria", "she suggested, walking over to the window". Discussing writing with Marlene, Gloria says "fiction both belongs to and creates fantasy, so why should it not be as wild as your wildest dreams?" "Well, I just like things to happen in a line, that's all", replies Marlene. One feels for Marlene, but also for Jeanette Winterson, bobbing in the sea of literature.

> *Emma Fisher, " . . . and before," in* The Times Literary Supplement, *No. 4309, November 1, 1985, p. 1228.*

## Dorothy Stannard

Retelling bits of the Bible to endow the protagonists with twentieth century sexual neuroses, fridge-freezers and colloquial expressions has been done many times before, not least by the Monty Python team, so *Boating for Beginners,* the story of Noah and the Flood according to Jeanette Winterson, didn't inspire. Information that somebody on *Watch the Woman,* that patronising magazine programme for women on Channel 4, had waved it as proof that women are funny (the sort of remark which no longer makes one flinch—just yawn) didn't help. But even up against these prejudices the book seemed well written, its humour nicely paced and the imaginative leaping not bad. Noah is a sort of racketeering god-father with three gormless sons, God is a camp petulant who started off as a giant ice-cream, wickedness is at about a 1985, consumer-ridden level. Somebody called Gloria wanders through the story like an Alice in Wonderland and Doris, who dusts Noah's house calls herself an "organic philosopher": "Decay is the key," she says, "once you've come to terms with decay not much can disappoint." In the end Noah, and his mistress, romantic fiction writer Bunny Mix, who helps him to rewrite the Book of Genesis according to the Authorised Version, and his vile sons sail off to inherit the earth, leaving the nicer characters to no doubt perish. What Ms. Winterson calls "gross reality" barging in, I suppose.

> *Dorothy Stannard, in a review of "Boating for Beginners," in* Punch, *Vol. 289, No. 7564, December 4, 1985, p. 111.*

## Nicholas Shrimpton

Leadership, and our attitude to leaders, are apt topics for fiction in this exhausted, post-electoral lull. Our would-be masters have completed their performances as would-be servants. We are left to contemplate our feelings about the state of being led.

Jeanette Winterson has turned to the early nineteenth century for her reflections on the subject, and to that most charismatic of statesmen, Napoleon. The hero of her new novel, *The Passion,* is a star-struck conscript who becomes the Emperor's butcher. From Boulogne to the gates of Moscow he kills chickens for the Imperial table, while the Emperor himself kills men. From this humble point of vantage Henry worships his leader, because his career of war and destruction enacts, on a vast stage, the revolutionary dream that it might be possible 'to tear down our long-honoured lives and . . . start again'.

As this suggests, the novel is more psychological or metaphysical than historical, and its language is constantly nudging it from the real to the fantastic. The troops drowned at Boulogne, for example, in the abortive invasion of England, have 'married the mermaids.' What starts as a snatch of slang grows, by repetition, into a transfigured world in which ideas can play at will.

This process becomes more obvious in the second section of the book. Villanelle is the daughter of a Venetian gondolier. From her father she has inherited webbed feet, and at crucial moments of the plot she is able to walk on water. For her, however, those crucial moments are not battles (though she too is caught up in the Napoleonic cataclysm, and meets Henri during the Retreat from Moscow) but episodes in the life of the heart. Against Henri's male story of public hero-worship is set a female narrative of private adoration, in the form of a tender lesbian love affair.

That contrast suggests a simple moral message, and the novel does not entirely resist it. Henri's violent life ends in a madhouse, where he ruefully observes that the longing for freedom which Bonaparte's military leadership promised to fulfil was only a distortion of a deeper longing for love. At such moments the technique can slip into the pat, the twee or the fey. But it can also be a procedure of immense fertility—an allusive psychological fantasia with roots in Virginia Woolf and modern *realismo magico,* here applied, with great zest, to large matters of moral argument and historical interpretation.

> Nicholas Shrimpton, *"Emperors and Mermaids,"* in The Observer, *June 14, 1987, p. 23.*

## Kathy Page

Jeanette Winterson slips easily from the past to the present, from the plausible to the fantastic and back again. Her first novel, *Oranges Are Not the Only Fruit,* was the largely autobiographical account of her upbringing by an adoptive mother who wanted her to be a missionary. The second, *Boating for Beginners*—drawing on a wealth of biblical influence—was set at the time of the Flood. Although very different, both were characterised by the wit and agility of the story-telling voice. Neither quality is lacking in *The Passion,* but this latest novel has a concentration of purpose that sets it apart from the others. The passion in question is not Christ's, neither is there more than passing reference to any kind of organised religion, yet this novel is written with an intensity and a degree of repetitiveness that give it a strongly evangelical flavour.

The action takes place during the Napoleonic wars and spans the continent of Europe, but *The Passion* is not concerned with history. There are people with webbed feet in it, but it is not a fairy story. It's a novel about one word: the noun of the title. 'Only connect the prose and the passion and both will be exalted,' Forster wrote in *Howards End;* this essentially poetic (and evangelical) aim is the driving force of Jeanette Winterson's book.

The word passion, with its breathy 's's and connotations of illicit desire, is a pleasure to read and hear in the mind's ear. In this book you will read it, and the imagery of conquest it trails in its wake, many, many times. Passion is a demon which the two protagonists, Henri and Villanelle, share. Like Napoleon himself, it's a ruthless commander and its effects are as devastating as the scourge of Europe. The passion is of the romantic type and lurks 'somewhere between fear and sex', also 'somewhere between god and the devil'. How does it arise? What common need does it satisfy in the essentially ordinary Henri and the exotic Villanelle? The book is not interested in such questions; it aims to convince without argument.

From his final resting place—solitary confinement in San Servelo—Henri writes: 'our desire will lift us out of ourselves more cleanly than anything divine.' Passion here is a matter of faith: submit and be saved. Though their stories are different, Henri and Villanelle speak with one and the same voice: 'I'm telling stories. Trust me,' they command by turns—the tone, like the emotion invoked, is relentless and hectoring.

Henri is Napoleon's cook. Venetian-born Villanelle is a transvestite and gambler; she loses her heart to a woman who beats her at cards. Disappointed that the intensity of her love is not returned, she marries. She travels the world with a brutal and repulsive husband who eventually sells her as a sexual slave to Bonaparte's generals. So it is that Henri and Villanelle meet in Russia. Moscow is burning; Henri has grown to hate Bonaparte as fiercely as once he loved him. Accompanied by Patrick, a lascivious priest gifted with telescopic sight in one eye, they desert.

On the long trek through endless winter to occuped Venice, 'the city of mazes', which (like another city often mentioned: 'the city of the interior') cannot be charted, many tales are told: a heart is found beating in a jar; Villanelle walks on water; lives are lost limb by limb and cards and tears turn to jewels. Despite this proliferation of stories, *The Passion* is a novel of atmosphere rather than incident and an invocation rather than an exploration. Jeanette Winterson is not in the business of creating or reworking myth to reveal psychological or social realities.

Passion, says Villanelle, is 'sweeter split strand by strand'. For the fainthearted—or, as Henri puts it, 'lukewarm people'—the best approach will be to take this hymn to desire strand by strand (there's a bookmark for the purpose) and read it for enjoyment of the writing. . . . Jeanette Winterson has worked the narrative into a glittering setting for her ominous meditations on the nature of passion, and the language she uses, whether solemn and latinate or brief and to the point, is vivid and tightly controlled. (pp. 26-7)

> Kathy Page, *"Heart and Stomach,"* in New Statesman, *Vol. 113, No. 2935, June 26, 1987, pp. 26-7.*

## Anne Duchêne

"I'm telling you stories. Trust me" is one leitmotif in Jeanette Winterson's new novel [*The Passion*]—her third since the Whitbread Prize in 1985 and the laborious larkiness of *Boating for Beginners* last year. Now, she quite overwhelms talk of "promise" with a book of great imaginative audacity and assurance.

The setting itself is a challenge: the Grande Armée after 1805, and a splendidly dark, brooding backcloth of Venice at the same period. There are two narrators. Villanelle is a red-haired Venetian girl who has webbed feet, like her boatman father, and has lost her heart—literally—to an older woman. The other and principal narrator, Henri, is a young French peasant, haphazardly educated and ambitious, who becomes personal chicken-cook (after Marengo, this is) to the Emperor. One of his army comrades is a defrocked Irish priest whose left eye can see for miles: employed as a lookout at Boulogne, he reports the weevils in the British troops' bread—"Don't believe that one", adds Henri. It is the priest who first talks of trusting the story-teller.

The two meet in burning Moscow and retreat privately,

disenchanted, back to Italy. In Venice, Henri steals back Villanelle's heart, found pumping away in a jar in her lover's wardrobe. So Villanelle swallows it, and has her heart again. (She does not give it to Henri, who loves her more than he loved Napoleon.) These fairy-tale elements need cause no anxiety, because they are beautifully embedded in the story.

The "passion" promised in the title is hard to isolate in a book written wholly with passionate enjoyment and control. Certainly, conventional sexual passion prickles in Villanelle's love-affair; but relatively briefly. Henri's devotion demands a fuller definition. Napoleon, of course, has a passion for greatness; and Henri's infatuation only dwindles as he learns its cost. Even Josephine makes some delicious incidental appearances—a lovely, elegant, wronged creature with a salving passion for horticulture.

All this is too coarsely schematic, though. We are repeatedly told, in another leitmotif, that "somewhere between fear and sex passion is"; but also, almost as often, that "religion lies between fear and sex". This correspondence is not developed. It is noticeable that the prose, which is in general buoyant and immediate and easy (Napoleon contemplating invasion, "scanning the seas like an ordinary man checks his rain-barrel") turns cloudy only when the talk is of "passion". . . .

A story about history and hero-worship, the plight of women, the pains of soldiering, the violence of youth, and about the sadness of the unfulfillable condition of humanity—whichever thread one chooses to pull out, it comes from a richly tangled skein of enquiry and assertion, which only falters at this one point, and is elsewhere embodied in brilliantly physical (and funny) detail. The author is still not thirty years old. It looks as if we shall very rapidly come to trust her when she tells us stories.

*Anne Duchêne, "After Marengo," in* The Times Literary Supplement, *No. 4395, June 26, 1987, p. 697.*

**Dorothy Stannard**

We know what Jeanette Winterson's strange folk-tale set in Napoleonic Europe is supposed to be about because at the end of it the two main characters, a spirited and independent woman and a shy, sensitive man, stand up and tell us. They become the chorus to their own story. But then, if they didn't, and we followed the old advice "Never trust the teller, trust the tale", it would be tempting to define *The Passion* as complete tosh when in fact Ms Winterson *is* trying to tell us something.

The novel's first fifty pages concern the background of Henri, a young Frenchman in charge of chicken in the kitchen of Napoleon, and his friendships with Patrick, a disgraced priest with a telescopic eye who can spot an undressed woman two parishes away, and Domino, a midget. Henri, so passive and adoring, is enthralled by Napoleon. He follows him faithfully—until he meets Villanelle.

Villanelle comes from Venice. . . . She cross-dresses and is in love with an elegant Venetian lady who has, literally, reached into her breast and stolen her heart.

Henri and Villanelle unaccountably meet in Moscow, decide to desert Napoleon and walk home to Venice. There Henri bids for her love (he is prepared to kill for her, as he was for Napoleon) but is beaten by the elegant Venetian.

The problem with *The Passion* is that it uses the conventions of the traditional folk-tale (short, declarative sentences, unexplained happenings and magic) and enjoys a freedom from the dull spadework of naturalistic fiction without communicating the universal wisdom and humanity usually inherent in this genre.

Ms Winterson cannot resist the incidental cheap joke, nor some surprisingly slushy sentiment. The result is that the novel, which proceeds with vigour and intelligence in parts, fails to convince. The obviously meaningful refrains—"Somewhere between fear and sex Passion is", "You play, you win, you play, you lose, you play", or worse, the supremely irritating and capricious "I'm telling you stories. Trust me"—ring hollow. Henri says at one point near the end "Words like passion and extasy, we learn them but they stay flat on the page." I don't think this novel does much to raise them.

*Dorothy Stannard, "Chorus Lines," in* Punch, *Vol. 293, No. 7644, July 1, 1987, p. 60.*

**Joseph Olshan**

The world of Jeanette Winterson's daring, unconventionally comic novel *Oranges Are Not the Only Fruit* centers on a pentecostal church congregation in the Midlands of England.

Its heroine, who shares the author's first name, begins this first-person narrative by describing how a vision led her adoptive mother to the orphanage where she was a foundling.

Once adopted, Jeanette ruefully discovers that her mother is a religious fanatic, "Old Testament through and through." Like William Blake, she has visions and dreams and she cannot always distinguish a flea's head from a king.

Luckily, Jeanette is strong-willed and has enough inner fiber not to be crushed by her mother's ecumenical steamrolling.

The two have a curious dynamic, and watching them together can be deliciously humorous. For example, when an attack of adenoids renders Jeanette temporarily deaf ("it struck me that life had gone very quiet"), her mother immediately assumes that she has been given to such rapture of the spirit that she is unable to communicate.

Her mother discourages other members of the church from speaking to Jeanette, who for a few weeks actually assumes the world is dumb. But then she tries to play her recorder and discovers that she is unable to hear any music.

Jeanette's mother attempts to educate her at home until the local board of education objects and orders her to attend school. By now she has been so indoctrinated with

Christian zealousness that she frightens her schoolfellows with tales of hell and demons and ends up becoming their scapegoat.

But she has begun to see the outside world in opposition to the insular world of her mother's church group. "Since I was born, I had assumed that the world ran on very simple lines, like a larger version of our church. Now I was finding that even the church was sometimes confused. This was a problem. But not one I chose to deal with for many years more."

The time required by prayer meetings, revival groups and proselytizing keeps Jeanette from making friends her own age. The only respite from her mother is the ladies of the church group, who make up this novel's font of well-drawn minor characters.

The most memorable is Elsie, an aging, toothless numerologist with whom Jeanette often spends the night. They share stories from Elsie's past. They eat oranges, which take on important meaning in the novel.

Until the end of the book, when her mother's vision of the world finally broadens, Jeanette is told that oranges are the only fruit worth eating. To her, this rigid belief comes to symbolize the blinkered existence of the pentecostals, who, among other things, cannot accept sexual love between two women. Unfortunately for them, Jeanette discovers that she is attracted to women.

By employing quirky anecdotes, which are told with romping humor, and by splicing various parables into the narrative, Winterson allows herself the dangerous luxury of writing a novel that refuses to rely on rousing plot devices.

The parables directly relate to the state of spiritual siege going on within Jeanette, as well as her sexual identity crisis.

The most significant of these tales are the story of Sir Percival, one of Arthur's knights, who begins to see that life has a purpose other than finding the Holy Grail, and of a young girl named Winnet, who becomes a sorcerer's apprentice and, after a time in the sorcerer's castle, forgets that she had a life before sorcery, as Jeanette has forgotten that she had a life before her mother's church. . . .

With off-beat honesty, Winterson has skillfully conjured up a range of idiosyncratic characters, who are served to us with a spice of Midlands speech.

Curiously, Jeanette's father is kept perpetually off-stage, either at work or watching sports competitions on television. One asks why Winterson employs him in the first place. However, this is a minor quibble in what is largely a fascinating debut. Despite all the adversity she is faced with, Jeanette is able to realize herself and eventually make peace with her fanatical mother. She is a *tour-de-force* character in a penetrating novel.

> *Joseph Olshan, "Rollicking 'Oranges' Uses Its Daring Humor to Get Religion," in* Chicago Tribune—Books, *November 8, 1987, p. 8.*

## Barbara O'Dair

Jeanette Winterson's first novel, **Oranges Are Not the Only Fruit,** is the story of a young English girl adopted as a baby by an evangelical churchlady. Winterson gives us little Jeanette, smart as a whip, with a likable deadpan take on the church teachings she's enmeshed in. Jeanette's first years are spent being groomed to become an even better acolyte than her mother, and she grows devotedly into the job till she's leading congregations with rousing propaganda for the Lord. That is, until the dirty deed. As a teenager, she gets booted out of the house on account of her penchant for sex of the girl-to-girl variety and her unwillingness to repent.

Far from elaborating on anguished years of a vague chrysalis that finally emerges as a brilliant monarch at the back of her lover's velvety lips, **Oranges** details a spirited and imaginative childhood, dense with variegated religious lore, all passion and piety, against the drab landscape of a northern English mill town in the stingy '50s. Jeanette traipses between church and prayer meetings, religious roadshows and weekend retreats. She also frequents Grimsby's sweetshop until her mother forbids her to go back: its two female proprietors "dealt in unnatural passions." "I thought she meant they put chemicals in their sweets."

Men don't fare well in this tale. Dad is a shadowy figure who works by night and sleeps by day. His function is to bolster the home while Mother saves the world; his participation is neither needed nor desired. Women-loving, on the other hand, is clear abomination. Early on, a stranger peers at Jeanette's palm and prophesies, "You'll never marry . . . not you, and you'll never be still." When her first girl-love is discovered and Jeanette is sent up before the church tribunal, Pastor Spratt tells her it's her demons they're after. "If I let them take away my demons," Jeanette thinks, "I'll have to give up what I've found."

Meanwhile, the relationship between starchy mother and sassy child is a delight:

> I heard my mother switch on the radio. "And now," said a voice, "a programme about the family life of snails." My mother shrieked. "Did you hear that?' she demanded, and poked her head round the kitchen door. "The family life of snails, it's an Abomination, it's like saying we come from monkeys." I thought about it. Mr and Mrs Snail at home on a wet Wednesday night; Mr Snail dozing quietly, Mrs Snail reading a book about difficult children. "I'm so worried doctor. He's so quiet, won't come out of his shell." "No mum," I replied, "it's not like that at all."

Winterson's style is delectable, sometimes poetically concise, . . . sometimes terse, epigrammatic (Jeanette to the orange demon who sits on her shoulder during her purge from the community: " 'But in the Bible you keep getting driven out.' 'Don't believe all you read.' . . . " 'What sex are you?' 'Doesn't matter does it? After all that's your problem' "). And Winterson occasionally takes off into epic sweeps, such as when Jeanette contemplates what she has done:

I miss God who was my friend. . . . As it is, I can't settle, I want someone who is fierce and will love me until death and know that love is as strong as death, and be on my side for ever and ever. I want someone who will destroy and be destroyed by me. There are many forms of love and affection, some people can spend their whole lives together without knowing each other's names. Naming is a difficult and time-consuming process; it concerns essences, and it means power. But on the wild nights who can call you home? . . . I would cross seas and suffer sunstroke and give away all I have, but not for a man, because they want to be the destroyer and never the destroyed. There are exceptions and I hope they are happy.

Jeanette gobbles orange slices from Mother's hand—a leitmotif overturned when she makes the definitive move away from prodding Mom to secret lover, forsaking the Promised Land for the Forbidden. When she embarks alone, her one fear "was the thought of having to work on a fruit stall. Spanish Navels, Juicy Jaffas, Ripe Sevilles." In the space of a quick 176 pages, this self-styled outcast, with her sly wit and seductive irony, has gone from terrorizing her classmates . . . to driving an ice-cream van and living the lesbian life. "At the heart [of the garden] an orange tree. All true quests end in this garden. . . . To eat of the fruit means to leave the garden because the fruit speaks of other things, other longings. So at dusk you say goodbye to the place you love . . . knowing you can never return by the same way as this . . . " Winterson's story is a kind of liberation theology, a swift, winning romp that leads to secret gardens.

Barbara O'Dair, "The Color Orange," in The Village Voice, Vol. 32, No. 47, November 24, 1987, p. 65.

## David Lodge

One of the privileges of maturity and distinction in the world of letters is the power to bestow accolades on younger writers. Such gestures are disinterested only in a materialistic sense. They are always interventions in literary politics, attempts to influence literary taste, rituals of succession, and they carry an intriguing element of risk for both parties. When Gore Vidal declares that the twenty-nine-year-old British novelist Jeanette Winterson is "the most interesting young writer I have read in twenty years"—words that her publishers predictably quote at every opportunity—one sits up and takes notice because he is laying his own literary judgment as well as her merit on the line.

Likewise, and for much the same reasons, such patronage could be a source of anxiety as well as encouragement for Jeanette Winterson. But one feels sure that the responsibility will not oppress her. The overwhelming impression of her work is one of remarkable self-confidence, and she evidently thrives on risk. The heroine of her latest novel [*The Passion*] is a croupier who sees life very much in terms of gambling:

Gambling is not a vice, it is an expression of our humanness.

We gamble. Some do it at the gaming table, some do not.

You play, you win, you play, you lose. You play.

*The Passion* is Jeanette Winterson's third novel, and about all it has in common with its two predecessors is a fondness for short declarative sentences and one-line paragraphs. Nevertheless, to respond to Mr. Vidal's assessment of her talent it is necessary to consider her work to date as a whole. The first novel, *Oranges Are Not the Only Fruit,* published in England in 1985 and in the US last year, was an episodic autobiographical novel of childhood and adolescence, familiar in structure but refreshingly distinctive in style and in the social milieu with which it deals. The heroine-narrator (called, with disarming transparency, Jeanette) is brought up in a working-class industrial community in the north of England by a dominating mother who belongs to a strict Pentecostal sect. The difficulties of growing up in a subculture so ideologically and linguistically out of touch with secular modern life are touchingly and amusingly rendered in the account of the heroine's early school days.

I wanted to please [the teacher], and trembling with anticipation I started my essay. . . . "This holiday I went to Colwyn Bay with our church camp."

The teacher nodded and smiled.

"It was very hot, and Auntie Betty, whose leg was loose anyway, got sunstroke and we thought she might die."

The teacher began to look a bit worried, but the class perked up.

"But she got better, thanks to my mother who stayed up all night struggling mightily."

"Is your mother a nurse?" asked teacher, with quiet sympathy.

"No, she just heals the sick."

Teacher frowned. "Well carry on then."

The strongest character in the book is the mercurial mother, who is in a constant temper with the irredeemably secular world around her and cherishes an ambition for her daughter to be a missionary. Jeanette acquiesces meekly enough in this plan until, after puberty, she discovers that she is attracted to other girls rather than to boys and that what her mother refers to darkly as "Unnatural Passions" is not artificial additives in candies. A series of lesbian escapades provoke punishment, rebellion, and, finally, flight.

The comic realism of *Oranges* is interrupted, from time to time, by fragments of invented fairy tales that serve as allegories for the heroine's progress toward liberation and self-knowledge. Jeanette Winterson's second novel, *Boating for Beginners,* published in the same year, breaks more radically with realism. Although it won no prizes and has not been published in America it gave me more simple pleasure than the other two, which did, and have. It is an extremely funny travesty of the Book of Genesis, which transfers the story of Noah to our own commercialized and media-ridden times:

> Noah was an ordinary man, bored and fat, running a thriving little pleasure boat company called Boating for Beginners. Gaudily painted cabin cruisers took droves of babbling tourists up and down the Tigris and Euphrates, sightseeing. . . . Noah worked hard and was not pleased to see the fruits of his labour slipping away into dubious community projects. That was the trouble with Nineveh: it had become a Socialist state full of immigrants, steel bands and Black Forest Gateau. . . . He reached for his heart pills; it was really getting a bit much. Suddenly a huge hand poked out of the sky, holding a leaflet. Trembling, Noah took it. It was yellow with black letters and it said, "I AM THAT I AM, YAWEH THE UNPRONOUNCE-ABLE."

There is a heroine called Gloria whose arguments with her mother (who speaks sententiously of "dropping a stitch in the jumper of life") recall the tussles between Jeanette and her mother in the earlier novel. Gloria goes to work for Noah, collecting animals for his "travelling stage epic about the world and how the Unpronounceable made it," written in collaboration with the romantic novelist Bunny Mix. Although the comedy is often blasphemous, it is based on affection for as well as familiarity with the Bible. There is a serious and eloquent passage in the authorial voice which is worth quoting at length:

> The Bible writers didn't care that they were bunching together sequences some of which were historical, some preposterous, and some downright manipulative. Faithful recording was not their business; faith was. They set it out in order to create a certain effect and did it so well that we're still arguing about it. . . . Believers are dangerous and mad and may even destroy the world in a different deluge if they deem it necessary to keep the faith. They are fanatics, and reasonable people will never deal with their excesses until reasonable people find a counter-myth in themselves and learn to fight fire with fire. It's very potent, that Punch and Judy show book. The Romantics didn't need it because they found their own fire, but every other quasi-revolt has gone back to it, because when the heart revolts it wants outrageous things that cannot possibly be factual. Robes and incense and larger-than-life and miracles and heroes. It's all there, it's heart-food, and the more we deprive ourselves of colours and folly, the more attractive that now legitimate folly will become.

This could be read as some kind of trailer or manifesto for *The Passion,* in which Jeanette Winterson has gone back to a famous episode in history—the rise and fall of Napoleon—and treated it freely, inventively, and obliquely, in order to produce "heart-food" for herself and her readers. It is a short novel, divided into four sections. The first, entitled "The Emperor," is narrated by a young boy-soldier, Henri, who becomes Napoleon's personal waiter during the preparations to invade England in 1804. It begins:

> It was Napoleon who had such a passion for chicken that he kept his chefs working around the clock. What a kitchen that was, with birds in every state of undress; some still cold and slung over hooks, some turning slowly on the spit, but most in wasted piles because the Emperor was busy.
>
> Odd to be so governed by an appetite. . . .

Whether Napoleon really ate nothing but chicken I don't know, but it is a measure of Jeanette Winterson's authority as a storyteller that one does not question it. She writes with astonishing poise and directness. Without any of the usual, laboriously researched detail of the orthodox historical novel, she places the reader convincingly in the tented kitchen, the sordid brothel, the seasick-making flat-bottomed barges that never made it to England.

The second section, "The Queen of Spades," seems wholly unrelated to the first. It is narrated by a young woman called Villanelle, the posthumous daughter of a Venetian boatman. Because her mother bungled the funeral rites, she is born with webbed feet. She works for a fat, repulsive butcher by day, and at the Casino by night, wearing male clothing partly for self-protection and partly because she enjoys cross-dressing. This leads her into an intrigue with a beautiful woman with whom she enjoys a brief, passionate affair while the latter's husband is away on business. She watches their loving reunion through a window, and rows sadly away into the lagoon. The section ends:

> The ancestors cry from about the water and in St. Mark's the organ begins. In between freezing and melting. In between love and despair. In between fear and sex, passion is. My oars lie flat on the water. It is New Year's Day, 1805.

The next section, "The Zero Winter," returns us to Henri's narrative and the rigors of Napoleon's Russian campaign. The cruelty and the cold are powerfully evoked:

> The Russians didn't even bother to fight the Grand Armée in any serious way, they kept on marching, burning villages behind them, leaving nothing to eat, nowhere to sleep. They marched into winter and we followed them. Into the Russian winter in our summer overcoats. Into the snow in our glued-together boots. When our horses died of the cold we slit their bellies and slept with our feet inside the guts. One man's horse froze around him; in the morning when he tried to take his feet out they were stuck, entombed in the brittle entrails. We couldn't free him, we had to leave him. He wouldn't stop screaming.

Eventually even Henri's loyalty to Napoleon cracks. With his friend Patrick, a defrocked Irish priest whose left eye has telescopic properties, and a *vivandière* (military prostitute) who turns up unexpectedly in a fur coat with pockets full of chicken joints, he deserts and walks back through the frozen wastes—to Venice. For the *vivandière* is Villanelle. It is revealed that she married the gross butcher (a character who crossed Henri's path in Boulogne), ran away from him and was recaptured, lost a wager for her freedom, and was sold into Napoleon's army as a prostitute. Henri falls in love with her and is puzzled why she never takes off her boots, even in bed, until, back in Venice, she gets them both out of a tight corner by walking on the water on her webbed feet. Henri ends up, like his fallen idol Napoleon, imprisoned on a rock, apparently content to sacrifice his freedom to secure Villanelle's.

In *The Passion,* Jeanette Winterson's bent for fantasy, which showed itself in the interpolated fairy tales of *Oranges Are Not the Only Fruit* and the Monty Pythonesque surrealism of *Boating for Beginners,* manifests itself as full-blown magic realism; webbed feet, telescopic eyes, a gold locket miraculously preserved in an icicle in the heat of a Venetian summer, and the heart that Villanelle literally left behind her, in the house of her Venetian lover. In an astonishing scene, Henri burgles the house in an effort to recover it for her. . . .

> [A] noise stopped me. A noise not like the sound of mice or beetles. A regular steady noise, like a heartbeat. . . . On my hands and knees I crawled under one of the clothes rails and found a silk shift wrapped round an indigo jar. The jar was throbbing. I did not dare to unstopper it. I did not dare to check this valuable, fabulous thing and I carried it, still in the shift, down the last two floors and out into the empty night.

> Villanelle was hunched in the boat staring at the water. . . . I heard her uncork the jar and a sound like gas escaping. Then she began to make terrible swallowing and choking noises and only my fear kept me sitting at the other end of the boat, perhaps hearing her die.

This is as good as Poe: it dares you to laugh and stares you down. But, like Poe, Jeanette Winterson sometimes seems a slapdash, lazy, and derivative writer. That powerful description of the soldier with his feet encased in the frozen corpse of his horse is spoiled by the hackneyed spine-chilling formula, "He wouldn't stop screaming." The short, declarative paragraphs do not always earn by the profundity of their meaning the lavish white space that surrounds them on the page:

> But darkness and death are not the same.

> The one is temporary, the other is not.

Fragments of modern poetry, like the last line of T. S. Eliot's "The Love Song of J. Alfred Prufrock," are anachronistically put into the mouths of the characters with no discernible reason except to contribute a spurious touch of class to the discourse:

> In our dreams we sometimes struggle from the oceans of desire up Jacob's ladder to that orderly place. Then human voices wake us and we drown.

In that interesting passage on the Bible in *Boating for Beginners,* quoted earlier, Jeanette Winterson observes that the Romantics freed themselves from the influence of the Bible by creating their own myths, and in *The Passion* she has continued her own flight from a repressive Christian upbringing by embracing the Romantic tradition of storytelling, the tradition of Poe, Mary Shelley, and Emily Brontë. Whereas the realist tradition reflects back to us a

familiar world subtly defamiliarized, and thus made more luminous or comprehensible or meaningful than it was before, the Romantic tradition deals with the unfamiliar, transgresses known limits, and transports the reader into new imaginative territory. There is a certain stylistic price to be paid for this adventurousness, and a certain danger to be faced. Marie Corelli belongs to the Romantic tradition, too. The Romantic novelist tends to be an intuitive, hit-or-miss writer, too impatient to search for *le mot juste* or test the ring of every sentence, like Flaubert or Joyce, and lacking in the ironical self-consciousness that saves a writer from bathos and pretentiousness. We know from her first two novels that Jeanette Winterson is not lacking in a sense of humor and a sense of the absurd, but these qualities are greatly attenuated in *The Passion,* and one must hope that she does not renounce them altogether in pursuit of romantic high seriousness. In other respects *The Passion* represents a remarkable advance in boldness and invention, compared to her previous novels, and suggests that Mr. Vidal's assessment of her ability is, though hyperbolically expressed, fundamentally sound. (pp. 25-6)

> *David Lodge, "Outrageous Things," in* The New York Review of Books, *Vol. XXXV, No. 14, September 29, 1988, pp. 25-6.*

## Nicci Gerrard

Evangelists don't lose their zeal, they just find other causes. At 12, the formidable young novelist Jeanette Winterson was preaching from the hustings and saving souls; at 16 she was found in bed with another woman and thrown out of her home and the Pentecostal Church. Her mother keeps a revolver in the duster drawer to scare away door-to-door salesmen and Jehovah's Witnesses and her enemies are the Devil, Next Door, Sex and Slugs. She called her daughter the "child of the Devil" when she read Jeanette's autobiographical first novel, *Oranges Are Not the Only Fruit.* But Jeanette is still fuelled by the evangelical fervour whose wrathful "thou shalt nots" she has struggled so successfully to escape.

Sitting in her garden with her two cats (MG—because she loves those particular cars and in fact owns one—and Hopeful—because she is) Jeanette Winterson comes across as relaxed and humorous rather than morally driven. But many years ago, her mother told her "you can change the world", and Jeanette still believes that. Her self-appointed task is to "challenge the way people think, not just about big things but about little daily things as well—to free them for a time from gravity".

Her first two novels—*Oranges Are Not the Only Fruit* and *Boating for Beginners*—are acerbic and touching comedies. The next two, *The Passion* and, now, *Sexing the Cherry,* are slim and poetic novels of magic realism. They are arresting precisely because they are unafraid of zestful morality, and enchanting because, like The Bible, they often make imaginative metaphors literal. *The Passion* is set in the Napoleonic Wars and ranges down the labyrinths of Venice and the vast wastes of Siberia. Its web-footed heroine literally loses her heart. *Sexing the Cherry* takes place during the epic ravages of the civil war, plague and Great Fire [of London]. In it, the grotesque and loyal dog woman, who can hold a dozen oranges in her mouth and who sucks a gallant would-be lover into her cavernous vagina, is literally heavier than an elephant. The protagonist, Jordan, is in search of the dancer (or perhaps "the dancing part of himself") who really does float. **Sexing the Cherry,** like its predecessor **The Passion,** combines sensuous detail, magic and lovely language. And it, too, meditates religiously upon the nature of reality and of the self ("I'm not looking for God, only for myself" says the restless Jordan, "and that is far more complicated").

There are two religious roles according to Winterson, who specialises in epigrammatic virtuousity: that of the priest and that of the prophet. The priests "have all the words written out already and only have to read them". The prophets, on the other hand, "are always on the edge, crying in the wilderness—and often what they say isn't wanted. Art should be shocking—otherwise, all you are left with is entertainment—like a baby with a dummy."

So, with engaging and slightly shocking candour, the novelist sets herself up as a prophet of Hampstead Heath. And for someone who so flagrantly transgressed the laws of her native church, she speaks in strangely biblical and rapturous prose about her ideals and ambitions. When **The Passion** was translated into several foreign languages, she felt "pride, yes, but above all joy—joy that more people would read my words". When she considers modern life, she condemns its continual noise and stress which "take the hallowed time out of life". When she calls herself an "optimist" it is because she "believes in miracles".

Perhaps it is, in Winterson's chivalric language, almost a miracle that she escaped from Pentecostal Evangelism and northern working class constraints. She has become, at 30, one of the most exciting and acclaimed authors of her generation. When she was a child, unnatural passions were chemicals put in sweets, and bedtime reading was Deuteronomy. There is a sense in which her scramble towards an unencumbered and self-supporting success resembles that of a "rebellious young man" rather than a young woman without role models.

From saving souls in Lancashire, she progressed to putting smiles on the faces of corpses in an undertaker's parlour, selling ice-cream, and working in a mental hospital. After studying English at Oxford she tried to get a job in advertising (but writing the words for a symphony for Schweppes floored her) and then in publishing (but was told she was too "wayward and headstrong"). Alone and fearful—"I had no back-up, no one to telephone, nowhere to go, and sometimes I wondered if I could keep it up"—she wrote **Oranges.** "What else could I do? What else can I do now? I've established that I'm unemployable." It was well-received, and won the 1985 Whitbread First Novel Award.

The saga is less manically bizarre after her first novel was published, and is charted by "prizes and successes" rather than colourful excursions into alien worlds. But she says she is becoming ever more frightened by the interior process of writing. "If you want to go on inventing the self, then you can never be satisfied with what you have already done. Each time it is an uncharted journey." And she hates the way the media now treats writers: "Writing is so private and interior, but when the book is published, everything changes. Nothing is private; everything can be divulged." . . .

In **Sexing the Cherry** Jordan pursues his "hidden life" which "was written invisibly, was squashed between the facts, was flying without me . . . " Winterson too has "a hidden life, while appearing to be open and candid". She revels in her concealment, calling her camouflage of self-revelation "a useful paradox". She talks tranquilly, and with arresting frankness, about her tantrums. They are directed against herself when she feels she has "failed language." . . .

She readily admits that she was damaged in her childhood, and discusses the process of "self-healing". She recalls her anti-social behaviour, and her stormy relationships. She questions her lack of guilt, a passion she dwells upon much in fiction. And all the while she warns you that she is glad to hide behind her apparent openness and her self-generated publicity. "Naked is the best disguise."

For the relaxed yet intense Jeanette Winterson is a consummate self-publicist, articulate and anecdotal. She has a way of fictionalising herself—making her life into a series of fables and self-consciously fantastical gestures. She has, for instance, bought herself a plot in Highgate Cemetery ("I tend it; it is like my second home"), and wanted to buy a coffin where she would keep her foreign editions, until her horrified friends accused her of being macabre. Warned by the muddled fall-out of the death of a close friend, and not wanting Mrs Winterson to collect the loot for a new gospel tent, she has also arranged her after-life, which includes a theatrical funeral service. "It will be a big do—lots of champagne. And I've left enough money for people to go on trips and forget about me." The details of the actual service remain secret—but it all ends with a hot air balloon. Behind the stories and gestures, the real self remains hidden.

There could be something faintly ludicrous about someone who thinks she is a "prophet crying in the wilderness". Yet with her quiet but almost tangible self-assurance, this "self-made" woman somehow pulls it off. Considering the question of whether or not she is arrogant, she pauses before replying: "I've always thought of arrogance as being pleased with oneself without just reason. I have reason to be pleased with myself. Of course I am pleased with myself. Against all the odds I have come from nowhere and been able to make a difference." (p. 13)

*Nicci Gerrard, "The Prophet," in* New Statesman & Society, *Vol. 2, No. 65, September 1, 1989, pp. 12-13.*

**Rose Tremain**

In one of the most successful passages in Jeanette Winterson's new novel [**Sexing the Cherry**], the protagonist, Jordan, finds himself in a clamorous place where words form a thick cloud over the city. 'Men and women in balloons fly up from the main square and, armed with mops and scrubbing brushes, do battle with the canopy of words trapped under the sun. [But] the words resist erasure.' She is describing the dilemma of the novelist in the late Eighties: we are in the literary greenhouse. The novel will die if we continue to add to the noxious emissions of tired stories. The only way to a healthier text is via the imagination. We must dream our way out.

Writers and critics are agreed, the post-modern novel can be more or less whatever we wish it to be, just as long as it offers a freshness of vision. Jeanette Winterson has asked all the right questions, and every page of this book testifies to her struggle to find answers to them. Invention pours out of her: dancing princesses and dancing weasels, a woman who turns into a lotus tree, a woman heavier than an elephant, a house without floors whose occupants fly around on pulleys, visions of sea and palm trees in the sighting of the first banana to reach England. 'Wondrous, wondrous, wondrous', as one character murmurs when the elephantine woman takes his member into her colossal mouth, and the vibrancy of certain passages does indeed make the reader marvel. But, disappointingly, neither rapture lasts. The huge incisors sever the penis. The reader is severed from the narrative so many times by its shifts of focus that indifference very soon sets in. Novels that tease and subvert the reader, as this one does (with more than a nod in the direction of Borges and Calvino and Salman Rushdie and even Angela Carter), succeed only if they work an enchantment on the teased and subverted. The reader must be so spellbound that he doesn't drop out of the game. And here lies the problem with *Sexing the Cherry:* for all its grand design, it fails to carry the reader along.

Set mainly in the 17th century, with a swift look at 1990 along the way, the book develops around the lives and dreams of the unnamed fat woman and her adopted son, Jordan. Named after a river, Jordan embarks on a series of journeys in search of himself. 'In the flood-tide he slipped away', says his mother, thus encouraging us to follow and reminding us that the great novels of both past and present, whatever their differences of form, have about them the power and the inevitability of great rivers: they cannot be resisted. But this novel is no such river. Breaks in the narrative are signalled by comical little drawings of pineapples and bananas (what is the origin, I wonder, of Jeanette Winterson's obsession with fruit?) and at each banana it is all too easy to slip and clamber out.

Most disappointing is the novel's failure to use history in a way that illuminates the present. The traumatising events of the mid-17th century—the execution of Charles I, the public hanging of the regicides, the plague and the Great Fire—are dutifully recorded, and we get a sniff at the filthy waters of the Thames, but this is all. There seems to be no attempt to inhabit the age, either in image or in language, so that in the end the choice of century seems arbitrary.

The most original pieces of writing in this novel have their origins, not in history, but in the fairytale, which is timeless. These are the 11 stories of the Twelve Dancing Prin-

cesses. Married by their father to 12 brothers (one of whom turns out to be a woman in disguise) every one of the princesses is now divorced. One by one, each tells the story of her marriage and how it ended. These short accounts have the economy and the disguised moral purpose of the fable. They're clever and witty and Jeanette Winterson's palpable enjoyment of her own power here makes them seductive reading. I particularly liked the feminist retelling of the Rapunzel story. Such discoveries are reminders that here is a writer with a quirky and original mind. What the book seems to lack is the ability to develop the large idea in a way that holds the reader firmly in its grasp.

*Rose Tremain, "Banana Skins," in* The Listener, *Vol. 122, No. 3131, September 14, 1989, p. 29.*

### Shena Mackay

"The Hopi, an Indian tribe, have a language as sophisticated as ours, but no tenses for past, present and future. The division does not exist. What does this say about time?" Questions about time and matter and the reality of the world are central to Jeanette Winterson's new novel [*Sexing the Cherry*], and she attempts to answer them in a narrative in which the seventeenth century dissolves into our own, and vice versa. . . . *Sexing the Cherry,* co-opting as a character the traveller and Royal Gardener, Tradescant the Younger, is a sort of *Botany for Beginners* meets Swift, Defoe, Hans Andersen and Mary Poppins, the New Physics and Green politics.

The novel takes its inspiration from a painting by an unknown artist, entitled "Mr Rose, the Royal Gardener, presents The Pineapple to Charles II". This pineapple, the first to be seen in England, is brought from Barbados by Jordan, the hero of the book, who sailed there with Tradescant. Jordan's taste for travelling and exotic fruit was kindled when, at the age of three, he was one of the incredulous witnesses to the unveiling of the first banana to reach these shores, which "resembled nothing more than the private parts of an oriental. It was yellow and livid and long." The description comes from Jordan's adoptive mother, known as the Dog Woman, whose obsession with "members", those belonging to Puritans, those bitten off, those thrust into pigs, is manifest throughout the text. The Dog Woman, who fished the infant Jordan out of the Thames, strides across foul-smelling, pestilential London covered in the bites and saliva of the pack of boarhounds which she breeds for racing and fighting. Men quake at the prospect of smothering between her gigantic breasts with nipples like walnuts, covered by a dress which has not been removed for five years. She can send an elephant flying into the sky and she can be weightless and invisible.

Taking the Old Testament literally, she exacts enthusiastic revenge for the execution of Charles I by popping hundreds of Puritan eyeballs with her thumbs and gathering a sackful of Puritan teeth. "It was not until the afternoon that the King appeared in his linen shirt, his beard trimmed and nothing of him shivering though many a spectator had fainted with cold." The Dog Woman's depiction of the death of the King points up one of the pitfalls of fictionalizing real events: the supersubtlety of assuming the reader knows that Charles wore *two* shirts lest his shivering be misinterpreted as fear risks robbing his end of much of its dignity and pathos.

Jordan is apprenticed to Tradescant, voyages with him, and pursues his own adventures, in the course of which he meets the Twelve Dancing Princesses, each of whom tells him her feminist tale. He falls in love with one of them, the tightrope-walker, Fortunata, and travels the world in pursuit of her. As he encounters strange lands and philosophies, the Dog Woman battles against Puritanism—personified by the hypocritical Worthies, Neighbour Firebrace and Preacher Scroggs; visits a brothel staffed by nuns with branding irons, and other houses, and helps to heap the bodies of plague victims into pits for burning. London, she decides, must be purged by fire. Quite by chance she is drinking with a group of bakers in Pudding Lane one night when the fire breaks out, and assists it with a vat of oil.

Then it is 1990, and a youth named Nicolas Jordan decides to go to sea. He is intrigued by a painting of the Royal Gardener presenting a pineapple to Charles II, and is obsessed also with a woman who is waging a campaign against the poisoning of rivers with mercury and phosphorus. She decides to burn down a chemical factory . . . . London is a pestilential city where the muted children of the polluted present jostle against the maimed casualties of the Civil War.

*Sexing the Cherry* contains passages of beautiful writing but its juxtaposition of fact, fantasy and didacticism never quite gives the impression of an artist in love with her material. The titular cherry, the result of a bit of early genetic engineering, the grafting of a Polstead Black on to a Morello, turns out to be female, but the significance of its sex is not clear. As with much of the book there may be more, or less, to that than meets the eye.

> *Shena Mackay, "The Exotic Fruits of Time,"*
> *in* The Times Literary Supplement, *No. 4511,*
> *September 15-21, 1989, p. 1006.*

## Jane Urquhart

Reading or listening to fairy tales as a child, I often wondered what took place during that vague, trackless period of time referred to, with ominous finality, as "happily ever after." I was troubled by the apparent emptiness of this state, by its total lack of narrative, and by the suspicion that after keeping house for a collection of dwarfs, being relentlessly pursued by an evil witch, and sleeping for years inside a glass coffin surrounded by an enchanted forest, domestic life with the awakening prince might be, well, a tad boring at best and at worst might resemble death.

Jeanette Winterson seems to have suffered from the same suspicion but has, in *Sexing the Cherry,* decided to do something about the quandary. Her narrative begins where others end, be they historical or mythical, and by

doing this she not only cheats both time and death, but also manages to keep the fairy tale going and all the magic alive.

Set in 17th-century London, near the banks of the Thames, *Sexing the Cherry* deals with such historical givens as the plague, the Great Fire, the rise of Puritanism, and the introduction of certain exotic, tropical fruits to England.

Using these events as springboards for her remarkable imagination, Winterson jumps gleefully into the sometimes grim, always bizarre territory of "happily ever after," where she combines philosophy, mysticism, farce, fable, and the telling of tall tales. . . .

*Sexing the Cherry* is essentially a picaresque novel, one in which we're presented with a cast of rogues and misfits who, it turns out, have much to impart. Consider, for instance, the gargantuan Dog Woman, an affable but murderous giantess who, literally, eats Puritans for breakfast but whose pleasure is singing. "My voice," she says, "is as slender as a reed, and my voice has no lard in it." Or the Twelve Dancing Princesses who tell tiny, perfect tales of how they lived happily ever after without their husbands. There is also a witch-like creature who appears to be made of leather and rags and who, the Dog Woman informs us, "has twice been mistaken for a side of beef wrapped in muslin." All of these unusual female characters are balanced by an array of humorous, mostly nefarious male characters, and by the gentle, saintly Jordan, son of the Dog Woman, whose love for the Twelfth Dancing Princess takes him on a series of incredible journeys.

Winterson, whose work is full of profound truths disguised as simple statements, is at her epigrammatic best on the subject of romantic love. "I fell in love once," the Dog Woman tells us, "if love be that cruelty which takes us straight to the gates of Paradise only to remind us that they are closed forever." In one of the villages that Jordan visits there are some who believe that love must be tamed and others who believe that "only passion frees the soul from its mud-hut, and that only by loosing the heart like a coursing hare and following it 'til sundown could a man or woman sleep quietly at night." A whore announces "that she hates her lovers-by-the-hour but still longs for someone to come along in a coach and feed her on mince pies." And another village is destroyed time and time again by epidemic outbreaks of love.

There are, admittedly, a few flaws in this delightful book. Occasionally, Winterson's influences are jarringly evident, as in her descriptions of cities so fantastical as to have been created by Italo Calvino himself, or in her retelling of fairy tales in the manner of British writer Angela Carter. The ending of this flight of fancy, moreover, brings us back to earth, and to the present, with a rather disappointing thud as Winterson engages in some vaguely preachy—albeit admirable—ruminations on the subject of ecology. But, despite this, *Sexing the Cherry* is a life-enhancing, gratifying book. And Winterson's use of language is superb. Like the grotesque Dog Woman on the banks of the Thames, she has a beautiful, clear voice.

*Sexing the Cherry* is "as slender as a reed" and it definitely "has no lard in it."

Jane Urquhart, "Jeanette Winterson's Fantastical Passion Fruit," in Quill and Quire, Vol. 56, No. 4, April, 1990, p. 29.

## Michiko Kakutani

The marvelous and the horrific, the mythic and the mundane overlap and intermingle in this wonderfully inventive new novel by the young English writer Jeanette Winterson.

Although *Sexing the Cherry* nominally takes place in 17th-century England, its hero—a young adventurer named Jordan—journeys not only around the world, but also through time and space, using his imagination to enter marvelous kingdoms that may or may not exist outside his mind. Like so many other mythic heroes, Jordan is an orphan, found floating down a river (in his case, the Thames), and adopted by a surrogate parent who raises him as her own until he is ready to set off on a quest—to find out his own identity and, in the process, to transform the world.

Jordan's adoptive mother, known as Dog Woman, is herself a kind of Rabelaisian creation. A giantess who outweighs the local circus elephant, she is hideously disfigured by smallpox and reeks from her decadelong refusal to bathe. She has spent her life alone, self-reliant and wary of love; she knows when she finds Jordan that he will eventually leave her, leave her and break her heart.

Indeed, Jordan has an epiphany at the age of 3 that makes him realize that it is his destiny to see the world: he has seen an herbalist exhibit "an edible fruit of the like never seen in England," and in this glimpse of a banana he has a vision of a "tree and the beach and the white waves below birds with wide wings"—a vision of the exotic lands he will one day visit.

In time, Jordan will apprentice himself to the King's gardener, a man named Tradescant who is pledged to bringing back wondrous new plants from around the world. He will sail the globe with Tradescant; and after Tradescant's death, he will take over the expeditions, charting the voyages and deciding "what was precious and what was not."

Some of the places that Jordan visits are real—France and Italy, Persia and Barbados, others are more magical, accessible not by way of ordinary navigation, but only by leaps of the imagination. In search of a dancer he loves named Fortunata, he journeys to the fairy-tale world of Grimm and beyond. He meets 12 princesses who fly, every night, to a floating city that is immune to the laws of gravity. He meets a group of nuns who fish for lost souls with shrimping nets. And he visits with a group of word-cleaners, people who fly up to the sky in balloons to "do battle with the canopy of words trapped under the sun." . . .

Perhaps most disturbing of all the places Jordan visits is a city—meant to resemble Puritan England—in which love is regarded as a plague. Smiling, kissing and the playing of music are banned here; mandolins, romantic ballads and bouquets exist only in glass cases in the little-visited Museum of Love. When another plague of love threatens to overcome the city, its ruling monk warns the populace that the penalty for love is death; the people take a vote and unanimously agree to die.

Juxtaposed with Jordan's reminiscences about his travels are Dog Woman's, vivid—and often grotesquely brutal—accounts of the battles at home between the Royalists and the followers of Oliver Cromwell. A fervent anti-Puritan, Dog Woman vigorously throws herself into battle: she spits on any passing Puritan and kills those who fight back. When a preacher reminds the Royalists of the biblical law "an eye for an eye and a tooth for a tooth," she exchanges murder for bodily assault. Within a month, she has a collection of 2,000 teeth and 119 eyeballs; she plants the teeth in her garden and feeds the eyeballs to her dogs.

In the course of giving the reader an account of their lives, both Dog Woman and Jordan make numerous digressions on the subjects of love, time and the nature of identity. There are paradoxes ("The earth is round and flat at the same time") and truisms ("The difference between the past and the future is that one has happened while the other has not") and words of advice ("Men are best left in groups by themselves where they will entirely wear themselves out in drunkenness and competition").

These stabs at philosophical speculation have a way of turning into windy effusions—abstract and pretentious. And Ms. Winterson's attempt, late in the novel, to create two new characters—a boyish sailor and an ardent environmentalist—who represent contemporary reincarnations of Jordan and Dog Woman feels similarly strained.

These, however, are minor problems in a book that eloquently attests to its author's powers of invention. Like Scheherazade, Ms. Winterson possesses an ability to dazzle the reader by creating wondrous worlds in which the usual laws of plausibility are suspended. She possesses the ability to combine the biting satire of Swift with the ethereal magic of Garcia Márquez, the ability to reinvent old myths even as she creates new ones of her own.

Michiko Kakutani, "A Journey through Time, Space and Imagination," in The New York Times, April 27, 1990, p. C33.

## Michael Gorra

"Oranges are not the only fruit," Nell Gwyn once said, knowing she had something sexier to sell to Covent Garden's 17th-century theatergoers in the days before she became a royal mistress. Indeed, as Jeanette Winterson demonstrates in *Sexing the Cherry,* they're not. The young British writer used the one-time orange girl's words as the title for her first novel, a somewhat autobiographical account of a lesbian orphan brought up in a fundamentalist sect. And her new book proffers not only the title's cherry but also the first pineapple ever seen in England, presented to Charles II in 1661, and a banana that in its London debut is taken to be "the private parts of an Oriental."

Fruit as a metaphor for sexuality—well, nothing new in

that. But for Ms. Winterson fruit is also something rich and sweet, an exotic juiciness hidden beneath the pineapple's unpalatable skin, a new marvel brought into our ken. *Sexing the Cherry* fuses history, fairy tale and metafiction into a fruit that's rather crisp, not terribly sweet, but of a memorably startling flavor. Set mostly in the 17th century, the novel employs two alternating narrators. One is the gigantic Dog Woman. an appealingly innocent murderess, puzzled by just what it is that attracts people about sex— for she's so enormous that experiencing it herself has proved impossible. The other is her adopted son, Jordan, a naturalist who wonders about the human applications of "the new fashion of grafting, which we had understood from France," the grafting through which a new kind of cherry tree has been created and given a sex—female— without parent or seed. And the novel itself grafts together not just those two voices, but different narrative modes as well.

"My neighbour, who is so blackened and hairless that she has twice been mistaken for a side of salt beef wrapped in muslin, airs herself abroad as a witch." That's the Dog Woman, so called because she breeds dogs for the fights and races in Hyde Park. Jordan's voice is less pungent and more meditative: "Every journey conceals another journey within its lines," he muses. "The path not taken and the forgotten angle. These are the journeys I wish to record. Not the ones I made, but the ones I might have made, or perhaps did make in some other place or time." Like his quest for a woman whom he sees one morning "climbing down from her window on a thin rope which she cut and reknotted a number of times during the descent"—a quest that leads to his discovery of 12 princesses who dance away each night to a weightless city in the sky. Or a journey through time itself, which Jordan believes to be rounded and curved like a globe, instead of flat and linear like a map—so that at the end of the novel we meet another Jordan and another Dog Woman in 1990, and find that nothing has changed in 300 years.

But Ms. Winterson alternates these metaphysical conceits with the Dog Woman's world of blood and pus and sweat. A Royalist, a Cavalier of the slums, she's long pondered the biblical motto "an eye for an eye and a tooth for a tooth," and one day decides to take it seriously. Soon she's got a bagful of both, all popped from Puritans, and moves on to work as an executioner at a brothel where the whores murder their puritanical Roundhead customers. Of course, all her victims are men. . . . At times, in fact, it seems that the only men in *Sexing the Cherry* worth saving are those who, like Jordan, have given cross-dressing a try. I note this, but curiously enough it didn't bother me as I read the novel. If Kingsley Amis can use women as objects for his misanthropy, I suppose Ms. Winterson can use men as a metaphor for a world based on a pestilential hypocrisy.

I do, however, question her success in producing her own kind of graft. Her prose is exquisite, although, like the best sort of fruitcake, it's too rich to take much of at a sitting. But the book seems disjointed. It needs, but never quite achieves, an integration of the Dog Woman's world and Jordan's speculations. The games it plays with gender

aren't made to relate to the ones it plays with time. And while the effect of *Sexing the Cherry* depends above all on novelty, the kinds of materials Ms. Winterson uses—the feminist revision of fairy tales, the reliance on historical pastiche, an insistence on the subjectivity of all truth— have paradoxically become so fashionably familiar that they begin to seem the clichés of post-modernism. It almost seems written to recipe: graft Italo Calvino onto Angela Carter, with an admixture of Peter Ackroyd.

But no—Ms. Winterson has her own strengths, above all an emotional intensity that Ms. Carter, for example, seems without. I think of two things that set her apart, two things that figure in all her work: a fascination with sexual ambiguity, cross-dressing and blurred genders on the one hand, and with foundling children on the other. And their combination gives her prose an exuberance cut with a melancholy knowledge of what it is to be hurt, and of how deep and enduring that hurt can be; a knowledge that's far more memorable, and unsettling, than any of the Dog Woman's murders. *Sexing the Cherry* may not be without parent or seed, but its taste is rich enough to make me look forward to whatever fruit may follow it.

> *Michael Gorra, "Gender Games in Restoration London," in* The New York Times Book Review, *April 29, 1990, p. 24.*

### Jeanette Winterson    (Interview with Suzanne Scott and Lynne M. Constantine)

[Scott and Constantine]: *We're always interested in what motivates people to write books. How did you come to be a writer?*

[Winterson]: It wasn't intentional! I never wanted to be a writer because it seemed to me you had to struggle for years and years and never get anywhere. Particularly, you never made any money. And if you were brought up poor, as I was, poverty is not an attraction. Scribbling in a garret is something only people with private incomes can do.

I did try to get various jobs when I left Oxford, but I was splendidly unsuccessful. Eventually, during my second go at trying to be an editor at Pandora Press, I was so bored and fed up when I realized I wasn't going to get the job that I began telling the person in charge various stories— some true and some apocryphal—about my early life and Pentecostal evangelism. She said to me, "If you can write it the way you tell it to me, I'll buy it." And that's how *Oranges Are Not the Only Fruit* came into being and how I came to be a writer.

*Exactly how autobiographical is* **Oranges?**

Well, if I were to tell you, you'd be the very first person I ever told. Everyone wants to know how autobiographical it is, and the truth is, I can't remember.

*An extraordinary fact about* **Oranges** *is that you do not come off as unsympathetic to Pentecostalism, despite a rather frank depiction of its grim and stultifying world view. Was that a way of writing the story, or is that the way you feel now?*

I learned very early on that bitterness is nobody's friend.

I'm not a bitter person. I find that both compassion and laughter have allowed me to get free from what was a rather dreadful upbringing. I always like to see the other side because there always is one.

Although in many ways I think the charismatic or evangelical movements are extremely dangerous, I also know that they believe sincerely in what they're about. And if you can't understand these people, you can never really portray them.

Oddly, people who read **Oranges** tend to come down resolutely on the side of the heroine even though she challenges the three things many people hold most dear—the normality of heterosexuality, the sanctity of the family, and the notion that the church is about love and not about power. I think this happens precisely because **Oranges** isn't bitter: There's enough space left for people to think it through.

*That's a hallmark of all three of your novels—a lot of space.*

I hope so, because I think that reading is not a passive act. It's a creative act. It's a relationship between the writer and a person the writer will probably never meet. I think it's very wrong to write in a way that leaves no room for the reader to maneuver. I don't want to get in the way. What I'd really like to do is to perform the Indian Rope Trick—go higher and higher and eventually disappear.

*There is a considerable stylistic leap between* **Oranges** *(1985) and* **The Passion** *(1987). How did that change come about?*

After a long silence and a lot of worry and anxiety. **Oranges** in England was a huge success, and I was taken aback by it. Whenever you do something that's a success, a hundred people pop up and say, "Why don't you do this next or that next?" Any good idea, and somebody wants to milk it to death. I was not prepared for that sort of interest in me because I am, in many respects, a retiring person. I wondered how I could possibly find my own voice again in the midst of all this noise. It often does silence writers. And I was being told who I was and how to write. I'd spent all my life trying to get out of people telling me what to do. So I sacked my agent and I wouldn't go back to the same publisher. In effect, I started again.

It was an enormous risk, but it paid off. When I was calculating, I said, "Well, all right, I could do what everybody says, and I'd be all right for a few years, then what would I have? Nothing. Whereas if I do it this way, and it does work, it will be absolutely mine."

**Sexing the Cherry** *(1989) follows in the same stylistic vein as* **The Passion.** *It's so dense and rich—how long did it take you to write it?*

I think writing is a process that starts long before the writer actually writes and probably goes on long afterward. It's rather like the way the Arabs weave rugs. They don't stop. They just cut them off at a certain spot on the loom. There is no particular beginning or end. So it was with **Sexing the Cherry.** It came out of notes of sorts, and the end of it ran into other projects.

*Your love of literature and fondness for literary allusion are*

*evident in both* **The Passion** *and* **Sexing the Cherry.** *What writers did you read as a child?*

That really came about when I went to Oxford and found out that there were far more books and writers than I had ever thought possible. As a child I was very narrow. I learned to read from the Bible. There weren't any other books in our house except for *Jane Eyre.* Actually, an addiction to the library started me reading. And because I had no guidance, I took just about anything off the shelves, usually because I liked the jackets. I read five or six books a week.

*What writers do you feel a particular affinity with?*

The writers who particularly influenced me are Italo Calvino and Virginia Woolf. A contemporary poet I like is Marilyn Hacker. I like them all for the same reasons. I look for a dedication to language and an economy of language—a thorough searching for the right word at the right place, without sloppiness, and a determination to hone a hard, bright image that the reader can keep over time. Very often if you read a lot of books, you forget plot and you forget character. But if the writer can leave in readers' minds just one image that they can turn over and over and draw on and take out and look at now and again, then the writer has succeeded. I'm very much a writer who enjoys poetry and takes the tenets of poetry into her own work.

*That fact is evident in your economical style of writing.*

I think it's rude to write long books. This is the late twentieth century, and never before has people's time been so compressed with so many demands made on it. It's not the nineteenth century, the heyday of the novel, where the choices for your leisure time were whether to play the piano or read the latest installment of Dickens. Now people have very little time. I think if you're going to say "Yes, read this book. Don't go to a movie. Don't go to the theater or the opera," then you've got to be offering something very special.

*That attitude toward the writer's responsibilities seems to be particularly an attitude of someone who did not grow up among the privileged classes.*

That's absolutely true. Because overwhelmingly still, writing is a middle-class, private-income domain—certainly in my country. And probably only when that truly breaks down will we begin to see exciting things happening in literature and start to hear voices that have previously been silent.

**The Passion** *is set in the Napoleonic era.* **Sexing the Cherry** *is set in the age of Cromwell. How did you come to be so interested in history?*

I've always been fascinated by history. When I was a kid, history books were among the ones I used to take out of the library. My interest may be because I have no discernible past: I don't know who my ancestors are or where I come from. I'm not tethered by family. So in that sense, I'm rather like Henri in **The Passion.** I can make up things about the past. The past is a playground adventure.

My interest is also expedient—how can you most readily

persuade people to come around to your point of view? I sometimes think that setting scenes in the present makes people too uncomfortable. Anything that you've got your nose right up against is going to be a great scene of emotions reaching boiling point. It's difficult to stand back. So what I do—which is what Shakespeare does in the comedies, and especially in *As You Like it*—is to create a space free from the problems of gravity. A place of escape. Free from the content of the everyday, or so it seems. People feel free to wander about, touch and look and smell. It's not frightening. And then, gradually, I begin to challenge the very things they thought they were escaping from.

*Why do you think the stories you tell have struck such a chord in so many readers, particularly women?*

I think because they're universal stories. Also, they include voices that aren't always heard. All of the characters are outsiders, who come at life at an angle. They're not privileged and wealthy, nor do they expect things from life. They're people for whom, at best, life is going to be a continual challenge. So often we have only the pat voices of people who are rather comfortable.

Another factor is that the characters in my stories come to a personal crossroads (the frontier of common sense) and have to decide whether or not to cross over into an unknown, risky world or whether to turn back into what is safe but unsatisfactory. I describe that crisis in my work because it is also in most people's lives.

I think, too, it's a question of language and the way you express your own stories. There are certainly subtle skills that a writer can employ to make sure the story locks in the mind. I can do that because, remember, I was an evangelist. Everyone out there to me is a soul to be saved. I think of my audience as the whole world.

*Do you find men responsive to your work as well?*

My books are published in fourteen languages, so I've received letters from men of all ages, persuasions, and classes. Many of them say, "Yes, I was in national service, I was a soldier, and I felt like Henri [in **The Passion**], but I couldn't tell anybody because they'd call me a girl."

Every so often I get men thundering up and down saying, "Oh, she's so horrible to us." But on the whole, the overwhelming majority of them breathe a great sigh of relief and say, "We're delighted to think of ourselves as Henri or as Jordan [in **Sexing the Cherry**] because it gives us space not to be a joke."

*You obviously come at your work from a very strong class perspective and from a strong feminist consciousness. Do you think of yourself as a feminist writer?*

I don't think of myself as a feminist writer. I think of myself as a feminist. I think every woman should think of herself as such—and probably every sane man, too. There is no proper alternative to it. And naturally it informs my whole life, my whole consciousness.

I would never put a woman in my books who is less than what I think a woman can be. In many ways, these books are about potential—about what people can achieve against overwhelming odds. The women I write about are strong, very controlled, in touch, and always at least one step ahead of the men in whatever context. I won't accept woman as the weaker sex. I don't bother to deal with it.

*There is a great deal of blurring of distinctions between the sexes in your work, with women and men cross-dressing and acting, in fact, as if they possess multiple selves of different sexes. Is that a legacy of Woolf?*

Yes, and of course Shakespeare, who is one of my great sources of inspiration. In Shakespeare, you find that the minute a girl puts on a pair of britches, another girl falls in love with her. As soon as a man puts on a frock, his best friend is drooling over him. People go by appearances and expectations. And one of the ways of challenging these is to turn them around in funny stories that say, "Is there really so much to gender? Do masculine and feminine models make a person self-contained?"

If you want to challenge things that make people feel uneasy—and a lot of people are uneasy with homosexuality or with the idea of a blurring of male and female—then you have to be a little bit clever and a little bit sly. If you start hitting them over the head with it, they'll turn off and start shouting at you. If you can make them laugh, if you can tell them the stories they want to read, then somewhere, sometime their brains are going to start ticking. And maybe one time when they start to open their mouths and be a prejudiced, popeyed idiot, they might think again. I want to seduce people into a different point of view. I don't want to bully them, because I don't think bully tactics work in any context. I think you could call it nonviolent direct action.

*And what kind of nonviolent direct actions are you working on now?*

At the moment, I'm doing an original screenplay called *Great Moments in Aviation*. As a matter of fact, I'm also learning to fly. It's great fun. A pilot who is a great admirer of my books offered to give me lessons. That would be hard to turn down, wouldn't it? Especially after all the flying in **Sexing the Cherry**.

The screenplay is about a young Black woman who comes from the Caribbean to Great Britain in the fifties, which was the first great wave of immigration for us, and which was encouraged and sponsored by the government. (That's a fact, by the way, which everyone has forgotten forty years later.) And the woman, for her own reasons, wants to learn to fly. Her whole life is spent reading about the great pioneers of aviation. They are her special saints, her heroes. Clearly, it's not going to work out for her. We know that a black woman coming to England in the fifties is not going to be trained as a pilot. But this too is about the triumph of the spirit. If something is denied to you, you can still find something else. You can't be crushed.

Because I love journeys, it all takes place on a boat during the eight-day crossing. When she finally arrives, she knows perfectly well that it won't be the way she imagined it. In fact, the film has three possible endings, all of which she tells. Her life can go in any of these directions, but whichever one it goes in, it's still her life.

*What wonderful optimism. Do you think of your work as optimistic?*

Yes, because I am very optimistic. I see things at once tragic and absurd. The two things run together. Every day I find there's something to celebrate about the human condition. People just won't lie down and shut up. It's right to look at the atrocities in our society wherever we find them, but it's also right to be in the spirit of celebration. I don't want people to feel crushed. I want them to feel that there is a way out—even if you have to build your own door. (pp. 24-6)

> *Jeanette Winterson, Suzanne Scott and Lynne M. Constantine, in an interview in* Belle Lettres: A Review of Books by Women, *Vol. 5, No. 4, Summer, 1990, pp. 24-6.*

## Charlotte Innes

Every decade or so a new group of so-called minority writers appear, quite suddenly it seems, at the center of the American literary scene—the abruptness of their arrival simply a reflection of some new warping of market forces and cultural bias. . . .

The latest group of writers just beginning to have their day in the literary sun are lesbians—that is, writers who are lesbian and whose work is obviously informed by their lesbianism. Of these, Jeanette Winterson is an outstanding example. With the publication of her fourth novel, ***Sexing the Cherry,*** Winterson recently received the E. M. Forster Award from the American Academy and Institute of Arts and Letters for the body of her work. (This is a $5,000 award, given annually to a young English writer, to be used for travel in the United States.) Her first and third novels also won prizes in England and praise here: ***Oranges Are Not the Only Fruit,*** an autobiographical coming-out story of a young lesbian raised by a family of Pentecostal Evangelists in northern England, and ***The Passion,*** a meditation on personal love and public hero-worship set in the Napoleonic era. (p. 64)

Winterson didn't spring from nowhere. There is a long if little-known tradition of lesbian fiction, ranging from treatment by French male authors in the nineteenth century, when lesbians were seen as exotic but doomed creatures, to the upbeat feminist works of the 1970s and 1980s published by small presses in the United States. Nevertheless, Winterson and a number of other writers (for example, Sarah Schulman and Margaret Erhart) appear to represent a new phase in lesbian fiction, one moving on from the themes of self-discovery and self-affirmation that have characterized the literature of the past twenty years, to engage a more complex reality.

What's exciting about Winterson is her grace as a writer with an impressive array of imaginative tools. In a style reminiscent of other fantasists, like Donald Barthelme or Italo Calvino, she takes the lesbian experience, presses it through a sieve of history, fairy tales, myth and literary allusion, mixes in a little social criticism and a lot of humor, and then shakes it to a froth on some other level of time and space. In that sense, ***Sexing the Cherry*** is Winterson's most ambitious creation so far. If some of its obsessions and imagery are familiar from her earlier works—discussions on the nature of time, gender and love, God, strong mothers, an affection for dogs, not to mention the use of fruit as a metaphor for the alien, the exotic or the sexually different—it is also her most metaphysical work, the furthest removed from conventional narrative and the most angrily political in tone. It is never heavy-handed, though, as Winterson charms the reader into accepting difficult concepts, like murder for revenge.

Set in two time periods—seventeenth-century Britain and the present day—***Sexing the Cherry*** is devoted to the adventures of the Dog Woman and her foundling son, Jordan, whom she fished like Moses from "the stinking Thames" and named for the biblical river. The Dog Woman (as her name suggests) breeds dogs. She is a giantess—so heavy that as a child she broke both her father's legs when she sat in his lap, and so ugly that when once she asked a man to kiss her, he fainted. But she is also brave and earthy, with a strong personal moral code and a disdain for the hypocritical, sexually repressed Puritans with whom she does battle and sometimes kills. Jordan is the opposite, a dreamy 19-year-old who travels with the King's gardener to exotic parts of the world in search of rare plant specimens and adventure. He learns about the grafting of cherry trees (hence the title) and later brings back the pineapple to the court of Charles II. The final quarter of the book introduces Jordan and the Dog Woman's modern alter egos: Nicholas Jordan, another sensitive youth, who joins the navy to be a hero; and a young female scientist conducting a one-woman protest against mercury pollution of the country's waterways.

This is the plot, but—this being a Winterson novel—only half the story. Fact and fantasy blur; the two time periods bump against each other. It's not even clear whether Jordan and the Dog Woman are real or fantasies in the minds of the modern characters. "I don't know if other worlds exist in space or time," says the scientist. "Perhaps this is the only one and the rest is rich imaginings. Either way it doesn't matter. We have to protect both possibilities."

That sense of possibility, the power of the imagination and where it can take us, is the sinew that binds the various episodes of the book together. Through Jordan's inner explorations and the Dog Woman's more concrete adventures, Winterson preaches free thought, unhampered by old assumptions. When a Royalist urges the Dog Woman to heed the Old Testament saying "An eye for an eye, a tooth for a tooth," she takes him seriously and amasses a sackful of both—from narrow-minded Puritans who give her trouble. In a brothel, she does further gory damage to those hypocritical clients who chastely make love to their wives through a hole in the sheet at home and then creep after prostitutes for their real sexual pleasure.

Jordan, meanwhile, tells of a city without gravity that sails above the earth, and the twelve dancing princesses who visit it secretly at night, floating upward through their windows. During the day they disguise their ability to float by wearing long gowns. But their father finds them out and, because he wants to marry them off to twelve princes, chains them all up by the ankle. Later, the princesses do live happily ever after, "but not with [their] husbands."

As Jordan continues his inner journey it becomes clear that to think freely he must have a strong sense of self, though at first he sees it as a quest for love. He falls for the youngest princess, a dancer, who unlike her sisters managed to escape marriage. But does she really exist? It's most likely that she too is a figment of his imagination, or even an aspect of himself. (pp. 64-5)

Ultimately, the characters in *Sexing the Cherry*, though powerfully described, are not people in a real sense but states of being. To be complete, either as men or women, Winterson seems to say, we need both the courage and directed anger of the Dog Woman and the imaginative powers and sensitivity of Jordan—as in the process of grafting, "whereby a plant, perhaps tender or uncertain, is fused into a hardier member of its strain . . . [to] produce a third kind, without seed or parent."

If Winterson's ideas don't always soar as high as her imagination, she is more than saved by fine, clean writing, a clear vision, an earthy sense of humor and the wisdom to see there are no easy solutions, no sure happiness. There is only the search for it. "How vast it all is, this matter of the mind," says Jordan. "Each journey conceals another journey within its lines: the path not taken and the forgotten angle. These are the journeys I wish to record." (p. 65)

> Charlotte Innes, "Rich Imaginings," in The Nation, New York, Vol. 251, No. 2, July 9, 1990, pp. 64-5.

**Rosellen Brown**

Here is a son describing his mother. It's surely a familiar picture. She "cares nothing for how she looks, only for what she does. She has never been in love, no, and never wanted to be either. She is self-sufficient and without self-doubt." A successful MBA, perhaps? A lawyer or some other frequent flyer and board-room familiar too busy for romance?

Not exactly. The book is Jeanette Winterson's *Sexing the Cherry;* the speaker is Jordan, a foundling boy pulled up from, then named for, a river, whose apparently self-sufficient mother turns out to be a giantess of fabulous size and might and appetite who lives alone with fifty dogs. This is the seventeenth century, the reign of Charles II, a time of Papists and Puritans, and all of England is in an ugly turmoil. In a time of uncivilized excess, the Dog Woman, who can (and must) dish out violence with the force of an army, accomplishes mythic defenses: at one point she plucks a musket ball out of her cleavage and complains that it's spoiled her best dress; later, simultaneously a sympathetic and a synthetic character, she plucks out 119 of her political enemies' eyeballs and severs heads (among other extremities) without regret. Given her rather indelicate physique, it is not surprising that she prefers the sins of excess to those of denial, and chastises the Puritans for denying the flesh. "Their women bind their breasts and cook plain food without salt, and the men are

so afraid of their member uprising that they keep it strapped between their legs with bandages."

But she is not, in fact, as self-sufficient as her size and bluster make her seem. For all that she may repulse the world with her ugliness, Dog Woman has a touching vulnerability, even a shred of vanity. Wearing a dress "with a wide skirt that would serve as a sail for some war-torn ship," and a dozen blankets sewn together for a shawl, she remarks that "despite my handicap, I cut something of a fine figure, I thought." Contrary to what her son thinks, she has loved—once only, with humiliating consequences—and now her heart belongs only to him. But even if he were to recognize that, it's clear he'd go on about his business of independence just the same.

Because, in spite of a story and structure that play wonderfully fast and loose with history, that take great delight (as do Winterson's previous novels) in devising occasions for cross-dressing, and in imagining a catalogue of violent rapes and reprisals common to their ribald age, the emotional duties of the sexes are at bottom nearly as traditional as Danielle Steel's: women lose and long for their children while young men break free to sail forth in search of love and adventure and, if they dare, themselves. Even the Dog Woman, imagining the instructions she owes her son, realizes that although she and the other women in her story tend rather casually to menace or detach the penises forever aimed in their directions, biting and chopping their way to safety, in fact the intimate organ he most needs to be warned to protect is his *heart*. Under layers of fetching embroidery Winterson is hiding an ancient, even sentimental, tale, a picaresque search for differing kinds of love.

While his mother stays at home in a country of stinking slums, brothels, wamps and violent politics, Jordan sails forth and almost instantly glimpses his ideal (of course from afar), a dancer named Fortunata who turns out to be one of the Twelve Dancing Princesses. Bitter though she was, even Anne Sexton never extended her continuing fairy tales to include the indignities and viciousness of the Princesses' forced marriages to these nightmare princes. One by one they tell their parodic stories: "That's my last husband painted on the wall . . . " "He walked in beauty . . . " There is a mermaid, there is Rapunzel, there is the Prince kissed into a frog. The long file of disappointed women displays their fates, many of which involve inspired and ugly violence against their horrific husbands, whose sins make a mighty contemporary music. Then, since this is a story of wish as well as self-fulfillment, they spin out their dreams of repair: to live happily with women, or alone, or to rejoin their sisters.

The Dancing Princesses become an emblem for Jordan's quest: since he is "giving (himself) the slip," journeying around the world obsessed with self-discovery, they represent his own slippery movement. They steal out to dance with abandon every night and return every morning with no memory of where they've been. Jordan, dragged up from a slimy river, is desperate to see who he was and who he might yet turn out to be, and knows he won't remember the half of it.

No identity is fixed in Jeanette Winterson's work. Disguises abound. Again the conventions of earlier centuries proved useful here, their socially approved evasions, their masks and cloaks and ill-lit spaces in which no one is easy to identify. In *Sexing the Cherry* both the banana and then the pineapple are first brought to England. (The former, Dog Woman thinks, resembles "the private parts of an Oriental.") Jordan learns from a master-botanist/adventurer the art of grafting, of combining strengths, and "wondered whether it was an art I might apply to myself," though "there are many in the church who condemn this practice as unnatural, holding that the Lord who made the world made its flora as he wished and in no other way." Thus he can graft two kinds of cherry and choose what sex to call the result; of course it is female.

Just as in Winterson's earlier *The Passion,* where Napoleon's Josephine brings the geranium to France, hybrids, changes, new forms, fluid boundaries, all are joyfully entertained as enrichments and improvements. *Oranges Are Not the Only Fruit* (an assertion attributed to Nell Gwyn), Winterson's first book, a vivid and funny and surprisingly good-natured autobiographical novel, puts forth fruit as the same symbol of sweet, strange, fleshy but satisfying novelty. (pp. 9-10)

Winterson's novels are rich and beguiling stuff, complex and exquisitely written and full of useful manipulations of history. It is impossible to read plummy prose like hers at this moment of flat-earth minimalism without rejoicing in its rhythm and daring leaps of allusiveness, if nothing else. Her didacticism, especially about boundarylessness— "Time has no meaning, space and place have no meaning . . . The journey is not linear, it is always back and forth, denying the calendar, the wrinkles and lines of the body"—would be harder to take, with its tinge of Shirley MacLaine optimism, if it weren't for the sheer joy and music of her sentences. ("In a single day the mind can make a millpond of the ocean.")

Michael Gorra, writing in the *New York Times,* sees Winterson with perfect clarity as a graft, with its own distinctive taste, of Angela Carter and Italo Calvino [see Gorra's excerpt]. Winterson, for example, dreams up a scheme whereby, to escape their creditors, people knock down their houses in a single night and rebuild them elsewhere; another family lives suspended over a pit, all their furniture held up on winches, "celebrating ceilings but denying floors." In this world of the willful, "for the people who had abandoned gravity, gravity had abandoned them." These could be newly dug-up chapters of Calvino's *Invisible Cities.*

To be honest, I found myself a good deal less than compelled by the intellectual schema of *Sexing the Cherry,* which ends by transforming Jordan, eddied forward in the flux of time, into a twentieth-century London adolescent

with an environmentalist's yen to save the Thames from mercury contamination. All times and identities run together in the final pages and exaggerate the inspired arbitrariness of much of Winterson's concoction.

If there is anything vaguely unsettling about this endlessly inventive fabulist's dreaming (though I can imagine this would endear it to many), it is the element of loosely cloaked in-joke wish-fulfillment that rides so near the surface. Granted, every writer creates characters and stories to play out inchoate fantasies and preoccupations of many kinds—memories worth revisiting, unresolved psychic wounds, a search for another way to ease conflicts. But Winterson plays out her vengeful hostility to men and marriage, her fascination with androgyny, and her compensatory vision of women as the stronger, more sane and even physically dominating sex, with an insistence that often makes her stories feel like pretexts.

For all their sensual luxe, these books are indeed, in the end, the creations of an Evangelical missionary's daughter. Though she may ice her cake with irresistible detail and nearly flawless prose, there is an obsessive (that is to say, compelled) quality to what lies beneath: I keep getting the feeling that, like one of her own characters perhaps, a sort of baker in red shoes, Winterson is driven to bake this cake—laced with the arsenic of sexual retribution but sweetened to go down with pleasure—over and over again.

But that pleasure is enormous; let my quibbles slow no one down on her way to the bookstore. Jeanette Winterson is the best relief we've had from a deadpan recitation of Life As It Is and Ever More Must Be since pineapples and cherries came to England, sweet, sour and dangerous with spines and pits to keep the careless on their guard. (p. 10)

*Rosellen Brown, "Fertile Imagination," in* The Women's Review of Books, *Vol. VII, No. 12, September, 1990, pp. 9-10.*

---

## FURTHER READING

Anshaw, Carol. "Fantastic Voyage." *The Village Voice Literary Supplement,* No. 86 (June 1990): 17.

    Interview focusing on Winterson's themes and her goals as a writer.

Marvel, Mark. "Jeanette Winterson: Trust Me. I'm Telling You Stories." *Interview* XX, No. 10 (October 1990): 162, 168.

    Interview concerning Winterson's personal life and past experiences, and their influence on her writing.

# Tobias Wolff

## 1945-

(Full name Tobias Jonathan Ansell Wolff) American short story writer, novelist, memoirist, editor, and journalist.

Wolff's understated, lyrical prose illuminates critical points in the lives of characters who discover flaws in the value system that has guided them. Often compared to works by Raymond Carver and Ann Beattie, Wolff's fiction features stark, ambivalent portrayals of contemporary existence. Wolff's works are often humorous and piercing exposés of hypocrisy; his characters—ranging from a young boy to an elderly married couple and soldiers in the Vietnam War—are generally failures, people with unfulfilled hopes whose loneliness leads them to behave dishonorably. While some critics fault Wolff for failing to resolve his plots, others commend his portrayal of the perpetual quest for order or purpose in human life.

*In the Garden of the North American Martyrs,* Wolff's highly praised first publication, contains twelve stories that focus upon lonely characters facing the consequences of past decisions. In the title story, an overly obsequious university teacher is interviewed for a position at a prestigious college in the East. When she discovers that she was never under serious consideration for the opening, she speaks out eloquently and controversially for the first time in her career. In "An Episode in the Life of Professor Brooke," a man discovers how far removed his values are from those of most people, and that he is unable to positively affect the lives of others through his work in academia. "Face to Face" depicts the failure of a romantic weekend vacation for a couple increasingly isolated from each other. Critics commended these stories for the wealth of metaphorical meaning beneath simple, natural language. Welch D. Everman commented: "Through these gracefully evoked tales, Wolff touches the heart of the human condition and speaks in a voice that is sincere, original yet familiar—a voice that sounds as if it must last."

Wolff's next publication, *The Barracks Thief,* concerns three American paratroopers stationed in North Carolina during the Vietnam War; they bond together through a shared temptation to allow an approaching forest fire to consume the ammunition dump they are guarding. Told retrospectively by a soldier named Bishop, *The Barracks Thief* explores the question of whether it is better to die young and tragically or to live a long, but dull, conventional life. Walter Kendrick remarked: "[The pathos of these people] resides in the way they blunder from one mistake to another, ignorant of their own motives and blind to consequences. . . . Mr. Wolff has boundless tolerance for the stupid sorrow of ordinary human entanglements." *The Barracks Thief* won the prestigious PEN/Faulkner Award for fiction in 1984.

*Back in the World,* Wolff's second collection of short fic-

tion, takes its title from the hopes of American Vietnam War veterans for clarity and purpose after their tour of duty. Other stories include "Coming Attractions," featuring a lonely 15-year-old girl who makes phone calls that reveal her lack of close relationships, even among her family. "The Missing Person" is a comical story concerning Father Leo, whose failures include his latest assignment at a parish that has little use for his spiritual guidance. In general, Wolff's stories include a character whose circumstances lead him or her to dissembling as a way of creating a new self or revealing hidden truths. Critics laud Wolff's inclusion of idiosyncratic, naturalistic details and his insight into the lives of a diverse range of characters.

*This Boy's Life: A Memoir* recounts Wolff's life from age ten, when he and his mother traveled from Florida to Utah, until he joined the Army as a young man. His experiences living with his mother and abusive step-father in Seattle, Washington, in the 1950s form the majority of the narrative. His unhappiness and feelings of powerlessness led the young Wolff to lying and petty thievery as a means for rebelling against his unreasonably strict step-father. *This Boy's Life* was most often compared with *The Duke of Deception,* the highly regarded memoirs of Wolff's brother Geoffrey. Both works are respected for their humorous, affectionate portrayal of less-than-ideal childhood experiences. Joel Conarroe commented: "[*This Boy's Life*] is literate and consistently entertaining—and richer, darker, and funnier than anything else Tobias Wolff has written."

(See also *CLC,* Vol. 39; and *Contemporary Authors* Vols. 114, 117.)

## PRINCIPAL WORKS

*In the Garden of the North American Martyrs* 1981 (short fiction)
*The Barracks Thief* 1984 (novel)
*Back in the World* 1985 (short fiction)
*This Boy's Life: A Memoir* 1989 (autobiography)

---

## James C. Dolan

If you're braced for stomach-wrenching tales of bloody disfigurement, relax and enter into the sometimes comic, always compassionate world of ordinary people who suffer twentieth-century martyrdoms of growing up, growing old, loving and lacking love, living with parents and lovers and wives and their own weaknesses. You can dig deep in Wolff's garden—if I might be forgiven playing with the title's metaphor; the twelve short stories in this fine collection [*In the Garden of the North American Martyrs*] ask for and surely reward re-reading.

One test of the great short-story writer is his ability to convince the reader of the "actuality" of his characters and of the world they inhabit in the fewest possible words: the telling detail that puts you there, the dialogue that evokes the subtle shadings of a real personality. Wolff has such an unerring eye, such a finely tuned ear that you will find yourself wanting to buttonhole friends to read them lines like: the middle-aged housewife in **"Next Door,"** threatened by yet another disturbance of her passionate neighbors, who says, "Maybe there's something on TV . . . See who's on Johnny." Or the aging hippie hitchhiker in **"Passengers"** who accosts her driver with, "I'm hungry, . . . let's score some pancakes." Or the commune dwellers in **"Poaching"** who argue over child care, cooking, and the "careless use of someone's Deutschegrammophon records."

Although Wolff focuses our attention, as a writer must, on the problematic experiences of his characters, there abides behind them for the reader an intuition of hope, the promise of the garden of the title. Wolff suggests an enveloping sense of a higher plane of values, something in terms of which his characters (or we) can bear their "martyrdoms." . . .

These stories are beautifully but unobtrusively crafted, both individually and as a group, to be what they so palpably are, yet to point beyond themselves—small victories, I suggest, of and for the imagination.

*James C. Dolan, in a review of "In the Garden of the North American Martyrs," in* Best Sellers, *Vol. 41, No. 8, November, 1981, p. 293.*

## Le Anne Schreiber

[*In the Garden of the North American Martyrs*], his first book, Tobias Wolff avoids the emotional and stylistic monotone that constricts so many collections of contemporary short stories. His range, sometimes within the same story, extends from fastidious realism to the grotesque and the lyrical. In these 12 stories, Wolff's characters include a teen-age boy who becomes a compulsive liar on the day his father dies, an elderly couple who try to maintain their dignity despite the travesties of a golden anniversary love cruise, and an obese man whose surreptitious eating makes him feel as duplicitous as a spy. He allows these characters scenes of flamboyant madness as well as quiet desperation, moments of slap-happiness as well as muted contentment.

At the end of **"Face to Face,"** a man and a woman drive home in silence after a weekend spent in the country "getting to know each other." He nurses a baffled sense of injury over her sexual unresponsiveness. She barely understands that she has just endured the kind of unconscious sexual sadism that might have been expected from someone who begins too many sentences with "You women." **"Face to Face"** is one of the most distressing things I have ever read. And it takes the precise measure of an emotion so familiar to women and yet so elusive that I imagine few have been able to articulate it to themselves, much less communicate it to a man. (p. 11)

Tobias Wolff risks every kind of ending, and that perhaps is the surest sign of a storyteller who is willing to stretch his talent. The extent of that talent is most apparent in **"An Episode in the Life of Professor Brooke."** Wolff begins with a description of one English professor observing another at church and contemplating the distaste he feels for his colleague whenever "the handlebars of his unnecessarily large moustache come into view." Within a few sentences you've developed a fix on both characters and start to anticipate the process of having all your presumptions confirmed by a steady accumulation of incriminating details—which, after all, is usually one of the more considerable satisfactions of tightly controlled fiction and closely observed life. But then Wolff begins to undermine our complacency of response. Because part of what he is up to in this unsettling collection is demonstrating how slippery the matter of passing judgment, moral or esthetic, can be.

The case at hand is Professor Brooke, a vigilantly moral man, so attuned to the possible consequences of conduct that he has become a seasoned connoisseur of unkindness. (And since much of this story is set at a regional Modern Language Association conference, the observable forms of turpitude are many and various.) When Brooke unwittingly embarrasses a woman from the local literary society by making fun of the little pennants with quotations from Bartlett's that she has stuck in the sandwiches on the M.L.A. refreshment table, he knows he has amends to make. And in his desire for expiation, he blunders into a one-night romance so incongruous and touching that one's sympathies ricochet back and forth with each line of dialogue:

> "I believe in being honest," Ruth said.
>
> "So do I," Brooke said, thinking that she was going to tell him about a boy friend or fiancé. He hoped so.
>
> Ruth said nothing. Instead she brought both of her hands up to her hair and lifted it off like a hat. . . . Ruth put the wig on a plaster bust that stood between a camel saddle and some foreign dolls on her bric-a-brac shelf. Then she faced Brooke. "Do you mind?" she asked. . . .
>
> "You look fine to me," Brooke said. "Exotic."
>
> "You think so? Well, frankly, I'd rather have hair. I got pretty sick a few years ago and this is all I had left. . . . Do you know 'Sunrise near Monterey'?"
>
> "Vaguely," Brooke said. He remembered that [the poem] ended with the command "Embrace!" He had thought it silly.
>
> "That was the first poem I read," Ruth said. "When I got to the end I read it again and again and I just knew I was going to live. And here I am."
>
> "You should write Dillon and tell him that."
>
> "I did. I made up a poem and sent it to him."
>
> . . . She began to recite [her poem] from memory. Brooke nodded to the beat, which was forced and obvious. He barely heard the words. He was thinking that nothing he had ever thought or said could make a woman want to live again. "That was beautiful," he said. . . .
>
> (pp. 11, 20)

Returning home the next day, Brooke decides to spare his wife knowledge of this evening.

> And Brooke's wife, unpacking his clothes, smelled perfume on his necktie. . . . There had to be an explanation, but no matter how long she sat on the edge of the bed and held her head in her hands and rocked back and forth she could not imagine what it might be. And her husband was so much himself that night, so merry and warm, that she felt unworthy of him. The doubt passed from her mind to her body; it became one of those flutters that stops you cold from time to time for a few years, and then goes away.

**"An Episode in the Life of Professor Brooke"** is 16 pages long, and it offers more complete satisfactions than most novels. There are five characters who take on a reality that lingers longer than the story does, including Brooke's wife, who has only that one, last, unspeakably sad paragraph. Some stories, like this one, unfold over hours; others span 20 years in as few pages, but Wolff's vision is so acute and his talent so refined that none of them seems sketchy. (p. 20)

*Le Anne Schreiber, "Controlled Fiction and Reckless Endings," in* The New York Times Book Review, *November 15, 1981, pp. 11, 20.*

**Brina Caplan**

As steel vaporizes in a beam of laser light, the substance of experience disintegrates when subjected to radical skepticism. Our conceptions of reality could be psychic inventions, the skeptic argues, neither more nor less so than our dreams. However much we protest this argument, we find it difficult to refute. No logical system finally establishes the distinction we make intuitively, at least when awake, between reality and dream. Worse, no formal reasoning proves that our mental reconstructions of the world—our images, symbols, languages—actually tell us about the world instead of, at best, about their own rules of order.

If our experiences and perceptions are simply exercises in self-reference, how much less reflective of reality must be the experiences and perceptions of characters in fiction, who are by definition illusions without existence beyond the printed page. Indeed, deconstructionist critics, viewing fiction in this light, see in it linguistic events rather than meaningful projections of reality and overhear a kind of speech that comments only on itself. The language—not the author—writes the text, they tell us; fiction is the set of changes possible in a self-enclosed system that, like a Rubik's cube, is at once variable and rigidly bound.

Although radical skepticism cannot be formally refuted, it can be opposed. Rather than academic polemicists or philosophers, however, the most convincing defenders of storytelling as an interpretive art are contemporary writers whose careful representation of detail implies that words mirror reality. Against a denial of all truth, they pit individual truths; against the impossibility of general meaning, they set the meaningfulness of small details—apparel, gestures, impulses, the individual character of human voices. Significant experience emerges, they assume, when the storyteller selects from an infinity of disparate and random possible events those that constitute a pattern of living. As the title of a Wallace Stevens poem has it, such writers pursue a knowledge of the world by following out "The Course of a Particular." (p. 152)

In realistic fiction, events do not speak for themselves; they require both a shaping grammar that controls incident and explains the convergence of circumstance and personal necessity. . . . Tobias Wolff scrutinizes the disorder of daily living to find significant order; in the best of the stories collected under the title ***In the Garden of the North American Martyrs,*** he informs us not only of what happened but of why it had to happen as it did.

His characters are various: a prep school freshman; a young mother deserted by her husband; a businessman with a precarious hold on his conscience and his job; an old couple defending property and propriety against obtrusive neighbors; a middle-aged Southerner uncertainly transplanted to a large Northern city. Distant in age, class and geography, these people have in common lives crowded with the results of previous choices. Amid possessions and routines, they pause before decisions that may fulfill their lives or merely clutter them further.

The heroine of ["**In the Garden of the North American Martyrs**"] finds herself making a decision of this sort at a time when circumstances have limited her possibilities to the bleak or the ridiculous. A teacher for fifteen years, Mary stabilized her academic career through extreme caution:

> Now and then she wondered whether she had been too careful. The things she said and wrote seemed flat to her, pulpy, as though someone else had squeezed the juice out of them. And once, while talking with a senior professor, Mary saw herself reflected in a window; she was leaning toward him and had her head turned so that her ear was right in front of his moving mouth. The sight disgusted her. Years later, when she had to get a hearing aid, Mary suspected that her deafness was a result of always trying to catch everything everyone said.

Even though bankruptcy closes the college and forces her to accept exile, lecturing to the fog-bound in a dank, obscure corner of Oregon, compliance still seems to Mary the appropriate course. Indeed, remembering her accommodating manner, a former colleague, a woman not known for impulsive generosity, invites her to interview for a job back East at her own urbane and sunny institution.

Not only compared with the dismal conditions of Mary's current job but in itself, the college seems perfect: "It looked so much like a college that movie-makers sometimes used it as a set. *Andy Hardy Goes to College* had been filmed there." Yet, during her visit, Mary detects something amiss. Her host and former colleague, Louise, refuses to discuss job prospects and monopolizes their conversations with complaints about her love life—mentioning only casually and at the last moment that Mary must address a formal assembly of faculty and students. In turn, the department chairman avoids the subject of her qualifications to opine instead about the local weather: " 'Of course it snows here, and you have your rain now and then, but it's a *dry* rain.' " Other members of the department do not speak to her at all. The mystery remains unresolved until Mary's tour of the campus confronts her with the power-plant dynamo; there, in "the depths of the service building" before the vast, humming machine, her student-guide explains,

> "People think the college is really old-fashioned . . . but it isn't. They let girls come here now, and some of the teachers are women. In fact, there's a statute that says they have to interview at least one woman for each opening."

No matter how successful her lecture, she is without hope, "brought here to satisfy a rule."

She speaks as scheduled—though not as planned—in the first authentic act of her academic career. Her lecture is spontaneous, visionary, lyric and simultaneously absurd; like a cog thrown into the works, Mary's pronouncements on justice and love disorder the machinery of expectation. (When distressed faculty members shout from the audience to quiet her, she avoids distraction by turning off her

hearing aid.) Her moment of private deliverance is, of course, also a moment of public farce; **"In the Garden of the North American Martyrs"** does not glorify spontaneity or suggest that moral choice dissolves the conditions that provoke it. Mary's story and the collection of stories that share its title make a claim far less optimistic: there is, Wolff implies, no such thing as meaningless choice. Every decision emerges from a consciousness which it both expresses and modifies. In fact, a hardened core of habits, old compromises and pragmatic adjustments continues to support a structure that, at its living edges, can reshape or extend itself in surprising ways.

Not every story makes the point convincingly, however. The hazard of realistic fiction lies in its engagement with surfaces, and at times Wolff evokes situations with a skill that verges on facility. **"Smokers,"** for example, offers a too-easy condemnation of adolescent social-climbing, while **"Worldly Goods"** teases at but does not unravel the complexities of a peculiarly self-isolated Southerner. In both cases, mirroring events has become an end in itself, and the result is sterile flashes of likeness. But when he chooses to, Wolff can do more than find the words for things; at his best, he can use words to test lives against accidental and self-selected conditions. When he concentrates on the interpenetration of mind and circumstance, then his perspective—however trivial the situation or purposefully alien the character—fixes our attention; for there the mirror has become a microscope and, in the words of Wallace Stevens, "Life's nonsense pierces us with strange relation." (pp. 154-55)

*Brina Caplan, "Particular Truths," in* The Nation, *New York, Vol. 234, No. 5, February 6, 1982, pp. 152-55.*

**Welch D. Everman**

*In the Garden of the North American Martyrs* is Tobias Wolff's stunning first collection of short fiction. Through these gracefully evoked tales, Wolff touches the heart of the human condition and speaks in a voice that is sincere, original yet familiar—a voice that sounds as if it must last.

His careful, simple prose style is often deceptive. His stories' complex levels of meaning are covered by a delicate veneer. His metaphors reach deep into the imagination. In **"Next Door,"** Wolff moves subtly in and out of the lives of his character. The sounds of domestic intranquility coming from next door lead the main character to think about other proximities, other geographies, which include the body of his invalid wife. He begins to think about those places that are not on the map, lost cities, "white trees in a land where no one has ever been." Perhaps all of these are really no further away from him than next door.

The characters on whom Wolff focuses manage to gain our sympathies, but slowly, slowly, Wolff reveals them to themselves and then to us. A pair of hunters let their wounded friend bleed and freeze as they expose their own pathetic selves to each other, lose track of themselves, and make a wrong turn on their way to the hospital. An English professor, entering the world of guilt and sorrow, is genuinely touched by a woman, hairless from chemotherapy treatments. He is moved that her life has been somehow saved by a poem (by a McKuenesque poet) that had given her the strength to survive. His experience challenges his own way of thinking, his own habit of passing judgments on other people, until he must become the one "to sit in the front of the church" and be watched by others. Wolff's characters, like the nameless narrator of **"Smokers,"** are "those who knew that something was wrong but didn't know what it was."

The author does not moralize, though his concerns are usually moral in nature. His characters are Every-men, like Davis in the brilliant story, **"Worldly Goods."** Davis, victimized in a harmless automobile accident, must deal with a claims adjuster, a modern version of Knowledge, who gives Davis the kind of advice he will need to get by in the world, that is, to screw before he himself is screwed. Davis stands on moral principle, but that is not enough. A friend tells him, "Nothing is good enough for you." Davis cannot see beyond the surface issues: he will drive his life the way he resolves to drive his maimed automobile "the way it was until it fell apart." And, ironically, his car is stolen from him, the way all our worldly goods are, in time, taken from us. In **"Passengers,"** this theme is reprised once again: if a person must change his ways, what if he "wasn't sure just what was wrong with his ways?" We may admire the heroine's ability to see through her pathetic lover in **"Face to Face,"** but what she sees never really goes beyond the heart of pity. We know that she is coming face to face with herself, deciding, as her lover has, "always to be alone." But does she know this? It is a process, writes Wolff, that might "take forever." For characters who can never "imagine things coming together," conversely, they must see things "always falling apart." How difficultly or belatedly they will come to know (as Vernon does in **"Poaching"**) if ever they have "been offered an olive branch and were not far from home."

So "Mend your lives." "Turn from power to love," the feeble history teacher of the title story advises us. And Wolff responds poetically: how do we do so in a world where our own hands seem to be things we are holding for someone else? To protect us is the insulating power of lies. As Wolff demonstrates in **"The Liar,"** lies, like fictions, sometimes bring people closer to the truths—in this case, that people do have something in common with each other in their relishing of lies *and* in their loathing of lies—"a shared fear."

Many of the stories of *In the Garden of the North American Martyrs* end on an introspective note. The narratives filter down to a moment alone with a character, who may be sitting alone in a closet, smoking a joint or lying on a blanket, dreaming up at the stars or lecturing passionately but with her hearing aid turned off. There they reflect and, maybe, learn. To us, they are speccks on a large photograph that, when enlarged, reveals expressions on faces that are troubling, fearful, and human.

*Welch D. Everman, in a review of "In the Garden of the North American Martyrs," in* The North American Review, *Vol. 267, No. 2, June, 1982, p. 60.*

**Dean Flower**

Tobias Wolff's short stories [collected in *In the Garden of the North American Martyrs*] depend so heavily on dialogue and limited points of view that they remind me of the early J. D. Salinger. Wolff has a fine ear for the clichés of hippie wisdom, the jargon of academic types, the formulas of parental criticism, and the evasions of the unhappily married. Children appear frequently in these stories, but the focus is more often on insecure and immature adults. The effect is less Salinger than, say, Raymond Carver, with its special emphasis on passivity and sublimation. Several of the stories are a delight to read aloud, notably **"Passengers,"** about a nervous young man who picks up a girl hitchhiking with guitar and large hairy dog, and **"The Liar,"** about a boy who fends off the world by his compulsive and usually morbid lying. But the immediately engaging and winning manner of Wolff's colloquial technique is deceptive. These stories repeatedly turn on moments of cruelty, cowardice, and impure guilt.

**"Hunters in the Snow"** features the sadistic Kenny, who teases his fat friend Tub to the breaking point, gets himself shot in the stomach, and spends the rest of the story bounced around in the rear of a pickup truck on the way to a hospital they never reach. The third hunter is Frank, a typical Wolff character in that he fails to take any stand, siding with Kenny at first and getting drunk with Tub later, apparently because the confusions of his personal life (an affair with the babysitter) have made him covertly vengeful. **"An Episode in the Life of Professor Brook"** exposes the cruelty of a young English professor who cuts down a fellow scholar in a panel discussion and then indulges himself in an overnight romance with an ignorant young poetess. Wolff charts this progression from unconscious arrogance to uneasy guilt to self-pity and deception so believably that you wonder at the end why anyone ever thought the humanities made people humane. In the title story a woman who teaches history at a West Coast college is flown to an eastern university for a job interview, only to learn that the position isn't open and she must deliver a lecture (not her own) to complete the charade of a "nationwide search." Instead of the canned lecture, however, she improvises from her research in American history a hair-raising account of how the Iroquois tormented their captives with red-hot hatchets, pitch, and boiling water. We are left in no doubt about who in the lecture room are the Iroquois and who is the captive martyr; but the stinging justice of her tirade only intensifies her hopeless position. The recurring predicament of a Wolff character seems to be fear of the self: fear of sexual aggression, of betraying half-hearted loyalties, of asserting authority. Between cruelties and fears, Wolff doesn't leave us enough to choose. He has narrowed his vision so far as to suggest gratuitous cruelty, and that needs to be tempered. (pp. 278-79)

*Dean Flower, in a review of "In the Garden of the North American Martyrs," in* The Hudson Review, *Vol. XXXV, No. 2, Summer, 1982, pp. 278-79.*

## Thomas Sutcliffe

Short stories are sometimes referred to as if they were an endangered species, urgently in need of acts of conservation by well-disposed publishers and fiction editors who can commission collections and anthologies. Reading *Hunters in the Snow* it is hard not to feel that in some cases benign neglect might be a more effective policy, leaving the genre to work out its own survival in the environment of glossy monthlies and literary reviews. It isn't that Tobias Wolff's collection contains a single story that shouldn't have been published at some time, somewhere. His melancholy and regretful accounts of the hazards of sociable solitude and the pitfalls of the urbane jungle might have contrasted well with the sophisticated enthusiasms of *Tri-Quarterly* or *Vogue*. A story about social emulation in an American prep school probably sounded an effective dissonance when printed in *Atlantic Monthly,* just as an account of the humiliations of the academic life would have an extra edge for the readership of *Anteus*. But when they are removed from their natural habitat, the effect of the stories is increasingly dispiriting; reading them is like touring a menagerie in which the cages all contain the same restless, morose animal.

None of Wolff's characters is really happy, and by and large they seem to be unhappy for similar reasons; loneliness, a vagueness about the best way to behave, and continuing distress at the inefficiency of mere politeness as a means of doing good. They resign themselves to their inertia, to grey fates dictated by other people's expectations and the consequences of decisions already taken. The prevailing conditions are gloomy and overcast, with intermittent rain and occasional mist.

In **"An Episode in the Life of Professor Brooke"** an inoffensive and honourable academic exposes himself to the conspiratorial solidarity of a disliked colleague after an innocent adventure at a literary seminar away from home. All his difficulties come about as a result of his desire not to hurt feelings. He tells his wife nothing, suffering his own deceit in order to spare her, but she smells perfume on his shirt; an unhappiness is compounded out of inexplicable circumstances and her justified faith in her husband's fidelity. . . . In **"Maiden Voyage"** an elderly man, dourly celebrating the golden anniversary of a routine marriage on a cruise, resists the relentless conviviality of the social director—a man who uses sentiment like Chemical Mace to bring his charges into line. For Tweed love is "the artillery of heaven. If two individuals can stock up a century of love between them, well as far as I personally am concerned the smartalecks will just have to go on home and think of something else to try and make us give up on." Called upon to explain the secret of his marriage, the old man himself offers a smartaleck reply: "Nothing to it. You just go from day to day and before you know it fifty years are up."

This philosophy of stolid impermeability is offered as one of the better resources for dealing with the world, and moments when the cloud lifts are seen either as bogus or simply illusory. The rain might get warmer for a while (it is actually described as doing this in one story) but it isn't going to stop. Wolff's characters would exact our pity if

there wasn't such a strong suggestion that pity could go off in our faces, that it is a condescending and unperceptive emotion which fails to take account of our own pitifulness. In the end it is hard not to feel a sense of downhearted acquiescence in the baleful spirit of the stories.

Perhaps this is just repeating the naive complaint of the widowed mother in **"The Liar"**, one of the best stories in the book. She is worried by her youngest son's compulsion to tell stories of appalling domestic tragedy to any stranger prepared to listen. It isn't just the lies that worry her, but their morbidity; for her the invention of misery is a poor addition to the world and a disturbance to be cured. (Told that the boy will outgrow this phase she asks "What if he doesn't. What if he just gets better at it?" (One answer would be that he will stop giving them to strangers for free, and with a bit of parental encouragement might, like Wolff, win an O. Henry prize and a grant from the National Endowment of Arts.)

Thomas Sutcliffe, "Things Falling Apart," in The Times Literary Supplement, No. 4137, July 30, 1982, p. 815.

## Michiko Kakutani

"We used to talk about how when we got back in the world we were going to do this and we were going to do that," says a character in one of Tobias Wolff's fine, angular stories. "Back in the world we were going to have it made. But ever since then it's been nothing but confusion." Though this happens to be a Vietnam veteran talking about the disillusion he experienced on returning home after the war, he might well be speaking for any one of Mr. Wolff's disaffected heroes. Frustrated, lonely and divorced from their youthful expectations, [the characters in *Back in the World* ] all drift through the present, trying to get by day to day, by telling assorted stories and lies. For them, as for Mr. Wolff lying—in this case, fiction-making—represents a way of imposing a narrative order on their lives, as well as a means of connecting with others and with their receding dreams.

Hooper, the hero of **"Soldier's Joy,"** considers making up a story about himself, so as to help comfort a distraught soldier in his command. And in **"The Missing Person"** a shabby priest concocts an outrageous tale about killing a man—just in order to have something to share with his new friend, a fast-talking con man with lots of tall tales about his past. Father Leo, writes Mr. Wolff, "believed about half of what he heard. That was fine with him. He didn't mind having his leg pulled. He thought it was the sort of thing men did in lumber camps and on ships— sitting around, swapping lies."

Jean, the 15-year-old shoplifter in **"Coming Attractions,"** lies to ward off boredom, to ward off fear and to protect her delicate father from distress, whereas Mark, the unemployed singer in **"Desert Breakdown, 1968,"** cherishes an elaborate fantasy in which he becomes a star, goes on stage to take a bow and then delivers a phony childhood reminiscence, designed to humiliate his anxious parents. . . .

As this volume of stories, along with a previous collection

(*In the Garden of the North American Martyrs*) and a prize-winning novella (*The Barracks Thief*) abundantly demonstrate, Mr. Wolff is a masterful storyteller, a natural raconteur, who is willing to take all sorts of technical risks. Sometimes those risks don't completely pay off: **"The Rich Brother,"** a kind of contemporary parable about Abel and Cain, set down in colloquial but slightly formalized prose, never quite manages to sketch in the moral ambiguities suggested by its action; **"Our Story Begins"**—which uses the frame device of a story within a story, overheard within another story—leaves the reader all too aware of the narrative machinery at work.

If such efforts fail to trace a perfect emotional arc, however, they are not without their pleasures; even the weakest stories in *Back in the World* are enlivened by gleaming moments that display Mr. Wolff's quick eye, his gift for meticulous observation. The sound of magazine pages being turned with the quick snap of anger; the glitter of a sparkly ceiling in a cheap Las Vegas hotel; the swollen look that too-white, too-new sneakers give to a young girl's feet—such details take on an understated metaphorical power in these stories. Indeed, Mr. Wolff shows he is as fluent in evoking mood through naturalistic descriptions of the mundane—"The woman had all the shades pulled down. It was like evening inside: dim, peaceful, cool. Krystal could make out the shapes of things but not their colors"—as he is in creating a Sam Shepard-esque sense of menace through the manipulation of bizarre images: a hearse, filled with partygoing kids, speeding through the desert; an old bicycle lying at the bottom of a chilly swimming pool.

In the end, though, what really makes the finest of these stories so compelling is the author's sympathy for his characters, his clear-eyed but generous sense of their weaknesses, their frustrations and disappointments. Most of the people in *Back in the World* are losers or lapsed dreamers, weary people who have passively allowed circumstance and blind chance to dictate the shape of their lives: in **"The Poor Are Always With Us,"** a garage mechanic throws away two cars—and his financial security—on a silly bet; in **"Desert Breakdown"** an aspiring singer desultorily contemplates abandoning his pregnant wife and child at a local gas station. Aimless about their future, oblivious to the consequences of their past actions, these people all inhabit that precarious emotional terrain where discouragement threatens to turn into despair and a sense of permanent dislocation. . . .

There is not a lot of hope for these people, but Mr. Wolff suggests the promise of some kind of redemption in their fumbling efforts to connect with one another, and even in their sad attempts to shore up their dignity with their pipe dreams and clumsy fictions. This is what enables these characters to go on, and it is also what invests these stories with the burnished glow of compassion.

> *Michiko Kakutani, in a review of "Back in the World," in* The New York Times, *October 2, 1985, p. C25.*

## Russell Banks

One comes to Tobias Wolff's *Back in the World* with dangerously raised expectations, for his two previous books, *In the Garden of the North American Martyrs* (a volume of short stories) and *The Barracks Thief* (a single long story), were exceptionally fine works of a fully mature writer. This collection of stories is mostly concerned with the inner lives of middle-class loners in the Sun Belt. They are lapsed materialists in a material world trying to ignite a spiritual flame despite being cut off from all traditional sources of the spirit—family, church, art, even politics. Most of Mr. Wolff's characters are motivated by unenlightened self-interest. They may be yuppies, but they are trapped and manipulated by the system, and that makes them sympathetic. Mr. Wolff views their entrapment as something to be both feared and pitied and their attempts at escape—through fantasy, drugs, exercise, electronic toys and casual sex—as dignified. These microchippers, real-estate speculators, compulsively exercising cocaine addicts and frantic adulterers are victims, not exotic objects of derision, and consequently one reads the stories with an open heart.

Even so, it must be said that this book is a considerable falling off for Mr. Wolff. *Back in the World* does not measure up to *The Barracks Thief* and *In the Garden of the North American Martyrs.* Whereas the earlier stories used digression to build a dialectic, to make something *happen,* these seem instead to meander into narrative cul-de-sacs. And whereas stories like *The Barracks Thief* and **"Hunters in the Snow"** or **"The Liar"** used exposition to create atmosphere and a sense of crisis, the more recent stories often seem gabby and self-indulgently reluctant to get on with the telling, as in the opening pages of **"The Missing Person,"** about a priest who, without any obvious skills, is drifting downward from one minor post to another until he finds his calling, as it were, raising funds for a small convent.

> The monsignor took Father Leo out to dinner at a seafood house and explained the situation to him. . . . Mother Vincent at Star of the Sea needed a new chaplain. Their last chaplain had married one of the nuns. It so happened, the monsignor said, looking into his wine, swirling it gently, that he had done several favors for Mother Vincent in his days at the chancery. In short, if Father Leo wanted the position he could have it. The monsignor lit a cigarette and looked out the window, over the water. Gulls were diving for scraps.

In *Back in the World* there's too much of this kind of writing, suetlike prose studded with an occasional image (like the gulls "diving for scraps"), inserted for literary flavor rather than for any dramatic purpose and serving only to make the obvious more obvious. There are frequent flashy but cheap effects here that make one withdraw from a story, puzzled and detached, exactly when one should be suspending disbelief and entering the author's fictional world. . . .

Two stories, **"Leviathan"** and **"The Rich Brother,"** are as fine as anything Mr. Wolff has written. **"Leviathan"** lets us enter the lives of Mitch and Bliss and Ted and Helen, who have reached their 30's but haven't noticed it yet. They're trim, tanned, affluent, smart and sexy, but, like the rest of us, they're mortal—aging clay. They do everything they can to avoid facing that fact, life's main fact, and the thing they most like to do is cocaine. The story, very funny and very sad, is a description of an all-night 30th birthday party for Helen, with only her husband, Ted, and her best friends, Bliss and Mitch. It is about Helen; she is the one who is able to glimpse what all four of them, stubbornly, desperately, have avoided seeing.

> They watched over Helen's shoulders as Helen bent down to sift the gleaming crystal. First she chopped it with a razor. Then she began to spread it out. Mitch and Bliss smiled up at her from the mirror, and Helen smiled back between them. Their faces were rosy with candlelight. They were the faces of three well-wishers, carolers, looking in at Helen through a window filling up with snow.

**"The Rich Brother"** is more complex. It is a retelling of the prodigal son parable, told from the point of view of the good son, who makes lots of money in real estate and then has to spend it taking care of his younger brother, an incompetent, gullible seeker after transcendence who keeps sliding helplessly from cult to commune to cult, calling his brother to rescue, house and feed him until he finds another group to join. The story is a small classic about family life in America, what's left of it.

These two stories, along with brilliant moments scattered throughout the others, keep ***Back in the World*** from disappointing one altogether. If anything, one awaits Mr. Wolff's next book with all the more eagerness.

> *Russell Banks, "Aging Clay and the Prodigal Son," in* The New York Times Book Review, *October 20, 1985, p. 9.*

**Jonathan Penner**

Tobias Wolff knows a lot. He knows about men and women and children, and about America in its variety. His people are kids, soldiers, wives, successful in business or failed in art. They're devotees of love, of drugs, of technology. Wolff's taste for experience seems, as a major writer's should seem, promiscuous.

All 10 of [the stories in ***Back in the World***] are told in the third person. This narrative mode permits an exterior view of even the central figure, which seems to be why Wolff employs it. He's disinclined to tell stories from the inside out, to present a world through the thoughts and feelings of a viewpoint character.

Instead, Wolff tries to create windows on the soul through speech and action. In pure form, that is the way of drama. In fiction it tends to be awkward, artificial, inefficient, and extraordinarily difficult.

Yet at his best Wolff turns the handicap into an added grace, making his method appear easy or even inevitable. The central character of **"Coming Attractions,"** 15-year-old Jean, works in a movie theater. After closing up for the night, she's waiting alone for her boss to come and drive her home.

We see inside her scarcely at all. But the pathos of her life, and the heroism with which she meets it, emerge through phone calls that we hear her make, followed by a series of inspired events.

This story, like several others collected here, combines a traditional emphasis on character with a contemporary looseness of plot. There's no clear forward march, no resolution, no comes-to-realize. Helpless to change her circumstances, Jean wages war within them. She is an existential heroine, who continues to act, no matter how ineffectively or irrelevantly, and thus to be. At the end, though nothing has changed in her, something has in us.

**"The Poor Are Always With Us,"** another grand story, takes place among computer engineers in Silicon Valley. The milieu is authentic: protagonist and antagonist meet when they bring their Porsches in for servicing. The audacious plot turns on a wager, the consequences of which change several lives. Here again, the inner world is illuminated through word and deed. . . .

Still, many of these stories do not seem adequately lit. Collectively, they show the limits of what exterior signs can tell us of people's brains and viscera. Only a partial humanity percolates through action and speech. Not even a writer as good as Wolff can eschew *he thought* and *he felt* forever.

The distress that his method creates is seen first of all in dialogue. Speech in fiction, in order to be efficient for the author's purposes, needs to be inefficient for the characters'. Wolff's dialogue falls easily into addresses, so eloquently explanatory that they look less like speech than like writing.

One sometimes feels, eerily, that the characters are aware of the reader's need for information. At times the ostensible viewpoint character becomes little more than a conveniently placed eye and ear, used by the author to let us eavesdrop on a story-within-the-story.

In **"Our Story Begins,"** a busboy walking home from work stops at a coffeehouse. There he overhears a story told by one patron to another—a story that continues for nine pages. Afterward, completing a kind of narrative sandwich, the busboy continues his walk home. He has (so far as Wolff lets us know) no response whatever to the overheard story. Any connection between it and his own story is obscure.

**"Leviathan,"** a close to generic story of four friends gathering for cocaine and confessions, lies at the nadir of this collection. The anecdotes are boring, the action thin. Yet even here, Wolff does so much well that his gifts are continually evident.

Those gifts are lavish. His ear is sharp for every kind of speech. He can be very funny. He can be lyrical. His people display consistency and irrelevance—that odd blend of the mechanical and the random that we embrace as free will. His decorative surfaces turn out to be weight-bearing. His details, innocently planted, germinate. ***Back in the***

*World* is a striking and an exciting collection by a writer unusually fine.

Jonathan Penner, "Tobias Wolff and the Taste for Experience," in Book World—The Washington Post, *November 3, 1985, p. 5.*

## Richard Eder

Like an ophthalmological surgeon with huge hands, Wolff presents the paradox of a big energy applied to microscopic artisanry. The stories in *Back in the World* fairly prance with a natural storyteller's repressed high spirits. The best of them are feverish and dramatic; there is a hint that the protagonist is getting ready to bust out of the stillness, that a week or two after the story ends, pity and terror and, who knows, even laughter will replace disquiet. Perhaps Wolff himself will move on.

Meanwhile, he writes with a lavish display of skill. His achievement is not any special originality of situation, character or point of view, but an impressive elaboration of models we already know. It can verge upon gilding the lily.

Certainly the first story in the collection, **"Coming Attractions,"** is a compelling variation on the theme of the lonely adolescent. Kathy works nights in a movie theater, cleaning up after the last show. She wanders about the empty house, picking up remnants of human habitation: a dropped sweater, a half-chewed ham-bone. Watch that ham-bone; it is enticingly excessive and out of place.

Because everything else fits almost too well. Waiting for her boss to give her a ride home, Kathy calls her father, three thousand miles away, and gets her stepmother who doesn't want to wake him, especially if it's about a problem. "He's more of a good news person," she says cheerfully. Kathy calls home, but her mother is out on a date and there's only her little brother, watching television, and as lonely as she is. She looks up a stranger in the phone book and chats with him for a while. The world isn't home to Kathy; she can't break through. So when she gets back, past midnight, and sees a bicycle at the bottom of the condo swimming pool, she dives in and pulls it out, almost drowning. When trapped in a maze, hurl yourself at its walls.

Salinger's adolescents have passed this way; Wolff's Kathy has her own desolation, more brilliance in some ways, less interior grace. Similarly, in a story about a saintly, incompetent priest whom the world regularly dumps upon, we get more than a hint of the hapless but alluring Guy Crouchback in Evelyn Waugh's war trilogy.

Father Leo, who dreams of being a missionary, drifts haplessly through the Catholic parishes of his city. He ends up as chaplain at a convent whose members are in a frenzy of theological modernization. Leo can find no lambs to save; nobody wants to be a lamb any more. One of the nuns married his predecessor; others have left or taken jobs in town. One is a disc jockey.

Wolff writes with delightful irony about Father Leo's unexpectedly successful team-work with an extroverted fund-raiser who treats him to expensive lunches and ultimately absconds. Leo remains an innocent; finally finding his lamb in a forlorn middle-aged woman who is looking for love but settles for charity.

If Wolff handles the notion of a Divine Fool descending in a manner reminiscent of Waugh, he lacks the former's chilly faith that this is just what is supposed to happen to Divine Fools. Treated with such chill, Crouchback emerged with a comical radiance; lacking it, Father Leo gets a sentimental softening.

On the other hand, Wolff's story about the duel between an aging boy-wonder of the electronics business, and a young and rigid technocrat, has a wildness that mounts steadily out of a casual encounter. The duel is a mad series of wagers. The older man keeps betting his automobiles and losing; the younger man wins while never managing to understand the agony of someone who once won all his bets, and never will again.

The notion of the crazed wager is not new; Roald Dahl did something of the kind in his tale of a rich man who bet his fortune against other people's fingers. But Wolff makes something more than a tale out of it. It is a parable, in a way, but sufficiently unpredictable to avoid a parable's sleekness.

Another story that emerges from disquiet into a kind of grand ominousness has a jobless young man driving his pregnant wife and child across the Western desert. When the car breaks down, the disaster manages to turn his apparent strength into childish weakness, and her apparent dependence into a magnificent adaptability. The story is less perfect, in some ways, than some of the others; yet it holds a promise of Wolff's continued growth, from surprise parties to real surprise.

Richard Eder, in a review of "Back in the World," in Los Angeles Times Book Review, *November 17, 1985, p. 3.*

## Matthew Gilbert

There is nothing more daunting than reviewing a book of short stories—especially one as heterogeneous as *Back in the World.* Each story is so distinct, so self-sufficient, that to extract common themes from the collection is to neglect its most outstanding quality. Tobias Wolff breathes life into ten discrete worlds, each containing characters who wrestle with profound personal conflicts.

Wolff goes at his characters from the outside, using concrete details to intimate psychological complexion. The stories occur back in the world. Wolff provides the setting, the characters, and their words in a detached, impersonal fashion; we judge the facts for ourselves. In this sense he is a realist: accuracy, not style, is his aim. He avoids abstract and connotative words to insure surface clarity.

Wolff often lets his characters tell their own stories; *Back in the World* contains a number of short narrative-within-the-narratives. In **"Soldier's Joy,"** for instance, the hero, Hooper, is an army man in occupational, emotional, and sexual decline. He has been demoted from Corporal to

PFC, and though he is having an affair with the supply sergeant's wife, "he wasn't exactly sure why he kept going back. It was just something he did, again and again."

When confronted with a suicidal soldier, the usually laconic Hooper uses the past to explain his own monotonous life: "Everything was clear [in Vietnam]. . . . You learned what you had to know and you forgot the rest. All this chickenshit. This clutter. You didn't spend every living minute of the day thinking about your own sorry-ass little self. Am I getting laid enough. What's wrong with my kid. Should I insulate the fucking house. . . . That's what kills you in the end."

Then there is Marty, the young woman in **"Sister"** who tries unsuccessfully to befriend two men in a park while her brother is away. Wolff has her say very little; in her desperate loneliness she does not believe herself worthy of defense. She is like her brother's dogs, "waiting, ears pricked for the least sound, sometimes whimpering to themselves, but mostly silent, tense, and still, watching the bright door the men have closed behind them."

Wolff also invests the settings of these stories with a life of their own. They embrace the main action and subtly become essential to the story. In **"Say Yes,"** the kitchen utensils seem to participate in the argument between husband and wife. In **"Soldier's Joy,"** the rain mirrors Hooper's peacetime passivity—"a light rain began to fall, but it stopped before he'd even turned the wipers on"—until he momentarily recalls Vietnam and feels the rain "stream down his face and neck."

The most impressive aspect of Wolff's storytelling is its focus. If there is a common theme in this collection, it is that most of the characters are seen at some decisive point in their lives, an eleventh hour during which they cannot be expected to act with logic and foresight. There is the moment in **"Desert Breakdown, 1968,"** when Mark must decide whether or not to abandon his pregnant wife and their son; the moment in **"Coming Attractions"** when Jean, the teenager who lies to gain attention from adults, risks her life to salvage a bicycle from the bottom of a swimming pool for her younger brother; the moment in **"Sister"** when Marty must face her lonely life after nearly being killed by a careening car. . . .

The stakes are high in these stories, risk is in the air. Yet Wolff himself takes the greatest risk: writing stories with such serious intent. He does so in a modest and just manner.

*Matthew Gilbert, in a review of "Back in the World," in* Boston Review, *Vol. X, No. 6, December, 1985, p. 27.*

### Thomas DePietro

Recent talk of a short story revival often ignores the obvious: more, not better, collections than ever before are being published. In fact, this marketplace vitality disguises a genre in malaise. Not the short story per se, but that popular species, practiced by Raymond Carver, Ann Beattie and Co., and accurately described by its hostile critics as "shrinking," "diminishing," and "dwindling."

Tobias Wolff, a recent PEN/Faulkner Award winner, writes the kind of short fiction that we might call, to paraphrase Carver, the what-we-talk-about-when-we-have-nothing-to-say story. His new collection, **Back in the World,** exemplifies the trendy "minimalist" mode with its conspicuous absence of subject matter. These stories, for all their surface detail, might well be set anywhere, and that's the point: the middle-American metaphysicians who people Wolff's tales are often loners, far from home, friendless and in search of something, though neither they nor we know what they hope to find. Time and again, his characters reach a kind of pseudo-epiphany, as in **"Sister,"** a vignette in which a young woman named "Marty," an Edgar Cayce enthusiast, goes out for an afternoon jog. Still slightly paranoid from the joint she smoked earlier, this believer in reincarnation has a spaced-out conversation with two guys in the park, and then almost gets run over chasing after a Frisbee. Back at her apartment steps, the lonely woman realizes there's no one to tell about this brush with death, nor anyone to assure her "that everything was going to be all right." This leads to the equally enigmatic insight "that there was never going to be anyone to tell her these things. She had no idea why this should be so; it was just something she knew."

Even the longer, hence somewhat more compelling, pieces (**"Soldier's Joy," "Our Story Begins,"** or **"The Rich Brother"**) end washed-out and proud of it. This is especially annoying in **"The Missing Person,"** the best of the lot, which begins with great promise. Fr. Leo, a young but old-fashioned priest, finds himself the pastor of a wild, post-Vatican II convent in financial and physical shambles. The dull clergyman and a smooth-talking fundraiser, the latter a likeable charlatan, celebrate their success at soliciting contributions with a junket to Las Vegas ("when you reach a certain point it's the logical place to come"). Amidst the high rollers and lounge lizards, Jerry disappears with the money he's been secretly embezzling from the convent. Bored Fr. Leo, out of his collar, befriends a lonely woman who, as if aware this story is going nowhere, provides what could serve as the epigraph to Wolff's entire collection: "Once I start something I have to finish it. I have to take it to the end and see how it turns out, even if it turns out awful." (pp. 487-88)

*Thomas DePietro, "Minimalists, Moralists and Manhattanites," in* The Hudson Review, *Vol. XXXIX, No. 3, Autumn, 1986, pp. 487-88.*

### Marianne Boruch

[A feeling of] finality has informed Tobias Wolff's carefully wrought stories through three collections now, most recently, **The Barracks Thief and Selected Stories,** which draws the strongest work from the first book (although at forty, Wolff seems a bit young to be worried into "selecting"), sending them out again with the new title piece, really a short novel. The stories selected force a retrospective (a small one anyway), and remind us once more of Wolff's near contradictory gifts: a respect for classic step-by-step character development, and a fondness for nearly shorting out its hard won predictability with an ending turn that brings a kind of epiphany, either rapid as Joyce would have it, or settling slowly as is Wolff's usual preference. William Gass has written somewhere that the structure of certain stories resembles a journey over snow, a hard-packed trail of it. We move easily, thinking everything safe until the ringing crack in the air stops us, and we turn to find the path we've trudged nothing at all, mere space. What we assumed solid all along was not; or rather, I suspect, we are braver to begin with, more innocent than we imagine.

In spite of what they do—thieves, liars, or plainer folk caught up in bad luck, tedium, confusion—Wolff's characters carry this wise innocence, something we as readers tend to catch, a charmed fever that registers in us as grief does with its distant falling quiet. For Mary, the main figure of **"In the Garden of the North American Martyrs,"** fate, like the initial reality of the snow trail, seems visible enough: she doesn't get the teaching position she seeks; more, she had no hope from the start. Everything moves orderly, with a clear, deadpan humor . . . toward this fact—the bland response of her would-be colleagues, the discovery of the affirmative action stipulation requiring female candidates, and so on. Clockwork. One feels the story pulsing ahead, as plainly as one notices bones under the skin when thinness goes past beauty into something half-savage. A murmuring, however, in deeper ground continues, the real fate buried (as the classic rule dictates) in the story's first sentence. "When she was young, Mary saw a brilliant and original man lose his job because he had expressed ideas that were offensive to the trustees of the college where they both taught." That this man's nerve will eventually be Mary's, after years of colorless lip service, is the story of the story, making the traceable outer husk of the piece—girl does not get job—mere catapult for her great leap. Now knowing the shabby reason for the college's invitation, Mary "comes to the end of her facts," launching joyously into a blood-curdling, politically unfashionable account of the Iroquois's torture of French missionaries. Our own joy in her recklessness is moral; there are bad guys here, real bullies, and through Mary's sudden indifference, we are avenged, shed of such evil too. This is catharsis—even with Wolff's comic edge—and one feels a physical relish before it, an ancestry back to the terrible myths of human power and powerlessness, a victory *anyway.*

Destiny, however, for Wolff's characters is not always so triumphant, though because his main figures are usually unmalicious sorts, and relatively thoughtful, hope seeps into the stories even when moral exhaustion stops the characters, makes them shake their heads or sit quietly in living rooms or in barracks. **"The Liar"** is told with a hindsight close to omniscience by its main character, James, about his adolescent mania to lie about his mother's good health—specific untruths about leukemia, TB, other disastrous ailments. These lies spring up after his father's death and Wolff works this crucial connection with typical generosity, taking time to reveal past moments between them: father and son camping, joking, reading aloud, sharing anger, more importantly, fear, and finally the death itself. Part of Wolff's authority is timing, *where* he chooses to enter the story. The lies have been coming

for months, and the mother is past rage as the boy is past guilt; both have reached that point of fatigue which sometimes marks the onset of tenderness. "Why do you do it?" asks the mother, finally, out of plain curiosity. "I don't know," says the boy. And the narrator, as though still perplexed, adds that "that was the truth." Her advice now is boiled down beyond self-defense to the very heart of concern. "You don't have to make all these things up, James," she tells him, picking at the hem of her skirt. "They'll happen anyway." She says he's cheating himself. "When you get to be my age, you won't know anything at all about life. All you'll know is what you've made up."

That James and his mother feel helpless before this compulsion for tragedy becomes the central mystery of the story, one they come to accept the way one accepts a machine that can't be fixed or stopped, but just lunges forward sputtering until it runs out of gas. James, for his part, is grateful for this patience, and it occurs to him suddenly that his mother's imagination is "superior" to his, for "she could imagine things as coming together, not falling apart."

Either, certainly, is invention—James might see this as quickly as we do—but a final mending, this "coming together," is a habit of traditional fiction: resolution which assumes direction from the start *is* a kind of eloquence, perhaps—here is the risk—even a kind of pomposity. So Wolff is careful in its delivery, so careful we hardly know what hits us with such power in the last scene—more lies, of course, but this time charged with beauty. To calm the waiting passengers on a dark, stalled bus, James impersonates a Tibetan translator. Against the blinding rain outside, he sings his fellow travelers quietly to sleep—this boy whose mother claims he cannot sing—in what, Wolff writes, "was surely an ancient and holy tongue."

Against Wolff's other work, as against the bulk of recent short fiction, another oddity of this story is its reliance on the conventional sources of survival, the family—here, however damaged, the parent-child relationship. This subject—and its eventual corollary, marriage—is a thing on which many contemporary writers have given up, or if they haven't, busy themselves tracing its unraveling which perhaps, if not more interesting, is at least more predictable. (pp. 102-04)

*Marianne Boruch, in a review of "The Barracks Thief and Selected Stories," in* New England Review and Bread Loaf Quarterly, *Vol. IX, No. 1, Autumn, 1986, pp. 102-04.*

## Donna Rifkind

The boyhood memoir is a beloved literary form, and a highly adaptable one. . . . It can be as sentimental as a fairy tale of as matter-of-fact as a Scout manual. To be effective, however, works in this otherwise unrestricted genre ought to observe one indispensable rule: They must be immediate. Readers must be able to sense an author's wholehearted participation in his own memories, or the entire project is likely to fail.

Tobias Wolff has attempted to meet this challenge with his

latest book, *This Boy's Life: A Memoir.* Mr. Wolff is the author of two short-story collections, *In the Garden of the North American Martyrs* (1981) and *Back in the World* (1985), in addition to a novelette entitled *The Barracks Thief* (1984). He also has received an astounding number of grants and awards, including a Guggenheim fellowship, two National Endowment for the Arts awards, a Wallace Stegner fellowship, and the PEN/Faulkner award for 1985. Mr. Wolff's career thus far, then, has amounted to an impressive exercise in grantsmanship combined with a supremely modest display of fiction-writing talent—a familiar formula in the contemporary publishing world.

*This Boy's Life* opens with 10-year-old Toby Wolff and his mother driving from Florida to Utah to "get away from a man my mother was afraid of and to get rich on uranium." They reach Salt Lake City long after the mining boom has ended; Toby's mother finds work as a secretary, and Toby, seeking a total escape, changes his name to Jack, after Jack London. When his mother's fearsome boyfriend tracks them down, they flee again to Seattle, where "Jack" begins to play at being a hoodlum, smashing windows and shoplifting.

Before long his mother, who has "a strange docility, almost paralysis, with men of the tyrant breed," meets a horrible little man called Dwight, who lives in the remote mountain town of Chinook, Wash. Jack, who has by now developed a rather serious attitude problem, is sent to live with Dwight and his three children, while Jack's mother remains in Seattle to decide whether to accept Dwight's marriage proposal. . . .

The dreaded marriage takes place, locking Jack in Chinook for good; he starts hitchhiking, lying, stealing money. For a while he entertains the idea of going to live with his uncle's family in Paris, but he gives it up, unable to leave his mother in Dwight's hands. In high school, Jack takes up smoking and drinking, and changes the marks on his report cards. "I wanted distinction," he explains, "and the respectable forms of it seemed to be eluding me. If I couldn't have it as a citizen I would have it as an outlaw."

In the end, Jack escapes his servitude to his stepfather through another dishonest act: He fakes his way into a scholarship at an Eastern preparatory school, concocting all of the necessary letters of recommendation himself. The book ends with a brief description of prep school life ("I did not do well at Hill . . . and to cover my fear I became one of the school wild-men") and a decision to join the Army: "It seemed to me when I got there that this was where I had been going all along, and where I might still redeem myself."

But of course the author's real redemption—never stated in the narrative yet implicit throughout—lies in the fact that at some point he stopped being a bad boy, an outlaw, and joined society by becoming a Famous Writer. In fact, this redemption may be said to exist in all literary memoirs: Whether they include talk of literature or not, boyhood-memory books like *This Boy's Life* justify their existence in print by the mature success of their authors. "See what a queer fish I was, how special I was, how closely I

observed my world," their authors seem to be saying; "look what happens in childhood to cause a writer to write."

Unfortunately, the suggestion of literary entitlement that runs through *This Boy's Life* also signals the book's main flaw. Mr. Wolff violates the rule of immediacy by writing in a flat, numb, overtly adult voice that cancels all the energy in his childhood misbehavior. He seems to have adopted this tone in an effort to avoid sentimentality, but he has succeeded in averting any hints of authentic emotion whatsoever. The reader is left with a colorless collection of details about growing up in the '50s and early '60s, but without the remotest means of being affected by the unhappy castaway that was the young Tobias Wolff.

> Donna Rifkind, "From Bad Boy to Big Time," in The Wall Street Journal, *January 3, 1989, p. A11.*

## Christopher Lehmann-Haupt

So absolutely clear and hypnotic is Tobias Wolff's painful memoir of growing up in the 1950's that a reader wants to take it apart and find some simple way to describe why it works so beautifully.

It's tempting, for example, to call *This Boy's Life* the story of a persecuted child who finally triumphs over his tormenters. After all, it's almost Dickensian the way the narrator's mother entrusts him to the care of the wheedling and malicious Dwight from tiny Chinook, in the state of Washington. The moment her back is turned, he begins to abuse Tobias—or Jack, as he preferred to be called as a child. . . .

Yet one can't feel too sorry for Jack, because there's not a trace of self-pity in his narrative, and the way he portrays Dwight is too full of humor and touches of sympathy, particularly in a scene where, in honor of Jack's mother's arrival, Dwight paints the entire inside of his house white, including the yellowing keys of the old Baldwin upright piano.

Besides, Jack gets his own back, by running wild when Dwight isn't watching him. He hangs out with the outlaws of his high school, cutting classes, getting drunk and altering his report card. He steals money from the customers on his paper route. He takes the family car for midnight joy rides. In fact it also occurs to the reader to call *This Boy's Life* a story of juvenile revenge on an uncomprehending adult world, like Rudyard Kipling's "Stalky and Co." or J. D. Salinger's *Catcher in the Rye*. But the author takes no satisfaction in his hero's cutting up. There's no anger or delight, and only the barest trace of bitterness.

Still another temptation is to call the book a fairy tale of a prince in exile. Jack knows instinctively that he is meant for something better than the squalid life into which his mother's failings have plunged him. He dreams of ascending to the life that his brother, Geoffrey Wolff, is living across the continent as a student at Princeton. He idealizes his father, the great pretender and con man whom Geoffrey will later memorialize in his own unforgettable memoir, *The Duke of Deception* (1979), and he lives for the day when he will be called to the throne.

Indeed, Jack is a burgeoning Duke himself, training in the art of deception. One doesn't bat an eye when he counterfeits the transcript and recommendations that he sends with his applications to a list of high-status Eastern prep schools. And one cheers him through the enchanting Gatsby-like scenes in which he wins a scholarship to the Hill School, gets prepped and outfitted for his new life, and sets off to become Tobias Jonathan von Ansell-Wolff III.

Except that of course it doesn't work. "I did not do well at Hill," he concludes. "How could I? I knew nothing. . . . In my last year I . . . was asked to leave. . . . I wore myself out with raging. Then I went into the army. . . . It seemed to me when I got there that this was where I had been going all along, and where I might still redeem myself. All I needed was a war. Careful what you pray for."

No, the more one reflects on the stinging honesty of *This Boy's Life,* the more it seems a mystery. Its clarity of vision is imposed by its grown-up narrator. The hero himself is inaccessible. As he declares near the end when yet another sympathizing adult tries to reach him: "I was not available to be reached. I was in hiding. I had left a dummy in my place to look sorry and make promises, but I was nowhere in the neighborhood. . . .

So the only simple explanation for *This Boy's Life* is that it is the portrait of an artist as a very young man. The narrator doesn't refer to his future as a writer, except once where he mentions sending Geoffrey a story he has written about "two wolves fighting to the death in the Yukon," and receiving in return words of praise and encouragement.

But he is clearly searching for a writer's persona in *This Boy's Life.* He is learning the arts of disguise and illusion. One is aware throughout the book that he will exercise them artfully in his two admirable story collections, *In the Garden of the North American Martyrs* (1981) and *Back in the World* (1985), and in his novella *The Barracks Thief,* which won the 1985 PEN/Faulkner Award. But perhaps the best evidence of his mastery lies in the superb storytelling that is in evidence here, and in the creation of the boy Jack, who teaches us something new about the alienated world of childhood.

> *Christopher Lehmann-Haupt, "Through a Dark Boyhood to a Place in the Sun," in* The New York Times, *January 12, 1989, p. C25.*

## Joel Conarroe

Tobias Wolff's first stepfather was not exactly a model parent. An alcoholic sadist who humiliated his young charge and regularly beat him up, he also stole his money and shot his dog. As if that weren't enough, he tried to strangle the boy's mother. Not a very nice fellow, and were he to show up in a novel we'd probably say that he lacked credibility, that the author had overegged the custard.

Life, though, has a habit of outdoing even extremist fiction, and while Dwight is presented to us [in *This Boy's Life*] not so much warts and all as all warts, he nevertheless achieves a certain bizarre plausibility. And yet for all his oddness he is not even the most incredible of Mr. Wolff's relatives. That honor belongs to his actual father, as we know from *The Duke of Deception,* a cathartic memoir published 10 years ago by the author's older brother, Geoffrey. With his fake coat of arms and nonexistent degrees from Oxford and Yale, where he was—that is, wasn't—Skull and Bones, Duke Wolff was a Gatsby-like con artist of considerable charm who somehow managed, despite his failings, to gain not only the rage but also the love of his oldest son.

Love, however, is not a word that leaps to mind when we consider the younger sibling's descriptions of his stepfather. Perhaps through sheer loathsomeness, Dwight is even more memorable than the numerous unsympathetic characters who appear in the author's novella *The Barracks Thief,* which won a PEN/Faulkner award, and his two books of disturbing and often brilliant stories, *In the Garden of the North American Martyrs* and *Back in the World.* The memoir as a whole, moreover, is literate and consistently entertaining—and richer, darker, and funnier than anything else Tobias Wolff has written. (pp. 1, 28)

Mr. Wolff's title plays variations on Philip Roth's *My Life as a Man* and on Edmund White's *A Boy's Own Story,* but where these products of inventive imaginations are fiction that resembles autobiography, *This Boy's Life* is apparently straight autobiography—the facts, attired in their exotic garments. The book, however, reads very much like a collection of short stories, each with its own beginning, middle and end. Lifted from their context, the individual chapters would be at home in the fiction pages of any good magazine.

And the tale itself? In 1955, when he was 10, Tobias and Rosemary, his mother, left Florida (having departed from Connecticut and the Duke some five years earlier) to get away from a man who was violent, a trait he shared with all the men in Rosemary's life, including her father, who beat her every day on the assumption that she must have done something wrong. The mother-son duo ends up in Chinook, Wash., a tiny village about three hours north of Seattle, where they settle into a domestic nightmare with the besotted Dwight and his three children. It is here that Tobias (who now calls himself Jack) gets an informal education in humiliation, betrayal and injustice, and learns how to fight, cheat, steal, gamble and, especially, lie. (He even plagiarizes his first confession to a priest, claiming as his own an acquaintance's minor transgressions.) This streetwise training in a hardscrabble world makes up the major part of the book.

His formal education, if it can be called that, is acquired at a place with the unpromising name of Concrete High School, an institution not calculated to make anyone forget Choate (brother Geoffrey's alma mater) or the Hill School, to which "Jack"—forging both his academic transcript and letters of recommendation—ultimately manages to get a scholarship, thus escaping Dwight's tyranny. . . .

In the course of conning his way out of Chinook, Toby wins over a Hill alumnus from Seattle, who outfits him with the Harris tweeds, Weejuns, and other sartorial necessities of a proper preppie. The boy's intellectual wardrobe, however, remains woefully shabby, and once at Hill our young forger fails miserably: "I knew nothing. My ignorance was so profound that entire class periods would pass without my understanding anything that was said." How, then, did this dishonest, disillusioned and culturally impoverished young man transform himself into the writer we read with admiration today? That, as he says at one point, is another story. I hope he will tell it.

As for this story, there may or may not be convincing reasons to believe everything Mr. Wolff tells us. He is, by his own admission, a fabricator who learned at his father's knee that it is pointless to stick with facts when fantasy is so much more rewarding. Mendacity is a central motif in his fiction, which is crowded with individuals who take liberties with the truth. In one story, for example, a depressed priest invents a murder he committed and persuades a colleague it really occurred; in another, a lonely girl calls a stranger on the phone and tells him he has won a prize. Lies give substance, however minimal, to empty lives.

And yet whatever liberties Mr. Wolff may have taken with the facts of his boyhood in this memoir (and he admits in the preface that memory has its own tale to tell), I found myself convinced by the sharply etched details and more than willing to suspend any disbelief. It is possible, to be sure, that Tobias Wolff is the Joe Isuzu of contemporary autobiography and *This Boy's Life* simply another of his fabrications. If that's the case, so be it—the book won me over. And that's the truth. (p. 28)

Joel Conarroe, "Fugitive Childhoods," in The New York Times Book Review, *January 15, 1989, pp. 1, 28.*

## Jonathan Yardley

Tobias Wolff has written in *This Boy's Life* a memoir of his childhood that cannot escape comparison with *The Duke of Deception,* his brother Geoffrey's memoir of *his* childhood: the volumes stand together on the shelf as bookends, holding between them the story of a marriage made anywhere except in heaven and of the two sons who somehow fought their way through unsettled upbringings to become writers of accomplishment and character. *The Duke of Deception* is the darker, deeper and—yes—funnier of the two, and thus a daunting object of sibling competition; but *This Boy's Life* is modest and charming and exact, and it recreates a 1950s boyhood with affection and verisimilitude.

Arthur and Rosemary Wolff separated about four decades ago, when Geoffrey was a teenager and Tobias still a young boy. Geoffrey went off with his father, a beguiling man whose capacity to deceive others was exceeded only by his capacity to deceive himself; he was a compulsive if ingratiating liar, and as those familiar with *The Duke of Deception* well know, he presented a model by which his elder son was both attracted and repelled. Toby mean-

while was placed in the charge of his mother, herself a person of much charm; the problems in her life had less to do with flights of fancy, though she had these from time to time, than with an unfortunate taste for men who offered her little except trouble.

As *This Boy's Life* begins she is fleeing one of these with Toby, who at the age of 10 has declared his distaste for his given name and his preference for being called Jack. They have left Florida and are headed, somewhat improbably, for Utah, which proves only a stopover on a flight plan that takes them on an inexorable path to Washington State and a man named Dwight: a strange, bitter, alcoholic, dreamy, abusive man who of course becomes Rosemary's second husband and Toby's stepfather.

To some extent then *This Boy's Life* is the story of what happens to a child when the peculiarities of a mother's romance place him at the mercy of a man who is neither his father nor his protector, but it is not a self-pitying lament and it is not really a tale of abuse and neglect. The mistreatment young Wolff received at Dwight's hands was more psychological than physical—which is hardly to say that it was therefore less hurtful—and his mother was so constant and loving a presence in his life that the twig, if bent for a time, was never broken.

Rather *This Boy's Life* is about growing up, as inevitably any such memoir must be, and more specifically about the ruses and deceits that maturation at times requires. To what extent Toby fooled himself is not made entirely clear in his memoir, but for much of his youth he was actively engaged in trying to fool others. When, before his mother's remarriage, he moved to the settlement of Chinook to live with Dwight and his children, he saw before him a golden opportunity to do precisely that:

> I had agreed to move to Chinook partly because I thought I had no choice. But there was more to it than that. Unlike my mother, I was fiercely conventional. I was tempted by the idea of belonging to a conventional family, and living in a house, and having a big brother and a couple of sisters . . . And in my heart I despised the life I led in Seattle. I was sick of it and had no idea how to change it. I thought that in Chinook . . . away from people who had already made up their minds about me, I could be different. I could introduce myself as a scholar-athlete, a boy of dignity and consequence, and without any reason to doubt me people would believe I was that boy, and thus allow me to be that boy. I recognized no obstacle to miraculous change but the incredulity of others. This was an idea that died hard, if it ever really died at all.

The obvious irony is that Dwight's household proved anything except conventional; Toby was fond of his stepbrother and step-sisters, but the demands Dwight placed on him were so strenuous and irrational that there was never a chance of regaining the father he had lost. More than that, Toby's desire to be accepted by his teachers and fellow students was in irreconcilable conflict with a rebellious urge that ultimately gained control. In league with a small band of like-minded juvenile delinquents, as in those days we called them, Toby became "a liar" and "a thief," who began by stealing candy and soon enough graduated to coins and bills; it was, as often happens with bright but troubled children, not merely a form of rebellion but also of self-expression and self-assertion. . . .

Wolff's is a story of guile and accommodation and pain and apprehension, and he tells it as such; no false triumphs or epiphanies are to be found here, no suggestion that what was to follow would be any less difficult than what had gone before. But it is also a story of mere boyhood in a certain time and place, and this too Wolff gives us with honesty and clarity. Not merely are there boyish escapades and awkward encounters with girls and embarrassing ones with adults, there also is the slow, reluctant discovery that the Northwest had earned his love and, throughout, the proud recognition that "I was my mother's son." That he remains as an adult, as *This Boy's Life* openly but unsentimentally acknowledges on every page; it's a nice book, and a fit companion for *The Duke of Deception.*

*Jonathan Yardley, "Adventures of a Younger Son," in* Book World—The Washington Post, *January 22, 1989, p. 3.*

## Richard Russo

As young Toby Wolff leaves home to meet a man who will interview him for admission to a prestigious prep school, his mother gives him some advice. "Don't try to impress him," she says. "Just be yourself." This isn't bad advice exactly, just impossible to follow, at least for an adolescent. And that is what Tobias Wolff's memoir, *This Boy's Life,* is about—the young man's dilemma of being "still half-created," and therefore lost in a world where the vast majority of advice is bad, where good role models are few, where culture reinforces his worst instincts, where patience, kindness and love haven't the magical powers we like to attribute to them.

I probably should mention here, since the reader will have no way of guessing it from these rather somber reflections, that Wolff's book happens to be wonderfully funny. Readers who are familiar with his fiction will recognize not only the familiar focus on lying, hypocrisy and betrayal but also the precise, wicked, ironic wit that allows the perversity, the downright depravity, of human nature to be the source of rollicking entertainment.

Like Mark Twain, Wolff always manages to render comic the most subversive of messages; and he apparently shares with Twain the belief that we learn corruption from our parents and educators. *This Boy's Life,* like *Huckleberry Finn,* is full of corrupt educators, both professional and parental.

Consider Mr. Mitchell, Toby's high school civics teacher, a World War II veteran who regales his students with dubious tales of personal heroics and brings to class for inspection not only German bayonets but also wallets taken from the bodies of fallen soldiers, complete with pictures of the soldiers' families inside. In Mr. Mitchell's opinion

we had fought on the wrong side. We should have gone into Moscow, not Berlin. . . . On our

final examination Mr. Mitchell asked, 'What is your favorite amendment?' We were ready for this question, and all of us gave the correct answer—'The Right to Bear Arms'—except for a girl who answered 'Freedom of Speech.' For this impertinence she failed not only the question but the whole test.

The most vivid character portrait in the book is Dwight, Toby's stepfather, an insecure bully, abject coward and epic hypocrite whose example is enough to guarantee that any kid growing up in his proximity will be a case study in arrested development. Dwight is not averse to abusing physically either Toby or his mother, but his deep maliciousness is rendered most effectively in his fine-tuned psychological cruelty toward the boy—refusing, for instance, to buy him sneakers so Toby has to play basketball on a slick gym floor in heavy brown street shoes.

We come to realize that Dwight's simple, unflagging purpose is to break the boy's spirit; and much of the fun of *This Boy's Life* lies in watching Dwight, who is as inept as he is cruel, get what he deserves. No one could possibly humiliate him as thoroughly as he repeatedly humiliates himself, and Wolff's memoir is, at one level, an exquisite act of surgically precise revenge. It's not just Dwight who goes under the knife either, but the entire culture of the '50s—scouting, *Boy's Life* magazine, the Mickey Mouse Club, the champagne music of Lawrence Welk, who "came on stage salaaming in every direction, crying out declarations of humility in his unctuous, brain-scalding Swedish kazoo of a voice."

The '50s, our country's decade of supposed innocence, were never all that innocent, Wolff suggests, but rather a profound narcotic lie that parallels male adolescence itself—which despite its superficial innocence is preoccupied with violence, sex, power and status.

As tough as Wolff is on a hypocritical culture and the sly, corrupt education he received as a boy, he is even tougher on himself, or the self he recreates. Unlike Huck Finn, young Toby is all too corruptible, learning the worst lessons too wisely and too well. A liar, a cheat, a thief, a betrayer of those who love and believe in him, young Toby is sometimes unable, sometimes unwilling, to grasp the simplest truths and realities about himself; and he vacillates between self-loathing and arrogance. . . .

The central beliefs of adolescence, Wolff's memoir insists, are that the self can be invented, the past discarded. That Gatsby-like faith is evident from the first page, where we encounter 10-year-old Toby and his brave, spirited mother on the run from the past—she to escape a failed marriage with Toby's father and an even more unfortunate liason with a violent man named Roy, Toby to distance himself from the perceptions of his classmates and friends. "I didn't come to Utah to be the same boy I'd been before," he tells us. . . .

Wolff leaves open the question of whether this desire to ignore the past and re-invent the self is rooted in nature or nurture. Throughout the book, young Toby is influenced almost randomly by newspaper accounts of murders, by newsreels of high-stepping Nazis in "snappy uniforms," by his mother, who "makes the world seem friendly," and by the men who abuse her. And if, until the end, Toby himself is a chameleon, he comes by it rightly—his absent father being a Jew who claims to be an Episcopalian and who has designed for himself an ancient family coat-of-arms.

Ironically, that foolish and peculiarly American faith that the past is meaningless and that, in America at least, you can be whatever (read "whoever") you want is in large measure responsible for the resilience we so admire about youth in general and this youth in particular. Giving up that faith is called growing up, the book seems to suggest—until we remember, as Wolff no doubt intends, that the writing of a memoir partakes of the same urge to re-create the self. "Memory," the author warns us in the book's preface, "has its own story to tell." And what a fine story.

> Richard Russo, "Seeking A Self," in Chicago Tribune—Books, *January 22, 1989, p. 3.*

## Katherine Dieckmann

There are times you shouldn't compete with your older sibling. Tobias Wolff's account of his childhood, *This Boy's Life,* is a perfect example. Tobias clearly has his big bro Geoffrey beat for fiction—his books ring true to disaffected lives in a tough, humorous prose that makes minimalist efforts on similar subjects feel like pallid substitutes. Geoffrey's novels lack the vigor and bite of Tobias's (to be nice about it), but his 1979 childhood recollection, *The Duke of Deception: Memories of My Father,* is a deft memoir of familial conflict and a classic of the genre.

Of course, Geoffrey got the better half of an exorcist's package: the Oedipal kick. The Wolff parents split up while the sons were still kids; their mother, Rosemary, by all accounts a mixed-up but loving woman, took Tobias, while Arthur, the boys' rigid, self-deceiving, confidence man of a father, kept Geoffrey. Never particularly close before the separation, the brothers reunited when Tobias was a teen in crisis (his childhood is marked by a penchant for troublemaking) and Geoffrey a student at Princeton, an incident recounted with surprisingly little feeling in both books.

Since *This Boy's Life* is inevitably a companion piece to *The Duke of Deception,* it's telling that Tobias Wolff seals off his book in boyhood, with few references to later life. He utilizes none of the familial information available to him from his brother's work. Though Wolff is a master of the well-cast sentence and telling incident, *This Boy's Life* feels hermetic and slight. For one thing, there's not much to come to terms with—or if there is, the author has successfully repressed it.

Life with the freewheeling Rosemary involves some drifting (in search of uranium in Utah, to a new house, "the most scabrous eyesore in West Seattle") and, finally, settling with a truly scurvy stepfather named Dwight, and his kids, in a barrackslike complex. Wolff's hatred of Dwight is profound enough to warrant a nyah nyah mention in his acknowledgments. "My first stepfather used to say that what I didn't know would fill a book. Well here it is." In-

deed, Dwight is truly hateful. Though his stepson is admittedly unruly and undisciplined. Dwight goes overboard, stealing Tobias's paper route earnings, berating and emasculating him, and trading the child's prize rifle in for a dog (which he later shoots). Such evil begs retribution, but none comes.

Chunks of *This Boy's Life* are entertaining: a description of watching the Mouseketeers on TV that perfectly captures boys perched between childhood and adolescence; the account of Tobias fudging his records to get into prep school (a sign that although his father is a troubling absence, the two at least have lying in common). And there's something inherently touching about a young boy alone with his mother—the way the burden of protection shifts from parent to child, then back again. But the well-told scenes and occasional touching moments never add up to anything close to a revelation. . . .

There's a moment towards the end of *This Boy's Life* where Tobias, in trouble for the umpteenth time, offers the following: "I believed that there was no difference between explanations and excuses, and that excuses were unmanly. So were feelings, especially complicated feelings. I didn't admit to them. I hardly knew I had them." Well, neither do we.

> Katherine Dieckmann, "Pop Art," in The Village Voice, *Vol. XXXIV, No. 5, January 31, 1989, p. 54.*

## John Clute

America is a land for the self-made man, the impostor, the teller of tales. From the beginnings of American literature, Huckleberry Finn and his brothers have been inventing themselves, lighting out for new territories they hope to carve in their own image; but a dark twin has always shadowed them, the confidence-man at the heart of the dream of freedom, for whom identity is a sleight-of-hand. As he grows into adulthood, Huck Finn must come to terms with that shadow; he must learn how to fabricate himself. Perhaps, like the young Tobias Wolff in *This Boy's Life,* he must become a liar.

Now in his forties, and the author of three cunning and successful volumes of fiction, Wolff knows a great deal about telling tales; and in his prefatory note he makes it clear that *This Boy's Life,* the story of a liar, is indeed a tale, "a book of memory" with "its own story to tell"; the shaping urgencies of re-creation—rather than any documentary proprieties—will govern its fabrication.

We begin *in medias res* and in flight. Tobias and his alluring mother have hit out from a bad scene in Florida—violent men attract her—and plan to get rich quick in Utah, where they've heard that uranium can be picked up off the ground. Their car has boiled over after climbing the spine of the continent, and they have stopped. A huge truck hurtles out of control past them down the steep Loveland Pass grade, for this is 1955, before the time of the Interstates; and topples hundreds of feet into a canyon. Shocked, Tobias's mother becomes tender with her son, who parlays this moment of weakness into a successful request for Colorado souvenirs before they leave Grand Junction, though he knows there is no money to spare. But her guard is down, and Tobias cannot stop himself. He is ten.

It is an anecdote which demonstrates more than Tobias's precocious skill at playing his audiences for profit; it also illuminates something of the deeply engaging craft of the older Wolff's way with a tale. In giving the impression that the accident and Tobias's manipulation of his mother make up a dramatic unit, he may tell no actual lie, but readers today might reasonably fail to know that in 1955 Grand Junction was many hours' drive westwards of the scene, and might well fail to notice Wolff hinting, on a later page, that the two travellers almost certainly stopped overnight there before slipping over the border into the hopelessness of Utah. Told with this lumbering exactitude, however, the anecdote would have seemed nearly pointless. Again and again, through polishings and elisions of this sort, and through an adroit manipulation of time, Wolff transforms inchoate raw materials into shining fable; about *This Boy's Life* there abides a sense of easy, limpid profundity.

That sense may not be wholly earned. The legerdemain is sometimes obtrusive, and the sheer professionalism of the book sometimes gives it an almost dandiacal tone, a glow that suffuses the most dreadful moments of young Tobias's perilous race into adulthood, making less than fully persuasive the moral lessons Wolff derives from that race. But the lessons are there to be absorbed. His mother drags him from Utah to Washington, tormenting him with her need for a new man, eventually making the worst possible kind of match with the brutal and hysterical Dwight, who fiercely resents his smart-aleck stepson, tortures him and steals his money. Tobias's violent father has long since disappeared, but the prestige of his East Coast connections continues to haunt the child with visions of a finer, more

powerful life; while Tobias is confined to high school in the ghastly town of Concrete, near Seattle, an older brother is attending Princeton.

The only safety for Tobias—the only way he can maintain any saving secret life—is to lie. Because the world offers him nothing to hold on to, he must create his own. He must pretend to become a psychopath (which is perhaps not very different from being one). He fabricates his past; he cheats, steals, bullies, runs rampage; finally, by forging his entire academic record, he gains admission to an exclusive prep school in Pennsylvania. After a slingshot preview of the gruelling years to come in that school and in the army, the book ends.

Because he is brilliant and compulsively audacious, Tobias comes much closer to real criminality, and to serious personality disorder, than most of his countrymen in the same fix—on the wrong side of the Divide. But *This Boy's Life* is also the story of the making of the man who could have written his book only by learning the lessons it imparts; and that story is an almost unalloyed triumph.

*John Clute, "States of Exile," in* The Times Literary Supplement, *No. 4493, May 12, 1989, p. 508.*

---

## FURTHER READING

Wolff, Tobias. "An Interview with Tobias Wolff" by Bonnie Lyons and Bill Oliver. *Contemporary Literature* 31, No. 1 (Spring 1990): 1-16.
    Wolff discusses *This Boy's Life* and his fiction.

□ Contemporary
Literary Criticism

Indexes

Literary Criticism Series
    Cumulative Author Index
Cumulative Nationality Index
Title Index, Volume 64

# This Index Includes References to Entries in These Gale Series

## Contemporary Literary Criticism

Presents excerpts of criticism on the works of novelists, poets, dramatists, short story writers, scriptwriters, and other creative writers who are now living or who have died since 1960.

## Twentieth-Century Literary Criticism

Contains critical excerpts by the most significant commentators on poets, novelists, short story writers, dramatists, and philosophers who died between 1900 and 1960.

## Nineteenth-Century Literature Criticism

Offers significant passages from criticism on authors who died between 1800 and 1899.

## Literature Criticism from 1400 to 1800

Compiles significant passages from the most noteworthy criticism on authors of the fifteenth through eighteenth centuries.

## Classical and Medieval Literature Criticism

Offers excerpts of criticism on the works of world authors from classical antiquity through the fourteenth century.

## Short Story Criticism

Compiles excerpts of criticism on short fiction by writers of all eras and nationalities.

## Children's Literature Review

Includes excerpts from reviews, criticism, and commentary on works of authors and illustrators who create books for children.

## Contemporary Authors Series

Encompasses five related series. *Contemporary Authors* provides biographical and bibliographical information on more than 95,000 writers of fiction, nonfiction, poetry, journalism, drama, motion pictures, and other fields. Each new volume contains sketches on authors not previously covered in the series. *Contemporary Authors New Revision Series* provides completely updated information on active authors covered in previously published volumes of *CA*. Only entries requiring significant change are revised for *CA New Revision Series*. *Contemporary Authors Permanent Series* consists of updated listings for deceased and inactive authors removed from the original volumes 9-36 when these volumes were revised. *Contemporary Authors Autobiography Series* presents specially commissioned autobiographies by leading contemporary writers. *Contemporary Authors Bibliographical Series* contains primary and secondary bibliographies as well as analytical bibliographical essays by authorities on major modern authors.

## Dictionary of Literary Biography

Encompasses four related series. *Dictionary of Literary Biography* furnishes illustrated overviews of authors' lives and works and places them in the larger perspective of literary history. *Dictionary of Literary Biography Documentary Series* illuminates the careers of major figures through a selection of literary documents, including letters, notebook and diary entries, interviews, book reviews, and photographs. *Dictionary of Literary Biography Yearbook* summarizes the past year's literary activity with articles on genres, major prizes, conferences, and other timely subjects and includes updated and new entries on individual authors. *Concise Dictionary of American Literary Biography* comprises six volumes of revised and updated sketches on major American authors that were originally presented in *Dictionary of Literary Biography*.

## Something about the Author Series

Encompasses three related series. *Something about the Author* contains heavily illustrated biographical sketches on juvenile and young adult authors and illustrators from all eras. *Something about the Author Autobiography Series* presents specially commissioned autobiographies by prominent authors and illustrators of books for children and young adults. *Authors & Artists for Young Adults* provides high school and junior high school students with profiles of their favorite creative artists in the mediums of print, film, television, drama, song lyrics, and cartoons.

## Yesterday's Authors of Books for Children

Contains heavily illustrated entries on children's writers who died before 1961. Complete in two volumes.

# Literary Criticism Series
# Cumulative Author Index

This index lists all author entries in the Gale Literary Criticism Series and includes cross-references to other Gale sources. References in the index are identified as follows:

**AAYA:** *Authors & Artists for Young Adults,* Volumes 1-3
**CAAS:** *Contemporary Authors Autobiography Series,* Volumes 1-11
**CA:** *Contemporary Authors* (original series), Volumes 1-131
**CABS:** *Contemporary Authors Bibliographical Series,* Volumes 1-3
**CANR:** *Contemporary Authors New Revision Series,* Volumes 1-31
**CAP:** *Contemporary Authors Permanent Series,* Volumes 1-2
**CA-R:** *Contemporary Authors* (revised editions), Volumes 1-44
**CDALB:** *Concise Dictionary of American Literary Biography,* Volumes 1-6
**CLC:** *Contemporary Literary Criticism,* Volumes 1-64
**CLR:** *Children's Literature Review,* Volumes 1-23
**CMLC:** *Classical and Medieval Literature Criticism,* Volumes 1-6
**DC:** *Drama Criticism,* Volume 1
**DLB:** *Dictionary of Literary Biography,* Volumes 1-101
**DLB-DS:** *Dictionary of Literary Biography Documentary Series,* Volumes 1-7
**DLB-Y:** *Dictionary of Literary Biography Yearbook,* Volumes 1980-1988
**LC:** *Literature Criticism from 1400 to 1800,* Volumes 1-15
**NCLC:** *Nineteenth-Century Literature Criticism,* Volumes 1-30
**PC:** *Poetry Criticism,* Volumes 2-2
**SAAS:** *Something about the Author Autobiography Series,* Volumes 1-11
**SATA:** *Something about the Author,* Volumes 1-62
**SSC:** *Short Story Criticism,* Volumes 1-7
**TCLC:** *Twentieth-Century Literary Criticism,* Volumes 1-40
**YABC:** *Yesterday's Authors of Books for Children,* Volumes 1-2

---

**A. E.** 1867-1935 . . . . . . . . . . . . . TCLC 3, 10
See also Russell, George William
See also DLB 19

**Abbey, Edward** 1927-1989 . . . . . . CLC 36, 59
See also CANR 2; CA 45-48;
obituary CA 128

**Abbott, Lee K., Jr.** 19??- . . . . . . . . . CLC 48

**Abe, Kobo** 1924- . . . . . . . . . . . . CLC 8, 22, 53
See also CANR 24; CA 65-68

**Abell, Kjeld** 1901-1961 . . . . . . . . . . . CLC 15
See also obituary CA 111

**Abish, Walter** 1931- . . . . . . . . . . . . . . CLC 22
See also CA 101

**Abrahams, Peter (Henry)** 1919- . . . . . CLC 4
See also CA 57-60

**Abrams, M(eyer) H(oward)** 1912-... CLC 24
See also CANR 13; CA 57-60; DLB 67

**Abse, Dannie** 1923- . . . . . . . . . . . . . CLC 7, 29
See also CAAS 1; CANR 4; CA 53-56;
DLB 27

**Achebe, (Albert) Chinua(lumogu)**
1930- . . . . . . . . CLC 1, 3, 5, 7, 11, 26, 51
See also CLR 20; CANR 6, 26; CA 1-4R;
SATA 38, 40

**Acker, Kathy** 1948- . . . . . . . . . . . . . . CLC 45
See also CA 117, 122

**Ackroyd, Peter** 1949- . . . . . . . . . CLC 34, 52
See also CA 123, 127

**Acorn, Milton** 1923- . . . . . . . . . . . . . . CLC 15
See also CA 103; DLB 53

**Adamov, Arthur** 1908-1970 . . . . . . CLC 4, 25
See also CAP 2; CA 17-18;
obituary CA 25-28R

**Adams, Alice (Boyd)** 1926- ... CLC 6, 13, 46
See also CANR 26; CA 81-84; DLB-Y 86

**Adams, Douglas (Noel)** 1952- ... CLC 27, 60
See also CA 106; DLB-Y 83

**Adams, Henry (Brooks)**
1838-1918 . . . . . . . . . . . . . . . . . TCLC 4
See also CA 104; DLB 12, 47

**Adams, Richard (George)**
1920- . . . . . . . . . . . . . . . . . CLC 4, 5, 18
See also CLR 20; CANR 3; CA 49-52;
SATA 7

**Adamson, Joy(-Friederike Victoria)**
1910-1980 . . . . . . . . . . . . . . . . . CLC 17
See also CANR 22; CA 69-72;
obituary CA 93-96; SATA 11;
obituary SATA 22

**Adcock, (Kareen) Fleur** 1934- . . . . . . CLC 41
See also CANR 11; CA 25-28R; DLB 40

**Addams, Charles (Samuel)**
1912-1988 . . . . . . . . . . . . . . . . . CLC 30
See also CANR 12; CA 61-64;
obituary CA 126

**Adler, C(arole) S(chwerdtfeger)**
1932- . . . . . . . . . . . . . . . . . . . . CLC 35
See also CANR 19; CA 89-92; SATA 26

**Adler, Renata** 1938- . . . . . . . . . . . . CLC 8, 31
See also CANR 5, 22; CA 49-52

**Ady, Endre** 1877-1919 . . . . . . . . . . . TCLC 11
See also CA 107

**Agee, James** 1909-1955 . . . . . . . . TCLC 1, 19
See also CA 108; DLB 2, 26;
CDALB 1941-1968

**Agnon, S(hmuel) Y(osef Halevi)**
1888-1970 . . . . . . . . . . . . . . CLC 4, 8, 14
See also CAP 2; CA 17-18;
obituary CA 25-28R

**Ai** 1947- . . . . . . . . . . . . . . . . . . . . . CLC 4, 14
See also CA 85-88

**Aickman, Robert (Fordyce)**
1914-1981 . . . . . . . . . . . . . . . . . CLC 57
See also CANR 3; CA 7-8R

Aiken, Conrad (Potter)
    1889-1973 ......... CLC 1, 3, 5, 10, 52
    See also CANR 4; CA 5-8R;
    obituary CA 45-48; SATA 3, 30; DLB 9,
    45

Aiken, Joan (Delano)   1924- ........ CLC 35
    See also CLR 1, 19; CANR 4; CA 9-12R;
    SAAS 1; SATA 2, 30

Ainsworth, William Harrison
    1805-1882 ................. NCLC 13
    See also SATA 24; DLB 21

Ajar, Emile   1914-1980
    See Gary, Romain

Akhmadulina, Bella (Akhatovna)
    1937- ....................... CLC 53
    See also CA 65-68

Akhmatova, Anna
    1888-1966 ....... CLC 11, 25, 64; PC 2
    See also CAP 1; CA 19-20;
    obituary CA 25-28R

Aksakov, Sergei Timofeyvich
    1791-1859 ................. NCLC 2

Aksenov, Vassily (Pavlovich)   1932-
    See Aksyonov, Vasily (Pavlovich)

Aksyonov, Vasily (Pavlovich)
    1932- .................... CLC 22, 37
    See also CANR 12; CA 53-56

Akutagawa Ryunosuke
    1892-1927 ................. TCLC 16
    See also CA 117

Alain-Fournier   1886-1914 ......... TCLC 6
    See also Fournier, Henri Alban
    See also DLB 65

Alarcon, Pedro Antonio de
    1833-1891 ................. NCLC 1

Alas (y Urena), Leopoldo (Enrique Garcia)
    1852-1901 ................. TCLC 29
    See also CA 113

Albee, Edward (Franklin III)
    1928- ... CLC 1, 2, 3, 5, 9, 11, 13, 25, 53
    See also CANR 8; CA 5-8R; DLB 7;
    CDALB 1941-1968

Alberti, Rafael   1902- ............ CLC 7
    See also CA 85-88

Alcott, Amos Bronson   1799-1888 .. NCLC 1
    See also DLB 1

Alcott, Louisa May   1832-1888 .... NCLC 6
    See also CLR 1; YABC 1; DLB 1, 42, 79;
    CDALB 1865-1917

Aldanov, Mark   1887-1957 ........ TCLC 23
    See also CA 118

Aldington, Richard   1892-1962 ...... CLC 49
    See also CA 85-88; DLB 20, 36

Aldiss, Brian W(ilson)
    1925- ................. CLC 5, 14, 40
    See also CAAS 2; CANR 5; CA 5-8R;
    SATA 34; DLB 14

Alegria, Fernando   1918- ........... CLC 57
    See also CANR 5; CA 11-12R

Aleixandre, Vicente   1898-1984 ... CLC 9, 36
    See also CANR 26; CA 85-88;
    obituary CA 114

Alepoudelis, Odysseus   1911-
    See Elytis, Odysseus

Aleshkovsky, Yuz   1929- ........... CLC 44
    See also CA 121, 128

Alexander, Lloyd (Chudley)   1924- .. CLC 35
    See also CLR 1, 5; CANR 1; CA 1-4R;
    SATA 3, 49; DLB 52

Alger, Horatio, Jr.   1832-1899 ..... NCLC 8
    See also SATA 16; DLB 42

Algren, Nelson   1909-1981 .... CLC 4, 10, 33
    See also CANR 20; CA 13-16R;
    obituary CA 103; DLB 9; DLB-Y 81, 82;
    CDALB 1941-1968

Alighieri, Dante   1265-1321 ....... CMLC 3

Allard, Janet   1975- ............... CLC 59

Allen, Edward   1948- ............... CLC 59

Allen, Roland   1939-
    See Ayckbourn, Alan

Allen, Woody   1935- ........... CLC 16, 52
    See also CANR 27; CA 33-36R; DLB 44

Allende, Isabel   1942- .......... CLC 39, 57
    See also CA 125

Allingham, Margery (Louise)
    1904-1966 .................. CLC 19
    See also CANR 4; CA 5-8R;
    obituary CA 25-28R; DLB 77

Allingham, William   1824-1889 ... NCLC 25
    See also DLB 35

Allston, Washington   1779-1843.... NCLC 2
    See also DLB 1

Almedingen, E. M.   1898-1971...... CLC 12
    See also Almedingen, Martha Edith von
    See also SATA 3

Almedingen, Martha Edith von   1898-1971
    See Almedingen, E. M.
    See also CANR 1; CA 1-4R

Alonso, Damaso   1898- ............ CLC 14
    See also CA 110; obituary CA 130

Alta   1942- ....................... CLC 19
    See also CA 57-60

Alter, Robert B(ernard)   1935- ...... CLC 34
    See also CANR 1; CA 49-52

Alther, Lisa   1944- .............. CLC 7, 41
    See also CANR 12; CA 65-68

Altman, Robert   1925- ............. CLC 16
    See also CA 73-76

Alvarez, A(lfred)   1929- .......... CLC 5, 13
    See also CANR 3; CA 1-4R; DLB 14, 40

Alvarez, Alejandro Rodriguez   1903-1965
    See Casona, Alejandro
    See also obituary CA 93-96

Amado, Jorge   1912- ........... CLC 13, 40
    See also CA 77-80

Ambler, Eric   1909- ............ CLC 4, 6, 9
    See also CANR 7; CA 9-12R; DLB 77

Amichai, Yehuda   1924- ...... CLC 9, 22, 57
    See also CA 85-88

Amiel, Henri Frederic   1821-1881 .. NCLC 4

Amis, Kingsley (William)
    1922- ....... CLC 1, 2, 3, 5, 8, 13, 40, 44
    See also CANR 8; CA 9-12R; DLB 15, 27

Amis, Martin   1949- ....... CLC 4, 9, 38, 62
    See also CANR 8, 27; CA 65-68; DLB 14

Ammons, A(rchie) R(andolph)
    1926- ......... CLC 2, 3, 5, 8, 9, 25, 57
    See also CANR 6; CA 9-12R; DLB 5

Anand, Mulk Raj   1905- ........... CLC 23
    See also CA 65-68

Anaya, Rudolfo A(lfonso)   1937- .... CLC 23
    See also CAAS 4; CANR 1; CA 45-48;
    DLB 82

Andersen, Hans Christian
    1805-1875 ............ NCLC 7; SSC 6
    See also CLR 6; YABC 1, 1

Anderson, Jessica (Margaret Queale)
    19??- ...................... CLC 37
    See also CANR 4; CA 9-12R

Anderson, Jon (Victor)   1940- ....... CLC 9
    See also CANR 20; CA 25-28R

Anderson, Lindsay   1923- .......... CLC 20
    See also CA 125

Anderson, Maxwell   1888-1959 ..... TCLC 2
    See also CA 105; DLB 7

Anderson, Poul (William)   1926- .... CLC 15
    See also CAAS 2; CANR 2, 15; CA 1-4R;
    SATA 39; DLB 8

Anderson, Robert (Woodruff)
    1917- ...................... CLC 23
    See also CA 21-24R; DLB 7

Anderson, Roberta Joan   1943-
    See Mitchell, Joni

Anderson, Sherwood
    1876-1941 ...... TCLC 1, 10, 24; SSC 1
    See also CAAS 3; CA 104, 121; DLB 4, 9;
    DLB-DS 1

Andrade, Carlos Drummond de
    1902-1987 .................. CLC 18
    See also CA 123

Andrewes, Lancelot   1555-1626 ....... LC 5

Andrews, Cicily Fairfield   1892-1983
    See West, Rebecca

Andreyev, Leonid (Nikolaevich)
    1871-1919 .................. TCLC 3
    See also CA 104

Andrezel, Pierre   1885-1962
    See Dinesen, Isak; Blixen, Karen
    (Christentze Dinesen)

Andric, Ivo   1892-1975 ............. CLC 8
    See also CA 81-84; obituary CA 57-60

Angelique, Pierre   1897-1962
    See Bataille, Georges

Angell, Roger   1920- .............. CLC 26
    See also CANR 13; CA 57-60

Angelou, Maya   1928- ....... CLC 12, 35, 64
    See also CANR 19; CA 65-68; SATA 49;
    DLB 38

Annensky, Innokenty   1856-1909 ... TCLC 14
    See also CA 110

Anouilh, Jean (Marie Lucien Pierre)
    1910-1987 ...... CLC 1, 3, 8, 13, 40, 50
    See also CA 17-20R; obituary CA 123

Anthony, Florence   1947-
    See Ai

Anthony (Jacob), Piers   1934- ...... CLC 35
    See also Jacob, Piers A(nthony)
    D(illingham)
    See also DLB 8

**Antoninus, Brother** 1912-
See Everson, William (Oliver)

**Antonioni, Michelangelo** 1912- ..... **CLC 20**
See also CA 73-76

**Antschel, Paul** 1920-1970...... **CLC 10, 19**
See also Celan, Paul
See also CA 85-88

**Anwar, Chairil** 1922-1949 ....... **TCLC 22**
See also CA 121

**Apollinaire, Guillaume**
1880-1918 ................. **TCLC 3, 8**
See also Kostrowitzki, Wilhelm Apollinaris
de

**Appelfeld, Aharon** 1932- ....... **CLC 23, 47**
See also CA 112

**Apple, Max (Isaac)** 1941-........ **CLC 9, 33**
See also CANR 19; CA 81-84

**Appleman, Philip (Dean)** 1926- ..... **CLC 51**
See also CANR 6; CA 13-16R

**Apuleius, (Lucius) (Madaurensis)**
125?-175?.................. **CMLC 1**

**Aquin, Hubert** 1929-1977......... **CLC 15**
See also CA 105; DLB 53

**Aragon, Louis** 1897-1982........ **CLC 3, 22**
See also CA 69-72; obituary CA 108;
DLB 72

**Arbuthnot, John** 1667-1735.......... **LC 1**

**Archer, Jeffrey (Howard)** 1940- .... **CLC 28**
See also CANR 22; CA 77-80

**Archer, Jules** 1915- ............. **CLC 12**
See also CANR 6; CA 9-12R; SAAS 5;
SATA 4

**Arden, John** 1930- .......... **CLC 6, 13, 15**
See also CAAS 4; CA 13-16R; DLB 13

**Arenas, Reinaldo** 1943- ........... **CLC 41**
See also CA 124, 128

**Aretino, Pietro** 1492-1556 .......... **LC 12**

**Arguedas, Jose Maria**
1911-1969 .............. **CLC 10, 18**
See also CA 89-92

**Argueta, Manlio** 1936-........... **CLC 31**

**Ariosto, Ludovico** 1474-1533........ **LC 6**

**Aristophanes**
c. 450 B. C.-c. 385 B. C. ...... **CMLC 4**

**Arlt, Roberto** 1900-1942 ........ **TCLC 29**
See also CA 123

**Armah, Ayi Kwei** 1939-......... **CLC 5, 33**
See also CANR 21; CA 61-64

**Armatrading, Joan** 1950-.......... **CLC 17**
See also CA 114

**Arnim, Achim von (Ludwig Joachim von**
**Arnim)** 1781-1831 ......... **NCLC 5**
See also DLB 90

**Arnold, Matthew** 1822-1888 ... **NCLC 6, 29**
See also DLB 32, 57

**Arnold, Thomas** 1795-1842 ...... **NCLC 18**
See also DLB 55

**Arnow, Harriette (Louisa Simpson)**
1908-1986 .......... **CLC 2, 7, 18**
See also CANR 14; CA 9-12R;
obituary CA 118; SATA 42, 47; DLB 6

**Arp, Jean** 1887-1966............... **CLC 5**
See also CA 81-84; obituary CA 25-28R

**Arquette, Lois S(teinmetz)** 1934-
See Duncan (Steinmetz Arquette), Lois
See also SATA 1

**Arrabal, Fernando** 1932- ... **CLC 2, 9, 18, 58**
See also CANR 15; CA 9-12R

**Arrick, Fran** 19??- ............... **CLC 30**

**Artaud, Antonin** 1896-1948 ..... **TCLC 3, 36**
See also CA 104

**Arthur, Ruth M(abel)** 1905-1979.... **CLC 12**
See also CANR 4; CA 9-12R;
obituary CA 85-88; SATA 7;
obituary SATA 26

**Artsybashev, Mikhail Petrarch**
1878-1927 .................. **TCLC 31**

**Arundel, Honor (Morfydd)**
1919-1973 ................... **CLC 17**
See also CAP 2; CA 21-22;
obituary CA 41-44R; SATA 4;
obituary SATA 24

**Asch, Sholem** 1880-1957 .......... **TCLC 3**
See also CA 105

**Ashbery, John (Lawrence)**
1927- ... **CLC 2, 3, 4, 6, 9, 13, 15, 25, 41**
See also CANR 9; CA 5-8R; DLB 5;
DLB-Y 81

**Ashton-Warner, Sylvia (Constance)**
1908-1984 ................... **CLC 19**
See also CA 69-72; obituary CA 112

**Asimov, Isaac** 1920-.... **CLC 1, 3, 9, 19, 26**
See also CLR 12; CANR 2, 19; CA 1-4R;
SATA 1, 26; DLB 8

**Astley, Thea (Beatrice May)**
1925- ...................... **CLC 41**
See also CANR 11; CA 65-68

**Aston, James** 1906-1964
See White, T(erence) H(anbury)

**Asturias, Miguel Angel**
1899-1974 ............... **CLC 3, 8, 13**
See also CAP 2; CA 25-28;
obituary CA 49-52

**Atheling, William, Jr.** 1921-1975
See Blish, James (Benjamin)

**Atherton, Gertrude (Franklin Horn)**
1857-1948 .................... **TCLC 2**
See also CA 104; DLB 9, 78

**Atwood, Margaret (Eleanor)**
1939- .... **CLC 2, 3, 4, 8, 13, 15, 25, 44;**
**SSC 2**
See also CANR 3, 24; CA 49-52; SATA 50;
DLB 53

**Aubin, Penelope** 1685-1731? ......... **LC 9**
See also DLB 39

**Auchincloss, Louis (Stanton)**
1917- ............. **CLC 4, 6, 9, 18, 45**
See also CANR 6; CA 1-4R; DLB 2;
DLB-Y 80

**Auden, W(ystan) H(ugh)**
1907-1973 ..... **CLC 1, 2, 3, 4, 6, 9, 11,**
**14, 43; PC 1**
See also CANR 5; CA 9-12R;
obituary CA 45-48; DLB 10, 20

**Audiberti, Jacques** 1899-1965 ...... **CLC 38**
See also obituary CA 25-28R

**Auel, Jean M(arie)** 1936-......... **CLC 31**
See also CANR 21; CA 103

**Augustine, St.** 354-430 .......... **CMLC 6**

**Austen, Jane** 1775-1817.... **NCLC 1, 13, 19**

**Auster, Paul** 1947-............... **CLC 47**
See also CANR 23; CA 69-72

**Austin, Mary (Hunter)**
1868-1934 ................. **TCLC 25**
See also CA 109; DLB 9

**Avison, Margaret** 1918-.......... **CLC 2, 4**
See also CA 17-20R; DLB 53

**Ayckbourn, Alan** 1939- .... **CLC 5, 8, 18, 33**
See also CA 21-24R; DLB 13

**Aydy, Catherine** 1937-
See Tennant, Emma

**Ayme, Marcel (Andre)** 1902-1967... **CLC 11**
See also CA 89-92; DLB 72

**Ayrton, Michael** 1921-1975........ **CLC 7**
See also CANR 9, 21; CA 5-8R;
obituary CA 61-64

**Azorin** 1874-1967 ................ **CLC 11**
See also Martinez Ruiz, Jose

**Azuela, Mariano** 1873-1952........ **TCLC 3**
See also CA 104

**"Bab"** 1836-1911
See Gilbert, (Sir) W(illiam) S(chwenck)

**Babel, Isaak (Emmanuilovich)**
1894-1941 ................ **TCLC 2, 13**
See also CA 104

**Babits, Mihaly** 1883-1941 ........ **TCLC 14**
See also CA 114

**Bacchelli, Riccardo** 1891-1985 ..... **CLC 19**
See also CA 29-32R; obituary CA 117

**Bach, Richard (David)** 1936-....... **CLC 14**
See also CANR 18; CA 9-12R; SATA 13

**Bachman, Richard** 1947-
See King, Stephen (Edwin)

**Bacovia, George** 1881-1957 ...... **TCLC 24**

**Bagehot, Walter** 1826-1877 ...... **NCLC 10**
See also DLB 55

**Bagnold, Enid** 1889-1981.......... **CLC 25**
See also CANR 5; CA 5-8R;
obituary CA 103; SATA 1, 25; DLB 13

**Bagryana, Elisaveta** 1893-......... **CLC 10**

**Bailey, Paul** 1937- ............... **CLC 45**
See also CANR 16; CA 21-24R; DLB 14

**Baillie, Joanna** 1762-1851 ........ **NCLC 2**

**Bainbridge, Beryl**
1933- .... **CLC 4, 5, 8, 10, 14, 18, 22, 62**
See also CANR 24; CA 21-24R; DLB 14

**Baker, Elliott** 1922-............. **CLC 8, 61**
See also CANR 2; CA 45-48

**Baker, Nicholson** 1957-........... **CLC 61**

**Baker, Russell (Wayne)** 1925-...... **CLC 31**
See also CANR 11; CA 57-60

**Bakshi, Ralph** 1938-.............. **CLC 26**
See also CA 112

**Bakunin, Mikhail (Alexandrovich)**
1814-1876 ................ **NCLC 25**

Author Index

Baldwin, James (Arthur)
1924-1987 . . . . . **CLC 1, 2, 3, 4, 5, 8, 13,
15, 17, 42, 50; DC 1**
See also CANR 3,24; CA 1-4R;
obituary CA 124; CABS 1; SATA 9, 54;
DLB 2, 7, 33; DLB-Y 87;
CDALB 1941-1968; AAYA 4

Ballard, J(ames) G(raham)
1930- . . . . . . . . **CLC 3, 6, 14, 36; SSC 1**
See also CANR 15; CA 5-8R; DLB 14

Balmont, Konstantin Dmitriyevich
1867-1943 . . . . . . . . . . . . . . . . . **TCLC 11**
See also CA 109

Balzac, Honore de
1799-1850 . . . . . . . . . . . **NCLC 5; SSC 5**

Bambara, Toni Cade   1939- . . . . . . . . **CLC 19**
See also CA 29-32R; DLB 38

Bandanes, Jerome   1937- . . . . . . . . . . **CLC 59**

Banim, John   1798-1842 . . . . . . . . . **NCLC 13**

Banim, Michael   1796-1874 . . . . . . **NCLC 13**

Banks, Iain   1954- . . . . . . . . . . . . . . . **CLC 34**
See also CA 123

Banks, Lynne Reid   1929- . . . . . . . . . **CLC 23**
See also Reid Banks, Lynne

Banks, Russell   1940- . . . . . . . . . . . . **CLC 37**
See also CANR 19; CA 65-68

Banville, John   1945- . . . . . . . . . . . . . **CLC 46**
See also CA 117, 128; DLB 14

Banville, Theodore (Faullain) de
1832-1891 . . . . . . . . . . . . . . . . . **NCLC 9**

Baraka, Imamu Amiri
1934- . . . . . . . . **CLC 1, 2, 3, 5, 10, 14, 33**
See also Jones, (Everett) LeRoi
See also DLB 5, 7, 16, 38;
CDALB 1941-1968

Barbellion, W. N. P.   1889-1919 . . . **TCLC 24**

Barbera, Jack   1945- . . . . . . . . . . . . . . **CLC 44**
See also CA 110

Barbey d'Aurevilly, Jules Amedee
1808-1889 . . . . . . . . . . . . . . . . . **NCLC 1**

Barbusse, Henri   1873-1935 . . . . . . . . **TCLC 5**
See also CA 105; DLB 65

Barea, Arturo   1897-1957 . . . . . . . . . **TCLC 14**
See also CA 111

Barfoot, Joan   1946- . . . . . . . . . . . . . . **CLC 18**
See also CA 105

Baring, Maurice   1874-1945 . . . . . . . . **TCLC 8**
See also CA 105; DLB 34

Barker, Clive   1952- . . . . . . . . . . . . . . **CLC 52**
See also CA 121

Barker, George (Granville)
1913- . . . . . . . . . . . . . . . . . . . . . **CLC 8, 48**
See also CANR 7; CA 9-12R; DLB 20

Barker, Howard   1946- . . . . . . . . . . . . **CLC 37**
See also CA 102; DLB 13

Barker, Pat   1943- . . . . . . . . . . . . . . . . **CLC 32**
See also CA 117, 122

Barlow, Joel   1754-1812 . . . . . . . . . **NCLC 23**
See also DLB 37

Barnard, Mary (Ethel)   1909- . . . . . . . **CLC 48**
See also CAP 2; CA 21-22

Barnes, Djuna (Chappell)
1892-1982 . . . **CLC 3, 4, 8, 11, 29; SSC 3**
See also CANR 16; CA 9-12R;
obituary CA 107; DLB 4, 9, 45

Barnes, Julian   1946- . . . . . . . . . . . . . **CLC 42**
See also CANR 19; CA 102

Barnes, Peter   1931- . . . . . . . . . . . . **CLC 5, 56**
See also CA 65-68; DLB 13

Baroja (y Nessi), Pio   1872-1956 . . . . **TCLC 8**
See also CA 104

Barondess, Sue K(aufman)   1926-1977
See Kaufman, Sue
See also CANR 1; CA 1-4R;
obituary CA 69-72

Barrett, (Roger) Syd   1946-
See Pink Floyd

Barrett, William (Christopher)
1913- . . . . . . . . . . . . . . . . . . . . . . . . **CLC 27**
See also CANR 11; CA 13-16R

Barrie, (Sir) J(ames) M(atthew)
1860-1937 . . . . . . . . . . . . . . . . . . . **TCLC 2**
See also CLR 16; YABC 1; CA 104;
DLB 10

Barrol, Grady   1953-
See Bograd, Larry

Barry, Philip (James Quinn)
1896-1949 . . . . . . . . . . . . . . . . . . **TCLC 11**
See also CA 109; DLB 7

Barth, John (Simmons)
1930- . . . . . . **CLC 1, 2, 3, 5, 7, 9, 10, 14,
27, 51**
See also CANR 5, 23; CA 1-4R; CABS 1;
DLB 2

Barthelme, Donald
1931-1989 . . . . . **CLC 1, 2, 3, 5, 6, 8, 13,
23, 46, 59; SSC 2**
See also CANR 20; CA 21-24R, 129;
SATA 7; DLB 2; DLB-Y 80

Barthelme, Frederick   1943- . . . . . . . . **CLC 36**
See also CA 114, 122; DLB-Y 85

Barthes, Roland   1915-1980 . . . . . . . . **CLC 24**
See also obituary CA 97-100

Barzun, Jacques (Martin)   1907- . . . . **CLC 51**
See also CANR 22; CA 61-64

Bashkirtseff, Marie   1859-1884 . . . **NCLC 27**

Bassani, Giorgio   1916- . . . . . . . . . . . . **CLC 9**
See also CA 65-68

Bataille, Georges   1897-1962 . . . . . . . **CLC 29**
See also CA 101; obituary CA 89-92

Bates, H(erbert) E(rnest)
1905-1974 . . . . . . . . . . . . . . . . . . . . **CLC 46**
See also CA 93-96; obituary CA 45-48

Baudelaire, Charles
1821-1867 . . . . . . . . . . **NCLC 6, 29; PC 1**

Baudrillard, Jean   1929- . . . . . . . . . . . **CLC 60**

Baum, L(yman) Frank   1856-1919 . . . **TCLC 7**
See also CLR 15; CA 108; SATA 18;
DLB 22

Baumbach, Jonathan   1933- . . . . . . **CLC 6, 23**
See also CAAS 5; CANR 12; CA 13-16R;
DLB-Y 80

Bausch, Richard (Carl)   1945- . . . . . . **CLC 51**
See also CA 101

Baxter, Charles   1947- . . . . . . . . . . . . **CLC 45**
See also CA 57-60

Baxter, James K(eir)   1926-1972 . . . . **CLC 14**
See also CA 77-80

Bayer, Sylvia   1909-1981
See Glassco, John

Beagle, Peter S(oyer)   1939- . . . . . . . . **CLC 7**
See also CANR 4; CA 9-12R; DLB-Y 80

Beard, Charles A(ustin)
1874-1948 . . . . . . . . . . . . . . . . . **TCLC 15**
See also CA 115; SATA 18; DLB 17

Beardsley, Aubrey   1872-1898 . . . . . **NCLC 6**

Beattie, Ann   1947- . . . **CLC 8, 13, 18, 40, 63**
See also CA 81-84; DLB-Y 82

Beattie, James   1735-1803 . . . . . . . **NCLC 25**

Beauvoir, Simone (Lucie Ernestine Marie
Bertrand) de
1908-1986 . . . **CLC 1, 2, 4, 8, 14, 31, 44,
50**
See also CANR 28; CA 9-12R;
obituary CA 118; DLB 72; DLB-Y 86

Becker, Jurek   1937- . . . . . . . . . . . . **CLC 7, 19**
See also CA 85-88; DLB 75

Becker, Walter   1950- . . . . . . . . . . . . . **CLC 26**

Beckett, Samuel (Barclay)
1906-1989 . . . . . **CLC 1, 2, 3, 4, 6, 9, 10,
11, 14, 18, 29, 57, 59**
See also CA 5-8R; DLB 13, 15

Beckford, William   1760-1844 . . . . **NCLC 16**
See also DLB 39

Beckman, Gunnel   1910- . . . . . . . . . . . **CLC 26**
See also CANR 15; CA 33-36R; SATA 6

Becque, Henri   1837-1899 . . . . . . . . **NCLC 3**

Beddoes, Thomas Lovell
1803-1849 . . . . . . . . . . . . . . . . . **NCLC 3**

Beecher, Catharine Esther
1800-1878 . . . . . . . . . . . . . . . . . **NCLC 30**
See also DLB 1

Beecher, John   1904-1980 . . . . . . . . . . **CLC 6**
See also CANR 8; CA 5-8R;
obituary CA 105

Beer, Johann   1655-1700 . . . . . . . . . . . **LC 5**

Beer, Patricia   1919?- . . . . . . . . . . . . . **CLC 58**
See also CANR 13; CA 61-64; DLB 40

Beerbohm, (Sir Henry) Max(imilian)
1872-1956 . . . . . . . . . . . . . . . . **TCLC 1, 24**
See also CA 104; DLB 34

Behan, Brendan
1923-1964 . . . . . . . . . . . . **CLC 1, 8, 11, 15**
See also CA 73-76; DLB 13

Behn, Aphra   1640?-1689 . . . . . . . . . . . **LC 1**
See also DLB 39, 80

Behrman, S(amuel) N(athaniel)
1893-1973 . . . . . . . . . . . . . . . . . . . . **CLC 40**
See also CAP 1; CA 15-16;
obituary CA 45-48; DLB 7, 44

Beiswanger, George Edwin   1931-
See Starbuck, George (Edwin)

Belasco, David   1853-1931 . . . . . . . . . **TCLC 3**
See also CA 104; DLB 7

Belcheva, Elisaveta   1893-
See Bagryana, Elisaveta

**Belinski, Vissarion Grigoryevich**
1811-1848 . . . . . . . . . . . . . . . . NCLC 5

**Belitt, Ben** 1911- . . . . . . . . . . . . . . . . CLC 22
See also CAAS 4; CANR 7; CA 13-16R;
DLB 5

**Bell, Acton** 1820-1849
See Bronte, Anne

**Bell, Currer** 1816-1855
See Bronte, Charlotte

**Bell, Madison Smartt** 1957- . . . . . . . . CLC 41
See also CA 111

**Bell, Marvin (Hartley)** 1937- . . . . . CLC 8, 31
See also CA 21-24R; DLB 5

**Bellamy, Edward** 1850-1898 . . . . . . NCLC 4
See also DLB 12

**Belloc, (Joseph) Hilaire (Pierre Sebastien Rene Swanton)**
1870-1953 . . . . . . . . . . . . . . . TCLC 7, 18
See also YABC 1; CA 106; DLB 19

**Bellow, Saul**
1915- . . . . . CLC 1, 2, 3, 6, 8, 10, 13, 15,
25, 33, 34, 63
See also CA 5-8R; CABS 1; DLB 2, 28;
DLB-Y 82; DLB-DS 3;
CDALB 1941-1968

**Belser, Reimond Karel Maria de** 1929-
See Ruyslinck, Ward

**Bely, Andrey** 1880-1934 . . . . . . . . . . TCLC 7
See also CA 104

**Benary-Isbert, Margot** 1889-1979 . . . CLC 12
See also CLR 12; CANR 4; CA 5-8R;
obituary CA 89-92; SATA 2;
obituary SATA 21

**Benavente (y Martinez), Jacinto**
1866-1954 . . . . . . . . . . . . . . . . TCLC 3
See also CA 106

**Benchley, Peter (Bradford)**
1940- . . . . . . . . . . . . . . . . . . . . . CLC 4, 8
See also CANR 12; CA 17-20R; SATA 3

**Benchley, Robert** 1889-1945 . . . . . . . TCLC 1
See also CA 105; DLB 11

**Benedikt, Michael** 1935- . . . . . . . . CLC 4, 14
See also CANR 7; CA 13-16R; DLB 5

**Benet, Juan** 1927- . . . . . . . . . . . . . . . CLC 28

**Benet, Stephen Vincent**
1898-1943 . . . . . . . . . . . . . . . . . . TCLC 7
See also YABC 1; CA 104; DLB 4, 48

**Benet, William Rose** 1886-1950 . . . TCLC 28
See also CA 118; DLB 45

**Benford, Gregory (Albert)** 1941- . . . . CLC 52
See also CANR 12, 24; CA 69-72;
DLB-Y 82

**Benjamin, Walter** 1892-1940 . . . . . . TCLC 39

**Benn, Gottfried** 1886-1956 . . . . . . . . TCLC 3
See also CA 106; DLB 56

**Bennett, Alan** 1934- . . . . . . . . . . . . . . CLC 45
See also CA 103

**Bennett, (Enoch) Arnold**
1867-1931 . . . . . . . . . . . . . . TCLC 5, 20
See also CA 106; DLB 10, 34

**Bennett, George Harold** 1930-
See Bennett, Hal
See also CA 97-100

**Bennett, Hal** 1930- . . . . . . . . . . . . . . . . CLC 5
See also Bennett, George Harold
See also DLB 33

**Bennett, Jay** 1912- . . . . . . . . . . . . . . CLC 35
See also CANR 11; CA 69-72; SAAS 4;
SATA 27, 41

**Bennett, Louise (Simone)** 1919- . . . . . CLC 28
See also Bennett-Coverly, Louise Simone

**Bennett-Coverly, Louise Simone** 1919-
See Bennett, Louise (Simone)
See also CA 97-100

**Benson, E(dward) F(rederic)**
1867-1940 . . . . . . . . . . . . . . . . . TCLC 27
See also CA 114

**Benson, Jackson J.** 1930- . . . . . . . . . CLC 34
See also CA 25-28R

**Benson, Sally** 1900-1972 . . . . . . . . . . CLC 17
See also CAP 1; CA 19-20;
obituary CA 37-40R; SATA 1, 35;
obituary SATA 27

**Benson, Stella** 1892-1933 . . . . . . . . TCLC 17
See also CA 117; DLB 36

**Bentley, E(dmund) C(lerihew)**
1875-1956 . . . . . . . . . . . . . . . . TCLC 12
See also CA 108; DLB 70

**Bentley, Eric (Russell)** 1916- . . . . . . . CLC 24
See also CANR 6; CA 5-8R

**Berger, John (Peter)** 1926- . . . . . . CLC 2, 19
See also CA 81-84; DLB 14

**Berger, Melvin (H.)** 1927- . . . . . . . . . CLC 12
See also CANR 4; CA 5-8R; SAAS 2;
SATA 5

**Berger, Thomas (Louis)**
1924- . . . . . . . CLC 3, 5, 8, 11, 18, 38
See also CANR 5; CA 1-4R; DLB 2;
DLB-Y 80

**Bergman, (Ernst) Ingmar** 1918- . . . . . CLC 16
See also CA 81-84

**Bergson, Henri** 1859-1941 . . . . . . . . TCLC 32

**Bergstein, Eleanor** 1938- . . . . . . . . . . CLC 4
See also CANR 5; CA 53-56

**Berkoff, Steven** 1937- . . . . . . . . . . . . . CLC 56
See also CA 104

**Bermant, Chaim** 1929- . . . . . . . . . . . . CLC 40
See also CANR 6; CA 57-60

**Bernanos, (Paul Louis) Georges**
1888-1948 . . . . . . . . . . . . . . . . . TCLC 3
See also CA 104; DLB 72

**Bernard, April** 19??- . . . . . . . . . . . . . CLC 59

**Bernhard, Thomas**
1931-1989 . . . . . . . . . . . . . CLC 3, 32, 61
See also CA 85-88,; obituary CA 127;
DLB 85

**Berriault, Gina** 1926- . . . . . . . . . . . . . CLC 54
See also CA 116

**Berrigan, Daniel J.** 1921- . . . . . . . . . . CLC 4
See also CAAS 1; CANR 11; CA 33-36R;
DLB 5

**Berrigan, Edmund Joseph Michael, Jr.**
1934-1983
See Berrigan, Ted
See also CANR 14; CA 61-64;
obituary CA 110

**Berrigan, Ted** 1934-1983 . . . . . . . . . CLC 37
See also Berrigan, Edmund Joseph Michael,
Jr.
See also DLB 5

**Berry, Chuck** 1926- . . . . . . . . . . . . . . CLC 17

**Berry, Wendell (Erdman)**
1934- . . . . . . . . . . . CLC 4, 6, 8, 27, 46
See also CA 73-76; DLB 5, 6

**Berryman, John**
1914-1972 . . . . . CLC 1, 2, 3, 4, 6, 8, 10,
13, 25, 62
See also CAP 1; CA 15-16;
obituary CA 33-36R; CABS 2; DLB 48;
CDALB 1941-1968

**Bertolucci, Bernardo** 1940- . . . . . . . . CLC 16
See also CA 106

**Bertran de Born** c. 1140-1215 . . . . . CMLC 5

**Besant, Annie (Wood)** 1847-1933 . . . TCLC 9
See also CA 105

**Bessie, Alvah** 1904-1985 . . . . . . . . . . CLC 23
See also CANR 2; CA 5-8R;
obituary CA 116; DLB 26

**Beti, Mongo** 1932- . . . . . . . . . . . . . . . CLC 27
See also Beyidi, Alexandre

**Betjeman, (Sir) John**
1906-1984 . . . . . . . . CLC 2, 6, 10, 34, 43
See also CA 9-12R; obituary CA 112;
DLB 20; DLB-Y 84

**Betti, Ugo** 1892-1953 . . . . . . . . . . . . . TCLC 5
See also CA 104

**Betts, Doris (Waugh)** 1932- . . . . CLC 3, 6, 28
See also CANR 9; CA 13-16R; DLB-Y 82

**Bialik, Chaim Nachman**
1873-1934 . . . . . . . . . . . . . . . . TCLC 25

**Bidart, Frank** 19??- . . . . . . . . . . . . . . CLC 33

**Bienek, Horst** 1930- . . . . . . . . . . . . . CLC 7, 11
See also CA 73-76; DLB 75

**Bierce, Ambrose (Gwinett)**
1842-1914? . . . . . . . . . . . . . . . . TCLC 1, 7
See also CA 104; DLB 11, 12, 23, 71, 74;
CDALB 1865-1917

**Billington, Rachel** 1942- . . . . . . . . . . CLC 43
See also CA 33-36R

**Binyon, T(imothy) J(ohn)** 1936- . . . . CLC 34
See also CA 111

**Bioy Casares, Adolfo** 1914- . . . . CLC 4, 8, 13
See also CANR 19; CA 29-32R

**Bird, Robert Montgomery**
1806-1854 . . . . . . . . . . . . . . . . NCLC 1

**Birdwell, Cleo** 1936-
See DeLillo, Don

**Birney (Alfred) Earle**
1904- . . . . . . . . . . . . . . . . CLC 1, 4, 6, 11
See also CANR 5, 20; CA 1-4R

**Bishop, Elizabeth**
1911-1979 . . . . . . CLC 1, 4, 9, 13, 15, 32
See also CANR 26; CA 5-8R;
obituary CA 89-92; CABS 2;
obituary SATA 24; DLB 5

**Bishop, John** 1935- . . . . . . . . . . . . . . . CLC 10
See also CA 105

**Bissett, Bill** 1939- . . . . . . . . . . . . . . . . CLC 18
See also CANR 15; CA 69-72; DLB 53

**Bitov, Andrei (Georgievich)** 1937- . . . CLC 57

**Biyidi, Alexandre** 1932-
See Beti, Mongo
See also CA 114, 124

**Bjornson, Bjornstjerne (Martinius)**
1832-1910 ............... **TCLC 7, 37**
See also CA 104

**Blackburn, Paul** 1926-1971 ...... **CLC 9, 43**
See also CA 81-84; obituary CA 33-36R;
DLB 16; DLB-Y 81

**Black Elk** 1863-1950 ............ **TCLC 33**

**Blackmore, R(ichard) D(oddridge)**
1825-1900 .................. **TCLC 27**
See also CA 120; DLB 18

**Blackmur, R(ichard) P(almer)**
1904-1965 ................. **CLC 2, 24**
See also CAP 1; CA 11-12;
obituary CA 25-28R; DLB 63

**Blackwood, Algernon (Henry)**
1869-1951 .................. **TCLC 5**
See also CA 105

**Blackwood, Caroline** 1931- ....... **CLC 6, 9**
See also CA 85-88; DLB 14

**Blair, Eric Arthur** 1903-1950
See Orwell, George
See also CA 104; SATA 29

**Blais, Marie-Claire**
1939- ............ **CLC 2, 4, 6, 13, 22**
See also CAAS 4; CA 21-24R; DLB 53

**Blaise, Clark** 1940-............... **CLC 29**
See also CAAS 3; CANR 5; CA 53-56R;
DLB 53

**Blake, Nicholas** 1904-1972
See Day Lewis, C(ecil)

**Blake, William** 1757-1827 ....... **NCLC 13**
See also SATA 30

**Blasco Ibanez, Vicente**
1867-1928 .................. **TCLC 12**
See also CA 110

**Blatty, William Peter** 1928-......... **CLC 2**
See also CANR 9; CA 5-8R

**Blessing, Lee** 1949-............... **CLC 54**

**Blish, James (Benjamin)**
1921-1975 .................. **CLC 14**
See also CANR 3; CA 1-4R;
obituary CA 57-60; DLB 8

**Blixen, Karen (Christentze Dinesen)**
1885-1962
See Dinesen, Isak
See also CAP 2; CA 25-28; SATA 44

**Bloch, Robert (Albert)** 1917-....... **CLC 33**
See also CANR 5; CA 5-8R; SATA 12;
DLB 44

**Blok, Aleksandr (Aleksandrovich)**
1880-1921 .................. **TCLC 5**
See also CA 104

**Bloom, Harold** 1930- ............. **CLC 24**
See also CA 13-16R; DLB 67

**Blount, Roy (Alton), Jr.** 1941- ..... **CLC 38**
See also CANR 10; CA 53-56

**Bloy, Leon** 1846-1917............ **TCLC 22**
See also CA 121

**Blume, Judy (Sussman Kitchens)**
1938- ................... **CLC 12, 30**
See also CLR 2, 15; CANR 13; CA 29-32R;
SATA 2, 31; DLB 52

**Blunden, Edmund (Charles)**
1896-1974 ................. **CLC 2, 56**
See also CAP 2; CA 17-18;
obituary CA 45-48; DLB 20

**Bly, Robert (Elwood)**
1926- .......... **CLC 1, 2, 5, 10, 15, 38**
See also CA 5-8R; DLB 5

**Bochco, Steven** 1944?-............. **CLC 35**

**Bodker, Cecil** 1927- .............. **CLC 21**
See also CLR 23; CANR 13; CA 73-76;
SATA 14

**Boell, Heinrich (Theodor)** 1917-1985
See Boll, Heinrich
See also CANR 24; CA 21-24R;
obituary CA 116

**Bogan, Louise** 1897-1970..... **CLC 4, 39, 46**
See also CA 73-76; obituary CA 25-28R;
DLB 45

**Bogarde, Dirk** 1921-.............. **CLC 19**
See also Van Den Bogarde, Derek (Jules
Gaspard Ulric) Niven
See also DLB 14

**Bogosian, Eric** 1953- ............. **CLC 45**

**Bograd, Larry** 1953-.............. **CLC 35**
See also CA 93-96; SATA 33

**Bohl de Faber, Cecilia** 1796-1877
See Caballero, Fernan

**Boiardo, Matteo Maria** 1441-1494 .... **LC 6**

**Boileau-Despreaux, Nicolas**
1636-1711 .................... **LC 3**

**Boland, Eavan (Aisling)** 1944-...... **CLC 40**
See also DLB 40

**Boll, Heinrich (Theodor)**
1917-1985 ... **CLC 2, 3, 6, 9, 11, 15, 27,
39**
See also Boell, Heinrich (Theodor)
See also DLB 69; DLB-Y 85

**Bolt, Robert (Oxton)** 1924- ........ **CLC 14**
See also CA 17-20R; DLB 13

**Bond, Edward** 1934-....... **CLC 4, 6, 13, 23**
See also CA 25-28R; DLB 13

**Bonham, Frank** 1914-............. **CLC 12**
See also CANR 4; CA 9-12R; SAAS 3;
SATA 1, 49

**Bonnefoy, Yves** 1923-........ **CLC 9, 15, 58**
See also CA 85-88

**Bontemps, Arna (Wendell)**
1902-1973 ................. **CLC 1, 18**
See also CLR 6; CANR 4; CA 1-4R;
obituary CA 41-44R; SATA 2, 44;
obituary SATA 24; DLB 48, 51

**Booth, Martin** 1944-.............. **CLC 13**
See also CAAS 2; CA 93-96

**Booth, Philip** 1925-............... **CLC 23**
See also CANR 5; CA 5-8R; DLB-Y 82

**Booth, Wayne C(layson)** 1921- ..... **CLC 24**
See also CAAS 5; CANR 3; CA 1-4R;
DLB 67

**Borchert, Wolfgang** 1921-1947 ..... **TCLC 5**
See also CA 104; DLB 69

**Borges, Jorge Luis**
1899-1986 ... **CLC 1, 2, 3, 4, 6, 8, 9, 10,
13, 19, 44, 48; SSC 4**
See also CANR 19; CA 21-24R; DLB-Y 86

**Borowski, Tadeusz** 1922-1951...... **TCLC 9**
See also CA 106

**Borrow, George (Henry)**
1803-1881 ................. **NCLC 9**
See also DLB 21, 55

**Bosschere, Jean de** 1878-1953..... **TCLC 19**
See also CA 115

**Boswell, James** 1740-1795.......... **LC 4**

**Bottoms, David** 1949-............. **CLC 53**
See also CANR 22; CA 105; DLB-Y 83

**Boucolon, Maryse** 1937-
See Conde, Maryse
See also CA 110

**Bourget, Paul (Charles Joseph)**
1852-1935 ................. **TCLC 12**
See also CA 107

**Bourjaily, Vance (Nye)** 1922- .... **CLC 8, 62**
See also CAAS 1; CANR 2; CA 1-4R;
DLB 2

**Bourne, Randolph S(illiman)**
1886-1918 ................. **TCLC 16**
See also CA 117; DLB 63

**Bova, Ben(jamin William)** 1932-.... **CLC 45**
See also CLR 3; CANR 11; CA 5-8R;
SATA 6; DLB-Y 81

**Bowen, Elizabeth (Dorothea Cole)**
1899-1973 ..... **CLC 1, 3, 6, 11, 15, 22;
SSC 3**
See also CAP 2; CA 17-18;
obituary CA 41-44R; DLB 15

**Bowering, George** 1935-........ **CLC 15, 47**
See also CANR 10; CA 21-24R; DLB 53

**Bowering, Marilyn R(uthe)** 1949-... **CLC 32**
See also CA 101

**Bowers, Edgar** 1924- .............. **CLC 9**
See also CANR 24; CA 5-8R; DLB 5

**Bowie, David** 1947- ............... **CLC 17**
See also Jones, David Robert

**Bowles, Jane (Sydney)** 1917-1973.... **CLC 3**
See also CAP 2; CA 19-20;
obituary CA 41-44R

**Bowles, Paul (Frederick)**
1910- ........ **CLC 1, 2, 19, 53; SSC 3**
See also CAAS 1; CANR 1, 19; CA 1-4R;
DLB 5, 6

**Box, Edgar** 1925-
See Vidal, Gore

**Boyd, William** 1952-........... **CLC 28, 53**
See also CA 114, 120

**Boyle, Kay** 1903- .. **CLC 1, 5, 19, 58; SSC 5**
See also CAAS 1; CA 13-16R; DLB 4, 9, 48

**Boyle, Patrick** 19??-.............. **CLC 19**

**Boyle, Thomas Coraghessan**
1948- ................... **CLC 36, 55**
See also CA 120; DLB-Y 86

**Brackenridge, Hugh Henry**
1748-1816 ................. **NCLC 7**
See also DLB 11, 37

**Bradbury, Edward P.** 1939-
See Moorcock, Michael

**Bradbury, Malcolm (Stanley)**
1932- .................... **CLC 32, 61**
See also CANR 1; CA 1-4R; DLB 14

Bradbury, Ray(mond Douglas)
1920- ........... CLC 1, 3, 10, 15, 42
See also CANR 2; CA 1-4R; SATA 11;
DLB 2, 8

Bradford, Gamaliel 1863-1932..... TCLC 36
See also DLB 17

Bradley, David (Henry), Jr. 1950- .. CLC 23
See also CANR 26; CA 104; DLB 33

Bradley, John Ed 1959-........... CLC 55

Bradley, Marion Zimmer 1930-..... CLC 30
See also CANR 7; CA 57-60; DLB 8

Bradstreet, Anne 1612-1672......... LC 4
See also DLB 24; CDALB 1640-1865

Bragg, Melvyn 1939- ............. CLC 10
See also CANR 10; CA 57-60; DLB 14

Braine, John (Gerard)
1922-1986 ............... CLC 1, 3, 41
See also CANR 1; CA 1-4R;
obituary CA 120; DLB 15; DLB-Y 86

Brammer, Billy Lee 1930?-1978
See Brammer, William

Brammer, William 1930?-1978 ..... CLC 31
See also obituary CA 77-80

Brancati, Vitaliano 1907-1954..... TCLC 12
See also CA 109

Brancato, Robin F(idler) 1936- ..... CLC 35
See also CANR 11; CA 69-72; SATA 23

Brand, Millen 1906-1980.......... CLC 7
See also CA 21-24R; obituary CA 97-100

Branden, Barbara 19??-........... CLC 44

Brandes, Georg (Morris Cohen)
1842-1927 ................. TCLC 10
See also CA 105

Brandys, Kazimierz 1916-......... CLC 62

Branley, Franklyn M(ansfield)
1915- ....................... CLC 21
See also CLR 13; CANR 14; CA 33-36R;
SATA 4

Brathwaite, Edward 1930-......... CLC 11
See also CANR 11; CA 25-28R; DLB 53

Brautigan, Richard (Gary)
1935-1984 .... CLC 1, 3, 5, 9, 12, 34, 42
See also CA 53-56; obituary CA 113;
SATA 56; DLB 2, 5; DLB-Y 80, 84

Brecht, (Eugen) Bertolt (Friedrich)
1898-1956 .......... TCLC 1, 6, 13, 35
See also CA 104; DLB 56

Bremer, Fredrika 1801-1865 ..... NCLC 11

Brennan, Christopher John
1870-1932 .................. TCLC 17
See also CA 117

Brennan, Maeve 1917-............. CLC 5
See also CA 81-84

Brentano, Clemens (Maria)
1778-1842 .................. NCLC 1
See also DLB 90

Brenton, Howard 1942-........... CLC 31
See also CA 69-72; DLB 13

Breslin, James 1930-
See Breslin, Jimmy
See also CA 73-76

Breslin, Jimmy 1930-........... CLC 4, 43
See also Breslin, James

Bresson, Robert 1907-............ CLC 16
See also CA 110

Breton, Andre 1896-1966... CLC 2, 9, 15, 54
See also CAP 2; CA 19-20;
obituary CA 25-28R; DLB 65

Breytenbach, Breyten 1939-..... CLC 23, 37
See also CA 113, 129

Bridgers, Sue Ellen 1942- ......... CLC 26
See also CANR 11; CA 65-68; SAAS 1;
SATA 22; DLB 52

Bridges, Robert 1844-1930........ TCLC 1
See also CA 104; DLB 19

Bridie, James 1888-1951 .......... TCLC 3
See also Mavor, Osborne Henry
See also DLB 10

Brin, David 1950-................ CLC 34
See also CANR 24; CA 102

Brink, Andre (Philippus)
1935- ................... CLC 18, 36
See also CA 104

Brinsmead, H(esba) F(ay) 1922- .... CLC 21
See also CANR 10; CA 21-24R; SAAS 5;
SATA 18

Brittain, Vera (Mary) 1893?-1970... CLC 23
See also CAP 1; CA 15-16;
obituary CA 25-28R

Broch, Hermann 1886-1951....... TCLC 20
See also CA 117; DLB 85

Brock, Rose 1923-
See Hansen, Joseph

Brodkey, Harold 1930-........... CLC 56
See also CA 111

Brodsky, Iosif Alexandrovich 1940-
See Brodsky, Joseph (Alexandrovich)
See also CA 41-44R

Brodsky, Joseph (Alexandrovich)
1940- ............ CLC 4, 6, 13, 36, 50
See also Brodsky, Iosif Alexandrovich

Brodsky, Michael (Mark) 1948- .... CLC 19
See also CANR 18; CA 102

Bromell, Henry 1947-............. CLC 5
See also CANR 9; CA 53-56

Bromfield, Louis (Brucker)
1896-1956 .................. TCLC 11
See also CA 107; DLB 4, 9

Broner, E(sther) M(asserman)
1930- ...................... CLC 19
See also CANR 8, 25; CA 17-20R; DLB 28

Bronk, William 1918-............. CLC 10
See also CANR 23; CA 89-92

Bronte, Anne 1820-1849......... NCLC 4
See also DLB 21

Bronte, Charlotte 1816-1855 .... NCLC 3, 8
See also DLB 21

Bronte, (Jane) Emily 1818-1848 .. NCLC 16
See also DLB 21, 32

Brooke, Frances 1724-1789 ......... LC 6
See also DLB 39

Brooke, Henry 1703?-1783 .......... LC 1
See also DLB 39

Brooke, Rupert (Chawner)
1887-1915 ................. TCLC 2, 7
See also CA 104; DLB 19

Brooke-Rose, Christine 1926- ...... CLC 40
See also CA 13-16R; DLB 14

Brookner, Anita 1928-...... CLC 32, 34, 51
See also CA 114, 120; DLB-Y 87

Brooks, Cleanth 1906- ............ CLC 24
See also CA 17-20R; DLB 63

Brooks, Gwendolyn
1917- ........... CLC 1, 2, 4, 5, 15, 49
See also CANR 1; CA 1-4R; SATA 6;
DLB 5, 76; CDALB 1941-1968

Brooks, Mel 1926-................ CLC 12
See also Kaminsky, Melvin
See also CA 65-68; DLB 26

Brooks, Peter 1938-.............. CLC 34
See also CANR 1; CA 45-48

Brooks, Van Wyck 1886-1963...... CLC 29
See also CANR 6; CA 1-4R; DLB 45, 63

Brophy, Brigid (Antonia)
1929-.................. CLC 6, 11, 29
See also CAAS 4; CANR 25; CA 5-8R;
DLB 14

Brosman, Catharine Savage 1934-.... CLC 9
See also CANR 21; CA 61-64

Broughton, T(homas) Alan 1936- ... CLC 19
See also CANR 2, 23; CA 45-48

Broumas, Olga 1949-............. CLC 10
See also CANR 20; CA 85-88

Brown, Charles Brockden
1771-1810 ................. NCLC 22
See also DLB 37, 59, 73;
CDALB 1640-1865

Brown, Christy 1932-1981......... CLC 63
See also CA 105; obituary CA 104

Brown, Claude 1937- ............. CLC 30
See also CA 73-76

Brown, Dee (Alexander) 1908- .. CLC 18, 47
See also CAAS 6; CANR 11; CA 13-16R;
SATA 5; DLB-Y 80

Brown, George Douglas 1869-1902
See Douglas, George

Brown, George Mackay 1921-.... CLC 5, 28
See also CAAS 6; CANR 12; CA 21-24R;
SATA 35; DLB 14, 27

Brown, Rita Mae 1944-........ CLC 18, 43
See also CANR 2, 11; CA 45-48

Brown, Rosellen 1939-............. CLC 32
See also CANR 14; CA 77-80

Brown, Sterling A(llen)
1901-1989 .............. CLC 1, 23, 59
See also CANR 26; CA 85-88;
obituary CA 27; DLB 48, 51, 63

Brown, William Wells
1816?-1884.............. NCLC 2; DC 1
See also DLB 3, 50

Browne, Jackson 1950- ........... CLC 21
See also CA 120

Browning, Elizabeth Barrett
1806-1861 ............... NCLC 1, 16
See also DLB 32

Browning, Robert
1812-1889 ............ NCLC 19; PC 2
See also YABC 1; DLB 32

Browning, Tod 1882-1962 ......... CLC 16
See also obituary CA 117

Bruccoli, Matthew J(oseph) 1931- .. **CLC 34**
See also CANR 7; CA 9-12R

Bruce, Lenny 1925-1966 .......... **CLC 21**
See also Schneider, Leonard Alfred

Brunner, John (Kilian Houston)
1934- ..................... **CLC 8, 10**
See also CAAS 8; CANR 2; CA 1-4R

Brutus, Dennis 1924- ............. **CLC 43**
See also CANR 2; CA 49-52

Bryan, C(ourtlandt) D(ixon) B(arnes)
1936- ......................... **CLC 29**
See also CANR 13; CA 73-76

Bryant, William Cullen
1794-1878 ................. **NCLC 6**
See also DLB 3, 43, 59; CDALB 1640-1865

Bryusov, Valery (Yakovlevich)
1873-1924 ................. **TCLC 10**
See also CA 107

Buchanan, George 1506-1582 ........ **LC 4**

Buchheim, Lothar-Gunther 1918- .... **CLC 6**
See also CA 85-88

Buchner, (Karl) Georg
1813-1837 ................. **NCLC 26**

Buchwald, Art(hur) 1925- .......... **CLC 33**
See also CANR 21; CA 5-8R; SATA 10

Buck, Pearl S(ydenstricker)
1892-1973 .............. **CLC 7, 11, 18**
See also CANR 1; CA 1-4R;
obituary CA 41-44R; SATA 1, 25; DLB 9

Buckler, Ernest 1908-1984 ........ **CLC 13**
See also CAP 1; CA 11-12;
obituary CA 114; SATA 47

Buckley, Vincent (Thomas)
1925-1988 ................... **CLC 57**
See also CA 101

Buckley, William F(rank), Jr.
1925- ................... **CLC 7, 18, 37**
See also CANR 1, 24; CA 1-4R; DLB-Y 80

Buechner, (Carl) Frederick
1926- .................. **CLC 2, 4, 6, 9**
See also CANR 11; CA 13-16R; DLB-Y 80

Buell, John (Edward) 1927- ........ **CLC 10**
See also CA 1-4R; DLB 53

Buero Vallejo, Antonio 1916- ... **CLC 15, 46**
See also CANR 24; CA 106

Bukowski, Charles 1920- .... **CLC 2, 5, 9, 41**
See also CA 17-20R; DLB 5

Bulgakov, Mikhail (Afanas'evich)
1891-1940 ................. **TCLC 2, 16**
See also CA 105

Bullins, Ed 1935- ............. **CLC 1, 5, 7**
See also CANR 24; CA 49-52; DLB 7, 38

Bulwer-Lytton, (Lord) Edward (George Earle
Lytton) 1803-1873 .......... **NCLC 1**
See also Lytton, Edward Bulwer
See also DLB 21

Bunin, Ivan (Alexeyevich)
1870-1953 ............. **TCLC 6; SSC 5**
See also CA 104

Bunting, Basil 1900-1985 .... **CLC 10, 39, 47**
See also CANR 7; CA 53-56;
obituary CA 115; DLB 20

Bunuel, Luis 1900-1983 .......... **CLC 16**
See also CA 101; obituary CA 110

Bunyan, John 1628-1688 ............ **LC 4**
See also DLB 39

Burgess (Wilson, John) Anthony
1917- ..... **CLC 1, 2, 4, 5, 8, 10, 13, 15,
22, 40, 62**
See also Wilson, John (Anthony) Burgess
See also DLB 14

Burke, Edmund 1729-1797 .......... **LC 7**

Burke, Kenneth (Duva) 1897- .... **CLC 2, 24**
See also CA 5-8R; DLB 45, 63

Burney, Fanny 1752-1840 ...... **NCLC 12**
See also DLB 39

Burns, Robert 1759-1796 ............ **LC 3**

Burns, Tex 1908?-
See L'Amour, Louis (Dearborn)

Burnshaw, Stanley 1906- ..... **CLC 3, 13, 44**
See also CA 9-12R; DLB 48

Burr, Anne 1937- ................. **CLC 6**
See also CA 25-28R

Burroughs, Edgar Rice
1875-1950 ............... **TCLC 2, 32**
See also CA 104; SATA 41; DLB 8

Burroughs, William S(eward)
1914- .......... **CLC 1, 2, 5, 15, 22, 42**
See also CANR 20; CA 9-12R; DLB 2, 8,
16; DLB-Y 81

Busch, Frederick 1941- ... **CLC 7, 10, 18, 47**
See also CAAS 1; CA 33-36R; DLB 6

Bush, Ronald 19??- ................ **CLC 34**

Butler, Octavia E(stelle) 1947- ..... **CLC 38**
See also CANR 12, 24; CA 73-76; DLB 33

Butler, Samuel 1835-1902 ...... **TCLC 1, 33**
See also CA 104; DLB 18, 57

Butor, Michel (Marie Francois)
1926- ............. **CLC 1, 3, 8, 11, 15**
See also CA 9-12R

Buzo, Alexander 1944- ............ **CLC 61**
See also CANR 17; CA 97-100

Buzzati, Dino 1906-1972 .......... **CLC 36**
See also obituary CA 33-36R

Byars, Betsy 1928- ............... **CLC 35**
See also CLR 1, 16; CANR 18; CA 33-36R;
SAAS 1; SATA 4, 46; DLB 52

Byatt, A(ntonia) S(usan Drabble)
1936- ...................... **CLC 19**
See also CANR 13; CA 13-16R; DLB 14

Byrne, David 1953?- .............. **CLC 26**

Byrne, John Keyes 1926-
See Leonard, Hugh
See also CA 102

Byron, George Gordon (Noel), Lord Byron
1788-1824 ............... **NCLC 2, 12**

Caballero, Fernan 1796-1877 ..... **NCLC 10**

Cabell, James Branch 1879-1958 ... **TCLC 6**
See also CA 105; DLB 9, 78

Cable, George Washington
1844-1925 ............. **TCLC 4; SSC 4**
See also CA 104; DLB 12, 74

Cabrera Infante, G(uillermo)
1929- ................ **CLC 5, 25, 45**
See also CANR 29; CA 85-88

Cage, John (Milton, Jr.) 1912- ..... **CLC 41**
See also CANR 9; CA 13-16R

Cain, G. 1929-
See Cabrera Infante, G(uillermo)

Cain, James M(allahan)
1892-1977 ............. **CLC 3, 11, 28**
See also CANR 8; CA 17-20R;
obituary CA 73-76

Caldwell, Erskine (Preston)
1903-1987 ........ **CLC 1, 8, 14, 50, 60**
See also CAAS 1; CANR 2; CA 1-4R;
obituary CA 121; DLB 9, 86

Caldwell, (Janet Miriam) Taylor (Holland)
1900-1985 .............. **CLC 2, 28, 39**
See also CANR 5; CA 5-8R;
obituary CA 116

Calhoun, John Caldwell
1782-1850 ................. **NCLC 15**
See also DLB 3

Calisher, Hortense 1911- .... **CLC 2, 4, 8, 38**
See also CANR 1, 22; CA 1-4R; DLB 2

Callaghan, Morley (Edward)
1903- .................. **CLC 3, 14, 41**
See also CA 9-12R; DLB 68

Calvino, Italo
1923-1985 .... **CLC 5, 8, 11, 22, 33, 39;
SSC 3**
See also CANR 23; CA 85-88;
obituary CA 116

Cameron, Carey 1952- ............. **CLC 59**

Cameron, Peter 1959- ............. **CLC 44**
See also CA 125

Campana, Dino 1885-1932 ........ **TCLC 20**
See also CA 117

Campbell, John W(ood), Jr.
1910-1971 .................. **CLC 32**
See also CAP 2; CA 21-22;
obituary CA 29-32R; DLB 8

Campbell, (John) Ramsey 1946- .... **CLC 42**
See also CANR 7; CA 57-60

Campbell, (Ignatius) Roy (Dunnachie)
1901-1957 .................. **TCLC 5**
See also CA 104; DLB 20

Campbell, Thomas 1777-1844 .... **NCLC 19**

Campbell, (William) Wilfred
1861-1918 .................. **TCLC 9**
See also CA 106

Camus, Albert
1913-1960 ... **CLC 1, 2, 4, 9, 11, 14, 32,
63**
See also CA 89-92; DLB 72

Canby, Vincent 1924- ............. **CLC 13**
See also CA 81-84

Canetti, Elias 1905- ......... **CLC 3, 14, 25**
See also CANR 23; CA 21-24R; DLB 85

Canin, Ethan 1960- ............... **CLC 55**

Cape, Judith 1916-
See Page, P(atricia) K(athleen)

Capek, Karel
1890-1938 .......... **TCLC 6, 37; DC 1**
See also CA 104

Capote, Truman
1924-1984 ..... **CLC 1, 3, 8, 13, 19, 34,
38, 58; SSC 2**
See also CANR 18; CA 5-8R;
obituary CA 113; DLB 2; DLB-Y 80, 84;
CDALB 1941-1968

Capra, Frank 1897-.............. CLC 16
See also CA 61-64

Caputo, Philip 1941-............. CLC 32
See also CA 73-76

Card, Orson Scott 1951- .... CLC 44, 47, 50
See also CA 102

Cardenal, Ernesto 1925-.......... CLC 31
See also CANR 2; CA 49-52

Carducci, Giosue 1835-1907...... TCLC 32

Carew, Thomas 1595?-1640 ........ LC 13

Carey, Ernestine Gilbreth 1908- .... CLC 17
See also CA 5-8R; SATA 2

Carey, Peter 1943-............ CLC 40, 55
See also CA 123, 127

Carleton, William 1794-1869...... NCLC 3

Carlisle, Henry (Coffin) 1926-...... CLC 33
See also CANR 15; CA 13-16R

Carlson, Ron(ald F.) 1947-........ CLC 54
See also CA 105

Carlyle, Thomas 1795-1881 ...... NCLC 22
See also DLB 55

Carman, (William) Bliss
1861-1929 .................. TCLC 7
See also CA 104

Carpenter, Don(ald Richard)
1931- ...................... CLC 41
See also CANR 1; CA 45-48

Carpentier (y Valmont), Alejo
1904-1980 ........... CLC 8, 11, 38
See also CANR 11; CA 65-68;
obituary CA 97-100

Carr, Emily 1871-1945........... TCLC 32
See also DLB 68

Carr, John Dickson 1906-1977 ...... CLC 3
See also CANR 3; CA 49-52;
obituary CA 69-72

Carr, Virginia Spencer 1929-....... CLC 34
See also CA 61-64

Carrier, Roch 1937-.............. CLC 13
See also DLB 53

Carroll, James (P.) 1943-.......... CLC 38
See also CA 81-84

Carroll, Jim 1951- .............. CLC 35
See also CA 45-48

Carroll, Lewis 1832-1898......... NCLC 2
See also Dodgson, Charles Lutwidge
See also CLR 2; DLB 18

Carroll, Paul Vincent 1900-1968.... CLC 10
See also CA 9-12R; obituary CA 25-28R;
DLB 10

Carruth, Hayden 1921- .... CLC 4, 7, 10, 18
See also CANR 4; CA 9-12R; SATA 47;
DLB 5

Carter, Angela (Olive) 1940-..... CLC 5, 41
See also CANR 12; CA 53-56; DLB 14

Carver, Raymond
1938-1988 ......... CLC 22, 36, 53, 55
See also CANR 17; CA 33-36R;
obituary CA 126; DLB-Y 84, 88

Cary, (Arthur) Joyce (Lunel)
1888-1957 ............... TCLC 1, 29
See also CA 104; DLB 15

Casanova de Seingalt, Giovanni Jacopo
1725-1798 .................. LC 13

Casares, Adolfo Bioy 1914-
See Bioy Casares, Adolfo

Casely-Hayford, J(oseph) E(phraim)
1866-1930 ................. TCLC 24
See also CA 123

Casey, John 1880-1964
See O'Casey, Sean

Casey, John 1939- .............. CLC 59
See also CANR 23; CA 69-72

Casey, Michael 1947-............. CLC 2
See also CA 65-68; DLB 5

Casey, Warren 1935- ............. CLC 12
See also Jacobs, Jim and Casey, Warren
See also CA 101

Casona, Alejandro 1903-1965 ...... CLC 49
See also Alvarez, Alejandro Rodriguez

Cassavetes, John 1929-........... CLC 20
See also CA 85-88, 127

Cassill, R(onald) V(erlin) 1919-... CLC 4, 23
See also CAAS 1; CANR 7; CA 9-12R;
DLB 6

Cassity, (Allen) Turner 1929- .... CLC 6, 42
See also CANR 11; CA 17-20R

Castaneda, Carlos 1935?-.......... CLC 12
See also CA 25-28R

Castelvetro, Lodovico 1505-1571..... LC 12

Castiglione, Baldassare 1478-1529 ... LC 12

Castro, Rosalia de 1837-1885 ..... NCLC 3

Cather, Willa (Sibert)
1873-1947 ...... TCLC 1, 11, 31; SSC 2
See also CA 104; SATA 30; DLB 9, 54;
DLB-DS 1; CDALB 1865-1917

Catton, (Charles) Bruce
1899-1978 .................. CLC 35
See also CANR 7; CA 5-8R;
obituary CA 81-84; SATA 2;
obituary SATA 24; DLB 17

Cauldwell, Frank 1923-
See King, Francis (Henry)

Caunitz, William 1935- .......... CLC 34

Causley, Charles (Stanley) 1917-..... CLC 7
See also CANR 5; CA 9-12R; SATA 3;
DLB 27

Caute, (John) David 1936-........ CLC 29
See also CAAS 4; CANR 1; CA 1-4R;
DLB 14

Cavafy, C(onstantine) P(eter)
1863-1933 ................. TCLC 2, 7
See also CA 104

Cavanna, Betty 1909-............. CLC 12
See also CANR 6; CA 9-12R; SATA 1, 30

Cayrol, Jean 1911-............... CLC 11
See also CA 89-92; DLB 83

Cela, Camilo Jose 1916-...... CLC 4, 13, 59
See also CAAS 10; CANR 21; CA 21-24R

Celan, Paul 1920-1970..... CLC 10, 19, 53
See also Antschel, Paul
See also DLB 69

Celine, Louis-Ferdinand
1894-1961 ..... CLC 1, 3, 4, 7, 9, 15, 47
See also Destouches,
Louis-Ferdinand-Auguste
See also DLB 72

Cellini, Benvenuto 1500-1571 ........ LC 7

Cendrars, Blaise 1887-1961 ........ CLC 18
See also Sauser-Hall, Frederic

Cernuda, Luis (y Bidon)
1902-1963 .................. CLC 54
See also CA 89-92

Cervantes (Saavedra), Miguel de
1547-1616 .................... LC 6

Cesaire, Aime (Fernand) 1913- .. CLC 19, 32
See also CANR 24; CA 65-68

Chabon, Michael 1965?-........... CLC 55

Chabrol, Claude 1930- ............ CLC 16
See also CA 110

Challans, Mary 1905-1983
See Renault, Mary
See also CA 81-84; obituary CA 111;
SATA 23; obituary SATA 36

Chambers, Aidan 1934- ........... CLC 35
See also CANR 12; CA 25-28R; SATA 1

Chambers, James 1948-
See Cliff, Jimmy

Chandler, Raymond 1888-1959 ... TCLC 1, 7
See also CA 104

Channing, William Ellery
1780-1842 ................. NCLC 17
See also DLB 1, 59

Chaplin, Charles (Spencer)
1889-1977 .................. CLC 16
See also CA 81-84; obituary CA 73-76;
DLB 44

Chapman, Graham 1941?- ......... CLC 21
See also Monty Python
See also CA 116; obituary CA 169

Chapman, John Jay 1862-1933 ..... TCLC 7
See also CA 104

Chappell, Fred 1936- ............. CLC 40
See also CAAS 4; CANR 8; CA 5-8R;
DLB 6

Char, Rene (Emile)
1907-1988 .......... CLC 9, 11, 14, 55
See also CA 13-16R; obituary CA 124

Charles I 1600-1649 ............... LC 13

Charyn, Jerome 1937- ........ CLC 5, 8, 18
See also CAAS 1; CANR 7; CA 5-8R;
DLB-Y 83

Chase, Mary (Coyle) 1907-1981
See also CA 77-80, 105; SATA 17, 29; DC 1

Chase, Mary Ellen 1887-1973....... CLC 2
See also CAP 1; CA 15-16;
obituary CA 41-44R; SATA 10

Chateaubriand, Francois Rene de
1768-1848 .................. NCLC 3

Chatterji, Bankim Chandra
1838-1894 ................. NCLC 19

Chatterji, Saratchandra
1876-1938 ................. TCLC 13
See also CA 109

Chatterton, Thomas 1752-1770 ....... LC 3

**Chatwin, (Charles) Bruce**
1940-1989 . . . . . . . . . . . . **CLC 28, 57, 59**
See also CA 85-88,; obituary CA 127

**Chayefsky, Paddy** 1923-1981 . . . . . . **CLC 23**
See also CA 9-12R; obituary CA 104;
DLB 7, 44; DLB-Y 81

**Chayefsky, Sidney** 1923-1981
See Chayefsky, Paddy
See also CANR 18

**Chedid, Andree** 1920- . . . . . . . . . . . . **CLC 47**

**Cheever, John**
1912-1982 . . . . . **CLC 3, 7, 8, 11, 15, 25,
64; SSC 1**
See also CANR 5, 27; CA 5-8R;
obituary CA 106; CABS 1; DLB 2;
DLB-Y 80, 82; CDALB 1941-1968

**Cheever, Susan** 1943- . . . . . . . . **CLC 18, 48**
See also CA 103; DLB-Y 82

**Chekhov, Anton (Pavlovich)**
1860-1904 . . . . . . **TCLC 3, 10, 31; SSC 2**
See also CA 104, 124

**Chernyshevsky, Nikolay Gavrilovich**
1828-1889 . . . . . . . . . . . . . . . . . **NCLC 1**

**Cherry, Caroline Janice** 1942-
See Cherryh, C. J.

**Cherryh, C. J.** 1942- . . . . . . . . . . . . . **CLC 35**
See also CANR 10; CA 65-68; DLB-Y 80

**Chesnutt, Charles Waddell**
1858-1932 . . . . . . . . . **TCLC 5, 39; SSC 7**
See also CA 106, 125; DLB 12, 50, 78

**Chester, Alfred** 1929?-1971 . . . . . . . . **CLC 49**
See also obituary CA 33-36R

**Chesterton, G(ilbert) K(eith)**
1874-1936 . . . . . . . . . . **TCLC 1, 6; SSC 1**
See also CA 104; SATA 27; DLB 10, 19,
34, 70

**Ch'ien Chung-shu** 1910- . . . . . . . . . . **CLC 22**

**Child, Lydia Maria** 1802-1880 . . . . **NCLC 6**
See also DLB 1, 74

**Child, Philip** 1898-1978 . . . . . . . . . . . **CLC 19**
See also CAP 1; CA 13-14; SATA 47

**Childress, Alice** 1920- . . . . . . . . . **CLC 12, 15**
See also CLR 14; CANR 3; CA 45-48;
SATA 7, 48; DLB 7, 38

**Chislett, (Margaret) Anne** 1943?- . . . **CLC 34**

**Chitty, (Sir) Thomas Willes** 1926- . . **CLC 11**
See also Hinde, Thomas
See also CA 5-8R

**Chomette, Rene** 1898-1981
See Clair, Rene
See also obituary CA 103

**Chopin, Kate (O'Flaherty)**
1851-1904 . . . . . . . . . . . . . . . . **TCLC 5, 14**
See also CA 104, 122; DLB 12;
CDALB 1865-1917

**Christie, (Dame) Agatha (Mary Clarissa)**
1890-1976 . . . . . . **CLC 1, 6, 8, 12, 39, 48**
See also CANR 10; CA 17-20R;
obituary CA 61-64; SATA 36; DLB 13

**Christie, (Ann) Philippa** 1920-
See Pearce, (Ann) Philippa
See also CANR 4; CA 7-8

**Christine de Pizan** 1365?-1431? . . . . . . . **LC 9**

**Chulkov, Mikhail Dmitrievich**
1743-1792 . . . . . . . . . . . . . . . . . . . **LC 2**

**Churchill, Caryl** 1938- . . . . . . . . **CLC 31, 55**
See also CANR 22; CA 102; DLB 13

**Churchill, Charles** 1731?-1764 . . . . . . . **LC 3**

**Chute, Carolyn** 1947- . . . . . . . . . . . . . **CLC 39**
See also CA 123

**Ciardi, John (Anthony)**
1916-1986 . . . . . . . . . . . . . **CLC 10, 40, 44**
See also CAAS 2; CANR 5; CA 5-8R;
obituary CA 118; SATA 1, 46; DLB 5;
DLB-Y 86

**Cicero, Marcus Tullius**
106 B.C.-43 B.C. . . . . . . . . . . . . . **CMLC 3**

**Cimino, Michael** 1943?- . . . . . . . . . . . **CLC 16**
See also CA 105

**Cioran, E. M.** 1911- . . . . . . . . . . . . . . **CLC 64**
See also CA 25-28R

**Clair, Rene** 1898-1981 . . . . . . . . . . . . **CLC 20**
See also Chomette, Rene

**Clampitt, Amy** 19??- . . . . . . . . . . . . . . **CLC 32**
See also CA 110

**Clancy, Tom** 1947- . . . . . . . . . . . . . . **CLC 45**
See also CA 125

**Clare, John** 1793-1864 . . . . . . . . . . . **NCLC 9**
See also DLB 55

**Clark, (Robert) Brian** 1932- . . . . . . . **CLC 29**
See also CA 41-44R

**Clark, Eleanor** 1913- . . . . . . . . . . **CLC 5, 19**
See also CA 9-12R; DLB 6

**Clark, John Pepper** 1935- . . . . . . . . . **CLC 38**
See also CANR 16; CA 65-68

**Clark, Mavis Thorpe** 1912?- . . . . . . **CLC 12**
See also CANR 8; CA 57-60; SAAS 5;
SATA 8

**Clark, Walter Van Tilburg**
1909-1971 . . . . . . . . . . . . . . . . . . **CLC 28**
See also CA 9-12R; obituary CA 33-36R;
SATA 8; DLB 9

**Clarke, Arthur C(harles)**
1917- . . . . . . **CLC 1, 4, 13, 18, 35; SSC 3**
See also CANR 2; CA 1-4R; SATA 13

**Clarke, Austin** 1896-1974 . . . . . . . . **CLC 6, 9**
See also CANR 14; CAP 2; CA 29-32;
obituary CA 49-52; DLB 10, 20, 53

**Clarke, Austin (Ardinel) C(hesterfield)**
1934- . . . . . . . . . . . . . . . . . . . **CLC 8, 53**
See also CANR 14; CA 25-28R; DLB 53

**Clarke, Gillian** 1937- . . . . . . . . . . . . . **CLC 61**
See also CA 106; DLB 40

**Clarke, Marcus (Andrew Hislop)**
1846-1881 . . . . . . . . . . . . . . . . . **NCLC 19**

**Clarke, Shirley** 1925- . . . . . . . . . . . . . **CLC 16**

**Clash, The** . . . . . . . . . . . . . . . . . . . . . **CLC 30**

**Claudel, Paul (Louis Charles Marie)**
1868-1955 . . . . . . . . . . . . . . . . **TCLC 2, 10**
See also CA 104

**Clavell, James (duMaresq)**
1924- . . . . . . . . . . . . . . . . . . . . **CLC 6, 25**
See also CANR 26; CA 25-28R

**Cleaver, (Leroy) Eldridge** 1935- . . . . **CLC 30**
See also CANR 16; CA 21-24R

**Cleese, John** 1939- . . . . . . . . . . . . . . **CLC 21**
See also Monty Python
See also CA 112, 116

**Cleland, John** 1709-1789 . . . . . . . . . . . **LC 2**
See also DLB 39

**Clemens, Samuel Langhorne**
1835-1910 . . . . . . **TCLC 6, 12, 19; SSC 6**
See also Twain, Mark
See also YABC 2; CA 104; DLB 11, 12, 23,
64, 74; CDALB 1865-1917

**Cliff, Jimmy** 1948- . . . . . . . . . . . . . . . **CLC 21**

**Clifton, Lucille** 1936- . . . . . . . . . . . . . **CLC 19**
See also CLR 5; CANR 2, 24; CA 49-52;
SATA 20; DLB 5, 41

**Clough, Arthur Hugh** 1819-1861 . . **NCLC 27**
See also DLB 32

**Clutha, Janet Paterson Frame** 1924-
See Frame (Clutha), Janet (Paterson)
See also CANR 2; CA 1-4R

**Coburn, D(onald) L(ee)** 1938- . . . . . . **CLC 10**
See also CA 89-92

**Cocteau, Jean (Maurice Eugene Clement)**
1889-1963 . . . . . . . . **CLC 1, 8, 15, 16, 43**
See also CAP 2; CA 25-28; DLB 65

**Codrescu, Andrei** 1946- . . . . . . . . . . . **CLC 46**
See also CANR 13; CA 33-36R

**Coetzee, J(ohn) M.** 1940- . . . . . . . **CLC 23, 33**
See also CA 77-80

**Cohen, Arthur A(llen)**
1928-1986 . . . . . . . . . . . . . . . . . **CLC 7, 31**
See also CANR 1, 17; CA 1-4R;
obituary CA 120; DLB 28

**Cohen, Leonard (Norman)**
1934- . . . . . . . . . . . . . . . . . . . . **CLC 3, 38**
See also CANR 14; CA 21-24R; DLB 53

**Cohen, Matt** 1942- . . . . . . . . . . . . . . . **CLC 19**
See also CA 61-64; DLB 53

**Cohen-Solal, Annie** 19??- . . . . . . . . . . **CLC 50**

**Colegate, Isabel** 1931- . . . . . . . . . . . . **CLC 36**
See also CANR 8, 22; CA 17-20R; DLB 14

**Coleridge, Samuel Taylor**
1772-1834 . . . . . . . . . . . . . . . . . **NCLC 9**

**Coles, Don** 1928- . . . . . . . . . . . . . . . . **CLC 46**
See also CA 115

**Colette (Sidonie-Gabrielle)**
1873-1954 . . . . . . . . . . . . . **TCLC 1, 5, 16**
See also CA 104; DLB 65

**Collett, (Jacobine) Camilla (Wergeland)**
1813-1895 . . . . . . . . . . . . . . . . **NCLC 22**

**Collier, Christopher** 1930- . . . . . . . . . **CLC 30**
See also CANR 13; CA 33-36R; SATA 16

**Collier, James L(incoln)** 1928- . . . . . **CLC 30**
See also CLR 3; CANR 4; CA 9-12R;
SATA 8

**Collier, Jeremy** 1650-1726 . . . . . . . . . . **LC 6**

**Collins, Hunt** 1926-
See Hunter, Evan

**Collins, Linda** 19??- . . . . . . . . . . . . . . **CLC 44**
See also CA 125

**Collins, Tom** 1843-1912
See Furphy, Joseph

**Collins, (William) Wilkie**
1824-1889 . . . . . . . . . . . . . . . **NCLC 1, 18**
See also DLB 18, 70

Collins, William   1721-1759 . . . . . . . . .  LC 4

Colman, George   1909-1981
See Glassco, John

Colter, Cyrus   1910- . . . . . . . . . . . .  CLC 58
See also CANR 10; CA 65-68; DLB 33

Colton, James   1923-
See Hansen, Joseph

Colum, Padraic   1881-1972 . . . . . . . .  CLC 28
See also CA 73-76; obituary CA 33-36R;
SATA 15; DLB 19

Colvin, James   1939-
See Moorcock, Michael

Colwin, Laurie   1945- . . . . . . . .  CLC 5, 13, 23
See also CANR 20; CA 89-92; DLB-Y 80

Comfort, Alex(ander)   1920- . . . . . . . . .  CLC 7
See also CANR 1; CA 1-4R

Compton-Burnett, Ivy
1892-1969 . . . . . . .  CLC 1, 3, 10, 15, 34
See also CANR 4; CA 1-4R;
obituary CA 25-28R; DLB 36

Comstock, Anthony   1844-1915 . . . .  TCLC 13
See also CA 110

Conde, Maryse   1937- . . . . . . . . . . . .  CLC 52
See also Boucolon, Maryse

Condon, Richard (Thomas)
1915- . . . . . . . . . . . .  CLC 4, 6, 8, 10, 45
See also CAAS 1; CANR 2, 23; CA 1-4R

Congreve, William   1670-1729 . . . . . . .  LC 5
See also DLB 39

Connell, Evan S(helby), Jr.
1924- . . . . . . . . . . . . . . . . .  CLC 4, 6, 45
See also CAAS 2; CANR 2; CA 1-4R;
DLB 2; DLB-Y 81

Connelly, Marc(us Cook)
1890-1980 . . . . . . . . . . . . . . . . . .  CLC 7
See also CA 85-88; obituary CA 102;
obituary SATA 25; DLB 7; DLB-Y 80

Conner, Ralph   1860-1937 . . . . . . . .  TCLC 31

Conrad, Joseph
1857-1924 . . . . . . . . .  TCLC 1, 6, 13, 25
See also CA 104; SATA 27; DLB 10, 34

Conroy, Pat   1945- . . . . . . . . . . . . . .  CLC 30
See also CANR 24; CA 85-88; DLB 6

Constant (de Rebecque), (Henri) Benjamin
1767-1830 . . . . . . . . . . . . . . .  NCLC 6

Cook, Michael   1933- . . . . . . . . . . . .  CLC 58
See also CA 93-96; DLB 53

Cook, Robin   1940- . . . . . . . . . . . . . .  CLC 14
See also CA 108, 111

Cooke, Elizabeth   1948- . . . . . . . . . . .  CLC 55

Cooke, John Esten   1830-1886 . . . . .  NCLC 5
See also DLB 3

Cooney, Ray   19??- . . . . . . . . . . . . . .  CLC 62

Cooper, J. California   19??- . . . . . . . .  CLC 56
See also CA 125

Cooper, James Fenimore
1789-1851 . . . . . . . . . . . . . .  NCLC 1, 27
See also SATA 19; DLB 3;
CDALB 1640-1865

Coover, Robert (Lowell)
1932- . . . . . . . . . . .  CLC 3, 7, 15, 32, 46
See also CANR 3; CA 45-48; DLB 2;
DLB-Y 81

Copeland, Stewart (Armstrong)
1952- . . . . . . . . . . . . . . . . . . . . .  CLC 26
See also The Police

Coppard, A(lfred) E(dgar)
1878-1957 . . . . . . . . . . . . . . . . .  TCLC 5
See also YABC 1; CA 114

Coppee, Francois   1842-1908 . . . . . .  TCLC 25

Coppola, Francis Ford   1939- . . . . . . .  CLC 16
See also CA 77-80; DLB 44

Corcoran, Barbara   1911- . . . . . . . . .  CLC 17
See also CAAS 2; CANR 11; CA 21-24R;
SATA 3; DLB 52

Corman, Cid   1924- . . . . . . . . . . . . . .  CLC 9
See also Corman, Sidney
See also CAAS 2; DLB 5

Corman, Sidney   1924-
See Corman, Cid
See also CA 85-88

Cormier, Robert (Edmund)
1925- . . . . . . . . . . . . . . . . . .  CLC 12, 30
See also CLR 12; CANR 5, 23; CA 1-4R;
SATA 10, 45; DLB 52

Corn, Alfred (Dewitt III)   1943- . . . . .  CLC 33
See also CA 104; DLB-Y 80

Cornwell, David (John Moore)
1931- . . . . . . . . . . . . . . . . . . .  CLC 9, 15
See also le Carre, John
See also CANR 13; CA 5-8R

Corso, (Nunzio) Gregory   1930- . . .  CLC 1, 11
See also CA 5-8R; DLB 5, 16

Cortazar, Julio
1914-1984 . . . . .  CLC 2, 3, 5, 10, 13, 15,
33, 34; SSC 7
See also CANR 12; CA 21-24R

Corvo, Baron   1860-1913
See Rolfe, Frederick (William Serafino
Austin Lewis Mary)

Cosic, Dobrica   1921- . . . . . . . . . . . .  CLC 14
See also CA 122

Costain, Thomas B(ertram)
1885-1965 . . . . . . . . . . . . . . . . .  CLC 30
See also CA 5-8R; obituary CA 25-28R;
DLB 9

Costantini, Humberto   1924?-1987 . . .  CLC 49
See also obituary CA 122

Costello, Elvis   1955- . . . . . . . . . . . . .  CLC 21

Cotter, Joseph Seamon, Sr.
1861-1949 . . . . . . . . . . . . . . . .  TCLC 28
See also CA 124; DLB 50

Couperus, Louis (Marie Anne)
1863-1923 . . . . . . . . . . . . . . . .  TCLC 15
See also CA 115

Courtenay, Bryce   1933- . . . . . . . . . . .  CLC 59

Cousteau, Jacques-Yves   1910- . . . . . .  CLC 30
See also CANR 15; CA 65-68; SATA 38

Coward, (Sir) Noel (Pierce)
1899-1973 . . . . . . . . . .  CLC 1, 9, 29, 51
See also CAP 2; CA 17-18;
obituary CA 41-44R; DLB 10

Cowley, Malcolm   1898-1989 . . . . . . .  CLC 39
See also CANR 3; CA 5-6R;
obituary CA 128; DLB 4, 48; DLB-Y 81

Cowper, William   1731-1800 . . . . . .  NCLC 8

Cox, William Trevor   1928- . . . . . .  CLC 9, 14
See also Trevor, William
See also CANR 4; CA 9-12R

Cozzens, James Gould
1903-1978 . . . . . . . . . . . . .  CLC 1, 4, 11
See also CANR 19; CA 9-12R;
obituary CA 81-84; DLB 9; DLB-Y 84;
DLB-DS 2; CDALB 1941-1968

Crabbe, George   1754-1832 . . . . . .  NCLC 26

Crace, Douglas   1944- . . . . . . . . . . . .  CLC 58

Crane, (Harold) Hart
1899-1932 . . . . . . . . . . . . . . .  TCLC 2, 5
See also CA 104; DLB 4, 48

Crane, R(onald) S(almon)
1886-1967 . . . . . . . . . . . . . . . . . .  CLC 27
See also CA 85-88; DLB 63

Crane, Stephen
1871-1900 . . . . .  TCLC 11, 17, 32; SSC 7
See also YABC 2; CA 109; DLB 12, 54, 78;
CDALB 1865-1917

Craven, Margaret   1901-1980 . . . . . . .  CLC 17
See also CA 103

Crawford, F(rancis) Marion
1854-1909 . . . . . . . . . . . . . . . .  TCLC 10
See also CA 107; DLB 71

Crawford, Isabella Valancy
1850-1887 . . . . . . . . . . . . . . . .  NCLC 12
See also DLB 92

Crayencour, Marguerite de   1903-1987
See Yourcenar, Marguerite

Creasey, John   1908-1973 . . . . . . . . . .  CLC 11
See also CANR 8; CA 5-8R;
obituary CA 41-44R; DLB 77

Crebillon, Claude Prosper Jolyot de (fils)
1707-1777 . . . . . . . . . . . . . . . . . . .  LC 1

Creeley, Robert (White)
1926- . . . . . . . .  CLC 1, 2, 4, 8, 11, 15, 36
See also CANR 23; CA 1-4R; DLB 5, 16

Crews, Harry (Eugene)
1935- . . . . . . . . . . . . . . . . .  CLC 6, 23, 49
See also CANR 20; CA 25-28R; DLB 6

Crichton, (John) Michael
1942- . . . . . . . . . . . . . . . . . .  CLC 2, 6, 54
See also CANR 13; CA 25-28R; SATA 9;
DLB-Y 81

Crispin, Edmund   1921-1978 . . . . . . .  CLC 22
See also Montgomery, Robert Bruce
See also DLB 87

Cristofer, Michael   1946- . . . . . . . . . .  CLC 28
See also CA 110; DLB 7

Croce, Benedetto   1866-1952 . . . . . .  TCLC 37
See also CA 120

Crockett, David (Davy)
1786-1836 . . . . . . . . . . . . . . . .  NCLC 8
See also DLB 3, 11

Croker, John Wilson   1780-1857 . .  NCLC 10

Cronin, A(rchibald) J(oseph)
1896-1981 . . . . . . . . . . . . . . . . .  CLC 32
See also CANR 5; CA 1-4R;
obituary CA 102; obituary SATA 25, 47

Cross, Amanda   1926-
See Heilbrun, Carolyn G(old)

Crothers, Rachel   1878-1953 . . . . . . .  TCLC 19
See also CA 113; DLB 7

**Crowley, Aleister** 1875-1947 ....... **TCLC 7**
See also CA 104

**Crowley, John** 1942-
See also CA 61-64; DLB-Y 82

**Crumb, Robert** 1943- ............. **CLC 17**
See also CA 106

**Cryer, Gretchen** 1936?- ........... **CLC 21**
See also CA 114, 123

**Csath, Geza** 1887-1919........... **TCLC 13**
See also CA 111

**Cudlip, David** 1933- ............. **CLC 34**

**Cullen, Countee** 1903-1946 ..... **TCLC 4, 37**
See also CA 108, 124; SATA 18; DLB 4,
48, 51; CDALB 1917-1929

**Cummings, E(dward) E(stlin)**
1894-1962 ........ **CLC 1, 3, 8, 12, 15**
See also CA 73-76; DLB 4, 48

**Cunha, Euclides (Rodrigues) da**
1866-1909 .................. **TCLC 24**
See also CA 123

**Cunningham, J(ames) V(incent)**
1911-1985 ................. **CLC 3, 31**
See also CANR 1; CA 1-4R;
obituary CA 115; DLB 5

**Cunningham, Julia (Woolfolk)**
1916- ....................... **CLC 12**
See also CANR 4, 19; CA 9-12R; SAAS 2;
SATA 1, 26

**Cunningham, Michael** 1952- ....... **CLC 34**

**Currie, Ellen** 19??- .............. **CLC 44**

**Dabrowska, Maria (Szumska)**
1889-1965 .................. **CLC 15**
See also CA 106

**Dabydeen, David** 1956?-........... **CLC 34**
See also CA 106

**Dacey, Philip** 1939- ............. **CLC 51**
See also CANR 14; CA 37-40R

**Dagerman, Stig (Halvard)**
1923-1954 .................. **TCLC 17**
See also CA 117

**Dahl, Roald** 1916-............ **CLC 1, 6, 18**
See also CLR 1, 7; CANR 6; CA 1-4R;
SATA 1, 26

**Dahlberg, Edward** 1900-1977... **CLC 1, 7, 14**
See also CA 9-12R; obituary CA 69-72;
DLB 48

**Daly, Elizabeth** 1878-1967........ **CLC 52**
See also CAP 2; CA 23-24;
obituary CA 25-28R

**Daly, Maureen** 1921-............. **CLC 17**
See also McGivern, Maureen Daly
See also SAAS 1; SATA 2

**Daniken, Erich von** 1935-
See Von Daniken, Erich

**Dannay, Frederic** 1905-1982
See Queen, Ellery
See also CANR 1; CA 1-4R;
obituary CA 107

**D'Annunzio, Gabriele**
1863-1938 ................ **TCLC 6, 40**
See also CA 104

**Dante (Alighieri)**
See Alighieri, Dante

**Danziger, Paula** 1944- ............ **CLC 21**
See also CLR 20; CA 112, 115; SATA 30,
36

**Dario, Ruben** 1867-1916 .......... **TCLC 4**
See also Sarmiento, Felix Ruben Garcia
See also CA 104

**Darley, George** 1795-1846........ **NCLC 2**

**Daryush, Elizabeth** 1887-1977.... **CLC 6, 19**
See also CANR 3; CA 49-52; DLB 20

**Daudet, (Louis Marie) Alphonse**
1840-1897 .................. **NCLC 1**

**Daumal, Rene** 1908-1944........ **TCLC 14**
See also CA 114

**Davenport, Guy (Mattison, Jr.)**
1927- .................. **CLC 6, 14, 38**
See also CANR 23; CA 33-36R

**Davidson, Donald (Grady)**
1893-1968 ............. **CLC 2, 13, 19**
See also CANR 4; CA 5-8R;
obituary CA 25-28R; DLB 45

**Davidson, John** 1857-1909....... **TCLC 24**
See also CA 118; DLB 19

**Davidson, Sara** 1943- ............. **CLC 9**
See also CA 81-84

**Davie, Donald (Alfred)**
1922- ............**CLC 5, 8, 10, 31**
See also CAAS 3; CANR 1; CA 1-4R;
DLB 27

**Davies, Ray(mond Douglas)** 1944- .. **CLC 21**
See also CA 116

**Davies, Rhys** 1903-1978........... **CLC 23**
See also CANR 4; CA 9-12R;
obituary CA 81-84

**Davies, (William) Robertson**
1913- ............ **CLC 2, 7, 13, 25, 42**
See also CANR 17; CA 33-36R; DLB 68

**Davies, W(illiam) H(enry)**
1871-1940 ................... **TCLC 5**
See also CA 104; DLB 19

**Davis, H(arold) L(enoir)**
1896-1960 .................. **CLC 49**
See also obituary CA 89-92; DLB 9

**Davis, Rebecca (Blaine) Harding**
1831-1910 ................... **TCLC 6**
See also CA 104; DLB 74

**Davis, Richard Harding**
1864-1916 .................. **TCLC 24**
See also CA 114; DLB 12, 23, 78, 79

**Davison, Frank Dalby** 1893-1970 ... **CLC 15**
See also obituary CA 116

**Davison, Peter** 1928- ............. **CLC 28**
See also CAAS 4; CANR 3; CA 9-12R;
DLB 5

**Davys, Mary** 1674-1732............ **LC 1**
See also DLB 39

**Dawson, Fielding** 1930- ............ **CLC 6**
See also CA 85-88

**Day, Clarence (Shepard, Jr.)**
1874-1935 .................. **TCLC 25**
See also CA 108; DLB 11

**Day, Thomas** 1748-1789............ **LC 1**
See also YABC 1; DLB 39

**Day Lewis, C(ecil)**
1904-1972 ............... **CLC 1, 6, 10**
See also CAP 1; CA 15-16;
obituary CA 33-36R; DLB 15, 20

**Dazai Osamu** 1909-1948 ........ **TCLC 11**
See also Tsushima Shuji

**De Crayencour, Marguerite** 1903-1987
See Yourcenar, Marguerite

**Deer, Sandra** 1940-................ **CLC 45**

**Defoe, Daniel** 1660?-1731 ........... **LC 1**
See also SATA 22; DLB 39

**De Hartog, Jan** 1914-.............. **CLC 19**
See also CANR 1; CA 1-4R

**Deighton, Len** 1929-........ **CLC 4, 7, 22, 46**
See also Deighton, Leonard Cyril
See also DLB 87

**Deighton, Leonard Cyril** 1929-
See Deighton, Len
See also CANR 19; CA 9-12R

**De la Mare, Walter (John)**
1873-1956................ **TCLC 4**
See also CLR 23; CA 110; SATA 16;
DLB 19

**Delaney, Shelagh** 1939- ........... **CLC 29**
See also CA 17-20R; DLB 13

**Delany, Mary (Granville Pendarves)**
1700-1788 .................. **LC 12**

**Delany, Samuel R(ay, Jr.)**
1942- ................... **CLC 8, 14, 38**
See also CA 81-84; DLB 8, 33

**De la Roche, Mazo** 1885-1961 ..... **CLC 14**
See also CA 85-88; DLB 68

**Delbanco, Nicholas (Franklin)**
1942-...................... **CLC 6, 13**
See also CAAS 2; CA 17-20R; DLB 6

**del Castillo, Michel** 1933- ......... **CLC 38**
See also CA 109

**Deledda, Grazia** 1871-1936 ....... **TCLC 23**
See also CA 123

**Delibes (Setien), Miguel** 1920- ... **CLC 8, 18**
See also CANR 1; CA 45-48

**DeLillo, Don**
1936- ........ **CLC 8, 10, 13, 27, 39, 54**
See also CANR 21; CA 81-84; DLB 6

**De Lisser, H(erbert) G(eorge)**
1878-1944 .................. **TCLC 12**
See also CA 109

**Deloria, Vine (Victor), Jr.** 1933-.... **CLC 21**
See also CANR 5, 20; CA 53-56; SATA 21

**Del Vecchio, John M(ichael)**
1947-...................... **CLC 29**
See also CA 110

**de Man, Paul** 1919-1983 .......... **CLC 55**
See also obituary CA 111; DLB 67

**De Marinis, Rick** 1934-........... **CLC 54**
See also CANR 9, 25; CA 57-60

**Demby, William** 1922-............. **CLC 53**
See also CA 81-84; DLB 33

**Denby, Edwin (Orr)** 1903-1983..... **CLC 48**
See also obituary CA 110

**Dennis, John** 1657-1734............ **LC 11**

**Dennis, Nigel (Forbes)** 1912-........ **CLC 8**
See also CA 25-28R; obituary CA 129;
DLB 13, 15

**De Palma, Brian** 1940-............ **CLC 20**
See also CA 109

**De Quincey, Thomas** 1785-1859 ... **NCLC 4**

**Deren, Eleanora** 1908-1961
See Deren, Maya
See also obituary CA 111

**Deren, Maya** 1908-1961........... **CLC 16**
See also Deren, Eleanora

**Derleth, August (William)**
1909-1971 .................. **CLC 31**
See also CANR 4; CA 1-4R;
obituary CA 29-32R; SATA 5; DLB 9

**Derrida, Jacques** 1930-............ **CLC 24**
See also CA 124, 127

**Desai, Anita** 1937- ........... **CLC 19, 37**
See also CA 81-84

**De Saint-Luc, Jean** 1909-1981
See Glassco, John

**De Sica, Vittorio** 1902-1974 ...... **CLC 20**
See also obituary CA 117

**Desnos, Robert** 1900-1945........ **TCLC 22**
See also CA 121

**Destouches, Louis-Ferdinand-Auguste**
1894-1961
See Celine, Louis-Ferdinand
See also CA 85-88

**Deutsch, Babette** 1895-1982 ....... **CLC 18**
See also CANR 4; CA 1-4R;
obituary CA 108; SATA 1;
obituary SATA 33; DLB 45

**Devenant, William** 1606-1649 ...... **LC 13**

**Devkota, Laxmiprasad**
1909-1959 ................. **TCLC 23**
See also CA 123

**DeVoto, Bernard (Augustine)**
1897-1955 ................. **TCLC 29**
See also CA 113; DLB 9

**De Vries, Peter**
1910- ........ **CLC 1, 2, 3, 7, 10, 28, 46**
See also CA 17-20R; DLB 6; DLB-Y 82

**Dexter, Pete** 1943-............ **CLC 34, 55**
See also CA 127

**Diamond, Neil (Leslie)** 1941-....... **CLC 30**
See also CA 108

**Dick, Philip K(indred)**
1928-1982 ................ **CLC 10, 30**
See also CANR 2, 16; CA 49-52;
obituary CA 106; DLB 8

**Dickens, Charles**
1812-1870 .......... **NCLC 3, 8, 18, 26**
See also SATA 15; DLB 21, 55, 70

**Dickey, James (Lafayette)**
1923- ........ **CLC 1, 2, 4, 7, 10, 15, 47**
See also CANR 10; CA 9-12R; CABS 2;
DLB 5; DLB-Y 82; DLB-DS 7

**Dickey, William** 1928-.......... **CLC 3, 28**
See also CANR 24; CA 9-12R; DLB 5

**Dickinson, Charles** 1952-.......... **CLC 49**

**Dickinson, Emily (Elizabeth)**
1830-1886 ........... **NCLC 21; PC 1**
See also SATA 29; DLB 1;
CDALB 1865-1917

**Dickinson, Peter (Malcolm de Brissac)**
1927- ................... **CLC 12, 35**
See also CA 41-44R; SATA 5; DLB 87

**Didion, Joan** 1934-..... **CLC 1, 3, 8, 14, 32**
See also CANR 14; CA 5-8R; DLB 2;
DLB-Y 81, 86; CDALB 1968-1987

**Dillard, Annie** 1945-............ **CLC 9, 60**
See also CANR 3; CA 49-52; SATA 10;
DLB-Y 80

**Dillard, R(ichard) H(enry) W(ilde)**
1937- ....................... **CLC 5**
See also CAAS 7; CANR 10; CA 21-24R;
DLB 5

**Dillon, Eilis** 1920-............... **CLC 17**
See also CAAS 3; CANR 4; CA 9-12R;
SATA 2

**Dinesen, Isak**
1885-1962 ........ **CLC 10, 29; SSC 7**
See also Blixen, Karen (Christentze
Dinesen)
See also CANR 22

**Disch, Thomas M(ichael)** 1940-... **CLC 7, 36**
See also CAAS 4; CANR 17; CA 21-24R;
SATA 54; DLB 8

**Disraeli, Benjamin** 1804-1881 ..... **NCLC 2**
See also DLB 21, 55

**Dixon, Paige** 1911-
See Corcoran, Barbara

**Dixon, Stephen** 1936-............ **CLC 52**
See also CANR 17; CA 89-92

**Doblin, Alfred** 1878-1957........ **TCLC 13**
See also Doeblin, Alfred

**Dobrolyubov, Nikolai Alexandrovich**
1836-1861 .................. **NCLC 5**

**Dobyns, Stephen** 1941-............ **CLC 37**
See also CANR 2, 18; CA 45-48

**Doctorow, E(dgar) L(aurence)**
1931- ........ **CLC 6, 11, 15, 18, 37, 44**
See also CANR 2; CA 45-48; DLB 2, 28;
DLB-Y 80; CDALB 1968-1987

**Dodgson, Charles Lutwidge** 1832-1898
See Carroll, Lewis
See also YABC 2

**Doeblin, Alfred** 1878-1957........ **TCLC 13**
See also CA 110; DLB 66

**Doerr, Harriet** 1910- ............. **CLC 34**
See also CA 117, 122

**Donaldson, Stephen R.** 1947-....... **CLC 46**
See also CANR 13; CA 89-92

**Donleavy, J(ames) P(atrick)**
1926- ........ **CLC 1, 4, 6, 10, 45**
See also CANR 24; CA 9-12R; DLB 6

**Donnadieu, Marguerite** 1914-
See Duras, Marguerite

**Donne, John** 1572?-1631 ...... **LC 10; PC 1**

**Donnell, David** 1939?- ............ **CLC 34**

**Donoso, Jose** 1924-........ **CLC 4, 8, 11, 32**
See also CA 81-84

**Donovan, John** 1928- ............. **CLC 35**
See also CLR 3; CA 97-100; SATA 29

**Doolittle, Hilda** 1886-1961
See H(ilda) D(oolittle)
See also CA 97-100; DLB 4, 45

**Dorfman, Ariel** 1942-............. **CLC 48**
See also CA 124

**Dorn, Ed(ward Merton)** 1929-... **CLC 10, 18**
See also CA 93-96; DLB 5

**Dos Passos, John (Roderigo)**
1896-1970 ... **CLC 1, 4, 8, 11, 15, 25, 34**
See also CANR 3; CA 1-4R;
obituary CA 29-32R; DLB 4, 9;
DLB-DS 1

**Dostoevski, Fedor Mikhailovich**
1821-1881 ....... **NCLC 2, 7, 21; SSC 2**

**Doughty, Charles (Montagu)**
1843-1926 ................. **TCLC 27**
See also CA 115; DLB 19, 57

**Douglas, George** 1869-1902....... **TCLC 28**

**Douglas, Keith** 1920-1944 ....... **TCLC 40**
See also DLB 27

**Douglass, Frederick** 1817-1895 .... **NCLC 7**
See also SATA 29; DLB 1, 43, 50;
CDALB 1640-1865

**Dourado, (Waldomiro Freitas) Autran**
1926- .................... **CLC 23, 60**
See also CA 25-28R

**Dove, Rita** 1952-................. **CLC 50**
See also CA 109

**Dowson, Ernest (Christopher)**
1867-1900 .................. **TCLC 4**
See also CA 105; DLB 19

**Doyle, (Sir) Arthur Conan**
1859-1930 ............... **TCLC 7, 26**
See also CA 104, 122; SATA 24; DLB 18,
70

**Dr. A** 1933-
See Silverstein, Alvin and Virginia B(arbara
Opshelor) Silverstein

**Drabble, Margaret**
1939- ........ **CLC 2, 3, 5, 8, 10, 22, 53**
See also CANR 18; CA 13-16R; SATA 48;
DLB 14

**Drayton, Michael** 1563-1631........ **LC 8**

**Dreiser, Theodore (Herman Albert)**
1871-1945 .......... **TCLC 10, 18, 35**
See also CA 106; SATA 48; DLB 9, 12;
DLB-DS 1; CDALB 1865-1917

**Drexler, Rosalyn** 1926- .......... **CLC 2, 6**
See also CA 81-84

**Dreyer, Carl Theodor** 1889-1968.... **CLC 16**
See also obituary CA 116

**Drieu La Rochelle, Pierre**
1893-1945 ................. **TCLC 21**
See also CA 117; DLB 72

**Droste-Hulshoff, Annette Freiin von**
1797-1848 ................. **NCLC 3**

**Drummond, William Henry**
1854-1907 ................. **TCLC 25**
See also DLB 92

**Drummond de Andrade, Carlos** 1902-1987
See Andrade, Carlos Drummond de

**Drury, Allen (Stuart)** 1918-........ **CLC 37**
See also CANR 18; CA 57-60

**Dryden, John** 1631-1700 ............ **LC 3**

**Duberman, Martin** 1930-........... **CLC 8**
See also CANR 2; CA 1-4R

**Dubie, Norman (Evans, Jr.)** 1945- .. **CLC 36**
See also CANR 12; CA 69-72

**Du Bois, W(illiam) E(dward) B(urghardt)**
1868-1963 ............ **CLC 1, 2, 13, 64**
See also CA 85-88; SATA 42; DLB 47, 50,
91; CDALB 1865-1917

**Dubus, Andre** 1936- .......... **CLC 13, 36**
See also CANR 17; CA 21-24R

**Ducasse, Isidore Lucien** 1846-1870
See Lautreamont, Comte de

**Duclos, Charles Pinot** 1704-1772 ..... **LC 1**

**Dudek, Louis** 1918- ........... **CLC 11, 19**
See also CANR 1; CA 45-48; DLB 88

**Dudevant, Amandine Aurore Lucile Dupin**
1804-1876
See Sand, George

**Duerrenmatt, Friedrich**
1921- .......... **CLC 1, 4, 8, 11, 15, 43**
See also CA 17-20R; DLB 69

**Duffy, Bruce** 19??- ............... **CLC 50**

**Duffy, Maureen** 1933- ............ **CLC 37**
See also CA 25-28R; DLB 14

**Dugan, Alan** 1923- .............. **CLC 2, 6**
See also CA 81-84; DLB 5

**Duhamel, Georges** 1884-1966 ....... **CLC 8**
See also CA 81-84; obituary CA 25-28R;
DLB 65

**Dujardin, Edouard (Emile Louis)**
1861-1949 ................. **TCLC 13**
See also CA 109

**Duke, Raoul** 1939-
See Thompson, Hunter S(tockton)

**Dumas, Alexandre (Davy de la Pailleterie)**
**(pere)** 1802-1870.......... **NCLC 11**
See also SATA 18

**Dumas, Alexandre (fils)**
1824-1895 ............. **NCLC 9; DC 1**

**Dumas, Henry** 1918-1968 ......... **CLC 62**

**Dumas, Henry (L.)** 1934-1968....... **CLC 6**
See also CA 85-88; DLB 41

**Du Maurier, Daphne** 1907- ... **CLC 6, 11, 59**
See also CANR 6; CA 5-8R;
obituary CA 128; SATA 27

**Dunbar, Paul Laurence**
1872-1906 ............... **TCLC 2, 12**
See also CA 104, 124; SATA 34; DLB 50,
54, 78; CDALB 1865-1917

**Duncan (Steinmetz Arquette), Lois**
1934- ...................... **CLC 26**
See also Arquette, Lois S(teinmetz)
See also CANR 2; CA 1-4R; SAAS 2;
SATA 1, 36

**Duncan, Robert (Edward)**
1919-1988 ... **CLC 1, 2, 4, 7, 15, 41, 55;**
**PC 2**
See also CANR 28; CA 9-12R;
obituary CA 124; DLB 5, 16

**Dunlap, William** 1766-1839 ....... **NCLC 2**
See also DLB 30, 37, 59

**Dunn, Douglas (Eaglesham)**
1942- ..................... **CLC 6, 40**
See also CANR 2; CA 45-48; DLB 40

**Dunn, Elsie** 1893-1963
See Scott, Evelyn

**Dunn, Stephen** 1939- ............. **CLC 36**
See also CANR 12; CA 33-36R

**Dunne, Finley Peter** 1867-1936.... **TCLC 28**
See also CA 108; DLB 11, 23

**Dunne, John Gregory** 1932-........ **CLC 28**
See also CANR 14; CA 25-28R; DLB-Y 80

**Dunsany, Lord (Edward John Moreton Drax**
**Plunkett)** 1878-1957......... **TCLC 2**
See also CA 104; DLB 10

**Durang, Christopher (Ferdinand)**
1949- ................... **CLC 27, 38**
See also CA 105

**Duras, Marguerite**
1914- ........ **CLC 3, 6, 11, 20, 34, 40**
See also CA 25-28R; DLB 83

**Durban, Pam** 1947-............... **CLC 39**
See also CA 123

**Durcan, Paul** 1944-............... **CLC 43**

**Durrell, Lawrence (George)**
1912-1990 .... **CLC 1, 4, 6, 8, 13, 27, 41**
See also CA 9-12R; DLB 15, 27

**Durrenmatt, Friedrich**
1921- .......... **CLC 1, 4, 8, 11, 15, 43**
See also Duerrenmatt, Friedrich
See also DLB 69

**Dutt, Toru** 1856-1877........... **NCLC 29**

**Dwight, Timothy** 1752-1817...... **NCLC 13**
See also DLB 37

**Dworkin, Andrea** 1946- ........... **CLC 43**
See also CANR 16; CA 77-80

**Dylan, Bob** 1941-.......... **CLC 3, 4, 6, 12**
See also CA 41-44R; DLB 16

**Eagleton, Terry** 1943-............. **CLC 63**

**East, Michael** 1916-
See West, Morris L.

**Eastlake, William (Derry)** 1917-..... **CLC 8**
See also CAAS 1; CANR 5; CA 5-8R;
DLB 6

**Eberhart, Richard** 1904-... **CLC 3, 11, 19, 56**
See also CANR 2; CA 1-4R; DLB 48;
CDALB 1941-1968

**Eberstadt, Fernanda** 1960-........ **CLC 39**

**Echegaray (y Eizaguirre), Jose (Maria Waldo)**
1832-1916 ................... **TCLC 4**
See also CA 104

**Echeverria, (Jose) Esteban (Antonino)**
1805-1851 ................ **NCLC 18**

**Eckert, Allan W.** 1931- ........... **CLC 17**
See also CANR 14; CA 13-16R; SATA 27,
29

**Eco, Umberto** 1932-........... **CLC 28, 60**
See also CANR 12; CA 77-80

**Eddison, E(ric) R(ucker)**
1882-1945 ................. **TCLC 15**
See also CA 109

**Edel, Leon (Joseph)** 1907-...... **CLC 29, 34**
See also CANR 1, 22; CA 1-4R

**Eden, Emily** 1797-1869 ......... **NCLC 10**

**Edgar, David** 1948-.............. **CLC 42**
See also CANR 12; CA 57-60; DLB 13

**Edgerton, Clyde** 1944- ........... **CLC 39**
See also CA 118

**Edgeworth, Maria** 1767-1849...... **NCLC 1**
See also SATA 21

**Edmonds, Helen (Woods)** 1904-1968
See Kavan, Anna
See also CA 5-8R; obituary CA 25-28R

**Edmonds, Walter D(umaux)** 1903- .. **CLC 35**
See also CANR 2; CA 5-8R; SAAS 4;
SATA 1, 27; DLB 9

**Edson, Russell** 1905- ............. **CLC 13**
See also CA 33-36R

**Edwards, G(erald) B(asil)**
1899-1976 ................. **CLC 25**
See also obituary CA 110

**Edwards, Gus** 1939-............. **CLC 43**
See also CA 108

**Edwards, Jonathan** 1703-1758........ **LC 7**
See also DLB 24

**Ehle, John (Marsden, Jr.)** 1925-.... **CLC 27**
See also CA 9-12R

**Ehrenburg, Ilya (Grigoryevich)**
1891-1967 ............ **CLC 18, 34, 62**
See also CA 102; obituary CA 25-28R

**Eich, Guenter** 1907-1971
See also CA 111; obituary CA 93-96

**Eich, Gunter** 1907-1971........... **CLC 15**
See also Eich, Guenter
See also DLB 69

**Eichendorff, Joseph Freiherr von**
1788-1857 ................... **NCLC 8**
See also DLB 90

**Eigner, Larry** 1927-............... **CLC 9**
See also Eigner, Laurence (Joel)
See also DLB 5

**Eigner, Laurence (Joel)** 1927-
See Eigner, Larry
See also CANR 6; CA 9-12R

**Eiseley, Loren (Corey)** 1907-1977.... **CLC 7**
See also CANR 6; CA 1-4R;
obituary CA 73-76

**Eisenstadt, Jill** 1963-.............. **CLC 50**

**Ekeloef, Gunnar (Bengt)** 1907-1968
See Ekelof, Gunnar (Bengt)
See also obituary CA 25-28R

**Ekelof, Gunnar (Bengt)** 1907-1968 .. **CLC 27**
See also Ekeloef, Gunnar (Bengt)

**Ekwensi, Cyprian (Odiatu Duaka)**
1921- ...................... **CLC 4**
See also CANR 18; CA 29-32R

**Eliade, Mircea** 1907-1986 ......... **CLC 19**
See also CA 65-68; obituary CA 119

**Eliot, George** 1819-1880.... **NCLC 4, 13, 23**
See also DLB 21, 35, 55

**Eliot, John** 1604-1690 .............. **LC 5**
See also DLB 24

**Eliot, T(homas) S(tearns)**
1888-1965 .... **CLC 1, 2, 3, 6, 9, 10, 13,**
**15, 24, 34, 41, 55, 57**
See also CA 5-8R; obituary CA 25-28R;
DLB 7, 10, 45, 63; DLB-Y 88

**Elkin, Stanley (Lawrence)**
1930- ........ **CLC 4, 6, 9, 14, 27, 51**
See also CANR 8; CA 9-12R; DLB 2, 28;
DLB-Y 80

**Elledge, Scott** 19??- .............. **CLC 34**

Elliott, George P(aul)  1918-1980..... CLC 2
  See also CANR 2; CA 1-4R;
  obituary CA 97-100

Elliott, Janice  1931-.............. CLC 47
  See also CANR 8; CA 13-16R; DLB 14

Elliott, Sumner Locke  1917-....... CLC 38
  See also CANR 2, 21; CA 5-8R

Ellis, A. E.  19??-................. CLC 7

Ellis, Alice Thomas  19??-......... CLC 40

Ellis, Bret Easton  1964-.......... CLC 39
  See also CA 118, 123

Ellis, (Henry) Havelock
  1859-1939 .................. TCLC 14
  See also CA 109

Ellis, Trey  1964-................. CLC 55

Ellison, Harlan (Jay)  1934-... CLC 1, 13, 42
  See also CANR 5; CA 5-8R; DLB 8

Ellison, Ralph (Waldo)
  1914- ................ CLC 1, 3, 11, 54
  See also CANR 24; CA 9-12R; DLB 2, 76;
  CDALB 1941-1968

Ellmann, Lucy  1956- ............. CLC 61
  See also CA 128

Ellmann, Richard (David)
  1918-1987 .................. CLC 50
  See also CANR 2; CA 1-4R;
  obituary CA 122; DLB-Y 87

Elman, Richard  1934-............. CLC 19
  See also CAAS 3; CA 17-20R

Eluard, Paul  1895-1952 ........... TCLC 7
  See also Grindel, Eugene

Elyot, (Sir) Thomas  1490?-1546 ..... LC 11

Elytis, Odysseus  1911-......... CLC 15, 49
  See also CA 102

Emecheta, (Florence Onye) Buchi
  1944- ................... CLC 14, 48
  See also CA 81-84

Emerson, Ralph Waldo
  1803-1882 .................. NCLC 1
  See also DLB 1, 59, 73; CDALB 1640-1865

Empson, William
  1906-1984 ....... CLC 3, 8, 19, 33, 34
  See also CA 17-20R; obituary CA 112;
  DLB 20

Enchi, Fumiko (Veda)  1905-1986 ... CLC 31
  See also obituary CA 121

Ende, Michael  1930-.............. CLC 31
  See also CLR 14; CA 118, 124; SATA 42;
  DLB 75

Endo, Shusaku  1923- ..... CLC 7, 14, 19, 54
  See also CANR 21; CA 29-32R

Engel, Marian  1933-1985.......... CLC 36
  See also CANR 12; CA 25-28R; DLB 53

Engelhardt, Frederick  1911-1986
  See Hubbard, L(afayette) Ron(ald)

Enright, D(ennis) J(oseph)
  1920- .................. CLC 4, 8, 31
  See also CANR 1; CA 1-4R; SATA 25;
  DLB 27

Enzensberger, Hans Magnus
  1929-..................... CLC 43
  See also CA 116, 119

Ephron, Nora  1941-........... CLC 17, 31
  See also CANR 12; CA 65-68

Epstein, Daniel Mark  1948- ........ CLC 7
  See also CANR 2; CA 49-52

Epstein, Jacob  1956-  ............. CLC 19
  See also CA 114

Epstein, Joseph  1937-............. CLC 39
  See also CA 112, 119

Epstein, Leslie  1938- ............. CLC 27
  See also CANR 23; CA 73-76

Erdman, Paul E(mil)  1932- ........ CLC 25
  See also CANR 13; CA 61-64

Erdrich, Louise  1954-.......... CLC 39, 54
  See also CA 114

Erenburg, Ilya (Grigoryevich)  1891-1967
  See Ehrenburg, Ilya (Grigoryevich)

Erickson, Steve  1950-............. CLC 64
  See also CA 129

Eseki, Bruno  1919-
  See Mphahlele, Ezekiel

Esenin, Sergei (Aleksandrovich)
  1895-1925 .................. TCLC 4
  See also CA 104

Eshleman, Clayton  1935-.......... CLC 7
  See also CAAS 6; CA 33-36R; DLB 5

Espriu, Salvador  1913-1985........ CLC 9
  See also obituary CA 115

Estleman, Loren D.  1952- ........ CLC 48
  See also CA 85-88

Evans, Marian  1819-1880
  See Eliot, George

Evans, Mary Ann  1819-1880
  See Eliot, George

Evarts, Esther  1900-1972
  See Benson, Sally

Everett, Percival L.  1957?- ........ CLC 57
  See also CA 129

Everson, Ronald G(ilmour)  1903-... CLC 27
  See also CA 17-20R; DLB 88

Everson, William (Oliver)
  1912-................... CLC 1, 5, 14
  See also CANR 20; CA 9-12R; DLB 5, 16

Evtushenko, Evgenii (Aleksandrovich)  1933-
  See Yevtushenko, Yevgeny

Ewart, Gavin (Buchanan)
  1916- ................... CLC 13, 46
  See also CANR 17; CA 89-92; DLB 40

Ewers, Hanns Heinz  1871-1943 ... TCLC 12
  See also CA 109

Ewing, Frederick R.  1918-
  See Sturgeon, Theodore (Hamilton)

Exley, Frederick (Earl)  1929- .... CLC 6, 11
  See also CA 81-84; DLB-Y 81

Ezekiel, Nissim  1924-............. CLC 61
  See also CA 61-64

Ezekiel, Tish O'Dowd  1943-....... CLC 34

Fagen, Donald  1948-.............. CLC 26

Fair, Ronald L.  1932-............. CLC 18
  See also CANR 25; CA 69-72; DLB 33

Fairbairns, Zoe (Ann)  1948- ....... CLC 32
  See also CANR 21; CA 103

Fairfield, Cicily Isabel  1892-1983
  See West, Rebecca

Fallaci, Oriana  1930-............. CLC 11
  See also CANR 15; CA 77-80

Faludy, George  1913-............. CLC 42
  See also CA 21-24R

Fante, John  1909-1983............ CLC 60
  See also CANR 23; CA 69-72;
  obituary CA 109; DLB-Y 83

Farah, Nuruddin  1945-............ CLC 53
  See also CA 106

Fargue, Leon-Paul  1876-1947 ..... TCLC 11
  See also CA 109

Farigoule, Louis  1885-1972
  See Romains, Jules

Farina, Richard  1937?-1966........ CLC 9
  See also CA 81-84; obituary CA 25-28R

Farley, Walter  1920- ............. CLC 17
  See also CANR 8; CA 17-20R; SATA 2, 43;
  DLB 22

Farmer, Philip Jose  1918-....... CLC 1, 19
  See also CANR 4; CA 1-4R; DLB 8

Farrell, J(ames) G(ordon)
  1935-1979 .................... CLC 6
  See also CA 73-76; obituary CA 89-92;
  DLB 14

Farrell, James T(homas)
  1904-1979 .............. CLC 1, 4, 8, 11
  See also CANR 9; CA 5-8R;
  obituary CA 89-92; DLB 4, 9; DLB-DS 2

Farrell, M. J.  1904-
  See Keane, Molly

Fassbinder, Rainer Werner
  1946-1982 .................. CLC 20
  See also CA 93-96; obituary CA 106

Fast, Howard (Melvin)  1914- ...... CLC 23
  See also CANR 1; CA 1-4R; SATA 7;
  DLB 9

Faulkner, William (Cuthbert)
  1897-1962 .... CLC 1, 3, 6, 8, 9, 11, 14,
                18, 28, 52; SSC 1
  See also CA 81-84; DLB 9, 11, 44;
  DLB-Y 86; DLB-DS 2

Fauset, Jessie Redmon
  1884?-1961................ CLC 19, 54
  See also CA 109; DLB 51

Faust, Irvin  1924-................. CLC 8
  See also CA 33-36R; DLB 2, 28; DLB-Y 80

Fearing, Kenneth (Flexner)
  1902-1961 ................... CLC 51
  See also CA 93-96; DLB 9

Federman, Raymond  1928- ...... CLC 6, 47
  See also CANR 10; CA 17-20R; DLB-Y 80

Federspiel, J(urg) F.  1931-......... CLC 42

Feiffer, Jules  1929-........... CLC 2, 8, 64
  See also CANR 30; CA 17-20R; SATA 8,
  61; DLB 7, 44; AAYA 3

Feinberg, David B.  1956-.......... CLC 59

Feinstein, Elaine  1930-............ CLC 36
  See also CAAS 1; CA 69-72; DLB 14, 40

Feldman, Irving (Mordecai)  1928-.... CLC 7
  See also CANR 1; CA 1-4R

Fellini, Federico  1920-............ CLC 16
  See also CA 65-68

Felsen, Gregor  1916-
  See Felsen, Henry Gregor

Felsen, Henry Gregor  1916- . . . . . . . CLC 17
See also CANR 1; CA 1-4R; SAAS 2;
SATA 1

Fenton, James (Martin)  1949- . . . . . . CLC 32
See also CA 102; DLB 40

Ferber, Edna  1887-1968 . . . . . . . . . . CLC 18
See also CA 5-8R; obituary CA 25-28R;
SATA 7; DLB 9, 28, 86

Ferlinghetti, Lawrence (Monsanto)
1919?- . . . . . . . . . CLC 2, 6, 10, 27; PC 1
See also CANR 3; CA 5-8R; DLB 5, 16;
CDALB 1941-1968

Ferrier, Susan (Edmonstone)
1782-1854 . . . . . . . . . . . . . . . . . NCLC 8

Feuchtwanger, Lion  1884-1958 . . . . . TCLC 3
See also CA 104; DLB 66

Feydeau, Georges  1862-1921 . . . . . . TCLC 22
See also CA 113

Ficino, Marsilio  1433-1499 . . . . . . . . LC 12

Fiedler, Leslie A(aron)
1917- . . . . . . . . . . . . . . . CLC 4, 13, 24
See also CANR 7; CA 9-12R; DLB 28, 67

Field, Andrew  1938- . . . . . . . . . . . . . CLC 44
See also CANR 25; CA 97-100

Field, Eugene  1850-1895 . . . . . . . . . NCLC 3
See also SATA 16; DLB 21, 23, 42

Fielding, Henry  1707-1754 . . . . . . . . . . LC 1
See also DLB 39, 84

Fielding, Sarah  1710-1768 . . . . . . . . . . LC 1
See also DLB 39

Fierstein, Harvey  1954- . . . . . . . . . . CLC 33
See also CA 123, 129

Figes, Eva  1932- . . . . . . . . . . . . . . . CLC 31
See also CANR 4; CA 53-56; DLB 14

Finch, Robert (Duer Claydon)
1900- . . . . . . . . . . . . . . . . . . . . CLC 18
See also CANR 9, 24; CA 57-60; DLB 88

Findley, Timothy  1930- . . . . . . . . . . CLC 27
See also CANR 12; CA 25-28R; DLB 53

Fink, Janis  1951-
See Ian, Janis

Firbank, Louis  1944-
See Reed, Lou
See also CA 117

Firbank, (Arthur Annesley) Ronald
1886-1926 . . . . . . . . . . . . . . . . . TCLC 1
See also CA 104; DLB 36

Fisher, Roy  1930- . . . . . . . . . . . . . . CLC 25
See also CANR 16; CA 81-84; DLB 40

Fisher, Rudolph  1897-1934 . . . . . . . TCLC 11
See also CA 107; DLB 51

Fisher, Vardis (Alvero)  1895-1968 . . . . CLC 7
See also CA 5-8R; obituary CA 25-28R;
DLB 9

FitzGerald, Edward  1809-1883 . . . . NCLC 9
See also DLB 32

Fitzgerald, F(rancis) Scott (Key)
1896-1940 . . . . TCLC 1, 6, 14, 28; SSC 6
See also CA 110, 123; DLB 4, 9, 86;
DLB-Y 81; DLB-DS 1;
CDALB 1917-1929

Fitzgerald, Penelope  1916- . . . CLC 19, 51, 61
See also CAAS 10; CA 85-88,; DLB 14

Fitzgerald, Robert (Stuart)
1910-1985 . . . . . . . . . . . . . . . . . CLC 39
See also CANR 1; CA 2R;
obituary CA 114; DLB-Y 80

FitzGerald, Robert D(avid)  1902- . . . CLC 19
See also CA 17-20R

Flanagan, Thomas (James Bonner)
1923- . . . . . . . . . . . . . . . . . CLC 25, 52
See also CA 108; DLB-Y 80

Flaubert, Gustave
1821-1880 . . . . . . . . . . . NCLC 2, 10, 19

Fleming, Ian (Lancaster)
1908-1964 . . . . . . . . . . . . . . . CLC 3, 30
See also CA 5-8R; SATA 9; DLB 87

Fleming, Thomas J(ames)  1927- . . . . CLC 37
See also CANR 10; CA 5-8R; SATA 8

Fletcher, John Gould  1886-1950 . . . TCLC 35
See also CA 107; DLB 4, 45

Flieg, Hellmuth
See Heym, Stefan

Flying Officer X  1905-1974
See Bates, H(erbert) E(rnest)

Fo, Dario  1929- . . . . . . . . . . . . . . . . CLC 32
See also CA 116

Follett, Ken(neth Martin)  1949- . . . . CLC 18
See also CANR 13; CA 81-84; DLB-Y 81

Fontane, Theodor  1819-1898 . . . . . NCLC 26

Foote, Horton  1916- . . . . . . . . . . . . . CLC 51
See also CA 73-76; DLB 26

Forbes, Esther  1891-1967 . . . . . . . . . CLC 12
See also CAP 1; CA 13-14;
obituary CA 25-28R; SATA 2; DLB 22

Forche, Carolyn  1950- . . . . . . . . . . . CLC 25
See also CA 109, 117; DLB 5

Ford, Ford Madox
1873-1939 . . . . . . . . TCLC 1, 15, 39
See also CA 104; DLB 34

Ford, John  1895-1973 . . . . . . . . . . . . CLC 16
See also obituary CA 45-48

Ford, Richard  1944- . . . . . . . . . . . . . CLC 46
See also CANR 11; CA 69-72

Foreman, Richard  1937- . . . . . . . . . . CLC 50
See also CA 65-68

Forester, C(ecil) S(cott)
1899-1966 . . . . . . . . . . . . . . . . . CLC 35
See also CA 73-76; obituary CA 25-28R;
SATA 13

Forman, James D(ouglas)  1932- . . . . CLC 21
See also CANR 4, 19; CA 9-12R; SATA 8,
21

Fornes, Maria Irene  1930- . . . . . . CLC 39, 61
See also CANR 28; CA 25-28R; DLB 7

Forrest, Leon  1937- . . . . . . . . . . . . . . CLC 4
See also CAAS 7; CA 89-92; DLB 33

Forster, E(dward) M(organ)
1879-1970 . . . . CLC 1, 2, 3, 4, 9, 10, 13,
15, 22, 45
See also CAP 1; CA 13-14;
obituary CA 25-28R; SATA 57; DLB 34

Forster, John  1812-1876 . . . . . . . . NCLC 11

Forsyth, Frederick  1938- . . . . . . CLC 2, 5, 36
See also CA 85-88; DLB 87

Forten (Grimke), Charlotte L(ottie)
1837-1914 . . . . . . . . . . . . . . . . TCLC 16
See also Grimke, Charlotte L(ottie) Forten
See also DLB 50

Foscolo, Ugo  1778-1827 . . . . . . . . . NCLC 8

Fosse, Bob  1925-1987 . . . . . . . . . . . . CLC 20
See also Fosse, Robert Louis

Fosse, Robert Louis  1925-1987
See Bob Fosse
See also CA 110, 123

Foster, Stephen Collins
1826-1864 . . . . . . . . . . . . . . . . . NCLC 26

Foucault, Michel  1926-1984 . . . . CLC 31, 34
See also CANR 23; CA 105;
obituary CA 113

Fouque, Friedrich (Heinrich Karl) de La
Motte  1777-1843 . . . . . . . . . . . NCLC 2

Fournier, Henri Alban  1886-1914
See Alain-Fournier
See also CA 104

Fournier, Pierre  1916- . . . . . . . . . . . . CLC 11
See also Gascar, Pierre
See also CANR 16; CA 89-92

Fowles, John (Robert)
1926- . . . . CLC 1, 2, 3, 4, 6, 9, 10, 15, 33
See also CANR 25; CA 5-8R; SATA 22;
DLB 14

Fox, Paula  1923- . . . . . . . . . . . . . . . CLC 2, 8
See also CLR 1; CANR 20; CA 73-76;
SATA 17; DLB 52

Fox, William Price (Jr.)  1926- . . . . . CLC 22
See also CANR 11; CA 17-20R; DLB 2;
DLB-Y 81

Foxe, John  1516?-1587 . . . . . . . . . . . . LC 14

Frame (Clutha), Janet (Paterson)
1924- . . . . . . . . . . . . . . . CLC 2, 3, 6, 22
See also Clutha, Janet Paterson Frame

France, Anatole  1844-1924 . . . . . . . . TCLC 9
See also Thibault, Jacques Anatole Francois

Francis, Claude  19??- . . . . . . . . . . . . CLC 50

Francis, Dick  1920- . . . . . . . . . CLC 2, 22, 42
See also CANR 9; CA 5-8R; DLB 87

Francis, Robert (Churchill)
1901-1987 . . . . . . . . . . . . . . . . . CLC 15
See also CANR 1; CA 1-4R;
obituary CA 123

Frank, Anne  1929-1945 . . . . . . . . . . TCLC 17
See also CA 113; SATA 42

Frank, Elizabeth  1945- . . . . . . . . . . . CLC 39
See also CA 121, 126

Franklin, (Stella Maria Sarah) Miles
1879-1954 . . . . . . . . . . . . . . . . . TCLC 7
See also CA 104

Fraser, Antonia (Pakenham)
1932- . . . . . . . . . . . . . . . . . . . . CLC 32
See also CA 85-88; SATA 32

Fraser, George MacDonald  1925- . . . . CLC 7
See also CANR 2; CA 45-48

Fraser, Sylvia  1935- . . . . . . . . . . . . . CLC 64
See also CANR 1, 16; CA 45-48

Frayn, Michael  1933- . . . . . . CLC 3, 7, 31, 47
See also CA 5-8R; DLB 13, 14

Fraze, Candida  19??- . . . . . . . . . . . . . CLC 50
See also CA 125

Frazer, Sir James George
  1854-1941 .................. TCLC **32**
  See also CA 118

Frazier, Ian  1951- ............... CLC **46**
  See also CA 130

Frederic, Harold  1856-1898 ...... NCLC **10**
  See also DLB 12, 23

Frederick the Great  1712-1786 ...... LC **14**

Fredman, Russell (Bruce)  1929-
  See also CLR 20

Fredro, Aleksander  1793-1876 ..... NCLC **8**

Freeling, Nicolas  1927- ........... CLC **38**
  See also CANR 1, 17; CA 49-52; DLB 87

Freeman, Douglas Southall
  1886-1953 .................. TCLC **11**
  See also CA 109; DLB 17

Freeman, Judith  1946- ............ CLC **55**

Freeman, Mary (Eleanor) Wilkins
  1852-1930 ............ TCLC **9**; SSC **1**
  See also CA 106; DLB 12, 78

Freeman, R(ichard) Austin
  1862-1943 ................... TCLC **21**
  See also CA 113; DLB 70

French, Marilyn  1929- ...... CLC **10, 18, 60**
  See also CANR 3; CA 69-72

Freneau, Philip Morin  1752-1832 .. NCLC **1**
  See also DLB 37, 43

Friedman, B(ernard) H(arper)
  1926- ....................... CLC **7**
  See also CANR 3; CA 1-4R

Friedman, Bruce Jay  1930- .... CLC **3, 5, 56**
  See also CANR 25; CA 9-12R; DLB 2, 28

Friel, Brian  1929- ........... CLC **5, 42, 59**
  See also CA 21-24R; DLB 13

Friis-Baastad, Babbis (Ellinor)
  1921-1970 .................. CLC **12**
  See also CA 17-20R; SATA 7

Frisch, Max (Rudolf)
  1911- ......... CLC **3, 9, 14, 18, 32, 44**
  See also CA 85-88; DLB 69

Fromentin, Eugene (Samuel Auguste)
  1820-1876 ................. NCLC **10**

Frost, Robert (Lee)
  1874-1963 ... CLC **1, 3, 4, 9, 10, 13, 15,
                      26, 34, 44**; PC **1**
  See also CA 89-92; SATA 14; DLB 54;
  DLB-DS 7; CDALB 1917-1929

Fry, Christopher  1907- ....... CLC **2, 10, 14**
  See also CANR 9; CA 17-20R; DLB 13

Frye, (Herman) Northrop  1912- .... CLC **24**
  See also CANR 8; CA 5-8R; DLB 67, 68

Fuchs, Daniel  1909- ............ CLC **8, 22**
  See also CAAS 5; CA 81-84; DLB 9, 26, 28

Fuchs, Daniel  1934- .............. CLC **34**
  See also CANR 14; CA 37-40R

Fuentes, Carlos
  1928- ...... CLC **3, 8, 10, 13, 22, 41, 60**
  See also CANR 10; CA 69-72

Fugard, Athol  1932- ... CLC **5, 9, 14, 25, 40**
  See also CA 85-88

Fugard, Sheila  1932- ............. CLC **48**
  See also CA 125

Fuller, Charles (H., Jr.)
  1939- ................. CLC **25**; DC **1**
  See also CA 108, 112; DLB 38

Fuller, John (Leopold)  1937- ....... CLC **62**
  See also CANR 9; CA 21-22R; DLB 40

Fuller, (Sarah) Margaret
  1810-1850 .................. NCLC **5**
  See also Ossoli, Sarah Margaret (Fuller
  marchesa d')
  See also DLB 1, 59, 73; CDALB 1640-1865

Fuller, Roy (Broadbent)  1912- .... CLC **4, 28**
  See also CA 5-8R; DLB 15, 20

Fulton, Alice  1952- ............... CLC **52**
  See also CA 116

Furphy, Joseph  1843-1912 ....... TCLC **25**

Futrelle, Jacques  1875-1912 ..... TCLC **19**
  See also CA 113

Gaboriau, Emile  1835-1873 ...... NCLC **14**

Gadda, Carlo Emilio  1893-1973 .... CLC **11**
  See also CA 89-92

Gaddis, William
  1922- ...... CLC **1, 3, 6, 8, 10, 19, 43**
  See also CAAS 4; CANR 21; CA 17-20R;
  DLB 2

Gaines, Ernest J.  1933- ...... CLC **3, 11, 18**
  See also CANR 6, 24; CA 9-12R; DLB 2,
  33; DLB-Y 80

Gale, Zona  1874-1938 ............ TCLC **7**
  See also CA 105; DLB 9, 78

Gallagher, Tess  1943- .......... CLC **18, 63**
  See also CA 106

Gallant, Mavis
  1922- ........... CLC **7, 18, 38**; SSC **5**
  See also CA 69-72; DLB 53

Gallant, Roy A(rthur)  1924- ....... CLC **17**
  See also CANR 4; CA 5-8R; SATA 4

Gallico, Paul (William)  1897-1976 ... CLC **2**
  See also CA 5-8R; obituary CA 69-72;
  SATA 13; DLB 9

Galsworthy, John  1867-1933 ...... TCLC **1**
  See also CA 104; DLB 10, 34

Galt, John  1779-1839 ........... NCLC **1**

Galvin, James  1951- ............. CLC **38**
  See also CANR 26; CA 108

Gamboa, Frederico  1864-1939 ..... TCLC **36**

Gann, Ernest K(ellogg)  1910- ...... CLC **23**
  See also CANR 1; CA 1-4R

Garcia Lorca, Federico
  1899-1936 ................. TCLC **1, 7**
  See also CA 104

Garcia Marquez, Gabriel (Jose)
  1928- .... CLC **2, 3, 8, 10, 15, 27, 47, 55**
  See also CANR 10; CA 33-36R

Gardam, Jane  1928- .............. CLC **43**
  See also CLR 12; CANR 2, 18; CA 49-52;
  SATA 28, 39; DLB 14

Gardner, Herb  1934- ............. CLC **44**

Gardner, John (Champlin, Jr.)
  1933-1982 .... CLC **2, 3, 5, 7, 8, 10, 18,
                      28, 34**; SSC **7**
  See also CA 65-68; obituary CA 107;
  obituary SATA 31, 40; DLB 2; DLB-Y 82

Gardner, John (Edmund)  1926- ..... CLC **30**
  See also CANR 15; CA 103

Garfield, Leon  1921- ............. CLC **12**
  See also CA 17-20R; SATA 1, 32

Garland, (Hannibal) Hamlin
  1860-1940 .................. TCLC **3**
  See also CA 104; DLB 12, 71, 78

Garneau, Hector (de) Saint Denys
  1912-1943 ................. TCLC **13**
  See also CA 111; DLB 88

Garner, Alan  1935- ............... CLC **17**
  See also CLR 20; CANR 15; CA 73-76;
  SATA 18

Garner, Hugh  1913-1979 .......... CLC **13**
  See also CA 69-72; DLB 68

Garnett, David  1892-1981 .......... CLC **3**
  See also CANR 17; CA 5-8R;
  obituary CA 103; DLB 34

Garrett, George (Palmer, Jr.)
  1929- .................. CLC **3, 11, 51**
  See also CAAS 5; CANR 1; CA 1-4R;
  DLB 2, 5; DLB-Y 83

Garrick, David  1717-1779 .......... LC **15**
  See also DLB 84

Garrigue, Jean  1914-1972 ......... CLC **2, 8**
  See also CANR 20; CA 5-8R;
  obituary CA 37-40R

Gary, Romain  1914-1980 .......... CLC **25**
  See also Kacew, Romain

Gascar, Pierre  1916- ............. CLC **11**
  See also Fournier, Pierre

Gascoyne, David (Emery)  1916- .... CLC **45**
  See also CANR 10; CA 65-68; DLB 20

Gaskell, Elizabeth Cleghorn
  1810-1865 .................. NCLC **5**
  See also DLB 21

Gass, William H(oward)
  1924- .......... CLC **1, 2, 8, 11, 15, 39**
  See also CA 17-20R; DLB 2

Gautier, Theophile  1811-1872 ..... NCLC **1**

Gaye, Marvin (Pentz)  1939-1984 ... CLC **26**
  See also obituary CA 112

Gebler, Carlo (Ernest)  1954- ....... CLC **39**
  See also CA 119

Gee, Maggie  19??- ............... CLC **57**

Gee, Maurice (Gough)  1931- ....... CLC **29**
  See also CA 97-100; SATA 46

Gelbart, Larry  1923?- .......... CLC **21, 61**
  See also CA 73-76

Gelber, Jack  1932- ........ CLC **1, 6, 14, 60**
  See also CANR 2; CA 1-4R; DLB 7

Gellhorn, Martha (Ellis)  1908- .. CLC **14, 60**
  See also CA 77-80; DLB-Y 82

Genet, Jean
  1910-1986 ... CLC **1, 2, 5, 10, 14, 44, 46**
  See also CANR 18; CA 13-16R; DLB 72;
  DLB-Y 86

Gent, Peter  1942- ................ CLC **29**
  See also CA 89-92; DLB 72; DLB-Y 82

George, Jean Craighead  1919 ...... CLC **35**
  See also CLR 1; CA 5-8R; SATA 2;
  DLB 52

George, Stefan (Anton)
  1868-1933 ................ TCLC **2, 14**
  See also CA 104

Gerhardi, William (Alexander) 1895-1977
    See Gerhardie, William (Alexander)

Gerhardie, William (Alexander)
    1895-1977 .................... CLC 5
    See also CANR 18; CA 25-28R;
    obituary CA 73-76; DLB 36

Gertler, T(rudy) 1946?- ........... CLC 34
    See also CA 116

Gessner, Friedrike Victoria 1910-1980
    See Adamson, Joy(-Friederike Victoria)

Ghelderode, Michel de
    1898-1962 ................. CLC 6, 11
    See also CA 85-88

Ghiselin, Brewster 1903- .......... CLC 23
    See also CANR 13; CA 13-16R

Ghose, Zulfikar 1935-............. CLC 42
    See also CA 65-68

Ghosh, Amitav 1943- ............. CLC 44

Giacosa, Giuseppe 1847-1906 ...... TCLC 7
    See also CA 104

Gibbon, Lewis Grassic 1901-1935... TCLC 4
    See also Mitchell, James Leslie

Gibbons, Kaye 1960- ............. CLC 50

Gibran, (Gibran) Kahlil
    1883-1931 ................. TCLC 1, 9
    See also CA 104

Gibson, William 1914- ............ CLC 23
    See also CANR 9; CA 9-12R; DLB 7

Gibson, William 1948- ......... CLC 39, 63
    See also CA 126

Gide, Andre (Paul Guillaume)
    1869-1951 ............ TCLC 5, 12, 36
    See also CA 104, 124; DLB 65

Gifford, Barry (Colby) 1946-....... CLC 34
    See also CANR 9; CA 65-68

Gilbert, (Sir) W(illiam) S(chwenck)
    1836-1911 ................... TCLC 3
    See also CA 104; SATA 36

Gilbreth, Ernestine 1908-
    See Carey, Ernestine Gilbreth

Gilbreth, Frank B(unker), Jr.
    1911- ....................... CLC 17
    See also CA 9-12R; SATA 2

Gilchrist, Ellen 1935-.......... CLC 34, 48
    See also CA 113, 116

Giles, Molly 1942- .............. CLC 39
    See also CA 126

Gilliam, Terry (Vance) 1940-
    See Monty Python
    See also CA 108, 113

Gilliatt, Penelope (Ann Douglass)
    1932-............... CLC 2, 10, 13, 53
    See also CA 13-16R; DLB 14

Gilman, Charlotte (Anna) Perkins (Stetson)
    1860-1935 ................ TCLC 9, 37
    See also CA 106

Gilmour, David 1944-
    See Pink Floyd

Gilpin, William 1724-1804....... NCLC 30

Gilroy, Frank D(aniel) 1925-........ CLC 2
    See also CA 81-84; DLB 7

Ginsberg, Allen
    1926- ......... CLC 1, 2, 3, 4, 6, 13, 36
    See also CANR 2; CA 1-4R; DLB 5, 16;
    CDALB 1941-1968

Ginzburg, Natalia 1916-...... CLC 5, 11, 54
    See also CA 85-88

Giono, Jean 1895-1970......... CLC 4, 11
    See also CANR 2; CA 45-48;
    obituary CA 29-32R; DLB 72

Giovanni, Nikki 1943- ..... CLC 2, 4, 19, 64
    See also CLR 6; CAAS 6; CANR 18;
    CA 29-32R; SATA 24; DLB 5, 41

Giovene, Andrea 1904-............. CLC 7
    See also CA 85-88

Gippius, Zinaida (Nikolayevna) 1869-1945
    See Hippius, Zinaida
    See also CA 106

Giraudoux, (Hippolyte) Jean
    1882-1944 ................. TCLC 2, 7
    See also CA 104; DLB 65

Gironella, Jose Maria 1917- ....... CLC 11
    See also CA 101

Gissing, George (Robert)
    1857-1903 ................ TCLC 3, 24
    See also CA 105; DLB 18

Gladkov, Fyodor (Vasilyevich)
    1883-1958 ................. TCLC 27

Glanville, Brian (Lester) 1931- ...... CLC 6
    See also CANR 3; CA 5-8R; SATA 42;
    DLB 15

Glasgow, Ellen (Anderson Gholson)
    1873?-1945................. TCLC 2, 7
    See also CA 104; DLB 9, 12

Glassco, John 1909-1981 .......... CLC 9
    See also CANR 15; CA 13-16R;
    obituary CA 102; DLB 68

Glasser, Ronald J. 1940?- ......... CLC 37

Glendinning, Victoria 1937-....... CLC 50
    See also CA 120

Glissant, Edouard 1928-.......... CLC 10

Gloag, Julian 1930- ............. CLC 40
    See also CANR 10; CA 65-68

Gluck, Louise (Elisabeth)
    1943-................. CLC 7, 22, 44
    See also CA 33-36R; DLB 5

Gobineau, Joseph Arthur (Comte) de
    1816-1882 ................. NCLC 17

Godard, Jean-Luc 1930-........... CLC 20
    See also CA 93-96

Godden, (Margaret) Rumer 1907-... CLC 53
    See also CLR 20; CANR 4, 27; CA 7-8R;
    SATA 3, 36

Godwin, Gail 1937-........ CLC 5, 8, 22, 31
    See also CANR 15; CA 29-32R; DLB 6

Godwin, William 1756-1836...... NCLC 14
    See also DLB 39

Goethe, Johann Wolfgang von
    1749-1832 ............... NCLC 4, 22

Gogarty, Oliver St. John
    1878-1957 ................. TCLC 15
    See also CA 109; DLB 15, 19

Gogol, Nikolai (Vasilyevich)
    1809-1852 ... NCLC 5, 15; DC 1; SSC 4

Gokceli, Yasar Kemal 1923-
    See Kemal, Yashar

Gold, Herbert 1924-....... CLC 4, 7, 14, 42
    See also CANR 17; CA 9-12R; DLB 2;
    DLB-Y 81

Goldbarth, Albert 1948-......... CLC 5, 38
    See also CANR 6; CA 53-56

Goldberg, Anatol 1910-1982 ....... CLC 34
    See also obituary CA 117

Goldemberg, Isaac 1945-.......... CLC 52
    See also CANR 11; CA 69-72

Golding, William (Gerald)
    1911- ..... CLC 1, 2, 3, 8, 10, 17, 27, 58
    See also CANR 13; CA 5-8R; DLB 15

Goldman, Emma 1869-1940...... TCLC 13
    See also CA 110

Goldman, William (W.) 1931-.... CLC 1, 48
    See also CA 9-12R; DLB 44

Goldmann, Lucien 1913-1970 ...... CLC 24
    See also CAP 2; CA 25-28

Goldoni, Carlo 1707-1793 .......... LC 4

Goldsberry, Steven 1949-.......... CLC 34

Goldsmith, Oliver 1728?-1774....... LC 2
    See also SATA 26; DLB 39

Gombrowicz, Witold
    1904-1969 ...........CLC 4, 7, 11, 49
    See also CAP 2; CA 19-20;
    obituary CA 25-28R

Gomez de la Serna, Ramon
    1888-1963 .................... CLC 9
    See also obituary CA 116

Goncharov, Ivan Alexandrovich
    1812-1891 .................... NCLC 1

Goncourt, Edmond (Louis Antoine Huot) de
    1822-1896 ................... NCLC 7

Goncourt, Jules (Alfred Huot) de
    1830-1870 ................... NCLC 7

Gontier, Fernande 19??-........... CLC 50

Goodman, Paul 1911-1972.... CLC 1, 2, 4, 7
    See also CAP 2; CA 19-20;
    obituary CA 37-40R

Gordimer, Nadine
    1923- ....... CLC 3, 5, 7, 10, 18, 33, 51
    See also CANR 3; CA 5-8R

Gordon, Adam Lindsay
    1833-1870 ................. NCLC 21

Gordon, Caroline
    1895-1981 .............. CLC 6, 13, 29
    See also CAP 1; CA 11-12;
    obituary CA 103; DLB 4, 9; DLB-Y 81

Gordon, Charles William 1860-1937
    See Conner, Ralph
    See also CA 109

Gordon, Mary (Catherine)
    1949-.................... CLC 13, 22
    See also CA 102; DLB 6; DLB-Y 81

Gordon, Sol 1923-............... CLC 26
    See also CANR 4; CA 53-56; SATA 11

Gordone, Charles 1925- .......... CLC 1, 4
    See also CA 93-96; DLB 7

Gorenko, Anna Andreyevna 1889?-1966
    See Akhmatova, Anna

**Gorky, Maxim**  1868-1936 . . . . . . . . TCLC 8
See also Peshkov, Alexei Maximovich

**Goryan, Sirak**  1908-1981
See Saroyan, William

**Gosse, Edmund (William)**
1849-1928 . . . . . . . . . . . . . . . . . TCLC 28
See also CA 117; DLB 57

**Gotlieb, Phyllis (Fay Bloom)**
1926- . . . . . . . . . . . . . . . . . . . . . . CLC 18
See also CANR 7; CA 13-16R; DLB 88

**Gould, Lois**  1938?- . . . . . . . . . . . . . CLC 4, 10
See also CA 77-80

**Gourmont, Remy de**  1858-1915 . . . . TCLC 17
See also CA 109

**Govier, Katherine**  1948- . . . . . . . . . . CLC 51
See also CANR 18; CA 101

**Goyen, (Charles) William**
1915-1983 . . . . . . . . . . . . CLC 5, 8, 14, 40
See also CANR 6; CA 5-8R;
obituary CA 110; DLB 2; DLB-Y 83

**Goytisolo, Juan**  1931- . . . . . . . CLC 5, 10, 23
See also CA 85-88

**Gozzi, (Conte) Carlo**  1720-1806 . . NCLC 23

**Grabbe, Christian Dietrich**
1801-1836 . . . . . . . . . . . . . . . . . NCLC 2

**Grace, Patricia**  1937- . . . . . . . . . . . . CLC 56

**Gracian y Morales, Baltasar**
1601-1658 . . . . . . . . . . . . . . . . . . LC 15

**Gracq, Julien**  1910- . . . . . . . . . . CLC 11, 48
See also Poirier, Louis
See also DLB 83

**Grade, Chaim**  1910-1982 . . . . . . . . . . CLC 10
See also CA 93-96; obituary CA 107

**Graham, Jorie**  1951- . . . . . . . . . . . . . CLC 48
See also CA 111

**Graham, R(obert) B(ontine) Cunninghame**
1852-1936 . . . . . . . . . . . . . . . . . TCLC 19

**Graham, W(illiam) S(ydney)**
1918-1986 . . . . . . . . . . . . . . . . . CLC 29
See also CA 73-76; obituary CA 118;
DLB 20

**Graham, Winston (Mawdsley)**
1910- . . . . . . . . . . . . . . . . . . . . . CLC 23
See also CANR 2, 22; CA 49-52;
obituary CA 118

**Granville-Barker, Harley**
1877-1946 . . . . . . . . . . . . . . . . . TCLC 2
See also CA 104

**Grass, Gunter (Wilhelm)**
1927- . . CLC 1, 2, 4, 6, 11, 15, 22, 32, 49
See also CANR 20; CA 13-16R; DLB 75

**Grau, Shirley Ann**  1929- . . . . . . . . CLC 4, 9
See also CANR 22; CA 89-92; DLB 2

**Graves, Richard Perceval**  1945- . . . . CLC 44
See also CANR 9, 26; CA 65-68

**Graves, Robert (von Ranke)**
1895-1985 . . . CLC 1, 2, 6, 11, 39, 44, 45
See also CANR 5; CA 5-8R;
obituary CA 117; SATA 45; DLB 20;
DLB-Y 85

**Gray, Alasdair**  1934- . . . . . . . . . . . . . CLC 41
See also CA 123

**Gray, Amlin**  1946- . . . . . . . . . . . . . . CLC 29

**Gray, Francine du Plessix**  1930- . . . . CLC 22
See also CAAS 2; CANR 11; CA 61-64

**Gray, John (Henry)**  1866-1934 . . . . TCLC 19
See also CA 119

**Gray, Simon (James Holliday)**
1936- . . . . . . . . . . . . . . . . . CLC 9, 14, 36
See also CAAS 3; CA 21-24R; DLB 13

**Gray, Spalding**  1941- . . . . . . . . . . . . CLC 49

**Gray, Thomas**  1716-1771 . . . . . . LC 4; PC 2

**Grayson, Richard (A.)**  1951- . . . . . . . CLC 38
See also CANR 14; CA 85-88

**Greeley, Andrew M(oran)**  1928- . . . . CLC 28
See also CAAS 7; CANR 7; CA 5-8R

**Green, Hannah**  1932- . . . . . . . . CLC 3, 7, 30
See also Greenberg, Joanne
See also CA 73-76

**Green, Henry**  1905-1974 . . . . . . . CLC 2, 13
See also Yorke, Henry Vincent
See also DLB 15

**Green, Julien (Hartridge)**  1900- . . CLC 3, 11
See also CA 21-24R; DLB 4, 72

**Green, Paul (Eliot)**  1894-1981 . . . . . CLC 25
See also CANR 3; CA 5-8R;
obituary CA 103; DLB 7, 9; DLB-Y 81

**Greenberg, Ivan**  1908-1973
See Rahv, Philip
See also CA 85-88

**Greenberg, Joanne (Goldenberg)**
1932- . . . . . . . . . . . . . . . . . CLC 3, 7, 30
See also Green, Hannah
See also CANR 14; CA 5-8R; SATA 25

**Greenberg, Richard**  1959?- . . . . . . . . CLC 57

**Greene, Bette**  1934- . . . . . . . . . . . . . CLC 30
See also CLR 2; CANR 4; CA 53-56;
SATA 8

**Greene, Gael**  19??- . . . . . . . . . . . . . . . CLC 8
See also CANR 10; CA 13-16R

**Greene, Graham (Henry)**
1904- . . . . . CLC 1, 3, 6, 9, 14, 18, 27, 37
See also CA 13-16R; SATA 20; DLB 13, 15;
DLB-Y 85

**Gregor, Arthur**  1923- . . . . . . . . . . . . . CLC 9
See also CANR 11; CA 25-28R; SATA 36

**Gregory, Lady (Isabella Augusta Persse)**
1852-1932 . . . . . . . . . . . . . . . . . TCLC 1
See also CA 104; DLB 10

**Grendon, Stephen**  1909-1971
See Derleth, August (William)

**Grenville, Kate**  1950- . . . . . . . . . . . . CLC 61
See also CA 118

**Greve, Felix Paul Berthold Friedrich**
1879-1948
See Grove, Frederick Philip
See also CA 104

**Grey, (Pearl) Zane**  1872?-1939 . . . . . TCLC 6
See also CA 104; DLB 9

**Grieg, (Johan) Nordahl (Brun)**
1902-1943 . . . . . . . . . . . . . . . . . TCLC 10
See also CA 107

**Grieve, C(hristopher) M(urray)**  1892-1978
See MacDiarmid, Hugh
See also CA 5-8R; obituary CA 85-88

**Griffin, Gerald**  1803-1840 . . . . . . . NCLC 7

**Griffin, Peter**  1942- . . . . . . . . . . . . . . CLC 39

**Griffiths, Trevor**  1935- . . . . . . . . . CLC 13, 52
See also CA 97-100; DLB 13

**Grigson, Geoffrey (Edward Harvey)**
1905-1985 . . . . . . . . . . . . . . . . . CLC 7, 39
See also CANR 20; CA 25-28R;
obituary CA 118; DLB 27

**Grillparzer, Franz**  1791-1872 . . . . . . NCLC 1

**Grimke, Charlotte L(ottie) Forten**  1837-1914
See Forten (Grimke), Charlotte L(ottie)
See also CA 117, 124

**Grimm, Jakob (Ludwig) Karl**
1785-1863 . . . . . . . . . . . . . . . . . NCLC 3
See also SATA 22; DLB 90

**Grimm, Wilhelm Karl**  1786-1859 . . NCLC 3
See also SATA 22; DLB 90

**Grimmelshausen, Johann Jakob Christoffel**
von  1621-1676 . . . . . . . . . . . . . . . LC 6

**Grindel, Eugene**  1895-1952
See also CA 104

**Grossman, Vasily (Semenovich)**
1905-1964 . . . . . . . . . . . . . . . . . CLC 41
See also CA 124, 130

**Grove, Frederick Philip**
1879-1948 . . . . . . . . . . . . . . . . . TCLC 4
See also Greve, Felix Paul Berthold
Friedrich

**Grumbach, Doris (Isaac)**
1918- . . . . . . . . . . . . . . . . CLC 13, 22, 64
See also CAAS 2; CANR 9; CA 5-8R

**Grundtvig, Nicolai Frederik Severin**
1783-1872 . . . . . . . . . . . . . . . . . NCLC 1

**Grunwald, Lisa**  1959- . . . . . . . . . . . . CLC 44
See also CA 120

**Guare, John**  1938- . . . . . . . . . . CLC 8, 14, 29
See also CANR 21; CA 73-76; DLB 7

**Gudjonsson, Halldor Kiljan**  1902-
See Laxness, Halldor (Kiljan)
See also CA 103

**Guest, Barbara**  1920- . . . . . . . . . . . . CLC 34
See also CANR 11; CA 25-28R; DLB 5

**Guest, Judith (Ann)**  1936- . . . . . . . CLC 8, 30
See also CANR 15; CA 77-80

**Guild, Nicholas M.**  1944- . . . . . . . . . CLC 33
See also CA 93-96

**Guillen, Jorge**  1893-1984 . . . . . . . . . . CLC 11
See also CA 89-92; obituary CA 112

**Guillen, Nicolas**  1902-1989 . . . . . . . . CLC 48
See also CA 116, 125; obituary CA 129

**Guillevic, (Eugene)**  1907- . . . . . . . . . . CLC 33
See also CA 93-96

**Guiraldes, Ricardo**  1886-1927 . . . . . TCLC 39

**Gunn, Bill**  1934-1989 . . . . . . . . . . . . . CLC 5
See also Gunn, William Harrison
See also DLB 38

**Gunn, Thom(son William)**
1929- . . . . . . . . . . . . . . . CLC 3, 6, 18, 32
See also CANR 9; CA 17-20R; DLB 27

**Gunn, William Harrison**  1934-1989
See Gunn, Bill
See also CANR 12, 25; CA 13-16R;
obituary CA 128

**Gurney, A(lbert) R(amsdell), Jr.**
1930- . . . . . . . . . . . . . . . . CLC 32, 50, 54
See also CA 77-80

Gurney, Ivor (Bertie)  1890-1937 . . . TCLC 33

Gustafson, Ralph (Barker)  1909- . . . . CLC 36
See also CANR 8; CA 21-24R; DLB 88

Guthrie, A(lfred) B(ertram), Jr.
1901- . . . . . . . . . . . . . . . . . . . . . CLC 23
See also CA 57-60; DLB 6

Guthrie, Woodrow Wilson  1912-1967
See Guthrie, Woody
See also CA 113; obituary CA 93-96

Guthrie, Woody  1912-1967 . . . . . . . . CLC 35
See also Guthrie, Woodrow Wilson

Guy, Rosa (Cuthbert)  1928- . . . . . CLC 26 13
See also CANR 14; CA 17-20R; SATA 14;
DLB 33

Haavikko, Paavo (Juhani)
1931- . . . . . . . . . . . . . . . . . . . CLC 18, 34
See also CA 106

Hacker, Marilyn  1942- . . . . . . . CLC 5, 9, 23
See also CA 77-80

Haggard, (Sir) H(enry) Rider
1856-1925 . . . . . . . . . . . . . . . . . TCLC 11
See also CA 108; SATA 16; DLB 70

Haig-Brown, Roderick L(angmere)
1908-1976 . . . . . . . . . . . . . . . . . . . CLC 21
See also CANR 4; CA 5-8R;
obituary CA 69-72; SATA 12; DLB 88

Hailey, Arthur  1920- . . . . . . . . . . . . . CLC 5
See also CANR 2; CA 1-4R; DLB-Y 82

Hailey, Elizabeth Forsythe  1938- . . . CLC 40
See also CAAS 1; CANR 15; CA 93-96

Haines, John  1924- . . . . . . . . . . . . . . CLC 58
See also CANR 13; CA 19-20R; DLB 5

Haldeman, Joe  1943- . . . . . . . . . . . . . CLC 61
See also CA 53-56; DLB 8

Haley, Alex (Palmer)  1921- . . . . . . CLC 8, 12
See also CA 77-80; DLB 38

Haliburton, Thomas Chandler
1796-1865 . . . . . . . . . . . . . . . . . NCLC 15
See also DLB 11

Hall, Donald (Andrew, Jr.)
1928- . . . . . . . . . . . . . . CLC 1, 13, 37, 59
See also CAAS 7; CANR 2; CA 5-8R;
SATA 23; DLB 5

Hall, James Norman  1887-1951 . . . TCLC 23
See also CA 123; SATA 21

Hall, (Marguerite) Radclyffe
1886-1943 . . . . . . . . . . . . . . . . . TCLC 12
See also CA 110

Hall, Rodney  1935- . . . . . . . . . . . . . . CLC 51
See also CA 109

Halpern, Daniel  1945- . . . . . . . . . . . . CLC 14
See also CA 33-36R

Hamburger, Michael (Peter Leopold)
1924- . . . . . . . . . . . . . . . . . . . CLC 5, 14
See also CAAS 4; CANR 2; CA 5-8R;
DLB 27

Hamill, Pete  1935- . . . . . . . . . . . . . . CLC 10
See also CANR 18; CA 25-28R

Hamilton, Edmond  1904-1977 . . . . . . . CLC 1
See also CANR 3; CA 1-4R; DLB 8

Hamilton, Gail  1911-
See Corcoran, Barbara

Hamilton, Ian  1938- . . . . . . . . . . . . . CLC 55
See also CA 106; DLB 40

Hamilton, Mollie  1909?-
See Kaye, M(ary) M(argaret)

Hamilton, (Anthony Walter) Patrick
1904-1962 . . . . . . . . . . . . . . . . . . CLC 51
See also obituary CA 113; DLB 10

Hamilton, Virginia (Esther)  1936- . . . CLC 26
See also CLR 1, 11; CANR 20; CA 25-28R;
SATA 4; DLB 33, 52

Hammett, (Samuel) Dashiell
1894-1961 . . . . . . . CLC 3, 5, 10, 19, 47
See also CA 81-84; DLB-DS 6

Hammon, Jupiter  1711?-1800? . . . . NCLC 5
See also DLB 31, 50

Hamner, Earl (Henry), Jr.  1923- . . . CLC 12
See also CA 73-76; DLB 6

Hampton, Christopher (James)
1946- . . . . . . . . . . . . . . . . . . . . . . CLC 4
See also CA 25-28R; DLB 13

Hamsun, Knut  1859-1952 . . . . . . TCLC 2, 14
See also Pedersen, Knut

Handke, Peter  1942- . . CLC 5, 8, 10, 15, 38
See also CA 77-80; DLB 85

Hanley, James  1901-1985 . . . CLC 3, 5, 8, 13
See also CA 73-76; obituary CA 117

Hannah, Barry  1942- . . . . . . . . . . CLC 23, 38
See also CA 108, 110; DLB 6

Hansberry, Lorraine (Vivian)
1930-1965 . . . . . . . . . . . . . . . . CLC 17, 62
See also CA 109; obituary CA 25-28R;
CABS 3; DLB 7, 38; CDALB 1941-1968

Hansen, Joseph  1923- . . . . . . . . . . . . CLC 38
See also CANR 16; CA 29-32R

Hansen, Martin  1909-1955 . . . . . . . TCLC 32

Hanson, Kenneth O(stlin)  1922- . . . . CLC 13
See also CANR 7; CA 53-56

Hardenberg, Friedrich (Leopold Freiherr) von
1772-1801
See Novalis

Hardwick, Elizabeth  1916- . . . . . . . . CLC 13
See also CANR 3; CA 5-8R; DLB 6

Hardy, Thomas
1840-1928 . . . TCLC 4, 10, 18, 32; SSC 2
See also CA 104, 123; SATA 25; DLB 18,
19

Hare, David  1947- . . . . . . . . . . . . CLC 29, 58
See also CA 97-100; DLB 13

Harlan, Louis R(udolph)  1922- . . . . . CLC 34
See also CANR 25; CA 21-24R

Harling, Robert  1951?- . . . . . . . . . . . CLC 53

Harmon, William (Ruth)  1938- . . . . . CLC 38
See also CANR 14; CA 33-36R

Harper, Frances Ellen Watkins
1825-1911 . . . . . . . . . . . . . . . . . TCLC 14
See also CA 111, 125; DLB 50

Harper, Michael S(teven)  1938- . . CLC 7, 22
See also CANR 24; CA 33-36R; DLB 41

Harris, Christie (Lucy Irwin)
1907- . . . . . . . . . . . . . . . . . . . . . CLC 12
See also CANR 6; CA 5-8R; SATA 6;
DLB 88

Harris, Frank  1856-1931 . . . . . . . . TCLC 24
See also CAAS 1; CA 109

Harris, George Washington
1814-1869 . . . . . . . . . . . . . . . . NCLC 23
See also DLB 3, 11

Harris, Joel Chandler  1848-1908 . . . TCLC 2
See also YABC 1; CA 104; DLB 11, 23, 42,
78, 91

Harris, John (Wyndham Parkes Lucas)
Beynon  1903-1969 . . . . . . . . . . CLC 19
See also Wyndham, John
See also CA 102; obituary CA 89-92

Harris, MacDonald  1921- . . . . . . . . . CLC 9
See also Heiney, Donald (William)

Harris, Mark  1922- . . . . . . . . . . . . . . CLC 19
See also CAAS 3; CANR 2; CA 5-8R;
DLB 2; DLB-Y 80

Harris, (Theodore) Wilson  1921- . . . . CLC 25
See also CANR 11, 27; CA 65-68

Harrison, Harry (Max)  1925- . . . . . . CLC 42
See also CANR 5, 21; CA 1-4R; SATA 4;
DLB 8

Harrison, James (Thomas)  1937-
See Harrison, Jim
See also CANR 8; CA 13-16R

Harrison, Jim  1937- . . . . . . . . CLC 6, 14, 33
See also Harrison, James (Thomas)
See also DLB-Y 82

Harrison, Tony  1937- . . . . . . . . . . . . CLC 43
See also CA 65-68; DLB 40

Harriss, Will(ard Irvin)  1922- . . . . . . CLC 34
See also CA 111

Harte, (Francis) Bret(t)
1836?-1902 . . . . . . . . . . . . . . . TCLC 1, 25
See also CA 104; SATA 26; DLB 12, 64,
74, 79; CDALB 1865-1917

Hartley, L(eslie) P(oles)
1895-1972 . . . . . . . . . . . . . . . . CLC 2, 22
See also CA 45-48; obituary CA 37-40R;
DLB 15

Hartman, Geoffrey H.  1929- . . . . . . . CLC 27
See also CA 117, 125; DLB 67

Haruf, Kent  19??- . . . . . . . . . . . . . . . CLC 34

Harwood, Ronald  1934- . . . . . . . . . . CLC 32
See also CANR 4; CA 1-4R; DLB 13

Hasek, Jaroslav (Matej Frantisek)
1883-1923 . . . . . . . . . . . . . . . . . . TCLC 4
See also CA 104, 129

Hass, Robert  1941- . . . . . . . . . . . . CLC 18, 39
See also CANR 30; CA 111

Hastings, Selina  19??- . . . . . . . . . . . . CLC 44

Hauptmann, Gerhart (Johann Robert)
1862-1946 . . . . . . . . . . . . . . . . . . TCLC 4
See also CA 104; DLB 66

Havel, Vaclav  1936- . . . . . . . . . . . CLC 25, 58
See also CA 104

Haviaras, Stratis  1935- . . . . . . . . . . CLC 33
See also CA 105

Hawkes, John (Clendennin Burne, Jr.)
1925- . . . . . . CLC 1, 2, 3, 4, 7, 9, 14, 15,
27, 49
See also CANR 2; CA 1-4R; DLB 2, 7;
DLB-Y 80

Hawking, Stephen (William)
1948- . . . . . . . . . . . . . . . . . . . . . CLC 63
See also CA 126, 129

Hawthorne, Julian  1846-1934 . . . . . TCLC 25

Hawthorne, Nathaniel
1804-1864 . . . NCLC 2, 10, 17, 23; SSC 3
See also YABC 2; DLB 1, 74;
CDALB 1640-1865

Hayashi Fumiko  1904-1951 . . . . . . TCLC 27

Haycraft, Anna  19??-
See Ellis, Alice Thomas
See also CA 122

Hayden, Robert (Earl)
1913-1980 . . . . . . . . . . . CLC 5, 9, 14, 37
See also CANR 24; CA 69-72;
obituary CA 97-100; CABS 2; SATA 19;
obituary SATA 26; DLB 5, 76;
CDALB 1941-1968

Hayman, Ronald  1932- . . . . . . . . . . . CLC 44
See also CANR 18; CA 25-28R

Haywood, Eliza (Fowler)  1693?-1756 . . LC 1
See also DLB 39

Hazlitt, William  1778-1830 . . . . . . NCLC 29

Hazzard, Shirley  1931- . . . . . . . . . . . CLC 18
See also CANR 4; CA 9-12R; DLB-Y 82

H(ilda) D(oolittle)
1886-1961 . . . . . . . . CLC 3, 8, 14, 31, 34
See also Doolittle, Hilda

Head, Bessie  1937-1986 . . . . . . . . . . . CLC 25
See also CANR 25; CA 29-32R;
obituary CA 119

Headon, (Nicky) Topper  1956?- . . . . CLC 30
See also The Clash

Heaney, Seamus (Justin)
1939- . . . . . . . . . . . CLC 5, 7, 14, 25, 37
See also CANR 25; CA 85-88; DLB 40

Hearn, (Patricio) Lafcadio (Tessima Carlos)
1850-1904 . . . . . . . . . . . . . . . . . . . . TCLC 9
See also CA 105; DLB 12, 78

Hearne, Vicki  1946- . . . . . . . . . . . . . . CLC 56

Hearon, Shelby  1931- . . . . . . . . . . . . . CLC 63
See also CANR 18; CA 25-28

Heat Moon, William Least  1939- . . . CLC 29

Hebert, Anne  1916- . . . . . . . . . CLC 4, 13, 29
See also CA 85-88; DLB 68

Hecht, Anthony (Evan)
1923- . . . . . . . . . . . . . . . . . CLC 8, 13, 19
See also CANR 6; CA 9-12R; DLB 5

Hecht, Ben  1894-1964 . . . . . . . . . . . . . CLC 8
See also CA 85-88; DLB 7, 9, 25, 26, 28, 86

Hedayat, Sadeq  1903-1951 . . . . . . . TCLC 21
See also CA 120

Heidegger, Martin  1889-1976 . . . . . . CLC 24
See also CA 81-84; obituary CA 65-68

Heidenstam, (Karl Gustaf) Verner von
1859-1940 . . . . . . . . . . . . . . . . . . . TCLC 5
See also CA 104

Heifner, Jack  1946- . . . . . . . . . . . . . . CLC 11
See also CA 105

Heijermans, Herman  1864-1924 . . . TCLC 24
See also CA 123

Heilbrun, Carolyn G(old)  1926- . . . . . CLC 25
See also CANR 1, 28; CA 45-48

Heine, Harry  1797-1856
See Heine, Heinrich

Heine, Heinrich  1797-1856 . . . . . . . NCLC 4
See also DLB 90

Heinemann, Larry C(urtiss)  1944- . . CLC 50
See also CA 110

Heiney, Donald (William)  1921- . . . . . CLC 9
See also Harris, MacDonald
See also CANR 3; CA 1-4R

Heinlein, Robert A(nson)
1907-1988 . . . . . . CLC 1, 3, 8, 14, 26, 55
See also CANR 1, 20; CA 1-4R;
obituary CA 125; SATA 9, 56; DLB 8

Heller, Joseph
1923- . . . . . . . . CLC 1, 3, 5, 8, 11, 36, 63
See also CANR 8; CA 5-8R; CABS 1;
DLB 2, 28; DLB-Y 80

Hellman, Lillian (Florence)
1905?-1984 . . . . . CLC 2, 4, 8, 14, 18, 34,
44, 52; DC 1
See also CA 13-16R; obituary CA 112;
DLB 7; DLB-Y 84

Helprin, Mark  1947- . . . . . CLC 7, 10, 22, 32
See also CA 81-84; DLB-Y 85

Hemans, Felicia  1793-1835 . . . . . . NCLC 29

Hemingway, Ernest (Miller)
1899-1961 . . . CLC 1, 3, 6, 8, 10, 13, 19,
30, 34, 39, 41, 44, 50, 61; SSC 1
See also CA 77-80; DLB 4, 9; DLB-Y 81,
87; DLB-DS 1; CDALB 1917-1929

Hempel, Amy  1951- . . . . . . . . . . . . . . CLC 39
See also CA 118

Henley, Beth  1952- . . . . . . . . . . . . . . CLC 23
See also Henley, Elizabeth Becker
See also CABS 3; DLB-Y 86

Henley, Elizabeth Becker  1952-
See Henley, Beth
See also CA 107

Henley, William Ernest
1849-1903 . . . . . . . . . . . . . . . . . . . TCLC 8
See also CA 105; DLB 19

Hennissart, Martha
See Lathen, Emma
See also CA 85-88

Henry, O.  1862-1910 . . . TCLC 1, 19; SSC 5
See also Porter, William Sydney
See also YABC 2; CA 104; DLB 12, 78, 79;
CDALB 1865-1917

Henry VIII  1491-1547 . . . . . . . . . . . . LC 10

Hentoff, Nat(han Irving)  1925- . . . . . CLC 26
See also CLR 1; CAAS 6; CANR 5, 25;
CA 1-4R; SATA 27, 42; AAYA 4

Heppenstall, (John) Rayner
1911-1981 . . . . . . . . . . . . . . . . . . . CLC 10
See also CANR 29; CA 1-4R;
obituary CA 103

Herbert, Frank (Patrick)
1920-1986 . . . . . . . . . . CLC 12, 23, 35, 44
See also CANR 5; CA 53-56;
obituary CA 118; SATA 9, 37, 47; DLB 8

Herbert, Zbigniew  1924- . . . . . . . . CLC 9, 43
See also CA 89-92

Herbst, Josephine  1897-1969 . . . . . . CLC 34
See also CA 5-8R; obituary CA 25-28R;
DLB 9

Herder, Johann Gottfried von
1744-1803 . . . . . . . . . . . . . . . . . . NCLC 8

Hergesheimer, Joseph
1880-1954 . . . . . . . . . . . . . . . . . TCLC 11
See also CA 109; DLB 9

Herlagnez, Pablo de  1844-1896
See Verlaine, Paul (Marie)

Herlihy, James Leo  1927- . . . . . . . . . . CLC 6
See also CANR 2; CA 1-4R

Hermogenes  fl.c. 175- . . . . . . . . . . . CMLC 6

Hernandez, Jose  1834-1886 . . . . . . NCLC 17

Herrick, Robert  1591-1674 . . . . . . . . . LC 13

Herriot, James  1916- . . . . . . . . . . . . . CLC 12
See also Wight, James Alfred
See also AAYA 1

Herrmann, Dorothy  1941- . . . . . . . . . CLC 44
See also CA 107

Hersey, John (Richard)
1914- . . . . . . . . . . . . . . CLC 1, 2, 7, 9, 40
See also CA 17-20R; SATA 25; DLB 6

Herzen, Aleksandr Ivanovich
1812-1870 . . . . . . . . . . . . . . . . . NCLC 10

Herzl, Theodor  1860-1904 . . . . . . . . TCLC 36

Herzog, Werner  1942- . . . . . . . . . . . . CLC 16
See also CA 89-92

Hesiod  c. 8th Century B.C.- . . . . . . CMLC 5

Hesse, Hermann
1877-1962 . . . . CLC 1, 2, 3, 6, 11, 17, 25
See also CAP 2; CA 17-18; SATA 50;
DLB 66

Heyen, William  1940- . . . . . . . . . CLC 13, 18
See also CAAS 9; CA 33-36R; DLB 5

Heyerdahl, Thor  1914- . . . . . . . . . . . . CLC 26
See also CANR 5, 22; CA 5-8R; SATA 2,
52

Heym, Georg (Theodor Franz Arthur)
1887-1912 . . . . . . . . . . . . . . . . . . . TCLC 9
See also CA 106

Heym, Stefan  1913- . . . . . . . . . . . . . . CLC 41
See also CANR 4; CA 9-12R; DLB 69

Heyse, Paul (Johann Ludwig von)
1830-1914 . . . . . . . . . . . . . . . . . . . TCLC 8
See also CA 104

Hibbert, Eleanor (Burford)  1906- . . . . CLC 7
See also CANR 9, 28; CA 17-20R; SATA 2

Higgins, George V(incent)
1939- . . . . . . . . . . . . . . . CLC 4, 7, 10, 18
See also CAAS 5; CANR 17; CA 77-80;
DLB 2; DLB-Y 81

Higginson, Thomas Wentworth
1823-1911 . . . . . . . . . . . . . . . . . . TCLC 36
See also DLB 1, 64

Highsmith, (Mary) Patricia
1921- . . . . . . . . . . . . . . . CLC 2, 4, 14, 42
See also CANR 1, 20; CA 1-4R

Highwater, Jamake  1942- . . . . . . . . . CLC 12
See also CLR 17; CAAS 7; CANR 10;
CA 65-68; SATA 30, 32; DLB 52;
DLB-Y 85

Hikmet (Ran), Nazim  1902-1963 . . . . CLC 40
See also obituary CA 93-96

Hildesheimer, Wolfgang  1916- . . . . . CLC 49
See also CA 101; DLB 69

Hill, Geoffrey (William)
1932- . . . . . . . . . . . . . . . CLC 5, 8, 18, 45
See also CANR 21; CA 81-84; DLB 40

Hill, George Roy 1922- . . . . . . . . . . CLC 26
See also CA 110, 122

Hill, Susan B. 1942- . . . . . . . . . . . . . . CLC 4
See also CANR 29; CA 33-36R; DLB 14

Hillerman, Tony 1925- . . . . . . . . . . . CLC 62
See also CANR 21; CA 29-32R; SATA 6

Hilliard, Noel (Harvey) 1929- . . . . . . CLC 15
See also CANR 7; CA 9-12R

Hilton, James 1900-1954 . . . . . . . . TCLC 21
See also CA 108; SATA 34; DLB 34, 77

Himes, Chester (Bomar)
    1909-1984 . . . . . . . . CLC 2, 4, 7, 18, 58
See also CANR 22; CA 25-28R;
   obituary CA 114; DLB 2, 76

Hinde, Thomas 1926- . . . . . . . . . . . CLC 6, 11
See also Chitty, (Sir) Thomas Willes

Hine, (William) Daryl 1936- . . . . . . . CLC 15
See also CANR 1, 20; CA 1-4R; DLB 60

Hinton, S(usan) E(loise) 1950- . . . . . CLC 30
See also CLR 3, 23; CA 81-84; SATA 19,
   58; AAYA 2

Hippius (Merezhkovsky), Zinaida
   (Nikolayevna) 1869-1945 . . . . . . TCLC 9
See also Gippius, Zinaida (Nikolayevna)

Hiraoka, Kimitake 1925-1970
See Mishima, Yukio
See also CA 97-100; obituary CA 29-32R

Hirsch, Edward (Mark) 1950- . . . CLC 31, 50
See also CANR 20; CA 104

Hitchcock, (Sir) Alfred (Joseph)
   1899-1980 . . . . . . . . . . . . . . . . . . . CLC 16
See also obituary CA 97-100; SATA 27;
   obituary SATA 24

Hoagland, Edward 1932- . . . . . . . . . CLC 28
See also CANR 2; CA 1-4R; SATA 51;
   DLB 6

Hoban, Russell C(onwell) 1925- . . CLC 7, 25
See also CLR 3; CANR 23; CA 5-8R;
   SATA 1, 40; DLB 52

Hobson, Laura Z(ametkin)
   1900-1986 . . . . . . . . . . . . . . . CLC 7, 25
See also CA 17-20R; obituary CA 118;
   SATA 52; DLB 28

Hochhuth, Rolf 1931- . . . . . . . . CLC 4, 11, 18
See also CA 5-8R

Hochman, Sandra 1936- . . . . . . . . . . CLC 3, 8
See also CA 5-8R; DLB 5

Hochwalder, Fritz 1911-1986 . . . . . . CLC 36
See also CA 29-32R; obituary CA 120

Hocking, Mary (Eunice) 1921- . . . . . CLC 13
See also CANR 18; CA 101

Hodgins, Jack 1938- . . . . . . . . . . . . . CLC 23
See also CA 93-96; DLB 60

Hodgson, William Hope
   1877-1918 . . . . . . . . . . . . . . . . TCLC 13
See also CA 111; DLB 70

Hoffman, Alice 1952- . . . . . . . . . . . . CLC 51
See also CA 77-80

Hoffman, Daniel (Gerard)
   1923- . . . . . . . . . . . . . . . CLC 6, 13, 23
See also CANR 4; CA 1-4R; DLB 5

Hoffman, Stanley 1944- . . . . . . . . . . . CLC 5
See also CA 77-80

Hoffman, William M(oses) 1939- . . . CLC 40
See also CANR 11; CA 57-60

Hoffmann, Ernst Theodor Amadeus
   1776-1822 . . . . . . . . . . . . . . . . . NCLC 2
See also SATA 27; DLB 90

Hoffmann, Gert 1932- . . . . . . . . . . . CLC 54

Hofmannsthal, Hugo (Laurenz August
   Hofmann Edler) von
   1874-1929 . . . . . . . . . . . . . . . . . TCLC 11
See also CA 106; DLB 81

Hogg, James 1770-1835 . . . . . . . . . . NCLC 4

Holbach, Paul Henri Thiry, Baron d'
   1723-1789 . . . . . . . . . . . . . . . . . . . LC 14

Holberg, Ludvig 1684-1754 . . . . . . . . . LC 6

Holden, Ursula 1921- . . . . . . . . . . . . CLC 18
See also CAAS 8; CANR 22; CA 101

Holderlin, (Johann Christian) Friedrich
   1770-1843 . . . . . . . . . . . . . . . . NCLC 16

Holdstock, Robert (P.) 1948- . . . . . . CLC 39

Holland, Isabelle 1920- . . . . . . . . . . CLC 21
See also CANR 10, 25; CA 21-24R;
   SATA 8

Holland, Marcus 1900-1985
See Caldwell, (Janet Miriam) Taylor
   (Holland)

Hollander, John 1929- . . . . . . CLC 2, 5, 8, 14
See also CANR 1; CA 1-4R; SATA 13;
   DLB 5

Holleran, Andrew 1943?- . . . . . . . . . CLC 38

Hollinghurst, Alan 1954- . . . . . . . . . CLC 55
See also CA 114

Hollis, Jim 1916-
See Summers, Hollis (Spurgeon, Jr.)

Holmes, John Clellon 1926-1988 . . . . CLC 56
See also CANR 4; CA 9-10R;
   obituary CA 125; DLB 16

Holmes, Oliver Wendell
   1809-1894 . . . . . . . . . . . . . . . . NCLC 14
See also SATA 34; DLB 1;
   CDALB 1640-1865

Holt, Victoria 1906-
See Hibbert, Eleanor (Burford)

Holub, Miroslav 1923- . . . . . . . . . . . . CLC 4
See also CANR 10; CA 21-24R

Homer c. 8th century B.C.- . . . . . . . CMLC 1

Honig, Edwin 1919- . . . . . . . . . . . . . CLC 33
See also CAAS 8; CANR 4; CA 5-8R;
   DLB 5

Hood, Hugh (John Blagdon)
   1928- . . . . . . . . . . . . . . . . . . CLC 15, 28
See also CANR 1; CA 49-52; DLB 53

Hood, Thomas 1799-1845 . . . . . . . . NCLC 16

Hooker, (Peter) Jeremy 1941- . . . . . . CLC 43
See also CANR 22; CA 77-80; DLB 40

Hope, A(lec) D(erwent) 1907- . . . . CLC 3, 51
See also CA 21-24R

Hope, Christopher (David Tully)
   1944- . . . . . . . . . . . . . . . . . . . . . CLC 52
See also CA 106

Hopkins, Gerard Manley
   1844-1889 . . . . . . . . . . . . . . . . NCLC 17
See also DLB 35, 57

Hopkins, John (Richard) 1931- . . . . . . CLC 4
See also CA 85-88

Hopkins, Pauline Elizabeth
   1859-1930 . . . . . . . . . . . . . . . . TCLC 28
See also DLB 50

Horgan, Paul 1903- . . . . . . . . . . CLC 9, 53
See also CANR 9; CA 13-16R; SATA 13;
   DLB-Y 85

Horovitz, Israel 1939- . . . . . . . . . . . CLC 56
See also CA 33-36R; DLB 7

Horwitz, Julius 1920-1986 . . . . . . . . CLC 14
See also CANR 12; CA 9-12R;
   obituary CA 119

Hospital, Janette Turner 1942- . . . . . CLC 42
See also CA 108

Hostos (y Bonilla), Eugenio Maria de
   1893-1903 . . . . . . . . . . . . . . . . TCLC 24
See also CA 123

Hougan, Carolyn 19??- . . . . . . . . . . . CLC 34

Household, Geoffrey (Edward West)
   1900-1988 . . . . . . . . . . . . . . . . . CLC 11
See also CA 77-80; obituary CA 126;
   SATA 14, 59; DLB 87

Housman, A(lfred) E(dward)
   1859-1936 . . . . . . . . . . TCLC 1, 10; PC 2
See also CA 104, 125; DLB 19

Housman, Laurence 1865-1959 . . . . . TCLC 7
See also CA 106; SATA 25; DLB 10

Howard, Elizabeth Jane 1923- . . . CLC 7, 29
See also CANR 8; CA 5-8R

Howard, Maureen 1930- . . . . . CLC 5, 14, 46
See also CA 53-56; DLB-Y 83

Howard, Richard 1929- . . . . . . CLC 7, 10, 47
See also CANR 25; CA 85-88; DLB 5

Howard, Robert E(rvin)
   1906-1936 . . . . . . . . . . . . . . . . . TCLC 8
See also CA 105

Howe, Fanny 1940- . . . . . . . . . . . . . CLC 47
See also CA 117; SATA 52

Howe, Julia Ward 1819-1910 . . . . . TCLC 21
See also CA 117; DLB 1

Howe, Tina 1937- . . . . . . . . . . . . . . CLC 48
See also CA 109

Howell, James 1594?-1666 . . . . . . . . . LC 13

Howells, William Dean
   1837-1920 . . . . . . . . . . . . . . TCLC 7, 17
See also CA 104; DLB 12, 64, 74, 79;
   CDALB 1865-1917

Howes, Barbara 1914- . . . . . . . . . . . CLC 15
See also CAAS 3; CA 9-12R; SATA 5

Hrabal, Bohumil 1914- . . . . . . . . . . CLC 13
See also CA 106

Hubbard, L(afayette) Ron(ald)
   1911-1986 . . . . . . . . . . . . . . . . . CLC 43
See also CANR 22; CA 77-80;
   obituary CA 118

Huch, Ricarda (Octavia)
   1864-1947 . . . . . . . . . . . . . . . . TCLC 13
See also CA 111; DLB 66

Huddle, David 1942- . . . . . . . . . . . . CLC 49
See also CA 57-60

Hudson, W(illiam) H(enry)
   1841-1922 . . . . . . . . . . . . . . . . TCLC 29
See also CA 115; SATA 35

**Hueffer, Ford Madox** 1873-1939
See Ford, Ford Madox

**Hughart, Barry** 1934-............ **CLC 39**

**Hughes, David (John)** 1930- ....... **CLC 48**
See also CA 116, 129; DLB 14

**Hughes, Edward James** 1930-
See Hughes, Ted

**Hughes, (James) Langston**
1902-1967 .... **CLC 1, 5, 10, 15, 35, 44;**
**PC 1; SSC 6**
See also CLR 17; CANR 1; CA 1-4R;
obituary CA 25-28R; SATA 4, 33;
DLB 4, 7, 48, 51, 86; CDALB 1929-1941

**Hughes, Richard (Arthur Warren)**
1900-1976 ................. **CLC 1, 11**
See also CANR 4; CA 5-8R;
obituary CA 65-68; SATA 8;
obituary SATA 25; DLB 15

**Hughes, Ted** 1930-..... **CLC 2, 4, 9, 14, 37**
See also CLR 3; CANR 1; CA 1-4R;
SATA 27, 49; DLB 40

**Hugo, Richard F(ranklin)**
1923-1982 .............. **CLC 6, 18, 32**
See also CANR 3; CA 49-52;
obituary CA 108; DLB 5

**Hugo, Victor Marie**
1802-1885 ............ **NCLC 3, 10, 21**
See also SATA 47

**Huidobro, Vicente** 1893-1948 ..... **TCLC 31**

**Hulme, Keri** 1947- ................. **CLC 39**
See also CA 125

**Hulme, T(homas) E(rnest)**
1883-1917 .................. **TCLC 21**
See also CA 117; DLB 19

**Hume, David** 1711-1776............. **LC 7**

**Humphrey, William** 1924-......... **CLC 45**
See also CA 77-80; DLB 6

**Humphreys, Emyr (Owen)** 1919-.... **CLC 47**
See also CANR 3, 24; CA 5-8R; DLB 15

**Humphreys, Josephine** 1945-.... **CLC 34, 57**
See also CA 121, 127

**Hunt, E(verette) Howard (Jr.)**
1918- ........................ **CLC 3**
See also CANR 2; CA 45-48

**Hunt, (James Henry) Leigh**
1784-1859 ................. **NCLC 1**

**Hunter, Evan** 1926- ........... **CLC 11, 31**
See also CANR 5; CA 5-8R; SATA 25;
DLB-Y 82

**Hunter, Kristin (Eggleston)** 1931-... **CLC 35**
See also CLR 3; CANR 13; CA 13-16R;
SATA 12; DLB 33

**Hunter, Mollie (Maureen McIlwraith)**
1922- ....................... **CLC 21**
See also McIlwraith, Maureen Mollie
Hunter

**Hunter, Robert** ?-1734.............. **LC 7**

**Hurston, Zora Neale**
1891-1960 ....... **CLC 7, 30, 61; SSC 4**
See also CA 85-88; DLB 51, 86

**Huston, John (Marcellus)**
1906-1987 .................... **CLC 20**
See also CA 73-76; obituary CA 123;
DLB 26

**Huxley, Aldous (Leonard)**
1894-1963 .. **CLC 1, 3, 4, 5, 8, 11, 18, 35**
See also CA 85-88; DLB 36

**Huysmans, Charles Marie Georges**
1848-1907
See Huysmans, Joris-Karl
See also CA 104

**Huysmans, Joris-Karl** 1848-1907 ... **TCLC 7**
See also Huysmans, Charles Marie Georges

**Hwang, David Henry** 1957-........ **CLC 55**
See also CA 127

**Hyde, Anthony** 1946?-............ **CLC 42**

**Hyde, Margaret O(ldroyd)** 1917- ... **CLC 21**
See also CLR 23; CANR 1; CA 1-4R;
SAAS 8; SATA 1, 42

**Ian, Janis** 1951- ................. **CLC 21**
See also CA 105

**Ibarguengoitia, Jorge** 1928-1983.... **CLC 37**
See also obituary CA 113, 124

**Ibsen, Henrik (Johan)**
1828-1906 .......... **TCLC 2, 8, 16, 37**
See also CA 104

**Ibuse, Masuji** 1898-............. **CLC 22**
See also CA 127

**Ichikawa, Kon** 1915-.............. **CLC 20**
See also CA 121

**Idle, Eric** 1943-................. **CLC 21**
See also Monty Python
See also CA 116

**Ignatow, David** 1914-...... **CLC 4, 7, 14, 40**
See also CAAS 3; CA 9-12R; DLB 5

**Ihimaera, Witi (Tame)** 1944-....... **CLC 46**
See also CA 77-80

**Ilf, Ilya** 1897-1937 .............. **TCLC 21**

**Immermann, Karl (Lebrecht)**
1796-1840 .................. **NCLC 4**

**Ingalls, Rachel** 19??-.............. **CLC 42**
See also CA 123, 127

**Ingamells, Rex** 1913-1955 ....... **TCLC 35**

**Inge, William (Motter)**
1913-1973 .............. **CLC 1, 8, 19**
See also CA 9-12R; DLB 7;
CDALB 1941-1968

**Innaurato, Albert** 1948-........ **CLC 21, 60**
See also CA 115, 122

**Innes, Michael** 1906-
See Stewart, J(ohn) I(nnes) M(ackintosh)

**Ionesco, Eugene**
1912- ........ **CLC 1, 4, 6, 9, 11, 15, 41**
See also CA 9-12R; SATA 7

**Iqbal, Muhammad** 1877-1938 ..... **TCLC 28**

**Irving, John (Winslow)**
1942- ................. **CLC 13, 23, 38**
See also CANR 28; CA 25-28R; DLB 6;
DLB-Y 82

**Irving, Washington**
1783-1859 ........ **NCLC 2, 19; SSC 2**
See also YABC 2; DLB 3, 11, 30, 59, 73,
74; CDALB 1640-1865

**Isaacs, Susan** 1943- .............. **CLC 32**
See also CANR 20; CA 89-92

**Isherwood, Christopher (William Bradshaw)**
1904-1986 ........ **CLC 1, 9, 11, 14, 44**
See also CA 13-16R; obituary CA 117;
DLB 15; DLB-Y 86

**Ishiguro, Kazuo** 1954- ...... **CLC 27, 56, 59**
See also CA 120

**Ishikawa Takuboku** 1885-1912 .... **TCLC 15**
See also CA 113

**Iskander, Fazil (Abdulovich)**
1929- ....................... **CLC 47**
See also CA 102

**Ivanov, Vyacheslav (Ivanovich)**
1866-1949 .................. **TCLC 33**
See also CA 122

**Ivask, Ivar (Vidrik)** 1927- ......... **CLC 14**
See also CANR 24; CA 37-40R

**Jackson, Jesse** 1908-1983 ......... **CLC 12**
See also CANR 27; CA 25-28R;
obituary CA 109; SATA 2, 29, 48

**Jackson, Laura (Riding)** 1901- ...... **CLC 7**
See also Riding, Laura
See also CANR 28; CA 65-68; DLB 48

**Jackson, Shirley** 1919-1965..... **CLC 11, 60**
See also CANR 4; CA 1-4R;
obituary CA 25-28R; SATA 2; DLB 6;
CDALB 1941-1968

**Jacob, (Cyprien) Max** 1876-1944 ... **TCLC 6**
See also CA 104

**Jacob, Piers A(nthony) D(illingham)** 1934-
See Anthony (Jacob), Piers
See also CA 21-24R

**Jacobs, Jim** 1942- and **Casey, Warren**
1942- ....................... **CLC 12**
See also CA 97-100

**Jacobs, Jim** 1942-
See Jacobs, Jim and Casey, Warren
See also CA 97-100

**Jacobs, W(illiam) W(ymark)**
1863-1943 ................. **TCLC 22**
See also CA 121

**Jacobsen, Josephine** 1908-......... **CLC 48**
See also CANR 23; CA 33-36R

**Jacobson, Dan** 1929- ........... **CLC 4, 14**
See also CANR 2, 25; CA 1-4R; DLB 14

**Jagger, Mick** 1944-............... **CLC 17**

**Jakes, John (William)** 1932- ....... **CLC 29**
See also CANR 10; CA 57-60; DLB-Y 83

**James, C(yril) L(ionel) R(obert)**
1901-1989 .................. **CLC 33**
See also CA 117, 125; obituary CA 128

**James, Daniel** 1911-1988
See Santiago, Danny
See also obituary CA 125

**James, Henry (Jr.)**
1843-1916 ......... **TCLC 2, 11, 24, 40**
See also CA 104, 132; DLB 12, 71, 74;
CDALB 1865-1917

**James, M(ontague) R(hodes)**
1862-1936 .................. **TCLC 6**
See also CA 104

**James, P(hyllis) D(orothy)**
1920- ...................... **CLC 18, 46**
See also CANR 17; CA 21-24R

**James, William** 1842-1910..... **TCLC 15, 32**
See also CA 109

Jami, Nur al-Din 'Abd al-Rahman
    1414-1492 .................... LC 9

Jandl, Ernst  1925- .............. CLC 34

Janowitz, Tama  1957- ........... CLC 43
    See also CA 106

Jarrell, Randall
    1914-1965 ....... CLC 1, 2, 6, 9, 13, 49
    See also CLR 6; CANR 6; CA 5-8R;
    obituary CA 25-28R; CABS 2; SATA 7;
    DLB 48, 52; CDALB 1941-1968

Jarry, Alfred  1873-1907....... TCLC 2, 14
    See also CA 104

Jeake, Samuel, Jr.  1889-1973
    See Aiken, Conrad

Jean Paul  1763-1825 ............ NCLC 7

Jeffers, (John) Robinson
    1887-1962 ........ CLC 2, 3, 11, 15, 54
    See also CA 85-88; DLB 45;
    CDALB 1917-1929

Jefferson, Thomas  1743-1826 .... NCLC 11
    See also DLB 31; CDALB 1640-1865

Jellicoe, (Patricia) Ann  1927- ...... CLC 27
    See also CA 85-88; DLB 13

Jenkins, (John) Robin  1912- ....... CLC 52
    See also CANR 1; CA 4R; DLB 14

Jennings, Elizabeth (Joan)
    1926- ..................... CLC 5, 14
    See also CAAS 5; CANR 8; CA 61-64;
    DLB 27

Jennings, Waylon  1937-........... CLC 21

Jensen, Laura (Linnea)  1948- ...... CLC 37
    See also CA 103

Jerome, Jerome K.  1859-1927..... TCLC 23
    See also CA 119; DLB 10, 34

Jerrold, Douglas William
    1803-1857 .................. NCLC 2

Jewett, (Theodora) Sarah Orne
    1849-1909 ......... TCLC 1, 22; SSC 6
    See also CA 108, 127; SATA 15; DLB 12,
    74

Jewsbury, Geraldine (Endsor)
    1812-1880 ................. NCLC 22
    See also DLB 21

Jhabvala, Ruth Prawer
    1927- .................. CLC 4, 8, 29
    See also CANR 2, 29; CA 1-4R

Jiles, Paulette  1943-........... CLC 13, 58
    See also CA 101

Jimenez (Mantecon), Juan Ramon
    1881-1958 .................. TCLC 4
    See also CA 104

Joel, Billy  1949-................ CLC 26
    See also Joel, William Martin

Joel, William Martin  1949-
    See Joel, Billy
    See also CA 108

Johnson, B(ryan) S(tanley William)
    1933-1973 .................. CLC 6, 9
    See also CANR 9; CA 9-12R;
    obituary CA 53-56; DLB 14, 40

Johnson, Charles (Richard)
    1948- ..................... CLC 7, 51
    See also CA 116; DLB 33

Johnson, Denis  1949-............. CLC 52
    See also CA 117, 121

Johnson, Diane  1934-........ CLC 5, 13, 48
    See also CANR 17; CA 41-44R; DLB-Y 80

Johnson, Eyvind (Olof Verner)
    1900-1976 .................. CLC 14
    See also CA 73-76; obituary CA 69-72

Johnson, James Weldon
    1871-1938 ................ TCLC 3, 19
    See also Johnson, James William
    See also CA 104, 125; DLB 51

Johnson, James William  1871-1938
    See Johnson, James Weldon
    See also SATA 31

Johnson, Joyce  1935-............. CLC 58
    See also CA 125

Johnson, Lionel (Pigot)
    1867-1902 .................. TCLC 19
    See also CA 117; DLB 19

Johnson, Marguerita  1928-
    See Angelou, Maya

Johnson, Pamela Hansford
    1912-1981 ............... CLC 1, 7, 27
    See also CANR 2; CA 1-4R;
    obituary CA 104; DLB 15

Johnson, Samuel  1709-1784........ LC 15
    See also DLB 39, 95

Johnson, Uwe
    1934-1984 ........... CLC 5, 10, 15, 40
    See also CANR 1; CA 1-4R;
    obituary CA 112; DLB 75

Johnston, George (Benson)  1913- ... CLC 51
    See also CANR 5, 20; CA 1-4R

Johnston, Jennifer  1930-........... CLC 7
    See also CA 85-88; DLB 14

Jolley, Elizabeth  1923-............. CLC 46

Jones, D(ouglas) G(ordon)  1929-.... CLC 10
    See also CANR 13; CA 113; DLB 53

Jones, David
    1895-1974 ......... CLC 2, 4, 7, 13, 42
    See also CA 9-12R; obituary CA 53-56;
    DLB 20

Jones, David Robert  1947-
    See Bowie, David
    See also CA 103

Jones, Diana Wynne  1934- ........ CLC 26
    See also CLR 23; CANR 4; CA 49-52;
    SATA 9

Jones, Gayl  1949-................ CLC 6, 9
    See also CA 77-80; DLB 33

Jones, James  1921-1977.... CLC 1, 3, 10, 39
    See also CANR 6; CA 1-4R;
    obituary CA 69-72; DLB 2

Jones, (Everett) LeRoi
    1934- ........ CLC 1, 2, 3, 5, 10, 14, 33
    See also Baraka, Amiri; Baraka, Imamu
    Amiri
    See also CA 21-24R

Jones, Madison (Percy, Jr.)  1925- ... CLC 4
    See also CANR 7; CA 13-16R

Jones, Mervyn  1922- .......... CLC 10, 52
    See also CAAS 5; CANR 1; CA 45-48

Jones, Mick  1956?-
    See The Clash

Jones, Nettie  19??-.............. CLC 34

Jones, Preston  1936-1979 ........ CLC 10
    See also CA 73-76; obituary CA 89-92;
    DLB 7

Jones, Robert F(rancis)  1934-....... CLC 7
    See also CANR 2; CA 49-52

Jones, Rod  1953- ................ CLC 50

Jones, Terry  1942?-
    See Monty Python
    See also CA 112, 116; SATA 51

Jong, Erica  1942-..........CLC 4, 6, 8, 18
    See also CANR 26; CA 73-76; DLB 2, 5, 28

Jonson, Ben(jamin)  1572-1637........ LC 6
    See also DLB 62

Jordan, June  1936-.......... CLC 5, 11, 23
    See also CLR 10; CANR 25; CA 33-36R;
    SATA 4; DLB 38

Jordan, Pat(rick M.)  1941- ........ CLC 37
    See also CANR 25; CA 33-36R

Josipovici, Gabriel (David)
    1940- ..................... CLC 6, 43
    See also CA 37-40R; DLB 14

Joubert, Joseph  1754-1824 ....... NCLC 9

Jouve, Pierre Jean  1887-1976...... CLC 47
    See also obituary CA 65-68

Joyce, James (Augustine Aloysius)
    1882-1941 ...... TCLC 3, 8, 16, 26, 35;
                                         SSC 3
    See also CA 104, 126; DLB 10, 19, 36

Jozsef, Attila  1905-1937.......... TCLC 22
    See also CA 116

Juana Ines de la Cruz  1651?-1695 .... LC 5

Julian of Norwich  1342?-1416?....... LC 6

Just, Ward S(wift)  1935-........ CLC 4, 27
    See also CA 25-28R

Justice, Donald (Rodney)  1925- .. CLC 6, 19
    See also CANR 26; CA 5-8R; DLB-Y 83

Kacew, Romain  1914-1980
    See Gary, Romain
    See also CA 108; obituary CA 102

Kacewgary, Romain  1914-1980
    See Gary, Romain

Kadare, Ismail  1936- ............. CLC 52

Kadohata, Cynthia  19??- .......... CLC 59

Kafka, Franz
    1883-1924 .... TCLC 2, 6, 13, 29; SSC 5
    See also CA 105, 126; DLB 81

Kahn, Roger  1927-................ CLC 30
    See also CA 25-28R; SATA 37

Kaiser, (Friedrich Karl) Georg
    1878-1945 .................. TCLC 9
    See also CA 106

Kaletski, Alexander  1946-......... CLC 39
    See also CA 118

Kallman, Chester (Simon)
    1921-1975 ................... CLC 2
    See also CANR 3; CA 45-48;
    obituary CA 53-56

Kaminsky, Melvin  1926-
    See Brooks, Mel
    See also CANR 16; CA 65-68

Kaminsky, Stuart  1934-........... CLC 59
    See also CA 73-76

Kane, Paul 1941-
See Simon, Paul

Kanin, Garson 1912-........... CLC 22
See also CANR 7; CA 5-8R; DLB 7

Kaniuk, Yoram 1930-........... CLC 19

Kant, Immanuel 1724-1804 ...... NCLC 27

Kantor, MacKinlay 1904-1977 ...... CLC 7
See also CA 61-64; obituary CA 73-76;
DLB 9

Kaplan, David Michael 1946- ...... CLC 50

Kaplan, James 19??-........... CLC 59

Karamzin, Nikolai Mikhailovich
1766-1826 ................. NCLC 3

Karapanou, Margarita 1946-....... CLC 13
See also CA 101

Karl, Frederick R(obert) 1927- ..... CLC 34
See also CANR 3; CA 5-8R

Kassef, Romain 1914-1980
See Gary, Romain

Katz, Steve 1935-............... CLC 47
See also CANR 12; CA 25-28R; DLB-Y 83

Kauffman, Janet 1945-........... CLC 42
See also CA 117; DLB-Y 86

Kaufman, Bob (Garnell)
1925-1986 ................. CLC 49
See also CANR 22; CA 41-44R;
obituary CA 118; DLB 16, 41

Kaufman, George S(imon)
1889-1961 ................. CLC 38
See also CA 108; obituary CA 93-96; DLB 7

Kaufman, Sue 1926-1977 ........ CLC 3, 8
See also Barondess, Sue K(aufman)

Kavan, Anna 1904-1968 ........ CLC 5, 13
See also Edmonds, Helen (Woods)
See also CANR 6; CA 5-8R

Kavanagh, Patrick (Joseph Gregory)
1905-1967 ................. CLC 22
See also CA 123; obituary CA 25-28R;
DLB 15, 20

Kawabata, Yasunari
1899-1972 ........... CLC 2, 5, 9, 18
See also CA 93-96; obituary CA 33-36R

Kaye, M(ary) M(argaret) 1909?-.... CLC 28
See also CANR 24; CA 89-92

Kaye, Mollie 1909?-
See Kaye, M(ary) M(argaret)

Kaye-Smith, Sheila 1887-1956..... TCLC 20
See also CA 118; DLB 36

Kazan, Elia 1909-........... CLC 6, 16, 63
See also CA 21-24R

Kazantzakis, Nikos
1885?-1957............. TCLC 2, 5, 33
See also CA 105

Kazin, Alfred 1915- ........... CLC 34, 38
See also CAAS 7; CANR 1; CA 1-4R

Keane, Mary Nesta (Skrine) 1904-
See Keane, Molly
See also CA 108, 114

Keane, Molly 1904- ............. CLC 31
See also Keane, Mary Nesta (Skrine)

Keates, Jonathan 19??-........... CLC 34

Keaton, Buster 1895-1966 ........ CLC 20

Keaton, Joseph Francis 1895-1966
See Keaton, Buster

Keats, John 1795-1821..... NCLC 8; PC 1

Keene, Donald 1922- ............ CLC 34
See also CANR 5; CA 1-4R

Keillor, Garrison 1942- ........... CLC 40
See also Keillor, Gary (Edward)
See also CA 111; DLB 87

Keillor, Gary (Edward)
See Keillor, Garrison
See also CA 111, 117

Kell, Joseph 1917-
See Burgess (Wilson, John) Anthony

Keller, Gottfried 1819-1890...... NCLC 2

Kellerman, Jonathan (S.) 1949-..... CLC 44
See also CA 106

Kelley, William Melvin 1937-...... CLC 22
See also CA 77-80; DLB 33

Kellogg, Marjorie 1922-........... CLC 2
See also CA 81-84

Kelly, M. T. 1947- ............. CLC 55
See also CANR 19; CA 97-100

Kelman, James 1946-............ CLC 58

Kemal, Yashar 1922- .......... CLC 14, 29
See also CA 89-92

Kemble, Fanny 1809-1893 ....... NCLC 18
See also DLB 32

Kemelman, Harry 1908-........... CLC 2
See also CANR 6; CA 9-12R; DLB 28

Kempe, Margery 1373?-1440? ........ LC 6

Kempis, Thomas á 1380-1471 ...... LC 11

Kendall, Henry 1839-1882....... NCLC 12

Keneally, Thomas (Michael)
1935- ...... CLC 5, 8, 10, 14, 19, 27, 43
See also CANR 10; CA 85-88

Kennedy, John Pendleton
1795-1870 ................. NCLC 2
See also DLB 3

Kennedy, Joseph Charles 1929-...... CLC 8
See also Kennedy, X. J.
See also CANR 4; CA 1-4R; SATA 14

Kennedy, William (Joseph)
1928-.......... CLC 6, 28, 34, 53
See also CANR 14; CA 85-88; DLB-Y 85;
AAYA 1

Kennedy, X. J. 1929- ........... CLC 8, 42
See also Kennedy, Joseph Charles
See also DLB 5

Kerouac, Jack
1922-1969 .... CLC 1, 2, 3, 5, 14, 29, 61
See also Kerouac, Jean-Louis Lebris de
See also DLB 2, 16; DLB-DS 3;
CDALB 1941-1968

Kerouac, Jean-Louis Lebris de 1922-1969
See Kerouac, Jack
See also CA 5-8R; obituary CA 25-28R;
CDALB 1941-1968

Kerr, Jean 1923-................ CLC 22
See also CANR 7; CA 5-8R

Kerr, M. E. 1927-............. CLC 12, 35
See also Meaker, Marijane
See also SAAS 1

Kerr, Robert 1970?-........... CLC 55, 59

Kerrigan, (Thomas) Anthony
1918- ..................... CLC 4, 6
See also CANR 4; CA 49-52

Kesey, Ken (Elton)
1935- .......... CLC 1, 3, 6, 11, 46, 64
See also CANR 22; CA 1-4R; DLB 2, 16;
CDALB 1968-1987

Kesselring, Joseph (Otto)
1902-1967 .................. CLC 45

Kessler, Jascha (Frederick) 1929-.... CLC 4
See also CANR 8; CA 17-20R

Kettelkamp, Larry 1933-.......... CLC 12
See also CANR 16; CA 29-32R; SAAS 3;
SATA 2

Kherdian, David 1931-........... CLC 6, 9
See also CAAS 2; CA 21-24R; SATA 16

Khlebnikov, Velimir (Vladimirovich)
1885-1922 ................. TCLC 20
See also CA 117

Khodasevich, Vladislav (Felitsianovich)
1886-1939 ................. TCLC 15
See also CA 115

Kielland, Alexander (Lange)
1849-1906 .................. TCLC 5
See also CA 104

Kiely, Benedict 1919-.......... CLC 23, 43
See also CANR 2; CA 1-4R; DLB 15

Kienzle, William X(avier) 1928- .... CLC 25
See also CAAS 1; CANR 9; CA 93-96

Killens, John Oliver 1916-......... CLC 10
See also CAAS 2; CANR 26; CA 77-80,
123; DLB 33

Killigrew, Anne 1660-1685........... LC 4

Kincaid, Jamaica 1949?- .......... CLC 43
See also CA 125

King, Francis (Henry) 1923-..... CLC 8, 53
See also CANR 1; CA 1-4R; DLB 15

King, Stephen (Edwin)
1947-.............. CLC 12, 26, 37, 61
See also CANR 1; CA 61-64; SATA 9, 55;
DLB-Y 80

Kingman, (Mary) Lee 1919-........ CLC 17
See also Natti, (Mary) Lee
See also CA 5-8R; SAAS 3; SATA 1

Kingsley, Sidney 1906-........... CLC 44
See also CA 85-88; DLB 7

Kingsolver, Barbara 1955-......... CLC 55

Kingston, Maxine Hong
1940-................ CLC 12, 19, 58
See also CANR 13; CA 69-72; SATA 53;
DLB-Y 80

Kinnell, Galway
1927-........... CLC 1, 2, 3, 5, 13, 29
See also CANR 10; CA 9-12R; DLB 5;
DLB-Y 87

Kinsella, Thomas 1928- ...... CLC 4, 19, 43
See also CANR 15; CA 17-20R; DLB 27

Kinsella, W(illiam) P(atrick)
1935- ................... CLC 27, 43
See also CAAS 7; CANR 21; CA 97-100

Kipling, (Joseph) Rudyard
1865-1936 ......... TCLC 8, 17; SSC 5
See also YABC 2; CA 105, 120; DLB 19, 34

**Kirkup, James** 1918- .............. **CLC 1**
See also CAAS 4; CANR 2; CA 1-4R;
SATA 12; DLB 27

**Kirkwood, James** 1930-1989 ........ **CLC 9**
See also CANR 6; CA 1-4R

**Kis, Danilo** 1935-1989 ............ **CLC 57**
See also CA 118, 129; brief entry CA 109

**Kivi, Aleksis** 1834-1872 ......... **NCLC 30**

**Kizer, Carolyn (Ashley)** 1925-... **CLC 15, 39**
See also CAAS 5; CANR 24; CA 65-68;
DLB 5

**Klappert, Peter** 1942-.............. **CLC 57**
See also CA 33-36R; DLB 5

**Klausner, Amos** 1939-
See Oz, Amos

**Klein, A(braham) M(oses)**
1909-1972 .................. **CLC 19**
See also CA 101; obituary CA 37-40R;
DLB 68

**Klein, Norma** 1938-1989 .......... **CLC 30**
See also CLR 2; CANR 15; CA 41-44R;
SAAS 1; SATA 7

**Klein, T.E.D.** 19??-............... **CLC 34**
See also CA 119

**Kleist, Heinrich von** 1777-1811.... **NCLC 2**

**Klima, Ivan** 1931-................. **CLC 56**
See also CANR 17; CA 25-28R

**Klimentev, Andrei Platonovich** 1899-1951
See Platonov, Andrei (Platonovich)
See also CA 108

**Klinger, Friedrich Maximilian von**
1752-1831 .................. **NCLC 1**

**Klopstock, Friedrich Gottlieb**
1724-1803 ................. **NCLC 11**

**Knebel, Fletcher** 1911-............ **CLC 14**
See also CAAS 3; CANR 1; CA 1-4R;
SATA 36

**Knight, Etheridge** 1931-........... **CLC 40**
See also CANR 23; CA 21-24R; DLB 41

**Knight, Sarah Kemble** 1666-1727 ..... **LC 7**
See also DLB 24

**Knowles, John** 1926- ...... **CLC 1, 4, 10, 26**
See also CA 17-20R; SATA 8; DLB 6

**Koch, C(hristopher) J(ohn)** 1932-... **CLC 42**

**Koch, Kenneth** 1925- ......... **CLC 5, 8, 44**
See also CANR 6; CA 1-4R; DLB 5

**Kochanowski, Jan** 1530-1584....... **LC 10**

**Kock, Charles Paul de**
1794-1871 ................. **NCLC 16**

**Koestler, Arthur**
1905-1983 ...... **CLC 1, 3, 6, 8, 15, 33**
See also CANR 1; CA 1-4R;
obituary CA 109; DLB-Y 83

**Kohout, Pavel** 1928-.............. **CLC 13**
See also CANR 3; CA 45-48

**Kolmar, Gertrud** 1894-1943....... **TCLC 40**

**Konigsberg, Allen Stewart** 1935-
See Allen, Woody

**Konrad, Gyorgy** 1933-.......... **CLC 4, 10**
See also CA 85-88

**Konwicki, Tadeusz** 1926-..... **CLC 8, 28, 54**
See also CA 101

**Kopit, Arthur (Lee)** 1937-.... **CLC 1, 18, 33**
See also CA 81-84; DLB 7

**Kops, Bernard** 1926-.............. **CLC 4**
See also CA 5-8R; DLB 13

**Kornbluth, C(yril) M.** 1923-1958.... **TCLC 8**
See also CA 105; DLB 8

**Korolenko, Vladimir (Galaktionovich)**
1853-1921 ................. **TCLC 22**
See also CA 121

**Kosinski, Jerzy (Nikodem)**
1933- ........ **CLC 1, 2, 3, 6, 10, 15, 53**
See also CANR 9; CA 17-20R; DLB 2;
DLB-Y 82

**Kostelanetz, Richard (Cory)** 1940- .. **CLC 28**
See also CA 13-16R

**Kostrowitzki, Wilhelm Apollinaris de**
1880-1918
See Apollinaire, Guillaume
See also CA 104

**Kotlowitz, Robert** 1924-............ **CLC 4**
See also CA 33-36R

**Kotzebue, August (Friedrich Ferdinand) von**
1761-1819 ................. **NCLC 25**

**Kotzwinkle, William** 1938-... **CLC 5, 14, 35**
See also CLR 6; CANR 3; CA 45-48;
SATA 24

**Kozol, Jonathan** 1936-............. **CLC 17**
See also CANR 16; CA 61-64

**Kozoll, Michael** 1940?-............ **CLC 35**

**Kramer, Kathryn** 19??-............ **CLC 34**

**Kramer, Larry** 1935- ............. **CLC 42**
See also CA 124, 126

**Krasicki, Ignacy** 1735-1801 ....... **NCLC 8**

**Krasinski, Zygmunt** 1812-1859 .... **NCLC 4**

**Kraus, Karl** 1874-1936............ **TCLC 5**
See also CA 104

**Kreve, Vincas** 1882-1954 ........ **TCLC 27**

**Kristofferson, Kris** 1936-.......... **CLC 26**
See also CA 104

**Krizanc, John** 1956-.............. **CLC 57**

**Krleza, Miroslav** 1893-1981......... **CLC 8**
See also CA 97-100; obituary CA 105

**Kroetsch, Robert (Paul)**
1927-.................. **CLC 5, 23,57**
See also CANR 8; CA 17-20R; DLB 53

**Kroetz, Franz Xaver** 1946- ........ **CLC 41**

**Kropotkin, Peter** 1842-1921....... **TCLC 36**
See also CA 119

**Krotkov, Yuri** 1917-.............. **CLC 19**
See also CA 102

**Krumgold, Joseph (Quincy)**
1908-1980 .................. **CLC 12**
See also CANR 7; CA 9-12R;
obituary CA 101; SATA 48;
obituary SATA 23

**Krutch, Joseph Wood** 1893-1970.... **CLC 24**
See also CANR 4; CA 1-4R;
obituary CA 25-28R; DLB 63

**Krylov, Ivan Andreevich**
1768?-1844................. **NCLC 1**

**Kubin, Alfred** 1877-1959 ........ **TCLC 23**
See also CA 112

**Kubrick, Stanley** 1928-............ **CLC 16**
See also CA 81-84; DLB 26

**Kumin, Maxine (Winokur)**
1925- ................. **CLC 5, 13, 28**
See also CANR 1, 21; CA 1-4R; SATA 12;
DLB 5

**Kundera, Milan** 1929- ..... **CLC 4, 9, 19, 32**
See also CANR 19; CA 85-88

**Kunitz, Stanley J(asspon)**
1905-................. **CLC 6, 11, 14**
See also CA 41-44R; DLB 48

**Kunze, Reiner** 1933-.............. **CLC 10**
See also CA 93-96; DLB 75

**Kuprin, Aleksandr (Ivanovich)**
1870-1938 ................. **TCLC 5**
See also CA 104

**Kureishi, Hanif** 1954-............. **CLC 64**

**Kurosawa, Akira** 1910-............ **CLC 16**
See also CA 101

**Kuttner, Henry** 1915-1958........ **TCLC 10**
See also CA 107; DLB 8

**Kuzma, Greg** 1944-................ **CLC 7**
See also CA 33-36R

**Kuzmin, Mikhail** 1872?-1936...... **TCLC 40**

**Labrunie, Gerard** 1808-1855
See Nerval, Gerard de

**Laclos, Pierre Ambroise Francois Choderlos**
de 1741-1803 .............. **NCLC 4**

**La Fayette, Marie (Madelaine Pioche de la**
**Vergne, Comtesse) de**
1634-1693 ................... **LC 2**

**Lafayette, Rene**
See Hubbard, L(afayette) Ron(ald)

**Laforgue, Jules** 1860-1887........ **NCLC 5**

**Lagerkvist, Par (Fabian)**
1891-1974 .......... **CLC 7, 10, 13, 54**
See also CA 85-88; obituary CA 49-52

**Lagerlof, Selma (Ottiliana Lovisa)**
1858-1940 ................. **TCLC 4, 36**
See also CLR 7; CA 108; SATA 15

**La Guma, (Justin) Alex(ander)**
1925-1985 ................. **CLC 19**
See also CA 49-52; obituary CA 118

**Lamartine, Alphonse (Marie Louis Prat) de**
1790-1869 ................. **NCLC 11**

**Lamb, Charles** 1775-1834........ **NCLC 10**
See also SATA 17

**Lamming, George (William)**
1927- ...................... **CLC 2, 4**
See also CANR 26; CA 85-88

**LaMoore, Louis Dearborn** 1908?-
See L'Amour, Louis (Dearborn)

**L'Amour, Louis (Dearborn)**
1908-1988 ................. **CLC 25, 55**
See also CANR 3; CA 1-4R;
obituary CA 125; DLB-Y 80

**Lampedusa, (Prince) Giuseppe (Maria**
**Fabrizio) Tomasi di**
1896-1957 ................. **TCLC 13**
See also CA 111

**Lampman, Archibald** 1861-1899 .. **NCLC 25**

**Lancaster, Bruce** 1896-1963........ **CLC 36**
See also CAP 1; CA 9-12; SATA 9

**Landis, John (David)** 1950- ........ **CLC 26**
See also CA 112

**Landolfi, Tommaso** 1908-1979... **CLC 11, 49**
See also obituary CA 117

**Landon, Letitia Elizabeth**
1802-1838 ................ **NCLC 15**

**Landor, Walter Savage**
1775-1864 ................ **NCLC 14**

**Landwirth, Heinz** 1927-
See Lind, Jakov
See also CANR 7; CA 11-12R

**Lane, Patrick** 1939- ............. **CLC 25**
See also CA 97-100; DLB 53

**Lang, Andrew** 1844-1912 ........ **TCLC 16**
See also CA 114; SATA 16

**Lang, Fritz** 1890-1976 ............ **CLC 20**
See also CA 77-80; obituary CA 69-72

**Langer, Elinor** 1939- ............ **CLC 34**
See also CA 121

**Lanier, Sidney** 1842-1881 ........ **NCLC 6**
See also SATA 18; DLB 64

**Lanyer, Aemilia** 1569-1645 ........ **LC 10**

**Lapine, James** 1949- ............. **CLC 39**

**Larbaud, Valery** 1881-1957 ........ **TCLC 9**
See also CA 106

**Lardner, Ring(gold Wilmer)**
1885-1933 ............... **TCLC 2, 14**
See also CA 104; DLB 11, 25

**Larkin, Philip (Arthur)**
1922-1985 ... **CLC 3, 5, 8, 9, 13, 18, 33,**
                                  **39, 64**
See also CANR 24; CA 5-8R;
obituary CA 117; DLB 27

**Larra (y Sanchez de Castro), Mariano Jose de**
1809-1837 ................ **NCLC 17**

**Larsen, Eric** 1941- ............... **CLC 55**

**Larsen, Nella** 1891-1964 .......... **CLC 37**
See also CA 125; DLB 51

**Larson, Charles R(aymond)** 1938-... **CLC 31**
See also CANR 4; CA 53-56

**Latham, Jean Lee** 1902-.......... **CLC 12**
See also CANR 7; CA 5-8R; SATA 2

**Lathen, Emma** .................... **CLC 2**
See also Hennissart, Martha; Latsis, Mary
J(ane)

**Latsis, Mary J(ane)**
See Lathen, Emma
See also CA 85-88

**Lattimore, Richmond (Alexander)**
1906-1984 .................... **CLC 3**
See also CANR 1; CA 1-4R;
obituary CA 112

**Laughlin, James** 1914- ........... **CLC 49**
See also CANR 9; CA 21-24R; DLB 48

**Laurence, (Jean) Margaret (Wemyss)**
1926-1987 .. **CLC 3, 6, 13, 50, 62; SSC 7**
See also CA 5-8R; obituary CA 121;
SATA 50; DLB 53

**Laurent, Antoine** 1952- ........... **CLC 50**

**Lautreamont, Comte de**
1846-1870 ................ **NCLC 12**

**Lavin, Mary** 1912- ...... **CLC 4, 18; SSC 4**
See also CA 9-12R; DLB 15

**Lawler, Raymond (Evenor)** 1922-... **CLC 58**
See also CA 103

**Lawrence, D(avid) H(erbert)**
1885-1930 .... **TCLC 2, 9, 16, 33; SSC 4**
See also CA 104, 121; DLB 10, 19, 36

**Lawrence, T(homas) E(dward)**
1888-1935 ................. **TCLC 18**
See also CA 115

**Lawson, Henry (Archibald Hertzberg)**
1867-1922 ................. **TCLC 27**
See also CA 120

**Laxness, Halldor (Kiljan)** 1902- .... **CLC 25**
See also Gudjonsson, Halldor Kiljan

**Laye, Camara** 1928-1980 ........ **CLC 4, 38**
See also CA 85-88; obituary CA 97-100

**Layton, Irving (Peter)** 1912- ..... **CLC 2, 15**
See also CANR 2; CA 1-4R

**Lazarus, Emma** 1849-1887 ........ **NCLC 8**

**Leacock, Stephen (Butler)**
1869-1944 ................... **TCLC 2**
See also CA 104

**Lear, Edward** 1812-1888 ......... **NCLC 3**
See also CLR 1; SATA 18; DLB 32

**Lear, Norman (Milton)** 1922- ...... **CLC 12**
See also CA 73-76

**Leavis, F(rank) R(aymond)**
1895-1978 ................... **CLC 24**
See also CA 21-24R; obituary CA 77-80

**Leavitt, David** 1961?-............. **CLC 34**
See also CA 116, 122

**Lebowitz, Fran(ces Ann)**
1951?- ................. **CLC 11, 36**
See also CANR 14; CA 81-84

**Le Carre, John** 1931-... **CLC 3, 5, 9, 15, 28**
See also Cornwell, David (John Moore)

**Le Clezio, J(ean) M(arie) G(ustave)**
1940- ....................... **CLC 31**
See also CA 116

**Leconte de Lisle, Charles-Marie-Rene**
1818-1894 ................ **NCLC 29**

**Leduc, Violette** 1907-1972......... **CLC 22**
See also CAP 1; CA 13-14;
obituary CA 33-36R

**Ledwidge, Francis** 1887-1917...... **TCLC 23**
See also CA 123; DLB 20

**Lee, Andrea** 1953- ............... **CLC 36**
See also CA 125

**Lee, Andrew** 1917-
See Auchincloss, Louis (Stanton)

**Lee, Don L.** 1942-................. **CLC 2**
See also Madhubuti, Haki R.
See also CA 73-76

**Lee, George Washington**
1894-1976 ................... **CLC 52**
See also CA 125; DLB 51

**Lee, (Nelle) Harper** 1926- ...... **CLC 12, 60**
See also CA 13-16R; SATA 11; DLB 6;
CDALB 1941-1968

**Lee, Lawrence** 1903- ............. **CLC 34**
See also CA 25-28R

**Lee, Manfred B(ennington)** 1905-1971
See Queen, Ellery
See also CANR 2; CA 1-4R, 11;
obituary CA 29-32R

**Lee, Stan** 1922-................. **CLC 17**
See also CA 108, 111

**Lee, Tanith** 1947-................ **CLC 46**
See also CA 37-40R; SATA 8

**Lee, Vernon** 1856-1935 ........... **TCLC 5**
See also Paget, Violet
See also DLB 57

**Lee-Hamilton, Eugene (Jacob)**
1845-1907 ................. **TCLC 22**

**Leet, Judith** 1935- ............... **CLC 11**

**Le Fanu, Joseph Sheridan**
1814-1873 .................. **NCLC 9**
See also DLB 21, 70

**Leffland, Ella** 1931- .............. **CLC 19**
See also CA 29-32R; DLB-Y 84

**Leger, (Marie-Rene) Alexis Saint-Leger**
1887-1975
See Perse, St.-John
See also CA 13-16R; obituary CA 61-64

**Le Guin, Ursula K(roeber)**
1929- ............... **CLC 8, 13, 22, 45**
See also CLR 3; CANR 9; CA 21-24R;
SATA 4, 52; DLB 8, 52

**Lehmann, Rosamond (Nina)** 1901- ... **CLC 5**
See also CANR 8; CA 77-80; DLB 15

**Leiber, Fritz (Reuter, Jr.)** 1910-.... **CLC 25**
See also CANR 2; CA 45-48; SATA 45;
DLB 8

**Leino, Eino** 1878-1926.......... **TCLC 24**

**Leiris, Michel** 1901-.............. **CLC 61**
See also CA 119, 128

**Leithauser, Brad** 1953-............ **CLC 27**
See also CA 107

**Lelchuk, Alan** 1938-.............. **CLC 5**
See also CANR 1; CA 45-48

**Lem, Stanislaw** 1921-........ **CLC 8, 15, 40**
See also CAAS 1; CA 105

**Lemann, Nancy** 1956-............. **CLC 39**
See also CA 118

**Lemonnier, (Antoine Louis) Camille**
1844-1913 ................. **TCLC 22**

**Lenau, Nikolaus** 1802-1850 ...... **NCLC 16**

**L'Engle, Madeleine** 1918- ......... **CLC 12**
See also CLR 1, 14; CANR 3, 21; CA 1-4R;
SATA 1, 27; DLB 52

**Lengyel, Jozsef** 1896-1975.......... **CLC 7**
See also CA 85-88; obituary CA 57-60

**Lennon, John (Ono)**
1940-1980 ............. **CLC 12, 35**
See also CA 102

**Lennon, John Winston** 1940-1980
See Lennon, John (Ono)

**Lennox, Charlotte Ramsay** 1729 or
1730-1804 ................. **NCLC 23**
See also DLB 39, 39

**Lennox, Charlotte Ramsay**
1729?-1804................. **NCLC 23**
See also DLB 39

**Lentricchia, Frank (Jr.)** 1940-...... **CLC 34**
See also CANR 19; CA 25-28R

**Lenz, Siegfried** 1926-............. **CLC 27**
See also CA 89-92; DLB 75

Leonard, Elmore 1925- ........ CLC 28, 34
See also CANR 12; CA 81-84

Leonard, Hugh 1926- ............ CLC 19
See also Byrne, John Keyes
See also DLB 13

Leopardi, (Conte) Giacomo (Talegardo
Francesco di Sales Saverio Pietro)
1798-1837 ................. NCLC 22

Lerman, Eleanor 1952- ............ CLC 9
See also CA 85-88

Lerman, Rhoda 1936- ............. CLC 56
See also CA 49-52

Lermontov, Mikhail Yuryevich
1814-1841 ................. NCLC 5

Leroux, Gaston 1868-1927 ....... TCLC 25
See also CA 108

Lesage, Alain-Rene 1668-1747 ....... LC 2

Leskov, Nikolai (Semyonovich)
1831-1895 ................. NCLC 25

Lessing, Doris (May)
1919- .... CLC 1, 2, 3, 6, 10, 15, 22, 40;
SSC 6
See also CA 9-12R; DLB 15; DLB-Y 85

Lessing, Gotthold Ephraim
1729-1781 ................... LC 8

Lester, Richard 1932- ............ CLC 20

Lever, Charles (James)
1806-1872 ................ NCLC 23
See also DLB 21

Leverson, Ada 1865-1936 ........ TCLC 18
See also CA 117

Levertov, Denise
1923- ........ CLC 1, 2, 3, 5, 8, 15, 28
See also CANR 3; CA 1-4R; DLB 5

Levi, Peter (Chad Tiger) 1931- ..... CLC 41
See also CA 5-8R; DLB 40

Levi, Primo 1919-1987 ........ CLC 37, 50
See also CANR 12; CA 13-16R;
obituary CA 122

Levin, Ira 1929- ................ CLC 3, 6
See also CANR 17; CA 21-24R

Levin, Meyer 1905-1981 ........... CLC 7
See also CANR 15; CA 9-12R;
obituary CA 104; SATA 21;
obituary SATA 27; DLB 9, 28; DLB-Y 81

Levine, Norman 1924- ............ CLC 54
See also CANR 14; CA 73-76

Levine, Philip 1928- .. CLC 2, 4, 5, 9, 14, 33
See also CANR 9; CA 9-12R; DLB 5

Levinson, Deirdre 1931- ........... CLC 49
See also CA 73-76

Levi-Strauss, Claude 1908- ........ CLC 38
See also CANR 6; CA 1-4R

Levitin, Sonia 1934- .............. CLC 17
See also CANR 14; CA 29-32R; SAAS 2;
SATA 4

Lewes, George Henry
1817-1878 ................. NCLC 25
See also DLB 55

Lewis, Alun 1915-1944 ........... TCLC 3
See also CA 104; DLB 20

Lewis, C(ecil) Day 1904-1972
See Day Lewis, C(ecil)

Lewis, C(live) S(taples)
1898-1963 ........ CLC 1, 3, 6, 14, 27
See also CLR 3; CA 81-84; SATA 13;
DLB 15

Lewis (Winters), Janet 1899- ....... CLC 41
See also Winters, Janet Lewis
See also DLB-Y 87

Lewis, Matthew Gregory
1775-1818 ................. NCLC 11
See also DLB 39

Lewis, (Harry) Sinclair
1885-1951 .......... TCLC 4, 13, 23,39
See also CA 104; DLB 9; DLB-DS 1;
CDALB 1917-1929

Lewis, (Percy) Wyndham
1882?-1957 ................ TCLC 2, 9
See also CA 104; DLB 15

Lewisohn, Ludwig 1883-1955 ...... TCLC 19
See also CA 73-76, 107;
obituary CA 29-32R

L'Heureux, John (Clarke) 1934- .... CLC 52
See also CANR 23; CA 15-16R

Lieber, Stanley Martin 1922-
See Lee, Stan

Lieberman, Laurence (James)
1935- ..................... CLC 4, 36
See also CANR 8; CA 17-20R

Li Fei-kan 1904-
See Pa Chin
See also CA 105

Lightfoot, Gordon (Meredith)
1938- ..................... CLC 26
See also CA 109

Ligotti, Thomas 1953- ............ CLC 44
See also CA 123

Liliencron, Detlev von
1844-1909 ................. TCLC 18
See also CA 117

Lima, Jose Lezama 1910-1976
See Lezama Lima, Jose

Lima Barreto, (Alfonso Henriques de)
1881-1922 ................. TCLC 23
See also CA 117

Lincoln, Abraham 1809-1865 ..... NCLC 18

Lind, Jakov 1927- .......... CLC 1, 2, 4, 27
See also Landwirth, Heinz
See also CAAS 4; CA 9-12R

Lindsay, David 1876-1945 ........ TCLC 15
See also CA 113

Lindsay, (Nicholas) Vachel
1879-1931 ................. TCLC 17
See also CA 114; SATA 40; DLB 54;
CDALB 1865-1917

Linney, Romulus 1930- ........... CLC 51
See also CA 1-4R

Li Po 701-763 ................. CMLC 2

Lipsyte, Robert (Michael) 1938- .... CLC 21
See also CLR 23; CANR 8; CA 17-20R;
SATA 5

Lish, Gordon (Jay) 1934- .......... CLC 45
See also CA 113, 117

Lispector, Clarice 1925-1977 ....... CLC 43
See also obituary CA 116

Littell, Robert 1935?- ............. CLC 42
See also CA 109, 112

Liu E 1857-1909 ............... TCLC 15
See also CA 115

Lively, Penelope 1933- ........ CLC 32, 50
See also CLR 7; CA 41-44R; SATA 7;
DLB 14

Livesay, Dorothy 1909- ......... CLC 4, 15
See also CA 25-28R

Lizardi, Jose Joaquin Fernandez de
1776-1827 ................. NCLC 30

Llewellyn, Richard 1906-1983 ....... CLC 7
See also Llewellyn Lloyd, Richard (Dafydd
Vyvyan)
See also DLB 15

Llewellyn Lloyd, Richard (Dafydd Vyvyan)
1906-1983
See Llewellyn, Richard
See also CANR 7; CA 53-56;
obituary CA 111; SATA 11, 37

Llosa, Mario Vargas 1936-
See Vargas Llosa, Mario

Lloyd, Richard Llewellyn 1906-
See Llewellyn, Richard

Locke, John 1632-1704 ............. LC 7
See also DLB 31

Lockhart, John Gibson
1794-1854 ................. NCLC 6

Lodge, David (John) 1935- ........ CLC 36
See also CANR 19; CA 17-20R; DLB 14

Loewinsohn, Ron(ald William)
1937- ..................... CLC 52
See also CA 25-28R

Logan, John 1923- ................ CLC 5
See also CA 77-80, 124; DLB 5

Lo Kuan-chung 1330?-1400? ........ LC 12

Lombino, S. A. 1926-
See Hunter, Evan

London, Jack
1876-1916 ...... TCLC 9, 15, 39; SSC 4
See also London, John Griffith
See also SATA 18; DLB 8, 12, 78;
CDALB 1865-1917

London, John Griffith 1876-1916
See London, Jack
See also CA 110, 119

Long, Emmett 1925-
See Leonard, Elmore

Longbaugh, Harry 1931-
See Goldman, William (W.)

Longfellow, Henry Wadsworth
1807-1882 ................. NCLC 2
See also SATA 19; DLB 1, 59;
CDALB 1640-1865

Longley, Michael 1939- ........... CLC 29
See also CA 102; DLB 40

Lopate, Phillip 1943- ............. CLC 29
See also CA 97-100; DLB-Y 80

Lopez Portillo (y Pacheco), Jose
1920- ..................... CLC 46

Lopez y Fuentes, Gregorio
1897-1966 ................. CLC 32

Lord, Bette Bao 1938- ............ CLC 23
See also CA 107

**Lorde, Audre (Geraldine)** 1934-..... **CLC 18**
See also CANR 16, 26; CA 25-28R;
DLB 41

**Loti, Pierre** 1850-1923........... **TCLC 11**
See also Viaud, (Louis Marie) Julien

**Lovecraft, H(oward) P(hillips)**
1890-1937 ........ **TCLC 4, 22; SSC 3**
See also CA 104

**Lovelace, Earl** 1935-.............. **CLC 51**
See also CA 77-80

**Lowell, Amy** 1874-1925........ **TCLC 1, 8**
See also CA 104; DLB 54

**Lowell, James Russell** 1819-1891 .. **NCLC 2**
See also DLB 1, 11, 64; CDALB 1640-1865

**Lowell, Robert (Traill Spence, Jr.)**
1917-1977 ... **CLC 1, 2, 3, 4, 5, 8, 9, 11,**
**15, 37**
See also CANR 26; CA 9-12R;
obituary CA 73-76; CABS 2; DLB 5

**Lowndes, Marie (Adelaide) Belloc**
1868-1947 ................ **TCLC 12**
See also CA 107; DLB 70

**Lowry, (Clarence) Malcolm**
1909-1957 ............... **TCLC 6, 40**
See also CA 105, 131; DLB 15

**Loy, Mina** 1882-1966............. **CLC 28**
See also CA 113; DLB 4, 54

**Lucas, Craig**...................... **CLC 64**

**Lucas, George** 1944-.............. **CLC 16**
See also CA 77-80

**Lucas, Victoria** 1932-1963
See Plath, Sylvia

**Ludlam, Charles** 1943-1987..... **CLC 46, 50**
See also CA 85-88; obituary CA 122

**Ludlum, Robert** 1927- ......... **CLC 22, 43**
See also CANR 25; CA 33-36R; DLB-Y 82

**Ludwig, Ken** 19??- .............. **CLC 60**

**Ludwig, Otto** 1813-1865......... **NCLC 4**

**Lugones, Leopoldo** 1874-1938..... **TCLC 15**
See also CA 116

**Lu Hsun** 1881-1936 .............. **TCLC 3**

**Lukacs, Georg** 1885-1971.......... **CLC 24**
See also Lukacs, Gyorgy

**Lukacs, Gyorgy** 1885-1971
See Lukacs, Georg
See also CA 101; obituary CA 29-32R

**Luke, Peter (Ambrose Cyprian)**
1919- ...................... **CLC 38**
See also CA 81-84; DLB 13

**Lurie (Bishop), Alison**
1926-................ **CLC 4, 5, 18, 39**
See also CANR 2, 17; CA 1-4R; SATA 46;
DLB 2

**Lustig, Arnost** 1926-.............. **CLC 56**
See also CA 69-72; SATA 56

**Luther, Martin** 1483-1546........... **LC 9**

**Luzi, Mario** 1914-................ **CLC 13**
See also CANR 9; CA 61-64

**Lynn, Kenneth S(chuyler)** 1923-.... **CLC 50**
See also CANR 3; CA 1-4R

**Lytle, Andrew (Nelson)** 1902-...... **CLC 22**
See also CA 9-12R; DLB 6

**Lyttelton, George** 1709-1773........ **LC 10**

**Lytton, Edward Bulwer** 1803-1873
See Bulwer-Lytton, (Lord) Edward (George
Earle Lytton)
See also SATA 23

**Maas, Peter** 1929- ............... **CLC 29**
See also CA 93-96

**Macaulay, (Dame Emile) Rose**
1881-1958 .................. **TCLC 7**
See also CA 104; DLB 36

**MacBeth, George (Mann)**
1932-.................... **CLC 2, 5, 9**
See also CA 25-28R; SATA 4; DLB 40

**MacCaig, Norman (Alexander)**
1910-................... **CLC 36**
See also CANR 3; CA 9-12R; DLB 27

**MacCarthy, Desmond** 1877-1952 .. **TCLC 36**

**MacDermot, Thomas H.** 1870-1933
See Redcam, Tom

**MacDiarmid, Hugh**
1892-1978 ....... **CLC 2, 4, 11, 19, 63**
See also Grieve, C(hristopher) M(urray)
See also DLB 20

**Macdonald, Cynthia** 1928-...... **CLC 13, 19**
See also CANR 4; CA 49-52

**MacDonald, George** 1824-1905..... **TCLC 9**
See also CA 106; SATA 33; DLB 18

**MacDonald, John D(ann)**
1916-1986 .............. **CLC 3, 27, 44**
See also CANR 1, 19; CA 1-4R;
obituary CA 121; DLB 8; DLB-Y 86

**Macdonald, (John) Ross**
1915-1983 ...... **CLC 1, 2, 3, 14, 34, 41**
See also Millar, Kenneth

**MacEwen, Gwendolyn (Margaret)**
1941-1987 ................ **CLC 13, 55**
See also CANR 7, 22; CA 9-12R;
obituary CA 124; SATA 50; DLB 53

**Machado (y Ruiz), Antonio**
1875-1939 .................. **TCLC 3**
See also CA 104

**Machado de Assis, (Joaquim Maria)**
1839-1908 ................. **TCLC 10**
See also CA 107

**Machen, Arthur (Llewellyn Jones)**
1863-1947 .................. **TCLC 4**
See also CA 104; DLB 36

**Machiavelli, Niccolo** 1469-1527 ...... **LC 8**

**MacInnes, Colin** 1914-1976...... **CLC 4, 23**
See also CA 69-72; obituary CA 65-68;
DLB 14

**MacInnes, Helen (Clark)**
1907-1985 ................ **CLC 27, 39**
See also CANR 1; CA 1-4R;
obituary CA 65-68, 117; SATA 22, 44

**Macintosh, Elizabeth** 1897-1952
See Tey, Josephine
See also CA 110

**Mackenzie, (Edward Montague) Compton**
1883-1972 ................... **CLC 18**
See also CAP 2; CA 21-22;
obituary CA 37-40R; DLB 34

**Mac Laverty, Bernard** 1942-....... **CLC 31**
See also CA 116, 118

**MacLean, Alistair (Stuart)**
1922-1987 .......... **CLC 3, 13, 50, 63**
See also CANR 28; CA 57-60;
obituary CA 121; SATA 23, 50

**MacLeish, Archibald**
1892-1982 ............... **CLC 3, 8, 14**
See also CA 9-12R; obituary CA 106;
DLB 4, 7, 45; DLB-Y 82

**MacLennan, (John) Hugh**
1907- ..................... **CLC 2, 14**
See also CA 5-8R

**MacLeod, Alistair** 1936- ......... **CLC 56**
See also CA 123; DLB 60

**Macleod, Fiona** 1855-1905
See Sharp, William

**MacNeice, (Frederick) Louis**
1907-1963 ............ **CLC 1, 4, 10, 53**
See also CA 85-88; DLB 10, 20

**Macpherson, (Jean) Jay** 1931-...... **CLC 14**
See also CA 5-8R; DLB 53

**MacShane, Frank** 1927-........... **CLC 39**
See also CANR 3; CA 11-12R

**Macumber, Mari** 1896-1966
See Sandoz, Mari (Susette)

**Madach, Imre** 1823-1864........ **NCLC 19**

**Madden, (Jerry) David** 1933- .... **CLC 5, 15**
See also CAAS 3; CANR 4; CA 1-4R;
DLB 6

**Madhubuti, Haki R.** 1942-.......... **CLC 6**
See also Lee, Don L.
See also CANR 24; CA 73-76; DLB 5, 41

**Maeterlinck, Maurice** 1862-1949 ... **TCLC 3**
See also CA 104

**Mafouz, Naguib** 1912-
See Mahfuz, Najib

**Maginn, William** 1794-1842....... **NCLC 8**

**Mahapatra, Jayanta** 1928-......... **CLC 33**
See also CANR 15; CA 73-76

**Mahfuz Najib** 1912-........... **CLC 52, 55**
See also DLB-Y 88

**Mahon, Derek** 1941-.............. **CLC 27**
See also CA 113; DLB 40

**Mailer, Norman**
1923- ...... **CLC 1, 2, 3, 4, 5, 8, 11, 14,**
**28, 39**
See also CA 9-12R; CABS 1; DLB 2, 16,
28; DLB-Y 80, 83; DLB-DS 3

**Maillet, Antonine** 1929-........... **CLC 54**
See also CA 115, 120; DLB 60

**Mais, Roger** 1905-1955 ........... **TCLC 8**
See also CA 105

**Maitland, Sara (Louise)** 1950-...... **CLC 49**
See also CANR 13; CA 69-72

**Major, Clarence** 1936-,...... **CLC 3, 19, 48**
See also CAAS 6; CANR 13; CA 21-24R;
DLB 33

**Major, Kevin** 1949- .............. **CLC 26**
See also CLR 11; CANR 21; CA 97-100;
SATA 32; DLB 60

**Malamud, Bernard**
    1914-1986 . . . . . **CLC 1, 2, 3, 5, 8, 9, 11,
                                    18, 27, 44**
    See also CA 5-8R; obituary CA 118;
    CABS 1; DLB 2, 28; DLB-Y 80, 86;
    CDALB 1941-1968

**Malherbe, Francois de** 1555-1628 . . . . . **LC 5**

**Mallarme, Stephane** 1842-1898 . . . . **NCLC 4**

**Mallet-Joris, Francoise** 1930- . . . . . . **CLC 11**
    See also CANR 17; CA 65-68

**Maloff, Saul** 1922- . . . . . . . . . . . . . . . **CLC 5**
    See also CA 33-36R

**Malone, Louis** 1907-1963
    See MacNeice, (Frederick) Louis

**Malone, Michael (Christopher)**
    1942- . . . . . . . . . . . . . . . . . . . . . . . **CLC 43**
    See also CANR 14; CA 77-80

**Malory, (Sir) Thomas** ?-1471 . . . . . . . **LC 11**
    See also SATA 33

**Malouf, David** 1934- . . . . . . . . . . . . . **CLC 28**

**Malraux, (Georges-) Andre**
    1901-1976 . . . . . . **CLC 1, 4, 9, 13, 15, 57**
    See also CAP 2; CA 21-24;
    obituary CA 69-72; DLB 72

**Malzberg, Barry N.** 1939- . . . . . . . . . . **CLC 7**
    See also CAAS 4; CANR 16; CA 61-64;
    DLB 8

**Mamet, David (Alan)**
    1947-  . . . . . . . . . . **CLC 9, 15, 34, 46**
    See also CANR 15; CA 81-84, 124; DLB 7

**Mamoulian, Rouben** 1898- . . . . . . . . . **CLC 16**
    See also CA 25-28R

**Mandelstam, Osip (Emilievich)**
    1891?-1938? . . . . . . . . . . . . . . . . **TCLC 2, 6**
    See also CA 104

**Mander, Jane** 1877-1949 . . . . . . . . **TCLC 31**

**Mandiargues, Andre Pieyre de**
    1909- . . . . . . . . . . . . . . . . . . . . . . . **CLC 41**
    See also CA 103

**Mangan, James Clarence**
    1803-1849 . . . . . . . . . . . . . . . . . **NCLC 27**

**Manley, (Mary) Delariviere**
    1672?-1724 . . . . . . . . . . . . . . . . . . . **LC 1**
    See also DLB 39

**Mann, (Luiz) Heinrich** 1871-1950 . . . **TCLC 9**
    See also CA 106; DLB 66

**Mann, Thomas**
    1875-1955 . . . . . . **TCLC 2, 8, 14, 21, 35;
                                            SSC 5**
    See also CA 104, 128; DLB 66

**Manning, Frederic** 1882-1935 . . . . . **TCLC 25**

**Manning, Olivia** 1915-1980 . . . . . . **CLC 5, 19**
    See also CA 5-8R; obituary CA 101

**Mano, D. Keith** 1942- . . . . . . . . . . **CLC 2, 10**
    See also CAAS 6; CANR 26; CA 25-28R;
    DLB 6

**Mansfield, Katherine**
    1888-1923 . . . . . . . . . . . . . **TCLC 2, 8, 39**
    See also CA 104

**Manso, Peter** 1940- . . . . . . . . . . . . . . **CLC 39**
    See also CA 29-32R

**Manzoni, Alessandro** 1785-1873 . . **NCLC 29**

**Mapu, Abraham (ben Jekutiel)**
    1808-1867 . . . . . . . . . . . . . . . . . **NCLC 18**

**Marat, Jean Paul** 1743-1793 . . . . . . . **LC 10**

**Marcel, Gabriel (Honore)**
    1889-1973 . . . . . . . . . . . . . . . . . . **CLC 15**
    See also CA 102; obituary CA 45-48

**Marchbanks, Samuel** 1913-
    See Davies, (William) Robertson

**Marie de l'Incarnation** 1599-1672 . . . . **LC 10**

**Marinetti, F(ilippo) T(ommaso)**
    1876-1944 . . . . . . . . . . . . . . . . . . **TCLC 10**
    See also CA 107

**Marivaux, Pierre Carlet de Chamblain de**
    (1688-1763) . . . . . . . . . . . . . . . . . . **LC 4**

**Markandaya, Kamala** 1924- . . . . . . **CLC 8, 38**
    See also Taylor, Kamala (Purnaiya)

**Markfield, Wallace (Arthur)** 1926- . . . **CLC 8**
    See also CAAS 3; CA 69-72; DLB 2, 28

**Markham, Robert** 1922-
    See Amis, Kingsley (William)

**Marks, J.** 1942-
    See Highwater, Jamake

**Marley, Bob** 1945-1981 . . . . . . . . . . . **CLC 17**
    See also Marley, Robert Nesta

**Marley, Robert Nesta** 1945-1981
    See Marley, Bob
    See also CA 107; obituary CA 103

**Marlowe, Christopher** 1564-1593
    See also DLB 62; DC 1

**Marmontel, Jean-Francois**
    1723-1799 . . . . . . . . . . . . . . . . . . . . **LC 2**

**Marquand, John P(hillips)**
    1893-1960 . . . . . . . . . . . . . . . . . **CLC 2, 10**
    See also CA 85-88; DLB 9

**Marquez, Gabriel Garcia** 1928-
    See Garcia Marquez, Gabriel

**Marquis, Don(ald Robert Perry)**
    1878-1937 . . . . . . . . . . . . . . . . . . . **TCLC 7**
    See also CA 104; DLB 11, 25

**Marryat, Frederick** 1792-1848 . . . . **NCLC 3**
    See also DLB 21

**Marsh, (Dame Edith) Ngaio**
    1899-1982 . . . . . . . . . . . . . . . . . **CLC 7, 53**
    See also CANR 6; CA 9-12R; DLB 77

**Marshall, Garry** 1935?- . . . . . . . . . . . **CLC 17**
    See also CA 111

**Marshall, Paule** 1929- . . . . . **CLC 27; SSC 3**
    See also CANR 25; CA 77-80; DLB 33

**Marsten, Richard** 1926-
    See Hunter, Evan

**Martin, Steve** 1945?- . . . . . . . . . . . . . **CLC 30**
    See also CA 97-100

**Martin du Gard, Roger**
    1881-1958 . . . . . . . . . . . . . . . . . . **TCLC 24**
    See also CA 118

**Martineau, Harriet** 1802-1876 . . . . **NCLC 26**
    See also YABC 2; DLB 21, 55

**Martinez Ruiz, Jose** 1874-1967
    See Azorin
    See also CA 93-96

**Martinez Sierra, Gregorio**
    1881-1947 . . . . . . . . . . . . . . . . . . . **TCLC 6**
    See also CA 104, 115

**Martinez Sierra, Maria (de la O'LeJarraga)**
    1880?-1974 . . . . . . . . . . . . . . . . . . **TCLC 6**
    See also obituary CA 115

**Martinson, Harry (Edmund)**
    1904-1978 . . . . . . . . . . . . . . . . . . **CLC 14**
    See also CA 77-80

**Marvell, Andrew** 1621-1678 . . . . . . . . . **LC 4**

**Marx, Karl (Heinrich)**
    1818-1883 . . . . . . . . . . . . . . . . . **NCLC 17**

**Masaoka Shiki** 1867-1902 . . . . . . . **TCLC 18**

**Masefield, John (Edward)**
    1878-1967 . . . . . . . . . . . . . . **CLC 11, 47**
    See also CAP 2; CA 19-20;
    obituary CA 25-28R; SATA 19; DLB 10,
    19

**Maso, Carole** 19??- . . . . . . . . . . . . . . . **CLC 44**

**Mason, Bobbie Ann**
    1940- . . . . . . . . . . . . . **CLC 28, 43; SSC 4**
    See also CANR 11; CA 53-56; SAAS 1;
    DLB-Y 87

**Mason, Nick** 1945- . . . . . . . . . . . . . . . **CLC 35**
    See also Pink Floyd

**Mason, Tally** 1909-1971
    See Derleth, August (William)

**Masters, Edgar Lee**
    1868?-1950 . . . . . . . . . **TCLC 2, 25; PC 1**
    See also CA 104; DLB 54;
    CDALB 1865-1917

**Masters, Hilary** 1928- . . . . . . . . . . . . . **CLC 48**
    See also CANR 13; CA 25-28R

**Mastrosimone, William** 19??- . . . . . . **CLC 36**

**Matheson, Richard (Burton)**
    1926- . . . . . . . . . . . . . . . . . . . . . . . **CLC 37**
    See also CA 97-100; DLB 8, 44

**Mathews, Harry** 1930- . . . . . . . . . . **CLC 6, 52**
    See also CAAS 6; CANR 18; CA 21-24R

**Mathias, Roland (Glyn)** 1915- . . . . . . **CLC 45**
    See also CANR 19; CA 97-100; DLB 27

**Matthews, Greg** 1949- . . . . . . . . . . . . **CLC 45**

**Matthews, William** 1942- . . . . . . . . . . **CLC 40**
    See also CANR 12; CA 29-32R; DLB 5

**Matthias, John (Edward)** 1941- . . . . . . **CLC 9**
    See also CA 33-36R

**Matthiessen, Peter**
    1927- . . . . . . . . . . . . **CLC 5, 7, 11, 32, 64**
    See also CANR 21; CA 9-12R; SATA 27;
    DLB 6

**Maturin, Charles Robert**
    1780?-1824 . . . . . . . . . . . . . . . . . **NCLC 6**

**Matute, Ana Maria** 1925- . . . . . . . . . **CLC 11**
    See also CA 89-92

**Maugham, W(illiam) Somerset**
    1874-1965 . . . . . . . . . . . . **CLC 1, 11, 15**
    See also CA 5-8R; obituary CA 25-28R;
    DLB 10, 36

**Maupassant, (Henri Rene Albert) Guy de**
    1850-1893 . . . . . . . . . . . **NCLC 1; SSC 1**

**Mauriac, Claude** 1914- . . . . . . . . . . . . **CLC 9**
    See also CA 89-92; DLB 83

**Mauriac, Francois (Charles)**
    1885-1970 . . . . . . . . . . . . . . **CLC 4, 9, 56**
    See also CAP 2; CA 25-28; DLB 65

**Mavor, Osborne Henry** 1888-1951
See Bridie, James
See also CA 104

**Maxwell, William (Keepers, Jr.)**
1908- . . . . . . . . . . . . . . . . . . . . . . **CLC 19**
See also CA 93-96; DLB-Y 80

**May, Elaine** 1932- . . . . . . . . . . . . . . . **CLC 16**
See also CA 124; DLB 44

**Mayakovsky, Vladimir (Vladimirovich)**
1893-1930 . . . . . . . . . . . . . . . **TCLC 4, 18**
See also CA 104

**Maynard, Joyce** 1953- . . . . . . . . . . . **CLC 23**
See also CA 111, 129

**Mayne, William (James Carter)**
1928- . . . . . . . . . . . . . . . . . . . . . . **CLC 12**
See also CA 9-12R; SATA 6

**Mayo, Jim** 1908?-
See L'Amour, Louis (Dearborn)

**Maysles, Albert** 1926- and **Maysles, David**
1926- . . . . . . . . . . . . . . . . . . . . . . **CLC 16**
See also CA 29-32R

**Maysles, Albert** 1926- . . . . . . . . . . . . **CLC 16**
See Maysles, Albert and Maysles,
David
See also CA 29-32R

**Maysles, David** 1932- . . . . . . . . . . . . **CLC 16**
See Maysles, Albert and Maysles,
David

**Mazer, Norma Fox** 1931- . . . . . . . . . **CLC 26**
See also CLR 23; CANR 12; CA 69-72;
SAAS 1; SATA 24

**McAuley, James (Phillip)**
1917-1976 . . . . . . . . . . . . . . . . . . **CLC 45**
See also CA 97-100

**McBain, Ed** 1926-
See Hunter, Evan

**McBrien, William** 1930- . . . . . . . . . . **CLC 44**
See also CA 107

**McCaffrey, Anne** 1926- . . . . . . . . . . . **CLC 17**
See also CANR 15; CA 25-28R; SATA 8;
DLB 8

**McCarthy, Cormac** 1933- . . . . . . . . **CLC 4, 57**
See also CANR 10; CA 13-16R; DLB 6

**McCarthy, Mary (Therese)**
1912-1989- . . . **CLC 1, 3, 5, 14, 24, 39, 59**
See also CANR 16; CA 5-8R;
obituary CA 129; DLB 2; DLB-Y 81

**McCartney, (James) Paul**
1942- . . . . . . . . . . . . . . . . . . . **CLC 12, 35**

**McCauley, Stephen** 19??- . . . . . . . . . **CLC 50**

**McClure, Michael** 1932- . . . . . . . . **CLC 6, 10**
See also CANR 17; CA 21-24R; DLB 16

**McCorkle, Jill (Collins)** 1958- . . . . . . **CLC 51**
See also CA 121; DLB-Y 87

**McCourt, James** 1941- . . . . . . . . . . . . **CLC 5**
See also CA 57-60

**McCoy, Horace** 1897-1955 . . . . . . . **TCLC 28**
See also CA 108; DLB 9

**McCrae, John** 1872-1918 . . . . . . . . **TCLC 12**
See also CA 109; DLB 92

**McCullers, (Lula) Carson (Smith)**
1917-1967 . . . . . . . . **CLC 1, 4, 10, 12, 48**
See also CANR 18; CA 5-8R;
obituary CA 25-28R; CABS 1; SATA 27;
DLB 2, 7; CDALB 1941-1968

**McCullough, Colleen** 1938?- . . . . . . . **CLC 27**
See also CANR 17; CA 81-84

**McElroy, Joseph (Prince)**
1930- . . . . . . . . . . . . . . . . . . . **CLC 5, 47**
See also CA 17-20R

**McEwan, Ian (Russell)** 1948- . . . . . . **CLC 13**
See also CANR 14; CA 61-64; DLB 14

**McFadden, David** 1940- . . . . . . . . . . **CLC 48**
See also CA 104; DLB 60

**McGahern, John** 1934- . . . . . . . **CLC 5, 9, 48**
See also CANR 29; CA 17-20R; DLB 14

**McGinley, Patrick** 1937- . . . . . . . . . . **CLC 41**
See also CA 120, 127

**McGinley, Phyllis** 1905-1978 . . . . . . **CLC 14**
See also CANR 19; CA 9-12R;
obituary CA 77-80; SATA 2, 44;
obituary SATA 24; DLB 11, 48

**McGinniss, Joe** 1942- . . . . . . . . . . . . **CLC 32**
See also CANR 26; CA 25-28R

**McGivern, Maureen Daly** 1921-
See Daly, Maureen
See also CA 9-12R

**McGrath, Patrick** 1950- . . . . . . . . . . **CLC 55**

**McGrath, Thomas** 1916- . . . . . . . **CLC 28, 59**
See also CANR 6; CA 9-12R, 130;
SATA 41

**McGuane, Thomas (Francis III)**
1939- . . . . . . . . . . . . . . **CLC 3, 7, 18, 45**
See also CANR 5, 24; CA 49-52; DLB 2;
DLB-Y 80

**McGuckian, Medbh** 1950- . . . . . . . . **CLC 48**
See also DLB 40

**McHale, Tom** 1941-1982 . . . . . . . . . **CLC 3, 5**
See also CA 77-80; obituary CA 106

**McIlvanney, William** 1936- . . . . . . . . **CLC 42**
See also CA 25-28R; DLB 14

**McIlwraith, Maureen Mollie Hunter** 1922-
See Hunter, Mollie
See also CA 29-32R; SATA 2

**McInerney, Jay** 1955- . . . . . . . . . . . . **CLC 34**
See also CA 116, 123

**McIntyre, Vonda N(eel)** 1948- . . . . . **CLC 18**
See also CANR 17; CA 81-84

**McKay, Claude** 1889-1948 . . . **TCLC 7; PC 2**
See also CA 104, 124; DLB 4, 45, 51

**McKuen, Rod** 1933- . . . . . . . . . . . . . **CLC 1, 3**
See also CA 41-44R

**McLuhan, (Herbert) Marshall**
1911-1980 . . . . . . . . . . . . . . . . . . **CLC 37**
See also CANR 12; CA 9-12R;
obituary CA 102; DLB 88

**McManus, Declan Patrick** 1955-
See Costello, Elvis

**McMillan, Terry** 1951- . . . . . . . . **CLC 50, 61**

**McMurtry, Larry (Jeff)**
1936- . . . . . . . . . . **CLC 2, 3, 7, 11, 27, 44**
See also CANR 19; CA 5-8R; DLB 2;
DLB-Y 80, 87; CDALB 1968-1987

**McNally, Terrence** 1939- . . . . . . **CLC 4, 7, 41**
See also CANR 2; CA 45-48; DLB 7

**McPhee, John** 1931- . . . . . . . . . . . . . **CLC 36**
See also CANR 20; CA 65-68

**McPherson, James Alan** 1943- . . . . . **CLC 19**
See also CANR 24; CA 25-28R; DLB 38

**McPherson, William** 1939- . . . . . . . . **CLC 34**
See also CA 57-60

**McSweeney, Kerry** 19??- . . . . . . . . . . **CLC 34**

**Mead, Margaret** 1901-1978 . . . . . . . . **CLC 37**
See also CANR 4; CA 1-4R;
obituary CA 81-84; SATA 20

**Meaker, M. J.** 1927-
See Kerr, M. E.; Meaker, Marijane

**Meaker, Marijane** 1927-
See Kerr, M. E.
See also CA 107; SATA 20

**Medoff, Mark (Howard)** 1940- . . . **CLC 6, 23**
See also CANR 5; CA 53-56; DLB 7

**Megged, Aharon** 1920- . . . . . . . . . . . . **CLC 9**
See also CANR 1; CA 49-52

**Mehta, Ved (Parkash)** 1934- . . . . . . . **CLC 37**
See also CANR 2, 23; CA 1-4R

**Mellor, John** 1953?-
See The Clash

**Meltzer, Milton** 1915- . . . . . . . . . . . . **CLC 26**
See also CLR 13; CA 13-16R; SAAS 1;
SATA 1, 50; DLB 61

**Melville, Herman**
1819-1891 . . . . . . **NCLC 3, 12, 29; SSC 1**
See also SATA 59; DLB 3, 74;
CDALB 1640-1865

**Membreno, Alejandro** 1972- . . . . . . . **CLC 59**

**Mencken, H(enry) L(ouis)**
1880-1956 . . . . . . . . . . . . . . . . . . **TCLC 13**
See also CA 105, 125; DLB 11, 29, 63;
CDALB 1917-1929

**Mercer, David** 1928-1980 . . . . . . . . . . **CLC 5**
See also CANR 23; CA 9-12R;
obituary CA 102; DLB 13

**Meredith, George** 1828-1909 . . . . . . **TCLC 17**
See also CA 117; DLB 18, 35, 57

**Meredith, William (Morris)**
1919- . . . . . . . . . . . . . . **CLC 4, 13, 22, 55**
See also CANR 6; CA 9-12R; DLB 5

**Merezhkovsky, Dmitri**
1865-1941 . . . . . . . . . . . . . . . . . . **TCLC 29**

**Merimee, Prosper**
1803-1870 . . . . . . . . . . . . **NCLC 6; SSC 7**

**Merkin, Daphne** 1954- . . . . . . . . . . . . **CLC 44**
See also CANR 123

**Merrill, James (Ingram)**
1926- . . . . . . . . **CLC 2, 3, 6, 8, 13, 18, 34**
See also CANR 10; CA 13-16R; DLB 5;
DLB-Y 85

**Merton, Thomas (James)**
1915-1968 . . . . . . . . . . . . **CLC 1, 3, 11, 34**
See also CANR 22; CA 5-8R;
obituary CA 25-28R; DLB 48; DLB-Y 81

**Merwin, W(illiam) S(tanley)**
1927- . . . . . . **CLC 1, 2, 3, 5, 8, 13, 18, 45**
See also CANR 15; CA 13-16R; DLB 5

**Metcalf, John** 1938- . . . . . . . . . . . . . . **CLC 37**
See also CA 113; DLB 60

Mew, Charlotte (Mary)
1870-1928 . . . . . . . . . . . . . . . . . TCLC 8
See also CA 105; DLB 19

Mewshaw, Michael 1943- . . . . . . . . . CLC 9
See also CANR 7; CA 53-56; DLB-Y 80

Meyer-Meyrink, Gustav 1868-1932
See Meyrink, Gustav
See also CA 117

Meyers, Jeffrey 1939- . . . . . . . . . . . CLC 39
See also CA 73-76

Meynell, Alice (Christiana Gertrude
Thompson) 1847-1922 . . . . . . . TCLC 6
See also CA 104; DLB 19

Meyrink, Gustav 1868-1932 . . . . . . TCLC 21
See also Meyer-Meyrink, Gustav

Michaels, Leonard 1933- . . . . . . . . CLC 6, 25
See also CANR 21; CA 61-64

Michaux, Henri 1899-1984 . . . . . . CLC 8, 19
See also CA 85-88; obituary CA 114

Michelangelo 1475-1564 . . . . . . . . . . . LC 12

Michener, James A(lbert)
1907- . . . . . . . . . . . CLC 1, 5, 11, 29, 60
See also CANR 21; CA 5-8R; DLB 6

Mickiewicz, Adam 1798-1855 . . . . . NCLC 3

Middleton, Christopher 1926- . . . . . . CLC 13
See also CANR 29; CA 13-16R; DLB 40

Middleton, Stanley 1919- . . . . . . . CLC 7, 38
See also CANR 21; CA 25-28R; DLB 14

Migueis, Jose Rodrigues 1901- . . . . . CLC 10

Mikszath, Kalman 1847-1910 . . . . . TCLC 31

Miles, Josephine (Louise)
1911-1985 . . . . . . . . CLC 1, 2, 14, 34, 39
See also CANR 2; CA 1-4R;
obituary CA 116; DLB 48

Mill, John Stuart 1806-1873 . . . . . NCLC 11
See also DLB 55

Millar, Kenneth 1915-1983 . . . . . . . . CLC 14
See also Macdonald, Ross
See also CANR 16; CA 9-12R;
obituary CA 110; DLB 2; DLB-Y 83;
DLB-DS 6

Millay, Edna St. Vincent
1892-1950 . . . . . . . . . . . . . . . . . . TCLC 4
See also CA 103; DLB 45;
CDALB 1917-1929

Miller, Arthur
1915- . . . . . . CLC 1, 2, 6, 10, 15, 26, 47;
DC 1
See also CANR 2, 30; CA 1-4R; CABS 3;
DLB 7; CDALB 1941-1968

Miller, Henry (Valentine)
1891-1980 . . . . . . . CLC 1, 2, 4, 9, 14, 43
See also CA 9-12R; obituary CA 97-100;
DLB 4, 9; DLB-Y 80; CDALB 1929-1941

Miller, Jason 1939?- . . . . . . . . . . . . . CLC 2
See also CA 73-76; DLB 7

Miller, Sue 19??- . . . . . . . . . . . . . . . CLC 44

Miller, Walter M(ichael), Jr.
1923- . . . . . . . . . . . . . . . . . . . CLC 4, 30
See also CA 85-88; DLB 8

Millhauser, Steven 1943- . . . . . . . CLC 21, 54
See also CA 108, 110, 111; DLB 2

Millin, Sarah Gertrude 1889-1968 . . CLC 49
See also CA 102; obituary CA 93-96

Milne, A(lan) A(lexander)
1882-1956 . . . . . . . . . . . . . . . . . TCLC 6
See also CLR 1; YABC 1; CA 104;
DLB 10, 77

Milner, Ron(ald) 1938- . . . . . . . . . . CLC 56
See also CANR 24; CA 73-76; DLB 38

Milosz Czeslaw
1911- . . . . . . . . . CLC 5, 11, 22, 31, 56
See also CANR 23; CA 81-84

Milton, John 1608-1674 . . . . . . . . . . . . LC 9

Miner, Valerie (Jane) 1947- . . . . . . . CLC 40
See also CA 97-100

Minot, Susan 1956- . . . . . . . . . . . . . CLC 44

Minus, Ed 1938- . . . . . . . . . . . . . . . CLC 39

Miro (Ferrer), Gabriel (Francisco Victor)
1879-1930 . . . . . . . . . . . . . . . . . TCLC 5
See also CA 104

Mishima, Yukio
1925-1970 . . . . CLC 2, 4, 6, 9, 27; DC 1;
SSC 4
See also Hiraoka, Kimitake

Mistral, Gabriela 1889-1957 . . . . . . . TCLC 2
See also CA 104

Mitchell, James Leslie 1901-1935
See Gibbon, Lewis Grassic
See also CA 104; DLB 15

Mitchell, Joni 1943- . . . . . . . . . . . . . CLC 12
See also CA 112

Mitchell (Marsh), Margaret (Munnerlyn)
1900-1949 . . . . . . . . . . . . . . . . TCLC 11
See also CA 109, 125; DLB 9

Mitchell, S. Weir 1829-1914 . . . . . TCLC 36

Mitchell, W(illiam) O(rmond)
1914- . . . . . . . . . . . . . . . . . . . . . CLC 25
See also CANR 15; CA 77-80; DLB 88

Mitford, Mary Russell 1787-1855 . . NCLC 4

Mitford, Nancy 1904-1973 . . . . . . . . CLC 44
See also CA 9-12R

Miyamoto Yuriko 1899-1951 . . . . . TCLC 37

Mo, Timothy 1950- . . . . . . . . . . . . . CLC 46
See also CA 117

Modarressi, Taghi 1931- . . . . . . . . . CLC 44
See also CA 121

Modiano, Patrick (Jean) 1945- . . . . . CLC 18
See also CANR 17; CA 85-88; DLB 83

Mofolo, Thomas (Mokopu)
1876-1948 . . . . . . . . . . . . . . . . TCLC 22
See also CA 121

Mohr, Nicholasa 1935- . . . . . . . . . . CLC 12
See also CLR 22; CANR 1; CA 49-52;
SAAS 8; SATA 8

Mojtabai, A(nn) G(race)
1938- . . . . . . . . . . . . . . . CLC 5, 9, 15, 29
See also CA 85-88

Moliere 1622-1673 . . . . . . . . . . . . . . . LC 10

Molnar, Ferenc 1878-1952 . . . . . . . TCLC 20
See also CA 109

Momaday, N(avarre) Scott
1934- . . . . . . . . . . . . . . . . . . . . CLC 2, 19
See also CANR 14; CA 25-28R; SATA 30,
48

Monroe, Harriet 1860-1936 . . . . . . . TCLC 12
See also CA 109; DLB 54, 91

Montagu, Elizabeth 1720-1800 . . . . NCLC 7

Montagu, Lady Mary (Pierrepont) Wortley
1689-1762 . . . . . . . . . . . . . . . . . . . LC 9

Montague, John (Patrick)
1929- . . . . . . . . . . . . . . . . . . . CLC 13, 46
See also CANR 9; CA 9-12R; DLB 40

Montaigne, Michel (Eyquem) de
1533-1592 . . . . . . . . . . . . . . . . . . . LC 8

Montale, Eugenio 1896-1981 . . . CLC 7, 9, 18
See also CANR 30; CA 17-20R;
obituary CA 104

Montgomery, Marion (H., Jr.)
1925- . . . . . . . . . . . . . . . . . . . . . . . CLC 7
See also CANR 3; CA 1-4R; DLB 6

Montgomery, Robert Bruce 1921-1978
See Crispin, Edmund
See also CA 104

Montherlant, Henri (Milon) de
1896-1972 . . . . . . . . . . . . . . . . CLC 8, 19
See also CA 85-88; obituary CA 37-40R;
DLB 72

Montisquieu, Charles-Louis de Secondat
1689-1755 . . . . . . . . . . . . . . . . . . . LC 7

Monty Python . . . . . . . . . . . . . . . . . CLC 21

Moodie, Susanna (Strickland)
1803-1885 . . . . . . . . . . . . . . . . . NCLC 14

Mooney, Ted 1951- . . . . . . . . . . . . . CLC 25

Moorcock, Michael (John)
1939- . . . . . . . . . . . . . . . CLC 5, 27, 58
See also CAAS 5; CANR 2, 17; CA 45-48;
DLB 14

Moore, Brian
1921- . . . . . . . . . CLC 1, 3, 5, 7, 8, 19, 32
See also CANR 1, 25; CA 1-4R

Moore, George (Augustus)
1852-1933 . . . . . . . . . . . . . . . . . TCLC 7
See also CA 104; DLB 10, 18, 57

Moore, Lorrie 1957- . . . . . . . . . . . CLC 39, 45
See also Moore, Marie Lorena

Moore, Marianne (Craig)
1887-1972 . . . CLC 1, 2, 4, 8, 10, 13, 19,
47
See also CANR 3; CA 1-4R;
obituary CA 33-36R; SATA 20; DLB 45;
CDALB 1929-1941

Moore, Marie Lorena 1957-
See Moore, Lorrie
See also CA 116

Moore, Thomas 1779-1852 . . . . . . . NCLC 6

Morand, Paul 1888-1976 . . . . . . . . . CLC 41
See also obituary CA 69-72; DLB 65

Morante, Elsa 1918-1985 . . . . . . . CLC 8, 47
See also CA 85-88; obituary CA 117

Moravia, Alberto
1907- . . . . . . . . . CLC 2, 7, 11, 18, 27, 46
See also Pincherle, Alberto

More, Hannah 1745-1833 . . . . . . . NCLC 27

More, Henry 1614-1687 . . . . . . . . . . . LC 9

More, (Sir) Thomas 1478-1535 . . . . . LC 10

Moreas, Jean 1856-1910 . . . . . . . . TCLC 18

Morgan, Berry 1919- . . . . . . . . . . . . CLC 6
See also CA 49-52; DLB 6

**Morgan, Edwin (George)**  1920- . . . . . **CLC 31**
See also CANR 3; CA 7-8R; DLB 27

**Morgan, (George) Frederick**
1922- . . . . . . . . . . . . . . . . . . . . . . . **CLC 23**
See also CANR 21; CA 17-20R

**Morgan, Janet**  1945- . . . . . . . . . . . . . **CLC 39**
See also CA 65-68

**Morgan, Lady**  1776?-1859 . . . . . . **NCLC 29**

**Morgan, Robin**  1941- . . . . . . . . . . . . . **CLC 2**
See also CA 69-72

**Morgenstern, Christian (Otto Josef Wolfgang)**
1871-1914 . . . . . . . . . . . . . . . . . **TCLC 8**
See also CA 105

**Moricz, Zsigmond**  1879-1942 . . . . . **TCLC 33**

**Morike, Eduard (Friedrich)**
1804-1875 . . . . . . . . . . . . . . . . **NCLC 10**

**Mori Ogai**  1862-1922. . . . . . . . . . . **TCLC 14**
See also Mori Rintaro

**Mori Rintaro**  1862-1922
See Mori Ogai
See also CA 110

**Moritz, Karl Philipp**  1756-1793 . . . . . . **LC 2**

**Morris, Julian**  1916-
See West, Morris L.

**Morris, Steveland Judkins**  1950-
See Wonder, Stevie
See also CA 111

**Morris, William**  1834-1896 . . . . . . . **NCLC 4**
See also DLB 18, 35, 57

**Morris, Wright (Marion)**
1910- . . . . . . . . . . . . . **CLC 1, 3, 7, 18, 37**
See also CANR 21; CA 9-12R; DLB 2;
DLB-Y 81

**Morrison, James Douglas**  1943-1971
See Morrison, Jim
See also CA 73-76

**Morrison, Jim**  1943-1971. . . . . . . . . **CLC 17**
See also Morrison, James Douglas

**Morrison, Toni**  1931- . . . . . **CLC 4, 10, 22, 55**
See also CANR 27; CA 29-32R; DLB 6, 33;
DLB-Y 81; CDALB 1968-1987; AAYA 1

**Morrison, Van**  1945- . . . . . . . . . . . . . **CLC 21**
See also CA 116

**Mortimer, John (Clifford)**
1923- . . . . . . . . . . . . . . . . . . . **CLC 28, 43**
See also CANR 21; CA 13-16R; DLB 13

**Mortimer, Penelope (Ruth)**  1918- . . . . **CLC 5**
See also CA 57-60

**Mosher, Howard Frank**  19??- . . . . . . **CLC 62**

**Mosley, Nicholas**  1923- . . . . . . . . . . **CLC 43**
See also CA 69-72; DLB 14

**Moss, Howard**
1922-1987 . . . . . . . . . . **CLC 7, 14, 45, 50**
See also CANR 1; CA 1-4R;
obituary CA 123; DLB 5

**Motion, Andrew (Peter)**  1952- . . . . . . **CLC 47**
See also DLB 40

**Motley, Willard (Francis)**
1912-1965 . . . . . . . . . . . . . . . . . . **CLC 18**
See also CA 117; obituary CA 106; DLB 76

**Mott, Michael (Charles Alston)**
1930- . . . . . . . . . . . . . . . . . . **CLC 15, 34**
See also CAAS 7; CANR 7, 29; CA 5-8R

**Mowat, Farley (McGill)**  1921- . . . . . **CLC 26**
See also CLR 20; CANR 4, 24; CA 1-4R;
SATA 3, 55; DLB 68; AAYA 1

**Mphahlele, Es'kia**  1919-
See Mphahlele, Ezekiel

**Mphahlele, Ezekiel**  1919-. . . . . . . . . **CLC 25**
See also CA 81-84

**Mqhayi, S(amuel) E(dward) K(rune Loliwe)**
1875-1945 . . . . . . . . . . . . . . . . . **TCLC 25**

**Mrozek, Slawomir**  1930- . . . . . . . . **CLC 3, 13**
See also CAAS 10; CANR 29; CA 13-16R

**Mtwa, Percy**  19??- . . . . . . . . . . . . . . **CLC 47**

**Mueller, Lisel**  1924-. . . . . . . . . . **CLC 13, 51**
See also CA 93-96

**Muir, Edwin**  1887-1959 . . . . . . . . . . **TCLC 2**
See also CA 104; DLB 20

**Muir, John**  1838-1914 . . . . . . . . . . **TCLC 28**

**Mujica Lainez, Manuel**
1910-1984 . . . . . . . . . . . . . . . . . **CLC 31**
See also CA 81-84; obituary CA 112

**Mukherjee, Bharati**  1940- . . . . . . . . **CLC 53**
See also CA 107; DLB 60

**Muldoon, Paul**  1951- . . . . . . . . . . . . **CLC 32**
See also CA 113, 129; DLB 40

**Mulisch, Harry (Kurt Victor)**
1927- . . . . . . . . . . . . . . . . . . . . . **CLC 42**
See also CANR 6, 26; CA 9-12R

**Mull, Martin**  1943-. . . . . . . . . . . . . . **CLC 17**
See also CA 105

**Munford, Robert**  1737?-1783. . . . . . . . **LC 5**
See also DLB 31

**Munro, Alice (Laidlaw)**
1931- . . . . . . . . **CLC 6, 10, 19, 50; SSC 3**
See also CA 33-36R; SATA 29; DLB 53

**Munro, H(ector) H(ugh)**  1870-1916
See Saki
See also CA 104; DLB 34

**Murasaki, Lady**  c. 11th century-. . . **CMLC 1**

**Murdoch, (Jean) Iris**
1919- . . . . . . **CLC 1, 2, 3, 4, 6, 8, 11, 15,
22, 31, 51**
See also CANR 8; CA 13-16R; DLB 14

**Murphy, Richard**  1927-. . . . . . . . . . . **CLC 41**
See also CA 29-32R; DLB 40

**Murphy, Sylvia**  19??-. . . . . . . . . . . . . **CLC 34**

**Murphy, Thomas (Bernard)**  1935-. . . **CLC 51**
See also CA 101

**Murray, Les(lie) A(llan)**  1938- . . . . . **CLC 40**
See also CANR 11, 27; CA 21-24R

**Murry, John Middleton**
1889-1957 . . . . . . . . . . . . . . . . . **TCLC 16**
See also CA 118

**Musgrave, Susan**  1951- . . . . . . . . **CLC 13, 54**
See also CA 69-72

**Musil, Robert (Edler von)**
1880-1942 . . . . . . . . . . . . . . . . . **TCLC 12**
See also CA 109; DLB 81

**Musset, (Louis Charles) Alfred de**
1810-1857 . . . . . . . . . . . . . . . . . **NCLC 7**

**Myers, Walter Dean**  1937- . . . . . . . . **CLC 35**
See also CLR 4, 16; CANR 20; CA 33-36R;
SAAS 2; SATA 27, 41; DLB 33; AAYA 4

**Nabokov, Vladimir (Vladimirovich)**
1899-1977 . . . . **CLC 1, 2, 3, 6, 8, 11, 15,
23, 44, 46, 64**
See also CANR 20; CA 5-8R;
obituary CA 69-72; DLB 2; DLB-Y 80;
DLB-DS 3; CDALB 1941-1968

**Nagy, Laszlo**  1925-1978. . . . . . . . . . . **CLC 7**
See also CA 129; obituary CA 112

**Naipaul, Shiva(dhar Srinivasa)**
1945-1985 . . . . . . . . . . . . . . . **CLC 32, 39**
See also CA 110, 112; obituary CA 116;
DLB-Y 85

**Naipaul, V(idiadhar) S(urajprasad)**
1932- . . . . . . . . . . **CLC 4, 7, 9, 13, 18, 37**
See also CANR 1; CA 1-4R; DLB-Y 85

**Nakos, Ioulia**  1899?-
See Nakos, Lilika

**Nakos, Lilika**  1899?- . . . . . . . . . . . . . **CLC 29**

**Nakou, Lilika**  1899?-
See Nakos, Lilika

**Narayan, R(asipuram) K(rishnaswami)**
1906- . . . . . . . . . . . . . . . . **CLC 7, 28, 47**
See also CA 81-84

**Nash, (Fredric) Ogden**  1902-1971 . . **CLC 23**
See also CAP 1; CA 13-14;
obituary CA 29-32R; SATA 2, 46;
DLB 11

**Nathan, George Jean**  1882-1958 . . . **TCLC 18**
See also CA 114

**Natsume, Kinnosuke**  1867-1916
See Natsume, Soseki
See also CA 104

**Natsume, Soseki**  1867-1916. . . . . **TCLC 2, 10**
See also Natsume, Kinnosuke

**Natti, (Mary) Lee**  1919-
See Kingman, (Mary) Lee
See also CANR 2; CA 7-8R

**Naylor, Gloria**  1950- . . . . . . . . . . **CLC 28, 52**
See also CANR 27; CA 107

**Neff, Debra**  1972-. . . . . . . . . . . . . . . **CLC 59**

**Neihardt, John G(neisenau)**
1881-1973 . . . . . . . . . . . . . . . . . . **CLC 32**
See also CAP 1; CA 13-14; DLB 9, 54

**Nekrasov, Nikolai Alekseevich**
1821-1878 . . . . . . . . . . . . . . . . **NCLC 11**

**Nelligan, Emile**  1879-1941. . . . . . . **TCLC 14**
See also CA 114; DLB 92

**Nelson, Willie**  1933-. . . . . . . . . . . . . **CLC 17**
See also CA 107

**Nemerov, Howard**  1920- . . . . **CLC 2, 6, 9, 36**
See also CANR 1, 27; CA 1-4R; CABS 2;
DLB 5, 6; DLB-Y 83

**Neruda, Pablo**
1904-1973 . . . . . **CLC 1, 2, 5, 7, 9, 28, 62**
See also CAP 2; CA 19-20;
obituary CA 45-48

**Nerval, Gerard de**  1808-1855. . . . . . **NCLC 1**

**Nervo, (Jose) Amado (Ruiz de)**
1870-1919 . . . . . . . . . . . . . . . . . **TCLC 11**
See also CA 109

**Neufeld, John (Arthur)**  1938- . . . . . . **CLC 17**
See also CANR 11; CA 25-28R; SAAS 3;
SATA 6

Neville, Emily Cheney 1919-....... CLC 12
See also CANR 3; CA 5-8R; SAAS 2;
SATA 1

Newbound, Bernard Slade 1930-
See Slade, Bernard
See also CA 81-84

Newby, P(ercy) H(oward)
1918-..................... CLC 2, 13
See also CA 5-8R; DLB 15

Newlove, Donald 1928-............ CLC 6
See also CANR 25; CA 29-32R

Newlove, John (Herbert) 1938-..... CLC 14
See also CANR 9, 25; CA 21-24R

Newman, Charles 1938-.......... CLC 2, 8
See also CA 21-24R

Newman, Edwin (Harold) 1919- .... CLC 14
See also CANR 5; CA 69-72

Newton, Suzanne 1936-........... CLC 35
See also CANR 14; CA 41-44R; SATA 5

Ngema, Mbongeni 1955- .......... CLC 57

Ngugi, James (Thiong'o)
1938-............... CLC 3, 7, 13, 36
See also Ngugi wa Thiong'o; Wa Thiong'o,
Ngugi
See also CANR 27; CA 81-84

Ngugi wa Thiong'o 1938-... CLC 3, 7, 13, 36
See also Ngugi, James (Thiong'o); Wa
Thiong'o, Ngugi

Nichol, B(arrie) P(hillip) 1944-..... CLC 18
See also CA 53-56; DLB 53

Nichols, John (Treadwell) 1940-.... CLC 38
See also CAAS 2; CANR 6; CA 9-12R;
DLB-Y 82

Nichols, Peter (Richard) 1927-... CLC 5, 36
See also CA 104; DLB 13

Nicolas, F.R.E. 1927-
See Freeling, Nicolas

Niedecker, Lorine 1903-1970.... CLC 10, 42
See also CAP 2; CA 25-28; DLB 48

Nietzsche, Friedrich (Wilhelm)
1844-1900 ............... TCLC 10, 18
See also CA 107, 121

Nievo, Ippolito 1831-1861 ....... NCLC 22

Nightingale, Anne Redmon 1943-
See Redmon (Nightingale), Anne
See also CA 103

Nin, Anais
1903-1977 ...... CLC 1, 4, 8, 11, 14, 60
See also CANR 22; CA 13-16R;
obituary CA 69-72; DLB 2, 4

Nissenson, Hugh 1933-........... CLC 4, 9
See also CANR 27; CA 17-20R; DLB 28

Niven, Larry 1938-................ CLC 8
See also Niven, Laurence Van Cott
See also DLB 8

Niven, Laurence Van Cott 1938-
See Niven, Larry
See also CANR 14; CA 21-24R

Nixon, Agnes Eckhardt 1927-...... CLC 21
See also CA 110

Nizan, Paul 1905-1940........... TCLC 40
See also DLB 72

Nkosi, Lewis 1936-............... CLC 45
See also CANR 27; CA 65-68

Nodier, (Jean) Charles (Emmanuel)
1780-1844 ................. NCLC 19

Nolan, Christopher 1965-......... CLC 58
See also CA 111

Nordhoff, Charles 1887-1947..... TCLC 23
See also CA 108; SATA 23; DLB 9

Norman, Marsha 1947- .......... CLC 28
See also CA 105; CABS 3; DLB-Y 84

Norris, (Benjamin) Frank(lin)
1870-1902 ................. TCLC 24
See also CA 110; DLB 12, 71;
CDALB 1865-1917

Norris, Leslie 1921-.............. CLC 14
See also CANR 14; CAP 1; CA 11-12;
DLB 27

North, Andrew 1912-
See Norton, Andre

North, Christopher 1785-1854
See Wilson, John

Norton, Alice Mary 1912-
See Norton, Andre
See also CANR 2; CA 1-4R; SATA 1, 43

Norton, Andre 1912- ............. CLC 12
See also Norton, Mary Alice
See also DLB 8, 52

Norway, Nevil Shute 1899-1960
See Shute (Norway), Nevil
See also CA 102; obituary CA 93-96

Norwid, Cyprian Kamil
1821-1883 ................. NCLC 17

Nossack, Hans Erich 1901-1978 ..... CLC 6
See also CA 93-96; obituary CA 85-88;
DLB 69

Nova, Craig 1945-................ CLC 7, 31
See also CANR 2; CA 45-48

Novak, Joseph 1933-
See Kosinski, Jerzy (Nikodem)

Novalis 1772-1801 ............. NCLC 13

Nowlan, Alden (Albert) 1933-...... CLC 15
See also CANR 5; CA 9-12R; DLB 53

Noyes, Alfred 1880-1958 .......... TCLC 7
See also CA 104; DLB 20

Nunn, Kem 19??-................. CLC 34

Nye, Robert 1939- ............. CLC 13, 42
See also CANR 29; CA 33-36R; SATA 6;
DLB 14

Nyro, Laura 1947- .............. CLC 17

Oates, Joyce Carol
1938-..... CLC 1, 2, 3, 6, 9, 11, 15, 19,
33, 52; SSC 6
See also CANR 25; CA 5-8R; DLB 2, 5;
DLB-Y 81; CDALB 1968-1987

O'Brien, Darcy 1939-............. CLC 11
See also CANR 8; CA 21-24R

O'Brien, Edna 1932-.... CLC 3, 5, 8, 13, 36
See also CANR 6; CA 1-4R; DLB 14

O'Brien, Fitz-James 1828?-1862.. NCLC 21
See also DLB 74

O'Brien, Flann
1911-1966 ....... CLC 1, 4, 5, 7, 10, 47
See also O Nuallain, Brian

O'Brien, Richard 19??-............ CLC 17
See also CA 124

O'Brien, (William) Tim(othy)
1946-.................. CLC 7, 19, 40
See also CA 85-88; DLB-Y 80

Obstfelder, Sigbjorn 1866-1900.... TCLC 23
See also CA 123

O'Casey, Sean
1880-1964 ........ CLC 1, 5, 9, 11, 15
See also CA 89-92; DLB 10

Ochs, Phil 1940-1976............. CLC 17
See also obituary CA 65-68

O'Connor, Edwin (Greene)
1918-1968 ................. CLC 14
See also CA 93-96; obituary CA 25-28R

O'Connor, (Mary) Flannery
1925-1964 ... CLC 1, 2, 3, 6, 10, 13, 15,
21; SSC 1
See also CANR 3; CA 1-4R; DLB 2;
DLB-Y 80; CDALB 1941-1968

O'Connor, Frank
1903-1966 ........ CLC 14, 23; SSC 5
See also O'Donovan, Michael (John)
See also CA 93-96

O'Dell, Scott 1903-............... CLC 30
See also CLR 1, 16; CANR 12; CA 61-64;
SATA 12; DLB 52

Odets, Clifford 1906-1963 ....... CLC 2, 28
See also CA 85-88; DLB 7, 26

O'Donovan, Michael (John)
1903-1966 ................... CLC 14
See also O'Connor, Frank
See also CA 93-96

Oe, Kenzaburo 1935-.......... CLC 10, 36
See also CA 97-100

O'Faolain, Julia 1932-....... CLC 6, 19, 47
See also CAAS 2; CANR 12; CA 81-84;
DLB 14

O'Faolain, Sean 1900- ..... CLC 1, 7, 14, 32
See also CANR 12; CA 61-64; DLB 15

O'Flaherty, Liam
1896-1984 .......... CLC 5, 34; SSC 6
See also CA 101; obituary CA 113; DLB 36;
DLB-Y 84

O'Grady, Standish (James)
1846-1928 ................. TCLC 5
See also CA 104

O'Grady, Timothy 1951- .......... CLC 59

O'Hara, Frank 1926-1966 ..... CLC 2, 5, 13
See also CA 9-12R; obituary CA 25-28R;
DLB 5, 16; CDALB 1929-1941

O'Hara, John (Henry)
1905-1970 ....... CLC 1, 2, 3, 6, 11, 42
See also CA 5-8R; obituary CA 25-28R;
DLB 9; DLB-DS 2; CDALB 1929-1941

O'Hara Family
See Banim, John and Banim, Michael

O'Hehir, Diana 1922-............. CLC 41
See also CA 93-96

Okigbo, Christopher (Ifenayichukwu)
1932-1967 ................... CLC 25
See also CA 77-80

Olds, Sharon 1942-............. CLC 32, 39
See also CANR 18; CA 101

Olesha, Yuri (Karlovich)
1899-1960 ................... CLC 8
See also CA 85-88

**Oliphant, Margaret (Oliphant Wilson)**
    1828-1897 ................ NCLC **11**
    See also DLB 18

**Oliver, Mary** 1935-............ CLC **19, 34**
    See also CANR 9; CA 21-24R; DLB 5

**Olivier, (Baron) Laurence (Kerr)**
    1907- ....................... CLC **20**
    See also CA 111, 129

**Olsen, Tillie** 1913- ............. CLC **4, 13**
    See also CANR 1; CA 1-4R; DLB 28;
    DLB-Y 80

**Olson, Charles (John)**
    1910-1970 ..... CLC **1, 2, 5, 6, 9, 11, 29**
    See also CAP 1; CA 15-16;
    obituary CA 25-28R; CABS 2; DLB 5, 16

**Olson, Theodore** 1937-
    See Olson, Toby

**Olson, Toby** 1937- ............... CLC **28**
    See also CANR 9; CA 65-68

**Ondaatje, (Philip) Michael**
    1943- ................. CLC **14, 29, 51**
    See also CA 77-80; DLB 60

**Oneal, Elizabeth** 1934-............ CLC **30**
    See also Oneal, Zibby
    See also CLR 13; CA 106; SATA 30

**Oneal, Zibby** 1934-............... CLC **30**
    See also Oneal, Elizabeth

**O'Neill, Eugene (Gladstone)**
    1888-1953 ............. TCLC **1, 6, 27**
    See also CA 110; DLB 7;
    CDALB 1929-1941

**Onetti, Juan Carlos** 1909-....... CLC **7, 10**
    See also CA 85-88

**O'Nolan, Brian** 1911-1966
    See O'Brien, Flann

**O Nuallain, Brian** 1911-1966
    See O'Brien, Flann
    See also CAP 2; CA 21-22;
    obituary CA 25-28R

**Oppen, George** 1908-1984 .... CLC **7, 13, 34**
    See also CANR 8; CA 13-16R;
    obituary CA 113; DLB 5

**Orlovitz, Gil** 1918-1973 ........... CLC **22**
    See also CA 77-80; obituary CA 45-48;
    DLB 2, 5

**Ortega y Gasset, Jose** 1883-1955 ... TCLC **9**
    See also CA 106, 130

**Ortiz, Simon J.** 1941-............. CLC **45**

**Orton, Joe** 1933?-1967....... CLC **4, 13, 43**
    See also Orton, John Kingsley
    See also DLB 13

**Orton, John Kingsley** 1933?-1967
    See Orton, Joe
    See also CA 85-88

**Orwell, George**
    1903-1950 ......... TCLC **2, 6, 15, 31**
    See also Blair, Eric Arthur
    See also DLB 15

**Osborne, John (James)**
    1929- ........... CLC **1, 2, 5, 11, 45**
    See also CANR 21; CA 13-16R; DLB 13

**Osborne, Lawrence** 1958- ........ CLC **50**

**Osceola** 1885-1962
    See Dinesen, Isak; Blixen, Karen
    (Christentze Dinesen)

**Oshima, Nagisa** 1932- ............ CLC **20**
    See also CA 116

**Oskison, John M.** 1874-1947...... TCLC **35**

**Ossoli, Sarah Margaret (Fuller marchesa d')**
    1810-1850
    See Fuller, (Sarah) Margaret
    See also SATA 25

**Ostrovsky, Alexander**
    1823-1886 ................. NCLC **30**

**Otero, Blas de** 1916- ............. CLC **11**
    See also CA 89-92

**Ovid** 43 B.C.-c. 18 A.D.
    See also PC 2

**Owen, Wilfred (Edward Salter)**
    1893-1918 ................ TCLC **5, 27**
    See also CA 104; DLB 20

**Owens, Rochelle** 1936-............. CLC **8**
    See also CAAS 2; CA 17-20R

**Owl, Sebastian** 1939-
    See Thompson, Hunter S(tockton)

**Oz, Amos** 1939- ... CLC **5, 8, 11, 27, 33, 54**
    See also CANR 27; CA 53-56

**Ozick, Cynthia** 1928-...... CLC **3, 7, 28, 62**
    See also CANR 23; CA 17-20R; DLB 28;
    DLB-Y 82

**Ozu, Yasujiro** 1903-1963.......... CLC **16**
    See also CA 112

**Pa Chin** 1904-.................... CLC **18**
    See also Li Fei-kan

**Pack, Robert** 1929-............... CLC **13**
    See also CANR 3; CA 1-4R; DLB 5

**Padgett, Lewis** 1915-1958
    See Kuttner, Henry

**Padilla, Heberto** 1932-............ CLC **38**
    See also CA 123

**Page, Jimmy** 1944-............... CLC **12**

**Page, Louise** 1955-............... CLC **40**

**Page, P(atricia) K(athleen)**
    1916- ..................... CLC **7, 18**
    See also CANR 4, 22; CA 53-56; DLB 68

**Paget, Violet** 1856-1935
    See Lee, Vernon
    See also CA 104

**Palamas, Kostes** 1859-1943 ....... TCLC **5**
    See also CA 105

**Palazzeschi, Aldo** 1885-1974 ...... CLC **11**
    See also CA 89-92; obituary CA 53-56

**Paley, Grace** 1922-........... CLC **4, 6, 37**
    See also CANR 13; CA 25-28R; DLB 28

**Palin, Michael** 1943- ............. CLC **21**
    See also Monty Python
    See also CA 107

**Palma, Ricardo** 1833-1919........ TCLC **29**
    See also CANR 123

**Pancake, Breece Dexter** 1952-1979
    See Pancake, Breece D'J

**Pancake, Breece D'J** 1952-1979 .... CLC **29**
    See also obituary CA 109

**Papadiamantis, Alexandros**
    1851-1911 ................. TCLC **29**

**Papini, Giovanni** 1881-1956....... TCLC **22**
    See also CA 121

**Paracelsus** 1493-1541.............. LC **14**

**Parini, Jay (Lee)** 1948- .......... CLC **54**
    See also CA 97-100

**Parker, Dorothy (Rothschild)**
    1893-1967 ............ CLC **15; SSC 2**
    See also CAP 2; CA 19-20;
    obituary CA 25-28R; DLB 11, 45. 86

**Parker, Robert B(rown)** 1932-...... CLC **27**
    See also CANR 1, 26; CA 49-52

**Parkin, Frank** 1940-.............. CLC **43**

**Parkman, Francis** 1823-1893..... NCLC **12**
    See also DLB 1, 30

**Parks, Gordon (Alexander Buchanan)**
    1912-..................... CLC **1, 16**
    See also CANR 26; CA 41-44R; SATA 8;
    DLB 33

**Parnell, Thomas** 1679-1718......... LC **3**

**Parra, Nicanor** 1914-.............. CLC **2**
    See also CA 85-88

**Pasolini, Pier Paolo**
    1922-1975 ................ CLC **20, 37**
    See also CA 93-96; obituary CA 61-64

**Pastan, Linda (Olenik)** 1932- ...... CLC **27**
    See also CANR 18; CA 61-64; DLB 5

**Pasternak, Boris**
    1890-1960 .......... CLC **7, 10, 18, 63**
    See also CA 127; obituary CA 116

**Patchen, Kenneth** 1911-1972 ... CLC **1, 2, 18**
    See also CANR 3; CA 1-4R;
    obituary CA 33-36R; DLB 16, 48

**Pater, Walter (Horatio)**
    1839-1894 ................. NCLC **7**
    See also DLB 57

**Paterson, Andrew Barton**
    1864-1941 ................. TCLC **32**

**Paterson, Katherine (Womeldorf)**
    1932- ................... CLC **12, 30**
    See also CLR 7; CANR 28; CA 21-24R;
    SATA 13, 53; DLB 52; AAYA 1

**Patmore, Coventry Kersey Dighton**
    1823-1896 ................. NCLC **9**
    See also DLB 35

**Paton, Alan (Stewart)**
    1903-1988 .......... CLC **4, 10, 25, 55**
    See also CANR 22; CAP 1; CA 15-16;
    obituary CA 125; SATA 11

**Paulding, James Kirke** 1778-1860.. NCLC **2**
    See also DLB 3, 59, 74

**Paulin, Tom** 1949- ............... CLC **37**
    See also CA 123; DLB 40

**Paustovsky, Konstantin (Georgievich)**
    1892-1968 .................. CLC **40**
    See also CA 93-96; obituary CA 25-28R

**Paustowsky, Konstantin (Georgievich)**
    1892-1968
    See Paustovsky, Konstantin (Georgievich)

**Pavese, Cesare** 1908-1950 ......... TCLC **3**
    See also CA 104

**Pavic, Milorad** 1929-............. CLC **60**

**Payne, Alan** 1932-
    See Jakes, John (William)

**Paz, Octavio**
    1914- ..... CLC **3, 4, 6, 10, 19, 51; PC 1**
    See also CA 73-76

Peacock, Molly 1947-. . . . . . . . . . . CLC 60
See also CA 103

Peacock, Thomas Love
1785-1886 . . . . . . . . . . . . . . . . NCLC 22

Peake, Mervyn 1911-1968 . . . . . . CLC 7, 54
See also CANR 3; CA 5-8R;
obituary CA 25-28R; SATA 23; DLB 15

Pearce, (Ann) Philippa 1920-. . . . . . CLC 21
See also Christie, (Ann) Philippa
See also CLR 9; CA 5-8R; SATA 1

Pearl, Eric 1934-
See Elman, Richard

Pearson, T(homas) R(eid) 1956- . . . . CLC 39
See also CA 120, 130

Peck, John 1941- . . . . . . . . . . . . . . . CLC 3
See also CANR 3; CA 49-52

Peck, Richard 1934-. . . . . . . . . . . . . CLC 21
See also CLR 15; CANR 19; CA 85-88;
SAAS 2; SATA 18; AAYA 1

Peck, Robert Newton 1928-. . . . . . . . CLC 17
See also CA 81-84; SAAS 1; SATA 21;
AAYA 3

Peckinpah, (David) Sam(uel)
1925-1984 . . . . . . . . . . . . . . . . . CLC 20
See also CA 109; obituary CA 114

Pedersen, Knut 1859-1952
See Hamsun, Knut
See also CA 104, 109, 119

Peguy, Charles (Pierre)
1873-1914 . . . . . . . . . . . . . . . . TCLC 10
See also CA 107

Pepys, Samuel 1633-1703. . . . . . . . . . LC 11

Percy, Walker
1916- . . . . . . . . CLC 2, 3, 6, 8, 14, 18, 47
See also CANR 1; CA 1-4R; DLB 2;
DLB-Y 80

Perec, Georges 1936-1982 . . . . . . . . CLC 56
See also DLB 83

Pereda, Jose Maria de
1833-1906 . . . . . . . . . . . . . . . . TCLC 16

Perelman, S(idney) J(oseph)
1904-1979 . . . CLC 3, 5, 9, 15, 23, 44, 49
See also CANR 18; CA 73-76;
obituary CA 89-92; DLB 11, 44

Peret, Benjamin 1899-1959 . . . . . . . TCLC 20
See also CA 117

Peretz, Isaac Leib 1852?-1915. . . . . TCLC 16
See also CA 109

Perez, Galdos Benito 1853-1920 . . . TCLC 27
See also CA 125

Perrault, Charles 1628-1703 . . . . . . . . LC 2
See also SATA 25

Perse, St.-John 1887-1975. . . . CLC 4, 11, 46
See also Leger, (Marie-Rene) Alexis
Saint-Leger

Pesetsky, Bette 1932-. . . . . . . . . . . . CLC 28

Peshkov, Alexei Maximovich 1868-1936
See Gorky, Maxim
See also CA 105

Pessoa, Fernando (Antonio Nogueira)
1888-1935 . . . . . . . . . . . . . . . . TCLC 27
See also CA 125

Peterkin, Julia (Mood) 1880-1961. . . CLC 31
See also CA 102; DLB 9

Peters, Joan K. 1945-. . . . . . . . . . . . CLC 39

Peters, Robert L(ouis) 1924-. . . . . . . CLC 7
See also CAAS 8; CA 13-16R

Petofi, Sandor 1823-1849. . . . . . . NCLC 21

Petrakis, Harry Mark 1923-. . . . . . . CLC 3
See also CANR 4, 30; CA 9-12R

Petrov, Evgeny 1902-1942. . . . . . . TCLC 21

Petry, Ann (Lane) 1908- . . . . . . CLC 1, 7, 18
See also CLR 12; CAAS 6; CANR 4;
CA 5-8R; SATA 5; DLB 76

Petursson, Halligrimur 1614-1674 . . . . LC 8

Philipson, Morris (H.) 1926-. . . . . . . CLC 53
See also CANR 4; CA 1-4R

Phillips, Jayne Anne 1952- . . . . . CLC 15, 33
See also CANR 24; CA 101; DLB-Y 80

Phillips, Robert (Schaeffer) 1938-. . . CLC 28
See also CANR 8; CA 17-20R

Pica, Peter 1925-
See Aldiss, Brian W(ilson)

Piccolo, Lucio 1901-1969. . . . . . . . . CLC 13
See also CA 97-100

Pickthall, Marjorie (Lowry Christie)
1883-1922 . . . . . . . . . . . . . . . . TCLC 21
See also CA 107; DLB 92

Pico della Mirandola, Giovanni
1463-1494 . . . . . . . . . . . . . . . . . . LC 15

Piercy, Marge
1936- . . . . . . . . CLC 3, 6, 14, 18, 27, 62
See also CAAS 1; CANR 13; CA 21-24R

Pilnyak, Boris 1894-1937? . . . . . . . TCLC 23

Pincherle, Alberto 1907- . . . . . . . CLC 11, 18
See also Moravia, Alberto
See also CA 25-28R

Pineda, Cecile 1942-. . . . . . . . . . . . . CLC 39
See also CA 118

Pinero, Miguel (Gomez)
1946-1988 . . . . . . . . . . . . . . . CLC 4, 55
See also CANR 29; CA 61-64;
obituary CA 125

Pinero, Sir Arthur Wing
1855-1934 . . . . . . . . . . . . . . . . TCLC 32
See also CA 110; DLB 10

Pinget, Robert 1919- . . . . . . . . CLC 7, 13, 37
See also CA 85-88; DLB 83

Pink Floyd. . . . . . . . . . . . . . . . . . . . CLC 35

Pinkwater, D(aniel) M(anus)
1941- . . . . . . . . . . . . . . . . . . . . CLC 35
See also Pinkwater, Manus
See also CLR 4; CANR 12; CA 29-32R;
SAAS 3; SATA 46; AAYA 1

Pinkwater, Manus 1941-
See Pinkwater, D(aniel) M(anus)
See also SATA 8

Pinsky, Robert 1940-. . . . . . . . CLC 9, 19, 38
See also CAAS 4; CA 29-32R; DLB-Y 82

Pinter, Harold
1930- . . . . . CLC 1, 3, 6, 9, 11, 15, 27, 58
See also CA 5-8R; DLB 13

Pirandello, Luigi 1867-1936. . . . . TCLC 4, 29
See also CA 104

Pirsig, Robert M(aynard) 1928- . . . CLC 4, 6
See also CA 53-56; SATA 39

Pisarev, Dmitry Ivanovich
1840-1868 . . . . . . . . . . . . . . . . NCLC 25

Pix, Mary (Griffith) 1666-1709. . . . . . LC 8
See also DLB 80

Plaidy, Jean 1906-
See Hibbert, Eleanor (Burford)

Plant, Robert 1948- . . . . . . . . . . . . . CLC 12

Plante, David (Robert)
1940-. . . . . . . . . . . . . . . . . CLC 7, 23, 38
See also CANR 12; CA 37-40R; DLB-Y 83

Plath, Sylvia
1932-1963 . . . . CLC 1, 2, 3, 5, 9, 11, 14,
17, 50, 51, 62; PC 1
See also CAP 2; CA 19-20; DLB 5, 6;
CDALB 1941-1968

Platonov, Andrei (Platonovich)
1899-1951 . . . . . . . . . . . . . . . . TCLC 14
See also Klimentov, Andrei Platonovich
See also CA 108

Platt, Kin 1911- . . . . . . . . . . . . . . . CLC 26
See also CANR 11; CA 17-20R; SATA 21

Plimpton, George (Ames) 1927-. . . . . CLC 36
See also CA 21-24R; SATA 10

Plomer, William (Charles Franklin)
1903-1973 . . . . . . . . . . . . . . . CLC 4, 8
See also CAP 2; CA 21-22; SATA 24;
DLB 20

Plumly, Stanley (Ross) 1939- . . . . . . CLC 33
See also CA 108, 110; DLB 5

Poe, Edgar Allan
1809-1849 . . . NCLC 1, 16; PC 1; SSC 1
See also SATA 23; DLB 3, 59, 73, 74;
CDALB 1640-1865

Pohl, Frederik 1919- . . . . . . . . . . . . CLC 18
See also CAAS 1; CANR 11; CA 61-64;
SATA 24; DLB 8

Poirier, Louis 1910-
See Gracq, Julien
See also CA 122, 126

Poitier, Sidney 1924?- . . . . . . . . . . . CLC 26
See also CA 117

Polanski, Roman 1933- . . . . . . . . . . CLC 16
See also CA 77-80

Poliakoff, Stephen 1952- . . . . . . . . . CLC 38
See also CA 106; DLB 13

Police, The. . . . . . . . . . . . . . . . . . . . CLC 26

Pollitt, Katha 1949- . . . . . . . . . . . . . CLC 28
See also CA 120, 122

Pollock, Sharon 19??-. . . . . . . . . . . . CLC 50
See also DLB 60

Pomerance, Bernard 1940-. . . . . . . . CLC 13
See also CA 101

Ponge, Francis (Jean Gaston Alfred)
1899-. . . . . . . . . . . . . . . . . . . CLC 6, 18
See also CA 85-88; obituary CA 126

Pontoppidan, Henrik 1857-1943 . . . TCLC 29
See also obituary CA 126

Poole, Josephine 1933-. . . . . . . . . . . CLC 17
See also CANR 10; CA 21-24R; SAAS 2;
SATA 5

Popa, Vasko 1922- . . . . . . . . . . . . . . CLC 19
See also CA 112

Pope, Alexander 1688-1744. . . . . . . . . LC 3

**Porter, Gene Stratton** 1863-1924 .. **TCLC 21**
See also CA 112

**Porter, Katherine Anne**
1890-1980 ..... **CLC 1, 3, 7, 10, 13, 15,**
**27; SSC 4**
See also CANR 1; CA 1-4R;
obituary CA 101; obituary SATA 23, 39;
DLB 4, 9; DLB-Y 80

**Porter, Peter (Neville Frederick)**
1929- .................. **CLC 5, 13, 33**
See also CA 85-88; DLB 40

**Porter, William Sydney** 1862-1910
See Henry, O.
See also YABC 2; CA 104; DLB 12, 78, 79;
CDALB 1865-1917

**Post, Melville D.** 1871-1930 ...... **TCLC 39**
See also brief entry CA 110

**Potok, Chaim** 1929- ....... **CLC 2, 7, 14, 26**
See also CANR 19; CA 17-20R; SATA 33;
DLB 28

**Potter, Dennis (Christopher George)**
1935- ...................... **CLC 58**
See also CA 107

**Pound, Ezra (Loomis)**
1885-1972 ..... **CLC 1, 2, 3, 4, 5, 7, 10,**
**13, 18, 34, 48, 50**
See also CA 5-8R; obituary CA 37-40R;
DLB 4, 45, 63; CDALB 1917-1929

**Povod, Reinaldo** 1959- ............ **CLC 44**

**Powell, Anthony (Dymoke)**
1905- ........... **CLC 1, 3, 7, 9, 10, 31**
See also CANR 1; CA 1-4R; DLB 15

**Powell, Padgett** 1952- ............ **CLC 34**
See also CA 126

**Powers, J(ames) F(arl)**
1917- ......... **CLC 1, 4, 8, 57; SSC 4**
See also CANR 2; CA 1-4R

**Pownall, David** 1938- ............ **CLC 10**
See also CA 89-92; DLB 14

**Powys, John Cowper**
1872-1963 ............ **CLC 7, 9, 15, 46**
See also CA 85-88; DLB 15

**Powys, T(heodore) F(rancis)**
1875-1953 ................... **TCLC 9**
See also CA 106; DLB 36

**Prager, Emily** 1952- .............. **CLC 56**

**Pratt, E(dwin) J(ohn)** 1883-1964.... **CLC 19**
See also obituary CA 93-96; DLB 92

**Premchand** 1880-1936 ........... **TCLC 21**

**Preussler, Otfried** 1923- ........... **CLC 17**
See also CA 77-80; SATA 24

**Prevert, Jacques (Henri Marie)**
1900-1977 .................. **CLC 15**
See also CANR 29; CA 77-80;
obituary CA 69-72; obituary SATA 30

**Prevost, Abbe (Antoine Francois)**
1697-1763 .................... **LC 1**

**Price, (Edward) Reynolds**
1933- ........ **CLC 3, 6, 13, 43, 50, 63**
See also CANR 1; CA 1-4R; DLB 2

**Price, Richard** 1949- ........... **CLC 6, 12**
See also CANR 3; CA 49-52; DLB-Y 81

**Prichard, Katharine Susannah**
1883-1969 .................. **CLC 46**
See also CAP 1; CA 11-12

**Priestley, J(ohn) B(oynton)**
1894-1984 ............. **CLC 2, 5, 9, 34**
See also CA 9-12R; obituary CA 113;
DLB 10, 34, 77; DLB-Y 84

**Prince (Rogers Nelson)** 1958?- ..... **CLC 35**

**Prince, F(rank) T(empleton)** 1912- .. **CLC 22**
See also CA 101; DLB 20

**Prior, Matthew** 1664-1721.......... **LC 4**

**Pritchard, William H(arrison)**
1932- ...................... **CLC 34**
See also CANR 23; CA 65-68

**Pritchett, V(ictor) S(awdon)**
1900- ............... **CLC 5, 13, 15, 41**
See also CA 61-64; DLB 15

**Probst, Mark** 1925- .............. **CLC 59**
See also CA 130

**Procaccino, Michael** 1946-
See Cristofer, Michael

**Prokosch, Frederic** 1908-1989.... **CLC 4, 48**
See also CA 73-76; obituary CA 128;
DLB 48

**Prose, Francine** 1947-............. **CLC 45**
See also CA 109, 112

**Proust, Marcel** 1871-1922 .. **TCLC 7, 13, 33**
See also CA 104, 120; DLB 65

**Pryor, Richard** 1940- ............. **CLC 26**
See also CA 122

**Przybyszewski, Stanislaw**
1868-1927 .................. **TCLC 36**
See also DLB 66

**Puig, Manuel** 1932- ....... **CLC 3, 5, 10, 28**
See also CANR 2; CA 45-48

**Purdy, A(lfred) W(ellington)**
1918- ................ **CLC 3, 6, 14, 50**
See also CA 81-84

**Purdy, James (Amos)**
1923- ......... **CLC 2, 4, 10, 28, 52**
See also CAAS 1; CANR 19; CA 33-36R;
DLB 2

**Pushkin, Alexander (Sergeyevich)**
1799-1837 ............... **NCLC 3, 27**

**P'u Sung-ling** 1640-1715 ............ **LC 3**

**Puzo, Mario** 1920- ......... **CLC 1, 2, 6, 36**
See also CANR 4; CA 65-68; DLB 6

**Pym, Barbara (Mary Crampton)**
1913-1980 ............ **CLC 13, 19, 37**
See also CANR 13; CAP 1; CA 13-14;
obituary CA 97-100; DLB 14; DLB-Y 87

**Pynchon, Thomas (Ruggles, Jr.)**
1937- ..... **CLC 2, 3, 6, 9, 11, 18, 33, 62**
See also CANR 22; CA 17-20R; DLB 2

**Quasimodo, Salvatore** 1901-1968 ... **CLC 10**
See also CAP 1; CA 15-16;
obituary CA 25-28R

**Queen, Ellery** 1905-1982 ........ **CLC 3, 11**
See also Dannay, Frederic; Lee, Manfred
B(ennington)

**Queneau, Raymond**
1903-1976 ........... **CLC 2, 5, 10, 42**
See also CA 77-80; obituary CA 69-72;
DLB 72

**Quin, Ann (Marie)** 1936-1973 ...... **CLC 6**
See also CA 9-12R; obituary CA 45-48;
DLB 14

**Quinn, Simon** 1942-
See Smith, Martin Cruz
See also CANR 6, 23; CA 85-88

**Quiroga, Horacio (Sylvestre)**
1878-1937 .................. **TCLC 20**
See also CA 117

**Quoirez, Francoise** 1935-
See Sagan, Francoise
See also CANR 6; CA 49-52

**Rabe, David (William)** 1940-... **CLC 4, 8, 33**
See also CA 85-88; CABS 3; DLB 7

**Rabelais, Francois** 1494?-1553....... **LC 5**

**Rabinovitch, Sholem** 1859-1916
See Aleichem, Sholom
See also CA 104

**Rachen, Kurt von** 1911-1986
See Hubbard, L(afayette) Ron(ald)

**Radcliffe, Ann (Ward)** 1764-1823 .. **NCLC 6**
See also DLB 39

**Radiguet, Raymond** 1903-1923 .... **TCLC 29**
See also DLB 65

**Radnoti, Miklos** 1909-1944 ....... **TCLC 16**
See also CA 118

**Rado, James** 1939- ............... **CLC 17**
See also CA 105

**Radomski, James** 1932-
See Rado, James

**Radvanyi, Netty Reiling** 1900-1983
See Seghers, Anna
See also CA 85-88; obituary CA 110

**Rae, Ben** 1935-
See Griffiths, Trevor

**Raeburn, John** 1941- .............. **CLC 34**
See also CA 57-60

**Ragni, Gerome** 1942- .............. **CLC 17**
See also CA 105

**Rahv, Philip** 1908-1973 ........... **CLC 24**
See also Greenberg, Ivan

**Raine, Craig** 1944- ............... **CLC 32**
See also CANR 29; CA 108; DLB 40

**Raine, Kathleen (Jessie)** 1908- ... **CLC 7, 45**
See also CA 85-88; DLB 20

**Rainis, Janis** 1865-1929.......... **TCLC 29**

**Rakosi, Carl** 1903- ............... **CLC 47**
See also Rawley, Callman
See also CAAS 5

**Ramos, Graciliano** 1892-1953 ..... **TCLC 32**

**Rampersad, Arnold** 19??-.......... **CLC 44**

**Ramuz, Charles-Ferdinand**
1878-1947 .................. **TCLC 33**

**Rand, Ayn** 1905-1982........ **CLC 3, 30, 44**
See also CANR 27; CA 13-16R;
obituary CA 105

**Randall, Dudley (Felker)** 1914-...... **CLC 1**
See also CANR 23; CA 25-28R; DLB 41

**Ransom, John Crowe**
1888-1974 ........ **CLC 2, 4, 5, 11, 24**
See also CANR 6; CA 5-8R;
obituary CA 49-52; DLB 45, 63

**Rao, Raja** 1909- .............. **CLC 25, 56**
See also CA 73-76

**Raphael, Frederic (Michael)**
1931- ..................... **CLC 2, 14**
See also CANR 1; CA 1-4R; DLB 14

**Rathbone, Julian** 1935- ........... **CLC 41**
See also CA 101

**Rattigan, Terence (Mervyn)**
1911-1977 .................... **CLC 7**
See also CA 85-88; obituary CA 73-76;
DLB 13

**Ratushinskaya, Irina** 1954- ....... **CLC 54**
See also CA 129

**Raven, Simon (Arthur Noel)**
1927- ....................... **CLC 14**
See also CA 81-84

**Rawley, Callman** 1903-
See Rakosi, Carl
See also CANR 12; CA 21-24R

**Rawlings, Marjorie Kinnan**
1896-1953 ................... **TCLC 4**
See also YABC 1; CA 104; DLB 9, 22

**Ray, Satyajit** 1921-............... **CLC 16**
See also CA 114

**Read, Herbert (Edward)** 1893-1968 .. **CLC 4**
See also CA 85-88; obituary CA 25-28R;
DLB 20

**Read, Piers Paul** 1941- ...... **CLC 4, 10, 25**
See also CA 21-24R; SATA 21; DLB 14

**Reade, Charles** 1814-1884 ........ **NCLC 2**
See also DLB 21

**Reade, Hamish** 1936-
See Gray, Simon (James Holliday)

**Reading, Peter** 1946- ............. **CLC 47**
See also CA 103; DLB 40

**Reaney, James** 1926- ............. **CLC 13**
See also CA 41-44R; SATA 43; DLB 68

**Rebreanu, Liviu** 1885-1944 ....... **TCLC 28**

**Rechy, John (Francisco)**
1934-...............**CLC 1, 7, 14, 18**
See also CAAS 4; CANR 6; CA 5-8R;
DLB-Y 82

**Redcam, Tom** 1870-1933 ......... **TCLC 25**

**Redgrove, Peter (William)**
1932-.....................**CLC 6, 41**
See also CANR 3; CA 1-4R; DLB 40

**Redmon (Nightingale), Anne**
1943- ....................... **CLC 22**
See also Nightingale, Anne Redmon
See also DLB-Y 86

**Reed, Ishmael**
1938-........ **CLC 2, 3, 5, 6, 13, 32, 60**
See also CANR 25; CA 21-24R; DLB 2, 5,
33

**Reed, John (Silas)** 1887-1920 ...... **TCLC 9**
See also CA 106

**Reed, Lou** 1944-................. **CLC 21**

**Reeve, Clara** 1729-1807 ......... **NCLC 19**
See also DLB 39

**Reid, Christopher** 1949-........... **CLC 33**
See also DLB 40

**Reid Banks, Lynne** 1929-
See Banks, Lynne Reid
See also CANR 6, 22; CA 1-4R; SATA 22

**Reiner, Max** 1900-
See Caldwell, (Janet Miriam) Taylor
(Holland)

**Reizenstein, Elmer Leopold** 1892-1967
See Rice, Elmer

**Remark, Erich Paul** 1898-1970
See Remarque, Erich Maria

**Remarque, Erich Maria**
1898-1970 ................... **CLC 21**
See also CA 77-80; obituary CA 29-32R;
DLB 56

**Remizov, Alexey (Mikhailovich)**
1877-1957 .................. **TCLC 27**
See also CA 125

**Renan, Joseph Ernest**
1823-1892 ................. **NCLC 26**

**Renard, Jules** 1864-1910 ......... **TCLC 17**
See also CA 117

**Renault, Mary** 1905-1983 .... **CLC 3, 11, 17**
See also Challans, Mary
See also DLB-Y 83

**Rendell, Ruth** 1930-........... **CLC 28, 48**
See also Vine, Barbara
See also CA 109; DLB 87

**Renoir, Jean** 1894-1979 ........... **CLC 20**
See also CA 129; obituary CA 85-88

**Resnais, Alain** 1922-.............. **CLC 16**

**Reverdy, Pierre** 1899-1960 ........ **CLC 53**
See also CA 97-100; obituary CA 89-92

**Rexroth, Kenneth**
1905-1982 ...... **CLC 1, 2, 6, 11, 22, 49**
See also CANR 14; CA 5-8R;
obituary CA 107; DLB 16, 48; DLB-Y 82;
CDALB 1941-1968

**Reyes, Alfonso** 1889-1959 ........ **TCLC 33**

**Reyes y Basoalto, Ricardo Eliecer Neftali**
1904-1973
See Neruda, Pablo

**Reymont, Wladyslaw Stanislaw**
1867-1925 .................. **TCLC 5**
See also CA 104

**Reynolds, Jonathan** 1942?- ...... **CLC 6, 38**
See also CANR 28; CA 65-68

**Reynolds, (Sir) Joshua** 1723-1792.... **LC 15**

**Reynolds, Michael (Shane)** 1937- ... **CLC 44**
See also CANR 9; CA 65-68

**Reznikoff, Charles** 1894-1976 ...... **CLC 9**
See also CAP 2; CA 33-36;
obituary CA 61-64; DLB 28, 45

**Rezzori, Gregor von** 1914-......... **CLC 25**
See also CA 122

**Rhys, Jean**
1890-1979 ...... **CLC 2, 4, 6, 14, 19, 51**
See also CA 25-28R; obituary CA 85-88;
DLB 36

**Ribeiro, Darcy** 1922- ............. **CLC 34**
See also CA 33-36R

**Ribeiro, Joao Ubaldo (Osorio Pimentel)**
1941- ...................... **CLC 10**
See also CA 81-84

**Ribman, Ronald (Burt)** 1932- ....... **CLC 7**
See also CA 21-24R

**Rice, Anne** 1941- ................ **CLC 41**
See also CANR 12; CA 65-68

**Rice, Elmer** 1892-1967.......... **CLC 7, 49**
See also CAP 2; CA 21-22;
obituary CA 25-28R; DLB 4, 7

**Rice, Tim** 1944- ................. **CLC 21**
See also CA 103

**Rich, Adrienne (Cecile)**
1929- .......... **CLC 3, 6, 7, 11, 18, 36**
See also CANR 20; CA 9-12R; DLB 5, 67

**Richard, Keith** 1943- .............. **CLC 17**
See also CA 107

**Richards, David Adam** 1950-....... **CLC 59**
See also CA 93-96; DLB 53

**Richards, I(vor) A(rmstrong)**
1893-1979 ................ **CLC 14, 24**
See also CA 41-44R; obituary CA 89-92;
DLB 27

**Richards, Keith** 1943-
See Richard, Keith
See also CA 107

**Richardson, Dorothy (Miller)**
1873-1957 ................... **TCLC 3**
See also CA 104; DLB 36

**Richardson, Ethel** 1870-1946
See Richardson, Henry Handel
See also CA 105

**Richardson, Henry Handel**
1870-1946 ................... **TCLC 4**
See also Richardson, Ethel

**Richardson, Samuel** 1689-1761 ....... **LC 1**
See also DLB 39

**Richler, Mordecai**
1931- .......... **CLC 3, 5, 9, 13, 18, 46**
See also CLR 17; CA 65-68; SATA 27, 44;
DLB 53

**Richter, Conrad (Michael)**
1890-1968 ................... **CLC 30**
See also CANR 23; CA 5-8R;
obituary CA 25-28R; SATA 3; DLB 9

**Richter, Johann Paul Friedrich** 1763-1825
See Jean Paul

**Riddell, Mrs. J. H.** 1832-1906..... **TCLC 40**

**Riding, Laura** 1901-............. **CLC 3, 7**
See also Jackson, Laura (Riding)

**Riefenstahl, Berta Helene Amalia**
1902-...................... **CLC 16**
See also Riefenstahl, Leni
See also CA 108

**Riefenstahl, Leni** 1902- ........... **CLC 16**
See also Riefenstahl, Berta Helene Amalia
See also CA 108

**Rilke, Rainer Maria**
1875-1926 ........ **TCLC 1, 6, 19; PC 2**
See also CA 104, 132; DLB 81

**Rimbaud, (Jean Nicolas) Arthur**
1854-1891 ................. **NCLC 4**

**Ringwood, Gwen(dolyn Margaret) Pharis**
1910-1984 ................... **CLC 48**
See also obituary CA 112

**Rio, Michel** 19??-................. **CLC 43**

**Ritsos, Yannis** 1909-......... **CLC 6, 13, 31**
See also CA 77-80

**Ritter, Erika** 1948?-.............. **CLC 52**

**Rivera, Jose Eustasio** 1889-1928... **TCLC 35**

**Rivers, Conrad Kent**   1933-1968...... **CLC 1**
See also CA 85-88; DLB 41

**Rizal, Jose**   1861-1896.......... **NCLC 27**

**Roa Bastos, Augusto**   1917-........ **CLC 45**

**Robbe-Grillet, Alain**
1922-...... **CLC 1, 2, 4, 6, 8, 10, 14, 43**
See also CA 9-12R; DLB 83

**Robbins, Harold**   1916-............. **CLC 5**
See also CANR 26; CA 73-76

**Robbins, Thomas Eugene**   1936-
See Robbins, Tom
See also CA 81-84

**Robbins, Tom**   1936-......... **CLC 9, 32, 64**
See also Robbins, Thomas Eugene
See also CANR 29; CA 81-84; DLB-Y 80

**Robbins, Trina**   1938-............. **CLC 21**

**Roberts, (Sir) Charles G(eorge) D(ouglas)**
1860-1943 ................... **TCLC 8**
See also CA 105; SATA 29; DLB 92

**Roberts, Kate**   1891-1985 .......... **CLC 15**
See also CA 107; obituary CA 116

**Roberts, Keith (John Kingston)**
1935- ....................... **CLC 14**
See also CA 25-28R

**Roberts, Kenneth**   1885-1957 ...... **TCLC 23**
See also CA 109; DLB 9

**Roberts, Michele (B.)**   1949-........ **CLC 48**
See also CA 115

**Robinson, Edwin Arlington**
1869-1935 ............. **TCLC 5; PC 1**
See also CA 104; DLB 54;
CDALB 1865-1917

**Robinson, Henry Crabb**
1775-1867 ................. **NCLC 15**

**Robinson, Jill**   1936-.............. **CLC 10**
See also CA 102

**Robinson, Kim Stanley**   19??-....... **CLC 34**
See also CA 126

**Robinson, Marilynne**   1944-........ **CLC 25**
See also CA 116

**Robinson, Smokey**   1940- .......... **CLC 21**

**Robinson, William**   1940-
See Robinson, Smokey
See also CA 116

**Robison, Mary**   1949-............. **CLC 42**
See also CA 113, 116

**Roddenberry, Gene**   1921-.......... **CLC 17**
See also CANR 110; SATA 45

**Rodgers, Mary**   1931-............. **CLC 12**
See also CLR 20; CANR 8; CA 49-52;
SATA 8

**Rodgers, W(illiam) R(obert)**
1909-1969 ................... **CLC 7**
See also CA 85-88; DLB 20

**Rodriguez, Claudio**   1934-......... **CLC 10**

**Roethke, Theodore (Huebner)**
1908-1963 ...... **CLC 1, 3, 8, 11, 19, 46**
See also CA 81-84; CABS 2; SAAS 1;
DLB 5; CDALB 1941-1968

**Rogers, Sam**   1943-
See Shepard, Sam

**Rogers, Thomas (Hunton)**   1931-.... **CLC 57**
See also CA 89-92

**Rogers, Will(iam Penn Adair)**
1879-1935 .................. **TCLC 8**
See also CA 105; DLB 11

**Rogin, Gilbert**   1929-.............. **CLC 18**
See also CANR 15; CA 65-68

**Rohan, Koda**   1867-1947.......... **TCLC 22**
See also CA 121

**Rohmer, Eric**   1920- .............. **CLC 16**
See also Scherer, Jean-Marie Maurice

**Rohmer, Sax**   1883-1959.......... **TCLC 28**
See also Ward, Arthur Henry Sarsfield
See also CA 108; DLB 70

**Roiphe, Anne (Richardson)**
1935-....................... **CLC 3, 9**
See also CA 89-92; DLB-Y 80

**Rolfe, Frederick (William Serafino Austin**
**Lewis Mary)**   1860-1913...... **TCLC 12**
See also CA 107; DLB 34

**Rolland, Romain**   1866-1944...... **TCLC 23**
See also CA 118; DLB 65

**Rolvaag, O(le) E(dvart)**
1876-1931 .................. **TCLC 17**
See also CA 117; DLB 9

**Romains, Jules**   1885-1972 .......... **CLC 7**
See also CA 85-88

**Romero, Jose Ruben**   1890-1952 ... **TCLC 14**
See also CA 114

**Ronsard, Pierre de**   1524-1585........ **LC 6**

**Rooke, Leon**   1934-............ **CLC 25, 34**
See also CANR 23; CA 25-28R

**Roper, William**   1498-1578.......... **LC 10**

**Rosa, Joao Guimaraes**   1908-1967... **CLC 23**
See also obituary CA 89-92

**Rosen, Richard (Dean)**   1949-....... **CLC 39**
See also CA 77-80

**Rosenberg, Isaac**   1890-1918....... **TCLC 12**
See also CA 107; DLB 20

**Rosenblatt, Joe**   1933-............ **CLC 15**
See also Rosenblatt, Joseph

**Rosenblatt, Joseph**   1933-
See Rosenblatt, Joe
See also CA 89-92

**Rosenfeld, Samuel**   1896-1963
See Tzara, Tristan
See also obituary CA 89-92

**Rosenthal, M(acha) L(ouis)**   1917-... **CLC 28**
See also CAAS 6; CANR 4; CA 1-4R;
SATA 59; DLB 5

**Ross, (James) Sinclair**   1908-....... **CLC 13**
See also CA 73-76; DLB 88

**Rossetti, Christina Georgina**
1830-1894 .................. **NCLC 2**
See also SATA 20; DLB 35

**Rossetti, Dante Gabriel**
1828-1882 .................. **NCLC 4**
See also DLB 35

**Rossetti, Gabriel Charles Dante**   1828-1882
See Rossetti, Dante Gabriel

**Rossner, Judith (Perelman)**
1935-..................... **CLC 6, 9, 29**
See also CANR 18; CA 17-20R; DLB 6

**Rostand, Edmond (Eugene Alexis)**
1868-1918 ................ **TCLC 6, 37**
See also CA 104, 126

**Roth, Henry**   1906-........... **CLC 2, 6, 11**
See also CAP 1; CA 11-12; DLB 28

**Roth, Joseph**   1894-1939.......... **TCLC 33**
See also DLB 85

**Roth, Philip (Milton)**
1933- ...... **CLC 1, 2, 3, 4, 6, 9, 15, 22,
31, 47**
See also CANR 1, 22; CA 1-4R; DLB 2, 28;
DLB-Y 82

**Rothenberg, James**   1931-.......... **CLC 57**

**Rothenberg, Jerome**   1931-....... **CLC 6, 57**
See also CANR 1; CA 45-48; DLB 5

**Roumain, Jacques**   1907-1944...... **TCLC 19**
See also CA 117

**Rourke, Constance (Mayfield)**
1885-1941 .................. **TCLC 12**
See also YABC 1; CA 107

**Rousseau, Jean-Baptiste**   1671-1741 ... **LC 9**

**Rousseau, Jean-Jacques**   1712-1778... **LC 14**

**Roussel, Raymond**   1877-1933 ..... **TCLC 20**
See also CA 117

**Rovit, Earl (Herbert)**   1927-........ **CLC 7**
See also CANR 12; CA 5-8R

**Rowe, Nicholas**   1674-1718......... **LC 8**

**Rowson, Susanna Haswell**
1762-1824 ................. **NCLC 5**
See also DLB 37

**Roy, Gabrielle**   1909-1983....... **CLC 10, 14**
See also CANR 5; CA 53-56;
obituary CA 110; DLB 68

**Rozewicz, Tadeusz**   1921-........ **CLC 9, 23**
See also CA 108

**Ruark, Gibbons**   1941- .............. **CLC 3**
See also CANR 14; CA 33-36R

**Rubens, Bernice**   192?- ......... **CLC 19, 31**
See also CA 25-28R; DLB 14

**Rudkin, (James) David**   1936- ...... **CLC 14**
See also CA 89-92; DLB 13

**Rudnik, Raphael**   1933-............. **CLC 7**
See also CA 29-32R

**Ruiz, Jose Martinez**   1874-1967
See Azorin

**Rukeyser, Muriel**
1913-1980 ........... **CLC 6, 10, 15, 27**
See also CANR 26; CA 5-8R;
obituary CA 93-96; obituary SATA 22;
DLB 48

**Rule, Jane (Vance)**   1931-.......... **CLC 27**
See also CANR 12; CA 25-28R; DLB 60

**Rulfo, Juan**   1918-1986............. **CLC 8**
See also CANR 26; CA 85-88;
obituary CA 118

**Runyon, (Alfred) Damon**
1880-1946 ................. **TCLC 10**
See also CA 107; DLB 11

**Rush, Norman**   1933-.............. **CLC 44**
See also CA 121, 126

**Rushdie, (Ahmed) Salman**
1947-............ **CLC 23, 31, 55, 59**
See also CA 108, 111

**Rushforth, Peter (Scott)**   1945- ..... **CLC 19**
See also CA 101**

Author Index

Ruskin, John 1819-1900......... TCLC 20
See also CA 114; SATA 24; DLB 55

Russ, Joanna 1937-............... CLC 15
See also CANR 11; CA 25-28R; DLB 8

Russell, George William 1867-1935
See A. E.
See also CA 104

Russell, (Henry) Ken(neth Alfred)
1927-........................ CLC 16
See also CA 105

Russell, Willy 1947-............. CLC 60

Rutherford, Mark 1831-1913..... TCLC 25
See also CA 121; DLB 18

Ruyslinck, Ward 1929-........... CLC 14

Ryan, Cornelius (John) 1920-1974 ... CLC 7
See also CA 69-72; obituary CA 53-56

Rybakov, Anatoli 1911?-....... CLC 23, 53
See also CA 126

Ryder, Jonathan 1927-
See Ludlum, Robert

Ryga, George 1932-............. CLC 14
See also CA 101; obituary CA 124; DLB 60

Séviné, Marquise de Marie de
Rabutin-Chantal 1626-1696..... LC 11

Saba, Umberto 1883-1957........ TCLC 33

Sabato, Ernesto 1911-......... CLC 10, 23
See also CA 97-100

Sachs, Marilyn (Stickle) 1927-..... CLC 35
See also CLR 2; CANR 13; CA 17-20R;
SAAS 2; SATA 3, 52

Sachs, Nelly 1891-1970 .......... CLC 14
See also CAP 2; CA 17-18;
obituary CA 25-28R

Sackler, Howard (Oliver)
1929-1982 .................. CLC 14
See also CA 61-64; obituary CA 108; DLB 7

Sade, Donatien Alphonse Francois, Comte de
1740-1814 .................. NCLC 3

Sadoff, Ira 1945-................. CLC 9
See also CANR 5, 21; CA 53-56

Safire, William 1929-............. CLC 10
See also CA 17-20R

Sagan, Carl (Edward) 1934-........ CLC 30
See also CANR 11; CA 25-28R; SATA 58

Sagan, Francoise
1935-............. CLC 3, 6, 9, 17, 36
See also Quoirez, Francoise
See also CANR 6; DLB 83

Sahgal, Nayantara (Pandit) 1927-... CLC 41
See also CANR 11; CA 9-12R

Saint, H(arry) F. 1941- ........... CLC 50

Sainte-Beuve, Charles Augustin
1804-1869 ................. NCLC 5

Sainte-Marie, Beverly 1941-1972?
See Sainte-Marie, Buffy
See also CA 107

Sainte-Marie, Buffy 1941-......... CLC 17
See also Sainte-Marie, Beverly

Saint-Exupery, Antoine (Jean Baptiste Marie
Roger) de 1900-1944 ......... TCLC 2
See also CLR 10; CA 108; SATA 20;
DLB 72

Saintsbury, George 1845-1933..... TCLC 31
See also DLB 57

Sait Faik (Abasiyanik)
1906-1954 ................. TCLC 23

Saki 1870-1916................. TCLC 3
See also Munro, H(ector) H(ugh)
See also CA 104

Salama, Hannu 1936-............. CLC 18

Salamanca, J(ack) R(ichard)
1922-..................... CLC 4, 15
See also CA 25-28R

Salinas, Pedro 1891-1951........ TCLC 17
See also CA 117

Salinger, J(erome) D(avid)
1919-....... CLC 1, 3, 8, 12, 56; SSC 2
See also CA 5-8R; DLB 2;
CDALB 1941-1968

Salter, James 1925-......... CLC 7, 52, 59
See also CA 73-76

Saltus, Edgar (Evertson)
1855-1921 ................. TCLC 8
See also CA 105

Saltykov, Mikhail Evgrafovich
1826-1889 ................. NCLC 16

Samarakis, Antonis 1919-.......... CLC 5
See also CA 25-28R

Sanchez, Florencio 1875-1910..... TCLC 37

Sanchez, Luis Rafael 1936-........ CLC 23

Sanchez, Sonia 1934-.............. CLC 5
See also CANR 24; CA 33-36R; SATA 22;
DLB 41

Sand, George 1804-1876.......... NCLC 2

Sandburg, Carl (August)
1878-1967 ... CLC 1, 4, 10, 15, 35; PC 2
See also CA 5-8R; obituary CA 25-28R;
SATA 8; DLB 17, 54; CDALB 1865-1917

Sandburg, Charles August 1878-1967
See Sandburg, Carl (August)

Sanders, (James) Ed(ward) 1939-... CLC 53
See also CANR 13; CA 15-16R, 103;
DLB 16

Sanders, Lawrence 1920-.......... CLC 41
See also CA 81-84

Sandoz, Mari (Susette) 1896-1966 .. CLC 28
See also CANR 17; CA 1-4R;
obituary CA 25-28R; SATA 5; DLB 9

Saner, Reg(inald Anthony) 1931- .... CLC 9
See also CA 65-68

Sannazaro, Jacopo 1456?-1530 ....... LC 8

Sansom, William 1912-1976....... CLC 2, 6
See also CA 5-8R; obituary CA 65-68

Santayana, George 1863-1952..... TCLC 40
See also CA 115; DLB 54, 71

Santiago, Danny 1911-............ CLC 33
See also CA 125

Santmyer, Helen Hooven
1895-1986 .................. CLC 33
See also CANR 15; CA 1-4R;
obituary CA 118; DLB-Y 84

Santos, Bienvenido N(uqui) 1911-... CLC 22
See also CANR 19; CA 101

Sappho c. 6th-century B.C.-....... CMLC 3

Sarduy, Severo 1937-.............. CLC 6
See also CA 89-92

Sargeson, Frank 1903-1982........ CLC 31
See also CA 106, 25-28R; obituary CA 106

Sarmiento, Felix Ruben Garcia 1867-1916
See Dario, Ruben
See also CA 104

Saroyan, William
1908-1981 ..... CLC 1, 8, 10, 29, 34, 56
See also CA 5-8R; obituary CA 103;
SATA 23; obituary SATA 24; DLB 7, 9;
DLB-Y 81

Sarraute, Nathalie
1902-........... CLC 1, 2, 4, 8, 10, 31
See also CANR 23; CA 9-12R; DLB 83

Sarton, Eleanore Marie 1912-
See Sarton, (Eleanor) May

Sarton, (Eleanor) May
1912-.................. CLC 4, 14, 49
See also CANR 1; CA 1-4R; SATA 36;
DLB 48; DLB-Y 81

Sartre, Jean-Paul (Charles Aymard)
1905-1980 ... CLC 1, 4, 7, 9, 13, 18, 24,
44, 50, 52
See also CANR 21; CA 9-12R;
obituary CA 97-100; DLB 72

Sassoon, Siegfried (Lorraine)
1886-1967 .................. CLC 36
See also CA 104; obituary CA 25-28R;
DLB 20

Saul, John (W. III) 1942-......... CLC 46
See also CANR 16; CA 81-84

Saura, Carlos 1932-.............. CLC 20
See also CA 114

Sauser-Hall, Frederic-Louis
1887-1961 .................. CLC 18
See also Cendrars, Blaise
See also CA 102; obituary CA 93-96

Savage, Thomas 1915-............. CLC 40
See also CA 126

Savan, Glenn 19??-............... CLC 50

Sayers, Dorothy L(eigh)
1893-1957 ................ TCLC 2, 15
See also CA 104, 119; DLB 10, 36, 77

Sayers, Valerie 19??-............. CLC 50

Sayles, John (Thomas)
1950-................... CLC 7, 10, 14
See also CA 57-60; DLB 44

Scammell, Michael 19??-.......... CLC 34

Scannell, Vernon 1922-........... CLC 49
See also CANR 8; CA 5-8R; DLB 27

Schaeffer, Susan Fromberg
1941-................... CLC 6, 11, 22
See also CANR 18; CA 49-52; SATA 22;
DLB 28

Schell, Jonathan 1943-............ CLC 35
See also CANR 12; CA 73-76

Schelling, Friedrich Wilhelm Joseph von
1775-1854 ................. NCLC 30
See also DLB 90

Scherer, Jean-Marie Maurice 1920-
See Rohmer, Eric
See also CA 110

Schevill, James (Erwin) 1920-....... CLC 7
See also CA 5-8R

**Schisgal, Murray (Joseph)** 1926-..... **CLC 6**
See also CA 21-24R

**Schlee, Ann** 1934-............... **CLC 35**
See also CA 101; SATA 36, 44

**Schlegel, August Wilhelm von**
1767-1845 ................. **NCLC 15**

**Schlegel, Johann Elias (von)**
1719?-1749..................... **LC 5**

**Schmidt, Arno** 1914-1979.......... **CLC 56**
See also obituary CA 109; DLB 69

**Schmitz, Ettore** 1861-1928
See Svevo, Italo
See also CA 104, 122

**Schnackenberg, Gjertrud** 1953-..... **CLC 40**
See also CA 116

**Schneider, Leonard Alfred** 1925-1966
See Bruce, Lenny
See also CA 89-92

**Schnitzler, Arthur** 1862-1931 ...... **TCLC 4**
See also CA 104; DLB 81

**Schorer, Mark** 1908-1977 .......... **CLC 9**
See also CANR 7; CA 5-8R;
obituary CA 73-76

**Schrader, Paul (Joseph)** 1946-...... **CLC 26**
See also CA 37-40R; DLB 44

**Schreiner (Cronwright), Olive (Emilie**
**Albertina)** 1855-1920......... **TCLC 9**
See also CA 105; DLB 18

**Schulberg, Budd (Wilson)**
1914-...................... **CLC 7, 48**
See also CANR 19; CA 25-28R; DLB 6, 26,
28; DLB-Y 81

**Schulz, Bruno** 1892-1942.......... **TCLC 5**
See also CA 115, 123

**Schulz, Charles M(onroe)** 1922-.... **CLC 12**
See also CANR 6; CA 9-12R; SATA 10

**Schuyler, James (Marcus)**
1923-...................... **CLC 5, 23**
See also CA 101; DLB 5

**Schwartz, Delmore**
1913-1966 ........... **CLC 2, 4, 10, 45**
See also CAP 2; CA 17-18;
obituary CA 25-28R; DLB 28, 48

**Schwartz, John Burnham** 1925- .... **CLC 59**

**Schwartz, Lynne Sharon** 1939-..... **CLC 31**
See also CA 103

**Schwarz-Bart, Andre** 1928-....... **CLC 2, 4**
See also CA 89-92

**Schwarz-Bart, Simone** 1938-........ **CLC 7**
See also CA 97-100

**Schwob, (Mayer Andre) Marcel**
1867-1905 ................. **TCLC 20**
See also CA 117

**Sciascia, Leonardo**
1921-1989 ............ **CLC 8, 9, 41**
See also CA 85-88

**Scoppettone, Sandra** 1936-...... **CLC 26**
See also CA 5-8R; SATA 9

**Scorsese, Martin** 1942- .......... **CLC 20**
See also CA 110, 114

**Scotland, Jay** 1932-
See Jakes, John (William)

**Scott, Duncan Campbell**
1862-1947 ................. **TCLC 6**
See also CA 104; DLB 92

**Scott, Evelyn** 1893-1963.......... **CLC 43**
See also CA 104; obituary CA 112; DLB 9,
48

**Scott, F(rancis) R(eginald)**
1899-1985 ................. **CLC 22**
See also CA 101; obituary CA 114; DLB 88

**Scott, Joanna** 19??-............... **CLC 50**
See also CA 126

**Scott, Paul (Mark)** 1920-1978.... **CLC 9, 60**
See also CA 81-84; obituary CA 77-80;
DLB 14

**Scott, Sir Walter** 1771-1832 ..... **NCLC 15**
See also YABC 2

**Scribe, (Augustin) Eugene**
1791-1861 ................. **NCLC 16**

**Scudery, Madeleine de** 1607-1701..... **LC 2**

**Sealy, I. Allan** 1951- ............. **CLC 55**

**Seare, Nicholas** 1925-
See Trevanian; Whitaker, Rodney

**Sebestyen, Igen** 1924-
See Sebestyen, Ouida

**Sebestyen, Ouida** 1924-........... **CLC 30**
See also CLR 17; CA 107; SATA 39

**Sedgwick, Catharine Maria**
1789-1867 ................. **NCLC 19**
See also DLB 1, 74

**Seelye, John** 1931-............... **CLC 7**
See also CA 97-100

**Seferiades, Giorgos Stylianou** 1900-1971
See Seferis, George
See also CANR 5; CA 5-8R;
obituary CA 33-36R

**Seferis, George** 1900-1971....... **CLC 5, 11**
See also Seferiades, Giorgos Stylianou

**Segal, Erich (Wolf)** 1937- ....... **CLC 3, 10**
See also CANR 20; CA 25-28R; DLB-Y 86

**Seger, Bob** 1945-................. **CLC 35**

**Seger, Robert Clark** 1945-
See Seger, Bob

**Seghers, Anna** 1900-1983....... **CLC 7, 110**
See also Radvanyi, Netty Reiling
See also DLB 69

**Seidel, Frederick (Lewis)** 1936-..... **CLC 18**
See also CANR 8; CA 13-16R; DLB-Y 84

**Seifert, Jaroslav** 1901-1986..... **CLC 34, 44**
See also CA 127

**Sei Shonagon** c. 966-1017?........ **CMLC 6**

**Selby, Hubert, Jr.** 1928- .....**CLC 1, 2, 4, 8**
See also CA 13-16R; DLB 2

**Senacour, Etienne Pivert de**
1770-1846 ................. **NCLC 16**

**Sender, Ramon (Jose)** 1902-1982 .... **CLC 8**
See also CANR 8; CA 5-8R;
obituary CA 105

**Seneca, Lucius Annaeus**
4 B.C.-65 A.D. .............. **CMLC 6**

**Senghor, Léopold Sédar** 1906-...... **CLC 54**
See also CA 116

**Serling, (Edward) Rod(man)**
1924-1975 .................. **CLC 30**
See also CA 65-68; obituary CA 57-60;
DLB 26

**Serpieres** 1907-
See Guillevic, (Eugene)

**Service, Robert W(illiam)**
1874-1958 ................. **TCLC 15**
See also CA 115; SATA 20

**Seth, Vikram** 1952-............... **CLC 43**
See also CA 121, 127

**Seton, Cynthia Propper**
1926-1982 ................. **CLC 27**
See also CANR 7; CA 5-8R;
obituary CA 108

**Seton, Ernest (Evan) Thompson**
1860-1946 ................. **TCLC 31**
See also CA 109; SATA 18; DLB 92

**Settle, Mary Lee** 1918- ........ **CLC 19, 61**
See also CAAS 1; CA 89-92; DLB 6

**Sevigne, Marquise de Marie de**
**Rabutin-Chantal** 1626-1696..... **LC 11**

**Sexton, Anne (Harvey)**
1928-1974 ... **CLC 2, 4, 6, 8, 10, 15, 53;**
**PC 2**
See also CANR 3; CA 1-4R;
obituary CA 53-56; CABS 2; SATA 10;
DLB 5; CDALB 1941-1968

**Shaara, Michael (Joseph)** 1929- .... **CLC 15**
See also CA 102; obituary CA 125;
DLB-Y 83

**Shackleton, C. C.** 1925-
See Aldiss, Brian W(ilson)

**Shacochis, Bob** 1951-............. **CLC 39**
See also CA 119, 124

**Shaffer, Anthony** 1926- .......... **CLC 19**
See also CA 110, 116; DLB 13

**Shaffer, Peter (Levin)**
1926-........... **CLC 5, 14, 18, 37, 60**
See also CANR 25; CA 25-28R; DLB 13

**Shalamov, Varlam (Tikhonovich)**
1907?-1982................. **CLC 18**
See also obituary CA 105

**Shamlu, Ahmad** 1925- ............ **CLC 10**

**Shammas, Anton** 1951-............. **CLC 55**

**Shange, Ntozake** 1948-....... **CLC 8, 25, 38**
See also CA 85-88; DLB 38

**Shapcott, Thomas W(illiam)** 1935- .. **CLC 38**
See also CA 69-72

**Shapiro, Karl (Jay)** 1913- ..**CLC 4, 8, 15, 53**
See also CAAS 6; CANR 1; CA 1-4R;
DLB 48

**Sharp, William** 1855-1905 ........ **TCLC 39**

**Sharpe, Tom** 1928-............... **CLC 36**
See also CA 114; DLB 14

**Shaw, (George) Bernard**
1856-1950 ............. **TCLC 3, 9, 21**
See also CA 104, 109, 119; DLB 10, 57

**Shaw, Henry Wheeler**
1818-1885 ................. **NCLC 15**
See also DLB 11

Shaw, Irwin 1913-1984...... **CLC 7, 23, 34**
See also CANR 21; CA 13-16R;
obituary CA 112; DLB 6; DLB-Y 84;
CDALB 1941-1968

Shaw, Robert 1927-1978 ........... **CLC 5**
See also CANR 4; CA 1-4R;
obituary CA 81-84; DLB 13, 14

Shawn, Wallace 1943- ............ **CLC 41**
See also CA 112

Sheed, Wilfrid (John Joseph)
1930- ............... **CLC 2, 4, 10, 53**
See also CA 65-68; DLB 6

Sheffey, Asa 1913-1980
See Hayden, Robert (Earl)

Sheldon, Alice (Hastings) B(radley)
1915-1987
See Tiptree, James, Jr.
See also CA 108; obituary CA 122

Shelley, Mary Wollstonecraft Godwin
1797-1851 ............... **NCLC 14**
See also SATA 29

Shelley, Percy Bysshe
1792-1822 ................. **NCLC 18**

Shepard, Jim 19??-................ **CLC 36**

Shepard, Lucius 19??-............. **CLC 34**
See also CA 128

Shepard, Sam
1943- ........ **CLC 4, 6, 17, 34, 41, 44**
See also CANR 22; CA 69-72; DLB 7

Shepherd, Michael 1927-
See Ludlum, Robert

Sherburne, Zoa (Morin) 1912-...... **CLC 30**
See also CANR 3; CA 1-4R; SATA 3

Sheridan, Frances 1724-1766........ **LC 7**
See also DLB 39, 84

Sheridan, Richard Brinsley
1751-1816 ............. **NCLC 5; DC 1**
See also DLB 89

Sherman, Jonathan Marc 1970?-.... **CLC 55**

Sherman, Martin 19??-............. **CLC 19**
See also CA 116

Sherwin, Judith Johnson 1936-... **CLC 7, 15**
See also CA 25-28R

Sherwood, Robert E(mmet)
1896-1955 ................... **TCLC 3**
See also CA 104; DLB 7, 26

Shiel, M(atthew) P(hipps)
1865-1947 ................... **TCLC 8**
See also CA 106

Shiga, Naoya 1883-1971........... **CLC 33**
See also CA 101; obituary CA 33-36R

Shimazaki, Haruki 1872-1943
See Shimazaki, Toson
See also CA 105

Shimazaki, Toson 1872-1943....... **TCLC 5**
See also Shimazaki, Haruki

Sholokhov, Mikhail (Aleksandrovich)
1905-1984 ................. **CLC 7, 15**
See also CA 101; obituary CA 112;
SATA 36

Sholom Aleichem 1859-1916 .... **TCLC 1, 35**
See also Rabinovitch, Sholem

Shreve, Susan Richards 1939-...... **CLC 23**
See also CAAS 5; CANR 5; CA 49-52;
SATA 41, 46

Shue, Larry 1946-1985............ **CLC 52**
See also obituary CA 117

Shulman, Alix Kates 1932- ...... **CLC 2, 10**
See also CA 29-32R; SATA 7

Shuster, Joe 1914- ............... **CLC 21**

Shute (Norway), Nevil 1899-1960... **CLC 30**
See also Norway, Nevil Shute
See also CA 102; obituary CA 93-96

Shuttle, Penelope (Diane) 1947-..... **CLC 7**
See also CA 93-96; DLB 14, 40

Siegel, Jerome 1914- ............. **CLC 21**
See also CA 116

Sienkiewicz, Henryk (Adam Aleksander Pius)
1846-1916 .................. **TCLC 3**
See also CA 104

Sigal, Clancy 1926-................ **CLC 7**
See also CA 1-4R

Sigourney, Lydia (Howard Huntley)
1791-1865 .................. **NCLC 21**
See also DLB 1, 42, 73

Siguenza y Gongora, Carlos de
1645-1700 ..................... **LC 8**

Sigurjonsson, Johann 1880-1919... **TCLC 27**

Sikelianos, Angeles 1884-1951..... **TCLC 39**

Silkin, Jon 1930- ............. **CLC 2, 6, 43**
See also CAAS 5; CA 5-8R; DLB 27

Silko, Leslie Marmon 1948- ....... **CLC 23**
See also CA 115, 122

Sillanpaa, Franz Eemil 1888-1964... **CLC 19**
See also CA 129; obituary CA 93-96

Sillitoe, Alan
1928- .......... **CLC 1, 3, 6, 10, 19, 57**
See also CAAS 2; CANR 8, 26; CA 9-12R;
DLB 14

Silone, Ignazio 1900-1978 .......... **CLC 4**
See also CAAS 2; CANR 26; CAP 2;
CA 25-28, 11-12R,; obituary CA 81-84

Silver, Joan Micklin 1935- ........ **CLC 20**
See also CA 114, 121

Silverberg, Robert 1935- ........... **CLC 7**
See also CAAS 3; CANR 1, 20; CA 1-4R;
SATA 13; DLB 8

Silverstein, Alvin 1933- ........... **CLC 17**
See also CANR 2; CA 49-52; SATA 8

Silverstein, Virginia B(arbara Opshelor)
1937- ..................... **CLC 17**
See also CANR 2; CA 49-52; SATA 8

Simak, Clifford D(onald)
1904-1988 ................. **CLC 1, 55**
See also CANR 1; CA 1-4R;
obituary CA 125; DLB 8

Simenon, Georges (Jacques Christian)
1903-1989 ....... **CLC 1, 2, 3, 8, 18, 47**
See also CA 85-88; obituary CA 129;
DLB 72

Simenon, Paul 1956?-
See The Clash

Simic, Charles 1938-....... **CLC 6, 9, 22, 49**
See also CAAS 4; CANR 12; CA 29-32R

Simmons, Charles (Paul) 1924-..... **CLC 57**
See also CA 89-92

Simmons, Dan 1948-............. **CLC 44**

Simmons, James (Stewart Alexander)
1933- ...................... **CLC 43**
See also CA 105; DLB 40

Simms, William Gilmore
1806-1870 ................. **NCLC 3**
See also DLB 3, 30, 59, 73

Simon, Carly 1945-.............. **CLC 26**
See also CA 105

Simon, Claude (Henri Eugene)
1913- ................**CLC 4, 9, 15, 39**
See also CA 89-92; DLB 83

Simon, (Marvin) Neil
1927- ...............**CLC 6, 11, 31, 39**
See also CA 21-24R; DLB 7

Simon, Paul 1941- ............... **CLC 17**
See also CA 116

Simonon, Paul 1956?-
See The Clash

Simpson, Louis (Aston Marantz)
1923-.................**CLC 4, 7, 9, 32**
See also CAAS 4; CANR 1; CA 1-4R;
DLB 5

Simpson, Mona (Elizabeth) 1957-... **CLC 44**
See also CA 122

Simpson, N(orman) F(rederick)
1919-...................... **CLC 29**
See also CA 11-14R; DLB 13

Sinclair, Andrew (Annandale)
1935-..................... **CLC 2, 14**
See also CAAS 5; CANR 14; CA 9-12R;
DLB 14

Sinclair, Mary Amelia St. Clair 1865?-1946
See Sinclair, May
See also CA 104

Sinclair, May 1865?-1946 ...... **TCLC 3, 11**
See also Sinclair, Mary Amelia St. Clair
See also DLB 36

Sinclair, Upton (Beall)
1878-1968 ...........**CLC 1, 11, 15, 63**
See also CANR 7; CA 5-8R;
obituary CA 25-28R; SATA 9; DLB 9

Singer, Isaac Bashevis
1904- .... **CLC 1, 3, 6, 9, 11, 15, 23, 38;**
　　　　　　　　　　　　　　　　**SSC 3**
See also CLR 1; CANR 1; CA 1-4R;
SATA 3, 27; DLB 6, 28, 52;
CDALB 1941-1968

Singer, Israel Joshua 1893-1944... **TCLC 33**

Singh, Khushwant 1915-........... **CLC 11**
See also CANR 6; CA 9-12R

Sinyavsky, Andrei (Donatevich)
1925-...................... **CLC 8**
See also CA 85-88

Sirin, V.
See Nabokov, Vladimir (Vladimirovich)

Sissman, L(ouis) E(dward)
1928-1976 ................. **CLC 9, 18**
See also CANR 13; CA 21-24R;
obituary CA 65-68; DLB 5

Sisson, C(harles) H(ubert) 1914-..... **CLC 8**
See also CAAS 3; CANR 3; CA 1-4R;
DLB 27

Sitwell, (Dame) Edith 1887-1964... **CLC 2, 9**
See also CA 9-12R; DLB 20

**Sjoewall, Maj**  1935-
See Wahloo, Per
See also CA 61-64, 65-68

**Sjowall, Maj**  1935-
See Wahloo, Per

**Skelton, Robin**  1925- . . . . . . . . . . . . **CLC 13**
See also CAAS 5; CA 5-8R; DLB 27, 53

**Skolimowski, Jerzy**  1938- . . . . . . . . **CLC 20**

**Skolimowski, Yurek**  1938-
See Skolimowski, Jerzy

**Skram, Amalie (Bertha)**
1847-1905 . . . . . . . . . . . . . . . . . **TCLC 25**

**Skrine, Mary Nesta**  1904-
See Keane, Molly

**Skvorecky, Josef (Vaclav)**
1924- . . . . . . . . . . . . . . . . . . . . **CLC 15, 39**
See also CAAS 1; CANR 10; CA 61-64

**Slade, Bernard**  1930- . . . . . . . . . **CLC 11, 46**
See also Newbound, Bernard Slade
See also DLB 53

**Slaughter, Carolyn**  1946- . . . . . . . . . . **CLC 56**
See also CA 85-88

**Slaughter, Frank G(ill)**  1908- . . . . . . **CLC 29**
See also CANR 5; CA 5-8R

**Slavitt, David (R.)**  1935- . . . . . . . . **CLC 5, 14**
See also CAAS 3; CA 21-24R; DLB 5, 6

**Slesinger, Tess**  1905-1945 . . . . . . . . **TCLC 10**
See also CA 107

**Slessor, Kenneth**  1901-1971 . . . . . . . . **CLC 14**
See also CA 102; obituary CA 89-92

**Slowacki, Juliusz**  1809-1849 . . . . . **NCLC 15**

**Smart, Christopher**  1722-1771 . . . . . . . **LC 3**

**Smart, Elizabeth**  1913-1986 . . . . . . . . **CLC 54**
See also CA 81-84; obituary CA 118;
DLB 88

**Smiley, Jane (Graves)**  1949- . . . . . . . **CLC 53**
See also CA 104

**Smith, A(rthur) J(ames) M(arshall)**
1902-1980 . . . . . . . . . . . . . . . . . . **CLC 15**
See also CANR 4; CA 1-4R;
obituary CA 102; DLB 88

**Smith, Betty (Wehner)**  1896-1972 . . . **CLC 19**
See also CA 5-8R; obituary CA 33-36R;
SATA 6; DLB-Y 82

**Smith, Cecil Lewis Troughton**  1899-1966
See Forester, C(ecil) S(cott)

**Smith, Charlotte (Turner)**
1749-1806 . . . . . . . . . . . . . . . . . **NCLC 23**
See also DLB 39

**Smith, Clark Ashton**  1893-1961 . . . . **CLC 43**

**Smith, Dave**  1942- . . . . . . . . . . . **CLC 22, 42**
See also Smith, David (Jeddie)
See also CAAS 7; CANR 1; DLB 5

**Smith, David (Jeddie)**  1942-
See Smith, Dave
See also CANR 1; CA 49-52

**Smith, Florence Margaret**  1902-1971
See Smith, Stevie
See also CAP 2; CA 17-18;
obituary CA 29-32R

**Smith, Iain Crichton**  1928- . . . . . . . . **CLC 64**
See also DLB 40

**Smith, John**  1580?-1631 . . . . . . . . . . . . **LC 9**
See also DLB 24, 30

**Smith, Lee**  1944- . . . . . . . . . . . . . . . . **CLC 25**
See also CA 114, 119; DLB-Y 83

**Smith, Martin Cruz**  1942- . . . . . . . . **CLC 25**
See also CANR 6; CA 85-88

**Smith, Martin William**  1942-
See Smith, Martin Cruz

**Smith, Mary-Ann Tirone**  1944- . . . . . **CLC 39**
See also CA 118

**Smith, Patti**  1946- . . . . . . . . . . . . . . **CLC 12**
See also CA 93-96

**Smith, Pauline (Urmson)**
1882-1959 . . . . . . . . . . . . . . . . . **TCLC 25**
See also CA 29-32R; SATA 27

**Smith, Rosamond**  1938-
See Oates, Joyce Carol

**Smith, Sara Mahala Redway**  1900-1972
See Benson, Sally

**Smith, Stevie**  1902-1971 . . . . **CLC 3, 8, 25, 44**
See also Smith, Florence Margaret
See also DLB 20

**Smith, Wilbur (Addison)**  1933- . . . . . **CLC 33**
See also CANR 7; CA 13-16R

**Smith, William Jay**  1918- . . . . . . . . . **CLC 6**
See also CA 5-8R; SATA 2; DLB 5

**Smolenskin, Peretz**  1842-1885 . . . . **NCLC 30**

**Smollett, Tobias (George)**  1721-1771 . . **LC 2**
See also DLB 39

**Snodgrass, W(illiam) D(e Witt)**
1926- . . . . . . . . . . . . . . . **CLC 2, 6, 10, 18**
See also CANR 6; CA 1-4R; DLB 5

**Snow, C(harles) P(ercy)**
1905-1980 . . . . . . . **CLC 1, 4, 6, 9, 13, 19**
See also CA 5-8R; obituary CA 101;
DLB 15, 77

**Snyder, Gary (Sherman)**
1930- . . . . . . . . . . . . . . **CLC 1, 2, 5, 9, 32**
See also CANR 30; CA 17-20R; DLB 5, 16

**Snyder, Zilpha Keatley**  1927- . . . . . . **CLC 17**
See also CA 9-12R; SAAS 2; SATA 1, 28

**Sobol, Joshua**  19??- . . . . . . . . . . . . . . **CLC 60**

**Soderberg. Hjalmar**  1869-1941 . . . . **TCLC 39**

**Sodergran, Edith**  1892-1923 . . . . . . . **TCLC 31**

**Sokolov, Raymond**  1941- . . . . . . . . . . **CLC 7**
See also CA 85-88

**Sologub, Fyodor**  1863-1927 . . . . . . . . **TCLC 9**
See also Teternikov, Fyodor Kuzmich
See also CA 104

**Solomos, Dionysios**  1798-1857 . . . **NCLC 15**

**Solwoska, Mara**  1929-
See French, Marilyn
See also CANR 3; CA 69-72

**Solzhenitsyn, Aleksandr I(sayevich)**
1918- . . . **CLC 1, 2, 4, 7, 9, 10, 18, 26, 34**
See also CA 69-72

**Somers, Jane**  1919-
See Lessing, Doris (May)

**Sommer, Scott**  1951- . . . . . . . . . . . . . **CLC 25**
See also CA 106

**Sondheim, Stephen (Joshua)**
1930- . . . . . . . . . . . . . . . . . . . **CLC 30, 39**
See also CA 103

**Sontag, Susan**  1933- . . . **CLC 1, 2, 10, 13, 31**
See also CA 17-20R; DLB 2, 67

**Sophocles**
c. 496? B.C.-c. 406? B.C. . . . . . **CMLC 2;**
**DC 1**

**Sorrentino, Gilbert**
1929- . . . . . . . . . . . . **CLC 3, 7, 14, 22, 40**
See also CANR 14; CA 77-80; DLB 5;
DLB-Y 80

**Soto, Gary**  1952- . . . . . . . . . . . . . . . . **CLC 32**
See also CA 119, 125; DLB 82

**Souster, (Holmes) Raymond**
1921- . . . . . . . . . . . . . . . . . . . . **CLC 5, 14**
See also CANR 13; CA 13-16R; DLB 88

**Southern, Terry**  1926- . . . . . . . . . . . . . **CLC 7**
See also CANR 1; CA 1-4R; DLB 2

**Southey, Robert**  1774-1843 . . . . . . **NCLC 8**
See also SATA 54

**Southworth, Emma Dorothy Eliza Nevitte**
1819-1899 . . . . . . . . . . . . . . . . **NCLC 26**

**Soyinka, Akinwande Oluwole**  1934-
See Soyinka, Wole

**Soyinka, Wole**  1934- . . **CLC 3, 5, 14, 36, 44**
See also CA 13-16R; DLB-Y 86

**Spackman, W(illiam) M(ode)**
1905- . . . . . . . . . . . . . . . . . . . . . . **CLC 46**
See also CA 81-84

**Spacks, Barry**  1931- . . . . . . . . . . . . . . **CLC 14**
See also CA 29-32R

**Spanidou, Irini**  1946- . . . . . . . . . . . . . **CLC 44**

**Spark, Muriel (Sarah)**
1918- . . . . . . . . **CLC 2, 3, 5, 8, 13, 18, 40**
See also CANR 12; CA 5-8R; DLB 15

**Spencer, Elizabeth**  1921- . . . . . . . . . . **CLC 22**
See also CA 13-16R; SATA 14; DLB 6

**Spencer, Scott**  1945- . . . . . . . . . . . . . . **CLC 30**
See also CA 113; DLB-Y 86

**Spender, Stephen (Harold)**
1909- . . . . . . . . . . . . . . **CLC 1, 2, 5, 10, 41**
See also CA 9-12R; DLB 20

**Spengler, Oswald**  1880-1936 . . . . . . **TCLC 25**
See also CA 118

**Spenser, Edmund**  1552?-1599 . . . . . . . . **LC 5**

**Spicer, Jack**  1925-1965 . . . . . . . . . **CLC 8, 18**
See also CA 85-88; DLB 5, 16

**Spielberg, Peter**  1929- . . . . . . . . . . . . . **CLC 6**
See also CANR 4; CA 5-8R; DLB-Y 81

**Spielberg, Steven**  1947- . . . . . . . . . . . **CLC 20**
See also CA 77-80; SATA 32

**Spillane, Frank Morrison**  1918-
See Spillane, Mickey
See also CA 25-28R

**Spillane, Mickey**  1918- . . . . . . . . . **CLC 3, 13**
See also Spillane, Frank Morrison

**Spinoza, Benedictus de**  1632-1677 . . . . **LC 9**

**Spinrad, Norman (Richard)**  1940- . . . **CLC 46**
See also CANR 20; CA 37-40R; DLB 8

**Spitteler, Carl (Friedrich Georg)**
1845-1924 . . . . . . . . . . . . . . . . . **TCLC 12**
See also CA 109

**Spivack, Kathleen (Romola Drucker)**
1938- . . . . . . . . . . . . . . . . . . . . . . **CLC 6**
See also CA 49-52

**Spoto, Donald** 1941-.............. **CLC 39**
See also CANR 11; CA 65-68

**Springsteen, Bruce** 1949-.......... **CLC 17**
See also CA 111

**Spurling, Hilary** 1940-............ **CLC 34**
See also CANR 25; CA 104

**Squires, (James) Radcliffe** 1917-.... **CLC 51**
See also CANR 6, 21; CA 1-4R

**Stael-Holstein, Anne Louise Germaine Necker,
Baronne de** 1766-1817....... **NCLC 3**

**Stafford, Jean** 1915-1979...... **CLC 4, 7, 19**
See also CANR 3; CA 1-4R;
obituary CA 85-88; obituary SATA 22;
DLB 2

**Stafford, William (Edgar)**
1914-.................. **CLC 4, 7, 29**
See also CAAS 3; CANR 5, 22; CA 5-8R;
DLB 5

**Stannard, Martin** 1947-........... **CLC 44**

**Stanton, Maura** 1946-............ **CLC 9**
See also CANR 15; CA 89-92

**Stapledon, (William) Olaf**
1886-1950.................**TCLC 22**
See also CA 111; DLB 15

**Starbuck, George (Edwin)** 1931-.... **CLC 53**
See also CANR 23; CA 21-22R

**Stark, Richard** 1933-
See Westlake, Donald E(dwin)

**Stead, Christina (Ellen)**
1902-1983.............**CLC 2, 5, 8, 32**
See also CA 13-16R; obituary CA 109

**Steele, Timothy (Reid)** 1948-....... **CLC 45**
See also CANR 16; CA 93-96

**Steffens, (Joseph) Lincoln**
1866-1936.................**TCLC 20**
See also CA 117; SAAS 1

**Stegner, Wallace (Earle)** 1909-... **CLC 9, 49**
See also CANR 1, 21; CA 1-4R; DLB 9

**Stein, Gertrude** 1874-1946... **TCLC 1, 6, 28**
See also CA 104; DLB 4, 54, 86;
CDALB 1917-1929

**Steinbeck, John (Ernst)**
1902-1968..... **CLC 1, 5, 9, 13, 21, 34,
45, 59**
See also CANR 1; CA 1-4R;
obituary CA 25-28R; SATA 9; DLB 7, 9;
DLB-DS 2; CDALB 1929-1941

**Steinem, Gloria** 1934-............. **CLC 63**
See also CANR 28; CA 53-56

**Steiner, George** 1929-............. **CLC 24**
See also CA 73-76; DLB 67

**Steiner, Rudolf(us Josephus Laurentius)**
1861-1925 .................. **TCLC 13**
See also CA 107

**Stendhal** 1783-1842............. **NCLC 23**

**Stephen, Leslie** 1832-1904....... **TCLC 23**
See also CANR 9; CA 21-24R, 123;
DLB 57

**Stephens, James** 1882?-1950....... **TCLC 4**
See also CA 104; DLB 19

**Stephens, Reed**
See Donaldson, Stephen R.

**Steptoe, Lydia** 1892-1982
See Barnes, Djuna

**Sterling, George** 1869-1926...... **TCLC 20**
See also CA 117; DLB 54

**Stern, Gerald** 1925- .............. **CLC 40**
See also CA 81-84

**Stern, Richard G(ustave)** 1928-... **CLC 4, 39**
See also CANR 1, 25; CA 1-4R; DLB 87

**Sternberg, Jonas** 1894-1969
See Sternberg, Josef von

**Sternberg, Josef von** 1894-1969..... **CLC 20**
See also CA 81-84

**Sterne, Laurence** 1713-1768......... **LC 2**
See also DLB 39

**Sternheim, (William Adolf) Carl**
1878-1942 ................. **TCLC 8**
See also CA 105

**Stevens, Mark** 19??-.............. **CLC 34**

**Stevens, Wallace** 1879-1955..... **TCLC 3, 12**
See also CA 104, 124; DLB 54

**Stevenson, Anne (Katharine)**
1933-..................... **CLC 7, 33**
See also Elvin, Anne Katharine Stevenson
See also CANR 9; CA 17-18R; DLB 40

**Stevenson, Robert Louis**
1850-1894 ............... **NCLC 5, 14**
See also CLR 10, 11; YABC 2; DLB 18, 57

**Stewart, J(ohn) I(nnes) M(ackintosh)**
1906-................. **CLC 7, 14, 32**
See also CAAS 3; CA 85-88

**Stewart, Mary (Florence Elinor)**
1916-.................... **CLC 7, 35**
See also CANR 1; CA 1-4R; SATA 12

**Stewart, Will** 1908-
See Williamson, Jack
See also CANR 23; CA 17-18R

**Still, James** 1906-................ **CLC 49**
See also CANR 10, 26; CA 65-68;
SATA 29; DLB 9

**Sting** 1951-
See The Police

**Stitt, Milan** 1941-................ **CLC 29**
See also CA 69-72

**Stoker, Abraham**
See Stoker, Bram
See also CA 105; SATA 29

**Stoker, Bram** 1847-1912 .......... **TCLC 8**
See also Stoker, Abraham
See also SATA 29; DLB 36, 70

**Stolz, Mary (Slattery)** 1920-....... **CLC 12**
See also CANR 13; CA 5-8R; SAAS 3;
SATA 10

**Stone, Irving** 1903-1989........... **CLC 7**
See also CAAS 3; CANR 1; CA 1-4R, 129;
SATA 3

**Stone, Robert (Anthony)**
1937?-................. **CLC 5, 23, 42**
See also CANR 23; CA 85-88

**Stoppard, Tom**
1937-... **CLC 1, 3, 4, 5, 8, 15, 29, 34, 63**
See also CA 81-84; DLB 13; DLB-Y 85

**Storey, David (Malcolm)**
1933-.................**CLC 2, 4, 5, 8**
See also CA 81-84; DLB 13, 14

**Storm, Hyemeyohsts** 1935-......... **CLC 3**
See also CA 81-84

**Storm, (Hans) Theodor (Woldsen)**
1817-1888 .................. **NCLC 1**

**Storni, Alfonsina** 1892-1938....... **TCLC 5**
See also CA 104

**Stout, Rex (Todhunter)** 1886-1975 ... **CLC 3**
See also CA 61-64

**Stow, (Julian) Randolph** 1935- .. **CLC 23, 48**
See also CA 13-16R

**Stowe, Harriet (Elizabeth) Beecher**
1811-1896 .................. **NCLC 3**
See also YABC 1; DLB 1, 12, 42, 74;
CDALB 1865-1917

**Strachey, (Giles) Lytton**
1880-1932 .................. **TCLC 12**
See also CA 110

**Strand, Mark** 1934-......... **CLC 6, 18, 41**
See also CA 21-24R; SATA 41; DLB 5

**Straub, Peter (Francis)** 1943-...... **CLC 28**
See also CA 85-88; DLB-Y 84

**Strauss, Botho** 1944- .............. **CLC 22**

**Straussler, Tomas** 1937-
See Stoppard, Tom

**Streatfeild, (Mary) Noel** 1897- ..... **CLC 21**
See also CA 81-84; obituary CA 120;
SATA 20, 48

**Stribling, T(homas) S(igismund)**
1881-1965 .................. **CLC 23**
See also obituary CA 107; DLB 9

**Strindberg, (Johan) August**
1849-1912 ............. **TCLC 1, 8, 21**
See also CA 104

**Stringer, Arthur** 1874-1950....... **TCLC 37**
See also DLB 92

**Strugatskii, Arkadii (Natanovich)**
1925-..................... **CLC 27**
See also CA 106

**Strugatskii, Boris (Natanovich)**
1933-..................... **CLC 27**
See also CA 106

**Strummer, Joe** 1953?-
See The Clash

**Stuart, (Hilton) Jesse**
1906-1984 ........ **CLC 1, 8, 11, 14, 34**
See also CA 5-8R; obituary CA 112;
SATA 2; obituary SATA 36; DLB 9, 48;
DLB-Y 84

**Sturgeon, Theodore (Hamilton)**
1918-1985 ................ **CLC 22, 39**
See also CA 81-84; obituary CA 116;
DLB 8; DLB-Y 85

**Styron, William**
1925-......... **CLC 1, 3, 5, 11, 15, 60**
See also CANR 6; CA 5-8R; DLB 2;
DLB-Y 80; CDALB 1968-1987

**Sudermann, Hermann** 1857-1928 .. **TCLC 15**
See also CA 107

**Sue, Eugene** 1804-1857 .......... **NCLC 1**

**Sukenick, Ronald** 1932-..... **CLC 3, 4, 6, 48**
See also CAAS 8; CA 25-28R; DLB-Y 81

**Suknaski, Andrew** 1942- .......... **CLC 19**
See also CA 101; DLB 53

**Sully Prudhomme, Rene**
1839-1907 ................. **TCLC 31**

**Su Man-shu** 1884-1918.......... **TCLC 24**
See also CA 123

**Summers, Andrew James** 1942-
See The Police

**Summers, Andy** 1942-
See The Police

**Summers, Hollis (Spurgeon, Jr.)**
1916-....................... **CLC 10**
See also CANR 3; CA 5-8R; DLB 6

**Summers, (Alphonsus Joseph-Mary Augustus)**
**Montague** 1880-1948....... **TCLC 16**
See also CA 118

**Sumner, Gordon Matthew** 1951-
See The Police

**Surtees, Robert Smith**
1805-1864 ................ **NCLC 14**
See also DLB 21

**Susann, Jacqueline** 1921-1974....... **CLC 3**
See also CA 65-68; obituary CA 53-56

**Suskind, Patrick** 1949-............ **CLC 44**

**Sutcliff, Rosemary** 1920-......... **CLC 26**
See also CLR 1; CA 5-8R; SATA 6, 44

**Sutro, Alfred** 1863-1933........... **TCLC 6**
See also CA 105; DLB 10

**Sutton, Henry** 1935-
See Slavitt, David (R.)

**Svevo, Italo** 1861-1928........ **TCLC 2, 35**
See also Schmitz, Ettore

**Swados, Elizabeth** 1951- ......... **CLC 12**
See also CA 97-100

**Swados, Harvey** 1920-1972........ **CLC 5**
See also CANR 6; CA 5-8R;
obituary CA 37-40R; DLB 2

**Swarthout, Glendon (Fred)** 1918-... **CLC 35**
See also CANR 1; CA 1-4R; SATA 26

**Swenson, May** 1919-1989..... **CLC 4, 14, 61**
See also CA 5-8R; obituary CA 130;
SATA 15; DLB 5

**Swift, Graham** 1949- ............. **CLC 41**
See also CA 117, 122

**Swift, Jonathan** 1667-1745.......... **LC 1**
See also SATA 19; DLB 39

**Swinburne, Algernon Charles**
1837-1909 ............... **TCLC 8, 36**
See also CA 105; DLB 35, 57

**Swinfen, Ann** 19??-............... **CLC 34**

**Swinnerton, Frank (Arthur)**
1884-1982 .................. **CLC 31**
See also obituary CA 108; DLB 34

**Symons, Arthur (William)**
1865-1945 ................ **TCLC 11**
See also CA 107; DLB 19, 57

**Symons, Julian (Gustave)**
1912- ................. **CLC 2, 14, 32**
See also CAAS 3; CANR 3; CA 49-52;
DLB 87

**Synge, (Edmund) John Millington**
1871-1909 ............... **TCLC 6, 37**
See also CA 104; DLB 10, 19

**Syruc, J.** 1911-
See Milosz, Czeslaw

**Szirtes, George** 1948-............. **CLC 46**
See also CANR 27; CA 109

**Tabori, George** 1914-............ **CLC 19**
See also CANR 4; CA 49-52

**Tagore, (Sir) Rabindranath**
1861-1941 .................. **TCLC 3**
See also Thakura, Ravindranatha
See also CA 120

**Taine, Hippolyte Adolphe**
1828-1893 ................ **NCLC 15**

**Talese, Gaetano** 1932-
See Talese, Gay

**Talese, Gay** 1932-................ **CLC 37**
See also CANR 9; CA 1-4R

**Tallent, Elizabeth (Ann)** 1954- ..... **CLC 45**
See also CA 117

**Tally, Ted** 1952-.................. **CLC 42**
See also CA 120, 124

**Tamayo y Baus, Manuel**
1829-1898 ................. **NCLC 1**

**Tammsaare, A(nton) H(ansen)**
1878-1940 ................ **TCLC 27**

**Tan, Amy** 1952- .................. **CLC 59**

**Tanizaki, Jun'ichiro**
1886-1965 ........... **CLC 8, 14, 28**
See also CA 93-96; obituary CA 25-28R

**Tarbell, Ida** 1857-1944........... **TCLC 40**
See also CA 122; DLB 47

**Tarkington, (Newton) Booth**
1869-1946 .................. **TCLC 9**
See also CA 110; SATA 17; DLB 9

**Tasso, Torquato** 1544-1595 ......... **LC 5**

**Tate, (John Orley) Allen**
1899-1979 .... **CLC 2, 4, 6, 9, 11, 14, 24**
See also CA 5-8R; obituary CA 85-88;
DLB 4, 45, 63

**Tate, James** 1943-........... **CLC 2, 6, 25**
See also CA 21-24R; DLB 5

**Tavel, Ronald** 1940-............... **CLC 6**
See also CA 21-24R

**Taylor, C(ecil) P(hillip)** 1929-1981 .. **CLC 27**
See also CA 25-28R; obituary CA 105

**Taylor, Edward** 1644?-1729 ........ **LC 11**
See also DLB 24

**Taylor, Eleanor Ross** 1920-......... **CLC 5**
See also CA 81-84

**Taylor, Elizabeth** 1912-1975 ... **CLC 2, 4, 29**
See also CANR 9; CA 13-16R; SATA 13

**Taylor, Henry (Splawn)** 1917-...... **CLC 44**
See also CAAS 7; CA 33-36R; DLB 5

**Taylor, Kamala (Purnaiya)** 1924-
See Markandaya, Kamala
See also CA 77-80

**Taylor, Mildred D(elois)** 1943- ..... **CLC 21**
See also CLR 9; CANR 25; CA 85-88;
SAAS 5; SATA 15; DLB 52

**Taylor, Peter (Hillsman)**
1917- ....... **CLC 1, 4, 18, 37, 44, 50**
See also CANR 9, CA 13-16R; DLB-Y 81

**Taylor, Robert Lewis** 1912-........ **CLC 14**
See also CANR 3; CA 1-4R; SATA 10

**Teasdale, Sara** 1884-1933........... **TCLC 4**
See also CA 104; SATA 32; DLB 45

**Tegner, Esaias** 1782-1846........ **NCLC 2**

**Teilhard de Chardin, (Marie Joseph) Pierre**
1881-1955 ................... **TCLC 9**
See also CA 105

**Tennant, Emma** 1937- ........ **CLC 13, 52**
See also CAAS 9; CANR 10; CA 65-68;
DLB 14

**Tennyson, Alfred** 1809-1892 ..... **NCLC 30**
See also DLB 32

**Teran, Lisa St. Aubin de** 19??- ..... **CLC 36**

**Terkel, Louis** 1912-
See Terkel, Studs
See also CANR 18; CA 57-60

**Terkel, Studs** 1912- .............. **CLC 38**
See also Terkel, Louis

**Terry, Megan** 1932-............... **CLC 19**
See also CA 77-80; CABS 3; DLB 7

**Tertz, Abram** 1925-
See Sinyavsky, Andrei (Donatevich)

**Tesich, Steve** 1943?-.............. **CLC 40**
See also CA 105; DLB-Y 83

**Tesich, Stoyan** 1943?-
See Tesich, Steve

**Teternikov, Fyodor Kuzmich** 1863-1927
See Sologub, Fyodor
See also CA 104

**Tevis, Walter** 1928-1984 .......... **CLC 42**
See also CA 113

**Tey, Josephine** 1897-1952 ........ **TCLC 14**
See also Mackintosh, Elizabeth

**Thackeray, William Makepeace**
1811-1863 ............ **NCLC 5, 14, 22**
See also SATA 23; DLB 21, 55

**Thakura, Ravindranatha** 1861-1941
See Tagore, (Sir) Rabindranath
See also CA 104

**Thelwell, Michael (Miles)** 1939-.... **CLC 22**
See also CA 101

**Theroux, Alexander (Louis)**
1939-..................... **CLC 2, 25**
See also CANR 20; CA 85-88

**Theroux, Paul**
1941-......... **CLC 5, 8, 11, 15, 28, 46**
See also CANR 20; CA 33-36R; SATA 44;
DLB 2

**Thesen, Sharon** 1946-............. **CLC 56**

**Thibault, Jacques Anatole Francois**
1844-1924
See France, Anatole
See also CA 106

**Thiele, Colin (Milton)** 1920- ....... **CLC 17**
See also CANR 12; CA 29-32R; SAAS 2;
SATA 14

**Thomas, Audrey (Grace)**
1935- .................. **CLC 7, 13, 37**
See also CA 21-24R; DLB 60

**Thomas, D(onald) M(ichael)**
1935- ................. **CLC 13, 22, 31**
See also CANR 17; CA 61-64; DLB 40

**Thomas, Dylan (Marlais)**
1914-1953 ..... **TCLC 1, 8; PC 2; SSC 3**
See also CA 104, 120; SATA 60; DLB 13,
20

**Thomas, Edward (Philip)**
    1878-1917 . . . . . . . . . . . . . . . . . **TCLC 10**
    See also CA 106; DLB 19

**Thomas, John Peter**   1928-
    See Thomas, Piri

**Thomas, Joyce Carol**   1938- . . . . . . . . **CLC 35**
    See also CLR 19; CA 113, 116; SAAS 7;
    SATA 40; DLB 33

**Thomas, Lewis**   1913- . . . . . . . . . . . . . **CLC 35**
    See also CA 85-88

**Thomas, Piri**   1928- . . . . . . . . . . . . . . **CLC 17**
    See also CA 73-76

**Thomas, R(onald) S(tuart)**
    1913- . . . . . . . . . . . . . . . . **CLC 6, 13, 48**
    See also CAAS 4; CA 89-92; DLB 27

**Thomas, Ross (Elmore)**   1926- . . . . . . **CLC 39**
    See also CANR 22; CA 33-36R

**Thompson, Ernest**   1860-1946
    See Seton, Ernest (Evan) Thompson

**Thompson, Francis (Joseph)**
    1859-1907 . . . . . . . . . . . . . . . . . . **TCLC 4**
    See also CA 104; DLB 19

**Thompson, Hunter S(tockton)**
    1939- . . . . . . . . . . . . . . . . **CLC 9, 17, 40**
    See also CANR 23; CA 17-20R

**Thompson, Judith**   1954- . . . . . . . . . . . **CLC 39**

**Thomson, James**   1834-1882 . . . . . . **NCLC 18**
    See also DLB 35

**Thoreau, Henry David**
    1817-1862 . . . . . . . . . . . . . . . **NCLC 7, 21**
    See also DLB 1; CDALB 1640-1865

**Thurber, James (Grover)**
    1894-1961 . . . . . . . **CLC 5, 11, 25; SSC 1**
    See also CANR 17; CA 73-76; SATA 13;
    DLB 4, 11, 22

**Thurman, Wallace**   1902-1934 . . . . . . **TCLC 6**
    See also CA 104, 124; DLB 51

**Tieck, (Johann) Ludwig**
    1773-1853 . . . . . . . . . . . . . . . . . . **NCLC 5**
    See also DLB 90

**Tillinghast, Richard**   1940- . . . . . . . . . **CLC 29**
    See also CANR 26; CA 29-32R

**Timrod, Henry**   1828-1867 . . . . . . . **NCLC 25**

**Tindall, Gillian**   1938- . . . . . . . . . . . . . **CLC 7**
    See also CANR 11; CA 21-24R

**Tiptree, James, Jr.**   1915-1987 . . . **CLC 48, 50**
    See also Sheldon, Alice (Hastings) B(radley)
    See also DLB 8

**Tocqueville, Alexis (Charles Henri Maurice**
    **Clerel, Comte) de**   1805-1859 . . **NCLC 7**

**Tolkien, J(ohn) R(onald) R(euel)**
    1892-1973 . . . . . . . **CLC 1, 2, 3, 8, 12, 38**
    See also CAP 2; CA 17-18;
    obituary CA 45-48; SATA 2, 24, 32;
    obituary SATA 24; DLB 15

**Toller, Ernst**   1893-1939 . . . . . . . . . . **TCLC 10**
    See also CA 107

**Tolson, Melvin B(eaunorus)**
    1900?-1966 . . . . . . . . . . . . . . . . . . **CLC 36**
    See also CA 124; obituary CA 89-92;
    DLB 48, 124

**Tolstoy, (Count) Alexey Nikolayevich**
    1883-1945 . . . . . . . . . . . . . . . . . . **TCLC 18**
    See also CA 107

**Tolstoy, (Count) Leo (Lev Nikolaevich)**
    1828-1910 . . . . . . . . **TCLC 4, 11, 17, 28**
    See also CA 104, 123; SATA 26

**Tomlin, Lily**   1939- . . . . . . . . . . . . . . **CLC 17**

**Tomlin, Mary Jean**   1939-
    See Tomlin, Lily
    See also CA 117

**Tomlinson, (Alfred) Charles**
    1927- . . . . . . . . . . . . **CLC 2, 4, 6, 13, 45**
    See also CA 5-8R; DLB 40

**Toole, John Kennedy**
    1937-1969 . . . . . . . . . . . . . . . **CLC 19, 64**
    See also CA 104; DLB-Y 81

**Toomer, Jean**
    1894-1967 . . . . . **CLC 1, 4, 13, 22; SSC 1**
    See also CA 85-88; DLB 45, 51

**Torrey, E. Fuller**   19??- . . . . . . . . . . . . **CLC 34**
    See also CA 119

**Tournier, Michel**   1924- . . . . . . **CLC 6, 23, 36**
    See also CANR 3; CA 49-52; SATA 23;
    DLB 83

**Townsend, Sue**   1946- . . . . . . . . . . . . . **CLC 61**
    See also CA 119, 127; SATA 48, 55

**Townshend, Peter (Dennis Blandford)**
    1945- . . . . . . . . . . . . . . . . . . **CLC 17, 42**
    See also CA 107

**Tozzi, Federigo**   1883-1920 . . . . . . . **TCLC 31**

**Trakl, Georg**   1887-1914 . . . . . . . . . . **TCLC 5**
    See also CA 104

**Transtromer, Tomas (Gosta)**
    1931- . . . . . . . . . . . . . . . . . . . . . **CLC 52**
    See also CA 117

**Traven, B.**   1890-1969 . . . . . . . . . . **CLC 8, 11**
    See also CAP 2; CA 19-20;
    obituary CA 25-28R; DLB 9, 56

**Tremain, Rose**   1943- . . . . . . . . . . . . . **CLC 42**
    See also CA 97-100; DLB 14

**Tremblay, Michel**   1942- . . . . . . . . . . . **CLC 29**
    See also CA 116; DLB 60

**Trevanian**   1925- . . . . . . . . . . . . . . . . **CLC 29**
    See also CA 108

**Trevor, William**   1928- . . . . . **CLC 7, 9, 14, 25**
    See also Cox, William Trevor
    See also DLB 14

**Trifonov, Yuri (Valentinovich)**
    1925-1981 . . . . . . . . . . . . . . . . . . **CLC 45**
    See also obituary CA 103, 126

**Trilling, Lionel**   1905-1975 . . . . **CLC 9, 11, 24**
    See also CANR 10; CA 9-12R;
    obituary CA 61-64; DLB 28, 63

**Trogdon, William**   1939-
    See Heat Moon, William Least
    See also CA 115, 119

**Trollope, Anthony**   1815-1882 . . . . . **NCLC 6**
    See also SATA 22; DLB 21, 57

**Trollope, Frances**   1780-1863 . . . . . **NCLC 30**
    See also DLB 21

**Trotsky, Leon (Davidovich)**
    1879-1940 . . . . . . . . . . . . . . . . . . **TCLC 22**
    See also CA 118

**Trotter (Cockburn), Catharine**
    1679-1749 . . . . . . . . . . . . . . . . . . . . **LC 8**
    See also DLB 84

**Trow, George W. S.**   1943- . . . . . . . . . **CLC 52**
    See also CA 126

**Troyat, Henri**   1911- . . . . . . . . . . . . . . **CLC 23**
    See also CANR 2; CA 45-48

**Trudeau, G(arretson) B(eekman)**   1948-
    See Trudeau, Garry
    See also CA 81-84; SATA 35

**Trudeau, Garry**   1948- . . . . . . . . . . . . . **CLC 12**
    See also Trudeau, G(arretson) B(eekman)

**Truffaut, Francois**   1932-1984 . . . . . . . **CLC 20**
    See also CA 81-84; obituary CA 113

**Trumbo, Dalton**   1905-1976 . . . . . . . . **CLC 19**
    See also CANR 10; CA 21-24R;
    obituary CA 69-72; DLB 26

**Trumbull, John**   1750-1831 . . . . . . . **NCLC 30**
    See also DLB 31

**Tryon, Thomas**   1926- . . . . . . . . . . . **CLC 3, 11**
    See also CA 29-32R

**Ts'ao Hsueh-ch'in**   1715?-1763 . . . . . . . . **LC 1**

**Tsushima Shuji**   1909-1948
    See Dazai Osamu
    See also CA 107

**Tsvetaeva (Efron), Marina (Ivanovna)**
    1892-1941 . . . . . . . . . . . . . . . **TCLC 7, 35**
    See also CA 104, 128

**Tunis, John R(oberts)**   1889-1975 . . . **CLC 12**
    See also CA 61-64; SATA 30, 37; DLB 22

**Tuohy, Frank**   1925- . . . . . . . . . . . . . . **CLC 37**
    See also DLB 14

**Tuohy, John Francis**   1925-
    See Tuohy, Frank
    See also CANR 3; CA 5-8R

**Turco, Lewis (Putnam)**   1934- . . . **CLC 11, 63**
    See also CANR 24; CA 13-16R; DLB-Y 84

**Turgenev, Ivan**
    1818-1883 . . . . . . . . . . . **NCLC 21; SSC 7**

**Turner, Frederick**   1943- . . . . . . . . . . . **CLC 48**
    See also CANR 12; CA 73-76; DLB 40

**Tutuola, Amos**   1920- . . . . . . . . **CLC 5, 14, 29**
    See also CA 9-12R

**Twain, Mark**
    1835-1910 . . . **TCLC 6, 12, 19, 36; SSC 6**
    See also Clemens, Samuel Langhorne
    See also YABC 2; DLB 11, 12, 23, 64, 74

**Tyler, Anne**
    1941- . . . . . . . . **CLC 7, 11, 18, 28, 44, 59**
    See also CANR 11; CA 9-12R; SATA 7;
    DLB 6; DLB-Y 82

**Tyler, Royall**   1757-1826 . . . . . . . . . . **NCLC 3**
    See also DLB 37

**Tynan (Hinkson), Katharine**
    1861-1931 . . . . . . . . . . . . . . . . . . **TCLC 3**
    See also CA 104

**Tytell, John**   1939- . . . . . . . . . . . . . . **CLC 50**
    See also CA 29-32R

**Tzara, Tristan**   1896-1963 . . . . . . . . . . **CLC 47**
    See also Rosenfeld, Samuel

**Uhry, Alfred**   1947?- . . . . . . . . . . . . . . **CLC 55**
    See also CA 127

**Unamuno (y Jugo), Miguel de**
    1864-1936 . . . . . . . . . . . . . . . . **TCLC 2, 9**
    See also CA 104

**Underwood, Miles**   1909-1981
    See Glassco, John

**Undset, Sigrid** 1882-1949......... TCLC 3
See also CA 104

**Ungaretti, Giuseppe**
1888-1970 ............. CLC 7, 11, 15
See also CAP 2; CA 19-20;
obituary CA 25-28R

**Unger, Douglas** 1952-............ CLC 34
See also CA 130

**Unger, Eva** 1932-
See Figes, Eva

**Updike, John (Hoyer)**
1932-...... CLC 1, 2, 3, 5, 7, 9, 13, 15,
23, 34, 43
See also CANR 4; CA 1-4R; CABS 2;
DLB 2, 5; DLB-Y 80, 82; DLB-DS 3

**Urdang, Constance (Henriette)**
1922-........................ CLC 47
See also CANR 9, 24; CA 21-24R

**Uris, Leon (Marcus)** 1924-....... CLC 7, 32
See also CANR 1; CA 1-4R; SATA 49

**Ustinov, Peter (Alexander)** 1921-.... CLC 1
See also CANR 25; CA 13-16R; DLB 13

**Vaculik, Ludvik** 1926-............. CLC 7
See also CA 53-56

**Valenzuela, Luisa** 1938-........... CLC 31
See also CA 101

**Valera (y Acala-Galiano), Juan**
1824-1905 .................. TCLC 10
See also CA 106

**Valery, Paul (Ambroise Toussaint Jules)**
1871-1945 ................ TCLC 4, 15
See also CA 104, 122

**Valle-Inclan (y Montenegro), Ramon (Maria)**
del 1866-1936................ TCLC 5
See also CA 106

**Vallejo, Cesar (Abraham)**
1892-1938 ................... TCLC 3
See also CA 105

**Van Ash, Cay** 1918-............... CLC 34

**Vance, Jack** 1916?-................ CLC 35
See also DLB 8

**Vance, John Holbrook** 1916?-
See Vance, Jack
See also CANR 17; CA 29-32R

**Van Den Bogarde, Derek (Jules Gaspard
Ulric) Niven** 1921-
See Bogarde, Dirk
See also CA 77-80

**Vandenburgh, Jane** 19??-.......... CLC 59

**Vanderhaeghe, Guy** 1951- ......... CLC 41
See also CA 113

**Van der Post, Laurens (Jan)** 1906-... CLC 5
See also CA 5-8R

**Van de Wetering, Janwillem**
1931-........................ CLC 47
See also CANR 4; CA 49-52

**Van Dine, S. S.** 1888-1939....... TCLC 23

**Van Doren, Carl (Clinton)**
1885-1950 .................. TCLC 18
See also CA 111

**Van Doren, Mark** 1894-1972..... CLC 6, 10
See also CANR 3; CA 1-4R;
obituary CA 37-40R; DLB 45

**Van Druten, John (William)**
1901-1957 .................. TCLC 2
See also CA 104; DLB 10

**Van Duyn, Mona** 1921-....... CLC 3, 7, 63
See also CANR 7; CA 9-12R; DLB 5

**Van Itallie, Jean-Claude** 1936- ...... CLC 3
See also CAAS 2; CANR 1; CA 45-48;
DLB 7

**Van Ostaijen, Paul** 1896-1928..... TCLC 33

**Van Peebles, Melvin** 1932- ...... CLC 2, 20
See also CA 85-88

**Vansittart, Peter** 1920-............ CLC 42
See also CANR 3; CA 1-4R

**Van Vechten, Carl** 1880-1964 ...... CLC 33
See also obituary CA 89-92; DLB 4, 9, 51

**Van Vogt, A(lfred) E(lton)** 1912-..... CLC 1
See also CANR 28; CA 21-24R; SATA 14;
DLB 8

**Varda, Agnes** 1928- .............. CLC 16
See also CA 116, 122

**Vargas Llosa, (Jorge) Mario (Pedro)**
1936-....... CLC 3, 6, 9, 10, 15, 31, 42
See also CANR 18; CA 73-76

**Vassilikos, Vassilis** 1933-......... CLC 4, 8
See also CA 81-84

**Vaughn, Stephanie** 19??- .......... CLC 62

**Vazov, Ivan** 1850-1921.......... TCLC 25
See also CA 121

**Veblen, Thorstein Bunde**
1857-1929 .................. TCLC 31
See also CA 115

**Verga, Giovanni** 1840-1922 ....... TCLC 3
See also CA 104, 123

**Verhaeren, Emile (Adolphe Gustave)**
1855-1916 .................. TCLC 12
See also CA 109

**Verlaine, Paul (Marie)**
1844-1896 ............. NCLC 2; PC 2

**Verne, Jules (Gabriel)** 1828-1905 ... TCLC 6
See also CA 110; SATA 21

**Very, Jones** 1813-1880........... NCLC 9
See also DLB 1

**Vesaas, Tarjei** 1897-1970.......... CLC 48
See also obituary CA 29-32R

**Vian, Boris** 1920-1959 ........... TCLC 9
See also CA 106; DLB 72

**Viaud, (Louis Marie) Julien** 1850-1923
See Loti, Pierre
See also CA 107

**Vicker, Angus** 1916-
See Felsen, Henry Gregor

**Vidal, Eugene Luther, Jr.** 1925-
See Vidal, Gore

**Vidal, Gore**
1925-........ CLC 2, 4, 6, 8, 10, 22, 33
See also CANR 13; CA 5-8R; DLB 6

**Viereck, Peter (Robert Edwin)**
1916-........................ CLC 4
See also CANR 1; CA 1-4R; DLB 5

**Vigny, Alfred (Victor) de**
1797-1863 .................. NCLC 7

**Vilakazi, Benedict Wallet**
1905-1947 .................. TCLC 37

**Villiers de l'Isle Adam, Jean Marie Mathias
Philippe Auguste, Comte de,**
1838-1889 .................. NCLC 3

**Vinci, Leonardo da** 1452-1519...... LC 12

**Vine, Barbara** 1930-.............. CLC 50
See also Rendell, Ruth

**Vinge, Joan (Carol) D(ennison)**
1948-....................... CLC 30
See also CA 93-96; SATA 36

**Visconti, Luchino** 1906-1976....... CLC 16
See also CA 81-84; obituary CA 65-68

**Vittorini, Elio** 1908-1966...... CLC 6, 9, 14
See also obituary CA 25-28R

**Vizinczey, Stephen** 1933-.......... CLC 40

**Vliet, R(ussell) G(ordon)**
1929-1984 .................. CLC 22
See also CANR 18; CA 37-40R;
obituary CA 112

**Voight, Ellen Bryant** 1943-........ CLC 54
See also CANR 11; CA 69-72

**Voigt, Cynthia** 1942- ............. CLC 30
See also CANR 18; CA 106; SATA 33, 48;
AAYA 3

**Voinovich, Vladimir (Nikolaevich)**
1932-.................... CLC 10, 49
See also CA 81-84

**Voltaire** 1694-1778............... LC 14

**Von Daeniken, Erich** 1935-
See Von Daniken, Erich
See also CANR 17; CA 37-40R

**Von Daniken, Erich** 1935-......... CLC 30
See also Von Daeniken, Erich

**Vonnegut, Kurt, Jr.**
1922-...... CLC 1, 2, 3, 4, 5, 8, 12, 22,
40, 60
See also CANR 1; CA 1-4R; DLB 2, 8;
DLB-Y 80; DLB-DS 3;
CDALB 1968-1987

**Vorster, Gordon** 1924-............ CLC 34

**Voznesensky, Andrei** 1933-... CLC 1, 15, 57
See also CA 89-92

**Waddington, Miriam** 1917- ........ CLC 28
See also CANR 12, 30; CA 21-24R;
DLB 68

**Wagman, Fredrica** 1937- .......... CLC 7
See also CA 97-100

**Wagner, Richard** 1813-1883....... NCLC 9

**Wagner-Martin, Linda** 1936-...... CLC 50

**Wagoner, David (Russell)**
1926-.................... CLC 3, 5, 15
See also CAAS 3; CANR 2; CA 1-4R;
SATA 14; DLB 5

**Wah, Fred(erick James)** 1939-...... CLC 44
See also CA 107; DLB 60

**Wahloo, Per** 1926-1975 ........... CLC 7
See also CA 61-64

**Wahloo, Peter** 1926-1975
See Wahloo, Per

**Wain, John (Barrington)**
1925-.............CLC 2, 11, 15, 46
See also CAAS 4; CANR 23; CA 5-8R;
DLB 15, 27

**Wajda, Andrzej** 1926-............. CLC 16
See also CA 102

**Wakefield, Dan** 1932- .............. CLC 7
See also CAAS 7; CA 21-24R

**Wakoski, Diane**
1937- ........... CLC 2, 4, 7, 9, 11, 40
See also CAAS 1; CANR 9; CA 13-16R;
DLB 5

**Walcott, Derek (Alton)**
1930- .......... CLC 2, 4, 9, 14, 25, 42
See also CANR 26; CA 89-92; DLB-Y 81

**Waldman, Anne** 1945- ............. CLC 7
See also CA 37-40R; DLB 16

**Waldo, Edward Hamilton** 1918-
See Sturgeon, Theodore (Hamilton)

**Walker, Alice**
1944- ...... CLC 5, 6, 9, 19, 27, 46, 58;
SSC 5
See also CANR 9, 27; CA 37-40R;
SATA 31; DLB 6, 33; CDALB 1968-1988

**Walker, David Harry** 1911- ........ CLC 14
See also CANR 1; CA 1-4R; SATA 8

**Walker, Edward Joseph** 1934-
See Walker, Ted
See also CANR 12; CA 21-24R

**Walker, George F.** 1947- ....... CLC 44, 61
See also CANR 21; CA 103; DLB 60

**Walker, Joseph A.** 1935- ......... CLC 19
See also CANR 26; CA 89-92; DLB 38

**Walker, Margaret (Abigail)**
1915- .................... CLC 1, 6
See also CANR 26; CA 73-76; DLB 76

**Walker, Ted** 1934- ............... CLC 13
See also Walker, Edward Joseph
See also DLB 40

**Wallace, David Foster** 1962- ....... CLC 50

**Wallace, Irving** 1916- .......... CLC 7, 13
See also CAAS 1; CANR 1; CA 1-4R

**Wallant, Edward Lewis**
1926-1962 ................ CLC 5, 10
See also CANR 22; CA 1-4R; DLB 2, 28

**Walpole, Horace** 1717-1797 ......... LC 2
See also DLB 39

**Walpole, (Sir) Hugh (Seymour)**
1884-1941 .................. TCLC 5
See also CA 104; DLB 34

**Walser, Martin** 1927- ............. CLC 27
See also CANR 8; CA 57-60; DLB 75

**Walser, Robert** 1878-1956 ....... TCLC 18
See also CA 118; DLB 66

**Walsh, Gillian Paton** 1939-
See Walsh, Jill Paton
See also CA 37-40R; SATA 4

**Walsh, Jill Paton** 1939- ........... CLC 35
See also CLR 2; SAAS 3

**Wambaugh, Joseph (Aloysius, Jr.)**
1937- .................... CLC 3, 18
See also CA 33-36R; DLB 6; DLB-Y 83

**Ward, Arthur Henry Sarsfield** 1883-1959
See Rohmer, Sax
See also CA 108

**Ward, Douglas Turner** 1930- ....... CLC 19
See also CA 81-84; DLB 7, 38

**Warhol, Andy** 1928-1987 .......... CLC 20
See also CA 89-92; obituary CA 121

**Warner, Francis (Robert le Plastrier)**
1937- ...................... CLC 14
See also CANR 11; CA 53-56

**Warner, Marina** 1946- ............ CLC 59
See also CANR 21; CA 65-68

**Warner, Rex (Ernest)** 1905-1986 .... CLC 45
See also CA 89-92; obituary CA 119;
DLB 15

**Warner, Sylvia Townsend**
1893-1978 .................. CLC 7, 19
See also CANR 16; CA 61-64;
obituary CA 77-80; DLB 34

**Warren, Mercy Otis** 1728-1814... NCLC 13
See also DLB 31

**Warren, Robert Penn**
1905-1989 ... CLC 1, 4, 6, 8, 10, 13, 18,
39, 53, 59; SSC 4
See also CANR 10; CA 13-16R. 129. 130;
SATA 46; DLB 2, 48; DLB-Y 80;
CDALB 1968-1987

**Warton, Thomas** 1728-1790 ........ LC 15

**Washington, Booker T(aliaferro)**
1856-1915 .................. TCLC 10
See also CA 114, 125; SATA 28

**Wassermann, Jakob** 1873-1934 ..... TCLC 6
See also CA 104; DLB 66

**Wasserstein, Wendy** 1950- ...... CLC 32, 59
See also CA 121; CABS 3

**Waterhouse, Keith (Spencer)**
1929- ...................... CLC 47
See also CA 5-8R; DLB 13, 15

**Waters, Roger** 1944-
See Pink Floyd

**Wa Thiong'o, Ngugi**
1938- ................ CLC 3, 7, 13, 36
See also Ngugi, James (Thiong'o); Ngugi wa
Thiong'o

**Watkins, Paul** 1964- ............. CLC 55

**Watkins, Vernon (Phillips)**
1906-1967 .................. CLC 43
See also CAP 1; CA 9-10;
obituary CA 25-28R; DLB 20

**Waugh, Auberon (Alexander)** 1939-.. CLC 7
See also CANR 6, 22; CA 45-48; DLB 14

**Waugh, Evelyn (Arthur St. John)**
1903-1966 ... CLC 1, 3, 8, 13, 19, 27, 44
See also CANR 22; CA 85-88;
obituary CA 25-28R; DLB 15

**Waugh, Harriet** 1944- ............ CLC 6
See also CANR 22; CA 85-88

**Webb, Beatrice (Potter)**
1858-1943 .................. TCLC 22
See also CA 117

**Webb, Charles (Richard)** 1939- ...... CLC 7
See also CA 25-28R

**Webb, James H(enry), Jr.** 1946- .... CLC 22
See also CA 81-84

**Webb, Mary (Gladys Meredith)**
1881-1927 .................. TCLC 24
See also CA 123; DLB 34

**Webb, Phyllis** 1927- .............. CLC 18
See also CANR 23; CA 104; DLB 53

**Webb, Sidney (James)**
1859-1947 .................. TCLC 22
See also CA 117

**Webber, Andrew Lloyd** 1948- ...... CLC 21

**Weber, Lenora Mattingly**
1895-1971 .................. CLC 12
See also CAP 1; CA 19-20;
obituary CA 29-32R; SATA 2;
obituary SATA 26

**Webster, Noah** 1758-1843 ....... NCLC 30
See also DLB 1, 37, 42, 43, 73

**Wedekind, (Benjamin) Frank(lin)**
1864-1918 .................. TCLC 7
See also CA 104

**Weidman, Jerome** 1913-............ CLC 7
See also CANR 1; CA 1-4R; DLB 28

**Weil, Simone** 1909-1943......... TCLC 23
See also CA 117

**Weinstein, Nathan Wallenstein** 1903?-1940
See West, Nathanael
See also CA 104

**Weir, Peter** 1944-................. CLC 20
See also CA 113, 123

**Weiss, Peter (Ulrich)**
1916-1982 .............. CLC 3, 15, 51
See also CANR 3; CA 45-48;
obituary CA 106; DLB 69

**Weiss, Theodore (Russell)**
1916- .................... CLC 3, 8, 14
See also CAAS 2; CA 9-12R; DLB 5

**Welch, (Maurice) Denton**
1915-1948 .................. TCLC 22
See also CA 121

**Welch, James** 1940-......... CLC 6, 14, 52
See also CA 85-88

**Weldon, Fay**
1933- ......... CLC 6, 9, 11, 19, 36, 59
See also CANR 16; CA 21-24R; DLB 14

**Wellek, Rene** 1903- .............. CLC 28
See also CAAS 7; CANR 8; CA 5-8R;
DLB 63

**Weller, Michael** 1942- ......... CLC 10, 53
See also CA 85-88

**Weller, Paul** 1958- ............... CLC 26

**Wellershoff, Dieter** 1925-.......... CLC 46
See also CANR 16; CA 89-92

**Welles, (George) Orson**
1915-1985 .................. CLC 20
See also CA 93-96; obituary CA 117

**Wellman, Manly Wade** 1903-1986 .. CLC 49
See also CANR 6, 16; CA 1-4R;
obituary CA 118; SATA 6, 47

**Wells, Carolyn** 1862-1942 ....... TCLC 35
See also CA 113; DLB 11

**Wells, H(erbert) G(eorge)**
1866-1946 ...... TCLC 6, 12, 19; SSC 6
See also CA 110, 121; SATA 20; DLB 34,
70

**Wells, Rosemary** 1943-............ CLC 12
See also CLR 16; CA 85-88; SAAS 1;
SATA 18

**Welty, Eudora (Alice)**
1909- .... CLC 1, 2, 5, 14, 22, 33; SSC 1
See also CA 9-12R; CABS 1; DLB 2;
DLB-Y 87; CDALB 1941-1968

**Wen I-to** 1899-1946 ............. TCLC 28

**Werfel, Franz (V.)** 1890-1945 . . . . . . TCLC 8
See also CA 104; DLB 81

**Wergeland, Henrik Arnold**
1808-1845 . . . . . . . . . . . . . . . . . NCLC 5

**Wersba, Barbara** 1932- . . . . . . . . . . . CLC 30
See also CLR 3; CANR 16; CA 29-32R;
SAAS 2; SATA 1, 58; DLB 52

**Wertmuller, Lina** 1928- . . . . . . . . . . . CLC 16
See also CA 97-100

**Wescott, Glenway** 1901-1987 . . . . . . . CLC 13
See also CANR 23; CA 13-16R;
obituary CA 121; DLB 4, 9

**Wesker, Arnold** 1932- . . . . . . . . CLC 3, 5, 42
See also CAAS 7; CANR 1; CA 1-4R;
DLB 13

**Wesley, Richard (Errol)** 1945- . . . . . . CLC 7
See also CA 57-60; DLB 38

**Wessel, Johan Herman** 1742-1785 . . . . LC 7

**West, Anthony (Panther)**
1914-1987 . . . . . . . . . . . . . . . . . . CLC 50
See also CANR 3, 19; CA 45-48; DLB 15

**West, Jessamyn** 1907-1984 . . . . . . CLC 7, 17
See also CA 9-12R; obituary CA 112;
obituary SATA 37; DLB 6; DLB-Y 84

**West, Morris L(anglo)** 1916- . . . . CLC 6, 33
See also CA 5-8R; obituary CA 124

**West, Nathanael** 1903?-1940 . . . . TCLC 1, 14
See also Weinstein, Nathan Wallenstein
See also CA 125, 140; DLB 4, 9, 28

**West, Paul** 1930- . . . . . . . . . . . . . . CLC 7, 14
See also CAAS 7; CANR 22; CA 13-16R;
DLB 14

**West, Rebecca** 1892-1983 . . CLC 7, 9, 31, 50
See also CANR 19; CA 5-8R;
obituary CA 109; DLB 36; DLB-Y 83

**Westall, Robert (Atkinson)** 1929- . . . CLC 17
See also CLR 13; CANR 18; CA 69-72;
SAAS 2; SATA 23

**Westlake, Donald E(dwin)**
1933- . . . . . . . . . . . . . . . . . . . . CLC 7, 33
See also CANR 16; CA 17-20R

**Westmacott, Mary** 1890-1976
See Christie, (Dame) Agatha (Mary
Clarissa)

**Whalen, Philip** 1923- . . . . . . . . . . . CLC 6, 29
See also CANR 5; CA 9-12R; DLB 16

**Wharton, Edith (Newbold Jones)**
1862-1937 . . . . . . . TCLC 3, 9, 27; SSC 6
See also CA 104; DLB 4, 9, 12, 78;
CDALB 1865-1917

**Wharton, William** 1925- . . . . . . . . CLC 18, 37
See also CA 93-96; DLB-Y 80

**Wheatley (Peters), Phillis**
1753?-1784 . . . . . . . . . . . . . . . . . . . LC 3
See also DLB 31, 50; CDALB 1640-1865

**Wheelock, John Hall** 1886-1978 . . . . CLC 14
See also CANR 14; CA 13-16R;
obituary CA 77-80; DLB 45

**Whelan, John** 1900-
See O'Faolain, Sean

**Whitaker, Rodney** 1925-
See Trevanian

**White, E(lwyn) B(rooks)**
1899-1985 . . . . . . . . . . . . CLC 10, 34, 39
See also CLR 1; CANR 16; CA 13-16R;
obituary CA 116; SATA 2, 29, 44;
obituary SATA 44; DLB 11, 22

**White, Edmund III** 1940- . . . . . . . . . CLC 27
See also CANR 3, 19; CA 45-48

**White, Patrick (Victor Martindale)**
1912- . . . . . . . . . . . CLC 3, 4, 5, 7, 9, 18
See also CA 81-84

**White, T(erence) H(anbury)**
1906-1964 . . . . . . . . . . . . . . . . . . CLC 30
See also CA 73-76; SATA 12

**White, Terence de Vere** 1912- . . . . . . CLC 49
See also CANR 3; CA 49-52

**White, Walter (Francis)**
1893-1955 . . . . . . . . . . . . . . . . . TCLC 15
See also CA 115, 124; DLB 51

**White, William Hale** 1831-1913
See Rutherford, Mark
See also CA 121

**Whitehead, E(dward) A(nthony)**
1933- . . . . . . . . . . . . . . . . . . . . . . CLC 5
See also CA 65-68

**Whitemore, Hugh** 1936- . . . . . . . . . . CLC 37

**Whitman, Sarah Helen**
1803-1878 . . . . . . . . . . . . . . . . NCLC 19
See also DLB 1

**Whitman, Walt** 1819-1892 . . . . . . . . NCLC 4
See also SATA 20; DLB 3, 64;
CDALB 1640-1865

**Whitney, Phyllis A(yame)** 1903- . . . . CLC 42
See also CANR 3, 25; CA 1-4R; SATA 1,
30

**Whittemore, (Edward) Reed (Jr.)**
1919- . . . . . . . . . . . . . . . . . . . . . . CLC 4
See also CAAS 8; CANR 4; CA 9-12R;
DLB 5

**Whittier, John Greenleaf**
1807-1892 . . . . . . . . . . . . . . . . . NCLC 8
See also DLB 1; CDALB 1640-1865

**Wicker, Thomas Grey** 1926-
See Wicker, Tom
See also CANR 21; CA 65-68

**Wicker, Tom** 1926- . . . . . . . . . . . . . . CLC 7
See also Wicker, Thomas Grey

**Wideman, John Edgar**
1941- . . . . . . . . . . . . . . . CLC 5, 34, 36
See also CANR 14; CA 85-88; DLB 33

**Wiebe, Rudy (H.)** 1934- . . . . . . CLC 6, 11, 14
See also CA 37-40R; DLB 60

**Wieland, Christoph Martin**
1733-1813 . . . . . . . . . . . . . . . . NCLC 17

**Wieners, John** 1934- . . . . . . . . . . . . . CLC 7
See also CA 13-16R; DLB 16

**Wiesel, Elie(zer)** 1928- . . . . . CLC 3, 5, 11, 37
See also CAAS 4; CANR 8; CA 5-8R;
SATA 56; DLB 83; DLB-Y 87

**Wiggins, Marianne** 1948- . . . . . . . . . CLC 57

**Wight, James Alfred** 1916-
See Herriot, James
See also CA 77-80; SATA 44

**Wilbur, Richard (Purdy)**
1921- . . . . . . . . . . . . CLC 3, 6, 9, 14, 53
See also CANR 2; CA 1-4R; CABS 2;
SATA 9; DLB 5

**Wild, Peter** 1940- . . . . . . . . . . . . . . . CLC 14
See also CA 37-40R; DLB 5

**Wilde, Oscar (Fingal O'Flahertie Wills)**
1854-1900 . . . . . . . . . . . . . TCLC 1, 8, 23
See also CA 104, 119; SATA 24; DLB 10,
19, 34, 57

**Wilder, Billy** 1906- . . . . . . . . . . . . . . CLC 20
See also Wilder, Samuel
See also DLB 26

**Wilder, Samuel** 1906-
See Wilder, Billy
See also CA 89-92

**Wilder, Thornton (Niven)**
1897-1975 . . . . . CLC 1, 5, 6, 10, 15, 35;
           DC 1
See also CA 13-16R; obituary CA 61-64;
DLB 4, 7, 9

**Wiley, Richard** 1944- . . . . . . . . . . . . . CLC 44
See also CA 121, 129

**Wilhelm, Kate** 1928- . . . . . . . . . . . . . CLC 7
See also CAAS 5; CANR 17; CA 37-40R;
DLB 8

**Willard, Nancy** 1936- . . . . . . . . . . . CLC 7, 37
See also CLR 5; CANR 10; CA 89-92;
SATA 30, 37; DLB 5, 52

**Williams, C(harles) K(enneth)**
1936- . . . . . . . . . . . . . . . . . . . CLC 33, 56
See also CA 37-40R; DLB 5

**Williams, Charles (Walter Stansby)**
1886-1945 . . . . . . . . . . . . . . . TCLC 1, 11
See also CA 104

**Williams, Ella Gwendolen Rees** 1890-1979
See Rhys, Jean

**Williams, (George) Emlyn**
1905-1987 . . . . . . . . . . . . . . . . . . CLC 15
See also CA 104, 123; DLB 10, 77

**Williams, Hugo** 1942- . . . . . . . . . . . . CLC 42
See also CA 17-20R; DLB 40

**Williams, John A(lfred)** 1925- . . . . CLC 5, 13
See also CAAS 3; CANR 6, 26; CA 53-56;
DLB 2, 33

**Williams, Jonathan (Chamberlain)**
1929- . . . . . . . . . . . . . . . . . . . . . CLC 13
See also CANR 8; CA 9-12R; DLB 5

**Williams, Joy** 1944- . . . . . . . . . . . . . CLC 31
See also CANR 22; CA 41-44R

**Williams, Norman** 1952- . . . . . . . . . . CLC 39
See also CA 118

**Williams, Paulette** 1948-
See Shange, Ntozake

**Williams, Tennessee**
1911-1983 . . . . CLC 1, 2, 5, 7, 8, 11, 15,
          19, 30, 39, 45
See also CA 5-8R; obituary CA 108; DLB 7;
DLB-Y 83; DLB-DS 4;
CDALB 1941-1968

**Williams, Thomas (Alonzo)** 1926- . . . CLC 14
See also CANR 2; CA 1-4R

**Williams, Thomas Lanier** 1911-1983
See Williams, Tennessee

**Williams, William Carlos**
1883-1963 .... CLC **1, 2, 5, 9, 13, 22, 42**
See also CA 89-92; DLB 4, 16, 54, 86

**Williamson, David** 1932- ......... CLC **56**

**Williamson, Jack** 1908- ........... CLC **29**
See also Williamson, John Stewart
See also DLB 8

**Williamson, John Stewart** 1908-
See Williamson, Jack
See also CANR 123; CA 17-20R

**Willingham, Calder (Baynard, Jr.)**
1922- ...................... CLC **5, 51**
See also CANR 3; CA 5-8R; DLB 2, 44

**Wilson, A(ndrew) N(orman)** 1950- .. CLC **33**
See also CA 112, 122; DLB 14

**Wilson, Andrew** 1948-
See Wilson, Snoo

**Wilson, Angus (Frank Johnstone)**
1913- ............. CLC **2, 3, 5, 25, 34**
See also CANR 21; CA 5-8R; DLB 15

**Wilson, August** 1945- ....... CLC **39, 50, 63**
See also CA 115, 122

**Wilson, Brian** 1942- .............. CLC **12**

**Wilson, Colin** 1931- ............ CLC **3, 14**
See also CAAS 5; CANR 1, 122; CA 1-4R;
DLB 14

**Wilson, Edmund**
1895-1972 .......... CLC **1, 2, 3, 8, 24**
See also CANR 1; CA 1-4R;
obituary CA 37-40R; DLB 63

**Wilson, Ethel Davis (Bryant)**
1888-1980 ................... CLC **13**
See also CA 102; DLB 68

**Wilson, John** 1785-1854.......... NCLC **5**

**Wilson, John (Anthony) Burgess** 1917-
See Burgess, Anthony
See also CANR 2; CA 1-4R

**Wilson, Lanford** 1937- ....... CLC **7, 14, 36**
See also CA 17-20R; DLB 7

**Wilson, Robert (M.)** 1944- ....... CLC **7, 9**
See also CANR 2; CA 49-52

**Wilson, Sloan** 1920- .............. CLC **32**
See also CANR 1; CA 1-4R

**Wilson, Snoo** 1948-............... CLC **33**
See also CA 69-72

**Wilson, William S(mith)** 1932- ..... CLC **49**
See also CA 81-84

**Winchilsea, Anne (Kingsmill) Finch, Countess**
of 1661-1720................. LC **3**

**Winters, Janet Lewis** 1899-
See Lewis (Winters), Janet
See also CAP 1; CA 9-10

**Winters, (Arthur) Yvor**
1900-1968 .............. CLC **4, 8, 32**
See also CAP 1; CA 11-12;
obituary CA 25-28R; DLB 48

**Winterson, Jeannette** 1959- ........ CLC **64**

**Wiseman, Frederick** 1930- ........ CLC **20**

**Wister, Owen** 1860-1938 ......... TCLC **21**
See also CA 108; DLB 9, 78

**Witkiewicz, Stanislaw Ignacy**
1885-1939 .................. TCLC **8**
See also CA 105; DLB 83

**Wittig, Monique** 1935?- ........... CLC **22**
See also CA 116; DLB 83

**Wittlin, Joseph** 1896-1976......... CLC **25**
See also Wittlin, Jozef

**Wittlin, Jozef** 1896-1976
See Wittlin, Joseph
See also CANR 3; CA 49-52;
obituary CA 65-68

**Wodehouse, (Sir) P(elham) G(renville)**
1881-1975 ... CLC **1, 2, 5, 10, 22; SSC 2**
See also CANR 3; CA 45-48;
obituary CA 57-60; SATA 22; DLB 34

**Woiwode, Larry (Alfred)** 1941-... CLC **6, 10**
See also CANR 16; CA 73-76; DLB 6

**Wojciechowska, Maia (Teresa)**
1927- ...................... CLC **26**
See also CLR 1; CANR 4; CA 9-12R;
SAAS 1; SATA 1, 28

**Wolf, Christa** 1929- ........ CLC **14, 29, 58**
See also CA 85-88; DLB 75

**Wolfe, Gene (Rodman)** 1931-....... CLC **25**
See also CAAS 9; CANR 6; CA 57-60;
DLB 8

**Wolfe, George C.** 1954- .......... CLC **49**

**Wolfe, Thomas (Clayton)**
1900-1938 .......... TCLC **4, 13, 29**
See also CA 104; DLB 9; DLB-Y 85;
DLB-DS 2

**Wolfe, Thomas Kennerly, Jr.** 1931-
See Wolfe, Tom
See also CANR 9; CA 13-16R

**Wolfe, Tom** 1931-... CLC **1, 2, 9, 15, 35, 51**
See also Wolfe, Thomas Kennerly, Jr.

**Wolff, Geoffrey (Ansell)** 1937- ..... CLC **41**
See also CA 29-32R

**Wolff, Tobias (Jonathan Ansell)**
1945- ..................... CLC **39, 64**
See also CA 114, 117

**Wolfram von Eschenbach**
c. 1170-c. 1220 .............. CMLC **5**

**Wolitzer, Hilma** 1930- ............ CLC **17**
See also CANR 18; CA 65-68; SATA 31

**Wollstonecraft (Godwin), Mary**
1759-1797 .................. LC **5**
See also DLB 39

**Wonder, Stevie** 1950- ............. CLC **12**
See also Morris, Steveland Judkins

**Wong, Jade Snow** 1922-........... CLC **17**
See also CA 109

**Woodcott, Keith** 1934-
See Brunner, John (Kilian Houston)

**Woolf, (Adeline) Virginia**
1882-1941 ....... TCLC **1, 5, 20; SSC 7**
See also CA 130; brief entry CA 104;
DLB 36

**Woollcott, Alexander (Humphreys)**
1887-1943 ................. TCLC **5**
See also CA 105; DLB 29

**Wordsworth, Dorothy**
1771-1855 ................. NCLC **25**

**Wordsworth, William** 1770-1850.. NCLC **12**

**Wouk, Herman** 1915-......... CLC **1, 9, 38**
See also CANR 6; CA 5-8R; DLB-Y 82

**Wright, Charles** 1935- ....... CLC **6, 13, 28**
See also CAAS 7; CA 29-32R; DLB-Y 82

**Wright, Charles (Stevenson)** 1932- .. CLC **49**
See also CA 9-12R; DLB 33

**Wright, James (Arlington)**
1927-1980 ........... CLC **3, 5, 10, 28**
See also CANR 4; CA 49-52;
obituary CA 97-100; DLB 5

**Wright, Judith** 1915- .......... CLC **11, 53**
See also CA 13-16R; SATA 14

**Wright, L(auren) R.** 1939-......... CLC **44**

**Wright, Richard (Nathaniel)**
1908-1960 ... CLC **1, 3, 4, 9, 14, 21, 48;
SSC 2**
See also CA 108; DLB 76; DLB-DS 2

**Wright, Richard B(ruce)** 1937- ...... CLC **6**
See also CA 85-88; DLB 53

**Wright, Rick** 1945-
See Pink Floyd

**Wright, Stephen** 1946- ............. CLC **33**

**Wright, Willard Huntington** 1888-1939
See Van Dine, S. S.
See also CA 115

**Wright, William** 1930- ............ CLC **44**
See also CANR 7, 23; CA 53-56

**Wu Ch'eng-en** 1500?-1582? ......... LC **7**

**Wu Ching-tzu** 1701-1754 ............ LC **2**

**Wurlitzer, Rudolph** 1938?-..... CLC **2, 4, 15**
See also CA 85-88

**Wycherley, William** 1640?-1716 ...... LC **8**
See also DLB 80

**Wylie (Benet), Elinor (Morton Hoyt)**
1885-1928 ................... TCLC **8**
See also CA 105; DLB 9, 45

**Wylie, Philip (Gordon)** 1902-1971... CLC **43**
See also CAP 2; CA 21-22;
obituary CA 33-36R; DLB 9

**Wyndham, John** 1903-1969 ........ CLC **19**
See also Harris, John (Wyndham Parkes
Lucas) Beynon

**Wyss, Johann David** 1743-1818 .. NCLC **10**
See also SATA 27, 29

**Yanovsky, Vassily S(emenovich)**
1906-1989 ................. CLC **2, 18**
See also CA 97-100; obituary CA 129

**Yates, Richard** 1926- ......... CLC **7, 8, 23**
See also CANR 10; CA 5-8R; DLB 2;
DLB-Y 81

**Yeats, William Butler**
1865-1939 ......... TCLC **1, 11, 18, 31**
See also CANR 10; CA 104; DLB 10, 19

**Yehoshua, A(braham) B.**
1936- .................... CLC **13, 31**
See also CA 33-36R

**Yep, Laurence (Michael)** 1948-..... CLC **35**
See also CLR 3, 17; CANR 1; CA 49-52;
SATA 7; DLB 52

**Yerby, Frank G(arvin)** 1916-... CLC **1, 7, 22**
See also CANR 16; CA 9-12R; DLB 76

**Yevtushenko, Yevgeny (Alexandrovich)**
1933- ............. CLC **1, 3, 13, 26, 51**
See also CA 81-84

**Yezierska, Anzia** 1885?-1970...... **CLC 46**
See also CA 126; obituary CA 89-92;
DLB 28

**Yglesias, Helen** 1915-.......... **CLC 7, 22**
See also CANR 15; CA 37-40R

**Yorke, Henry Vincent** 1905-1974
See Green, Henry
See also CA 85-88; obituary CA 49-52

**Young, Al** 1939-................. **CLC 19**
See also CANR 26; CA 29-32R; DLB 33

**Young, Andrew** 1885-1971......... **CLC 5**
See also CANR 7; CA 5-8R

**Young, Edward** 1683-1765.......... **LC 3**

**Young, Neil** 1945-................ **CLC 17**
See also CA 110

**Yourcenar, Marguerite**
1903-1987 ............. **CLC 19, 38, 50**
See also CANR 23; CA 69-72; DLB 72;
DLB-Y 88

**Yurick, Sol** 1925-................. **CLC 6**
See also CANR 25; CA 13-16R

**Zamyatin, Yevgeny Ivanovich**
1884-1937 ............... **TCLC 8, 37**
See also CA 105

**Zangwill, Israel** 1864-1926....... **TCLC 16**
See also CA 109; DLB 10

**Zappa, Francis Vincent, Jr.** 1940-
See Zappa, Frank
See also CA 108

**Zappa, Frank** 1940- .............. **CLC 17**
See also Zappa, Francis Vincent, Jr.

**Zaturenska, Marya** 1902-1982.... **CLC 6, 11**
See also CANR 22; CA 13-16R;
obituary CA 105

**Zelazny, Roger** 1937-............. **CLC 21**
See also CANR 26; CA 21-24R; SATA 39,
59; DLB 8

**Zhdanov, Andrei A(lexandrovich)**
1896-1948 .................. **TCLC 18**
See also CA 117

**Ziegenhagen, Eric** 1970-.......... **CLC 55**

**Zimmerman, Robert** 1941-
See Dylan, Bob

**Zindel, Paul** 1936- .............. **CLC 6, 26**
See also CLR 3; CA 73-76; SATA 16, 58;
DLB 7, 52

**Zinoviev, Alexander** 1922-......... **CLC 19**
See also CAAS 10; CA 116

**Zola, Emile** 1840-1902...... **TCLC 1, 6, 21**
See also CA 104

**Zoline, Pamela** 1941-............. **CLC 62**

**Zorrilla y Moral, Jose** 1817-1893.. **NCLC 6**

**Zoshchenko, Mikhail (Mikhailovich)**
1895-1958 .................. **TCLC 15**
See also CA 115

**Zuckmayer, Carl** 1896-1977....... **CLC 18**
See also CA 69-72; DLB 56

**Zukofsky, Louis**
1904-1978 ....... **CLC 1, 2, 4, 7, 11, 18**
See also CA 9-12R; obituary CA 77-80;
DLB 5

**Zweig, Paul** 1935-1984........ **CLC 34, 42**
See also CA 85-88; obituary CA 113

**Zweig, Stefan** 1881-1942 ........ **TCLC 17**
See also CA 112; DLB 81

# *CLC* Cumulative Nationality Index

## ALBANIAN
Kadare, Ismail  **52**

## ALGERIAN
Camus, Albert  **1, 2, 4, 9, 11, 14, 32, 63**
Cohen-Solal, Annie  **50**

## AMERICAN
Abbey, Edward  **36, 59**
Abbott, Lee K., Jr.  **48**
Abish, Walter  **22**
Abrahams, Peter  **4**
Abrams, M. H.  **24**
Acker, Kathy  **45**
Adams, Alice  **6, 13, 46**
Addams, Charles  **30**
Adler, C. S.  **35**
Adler, Renata  **8, 31**
Ai  **4, 14**
Aiken, Conrad  **1, 3, 5, 10, 52**
Albee, Edward  **1, 2, 3, 5, 9, 11, 13, 25, 53**
Alexander, Lloyd  **35**
Algren, Nelson  **4, 10, 33**
Allard, Janet  **59**
Allen, Edward  **59**
Allen, Woody  **16, 52**
Alta  **19**
Alter, Robert B.  **34**
Alther, Lisa  **7, 41**
Altman, Robert  **16**
Ammons, A. R.  **2, 3, 5, 8, 9, 25, 57**
Anaya, Rudolfo A.  **23**
Anderson, Jon  **9**
Anderson, Poul  **15**
Anderson, Robert  **23**
Angell, Roger  **26**
Angelou, Maya  **12, 35, 64**
Anthony, Piers  **35**
Apple, Max  **9, 33**

Appleman, Philip  **51**
Archer, Jules  **12**
Arnow, Harriette  **2, 7, 18**
Arrick, Fran  **30**
Ashbery, John  **2, 3, 4, 6, 9, 13, 15, 25, 41**
Asimov, Isaac  **1, 3, 9, 19, 26**
Auchincloss, Louis  **4, 6, 9, 18, 45**
Auden, W. H.  **1, 2, 3, 4, 6, 9, 11, 14, 43**
Auel, Jean M.  **31**
Auster, Paul  **47**
Bach, Richard  **14**
Baker, Elliott  **8**
Baker, Nicholson  **61**
Baker, Russell  **31**
Bakshi, Ralph  **26**
Baldwin, James  **1, 2, 3, 4, 5, 8, 13, 15, 17, 42, 50**
Bambara, Toni Cade  **19**
Bandanes, Jerome  **59**
Banks, Russell  **37**
Baraka, Imamu Amiri  **1, 2, 3, 5, 10, 14, 33**
Barbera, Jack  **44**
Barnard, Mary  **48**
Barnes, Djuna  **3, 4, 8, 11, 29**
Barrett, William  **27**
Barth, John  **1, 2, 3, 5, 7, 9, 10, 14, 27, 51**
Barthelme, Donald  **1, 2, 3, 5, 6, 8, 13, 23, 46, 59**
Barthelme, Frederick  **36**
Barzun, Jacques  **51**
Baumbach, Jonathan  **6, 23**
Bausch, Richard  **51**
Baxter, Charles  **45**
Beagle, Peter S.  **7**
Beattie, Ann  **8, 13, 18, 40, 63**
Becker, Walter  **26**
Beecher, John  **6**
Behrman, S. N.  **40**
Belitt, Ben  **22**

Bell, Madison Smartt  **41**
Bell, Marvin  **8, 31**
Bellow, Saul  **1, 2, 3, 6, 8, 10, 13, 15, 25, 33, 34, 63**
Benary-Isbert, Margot  **12**
Benchley, Peter  **4, 8**
Benedikt, Michael  **4, 14**
Benford, Gregory  **52**
Bennett, Hal  **5**
Bennett, Jay  **35**
Benson, Jackson J.  **34**
Benson, Sally  **17**
Bentley, Eric  **24**
Berger, Melvin  **12**
Berger, Thomas  **3, 5, 8, 11, 18, 38**
Bergstein, Eleanor  **4**
Bernard, April  **59**
Berriault, Gina  **54**
Berrigan, Daniel J.  **4**
Berrigan, Ted  **37**
Berry, Chuck  **17**
Berry, Wendell  **4, 6, 8, 27, 46**
Berryman, John  **1, 2, 3, 4, 6, 8, 10, 13, 25, 62**
Bessie, Alvah  **23**
Betts, Doris  **3, 6, 28**
Bidart, Frank  **33**
Bishop, Elizabeth  **1, 4, 9, 13, 15, 32**
Bishop, John  **10**
Blackburn, Paul  **9, 43**
Blackmur, R. P.  **2, 24**
Blaise, Clark  **29**
Blatty, William Peter  **2**
Blessing, Lee  **54**
Blish, James  **14**
Bloch, Robert  **33**
Bloom, Harold  **24**
Blount, Roy, Jr.  **38**
Blume, Judy  **12, 30**

Bly, Robert   **1, 2, 5, 10, 15, 38**
Bochco, Steven   35
Bogan, Louise   **4, 39, 46**
Bogosian, Eric   45
Bograd, Larry   35
Bonham, Frank   12
Bontemps, Arna   **1, 18**
Booth, Philip   23
Booth, Wayne C.   24
Bottoms, David   53
Bourjaily, Vance   **8, 62**
Bova, Ben   45
Bowers, Edgar   9
Bowles, Jane   3
Bowles, Paul   **1, 2, 19, 53**
Boyle, Kay   **1, 5, 19, 58**
Boyle, T. Coraghessan   **36, 55**
Bradbury, Ray   **1, 3, 10, 15, 42**
Bradley, David, Jr.   23
Bradley, John Ed   55
Bradley, Marion Zimmer   30
Brammer, William   31
Brancato, Robin F.   35
Brand, Millen   7
Branden, Barbara   44
Branley, Franklyn M.   21
Brautigan, Richard   **1, 3, 5, 9, 12, 34, 42**
Brennan, Maeve   5
Breslin, Jimmy   **4, 43**
Bridgers, Sue Ellen   26
Brin, David   34
Brodkey, Harold   56
Brodsky, Joseph   **4, 6, 13, 36, 50**
Brodsky, Michael   19
Bromell, Henry   5
Broner, E. M.   19
Bronk, William   10
Brooks, Cleanth   24
Brooks, Gwendolyn   **1, 2, 4, 5, 15, 49**
Brooks, Mel   12
Brooks, Peter   34
Brooks, Van Wyck   29
Brosman, Catharine Savage   9
Broughton, T. Alan   19
Broumas, Olga   10
Brown, Claude   **30, 59**
Brown, Dee   **18, 47**
Brown, Rita Mae   **18, 43**
Brown, Rosellen   32
Brown, Sterling A.   **1, 23, 59**
Browne, Jackson   21
Browning, Tod   16
Bruccoli, Matthew J.   34
Bruce, Lenny   21
Bryan, C. D. B.   29
Buchwald, Art   33
Buck, Pearl S.   **7, 11, 18**
Buckley, William F., Jr.   **7, 18, 37**
Buechner, Frederick   **2, 4, 6, 9**
Bukowski, Charles   **2, 5, 9, 41**
Bullins, Ed   **1, 5, 7**
Burke, Kenneth   **2, 24**
Burnshaw, Stanley   **3, 13, 44**
Burr, Anne   6
Burroughs, William S.   **1, 2, 5, 15, 22, 42**
Busch, Frederick   **7, 10, 18, 47**
Bush, Ronald   34
Butler, Octavia E.   38
Byars, Betsy   35
Byrne, David   26
Cage, John   41
Cain, James M.   **3, 11, 28**

Caldwell, Erskine   **1, 8, 14, 50, 60**
Caldwell, Taylor   **2, 28, 39**
Calisher, Hortense   **2, 4, 8, 38**
Cameron, Carey   59
Cameron, Peter   44
Campbell, John W., Jr.   32
Canby, Vincent   13
Canin, Ethan   55
Capote, Truman   **1, 3, 8, 13, 19, 34, 38, 58**
Capra, Frank   16
Caputo, Philip   32
Card, Orson Scott   **44, 47, 50**
Carey, Ernestine Gilbreth   17
Carlisle, Henry   33
Carlson, Ron   54
Carpenter, Don   41
Carr, John Dickson   3
Carr, Virginia Spencer   34
Carroll, James   38
Carroll, Jim   35
Carruth, Hayden   **4, 7, 10, 18**
Carver, Raymond   **22, 36, 53, 55**
Casey, John   59
Casey, Michael   2
Casey, Warren   12
Cassavetes, John   20
Cassill, R. V.   **4, 23**
Cassity, Turner   **6, 42**
Catton, Bruce   35
Caunitz, William   34
Cavanna, Betty   12
Chabon, Michael   55
Chappell, Fred   40
Charyn, Jerome   **5, 8, 18**
Chase, Mary Ellen   2
Chayefsky, Paddy   23
Cheever, John   **3, 7, 8, 11, 15, 25, 64**
Cheever, Susan   **18, 48**
Cherryh, C. J.   35
Chester, Alfred   49
Childress, Alice   **12, 15**
Chute, Carolyn   39
Ciardi, John   **10, 40, 44**
Cimino, Michael   16
Clampitt, Amy   32
Clancy, Tom   45
Clark, Eleanor   **5, 19**
Clark, Walter Van Tilburg   28
Clarke, Shirley   16
Clavell, James   **6, 25**
Cleaver, Eldridge   30
Clifton, Lucille   19
Coburn, D. L.   10
Codrescu, Andrei   46
Cohen, Arthur A.   **7, 31**
Collier, Christopher   30
Collier, James L.   30
Collins, Linda   44
Colter, Cyrus   58
Colum, Padraic   28
Colwin, Laurie   **5, 13, 23**
Condon, Richard   **4, 6, 8, 10, 45**
Connell, Evan S., Jr.   **4, 6, 45**
Connelly, Marc   7
Conroy, Pat   30
Cook, Robin   14
Cooke, Elizabeth   55
Cooper, J. California   56
Coover, Robert   **3, 7, 15, 32, 46**
Coppola, Francis Ford   16
Corcoran, Barbara   17

Corman, Cid   9
Cormier, Robert   **12, 30**
Corn, Alfred   33
Corso, Gregory   **1, 11**
Costain, Thomas B.   30
Cowley, Malcolm   39
Cozzens, James Gould   **1, 4, 11**
Crace, Douglas   58
Crane, R. S.   27
Creeley, Robert   **1, 2, 4, 8, 11, 15, 36**
Crews, Harry   **6, 23, 49**
Crichton, Michael   **2, 6, 54**
Cristofer, Michael   28
Crowley, John   57
Crumb, Robert   17
Cryer, Gretchen   21
Cudlip, David   34
Cummings, E. E.   **1, 3, 8, 12, 15**
Cunningham, J. V.   **3, 31**
Cunningham, Julia   12
Cunningham, Michael   34
Currie, Ellen   44
Dacey, Philip   51
Dahlberg, Edward   **1, 7, 14**
Daly, Elizabeth   52
Daly, Maureen   17
Danziger, Paula   21
Davenport, Guy   **6, 14, 38**
Davidson, Donald   **2, 13, 19**
Davidson, Sara   9
Davis, H. L.   49
Davison, Peter   28
Dawson, Fielding   6
De Man, Paul   55
De Palma, Brian   20
De Vries, Peter   **1, 2, 3, 7, 10, 28, 46**
Deer, Sandra   45
Del Vecchio, John M.   29
Delany, Samuel R.   **8, 14, 38**
Delbanco, Nicholas   **6, 13**
DeLillo, Don   **8, 10, 13, 27, 39, 54**
Deloria, Vine, Jr.   21
DeMarinis, Rick   54
Demby, William   53
Denby, Edwin   48
Deren, Maya   16
Derleth, August   31
Deutsch, Babette   18
Dexter, Pete   **34, 55**
Diamond, Neil   30
Dick, Philip K.   **10, 30**
Dickey, James   **1, 2, 4, 7, 10, 15, 47**
Dickey, William   **3, 28**
Dickinson, Charles   49
Didion, Joan   **1, 3, 8, 14, 32**
Dillard, Annie   **9, 60**
Dillard, R. H. W.   5
Disch, Thomas M.   **7, 36**
Dixon, Stephen   52
Dobyns, Stephen   37
Doctorow, E. L.   **6, 11, 15, 18, 37, 44**
Doerr, Harriet   34
Donaldson, Stephen R.   46
Donleavy, J. P.   **1, 4, 6, 10, 45**
Donovan, John   35
Dorn, Ed   **10, 18**
Dos Passos, John   **1, 4, 8, 11, 15, 25, 34**
Dove, Rita   50
Drexler, Rosalyn   **2, 6**
Drury, Allen   37
Du Bois, W. E. B.   **1, 2, 13, 64**
Duberman, Martin   8

Dubie, Norman  36
Dubus, André  13, 36
Duffy, Bruce  50
Dugan, Alan  2, 6
Dumas, Henry  6, 62
Duncan, Robert  1, 2, 4, 7, 15, 41, 55
Duncan Lois  26
Dunn, Stephen  36
Dunne, John Gregory  28
Durang, Christopher  27, 38
Durban, Pam  39
Dworkin, Andrea  43
Dylan, Bob  3, 4, 6, 12
Eastlake, William  8
Eberhart, Richard  3, 11, 19, 56
Eberstadt, Fernanda  39
Eckert, Allan W.  17
Edel, Leon  29, 34
Edgerton, Clyde  39
Edmonds, Walter D.  35
Edson, Russell  13
Edwards, Gus  43
Ehle, John  27
Eigner, Larry  9
Eiseley, Loren  7
Eisenstadt, Jill  50
Eliade, Mircea  19
Eliot, T. S.  1, 2, 3, 6, 9, 10, 13, 15, 24, 34,
    41, 55, 57
Elkin, Stanley  4, 6, 9, 14, 27, 51
Elledge, Scott  34
Elliott, George P.  2
Ellis, Bret Easton  39
Ellis, Trey  55
Ellison, Harlan  1, 13, 42
Ellison, Ralph  1, 3, 11, 54
Ellmann, Lucy  61
Ellmann, Richard  50
Elman, Richard  19
Ephron, Nora  17, 31
Epstein, Daniel Mark  7
Epstein, Jacob  19
Epstein, Joseph  39
Epstein, Leslie  27
Erdman, Paul E.  25
Erdrich, Louise  39, 54
Erickson, Steve  64
Eshleman, Clayton  7
Estleman, Loren D.  48
Everett, Percival L.  57
Everson, William  1, 5, 14
Exley, Frederick  6, 11
Ezekiel, Tish O'Dowd  34
Fagen, Donald  26
Fair, Ronald L.  18
Fante, John  CLC-60
Fariña, Richard  9
Farley, Walter  17
Farmer, Philip José  1, 19
Farrell, James T.  1, 4, 8, 11
Fast, Howard  23
Faulkner, William  1, 3, 6, 8, 9, 11, 14, 18,
    28, 52
Fauset, Jessie Redmon  19, 54
Faust, Irvin  8
Fearing, Kenneth  51
Federman, Raymond  6, 47
Feiffer, Jules  2, 8, 64
Feinberg, David B.  59
Feldman, Irving  7
Felsen, Henry Gregor  17
Ferber, Edna  18

Ferlinghetti, Lawrence  2, 6, 10, 27
Fiedler, Leslie A.  4, 13, 24
Field, Andrew  44
Fierstein, Harvey  33
Fisher, Vardis  7
Fitzgerald, Robert  39
Flanagan, Thomas  25, 52
Fleming, Thomas J.  37
Foote, Horton  51
Forbes, Esther  12
Forché, Carolyn  25
Ford, John  16
Ford, Richard  46
Foreman, Richard  50
Forman, James D.  21
Fornes, Maria Irene  39, 61
Forrest, Leon  4
Fosse, Bob  20
Fox, Paula  2, 8
Fox, William Price  22
Francis, Robert  15
Frank, Elizabeth  39
Fraze, Candida  50
Frazier, Ian  46
Freeman, Judith  55
French, Marilyn  10, 18, 60
Friedman, B. H.  7
Friedman, Bruce Jay  3, 5, 56
Frost, Robert  1, 3, 4, 9, 10, 13, 15, 26, 34,
    44
Fuchs, Daniel (1934-)  34
Fuchs, Daniel (1909-)  8, 22
Fuller, Charles  25
Fulton, Alice  52
Gaddis, William  1, 3, 6, 8, 10, 19, 43
Gaines, Ernest J.  3, 11, 18
Gallagher, Tess  18, 63
Gallant, Roy A.  17
Gallico, Paul  2
Galvin, James  38
Gann, Ernest K.  23
Gardner, Herb  44
Gardner, John (Champlin, Jr.)  2, 3, 5, 7, 8,
    10, 18, 28, 34
Garrett, George  3, 11, 51
Garrigue, Jean  2, 8
Gass, William H.  1, 2, 8, 11, 15, 39
Gaye, Marvin  26
Gelbart, Larry  21, 61
Gelber, Jack  1, 6, 14
Gellhorn, Martha  14, 60
Gent, Peter  29
George, Jean Craighead  35
Gertler, T.  34
Ghiselin, Brewster  23
Gibbons, Kaye  50
Gibson, William (1948-)  39, 63
Gibson, William (1914-)  23
Gifford, Barry  34
Gilbreth, Frank B., Jr.  17
Gilchrist, Ellen  34, 48
Giles, Molly  39
Gilroy, Frank D.  2
Ginsberg, Allen  1, 2, 3, 4, 6, 13, 36
Giovanni, Nikki  2, 4, 19, 64
Glasser, Ronald J.  37
Glück, Louise  7, 22, 44
Godwin, Gail  5, 8, 22, 31
Gold, Herbert  4, 7, 14, 42
Goldbarth, Albert  5, 38
Goldman, William  1, 48
Goldsberry, Steven  34

Goodman, Paul  1, 2, 4, 7
Gordon, Caroline  6, 13, 29
Gordon, Mary  13, 22
Gordon, Sol  26
Gordone, Charles  1, 4
Gould, Lois  4, 10
Goyen, William  5, 8, 14, 40
Graham, Jorie  48
Grau, Shirley Ann  4, 9
Gray, Amlin  29
Gray, Francine du Plessix  22
Gray, Spalding  49
Grayson, Richard  38
Greeley, Andrew M.  28
Green, Paul  25
Greenberg, Joanne  3, 7, 30
Greenberg, Richard  57
Greene, Bette  30
Greene, Gael  8
Gregor, Arthur  9
Griffin, Peter  39
Grumbach, Doris  13, 22, 64
Grunwald, Lisa  44
Guare, John  8, 14, 29
Guest, Barbara  34
Guest, Judith  8, 30
Guild, Nicholas M.  33
Gunn, Bill  5
Gurney, A. R., Jr.  32, 50, 54
Guthrie, A. B., Jr.  23
Guthrie, Woody  35
Guy, Rosa  26
H. D.  3, 8, 14, 31, 34
Hacker, Marilyn  5, 9, 23
Hailey, Elizabeth Forsythe  40
Haines, John  58
Haldeman, Joe  61
Haley, Alex  8, 12
Hall, Donald  1, 13, 37, 59
Halpern, Daniel  14
Hamill, Pete  10
Hamilton, Edmond  1
Hamilton, Ian  55
Hamilton, Virginia  26
Hammett, Dashiell  3, 5, 10, 19, 47
Hamner, Earl, Jr.  12
Hannah, Barry  23, 38
Hansberry, Lorraine  17, 62
Hansen, Joseph  38
Hanson, Kenneth O.  13
Hardwick, Elizabeth  13
Harlan, Louis R.  34
Harling, Robert  53
Harmon, William  38
Harper, Michael S.  7, 22
Harris, MacDonald  9
Harris, Mark  19
Harrison, Harry  42
Harrison, Jim  6, 14, 33
Harriss, Will  34
Hartman, Geoffrey H.  27
Haruf, Kent  34
Hass, Robert  18, 39
Haviaras, Stratis  33
Hawkes, John  1, 2, 3, 4, 7, 9, 14, 15, 27,
    49
Hayden, Robert  5, 9, 14, 37
Hayman, Ronald  44
Hearne, Vicki  56
Hearon, Shelby  63
Heat Moon, William Least  29
Hecht, Anthony  8, 13, 19

Hecht, Ben  8
Heifner, Jack  11
Heilbrun, Carolyn G.  25
Heinemann, Larry  50
Heinlein, Robert A.  1, 3, 8, 14, 26, 55
Heller, Joseph  1, 3, 5, 8, 11, 36, 63
Hellman, Lillian  2, 4, 8, 14, 18, 34, 44, 52
Helprin, Mark  7, 10, 22, 32
Hemingway, Ernest  1, 3, 6, 8, 10, 13, 19,
   30, 34, 39, 41, 44, 50, 61
Hempel, Amy  39
Henley, Beth  23
Hentoff, Nat  26
Herbert, Frank  12, 23, 35, 44
Herbst, Josephine  34
Herlihy, James Leo  6
Herrmann, Dorothy  44
Hersey, John  1, 2, 7, 9, 40
Heyen, William  13, 18
Higgins, George V.  4, 7, 10, 18
Highsmith, Patricia  2, 4, 14, 42
Highwater, Jamake  12
Hill, George Roy  26
Hillerman, Tony  62
Himes, Chester  2, 4, 7, 18, 58
Hinton, S. E.  30
Hirsch, Edward  31, 50
Hoagland, Edward  28
Hoban, Russell C.  7, 25
Hobson, Laura Z.  7, 25
Hochman, Sandra  3, 8
Hoffman, Alice  51
Hoffman, Daniel  6, 13, 23
Hoffman, Stanley  5
Hoffman, William M.  40
Holland, Isabelle  21
Hollander, John  2, 5, 8, 14
Holleran, Andrew  38
Holmes, John Clellon  56
Honig, Edwin  33
Horgan, Paul  9, 53
Horovitz, Israel  56
Horwitz, Julius  14
Hougan, Carolyn  34
Howard, Maureen  5, 14, 46
Howard, Richard  7, 10, 47
Howe, Fanny  47
Howe, Tina  48
Howes, Barbara  15
Hubbard, L. Ron  43
Huddle, David  49
Hughart, Barry  39
Hughes, Langston  1, 5, 10, 15, 35, 44
Hugo, Richard F.  6, 18, 32
Humphrey, William  45
Humphreys, Josephine  34, 57
Hunt, E. Howard  3
Hunter, Evan  11, 31
Hunter, Kristin  35
Hurston, Zora Neale  7, 30, 61
Huston, John  20
Hwang, David Henry  55
Hyde, Margaret O.  21
Ian, Janis  21
Ignatow, David  4, 7, 14, 40
Ingalls, Rachel  42
Inge, William  1, 8, 19
Innaurato, Albert  21, 60
Irving, John  13, 23, 38
Isaacs, Susan  32
Ivask, Ivar  14
Jackson, Jesse  12

Jackson, Shirley  11, 60
Jacobs, Jim  12
Jacobsen, Josephine  48
Jakes, John  29
Janowitz, Tama  43
Jarrell, Randall  1, 2, 6, 9, 13, 49
Jeffers, Robinson  2, 3, 11, 15, 54
Jennings, Waylon  21
Jensen, Laura  37
Joel, Billy  26
Johnson, Charles  7, 51
Johnson, Denis  52
Johnson, Diane  5, 13, 48
Johnson, Joyce  58
Jones, Gayl  6, 9
Jones, James  1, 3, 10, 39
Jones, Madison  4
Jones, Nettie  34
Jones, Preston  10
Jones, Robert F.  7
Jong, Erica  4, 6, 8, 18
Jordan, June  5, 11, 23
Jordan, Pat  37
Just, Ward S.  4, 27
Justice, Donald  6, 19
Kadohata, Cynthia  59
Kahn, Roger  30
Kaletski, Alexander  39
Kallman, Chester  2
Kaminsky, Stuart  59
Kanin, Garson  22
Kantor, MacKinlay  7
Kaplan, David Michael  50
Kaplan, James  59
Karl, Frederick R.  34
Katz, Steve  47
Kauffman, Janet  42
Kaufman, Bob  49
Kaufman, George S.  38
Kaufman, Sue  3, 8
Kazan, Elia  6, 16, 63
Kazin, Alfred  34, 38
Keaton, Buster  20
Keene, Donald  34
Keillor, Garrison  40
Kellerman, Jonathan  44
Kelley, William Melvin  22
Kellogg, Marjorie  2
Kemelman, Harry  2
Kennedy, William  6, 28, 34, 53
Kennedy, X. J.  8, 42
Kerouac, Jack  1, 2, 3, 5, 14, 29, 61
Kerr, Jean  22
Kerr, M. E.  12, 35
Kerr, Robert  55, 59
Kerrigan, Anthony  4, 6
Kesey, Ken  1, 3, 6, 11, 46, 64
Kesselring, Joseph  45
Kessler, Jascha  4
Kettelkamp, Larry  12
Kherdian, David  6, 9
Kienzle, William X.  25
Killens, John Oliver  10
Kincaid, Jamaica  43
King, Stephen  12, 26, 37, 61
Kingman, Lee  17
Kingsley, Sidney  44
Kingsolver, Barbara  55
Kingston, Maxine Hong  12, 19, 58
Kinnell, Galway  1, 2, 3, 5, 13, 29
Kirkwood, James  9
Kizer, Carolyn  15, 39

Klappert, Peter  57
Klein, Norma  30
Klein, T. E. D.  34
Knebel, Fletcher  14
Knight, Etheridge  40
Knowles, John  1, 4, 10, 26
Koch, Kenneth  5, 8, 44
Kopit, Arthur  1, 18, 33
Kosinski, Jerzy  1, 2, 3, 6, 10, 15, 53
Kostelanetz, Richard  28
Kotlowitz, Robert  4
Kotzwinkle, William  5, 14, 35
Kozol, Jonathan  17
Kozoll, Michael  35
Kramer, Kathryn  34
Kramer, Larry  42
Kristofferson, Kris  26
Krumgold, Joseph  12
Krutch, Joseph Wood  24
Kubrick, Stanley  16
Kumin, Maxine  5, 13, 28
Kunitz, Stanley J.  6, 11, 14
Kuzma, Greg  7
L'Amour, Louis  25, 55
Lancaster, Bruce  36
Landis, John  26
Langer, Elinor  34
Lapine, James  39
Larsen, Eric  55
Larsen, Nella  37
Larson, Charles R.  31
Latham, Jean Lee  12
Lattimore, Richmond  3
Laughlin, James  49
Le Guin, Ursula K.  8, 13, 22, 45
Lear, Norman  12
Leavitt, David  34
Lebowitz, Fran  11, 36
Lee, Andrea  36
Lee, Don L.  2
Lee, George Washington  52
Lee, Harper  12, 60
Lee, Lawrence  34
Lee, Stan  17
Leet, Judith  11
Leffland, Ella  19
Leiber, Fritz  25
Leithauser, Brad  27
Lelchuk, Alan  5
Lemann, Nancy  39
L'Engle, Madeleine  12
Lentricchia, Frank  34
Leonard, Elmore  28, 34
Lerman, Eleanor  9
Lerman, Rhoda  56
Lester, Richard  20
Levertov, Denise  1, 2, 3, 5, 8, 15, 28
Levin, Ira  3, 6
Levin, Meyer  7
Levine, Philip  2, 4, 5, 9, 14, 33
Levinson, Deirdre  49
Levitin, Sonia  17
Lewis, Janet  41
L'Heureux, John  52
Lieber, Joel  6
Lieberman, Laurence  4, 36
Ligotti, Thomas  44
Linney, Romulus  51
Lipsyte, Robert  21
Lish, Gordon  45
Littell, Robert  42
Loewinsohn, Ron  52

Logan, John  5
Lopate, Phillip  29
Lord, Bette Bao  23
Lorde, Audre  18
Lowell, Robert  1, 2, 3, 4, 5, 8, 9, 11, 15, 37
Loy, Mina  28
Lucas, Craig  64
Lucas, George  16
Ludlam, Charles  46, 50
Ludlum, Robert  22, 43
Ludwig, Ken  60
Lurie, Alison  4, 5, 18, 39
Lynn, Kenneth S.  50
Lytle, Andrew  22
Maas, Peter  29
Macdonald, Cynthia  13, 19
MacDonald, John D.  3, 27, 44
Macdonald, Ross  1, 2, 3, 14, 34, 41
MacInnes, Helen  27, 39
MacLeish, Archibald  3, 8, 14
MacShane, Frank  39
Madden, David  5, 15
Madhubuti, Haki R.  6
Mailer, Norman  1, 2, 3, 4, 5, 8, 11, 14, 28, 39
Major, Clarence  3, 19, 48
Malamud, Bernard  1, 2, 3, 5, 8, 9, 11, 18, 27, 44
Maloff, Saul  5
Malone, Michael  43
Malzberg, Barry N.  7
Mamet, David  9, 15, 34, 46
Mamoulian, Rouben  16
Mano, D. Keith  2, 10
Manso, Peter  39
Markfield, Wallace  8
Marquand, John P.  2, 10
Marshall, Garry  17
Marshall, Paule  27
Martin, Steve  30
Maso, Carole  44
Mason, Bobbie Ann  28, 43
Masters, Hilary  48
Mastrosimone, William  36
Matheson, Richard  37
Mathews, Harry  6, 52
Matthews, William  40
Matthias, John  9
Matthiessen, Peter  5, 7, 11, 32, 64
Maxwell, William  19
May, Elaine  16
Maynard, Joyce  23
Maysles, Albert  16
Maysles, David  16
Mazer, Norma Fox  26
McBrien, William  44
McCaffrey, Anne  17, 59
McCarthy, Cormac  4, 57, 59
McCarthy, Mary  1, 3, 5, 14, 24, 39
McCauley, Stephen  50
McClure, Michael  6, 10
McCorkle, Jill  51
McCourt, James  5
McCullers, Carson  1, 4, 10, 12, 48
McElroy, Joseph  5, 47
McGinley, Phyllis  14
McGinniss, Joe  32
McGrath, Thomas  28, 59
McGuane, Thomas  3, 7, 18, 45
McHale, Tom  3, 5
McInerney, Jay  34
McIntyre, Vonda N.  18

McKuen, Rod  1, 3
McMillan, Terry  50, 61
McMurtry, Larry  2, 3, 7, 11, 27, 44
McNally, Terrence  4, 7, 41
McPhee, John  36
McPherson, James Alan  19
McPherson, William  34
Mead, Margaret  37
Medoff, Mark  6, 23
Mehta, Ved  37
Meltzer, Milton  26
Membreno, Alejandro  59
Meredith, William  4, 13, 22, 55
Merkin, Daphne  44
Merrill, James  2, 3, 6, 8, 13, 18, 34
Merton, Thomas  1, 3, 11, 34
Merwin, W. S.  1, 2, 3, 5, 8, 13, 18, 45
Mewshaw, Michael  9
Meyers, Jeffrey  39
Michaels, Leonard  6, 25
Michener, James A.  1, 5, 11, 29, 60
Miles, Josephine  1, 2, 14, 34, 39
Miller, Arthur  1, 2, 6, 10, 15, 26, 47
Miller, Henry  1, 2, 4, 9, 14, 43
Miller, Jason  2
Miller, Sue  44
Miller, Walter M., Jr.  4, 30
Millhauser, Steven  21, 54
Milner, Ron  56
Miner, Valerie  40
Minot, Susan  44
Minus, Ed  39
Modarressi, Taghi  44
Mohr, Nicholasa  12
Mojtabai, A. G.  5, 9, 15, 29
Momaday, N. Scott  2, 19
Montague, John  46
Montgomery, Marion  7
Mooney, Ted  25
Moore, Lorrie  39, 45
Moore, Marianne  1, 2, 4, 8, 10, 13, 19, 47
Morgan, Berry  6
Morgan, Frederick  23
Morgan, Robin  2
Morris, Wright  1, 3, 7, 18, 37
Morrison, Jim  17
Morrison, Toni  4, 10, 22, 55
Mosher, Howard Frank  62
Moss, Howard  7, 14, 45, 50
Motley, Willard  18
Mueller, Lisel  13, 51
Mukherjee, Bharati  53
Mull, Martin  17
Murphy, Sylvia  34
Myers, Walter Dean  35
Nabokov, Vladimir  1, 2, 3, 6, 8, 11, 15, 23, 44, 46, 64
Nash, Ogden  23
Naylor, Gloria  28, 52
Neff, Debra  56
Neihardt, John G.  32
Nelson, Willie  17
Nemerov, Howard  2, 6, 9, 36
Neufeld, John  17
Neville, Emily Cheney  12
Newlove, Donald  6
Newman, Charles  2, 8
Newman, Edwin  14
Newton, Suzanne  35
Nichols, John  38
Niedecker, Lorine  10, 42
Nin, Anaïs  1, 4, 8, 11, 14, 60

Nissenson, Hugh  4, 9
Niven, Larry  8
Nixon, Agnes Eckhardt  21
Norman, Marsha  28
Norton, Andre  12
Nova, Craig  7, 31
Nunn, Kem  34
Nyro, Laura  17
Oates, Joyce Carol  1, 2, 3, 6, 9, 11, 15, 19, 33, 52
O'Brien, Darcy  11
O'Brien, Tim  7, 19, 40
Ochs, Phil  17
O'Connor, Edwin  14
O'Connor, Flannery  1, 2, 3, 6, 10, 13, 15, 21
O'Dell, Scott  30
Odets, Clifford  2, 28
O'Grady, Timothy  59
O'Hara, Frank  2, 5, 13
O'Hara, John  1, 2, 3, 6, 11, 42
O'Hehir, Diana  41
Olds, Sharon  32, 39
Oliver, Mary  19, 34
Olsen, Tillie  4, 13
Olson, Charles  1, 2, 5, 6, 9, 11, 29
Olson, Toby  28
Oneal, Zibby  30
Oppen, George  7, 13, 34
Orlovitz, Gil  22
Ortiz, Simon J.  45
Owens, Rochelle  8
Ozick, Cynthia  3, 7, 28, 62
Pack, Robert  13
Paley, Grace  4, 6, 37
Pancake, Breece D'J  29
Parini, Jay  54
Parker, Dorothy  15
Parker, Robert B.  27
Parks, Gordon  1, 16
Pastan, Linda  27
Patchen, Kenneth  1, 2, 18
Paterson, Katherine  12, 30
Peacock, Molly  60
Pearson, T. R.  39
Peck, John  3
Peck, Richard  21
Peck, Robert Newton  17
Peckinpah, Sam  20
Percy, Walker  2, 3, 6, 8, 14, 18, 47
Perelman, S. J.  3, 5, 9, 15, 23, 44, 49
Pesetsky, Bette  28
Peterkin, Julia  31
Peters, Joan K.  39
Peters, Robert L.  7
Petrakis, Harry Mark  3
Petry, Ann  1, 7, 18
Philipson, Morris  53
Phillips, Jayne Anne  15, 33
Phillips, Robert  28
Piercy, Marge  3, 6, 14, 18, 27, 62
Pineda, Cecile  39
Pinkwater, D. M.  35
Pinsky, Robert  9, 19, 38
Pirsig, Robert M.  4, 6
Plante, David  7, 23, 38
Plath, Sylvia  1, 2, 3, 5, 9, 11, 14, 17, 50, 51, 62
Platt, Kin  26
Plimpton, George  36
Plumly, Stanley  33
Pohl, Frederik  18

Nationality Index

Poitier, Sidney  26
Pollitt, Katha  28
Pomerance, Bernard  13
Porter, Katherine Anne  1, 3, 7, 10, 13, 15, 27
Potok, Chaim  2, 7, 14, 26
Pound, Ezra  1, 2, 3, 4, 5, 7, 10, 13, 18, 34, 48, 50
Povod, Reinaldo  44
Powell, Padgett  34
Powers, J. F.  1, 4, 8, 57
Prager, Emily  56
Price, Reynolds  3, 6, 13, 43, 50, 63
Price, Richard  6, 12
Prince  35
Pritchard, William H.  34
Probst, Mark  59
Prokosch, Frederic  4, 48
Prose, Francine  45
Pryor, Richard  26
Purdy, James  2, 4, 10, 28, 52
Puzo, Mario  1, 2, 6, 36
Pynchon, Thomas  2, 3, 6, 9, 11, 18, 33, 62
Queen, Ellery  3, 11
Rabe, David  4, 8, 33
Rado, James  17
Raeburn, John  34
Ragni, Gerome  17
Rahv, Philip  24
Rakosi, Carl  47
Rampersad, Arnold  44
Rand, Ayn  3, 30, 44
Randall, Dudley  1
Ransom, John Crowe  2, 4, 5, 11, 24
Raphael, Frederic  2, 14
Rechy, John  1, 7, 14, 18
Redmon, Anne  22
Reed, Ishmael  2, 3, 5, 6, 13, 32, 60
Reed, Lou  21
Remarque, Erich Maria  21
Rexroth, Kenneth  1, 2, 6, 11, 22, 49
Reynolds, Jonathan  6, 38
Reynolds, Michael  44
Reznikoff, Charles  9
Ribman, Ronald  7
Rice, Anne  41
Rice, Elmer  7, 49
Rich, Adrienne  3, 6, 7, 11, 18, 36
Richter, Conrad  30
Riding, Laura  3, 7
Ringwood, Gwen Pharis  48
Robbins, Harold  5
Robbins, Tom  9, 32, 64
Robbins, Trina  21
Robinson, Jill  10
Robinson, Kim Stanley  34
Robinson, Marilynne  25
Robinson, Smokey  21
Robison, Mary  42
Roddenberry, Gene  17
Rodgers, Mary  12
Roethke, Theodore  1, 3, 8, 11, 19, 46
Rogers, Thomas  57
Rogin, Gilbert  18
Roiphe, Anne  3, 9
Rooke, Leon  25, 34
Rosen, Richard  39
Rosenthal, M. L.  28
Rossner, Judith  6, 9, 29
Roth, Henry  2, 6, 11
Roth, Philip  1, 2, 3, 4, 6, 9, 15, 22, 31, 47
Rothenberg, Jerome  6, 57

Rovit, Earl  7
Ruark, Gibbons  3
Rudnik, Raphael  7
Rukeyser, Muriel  6, 10, 15, 27
Rule, Jane  27
Rush, Norman  44
Russ, Joanna  15
Ryan, Cornelius  7
Sachs, Marilyn  35
Sackler, Howard  14
Sadoff, Ira  9
Safire, William  10
Sagan, Carl  30
Saint, H. F.  50
Sainte-Marie, Buffy  17
Salamanca, J. R.  4, 15
Salinger, J. D.  1, 3, 8, 12, 56
Salter, James  7, 52, 59
Sandburg, Carl  1, 4, 10, 15, 35
Sanders, Ed  53
Sanders, Lawrence  41
Sandoz, Mari  28
Saner, Reg  9
Santiago, Danny  33
Santmyer, Helen Hooven  33
Santos, Bienvenido N.  22
Saroyan, William  1, 8, 10, 29, 34, 56
Sarton, May  4, 14, 49
Saul, John  46
Savage, Thomas  40
Savan, Glenn  50
Sayers, Valerie  50
Sayles, John  7, 10, 14
Schaeffer, Susan Fromberg  6, 11, 22
Schell, Jonathan  35
Schevill, James  7
Schisgal, Murray  6
Schnackenberg, Gjertrud  40
Schorer, Mark  9
Schrader, Paul  26
Schulberg, Budd  7, 48
Schulz, Charles M.  12
Schuyler, James  5, 23
Schwartz, Delmore  2, 4, 10, 45
Schwartz, John Burnham  59
Schwartz, Lynne Sharon  31
Scoppettone, Sandra  26
Scorsese, Martin  20
Scott, Evelyn  43
Scott, Joanna  50
Sebestyen, Ouida  30
Seelye, John  7
Segal, Erich  3, 10
Seger, Bob  35
Seidel, Frederick  18
Selby, Hubert, Jr.  1, 2, 4, 8
Serling, Rod  30
Seton, Cynthia Propper  27
Settle, Mary Lee  19, 61
Sexton, Anne  2, 4, 6, 8, 10, 15, 53
Shaara, Michael  15
Shacochis, Bob  39
Shange, Ntozake  8, 25, 38
Shapiro, Karl  4, 8, 15, 53
Shaw, Irwin  7, 23, 34
Shawn, Wallace  41
Sheed, Wilfrid  2, 4, 10, 53
Shepard, Jim  36
Shepard, Lucius  34
Shepard, Sam  4, 6, 17, 34, 41, 44
Sherburne, Zoa  30
Sherman, Jonathan Marc  55

Sherman, Martin  19
Sherwin, Judith Johnson  7, 15
Shreve, Susan Richards  23
Shue, Larry  52
Shulman, Alix Kates  2, 10
Shuster, Joe  21
Siegel, Jerome  21
Sigal, Clancy  7
Silko, Leslie Marmon  23
Silver, Joan Micklin  20
Silverberg, Robert  7
Silverstein, Alvin  17
Silverstein, Virginia B.  17
Simak, Clifford  55
Simic, Charles  6, 9, 22, 49
Simmons, Charles  57
Simmons, Dan  44
Simon, Carly  26
Simon, Neil  6, 11, 31, 39
Simon, Paul  17
Simpson, Louis  4, 7, 9, 32
Simpson, Mona  44
Sinclair, Upton  1, 11, 15, 63
Singer, Isaac Bashevis  1, 3, 6, 9, 11, 15, 23, 38
Sissman, L. E.  9, 18
Slade, Bernard  11, 46
Slaughter, Frank G.  29
Slavitt, David  5, 14
Smiley, Jane  53
Smith, Betty  19
Smith, Clark Ashton  43
Smith, Dave  22, 42
Smith, Lee  25
Smith, Martin Cruz  25
Smith, Mary-Ann Tirone  39
Smith, Patti  12
Smith, William Jay  6
Snodgrass, W. D.  2, 6, 10, 18
Snyder, Gary  1, 2, 5, 9, 32
Snyder, Zilpha Keatley  17
Sokolov, Raymond  7
Sommer, Scott  25
Sondheim, Stephen  30, 39
Sontag, Susan  1, 2, 10, 13, 31
Sorrentino, Gilbert  3, 7, 14, 22, 40
Soto, Gary  32
Southern, Terry  7
Spackman, W. M.  46
Spacks, Barry  14
Spanidou, Irini  44
Spencer, Elizabeth  22
Spencer, Scott  30
Spicer, Jack  8, 18
Spielberg, Peter  6
Spielberg, Steven  20
Spillane, Mickey  3, 13
Spinrad, Norman  46
Spivack, Kathleen  6
Spoto, Donald  39
Springsteen, Bruce  17
Squires, Radcliffe  51
Stafford, Jean  4, 7, 19
Stafford, William  4, 7, 29
Stanton, Maura  9
Starbuck, George  53
Steele, Timothy  45
Stegner, Wallace  9, 49
Steinbeck, John  1, 5, 9, 13, 21, 34, 45, 59
Steinem, Gloria  63
Steiner, George  24
Stern, Gerald  40

Stern, Richard G.  **4, 39**
Sternberg, Josef von  **20**
Stevens, Mark  **34**
Stevenson, Anne  **7, 33**
Still, James  **49**
Stitt, Milan  **29**
Stolz, Mary  **12**
Stone, Irving  **7**
Stone, Robert  **5, 23, 42**
Storm, Hyemeyohsts  **3**
Stout, Rex  **3**
Strand, Mark  **6, 18, 41**
Straub, Peter  **28**
Stribling, T. S.  **23**
Stuart, Jesse  **1, 8, 11, 14, 34**
Sturgeon, Theodore  **22, 39**
Styron, William  **1, 3, 5, 11, 15, 60**
Sukenick, Ronald  **3, 4, 6, 48**
Summers, Hollis  **10**
Susann, Jacqueline  **3**
Swados, Elizabeth  **12**
Swados, Harvey  **5**
Swarthout, Glendon  **35**
Swenson, May  **4, 14, 61**
Talese, Gay  **37**
Tallent, Elizabeth  **45**
Tally, Ted  **42**
Tan, Amy  **59**
Tate, Allen  **2, 4, 6, 9, 11, 14, 24**
Tate, James  **2, 6, 25**
Tavel, Ronald  **6**
Taylor, Eleanor Ross  **5**
Taylor, Henry  **44**
Taylor, Mildred D.  **21**
Taylor, Peter  **1, 4, 18, 37, 44, 50**
Taylor, Robert Lewis  **14**
Terkel, Studs  **38**
Terry, Megan  **19**
Tesich, Steve  **40**
Tevis, Walter  **42**
Theroux, Alexander  **2, 25**
Theroux, Paul  **5, 8, 11, 15, 28, 46**
Thomas, Audrey  **7, 13, 37**
Thomas, Joyce Carol  **35**
Thomas, Lewis  **35**
Thomas, Piri  **17**
Thomas, Ross  **39**
Thompson, Hunter S.  **9, 17, 40**
Thurber, James  **5, 11, 25**
Tillinghast, Richard  **29**
Tiptree, James, Jr.  **48, 50**
Tolson, Melvin B.  **36**
Tomlin, Lily  **17**
Toole, John Kennedy  **19, 64**
Toomer, Jean  **1, 4, 13, 22**
Torrey, E. Fuller  **34**
Traven, B.  **8, 11**
Trevanian  **29**
Trilling, Lionel  **9, 11, 24**
Trow, George W. S.  **52**
Trudeau, Garry  **12**
Trumbo, Dalton  **19**
Tryon, Thomas  **3, 11**
Tunis, John R.  **12**
Turco, Lewis  **11, 63**
Tyler, Anne  **7, 11, 18, 28, 44, 59**
Tytell, John  **50**
Uhry, Alfred  **55**
Unger, Douglas  **34**
Updike, John  **1, 2, 3, 5, 7, 9, 13, 15, 23, 34, 43**
Urdang, Constance  **47**

Uris, Leon  **7, 32**
Van Ash, Cay  **34**
Van Doren, Mark  **6, 10**
Van Duyn, Mona  **3, 7, 63**
Van Peebles, Melvin  **2, 20**
Van Vechten, Carl  **33**
Vance, Jack  **35**
Vandenburgh, Jane  **59**
Vaughn, Stephanie  **62**
Vidal, Gore  **2, 4, 6, 8, 10, 22, 33**
Viereck, Peter  **4**
Vinge, Joan D.  **30**
Vliet, R. G.  **22**
Voigt, Cynthia  **30**
Voigt, Ellen Bryant  **54**
Vonnegut, Kurt, Jr.  **1, 2, 3, 4, 5, 8, 12, 22, 40, 60**
Wagman, Frederica  **7**
Wagner-Martin, Linda  **50**
Wagoner, David  **3, 5, 15**
Wakefield, Dan  **7**
Wakoski, Diane  **2, 4, 7, 9, 11, 40**
Waldman, Anne  **7**
Walker, Alice  **5, 6, 9, 19, 27, 46, 58**
Walker, Joseph A.  **19**
Walker, Margaret  **1, 6**
Wallace, David Foster  **50**
Wallace, Irving  **7, 13**
Wallant, Edward Lewis  **5, 10**
Wambaugh, Joseph  **3, 18**
Ward, Douglas Turner  **19**
Warhol, Andy  **20**
Warren, Robert Penn  **1, 4, 6, 8, 10, 13, 18, 39, 53, 59**
Wasserstein, Wendy  **32, 59**
Watkins, Paul  **55**
Webb, Charles  **7**
Webb, James H., Jr.  **22**
Weber, Lenora Mattingly  **12**
Weidman, Jerome  **7**
Weiss, Theodore  **3, 8, 14**
Welch, James  **6, 14, 52**
Wellek, René  **28**
Weller, Michael  **10, 53**
Welles, Orson  **20**
Wellman, Manly Wade  **49**
Wells, Rosemary  **12**
Welty, Eudora  **1, 2, 5, 14, 22, 33**
Wersba, Barbara  **30**
Wescott, Glenway  **13**
Wesley, Richard  **7**
West, Jessamyn  **7, 17**
West, Paul  **7, 14**
Westlake, Donald E.  **7, 33**
Whalen, Philip  **6, 29**
Wharton, William  **18, 37**
Wheelock, John Hall  **14**
White, E. B.  **10, 34, 39**
White, Edmund III  **27**
Whitney, Phyllis A.  **42**
Whittemore, Reed  **4**
Wicker, Tom  **7**
Wideman, John Edgar  **5, 34, 36**
Wieners, John  **7**
Wiesel, Elie  **3, 5, 11, 37**
Wiggins, Marianne  **57**
Wilbur, Richard  **3, 6, 9, 14, 53**
Wild, Peter  **14**
Wilder, Billy  **20**
Wilder, Thornton  **1, 5, 6, 10, 15, 35**
Wiley, Richard  **44**
Wilhelm, Kate  **7**

Willard, Nancy  **7, 37**
Williams, C. K.  **33, 56**
Williams, John A.  **5, 13**
Williams, Jonathan  **13**
Williams, Joy  **31**
Williams, Norman  **39**
Williams, Tennessee  **1, 2, 5, 7, 8, 11, 15, 19, 30, 39, 45**
Williams, Thomas  **14**
Williams, William Carlos  **1, 2, 5, 9, 13, 22, 42**
Williamson, Jack  **29**
Willingham, Calder  **5, 51**
Wilson, August  **39, 50, 63**
Wilson, Brian  **12**
Wilson, Edmund  **1, 2, 3, 8, 24**
Wilson, Lanford  **7, 14, 36**
Wilson, Robert  **7, 9**
Wilson, Sloan  **32**
Wilson, William S.  **49**
Winters, Yvor  **4, 8, 32**
Wiseman, Frederick  **20**
Wodehouse, P. G.  **1, 2, 5, 10, 22**
Woiwode, Larry  **6, 10**
Wojciechowska, Maia  **26**
Wolfe, Gene  **25**
Wolfe, George C.  **49**
Wolfe, Tom  **1, 2, 9, 15, 35, 51**
Wolff, Geoffrey  **41**
Wolff, Tobias  **39, 64**
Wolitzer, Hilma  **17**
Wonder, Stevie  **12**
Wong, Jade Snow  **17**
Wouk, Herman  **1, 9, 38**
Wright, Charles (Stevenson)  **49**
Wright, Charles  **6, 13, 28**
Wright, James  **3, 5, 10, 28**
Wright, Richard  **1, 3, 4, 9, 14, 21, 48**
Wright, Stephen  **33**
Wright, William  **44**
Wurlitzer, Rudolph  **2, 4, 15**
Wylie, Philip  **43**
Yates, Richard  **7, 8, 23**
Yep, Laurence  **35**
Yerby, Frank G.  **1, 7, 22**
Yglesias, Helen  **7, 22**
Young, Al  **19**
Yurick, Sol  **6**
Zappa, Frank  **17**
Zaturenska, Marya  **6, 11**
Zelazny, Roger  **21**
Ziegenhagen, Eric  **55**
Zindel, Paul  **6, 26**
Zoline, Pamela  **62**
Zukofsky, Louis  **1, 2, 4, 7, 11, 18**
Zweig, Paul  **34, 42**

### ARGENTINIAN
Bioy Casares, Adolfo  **4, 8, 13**
Borges, Jorge Luis  **1, 2, 3, 4, 6, 8, 9, 10, 13, 19, 44, 48**
Cortázar, Julio  **2, 3, 5, 10, 13, 15, 33, 34**
Costantini, Humberto  **49**
Mujica Láinez, Manuel  **31**
Puig, Manuel  **3, 5, 10, 28**
Sabato, Ernesto  **10, 23**
Valenzuela, Luisa  **31**

### ARMENIAN
Mamoulian, Rouben  **16**

**AUSTRALIAN**
Anderson, Jessica  37
Astley, Thea  41
Brinsmead, H. F.  21
Buckley, Vincent  57
Buzo, Alexander  61
Carey, Peter  40, 55
Clark, Mavis Thorpe  12
Courtenay, Bryce  59
Davison, Frank Dalby  15
Elliott, Sumner Locke  38
FitzGerald, Robert D.  19
Grenville, Kate  61
Hall, Rodney  51
Hazzard, Shirley  18
Hope, A. D.  3, 51
Hospital, Janette Turner  42
Jolley, Elizabeth  46
Jones, Rod  50
Keneally, Thomas  5, 8, 10, 14, 19, 27, 43
Koch, C. J.  42
Lawler, Raymond (Evenor)  58
Malouf, David  28
Matthews, Greg  45
McAuley, James  45
McCullough, Colleen  27
Murray, Les A.  40
Porter, Peter  5, 13, 33
Prichard, Katharine Susannah  46
Shapcott, Thomas W.  38
Slessor, Kenneth  14
Stead, Christina  2, 5, 8, 32
Stow, Randolph  23, 48
Thiele, Colin  17
Weir, Peter  20
West, Morris L.  6, 33
White, Patrick  3, 4, 5, 7, 9, 18
Williamson, David  56
Wright, Judith  11, 53

**AUSTRIAN**
Adamson, Joy  17
Bernhard, Thomas  3, 32, 61
Canetti, Elias  3, 14, 25
Gregor, Arthur  9
Handke, Peter  5, 8, 10, 15, 38
Hochwälder, Fritz  36
Jandl, Ernst  34
Lang, Fritz  20
Lind, Jakov  1, 2, 4, 27
Sternberg, Josef von  20
Wellek, René  28
Wilder, Billy  20

**BELGIAN**
Ghelderode, Michel de  6, 11
Lévi-Strauss, Claude  38
Mallet-Joris, Françoise  11
Michaux, Henri  8, 19
Sarton, May  4, 14, 49
Simenon, Georges  1, 2, 3, 8, 18, 47
Tytell, John  50
Van Itallie, Jean-Claude  3
Yourcenar, Marguerite  19, 38, 50

**BRAZILIAN**
Amado, Jorge  13, 40
Andrade, Carlos Drummond de  18
Dourado, Autran  23, 60
Lispector, Clarice  43
Ribeiro, Darcy  34
Ribeiro, João Ubaldo  10

Rosa, João Guimarães  23

**BULGARIAN**
Bagryana, Elisaveta  10

**CAMEROONIAN**
Beti, Mongo  27

**CANADIAN**
Acorn, Milton  15
Aquin, Hubert  15
Atwood, Margaret  2, 3, 4, 8, 13, 15, 25, 44
Avison, Margaret  2, 4
Barfoot, Joan  18
Bellow, Saul  1, 2, 3, 6, 8, 10, 13, 15, 25, 33, 34
Birney, Earle  1, 4, 6, 11
Bissett, Bill  18
Blais, Marie-Claire  2, 4, 6, 13, 22
Blaise, Clark  29
Bowering, George  15, 47
Bowering, Marilyn R.  32
Buckler, Ernest  13
Buell, John  10
Callaghan, Morley  3, 14, 41
Carrier, Roch  13
Child, Philip  19
Chislett, Anne  34
Cohen, Leonard  3, 38
Cohen, Matt  19
Coles, Don  46
Cook, Michael  58
Craven, Margaret  17
Davies, Robertson  2, 7, 13, 25, 42
De la Roche, Mazo  14
Donnell, David  34
Dudek, Louis  11, 19
Engel, Marian  36
Everson, Ronald G.  27
Faludy, George  42
Finch, Robert  18
Findley, Timothy  27
Fraser, Sylvia  64
Frye, Northrop  24
Gallant, Mavis  7, 18, 38
Garner, Hugh  13
Glassco, John  9
Gotlieb, Phyllis  18
Govier, Katherine  51
Gustafson, Ralph  36
Haig-Brown, Roderick L.  21
Hailey, Arthur  5
Harris, Christie  12
Hébert, Anne  4, 13, 29
Hine, Daryl  15
Hodgins, Jack  23
Hood, Hugh  15, 28
Hospital, Janette Turner  42
Hyde, Anthony  42
Jacobsen, Josephine  48
Jiles, Paulette  13, 58
Johnston, George  51
Jones, D. G.  10
Kelly, M. T.  55
Kinsella, W. P.  27, 43
Klein, A. M.  19
Krizanc, John  57
Kroetsch, Robert  5, 23, 57
Lane, Patrick  25
Laurence, Margaret  3, 6, 13, 50, 62
Layton, Irving  2, 15
Levine, Norman  54

Lightfoot, Gordon  26
Livesay, Dorothy  4, 15
Mac Ewen, Gwendolyn  13, 55
Mac Leod, Alistair  56
MacLennan, Hugh  2, 14
Macpherson, Jay  14
Maillet, Antonine  54
Major, Kevin  26
McFadden, David  48
McLuhan, Marshall  37
Metcalf, John  37
Mitchell, Joni  12
Mitchell, W. O.  25
Moore, Brian  1, 3, 5, 7, 8, 19, 32
Morgan, Janet  39
Mowat, Farley  26
Munro, Alice  6, 10, 19, 50
Musgrave, Susan  13, 54
Newlove, John  14
Nichol, B. P.  18
Nowlan, Alden  15
Ondaatje, Michael  14, 29, 51
Page, P. K.  7, 18
Pollack, Sharon  50
Pratt, E. J.  19
Purdy, A. W.  3, 6, 14, 50
Reaney, James  13
Richards, David Adam  59
Richler, Mordecai  3, 5, 9, 13, 18, 46
Ringwood, Gwen Pharis  48
Ritter, Erika  52
Rooke, Leon  25, 34
Rosenblatt, Joe  15
Ross, Sinclair  13
Roy, Gabrielle  10, 14
Rule, Jane  27
Ryga, George  14
Scott, F. R.  22
Skelton, Robin  13
Slade, Bernard  11, 46
Smart, Elizabeth  54
Smith, A. J. M.  15
Souster, Raymond  5, 14
Suknaski, Andrew  19
Thesen, Sharon  56
Thomas, Audrey  7, 13, 37
Thompson, Judith  39
Tremblay, Michel  29
Vanderhaeghe, Guy  41
Vizinczey, Stephen  40
Waddington, Miriam  28
Wah, Fred  44
Walker, David Harry  14
Walker, George F.  44, 61
Webb, Phyllis  18
Wiebe, Rudy  6, 11, 14
Wilson, Ethel Davis  13
Wright, L. R.  44
Wright, Richard B.  6
Young, Neil  17

**CHILEAN**
Alegria, Fernando  57
Allende, Isabel  39, 57
Donoso, José  4, 8, 11, 32
Dorfman, Ariel  48
Neruda, Pablo  1, 2, 5, 7, 9, 28, 62
Parra, Nicanor  2

**CHINESE**
Ch'ien Chung-shu  22
Lord, Bette Bao  23

Mo, Timothy  46
Pa Chin  18
Peake, Mervyn  7
Wong, Jade Snow  17

**COLOMBIAN**
García Márquez, Gabriel  2, 3, 8, 10, 15, 27, 47, 55

**CUBAN**
Arenas, Reinaldo  41
Cabrera Infante, G.  5, 25, 45
Carpentier, Alejo  8, 11, 38
Fornes, Maria Irene  39
Guillén, Nicolás  48
Lezama Lima, José  4, 10
Padilla, Heberto  38
Sarduy, Severo  6

**CZECHOSLOVAKIAN**
Havel, Václav  25, 58
Hrabal, Bohumil  13
Klima, Ivan  56
Kohout, Pavel  13
Kundera, Milan  4, 9, 19, 32
Lustig, Arnost  56
Seifert, Jaroslav  34, 44
Škvorecký, Josef  15, 39
Vaculík, Ludvík  7

**DANISH**
Abell, Kjeld  15
Bødker, Cecil  21
Dinesen, Isak  10, 29
Dreyer, Carl Theodor  16

**DUTCH**
De Hartog, Jan  19
Mulisch, Harry  42
Ruyslinck, Ward  14
Van de Wetering, Janwillem  47

**EGYPTIAN**
Chedid, Andrée  47
Mahfūz, Najīb  52, 55

**ENGLISH**
Ackroyd, Peter  34, 52
Adams, Douglas  27, 60
Adams, Richard  4, 5, 18
Adcock, Fleur  41
Aickman, Robert  57
Aiken, Joan  35
Aldington, Richard  49
Aldiss, Brian W.  5, 14, 40
Allingham, Margery  19
Almedingen, E. M.  12
Alvarez, A.  5, 13
Ambler, Eric  4, 6, 9
Amis, Kingsley  1, 2, 3, 5, 8, 13, 40, 44
Amis, Martin  4, 9, 38, 62
Anderson, Lindsay  20
Anthony, Piers  35
Archer, Jeffrey  28
Arden, John  6, 13, 15
Armatrading, Joan  17
Arthur, Ruth M.  12
Arundel, Honor  17
Auden, W. H.  1, 2, 3, 4, 6, 9, 11, 14, 43
Ayckbourn, Alan  5, 8, 18, 33
Ayrton, Michael  7
Bagnold, Enid  25

Bailey, Paul  45
Bainbridge, Beryl  4, 5, 8, 10, 14, 18, 22, 62
Ballard, J. G.  3, 6, 14, 36
Banks, Lynne Reid  23
Barker, Clive  52
Barker, George  8, 48
Barker, Howard  37
Barker, Pat  32
Barnes, Julian  42
Barnes, Peter  5, 56
Bates, H. E.  46
Beer, Patricia  58
Bennett, Alan  45
Berger, John  2, 19
Berkoff, Steven  56
Bermant, Chaim  40
Betjeman, John  2, 6, 10, 34, 43
Billington, Rachel  43
Binyon, T. J.  34
Blunden, Edmund  2, 56
Bogarde, Dirk  19
Bolt, Robert  14
Bond, Edward  4, 6, 13, 23
Booth, Martin  13
Bowen, Elizabeth  1, 3, 6, 11, 15, 22
Bowie, David  17
Boyd, William  28, 53
Bradbury, Malcolm  32, 61
Bragg, Melvyn  10
Braine, John  1, 3, 41
Brenton, Howard  31
Brittain, Vera  23
Brooke-Rose, Christine  40
Brophy, Brigid  6, 11, 29
Brunner, John  8, 10
Bryce, Courtenay  59
Bunting, Basil  10, 39, 47
Burgess, Anthony  1, 2, 4, 5, 8, 10, 13, 15, 22, 40, 62
Byatt, A. S.  19
Caldwell, Taylor  2, 28, 39
Campbell, Ramsey  42
Carter, Angela  5, 41
Caute, David  29
Chambers, Aidan  35
Chaplin, Charles  16
Chatwin, Bruce  28, 57, 59
Christie, Agatha  1, 6, 8, 12, 39, 48
Churchill, Caryl  31, 55
Clark, Brian  29
Clarke, Arthur C.  1, 4, 13, 18, 35
Clash, The  30
Clavell, James  6, 25
Colegate, Isabel  36
Comfort, Alex  7
Compton-Burnett, Ivy  1, 3, 10, 15, 34
Cooney, Ray  62
Costello, Elvis  21
Coward, Noël  1, 9, 29, 51
Creasey, John  11
Crispin, Edmund  22
Dahl, Roald  1, 6, 18
Daryush, Elizabeth  6, 19
Davie, Donald  5, 8, 10, 31
Davics, Ray  21
Davies, Rhys  23
Day Lewis, C.  1, 6, 10
Deighton, Len  4, 7, 22, 46
Delaney, Shelagh  29
Dennis, Nigel  8
Dickinson, Peter  12, 35

Drabble, Margaret  2, 3, 5, 8, 10, 22, 53
du Maurier, Daphne  6, 11, 59
Duffy, Maureen  37
Durrell, Lawrence  1, 4, 6, 8, 13, 27, 41
Eagleton, Terry  63
Edgar, David  42
Edwards, G. B.  25
Eliot, T. S.  1, 2, 3, 6, 9, 10, 13, 15, 24, 34, 41, 55, 57
Elliott, Janice  47
Ellis, A. E.  7
Ellis, Alice Thomas  40
Empson, William  3, 8, 19, 33, 34
Enright, D. J.  4, 8, 31
Ewart, Gavin  13, 46
Fairbairns, Zoë  32
Farrell, J. G.  6
Feinstein, Elaine  36
Fenton, James  32
Figes, Eva  31
Fisher, Roy  25
Fitzgerald, Penelope  19, 51, 61
Fleming, Ian  3, 30
Follett, Ken  18
Forester, C. S.  35
Forster, E. M.  1, 2, 3, 4, 9, 10, 13, 15, 22, 45
Forsyth, Frederick  2, 5, 36
Fowles, John  1, 2, 3, 4, 6, 9, 10, 15, 33
Francis, Dick  2, 22, 42
Fraser, Antonia  32
Fraser, George MacDonald  7
Frayn, Michael  3, 7, 31, 47
Freeling, Nicolas  38
Fry, Christopher  2, 10, 14
Fugard, Sheila  48
Fuller, John  62
Fuller, Roy  4, 28
Gardam, Jane  43
Gardner, John (Edmund)  30
Garfield, Leon  12
Garner, Alan  17
Garnett, David  3
Gascoyne, David  45
Gee, Maggie  57
Gerhardie, William  5
Gilliatt, Penelope  2, 10, 13, 53
Glanville, Brian  6
Glendinning, Victoria  50
Gloag, Julian  40
Godden, Rumer  53
Golding, William  1, 2, 3, 8, 10, 17, 27, 58
Graham, Winston  23
Graves, Richard P.  44
Graves, Robert  1, 2, 6, 11, 39, 44, 45
Gray, Simon  9, 14, 36
Green, Henry  2, 13
Greene, Graham  1, 3, 6, 9, 14, 18, 27, 37
Griffiths, Trevor  13, 52
Grigson, Geoffrey  7, 39
Gunn, Thom  3, 6, 18, 32
Haig-Brown, Roderick L.  21
Hailey, Arthur  5
Hall, Rodney  51
Hamburger, Michael  5, 14
Hamilton, Patrick  51
Hampton, Christopher  4
Hare, David  29, 58
Harrison, Tony  43
Hartley, L. P.  2, 22
Harwood, Ronald  32
Hastings, Selina  44

Nationality Index

Hawking, Stephen  63
Heppenstall, Rayner  10
Herriot, James  12
Hibbert, Eleanor  7
Hill, Geoffrey  5, 8, 18, 45
Hill, Susan B.  4
Hinde, Thomas  6, 11
Hitchcock, Alfred  16
Hocking, Mary  13
Holden, Ursula  18
Holdstock, Robert  39
Hollinghurst, Alan  55
Hooker, Jeremy  43
Hopkins, John  4
Household, Geoffrey  11
Howard, Elizabeth Jane  7, 29
Hughes, Richard  1, 11
Hughes, Ted  2, 4, 9, 14, 37
Huxley, Aldous  1, 3, 4, 5, 8, 11, 18, 35
Ingalls, Rachel  42
Isherwood, Christopher  1, 9, 11, 14, 44
Ishiguro, Kazuo  27, 56, 59
Jacobson, Dan  4, 14
Jagger, Mick  17
James, P. D.  18, 46
Jellicoe, Ann  27
Jennings, Elizabeth  5, 14
Jhabvala, Ruth Prawer  4, 8, 29
Johnson, B. S.  6, 9
Johnson, Pamela Hansford  1, 7, 27
Jolley, Elizabeth  46
Jones, David  2, 4, 7, 13, 42
Jones, Diana Wynne  26
Jones, Mervyn  10, 52
Josipovici, Gabriel  6, 43
Kavan, Anna  5, 13
Kaye, M. M.  28
Keates, Jonathan  34
King, Francis  8, 53
Koestler, Arthur  1, 3, 6, 8, 15, 33
Kops, Bernard  4
Kureishi, Hanif  64
Larkin, Philip  3, 5, 8, 9, 13, 18, 33, 39, 64
Le Carré, John  3, 5, 9, 15, 28
Leavis, F. R.  24
Lee, Tanith  46
Lehmann, Rosamond  5
Lennon, John  12, 35
Lessing, Doris  1, 2, 3, 6, 10, 15, 22, 40
Levertov, Denise  1, 2, 3, 5, 8, 15, 28
Levi, Peter  41
Lewis, C. S.  1, 3, 6, 14, 27
Lively, Penelope  32, 50
Lodge, David  36
Loy, Mina  28
Luke, Peter  38
MacInnes, Colin  4, 23
Mackenzie, Compton  18
Macpherson, Jay  14
Maitland, Sara  49
Manning, Olivia  5, 19
Markandaya, Kamala  8, 38
Masefield, John  11, 47
Maugham, W. Somerset  1, 11, 15
Mayne, William  12
McCartney, Paul  12, 35
McEwan, Ian  13
McGrath, Patrick  55
Mercer, David  5
Metcalf, John  37
Middleton, Christopher  13
Middleton, Stanley  7, 38

Mitford, Nancy  44
Mo, Timothy  46
Monty Python  21
Moorcock, Michael  5, 27, 58
Mortimer, John  28, 43
Mortimer, Penelope  5
Mosley, Nicholas  43
Motion, Andrew  47
Mott, Michael  15, 34
Murdoch, Iris  1, 2, 3, 4, 6, 8, 11, 15, 22, 31, 51
Naipaul, V. S.  4, 7, 9, 13, 18, 37
Newby, P. H.  2, 13
Nichols, Peter  5, 36
Nye, Robert  13, 42
O'Brien, Richard  17
O'Faolain, Julia  6, 19, 47
Olivier, Laurence  20
Orton, Joe  4, 13, 43
Osborne, John  1, 2, 5, 11, 45
Osborne, Lawrence  50
Page, Jimmy  12
Page, Louise  40
Parkin, Frank  43
Paulin, Tom  37
Peake, Mervyn  7, 54
Pearce, Philippa  21
Pink Floyd  35
Pinter, Harold  1, 3, 6, 9, 11, 15, 27, 58
Plant, Robert  12
Poliakoff, Stephen  38
Police, The  26
Poole, Josephine  17
Potter, Dennis  58
Powell, Anthony  1, 3, 7, 9, 10, 31
Pownall, David  10
Powys, John Cowper  7, 9, 15, 46
Priestley, J. B.  2, 5, 9, 34
Prince, F. T.  22
Pritchett, V. S.  5, 13, 15, 41
Pym, Barbara  13, 19, 37
Quin, Ann  6
Raine, Craig  32
Raine, Kathleen  7, 45
Rathbone, Julian  41
Rattigan, Terence  7
Raven, Simon  14
Read, Herbert  4
Read, Piers Paul  4, 10, 25
Reading, Peter  47
Redgrove, Peter  6, 41
Reid, Christopher  33
Renault, Mary  3, 11, 17
Rendell, Ruth  28, 48, 50
Rhys, Jean  2, 4, 6, 14, 19, 51
Rice, Tim  21
Richard, Keith  17
Richards, I. A.  14, 24
Roberts, Keith  14
Roberts, Michèle  48
Rudkin, David  14
Rushdie, Salman  23, 31, 55, 59
Rushforth, Peter  19
Russell, Ken  16
Russell, Willy  60
Sansom, William  2, 6
Sassoon, Siegfried  36
Scammell, Michael  34
Scannell, Vernon  49
Schlee, Ann  35
Scott, Paul  9, 60
Shaffer, Anthony  19

Shaffer, Peter  5, 14, 18, 37, 60
Sharpe, Tom  36
Shaw, Robert  5
Sheed, Wilfrid  2, 4, 10, 53
Shute, Nevil  30
Shuttle, Penelope  7
Silkin, Jon  2, 6, 43
Sillitoe, Alan  1, 3, 6, 10, 19, 57
Simpson, N. F.  29
Sinclair, Andrew  2, 14
Sisson, C. H.  8
Sitwell, Edith  2, 9
Slaughter, Carolyn  56
Smith, Stevie  3, 8, 25, 44
Snow, C. P.  1, 4, 6, 9, 13, 19
Spender, Stephen  1, 2, 5, 10, 41
Spurling, Hilary  34
Stannard, Martin  44
Stewart, J. I. M.  7, 14, 32
Stewart, Mary  7, 35
Stoppard, Tom  1, 3, 4, 5, 8, 15, 29, 34, 63
Storey, David  2, 4, 5, 8
Streatfeild, Noel  21
Sutcliff, Rosemary  26
Swift, Graham  41
Swinfen, Ann  34
Swinnerton, Frank  31
Symons, Julian  2, 14, 32
Szirtes, George  46
Taylor, Elizabeth  2, 4, 29
Tennant, Emma  13, 52
Teran, Lisa St. Aubin de  36
Thomas, D. M.  13, 22, 31
Tindall, Gillian  7
Tolkien, J. R. R.  1, 2, 3, 8, 12, 38
Tomlinson, Charles  2, 4, 6, 13, 45
Townsend, Sue  61
Townshend, Peter  17, 42
Tremain, Rose  42
Tuohy, Frank  37
Ustinov, Peter  1
Vansittart, Peter  42
Wain, John  2, 11, 15, 46
Walker, Ted  13
Walsh, Jill Paton  35
Warner, Francis  14
Warner, Marina  59
Warner, Rex  45
Warner, Sylvia Townsend  7, 19
Waterhouse, Keith  47
Waugh, Auberon  7
Waugh, Evelyn  1, 3, 8, 13, 19, 27, 44
Waugh, Harriet  6
Webber, Andrew Lloyd  21
Weldon, Fay  6, 9, 11, 19, 36, 59
Weller, Paul  26
Wesker, Arnold  3, 5, 42
West, Anthony  50
West, Paul  7, 14
West, Rebecca  7, 9, 31, 50
Westall, Robert  17
White, T. H.  30
Whitehead, E. A.  5
Whitemore, Hugh  37
Williams, Hugo  42
Wilson, A. N.  33
Wilson, Angus  2, 3, 5, 25, 34
Wilson, Colin  3, 14
Wilson, Snoo  33
Winterson, Jeannette  64
Wodehouse, P. G.  1, 2, 5, 10, 22
Wyndham, John  19

Young, Andrew  5

**ESTONIAN**
Ivask, Ivar  14

**FIJIAN**
Prichard, Katharine Susannah  46

**FINNISH**
Haavikko, Paavo  18, 34
Salama, Hannu  18
Sillanpää, Franz Eemil  19

**FRENCH**
Adamov, Arthur  4, 25
Anouilh, Jean  1, 3, 8, 13, 40, 50
Aragon, Louis  3, 22
Arrabal, Fernando  2, 9, 18
Audiberti, Jacques  38
Aymé, Marcel  11
Barthes, Roland  24
Bataille, Georges  29
Baudrillard, Jean  CLC-60
Beauvoir, Simone de  1, 2, 4, 8, 14, 31, 44, 50
Beckett, Samuel  1, 2, 3, 4, 6, 9, 10, 11, 14, 18, 29, 57
Bonnefoy, Yves  9, 15, 58
Bresson, Robert  16
Breton, André  2, 9, 15, 54
Butor, Michel  1, 3, 8, 11, 15
Cayrol, Jean  11
Céline, Louis-Ferdinand  1, 3, 4, 7, 9, 15, 47
Cendrars, Blaise  18
Chabrol, Claude  16
Char, René  9, 11, 14, 55
Chedid, Andrée  47
Clair, René  20
Cocteau, Jean  1, 8, 15, 16, 43
Cousteau, Jacques-Yves  30
Del Castillo, Michel  38
Derrida, Jacques  24
Duhamel, Georges  8
Duras, Marguerite  3, 6, 11, 20, 34, 40
Federman, Raymond  6, 47
Foucault, Michel  31, 34
Francis, Claude  50
Gary, Romain  25
Gascar, Pierre  11
Genet, Jean  1, 2, 5, 10, 14, 44, 46
Giono, Jean  4, 11
Godard, Jean-Luc  20
Goldmann, Lucien  24
Gontier, Fernande  50
Gracq, Julien  11, 48
Gray, Francine du Plessix  22
Green, Julien  3, 11
Guillevic  33
Ionesco, Eugène  1, 4, 6, 9, 11, 15, 41
Jouve, Pierre Jean  47
Laurent, Antoine  50
Le Clézio, J. M. G.  31
Leduc, Violette  22
Leiris, Michel  61
Lévi-Strauss, Claude  38
Mallet-Joris, Françoise  11
Malraux, André  1, 4, 9, 13, 15, 57
Mandiargues, André Pieyre de  41
Marcel, Gabriel  15
Mauriac, Claude  9
Mauriac, François  4, 9, 56

Merton, Thomas  1, 3, 11, 34
Modiano, Patrick  18
Montherlant, Henri de  8, 19
Morand, Paul  41
Perec, Georges  56
Perse, St.-John  4, 11, 46
Pinget, Robert  7, 13, 37
Ponge, Francis  6, 18
Prévert, Jacques  15
Queneau, Raymond  2, 5, 10, 42
Renoir, Jean  20
Resnais, Alain  16
Reverdy, Pierre  53
Rio, Michel  43
Robbe-Grillet, Alain  1, 2, 4, 6, 8, 10, 14, 43
Rohmer, Eric  16
Romains, Jules  7
Sagan, Françoise  3, 6, 9, 17, 36
Sarduy, Severo  6
Sarraute, Nathalie  1, 2, 4, 8, 10, 31
Sartre, Jean-Paul  1, 4, 7, 9, 13, 18, 24, 44, 50, 52
Schwarz-Bart, André  2, 4
Schwarz-Bart, Simone  7
Simenon, Georges  1, 2, 3, 8, 18, 47
Simon, Claude  4, 9, 15, 39
Steiner, George  24
Tournier, Michel  6, 23, 36
Troyat, Henri  23
Truffaut, François  20
Tzara, Tristan  47
Varda, Agnès  16
Wittig, Monique  22
Yourcenar, Marguerite  19, 38, 50

**GERMAN**
Becker, Jurek  7, 19
Benary-Isbert, Margot  12
Bienek, Horst  7, 11
Böll, Heinrich  2, 3, 6, 9, 11, 15, 27, 39
Buchheim, Lothar-Günther  6
Dürrenmatt, Friedrich  1, 4, 8, 11, 15, 43
Eich, Günter  15
Ende, Michael  31
Enzensberger, Hans Magnus  43
Fassbinder, Rainer Werner  20
Figes, Eva  31
Grass, Günter  1, 2, 4, 6, 11, 15, 22, 32, 49
Hamburger, Michael  5, 14
Heidegger, Martin  24
Herzog, Werner  16
Hesse, Hermann  1, 2, 3, 6, 11, 17, 25
Heym, Stefan  41
Hildesheimer, Wolfgang  49
Hochhuth, Rolf  4, 11, 18
Hofmann, Gert  54
Johnson, Uwe  5, 10, 15, 40
Kroetz, Franz Xaver  41
Kunze, Reiner  10
Lenz, Siegfried  27
Levitin, Sonia  17
Mueller, Lisel  13, 51
Nossack, Hans Erich  6
Preussler, Otfried  17
Remarque, Erich Maria  21
Riefenstahl, Leni  16
Sachs, Nelly  14
Schmidt, Arno  56
Seghers, Anna  7
Strauss, Botho  22
Süskind, Patrick  44

Walser, Martin  27
Weiss, Peter  3, 15, 51
Wellershoff, Dieter  46
Wolf, Christa  14, 29, 58
Zuckmayer, Carl  18

**GHANAIAN**
Armah, Ayi Kwei  5, 33

**GREEK**
Broumas, Olga  10
Elytis, Odysseus  15, 49
Haviaras, Stratis  33
Karapánou, Margaríta  13
Nakos, Lilika  29
Ritsos, Yannis  6, 13, 31
Samarakis, Antonis  5
Seferis, George  5, 11
Spanidou, Irini  44
Vassilikos, Vassilis  4, 8

**GUADELOUPEAN**
Condé, Maryse  52
Schwarz-Bart, Simone  7

**GUATEMALAN**
Asturias, Miguel Ángel  3, 8, 13

**GUINEAN**
Laye, Camara  4, 38

**GUYANESE**
Harris, Wilson  25

**HUNGARIAN**
Faludy, George  42
Koestler, Arthur  1, 3, 6, 8, 15, 33
Konrád, György  4, 10
Lengyel, József  7
Lukács, Georg  24
Nagy, László  7
Szirtes, George  46
Tabori, George  19
Vizinczey, Stephen  40
Wiesel, Elie  3, 5, 11, 37

**ICELANDIC**
Laxness, Halldór  25

**INDIAN**
Anand, Mulk Raj  23
Desai, Anita  19, 37
Ezekiel, Nissim  61
Ghosh, Amitav  44
Mahapatra, Jayanta  33
Markandaya, Kamala  8, 38
Mehta, Ved  37,
Mukherjee, Bharati  53
Narayan, R. K.  7, 28, 47
Rao, Raja  25, 56
Ray, Satyajit  16
Rushdie, Salman  23, 31, 55, 59
Sahgal, Nayantara  41
Sealy, I. Allan  55
Seth, Vikram  43
Singh, Khushwant  11

**IRANIAN**
Modarressi, Taghi  44
Shamlu, Ahmad  10

## IRISH

Banville, John  46
Beckett, Samuel  1, 2, 3, 4, 6, 9, 10, 11, 14, 18, 29, 57
Behan, Brendan  1, 8, 11, 15
Blackwood, Caroline  6, 9
Boland, Eavan  40
Bowen, Elizabeth  1, 3, 6, 11, 15, 22
Boyle, Patrick  19
Brennan, Maeve  5
Brown, Christy  63
Carroll, Paul Vincent  10
Clarke, Austin  6, 9
Dillon, Eilís  17
Donleavy, J. P.  1, 4, 6, 10, 45
Durcan, Paul  43
Friel, Brian  5, 42, 59
Gébler, Carlo  39
Hanley, James  3, 5, 8, 13
Heaney, Seamus  5, 7, 14, 25, 37
Johnston, Jennifer  7
Kavanagh, Patrick  22
Keane, Molly  31
Kiely, Benedict  23, 43
Kinsella, Thomas  4, 19
Lavin, Mary  4, 18
Leonard, Hugh  19
Longley, Michael  29
Mac Laverty, Bernard  31
MacNeice, Louis  1, 4, 10, 53
Mahon, Derek  27
McGahern, John  5, 9
McGinley, Patrick  41
McGuckian, Medbh  48
Montague, John  13, 46
Moore, Brian  1, 3, 5, 7, 8, 19, 32
Morrison, Van  21
Muldoon, Paul  32
Murphy, Richard  41
Murphy, Thomas  51
Nolan, Christopher  58
O'Brien, Edna  3, 5, 8, 13, 36
O'Brien, Flann  1, 4, 5, 7, 10, 47
O'Casey, Sean  1, 5, 9, 11, 15
O'Connor, Frank  14, 23
O'Faolain, Julia  6, 19, 47
O'Faoláin, Seán  1, 7, 14, 32
O'Flaherty, Liam  5, 34
Paulin, Tom  37
Rodgers, W. R.  7
Simmons, James  43
Trevor, William  7, 9, 14, 25,
White, Terence de Vere  49

## ISRAELI

Agnon, S. Y.  4, 8, 14
Amichai, Yehuda  9, 22, 57
Appelfeld, Aharon  23, 47
Kaniuk, Yoram  19
Levin, Meyer  7
Megged, Aharon  9
Oz, Amos  5, 8, 11, 27, 33, 54
Shamas, Anton  55
Sobol, Joshua  60
Yehoshua, A. B.  13, 31

## ITALIAN

Antonioni, Michelangelo  20
Bacchelli, Riccardo  19
Bassani, Giorgio  9
Bertolucci, Bernardo  16
Buzzati, Dino  36

Calvino, Italo  5, 8, 11, 22, 33, 39
De Sica, Vittorio  20
Eco, Umberto  28, 60
Fallaci, Oriana  11
Fellini, Federico  16
Fo, Dario  32
Gadda, Carlo Emilio  11
Ginzburg, Natalia  5, 11, 54
Giovene, Andrea  7
Landolfi, Tommaso  11, 49
Levi, Primo  37, 50
Luzi, Mario  13
Montale, Eugenio  7, 9, 18
Morante, Elsa  8, 47
Moravia, Alberto  2, 7, 11, 18, 27, 46
Palazzeschi, Aldo  11
Pasolini, Pier Paolo  20, 37
Piccolo, Lucio  13
Quasimodo, Salvatore  10
Silone, Ignazio  4
Ungaretti, Giuseppe  7, 11, 15
Visconti, Luchino  16
Vittorini, Elio  6, 9, 14
Wertmüller, Lina  16

## JAMAICAN

Bennett, Louise  28
Cliff, Jimmy  21
Marley, Bob  17
Thelwell, Michael  22

## JAPANESE

Abé, Kōbō  8, 22, 53
Enchi, Fumiko  31
Endo, Shusaku  7, 14, 19, 54
Ibuse, Masuji  22
Ichikawa, Kon  20
Ishiguro, Kazuo  56
Kawabata, Yasunari  2, 5, 9, 18
Kurosawa, Akira  16
Mishima, Yukio  2, 4, 6, 9, 27
Ōe, Kenzaburō  10, 36
Oshima, Nagisa  20
Ozu, Yasujiro  16
Shiga, Naoya  33
Tanizaki, Jun'ichirō  8, 14, 28

## KENYAN

Ngugi wa Thiong'o  3, 7, 13, 36

## MEXICAN

Fuentes, Carlos  3, 8, 10, 13, 22, 41, 60
Ibargüengoitia, Jorge  37
López Portillo, José  46
López y Fuentes, Gregorio  32
Paz, Octavio  3, 4, 6, 10, 19, 51
Rulfo, Juan  8

## MOROCCAN

Arrabal, Fernando  2, 9, 18, 58

## NEW ZEALAND

Adcock, Fleur  41
Ashton-Warner, Sylvia  19
Baxter, James K.  14
Frame, Janet  2, 3, 6, 22
Gee, Maurice  29
Grace, Patricia  56
Hilliard, Noel  15
Hulme, Keri  39
Ihimaera, Witi  46
Marsh, Ngaio  7, 53

Sargeson, Frank  31

## NICARAGUAN

Cardenal, Ernesto  31

## NIGERIAN

Achebe, Chinua  1, 3, 5, 7, 11, 26, 51
Clark, John Pepper  38
Ekwensi, Cyprian  4
Emecheta, Buchi  14, 48
Okigbo, Christopher  25
Soyinka, Wole  3, 5, 14, 36, 44
Tutuola, Amos  5, 14, 29

## NORWEGIAN

Friis-Baastad, Babbis  12
Heyerdahl, Thor  26

## PAKISTANI

Ghose, Zulfikar  42

## PALESTINIAN

Bakshi, Ralph  26

## PARAGUAYAN

Roa Bastos, Augusto  45

## PERUVIAN

Arguedas, José María  10, 18
Goldemberg, Isaac  52
Vargas Llosa, Mario  3, 6, 9, 10, 15, 31, 42

## POLISH

Agnon, S. Y.  4, 8, 14
Becker, Jurek  7, 19
Bermant, Chaim  40
Bienek, Horst  7, 11
Brandys, Kazimierz  62
Dąbrowska, Maria  15
Gombrowicz, Witold  4, 7, 11, 49
Herbert, Zbigniew  9, 43
Konwicki, Tadeusz  8, 28, 54
Kosinski, Jerzy  1, 2, 3, 6, 10, 15, 53
Lem, Stanislaw  8, 15, 40
Miłosz, Czesław  5, 11, 22, 31, 56
Mrozek, Sławomir  3, 13
Polanski, Roman  16
Różewicz, Tadeusz  9, 23
Singer, Isaac Bashevis  1, 3, 6, 9, 11, 15, 23, 38
Skolimowski, Jerzy  20
Wajda, Andrzej  16
Wittlin, Joseph  25
Wojciechowska, Maia  26

## PORTUGUESE

Miguéis, José Rodrigues  10

## PUERTO RICAN

Piñero, Miguel  4, 55
Sánchez, Luis Rafael  23

## RUMANIAN

Appelfeld, Aharon  23, 47
Celan, Paul  10, 19, 53
Cioran, E. M.  64
Codrescu, Andrei  46
Ionesco, Eugène  1, 4, 6, 9, 11, 15, 41
Rezzori, Gregor von  25
Tzara, Tristan  47

**RUSSIAN**
Akhmadulina, Bella  53
Akhmatova, Anna  11, 25, 64
Aksyonov, Vasily  22, 37
Aleshkovsky, Yuz  44
Almedingen, E. M.  12
Bitov, Andrei  57
Brodsky, Joseph  4, 6, 13, 36, 50
Ehrenburg, Ilya  18, 34, 62
Eliade, Mircea  19
Gary, Romain  25
Goldberg, Anatol  34
Grade, Chaim  10
Grossman, Vasily  41
Iskander, Fazil  47
Kaletski, Alexander  39
Krotkov, Yuri  19
Nabokov, Vladimir  1, 2, 3, 6, 8, 11, 15, 23,
    44, 46, 64
Olesha, Yuri  8
Pasternak, Boris  7, 10, 18, 63
Paustovsky, Konstantin  40
Rahv, Philip  24
Rand, Ayn  3, 30, 44
Ratushinskaya, Irina  54
Rybakov, Anatoli  23, 53
Shalamov, Varlam  18
Sholokhov, Mikhail  7, 15
Sinyavsky, Andrei  8
Solzhenitsyn, Aleksandr I.  1, 2, 4, 7, 9, 10,
    18, 24, 26, 34
Strugatskii, Arkadii  27
Strugatskii, Boris  27
Trifonov, Yuri  45
Troyat, Henri  23
Voinovich, Vladimir  10, 49
Voznesensky, Andrei  1, 15, 57
Yanovsky, Vassily S.  2, 18
Yevtushenko, Yevgeny  1, 3, 13, 26, 51
Yezierska, Anzia  46
Zaturenska, Marya  6, 11
Zinoviev, Alexander  19

**SALVADORAN**
Argueta, Manlio  31

**SCOTTISH**
Banks, Iain  34
Brown, George Mackay  5, 48
Cronin, A. J.  32
Dunn, Douglas  6, 40
Graham, W. S.  29
Gray, Alasdair  41
Hunter, Mollie  21
Jenkins, Robin  52
Kelman, James  58
MacBeth, George  2, 5, 9
MacCaig, Norman  36
MacDiarmid, Hugh  2, 4, 11, 19, 63
MacInnes, Helen  27, 39
MacLean, Alistair  3, 13, 50, 63
McIlvanney, William  42
Morgan, Edwin  31
Smith, Iain Crichton  64
Spark, Muriel  2, 3, 5, 8, 13, 18, 40
Taylor, C. P.  27
Walker, David Harry  14
Young, Andrew  5

**SENGALESE**
Senghor, Léopold Sédar  54

**SICILIAN**
Sciascia, Leonardo  8, 9, 41

**SOMALIAN**
Farah, Nuruddin  53

**SOUTH AFRICAN**
Breytenbach, Breyten  23, 37
Brink, André  18, 36
Brutus, Dennis  43
Coetzee, J. M.  23, 33
Fugard, Athol  5, 9, 14, 25, 40
Fugard, Sheila  48
Gordimer, Nadine  3, 5, 7, 10, 18, 33, 51
Harwood, Ronald  32
Head, Bessie  25
Hope, Christopher  52
La Guma, Alex  19
Millin, Sarah Gertrude  49
Mphahlele, Ezekiel  25
Mtwa, Percy  47
Ngema, Mbongeni  57
Nkosi, Lewis  45
Paton, Alan  4, 10, 25, 55
Plomer, William  4, 8
Prince, F. T.  22
Smith, Wilbur  33
Van der Post, Laurens  5
Vorster, Gordon  34

**SPANISH**
Alberti, Rafael  7
Aleixandre, Vicente  9, 36
Alonso, Dámaso  14
Azorín  11
Benet, Juan  28
Buero Vallejo, Antonio  15, 46
Buñuel, Luis  16
Casona, Alejandro  49
Cela, Camilo José  4, 13, 59
Cernuda, Luis  54
Del Castillo, Michel  38
Delibes, Miguel  8, 18
Donoso, José  4, 8, 11, 32
Espriu, Salvador  9
Gironella, José María  11
Gómez de la Serna, Ramón  9
Goytisolo, Juan  5, 10, 23
Guillén, Jorge  11
Matute, Ana María  11
Otero, Blas de  11
Rodríguez, Claudio  10
Saura, Carlos  20
Sender, Ramón  8

**SWEDISH**
Beckman, Gunnel  26
Bergman, Ingmar  16
Ekelöf, Gunnar  27
Johnson, Eyvind  14
Lagerkvist, Pär  7, 10, 13, 54
Martinson, Harry  14
Tranströmer, Tomas  52
Wahlöö, Per  7
Weiss, Peter  3, 15, 51

**SWISS**
Cendrars, Blaise  18
Dürrenmatt, Friedrich  1, 4, 8, 11, 15, 43
Federspiel, J. F.  42
Frisch, Max  3, 9, 14, 18, 32, 44
Hesse, Hermann  1, 2, 3, 6, 11, 17, 25

Pinget, Robert  7, 13, 37
Von Däniken, Erich  30

**TURKISH**
Hikmet, Nâzim  40
Kemal, Yashar  14, 29

**URUGUAYAN**
Onetti, Juan Carlos  7, 10

**WELSH**
Abse, Dannie  7, 29
Clarke, Gillian  61
Dahl, Roald  1, 6, 18
Davies, Rhys  23
Francis, Dick  2, 22, 42
Hughes, Richard  1, 11
Humphreys, Emyr  47
Jones, David  2, 4, 7, 13, 42
Levinson, Deirdre  49
Llewellyn, Richard  7
Mathias, Roland  45
Norris, Leslie  14
Roberts, Kate  15
Rubens, Bernice  19, 31
Thomas, R. S.  6, 13, 48
Watkins, Vernon  43
Williams, Emlyn  15

**WEST INDIAN**
Armatrading, Joan  17
Césaire, Aimé  19, 32
Dabydeen, David  34
Edwards, Gus  43
Glissant, Édouard  10
Guy, Rosa  26
James, C. L. R.  33
Kincaid, Jamaica  43
Lovelace, Earl  51
Naipaul, Shiva  32, 39
Naipaul, V. S.  4, 7, 9, 13, 18, 37
Rhys, Jean  2, 4, 6, 14, 19, 51
Walcott, Derek  2, 4, 9, 14, 25, 42

**YUGOSLAVIAN**
Andrić, Ivo  8
Ćosić, Dobrica  14
Kiš,Danilo  57
Krleža, Miroslav  8
Pavic, Milorad  60
Popa, Vasko  19
Simic, Charles  6, 9, 22, 49
Tesich, Steve  40

# *CLC-64* Title Index

"Aberdeen" (Smith)  **64**:395-96
"About That Mile" (Smith)  **64**:397
"Absences" (Larkin)  **64**:260, 262, 266
*Ackroyd* (Feiffer)  **64**:151-52, 157-58, 162
*Ada; or Ardor: A Family Chronicle* (Nabokov)  **64**:348, 350-51
"Adulthood" (Giovanni)  **64**:185
"After the War" (Smith)  **64**:388
"An Afterword to *Lolita* (Nabokov)  **64**:348
"Age" (Larkin)  **64**:262
*All God's Children Need Traveling Shoes* (Angelou)  **64**:35-8
"All I Gotta Do" (Giovanni)  **64**:187-88
"Ambulances" (Larkin)  **64**:266
*And Still I Rise* (Angelou)  **64**:32
"And the Wave Sings because It Is Moving" (Larkin)  **64**:282
"The Angel of the Bridge" (Cheever)  **64**:57, 61-3, 65
*Anno Domini MCMXXI* (Akhmatova)  **64**:5, 10
"Annus Mirabilis" (Larkin)  **64**:282
*Another Roadside Attraction* (Robbins)  **64**:371-73, 376-78, 382
"An Answer to Some Questions on How I Write" (Giovanni)  **64**:196
*Anthony Rose* (Feiffer)  **64**:163
"An April Sunday" (Larkin)  **64**:258
"Arrivals, Departures" (Larkin)  **64**:262, 266
"An Arundel Tomb" (Larkin)  **64**:263, 277, 279
*At Grass* (Larkin)  **64**:260, 262, 266, 269-70, 279
*At Play in the Fields of the Lord* (Matthiessen)  **64**:302-04, 307, 309, 311, 321, 327-28
"At the Fair" (Smith)  **64**:391-92
"At the Sale" (Smith)  **64**:395
"Aubade" (Larkin)  **64**:259-60, 263, 266-67, 272, 280, 285

"Autumn" (Larkin)  **64**:258
*Back in the World* (Wolff)  **64**:450-54, 456-57
*The Barracks Thief and Selected Stories* (Wolff)  **64**:451, 454, 456-57
"Beautiful Black Men (with compliments and apologies to all not mentioned by name)" (Giovanni)  **64**:185, 187
"The Beginning is Zero" (Giovanni)  **64**:183
*Belaya Staya* (*White Flock*) (Akhmatova)  **64**:3-4, 8-9
*Berlin Solstice* (Fraser)  **64**:178
"Best Society" (Larkin)  **64**:258, 263
"Beyond the Novel" (Cioran)  **64**:82, 84, 97
*Black Feeling, Black Talk, Black Judgement* (*Black Feeling, Black Talk*; *Black Judgement*) (Giovanni)  **64**:182, 185-86, 188, 190-91, 195
*Black Feeling, Black Talk/Black Judgement* (Giovanni)
See *Black Feeling, Black Talk, Black Judgement*
*The Black Flame* (Du Bois)  **64**:117, 119
"Black Poems, *Poseurs* and Powe" (Giovanni)  **64**:183
*Black Reconstruction: An Essay toward a History of the Part Which Black Folk Played in the Attempt to Reconstruct Democracy in America, 1860-1880* (Du Bois)  **64**:105-07, 116
"A Blind Negro Singer" (Smith)  **64**:398
*Blue Meridian: The Search for the Great White Shark* (Matthiessen)  **64**:305-06, 309
*Blue Window* (Lucas)  **64**:288-89, 292, 295-96
*Boating for Beginners* (Winterson)  **64**:427-29, 432-34
"Born Yesterday" (Larkin)  **64**:282
"The Brigadier and the Golf Widow" (Cheever)  **64**:57

*The Brigadier and the Golf Widow* (Cheever)  **64**:60, 62
"Broadcast" (Larkin)  **64**:263
"The Brothers" (Smith)  **64**:391
*The Buddha of Suburbia* (Kureishi)  **64**:249-53
"The Building" (Larkin)  **64**:266, 280, 282
*Bullet Park* (Cheever)  **64**:49-50, 57-9
"The Burden of Black Women" (Du Bois)  **64**:114, 116
"The Butterfly" (Giovanni)  **64**:187
"By Ferry to the Island" (Smith)  **64**:388, 393, 398
"By the Sea" (Smith)  **64**:390, 393
*By the Seashore* (Akhmatova)  **64**:11
"The Calling of Names" (Angelou)  **64**:32
*The Candy Factory* (Fraser)  **64**:167-69, 171-75
"The Card Players" (Larkin)  **64**:275
*Carnal Knowledge* (Feiffer)  **64**:149-50, 159, 161, 163-64
*A Casual Affair: A Modern Fairytale* (Fraser)  **64**:169-71
"Categories" (Giovanni)  **64**:186-87
"The Centerpiece" (Matthiessen)  **64**:321, 323-24
*Chamber Music* (Grumbach)  **64**:198-200
"Children of the Moon" (Du Bois)  **64**:110-11
"Chinese Poem" (Smith)  **64**:400
"Church Going" (Larkin)  **64**:261, 265, 269-70, 277, 282-83
*La chute dans le temps* (*The Fall into Time*) (Cioran)  **64**:82-5, 87-8, 92
*Chyotki* (*Rosary*) (Akhmatova)  **64**:3, 8-9, 11
"Clancy in the Tower of Babel" (Cheever)  **64**:65
"Cleopatra" (Akhmatova)  **64**:16
*Collected Poems* (Larkin)  **64**:256-87
"Come Then to Prayers" (Larkin)  **64**:282
"Coming" (Larkin)  **64**:262, 266, 274

"Coming Attractions" (Wolff)  **64**:450, 452-54

*The Complete Poems of Anna Akhmatova* (Akhmatova)  **64**:17-20

*A Confederacy of Dunces* (Toole)  **64**:404-24

*Consider the Lilies* (Smith)  **64**:389, 393

"Contrasts" (Smith)  **64**:396

"Cotton Candy" (Giovanni)  **64**:195

*Cotton Candy on a Rainy Day* (Giovanni) **64**:188, 191, 194-95

"Counting" (Larkin)  **64**:262

"The Country Husband" (Cheever)  **64**:53-4

"Courage" (Akhmatova)  **64**:15

*Crawling Arnold* (Feiffer)  **64**:159-60

"Criteria for Negro Art" (Du Bois)  **64**:120, 123

"The Crucifixion" (Akhmatova)  **64**:12

"The Cry" (Smith)  **64**:392

"Culloden and After" (Smith)  **64**:394

"Cut Grass" (Larkin)  **64**:282

"The Dance" (Larkin)  **64**:258, 260, 263-64, 280-81

"Dante" (Akhmatova)  **64**:16

*Dar* (*The Gift*) (Nabokov)  **64**:366

*Dark Princess* (Du Bois)  **64**:113-14, 117-18

*Darkwater: Voices from within the Veil* (Du Bois)  **64**:104, 116

"A Day in Africa" (Du Bois)  **64**:114, 117

"Days" (Larkin)  **64**:268-69, 271, 285

*Days between Stations* (Erickson)  **64**:137-40, 142, 144

"Dealing with the Mystics" (Cioran)  **64**:79, 82

"The Death of Justina" (Cheever)  **64**:48, 53, 57

"December of My Springs" (Giovanni) **64**:191

"Deceptions" (Larkin)  **64**:262, 266, 268, 270

"Deep Analysis" (Larkin)  **64**:282

"Deer on the High Hills" ("Deer on the High Hills—A Meditation") (Smith)  **64**:388, 394, 396, 398

"Deer on the High Hills—A Meditation" (Smith)
See "Deer on the High Hills"

*The Defense* (Nabokov)  **64**:348, 366

"The Demiurge" (Cioran)  **64**:80, 89, 94

"Desert Breakdown, 1968" (Wolff)  **64**:450-51, 454

*Despair* (Nabokov)  **64**:351, 366

"Detroit Conference of Unity and Art" (Giovanni)  **64**:194

"Dockery and Son" (Larkin)  **64**:260, 264, 266, 268

"Don't Have a Baby till You Read This" (Giovanni)  **64**:183

*Drawn and Quartered* (Cioran)
See *Écartèlement*

*The Dream* (Smith)  **64**:401-02

"Dreams" (Giovanni)  **64**:185

*Dusk of Dawn* (Du Bois)  **64**:127

"The earth eats everything" (Smith)  **64**:393

*Écartèlement* (*Drawn and Quartered*) (Cioran) **64**:94-6

"The Edge of the World" (Cheever)  **64**:66

"Ego Tripping" (Giovanni)  **64**:195

*Elliot Loves* (Feiffer)  **64**:163-64

*The Emperor's Virgin* (Fraser)  **64**:170

*The Enchanter/The Magician* (Nabokov)
See *Volshebnik*

"Encounters with Suicide" (Cioran)  **64**:89, 94

"The Enormous Radio" (Cheever)  **64**:65

"An Episode in the Life of Professor Brooke" (Wolff)  **64**:446-47, 449-50

"Essential Beauty" (Larkin)  **64**:269

*Even Cowgirls Get the Blues* (Robbins) **64**:371-73, 377-80, 382-83

*Evening* (Akhmatova)
See *Vecher*

"The Exorcism" (Smith)  **64**:391

"Expelled" (Cheever)  **64**:66

"The Explosion" (Larkin)  **64**:266, 280, 285

*The Eye* (Nabokov)  **64**:348

"Face to Face" (Wolff)  **64**:446, 449

*Falconer* (Cheever)  **64**:49-51, 57, 59, 65-8

"The Fall" (Smith)  **64**:390

*The Fall into Time* (Cioran)
See *La chute dans le temps*

*The Fantasy Poets: Philip Larkin* (Larkin) **64**:257

"Far Out" (Larkin)  **64**:258

*Far Tortuga* (Matthiessen)  **64**:307, 309, 311-14, 316, 320, 324-25, 327-28

*Feiffer: Jules Feiffer's America from Eisenhower to Reagan* (Feiffer)  **64**:156

*Feiffer on Civil Rights* (Feiffer)  **64**:153

*Feiffer on Nixon: The Cartoon Presidency* (Feiffer)  **64**:153

*Feiffer's Album* (Feiffer)  **64**:158

*Feiffer's Marriage Manual* (Feiffer)  **64**:158

"The Fifth Day" (Matthiessen)  **64**:321, 323-24

"Finis Not Tragedy" (Smith)  **64**:399

"The Five-Forty-Eight" (Cheever)  **64**:48, 65

"For Angus MacLeod" (Smith)  **64**:389

"For Keats" (Smith)  **64**:399

"For My Mother" ("To My Mother") (Smith) **64**:389, 393, 396

"For Sandra" (Giovanni)  **64**:182, 193-94

"For Sydney Bechet" (Larkin)  **64**:278

"For the Unknown Seamen of the 1939-45 War Buried in Iona Churchyard" (Smith) **64**:388, 393

"Forced Retirement" (Giovanni)  **64**:191

"The Forethought" (Du Bois)  **64**:132

"Forget What Did" (Larkin)  **64**:282

"Four Introductions" (Giovanni)  **64**:196

"Friday Night in the Royal Station Hotel" (Larkin)  **64**:266

*From Bourgeois Land* (Smith)  **64**:390, 395, 398-99

*Gather Together in My Name* (Angelou) **64**:24, 27, 29-30, 34, 36, 38-9

"Gde, vysokaya, tvoy tsyganyonok" ("Where, Tall Girl, Is Your Gypsy Babe") (Akhmatova)  **64**:9

"Gemini—A Prolonged Autobiographical Statement on Why" (Giovanni)  **64**:184

*Gemini: An Extended Autobiographical Statement on My First Twenty-Five Years of Being a Black Poet* (Giovanni)  **64**:183-85, 187-89, 191-92

"The Geometry of Love" (Cheever)  **64**:46-8

*The Gift* (Nabokov)
See *Dar*

*A Girl in Winter* (Larkin)  **64**:260, 280

*God Bless* (Feiffer)  **64**:149-50

"Going" (Larkin)  **64**:257, 259, 261, 274

"Going, Going" (Larkin)  **64**:266, 274

"Goodbye My Brother" (Cheever)  **64**:53, 65

"Grace Notes" (Smith)  **64**:397

*Grown Ups* (Feiffer)  **64**:155-56, 161-64

"Habits" (Giovanni)  **64**:195

"Haig" (Smith)  **64**:388

*Hamlet in Autumn* (Smith)  **64**:399

"Heads in the Women's Ward" (Larkin) **64**:264

*The Heart of a Woman* (Angelou)  **64**:24-5, 27, 33, 36, 39

"The Heiress" (Akhmatova)  **64**:13

"Here" (Larkin)  **64**:266, 276, 279

"The Hermit" (Smith)  **64**:391

*The Hermit and Other Stories* (Smith)  **64**:391

"High Windows" (Larkin)  **64**:265, 269, 272, 282, 284

*High Windows* (Larkin)  **64**:259, 263-64, 270-72, 275, 277-78, 280, 285

"A Highland Girl Studying Poetry" (Smith)
See "A Young Highland Girl Studying Poetry"

"Highland Portrait" (Smith)  **64**:394

*Histoire et utopie* (*History and Utopia*) (Cioran) **64**:97-9

"A Historical Footnote to Consider Only when All Else Fails" (Giovanni)  **64**:191

*History and Utopia* (Cioran)
See *Histoire et utopie*

*Hold Me!* (Feiffer)  **64**:151, 159, 164

"Homage to a Government" (Larkin)  **64**:274

"Homage to Shakespeare" (Cheever)  **64**:66

"Home Is So Sad" (Larkin)  **64**:266

"Horse Latitudes" (Matthiessen)  **64**:321, 324

"The Housebreaker of Shady Hill" (Cheever) **64**:48

*The Housebreaker of Shady Hill and Other Stories* (Cheever)  **64**:54

"How Distant" (Larkin)  **64**:282

"Hume" (Smith)  **64**:398

"Hunters in the Snow" (Wolff)  **64**:449, 451

*Hunters in the Snow* (Wolff)
See *In the Garden of the North American Martyrs*

"I Build an Orange Church" (Smith)  **64**:394

"I Hear the Oriole's Voice" (Akhmatova) **64**:16

*I Know Why the Caged Bird Sings* (Angelou) **64**:24-5, 27-30, 34-9

"I Pressed My Hands Together..." (Akhmatova)  **64**:8

"I Remember, I Remember" (Larkin)  **64**:266

*I Shall Not Be Moved* (Angelou)  **64**:40

"I Visited the Poet..." (Akhmatova)  **64**:20

"I Want to Sing" (Giovanni)  **64**:191

"If, My Darling" (Larkin)  **64**:260, 262, 266

"If You Are About to Die Now" (Smith) **64**:393

"The Importance of Elsewhere" (Larkin) **64**:262

"The Impulse" (Smith)  **64**:391

"In Luss Churchyard" (Smith)  **64**:388, 397

"In the Dark" (Smith)  **64**:399

*In the Garden of the North American Martyrs* (*Hunters in the Snow*) (Wolff)  **64**:446-49, 450-51, 456-57

"In the Garden of the North American Martyrs" (Wolff)  **64**:448, 455

"In the Middle" (Smith)  **64**:392, 400

*In the Middle* (Smith)  **64**:394

*In the Middle of the Wood* (Smith)  **64**:401

*In the Spirit of Crazy Horse* (Matthiessen) **64**:315, 325

"The Incident" (Smith)  **64**:391

*Indian Country* (Matthiessen)  **64**:315-16, 325

*Invitation to a Beheading* (Nabokov)  **64**:350-51

*Jill* (Larkin)  **64**:260, 280

*Jitterbug Perfume* (Robbins)   **64**:377, 381-82, 384

*John Brown* (Du Bois)   **64**:103

"John Knox" (Smith)   **64**:397

"The Judgment" (Akhmatova)   **64**:12

*Just Give Me a Cool Drink of Water 'fore I Diiie* (Angelou)   **64**:32

*Kesey's Garage Sale* (Kesey)   **64**:231

"Kierkegaard" (Smith)   **64**:397

*Killing Mr. Watson* (Matthiessen)   **64**:325-29

*The King and Me* (Kureishi)   **64**:246

*King, Queen, Knave* (Nabokov)   **64**:348

*Knock Knock* (Feiffer)   **64**:149-50, 159, 161

"Kogda v mrachneyshey iz stolits" ("When in the Gloomiest of Capitals") (Akhmatova)   **64**:9

*The Ladies* (Grumbach)   **64**:198-201

"The Large Cool Store" (Larkin)   **64**:269, 276

"Last Will and Testament" (Larkin)   **64**:261

"Late in the Season" (Matthiessen)   **64**:321, 324

"Latest Face" (Larkin)   **64**:262

*Laughter in the Dark* (Nabokov)   **64**:348

"The Law and the Grace" (Smith)   **64**:398

*The Law and the Grace* (Smith)   **64**:394, 398

*Leap Year* (Erickson)   **64**:142-43, 145

"Learning from the Tyrants" (Cioran)   **64**:98

"Leaving the Cherries" (Smith)   **64**:391

"Legacies" (Giovanni)   **64**:187

*The Less Deceived* (Larkin)   **64**:259, 267-68, 270-71, 278-80

"Letter to a Bourgeois Friend Whom Once I Loved (and Maybe Still Do if Love Is Valid)" (Giovanni)   **64**:194

"Letter to a Faraway Friend" (Cioran)   **64**:99

"Letter to a Friend About Girls" (Larkin)   **64**:280

"Leviathan" (Wolff)   **64**:451-52

"The Liar" (Wolff)   **64**:449-51, 454

"The Life I Led" (Giovanni)   **64**:191

"The Life with a Hole in It" (Larkin)   **64**:272

"Lines on a Young Lady's Photograph Album" (Larkin)   **64**:267, 279

"A Litany of Atlanta" (Du Bois)   **64**:114, 116

*Little Murders* (Feiffer)   **64**:148-50, 159-64

"Livings" (Larkin)   **64**:261, 268

*Lolita* (Nabokov)   **64**:332-69

*The Long River* (Smith)   **64**:397

*Longtime Companion* (Lucas)   **64**:296

"Lot's Wife" (Akhmatova)   **64**:16

"Love Again" (Larkin)   **64**:263, 277, 281

"Love: Is a Human Condition" (Giovanni)   **64**:192

*Love Poems and Elegies* (Smith)   **64**:393, 399

*Love Song of a Puritan* (Smith)   **64**:388

"Lumumba Lives" (Matthiessen)   **64**:322, 325

"Luss Village" (Smith)   **64**:397

*The Magician's Girl* (Grumbach)   **64**:201-05

"Maiden Voyage" (Wolff)   **64**:450

"Many famous feet have trod" (Larkin)   **64**:259

"The March Past" (Larkin)   **64**:262

"Marriages" (Larkin)   **64**:262, 283

*Mary* (Nabokov)
  See *Mashen'ka*

*Mashen'ka* (*Mary*) (Nabokov)   **64**:348

*Le mauvais démiurge* (*The New Gods*) (Cioran)   **64**:88-9, 93-4

"Meditation Addressed to Hugh MacDiarmid" (Smith)   **64**:397

"Mene, Mene, Tekel, Upharsin" (Cheever)   **64**:65

*Men's Lives: The Surfmen and Baymen of the South Fork* (Matthiessen)   **64**:317-19, 325, 327

"Metamorphoses" (Cheever)   **64**:65

"Midnight Turning Gray" (Matthiessen)   **64**:321, 324-25

*Midnight Turning Gray* (Matthiessen)   **64**:321

"Midnight Verses" (Akhmatova)   **64**:13

"Mirrors" (Giovanni)   **64**:192

*The Missing Person* (Grumbach)   **64**:198

"The Missing Person" (Wolff)   **64**:450-51, 454

"The Missionary" (Smith)   **64**:392

"Mr. Bleaney" (Larkin)   **64**:263, 272

"Mr. Heine" (Smith)   **64**:392

"Mr. Trill in Hades" (Smith)   **64**:401

"Money" (Larkin)   **64**:282

*Murdo and Other Stories* (Smith)   **64**:391

"The Muse" (Akhmatova)   **64**:16

*My Beautiful Laundrette* (Kureishi)   **64**:246-52, 254

*My Father's House: A Memoir of Incest and Healing* (Fraser)   **64**:179-80

"My House" (Giovanni)   **64**:187, 194

*My House* (Giovanni)   **64**:186-87, 191, 194

"My Poem" (Giovanni)   **64**:182, 186

"Mythological Introduction" (Larkin)   **64**:262, 282

"Naturally the Foundation Will Bear Your Expenses" (Larkin)   **64**:272-74

*The Negro* (Du Bois)   **64**:116, 131

"The Negro in Art" (Du Bois)   **64**:124

*The Neon Bible* (Toole)   **64**:412, 415-17, 421-24

"The New Gods" (Cioran)   **64**:89, 94

*The New Gods* (Cioran)
  See *Le mauvais démiurge*

"New Year Poem" (Larkin)   **64**:282, 285

"Next Door" (Wolff)   **64**:446, 448

"Nikki-Rosa" (Giovanni)   **64**:191

*Nine-Headed Dragon River: Zen Journals, 1969-1982* (Matthiessen)   **64**:316-21, 326

"No Road" (Larkin)   **64**:258, 260, 262, 266

*The North Ship* (Larkin)   **64**:257-61, 266-68, 270, 278

"Northern Elegies" (Akhmatova)   **64**:5

"A Note on Puritans" (Smith)   **64**:396

"The Notebooks of Robinson Crusoe" (Smith)   **64**:389-90

*The Notebooks of Robinson Crusoe* (Smith)   **64**:389-90, 400

"Nothing to Be Said" (Larkin)   **64**:271

"November, 1961" (Smith)   **64**:388

*Now Sheba Sings the Song* (Angelou)   **64**:38

"O City of Broken Dreams" (Cheever)   **64**:65

"O Youth and Beauty!" (Cheever)   **64**:46, 48

"Odyssey of Rancor" (Cioran)   **64**:98

"Of Alexander Crummell" (Du Bois)   **64**:130

"Of Liberation" (Giovanni)   **64**:182-83

"Of Love: A Testimony" (Cheever)   **64**:65

"Of the Coming of John" (Du Bois)   **64**:117-18, 130, 133

"Of the Faith of the Fathers" (Du Bois)   **64**:134

"Of the Passing of the First-Born" (Du Bois)   **64**:130, 133

"Of the Quest of the Golden Fleece" (Du Bois)   **64**:110

"Of the Sorrow Songs" (Du Bois)   **64**:130

"Of the Wings of Atlanta" (Du Bois)   **64**:110, 130

*Oh Pray My Wings Are Gonna Fit Me Well* (Angelou)   **64**:32

*Oh, What a Paradise It Seems* (Cheever)   **64**:49-52, 57, 59

"The Old Fools" (Larkin)   **64**:266, 270, 285

"Old Woman" (Smith)   **64**:388-89, 393-94, 398

"Old Woman with Flowers" (Smith)   **64**:393

"On a Book Entitled *Lolita*" (Nabokov)   **64**:344, 365

"On a Winded Civilization" (Cioran)   **64**:76, 78, 82, 96

"On Being Asked What It's Like to Be Black" (Giovanni)   **64**:183

"On Being Twenty-Six" (Larkin)   **64**:258, 260

"On Sickness" (Cioran)   **64**:88

"On the River Styx" (Matthiessen)   **64**:322-23, 325

*On the River Styx and Other Stories* (Matthiessen)   **64**:321-22, 324-25, 327

*One Flew over the Cuckoo's Nest* (Kesey)   **64**:206-44

*Oranges Are Not the Only Fruit* (Winterson)   **64**:426-27, 429-32, 434-35, 439-40, 442, 444

"Orpheus" (Smith)   **64**:399-400

*Orpheus and Other Poems* (Smith)   **64**:399

"Our Grandmothers" (Angelou)   **64**:41

"Our Story Begins" (Wolff)   **64**:451-52, 454

*Outskirts* (Kureishi)   **64**:246

*Pale Fire* (Nabokov)   **64**:348, 366

"Paleontology" (Cioran)   **64**:89, 94

*Pandora* (Fraser)   **64**:166-68, 171, 175-77

*Partisans* (Matthiessen)   **64**:327

"Passengers" (Wolff)   **64**:446, 449

*The Passion* (Winterson)   **64**:428-30, 432-35, 440-42, 444

"A People of Solitaries" (Cioran)
  See "Un peuple de solitaires"

"Un peuple de solitaires" ("A People of Solitaries") (Cioran)   **64**:74, 82, 84, 98

*The Philadelphia Negro* (Du Bois)   **64**:115, 128, 131

*Pictures at a Prosecution* (Feiffer)   **64**:153

"Pigeons" (Larkin)   **64**:271, 280

"Places, Loved Ones" (Larkin)   **64**:272

*Plantain* (Akhmatova)   **64**:10

*Pnin* (Nabokov)   **64**:351

"Poaching" (Wolff)   **64**:446, 449

"Poem (No Name No. 3)" (Giovanni)   **64**:182

"Poem" (Smith)   **64**:395

"Poem for Aretha" (Giovanni)   **64**:186

"Poem of Lewis" (Smith)   **64**:396-97

*Poem without a Hero* (Akhmatova)
  See *Poema bez geroia*

*Poema bez geroia* (*Poem without a Hero*) (Akhmatova)   **64**:11, 13-15, 18-19

"Poems about St. Petersburg, II" (Akhmatova)   **64**:9

*Poems of Akhmatova* (Akhmatova)   **64**:13-14

"Poetry of Departures" (Larkin)   **64**:272

"The Poor Are Always with Us" (Wolff)   **64**:451-52

"Poppies" (Smith)   **64**:388

"The Pot of Gold" (Cheever)   **64**:65

"Prayer" (Akhmatova)   **64**:4

*Précis de décomposition* (*A Short History of Decay*) (Cioran)   **64**:73, 91-2

*Prelude to a Kiss* (Lucas)   **64**:294-99

*The Quest of the Silver Fleece* (Du Bois)   **64**:110, 114, 117-18

*Race Rock* (Matthiessen)   **64**:309, 327

*Raditzer* (Matthiessen)   **64**:309, 327

"The Rainbow Sign" (Kureishi)   **64**:247-48

*The Real Life of Sebastian Knight* (Nabokov) **64**:348, 366
"Real People in a Real Place" (Smith) **64**:400
"Reasons for Attendance" (Larkin) **64**:258, 277
*Reckless* (Lucas) **64**:290-96
"Reconstruction and Its Benefits" (Du Bois) **64**:107
"Records" (Giovanni) **64**:191
*Re:Creation* (Giovanni) **64**:186, 188, 195
"Reference Back" (Larkin) **64**:282
"Reflections on My Profession" (Giovanni) **64**:196
*Requiem* (Akhmatova) **64**:6, 11-20
*Required Writing* (Larkin) **64**:282, 284
"Return to Lewis" (Smith) **64**:396
"Revolutionary Dreams" (Giovanni) **64**:186
"Revolutionary Music" (Giovanni) **64**:186
"Revolutionary Tale" (Giovanni) **64**:183
"The Rich Brother" (Wolff) **64**:451-52, 454
"The Riddle of the Sphinx" (Du Bois) **64**:109, 112, 116
*Rosary* (Akhmatova)
   See *Chyotki*
"The Rose Bush" (Giovanni) **64**:191
*Rubicon Beach* (Erickson) **64**:138-40, 142, 144
"Russia and the Virus of Liberty" (Cioran) **64**:98
*Sacred Cows and Other Edibles* (Giovanni) **64**:195-96
"Sad Steps" (Larkin) **64**:272, 276, 282
"Sadie" (Matthiessen) **64**:321-22, 324
*Sal Si Puedes: Cesar Chavez and the New American Revolution* (Matthiessen) **64**:303-04
*Sammy and Rosie Get Laid* (Kureishi) **64**:248-51, 254-55
*Sammy and Rosie Get Laid: The Script and the Diary* (Kureishi) **64**:249, 254
*Sand Rivers* (Matthiessen) **64**:310-11, 326
"Say Yes" (Wolff) **64**:454
"School Teacher" (Smith) **64**:389
"Schoolmaster" (Larkin) **64**:261
"The Scream" (Smith) **64**:392
"Seduction" (Giovanni) **64**:186-87, 194-95
*Selected Poems, 1955-1980* (Smith) **64**:393-96
"Self's the Man" (Larkin) **64**:267-68, 282
*The Seventh Book* (Akhmatova) **64**:21
*Sexing the Cherry* (Winterson) **64**:434-44
"Shall Gaelic Die?" (Smith) **64**:395-96
*A Short History of Decay* (Cioran)
   See *Précis de décomposition*
"Show Saturday" (Larkin) **64**:265, 282, 284-85
*Singin' and Swingin' and Gettin' Merry Like Christmas* (Angelou) **64**:24, 27, 29-31, 36, 39
"Sister" (Wolff) **64**:454
"Skeptic and Barbarian" (Cioran) **64**:88
*Skinny Legs and All* (Robbins) **64**:380-84
"A slight relax of air where cold was" (Larkin) **64**:258
"Smokers" (Wolff) **64**:448-49
*The Snow Leopard* (Matthiessen) **64**:308-11, 316-17, 320, 325-27
"Solar" (Larkin) **64**:265, 268-69, 285
"Soldier's Joy" (Wolff) **64**:450, 453-54
"The Soldier's Wish" (Smith) **64**:388
"Some Blind Alleys: A Letter" (Cioran) **64**:78, 99

"Something to Be Said for Silence" (Giovanni) **64**:191
*Sometimes a Great Notion* (Kesey) **64**:216
"The Song of the Final Meeting" (Akhmatova) **64**:8
"Song of the Smoke" (Du Bois) **64**:114
"The Sorrows of Gin" (Cheever) **64**:47, 65
*The Souls of Black Folk* (Du Bois) **64**:103-05, 110, 116-17, 127-34
"The Souls of White Folk" (Du Bois) **64**:104
"The space-ship" (Smith) **64**:393
"Spiritual View of Lena Horne" (Giovanni) **64**:183
"Spring" (Larkin) **64**:262, 266
"The Star of Ethiopia" (Du Bois) **64**:111
*The Star of Ethiopia* (Du Bois) **64**:111, 121
"Statement By a Responsible Spinster" (Smith) **64**:394
"Statue at Tsarskoye Selo" (Akhmatova) **64**:9
*Still Life with Woodpecker* (Robbins) **64**:377, 381-83
"A Stone Church Damaged by a Bomb" (Larkin) **64**:261, 282
*The Stories of John Cheever* (Cheever) **64**:66
"The Story of Africa" (Du Bois) **64**:112
"Strangled Thoughts" (Cioran) **64**:89, 94
"Studies in Power" (Smith) **64**:398
"A Study of Reading Habits" (Larkin) **64**:266
"Style as Risk" (Cioran) **64**:75, 78-9
"Sunday Morning Walk" (Smith) **64**:388, 394
"Sunny Prestatyn" (Larkin) **64**:262, 269-70
*The Suppression of the African Slave-Trade to the United States of America, 1638-1870* (Du Bois) **64**:128
"The Swimmer" (Cheever) **64**:46, 48, 53, 63, 66
*Syllogismes de l'amertume* (Cioran) **64**:73
"Sympathy in White Major" (Larkin) **64**:283
"The Tale of the Black Ring" (Akhmatova) **64**:16, 20
*Tantrum* (Feiffer) **64**:153
*The Temptation to Exist* (Cioran)
   See *La tentation d'exister*
*La tentation d'exister* (*The Temptation to Exist*) (Cioran) **64**:73-5, 77-84, 87, 90, 92-3, 96-9
"These Yet to Be United States" (Angelou) **64**:40
"Thinking against Oneself" (Cioran) **64**:96-7, 99
"This Be the Verse" (Larkin) **64**:282
*This Boy's Life* (Wolff) **64**:456-61
"This island formed you" (Smith) **64**:393
*Thistles and Roses* (Smith) **64**:393-94, 397-98
*Those Who Ride the Night Winds* (Giovanni) **64**:192
*Three Postcards* (Lucas) **64**:289-90, 292
"Three Sonnets" (Smith) **64**:398
"To A Man" (Angelou) **64**:33-4
"To Autumn" (Smith) **64**:399
"To My Mother" (Smith)
   See "For My Mother"
"To My Wife" (Larkin) **64**:262
"To the Sea" (Larkin) **64**:277, 280, 282, 284
"Toads" (Larkin) **64**:266, 272, 282
"Toads Revisited" (Larkin) **64**:282
*Tomorrow-Today* (Kureishi) **64**:246
"Torch Song" (Cheever) **64**:65
*Tours of the Black Clock* (Erickson) **64**:139-42, 144-45
*Towards the Human* (Smith) **64**:400
"Travelin Man" (Matthiessen) **64**:321, 323-24

*The Tree Where Man Was Born* (Matthiessen) **64**:306-07, 309
"The Trees" (Larkin) **64**:258, 266
*The Trouble with Being Born* (Cioran) **64**:90, 98
"The True Import of Present Dialogue, Black vs. Negro" (Giovanni) **64**:182, 185, 188, 191, 193
"True Tenderness" (Akhmatova) **64**:11
"Two Portraits of Sex" (Larkin) **64**:262, 282
"Ugly Honkies, or The Election Game and How to Win It" (Giovanni) **64**:183
"The Undelivered" (Cioran) **64**:89, 94
*Under the Mountain Wall: A Chronicle of Two Seasons of the Stone Age* (Matthiessen) **64**:309
"Unfinished Poem" (Larkin) **64**:276-77
"Unresting Death" (Larkin) **64**:258
*Vecher* (*Evening*) (Akhmatova) **64**:3, 8, 21
"Vers de Société" (Larkin) **64**:258, 263, 270, 282
"The Village" (Smith) **64**:402
*The Village* (Smith) **64**:402
"A Vision of the World" (Cheever) **64**:53, 58, 60-3
"The Visit" (Smith) **64**:392
*Volshebnik* (*The Enchanter; The Magician*) (Nabokov) **64**:366
"Wants" (Larkin) **64**:260, 266
*The Wapshot Chronicle* (Cheever) **64**:44, 48, 57, 65-7
*The Wapshot Scandal* (Cheever) **64**:44, 48-9, 57-9, 66
"Water" (Larkin) **64**:268, 282-84
*Way of All the Earth* (Akhmatova) **64**:13
*The Way Some People Live* (Cheever) **64**:66
"Wedding Wind" (Larkin) **64**:259, 282
"When first we faced" (Larkin) **64**:258
"When I Die" (Giovanni) **64**:191
"When I Nap" (Giovanni) **64**:187
"When in the Gloomiest of Capitals" (Akhmatova)
   See "Kogda v mrachneyshey iz stolits"
"Where, Tall Girl, Is Your Gypsy Babe" (Akhmatova)
   See "Gde, vysokaya, tvoy tsyganyonok"
"While Reading Hamlet" (Akhmatova) **64**:15
*White Flock* (Akhmatova)
   See *Belaya Staya*
*The White House Murder Case* (Feiffer) **64**:150, 160
*The White Noon* (Smith) **64**:397
"The Whitsun Weddings" (Larkin) **64**:265-66, 269-71, 275, 282-84
*The Whitsun Weddings* (Larkin) **64**:259-60, 269-72, 278-80, 283
"The Widow" (Smith) **64**:389, 394
"Wild Oats" (Larkin) **64**:272
*Wildlife in America* (Matthiessen) **64**:309
"Winter" (Giovanni) **64**:194
"Wires" (Larkin) **64**:262
"The Wolves of Aguila" (Matthiessen) **64**:321, 323-24
*The Women and the Men* (Giovanni) **64**:188-89, 191
"The Wonder Woman" (Giovanni) **64**:185-87
"A Word for Me...Also" (Giovanni) **64**:192
"The Workman" (Smith) **64**:390
*The World and Africa* (Du Bois) **64**:118
"The World of Apples" (Cheever) **64**:50, 53
*World War I* (Smith) **64**:388
"Worldly Goods" (Wolff) **64**:448-49

"Wreath for the Dead" (Akhmatova)   **64**:6
*XX Poems* (Larkin)   **64**:257
"You Lived in Glasgow" (Smith)   **64**:393
"A Young Highland Girl Studying Poetry"
   ("A Highland Girl Studying Poetry")
   (Smith)   **64**:387, 396-97

Title Index